South India & Kerala

Maharashtra
p82

Mumbai
p44

**Telangana &
Andhra Pradesh**
p228

Goa
p117

Karnataka
p170

**Andaman
Islands**
p417

Tamil Nadu
p333

Kerala
p259

Isabella Noble,
Michael Benanav, Paul Harding, Kevin Raub, Iain Stewart

Contents

PLAN YOUR TRIP

Welcome to South
India & Kerala 4

South India &
Kerala Map 6

South India &
Kerala's Top 12 8

Need to Know 14

What's New 16

If You Like 17

Month by Month....... 20

Itineraries 26

Booking Trains 29

Yoga, Spas &
Spiritual Pursuits...... 31

Volunteering 35

Travel with Children.... 37

Regions at a Glance.... 40

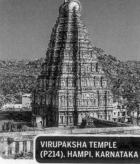
VIRUPAKSHA TEMPLE
(P214), HAMPI, KARNATAKA

NATALIIA SOKOLOVSKA / SHUTTERSTOCK ©

PALOLEM BEACH (P155), GOA

GUZEL GASHIGULLINA / SHUTTERSTOCK ©

ON THE ROAD

MUMBAI
(BOMBAY) 44

MAHARASHTRA.... 82
Northern Maharashtra.. 84
Nashik 84
Around Nashik 88
Aurangabad............ 88
Ellora 92
Ajanta................. 95
Jalgaon................ 98
Nagpur................ 98
Around Nagpur........ 100
Southern Maharashtra .101
Konkan Coast 101
Matheran............. 105
Lonavla............... 106
Pune 108
Around Pune........... 113
Kolhapur 114
Mahabaleshwar 115

GOA.................117
Panaji & Central Goa .. 120
Panaji 120
Old Goa 126
North Goa 127
Mapusa 127
Candolim 128
Calangute & Baga 131
Anjuna 135
Assagao 139
Vagator & Chapora 140
Morjim 144
Asvem................ 145
Mandrem 146
Arambol (Harmal) 147
South Goa 150
Margao............... 150
Colva................. 151
Benaulim 152
Agonda 153

Palolem 155
Patnem............... 160

KARNATAKA 170
Bengaluru (Bangalore). .172
Southern Karnataka ...187
Hesaraghatta 187
Mysuru (Mysore) 187
Around Mysuru........ 198
Bandipur National Park.. 199
Nagarhole
National Park 200
Kodagu (Coorg) Region.. 201
Hassan 203
Belur 204
Halebid...............205
Sravanabelagola.......205
Karnataka Coast......206
Mangaluru (Mangalore)..206
Dharmasthala 208
Udupi 208
Malpe 209
Gokarna 209
Central Karnataka 213
Hampi................ 213
Anegundi 220
Hosapete (Hospet) 221
Hubballi (Hubli) 221
Northern Karnataka... 221
Badami................ 221
Around Badami........223
Vijapura (Bijapur)......224
Bidar.................227

TELANGANA & ANDHRA
PRADESH......... 228
Telangana........... 230
Hyderabad............230
Bhongir 248
Warangal 248
Palampet............. 248
Andhra Pradesh 249
Vijayawada........... 249

Contents

Amaravathi 251
Nagarjunakonda 251
Visakhapatnam 252
Around Visakhapatnam . . 255
Tirumala & Tirupati 256
Around Tirumala
& Tirupati 258

KERALA 259

Southern Kerala 261
Thiruvananthapuram
(Trivandrum) 261
Kovalam 266
Varkala 271
Kollam (Quilon) 276
Around Kollam 278
Alappuzha (Alleppey) . . . 278
Marari & Kattoor 283
Kottayam 284
Kumarakom 285
**Kerala's
Western Ghats 286**
Periyar Tiger Reserve . . . 287
Munnar 292
Around Munnar 296
Central Kerala 297
Kochi (Cochin) 297
Around Kochi 311
Thrissur (Trichur) 312
Around Thrissur 314
Northern Kerala 314
Kozhikode (Calicut) 314
Wayanad Region 317
Kannur & Around 320
Bekal & Around 322
Lakshadweep 323

TAMIL NADU 333

Chennai (Madras) 335
Northern Tamil Nadu . . 353
East Coast Road 353
Mamallapuram
(Mahabalipuram) 355

Kanchipuram 359
Tiruvannamalai 362
Puducherry
(Pondicherry) 364
Auroville 373
Central Tamil Nadu . . . 374
Chidambaram 374
Tharangambadi
(Tranquebar) 375
Kumbakonam 376
Thanjavur (Tanjore) 378
Trichy (Tiruchirappalli) . . 382
Southern Tamil Nadu . . 386
Chettinadu 386
Madurai 389
Rameswaram 393
Kanyakumari
(Cape Comorin) 395
The Western Ghats 398
Kodaikanal (Kodai) 399
Coimbatore 404
Coonoor 406
Kotagiri 407
Ooty
(Udhagamandalam) 409
Mudumalai
Tiger Reserve 414
Anamalai Tiger Reserve
(Indira Gandhi
Wildlife Sanctuary &
National Park) 415

**ANDAMAN
ISLANDS 417**
Port Blair 421
Around Port Blair 425
Havelock Island
(Swaraj Dweep) 426
Neil Island
(Shaheed Dweep) 431
Middle & North
Andaman 434
Little Andaman 436

UNDERSTAND

South India Today 440
History 443
The Way Of Life 458
Spiritual India 465
Delicious India 472
**The Great
Indian Bazaar 483**
The Arts 490
**Architectural
Splendour 494**
Wildlife & Landscape . . 497

SURVIVAL GUIDE

Scams 504
Women & Solo
Travellers 506
Directory A-Z 508
Transport 521
Health 530
Language 535
Index 547
Map Legend 558

SPECIAL FEATURES

**Ancient & Historic
Sites colour feature . . . 162**

Mysuru Palace in 3D . . 190

Kerala colour feature . . 325

Delicious India 472

Welcome to South India & Kerala

Like a giant wedge plunging into the ocean, South India is the subcontinent's steamy heartland – a lush contrast to the peaks and plains up north.

A Fabulous Heritage

Wherever you go in the south you'll uncover splendid relics of the many civilisations that have inhabited this land over two millennia. The spectacular rock-cut shrines carved out by Buddhists, Hindus and Jains at Ajanta and Ellora; the palaces, tombs, forts and mosques of Muslim dynasties on the Deccan plateau; Tamil Nadu's inspired Pallava sculptures and towering Chola temples; the magical ruins of the Vijayanagar capital at Hampi...and so much more that you'd need a multitude of incarnations to see it all. It's a diverse cultural treasure trove with few parallels, in the land that also gave birth to yoga.

Luscious Landscapes

Thousands of kilometres of cascading coastline frame fertile plains, glinting backwaters and rolling hills in South India – a constantly changing landscape kept glisteningly green by the double-barrelled monsoon. The palm-strung strands and inland waterways of the west give way to spice gardens, emerald tea plantations, tropical forests and cool hill-station retreats in the Western Ghats. The drier Deccan 'plateau' is far from flat, criss-crossed by numerous craggy ranges and often spattered with dramatic, fort-topped outcrops. Across the region, protected wild forests shelter a world of wildlife, from elephants and tigers to monkeys, deer and sloth bears.

Culinary Delights

South India's glorious culinary variety and melange of dining options are an adventure in their own right. Some of India's most famous and traditional staples hail from here: large papery dosas (savoury crêpes) and fluffy *idlis* (fermented rice cakes) are the backbone of South Indian cooking. Mouth-watering Mumbai is India's top destination for gastronomic indulgence, be it hole-in-the-wall street food or haute-cuisine wizardry. Goa's spicy, Portuguese-influenced cuisine is fiery inventive fusion at its finest; Kerala's coconut-infused seafood is the stuff of legend; and, everywhere you travel, the humble South Indian *kaapi* (filter coffee) keeps things ticking over.

Sophisticated Cities

The south's vibrant cities are the pulse of a country that is fast-forwarding through the 21st century while also at times remaining staunchly traditional. From in-yer-face Mumbai and increasingly sophisticated Chennai to historic Hyderabad, IT capital Bengaluru (Bangalore) and charming, colonial-era Kochi (Cochin) and Puducherry (Pondicherry), southern cities are great for browsing teeming markets, soaking up local history and indulging in India's more fashionable side – from arty coffee houses and chic boutiques to an explosion of hipsterised microbreweries and cocktail bars.

Why I Love South India & Kerala

By Isabella Noble, Writer

My first taste of South India was a masala dosa at Shimla's Indian Coffee House, and I knew then that the south was calling. Whether it's Kerala's fiery sunsets, Tamil Nadu's incense-cloaked temples, the forested Western Ghats or the glint of a sparkly sari in a heaving bazaar, the many, multifaceted charms of the south unravel subtly, like the intricate spices of its cuisines. I'll always have a soft spot for palm-studded, backwater-laced Kerala; the Andamans' turquoise shallows; and architecturally fascinating Chettinadu. South India may be hot and often hectic, but it never fails to surprise and broaden the mind – and, inevitably, lure you back.

For more about our writers, see p559

Above: Tea plantations near Munnar (p292), Kerala

South India & Kerala

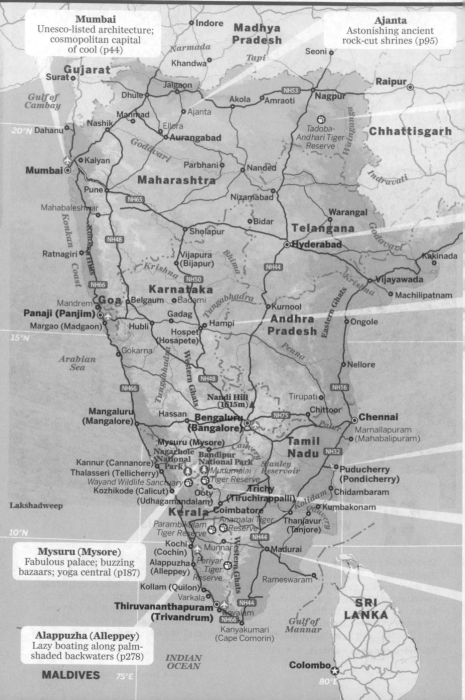

Mumbai
Unesco-listed architecture; cosmopolitan capital of cool (p44)

Ajanta
Astonishing ancient rock-cut shrines (p95)

Mysuru (Mysore)
Fabulous palace; buzzing bazaars; yoga central (p187)

Alappuzha (Alleppey)
Lazy boating along palm-shaded backwaters (p278)

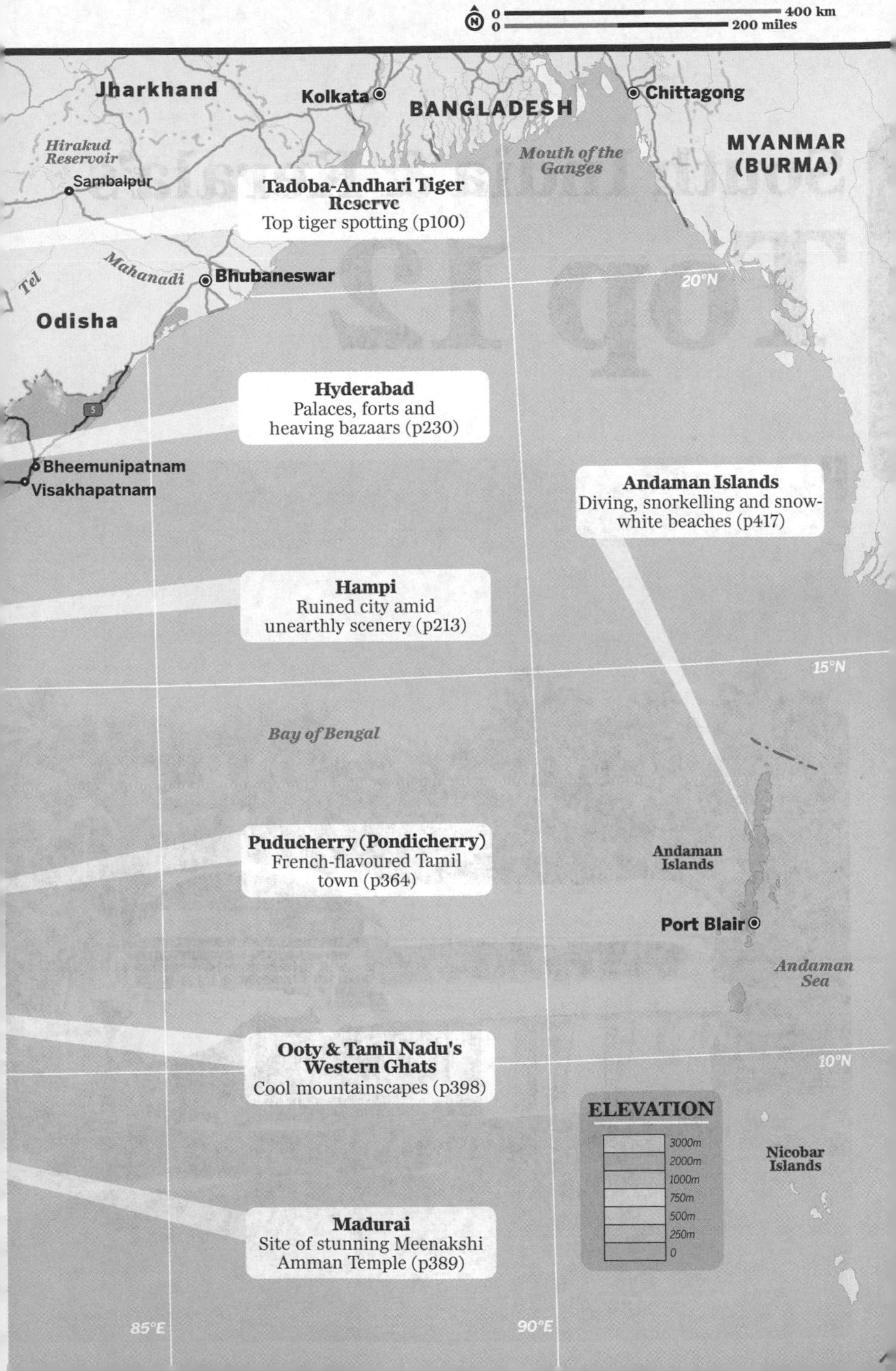

N 0 [scale bar] 400 km
0 [scale bar] 200 miles

Jharkhand

Kolkata ◎   **BANGLADESH**   ◎ **Chittagong**

Hirakud Reservoir
● Sambalpur

Tadoba-Andhari Tiger Reserve
Top tiger spotting (p100)

Mouth of the Ganges

MYANMAR (BURMA)

Mahanadi
Tel
◎ **Bhubaneswar**

Odisha

20°N

Hyderabad
Palaces, forts and heaving bazaars (p230)

○ **Bheemunipatnam**
○ **Visakhapatnam**

Andaman Islands
Diving, snorkelling and snow-white beaches (p417)

Hampi
Ruined city amid unearthly scenery (p213)

15°N

Bay of Bengal

Puducherry (Pondicherry)
French-flavoured Tamil town (p364)

Andaman Islands

Port Blair ◎

Andaman Sea

Ooty & Tamil Nadu's Western Ghats
Cool mountainscapes (p398)

10°N

ELEVATION

	3000m
	2000m
	1000m
	750m
	500m
	250m
	0

Nicobar Islands

Madurai
Site of stunning Meenakshi Amman Temple (p389)

85°E

90°E

South India & Kerala's
Top 12

Kerala's Beautiful Backwaters

1 Around 900km of interconnected rivers, twinkling lakes and glassy lagoons lined with lush tropical flora converge in Kerala's sublime backwaters. And there's no more serene and intimate way to experience them than aboard a teak-and-palm-thatch houseboat (pictured), a silently roaming kayak or a punt-powered canoe from Alappuzha (Alleppey; p278). Float along the water as the sun sinks behind whispering palms, feast on gloriously fresh seafood, pop into tiny water-ringed villages, witness the sun rising above rippling waves – and forget about life on land for a while.

Golden Goa

2 Silken sand, gently crashing waves, rich coconut groves, flaming-pink sunsets – if there's one place in India that effortlessly fulfils every beach paradise cliché, it's Goa. With few exceptions Goa's beaches, from mellow Mandrem (p146) to charming Palolem (p155), are a riot of activity, with a constant cavalcade of roaming sarong vendors, stacks of ramshackle beachside eateries and oiled bodies slowly baking on row after row of sun lounges. Goa is also loved for its inland spice plantations, flavour-filled seafood-fired cuisine and fine heritage buildings, most notably handsome Portuguese-era cathedrals.

Vagator Beach p140

Enigmatic Hampi

3 Today's surreal boulderscape of Hampi (p213) was once glorious Vijayanagar, capital of a powerful Hindu empire. Still glorious in ruin, its temples and royal structures combine with the terrain in mystical ways: giant rocks balance on skinny pedestals near an ancient elephant garage; temples tuck into crevices between boulders; and round coracle boats float by rice paddies, palm groves and bathing buffalo, near a gargantuan bathtub for a queen. As the sunset casts a rosy glow over this extraordinary landscape, you might just forget what planet you're on.

Maharashtra's Astounding Ancient Caves

4 The 2nd-century-BC Buddhist monks who created the Ajanta caves (pictured; p95) had an eye for the dramatic, as the rock-cut shrines and monasteries punctuating a horseshoe-shaped cliff attest. Centuries later, monks added exquisite carvings and paintings. Along an escarpment at Ellora (p92), less than 150km to the southwest, Hindus, Jains and Buddhists spent five centuries carving out another 34 elaborate shrines and monasteries, plus Kailasa Temple, the world's biggest monolithic structure.

PHOTOSO.KZ / SHUTTERSTOCK ©

CASPERITRA STUDIO / SHUTTERSTOCK ©

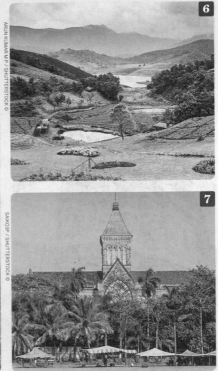

Out in the Wild

5 Disappearing into the wild jungles, bush and hills of South India, where dozens of parks and protected spaces await, is always a thrill. Maharashtra's Tadoba-Andhari Tiger Reserve (pictured; p100) has some of India's best tiger-spotting chances, while Mudumalai Tiger Reserve as one of the country's highest tiger population densities. Nagarhole National Park, Periyar Tiger Reserve and Wayanad Wildlife Sanctuary are top wildelephant territory. In almost any park you can expect to spy a range of deer, buffalo, primates and plenty of birds; and the landscapes themselves are always soulstirringly stunning.

Ooty & the Western Ghats

6 The palm-fringed beaches, pancake-flat plains and temple-tastic cities are all well and good, but it gets hot down there! India's princes and British colonials retreated to cool mountain towns such as Ooty (Udhagamandalam; p409), Kodaikanal (p399), Coonoor (p406) and Kotagiri (p407) to escape the relentless lowland heat. Today, Tamil Nadu's hill stations still serve up plenty of crisp air, shady forests, scenic viewpoints, sprawling tea plantations and quirky echoes-of-the-Raj charm.

Mumbai's Architectural Gems

7 Mumbai (p44) has long embraced global influences and made them its own. The result is a heady architectural melange of buildings with a raft of design influences. Modern towers lend the city its cosmopolitan air, but it's the eclectic, newly Unesco-listed art deco and Victorian-era structures – with Indo-Saracenic, Venetian Gothic and other old flourishes (pictured) – that have made Mumbai the flamboyant beauty it is. All those spires, arches and puffy onion domes, offset by lofty palms and leafy banyans, complete this head-spinning cocktail.

MILOSK50 / SHUTTERSTOCK ©

NICO TARAMAZ / SHUTTERSTOCK ©

JAS PHOTO / SHUTTERSTOCK ©

Tamil Temples

8 Opening through soaring, intricately carved *gopurams* (gateway towers), Tamil Nadu's temples are a feast of deftly crafted pillars, vibrantly painted murals and glittering tanks of holy water. Madurai's joyful Meenakshi Amman Temple (pictured; p389), surrounded by 12 lofty *gopurams* encrusted with thousands of technicolor deities, demons and heroes, is rightly considered the high point of South India's spectacular temple architecture. It's closely rivalled by the elegant, World Heritage–listed Brihadishwara Temple at Thanjavur (Tanjore), dating back to the 11th century.

Historic Hyderabad

9 Bustling Hyderabad (p230) tempts history lovers with its fascinating past and oodles of historic attractions, including massive Golconda Fort, the graceful Charminar mosque-monument, and the magnificent tombs and palaces of bygone rulers, such as the majestic Qutb Shahi Tombs (pictured; p235), now nominated for World Heritage status. But it's also a city of dizzying bazaars, *qawwali* devotional song and deliciously inventive cuisine, acclaimed for its traditional Mughal-style spicy kebabs and biryanis and unique Ramadan dishes.

Puducherry Savoir Faire

10 A seaside pocket of France surrounded by Tamil Nadu? *Pourquoi pas?* In this former French colony, mango-yellow houses line cobbled *rues,* imposing cathedrals are adorned with architectural *frou-frou,* and the croissants are the real deal. But Puducherry (Pondicherry; p364) is also a classic Indian town – with all the history and hubbub that involves – and a popular retreat, with the Sri Aurobindo Ashram at its heart and its offshoot Auroville nearby. Turns out that yoga, *pain au chocolat,* heritage hotels, Hindu deities and colonial-era architecture make for a *très* atmospheric mix.

Majestic Mysuru

11 Welcome to Mysuru (Mysore; p187) – a city whose name describes the spot where a brave goddess conquered a ferocious demon. Apart from its history and flamboyant palaces, it's a place for leisurely wanders through ancient bazaars filled with intoxicating aromas of sandalwood and fresh flowers. Mysuru is also a world-renowned yoga centre, famous for ashtanga yoga, and is known for its energetic festivals. Dussehra, celebrating the triumph of good over evil, is one of the most spectacular occasions, with the dazzling illumination of the 1912 Mysuru Palace (pictured; p188).

Andaman Island Eden

12 If lazing on beaches and diving into the deep is your thing, seek out the blissfully distant Andaman Islands. A world away from India's urban jungles, this slice of paradise has so far largely managed to retain its untouched beauty. The inhabitants are a mix of South and Southeast Asian settlers, as well as indigenous tribal groups. The islands, especially Havelock (Swaraj Dweep; pictured; p426), are blessed with aquamarine waters and white shores backed by impassable rainforest, offering outstanding snorkelling and diving. Permit restrictions were eased in 2018.

FOOFA JEARNMSIL / SHUTTERSTOCK ©

NICKOLAY STANEV / SHUTTERSTOCK ©

Need to Know

For more information, see Survival Guide (p503)

Currency
Indian rupee (₹)

Language
Tamil, Kannada, Konkani, Malayalam, Marathi and Telugu, in addition to Hindi and English

Visas
Many nationalities can obtain 60-day visas through India's e-Visa scheme. For longer trips, most people get a six-month tourist visa, valid from the date of issue (not arrival).

Money
ATMs are widely available; credit/debit cards are accepted in midrange hotels, shops and restaurants, but it remains a cash-based economy.

Mobile Phones
Roaming connections are excellent in urban areas, poor in the countryside and hills. Local prepaid SIMs are widely available but you'll have to wait 24 hours for activation.

Time
Indian Standard Time (GMT/UTC plus 5½ hours)

When to Go

Mumbai
GO Nov–Feb

Hyderabad
GO Nov–Mar

Panaji
GO Nov–Mar

Chennai
GO Dec–Mar

Thiruvananthapuram
GO Nov–Mar

Desert, dry climate
Tropical climate, rain year-round
Tropical climate, wet & dry seasons
Warm to hot summers, mild winters

High Season (Nov–Mar)
➡ Pleasant weather – warm days, coolish nights.

➡ Peak tourists. Peak prices. Peak festivals.

➡ December and January bring chilly nights in the hills and further north.

➡ Temperatures climb steadily from February.

Shoulder (Apr & Aug–Oct)
➡ Monsoon showers persist through to September.

➡ The eastern coast, Andamans and southern Kerala see heavy rain and sometimes cyclones from October to early December.

➡ Festivals abound.

Low Season (May–Jul)
➡ May and June are scorching. Competitive hotel prices.

➡ From June, the monsoon sweeps south to north, bringing draining humidity.

➡ Beat the heat (but not the crowds) in the cooler hills.

Useful Websites

Incredible India (www.incredibleindia.org) Official India tourism site.

Lonely Planet (www.lonelyplanet.com/india) Destination information, hotel bookings, traveller forum and more.

Templenet (www.templenet.com) Temple talk.

Rediff News (www.rediff.com/news) Portal for India-wide news.

The Alternative (www.thealternative.in) A green and socially conscious take on travel and Indian life.

Blogs and local media are also very handy resources.

Important Numbers

Country code	📞91
International access code	📞00
Emergency (police, fire and ambulance)	📞112
Toll-free tourist helpline	📞1800 111363

Exchange Rates

Australia	A$1	₹49
Canada	C$1	₹52
Euro zone	€1	₹80
Japan	¥100	₹63
New Zealand	NZ$1	₹47
UK	UK£1	₹89
US	US$1	₹69

For current exchange rates, see www.xe.com.

Daily Costs

Budget: Less than ₹2500

➡ Hostel dorm bed: ₹400–₹1000

➡ All-you-can-eat thali (traditional plate meal): ₹80–₹300

➡ Transport: ₹200–₹600

Midrange: ₹2500–₹7500

➡ Double hotel/homestay room: ₹1500–₹5000

➡ Meal in a midrange restaurant: ₹300–₹1000

➡ Admission to sights and museums: ₹200–₹800

➡ 2AC train travel: ₹700–₹2000

Top end: More than ₹7500

➡ Boutique/heritage hotel room: from ₹5500

➡ Dinner with wine: ₹2000–₹4000

➡ Renting a car and driver: per day ₹2000–₹3000

➡ Guided tour or cooking class: ₹1200–₹3000

Opening Hours

Some outdoor-centric spots may close or alter their hours during the monsoon months (June to September).

Banks 10am to 4pm Monday to Friday, to 1pm Saturday

Bars noon to 11pm (as late as 1.30am in Mumbai)

Markets 7am to 8pm, but very variable

Restaurants 8am or 9am to 10pm or 11pm (but variable; some restaurants close between 3pm and 7pm, and others in metro cities may stay open until 1.30am)

Shops 10am or 11am to 8pm or 9pm (some close Sunday)

Arriving in South India

Chhatrapati Shivaji Maharaj International Airport, Mumbai Prepaid taxis cost ₹670/810 (non-AC/AC) to Colaba and Fort; ₹400/480 to Bandra. Off-peak UberGo costs ₹250 to ₹560. Suburban trains to Fort (from ₹10) run from Andheri, a ₹50 to ₹70 autorickshaw from the airport.

Kempegowda International Airport, Bengaluru Metered AC taxis to central Bengaluru cost ₹750 to ₹1000; Uber/Ola rates are ₹550 to ₹650. Air-con buses run regularly to the city (₹170 to ₹260); Flybus travels to Mysuru, Tirupati and other destinations.

Cochin International Airport, Kochi Air-con buses run to/from Fort Cochin (₹88) via Ernakulam or Vyttila. Prepaid/app taxis cost ₹880/700 (Ernakulam), ₹1250/1000 (Fort Cochin).

Chennai International Airport Prepaid taxis to central Chennai cost ₹450 to ₹650; Ola and Uber around ₹300. Metro Rail (₹50 to ₹70) whisks you to Teynampet, Egmore, CMBT and Central Railway Station.

Getting Around

Air Larger cities have affordable flights to other Indian cities.

Bus Buses go everywhere, at similar speeds to trains. Some routes are served 24 hours but others just one or two a day.

Car and driver Convenient option for multistop trips or trips to out-of-the-way places.

Motorcycle Many travellers hire scooters or motorcycles to zip around.

Train Railways criss-cross the country, with frequent, inexpensive services on most routes.

For much more on **getting around**, see p522

What's New

Airports Everywhere

Kannur's international airport, which took off in 2018, is opening up northern Kerala, while a greenfield international airport at Mopa, North Goa, is slated for mid-2020. Hampi now has domestic links from upgraded Jindal Vijaynagar airport (p220).

Third-Wave Coffee

Proper espresso has landed at Mumbai's Koinonia Coffee Roasters (p72) and Blue Tokai (p71), and the likes of Third Wave Coffee Roasters (p182) are bringing forward-thinking coffee culture to Bengaluru (Bangalore). Kochi's (Cochin's) arty coffee scene has exploded in recent years.

Hassle-Free Andamans

Permit requirements for the Andaman Islands (p419) were eased in 2018. Throw in two luxury destination properties – Taj Exotica (p429) and Jalakara (p429) – and these far-flung isles feel more seductive than ever.

Hostel Heaven

South India's backpacker-hostel boom powers on (p510): Zostel in Kochi, Alappuzha (Alleppey), Gokarna and Chennai; Chettinad Packer in Chettinadu; Backpacker Panda in Goa and Mumbai; Rainbow Lining and Wonderland Hostel in Goa; Beehive Hostel in Mysuru (Mysore); and Varkala's Lost Hostel, among others.

Dhanushkodi

A new paved road whisks you across golden dunes to the evocatively ruined village of Dhanushkodi (p394) on India's southeasternmost tip.

Goa Craft Beer

Goa's love of beer (p479) has brought the craft movement to its tropical shores, with fresh microbreweries flaunting their brews.

Taxi Apps

Uber and Ola Cabs (p526) have revolutionised city travel across India. Both are banned in Goa, but Goa Tourism launched its own competitor app, Goa Miles (p119), in 2018.

Mumbai Flavours

Hot arrivals on Mumbai's dizzying, dazzling dining scene include Southeast Asian–inspired Miss T (p65), courtesy of culinary royalty the Colaba Cartel, and home-dining pop-up sensation Bohri Kitchen (p63).

Nashik Nights

Nashik's wine scene continues to blossom, and you can now sleep off tastings at The Source at Sula (p85), on the site of award-winning Sula Vineyards' original winery.

Heritage Homestays

Thiruvananthapuram's (Trivandrum's) fabulous Padmavilasom Palace (p264), reborn in 2018, delights with boutique sleeps in a 150-year-old royal Travancore home.

Mumbai–Goa Cruises

A luxury thrice-weekly cruise-ship-ferry between Mumbai and Goa, Angriya Cruises (p80), kicked off sailings in 2018.

For more recommendations and reviews, see lonelyplanet.com/India

If You Like...

Beaches

South India is home to the country's most breathtaking stretches of coastline.

Kerala Cliff-framed Varkala, up-and-coming Marari, and secluded, palm-fringed Thottada and Bekal are absolute visions. (p326)

Goa Despite the crowds, Goa's beaches still shine: Cola, Agonda, Palolem and Mandrem are among the prettiest. (p117)

Andaman Islands Pristine tropical beaches far away from everything on Havelock (Swaraj Dweep), Neil (Shaheed Dweep) and Little Andaman. (p417)

Mumbai Hit Chowpatty Beach for local *bhelpuri*, people-watching and blazing-pink sunsets. (p51)

Maharashtra The Konkan Coast's sun-soaked sands are less crowded than those of its neighbours, especially around Ganpatipule. (p103)

Kovalam (Covelong) A beachy surf, yoga and water-sports scene near Mamallapuram (Mahabalipuram) in Tamil Nadu. (p354)

Temples & Ruins

Nowhere does grand temples like the subcontinent. From Tamil Nadu's psychedelic Hindu towers to the faded splendour of the Buddhist caves of Ajanta and Ellora, the range is as vast as it is sublime.

Hampi Mighty Vijayanagar's rosy-hued temples and crumbling palaces are strewn among otherworldly boulders and hills. (p213)

Meenakshi Amman Temple Fantastical structure that soars skyward in riotous rainbows of sculpted deities in Madurai (Tamil Nadu). (p389)

Thanjavur (Tanjore) The greatest heights of Chola (and Tamil) temple architecture. (p378)

Ajanta Magnificent, Unesco-listed Maharashtrian rock-cut temples, revered for their spiritual significance and architectural prowess. (p95)

Ellora Five centuries of extraordinary rock-cut temples chiselled by generations of Buddhist, Hindu and Jain monks in Maharashtra. (p92)

Mamallapuram (Mahabalipuram) Exquisite medieval relief carvings, sculpted by Pallava artisans, and rock-cut temples dot this seaside Tamil town. (p355)

Forts & Palaces

South India's history is a uniquely colourful tapestry of wrangling dynasties interwoven with influxes of seafaring traders. Their legacy lives on in a remarkable collection of palaces and forts.

Mysuru Palace A spectacular royal confection of rare artworks, stained glass, mosaics and beautifully carved wood. (p188)

Daulatabad Fort A magnificent Maharashtrian hilltop fortress constructed by Yadava kings throughout the 12th century. (p92)

Hyderabad Golconda Fort complements the opulent palaces and ethereal royal tombs of the city of pearls. (p230)

Janjira A remarkably preserved island fortress built off the Konkan Coast in 1571. (p101)

Bidar Fort So weathered and peaceful, it's shocking that this marvellous 15th-century complex once commanded a powerful sultanate. (p227)

Gingee Fort Choose from three ruined citadels on the Tamil Nadu plains. (p363)

Meditation & Yoga

The art of well-being has long been ardently cultivated in the south. Numerous courses and treatments strive to heal mind, body and spirit, with meditation and yoga especially abundant.

Mysuru Home of ashtanga yoga; one of India's most popular places to practise and get certified. (p194)

Goa Yoga, meditation and other spiritual-health pursuits are taught and practised chiefly between October and April. (p117)

Krishnamacharya Yoga Mandiram Well-known and highly regarded yoga courses, yoga therapy and intensive teacher training in Chennai. (p341)

Sivananda Yoga Vedanta Dhanwantari Ashram Yoga courses at Kerala's respected ashram. Kerala, Kovalam, Varkala and Kochi have popular classes, too. (p266)

Vipassana International Academy Intensive meditation courses at one of the world's largest *vipassana* meditation centres, in Igatpuri, Maharashtra. (p88)

Gokarna Drop-in classes in a wonderful, natural beachy environment. (p211)

Isha Yoga Center Yoga courses and meditation at a renowned ashram near Coimbatore. (p404)

International Centre for Yoga Education & Research Yoga training at an established Puducherry (Pondicherry) school. (p367)

Nature

South India offers plenty of opportunities to search for wild things in wild places.

Wayanad Wildlife Sanctuary Remote, beautiful, unspoilt Keralan sanctuary with good chances of spotting wild elephants. (p317)

Nagarhole National Park Little-visited Karnataka park good for elephant sightings and – if you're lucky! – a tiger or two. (p200)

Tadoba-Andhari Tiger Reserve Top Indian tiger territory, plus gaurs, chital deer, nilgai antelope, sloth bears and leopards. (p100)

Periyar Tiger Reserve Popular Keralan sanctuary with gaurs, sambar deer, around 2000 elephants and a few tigers. (p287)

Mudumalai Tiger Reserve Tamil Nadu's favourite wildlife spot: deer, gaurs, wild boars, langurs, wild elephants and a good number of (elusive) tigers. (p414)

Bandipur National Park Another much-loved Karnataka reserve. (p199)

Bazaars

Megamalls may be popping up like monsoon frogs in southern cities, but the traditional outdoor bazaars – their tangled lanes lined with everything from freshly ground spices and floral garlands to kitchen utensils and colourful saris – can't be beat.

Goa Anjuna and Baga flea markets mesmerise; Margao, Mapusa and Panaji (Panjim) bazaars make for atmospheric wandering. (p117)

Mumbai Wonderful old markets are conveniently themed: Mangaldas (fabric), Zaveri (jewellery), Crawford (food) and Chor (antiques). (p73)

Mysuru (Mysore) The centuries-old Devaraja Market is filled with millions of flowers, fruits and spices. (p189)

Hyderabad Historic Charminar-area bazaars hawk everything from pearls and lac bangles to livestock and wedding outfits. (p244)

Chennai George Town's frenzied bazaar streets each flog their own particular products, from paper to jewellery. (p349)

City Sophistication

It's true that most Indians live in villages, but the southern cities have vibrant arts scenes, terrific multi-cuisine restaurants and oodles of style.

Mumbai Fashion, film, art, dining, nightlife against a backdrop of fanciful architecture and scenic water views. (p44)

Hyderabad The architecture of bygone dynasties sits across town from a refined food, nightlife and arts scene. (p230)

Bengaluru (Bangalore) Liberal and modern IT industry nucleus, superb for drinking, dining and shopping. (p172)

Nashik Surrounded by gorgeous vineyards, India's wine-country capital lures juice-loving city sophisticates. (p84)

Puducherry (Pondicherry) Lively coastal town known for its charmingly faded French flavour, boho boutiques and arty cafes. (p364)

Chennai Long-standing urban hub which now hosts sophisticated luxury hotels, contemporary restaurants, boutiques and nightspots. (p335)

Pune Progressive Pune relishes in its juxtapositional relationship between cutting-edge capitalism and age-old spirituality. (p108)

Kochi (Cochin) A growing arts, cafe and shopping scene graces Kerala's central historical hub. (p297)

Hill Stations

The colonial-era tradition of heading for the cool, green elevations of South India's Western Ghats when the plains get just too hot is alive and well among honeymooners, families and pretty much everyone else.

Ooty (Udhagamandalam) Tamil Nadu's 'Queen of Hill Stations' combines Indian bustle with Raj-era bungalows and a miniature train. (p409)

Kodaikanal (Kodai) A smaller, quirkier, more scenic alternative to Ooty, centred on a pretty lake surrounded by *shola* (virgin forest). (p399)

Munnar Trek through jade-green Keralan tea plantations, then meet a local family at an out-of-town homestay. (p292)

Matheran A scenic and vehicle-free weekend retreat for Mumbaikars. (p105)

Kodagu (Coorg) Coffee and spices scent the fresh mountain air of this Karnataka region, with Madikeri its hub. (p201)

Coonoor Heritage hotels, tea plantations and hilly hikes await in the Nilgiri Hills near Ooty. (p406)

Traveller Enclaves

Sometimes you just want to stop moving for a bit and relax and swap stories with fellow travellers.

Hampi The stunning beauty of Hampi's landscape and architecture sucks everyone in for a while. (p213)

Anjuna Goa is one big traveller enclave, but Anjuna, Palolem and cheaper Arambol are its current epicentres. (p135)

Gokarna Cosy, beautiful and relaxed beaches that form part of a sacred village in Karnataka. (p209)

Mamallapuram (Mahabalipuram) Cheap accommodation, striking ancient architecture and a booming surf scene on Tamil Nadu's coast. (p355)

Colaba Mumbai's boisterous melange of street stalls, classic watering holes, budget accommodation and bucket-list tourist sights. (p47)

Varkala Charming guesthouses, yoga *shalas* and traveller-packed cafes cling to cliffs above surf-tastic waves in Kerala. (p271)

Water Sports

Diving, snorkelling, surfing, SUP, kayaking and an array of other water sports are growing rapidly along South India's coasts.

Andaman Islands World-class diving and snorkelling in crystal-clear, coral- and marine-life-rich waters – 1370km east of mainland India. (p417)

Tamil Nadu Surf's up in Kovalam, Mamallapuram and Puducherry; Rameswaram has kitesurfing, kayaking, snorkelling, SUP and more. (p333)

Goa Gentle waves perfect for beginner surfers at Aswem and Agonda, and scuba diving at Grande Island. (p133)

Malvan India's little diving-destination-that-could: caves, coral, marine life and a top-class scuba school. (p104)

Lakshadweep Pristine lagoons and unspoilt coral reefs 300km off Kerala have wonderful diving and snorkelling. (p323)

Varkala Surfing, kayaking and SUP from this temple/traveller town in southern Kerala. (p271)

Boat Trips

Seeing South India from the water offers a whole new angle on its attractions.

Alappuzha (Alleppey) Houseboat, kayak or canoe drifting from Kerala's backwaters hub is one of South India's most cinematic experiences. (p279)

Kollam (Quilon) Observe village life on punted canoe rides through networks of canals around Munroe Island (Kerala). (p276)

Goa Dolphin- and croc-spotting tours on the Mandovi River. (p121)

Andaman Islands See coral-rich Mahatma Gandhi Marine National Park, and travel between ravishing islands by local ferry. (p425)

Malvan Take a trip along Maharashtra's little-known but beautiful Karli River backwaters. (p104)

Elephanta Island Catch a different perspective on Mumbai's iconic harbour while returning from this Unesco World Heritage Site. (p54)

Local Festivals

As well as embracing a range of countrywide festivals, South India has many vibrant locally celebrated events, from sacred temple processions to flamboyant beachside affairs.

Nehru Trophy Boat Race A lively showdown between elegant 40m-long canoes in Alleppey, Kerala. (p279)

Chennai Festival of Music & Dance For a month, Chennai fills up on Carnatic (and some non-Carnatic) music, dance and drama. (p336)

Pongal Decorated cows feast on *pongal* (a rice, sugar, dhal and milk concoction) in Tamil Nadu. (p20)

Goa Carnival This four-day fiesta kicks off Lent with colourful parades, concerts and plenty of merrymaking. (p20)

Ganesh Chaturthi Mumbai buzzes for the ceremonial dunking of statues of Hindu god Ganesh into the Arabian Sea. (p47)

Dussehra Mysuru Palace is spectacularly lit up at night, while the town puts on cultural events. (p84)

Month by Month

TOP EVENTS

Pongal, January

Carnival, February or March

Ganesh Chaturthi, August or September

Navratri & Dussehra, September or October

Diwali, October or November

January

The postmonsoon cool lingers, although it never gets truly cool in India's most southerly states. Pleasant weather and several festivals make this a popular time to travel (book ahead!).

✦ Sankranti

Sankranti, the Hindu festival marking the sun's passage into Capricorn and the end of the harvest, is celebrated on 14 or 15 January with mass kite-flying in Maharashtra, Telangana and Andhra Pradesh (among other states).

✦ Pongal

Aligned with Sankranti, Tamil Nadu's Pongal (p336) marks the end of the harvest. Families prepare pots of *pongal* (rice, sugar, dhal and milk), symbolic of prosperity and abundance, then feed them to decorated cows. The controversial *jallikattu* (bull taming) is popular during Pongal.

✦ Free India

Republic Day commemorates the founding of the Republic of India on 26 January 1950.

✦ Vasant Panchami

On Vasant Panchami, the 'fifth day of spring', Hindus (especially students) dress in yellow and place books, instruments and other educational objects in front of idols of Saraswati, the goddess of learning, to receive her blessing. May fall in February.

February

The weather is comfortable in most areas, with summer heat starting to percolate. Still peak travel season.

☆ SulaFest

In Maharashtra, Nashik's biggest party is SulaFest (p84), three wine-fuelled days at Sula Vineyards – one of India's best boutique music festivals.

✦ Maha Shivaratri

Held in February or March, Shivaratri, a day of Hindu fasting, recalls the *tandava* (cosmic victory dance) of Lord Shiva. Temple processions are followed by the chanting of mantras and the anointing of linga (phallic images of Shiva). Upcoming dates: 21 February 2020, 11 March 2021.

✦ Carnival in Goa

Carnival, the four-day party kicking off Lent, is particularly big in Goa (p120), especially in Panaji (Panjim). Sabado Gordo (Fat Saturday) starts it off with elaborate parades, and the revelry continues with street parties, concerts and merrymaking. Might also fall in March.

March

The last month of the travel high season, March is full-on hot in most of South India.

LUNAR & ISLAMIC CALENDARS

Many festivals follow the astrological-based Indian lunar calendar or the Islamic calendar (which moves about 11 days earlier each year, and changes annually relative to the Gregorian calendar). Check online or contact local tourist offices for exact festival dates.

Holi

Holi (www.holifestival.org), an ecstatic Hindu celebration at the beginning of spring (February/March), is associated with Krishna but also celebrates fertility, love, and good conquering evil. Mumbaikars and other southerners embrace this northern festival by throwing coloured water and *gulal* (powder) at everyone and everything. Upcoming dates: 9 March 2020, 28 March 2021.

April

The heat has well and truly arrived in South India; with the rise in temperature come competitive travel deals and a drop in tourist traffic.

Mahavir's Birthday

In March or April, Mahavir Jayanti commemorates the birth of Jainism's 24th and most important *tirthankar* (teacher and enlightened being). Temples are decorated, Mahavir statues given ritual baths, processions held and offerings given to the poor.

Rama's Birthday

During Ramanavami (one to nine days) in March or April, Hindus celebrate Rama's birth with processions, music, fasting and feasting, enactments of the Ramayana, and ceremonial weddings of Rama and Sita idols. Upcoming dates: 2 April 2020, 21 April 2021.

Ramadan (Ramazan)

Thirty days of dawn-to-dusk fasting mark the ninth month of the Islamic calendar. Ramadan begins around 24 April 2020 and 13 April 2021.

May

In most of the country it's *hot*, which makes it high season in Ooty (Udhagamandalam), Kodaikanal (Kodai) and other southern hill stations. Festivals slow down as humidity builds.

Thrissur Pooram

In April or May, Kerala's biggest Hindu temple festival (p261) sees parades of caparisoned elephants through town.

Eid al-Fitr

Muslims celebrate the end of Ramadan with three days of festivities (prayers, shopping, gift-giving). Around 24 May 2020 and 13 May 2021.

June

The monsoon begins in most areas, and where it doesn't you've got premonsoon extreme heat, so June isn't a popular travel month in South India.

July

It's really raining almost everywhere, with many remote roads being washed out. Consider doing a rainy-season meditation or ayurveda retreat, an ancient Indian tradition.

Naag Panchami

Naag Panchami, particularly vibrant in Pune and Kolhapur (Maharashtra) and Karnataka, is dedicated to Ananta, the serpent upon whose coils Vishnu rested between universes. Women fast at home, while serpents are venerated as totems. Upcoming dates: 25 July 2020 and 13 August 2021.

Eid al-Adha

Muslims commemorate Ibrahim's readiness to sacrifice his son to God by slaughtering a goat or sheep and sharing it. Around 31 July 2020 and 19 July 2021.

August

It's still high monsoon season, with some tourist-oriented businesses closed. Some folks swear by visiting tropical areas like Kerala or Goa at this time of year for the lush, glistening jungle.

Janmastami

Marking Krishna's birthday, Janmastami celebrations range from fasting and *puja* (prayers) to drawing elaborate *rangoli* (rice-paste designs) outside homes. Upcoming dates: 11 August 2020 and 30 August 2021.

Nehru Trophy Boat Race

On the second Saturday of August, the fiercely contested Nehru Trophy Boat Race sees 40m-long snake boats go head-to-head, powered by up to 100 rowers each, on Punnamada Lake near Alappuzha (Alleppey, Kerala; p261)

Independence Day

This public holiday, on 15 August, marks the anniversary of India's independence from Britain in 1947. Festivities include flag-hoisting ceremonies, parades and patriotic cultural programmes.

✨ Parsi New Year

Parsis celebrate Pateti, the last day of the Zoroastrian year, followed by the new year, especially in Mumbai. Houses are cleaned and decorated with flowers and *rangoli,* families dress up and eat special dishes, and offerings are made at the Fire Temple.

✨ Ganesh Chaturthi

Hindus, especially in Mumbai, celebrate the birth of the elephant-headed god (p47) for up to 10 days in August or September by displaying decorative statues then parading them around before ceremonially depositing them in rivers, lakes or the sea. Ganesh Chaturthi falls around 22 August 2020 and 10 September 2021.

✨ Ashura

Shiite Muslims commemorate the martyrdom of Prophet Mohammed's grandson Imam Hussain on the 10th day of the Islamic holy month of Muharram with beautiful processions, especially in Hyderabad. Around 28 August 2020 and 18 August 2021. Ashura also marks the day Noah left the ark, and the day Moses was saved from the Egyptians.

✨ Onam

Kerala's biggest cultural celebration, Onam (p261) is a 10-day Hindu soirée held at the beginning of the first month of the Malayalam calendar in August or September, glorifying the golden age of mythical King Mahabali. Upcoming dates: 30 August 2020, 21 August 2021.

September

The rain begins to ease off, but, with temperatures still relatively high, the moisture-filled air can create a fatiguing steam-bath-like environment.

October

The southeast coast (and southern Kerala) can still be rainy, but this is when South India starts to get its travel mojo on.

✨ Gandhi Jayanti

The national holiday of Gandhi Jayanti (2 October) is a solemn celebration of Mohandas Gandhi's birth, with prayer meetings at his cremation site in Delhi, and no alcohol on sale countrywide.

✨ Navratri

The Hindu 'Festival of Nine Nights' leading up to Dussehra celebrates the goddess Durga in all her incarnations. Festivities, in September or October, are particularly vibrant in Maharashtra. Most areas will celebrate around 17 October 2020, and 7 October 2021, but in some places, Dussehra events start well before, coinciding (confusingly!) with Navratri.

✨ Dussehra

Colourful Dussehra (p172), big in Mysuru (Mysore), celebrates the triumph of good over evil. In South India, it's centred on Durga's defeat of the demon Mahishasura; in the north and west, including Maharashtra, the focus is Rama's victory over Ravana. Around 8 October

2019, 25 October 2020 and 14 October 2021.

✨ Diwali

In the lunar month of Kartika, Hindus celebrate five-day Diwali, with gifts, fireworks, *rangoli,* and burning lanterns to lead Lord Rama home from exile. In the south, it's often associated with Krishna's victory over Naraka. Upcoming dates: 27 October 2019, 14 November 2020, 4 November 2021.

November

The northeast monsoon is sweeping Tamil Nadu and Kerala, but the tourist season is in swing and temperatures are pleasant enough.

✨ Eid-Milad-un-Nabi

The Islamic festival of Eid-Milad-un-Nabi celebrates the birth of the Prophet Mohammed with prayers and processions. Around 10 November 2019, 29 October 2020, 19 October 2021.

✨ Guru Nanak's Birthday

Nanak Jayanti, birthday of Guru Nanak, founder of Sikhism, is celebrated with prayer, *kirtan* (devotional singing) and processions for three days. Around 12 November 2019, 30 November 2020 and 19 November 2021.

☆ International Film Festival of India

The International Film Festival of India (www.iffi. nic.in), the country's biggest movie jamboree, attracts Bollywood's finest to Panaji, Goa, for premieres, parties and screenings.

Top: Revellers celebrating Ganesh Chaturthi, Mumbai

Bottom: *Kolam* (rice-flower design) decoration on display during Pongal (p20)

December

December is peak tourist season for a reason: the weather is lovely, the humidity lower than usual and the mood festive.

🎎 Feast of St Francis Xavier

On 3 December, thousands of pilgrims descend on Old Goa to honour the shrivelled remains of St Francis Xavier, marking the start of a week-long festival (p120).

🎎 Karthikai Deepam

Celebrating Shiva's restoration of light to the world, this 10-day festival (p336) is especially massive at Tiruvannamalai. Throngs of pilgrims arrive for the full-moon night. Upcoming dates: 10 December 2019, 29 November 2020 and 19 November 2021.

🎎 Christmas Day

Christians celebrate the birth of Jesus Christ on 25 December. The festivities are especially big in Goa and Kerala, with music, elaborate decorations and special masses, while Mumbai's Catholic neighbourhoods become festivals of lights.

☆ Kochi–Muziris Biennale

Kicking off every other December (2020, 2022 etc), the four-month Kochi–Muziris Biennale (p261) pulls Indian and international creatives to historic Fort Cochin for a major contemporary arts celebration.

South India & Kerala: Off the Beaten Track

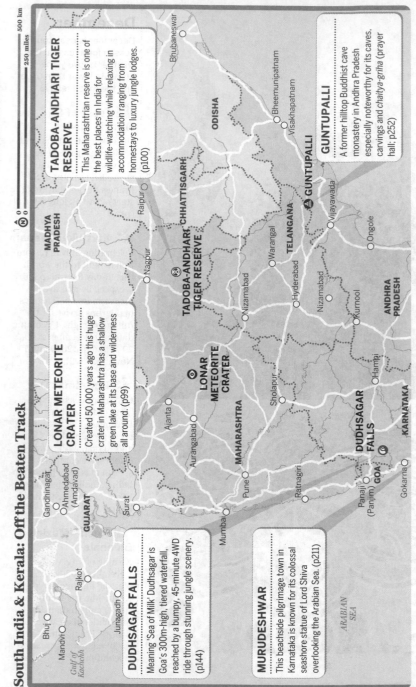

TADOBA-ANDHARI TIGER RESERVE

This Maharashtrian reserve is one of the best places in India for wildlife-watching while relaxing in accommodation ranging from homestays to luxury jungle lodges. (p100)

LONAR METEORITE CRATER

Created 50,000 years ago this huge crater in Maharashtra has a shallow green lake at its base and wilderness all around. (p99)

DUDHSAGAR FALLS

Meaning 'Sea of Milk' Dudhsagar is Goa's 300m-high, tiered waterfall, reached by a bumpy, 45-minute 4WD ride through stunning jungle scenery. (p144)

MURUDESHWAR

This beachside pilgrimage town in Karnataka is known for its colossal seashore statue of Lord Shiva overlooking the Arabian Sea. (p211)

GUNTUPALLI

A former hilltop Buddhist cave monastery in Andhra Pradesh especially noteworthy for its caves, carvings and *chaitya-griha* (prayer hall; p252)

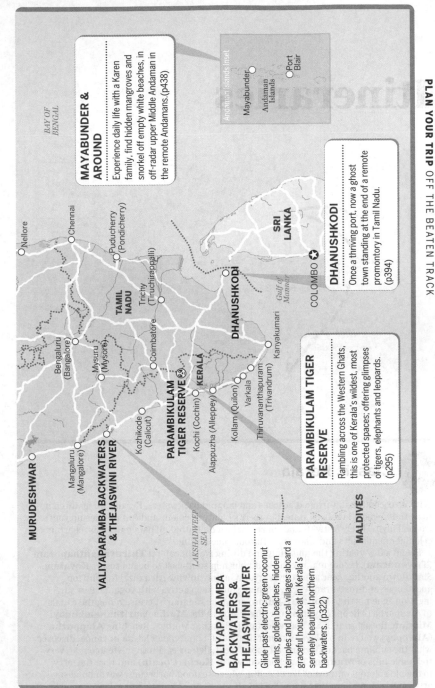

MAYABUNDER & AROUND

Experience daily life with a Karen family, find hidden mangroves and snorkel off empty white beaches, in off-radar upper Middle Andaman in the remote Andamans. (p438)

DHANUSHKODI

Once a thriving port, now a ghost town standing at the end of a remote promontory in Tamil Nadu. (p394)

PARAMBIKULAM TIGER RESERVE

Rambling across the Western Ghats, this is one of Kerala's wildest, most protected spaces; offering glimpses of tigers, elephants and leopards. (p295)

VALIYAPARAMBA BACKWATERS & THEJASWINI RIVER

Glide past electric-green coconut palms, golden beaches, hidden temples and local villages aboard a graceful houseboat in Kerala's serenely beautiful northern backwaters. (p322)

MURUDESHWAR

VALIYAPARAMBA BACKWATERS & THEJASWINI RIVER

PARAMBIKULAM TIGER RESERVE

DHANUSHKODI

Andaman Islands inset

Mayabunder

Andaman Islands

Port Blair

BAY OF BENGAL

Nellore

Chennai

Puducherry (Pondicherry)

Trichy (Tiruchirappalli)

TAMIL NADU

Bengaluru (Bangalore)

Mysuru (Mysore)

Coimbatore

Mangaluru (Mangalore)

Kozhikode (Calicut)

KERALA

Kochi (Cochin)

Alappuzha (Alleppey)

Kollam (Quilon)

Varkala

Thiruvananthapuram (Trivandrum)

Kanyakumari

Gulf of Mannar

COLOMBO

SRI LANKA

LAKSHADWEEP SEA

MALDIVES

Itineraries

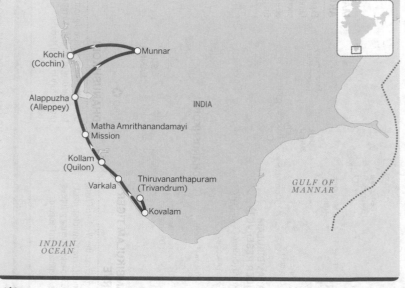

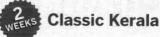 **Classic Kerala**

With its coconut-palm-fringed beaches and languid backwaters, Kerala can justly claim to be India's most laid-back state. But there's plenty of colour and fun to spice up your tropical idyll – lively festivals and snake-boat races, Kathakali dance-dramas, charming colonial-era quarters and a famously flavoursome cuisine.

Spend a day visiting the museums and dining well in capital **Thiruvananthapuram (Trivandrum)**, before making the half-hour hop southeast to beach resort **Kovalam**. Shift down another gear at nearby **Varkala**, a holy town with a dizzying clifftop guesthouse-and-restaurant enclave, where you'll keep active with yoga, SUP or surfing. Continue north to **Kollam (Quilon)** and take the tourist cruise along the canals to Alappuzha (Alleppey) with an overnight stop at the **Matha Amrithanandamayi Mission**, the ashram of Kerala's celebrated 'Hugging Mother'. Reaching **Alappuzha (Alleppey)**, you're in backwaters central; aboard a houseboat, kayak or canoe, discover what the sublime backwaters are all about. Next, detour east into the tea-coated, very trekkable hills of **Munnar**. Travel back down to **Kochi (Cochin)** and take the ferry to the old colonial outpost of Fort Cochin, where seafood barbecues, warm homestays, arty cafes, colonial-era mansions, Kathakali shows and the intriguing Jewish quarter at Mattancherry fill a fascinating few days.

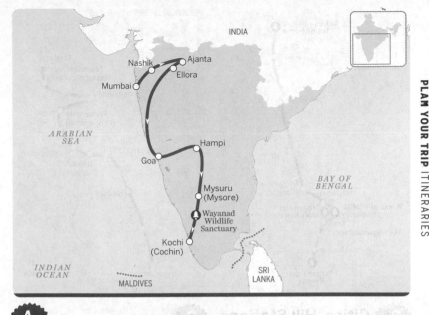

4 WEEKS Goa, Caves & Cities

City lights, historic sites, beachy bliss, jungle adventure and a touch of colonial-era quaintness – this trip will give you a flavour of all that's fantastic about the south.

Begin in cosmopolitan **Mumbai**, Bollywood's beating heart and home to some of the nation's finest spots to shop, eat and drink. Take a sunset stroll along Marine Drive, a curvaceous oceanside promenade dubbed the 'Queen's Necklace' because of its sparkling night lights, finishing with *bhelpuri* (fried rounds of dough with rice, lentils and chutney) on Chowpatty Beach. Catch a ferry to Elephanta Island from Mumbai's historic Gateway of India to explore its stunning rock-cut temples and the triple-faced sculpture of Lord Shiva.

Next, make your way to the dazzling vineyards of Indian wine country around **Nashik**, sipping award-winning creations at Grover Zampa or Sula Vineyards, an outside-the-box Indian experience. Continue northeast to explore the ancient cave art at **Ajanta** and **Ellora**, situated within 150km of each other near Aurangabad. The incredible frescoed Buddhist caves of Ajanta are clustered along a horseshoe-shaped gorge, while the rock-cut caves of Ellora – containing a mix of Hindu, Jain and Buddhist shrines – are set on a 2km escarpment. Next up: the tropical beach haven of **Goa** for some soul-reviving seaside therapy. Wander through lush spice plantations, visit Portuguese-era cathedrals in Old Goa, shop at Anjuna's colourful flea market and take your pick from dozens of fabulous beach spots, before travelling east to the traveller hot spot of **Hampi** in neighbouring Karnataka. Ramble around Hampi's enigmatic boulder-strewn landscape and imagine what life here was like when it was a centre of the mighty Vijayanagar empire. Make the long trip down to **Mysuru (Mysore)** to explore Mysuru Palace, one of India's grandest royal buildings, learn about ashtanga yoga and shop for silk and sandalwood in its colourful markets. From Mysuru it's an exciting bus or taxi ride across the Western Ghats into Kerala and **Wayanad Wildlife Sanctuary**, a pristine forest and jungle reserve and one of the best places in the south to spot wild elephants. Finally, take the hair-raising road down to the coast and make your way south to **Kochi**, Kerala's intriguing colonial-era city, where a blend of Portuguese, Dutch and British history combines with wonderful homestays, creative cafes and a buzzing traveller scene.

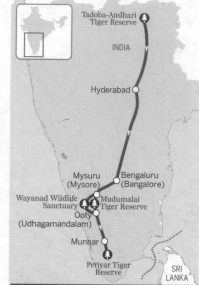

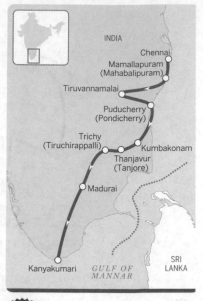

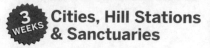

Cities, Hill Stations & Sanctuaries

3 WEEKS

An offbeat trip through the contrasting cities, wildlife reserves and hill stations of the Deccan and Western Ghats.

Start with Maharashtra's little-visited but fantastic **Tadoba-Andhari Tiger Reserve**, offering some of the best prospects for sighting wild tigers, before heading south to the wonderful princely capital **Hyderabad** with its centuries-old Islamic monuments and labyrinthine bazaars. Continue south to the culinary and shopping delights of India's 21st-century IT capital, **Bengaluru (Bangalore)**. On to the royal city of **Mysuru**. Gawp at ubergrand Mysuru Palace and try ashtanga yoga. Head south to Tamil Nadu's **Mudumalai Tiger Reserve** or Kerala's **Wayanad Wildlife Sanctuary**, where you can spot wild elephants and take jungle safaris, then on to the cool hill town of **Ooty (Udhagamandalam)**, one of India's most-loved holiday retreats. Take the toy train to Mettupalayam, near Coimbatore, then cross into Kerala and the tea-covered hills of **Munnar**, with fine hiking and secluded mountain accommodation. Finish with trekking and more chances of a tiger or elephant sighting at **Periyar Tiger Reserve**.

Sacred Tamil Nadu

2 WEEKS

A journey through Tamil Nadu is a trip into South India's spiritual soul.

Delve into the rich history of **Chennai** with a wander around the Government Museum before visiting the ancient Kapaleeshwarar and Parthasarathy temples. Travel south to beachside **Mamallapuram (Mahabalipuram)** and its rock-cut shrines. Move inland to **Tiruvannamalai**, where the Arunachaleshwar Temple is one of India's largest sacred complexes. Trade in temples for flamboyant cathedrals over a few days in the delightful old French seaside colony of **Puducherry (Pondicherry)** before heading back inland to the stunning Unesco World Heritage–listed medieval temples around **Kumbakonam** and **Thanjavur (Tanjore)**. Continue to **Trichy (Tiruchirappalli)**, home to the spectacular Rock Fort Temple and the Sri Ranganathaswamy Temple, probably India's biggest temple. Then head south to **Madurai** and the incredible Meenakshi Amman Temple, widely reckoned the pinnacle of South Indian temple architecture. If you like, wind down at **Kanyakumari**, the southern tip of India, with its temple to the virgin sea goddess Kumari, or continue west into Kerala.

Plan Your Trip
Booking Trains

In India, riding the rails has a romance all of its own. The Indian rail network snakes almost all over the country, trains run almost all the time, and there are seats to suit every size of wallet. However, booking can be a hassle – particularly from outside the country.

Train Reservations

Travellers to India have several options when it comes to making reservations. You can book online or with an Indian travel agent from outside India iving you the re-assurance of knowing that the train you want to travel on won't be booked out on the day you want to travel. Alternatively, you can leave booking till you arrive, and take the chance that a seat might be available.

However you book, you must make a reservation for chair-car, executive-chair-car, sleeper, 1AC, 2AC and 3AC carriages. Book well ahead for overnight journeys or travel during holidays and festivals.

Waiting until the day of travel to book is not recommended, though on short journeys, buying a general 2nd-class ticket for the next available train is a handy, cheap option, though you may have to stand.

Reserved tickets show your seat/berth and carriage number. Carriage numbers are written on the side of the train and a list of names and berths is usually posted on the side of each reserved carriage.

Booking Online

Booking online should be the easiest way to buy tickets – though it still isn't quite as straightforward as you'd expect, and the reservation system is only open from 12.30am to 11.45pm (IST). Bookings open 120 days before departure for long-distance trains, sometimes less for short-haul trips.

Train Classes

Air-Conditioned 1st Class (1AC)
The most expensive class, with two- or four-berth compartments with locking doors and meals included.

Air-Conditioned 2-Tier (2AC)
Two-tier berths arranged in groups of four and two in an open-plan carriage. Bunks convert to seats by day and curtains offer some privacy.

Air-Conditioned 3-Tier (3AC)
Three-tier berths arranged in groups of six in an open-plan carriage with no curtains.

Air-Conditioned Executive Chair (ECC)
Comfortable, reclining chairs and plenty of space; usually on Shatabdi express trains.

Air-Conditioned Chair (CC)
Similar to the executive-chair carriage but with less-fancy seating.

Sleeper Class (SL)
Open-plan carriages with three-tier bunks and no air-con, but the open windows afford great views.

Unreserved/Reserved 2nd Class (II/SS or 2S)
Known as 'general' class; shared, padded bench seats and usually too many people to fill them, but no reservations are necessary.

RAILWAY RAZZLE DAZZLE

You can live like a maharaja on one of India's luxury train tours, with accommodation on board, tours and meals included in the ticket price. As well as the following, consider the Golden Chariot (www.goldenchariottrain.com), a luxurious round-trip journey from Bengaluru (Bangalore); the train was under renovation at time of writing but is due to resume service in 2019.

Palace on Wheels (www.palaceonwheels.net) Eight- to 10-day tours of Rajasthan, departing from Delhi. Trains run on fixed dates from September to April; the fare per person for seven nights in a single/double cabin starts at US$4550/3500. Try to book 10 months in advance.

Royal Rajasthan on Wheels (www.royal-rajasthan-on-wheels.com) Another epic luxury ride from Delhi through Rajasthan. Lavish one-week trips take place from September to April. The fare per single/double cabin for seven nights starts at US$6055/9100, plus taxes.

Deccan Odyssey (www.deccan-odyssey-india.com) Seven-night whirls around Maharashtra, Goa and beyond cost from US$6100/8750 per single/double.

Mahaparinirvan Express (aka Buddhist Circuit Special; www.irctcbuddhisttrain.com) An eight-day trip from Delhi running from September to March and visiting India's key Buddhist sites, plus the Taj Mahal, and Lumbini in Nepal. Rates begin at US$945 per person. Note: you'll need a Nepali visa and a double/multiple-entry Indian visa (not included in the price).

The government-run Indian Railway Catering & Tourism Corp (IRCTC; www.irctc.co.in) takes bookings for regular and luxury trains. Using the site involves a frustrating, complex registration process, and many travellers have reported problems using international cards (though this may change). An IRCTC number may be needed for other booking sites.

An Indian mobile SIM will make life less frustrating when booking online; however, foreigners can verify their IRCTC account from abroad by entering a foreign mobile number, which will trigger an email from IRCTC allowing you to enter a verification code for your mobile (for which there's a small fee) after submitting a registration form. Enquiries should be directed to care@irctc.co.in.

The following are useful for online international bookings, all with user-friendly booking apps.

12Go (www.12go.asia) Handy ticketing agency, though only for India's 1000 most popular routes; accepts international cards.

Cleartrip (www.cleartrip.com) A reliable private agency; accepts international cards but requires an IRCTC registration, linked to your Cleartrip account.

Make My Trip (www.makemytrip.com) Reputable private agency; accepts international credit cards.

Booking on Arrival

If you plan to leave booking trains until you arrive in India, it pays to familiarise yourself with the routes you might travel before you get to the country. Booking in person at train stations is much easier if you have a train number and know the correct station names to list on the reservation form.

On arrival, pick up a copy of *Trains at a Glance*, a booklet sold at station news stands listing most of India's train routes, or check routes on the Indian Railways website (www.indianrailways.gov.in). See (p528) for more ticket-booking information.

Plan Your Trip

Yoga, Spas & Spiritual Pursuits

Birthplace of at least three religions, India offers a profound spiritual journey for those so inclined. Even sceptical travellers can enjoy spas, ayurvedic centres and yoga schools.

Ayurveda

Ayurveda – ancient Indian herbal medicine – aims to restore balance in the body.

Goa

Shanti Ayurvedic Massage Centre, Mandrem (p146)

Palm Trees Ayurvedic Heritage, Patnem (p161)

Karnataka

SwaSwara, Gokarna (p212) Therapies and artistic pursuits.

Arya Ayurvedic Panchakarma Centre, Gokarna (p212) Beachside ayurveda.

Ayurvedagram, Bengaluru (Bangalore; p177) In a fine garden setting.

Indus Valley Ayurvedic Centre, Mysuru (Mysore; p192) Therapies from ancient scriptures.

Swaasthya Ayurveda Retreat Village, Kodagu (Coorg; p202) Retreats and therapies.

Kerala

Ayurdara, Kochi (Cochin; p299) Waterside treatments of one to three weeks.

Neeleshwar Hermitage, Bekal (p323) Five-star ayurvedic beachfront hideaway.

Dr Franklin's Panchakarma Institute, Chowara (p270) South of Kovalam.

An Introduction

Ashrams

India has hundreds of ashrams – places of communal living established around the philosophies of a guru (spiritual guide or teacher).

Ayurveda

Ayurveda is the ancient science of Indian herbal medicine and holistic healing, based on natural plant extracts, massage and therapies for body and mind.

Meditation

Many centres in Buddhist areas offer training in *vipassana* (mindfulness meditation) and Buddhist philosophy; many require vows of silence and abstinence from tobacco, alcohol and sex.

Spa Treatments

South India's spas offer an enticing mix of international therapies and local ayurveda-based techniques.

Yoga

Yoga's roots lie firmly in India; you'll find hundreds of schools to suit all levels.

Harivihar, Kozhikode (Calicut; p315) At a 19th-century royal residence.

AyurSoul, Varkala (p273) Treatments, packages and accommodation.

Mumbai

Yogacara (p55) Ayurveda and massage.

Tamil Nadu

Sita, Puducherry (Pondicherry; p366) Ayurveda and yoga.

Yoga

You can practise yoga everywhere, from beach resorts and mountain retreats to serious-study schools.

Andaman Islands

Jalakara, Havelock Island (Swaraj Dweep; p429) Poolside yoga and massage at an exclusive boutique hotel.

Goa

Bamboo Yoga Retreat, Patnem (p161) Beachside yoga.

Himalaya Yoga Valley, Mandrem (p146) Popular teacher training.

Himalayan Iyengar Yoga Centre, Arambol (Harmal; p147) Reputable courses.

Swan Yoga Retreat, Assagao (p141) Retreat in a soothing jungle location.

Anand Yoga Village, Palolem (p155) Drop-in classes plus teacher training.

Karnataka

Mysuru is the birthplace of ashtanga yoga; there are centres across Karnataka.

IndeaYoga, Mysuru (p194) Hatha and ashtanga.

Namaste Yoga Farm, Gokarna (p212) Yoga in a leafy setting.

Yoga Bharata, Mysuru (p194) Ashtanga and hatha.

Soukya, Bengaluru (p177) Yoga and ayurveda on an organic farm.

Shankar Prasad, Gokarna (p211) In a century-old home.

Kerala

Kovalam, Varkala and Fort Cochin are especially popular for yoga, with lots of drop-in classes. Most hotels and guesthouses offer yoga and ayurveda.

Sivananda Yoga Vedanta Dhanwantari Ashram (p266) Respected hatha courses, at Neyyar Dam near Thiruvananthapuram (Trivandrum).

Soul & Surf, Varkala (p273) Rooftop yoga, retreats and meditation, plus surfing.

Secret Beach Yoga Homestay, Kattoor (p283) Personalised yoga and *kalarippayat* (a martial art).

Maharashtra

Kaivalyadhama Yoga Institute & Research Center, Lonavla (p107) Yogic healing.

Mumbai

Yoga Institute (p55) Daily and longer-term programmes.

Yogacara (p55) Iyengar and hatha.

Tamil Nadu

International Centre for Yoga Education & Research, Puducherry (p367) Introductory courses and advanced training.

Krishnamacharya Yoga Mandiram, Chennai (p341) Yoga courses, therapy and training.

Sivananda Vedanta Yoga Centre, Madurai (p391) Drop-in yoga and rigorous courses.

Isha Yoga Center, Poondi (p404) Established courses near Coimbatore.

Meditation

Whether for introduction or advanced study, there are South India–wide courses and retreats.

Maharashtra

Vipassana International Academy, Igatpuri (p88) Renowned 10-day *vipassana* courses.

Mumbai

Global Vipassana Pagoda, Gorai Island (p51) *Vipassana* courses (10 days).

PIKOSO.KZ / SHUTTERSTOCK ©

DMITRY RUKHLENKO / SHUTTERSTOCK ©

Top: Meditating
in Hampi (p213),
Karnataka

Bottom: Beach yoga in
Kerala (p259)

Telangana & Andhra Pradesh

Numerous Burmese-style *vipassana* courses.

Dhamma Nagajjuna, Nagarjunakonda (p251)

Vipassana International Meditation Centre, Hyderabad (p236)

Ashrams

Many ashrams (places of striving) are headed by charismatic gurus. Some tread a fine line between spiritual community and personality cult. Many gurus have amassed fortunes collected from devotees; others have been accused of sexually exploiting followers. Always check the reputation of any ashram you're considering joining.

Most ashrams offer philosophy, yoga and/or meditation courses. Visitors are usually required to follow strict rules, and a donation to cover your expenses is appropriate.

Kerala

Matha Amrithanandamayi Mission, Amrithapuri (p278) Famed for its female guru Amma, 'The Hugging Mother'.

Maharashtra

Osho International Meditation Resort, Pune (p109) Follows the sometimes controversial teachings of Osho.

Sevagram Ashram, Sevagram (p101) Founded by Gandhi.

Tamil Nadu

Sri Aurobindo Ashram, Puducherry (p364) Founded by Sri Aurobindo.

Sri Ramana Ashram, Tiruvannamalai (p362) Established by Sri Ramana Maharshi.

Spa Treatments

From solo practitioners to opulent retreats, South India is full of spas. Be wary of dodgy one-on-one massages by private (often unqualified) operators; seek recommendations locally and trust your instincts.

Andaman Islands

Barefoot at Havelock, Havelock Island (p429) Ayurvedic and Western-style treatments.

Goa

All five-star hotels and many midrange resorts in Goa have professional spa services.

Karnataka

Emerge Spa, Mysuru (p189) Pampering ayurvedic treatments.

Meraki, Bengaluru (p177) Professional spa.

Kerala

Taj Bekal Resort & Spa, Bekal (p323) Secluded luxury spa.

Jiva Spa, Kovalam (p202) Treatments, yoga and meditation at luxe Taj Group resort.

Niraamaya Retreats Surya Samudra, Pulinkudi (p270) Top-end ayurvedic spa near Kovalam.

Mumbai

Palms Spa (p55) Renowned Colaba spa.

Tamil Nadu

Hyatt Regency, Chennai (p344) Glitzy hotel spa.

Palais de Mahé, Puducherry (p370) Massage and ayurveda in a colonial-era mansion.

Plan Your Trip
Volunteering

For all India's beauty, rich culture and history, poverty and hardship are unavoidable facts of life. Many travellers feel motivated to help, and charities and aid organisations across the country welcome committed volunteers.

Aid Programs in South India

India faces considerable challenges and there are numerous opportunities for volunteers in the south. It may be possible to find a placement after you arrive, but charities and nongovernment organisations (NGOs) almost always prefer volunteers who have applied in advance and been approved for the kind of work involved (which may require specific visas, background checks or vaccinations). **Responsible Volunteering** (www.responsible volunteering.co.uk) is a useful resource.

As well as international organisations, local charities and NGOs have opportunities, though it can be difficult to assess the work that these organisations are doing. For listings of local agencies, check **NGOs India** (www.ngosindia.com) or contact the Delhi-based **Concern India Foundation** (☎011-26210998; www.concernindia foundation.org).

Note that Lonely Planet does not endorse any organisation that we do not work with directly, so it is essential that you do your own thorough research to assess the standards and suitability of a project before agreeing to volunteer with an organisation.

Community

Many community volunteer projects work to provide health care and education to villages.

How to Volunteer

Choosing an Organisation

Consider how your skills will benefit the people you are trying to help, and choose an organisation that can specifically benefit from your abilities. Short-term volunteer opportunities that do not require any specific skills are suspect.

Time Required

Think realistically about how much time you can devote to a project. You're more likely to be of help if you commit for at least a month; experts recommend at least a three-month commitment.

Money

Giving your time for free is only part of the story; most organisations expect volunteers to cover their own accommodation, food and transport.

Working Nine to Five

Make sure you understand what you are signing up for; many organisations expect volunteers to work full time, five days a week.

Transparency

Ensure that the organisation you choose is reputable and transparent about how it spends its money. Where possible, get feedback from former volunteers.

Research

Read up, plan your time and contact your chosen organisation in advance.

Karnataka

Kishkinda Trust, Hampi (p220) Volunteers assist with sustainable community development.

Mumbai

Slum Aid (☑in UK +44 0790 896 7375; www.slum aid.org) Works in Mumbai slums to improve lives; placements from two weeks to six months.

Working with Women & Children

Note that ethical organisations which provide support for disadvantaged children should require background checks. **Child Safe Movement** (http://thinkchildsafe.org) is a handy resource.

Goa

El Shaddai, Assagao (p139) Placements helping impoverished and homeless children; one-month minimum.

Mango Tree Goa (☑9604654588; www.mango treegoa.org) Opportunities in Mapusa for volunteer nurses and teaching assistants to help impoverished children.

Tamil Nadu

RIDE (p361) Works to empower village women and welcomes volunteers in Kanchipuram.

Environment & Conservation

Andaman Islands

ANET, Wandoor (p425) Sporadic specialised volunteer openings for environment-focused projects.

Reef Watch Marine Conservation, Chidiya Tapu (p426) Marine conservation nonprofit organisation accepting volunteers (one week minimum); contact the team to find a project match for your skills.

Karnataka

Rainforest Retreat, Kodagu (Coorg; p202) Organic farming, sustainable agriculture and waste management at this lush spice-plantation hideaway; openings for volunteers.

Kerala

Kaiya House, Varkala (p273) Ecoconscious guesthouse that organises beach clean-ups.

Maharashtra

Nimbkar Agricultural Research Institute (Nari; ☑9168937964; www.nariphaltan.org; Phaltan) Offers internships in sustainable agriculture lasting two to six months for agriculture, engineering and science graduates in Phaltan.

Tamil Nadu

Keystone Foundation, Kotagiri (p408) Opportunities to help improve environmental conditions, working with indigenous communities (minimum one month).

Working with Animals

From stray dogs to rescued reptiles, opportunities for volunteering with animals in need in South India are plentiful. Some local operations welcome drop-in volunteers to assist with walking, feeding, grooming and playing with animals.

Goa

Goa Animal Welfare Trust, Curchorem (☑0832-2653677, 9763681525; www.gawt.org; Curchorem) GAWT tackles animal cruelty and treats, sterilises and shelters animals; volunteers welcome.

International Animal Rescue, Assagao (p140) Well-established animal-rescue operation with short-term volunteering opportunities.

Mumbai

Welfare of Stray Dogs (☑022-64222838; www. wsdindia.org) Volunteers can work with the animals, manage stores or educate kids in school programs.

Tamil Nadu

Arunachala Animal Sanctuary, Tiruvannamalai (p362) Short- and long-term openings at a 200-animal dog- and cat-rescue operation.

Madras Crocodile Bank, Vadanemmeli (p354) A reptile conservation centre with placements for volunteers (minimum two weeks).

AGENCIES OVERSEAS

Indicorps (www.indicorps.org) Matches volunteers to projects across India, particularly in social development; Ahmedabad-based.

Voluntary Service Overseas (VSO; www.vsointernational.org) British organisation offering long-term professional placements worldwide.

Workaway (www.workaway.info) Connects people with hotels, guesthouses, organic farms, restaurants and more, where they will get free accommodation and food in return for working several days a week.

Plan Your Trip
Travel with Children

Fascinating and thrilling: India can be every bit as exciting for children as it is for their wide-eyed parents. The scents, sights and sounds of the friendly, beachy south will inspire and challenge young enquiring minds, and, with careful preparation and vigilance, a lifetime of vivid memories can be sown.

South India for Kids

In many respects, travel with children in India can be a delight, and warm welcomes are frequent. Locals will thrill at taking photographs beside your bouncing baby, and there's an endless stream of family-friendly activities and sights to keep kids busy. But, while all this is fabulous for outgoing children, it may prove tiring, or even disconcerting, for younger kids and those with more retiring dispositions.

As a parent on the road in India, the key is to stay alert to your children's needs and remain firm in fulfilling them, even if you feel you may offend a well-meaning local by doing so. The attention children will inevitably receive is almost always good-natured; kids are the centre of life in many Indian households (and holidays!), and your own will be treated just the same, but it can be invasive and tiring for kids, and being touched by strangers can bring hygiene issues. If necessary a polite 'no' should do the trick.

Hotels will almost always provide an extra bed or two, and there are plenty of restaurants with familiar continental-style menus (from pancakes to pastas) as well as pan-Indian favourites that can dial down the heat for less adventurous taste buds.

South India's beaches are a major attraction for families, with Goa's sands generally considered the most child-friendly, but kids

Best Regions for Kids

Goa
Palm-fringed, white-sand beaches, inexpensive local food and short travel times make Goa India's most family-friendly state, with apartments, huts, resorts and guesthouses to suit all budgets.

Kerala
Canoe and houseboat adventures, surf beaches, Arabian Sea sunsets, snake-boat races and wildlife-spotting: from the Ghats down to the sparkling coast, Kerala offers family-friendly action and relaxation in equal measure.

Karnataka
Hampi's magical World Heritage–listed ruins bewitch travellers of all ages, there's beach bliss at Gokarna, and who wouldn't get excited about searching for wild elephants and hoping to glimpse a tiger or leopard in Bandipur and Nagarhole National Parks?

can also thrive at the region's spectacular wildlife reserves, glittering megamalls, scenic spice and tea plantations, lively bazaars, hands-on cooking classes, and backwaters trips aboard houseboats, kayaks and canoes.

Children's Highlights

Best Natural Encounters

Elephants Kids will love spotting wild elephants on jeep safaris in Wayanad (p317) and Periyar (p287), Kerala; Bandipur (p199) and Nagarhole (p200), Karnataka; and Mudumalai (p414), Tamil Nadu.

Dolphins, Goa Splash out on a dolphin-spotting boat trip from almost any Goan beach to see them cavorting in the waves.

Tigers, Tadoba-Andhari Tiger Reserve (p100) Look for tigers on outstanding wildlife-sighting jeep safaris in this little-visited Maharashtra reserve.

Underwater creatures, Havelock Island (Swaraj Dweep; p426) Head out snorkelling or, for older kids, scuba diving in glassy, warm teal waters off the Andaman Islands.

Best Beaches

Do take care when swimming off South India's beaches: there can be strong undertows.

Palolem, Goa (p155) Hole up in a palm-thatched seafront hut and watch your kids cavort at Palolem's beautiful beach, featuring kayaking, SUP and Goa's safest waters.

Arambol (Harmal), Goa (p147) Popular with backpackers, long-stayers and families for wide-ranging accommodation, safe swimming, water sports and surfing.

Havelock Island, Andaman Islands (p426) Splash about and snorkel in the shallows at languid Havelock Island, reached by ferry; for older kids, there's fantastical diving.

Gokarna, Karnataka (p209) Low-key family fun on pristine golden sands at Kudle and Om Beaches.

Kovalam (p266) and **Varkala** (p271), **Kerala** Play on honey-coloured beaches at these two developed seaside resorts, but be careful with the currents.

Funnest Forms of Transport

Autorickshaw, anywhere Hurtle at top speed in these snap-happy, child-scale vehicles.

Houseboat, Alappuzha (Alleppey; p279) Hop on a houseboat to luxuriously cruise Kerala's beautiful backwaters, or keep it simple with a kayak or canoe. If you hit town on the second Saturday in August, take the kids to see the spectacular Nehru Trophy Boat Race (p279).

Nilgiri Mountain Railway, Ooty (Udhagamandalam; p529) Roll through the gorgeous Nilgiris on Tamil Nadu's superscenic Unesco-listed 'toy' train.

Hand-pulled rickshaw, Matheran (p106) Kids can roam this monkey-patrolled Maharashtra hill station on horseback or in traditional hand-pulled rickshaws.

Bicycle, Kochi (p300) Take a two-wheel tour around the (relatively) calm, flat historical streets of Fort Cochin.

Planning

For all-round information and advice, check out Lonely Planet's *Travel with Children* and visit the Thorn Tree travel forum at lonelyplanet.com.

Before You Go

➡ Look at climate charts: choose your dates to avoid the extremes of temperature that may put younger children at risk.

➡ Visit your doctor well in advance to discuss vaccinations, health advisories and other heath-related issues involving your children.

Eating

➡ You may have to work hard to find something to satisfy sensitive childhood palates, but if you're travelling in South India's more family-friendly regions, such as Goa, Kerala or the big cities (where there are plenty of familiar continental dishes), you'll find it easier to feed your brood.

➡ Portable snacks such as bananas, samosas, *puri* (puffy dough pockets) and packaged biscuits are easily available.

➡ Adventurous eaters and vegetarian children will delight in paneer (unfermented cheese) dishes, simple dhals (mild lentil curries), creamy kormas, buttered naans (tandoori breads), *parathas* (flaky breads), pilaus (rice dishes), lassis (yoghurt drinks) and Tibetan *momos* (steamed or fried dumplings).

➡ Few children, no matter how culinarily unadventurous, can resist the finger-food fun of a vast South Indian dosa (paper-thin savoury crêpe).

WHAT TO PACK

You can get some of these items in many parts of India, but prices are often at a premium and brands may not be those you recognise.

➡ For babies or toddlers: disposable or washable nappies (diapers), nappy rash cream (calendula cream works well against heat rash too), extra bottles, a good stock of wet wipes, infant formula and canned, bottled or rehydratable food.

➡ A fold-up baby bed or the lightest possible travel cot you can find (some companies make pop-up tent-style beds), as hotel cots may prove precarious.

➡ Don't take a pushchair/stroller–it's impractical to use and pavements are often scarce. A better option is a backpack or baby carrier, so they're lifted up and out of the daunting throng.

➡ A few less-precious toys that won't be mourned if lost or damaged.

➡ A swimming jacket, life jacket or water wings for the sea or pool.

➡ Good sturdy footwear.

➡ Audiobooks or tablets loaded with games, films and music – and headphones!

➡ Child-friendly insect repellent, hats and sun lotion.

Accommodation

➡ South India offers such an array of accommodation – from beach huts to heritage boutiques to five-star fantasies – that you're bound to find something to suit the whole family.

➡ Swish upmarket hotels are almost always child-friendly, but so are many upper midrange hotels, whose staff can usually rustle up extra mattresses. Some places won't mind cramming several children into a regular-sized double room along with their parents; there are often interconnecting rooms for families, too.

➡ The very best five-stars come equipped with children's pools, games rooms, kids' clubs and babysitting services. An occasional night in with a warm bubble bath, room service, macaroni cheese and a film will revive even the most disgruntled young traveller's spirits.

On the Road

➡ Travel in India, be it by taxi, bus, train or air, can be arduous for the whole family. Concepts such as clean public toilets, changing rooms, safe playgrounds etc are rare in much of the country. Public transport is often extremely overcrowded. Plan fun, easy days to follow longer journeys.

➡ Pack plenty of diversions. Tablets stocked with films make invaluable travel companions, as do audiobooks and the good old-fashioned storybooks, cheap toys and games widely available across India.

➡ If you're hiring a car and driver (a sensible, flexible option) and require safety capsules, child restraints or booster seats, you'll need to make this absolutely clear to the hiring company as early as possible. Don't expect to find these items readily available. And finally, never be afraid to tell your driver to *slow down*, stop checking their phone and drive responsibly.

Health

➡ The availability of decent health care varies widely across South India.

➡ Talk to your doctor about where you will be travelling to get advice on vaccinations and what to include in your first-aid kit.

➡ Access to health care is significantly better in traveller-frequented parts of South India, such as Goa or Kerala, where it's almost always easy to track down a doctor at short notice. Most hotels can recommend reliable doctors.

➡ Prescriptions are quickly and cheaply filled over the counter at numerous pharmacies, which often congregate near hospitals.

➡ Diarrhoea can be very serious in young children. Seek medical help if persistent or accompanied by fever; rehydration is essential, so pack rehydration sachets or similar.

➡ Heat rash and skin complaints such as impetigo, insect bites and stings can be treated with a well-equipped first-aid kit.

➡ Keep kids away from stray animals and try to ensure they understand the dangers of rabies; rabies vaccinations are worth considering.

➡ Wash hands frequently or use hand sanitiser to prevent upset stomachs.

Regions at a Glance

South India is a wonderfully diverse patchwork of states. The vernaculars are varied, the customs are distinctive, there's an astonishing (and delectable) range of culinary choices and the topography is spectacularly manifold. A mind-melting mix of state of the art and timeless tradition, the south rewards you with an invigorating, all-out sensory assault, regardless of your chosen destination.

For travellers, South India's remarkable diversity is most often apparent in its extraordinary wealth of architecture, cuisine, wildlife, landscapes, festivals, handicrafts and performing arts. And then there's spirituality – the heart, indeed, of the entire nation – which faithfully beats all the way from the jagged peaks of the snowy Himalaya to the lush, steamy jungles of the deep south.

Mumbai

Architecture
Cuisine
Nightlife

Colonial-Era Relics

The British left behind striking colonial-era architecture in Mumbai, highlighted by the Unesco-listed Chhatrapati Shivaji Maharaj Terminus, the High Court and the University of Mumbai.

Culture & Cuisine

Mumbai's collision of cultures makes it a haven for food lovers. Flavours from all over India vie for taste-bud attention with cuisines imported from the world over. Yum.

Bollywood & Booze

As India's financial powerhouse and home to the world's most prolific film industry, Mumbai parties hard. The subcontinent's wildest bars, hottest clubs and exclusive Bollywood bashes showcase a tipsier, more liberal side of India.

p44

Maharashtra

Caves
Beaches
Wine

Rock-Carved Cave Temples

The Unesco sites of Ajanta and Ellora house the most exquisite collection of cave paintings and rock sculptures A miraculous feats of architecture and engineering.

Sun-Toasted Konkan Sands

Strung out along Maharashtra's Konkan Coast are secluded and beautiful beaches custom-made for romantics, adventurers, loners and philosophers alike, with low-key fishing villages and splendid forts to enliven the mix.

Nashik's Up & Coming Vineyards

Nashik, the *grand cru* of India's blossoming wine industry, proudly flaunts a few world-class drops in the many excellent (and gorgeous!) vineyards sprinkled across the surrounding countryside.

p82

Goa

Beaches
Food
Architecture

Golden Goan Shores

Goa's stunning beachscapes are so beautiful that even the most hardcore, off-the-beaten-track travellers can't resist them. Many are backed by shady palm-tree groves and dotted with vibrant seasonal huts.

Fiery Seafood

Goa has a long tradition of preparing fresh seafood in brilliant ways, often with the ubiquitous coconut and a Portuguese influence. Sometimes it's the random shack on the beach that does it best.

Old-World Portuguese Relics

Mansions in Chandor, houses in Panaji (Panjim), Old Goa's grand religious structures, and little homes and churches scattered across the state are pure eye candy.

p117

Karnataka

Temples
National Parks
Cuisine

Architecturally Diverse Shrines

From the Hoysala beauties at Belur, Halebid and Somnathpur to the electric Virupaksha Temple in Hampi, Karnataka is strewn with temples that overwhelm with their atmosphere and ritual finery.

Biospheres & Bengals

The Nilgiri Biosphere Reserve hosts some of the most pristine forests in India, and there's abundant wildlife to be sighted in beloved national parks such as Bandipur and Nagarhole.

Masalas & Craft Brews

Start off with the delectable Udupi vegetarian thali, then move on to some fiery Mangalorean seafood, and finally wash it all down with fresh ale in beer-town Bengaluru (Bangalore).

p170

Telangana & Andhra Pradesh

Religious Sites
Food
Beaches

Multicultural Sanctums

Grand Islamic architecture graces Hyderabad, Hindus flock to the Venkateshwara Temple at Tirumala and the ancient ruins of once-flourishing Buddhist centres lie sprinkled around.

Hyderabadi Bonanza

Biryani is a local obsession, and the intricate flavours will leave you salivating long after your departure. Meanwhile, Hyderabadi *haleem* (a thick meat, lentil and wheat stew) has been patented so that it can't be served unless it meets strict quality standards.

Holidaying with Locals

Visakhapatnam has a sweeping stretch of sandy coastline, where tourism is geared towards the domestic market.

p228

Kerala

Backwaters
Wildlife
Food

Tranquil Inland Waterways

Kerala's vast lakes, lagoons and canals unravel inland as blissful backwaters. One of India's most relaxing and beautiful experiences is to explore them by boat.

Jungle Explorations

Kerala has a concentration of ethereal inland wildlife reserves where, amid lush mountainscapes, you might spot wild elephants, gaurs, deer, boars, numerous birds and, if you're incredibly lucky, even a tiger.

Coconut-Laced Spice Bounty

Kerala's table is born of a melting pot of influences, history and remarkable geography that has earned it the nickname 'Land of Spices'. Deftly spiced local cuisine is flavoured with coconut and gorgeously presented on banana leaves.

p259

Tamil Nadu

Temples
Hill Stations
Heritage Hotels

Towers & Pavilions

The astounding architecture, rituals and festivals of Tamil Nadu's Hindu temples draw pilgrims from across the country; major temples have soaring *gopurams* (gateway towers), sparkling tanks and intricately carved pillared *mandapas* (pavilions).

Colonial-Era Hilltop Refuges

The refreshing hill stations of the Western Ghats offer cool weather, mountain vistas, leisurely walks and colonial-era guesthouses.

Dignified Digs

Exquisitely restored spots to lay your head include romantic heritage houses in Puducherry's (Pondicherry's) French Quarter, colonial-era bungalows in the hill stations and fantastical Chettiar mansions in the south.

p333

Andaman Islands

Diving & Snorkelling
Beaches
Wildlife

Water & Coral

Apart from terrific snorkelling possibilities, this outstanding diving destination offers easy ocean dips for first-timers as well as more challenging dives for experts.

White Sands & Aqua Seas

Blessed with some of India's most beautiful beaches, the Andamans are a dreamy place to sink your toes into squeaky-soft white sand, splash about in warm teal waters and drink in the hot-pink sunsets.

Local Species

From rainbows of fish to crab-eating macaques, Andaman wild pigs and the fabulous Nicobar pigeon, the islands are home to an extraordinary mix of wildlife, much of it endemic. Turtles famously nest on Kalipur Beach.

p417

On the
Road

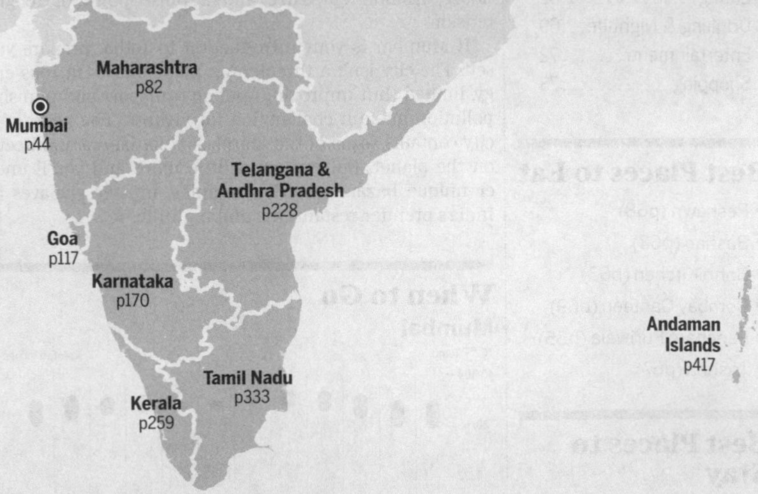

Maharashtra
p82

Mumbai
p44

**Telangana &
Andhra Pradesh**
p228

Goa
p117

Karnataka
p170

**Andaman
Islands**
p417

Tamil Nadu
p333

Kerala
p259

Mumbai (Bombay)

022 / POPULATION 21.1 MILLION

Includes ➡

History 46
Sights 47
Activities 55
Courses 55
Tours. 55
Sleeping. 56
Eating 62
Drinking & Nightlife . . .69
Entertainment. 72
Shopping 73

Best Places to Eat

➡ Peshawri (p68)

➡ Bastian (p68)

➡ Bohri Kitchen (p63)

➡ Bombay Canteen (p69)

➡ Pancham Puriwala (p65)

➡ Trishna (p67)

Best Places to Stay

➡ Taj Mahal Palace, Mumbai (p57)

➡ Abode Bombay (p57)

➡ Residency Hotel (p58)

➡ Sea Shore Hotel (p57)

➡ Juhu Residency (p58)

Why Go?

Mumbai, formerly Bombay, is big. It's full of dreamers and hard-labourers, starlets and gangsters, stray dogs and exotic birds, artists and servants, fisherfolk and *crorepatis* (millionaires), and lots and lots of people. It has India's most prolific film industry, some of Asia's biggest slums (as well as the world's most expensive home) and the largest tropical forest in an urban zone. Mumbai is India's financial powerhouse, fashion epicentre and a pulse point of religious tension.

If Mumbai is your introduction to India, prepare yourself. The city isn't a threatening place but its furious energy, limited (but improving) public transport and punishing pollution make it challenging for visitors. The heart of the city contains some of the grandest colonial-era architecture on the planet, but explore a little more and you'll uncover unique bazaars, hidden temples, hipster enclaves and India's premier restaurants and nightlife.

When to Go
Mumbai

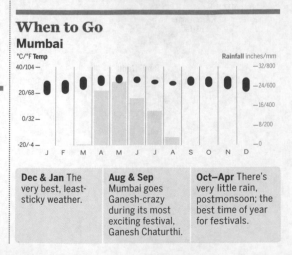

Dec & Jan The very best, least-sticky weather.

Aug & Sep Mumbai goes Ganesh-crazy during its most exciting festival, Ganesh Chaturthi.

Oct–Apr There's very little rain, postmonsoon; the best time of year for festivals.

Mumbai Highlights

❶ Chhatrapati Shivaji Maharaj Terminus (p49) Marvelling at the magnificent Unesco-listed colonial-era architecture, including this monumental train station.

❷ Sassoon Docks (p49) Waging war on your senses at Mumbai's cinematic fishing docks.

❸ Restaurants (p68) Dining like a maharaja at one of India's best restaurants, such as Peshawri.

❹ Iskcon Temple (p51) Feeling the love with the Krishna crowd at this unique temple.

❺ Dharavi Slum (p56) Touring through the self-sufficient world of Asia's largest shanty town.

❻ Taj Mahal Palace (p47) Staying at one of the world's most iconic hotels, or dropping in for a drink at its bar, Mumbai's first.

❼ Dr Bhau Daji Lad Mumbai City Museum (p50) Ogling this museum's gorgeous Renaissance-revival interiors.

❽ Elephanta Island (p54) Beholding the commanding triple-headed Shiva on this Mumbai Harbour island.

❾ Girgaum Chowpatty (p51) Snacking on *bhelpuri* (puffed rice and spices) among playing kids, big balloons and a hot-pink sunset.

History

Koli fisherfolk have inhabited the seven islands that form Mumbai from as far back as the 2nd century BC. Remnants of this culture remain huddled along the city shoreline today. A succession of Hindu dynasties held sway over the islands from the 6th century AD until the Muslim Sultans of Gujarat annexed the area in the 14th century, eventually ceding it to Portugal in 1534. The only memorable contribution the Portuguese made to the area was christening it Bom Baia (Good Bay). They handed control to the English government in 1665, which leased the islands to the East India Company.

Bombay flourished as a trading port. The city's fort was completed in the 1720s, and a century later ambitious land-reclamation projects joined the islands into today's single landmass. The city continued to grow, and in the 19th century the fort walls were dismantled and massive building works transformed the city in grand colonial style. When Bombay became the principal supplier of cotton to Britain during the American Civil War, the population soared and trade boomed as money flooded into the city.

Bombay was a major player in the independence movement, and the Quit India campaign was launched here in 1942 by Mahatma Gandhi. The city became capital of the Bombay presidency after Independence, but in 1960 Maharashtra and Gujarat were divided along linguistic lines – and Bombay became the capital of Maharashtra.

The rise of the pro-Marathi, pro-Hindu regionalist movement in the 1980s, spearheaded by the Shiv Sena (literally 'Shivaji's Army'), shattered the city's multicultural mould when it was accused of actively discriminating against Muslims and non-Maharashtrians. Communalist tensions increased, and the city's cosmopolitan self-image took a battering when 900 people were killed in riots in late 1992 and 1993. The riots were followed by a dozen retaliatory bombings which killed 257 people and damaged the Bombay Stock Exchange.

Shiv Sena's influence saw the names of many streets and public buildings – as well as the city itself – changed from their colonial monikers. In 1996 the city officially became Mumbai (derived from the Hindu goddess Mumba). The airport, Victoria Terminus and Prince of Wales Museum were all renamed after Chhatrapati Shivaji, the great Maratha leader.

MUMBAI IN...

Two Days

Begin at one of Mumbai's architectural masterpieces, the Chhatrapati Shivaji Maharaj Vastu Sangrahalaya museum (p49), before grabbing lunch Gujarati-style at Samrat (p66).

In the afternoon head to Colaba and tour the city's iconic sights, the Gateway of India (p48) and Taj Mahal Palace hotel (p57). That evening, drink cocktails and fine-dine at Miss T (p65) or chow down at Bademiya Seekh Kebab Stall (p62), followed by a nightcap at hip Colaba Social (p71).

The next day, take in the granddaddy of Mumbai's colonial-era giants, Chhatrapati Shivaji Terminus (p49), and **Crawford Market** (Mahatma Jyotiba Phule Mandai; Map p52; cnr DN & Lokmanya Tilak Rds, Fort; ⊙10am-8pm, to noon Sun) and its maze of bazaars, hidden temples and unique street life. Lunch at Revival (p68), then wander the tiny lanes of Khotachiwadi (p51), followed by beach *bhelpuri* (puffed rice tossed with fried rounds of dough, lentils, onions, herbs and chutneys) at Girgaum Chowpatty (p51). Need a drink? Hip nightlife hub Lower Parel beckons with craft beers at Toit Tap Room (p70) followed by dinner at sceney Bombay Canteen (p69) or Koko (p69).

Four Days

Sail to Unesco-listed Elephanta Island (p54), returning for lunch in artsy Kala Ghoda at Burma Burma (p67). In the evening head north for exquisite seafood at Bastian (p68), followed by serious bar action in Bandra.

Spend your last day at Mahalaxmi Dhobi Ghat (p51), **Shree Mahalaxmi Temple** (Map p52; www.mahalakshmi-temple.com; off Bhulabhai Desai Marg; ⊙6am-10pm) and Haji Ali Dargah (p50); or Sanjay Gandhi National Park (p77) for a peaceful forest walk. End with modern Indian fare at Bombay Canteen (p69).

Religious tensions deepened and became intertwined with national religious conflicts and India's relations with Pakistan. A series of bomb attacks on trains killed over 200 in July 2006. Then, in November 2008, a coordinated series of devastating attacks (by Pakistani gunmen) targeted landmark buildings across the city, as the Taj Mahal Palace hotel burned, passengers were gunned down inside the Chhatrapati Shivaji railway station and 10 people were killed inside the Leopold Cafe backpacker haunt.

In late 2012, when the Sena's charismatic founder Bal Thackeray died (500,000 attended his funeral), the Shiv Sena mission begin to falter, and in the 2014 assembly elections, President Modi's Bharatiya Janata Party (BJP) became the largest party in Mumbai.

Mumbaikars are a resilient bunch. Increased security is very much part of everyday life today and the city's status as the engine room of the Indian economy remains unchallenged. However, Mumbai politicians certainly have their work cut out, with the megacity's feeble public transport, gridlocked streets, pollution and housing crisis all in desperate need of attention.

⊙ Sights

Mumbai is an island – originally seven before land reclaiming sewed them together – connected by bridges to the mainland. The city's commercial and cultural centre is at the southern, claw-shaped end of the island known as South Mumbai. The southernmost peninsula is Colaba, traditionally the travellers' nerve centre, with many of the major attractions.

North of Colaba is the busy commercial area known as Fort, where the British fort once stood. This part of the city is bordered on the west by a series of interconnected grassy areas known as maidans (may-*dahns*).

Continuing north you enter 'the suburbs', which contain the airport and many of Mumbai's best restaurants, shops and nightspots. The upmarket districts of Bandra, Juhu and Lower Parel are key areas (the bohemians and hippies that used to claim Bandra have now moved further north to Andheri West and Vesova).

⊙ Colaba

Along the city's southernmost peninsula, Colaba is a bustling district packed with elegant art deco and colonial-era mansions, budget-to-midrange lodgings, bars and res-

TOP FESTIVALS

Mumbai Sanskruti (www.asiaticsociety. org.in; ⊙ Jan) This free, two-day celebration of Hindustani classical music is held on the steps of the gorgeous Asiatic Society Library in the Fort area.

Kala Ghoda Arts Festival (www. kalaghodaassociation.com; ⊙ Feb) Getting bigger and more sophisticated each year, this two-week-long art fest held in Kala Ghoda and the Fort area sees tons of performances and exhibitions.

Elephanta Festival (www.maharashtra tourism.gov.in; Elephanta Island; ⊙ Feb) Unesco-listed Elephanta Island comes to life with dancers, musicians and dramatists over the two-day classical-music and dance festival, usually in February.

Nariyal Poornima (⊙ Aug) This Koli celebration in Colaba marks the start of the fishing season and the retreat of monsoon winds.

Ganesh Chaturthi (www.ganesh chaturthi.com; ⊙ Aug/Sep) Mumbai gets totally swept up by this 10- to 12-day celebration of the elephant-headed Hindu god Ganesh. On the festival's first, third, fifth, seventh and 11th days, families and communities take their Ganesh statues to the seashore at Chowpatty and Juhu beaches and auspiciously submerge them.

Jio Mami Mumbai Film Festival (MFF; www.mumbaifilmfestival.com; ⊙ Oct/ Nov) New films from the subcontinent and beyond are screened at the week-long MFF at cinemas across Mumbai.

taurants, street stalls and a fisherfolk quarter. Colaba Causeway (Shahid Bhagat Singh Marg) dissects the district. If you're here in August, look out for the Koli festival Nariyal Poornima.

★Taj Mahal Palace, Mumbai　LANDMARK
(Map p48; https://taj.tajhotels.com; Apollo Bunder) Mumbai's most famous landmark, this stunning hotel is a fairy-tale blend of Islamic and Renaissance styles, and India's second-most-photographed monument. It was built in 1903 by the Parsi industrialist JN Tata, supposedly after he was refused entry to nearby European hotels on account of

Colaba

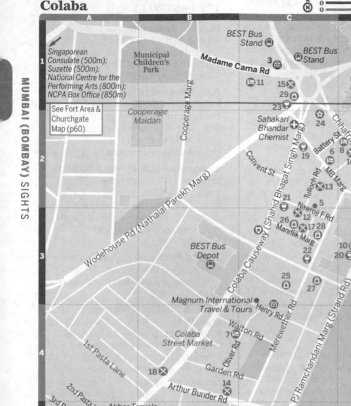

Today the Taj fronts the harbour and Gateway of India, but it was originally designed to face the city (the entrance has been changed).

Gateway of India MONUMENT
(Map p48; Apollo Bunder) This bold basalt arch of colonial triumph faces out to Mumbai Harbour from the tip of Apollo Bunder. Incorporating Islamic styles of 16th-century Gujarat, it was built to commemorate the 1911 royal visit of King George V, but wasn't completed until 1924. Ironically, the British builders of the gateway used it just 24 years later to parade the last British regiment as India marched towards independence.

being 'a native'. Dozens were killed inside the hotel when it was targeted during the 2008 terrorist attacks, and images of its burning facade were beamed worldwide. The fully restored hotel reopened on Independence Day 2010.

Much more than an iconic building, the Taj's history is intrinsically linked with the nation: it was the first hotel in India to employ women, the first to have electricity (and fans), and it also housed freedom fighters (for no charge) during the struggle for independence.

Coraba

◎ **Top Sights**
1 Taj Mahal Palace, Mumbai.....................D3

◎ **Sights**
2 Gateway of India................................D3
3 National Gallery of Modern Art C1

◎ **Activities, Courses & Tours**
4 Palms Spa D2
5 Reality Tours & Travel..........................C2

◎ **Sleeping**
6 Abode Bombay.................................C2
7 Backpacker Panda...........................B4
8 Hotel Suba Palace............................D2
9 Sea Shore Hotel C5
10 Taj Mahal Palace, Mumbai..................D3
11 YWCA...C1

◎ **Eating**
12 Bademiya Restaurant.........................C3
13 Bademiya Seekh Kebab Stall..............C2
14 Basilico...B4
15 Bombay Vintage.................................C1
16 Indigo Delicatessen............................D2
17 Miss T...C3
Table ....(see 8)

18 Theobroma..B4

◎ **Drinking & Nightlife**
19 Cafe Mondegar....................................C2
20 Harbour Bar...D3
21 Leopold Café C2
22 Social..C3
23 Woodside Inn.......................................C1

◎ **Entertainment**
24 Regal Cinema C2

◎ **Shopping**
25 Clove...C3
26 Cottonworld...C3
27 Good Earth..C3
28 Nappa Dori...C3
29 Phillips...C1

◎ **Information**
30 MTDC Booth..D2

◎ **Transport**
Launches to Elephanta Island......(see 31)
31 Launches to Mandwa............................D3
Maldar Catamarans....................(see 30)
PNP..(see 30)

★**Sassoon Docks** WATERFRONT
(Sassoon Dock Rd; ⊙24hr) No sense is left unaffected at Mumbai's incredibly atmospheric fishing docks, dating to 1875, the oldest and largest wholesale fish market in Mumbai. A scene of intense and pungent activity begins around 5am, when colourfully clad Koli fisherfolk sort the catch unloaded from fishing trawlers at the quay, and carries on throughout the morning.

◎ Fort Area & Churchgate

Lined up in a row and vying for your attention with aristocratic pomp, many of Mumbai's majestic Victorian buildings pose on the edge of Oval Maidan. This land, and the Cross and Azad Maidans immediately to the north, were all on the oceanfront in those days, and this series of grandiose structures faced west directly to the Arabian Sea.

Kala Ghoda (Black Horse) is a hip, atmospheric subneighbourhood of Fort just north of Colaba (see the neighbourhood's new Spirit of Kala Ghoda monument, erected in 2017, which might strike some as notable for being a riderless horse). It contains many of Mumbai's museums, galleries and design boutiques alongside a wealth of colonial-era buildings and some of the city's best restaurants and cafes.

★**Chhatrapati Shivaji**
Maharaj Terminus HISTORIC BUILDING
(Victoria Terminus (VT); Map p60; Chhatrapati Shivaji Terminus Area, Fort) Imposing, exuberant and overflowing with people, this monumental train station is the city's most extravagant Gothic building and an aphorism of colonial-era India. It's a meringue of Victorian, Hindu and Islamic styles whipped into an imposing Dalí-esque structure of buttresses, domes, turrets, spires and stained glass. It's also known as CSMT.

★**Chhatrapati Shivaji**
Maharaj Vastu Sangrahalaya MUSEUM
(Prince of Wales Museum; Map p60; www.csmvs. in; 159-161 MG Rd, Fort; Indian/foreigner ₹83/500, mobile/camera ₹50/100; ⊙10.15am-6pm) Mumbai's biggest and best museum displays a mix of India-wide exhibits. The domed behemoth, an intriguing hodgepodge of Islamic, Hindu and British architecture, is a flamboyant Indo-Saracenic design by George Wittet (who also designed the Gateway of India). Its vast collection includes impressive Hindu and Buddhist sculpture, terracotta figurines from the Indus Valley, Indian miniature paintings and some particularly vicious-looking weaponry.

Keneseth Eliyahoo Synagogue
SYNAGOGUE

(Map p60; Dr VB Gandhi Marg, Kala Ghoda; ☉11am-6pm Sun-Thu) Built in 1884, and tenderly maintained by the city's dwindling Jewish community, this white and indigo-trimmed synagogue emerged from under years of scaffolding in 2019, restored to its original 19th-century color scheme. It now dazzles inside with neoclassical splendour, awash in Burmese teak furnishings and Victorian stained glass. Staff are friendly, but it's protected by very heavy security – bring a copy of your passport to gain entry.

Marine Dr
WATERFRONT

(Map p60; Netaji Subhashchandra Bose Rd; ☉24hr) Built on reclaimed land in 1920 and a part of Mumbai's recently crowned Victorian Gothic and Art Deco Ensembles Unesco World Heritage Site, Marine Dr arcs along the shore of the Arabian Sea from Nariman Point past Girgaum Chowpatty and continues to the foot of Malabar Hill. Lined with flaking art deco apartments, it's one of Mumbai's most popular promenades and sunset-watching spots. Its twinkling nighttime lights have earned it the nickname 'the Queen's Necklace'.

University of Mumbai
HISTORIC BUILDING

(Bombay University; Map p60; www.mu.ac.in; Bhaurao Patil Marg) Looking like a 15th-century French-Gothic mansion plopped incongruously among Mumbai's palm trees, this structure was designed by Gilbert Scott of London's St Pancras station fame. There's an exquisite University Library and Convocation Hall, as well as the 84m-high Rajabai Clock Tower, decorated with detailed carvings. Since the 2008 terror attacks there has been no public access to the grounds, though pressure is beginning to be put on the vice chancellor to open the campus (check ahead).

Jehangir Art Gallery
GALLERY

(Map p60; www.jehangirartgallery.com; 161B MG Rd, Kala Ghoda; ☉11am-7pm) FREE Renovated in recent years, this excellent gallery hosts exhibitions across several galleries of all types of visual arts by Mumbaikar, national and international artists.

National Gallery of Modern Art
MUSEUM

(NGMA; Map p48; www.ngmaindia.gov.in; MG Rd; Indian/foreigner ₹20/500; ☉11am-6pm Tue-Sun) Well-curated shows of Indian and international artists in a bright and spacious five-floor exhibition space.

DAG
GALLERY

(Delhi Art Gallery; Map p60; www.discover dag.com; 58 Dr VB Gandhi Marg, Kala Ghoda; ☉10.30am-7pm Mon-Sat) FREE This top gallery is spread over three floors of a beautifully restored cream-coloured colonial-era structure. Its quarterly-changing exhibitions are curated from the largest collection of 20th-century modern Indian art in the world and its wares are showcased in museums throughout India as well as additional galleries in New Delhi and New York.

St Thomas' Cathedral
CHURCH

(Map p60; 3 Veer Nariman Rd, Churchgate; ☉7am-6pm) This charming cathedral, begun in 1672 and finished in 1718, is the oldest British-era building standing in Mumbai and the city's first Anglican church: it was once the eastern gateway of the East India Company's fort (the 'Churchgate' itself). The cathedral is a marriage of Byzantine and colonial-era architecture, and its airy interior is full of grandiose colonial memorials.

⊙ Kalbadevi to Mahalaxmi

★ Dr Bhau Daji Lad Mumbai City Museum
MUSEUM

(Map p52; www.bdlmuseum.org; Dr Babasaheb Ambedkar Rd; Indian/foreigner ₹10/100, audio guides ₹30/50; ☉10am-6pm Thu-Tue) This gorgeous museum, built in Renaissance revival style in 1872 as the Victoria & Albert Museum, contains 3500-plus objects centring on Mumbai's history – photography, maps, textiles, books, manuscripts, *bidriware* (Bidar's metalwork), lacquerware, weaponry and exquisite pottery. The landmark building was renovated in 2008, with its Minton-tile floors, gilded ceiling mouldings, ornate columns, chandeliers and staircases all gloriously restored.

Haji Ali Dargah
MOSQUE

(Map p52; www.hajialidargah.in; off V Desai Chowk; ☉5.30am-10pm) FREE Floating like a sacred mirage off the coast, this Indo-Islamic shrine located on an offshore inlet is a striking sight. Built in the 19th century, it contains the tomb of the Muslim saint Pir Haji Ali Shah Bukhari. Legend has it that Haji Ali died while on a pilgrimage to Mecca and his casket miraculously floated back to this spot.

It's only possible to visit the shrine at low tide, via a long causeway (check tide times locally). Thousands of pilgrims, especially on Thursday and Friday (when there may be *qawwali;* devotional singing), cross it daily, many donating to beggars who line the

WORTH A TRIP

KHOTACHIWADI

This storied *wadi* (hamlet), **Khotachiwadi** (Map p52) is a heritage village nearly 180 years old, is clinging onto Mumbai life as it was before high-rises. A Christian enclave of elegant two-storey Portuguese-style wooden mansions (of which only 23 out of 65 have survived), it's 500m northeast of Girgaum Chowpatty, lying amid Mumbai's predominantly Hindu and Muslim neighbourhoods. The winding lanes allow a wonderful glimpse into a quiet(ish) life away from noisier Mumbai.

It's not large, but you can spend a while wandering the alleyways and admiring the old homes and, around Christmas, their decorations. You can also plan an East Indian feast in advance or sleep at the home of celebrated fashion designer, Khotachiwadi activist and amateur chef James Ferreira (www.jamesferreira.co.in – find his rooms on Airbnb).

To find Khotachiwadi, head for **St Teresa's Church** (Map p52; cnr Jagannath Shankarsheth (JSS) Marg & Rajarammohan Roy (RR) Marg), on the corner of Jagannath Shankarsheth Marg (JSS Marg) and Rajarammohan Roy Marg (RR Rd/Charni Rd), then head directly opposite the church on JSS Marg and duck down the third lane on your left (look for the faded Khotachiwadi wall stencil map that says 'Khotachiwadi Imaginaries').

way. Sadly, parts of the shrine are in a poor state, damaged by storms and the saline air, though a renovation plan exists. It's visited by people of all faiths.

Mahalaxmi Dhobi Ghat   GHAT
(Map p52; Bapurao Jagtap Marg, Mahalaxmi; ⊙4.30am-dusk) This 140-year-old dhobi ghat (place where clothes are washed) is Mumbai's biggest human-powered washing machine: every day hundreds of people beat the dirt out of thousands of kilograms of soiled Mumbai clothes and linen in 1026 open-air troughs. The best view is from the bridge across the railway tracks near Mahalaxmi train station.

Girgaum Chowpatty   BEACH
(Map p52) This city beach is a favourite evening spot for courting couples, families, political rallies and anyone out to enjoy what passes for fresh air. Evening *bhelpuri* (puffed rice tossed with fried rounds of dough, lentils, onions, herbs and chutneys) at the throng of stalls at the beach's southern end is an essential part of the Mumbai experience. Forget about taking a dip: the water's toxic. On the 10th day of the Ganesh Chaturthi festival (p47) millions flock here to submerge huge Ganesh statues: it's joyful mayhem.

⊙ Western Suburbs

★**Iskcon Temple**   HINDU TEMPLE
(Map p64; www.iskconmumbai.com; Hare Krishna Land, Sri Mukteshwar Devalaya Rd, Juhu; ⊙4.30am-1pm & 4-9pm) Iskcon Juhu plays a key part in the Hare Krishna story, as founder AC Bhaktivedanta Swami Prabhupada

spent extended periods here (you can visit his modest living quarters-cum-museum in the adjacent building; 10.30am to 12.30pm and 5.30pm to 8.30pm). The temple compound comes alive during prayer time as the faithful whip themselves into a devotional frenzy of joy, with *kirtan* dancing accompanied by crashing hand symbols and drumbeats.

Juhu Beach   BEACH
(Map p64; Juhu Tara Rd, Juhu) This sprawling suburban beach draws legions of Indian families and courting couples frolicking in the Arabian Sea for 6km all the way to Versova. As far as beaches go, it's no sun-toasted Caribbean dream, but it's a fun place to have a drink or try some Mumbai street food from the nearby stalls. It's particularly vibrant during Ganesh Chaturthi (p47).

Gilbert Hill   MOUNTAIN
(Map p64; Sagar City, Andheri West; ⊙24hr) Smack dab among the residential apartment blocks of Andheri West sits this 61m-tall black basalt mountain that resembles a chocolate molten cake (unsurprisingly, as it was formed as result of Mesozoic era molten lava squeeze – it's 66 million years old. Climb the steep rock-carved staircase for panoramic views and the two Hindu temples set around a garden.

⊙ Gorai Island

Global Vipassana Pagoda   BUDDHIST TEMPLE
(☏022-62427500; www.globalpagoda.org; Global Pagoda Rd, Borivali West; ⊙9am-7pm, meditation classes 9.30am-6.30pm) Rising up like a

MUMBAI (BOMBAY)

Kalbadevi to Mahalaxmi

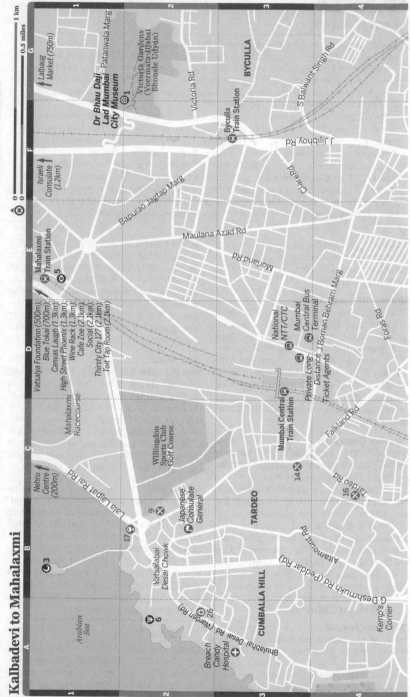

Arabian Sea

Nehru Centre (200m)

Vatsalya Foundation (500m); Blue Tokai (700m); Canvas Laugh (1.3km); High Street Phoenix (1.3km); Wine Rack (1.3km); Cafe Zoe (2.1km); Social (2.1km); Thirsty City 127 (2.1km); Toit Tap Room (2.2km)

Israeli Consulate (1.2km)

↑ Lalbaug Market (750m)

BYCULLA

Dr Bhau Daji Lad Mumbai City Museum

Victoria Gardens (Veermata Jijabai Bhonsle Udyan)

Patanwala Marg

Victoria Rd

Byculla Train Station

Jijibhoy Rd

S Balwant Singh Rd

Clare Rd

Bapurao Jagtap Marg

Maulana Azad Rd

Morland Rd

Mahalaxmi Train Station

Mahalaxmi Racecourse

Foras Rd

National NTT/CTC

Mumbai Central Bus Terminal

J Bonian Behram Marg

Private Long-Distance Ticket Agents

Mumbai Central Train Station

Falkland Rd

Willingdon Sports Club Golf Course

Japanese Consulate General

TARDEO

Lala Lajpat Rai Rd

Tardeo Rd

Vatsalabai Desai Chowk

CUMBALLA HILL

Deshmukh Rd (Peddar Rd)

Altamount Rd

G

Kemp's Corner

Breach Candy Hospital

Bhulabhai Desai Rd (Warden Rd)

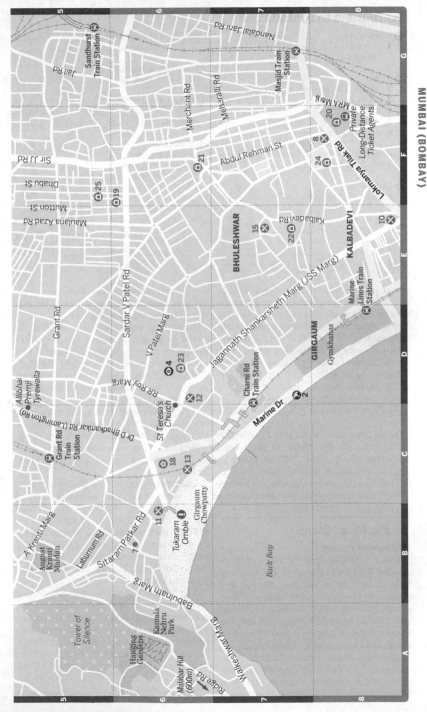

Kalbadevi to Mahalaxmi

◎ **Top Sights**
1 Dr Bhau Daji Lad Mumbai City
   Museum...................................G2

◎ **Sights**
2 Girgaum Chowpatty............................D7
3 Haji Ali Dargah...B1
4 Khotachiwadi...D6
5 Mahalaxmi Dhobi Ghat..........................E1
6 Shree Mahalaxmi Temple.....................A2

⊕ **Activities, Courses & Tours**
7 Bharatiya Vidya Bhavan........................B6

⊗ **Eating**
8 Badshah Cold Drinks............................ F8
9 Cafe Noorani...B2
10 Kyani & Co...E8
11 New Kulfi Centre....................................B6
12 Panshikar...D6
13 Revival...C6
14 Sardar..C3

15 Shree Thakkar Bhojanalay.....................E7
16 Swati Snacks...C4

◎ **Drinking & Nightlife**
17 Haji Ali Juice Centre B2

◎ **Entertainment**
   Quarter...(see 18)
18 Royal Opera House................................. C6

◎ **Shopping**
19 Chor Bazaar..F6
20 Crawford Market.....................................F8
21 Haji Mohammad Bashir Oil
   Shop..F6
22 M/S KN Ajani..E7
23 No Borders..D6
24 No-Mad Fabric Shop F8
   Play Clan..(see 18)
25 Poster Stuff..F5
26 Shrujan..A2

mirage from polluted Gorai Creek is this breathtaking, golden 96m-high stupa modelled on Myanmar's Shwedagon Pagoda. Its dome, which houses relics of Buddha, was built entirely without supports using an ancient technique of interlocking stones, and the meditation hall beneath it seats 8000.

There's an art gallery dedicated to the life of the Buddha and his teaching. Twenty-minute meditation classes are held daily; an on-site meditation centre also offers 10-day courses.

To get here, take a train from Churchgate to Borivali (exit the station at the 'West' side), then take bus 294 (₹10), an autorickshaw (₹60 to ₹65) or an Uber (₹420 or so) to the ferry landing, where Esselworld ferries (return ₹50) depart every 30 minutes. The last ferry to the pagoda is at 5.30pm.

◎ Elephanta Island

★**Elephanta Island**   HINDU TEMPLE
(Gharapuri; Indian/foreigner ₹40/600; ☺caves 9am-5pm Tue-Sun) Northeast of the Gateway of India in Mumbai Harbour, the rock-cut temples on Gharapuri, better known as Elephanta Island, are a Unesco World Heritage Site. Created between AD 450 and 750, the labyrinth of cave temples represent some of India's most impressive temple carving.

The main Shiva-dedicated temple is an intriguing latticework of courtyards, halls, pillars and shrines; its magnum opus is a 6m-tall statue of Sadhashiva, depicting a three-faced Shiva as the destroyer, creator and preserver of the universe, his eyes closed in eternal contemplation.

It was the Portuguese who dubbed the island Elephanta because of a large stone elephant near the shore (this collapsed in 1814 and was moved by the British to Mumbai's Jijamata Udyan). There's a small museum on-site, with informative pictorial panels on the origin of the caves.

Pushy, expensive guides are available – but you don't really need one as Pramod Chandra's *A Guide to the Elephanta Caves,* widely for sale, is more than sufficient.

The Elephanta Festival (p47) is held here in February.

Launches (Map p48; Apollo Bunder, Colaba; economy/deluxe ₹145/200) head to Gharapuri from the Gateway of India every half hour from 9am to 3.30pm. Buy tickets from the **MTDC booth** (Maharashtra Tourism Development Corporation; Map p48; ☎ 022-22841877; www.maharashtratourism.gov.in; ☺9am-3pm Tue-Sun) at Apollo Bunder. The voyage takes about an hour.

The ferries dock at the end of a concrete pier, from where you can walk or take the miniature train (₹10) to the stairway leading up to the caves (it's lined with souvenir stalls and patrolled by pesky monkeys). A passenger tax (₹5) is also charged. Wear good shoes (those opting to walk are looking at 1.2km). *Doli*-carriers charge ₹1200 to carry up the aged or disabled.

⚡ Activities

Mumbai has surprisingly good butterfly- and birdwatching opportunities. Sanjay Gandhi National Park (p77) is popular for woodland birds, while the mangroves of Godrej (13km east of Bandra) are rich in waders. The **Bombay Natural History Society** (BNHS; Map p60; ⌨ 022-22821811; www.bnhs.org; Hornbill House, Colaba Causeway, Fort; ⊙ 9.30am-5.30pm Mon-Fri) runs excellent trips every weekend.

Outbound Adventure   OUTDOORS

(⌨ 9820195115;   www.outboundadventure.com) Runs one-day rafting trips on the Ulhas River from July to early September (₹2300 per person). After a good rain, rapids can get up to Grade III+, though usually the rafting is calmer. Also organises guided nature walks, birdwatching, camping (from ₹2000 per person per day) and canoeing trips in the Western Ghats.

Antara Day Spa   SPA

(⌨ 022-66117777;   https://theclubmumbai.com/room/antara-spa; 197 DN Nagar, Andheri West; 1hr massage from ₹2500; ⊙ 10am-7.30pm) Midrange day spa on private club grounds with skilled therapists offering a range of therapies and treatments, including Swedish, Thai and hot-stone massages. Nonguests must pay a ₹100/120 (week/weekend) entry fee. Weekdays between 10.30am and 4pm nets a 30% discount on massages.

Palms Spa   SPA

(Map p48;   ⌨ 022-66349898;   www.thepalms spaindia.com; ground fl, Dhanraj Mahal, Chhatrapati Shivaji Marg, Colaba; 1hr massage from ₹3400; ⊙ 10am-10pm) Indulge in a rub, scrub or tub at this long-standing Colaba spa. The exfoliating lemongrass and green-tea scrub is ₹2500.

Vatsalya Foundation   VOLUNTEERING

(⌨ 022-24962115;   www.thevatsalyafoundation. org; Anand Niketan, King George V Memorial, off Dr E Moses Rd, Mahalaxmi) Works with Mumbai's street children; there are long- and short-term opportunities in teaching English, computer skills and sports.

Lok Seva Sangam   VOLUNTEERING

(⌨ 022-24070718; http://loksevasangam.org; D/1 Everard Nagar Eastern Express Hwy, Sion) Lok Seva Sangam has been working to improve lives in the city's slums since 1976. Medical staff who can speak Hindi/Marathi or those with fundraising skills are needed.

Yogacara   YOGA

(Map p64; ⌨ 022-26511464; www.yogacara.in; 1st fl, SBI Bldg, 18A New Kant Wadi Rd, Bandra West; ⊙ yoga per class ₹700, massage 1hr from ₹1850, unlimited per week/month ₹1900/5600) Classic hatha and Iyengar yoga institute, with excellent massages and treatments; the Abhyangam rejuvenating massage is recommended. Ayurvedic cooking, meditation and chakra-healing classes are also offered sporadically.

🍴 Courses

★ Flavour Diaries   FOOD & DRINK

(Map p64;   ⌨ 9820143404;   www.flavourdiaries. com; 3rd fl, Rohan Plaza, 5th Rd, Khar West; session from ₹4000; ⊙ 11am-6pm) If you fancy some good food and a chance to make friends with local Mumbaikars, head to Flavour Diaries in Khar. This interactive cooking studio is spearheaded by renowned UK-born international chef Anjali Pathak, and courses cover everything from Asian and Indian cuisine to American, European and Mediterranean specialities.

★ Yoga Institute   YOGA

(Map p64;   ⌨ 022-26122185;   www.theyoga institute.org; Shri Yogendra Marg, Prabhat Colony, Santa Cruz East; courses per 1st/2nd month from ₹700/500) At its peaceful leafy campus near Santa Cruz, the respected Yoga Institute has daily classes as well as weekend and week-long programs, and longer residential courses including teacher training (with the seven-day course a prerequisite).

🧭 Tours

★ Khaki Tours   OUTDOORS

(Map p60; ⌨ 8828100111; www.khakitours.com; 3rd fl, Hari Chambers, 58/64 Shadid Bhagat Singh Marg, Fort; walks from ₹4000, jeep rides from ₹10,000; ⊙ 9am-5pm) The best way to get under the skin of Mumbai is to meet and strike up a conversation with a true Mumbaikar. The tours developed by Bharat Gothoskar (and led by city ambassadors with regular day jobs) – city walks, food tours, sailing outings, 'urban safaris' by private jeep – showcase an unseen side of Mumbai in the name of awesomely coined 'heritage evangelism'.

★ Reality Tours & Travel   TOURS

(Map p48;   ⌨ 9820822253;   www.realitytours andtravel.com; 1/26 Unique Business Service Centre, Akber House, Nowroji Fardonji Rd, Colaba; most tours ₹750-1700; ⊙ 8am-9pm) 🖉 Compelling

DHARAVI SLUM

Mumbaikars were ambivalent about the stereotypes in 2008's *Slumdog Millionaire,* but slums are very much a part of – some would say the foundation of – Mumbai city life. An astonishing 60% of Mumbai's population lives in slums, and one of the city's largest slums is Dharavi, originally inhabited by fisherfolk when the area was still creeks, swamps and islands. It became attractive to migrant workers from South Mumbai and beyond when the swamp began to fill in due to natural and artificial causes. It now incorporates 2.2 sq km of land sandwiched between Mumbai's two major railway lines, and is home to perhaps as many as a million people.

While it may look a bit shambolic from the outside, the maze of dusty alleys and sewer-lined streets of this city-within-a-city is actually a collection of abutting settlements. Some parts of Dharavi have mixed populations, but in other parts inhabitants from different regions of India, and with different trades, have set up homes and tiny factories. Potters from Saurashtra (Gujarat) live in one area, Muslim tanners in another; embroidery workers from Uttar Pradesh work alongside metalsmiths; while other workers recycle plastics as women dry pappadams in the searing sun. Some of these thriving industries, as many as 20,000 in all, export their wares, and the annual turnover of business from Dharavi is thought to exceed US$700 million.

Up close, life in the slums is fascinating to witness. Residents pay rent, most houses have kitchens and electricity, and building materials range from flimsy corrugated-iron shacks to permanent multistorey concrete structures. Perhaps the biggest issue facing Dharavi residents is sanitation, as water supply is irregular – every household has a 200L drum for water storage. Very few dwellings have a private toilet or bathroom, so some neighbourhoods have constructed their own (to which every resident must contribute financially) while other residents are forced to use run-down public facilities.

Many families have been here for generations, and education achievements are higher than in many rural areas: around 15% of children complete higher education and find white-collar jobs. Many choose to stay, though, in the neighbourhood they grew up in.

Slum tourism is a polarising subject, so you'll have to decide for yourself. If you opt to visit, the award-winning Reality Tours & Travel (p55) has an illuminating tour (from ₹900), and puts 80% of profits back into Dharavi social programs. They can also now arrange a meal with a local family for further insight. Photography is strictly forbidden.

Some tourists opt to visit on their own, which is OK as well – just don't take photos. Take the train from Churchgate station to Mahim, exit on the west side and cross the bridge into Dharavi.

To learn more about Mumbai's slums, check out Katherine Boo's 2012 book *Behind the Beautiful Forevers,* about life in Annawadi, a slum near the airport, and *Rediscovering Dharavi* (2000), Kalpana Sharma's sensitive and engrossing history of Dharavi's people, culture and industry.

tours of the Dharavi slum, with 80% of post-tax profits going to the agency's own NGO, Reality Gives (www.realitygives.org). Street-food, pottery, market, bicycle and sightseeing tours are also excellent.

Bombay Heritage Walks　　WALKING
(☑9821887321; www.bombayheritagewalks.com; per 2hr tour (up to 5 people) from ₹3750) Started by two enthusiastic architects and operating with a slew of architects, journalists and art historians, BHW has terrific tours of heritage neighbourhoods.

Mumbai Magic Tours　　TOURS
(☑9867707414; www.mumbaimagic.com; 2hr tour per 2/4 people from ₹1750/1500; ⊙10am-5pm Mon-Fri, to 2pm Sat) Designed by the authors of the fabulous blog Mumbai Magic (www.mumbai-magic.blogspot.com), these city tours focus on Mumbai's quirks, culture, community, food, bazaars, festivals, Jewish heritage and more.

🛏 Sleeping

Mumbai has the most expensive accommodation in India and you'll never quite feel like you're getting your money's worth.

Colaba is compact, has the liveliest tourist scene and many budget and midrange options, but hassles are greater there (hash dealers, beggars). The neighbouring Fort area is convenient for the main train stations and hip dining and shopping epicentre. Most top-end places are along Marine Dr and in the western suburbs.

⌂ Colaba

Backpacker Panda   HOSTEL $
(Map p48; 9607900991; www.backpacker panda.com; 15 Walton Rd; dm ₹800-1200, d with AC ₹2600-4200; ❋@🛜) Mumbai's best hostel fills four floors of a crusty, can't-miss-it grey-and-pastel-rosé residential building in Colaba, with tiled stairwells and other heritage accents. Four-, six- and eight-bed dorm configurations are spacious and boast air-con and lockers; private rooms are disappointingly simple, but all have fantastic modern bathrooms, a trend seen in the common bathrooms as well.

There's a rooftop lounge and game room as well as a smoking area, plus filtered water on every floor. No breakfast is served. The huge Garage Inc. Public House is in the same building. Also in **Andheri** (Map p64; 022-28367141; Shaheed Bhagat Singh Society; dm with AC ₹650-750; ❋🛜).

Sea Shore Hotel   GUESTHOUSE $
(Map p48; 022-22874237; 4th fl, 1/49 Kamal Mansion, Arthur Bunder Rd; s/d without bathroom ₹700/1230; 🛜) This place is really making an effort, with small but immaculately clean and inviting rooms, all with flat-screen TVs, set off a railway-carriage-style corridor. Half the rooms even have harbour views (the others don't have a window). The modish communal bathrooms are well scrubbed and have a little gleam and sparkle. Wi-fi in the reception and *some* rooms.

★ YWCA   GUESTHOUSE $$
(Map p48; 022-22025053; www.ywcaic.info; 18 Madame Cama Rd; s/d/tr with AC incl breakfast & dinner ₹2678/4457/6478; ❋🛜) Efficiently managed, and within walking distance of all the sights in Colaba and Fort, the YWCA is a good deal and justifiably popular. The spacious, well-maintained rooms boast desks, wardrobes and multichannel TVs. Tariffs include a buffet breakfast, dinner, a daily newspaper and bed tea. In addition to the room rates there's a one-time ₹59 membership fee.

★ Abode Bombay   BOUTIQUE HOTEL $$$
(Map p48; 8080234066; www.abodeboutique hotels.com; 1st fl, Lansdowne House, MB Marg; d with AC incl breakfast ₹5310-14,975; ❋🛜) A terrific 20-room boutique hotel, stylishly designed with colonial-style and art deco furniture, reclaimed teak flooring and original artwork; the luxury rooms have glorious free-standing bathtubs. Staff are very switched on to travellers' needs, and breakfast is excellent, with fresh juice and delicious local and international choices. A little tricky to find, it's located behind the Regal Cinema.

★ Taj Mahal Palace, Mumbai   HERITAGE HOTEL $$$
(Map p48; 022-66653366; https://taj.taj hotels.com; Apollo Bunder; s/d tower from ₹13,000/15,000, palace from ₹25,000/27,000; ❋@🛜☰) The grande dame of Mumbai is one of the world's most iconic hotels and has hosted a roster of presidents and royalty. Sweeping arches, staircases and domes, and a glorious garden and pool ensure an unforgettable stay. Rooms in the adjacent tower lack the period details of the palace itself, but many have spectacular, full-frontal Gateway of India views. With a myriad of excellent in-house eating and drinking options, plus spa and leisure facilities, it can be a wrench to leave the hotel premises. There's even a small but discernibly curated art gallery. Heritage walks at 3.30pm daily (for guests) provide illuminating context about the hotel's role in the city's history.

Hotel Suba Palace   HOTEL $$$
(Map p48; 022-22020636; www.subahotels. com/hotel/suba-palace; Battery St; s/d with AC incl breakfast from ₹5900/7320; ❋🛜) 'Palace' is pushing it slightly, but this modern, brilliantly located little place is certainly a comfortable choice with its contemporary decor: neutral tones from a 2015 upgrade keep the tasteful rooms teetering on modern. There's a good in-house restaurant, and foodie destination the Table (p63) shares the same location.

🛏 Fort Area & Churchgate

Traveller's Inn   HOTEL **$**
(Map p60; ☑022-22644685; www.hoteltravellers inn.co; 26 Adi Marzban Path, Fort; dm with/without AC ₹700/600, d with/without AC ₹2300/1800; ❋@🤚) On a quiet, tree-lined street, this small hotel is a very sound choice. It has clean, if tiny, rooms with cable TV and king-sized beds that represent good value. The two dorms are cramped (the non-AC one Hades-hot in summer; the AC one requires a minimum of three people) but are a steal for Mumbai. A new mosaic-floored hang-out space catches a nice breeze.

The location's excellent and staff are helpful. Breakfast is ₹100.

⭐**Residency Hotel**   HOTEL **$$**
(Map p60; ☑022-22625525; www.residencyhotel. com; 26 Rustom Sidhwa Marg, Fort; s/d with AC incl breakfast from ₹5080/5550; ❋@🤚) The Residency is the kind of dependable place where you can breathe a sigh of relief after a long journey and be certain you'll be looked after well. It's fine value, too, with contemporary rooms, some boasting mood lighting, minibars, flat-screen TVs and hip en suite bathrooms. Best of all, staff are friendly, polite and understand the nuance of unforced hospitality. Its Fort location is also excellent, though noise is will be an issue through 2022 due to metro-station construction right outside its door. The best-run midranger in Mumbai.

🛏 Western & Northern Suburbs

Cohostel   HOSTEL **$**
(Map p64; ☑9856564545; bandra@cohostels. com; 43 Chapel Rd, Bandra West; dm incl breakfast ₹800-1000; ❋🤚) Village-like Ranwar along Chapel Rd leads to Bandra's first noteworthy hostel, which occupies the top floor of a pre-Partition bungalow. Six six-bed dorms feature Australian-pine dorm beds, lockers, air-con and private baths, one of which is female-only. But it's the airy, spacious rooftop and kitchen (induction stovetops!) where you'll want to hang out. Coffee and tea are made to order.

⭐**Juhu Residency**   BOUTIQUE HOTEL **$$**
(Map p64; ☑022-67834949; www.facebook.com/ JuhuResidency; 148B Juhu Tara Rd, Juhu; d with AC incl breakfast from ₹5900; ❋@🤚) The aroma of sweet lemongrass greets you in the lobby at this excellent 18-room boutique hotel with an inviting atmosphere – and a fine location, five minutes' walk from Juhu beach.

The chocolate-and-coffee colour scheme in the modish hotel works well, each room boasting marble floors, dark woods, artful bedspreads and flat-screen TVs. To top it all off, free airport pickups are included.

Iskcon   GUESTHOUSE **$$**
(Map p64; ☑022-26206860; www.iskcon mumbai.com/guest-house; Hare Krishna Land, Sri Mukteshwar Devalaya Rd, Juhu; s/d with AC ₹3550/4050, without AC ₹3150/3450; ❋🤚) An intriguing place to stay inside Juhu's lively Iskcon complex. Though the hotel building is a slightly soulless concrete block, some rooms enjoy vistas over the Hare Krishna temple compound. Spartan decor is offset by the odd decorative flourish such as Gujarati *sankheda* (lacquered country wood) furniture, and staff are very welcoming.

Anand Hotel   HOTEL **$$**
(Map p64; ☑022-26203372; anandpremises @gmail.com; Gandhigram Rd, Juhu; s/d with AC from ₹2464/4130; ❋🤚) Yes, the decor's in 50 shades of beige but the Anand's rooms are comfortable, spacious and represent decent value, considering the prime location on a quiet street next to Juhu beach. The excellent in-house Dakshinayan restaurant (p68) scores highly for authentic, inexpensive meals, too. It's a particularly good deal for solo travellers.

⭐**ITC Maratha**   HOTEL **$$$**
(Map p64; ☑022-28303030; www.itchotels.in; Sahar Rd, Andheri East; s/d incl breakfast from ₹15,360/17,900; ❋@🤚❄) 𝒫 This five-star, Leadership in Energy and Environmental Design (LEED) Platinum-certified hotel channels the most luxurious local character. The details are extraordinary: Muhammed Ali Rd–inspired *jharokas* (lattice windows) around the atrium, Maratha-influenced Resident's Bar (a guest-only level overlooking public areas), Warli painting–inspired tower rooms with fiery orange marble. The rooms, awash in lush colour schemes, exude Indian opulence. Peshawri (p68), Mumbai's most memorable Northwest Frontier restaurant, is located here.

⭐**Taj Santacruz**   BOUTIQUE HOTEL **$$$**
(Map p64; ☑022-62115211; https://taj.tajhotels. com/en-in/taj-santacruz-mumbai; Chhatrapati Shivaji International Airport (T1), Airport Rd, Santa Cruz East; s/d from ₹12,000/14,000; ❋@🤚) Forget the 3500 hand-blown chandelier bulbs or the 75-species aquarium in the lobby of this newer hotel connected to the domestic airport

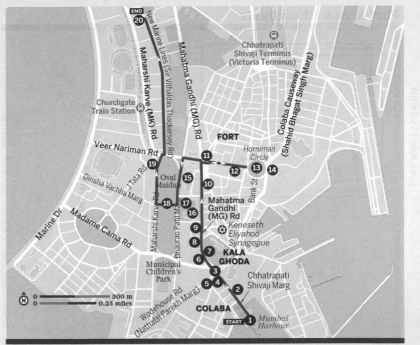

🏃 City Walk
Architectural Mumbai

START GATEWAY OF INDIA
END LIBERTY CINEMA
LENGTH 3.5KM; 1¾ HOURS

Mumbai's defining feature is its mix of colonial-era and art deco architecture. Starting from the ❶ **Gateway of India** (p48), walk up Chhatrapati Shivaji Marg past the art deco residential-commercial complex ❷ **Dhunraj Mahal**, towards ❸ **Regal Circle**. Walk the circle for views of the surrounding buildings, including the art deco ❹ **Regal Cinema** and ❺ **Majestic Hotel**, now the Sahakari Bhandar cooperative store. Continue up Mahatma Gandhi (MG) Rd, past the beautifully restored facade of the ❻ **National Gallery of Modern Art** (p50). Opposite is landmark ❼ **Chhatrapati Shivaji Maharaj Vastu Sangrahalaya** (p49), built in glorious Indo-Saracenic style. Back across the road is the 'Romanesque Transitional' ❽ **Elphinstone College** and the ❾ **David Sassoon Library & Reading Room** where members escape the afternoon heat lazing on planters' chairs on the upper balcony. Continue north to admire the vertical deco stylings of the ❿ **New India Assurance Company Building**.

On an island ahead lies ⓫ **Flora Fountain**, depicting the Roman goddess of flowers. Turn east down Veer Nariman Rd, walking towards ⓬ **St Thomas' Cathedral** (p50). Ahead lies the stately ⓭ **Horniman Circle**, an arcaded ring of buildings laid out in the 1860s around a beautifully kept botanical garden. It's overlooked by the neoclassical ⓮ **Town Hall**, home to the Asiatic Society library. Backtrack to Flora Fountain, continuing west and turning south onto Bhaurao Patil Marg to see the august ⓯ **High Court** (Map p60; www.bombayhighcourt.nic.in; Eldon Rd; ⊙10.30am-5.30pm) and ornate ⓰ **University of Mumbai** (p50). The university's 84m-high ⓱ **Rajabai Clock Tower** (p50) is off limits for visitors, but is best observed from within the ⓲ **Oval Maidan**. Turn around to compare the colonial edifices with the row of art deco beauties lining Maharshi Karve (MK) Rd – notably the wedding-cake tower of the ⓳ **Eros cinema** (Map p60; www.eroscinema.co.in; Maharshi Karve Rd, Churchgate). Divert east to New Marine Lines and head 1km north to the ⓴ **Liberty Cinema**, a dazzling, 1200-capacity single-screen art deco gem opened in 1949.

Fort Area & Churchgate

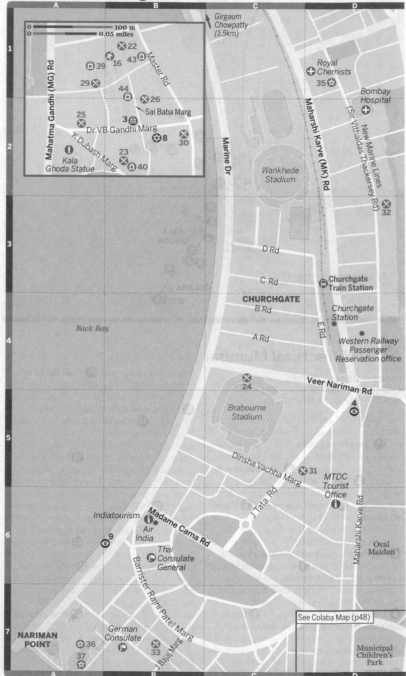

Girgaum
Chowpatty
(1.5km)

Inset map:

100 m
0.05 miles

🍴 22
16 43
🔒 39
Master Rd
29 ✕
44
🔒 ✕ 26
Sai Baba Marg
25 ✕
3 🏛
Dr VB Gandhi Marg
8
30
23
🔒 40
Mahatma Gandhi (MG) Rd
K Dubash Marg
🛈 Kala Ghoda Statue

Main map:

Royal Chemists
35
Bombay Hospital
Maharshi Karve (MK) Rd
New Marine Lines (Sir Vithaldas Thackersey Rd)
32

Marine Dr

Wankhede Stadium

D Rd

C Rd
Churchgate Train Station
CHURCHGATE
B Rd
Churchgate Station
A Rd
E Rd
Western Railway Passenger Reservation office

Back Bay

24
Veer Nariman Rd
4

Brabourne Stadium

Dinsha Vachha Marg
31
MTDC Tourist Office
Maharshi Karve Rd
Oval Maidan

Indiatourism
9
Air India
Madame Cama Rd
Thai Consulate General
J Tata Rd

Barrister Rajni Patel Marg

NARIMAN POINT
German Consulate
36
37
33
J Bajaj Marg

See Colaba Map (p48)

Municipal Children's Park

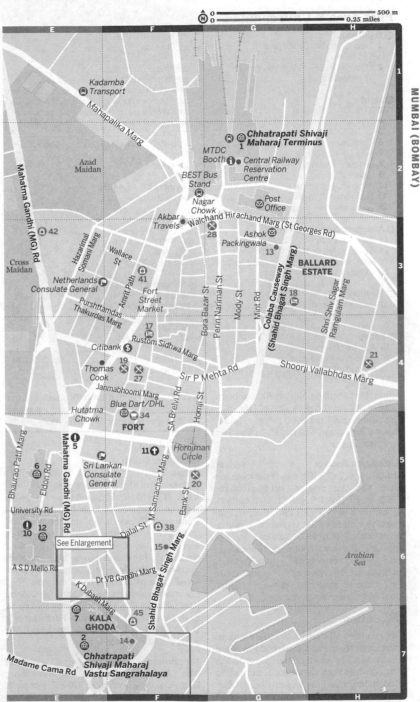

0
500 m
0
0.25 miles

E **F** **G** **H**

Kadamba
Transport

Mahapalika Marg

Azad
Maidan

Chhatrapati Shivaji
Maharaj Terminus
1

MTDC
Booth
Central Railway
Reservation
Centre

BEST Bus
Stand

Nagar
Chowk

Post
Office

Akbar
Travels

Walchand Hirachand Marg (St Georges Rd)

42

Ashok
Packingwala
13

Cross
Maidan

Netherlands
Consulate General

Hazarimal
Somani Marg

Wallace
St

Amrit Path

Fort
Street
Market

41

BALLARD
ESTATE

Colaba Causeway
(Shahid Bhagat Singh Marg)

18

Shri Shiv Sagar
Ramgulam Marg

Purshttamdas
Thakurdas Marg

Bora Bazar St

Perin Nariman St

Mody St

Mint Rd

17

Rustom Sidhwa Marg

Citibank

19

Thomas
Cook

27

Sir P Mehta Rd

Shoorji Vallabhdas Marg

21

Janmabhoomi Marg

Blue Dart/DHL

34

SA Brelvi Rd

Homji St

Hutatma
Chowk

FORT

Horniman
Circle

Bhaurao Patil Marg

Mahatma Gandhi (MG) Rd

5

Sri Lankan
Consulate
General

11

M Samachar Marg

Bank St

20

Eldon Rd

6

University Rd

10
12

Dalal St

38

15

Mahatma Gandhi (MG) Rd

A S D Mello Rd

See Enlargement

Dr VB Gandhi Marg

K Dubash Marg

Shahid Bhagat Singh Marg

Arabian
Sea

7 **KALA
GHODA**

45

2
14

Madame Cama Rd

Chhatrapati
Shivaji Maharaj
Vastu Sangrahalaya

Fort Area & Churchgate

◉ **Top Sights**
1 Chhatrapati Shivaji Maharaj
  Terminus G2
2 Chhatrapati Shivaji Maharaj Vastu
  Sangrahalaya E7

◎ **Sights**
3 DAG B2
4 Eros D5
5 Flora Fountain E5
6 High Court E5
7 Jehangir Art Gallery E7
8 Keneseth Eliyahoo Synagogue B2
9 Marine Dr B6
10 Rajabai Clock Tower E6
11 St Thomas' Cathedral F5
12 University of Mumbai E6

◐ **Activities, Courses & Tours**
13 Bollywood Tours G3
14 Bombay Natural History Society ... F7
15 Khaki Tours F6
16 Welfare of Stray Dogs B1

◉ **Sleeping**
17 Residency Hotel F4
18 Traveller's Inn G3

◈ **Eating**
19 A Taste of Kerala F4
20 Bademiya Restaurant F5
21 Britannia & Co. H4

22 Burma Burma B1
23 Chetana B2
24 K Rustom C4
25 Khyber A2
26 La Folie du Chocolate B2
27 Mahesh Lunch Home F4
28 Pancham Puriwala G3
29 Pantry A1
30 Rue du Liban B2
31 Samrat C5
32 SNDT to Cross Maiden Khao Gali D3
33 Suzette B7
  Trishna .... (see 26)

◉ **Drinking & Nightlife**
34 Raju Ki Chai F5

◉ **Entertainment**
35 Liberty Cinema D1
36 National Centre for the Performing
  Arts A7
37 NCPA Box Office A7

◉ **Shopping**
38 Bombay Paperie F6
39 Bombay Shirt Company A1
40 Chetana Book Centre B2
41 Chimanlals F3
42 Fashion Street E3
43 Kulture Shop B1
44 Nicobar B1
45 Sabyasachi F7

terminal. At the lap-of-luxury Taj Santacruz it's all about the gorgeous Tree of Life art installation forged from 4000 pieces of broken glass (a Rajasthani technique) in the Tiqri bar and restaurant.

Hotel Regal Enclave   HOTEL $$$
(Map p64; ☑ 022-67261111; www.regalenclave.com; 4th Rd, Khar West; d with AC incl breakfast from ₹7670; ❉❀🔊) Hotel Regal Enclave enjoys a stellar location in a leafy part of Khar, right near the station (some rooms have railway views) and close to all of Bandra's best eating, drinking and shopping. Rooms are spacious and comfortable – save the tight bathrooms – with pleasant if unoriginal decor (excluding the eight renovated rooms). Rates include airport pickup or drop-off.

✕ Eating

Flavours from all over India collide with international trends and taste buds in Mumbai. Colaba has most of the cheap tourist haunts, while Fort, Churchgate, Lower Parel, Mahalaxmi and the western suburbs are more upscale and trendy; it's these hoods where you'll find Mumbai's most international, expensive restaurants and see-and-be-seen gastronomic destinations.

✕ Colaba

Bademiya Seekh Kebab Stall   MUGHLAI, FAST FOOD $
(Map p48; www.bademiya.com; Tulloch Rd; light meals ₹130-250; ☺5pm-4am) These side-by-side, outrageously popular late-night street stalls (split between veg and nonveg) are in Bademiya's original location, where they remain a key Colaba hang-out for their trademark buzz and bustle and delicious meat-heavy menu. Expect spicy, fresh-grilled kebabs and tikka rolls hot off the grill. They also have sit-down restaurants in **Colaba** (Map p48; 19A Ram Mention, Nawroji Furdunji St; meals ₹80-370; ☺1pm-2am) and **Fort** (Map p60; ☑ 022-22655657; Botawala Bldg, Horniman Circle; mains ₹180-410; ☺noon-1am).

Theobroma   CAFE $$
(Map p48; www.theobroma.in; 24 Cusrow Baug, Colaba Causeway; confections ₹70-250, light meals ₹125-240; ☺9am-midnight; 🔊) Perfectly ex-

ecuted cakes, tarts and brownies go well with the coffee at this staple Mumbai patisserie. The pastries change regularly; if you're lucky, you'll find popular decadence like the chocolate-opium pastry, but it's all great. For brunch have the *akoori* (Parsi-style scrambled eggs) with green mango. The **Bandra branch** (Map p64; 33rd Rd, near Linking Rd; confections ₹70-250; ⊙8am-midnight; 🖭) is big and airy, though with a smaller menu.

Bombay Vintage   INDIAN $$

(Map p48; 🖭022-22880017; www.facebook.com/bombayvintage; Regal Circle, Oriental Mansion Bldg, Madame Cama Rd; mains ₹350-970; ⊙noon-midnight; 🖭) Brought to you by the same hospitality team as Woodside Inn (p70), Miss T (p65) and **Pantry** (Map p60; www.thepantry.in; ground fl, Yashwanth Chambers, Military Square Ln, B Bharucha Marg, Kala Ghoda; breakfast ₹1275-345, mains ₹320-600; ⊙8.30am-11pm; 🖭) 🌶, this cool throwback restaurant resurrects Bombay recipes of yore, often elevated versions of back-alley street food and dive-bar grub. Either way, you don't see a lot of options on this menu that pop up elsewhere, which is a refreshing change of pace for Colaba.

★ Bohri Kitchen   BOHRI $$$

(🖭9819447438; www.thebohrikitchen.com; ₹1500; ⊙12.30pm Fri & Sat) Served up in a family home, this weekend-only pop-up dining experience was cooked up by former Google employee Munaf Kapadia. It showcases both the spectacular home cooking of his mother, Nafisa, and the unique cuisine of the Bohra Muslim community, which draws on influences from as far afield as Yemen and Gujarat. The concept was so successful that the Maharashtra Government even lifted the idea for an initiative to empower local communities and increase tourism through visitors' bellies! Predictably, the seven-course, home-dining experience is easily one of Mumbai's most magical. Nafisa's smoked mutton *kheema* samosas and 48-hour *raan* are always included in the weekly-changing menu, which is announced on Facebook.

You must book ahead and pay a deposit – this is not a traditional restaurant! – and the address is revealed 24 hours in advance. Then settle in for a special afternoon with the Kapadia family.

Indigo Delicatessen   CAFE $$$

(Map p48; www.indigodeli.com; Pheroze Bldg, Chhatrapati Shivaji Marg; mains ₹665-710; ⊙8.30am-12.30am; 🖭) A bustling and fashionable cafe-restaurant with cool tunes and wooden tables. The menu includes all-day breakfasts (₹300 to ₹710) and straightforward international classics like pork ribs, thin-crust pizza and inventive sandwiches. It's always busy, so service can get stretched.

Table   FUSION $$$

(Map p48; 🖭022-22825000; www.thetable.in; Kalapesi Trust Bldg, Apollo Bunder Marg; small plates ₹575-1200, mains ₹700-1375; ⊙noon-4pm & 11.30pm-1am, tea 4.30-6.30pm Mon-Sat, noon-4pm Sun; 🖭) The market-fresh, globally inspired fusion menu, most of which was designed by former San Francisco chef Alex Sanchez, changes daily and does everything

THE PARSIS

Mumbai is home to the world's largest surviving community of Parsis, people of the ancient Zoroastrian faith, who fled Iran in the 10th century to escape religious persecution by the new Muslim rulers of Persia. 'Parsi' literally means Persian. Zoroastrians believe in a single deity, Ahura Mazda, who is worshipped at *agiari* (fire temples) across Mumbai, which non-Parsis are forbidden to enter. Parsi funeral rites are unique: the dead are laid out on open-air platforms to be picked over by vultures. The most renowned of these, the Tower of Silence, is located below the Hanging Gardens in Malabar Hill, yet screened by trees and hidden from public view.

The Mumbai Parsi community is extremely influential and successful, with a 98.6% literacy rate (the highest in the city). Famous Parsis include the Tata family (India's foremost industrialists), author Rohinton Mistry and Freddie Mercury. The best way for travellers to dig into the culture is by visiting one of the city's Parsi cafes. These atmospheric time capsules of a bygone era are a dying breed, but several sail on, including the excellent Britannia & Co. (p66) restaurant, **Kyani and Co** (Map p52; 657 JSS Marg, Jer Mahal Estate, Marine Lines; snacks ₹10-180; ⊙7am-8.30pm Mon-Sat, to 6pm Sun) and tourist hotbed Cafe Mondegar (p70).

Western Suburbs

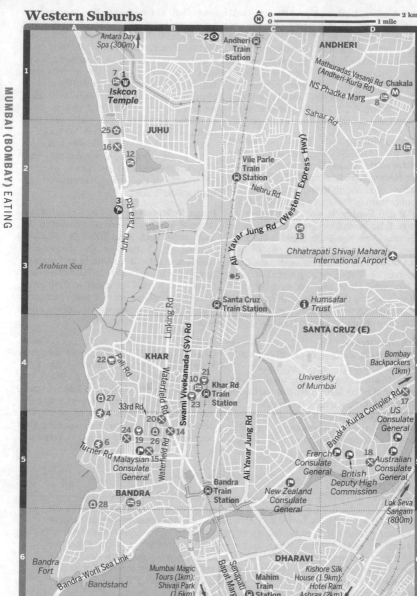

0 — 2 km
0 — 1 mile

Antara Day Spa (300m)

2 Andheri Train Station

ANDHERI

Mathuradas Vasanji Rd (Andheri-Kurla Rd)

Chakala

NS Phadke Marg

8

7 1
Iskcon Temple

Sahar Rd

25

JUHU

16

12

Vile Parle Train Station

Nehru Rd

11

3

Juhu Tara Rd

Ali Yavar Jung Rd (Western Express Hwy)

13

Arabian Sea

Chhatrapati Shivaji Maharaj International Airport

5

Linking Rd

Santa Cruz Train Station

Humsafar Trust

SANTA CRUZ (E)

KHAR

22

Pali Rd

Swami Vivekanada (SV) Rd

Waterfield Rd

10 21

Khar Rd Train Station

23

University of Mumbai

Bombay Backpackers (1km)

Bandra-Kurla Complex Rd

17

US Consulate General

27

33rd Rd

4

20

24 19 26 14

Ali Yavar Jung Rd

French Consulate General

18

British Deputy High Commission

Australian Consulate General

6 15

Turner Rd

Malaysian Consulate General

Bandra Train Station

New Zealand Consulate General

Lok Seva Sangam (800m)

BANDRA

28 9

Bandra Fort

Bandra-Worli Sea Link

Bandstand

Mumbai Magic Tours (1km); Shivaji Park (1.6km)

Senapati Bapat Marg

DHARAVI

Mahim Train Station

Kishore Silk House (1.9km); Hotel Ram Ashray (2km)

in its power to satisfy your cravings for a curry-free evening out. There's a lot to love: a crunchy kale salad with Iranian dates and toasted pistachios, zucchini spaghetti with almonds and Parmesan, and house-made black-truffle *taglierini*.

Basilico   MEDITERRANEAN **$$$**
(Map p48; www.cafebasilico.com; Sentinel House, Arthur Bunder Rd; mains ₹320-680; ⊙9am-12.30am; ☎) Euro-style Basilico does decadent sweets and especially creative fare when it comes to vegans and vegetarians. There are exquisite salads (from ₹330) like quinoa, organic av-

Western Suburbs

◉ **Top Sights**
1 Iskcon Temple B1

◉ **Sights**
2 Gilbert Hill...B1
3 Juhu Beach A2

◉ **Activities, Courses & Tours**
Flavour Diaries............................(see 23)
4 Yoga House A5
5 Yoga Institute C3
6 Yogacara A5

◉ **Sleeping**
7 Anand Hotel A1
8 Backpacker Panda.............................. D1
9 Cohostel B5
10 Hotel Regal Enclave B4
Iskcon ....(see 1)
11 ITC Maratha...D2
12 Juhu Residency B2
13 Taj Santacruz......................................C3

◉ **Eating**
14 Bastian...B5
Dakshinayan ....(see 7)

15 Hoppumm...B5
Kitchen Garden by Suzette ....(see 19)
16 Mahesh Lunch Home...........................A2
17 Masala Library.....................................D4
18 O Pedro..D5
Peshawri ....(see 11)
Prithvi Cafe ....(see 25)
19 Suzette...B5
20 Theobroma..B5

◉ **Drinking & Nightlife**
Bonobo..(see 20)
21 Doolally Taproom B4
Gateway Taproom..........................(see 18)
22 Koinonia Coffee Roasters....................A4
23 Social...B4
24 Toto's Garage.......................................B5

◉ **Entertainment**
25 Prithvi Theatre A2

◉ **Shopping**
26 Bombay Shirt Company B5
27 Indian Hippy A4
28 Kulture Shop A5

MUMBAI (BOMBAY) EATING

ocado and papaya, and numerous other interesting options like veg Moroccan tagine. It draws a top-end Indian crowd. If you can walk past that hazelnut chocolate crunch cake without biting, you're better than us.

Miss T SOUTHEAST ASIAN $$$
(Map p48; ☑022-22801144; www.miss-t.in; 4 Mandalik Marg, Apollo Bunder; mains for 2 ₹700-2500; ◷noon-3pm & 7.30pm-1am, bar from 6pm; 🛜) The Colaba Cartel, an impressive team of Mumbai foodies with a proven culinary track record including Pantry (p63), Woodside Inn (p70) and Table (p63), is the mind and manner behind Mumbai's coolest new restaurant. In a historic Mandalik Rd bungalow, Miss T's kitchen magicians include an executive chef from Hoi An (Vietnam) who draws menu inspiration equally from his neighbours (Thailand, Myanmar, Laos).

🍴 Fort Area & Churchgate

K Rustom SWEETS $
(Map p60; 87 Stadium House, Veer Nariman Rd, Churchgate; desserts ₹40-70; ◷9.30am-11pm Mon-Sat, 3-7pm Sun) K Rustom has nothing but a few metal freezers, but the ice-cream sandwiches here have been pleasing Mumbaikar palates since 1953. Pick from 50 flavours; roasted almond crunch is the bestseller.

Pancham Puriwala NORTH INDIAN $
(Map p60; 8/10 Perin Nariman St, Ballard Estate; mains ₹40-150; ◷8.30am-midnight) Located just outside CSMT, this budget eatery is a heritage icon, serving *puri bhaji* (puffed-up bread with a potato-and-pea curry) for over a century. The interiors are not fancy – there's no AC and diners sit on plain stainless benches – but the fun lies in listening to the stories of its owners, who set up this restaurant before the first train services started in India.

**SNDT to Cross
Maiden Khao Gali** STREET FOOD $
(Map p60; Vitthaldas Thackersey Marg, Marine Lines; mains from ₹20-120; ◷11am-11pm) A heaven for food lovers, Mumbai's famous *khau galis* (literally 'eat lanes') pack in some tantalising street treats, serving up a potpourri of cuisines and historic influences. Students and office workers are lured to the *khau galli* running from SNDT to Cross Maidan by the popular Bombay Sandwich (a toastie made with cheese, chutney and masala spices) and Frankie (a roti rolled with vegetables).

⭐ **Shree Thakkar Bhojanalay** INDIAN $$
(Map p52; ☑022-22011232; www.facebook.com/shreethaker1945; 31 Dadisheth Agyari Ln, Marine Lines; thali week/weekend ₹500/600; ◷11.30am-3pm & 7-10.30pm Mon-Sat, 11.30am-3.30pm Sun) With a cult following and festive lavender

STREET EATS

Mumbai's street cuisine is vaster than many Western culinary traditions. Stalls tend to get started in late afternoon, when chai complements much of the fried deliciousness; items are ₹10 to ₹80.

Most street food is vegetarian. Chowpatty Beach is a great place to try Mumbai's famous *bhelpuri* (puffed rice tossed with fried rounds of dough, lentils, onions, herbs and chutneys). Stalls offering samosas, *pav bhaji* (spiced vegetables and bread), *vada pav* (deep-fried spiced lentil-ball sandwich), *bhurji pav* (scrambled eggs and bread) and *dabeli* (a mixture of potatoes, spices, peanuts and pomegranate, also on bread) are spread through the city.

For a meaty meal, Mohammed Ali and Merchant Rds in Kalbadevi are famous for kebabs. In Colaba, Bademiya Seekh Kebab Stall (p62) is a late-night Mumbai rite of passage, renowned for its chicken tikka rolls.

The office workers' district on the north side of Kala Ghoda is another good hunting ground for street snacks.

tables to boot, this thali mainstay – one of the oldest in the city – puts on the full-court flavour with its never-ending Gujarati/Rajasthani set meals, full of *farsans* (bite-size snacks) and scrumptious veg curries. The air-con environs are a welcome retreat from the busy congestion below. It has been open since 1945.

La Folie du Chocolate   CAFE $$

(Map p60; www.lafolie.in; 16 Commerce House, Rope Walk Ln, Kala Ghoda; cakes ₹240-300; ⊙9am-11.30pm) Chocoholics and cake fetishists look no further – this minuscule Kala Ghoda place will seduce and hook you. Owner Sanjana Patel spent seven years in France studying the art of pastry- and chocolate-making, which was obviously time well spent. Try the Intense Caramel with Haitian chocolate mousse, burnt caramel crème brûlée and butterscotch praline. Koinonia coffee is served – even in keto-butter style.

Samrat   GUJARATI $$

(Map p60; www.prashantcaterers.com/samrat; Prem Court bldg, J Tata Rd, Churchgate; thali lunch/dinner ₹345/450; ⊙noon-11pm) Samrat has an à la carte menu but most rightly opt for the famous Gujarati thali – a cavalcade of taste and texture, sweetness and spice that includes numerous curries and chutneys, curd, rotis and other bits and pieces. Samrat is air-conditioned and beer is available.

A Taste of Kerala   KERALAN $$

(Map p60; Prospect Chambers Annex, Pitha St, Fort; mains ₹105-455, thali from ₹120-160; ⊙9am-midnight) An inexpensive Keralan eatery with lots of coconut and southern goodness on the menu. Try one of the epic thalis, served on a banana leaf and priced higher at ₹250 on Sundays. There are also seafood specials like prawn-pepper masala. Don't skip the *payasam* (rice pudding with jaggery and coconut milk) for dessert.

Britannia & Co.   PARSI $$

(Map p60; Wakefield House, 11 Sport Rd, Ballard Estate; mains ₹200-950; ⊙noon-4pm Mon-Fri, to 10pm Sat) This Parsi institution is the domain of 97-year-old Boman Kohinoor, who will warm your heart with his stories (and he still takes the orders!). The signature dishes are the *dhansak* (meat with curried lentils and rice) and the berry *pulao* – spiced and boneless mutton or chicken, veg or egg, buried in basmati rice and tart barberries imported from Iran. Cash only.

Rue du Liban   LEBANESE $$

(Map p60; ☑022-30151205; 43, Sasoon Bldg, VB Gandhi Marg, Kala Ghoda; small plates ₹550-800, mains ₹850-950; ⊙noon-4pm & 7pm-midnight) Moodily lit, art deco-era Beirut-inspired interiors complement the hyperauthentic dishes of the Levant in this sexy Kala Ghoda newcomer. The hummus? Texture-perfect, a precedent followed with lovely *moutabel* (charred eggplant puree with pomegranate, spring onion and sumac), the crunchy, Middle Eastern–authentic falafel, and a long list of excellent hot and cold meze.

Suzette   FRENCH $$

(Map p60; www.facebook.com/suzette.cafe; Atlanta Bldg, Vinayak K Shah Marg, Nariman Point; meals ₹390-700; ⊙9am-10.30pm Mon-Sat, 11am-5.30pm Sun; 🛜) 🍴 Relaxed Parisian-style place steeped where possible in organically sourced ingredients. Delectable crêpes, croques, salads, juices and soothing lounge music attract flocks of foreigners in need of a curry recess. On the crêpe front, sweet tooths should try the organic jaggery (₹120); for a savoury flavour, order a croque feta with tomato, mozzarella, creamed spinach and feta (₹490).

The **Bandra West branch** (Map p64; St John St, Pali Naka; mains 120-760; ☺9am-10.30pm) 🌿 has outdoor seating and is open daily.

★Khyber
MUGHLAI, INDIAN $$$
(Map p60; ☑022-40396666; www.khyber restaurant.com; 145 MG Rd; mains ₹590-1110; ☺12.30-4pm & 7.30-11.30pm) The much-acclaimed Khyber has a Northwest Frontier–themed design that incorporates murals depicting turbaned Mughal royalty, lots of exposed brickwork and oil lanterns – just the sort of place an Afghan warlord might feel at home. The meat-centric menu features gloriously tender kebabs, rich curries and lots of tandoori favourites roasted in the Khyber's famous red-masala sauce.

★Trishna
SEAFOOD $$$
(Map p60; ☑022-22703214; Ropewalk Ln, Kala Ghoda; mains ₹460-1830; ☺noon-3.30pm & 6.30pm-midnight) Behind a modest entrance on a quiet Kala Ghoda lane is this often-lauded, intimate South Indian seafood restaurant. It's not a trendy place – the decor is old school, the seating a little cramped and the menu perhaps too long – but the cooking is superb. Witness the Hyderabadi fish tikka, jumbo prawns with green-pepper sauce, and the outstanding king crab and lobster dishes.

Burma Burma
BURMESE $$$
(Map p60; ☑022-40036600; www.burma burma.in; Oak Ln, off MG Rd, Kala Ghoda; meals ₹360-490; ☺noon-2.45pm & 7-11pm; 🛜) A sleek, stylish restaurant that marries contemporary design with a few traditional artefacts (prayer wheels line one wall), providing a beautiful setting for the cuisine of Myanmar (Burma). The menu is well priced, intricate and ambitious, with inventive salads (the pickled tea leaf is extraordinary), curries and soups: *Oh No Khow Suey* is a glorious coconut-enriched noodle broth. No alcohol.

Mahesh Lunch Home
SEAFOOD $$$
(Map p60; ☑022-22023965; www.mahesh lunchhome.com; 8B Cowasji Patel Rd, Fort; mains ₹200-750; ☺11.30am-4pm & 6-11pm) A great place to try Mangalorean or Chinese-style seafood in Mumbai. It's renowned for its ladyfish, pomfret, lobster, crab (try it with butter garlic pepper sauce) and anything else out of the sea.

There's also a bigger **Juhu branch** (Map p64; ☑022-66955554; Juhu Tara Rd; mains ₹275-1475; ☺12-3.30pm & 7pm-12.30am; 🛜) with an extended menu.

✕ Kalbadevi to Mahalaxmi

Badshah Cold Drinks
INDIAN $
(Map p52; www.badshahcolddrinks.com; 52/156 Umrigar Bldg, Lokmanya Tilak Marg, Lohar Chawl; snacks & drinks ₹38-240; ☺7am-12.30am) Opposite Crawford Market, Badshah has been serving snacks, fruit juices and its famous *falooda* (rose-flavoured drink of milk, cream, nuts and vermicelli), *kulfi falooda* (with ice cream) and *kesar pista falooda* (with saffron and pistachios) to hungry bargain hunters since 1905. A must.

New Kulfi Centre
ICE CREAM $
(Map p52; 556 Marina Mansion, Sukh Sagar, Sardar V Patel Rd, Girgaon; kulfi per 100g ₹50-100; ☺9.30am-1am) Serves 36 flavours of the best *kulfi* (Indian firm-textured ice cream) you'll have anywhere. Killer flavours include pistachio, *malai* (cream) and mango.

Swati Snacks
FAST FOOD $
(Map p52; www.swatisnacks.com; 248, Karai Estate, Tardeo Rd, Tardeo; snacks ₹20-310, mains ₹135-315; ☺noon-10.45pm) Get in line for the upscale street food at this Mumbaikar classic, dishing up mostly Gujarati specialities since 1963. Amid minimalist, industrial aluminium diner-like tables offset by wooden banquettes, tasty treats like *panki chatni* (banana leaf–steamed savoury-rice pancakes), *mung dal chilla* (mung-dal pancakes) and *sabudana khichdi* (soaked sago cooked with coconut, green chilli and spices) are worth the wait.

Sardar
STREET FOOD $
(Map p52; 166A Tardeo Rd Junction, Tulsiwadi; pav bhaji from ₹140; ☺noon-2am) If you're spooked about Indian street food, try one of the city's most beloved street staples, *pav bhaji,* at this Mumbai institution. The curried-veg mix is cooked to death on a series of scalding *tawas* (hotplates) and served with a butter floater the size of a Bollywood ego. Get in line; the entire restaurant turns over at once.

Panshikar
INDIAN $
(Map p52; www.panshikarfoods.com; Mohan Bldg, Jagannath Shankar Sheth Rd, Girgaon; snacks ₹40-80; ☺9am-9pm-Sat) This clean and wonderful cheapie near Khotachiwadi is an excellent spot for snacks any time of day, but it all goes down especially well at breakfast. *Sub-udani wadi* (fried pearl-tapioca balls), *misal pav* (spicy bean sprouts and pulses), *pota-to wada* (mashed-potato patty), *kothimbir vadi* (crispy gram flour, coriander leaves and spices) – it's all excellent.

Wash it down with a masala chai or *kokum sharbat* (kokum juice).

★ **Revival** INDIAN $$
(Map p52; 39B Chowpatty Seaface, Chowpatty; thali ₹450; ◷ noon-3.30pm & 7-11.30pm; 🐾) Waiters at this thali mecca saunter around Chowpatty sea-view digs in silken dhotis, filling your plates with dozens of delectable (veg-only) curries, sides, chutneys, rotis and rice dishes in an all-you-can-eat gastronomic onslaught. The dishes change daily and, all said and done, is probably Mumbai's best thali.

Cafe Noorani MUGHLAI $$
(Map p52; www.cafenoorani.com; Tardeo Rd, Haji Ali Circle; mains ₹80-575; ◷ 8am-midnight) Inexpensive, old-school eatery that's a requisite stop before or after visiting Haji Ali Dargah (p50). Mughlai and Punjabi staples dominate, with kebabs chargrilled to perfection and great biryani; try the chicken tikka biryani (₹330).

🍴 Western Suburbs

★ **Hotel Ram Ashraya** SOUTH INDIAN $
(Bhandarkar Rd, King's Circle, Matunga East; light meals ₹40-90; ◷ 5am-9.30pm) In the Tamil enclave of King's Circle, 80-year-old Ram Ashraya is beloved by southern families for its spectacular dosas, *idli* (spongy, round, fermented rice cake) and *uttapa* (pancake with toppings). Filter coffee is strong and flavoursome. The menu changes daily. It's just outside Matunga Rd train station's east exit and draws Mumbaikars of all persuasions.

Hoppumm SRI LANKAN $
(Map p64; 8, Rafi Mansion, 28th Rd, Bandra West; mains ₹180-300; ◷ 11.30-3.30pm & 7.30-11.30pm) 🌿 Mumbai's best new budget eats are served up in this tiny – four tables and a counter – hipsterised Sri Lankan joint. It does absolutely delicious prawn *moilee* (seafood curry) and Ceylon roasted-chicken curries, served in hoppers (bowl-shaped, *appam* pancakes made from fermented rice flour and coconut milk) served alongside Keralan chutney-and-onion sambal. Portions aren't huge, so don't be afraid to order two items.

★ **Dakshinayan** SOUTH INDIAN $$
(Map p64; Anand Hotel, Gandhi Gram Rd, Juhu; mains ₹100-280; ◷ 11am-11pm Mon-Fri, from 8am Sat & Sun) With *rangoli* (elaborate designs) on the walls, servers in lungis, and sari-clad women lunching (*chappals* – sandals – off under the table), Dakshinayan channels

Tamil Nadu. There are delicately textured dosas, *idli* and *uttapam*, village-fresh chutneys and perhaps the best *rasam* (tomato soup with spices and tamarind) in Mumbai. Finish off with a South Indian filter coffee, served in a stainless-steel set.

Chilli-heads should order *molagapudi idli*, a dozen *idli* coated in 'gunpowder' (potent spices).

★ **Kitchen Garden by Suzette** CAFE $$
(Map p64; www.facebook.com/KitchenGarden bySuzette; 9 Gasper Enclave, St John's St, Bandra West; light meals ₹360-770; ◷ 9am-11pm; 🐾) 🌿 From the same French trio that brought us Suzette (p66) comes this superb organic cafe, a haven of health and homesick-remedying salads, sandwiches, cold-press juices and coffee sourced from local cooperatives and organic farms around Maharashtra and worldwide. The burrata, made by an American Indian Hare Krishna in Gujarat, is outstanding, but then again, so is everything.

O Pedro GOAN $$$
(Map p64; ☎ 022-26534700; www.opedro mumbai.com; BKC Bldg, No 2, Bandra Kurla Complex, Bandra East; mains ₹295-1400; 🐾) The first restaurant that makes it worth venturing into the Bandra Kurla Complex just to eat. The elevated Goan dishes are fantastic: spicy chorizo *bhakri* tacos, creamy seabass ceviche with tamarind, stir-fried prawn *sukhhe* with fresh coconut, Goa chillies and tamarind, fried *rawas* stuffed with green chilli-coconut chutney – it's all an explosion of flavour and spice and everything nice.

★ **Peshawri** NORTH INDIAN $$$
(Map p64; ☎ 022-28303030; www.itchotels.in; ITC Maratha, Sahar Rd, Andheri East; mains ₹1600-3225; ◷ 12.45-2.45pm & 7-11.45pm) Make this Northwest Frontier restaurant, outside the international airport, your first or last stop in Mumbai. It's a carbon copy of Delhi's famous Bukhara (☎ 011-26112233; ITC Maurya, Sardar Patel Marg; mains ₹1500-3000; ◷ 12.30-2.45pm & 7-11.30pm; Ⓜ Durgabai Deshmukh South Campus), with the same menu and decor. Folks flock here for the buttery dhal *bukhara*, a 24-hour simmered black dhal (₹945), but don't miss kebabs. Try the Murgh Malai (marinated tandoor-grilled chicken) and *raan* (impossibly succulent slow-roasted lamb hock).

★ **Bastian** SEAFOOD $$$
(Map p64; www.facebook.com/bastianmumbai; B/1, New Kamal Bldg, Linking Rd, Bandra West;

DABBA-WALLAHS

A small miracle of logistics, Mumbai's 5000 *dabba-wallahs* (literally 'food-container person'; also called tiffin wallahs) work tirelessly to deliver hot lunches to office workers throughout the city (and to the poor later on in the evenings, a 2015 initiative).

Lunch boxes are picked up each day from restaurants and homes and carried on heads, bicycles and trains to a centralised sorting station. A sophisticated system of numbers and colours (many wallahs don't read) identifies the destination of each lunch. More than 200,000 meals are delivered – always on time, come (monsoon) rain or (searing) shine.

This system has been used for over a century and there's only about one mistake per six million deliveries. (In a 2002 analysis, *Forbes Magazine* found that the *dabba-wallahs* had a six-sigma, or 99.999999%, reliability rating.) The system was also the subject of a Harvard Business School study in 2010 and a hit feature film in 2013 (*The Lunchbox*).

Look for these master messengers midmorning at Churchgate and Chhatrapati Shivaji Maharaj Terminus (CSMT) stations.

mains for 2 ₹1100-3200; ⊙noon-3pm & 7pm-midnight; ☎) All the praise bestowed upon this trendy seafooder is indisputably warranted. Chinese-Canadian chef Boo Kwang Kim and his culinary sidekick, American-Korean Kelvin Cheung, have forged an East-meets-West gastronomic dream. Go with the market-fresh side menu: choose your catch (prawns, fish, mud crab or lobster) then pick from an insanely difficult list of impossibly tasty pan-Asian sauces.

★ **Bombay Canteen**   INDIAN $$$
(☑022-49666666; www.thebombaycanteen.com; Process House, Kamala Mills, SB Marg, Lower Parel; small plates ₹225-650, mains ₹450-975; ⊙noon-1am; ☎) Bombay Canteen is one of Mumbai's hottest restaurants, courtesy of former New York chef and *Top Chef Masters* winner Floyd Cardoz, and executive chef Thomas Zacharias, who spent time at New York's three-Michelin-star Le Bernardin. India-wide regional dishes and traditional flavours dominate – Kejriwal toast, Goan pulled-pork-vindaloo tacos, mustard chicken curry – each dish an explosion of texture and flavour.

Koko   SUSHI $$$
(☑8451011124; www.facebook.com/KOKOAsian Gastropub; C2, Trade World, ground fl, Kamala Mills, SB Rd, Lower Parel; sushi rolls ₹900-1350, mains ₹590-3100; ⊙12.30-4.30pm & 7pm-12.30am Mon-Thu, to 1am Fri & Sat; ☎) Creative cocktails at this hot Asian gastrobar include the Tom Yum Cup (basically a tom yam soup laced with vodka), mixed by genuinely talented and friendly bartenders at the lengthy Burmese teak bar. Fantastic sushi – try the wild Japanese salmon truffle roll – and pan-Asian

dishes come from Eric Sifu, a Chinese chef from Malaysia with Michelin on his resume. Reservations essential; style recommended.

Masala Library   MODERN INDIAN $$$
(Map p64; ☑022-66424142; www.masalalibrary. co.in; ground fl, First International Financial Centre, G Block, BKC Rd, Bandra East; mains ₹575-1250, tasting menu ₹2500-2700, with wine ₹4250-4450; ⊙noon-2.15pm & 7-11pm) Daring and imaginative Masala Library dangles the contemporary Indian carrot to foodies and gastronauts, challenging them to rethink their notions of subcontinent cuisine. The tasting menus are an exotic culinary journey – think wild-dehydrated-mushroom chai with truffle-oil crumbs; langoustine *moilee* (seafood curry) with gunpowder mash; and a betel-leaf fairy floss to finish. Reservations essential.

🔴 Drinking & Nightlife

Colaba is rich in unpretentious pub-like joints (but also has some very classy places), while Bandra, Juhu and Andheri are home turf for the film and model set. Lower Parel has become a gourmet-dining hub, while the best craft-beer places are now way the hell up in Andheri. Wednesday and Thursday are big nights at some clubs, as well as the traditional Friday and Saturday; there's usually a cover charge. Dress codes apply, so don't rock up in shorts and sandals. Many places deny entry to men on their own. The trend in Mumbai is towards resto-lounges as opposed to full-on nightclubs. You're also technically supposed to have a licence to drink in Maharashtra; some bars require you to buy a temporary one, for a nominal fee, though we've never been asked.

CRAFT BREW MUMBAI

Few visitors to India would argue that an ice-cold Kingfisher in a dingy, smoke-filled bar isn't a quintessential Indian experience, but craft-beer connoisseurs might also add that India's ubiquitous native lager gets old pretty quick. And then there's those distinctly disgusting YouTube videos of oily, urine-coloured *something* being drained from beer bottles before drinking (it's usually glycerine, widely used in Indian beers as a preservative). Cheers? Not really.

While certainly late to the craft-brew boozefest, Mumbai has finally embraced hop-heavy IPAs, roasty, chocolatey porters and refreshing saisons, thanks to the city's very own craft-beer wallah, American expat Greg Kroitzsh. Kroitzsh opened Mumbai's first microbrewery, the now-shuttered Barking Deer, in 2013, and the taps began flowing in Mumbai as they already had been for some time in craftier Indian cities like Pune, Bangalore and Gurgaon.

Fancy a pint? Hoptimists now head north. In Andheri West, Independence Brewing Company (p71) and **Brewbot** (www.brewbot.in; Morya Landmark 1, off New Link Rd; pint ₹295; ☺4pm-1am Mon-Fri, noon-1am Sat; 🕏), and the 16-tap **Woodside Inn** (Map p48; www.facebook.com/Woodsideinn; Indian Mercantile Mansion, Wodehouse Rd; ☺11am-1.30am; 🕏) in Colaba, are within pub-crawl range of each other and are worth the journey, as is the good-time Doolally Taproom (p71) in Khar (also in Andheri and Kemps Corner) and the **Gateway Taproom** (Map p64; www.gatewaybrewery.com; BKC Bldg, No 3, G Block Bandra Kurla Complex; ☺noon-1.30am; 🕏) in Bandra East. In Lower Parel, **Toit Tap Room** (www.toit.in; Zeba Centre, Mathuradas Mill Compound, Senapati Bapat Marg; ☺noon-1.30am; 🕏) – a Bangalore transplant – is one of Mumbai's liveliest beer destinations; and Thirsty City 127 (p71) does tasty work next door in a more upscale ambience with the ex-Barking Deer brewer and a Sheffielder master brewer.

It's only a matter of time before taps start flowing in Fort and Colaba as well. The best of the production-only craft beer includes Pune's Great State Ale Works (www.facebook.com/greatstate.aleworks), which often holds tap takeovers in Mumbai (its salted kokum ale is one of India's best craft brews). White Owl (www.whiteowl.in), which has closed its excellent taproom to concentrate on bottling, is also worth seeking out.

The city's signature brew has quickly become Belgian Wit – citrusy and refreshing, it's a perfect accompaniment for hot and humid Mumbai.

🍸 Colaba

Cafe Mondegar
PUB

(Map p48; www.facebook.com/cafemondegar; Metro House, 5A Colaba Causeway; ☺7.30am-11.30pm) Iranian-founded 'Mondy's' has been drawing a heady mix of foreigners and locals since 1871. It's first and foremost a rowdy bar serving ice-cold mugs of Kingfisher (₹220), but don't discount its wide range of American, English and Parsi breakfast choices (₹130 to ₹350).

Harbour Bar
BAR

(Map p48; www.tajhotels.com/en-in/taj/taj-mahal-palace-mumbai/restaurants; Taj Mahal Palace, Apollo Bunder; ☺11am-11.45pm) With unmatched views of the Gateway of India and harbour, this timeless bar inside the Taj Mahal Palace is an essential visit. Drinks aren't uberexpensive (from ₹500/700/750 for a beer/wine/cocktail) given the surrounds and the fact that they come with very generous portions of nibbles, including jumbo cashews.

Leopold Café
BAR

(Map p48; www.leopoldcafe.com; cnr Colaba Causeway & Nawroji F Rd; ☺7.30am-1am) Love it or hate it, most tourists end up at this clichéd Mumbai travellers' institution at one time or another. Around since 1871, Leopold's has wobbly ceiling fans, a rambunctious atmosphere conducive to swapping tales with strangers, and an upstairs DJ most nights from 8pm.

Hammer & Song
COCKTAIL BAR

(www.flamboyante.in; Shop 10, The Arcade, World Trade Centre, Cuffe Parade; ☺noon-1.30am; 🕏) Off the tourist trail and full of Mumbai's beautiful set, this new bar tucked away inside Cuffe Parade's World Trade Centre is a fun night out, with an emphasis on craft beer and craft cocktails (barrel-aged old-fashioneds, for example) set to a DJ/live saxophonist tag team most nights. The crowd skews upscale and the seats are notably comfy – settle in.

Mixologist Ayush Arora trained at the European Bartender School in Australia.

★ Social
BAR
(Map p48; www.socialoffline.in; ground fl, Glen Rose Bldg, BK Boman Behram Marg, Apollo Bunder; ☺9am-1.30am; 🔊) Colaba is the best of the locations of the hip Social chain, which combines a restaurant/bar with a collaborative work space. The happening bar nails the cocktails (from ₹295) – the Acharroska is the perfect marriage of Indian pungency and Brazilian sweetness.

The food (mains ₹190 to ₹490) spans everything from Bollywoodised fish and chips and *poutine* (French fries and cheese curds topped with gravy) to Thai thalis and great Parsi dishes for breakfast. There are also Social locations at **Todi Mill** (www.social offline.in; 242 Mathuradas Mill Compound, ☺9am-1am; 🔊) in Lower Parel and **Khar** (Map p64; www.socialoffline.in; Rohan Plaza, 5th Rd, Ram Krishna Nagar; cocktails from ₹295; ☺9am-1am; 🔊).

Fort Area & Churchgate

Raju Ki Chai
TEAHOUSE
(Map p60; www.facebook.com/rajukichai; Shop 4, Kamar Bldg, Cowasji Patel Rd, Kala Ghoda; ☺9am-midnight Mon-Sat, from 2pm Sun) It's nearly impossible to saunter past this tiny brick-and-mortar chai joint – its colourful facade and vibrant interiors lure you in like an industrial-strength magnetic kaleidoscope. Taking street chai to a welcoming new level without disregarding tradition, the concoctions here (₹35 to ₹50) are served in customary clay cups, but not discarded on the pavement as at street stalls.

Kalbadevi to Mahalaxmi

★ Haji Ali Juice Centre
JUICE BAR
(Map p52; www.hajialijuicecentre.in; Lala Lajpat Rai Rd, Haji Ali Circle; ☺5am-1.30am) Serves fresh juices and milkshakes (₹50 to ₹400), mighty fine *falooda* and fruit salads. Strategically placed at the entrance to Haji Ali mosque, it's a great place to cool off after a visit. Try the Triveni, a gorgeous trifecta of mango, strawberry and kiwi (₹270).

Blue Tokai
COFFEE
(www.bluetokaicoffee.com; Unit 20-22, Laxmi Woollen Mill, Dr E Moses Marg, Mahalaxmi; ☺9am-9pm; 🔊) 🖋 Coffee's Third Wave has finally arrived in India. This speciality coffeehouse, one of four Mumbai locations, roasts its 100% Indian, traceable single-estate Arabica beans from farms like Vethilaikodaikanal (Tamil Nadu) and Thogarihunkal (Karnataka). It then brews them into espresso (from ₹100), cortados and flat whites (on the hot side) and pourovers and nitro (on the cold side). Coffee connoisseurs unite!

Western Suburbs

★ Independence Brewing Company
CRAFT BEER
(www.independencebrewco.com; Boolani Estate Owners Premises Co-Op, New Link Rd, Andheri West; pints ₹400; ☺1pm-1am Mon-Sat, noon-1am Sun; 🔊) A California-trained Indian master brewer oversees the craft at this trendy new Andheri West taproom from Pune-based Independence Brewing Company. Nine of the 10 taps are devoted to IBC brews, like four-grain saison, juicy Indian Pale Ales (IPAs), occasional sours and one of India's only double IPAs. There's Bollywoodised bar food to go along with it (grilled pickled paneer sandwiches, hot paprika wings).

★ Doolally Taproom
CRAFT BEER
(Map p64; www.doolally.in; Rajkutir 10A, E854, 3rd Rd, Khar West; pints ₹300; ☺7am-1am; 🔊) This Pune transplant, the vision of German brewmaster Oliver Schauf, was India's craft-beer pioneer. The fresh IPA, tangy Belgian Wit and apple cider are staples among the weekly changing 11 taps; and there are gourmet burgers and fat, hand-cut fries. It's steps from Khar station.

Wine Rack
WINE BAR
(www.facebook.com/TheWineRackMumbai; ground fl, High Street Phoenix,Tulsi Pipe Rd, Lower Parel; ☺noon-1am; 🔊) Sorely needed and refreshingly well done, Mumbai's first take on a serious wine bar should please connoisseurs. Part shop (over 300 bottles), part bar (48 wines by the glass, 21 of which are Indian; ₹325 to ₹995), it draws a sophisticated crowd, though not quite as sexy as the backdrop bar mural would suggest. Impressively stocked bar as well.

★ Thirsty City 127
BAR
(www.facebook.com/pg/thirstycity127; Todi Mills, Mathuradas Mill Compound, Tulsi Pipe Rd, Lower Parel; ☺6pm-1.30am Tue-Sun; 🔊) The former space of Mumbai's first microbrewery has been revamped into a slick craft beer and cocktail destination under the direction of Indian beer maven/visual artist Vir Kotak.

The striking space catches attention with copper-plated fermentation tanks, velvet and turquoise banquettes, but the swill reigns: eight taps (solid Neipa, Kölsch, Hefeweizen, etc served in Teku glassware) and cocktails (₹800) themed by beer ingredients.

★Cafe Zoe   BAR
(www.cafezoe.in; Mathurdas Mills Compound, NM Joshi Marg, Lower Parel; ⊙7.30am-1.30am; 🐾) Exposed brick and railing dominate the bilevel hipster hideaway inside a redeveloped cotton mill at Mathurdas Mills Compound. Forty wines by the glass, along with strong, well-mixed cocktails (₹700 to ₹1200) – like black grape caipiroskas and sage and lime martinis – ensure a lively crowd, who mingle alongside the old B&W photos of the space's former life dotting the walls.
Live jazz on Wednesdays at 9pm.

★Toto's Garage   BAR
(Map p64; ☑022-26005494; 30th Rd, Bandra West; ⊙6pm-1am) A highly sociable, down-to-earth local dive done up in a car-mechanic theme, where you can go in your dirty clothes, drink draught beer (₹200 a glass) and listen to classic rock. Check out the up-ended VW Beetle above the bar. It's always busy and caters to all kinds.

★Bonobo   BAR
(Map p64; www.facebook.com/Bonobo Bandra; Kenilworth Mall, 33rd Rd, off Linking Rd, Bandra West; ⊙6pm-1am) This bar champions underground and alternative music. DJs spin drum and bass and electronica, big beats and funky tech-house, and musicians play folk and blues. There's a great rooftop terrace and better-than-average craft beer on tap (Gateway and Brewbot). It's always a fun night out with a wildly eclectic crowd.

★Koinonia Coffee Roasters   COFFEE
(Map p64; www.koinoniacoffeeroasters.com; 66 Chuim Village Rd, Chuim Village, Khar West; ⊙7am-10pm; 🐾) Mumbai's best speciality coffee is served in this tiny Third Wave coffeehouse in atmospheric Chium Village. Single-origin Indian estate coffee is roasted in-house with a top-end Probat roaster. It comes cold-brewed, via Clever and Aeropress methods, as exquisite espresso (₹140), or with a dollop of ice cream from the affogato bar. Selections include salted caramel, Pondicherry vanilla or dark chocolate Italian truffle oil.

☆ Entertainment

Mumbai has an exciting live-music scene, some terrific theatres, an emerging network of comedy clubs and, of course, cinemas and sporting action.

Consult Time Out Mumbai (www.timeout.com/mumbai) and Insider (https://insider.in/mumbai) for events and/or live-music listings. Unfortunately, Hindi films aren't shown with English subtitles. You can book movies, theatre and sporting events online with Book My Show (https://in.bookmyshow.com).

★Royal Opera House   OPERA
(Map p52; ☑022-23668888; www.royalopera house.in; Mama Parmanand Marg, Girgaon; ⊙10am-6pm) India's only surviving opera house reopened to suitably dramatic fanfare with a 2016 performance by Mumbai-born British soprano Patricia Rozario, after a meticulous six-year restoration project that saw the regal address returned to full British-rule glory. Architect Abha Narain Lambah combed through old photographs of gilded ceilings, stained-glass windows and a baroque Indo-European foyer to restore the three-level auditorium.

Quarter   LIVE MUSIC
(Map p52; ☑8329110638; www.thequarter.in; Mathew Rd, Royal Opera House, Girgaon; ⊙10pm-1am) The Royal Opera House's signature entertainment venue (besides the Opera House itself, that is), the Quarter counts unique spaces like an airy, glass-fronted cafe and mozzarella bar, a Creole-cuisine-inspired restaurant and, most interestingly, a live-music venue evocative of a 1950s art deco jazz bar.

Canvas Laugh   COMEDY
(www.canvaslaughclub.com; 3rd fl, Palladium Mall, High Street Phoenix, Lower Parel; tickets ₹200-750) A popular comedy club that hosts around 50 shows per month, with twice-nightly programs on weekends (most comedians use English). It's 900m west of Lower Parel train station inside the High Street Phoenix shopping complex. Book tickets online.

National Centre for
the Performing Arts   THEATRE, LIVE MUSIC
(NCPA; Map p60; www.ncpamumbai.com; NCPA Marg, Nariman Point) This vast cultural centre is the hub of Mumbai's highbrow music, theatre and dance scene. In any given week, it might host experimental plays, poetry readings, photography exhibitions, a jazz band

QUEER MUMBAI

Although homosexuality was decriminalised by India's highest court in 2018, Mumbai's LGBTIQ scene is still quite underground, especially for women, but it's gaining momentum. No dedicated LGBTIQ bars/clubs have opened yet, but gay-friendly 'safe house' venues often host private gay parties (announced on Gay Bombay, www.gaybombay.org).

Gay Bombay is a great place to start, with event listings including meetups in Bandra, GB-hosted bar and film nights (including somewhat-regular gay Saturday nights at Liquid Lounge in Girgaum Chowpatty), plus hiking trips, picnics and other queer-community info. Following are some other useful resources.

Gaylaxy (www.gaylaxymag.com) India's best gay e-zine; well worth consulting and has lots of Mumbai content.

Gaysi (www.gaysifamily.com) Mumbai-based lifestyle e-zine.

Humsafar Trust (Map p64; ☑ 022-26673800; www.humsafar.org; 3rd fl, Manthan Plaza Nehru Rd, Vakola Santa Cruz East; ⊙10am-6.30pm Mon-Fri) Mumbai's most well-known LGBTIQ community organisation. It's also closely connected to the erratically published but pioneering magazine Bombay Dost (www.bombaydost.co.in).

Kashish Mumbai International Queer Film Festival (☑022-28618239; www.mumbai queerfest.com; ⊙May) Excellent annual event with a mix of Indian and foreign films; in 2018, 140 films from 45 countries were featured, including 33 LGBTIQ films from India.

LABIA (Lesbian & Bisexuals in Action; www.sites.google.com/site/labiacollective/home) Lesbian and bi support group based in Mumbai; provides a counselling service for women.

Queer Azaadi Mumbai (www.facebook.com/qam.mumbaipride) Organises Mumbai's Pride Parade (www.mumbaipride.in), which is usually held in early February.

Queer Ink (www.queer-ink.com) Online publisher with excellent books, DVDs and merchandise. Also hosts a monthly arts event with speakers, workshops, poetry, comedy, music and a marketplace.

RAGE-by D'kloset Gay parties and events organised via Instagram (www.instagram.com/ragebydkloset).

Salvation Star Community on Facebook (www.facebook.com/SalvationStar) and Twitter (@SalvationStar) that organises and promotes queer events and parties.

from Chicago or Indian classical music. Many performances are free. The **box office** (Map p60; ☑022-66223724; ⊙9am-7pm) is at the end of NCPA Marg.

Prithvi Theatre　　　　　THEATRE
(Map p64; ☑022-26149546; www.prithvitheatre. org; Juhu Church Rd, Juhu) A Juhu institution that's a great place to see both Hindi- and English-language theatre or an art-house film, with the **Prithvi Cafe** (light meals ₹40-180; ⊙10am-10.30pm) for drinks. Its excellent theatre festival in November showcases contemporary Indian theatre and includes international productions.

Regal Cinema　　　　　CINEMA
(Map p48; ☑022-22021017; www.regalcinema. in; Colaba Causeway, Regal Circle, Apollo Bunder, Colaba; tickets ₹80-250) A faded art deco masterpiece – Mumbai's oldest – that's good for Hollywood and Indian blockbusters.

Dating to 1933, it was the first centrally air-conditioned theatre in Asia.

Liberty Cinema　　　　　CINEMA
(Map p60; ☑022-22084521; www.facebook.com/ TheLibertyCinema; 41/42 New Marine Lines, Fort; ⊙tickets ₹100-200) The stunning art deco Liberty was once the queen of Hindi film – think red-carpet openings with Dev Anand. It fell on hard times in recent years, but is on the rebound and is now hosting films again. It's near Bombay Hospital.

🔒 Shopping

Mumbai is India's great marketplace, with some of the country's best shopping. Spend a day at the markets north of CSMT for the classic Mumbai shopping experience. Booksellers set up daily on the footpaths along the main thoroughfare between Colaba and Fort. Snap up a bargain backpacking wardrobe at **Fashion Street** (Map p60; MG Rd, Marine Lines;

⊕ hours vary). Kemp's Corner and Kala Ghoda have good shops for designer threads.

🔒 Colaba

Cottonworld
CLOTHING

(Map p48; www.cottonworld.net; Mandlik Marg; ⊕ 10.30am-8pm) A great shop for stylish Indian-Western-hybrid goods made from cotton, linen and natural materials. Think Indian Gap, but cooler.

Phillips
ANTIQUES

(Map p48; www.phillipsantiques.com; Wodehouse Rd; ⊕ 10am-7pm Mon-Sat) Art deco and colonial-era furniture, wooden ceremonial masks, silver, Victorian glass, plus high-quality reproductions of old photos, maps and paintings.

Clove
CONCEPT STORE

(Map p48; www.clovethestore.com; Churchill Chambers, JA Allana Marg; ⊕ 11am-8pm) Under the discerning eye of gourmet entrepreneur Samyukta Nair, this Colaba concept store occupies a late-19th-century art deco building chock-full of homegrown designer homewares (gorgeous coffee mugs, copper and clay dishware), jewellery, small-batch body scrubs and top-end designer *chappals* (sandals), *anarkali* (umbrella-flared dresses) and tunics for women, plus sleepwear for both sexes and children.

Nappa Dori
DESIGN

(Map p48; www.nappadori.com; Shop 2, Sunny House, Merewether Rd; ⊕ 10.30am-9pm) This very hip designer-leather shop from Delhi features a near-all-India lineup of carefully curated wallets, passport holders, truck-style travel cases, notebooks and other stylish writing and travel essentials (only the Novesta shoes aren't Indian, they hail from Slovakia). Discerning travellers and writers – take a look.

🔒 Fort Area & Churchgate

★ Sabyasachi
CLOTHING

(Map p60; www.sabyasachi.com; Ador House, 6 K Dubash Marg, Fort; ⊕ 11am-7pm Mon-Sat) It's worth popping in to this high-end traditional garment shop to see the space itself, a gorgeous, cavernous, rose-oil-scented stunner chock-full of owner and designer Sabyasachi Mukherjee's collection of chandeliers, antiques, ceramics, paintings and carpets. As far as retail goes, it's unlike anything you have ever seen.

★ Kulture Shop
DESIGN

(Map p60; www.kultureshop.in; 9 Examiner Press, 115 Nagindas Master Rd, Kala Ghoda; ⊕ 11am-8pm) Mumbai's coolest design shop has thankfully arrived in South Mumbai! Fittingly, the Pop Art cool kid from **Bandra** (Map p64; 241 Hill Rd, Bandra West; ⊕ 11am-8pm) has set up shop in Kala Ghoda, where its thought-provoking and conceptually daring art prints, notebooks, coffee mugs, stationery, T-shirts and other immensely desirable objets d'art from a cutting-edge collective of Indian artists will leave your head spinning.

Chimanlals
ARTS & CRAFTS

(Map p60; www.chimanlals.com; A2 Taj Bldg, Wallace St, Fort; ⊕ 9.30am-6pm Mon-Fri, to 5.30pm Sat) The beautiful traditional printed papers here will make you start writing letters.

Nicobar
HOMEWARES, CLOTHING

(Map p60; www.nicobar.com; 10 Ropewalk Ln, Kala Ghoda; ⊕ 11am-8pm) This new and excellent high-end boutique from the same folks who brought us **Good Earth** (Map p48; www.goodearth.in; 2 Reay House, Colaba; ⊕ 11am-8pm) is a great spot to pick up carefully curated homewares, travel totes and select Indian hipsterware.

MUMBAI FOR CHILDREN
....

Kidzania (www.kidzania.in; 3rd fl, R City, LBS Marg, Ghatkopar West; child/adult from ₹1000/500; ⊕ 10am-8pm Tue-Fri, 10am-3pm & 4-9pm Sat & Sun) Kidzania is predictably one of Mumbai's kid-tastic attractions, an educational activity centre where kids can learn all about piloting a plane, fighting fires, policing and get stuck into lots of art- and craft-making. It's on the outskirts on the city, 10km northeast of the Bandra Kurla Complex.

Esselworld (☑ 022-61589888; www.esselworld.in; Global Pagoda Rd, Borivali West; adult/child from ₹1050/750, with Water Kingdom ₹1390/950; ⊕ 11am-6pm Mon-Thu, to 7pm Fri & Sat) This Gorai Island amusement park is well maintained and has lots of rides, slides and shade. Ferries leave every 15 minutes (₹50) from Borivali jetty at Gorai Creek, best reached by bus 294 from Borivali Station.

Bombay Shirt Company CLOTHING
(Map p60; ☑022-40043455; www.bombayshirts.com; ground fl, 3 Sassoon Bldg, Fabindia Ln, Kala Ghoda; shirts from ₹2000; ⊙10.30am-9pm) A trendy, bespoke shirt tailor for men and women. You can customise everything – collars, buttons, cuffs and twill tapes. The results are stunning and the prices a fraction of those back home (unless home is Vietnam). Shirts take two weeks, and the business will deliver or ship internationally. It's also in **Bandra** (Map p64; ☑022-26056125; www.bombayshirts.com; ground fl, Kamal Vishrantee Kutir, 24th Rd;; shirts from ₹2000; ⊙10.30am-9pm).

Bombay Paperie ARTS & CRAFTS
(Map p60; ☑022-66358171; www.bombaypaperie.com; 63 Bombay Samachar Marg, Fort; ⊙10.30am-6pm Mon-Sat) Championing a dying art, this fascinating shop sells handmade, cotton-based paper crafted into charming cards, sculptures and lampshades.

Chetana Book Centre BOOKS
(Map p60; www.chetana.com; 34 K Dubash Marg, Kala Ghoda; ⊙10.30am-7.30pm Mon-Sat, 11.30-7pm Sun) This great spirituality bookshop has lots of books on Hinduism, yoga and philosophy, and the attached **restaurant** (thalis ₹500-635; ⊙12.30-3pm, 4-7pm & 7.30 to 11pm) does excellent Gujarati and Rajasthani thalis (₹499 to ₹635).

🔒 Kalbadevi to Mahalaxmi

⭐**Chor Bazaar** ANTIQUES
(Map p52; Mutton St, Kumbharwada; ⊙10am-9pm) Chor Bazaar is known for antiques, though be wary of reproductions. The main area of activity is Mutton St, where shops specialise in these 'antiques' and miscellaneous junk. Dhabu St, to the east, is lined with fine leather goods. It's an atmospheric spot for an afternoon browse, especially if you are looking for household trinkets and other nontouristy bric-a-brac.

⭐**Haji Mohammad
Bashir Oil Shop** HEALTH & WELLNESS
(Map p52; 426A Hamidiya Masjid, Bapu Khote Rd, Bhuleshwar; ⊙10am-10.30pm Mon-Sat, 9am-9pm Sun) Worth a visit as much for the spectacle if not to buy, this near-century-old traditional oil shop still hand-presses its medicinal, cooking and massage oils (often to order) with a sesame wood and metal press. The menu reaches long and wide (turmeric, avocado, sandalwood, neem, tulsi, almond, jojoba, cardamom – the list goes on and on, priced per kilo from ₹400 to ₹25,000).

BOLLYWOOD DREAMS
•••••••••••••••••••••••••••••••

BOLLYWOOD DREAMS

Mumbai is the glittering epicentre of India's gargantuan Hindi-language film industry. The Lumière brothers screened the first film ever shown in India at the Watson Hotel in Mumbai in 1896, and beginning with the 1913 silent epic *Raja Harishchandra* (with an all-male cast, some in drag) and the first talkie, *Alam Ara* (1931), Bollywood now churns out more than 1000 films a year – doubling Hollywood's output, and not surprising considering it has a captive audience of one-sixth of the world's population.

Every part of India has its regional film industry, but Bollywood continues to entrance the nation with its escapist formula in which all-singing, all-dancing lovers fight and conquer the forces keeping them apart. These days, Hollywood-inspired thrillers and action extravaganzas vie for moviegoers' attention alongside the more family-oriented saccharine formulas.

Bollywood stars can attain near-god-like status in India and star-spotting is a favourite pastime in Mumbai's posher establishments. You can also see the stars' homes as well as a film/TV studio with **Bollywood Tours** (Map p60; ☑9820255202; www.bollywoodtours.in; 8 Lucky House, Goa St, Fort; per person half-/full-day tour ₹8140/12,580; ⊙9am-6pm Mon-Fri, to 5pm Sat), but you're not guaranteed to see a dance number and you may spend much of the tour in traffic.

It's attached to the lovely Hamidiyah Masjid (mosque).

⭐**Play Clan** GIFTS & SOUVENIRS
(Map p52; www.theplayclan.com; Shop 1 & 2, Royal Opera House, Parmanand Marg, Girguam; ⊙11am-7pm) Kitschy, design-y goods such as stylish embroidered T-shirts, funky coffee mugs and coasters, and superhip graphic art, including beaded embroidered art and illustrative wood prints that are pricey but unique.

M/S KN Ajani HOMEWARES
(Map p52; Shop 102, Krishna Galli, Swadeshi Market, Kalbadevi Rd, Kalbadevi; ⊙noon-7pm Mon-Sat) One of Mumbai's oldest shops and born of a dying breed, this family-run retailer kicked off in 1918. Today, friendly grandson Paresh still hawks the family jewels: brass,

carbon-steel and aluminium scissors, nutcrackers, locks and knives inside the otherwise textile-driven Swadeshi Market. It's certainly not a conventional souvenir, but it's immensely satisfying to not buy your scissors at an office-supply shop.

No-Mad Fabric Shop   HOMEWARES
(Map p52; ☑022-22091787; www.no-mad.in; 3C-209, 1st fl, Mangaldas Market bldg, Kitchen Garden Ln; ⊙11am-7pm Mon-Sat) One of Mumbai's hottest new brands, this small showroom, overseen by Nandi the Holy Cow in logo, art and design, is an interior-design oasis in Mangaldas Market. Pick up colourful, India-inspired cocktail napkins, handbags, pillow covers, throws, candles, incense, and copper and brass serving trays, among other stylish items.

No Borders   CLOTHING
(Map p52; www.facebook.com/noborderssshop; 47G, 1st fl, Khotachi Wadi Ln, Kotachiwadi; ⊙11am-7pm Tue-Sun) This top-end shop occupies the former studio of fashion designer James Ferreira, located inside his 200-year-old Kotachiwadi bungalow. It curates designer threads from ethnic South Asian tastemakers as well as contemporary Indian, Norwegian and Israeli fashion designers, among others.

Lalbaug Market   SPICES
(Putibal Chawl, Dr Baba Saheb Ambedkar Rd, Lalbaug; ⊙11am-4.30pm Mon, 9am-7pm Tue-Sun) You could buy your packaged-for-tourists spices at hassle-y Crawford Market; or, go where Mumbaikars go, which is this fragrant market in Dadar that's considered top-rate for fresh, unadulterated hand-ground powdered goodness, fresh chillies and other chef essentials.

Shrujan   ARTS & CRAFTS
(Map p52; ☑022-23521693; www.shrujan.org; Krishnabad Bldg, 43 Bhulabhai Desai Marg, Breach Candy; ⊙10am-7.30pm Mon-Sat) 🍃 Selling the intricate embroidery work of women in villages across Kutch, Gujarat, the nonprofit Shrujan aims to help women earn a livelihood while preserving the spectacular embroidery of the area. The sophisticated clothing, wall hangings and purses make great gifts.

Poster Stuff   ART
(Map p52; ☑8976605743; 113 Mutton St, Kumbharwada; ⊙11am-9pm) Haji Abu's small Chor Bazaar shop offers a cornucopia of vintage Bollywood posters, lobby cards and show cards dating to the 1930s (originals and reprints), some 500,000 in total curated from his grandfather's much larger collection.

Prices start at ₹400 on up to ₹400,000. For Bollywood art buffs, this is your Holy Grail.

🏠 Western Suburbs

⭐ Indian Hippy   ART
(Map p64; ☑8080822022; www.hippy.in; 17C Sherly Rajan Rd, off Carter Rd, Bandra West; portraits ₹7500-15,000; ⊙by appointment) Indian Hippy will put your name in lights, with custom-designed Bollywood posters hand-painted on canvas by the original studio artists (a dying breed since the advent of digital illustrating). Bring or email a photo and your imagination (or let staff guide you). Also sells vinyl LP record clocks, vintage posters and all manner of frankly bizarre Bollywood-themed products. Ships worldwide.

Kishore Silk House   CLOTHING, HANDICRAFTS
(Dedhia Estate, 5/353 Bhandarkar Rd, Matunga East; ⊙10am-8.30pm Tue-Sun) Handwoven saris (from ₹300) and dhotis (from ₹250) from Tamil Nadu and Kerala.

High Street Phoenix   MALL
(www.highstreetphoenix.com; 462 Senapati Bapat Marg, Lower Parel; ⊙11am-10pm) High Street Phoenix, one of India's first and largest shopping malls, and its mall-within-a-mall, luxury-oriented Palladium, is an indoor/outdoor retail orgy that hosts top shops, great restaurants, fun bars and clubs, a 20-lane bowling alley and an IMAX cineplex. It's also where you go when you want a few horn-free hours.

ℹ️ Information

DANGERS & ANNOYANCES
For a city of its size, Mumbai affords few serious dangers and annoyances. However, it's worth being mindful of the following points:
➡ The city has a well-documented history of terrorism. Be vigilant – if you notice something off, or tell-tale signs like unattended bags, tell the police as soon as possible.
➡ Be alert for pickpocketing in crowded areas like Crawford Market, Mahalaxmi Temple, the Gateway of India and on crowded trains.

INTERNET ACCESS
While cybercafes are increasingly scarce, all but the simplest hotels, restaurants, cafes and bars now have wi-fi. Commercial establishments generally require a connection via social-media accounts or via a mobile-phone number, to which a unique one-time password (OPT) is sent.

The Maharashtra government also supports a wide network of over 500 public hot spots known as Aaple Sarkar Mumbai Wi-Fi. Check out www.

WORTH A TRIP

SANJAY GANDHI NATIONAL PARK

It's hard to believe that within 1½ hours of the teeming metropolis you can be surrounded by this 104-sq-km protected tropical **forest** (☑022-28868686; https://sgnp.maharashtra.gov. in; Borivali; adult/child ₹53/28, vehicle ₹177-266; ☺7.30am-6pm Tue-Sun, last entry 4pm). Here, bright flora, birds, butterflies and elusive wild leopards replace pollution and concrete, all surrounded by forested hills on the city's northern edge. Urban development has muscled in on the fringes of the park, but its heart is very peaceful.

The park's most intriguing option, the **Kanheri Caves** (https://sgnp.maharashtra.gov.in; Borivali; Indian/foreigner ₹25/300; ☺9am-5pm Tue-Sun) is a set of 109 dwellings and monastic structures for Buddhist monks 6km inside the park. The caves, not all of which are accessible, were developed over 1000 years, beginning in the 1st century BC, as part of a sprawling monastic university complex. Avoid the zoo-like lion and tiger 'safari' as the animals are in cages and enclosures.

Inside the park's main northern entrance is an information centre with a small exhibition on the park's wildlife. The best time to see birds is October to April and butterflies from August to November. Activities can now also be booked online.

The nearest station is Borivali, served by trains on the Western Railway line from Churchgate station (₹15 to ₹165, 30 minutes, frequent).

aaplesarkar.maharashtra.gov.in/file/Mumbai-Wifi-hotspots.pdf to locate the one nearest you.
RailWire (www.railwire.co.in) also offers a signal at select train stations, part of an over 700-station initiative throughout India.

MEDICAL SERVICES

Bombay Hospital (Map p60; ☑022-22067676; www.bombayhospital.com; 12 New Marine Lines, Marine Lines; ☺24hr) A private hospital with the latest medical technology and equipment.

Breach Candy Hospital (Map p52; ☑022-23672888, emergency 022-23667809; www.breachcandyhospital.org; 60A, Bhulabhai Desai Marg, Breach Candy) The best hospital in Mumbai, if not India. It's 2km northwest of Girgaum Chowpatty.

Royal Chemists (Map p60; www.royalchemists.com; 89A Queen's Chambers, Maharshi Karve Rd, Marine Lines; ☺8.30am-8.30pm Mon-Sat) Has delivery services.

Sahakari Bhandar Chemist (Map p48; Colaba Chamber, ground fl, Colaba Causeway, Colaba; ☺10am-8.30pm)

MONEY

ATMs are everywhere, and foreign-exchange offices are also plentiful. There are numerous Citibank branches, including a handy **Fort branch** (Map p60; Bombay Mutual Bldg, 293 Dr Dadabhai Naoroji Rd, Fort), which is handy for its larger, ₹20,000 withdrawal limits. Thomas Cook (p78) has a branch in the Fort area with foreign exchange.

POST

Post office (GPO; Map p60; www.indiapost.gov. in; Walchand Hirachand Marg, Fort; ☺9am-8pm Mon-Sat, to 4pm Sun) The main post office is an imposing building beside CSMT. Opposite gate 4 of the post office in front of Marine Supply is **Ashok Packingwala** (Map p60; ☑9323693870; opp GPO, Gate 4, Walchand Hirachand Marg, Fort) – parcel-wallahs who will stitch up your parcel (for between ₹60 and ₹300). There's also a convenient branch in **Colaba** (Map p48; Henry Rd; ☺10am-5pm Mon-Fri, to 1pm Sat).

Blue Dart/DHL (Map p60; ☑022-22049333; www.bluedart.com; ground fl, Shri Mahavir Chamber, Cawasji Patel St, Fort; ☺9am-9pm Mon-Sat) International courier services.

TOURIST INFORMATION

Indiatourism (Government of India Tourist Office; Map p60; ☑022-22074333; www.incredibleindia.com; ground fl, Air India Bldg, Vidhan Bhavan Marg, Narimen Point; ☺8.30am-6pm Mon-Fri, to 2pm Sat) Provides information for the entire country, as well as contacts for Mumbai guides and homestays.

MTDC Tourist Office (Maharashtra Tourism Development Corporation; Map p60; ☑022-22845678; www.maharashtratourism.gov.in; 4th fl, Apeejay House, 3 Dinsha Vachha Marg, Churchgate; ☺9am-5.30pm Mon-Sat, closed 2nd & 4th Sat of month) The MTDC's head office has helpful staff and lots of pamphlets and information on Maharashtra, as well as bookings for MTDC hotels. It's also the only MTDC office of note that accepts credit cards. There are additional booths at Apollo Bunder (p54) and **Chhatrapati Shivaji Maharaj Terminus** (Maharashtra Tourism Development Corporation; Map p60; ☑022-22622859; www.maharashtratourism.gov.in; Chhatrapati Shivaji Maharaj Terminus, Fort; ☺10am-5.30pm Mon-Sat, closed 2nd & 4th Sat of month).

TRAVEL AGENCIES

Akbar Travels (Map p48; ☑ 022-22823434; www.akbartravels.com; 30 Alipur Trust Bldg, Colaba Causeway, Colaba; ☺10am-10pm) Extremely helpful and can long-distance book car/drivers and buses. There's another branch in Fort (Map p60; ☑ 022-22633434; 167/169 Dr Dadabhai Naoroji Rd, Fort; ☺10am-7pm Mon-Sat).

Magnum International Travel & Tours (Map p48; ☑ 022-61559700; www.magnum international.com; 10 Henry Rd, Colaba; ☺10am-6pm Mon-Fri, to 1pm Sat) Handy Colaba travel agency.

Thomas Cook (Map p60; ☑ 022-48795009; www.thomascook.in; 324 Dr Dadabhai Naoroji Rd, Fort; ☺ 9.30am-6pm Mon-Sat) Flight and hotel bookings, plus foreign exchange.

ℹ Getting There & Away

AIR

Mumbai's carbon-neutral **Chhatrapati Shivaji Maharaj International Airport** (Map p64; ☑ 022-66851010; www.csia.in; Santa Cruz East), about 30km from the city centre, was recently modernised to the tune of US$2 billion. Now handling all international arrivals is the impressive, remodelled international Terminal 2 (T2), which includes India's largest public-art program (a skylighted, 3.2km multistorey Art Wall along moving walkways, boasting over 5000 pieces of art from every corner of India). The international terminal has its own app (Android/iPhone; Mumbai T2 App).

Domestic flights operate out of both the new T2 and the older Terminal 1 (T1), also known locally as Santa Cruz Airport, 5km away. An interterminal fixed-rate taxi service (non-AC/AC ₹230/260 from T1 to T2, ₹230/250 from T2 to T1) operates between the terminals. Both terminals have ATMs and foreign-exchange counters, and T2 also houses the luxurious **Niranta Transit Hotel** (☑ 022-67296729; www.nirantahotels.

com; s/d 4 hrs ₹5510/5900, 7 hrs ₹7080/7670, 24 hrs 11,529/13,800; @ ☎). There's left luggage near the hotel.

Air India (Map p60; ☑ 1800-1801407, 022-22023031; www.airindia.com; Air India Bldg, cnr Marine Dr & Madame Cama Rd, Nariman Point; ☺ 9.15am-6.30pm Mon-Thu, 9.15am-6.15pm Fri, 9.15am-1pm & 1.45-5pm Sat), Jet Airways (www. jetairways.com) and Vistara (www.airvistara. com) operate out of T2, while GoAir (www.goair. in), IndiGo (www.goindigo.in) and SpiceJet (www. spicejet.com), among others, operate out of T1 – be sure to check ahead for any changes on the ground. Travel agencies and the airlines' websites are usually best for booking flights.

BUS

Numerous private operators and state governments run long-distance buses to and from Mumbai.

Long-distance government-run buses depart from the **Mumbai Central bus terminal** (Map p52; ☑ 1800-221250, enquiries 022-23024076; Jehangir Boman Behram Marg, RBI Staff Colony) right by Mumbai Central train station. They're cheaper and more frequent than private services, but standards are usually lower with the exception of semiluxury ShivShahi and luxury Shivneri services (always look for those first). The website of the **Maharashtra State Road Transport Corporation** (MSRTC; ☑ 022-23023900; www.msrtc.gov.in) has online schedules and booking at https://public.msrtcors. com/ticket_booking/index.php, though you'll need a resident to book for you if you don't have an Indian credit card.

Private buses are usually more comfortable and simpler to book (if a bit more costly). Many normally depart from Dr Anadrao Nair Rd near Mumbai Central train station, but that has stopped due to metro construction without any timeline for ever returning. If you are in that area, **National NTT/CTC** (Map p52; ☑ 022-23015652; Dr Anadrao Nair Rd, RBI Staff Colony; ☺6am-

MAJOR LONG-DISTANCE BUS ROUTES

DESTINATION	PRIVATE NON-AC/AC SLEEPER (₹)	GOVERNMENT NON-AC (₹)	DURATION (HR)
Ahmedabad	500-2000/670-2500	N/A	7-12
Aurangabad	650-1100/550-2500	from 560 (four daily)	9-11
Hyderabad	1200-2000/1310-3000	N/A	16
Mahabaleshwar	1550/450-1349	from 300 (four daily)	7-8
Murud	2500 (seats only)	from 210 (eight daily)	8-10
Nashik	350-1500/400-2510	from 240 (12 per day, 6am-10.45pm)	13-16
Panaji (Panjim)	475-1500/1430-2500	N/A	14-16
Pune	600-2000/350-3000	from 210 (half-hourly, 6.35am-12.30am)	3-5
Udaipur	600-1400/1210-1810	N/A	14-17

11pm) remains open behind the metro construction and is a reliable ticketing agent.

The most centralised place to catch private buses these days is around Dadar TT Circle (Dadar East) under the flyover of the same name (free transport is usually provided to both by ticketing agents), but with the exception of the **MSRTC Shivneri buses to Pune** (www.msrtc. org.in; Dadar TT Flyover, Dadar East), you are going to need help to find your bus. The flyover is lined on both sides with private ticketing agents – make sure you arrive early and get specific indications from them where to find your bus. **Neeta Tours & Travels** (🗹 022-24162565; www.neeta bus.in; Shop 9, opp Dadar Post Office, Dr Ambed-kar Rd, Dadar East) is a good place to start.

Internet ticketing resources such as redBus (www.redbus.in) are in play, though some sites still require Indian mobile numbers and/or do-mestic payment options – most foreigners will still need to visit the ticketing agents (or have an Indian friend buy your ticket). Be sure to check your departure point (often called 'pickup point') as the reality is that private bus companies de-part from numerous points around the city.

In addition to **Dr Anadrao Nair Road** (Map p52; RBI Staff Colony) near Mumbai Central bus station and along both sides of Dr Baba Saheb Ambedkar Rd near the **Dadar TT Flyover** (Dr Baba Saheb Ambedkar Rd) in Dadar East, you'll also find private long-distance ticket agents near **Paltan Road** (Map p52; Sitaram Bldg, F-Block, opp Paltan Rd) in Fort.

Private buses to Goa are more convenient; these vary in price from as little as ₹760 (a bad choice) to ₹3000. Many leave from way out in the suburbs, but government-run **Kadamba Transport** (Map p60; 🗹 9969561146; www. goakadamba.com; 5 Mahapalika Marg, Fort; ⊗7.30am-5.30pm Mon-Sat) is convenient for the centre, leaving from in front of Azad Maidan. The trip takes 14 hours.

Fares to popular destinations (like Goa) are up to 75% higher during holiday periods.

TRAIN

Three train systems operate out of Mumbai, but the most important services for travellers are Central Railway and Western Railway. Tickets for either system can be bought from any station that has computerised ticketing.

Central Railway (www.cr.indianrailways.gov. in) – handling services to the east, south, plus a few trains to the north – operates from CSMT (also known as 'VT'). Foreign-tourist-quota tick-ets and Indrail passes can be bought at Counter 4 of the **reservation centre** (Map p60; 🗹139; www.cr.indianrailways.gov.in; Chhatrapati Shivaji Maharaj Terminus Area, Fort; ⊗8am-8pm Mon-Sat, to 2pm Sun). There is a prepaid taxi scheme near the MTDC tourist information booth (p77).

It's ₹160 to Colaba, ₹360 to Bandra, ₹430 to the domestic terminal and ₹500 to the international terminal.

Some Central Railway trains depart from Dadar (D), a few stations north of CSMT, or Lokmanya Tilak (LTT), 16km north of CSMT.

Western Railway (www.wr.indianrailways. gov.in) has services to the north from Mumbai Central train station, usually called Bombay Central (BCT). The **passenger reservation office** (Map p60; 🗹139; www.wr.indianrailways. gov.in; Station Bldg, Vithaldas Thackersey Marg, Churchgate; ⊗8am-8pm Mon-Sat, to 2pm Sun), opposite Churchgate station, has foreign-tourist-quota tickets.

Mumbai's local rail infrastructure has come under fire in recent years. The collapse of And-heri's Gokhale overbridge connecting Andheri West and East stations in 2018 killed two, a stampede killed 23 at Prabhadevi station in 2017, and there was a skywalk cave-in at Charni Road, also in 2017. A system-wide structural audit was underway at the time of writing – and for good reason, as 18,847 people have died riding the rails since 2013!

ℹ️ Getting Around

M-Indicator (http://m-indicator.soft112.com) is an invaluable app for Mumbai public transit – from train schedules to rickshaw fares it covers the whole shebang.

TO/FROM THE AIRPORT
Terminal 1

Autorickshaw If it's not rush hour (7am to 11am and 4pm to 8pm), catch an autorickshaw (between ₹25 and ₹48) to Vile Parle station, where you can get a train to Churchgate (from ₹10, 45 minutes).

Ride-share An off-peak UberGo from the airport runs ₹220 to Bandra Kurla Complex or Bandra West, ₹400 to Fort and ₹425 to Colaba. The Uber and Ola pickup point is a straight shot out the arrivals door to sections Z1–7 in the parking lot (Uber can hot-spot those without a connec-tion from their information booth).

Taxi There's a prepaid taxi counter in the arriv-als hall. A non-AC/AC taxi with one bag costs ₹570/695 to Colaba or Fort and ₹295/350 to Bandra (a bit more at night).

Terminal 2

Autorickshaw Although available, they only go as far south as Bandra; walk out of the terminal and follow the signs. Prices are ₹50 to ₹60 to Vila Parle, ₹50 to ₹70 to Andheri (a traffic warden should keep them honest).

Prepaid taxi Set-fare taxis cost ₹670/810 (non-AC/AC; including one piece of luggage) to Colaba and Fort and ₹400/480 to Bandra. The journey to Colaba takes about an hour at night (via the Sea Link) and 1½ to two hours during the day.

Ride-share Uber and Ola have specific pickup points at the P7 West and East levels respectively; and information booths can hot-spot those without a connection on arrival in order to get you on the road. An off-peak UberGo from the airport runs ₹250 to Bandra Kurla Complex, ₹260 to Bandra West, ₹460 to Fort and ₹560 to Colaba. A ₹105 pickup fee is automatically embedded into the fare.

Train If you arrive during the day (but not during rush hour, and are not weighed down with luggage), consider the train: take an autorickshaw to Andheri train station and then the Churchgate or CSMT train (from ₹10, 45 minutes).

Taxi The trip from South Mumbai to the international airport in an AC taxi should cost from ₹700 to ₹750, plus the ₹70 toll if you take the time-saving Sea Link Bridge. Allow two hours for the trip if you travel between 4pm and 8pm; 45 minutes to 1½ hours otherwise.

BOAT

PNP (Map p48; ☑ 022-22885220; Apollo Bunder, Colaba) and **Maldar Catamarans** (Map p48; ☑ 022-23734841; Apollo Bunder, Colaba) run regular ferries to Mandwa (one way ₹135 to ₹185), useful for access to Murud-Janjira and other parts of the Konkan Coast, avoiding the long bus trip out of Mumbai. Buy tickets at their Taj Gateway Plaza offices.

Launches to Elephanta Island (p54) head to Gharapuri from the Gateway of India every 30 minutes from 9am to 3.30pm (one hour). Buy tickets from the MTDC booth (p54) at the Taj Gateway Plaza. **Launches** (Map p48; Apollo Bunder, Colaba) also run to Mandwa. Buy tickets with PNP and Maldar Catamarans.

An overnight luxury cruise liner – the country's first such domestic operation – set sail in late 2018. **Angriya Cruises** (☑ 8314810440; www. angriyacruises.com; Victoria Docks 15, Purple Gate, off Ferry Wharf, Mazagão; d with/without window from ₹6800/5300), connecting Mumbai with Goa, departs Monday, Wednesday and Friday at 4pm from Victoria Docks just north of Fort, arriving by 10am the following day in Mormugao, 30km south of Panaji.

BUS

M-Indicator has a useful 'search bus routes' facility for hardcore shoestringers and masochists – you'll also need to read the buses' Devanagari numerals on older buses and beware of pickpockets. Fares start at ₹8. Check routes and timetables at http://routenetwork. bestundertaking.com.

BEST (www.bestundertaking.com) bus stands are numerous but include the **east** (Map p48; MG Rd, Colaba) and **west** (Map p48; MG Rd, Colaba) sides of Mahatma Gandhi (MG) Rd and at **CSMT** (Map p60; Chhatrapati Shivaji Maharaj Terminus Area, Fort); as well as **Colaba depot** (Map p48; Colaba Causeway).

METRO

Line 1 of the Mumbai Metro (www.reliance mumbaimetro.com) opened in 2014, the first of a long-phase project expected to finish by 2025. It connects 12 stations in the far northern suburbs to Ghatkopar Station in the east, mostly well away from anywhere of interest to visitors save the growing nightlife hubs of Andheri West and Versova, accessed by DN Nagar and Versova stations respectively. However, Line 1 of the monorail should have been extended south as far as Jacob Circle (5km north of CSMT) by the time you read this (after missing years of deadlines), bringing it past nightlife hub Lower Parel.

Single fares are based on distance and cost between ₹10 and ₹40, with monthly Trip Passes (₹750 to ₹1350) also available. Access to stations is by escalator, carriages are air-conditioned, and there are seats reserved for women and the disabled.

Line 3 (aka Colaba–Bandra–SEEPZ) will be a 33.5km, 27-station underground line connecting Cuffe Parade south of Colaba, Fort, all the main railway terminals, Dadar, Bandra Kurla Complex, Bandra, both airport terminals and on to Andheri. It will be of most interest to tourists but won't open until at least 2021. Station construction is currently wreaking havoc on main thoroughfares around all of these areas, causing major traffic issues and other navigation problems.

TAXI & AUTORICKSHAW

Mumbai's black-and-yellow taxis are very inexpensive and the most convenient way to get around southern Mumbai; drivers *almost* always use the meter without prompting. The minimum fare is ₹22 (for up to 1.5km); a 5km trip costs about ₹80. Meru Cabs (www.meru.in) is a reliable taxi service in Mumbai. Book online or via app, including outstation (long-distance) trips.

Ride-share apps in play include Uber (www. uber.com) and Ola (www.olacabs.com); the latter is good for booking autorickshaws as well – no more rickshaw-wallah price gouging (bear in mind with Ola, you will need to give the driver a one-time password – OTP – set when booking in order to commence the ride).

Autorickshaws are the name of the game north of Bandra. The minimum fare is ₹18, up to 1.5km; a 3km trip is about ₹36 during daylight hours.

Both taxis and autorickshaws tack 50% onto the fare between midnight and 5am; and a possible ₹2 fare hike for both was being bandied about at the time of research. Tip: Mumbaikars tend to navigate by landmarks, not street names (especially new names), so have some details before heading out.

TRAIN

Mumbai's suburban train network is one of the world's busiest; forget travelling during rush hours (7am to 11am and 4pm to 8pm). Trains run from 4.15am to 1am and there are two main lines of most interest to travellers: Western Line and Central Line.

Western Line The most useful; operates out of Churchgate north to Charni Rd (for Girgaum Chowpatty), Mumbai Central, Mahalaxmi (for the Dhobi Ghat), Bandra, Vile Parle (for the domestic airport), Andheri (for the international airport) and Borivali (for Sanjay Gandhi National Park), among others. Make sure you don't catch an express train when you need a slow train – the screens dictate this by an 'S' (Slow) or 'F' (Fast) under 'Mode'.

Mumbai's first AC local train was also introduced on this line in late 2017, running at least five times per day Monday through Friday (8.54am, 11.50am, 2.55pm & 7.49pm to Virar plus an additional 5.49pm departure as far as Borivali).

Central Line Runs from CSMT to Byculla (for Veermata Jijabai Bhonsle Udyan, formerly Victoria Gardens), Dadar and as far as Neral (for Matheran).

From Churchgate 2nd-/1st-class fares are ₹5/50 to Mumbai Central, ₹10/105 to Vile Parle and ₹15/140 to Borivali. 'Tourist tickets' permit unlimited travel in 2nd/1st class for one (₹75/275), two (₹115/445) or five (₹135/510) days. AC fares from Churchgate are ₹60 to Mumbai Central, ₹85 to Bandra, ₹125 to Andheri and ₹165 to Borivali.

To avoid the queues, buy a rechargeable **SmartCard** (₹100, ₹50 of which is retained in credit, ₹50 of which is a refundable deposit), good for use on either train line, then print out your tickets at the numerous automatic ticket vending machines (ATVMs) before boarding. (Place your card on the reader, touch the zone of your station, pick the specific station, choose the amount of tickets, choose 'Buy Ticket' and then 'Print'.) Mobile ticketing is also available via the UTS app (Android; www.utsonmobile. indianrail.gov.in) but set-up is more trouble than its worth for nonresidents.

Watch your valuables, and women, stick to the ladies-only carriages except late at night, when it's more important to avoid empty cars.

MAJOR TRAINS FROM MUMBAI

DESTINATION	TRAIN NO & NAME	SAMPLE FARE (₹)	DURA-TION (HR)	DEPARTURE
Agra	12137 Punjab Mail	585/1555/2250/3855 (A)	22	7.35pm CSMT
Ahmedabad	12901 Gujarat Mail	315/815/1150/1940 (A)	8½	10.05pm BCT
	12009 Shatabdi Exp	1030/1885 East	6½	6.25am BCT
Aurangabad	11401 Nandigram Exp	235/630/900/1510 (A)	7	4.35pm CSMT
	17617 Tapovan Exp	140/505 (C)	7	6.15am CSMT
Bengaluru	11301 Udyan Exp	500/1355/1975/3370 (A)	24	8.10am CSMT
Chennai	12163 Chennai Exp	570/1505/2175/3720 (A)	23½	8.30pm CSMT
Delhi	12951 Mumbai Rajdhani	2725/4075/4730 (D)	15¾	5pm BCT
Hyderabad	12701 Hussainsagar Exp	425/1075/1555/2625 (A)	14½	9.50pm CSMT
Indore	12961 Avantika Exp	440/1165/1660/2815 (A)	14	7.10pm BCT
Jaipur	12955 Mumbai Central Jaipur Superfast Exp (MMCT JP SF)	535/1420/2050/3495 (A)	18	6.50pm BCT
Kochi	16345 Netravati Exp	615/1655/2430 (B)	27	11.40am LTT
Madgaon (Goa)	10103 Mandovi Exp	390/1070/1540/2610 (A)	13	7.10am CSMT
	12133 Mangalore Exp	420/1150/1590 (B)	10¾	10.02pm CSMT
	11085 Mao Doubledecker	840 (F)	12	5.33am Wed, Fri & Sun LTT
Pune	11301 Udyan Exp	140/495/700/1165 (A)	3½	8.10am CSMT

Station abbreviations: CSMT (Chhatrapati Shivaji Maharaj Terminus); BCT (Mumbai Central); LTT (Lokmanya Tilak)

Fares: (A) sleeper/3AC/2AC/1AC; (B) sleeper/3AC/2AC; (C) second class/CC; (D) 3AC/2AC/1AC; East CC/Exec CC; (F) CC

Maharashtra

Includes ➡

Nashik 84
Aurangabad 88
Ellora 92
Ajanta 95
Jalgaon 98
Nagpur 98
Konkan Coast 101
Matheran 105
Lonavla 106
Pune 108
Kolhapur 114
Mahabaleshwar 115

Best Places to Eat

➡ Savya Rasa (p110)

➡ Malaka Spice (p111)

➡ Sadhana (p87)

➡ Bhoj (p91)

➡ Grapevine (p115)

Best Places to Stay

➡ The Machan (p107)

➡ Beyond by Sula (p85)

➡ Tiger Trails Jungle Lodge (p100)

➡ Anandvan Resort (p88)

➡ Dune Barr House (p106)

Why Go?

India's third-largest and second-most populous state, Maharashtra is showcase of many of India's iconic attractions. There are palm-fringed beaches; lofty, cool-green mountains; Unesco World Heritage Sites; and bustling cosmopolitan cities (and gorgeous vineyards in which to escape them). In the far east of the state are some of the nation's most impressive national parks, including Tadoba-Andhari Tiger Reserve.

Inland lie the extraordinary cave temples of Ellora and Ajanta, undoubtedly Maharashtra's greatest monuments, hewn by hand from solid rock. Matheran, a colonial-era hill station served by a toy train, has a certain allure, while pilgrims and inquisitive souls are drawn to cosmopolitan Pune, a city famous for its 'sex guru' and alternative spiritualism. Westwards, the romantic Konkan Coast, fringing the Arabian Sea, is lined with spectacular, crumbling forts and sandy beaches; some of the best are around pretty Malvan, which is fast becoming one of India's premier diving centres.

When to Go
Nashik

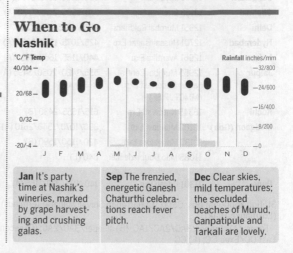

Jan It's party time at Nashik's wineries, marked by grape harvesting and crushing galas.

Sep The frenzied, energetic Ganesh Chaturthi celebrations reach fever pitch.

Dec Clear skies, mild temperatures; the secluded beaches of Murud, Ganpatipule and Tarkali are lovely.

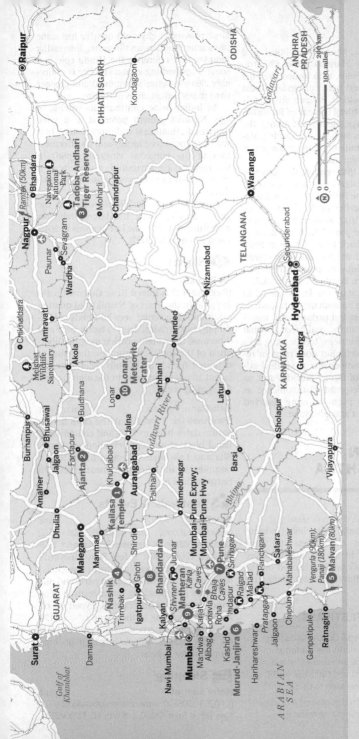

Maharashtra Highlights

1 Kailasa Temple (p93) Being amazed by the intricate beauty in the Ellora temples.

2 Ajanta (p96) Wandering through ancient cave galleries and admiring sublime ancient Buddhist art.

3 Tadoba-Andhari Tiger Reserve (p100) Searching for big cats inside this tiger reserve.

4 Nashik (p84) Sipping on a glass of Chenin Blanc or Cabernet-Shiraz in this gorgeous wine country.

5 Malvan (104) Diving or snorkelling in the big blue.

6 Murud-Janjira (p101) Wondering at the might of a lost civilisation at the colossal over-water Janjira Fort.

7 Pune (p108) Delving into new-age spiritualism and modern Indian cuisine.

8 Bhandardara (p88) Riding out a monsoon amid dramatic mountain scenery.

9 Matheran (p105) Exploring the spectacular hill station viewpoints.

10 Lonar Meteorite Crater (p99) Contemplating Mother Nature's wrath at a quirky, primordial crater.

History

Maharashtra was given its political and ethnic identity by Maratha leader Chhatrapati Shivaji (1627–80), who lorded over the Deccan plateau and much of western India from his stronghold at Raigad. Still highly respected today, Shivaji is credited for instilling a strong, independent spirit among the region's people, as well as establishing Maharashtra as a dominant player in the power relations of medieval India.

From the early 18th century, the state was under the administration of a succession of ministers called the Peshwas, who ruled until 1819, ceding thereafter to the British. After Independence in 1947, western Maharashtra and Gujarat were joined to form Bombay state. But it was back to the future in 1960, when modern Maharashtra was formed with the exclusion of Gujarati-speaking areas and with Mumbai (then Bombay) as its capital.

Since then the state has forged ahead to become one of the nation's most prosperous, with India's largest industrial sector, mainly thanks to agriculture, coal-based thermal energy, nuclear electricity, technology parks and software exports. But poor rains in recent years have hampered crop yields, leading to a number of farmer suicides and, as a byproduct, widespread caste violence as Maratha activists push for more reserved jobs in government and education.

NORTHERN MAHARASHTRA

Nashik

☑ 0253 / POP 1.57 MILLION / ELEV 565M

Located on the banks of the holy Godavari River, Nashik (or Nasik) gets its name from the episode in the Ramayana where Lakshmana, Rama's brother, hacked off the *nasika* (nose) of Ravana's sister. Today this

---

TOP STATE FESTIVALS

Dussehra (☉ Sep & Oct) A Hindu festival, but it also marks the Buddhist celebration of the anniversary of the famous humanist and Dalit leader BR Ambedkar's conversion to Buddhism.

Naag Panchami (☉ Jul/Aug) A traditional snake-worshipping festival.

---

large provincial city's old quarter has some intriguing wooden architecture, interesting temples that reference the Hindu epic and some huge bathing ghats. The city is noticeably cleaner, better maintained and greener than many Indian cities of its size.

As Indian wine continues its coming of age, Nashik's growth potential as a wine tourism destination is wide open. India's best wines are produced locally and an afternoon touring the gorgeous vineyards (p86) in the countryside surrounding the city is a great reason to point your nose in Nashik's direction.

Every 12 years Nashik plays host to the grand Kumbh Mela, the largest religious gathering on Earth (the last one was in 2015, the next one is in 2027).

⊙ Sights

★ Ramkund   GHAT

(Panchavati) This sacred River Godavari bathing ghat in the heart of Nashik's old quarter, a Kumbh Mela venue, sees hundreds of Hindu pilgrims arriving daily to bathe, pray and – because the waters provide moksha (liberation of the soul) – to immerse the ashes of departed friends and family. There's an adjacent market that adds to the alluring and fascinating scene.

Kala Rama Temple   HINDU TEMPLE

(Panchavati Rd; ☉ 5am-10pm) The city's holiest shrine dates back to 1794 and contains unusual black stone representations of Rama, Sita and Lakshmana. Legend has it that it occupies the site where Lakshmana sliced off Surpanakha's nose.

☼ Festivals & Events

SulaFest   WINE

(www.sulafest.com; Sula Vineyards, Gat 36/2, Govardhan Village, off Gangapur-Savargaon Rd; 1-/2-day pass ₹2600/4300; ☉ Feb) Sula Vineyard's SulaFest, which takes place the first weekend of February, is Nashik's biggest party and one of India's best boutique music festivals. The winery swarms with revellers, hyped up on juice and partying to the sound of over 120 live bands and internationally acclaimed DJs on three stages. Check https://in.bookmy show.com for tickets.

🛏 Sleeping

Hotel Samrat   HOTEL $

(☑ 0253-2306100; www.hotelsamratnasik.com; Old Agra Rd; d from ₹1000, s/d with AC ₹1790/2130;

Nashik

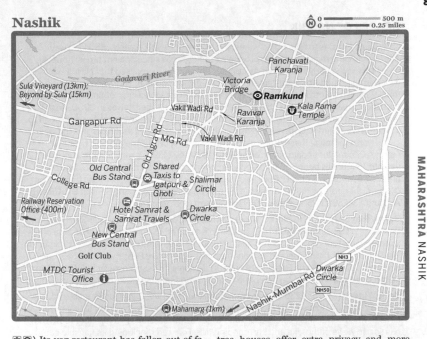

❄️🛜) Its veg restaurant has fallen out of favour as a local hotspot, but Samrat's hotel still offers superb value, with comfortable rooms, some of which have large windows and pine furniture. Located right next to the bus stand, with a private bus agent on its doorstep, it's a sensible choice. Wi-fi is speedy but requires maddening hoop jumping to connect.

Ginger HOTEL $$
(☑0253-6616333; www.gingerhotels.com; Plot P20, Satpur MIDC, Trimbak Rd; s/d ₹2580/3130; ❄️🛜) Primarily a business hotel, this hip Indian chain hotel features DIY services, but there are conveniences aplenty. Though the hotel itself is less lively than some other Ginger hotels in India, the 92 fresh and inviting rooms have blonde wood, high cleanliness standards and swish en suites. It's around 4.5km west of the central district.

★The Source at Sula BOUTIQUE HOTEL $$$
(☑7875555735; www.sulawines.com; Gat 36/2, off Gangapur-Savargaon Rd, Govardhan Village; d/ste from ₹9140/11,750; ❄️🛜🏊) 🍴 Sula's new 31-room, Tuscan-inspired resort occupies the converted facilities of the brand's original winery. Extremely comfortable rooms are decked out in French countryside chic with unobtrusive Indian touches (many with vineyard, pool or cobblestone courtyard views) and spacious bathrooms. Four acacia-wood

tree houses offer extra privacy and more rustic-chic decor. There is also a spa (grapeseed oil massage ₹3100).

★Beyond by Sula RESORT $$$
(☑7875555725; www.sulawines.com; Gangavarhe; d incl breakfast ₹10,240; ❄️🛜🏊) Sula Vineyard's seven-room flagship resort sits a few kilometres from the winery (hence the name: Beyond) near the edges of the beautiful Gangapur Dam backwaters. Uber-contemporary rooms feature polished concrete flooring and huge windows framing the picturesque setting, which culminates in the massive three-bedroom Sky Villa (₹38,400), a modern, architecturally fascinating space evoking the modernist luxury resorts of Patagonia.

★Vallonné Vineyards GUESTHOUSE $$$
(☑9819129455; www.vallonnevineyards.com; Gat 504, Kavnai Shivar; d lawn/vineyard view incl breakfast ₹6500/7500) First and foremost a boutique winery known for its Cabernet Sauvignon and Vin de Passerillage dessert wine (tastings ₹400; 11am to 4.30pm), not to mention the fantastic Malaka Spice (p87) restaurant, Valloné also has two vineyard-view rooms that offer the most extraordinary vistas of any Nashik wine country hotel. Don't expect hotel services, however – though the views make up for this.

GRAPES OF NASHIK

From wimpy raisins to full-bodied wines, the grapes of Nashik have come a long way. The surrounding region had been producing table grapes since ancient times; however, it was only in the early 1990s that a couple of entrepreneurs realised that Nashik, with its fertile soils and temperate climate, harboured good conditions for wine cultivation. In 1997 industry pioneer Sula Vineyards fearlessly invested in a crop of Sauvignon Blanc and Chenin Blanc and the first batch of domestic wines hit the shelves in 2000. Nashik hasn't looked back. These days the wine list in most of Nashik's wineries has stretched to include Shiraz, Merlot, Cabernet, Semillon and Zinfandel as well as a few sparkling wines.

It's worth sampling these drops first-hand by visiting one of the region's beautiful estates. Oenophiles should enlist **Wine Friend** (☑ 9822439051; www.winefriend.in; full-day tour ₹6000, plus tasting fees), the only experienced guide doing wine speciality tours around Nashik's vineyards (₹6000 plus tasting fees). Alternatively, cars can be hired on Ola for eight hours at ₹1450; or try the friendly and English-speaking Sanil at **SCK Rent-A-Car** (☑ 8888080525; scktravels2015@gmail.com) for a horn-free ride.

Sula Vineyards (☑ 9970090010; www.sulawines.com; Gat 36/2, off Gangapur-Savargaon Rd, Govardhan Village; tastings ₹400; ☉ 11am-11pm) 🍷 Located 15km west of Nashik, Sula offers a professional tour (around 45 minutes) of its impressive estate and high-tech facilities. This is rounded off with themed six wine-tasting sessions like Beat the Heat (₹400; all whites and sparkling) and Best of Sula (₹400; features its best drops, including two from its top-end Rasa line). The tasting patio here has commanding views of the countryside.

York Winery (☑ 0253-2230701; www.yorkwinery.com; Gat 15/2, Gangapur-Savargaon Rd, Gangavarhe Village; 5/7 wines ₹150/250; ☉ noon-10pm) A further kilometre from Sula Vineyards, family-owned York Winery offers tours and wine-tasting sessions in a top-floor room that has scenic views of the lake and surrounding hills. Four reds, including its flagship barrel-aged Cab Shiraz, three whites, a rosé and two sparklings are produced. There's a large garden where Western snacks (olives, cheeses) are offered.

Soma Vine Village (☑ 7028066016; www.somavinevillage.com; Gat 1, Gangavarhe; 5 wines ₹350; ☉ 11.30am-6.30pm) One of Nashik's newer wineries, Soma Vine Village, 17km west of the city centre on the same road as Sula and York, offers 45-minute tours that end in a sampling plucked from its 11-wine portfolio, including its award-winning Chenin Blanc Gold and its rosé dessert wine, both excellent.

Chandon (☑ 9561065030; www.chandon.co.in; Gat 652/653, Taluka-Dindori Village; tastings ₹500; ☉ 10am-6pm Mon-Fri) Nashik's newest winery is a world-class facility on meticulously manicured grounds that easily rank as Nashik's most peaceful and beautiful. Tastings (₹500, recoupable with purchase) feature India's leading sparkling wines, Chandon Brut (Chenin Blanc/Chardonnay/Pinot Noir) and Brut Rosé (Shiraz/Pinot Noir). Sip your bubbly in the upscale contemporary lounge, wine gallery or on the tremendously picturesque terrace. It's 26km north of Nashik.

Grover Zampa (☑ 02553-204379; www.groverzampa.in; Gat 967/1026, Village Sanjegaon, Tallgatpuri; 5/7 wines ₹500/650; ☉ 10am-5.30pm, tours 10.30am, 2.30pm & 4pm) It first produced juice with imported French vines at its Karnataka estate in 1992. Today, it's India's oldest surviving winery and easily its most lauded (74 international awards between 2014 and 2016 alone). Tours and tastings at its Nashik estate, 53km southwest of the city, take place in its cinematic cave. The Soireé Brut Rosé and the top-end Chêne Grand Réserve Tempranillo-Shiraz are fantastic. If you come out this way, do dine at nearby Malaka Spice (p87), Nashik's best and most scenic wine-country restaurant, and crash overnight at Valloné Vineyards (p85).

The Vern at BLVD   BOUTIQUE HOTEL **$$$**
(☑ 0253-6644000; www.blvdnashik.com; 1st Level, BLVD, P20, Trimbak Rd, MIDC; s/d from ₹5900/7080; ❄🔊) Nashik's newest digs are part of an entertainment complex featuring restaurants, bars and banquet halls. An elevator shaft complete with vertical garden leads to carpeted hallways and extremely comfortable and modern rooms, sleekly outfitted with flat-screen TVs and grey marble

bathrooms. For Nashik city proper, it's a step up from the mostly mundane, business-oriented offerings elsewhere.

✘ Eating & Drinking

★ Sadhana BREAKFAST $

(www.sadhanamisal.com; Hardev Baug, Gangapur-Satpur Link Rd, Barden Phata; meals ₹90-100; ⊕8am-3pm) This rustic institution on the edge of town serves Nashik's best breakfast of champions, *misal pav* – an unusual Maharashtrian dish prepared with bean sprouts and pulses, topped with flattened puffed rice, crunchy chickpea flour noodles, onions, lemon and coriander and served with a buttered bun – to the tune of up to 5000 people on weekends. Cash only. Unmissable.

Grab an Uber (₹125 or so) to get here.

★ Divtya Budhlya Wada MAHARASHTRIAN $$

(Anadwali, Gangapur Rd; mains ₹160-310, thalis ₹210-350; ⊕11am-3.30pm & 7-11pm) If you're looking for a spicy kick in the gut, this local hotspot is the place to come for authentic Maharashtrian food that'll make your nose run. Under an atmospheric, lantern-lit bamboo canopy, locals devour the special mutton thali (₹290; could be more generous) and rustic à la carte countryside dishes bone-in, grease, fat and all. Tasty stuff.

It's located 5km northwest of the centre – order an Uber for ₹85 or so. Signed in Marathi only.

★ Malaka Spice ASIAN $$$

(www.malakaspice.com; Vallonné Vineyard, Gat 504, Kavnai Shiver; mains ₹360-660; ⊕11.30am-11.30pm) This excellent branch of Pune's best restaurant is hands-down the most scenic spot to dine in Nashik wine country, with postcard-perfect views across Vallonné Vineyard, Lake Mukane and the dramatic Sahyadris mountains beyond. Tack on a cavalcade of Southeast Asian flavors and a Slow Food, stay-local philosophy and it all adds up to a dining destination worth travelling for.

The Foundry CLUB

(www.blvdnashik.com; 2nd level, BLVD, P20, Trimbak Rd, MIDC; ⊕7.30pm-midnight Sat) Nightlife is scarce in Nashik – it's primarily a spiritual city, despite the surrounding vineyards – but this new, small club inside multipurpose BLVD (pronounce the letters, not 'boulevard') is the hotspot of choice. Pounding techno ricochets off the unfinished concrete dance floor and across a bevy of Bollywood

and international movie posters, exposed air ducts and other industrial-savvy design touches.

ⓘ Information

MTDC Tourist Office (Maharashtra Tourism Development Corporation; ☑0253-2570059; www.maharashtratourism.gov.in; T/I, Golf Club, Old Agra Rd, Matoshree Nagar; ⊕9.45am-6.45pm Mon-Sat, closed 2nd & 4th Sat)

ⓘ Getting There & Away

BUS

The **New Central Bus Stand** (New CBS; ☑0253-2309308; Thakkar Bazar) has services to Aurangabad (non-AC/AC ₹250/425, 4½ hours, hourly, 5am to 12.15am) and Pune (non-AC/AC ₹300/410, 4½ hours, hourly, 4.30am to 1am).

Nashik's **Old Central Bus Stand** (Old CBS; ☑0253-2309310; Police Staff Colony) has buses to Ghoti (₹120, one hour, every two hours, 5am to 10pm), Igatpuri (₹140, one hour, every two hours, 5am to 10pm) and Trimbak (₹40, 45 minutes, every 30 minutes, 4.15am to 11pm). South of town, the **Mahamarg Bus Stand** (Gaikwad Nagar) has services to Mumbai (non-AC/AC ₹220/365, 4½ hours, hourly, 6am to 8pm) and Shirdi (non-AC/AC ₹150/200, 2½ hours, hourly, 6am to 7.30pm).

Private buses head to Ahmedabad (non-AC/AC sleeper from ₹1000/1200, 12 hours, 10 to 15 per day), Kolhapur (AC sleeper from ₹600, 10 hours, 10 daily, 7.30pm to 9pm), Mumbai (from ₹500, four hours, hourly), Pune (from ₹300/450, six hours, hourly) and Nagpur (AC sleeper ₹2200, 12 hours, five daily, 5pm to 7pm). Handy private bus agent **Samrat Travels** (☑92604484820; Hotel Samrat, Old Agra Rd) sits just outside Hotel Samrat.

Many private buses depart from **Dwarka Circle** (Dwarka Circle) and most Mumbai-bound buses terminate at Dadar TT Circle in Mumbai.

TRAIN

The **Nashik Rd train station** (NK; Iali Gaon) is 8km southeast of the town centre, but a useful **railway reservation office** (1st fl, Palika Bazaar, Sharanpur Rd; ⊙ 8am-8pm Mon-Sat, to 2pm Sun) is 500m west of the Old Central Bus Stand. There are over 25 daily trains to Mumbai so you won't have to wait long; these include the daily Pushpak Express (1st/2AC/sleeper ₹1245/745/170, 4½ hours, 3.15pm). Connections to Aurangabad are not good, with only four daily departures; try the Tapovan Express (2nd class/chair ₹85/325, 3½ hours, 9.50am). An Uber to/from the station to Panchavati costs around ₹175.

Around Nashik

Bhandardara

The picturesque village of Bhandardara is nestled deep in the folds of the Sahyadris, about 70km from Nashik. A surprisingly undiscovered place surrounded by craggy mountains, it is one of Maharashtra's best escapes from the bustle of urban India and one of its most cinematic and bucolic retreats. The lush mountain scenery, especially during the monsoon, is extraordinary.

Most of Bhandardara's habitation is set around Arthur Lake, a loosely horseshoe-shaped reservoir fed by the waters of the Pravara River, which is one of India's largest. The lake is barraged on one side by the imposing Wilson Dam, a colonial-era structure dating back to 1910. Hikers should consider a trek to the summit of Mt Kalsubai, which at 1646m was once used as an observation point by the Marathas. Alternatively, you could hike to the ruins of the Ratangad Fort, another of Shivaji's erstwhile strongholds; or to several Bollywood-preferred waterfalls like Randha or Umbrella falls. Guided highlight tours cost ₹700 – guides usually congregate outside **Anandvan Resort** (☑ 02424-257320; www.anandvanresorts. com; Ghatghar Rd, Village Shendi; ❋ ☎).

Bhandardara can be accessed by taking a local bus from Nashik's Old Central Bus Stand (p87) to Ghoti (₹120, one hour, every two hours, 5am to 10pm), from where **shared taxis** (Bhandardara Rd) carry on the remaining kilometres to Bhandardara (₹50, 45 minutes, 7am to 5.30pm). An outstation Mini Ola from Nashik runs around ₹1650. You can also grab a seat in a **shared taxi** (CBS Rd, Shalimar) (per person ₹50, 30 minutes, 8am to 10pm) to Ghoti from next door to Hotel Priya in Nashik.

From Mumbai, take a local fast Central Line train from CST to the end of the line at Kasara (₹30, 2¼ hours); from where buses to Sherdi village (Bhandardara) coordinate with the train (₹60, two hours).

Igatpuri

Located about 44km south of Nashik, Igatpuri is home to the headquarters of the world's largest *vipassana* meditation institution, the **Vipassana International Academy** (☑ 02553-244076; www.giri.dhamma.org; Dhamma Giri, Igatpuri; donations accepted; ⊙ visitors centre 9.30am-4.30pm). Ten-day residential courses (advance bookings compulsory) are held throughout the year, though teachers warn that it requires rigorous discipline. Visitors can watch a 20-minute intro video or take part in a 10-minute mini Anapana meditation session.

Basic accommodation, food and meditation instruction are provided free of charge, but donations upon completion are accepted.

This strict form of meditation was first taught by Gautama Buddha in the 6th century BC and was reintroduced to India by teacher SN Goenka in the 1960s.

Buses (₹140, one hour, every two hours, 5am to 10.30pm) and shared taxis (p88) (per person ₹60, one hour, 6am to 10pm) for Igatpuri depart next door to Hotel Priya in Nashik. Numerous daily trains call at Igatpuri from Nashik Rd station and Mumbai's CST.

Aurangabad

☑ 0240 / POP 1.28 MILLION / ELEV 515M

Aurangabad laid low through most of the tumultuous history of medieval India and only hit the spotlight when the last Mughal emperor, Aurangzeb, made the city his capital from 1653 to 1707. With the emperor's death came the city's rapid decline, but the brief period of glory saw the building of some fascinating monuments, including Bibi-qa-Maqbara (p89), a Taj Mahal replica, and these continue to draw a steady trickle of visitors. Alongside other historic relics, such as a group of ancient Buddhist caves (p90), these Mughal relics make Aurangabad a good choice for a weekend excursion from Mumbai. But the real reason for traipsing here is because the town is an excellent base for exploring the World Heritage Sites of Ellora and Ajanta.

Silk fabrics were once Aurangabad's chief revenue generator and the town is still

Aurangabad

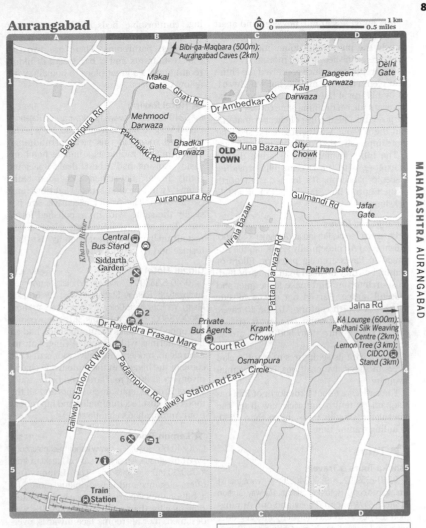

Bibi-qa-Maqbara (500m);
Aurangabad Caves (2km)

known across the world for its hand-woven
Himroo and Paithani saris.

◎ Sights

★ Bibi-qa-Maqbara MONUMENT
(Begumpura; Indian/foreigner ₹40/300; ⊙ 6am-
8pm) Built by Aurangzeb's son Azam Khan in
1679 as a mausoleum for his mother Rabia-
ud-Daurani, Bibi-qa-Maqbara is widely
known as the poor man's Taj. With its four
minarets flanking a central onion-domed
mausoleum, the white structure certainly
does bear a striking resemblance to Agra's
Taj Mahal.

Aurangabad

◉ Activities, Courses & Tours
Ashoka Tours & Travels .... (see 3)

⬛ Sleeping
1 Ginger Hotel B5
2 Hotel Green Olive B3
3 Hotel Panchavati B4
4 Hotel Raviraj B3

⊗ Eating
5 Bhoj B3
6 Tandoor B5

❶ Information
7 Indiatourism A5
  MTDC Tourist Office .... (see 7)

It is much less grand, however, and apart from having a few marble adornments, namely the plinth and dome, much of the structure is finished in lime mortar.

Apparently the prince conceived the entire mausoleum in white marble, but was thwarted by his frugal father who opposed his extravagant idea of draining state coffers for the purpose. Despite the use of cheaper material and the obvious weathering, it's a sight far more impressive than the average gravestone.

The Bibi's formal gardens are a delight to explore, with the Deccan hills providing a scenic backdrop. It's located 3km north of the Central Bus Stand – a ₹50 or so Ola rickshaw ride.

Aurangabad Caves   CAVE
(Grishneswar Temple Rd; Indian/foreigner ₹40/300; ☺6am-6pm) Architecturally speaking, the Aurangabad Caves aren't a patch on Ellora or Ajanta, but they do shed light on early Buddhist architecture and make for a quiet and peaceful outing. Carved out of the hillside in the 6th or 7th century AD, the 10 caves, comprising two groups 1km apart (retain your ticket for entry into both sets), are all Buddhist.

Cave 7, with its sculptures of scantily clad lovers in suggestive positions, is a perennial favourite.

The caves are about 2km north of Bibi-qa-Maqbara. A return autorickshaw from the mausoleum shouldn't cost more than ₹250, including waiting time.

☞ Tours

Ashoka Tours & Travels   TOURS
(☏0240-2359102, 9890340816; www.tourist aurangabad.com; Hotel Panchavati, Railway Station Rd West; ☺7am-9pm) The stand-out Aurangabad agency, with excellent city and regional tours and decent car hire at fair rates. Prices for an air-con car with up to four people are ₹1550 for Ellora and ₹2550 for Ajanta. Run by Ashok T Kadam, a knowledgeable former–autorickshaw driver.

🛏 Sleeping

★Hotel Panchavati   HOTEL $
(☏0240-2328755; www.hotelpanchavati.com; Railway Station Rd West; s/d ₹1000/1260, d with AC ₹1400; ❋@🛜) A traveller-oriented budget hotel, the Panchavati is run by ever-helpful, switched-on management who understand travellers' needs. Rooms are compact but thoughtfully appointed, with crown mould-

ing, comfortable beds (with paisley-style bedspreads); thick bath towels and newly renovated bathrooms. There are two decent restaurants and a 'bar' (read: drinking room) and it's a great place to hook up with fellow travellers.

★Hotel Raviraj   HOTEL $
(☏0240-2352124; www.hotelraviraj.in; Rajendra Prasad Marg; d with AC from ₹1680; ❋🛜) The standard rooms at this pleasant midrange option masquerading as a budget hotel are easily Aurangabad's best deal. Spacious, comfy linens, flat-screen TVs, good bathrooms (with motion-sensor lighting) and (weak) wi-fi. The pricier executives are basically the same, with more polished furniture. Tack on a friendly staff, a leafy foyer, restaurant/bar and beer-friendly 1st-floor terrace and it's tough to beat.

Ginger Hotel   HOTEL $$
(☏0240-6713300; www.gingerhotels.com/ginger-aurangabad; Railway Station Rd East (Dr Bhapkar Marg), Venkateshwar Colony; s/d incl breakfast from ₹3000/3500; ❋@🛜) This 2018 newcomer has upped the stakes in Aurangabad's budget hotel offerings with upgraded Ginger attributes: clean, modern, attractive rooms that are some of the biggest in the nationwide chain's inventory at 30 sq m. Hardwood floors, modern bathrooms, split air-con units and all the mod cons ensure a minimalist and hip retreat from Aurangabad's chaotic streets.

★Lemon Tree   HOTEL $$$
(☏0240-6603030; www.lemontreehotels.com; R7/2 Chikalthana, Airport Rd; s/d incl breakfast from ₹7780/10,140; ❋@🛜🏊) The Lemon Tree offers elegance and class, looking more like a billionaire's luxury whitewashed Mediterranean villa than an Indian hotel. It's well designed, too: all rooms face inwards, overlooking perhaps the best pool on the Decca plateau – all 50m of it. The artsy standard rooms, though not large, are brightened by vivid tropical tones offset against snow-white walls.

Located near the airport, 6km from the centre. You'll find good dining choices here, too, from local cuisine to an Asian noodle bar, and a nice bar with pool, foosball and *carom* (similar to billiards) games.

Hotel Green Olive   HOTEL $$$
(☏0240-2329490; www.hotelgreenolive.com; 13/3 Bhagya Nagar, CBS Rd; s/d from ₹4130/5310; ❋🛜) Cramped bathrooms aside, this boutique-ish business hotel offers stylish, well-equipped

and well-maintained rooms. The friendly staff here look after guests commendably and can organise transport and tours; there's a good bar and restaurant on the premises serving Maharashtrian thalis.

✖ Eating & Drinking

★ Green Leaf
INDIAN $$

(www.greenleafpureveg.com; Shop 6-9, Fame Tapadiya Multiplex, Town Centre; mains ₹160-330; ⊙noon-11pm; 🖘) Aurangabad's favourite modern vegetarian is loved for delectable pure-veg dishes that really pop with flavour (try the veg handi or off-menu paneer Hyderabadi) and come with spice level indicators (one chilli pepper equals medium – they don't offer an explanation for the four chilli pepper offerings...). It's 400m north of CIDCO Bus Stand.

★ Bhoj
INDIAN $$

(Railway Station Rd West; thali ₹260; ⊙11am-3pm & 7-11pm) Rightly famous for its delicious, unlimited Rajasthani and Gujarati thalis, Bhoj is a wonderful place to refuel and relax after a hard day on the road (or rails). It's on the 1st floor of a somewhat scruffy little shopping arcade, but the decor, ambience, service and presentation are all first-rate. Arguably the best thali in Maharashtra outside Mumbai.

Tandoor
NORTH INDIAN $$

(Railway Station Rd East, Shyam Chambers; mains ₹130-470; ⊙11am-11pm) Offers fine tandoori dishes, flavoursome North Indian veg and nonveg options, and an extensive beer list (for Aurangabad) in a weirdly Pharaonic atmosphere. Try the wonderful sizzler kebabs. A few Chinese dishes are also on offer, but patrons clearly prefer the dishes coming out of...well...the tandoor. Fully licensed.

HIMROO WEAVING

Himroo material is a traditional Aurangabad speciality made from cotton, silk and metallic threads. Most of today's Himroo shawls and saris are produced using power looms, but some showrooms still stock hand-loomed cloth.

Himroo saris start at around ₹1500 for a cotton and silk blend. Paithani saris, which are of superior quality, range from ₹9000 to ₹20,000 – but some of them take more than a year to make. If you're buying, make sure you get authentic Himroo, not 'Aurangabad silk'.

KA Lounge
BAR

(Satya Dharam Complex, Akashwari Cir, Jalna Rd; ⊙10am-11.30pm; 🖘) Aurangabad's one and only trendy bar-restaurant caters to the city's upwardly hip who knock back cocktails (₹350 to ₹450) – like the cool burning basil and green chilli mojito – from cosy lounge seating amid exposed brick walls. You can easily make an evening of it; the modern fusion menu (mains ₹150 to ₹690) features interesting Indian/Asian/Continental-hybrid cuisine.

🛍 Shopping

Paithani Silk Weaving Centre
TEXTILES

(📞9970092700; www.paithanisilk.com; 54, P-1, Town Centre, Lokmat Nagar; ⊙9.30am-9pm) One of the best places to come and watch weavers at work is the Paithani Silk Weaving Centre where you'll find good-quality products for sale. It's about 6km east of Kranti Chowk (opposite MGM Medical College), so take a taxi.

ℹ Information

Indiatourism (Government of India Tourism; 📞0240-2364999; www.incredibleindia.org; MTDC Holiday Resort, Railway Station Rd East; ⊙10.30am-5.30pm Mon-Fri)

MTDC Tourist Office (Maharashtra Tourism Development Corporation; 📞0240-2343169; www.maharashtratourism.gov.in; MTDC Holiday Resort, Railway Station Rd East; ⊙10am-5.30pm Mon-Sat, closed 2nd & 4th Sat)

Post Office (www.indiapost.gov.in; Buddi Ln, Naralibag; ⊙10am-5pm Mon-Fri, to 1pm Sat)

ℹ Getting There & Away

BUS

Buses leave about every half-hour from the **Central Bus Stand** (📞0240-2242164; Railway Station Rd West) to Pune (non-AC/AC ₹400/775, 5½ hours, 5am to 6pm) and hourly to Nashik (non-AC/AC ₹350/425, 4½ hours, 5am to 10pm). **Private bus agents** (Dr Rajendra Prasad Marg) are clustered on Dr Rajendra Prasad Marg and Court Rd; a few sit closer to the bus stand. Deluxe overnight bus destinations include Mumbai (AC sleeper ₹800 to ₹1450, 7½ to 9½ hours), Ahmedabad (non-AC/AC sleeper from ₹850/1200, 13 to 15 hours) and Nagpur (AC sleeper ₹1000 to ₹2900, non-AC from ₹1100, 8½ to 10 hours). Buses depart from three locations around town, including opposite Hotel Panchavati and next to DMart.

Ordinary buses head to Ellora from the Central Bus Stand every half-hour (non-AC/AC ₹37/345, 30 minutes, 5.30am to 8pm) and to Jalgaon (non-AC ₹200, four hours, 5.45am to 8pm) via

DON'T MISS

DAULATABAD FORT

No trip to Aurangabad is complete without a pit stop at the ruined but truly magnificent hilltop fortress of **Daulatabad Fort** (NH52; Indian/foreigner ₹25/300; ⊘ 6am-6pm), about 15km away from town en route to Ellora, which sits atop a 200m-high craggy outcrop known as Devagiri (Hill of the Gods). A 5km battlement surrounds this ancient fort, a most beguiling structure built by the Yadava kings through the 12th century and originally conceived as an impregnable fort.

In 1328, it was renamed Daulatabad, the City of Fortune, by Delhi sultan Mohammed Tughlaq, who decided to shift his kingdom's capital to this citadel from Delhi. Known for his eccentric ways, Tughlaq even marched the entire population of Delhi 1100km south to populate it. Ironically, Daulatabad – despite being better positioned strategically than Delhi – soon proved untenable as a capital due to an acute water crisis and Tughlaq forced its weary inhabitants to slope all the way back to Delhi, which had by then been reduced to a ghost town.

The climb to the summit takes about an hour, and leads past an ingenious series of defences, including multiple doorways designed with odd angles and spike-studded doors to prevent elephant charges. A tower of victory, known as the Chand Minar (Tower of the Moon), built in 1435, soars 60m above the ground to the right; it's closed to visitors. Higher up, you can walk into the Chini Mahal, where Abul Hasan Tana Shah, king of Golconda, was held captive for 12 years before his death in 1699. Nearby, there's a 6m cannon, cast from five different metals and engraved with Aurangzeb's name.

Part of the ascent goes through a pitch-black, bat-infested, water-seeping, spiralling tunnel. Guides (₹1600 up to five people) are available near the ticket counter to show you around and their torch-bearing assistants will lead you through the dark passageway for a small tip. On the way down you'll be left to your own devices, so carry a torch.

As the fort is in ruins (with crumbling staircases and sheer drops) and involves a steep ascent, the elderly, children and those suffering from vertigo or claustrophobia will find it a tough challenge. Bring water and allow 2½ hours to explore the structure.

There is little in the way of accommodation at Daulatabad – people bed down in Aurangabad or Ellora. For meals, the entrance to the fort is swarming with dhabas (casual eateries) and fresh fruit and flavoured crushed-ice stalls.

Ellora-bound buses departing the MSRTC bus stand every half-hour (non-AC ₹20, 30 minutes, 5.30am to 8pm) can drop you at the entrance. The stop for buses back to Aurangabad is 500m south of the Fort entrance on the NH52. Rickshaws charge ₹30 (sharing) or ₹100 back to Aurangabad.

Fardapur (₹180, three hours), which is the drop-off point for Ajanta.

From the **CIDCO Bus Stand** (☏ 0240-2240149; Airport Rd), by the Lemon Tree hotel junction, 12 direct buses leave for the Lonar meteorite crater every 45 minutes to one hour (₹200, 4½ hours) between 4.45am and 4.45pm.

TRAIN

Aurangabad's **train station** (AWB; Railway Station Rd East) is not on a main line, but it has four daily direct trains to/from Mumbai. The Tapovan Express (2nd class/chair ₹235/505, 7½ hours) departs Aurangabad at 2.35pm. The Janshatabdi Express (2nd class/chair ₹170/585, 6½ hours) departs Aurangabad at 6am. For Hyderabad, trains include the Ajanta Express (sleeper/2AC ₹300/1165, 10 hours, 10.45pm). To reach northern or eastern India, take a bus to Jalgaon and board a train there.

Ellora

☏ 02437

Give a man a hammer and chisel and he'll create art for posterity. Come to the Unesco World Heritage Site **Ellora cave temples** (Ellora Cave Rd; Indian/foreigner ₹40/600; ⊘ 6am-6pm Wed-Mon), located 30km from Aurangabad, and you'll know exactly what we mean. The epitome of ancient Indian rock-cut architecture, these caves were chipped out laboriously over five centuries by generations of Buddhist, Hindu and Jain monks. Monasteries, chapels, temples – the caves served every purpose and they were stylishly embellished with a profusion of remarkably detailed sculptures.

Undoubtedly Ellora's shining moment is the awesome Kailasa Temple (Cave 16), the world's largest monolithic sculpture, hewn top to bottom against a rocky slope by 7000 labourers over a period of 150 years. Dedicated to Lord Shiva, it is clearly among the best that ancient Indian architecture has to offer.

◉ Sights

Ellora has 34 caves in all: 12 Buddhist (AD 600–800), 17 Hindu (AD 600–900) and five Jain (AD 800–1000) – though the exact time scales of these caves' construction is the subject of academic debate.

Unlike the caves at Ajanta, which are carved into a sheer rock face, the Ellora caves line a 2km-long escarpment, the gentle slope of which allowed architects to build elaborate courtyards in front of the shrines and render them with sculptures of a surreal quality.

The established academic theory is that Ellora represents the renaissance of Hinduism under the Chalukya and Rashtrakuta dynasties, the subsequent decline of Indian Buddhism and a brief resurgence of Jainism under official patronage. However, due to the absence of inscriptional evidence, it's been impossible to accurately date most of Ellora's monuments – some scholars argue that some Hindu temples predate those in the Buddhist group. What is certain is that their coexistence at one site indicates a lengthy period of religious tolerance.

Official guides can be hired at the ticket office in front of the Kailasa Temple for ₹1370 (up to five people). Guides have an extensive knowledge of cave architecture so are worth the investment. If your tight itinerary forces you to choose between Ellora or Ajanta, Ellora wins hands down in terms of architecture (though Ajanta's setting is more beautiful and more of a pleasure to explore).

Ellora is very popular with domestic tourists; if you can visit on a weekday, it's far less crowded. Worth visiting if open for its impressive displays (it was closed during research) is the **Ellora Visitor Centre** (NH211; ⊗ 9am-5pm Wed-Mon).

★ **Kailasa Temple**   HINDU TEMPLE
One of India's greatest monuments, this astonishing temple, carved from solid rock, was built by King Krishna I in AD 760 to represent Mt Kailasa (Kailash), Shiva's Himalayan abode. To say that the assignment was daring would be an understatement. Three huge trenches were bored into the sheer cliff face, a process that entailed removing 200,000 tonnes of rock by hammer and chisel, before the temple could begin to take shape and its remarkable sculptural decoration could be added.

Covering twice the area of the Parthenon in Athens and being half as high again, Kailasa is an engineering marvel that was executed straight from the head with zero margin for error. Modern draughtspeople might have a lesson or two to learn here.

The temple houses several intricately carved panels, depicting scenes from the Ramayana, the Mahabharata and the adventures of Krishna. Also worth admiring are the immense monolithic pillars that stand in the courtyard, flanking the entrance on both sides, and the southeastern gallery that has 10 giant and fabulous panels depicting

MAHARASHTRA ELLORA

CANNABIS CONSERVATION

The remarkable preservation of Ellora's caves and paintings could be attributed to many things, but perhaps none more surprising than a healthy dose of hemp. While the jury is still out on whether the Buddhist, Hindu and Jain monks that called Ellora home over the centuries had a proclivity for smoking cannabis, archaeologists are sure they knew a thing or two about its preservation effects.

An 11-year study released in 2016 revealed that hemp, a variety of the *Cannabis sativa* plant (believed to be one of the world's oldest domesticated crops), has been discovered mixed in with the clay and lime plaster used at Ellora and is credited with being the secret ingredient that has slowed degradation at the Unesco World Heritage Site over the course of 1500 years.

Using electron microscopes, Fourier transforms, infrared spectroscopy and stereomicroscopic studies, chemists from the Archaeological Survey of India found that samples from Ellora contained 10% *Cannabis sativa*, which resulted in reduced levels of insect activity at Ellora – around 25% of the paintings at Ajanta have been destroyed, where hemp was not used. In addition to Ellora, hemp was also implemented by the Yadavas, who built Daulatabad Fort near Aurangabad in the 12th century.

Talk about high and mighty monuments!

Ellora Caves

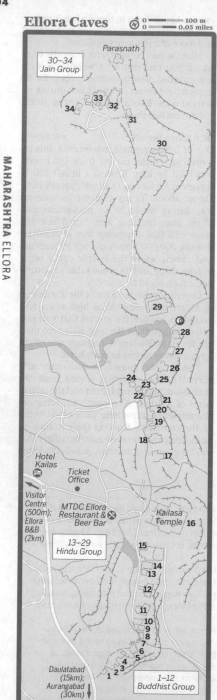

the different avatars (incarnations of a deity) of Lord Vishnu.

After you're done with the main enclosure, bypass the hordes of snack-munching day trippers to explore the temple's many dank, bat urine-soaked corners with their numerous forgotten carvings. Afterwards, hike the sturdier path up to the south of the complex (past the scaffolding) that takes you to the top perimeter of the 'cave', from where you can get a bird's-eye view of the entire temple complex.

Buddhist Caves
CAVE

Calm and contemplation infuse the 12 Buddhist caves, which stretch to the south of Kailasa. All are Buddhist *viharas* (monasteries) used for study and worship, but these multistoreyed structures also included cooking, living and sleeping areas. The one exception is Cave 10, which is a *chaitya* (assembly hall). While the earliest caves are simple, Caves 11 and 12 are more ambitious; both comprise three storeys and are on par with the more impressive Hindu temples.

Cave 1, the simplest vihara, may have been a granary. Cave 2 is notable for its ornate pillars and the imposing seated Buddha that faces the setting sun. Cave 3 and Cave 4 are unfinished and not well preserved.

Cave 5 is the largest vihara in this group at 18m wide and 36m long; the rows of stone benches hint that it may once have been an assembly hall.

Cave 6 is an ornate vihara with wonderful images of Tara, consort of the Bodhisattva Avalokitesvara, and of the Buddhist goddess of learning, Mahamayuri, looking remarkably similar to Saraswati, her Hindu equivalent. Cave 7 is an unadorned hall. Cave 8 is the first cave in which the sanctum is detached from the rear wall. Cave 9, located above Cave 8, is notable for its wonderfully carved fascia.

Cave 10 is the only chaitya in the Buddhist group and one of the finest in India. Its ceiling features ribs carved into the stonework; the grooves were once fitted with wooden panels. The balcony and upper gallery offer a closer view of the ceiling and a frieze depicting amorous couples. A decorative window gently illuminates an enormous figure of the teaching Buddha.

Cave 11, the Do Thal (Two Storey) Cave, is entered through its third basement level, not discovered until 1876. Like Cave 12, it possibly owes its size to competition with Hindu caves of the same period.

Cave 12, the huge Tin Thal (Three Storey) Cave, is entered through a courtyard. The locked shrine on the top floor contains a large Buddha figure flanked by his seven previous incarnations. The walls are carved with relief pictures. Note that the temples are closed on Tuesday.

Jain Caves
CAVE

The five Jain caves, the last created at Ellora, may lack the ambitious size of the best Hindu temples, but they are exceptionally detailed, with some remarkable paintings and carvings.

The caves are 1km north of the last Hindu temple (Cave 29) at the end of the bitumen road; an MSRTC bus departs from in front of Kailasa Temple and runs back and forth (₹20 return; 9.15am to 6pm).

🛏 Sleeping & Eating

Ellora B&B
GUESTHOUSE $

(☎9960589867, 9822534157; ellorabedandbreakfast@gmail.com; Ellora Village; s/d incl breakfast from ₹800/1000; 🛜) For a bit of rustic cultural immersion, good-hearted man about town Sadeek and his uncle Rafiq have four simple rooms in their village home, 2km from the caves (and the crowds). The three best rooms open out onto a breezy terrace with farmland and mountain views and feature renovated en suite bathrooms with sit-down flush toilets and 24-hour hot water.

Hotel Kailas
HOTEL $$

(☎02437-244446; www.hotelkailas.com; NH211; d with/without AC ₹4130/2570; 🌬🛜) The sole decent hotel near the site, with attractive air-con stone cottages set in leafy grounds. The restaurant (mains ₹70 to ₹280) is excellent, with a blackboard menu chalked up that includes sandwiches, breakfasts, curries and tandoori favourites. Wi-fi, however, sold in increments of three hours for ₹100, is ridiculous, though guests get one three-hour slot free.

MTDC Ellora
Restaurant & Beer Bar
INDIAN $

(www.maharashtratourism.gov.in; Ellora Cave Rd; mains/thali from ₹80/150; ⊙9am-5pm) Located within the temple complex, this is an easy place for lunch or a cold Kingfisher.

❶ Getting There & Away

Buses depart Aurangabad Central Bus Stand every half-hour (non-AC/AC ₹37/345, 30 minutes, 5.30am to 8pm); the last return bus departs from Ellora at 7pm. Share 4WDs are also an option, but get packed; they leave when full and stop outside the bus stand in Aurangabad (₹30). A full-day tour to Ellora, with stops en route, costs ₹1550 in an air-con car; try Ashoka Tours & Travels (p90). Autorickshaws ask for ₹800.

Ajanta
☑ 02438

Superbly set in a remote river valley 105km northeast of Aurangabad, the remarkable cave temples of Ajanta are this region's second World Heritage Site. Much older than Ellora, these secluded caves date from around the 2nd century BC to the 6th century AD and were among the earliest monastic institutions to be constructed in the country. Ironically, it was Ellora's rise that brought about Ajanta's downfall and historians believe the site was abandoned once the focus shifted to Ellora.

As the Deccan forest claimed and shielded the caves, with roots and shoots choking the sculptures, Ajanta remained deserted for about a millennium, until 1819 when a British hunting party led by officer John Smith stumbled upon it purely by chance.

◉ Sights

One of the primary reasons to visit Ajanta is to admire its renowned 'frescoes', actually temperas, which adorn many of the caves' interiors. With few other examples from ancient times matching their artistic excellence and fine execution, these paintings are of unfathomable heritage value.

Despite their age, the paintings in most caves remain finely preserved and many attribute it to their relative isolation from humanity for centuries. However, it would be a tad optimistic to say that decay hasn't set in.

It's believed that the natural pigments for these paintings were mixed with animal glue and vegetable gum to bind them to the dry surface. Many caves have small, craterlike

---

❶ PHOTO RULES

Flash photography is strictly prohibited within the caves, due to its adverse effect on the natural dyes used in the paintings. Authorities have installed rows of tiny pigment-friendly lights, which cast a faint glow within the caves, as additional lighting is required for glimpsing minute details, but you'll have to rely on long exposures for photographs.

Ajanta Caves

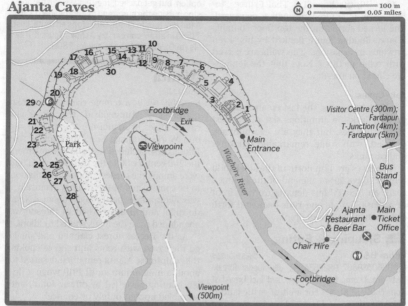

holes in their floors, which acted as palettes during paint jobs.

Two lookouts offer picture-perfect views of the whole horseshoe-shaped gorge. The first is a short walk beyond the river, crossed via a bridge below Cave 8. A further 40-minute uphill walk (not to be attempted during the monsoons) leads to the lookout from where the British party first spotted the caves.

Most buses ferrying tour groups don't arrive until noon. To avoid the crowds, stay locally in Fardapur or make an early start from Aurangabad.

While closed at time of research, the **Ajanta Visitor Centre** (Aurangabad-Jalgaon Hwy; ⊙9am-5.30pm Tue-Sun) is worth visiting if open for its displays, audio guides and cafe.

★ **Ajanta Caves** CAVE
(Indian/foreigner ₹40/600, video ₹25, authorised guide ₹1600; ⊙9am-5.30pm Tue-Sun) Ajanta's caves line a steep face of a horseshoe-shaped gorge bordering the Waghore River. Five of the caves are *chaityas* (assembly or prayer halls) while others are *viharas* (monasteries with attached residential cells). Caves 8, 9, 10, 12, 13 and part of 15 are early Buddhist caves, while the others date from around the 5th century AD (Mahayana period). In the austere early Buddhist school, the Buddha

was never represented directly but always alluded to by a symbol such as the footprint or wheel of law.

Cave 1 CAVE
Cave 1, a Mahayana *vihara*, was one of the last to be excavated and is the most beautifully decorated. This is where you'll find a rendition of the *Bodhisattva Padmapani*, the most famous and iconic of the Ajanta artworks. A verandah in front leads to a large congregation hall housing sculptures and narrative murals known for their splendid perspective and elaborate detailing of dress, daily life and facial expressions.

Cave 2 CAVE
Cave 2 is a late Mahayana *vihara* with deliriously ornamented columns and capitals and some fine paintings. The ceiling is decorated with geometric and floral patterns. The murals depict scenes from the Jataka tales, including Buddha's mother's dream of a six-tusked elephant, which heralded his conception.

Cave 4 CAVE
Cave 4 is the largest *vihara* at Ajanta and is supported by 28 pillars. Although never completed, the cave has some impressive sculptures, such as the four statues surrounding a huge central Buddha. There

are also scenes of people fleeing from the 'eight great dangers' to the protection of Avalokitesvara.

Cave 6
CAVE

Cave 6 is the only two-storey *vihara* at Ajanta, but parts of the lower storey have collapsed. Inside is a seated Buddha figure and an intricately carved door to the shrine. Upstairs the hall is surrounded by cells with fine paintings on the doorways.

Cave 7
CAVE

Cave 7 has an atypical design, with porches before the verandah leading directly to the four cells and the elaborately sculptured shrine.

Cave 9
CAVE

Cave 9 is one of the earliest *chaityas* at Ajanta. Although it dates from the early Buddhist period, the two figures flanking the entrance door were probably later Mahayana additions. Columns run down both sides of the cave and around the 3m-high dagoba (pagoda) at the far end.

Cave 10
CAVE

Cave 10 is thought to be the oldest cave (200 BC) and was the first one to be spotted by the British hunting party. Similar in design to Cave 9, it is the largest *chaitya*. The facade has collapsed and the paintings inside have been damaged, in some cases by graffiti dating from soon after their rediscovery. One of the pillars to the right bears the engraved name of Smith, who left his mark here for posterity.

Cave 16
CAVE

Cave 16, a *vihara*, contains some of Ajanta's finest paintings and is thought to have been the original entrance to the entire complex. The best known of these paintings is of the 'dying princess', Sundari, wife of the Buddha's half-brother Nanda, who is said to have fainted at the news her husband was renouncing the material life (and her) in order to become a monk.

Cave 17
CAVE

With carved dwarfs supporting the pillars, cave 17 has Ajanta's best-preserved and most varied paintings. Famous images include a princess applying make-up, a seductive prince using the old trick of plying his lover with wine, and the Buddha returning home from his enlightenment to beg from his wife and astonished son.

Cave 19
CAVE

Cave 19, a magnificent *chaitya,* has a remarkably detailed facade; its dominant feature is an impressive horseshoe-shaped window. Two fine, standing Buddha figures flank the entrance. Inside is a three-tiered dagoba with a figure of the Buddha on the front. Outside the cave, to the west, sits a striking image of the Naga king with seven cobra hoods around his head. His wife, hooded by a single cobra, sits by his side.

Cave 26
CAVE

A largely ruined *chaitya,* cave 26 is now dramatically lit and contains some fine sculptures that shouldn't be missed. On the left wall is a huge figure of the reclining Buddha, lying back in preparation for nirvana. Other scenes include a lengthy depiction of the Buddha's temptation by Maya.

🛏 Sleeping & Eating

MTDC Ajanta Tourist Resort   HOTEL **$$**
(☎02438-244230; www.maharashtratourism. gov.in; Aurangabad-Jalgaon Hwy, Fardapur; d with/ without AC ₹2130/1790; 🕸) This government hotel is pricey but the best option at Ajanta, set amid lawns in a peaceful location off the main road in Fardapur, 5km from the caves. Air-con rooms, in apple green structures, are spacious; non-AC rooms are less interesting but fine. There's a garden and restaurant with veg thalis (₹150 to ₹250).

★ Hotel Radhe Krishna   DHABA **$**
(Aurangabad-Jalgaon Hwy, Fardapur; mains ₹70-180, thalis from ₹180; ⊗24hr) The best of Fardapur's streetside *dhabas* (casual eatery serving basic meals), this excellent spot is fresh, cheap and satisfying. The famous cook, Babu, and his team get a big kick out of foreigners dropping in, and just watching these guys whip up various curries, thalis and a fry or two is pure entertainment.

ⓘ Getting There & Away

Buses from Aurangabad or Jalgaon will drop you at the Fardapur T-junction (where the highway meets the road to the caves), 4km from the site. From here, after paying an 'amenities' fee (₹10), walk to the departure point for the **buses** (with/ without AC ₹30/20; ⊗9am-6pm), which zoom up to the caves. Buses return half-hourly to the T-junction; the last bus is at 6pm. Note that the caves are closed on Monday.

All MSRTC (www.msrtc.gov.in) buses passing through Fardapur stop at the T-junction. After the caves close you can board buses to either

Aurangabad or Jalgaon outside the MTDC Holiday Resort in Fardapur, 1km down the main road towards Jalgaon. Taxis are available in Fardapur; ₹2000/3000 should get you to Jalgaon/Aurangabad.

The Aurangabad–Jalgaon Hwy was being expanded to four lanes at time of writing – expect faster drive times between the two and to Ajanta from either city in the near future.

Jalgaon

☎ 0257 / POP 468,300 / ELEV 208M

Apart from being a handy base for exploring Ajanta 60km away, the industrial city of Jalgaon is really nothing more than a convenient transit town. It has rail connections to all major cities across India.

🛏 Sleeping & Eating

★ Hotel Plaza   HOTEL $

(☎ 0257-2227354, 9370027354; hotelplaza_jal@ yahoo.com; Station Rd; dm ₹300, s/d from ₹650/950, d with AC ₹1500-2000; ❋@☎) This extremely well-managed and well-presented hotel is only a short hop from the station. Rooms vary in size and layout, but with whitewashed walls, a minimalist feel and bathrooms cleaner than a Jain temple, it's modestly boutique and brilliant value. Everything from the hospitality to the bed linens exceeds expectations.

Hotel Arya   INDIAN $

(Old Mamurabad Rd; mains ₹40-150; ☺11am-10.30pm) Delicious vegetarian food, particularly Punjabi cuisine, though a few Chinese and South Indian dishes are also offered. It's a short walk south along Station Rd, left at MG Rd and left at the clock tower. You may have to queue for a table at lunchtime.

ℹ Getting There & Away

Jalgaon's **train station** (JL; Station Rd) and **bus stand** (☎ 0257-2229774; Mahatma Gandhi Rd) are about 2km apart (₹30 by autorickshaw).

Several express trains connecting Mumbai (sleeper/2AC ₹280/1017, eight hours), Delhi (₹550/2020, 18 hours), Ahmedabad (₹340/1255, 10 hours) and Varanasi (₹485/1970, 20 hours) stop at Jalgaon Junction train station. Ten daily trains head for Nagpur (₹215/1015, five to nine hours).

Non-AC buses to Fardapur T-junction (₹82, 1½ hours), for access to Ajanta, depart every 30 minutes from the bus stand between 5am and 10pm, continuing to Aurangabad (₹235, four hours). There is also one daily AC departure to Nagpur (₹1200, nine hours, 1am).

Private bus companies on Station Rd offer AC sleeper services to Mumbai (₹800, 9½ hours) and Nagpur (₹750, nine hours). Try Durga Travels or Mahalaxmi Travels.

Nagpur

☎ 0712 / POP 2.43 MILLION / ELEV 305M

Way off the main tourist routes, the isolated city of Nagpur holds the distinction of being the dead geographical centre of India. It lacks must-see sights but is an important gateway to several reserves and parks including Tadoba-Andhari Tiger Reserve and Pench National Park. It's also close to the temples of Ramtek and the ashrams of Sevagram. Summer is the best time to taste the city's famous oranges, but the trade-off is unbearable heat.

🛏 Sleeping

Legend Inn   HOTEL $$

(☎ 0712-6658666; www.thelegendinn.com; 14 Modern Society, Wardha Rd; s/d incl breakfast from ₹4130/4720; ❋@☎) On the main highway for the Tadoba-Andhari Tiger Reserve, this is an efficiently run hotel, owned by an Indian mountaineering legend, with well-appointed rooms, a good restaurant, smoky bar and smiley staff (which might make up for the low water pressure). Free pick-ups from the airport, 1km away, are included, but the metro will eventually stop right outside its door.

Hotel Hardeo   HOTEL $$$

(☎ 0712-6684888; www.hardeohotel.com; Munje Marg, Sitabuldi; s/d incl breakfast from ₹3540/4130; ❋☎) The best hotel nearest the train station, this upper midrange, professionally run business hotel is 1.3km from the rails. The modern bathrooms, flat-screen LED TVs, lacquer-accented woods and soothing earth tones might just hit the spot after a long haul in sleeper class (as do the large dosas at breakfast). Prices include airport/railway station transfers.

🍴 Eating

★ Varadi That   MAHARASHTRIAN $

(Ganesh Chamber, Mehadiya Chowk, Dhantoli; mains ₹80-200; ☺11am-4pm & 7.30-11pm) No English inside or out, but this simple but super Maharashtrian stalwart is absolutely excellent for the state's fiery regional cuisine. Try *jhunka* (chickpea flour porridge with chillies and spices) and *kacha bharit* (a fire-roasted aubergine dish with chillies and spices similar to baba ghanoush, served

LONAR METEORITE CRATER

If you like offbeat adventures, travel to Lonar to explore a prehistoric natural wonder. About 50,000 years ago, a meteorite slammed into the earth here, leaving behind a massive crater 2km across and 170m deep (it's said to be the world's third largest). In scientific jargon, it's the only hypervelocity natural-impact crater in basaltic rock in the world. In lay terms, it's as tranquil and relaxing a spot as you could hope to find, with a shallow green lake at its base and wilderness all around, including aquatic birds. The lake water is supposedly alkaline and excellent for the skin. Scientists think the meteorite is still embedded about 600m below the southeastern rim of the crater.

The crater's edge is home to several Hindu temples as well as wildlife, including langurs, peacocks, deer and numerous birds.

The **MTDC Tourist Complex** (☑ 8806363498; rathod.dilip95@gmail. com; dm ₹250, d with AC ₹2015; ❈ 🛜) has a prime location just across the road from the crater and offers deluxe rooms that are in excellent shape, with stylish en suite bathrooms.

There are direct buses every 45 minutes to one hour between Lonar and the CIDCO bus stand in Aurangabad (₹200, 4½ hours, 4.45am to 4.45pm), but you'll need to catch the 7.30am departure at the latest unless you plan on spending the night. The last bus back from Lonar departs at 2pm.

It's also possible to visit Lonar on a day trip from Aurangabad or Jalgaon if you hire a car and driver and don't mind dishing out about ₹3060 (AC).

---

cold). Both can be scooped up with the house *bhakri* (sorghum bread). Cash only.

⭐ **Breakfast Story**   CAFE **$$**
(www.facebook.com/thebreakfastorynagpur; Sai Sagar Apt, Hingna Rd; mains ₹110-345; ⏲ 8am-2.30pm & 3.30-7pm Mon & Tue, Thu-Sat, 8am-3pm Sun; 🛜) This stylish all-day breakfast-only hotspot in a residential building 7km southwest of the centre is worth a diversion. English, American and Belgian breakfast combos, sandwiches, pancakes and waffles, along with daily chalkboard specials, are served up on artsy wooden tables covered in comics. Cassette tapes, newspapers and other pop art line the walls, completing the cosy, trendy atmosphere.

⭐ **Majestic Masala**   NORTH INDIAN **$$$**
(☑ 0712-6653666; www.tulihotels.com/tuli-imperial.html; Hotel Tuli Imperial, 37 Central Bazar Rd; mains ₹350-900; ⏲ noon-3pm & 7pm-midnight) Inside one of Nagpur's most regal hotels, this equally austere, incredibly atmospheric restaurant serves the delectable recipes of India's noble class, including rich Amritsari paneer dishes and tempting meat preparations not commonly seen (slow-fired lamb shanks, smoked mutton, Hyderbadi chicken with fenugreek), served on brass plateware. It's one of the city's top spots.

ℹ Information

MTDC Tourist Office (Maharashtra Tourism Development Corporation; ☑ 0712-2533325; www.maharashtratourism.gov.in; West High Court Rd, Civil Lines; ⏲ 10am-5pm Mon-Sat, closed 2nd & 4th Sat) Staff here can help with getting to national parks near Nagpur. There is also a **booth** (Arrivals Hall; ⏲ 9am-6pm Mon-Sat) at the airport.

ℹ Getting There & Away

AIR

Dr Babasaheb Ambedkar International Airport (☑ 0712-2807501; Sonegaon) is 8km southwest of the centre. Domestic airlines, including Air India (www.airindia.in), IndiGo (www.goindigo.in), Jet Airways (www.jetair ways.com) and GoAir (www.goair.in), fly direct to Prayagraj (Allahabad), Delhi, Mumbai, Kolkata, Hyderabad, Bengaluru, Indore, Chennai and Pune. Internationally, Qatar and Air Arabia fly to Doha and Sharjah, respectively.

BUS

The main **MSRTC/Ganesh Peth Bus Stand** (☑ 0712-2726221; Chopkar Rd) is 2km south of the train station. Ordinary buses head for Aurangabad (non-AC/ShivShahi ₹566/840, 17 daily, 4am to 8pm), Pune (non-AC/ShivShahi ₹1250/1370, 1pm, 4pm, 5pm and 6pm), Ramtek (₹60, 1½ hours, every 30 minutes, 6am to 10pm), Jalgaon (non-AC/ShivShahi sleeper ₹410/1210, nine hours, 7pm and 8.45pm) and Wardha (non-AC/ShivShahi ₹150/200, three hours, every 30 minutes, 5am to 4.30pm and 10.15pm).

WORTH A TRIP

TADOBA-ANDHARI TIGER RESERVE

The seldom-visited **Tadoba-Andhari Tiger Reserve** (Chandrapur; per entry week/weekend ₹4000/8000; ☺6am-10am & 3-6pm with seasonal variations), 150km south of Nagpur, is one of the best places to see tigers in India. Seeing fewer visitors than most other Indian forest reserves – it gets around 60% fewer visitors than neighbouring parks in Madhya Pradesh – this is a place where you can get up close to wildlife without having to jostle past truckloads of shutter-happy tourists. Rather than restrict access to certain zones of the park like other tiger parks in India, Tadoba-Andhari opted to limit the number of gypsy safaris per day instead (48) but give them free reign throughout the park. The results are excellent for wildlife-sighting opportunities. The park also remains open throughout the year, unlike many in India.

There are 15 legal lodges around Tadoba-Andhari Tiger Reserve, the majority of them in Moharli, ranging from resort homestays to more upscale options. For the best wildlife experience, however, it's tough to beat **Tiger Trails Jungle Lodge** (☎0712-6627649, 9763168010; www.tigertrails.in; Khutwanda Gate; s/d incl all meals from ₹9500/15,000; ❄☏☒) ⌖, located at Khutwanda with its own private gate.

Most visitors reach the park by private vehicle. The round trip from Nagpur can cost as much as ₹13,000 with a private driver, but an Ola Outstation in a prime sedan runs just ₹10 per kilometre, so ₹2620.

That said, to reach Khutwanda Gate on public transport, catch a bright and early Chandrapur-bound bus from Nagpur to Warora (non-AC/ShivShahi ₹150/200, three hours, every 30 minutes, 5am to 10pm), where you can catch the sole bus (10.45am) for the remaining 42km to Khutwanda gate (₹70, 1½ hours). The same bus returns the following day at 6am.

For Moharli, stay on the bus to Chandrapur (non-AC/ShvShahi ₹190/250, four hours) and catch a second bus on to Moharli (₹35, one hour, 6am, 8am, 10am, 2.30pm and 5.30pm). Returning to Chandrapur, buses depart Moharli at 7am, 10.30am, 1pm and 5.30pm.

There are government buses to Madhya Pradesh from the **MP Bus Stand** (☎0712-2533695; Sitabuldi), 350m south of the train station, to Khawasa (for access to Pench Tiger Reserve; ₹100, 1¾ hours, every 30 minutes, 6am to 10pm) that continue on to Jabalpur (₹300, six hours) but you'd be better off on private buses to the latter. **Saini Travels** (☎0712-6654321; www.sainitravels.com; 1149 Central Ave, Prem Bhawan; ☺8am-10pm) heads out at 8.30am and 11pm from Central Rd (AC seat/sleeper from ₹475/520, six hours).

Private buses leave from the Bhole Petrol Pump, 3km southwest of the train station. **Sanjay Travels** (☎0712-2528925; www.sanjay travels.in; near Bhole Petrol Pump, Nagpur-Aurangabad Hwy; ☺7.30am-10pm) books air-con seats and sleepers with the best companies, such as Purple (www.purplebus.in), to Mumbai (AC from ₹1210, 16 to 20 hours, 3pm, 4pm, 4.30pm and 5pm), Pune (AC from ₹1100, 15 hours, 12 daily, 3pm to 10.30pm), Aurangabad (non-AC/AC from ₹600/625, nine to 13 hours, hourly, 3pm to 10pm), Jalgaon (non-AC/AC from ₹720/900, nine hours, hourly, 4.30pm to 9.45pm) and Hyderabad (₹750 to ₹1000, 9pm and 10.30pm). For Jabalpur, **Nandan Bus** (☎0712-6641724; www.nandanbus.com;

Central Rd, Gitanjali Cinema Sq) goes daily at 2.30pm, 6pm, 6.30pm, 9.30pm and 11pm (non-AC/AC from ₹320/551, six to eight hours) from Central Ave.

TRAIN
From Mumbai's CST railway station, the CSMT NGP Duronto runs daily to **Nagpur Junction** (NGP; Sitabuldi; sleeper/2AC ₹705/2785, 11 hours, 8.15pm). From Nagpur it departs at 8.40pm and arrives at 8.05am the following morning. Heading north to Kolkata is the Gitanjali Express (sleeper/2AC ₹530/2020, 17½ hours, 7pm). Several expresses bound for Delhi and Mumbai stop at Jalgaon (sleeper/2AC ₹280/1015, eight hours) for the Ajanta Caves.

Around Nagpur

Ramtek

About 40km northeast of Nagpur, Ramtek is believed to be the place where Lord Rama, of the epic Ramayana, spent some time during his exile with his wife, Sita, and brother Lakshmana. The place is marked by a cluster of 10 or so ancient **temples** (☺6am-9pm), which sit atop the Hill of Rama and have their own population of resident langur monkeys.

Ramtek is beginning to fancy itself as a burgeoning adventure sports destination and Khindsi Lake is indeed a beautiful spot for kayaking, paragliding or hot-air ballooning. Mansar, 7km west of Ramtek, is an important archaeological site believed to be the 5th-century remains of Pravarapura, the capital ruled by the Vakataka King Pravarasena II.

Buses run between Ramtek and the Ganesh Peth Bus Stand (p99) in Nagpur (₹60, 1½ hours, every 30 minutes, 6am to 9pm).

Sevagram

About 85km from Nagpur, Sevagram (Village of Service) was chosen by Mahatma Gandhi as his base during the Indian Independence Movement. Throughout the freedom struggle, the village played host to several nationalist leaders, who would regularly come to visit the Mahatma at his **Sevagram Ashram** (☑07152-284754; www.gandhiashramsevagram. org; ☉6am-5.30pm). The overseers of this peaceful ashram, which is built on 40 hectares of farmland, have carefully restored the original huts where Gandhi lived and worked and which now house some of his personal effects. There is a small **museum** (Sevagram Ashram; ☉10am-6pm) as well.

In nearby Paunar village, just 3km from Sevagram, you'll find **Brahma Vidya Mandir** (☑07152-288388; Paunar; dm incl meals ₹250; ☉6am-noon & 2-7pm) founded by nationalist and Gandhi disciple Vinoba Bhave and run almost entirely by women. An experience here is steeped in *swarajya* (self-sufficiency) and is operated on a social system of consensus, with no central management.

Sevagram can be reached by taking a bus from Nagpur to Wardha (non-AC/AC ₹125/1100, three hours, every 30 minutes, 4.30am to 10.15pm), where you'll need to switch to a Sevagram-bound bus (₹10, 10 minutes), which drops you at Medical Sq, 1km from the ashram; or catch a shared autorickshaw (₹20).

SOUTHERN MAHARASHTRA

Konkan Coast

A little-developed shoreline running south from Mumbai all the way to Goa, this pic-

turesque strip of coast is peppered with picture-postcard beaches, fishing villages and magnificent ruined forts. Travelling through this tropical backwater can be sheer bliss, whether you're off to dabble in the sands with Mumbaikars in Ganpatipule, visiting the stunning Janjira Fort at Murud-Janjira or heading into the blue at Malvan, the last beach town of significance before the sands give way to Goa.

Murud-Janjira

☑02144

The sleepy fishing hamlet of Murud-Janjira – 165km from Mumbai – should be on any itinerary of the Konkan Coast. The relaxed pace of life, fresh seafood, stupendous offshore Janjira Fort (and the chance to feel the warm surf rush past your feet) make the trip here well worthwhile.

Murud-Janjira's beach is fun for a run or game of cricket with locals and it comes alive with street stalls and beach tomfoolery nightly. Alternatively, you could peer through the gates of the off-limits Ahmedganj Palace, estate of the Siddi Nawab of Murud, or scramble around the decaying mosque and tombs on the south side of town.

⊙ Sights

★ **Janjira Fort**   FORT
(Rajpuri; ☉7am-dusk) **FREE** The commanding, brooding fortress of Janjira, built on an island 500m offshore, is the most magnificent of the string of forts that line the Konkan coastline. This citadel was completed in 1571 by the Siddis, descendants of slaves from the Horn of Africa, and was the capital of a princely state.

Over the centuries Siddi alignment with Mughals provoked conflict with local kings, including Shivaji and his son Sambhaji, who attempted to scale the walls and tunnel to it, respectively. However, no outsider (including British, French and Portuguese colonists) ever made it past the fort's 12m-high granite walls which, when seen during high tide, seem to rise straight from the sea. Unconquered through history, the fort is finally falling to forces of nature as its mighty walls slowly crumble and wilderness reclaims its innards.

Still, there's a lot to see today, including the remarkable close-fitting stonework that's protected the citadel against centuries of attack by storms, colonists and gunpowder. You approach the fort via a brooding grey-stone gateway and can then explore its ramparts (complete with giant cannons) and 19 bastions, large parts of which are intact. Its inner keep, palaces and mosque are in ruins, though the fort's huge twin reservoirs remain. As many of the surviving walls and structures are in poor shape, tread carefully while you explore the site, which is unfortunately littered with rubbish.

The only way to reach Janjira is by boat (₹61 return, 20 minutes) from Rajpuri port. Boats depart with a minimum 20 people from 9am to 5pm Saturday to Thursday and 9am to noon and 2pm to 5pm Friday, and allow you 45 minutes to explore the fort. To get to Rajpuri from Murud-Janjira, take an autorickshaw (₹60 to ₹100) or hire a bicycle (warning: it involves quite an uphill slog).

🛏 Sleeping & Eating

Sea Shell Resort   HOTEL $$
(☑ 9833667985; www.seashellmurud.com; Darbar Rd; d with/without AC from ₹3190/2020; ❄ ❀) Set back from the coastal road across from the improvised beach cricket grounds, this cheery place has glistening, spacious and breezy sea-facing rooms with hot-water bathrooms (including rain-style showers and thick bath towels). There's a tiny pool as well. The owner's son, Zaid, works weekends and is incredibly friendly and helpful. Wi-fi frustratingly remains lobby only.

Golden Swan Beach Resort   HOTEL $$$
(☑ 9225591131; www.goldenswan.com; Darbar Rd; d incl breakfast from ₹5190; ❄ ❀ 🛜) Cute seafront cottages and rear rooms, soundtracked by a cacophony of resident swans, occupy fine beach real estate and afford distant views of Ahmedganj Palace and Kasa Fort. Some rooms feature loft beds and small patios ideal for sea-view beers, and all feature newly tiled bathrooms. A charming old bungalow houses rooms nearby, too. Rates increase on weekends.

Hotel Vinayak   SEAFOOD $$
(Darbar Rd; mains ₹75-450; ⏰ 7am-10pm) Its sea-facing terrace is the perfect place to tuck into a delicious and fiery Konkani thali (₹110 to ₹450), with fish curry, tawa (hotplate) fish fry, sol kadhi (pink-coloured, slightly sour digestive made from coconut milk and kokum fruit) and more. Fresh fish, prawn dishes and good breakfasts are also available.

ℹ Getting There & Around

Ferries and catamarans (₹125 to ₹165) from the Gateway of India in Mumbai cruise to Mandwa pier

between 8.15am and 8.15pm. The ticket includes a free shuttle bus to Alibag (30 minutes). Rickety local buses from Alibag head down the coast to Murud-Janjira (₹70, two hours, every 30 minutes to two hours). Alternatively, eight buses depart Mumbai Central bus stand between 6am and 1am and take almost six hours to reach Murud-Janjira (non-AC from ₹220). There are five buses a day to Pune from Murud-Janjira (non-AC from ₹180, seven hours, 7am, 8.45am, 9am, 2.15pm and 4pm).

In the other direction, buses depart Murud-Janjira's **bus stand** (☑ 02144-274044; Revdanda Murud Rd) for Alibag (₹70, two hours, every two hours, 5am to 11pm) – those at 6.30am, 10am, noon, 1pm and 7.30pm are express buses (1½ hours). Bear in mind if you are going to south Mumbai, the bus/ferry combo is the better option; for the western suburbs, airport etc, the bus is better.

The nearest railhead is at Roha, two hours away and poorly connected; and trying to reach Murud from the south (say, Ganpatipule) is equally frustrating (it can be done with a vicious combination of buses and ferries but it's not worth the effort – better to go from Mumbai!).

Bicycles (per hour ₹90) and cars (from ₹14 per kilometre) can be hired at the Golden Swan Beach Resort (p102).

Raigad Fort

Alone on a high and remote hilltop, 24km off Hwy 66, the enthralling **Raigad Fort** (Raigad; Indian/foreigner ₹25/300; ⏰ 6am-7pm) served as Shivaji's capital from 1648 until his death in 1680. The fort was later sacked by the British and some colonial structures added, but monuments such as the royal court, plinths of royal chambers, the main marketplace and Shivaji's tomb still remain – it's worth an excursion.

You can hike a crazy 1475 steps to the top, but for a more 'levitating' experience, take the vertigo-inducing **ropeway** (www.raigadropeway.com; Lower Station, Hirkaniwadi, Mahad; return ₹300; ⏰ 8am-6pm) – actually a cable car – which climbs up the cliff and offers a bird's-eye view of the deep gorges below. Be warned this is a very popular attraction with domestic tourists and you may have to wait up to an hour for a ride during holiday times. Guides (₹400) are available within the fort complex.

ℹ Getting There & Away

Autorickshaws shuttle up to the ropeway from the town of Mahad on Hwy 66 (look out for the 'Raigad Ropeway' sign) for ₹800 return including wait time. Mahad is 158km south of Mumbai and 88km from Murud-Janjira. The Mahad–Raigad road

ALL ABOARD THE KONKAN RAILWAY!

One in a long list of storied Indian train rides, the Konkan Railway hugs the southwest Indian coast along a 738km journey between Maharashtra, Goa and Karnataka. The line, which has hosted passenger trains since 1998, is considered the biggest and most expansive infrastructure project the country has undertaken (and completed) since Independence. So much so, the very idea was dismissed outright in the early 20th century by the British, who deemed the whole adventure an impossible task of construction and engineering, leaving it to the locals to finish the job over the course of several decades (10 of whom lost their lives in the disaster-plagued process).

Today, the ridiculously scenic route, chock-full of picturesque paddy fields, rolling green hills, craggy mountaintops, storybook sea views and numerous tunnels, waterfalls, viaducts and jungly landscapes, is made possible by 92 tunnels and 2000 bridges, including Panval Viaduct, India's highest (and Asia's third) viaduct at 64m tall.

Most travellers enjoy the Konkan ride on the Mandovi Express from Mumbai to Goa, but train enthusiasts can take in the whole shebang on the Mangalore Express, a 14-hour journey from Mumbai to Mangalore.

is paved and in good condition. Car and drivers charge from non-AC/AC ₹8/10 per km for a day trip (prices go up depending on type of car) here from Murud-Janjira. There is one AC bus from Mahad to Mahabaleshwar (₹110, two hours, 7am).

Ganpatipule

☑ 02357

The tiny beach resort of Ganpatipule has been luring a steady stream of beach lovers over the years with its warm waters and wonderful stretches of sand. Located about 375km from Mumbai, it's a village that snoozes through much of the year, except during holidays such as Diwali or Ganesh Chaturthi. These are times when hordes of boisterous tourists turn up to visit the seaside **Shree Ganpatipule Mandir** (www. ganpatipule.co.in; Ganpatipule Beach; ⊘ 6am-9pm), which houses a monolithic Ganesh (painted a bright orange). For more solitude, the sands just south of the main beach (such as Neware Beach) are both more spectacular than Ganpatipule and less crowded – have an autorickshaw take you there.

To reach Ganpatipule, you'll pass through the transport hub of Ratnagiri, home to the crumbling **Thibaw Palace** (Thibaw Palace Rd, Ratnagiri; adult/child ₹3/1; ⊘ 10am-5pm Tue-Sun) **FREE**, where the last Burmese king, Thibaw, was interned by the British.

🛏 Sleeping & Eating

MTDC Resort   HOTEL **$$**
(☑ 02357-235248; www.maharashtratourism.gov. in; d with/without AC from ₹2750/2240; 🅰🛜) Spread over prime beachfront, this huge operation is something of a holiday camp for Mumbaikar families. Its concrete rooms and cottages would benefit from a little updating, but all have magnificent full-frontal ocean views. It also packs in a decent restaurant that serves cold beer.

★**Bhau Joshi Bhojanalay**   MAHARASHTRIAN **$**
(mains ₹55-135; ⊘ 11.30am-3pm & 7.30-10.30pm) It's not the easiest place to eat (no English sign, nearly no English spoken and no napkins – so bring some baby wipes), but the delicious Maharashtrian food in this clean, orderly restaurant inland from the beach makes up for the struggles. Try the fantastic *baingan masala* (eggplant curry; ₹90). Jain and Punjabi dishes also on offer.

❶ Getting There & Away

From the small, unstaffed bus stand, there is one ordinary government bus to Pune daily (₹470, 8¼ hours, 6.45am). Regular buses head to Ratnagiri (₹33, 1¼ hours, every 30 minutes, 10am to 8pm). From there, you can pick up buses for destinations further afield such as Pune (non-AC/AC from ₹450/610, 9¼ hours, 6am, 7.45am, 11am, 7.15pm, 9.30pm and 10pm), Mumbai (non-AC/AC from ₹440/590, nine hours, 9.30am, 9pm and 10pm) and Kolhapur (non-AC/AC from ₹172/230, four hours, nine daily, 5.30am to 10.30pm).

There are also private buses to Mumbai (Volvo non-AC seat/AC sleeper from ₹600/900, 10 hours, 6.30pm, 7pm and 7.45pm) and Pune (Volvo AC sleeper from ₹800, nine hours, 6.45pm and 7pm).

From Ratnagiri's old bus stand, buses leave for Goa (semideluxe ₹380, six hours, 5.30am) and Kolhapur (non-AC/AC from ₹172/255, four hours, every 30 minutes, 5.30am to 7.30pm).

Ratnagiri train station is on the Konkan Railway line. From Ratnagiri, the Mandovi Express

MAHARASHTRA KONKAN COAST

goes daily to Mumbai (2nd class/sleeper/2AC ₹155/260/1000, 7¾ hours, 2.05pm). The return train heading for Goa (₹130/215/830, 5½ hours) is at 1.15pm.

Malvan

☎02365

A government tourism promo compares the emerging Malvan region to Tahiti, which is a tad ambitious, but it does have near-white sands, sparkling seas and jungle-fringed backwaters. Offshore there are coral reefs, sea caves and vibrant marine life that attracts divers, along with a world-class diving school.

Malvan town is one of the prettiest on the Konkan Coast. It's a mellow, bike-friendly place with a good stock of old wooden buildings, a busy little harbour and bazaar and a slow, tropical pace of life. Stretching directly south of the centre is lovely Tarkali Beach, home to many hotels and guesthouses.

Sights & Activities

Tarkali Beach BEACH

A golden arc south of Malvan, this crescent-shaped sandy beach is a vision of tropical I ndia, fringed by coconut palms and casuarina trees, plus the odd cow and camel. At dusk (between October and February) fisherfolk work together to haul in huge, kilometre-long nets that are impressively packed with thousands of *bangda* (mackerel), *tarli* (sardines), pomfret and/or *zinga* (prawns).

A rickshaw here from Malvan town is ₹150.

Sindhudurg Fort FORT

(₹5; ⏲8am-5.30pm) Built by Shivaji and dating from 1664, this monstrous fort lies on an offshore island and can be reached by frequent ferries (adult/child ₹90/50, 8am to 5.30pm), which depart with a minimum 20 people from Malvan's harbour. It's not as impressive as Janjira up the coast, and today lies mostly in ruins, but it remains a powerful presence. You can explore its ramparts and the coastal views are impressive. Boat operators allow you one hour on the island.

★IISDA DIVING

(Indian Institute of Scuba Diving & Aquatic Sports; ☎02365-248790; www.maharashtratourism.gov.in; Tarkali Beach; 1-/2-tank dive ₹4130/8260, PADI Open Water course ₹25,960; ⏲9am-6pm) This state-of-the-art PADI 5-Star diving centre, an initiative of Maharashtra Tourism, is India's finest, run by marine biologist and diving pro Dr Sarang Kulkarni. It offers professional instruction, a 20m-long pool for training, air-conditioned classrooms and comfortable sleeping quarters for students. IISDA is also a marine conservation centre. It's located 7km south of Malvan.

Sleeping & Eating

Vicky's Guest House GUESTHOUSE $

(☎9823423046; vickyfernandes11@gmail.com; near Heravi Batti, Dandi Beach; d with/without AC from ₹1500/1000; ❄📶) Down a quiet residential lane surrounded by lush palms 400m from Dandi Beach and steps form Malvan town, cool and mellow Vicky has five (more on the way) purpose-built rooms that don't look like much on arrival but are actually spacious, well equipped and extremely comfortable for the price. Vicky himself is super helpful and hospitable.

Visava Beach Resort RESORT $$

(☎9423304304; www.visavaresorttarkarli.com; Tarkali Beach; d ₹2500-3500; ❄📶) It's distinctly rustic, but this laid-back, family-run resort will charm a certain type of beach bum. The 11 rooms (12 more to come) aren't flashy but offer hot water, modern touches and idyllic porches with seating areas and swinging chairs. The sandy grounds are strewn with vegetation and coconut palms and it sits on a quieter, prettier stretch of Tarkali.

★Hotel Chaitanya KONKAN $$

(502 Dr Vallabh Marg; thalis ₹100-220, mains ₹70-450; ⏲11am-11pm) On Malvan's main drag, this great, family-run place specialises in Konkan cuisine including *bangda tikhale* (fish in thick coconut sauce), prawns *malvani* and very flavoursome crab masala; portions won't thrill you, but it's first-rate seafood. Its vegetarian dishes are also excellent. It's always packed with locals and has an air-con section.

Getting There & Away

The closest **train station** (KUDL; Railway Station Rd) is Kudal, 38km away. Frequent buses (₹35, one hour, 4.50am to 7.45pm) cover the route from **Malvan Bus Stand** (☎02365-252034; Shri Babi Hadkar Marg); alternatively, an autorickshaw is about ₹600. Malvan has ordinary buses to Kolhapur (non-AC from ₹210, five hours, 7am, 2.15pm and 3.15pm), Mumbai (AC ₹840, 12 hours, 8am), Panaji (AC from ₹150, four hours, 6.45am, 7.45am, 2.30pm and 3.15pm) and Ratnagiri (non-AC from ₹225, five hours, 6am, 7.45am and 11.15am). Slightly quicker to Goa are the blue-and-white Kadamba Goan government buses (₹200 to ₹250, 3½ hours, 7.45am, 2.15pm and 3pm) to Panaji, Margao and Vasco.

MALVAN MARINE NATIONAL PARK

The shoreline around Malvan is incredibly diverse, with rich wetlands, sandy and rocky beaches, mangroves and backwaters. But underwater it's arguably even more compelling, with coral patches and caves that shelter abundant marine life and extensive forests of *sargassum* seaweed that acts as a nursery for juvenile fish. Rocky offshore islands attract schools of snapper and large grouper, butterfly fish, yellow-striped fusilers, manta and sting rays and lobster. Pods of dolphins are regularly seen between October to May and the world's largest fish, the whale shark, even puts in an appearance every now and then.

Presently only a small section is protected as the Malvan Marine Sanctuary, which encompasses the Sindhudurg Fort; yet such is its rich diversity that marine biologists, including the director of the Indian Institute of Scuba Diving & Aquatic Sports (IISDA), Dr Sarang Kulkarni, feel it's essential that the boundaries are extended. A submerged plateau, the Angria Bank, exists 72 nautical miles off Malvan and clocks in at 40km long and 20km wide, with healthy coral and an abundance of sealife. It has been described as India's Great Barrier Reef. The Government of Maharashtra through IISDA has big plans to create world-class infrastructure to provide day trips and live-aboard excursions to Angria.

Plans are also in place for India's first tourism venture by submarine. Based in Vengurla, 51km north of Malvan, it is expected to offer underwater tours of the sanctuary by the end of 2019.

There are private bus agents on Dr Vallabh Marg selling more comfortable seats on Volvo buses to Mumbai and Pune, but these depart 33km inland from Malvan in Kasal and transport is not provided.

Malvan is only 80km from northern Goa; private drivers charge ₹3000 (non-AC) to ₹3500 (AC) for the two-hour trip. Heading north, it's ₹3500 to Ratnagiri and ₹4500 to Ganpatipule.

The region's new airport, Sindhudurg Chipi Airport, 16km southeast of Malvan at Parule-Chipi, was about to open at the time of research. Sitting just 62km northwest of Aswem Beach, it's also useful for Northern Goa.

Matheran

📞 02148 / POP 5750 / ELEV 803M

Matheran, literally 'Jungle Above', is a tiny patch of peace and quiet capping a craggy Sahyadri summit within spitting distance of Mumbai's heat and grime. Endowed with shady forests criss-crossed with foot trails and breathtaking lookouts, it still retains an elegance and colonial-era ambience, though creeping commercialism and illegal construction are marring its appeal (it could do without the Ferris wheel and wax museum, for example).

In the past, getting to Matheran was really half the fun. While speedier options were available by road, nothing beat arriving in town on the narrow-gauge toy train that chugged up to the heart of the settlement. However, derailment woes caused the suspension of the train in 2016, and it now mainly runs for just a 2km-stretch from Aman Lodge.

Motor vehicles are banned within Matheran, making it an ideal place to give your ears and lungs a rest and your feet some exercise.

👁 Sights & Activities

You can walk along shady forest paths to most of Matheran's viewpoints in a matter of hours; it's a place well suited to stress-free ambling. To catch the sunrise, head to Panorama Point, while Porcupine Point (also known as Sunset Point) is the most popular (read: packed) as the sun drops. Louisa Point and Little Chouk Point also have stunning views of the Sahyadris.

If you're here on a weekend or public holiday you might want to avoid the most crowded section around Echo Point, Charlotte Lake and Honeymoon Point, which get rammed with day trippers.

You can reach the valley below One Tree Hill down the path known as Shivaji's Ladder, supposedly trod upon by the Maratha leader himself.

🛏 Sleeping & Eating

Hope Hall Hotel HOTEL $
(📞 7066715973; www.hopehallmatheran.com; MG Rd; d from ₹1200) Run by a very hospitable family, this long-running place has been hosting happy travellers for years (though slow internet often derails their ability to register – and therefore accept – foreigners); the house dates back to 1875. Spacious rooms

with high ceilings and arty touches are in two blocks at the rear of the leafy garden. Good breakfasts and drinks are available.

MTDC Resort
LODGE $$

(☏ 02148-230277; www.maharashtratourism.gov.in; d ₹1680, with AC from ₹2576; ❀ ☎) This government-run place offers functional, economy rooms, disappointing family rooms and very attractive modern air-conditioned rooms in the Shruti Heritage Villa (₹3546). The downside is it's located next to the Dasturi car park, so you're away from the midtown action. There's a restaurant on-site.

★ Dune Barr House
HERITAGE HOTEL $$$

(Verandah in the Forest; ☏ 9152519989; www.dunewellnessgroup.com; Barr House; d incl breakfast ₹6000-8000; ☎) This deliciously preserved 150-year-old bungalow exudes undiluted nostalgia, with quaintly luxurious rooms. Reminisce about bygone times in the company of ornate candelabras, oriental rugs, antique teak furniture, Victorian canvases and grandfather clocks. The verandah has a lovely aspect over Matheran's wooded hillsides.

Shabbir Bhai
INDIAN $

(Merry Rd; mains ₹130-290; ☉ 9am-10.30pm) Known locally as the 'Byrianiwala', this funky joint has a full North Indian menu, but it's all about the spicy biryanis: spiced steamed rice with chicken, mutton and veg. To find it, take the footpath uphill beside the Jama Masjid on MG Rd and follow your nose.

ⓘ Information

Entry to Matheran costs ₹50 (₹25 for children), which you pay at the Dasturi car park.

ⓘ Getting There & Away

TAXI

Shared taxis (Neral Matheran Rd; ₹80) run from just outside the western entrance of Neral train station to Matheran's **Dasturi car park** (Neral-Matheran Rd; 30 minutes). Horses (₹350 to all hotels except Verandah in the Forest, which is ₹550) and hand-pulled rickshaws (₹700) wait here to whisk you (relatively speaking) to Matheran's main bazaar. The horse-wallahs are unionised and their prices are officially posted, but do not agree on a price until you have seen the board, which is located 50m *after* the Matheran ticket counter (hotel fares bottom-right in smaller font than the rest of the board). You can also walk this stretch (a somewhat inclined 2km) and your luggage can be hauled for around ₹250.

TRAIN

Matheran's toy train was suspended in 2016 after two derailments, but service was partially reinstated in early 2018. It now chugs between Matheran and **Neral Junction** (Ratnadeep Colony, Neral; 1st/2nd class ₹300/75) once daily, departing Neral at 6.40am, returning at 3.40pm (2.20pm on Mondays). Throughout the rest of the day, it merely ambles the 2km between Aman Lodge Station, located a few metres beyond Dasturi car park, and Matheran Station (1st/2nd class ₹300/45), serving little purpose – though it is helpful if you are lugging heavy bags. The first train departs at 9.02am (8.40am on weekends), and subsequent trains depart every 45 minutes to an hour until 3.05pm (6.05pm on weekends). From Matheran, departures start at 9.30am (8.15am on weekends) and run until 2.40pm (5.40pm on weekends).

From Mumbai's CST station there are two daily express trains stopping at Neral Junction at 7am and 8.40am, but they cannot be booked online as Neral and Mumbai are considered the same metropolitan area by IRCTC. You must book a further destination (Lonavla, for example; 2nd class/chair ₹75/260) and then hop down at Neral (1½ hours). Alternatively, numerous local trains ply the route between Mumbai CST and Dadar.

Lonavla

☏ 02114 / POP 57,400 / ELEV 625M

Lonavla is a raucous resort town about 106km southeast of Mumbai. Its main drag consists almost exclusively of garishly lit shops flogging *chikki*, the rock-hard, brittle sweet made in the area, and you get fun-for-the-whole-family kind of stuff like wax museums, go-karts and India's largest water park. But there are some pleasant side streets, serene residential areas and destination yoga places along with the pastoral surrounding countryside that means you can choose your own path here.

The main reason you'd want to come here is to visit the nearby Karla and Bhaja caves which, after those at Ellora and Ajanta, are the best in Maharashtra.

Hotels, restaurants and the main road to the caves lie north of the train station. Most of the Lonavla township and its markets are located south of the station.

⊙ Sights & Activities

★ Lion Point
VIEWPOINT

(Lonavla-Aamby Valley Rd, Hudco Colony; ☉ 24hr) This wildly panoramic viewpoint 12km south of Lonavla is one of the resort town's best non-kitschy sights. On a clear day, small waterfalls are visible among the lush green conical hills and the deep, cinematic valley, along with views across the Western Ghats. Locals flock here, many of whom climb over the railings for on-the-edge selfies (not recommended) when they are not munching on roasted corn and onion fritters from lines of vendors. Sunset and sunrise are, unsurprisingly, popular. Rickshaws charge ₹600 return from Lonavla with a bit of waiting to enjoy the view.

Nirvana Adventures PARAGLIDING
(☎ 022-26053724; www.flynirvana.com; 2-day learner course per person incl full board ₹12,000, tandem flights from ₹2500) Mumbai-based Nirvana Adventures offers paragliding courses and short tandem flights from its base camp in a charming rural setting near the town of Kamshet, 25km from Lonavla.

You'll need to hire your own transport to reach the base camp.

Kaivalyadhama Yoga Institute & Research Center YOGA
(☎ 8551092986, 02114-273039; www.kdham.com; Kaivalyadhama Ashram Kaivalyadhama; 40-day course incl full board US$1200) This progressive yoga centre is located in neatly kept grounds about 2km from Lonavla, en route to the Karla and Bhaja caves. Founded in 1924 by Swami Kuvalayananda, it combines yoga courses with naturopathic therapies. Courses cover full board, yoga classes, activities and lectures.

🛏 Sleeping

★ Ferreira Resort HOTEL $$
(☎ 02114-272689; www.ferreiraresort.in; DT Shahani Rd; s/d Mon-Thu ₹1680/2015, Fri-Sun ₹2015/2465, with AC Mon-Thu ₹1790/2240, Fri-Sun ₹2240/2465; ❄️🛜) It's certainly not a resort, but it is something of a rarity in Lonavla: a well-priced, family-run place in a quiet residential location that's close to the train station. Ten of the 15 clean but worn air-con rooms have a balcony and there's a little garden as well as room service.

★ The Machan BOUTIQUE HOTEL $$$
(☎ 7666622426; www.themachan.com; Private Rd, Atvan; tree houses Mon-Thu ₹11,520-38,400, Fri-Sun ₹44,800; ❄️🛜⚡) 🌿 This astonishing choice hidden away in forested mountains 16km south of Lonavla buries the competition for the state's best hotel. The 28 pine and red meranti wood tree houses rising 10 to 13m above the forest come in all shapes

and sizes, but every one is a postcard-perfect getaway from which you will probably need to be dragged at checkout.

The two-bedroom Starlight Villas are the stuff dreams are made of, with a fully retractable roof for stargazing, Victorian deep soaking bathtubs and hammocks on the patio with mountain views – not to mention a sizeable private pool in the forest and two bedrooms connected by a spiral staircase that's perfect for two couples (recycled woods and solar power where possible). Wonderful, home-style meals are taken outdoors and there's yoga, nature walks, bonfires and a spa. You are in the thick of it here with the scorpions, snakes and adorable Malabar giant squirrels. Book well in advance.

🍴 Eating & Drinking

★ Kinara Dhaba Village NORTH INDIAN, CHINESE $$$
(www.thekinaravillage.com; Vaksai Naka, Old Mumbai-Pune Hwy; mains ₹310-600; ⊙11am-11.30pm; 🅿️) A bit of a *dhaba* Disneyland, but therein lies the fun. About 5km east of Lonavla, near Karla and Bhaja caves, is this fun-for-all restaurant/entertainment venue. Dine under traditional *shamiana* huts amid festival lighting, camel and donkey rides, *jalebi* (deep-fried batter dunked in sugar syrup) carts, fish pedicure pools and Rajasthani astrologers. Live *ghazal* (Urdu love songs) nightly (7pm).

German Bakery Wunderbar CAFE
(Mumbai-Pune Rd, opposite Kumar Resort; ⊙7am-11pm) A youngish and hip crowd flocks to this Pune transplant for cocktails (₹190 to ₹310) and pitchers of Bira draught beer (₹630), as well as an expanded cafe menu (mains ₹220 to ₹450), all taken on a large, semi-open patio with wrought-iron deck furniture and milk-can bar stools.

ⓘ Getting There & Away

Neeta Tours & Travels (☎ 8652222640; www.neetabus.in; Valvan Dam, Old Mumbai Pune Hwy) offers numerous luxury air-con buses day and night to Mumbai (from ₹400, two hours, hourly, 7am to 1am) and Pune (from ₹250, two hours, hourly, 8.15am to 11.30pm) to its fancy station 3km northeast of the train station at Hotel Neeta's Inn.

All express trains from Mumbai's CST to Pune stop at **Lonavla** (LNL; Siddharth Nagar) (2nd class ₹65 to ₹90, chair ₹260 to ₹305, 2½ to three hours).

KARLA & BHAJA CAVES

The largest early *chaitya* (Buddhist temple) in India, **Karla Caves** (Indian/foreigner ₹30/300, video ₹25; ⊘9am-5pm) is reached by a 20-minute climb from a mini bazaar at the base of a hill. Completed in 80 BC, the *chaitya* is around 40m long and 15m high and sports a vaulted interior and intricately executed sculptures of Buddha, human and animal figures.

On the other side of the expressway from Karla Caves in a lush setting 3km off the main road, **Bhaja Caves** (Bhaja Caves Rd; Indian/foreigner ₹30/300, video ₹25; ⊘9am-5.30pm) is the greener and quieter of the region's caves. Thought to date from around 200 BC, 10 of the 18 caves here are *viharas* (Buddhist monasteries), while Cave 12 is an open *chaitya* containing a simple dagoba.

Karla is 11km east of Lonavla, and Bhaja 9km. Both can be visited on a local bus to the access point, from where it's about a 6km return walk on each side to the two sites – but that would be exhausting and hot. Autorickshaws charge around ₹1200 (depending on the day of the week) from Lonavla for the tour, including waiting time, but many refuse to go. Local cars go for ₹1200 to ₹1500 depending on your negotiation skills.

Pune

📝 020 / POP 5.14 MILLION / ELEV 535M

A thriving, vibrant metropolis, Pune is a centre of academia and business that epitomises 'New India' with its baffling mix of capitalism and spirituality (ancient and modern). It's also globally famous, or notorious, for an ashram, the Osho International Meditation Resort (p109), founded by the late guru Bhagwan Shree Rajneesh.

Pune was initially given pride of place by Shivaji and the ruling Peshwas, who made it their capital. The British took the city in 1817 and, thanks to its cool and dry climate, soon made it the Bombay Presidency's monsoon capital. Globalisation knocked on Pune's doors in the 1990s, following which it went in for an image overhaul. However, some colonial-era charm was retained in a few old buildings and residential areas, bringing about a pleasant coexistence of the old and new, which (despite the pollution and hectic traffic) makes Pune a worthwhile place to explore.

⊙ Sights

⭐ Raja Dinkar Kelkar Museum   MUSEUM

(www.facebook.com/rajakelkarmuseum; 1377/78 Kamal Kunj, Bajirao Rd, Shukrawar Peth; Indian/foreigner ₹50/200, mobile/camera ₹100/200; ⊘10am-6pm) An oddball of a museum that's one of Pune's true delights, housing only a fraction of the 20,000-odd objects of Indian daily life painstakingly collected by Dinkar Kelkar (who died in 1990). The quirky pan-Indian collection includes hundreds of hookah pipes, writing instruments, lamps, textiles, toys, entire doors and windows, kitchen utensils, furniture, puppets, ivory playing cards and betel-nut cutters.

⭐ Joshi's Museum of Miniature Railway   MUSEUM

(www.minirailways.com; 17/1 B/2 GA Kulkarni Rd, Kothrud; ₹90, minimum 4 people for 25min show; ⊘9am-5pm Mon-Wed & Fri, 9.30am-1pm Thu, 9am-4pm Sat, 5-8pm Sat & Sun) Inside the small Soudamini Instruments factory in eastern Pune is what is claimed to be India's only miniature city, the lifelong obsession of model train enthusiast Bhau Joshi. In short, it's one of the world's great model train layouts, a detailed, fully functional and passionate display of mechanical and engineering wow.

Aga Khan Palace   PALACE

(Pune Nagar Rd, Kalyani Nagar; Indian/foreigner ₹25/300; ⊘9am-5.30pm) The grand Aga Khan Palace is set in a peaceful wooded 6.5-hectare plot northeast of the centre. Built in 1892 by Sultan Aga Khan III, this graceful building was where Mahatma Gandhi and other prominent nationalist leaders were interned by the British following Gandhi's Quit India campaign in 1942.

The main palace now houses the **Gandhi National Memorial** (www.mkgandhi.org/museum/pune.htm; Aga Khan Palace, Pune Nagar Rd, Kalyani Nagar; ⊘9am-5.30pm) where you can peek into the room where the Mahatma used to stay. Photos and paintings exhibit moments in his extraordinary life. Both Kasturba Gandhi, the Mahatma's wife, and Mahadeobhai Desai, his secretary for 35 years, died here in confinement. You'll find their shrines (containing their ashes) in a quiet garden to the rear.

Osho Teerth Gardens
GARDENS

(www.osho.com; DH Dhunjibhoy Rd, Koregaon Park; ⊗ 6-9am & 3-6pm) The 5-hectare Osho Teerth Gardens are a verdant escape from urban living with giant bamboo, jogging trails, a gurgling brook and smooching couples. You don't have to be an Osho member – they're accessible to all.

Shaniwar Wada
FORT

(Shivaji Rd; Indian/foreigner ₹25/300; ⊗ 9am-5.30pm) The remains of this fortressed palace of the Peshwa rulers are located in the old part of the city. Built in 1732, Shaniwar Wada was destroyed by a fire in 1828, but the massive walls and ramparts remain, as does a mighty fortified gateway.

On Wednesday to Monday evenings there's a 40-minute sound-and-light show at 7pm (Marathi) and 8pm (Hindi), but not in English.

🏃 Activities

Osho International
Meditation Resort
MEDITATION

(☑ 020-66019999; www.osho.com; 17 Koregaon Park) Indelibly linked with Pune's identity, this iconic ashram-resort, located in a leafy, upscale northern suburb, has been drawing thousands of *sanyasins* (seekers) since the death of Osho in 1990. With its swimming pool, sauna and spa, 'zennis' and boutique guesthouse, it is, to some, the ultimate place to indulge in some luxe meditation.

🛌 Sleeping

Bombay Backpackers
HOSTEL $

(☑ 7028826713; www.bombaybackpackers.com; 40B, Lane C, Ragvilas Society, Koregaon Park; dm with/without AC ₹600/500, d ₹2200, all incl breakfast; ❄ 🤶) In a quiet residential location in Koregaon Park, Pune's edition of Bombay Backpackers features six- and 10-bed dorms, a basement common area and kitchen, and somewhat indifferent staff. The Osho-themed private rooms are quite spacious, with bamboo tables and chairs on hardwood floors, and are good value for the city.

Hotel Surya Villa
HOTEL $

(☑ 020-26124501; www.hotelsuryavilla.com; 294/1 German Bakery Ln, Koregaon Park; d with/without AC from ₹2240/1680; ❄ 🤶) The Surya's functional, tiled rooms are well kept and generously proportioned and, though a little spartan, they do have bathrooms with hot water, plus wi-fi and cable TV. It enjoys a good loca-

tion on a quiet street in Koregaon Park, close to popular cafes.

The Samrat Hotel
HOTEL $$

(☑ 020-26137964; www.thesamrathotel.com; 17 Wilson Garden; s/d incl breakfast from ₹2020/2470, with AC from ₹2800/3420; ❄ 🤶) It's not quite as grand as its fancy reception area would indicate, but with a central location just a few steps from the train station and spacious, well-maintained rooms, the 49-room Samrat represents good value. The staff are courteous and eager to please.

Hotel Lotus
HOTEL $$

(☑ 020-26139701; www.hotelsuryavilla.com; Lane 5, Koregaon Park; s/d with AC incl breakfast ₹2130/2690; ❄ 🤶) Hotel Lotus is good value for its quiet, Koregaon Park location and though the rooms are not that spacious, they are light and airy, and all but four have balconies. There's no restaurant, but it offers room service and there are plenty of good eating options close by.

★ Sunderban Resort & Spa
HOTEL $$$

(☑ 020-26124949; www.tghotels.com; 19 Koregaon Park; s/d incl breakfast from ₹4720/5900; ❄ 🤶) Set around a manicured lawn right next to the Osho resort, this renovated Art Deco bungalow effortlessly combines colonial-era class with boutique appeal. Deluxe rooms in the main building sport antique furniture, while even the cheapest options are beautifully presented and spacious. The best-value rooms are the lawn-facing studios, recently given a modern upgrade.

Osho Meditation
Resort Guesthouse
GUESTHOUSE $$$

(☑ 020-66019900; www.osho.com; Osho International Meditation Resort, 17 Koregaon Park; s/d ₹5310/5900; ❄ 🤶) This uber-chic, 60-room place will only allow you in if you come to meditate at the Osho International Meditation Resort. The rooms and common spaces are an elegant exercise in modern minimalist aesthetics with several very luxurious features – including purified fresh air supplied in all rooms.

🍴 Eating

German Bakery
BAKERY $$

(www.germanbakerypune.in; 292 North Main Rd, Koregaon Park; cakes ₹115-230, mains ₹180-440; ⊗ 7.45am-11.45pm; 🤶) A Pune institution famous for its traveller-geared grub and fusion food (such as vindaloo pork chops with garlic mash), including omelettes, cooked

Pune

breakfasts, Greek salads, espresso and lots of sweet treats (try the mango cheesecake). Located on a traffic-plagued corner.

★**Savya Rasa**   SOUTH INDIAN **$$$**
(☏ 9130095522; www.savyarasa.com; Gera Serenity Bldg, CTS No 15, Koregaon Park; mains ₹400-

800; ☺ noon-3pm & 7-11pm; ☏) This modern, fiercely regional South Indian restaurant champions the best of India's bottom half and isn't afraid to tell you if you are ordering the wrong bread with the wrong curry. Listen to the staff and you'll have one of the region's best meals.

Pune

⊙ Sights
1 Osho Teerth Gardens C2

⊕ Activities, Courses & Tours
2 Osho International Meditation
  Resort C2

⊜ Sleeping
3 Bombay Backpackers C1
4 Hotel Lotus D2
5 Hotel Surya Villa C1
6 Osho Meditation Resort
  Guesthouse C2
7 Sunderban Resort & Spa C2
8 The Samrat Hotel A3

⊗ Eating
  Dario's .... (see 7)
9 German Bakery C1
10 Malaka Spice D2
11 Savya Rasa C1

⊜ Drinking & Nightlife
12 Badshah B5
13 Botequim Cervejaria D2
14 Third Wave Coffee Roasters D1

⊜ Shopping
15 Bombay Store B5

★ **Malaka Spice**   ASIAN $$$
(www.malakaspice.com; Lane 5, North Main Rd,
Koregaon Park; mains ₹340-710; ⊙ 11.30am-
12.30am; ⚹ ⌨) ⚐ Maharashtra's shining
culinary moment is a fury of Southeast
Asian fantasticness; trying to choose one
dish among the delectable stir-fries, noodles
and curries – all strong on seafood, vegetar-
ian options, chicken, duck and mutton – is
futile. Dine alfresco under colourful tree
lights and relish the spicy and intricate fla-
vour cavalcade from star chefs reared on a
Slow Food, stay-local philosophy.

★ **Le Plaisir**   BISTRO $$$
(⌨ 020-25650106; www.facebook.com/pg/lep-
laisirpune; Rajkamal Survey No 759/125, Prabhat
Rd, Deccan Gymkhana; mains ₹290-420; ⊙ 9am-
9.45pm; ⌨) Foodies in the know often tout
this modern bistro on Pune's upscale west
side as the city's best place to eat. Sydney-
trained chef Siddarth Mahadik keeps it real
– nothing flashy, nothing fake is his mantra
– and his wholesome fusions creations are
well executed, artfully presented and taste
great. Worth a trip.

★ **Dario's**   ITALIAN $$$
(www.darios.in; Hotel Sunderban, Koregaon Park;
pasta ₹470-550, pizza ₹390-650; ⊙ 8am-11.30pm)
At the rear of Hotel Sunderban, this Ital-
ian-run veg paradise is one of Pune's most
elegant dining experiences, providing you
plant yourself in the gorgeous and intimate
courtyard for an alfresco meal. Homemade
pastas, very good pizzas and fine salads (try
the Bosco; ₹490), including wholewheat,
vegan and gluten-free options, fill the ex-
tensive menu of delectable remedies for
homesickness.

⊜ **Drinking & Nightlife**

★ **Independence**
Brewing Company   CRAFT BEER
(⌨ 020-66448308; www.independencebrewco.
com; Zero One, 79/1, Pingle Vasti, Mundhwa Rd,
Mundhwa; ⊙ 1pm-1.30am Mon-Sat, from noon
Sun) Reserve a table in the outstanding beer
garden at this industrially hip craft brewery
– Pune's finest – and you'll swear you're in
California. The eight taps change often –
look out for the Four Grain *saison* (a highly
carbonatred pale ale), Juicy IPA, sours, the
chocolate-bomb Ixcacao porter and Mahar-
ashtra's best (only?) Double IPA.

Badshah   JUICE BAR
(1 East St, Camp; juices ₹90-200; ⊙ 8am-11.30pm)
This institution for *faloodas* (rose-flavoured
drinks), *sharbats* (a chilled drink) and fresh
juices may have been born in Bombay, but it's
been at it in Pune for four decades as well.
It's tough to beat its signature *falooda* (with
cream and dry fruits) or a fresh *anar* (pome-
granate) enjoyed on its pleasant patio on a
hot day. Serves heftier Indian meals as well.

Botequim Cervejaria   BAR
(302 Power Plaza, Lane No 7, Koregaon Park;
⊙ 6.30pm-12.30am) The open-air rooftop at
this Brazilian-themed Koregaon Park new-
comer is a supreme drinking den, offering
10 craft beer options on draught, including
Pune's own excellent Great State Ale Works
(who do a fine, creamy Brazilian *chope* –
draught beer – and a New England IPA,
among others).

Third Wave Coffee Roasters   COFFEE
(www.thirdwavecoffee.in; 1 Vimal Kunj, North Main
Rd, Lane E, Koregaon Park; ⊙ 9am-11pm; ⌨) ⚐
This Bengaluru transplant has Punekars

OSHO: THE GURU OF SEX

Ever tried mixing spirituality with primal instincts and garnishing with oodles of expensive trinkets? Well, Bhagwan Shree Rajneesh (1931–90) certainly did. Osho, as he preferred to be called, was one of India's most flamboyant 'export gurus' to market the mystic East to the world and undoubtedly the most controversial.

Initially based in Pune, he followed no particular religion or philosophy and outraged many across the world with his advocacy of sex as a path to enlightenment. A darling of the international media, he quickly earned himself the epithet 'sex guru'. In 1981, Rajneesh took his curious blend of Californian pop psychology and Indian mysticism to the USA, where he set up an agricultural commune in Oregon. There, his ashram's notoriety, as well as its fleet of (material and thus valueless!) Rolls Royces grew, until raging local opposition following a bizarre, infamous food poisoning incident (designed to manipulate local elections) moved the authorities to charge Osho with immigration fraud. He was fined US$400,000 and deported.

An epic journey then began, during which Osho and his followers, in their search for a new base, were either deported from or denied entry into 21 countries. By 1987, he was back at his Pune ashram, where thousands of foreigners soon flocked for his nightly discourses and meditation sessions.

They still come from across the globe. Such is the demand for the resort's facilities that prices are continually on the rise, with luxury being redefined every day. Interestingly, despite Osho's discourse on how nobody should be poor, no money generated by the resort goes into helping the disadvantaged.

In recent years the Osho institute has embraced the digital age, with its online iOsho portal offering iMeditate programs, Osho radio and Osho library; subscriptions are required.

The whole wild ride was laid bare in 2018's *Wild Wild Country*, a six-episode Netflix documentary.

---

ditching traditional filter coffee for single origin, 100% Arabica Indian specialty espressos (₹110) and other now-ubiquitous Third Wave preparations (Aeropress, Chemex, Syphone etc). It's a big, modern space in Koregoan Park, conducive to working while enjoying creative lattes (Nutella & salted butter) or cold brews (guava chilli).

🔒 Shopping

⭐ Studio Coppre   HOMEWARES

(☑9168908484; www.studiocoppre.com; Beverly Estates, 852/4 Bhandarkar Rd, Lane No 12, Deccan Gymkhana; ☺10am-6pm Mon-Sat) 🖋 This craft revival project cofounded by four women champions the dying Indian art of handcrafted metalware from artisans in Pune, the Konkan Coast and Rajasthan. You'll want an extra suitcase for the gorgeous copper *mathar* bowls (with hand-beaten indentations), carafes, mugs, votives and vases, not to mention the hand-etched bronze thalis and trays, and beautiful decorative inlay boxes.

Bombay Store   GIFTS & SOUVENIRS

(www.thebombaystore.com; 322 MG Rd, Camp; ☺10am-9pm) Stocks quality handicrafts, souvenirs, quirky bags, cool accessories and contemporary furnishings, including Khadi cosmetics and kitschy Elephant Company clocks.

ℹ️ Information

Ruby Hall Clinic (☑020-66455100; www.rubyhall.com; 40 Sasoon Rd) One of Pune's best private hospitals, handily located near the train station.

For exchange services, there is a **Thomas Cook** (☑020-66007903; www.thomascook.in; Thakar House, 2418 General Thimmaya Rd, Camp; ☺9.30am-6.30pm Mon-Sat) branch on General Thimmaya Rd. ATMs are everywhere in Pune, including **Citibank** (www.citibank.com; Ground Onyx, North Main Rd, Tower 37, Koregoan Park), which allows a higher withdrawal limit than Indian banks (₹20,000).

Main Post Office (GPO Pune; www.indiapost.gov.in; Sadhu Vaswani Path; ☺10am-8pm Mon-Sat)

MTDC Tourist Office (Maharashtra Tourism Development Corporation; ☑020-26128169; www.maharashtratourism.gov.in; I Block, Central Bldg, Dr Annie Besant Rd; ☺10am-5pm Mon-Sat, closed 2nd & 4th Sat)

ⓘ Getting There & Away

AIR
The flashy new Chattrapati Sambhaji International Airport is currently under proposal at Purandar, 36km southeast of Pune. Until its fruition and completion, airlines including Air India (www.airindia.in), GoAir (www.goair.in), IndiGo (www.goindigo.in), Jet Airways (www.jetairways.com) and Spicejet (www.spicejet.com) fly daily from the **Pune International Airport** (PNQ; New Airport Rd, Lohgaon), 11km northeast of Koragoan Park, to Mumbai, Delhi, Jaipur, Bengaluru (Bangalore), Nagpur, Goa, Patna, and Chennai, among others. International destinations include Abu Dhabi and Dubai.

BUS
Pune has three bus stands. Maharashtra government buses leave the **Pune Station Bus Stand** (☑ 020-26126218; Agarkar Nagar) for Goa (AC ₹900, 10 hours, 5am, 5.45am, 4.30pm, 7.30pm and 9pm), while Goa government buses (Kadamba Transport) depart at 6.30pm, 7pm and 7.30pm (₹600 to ₹1000). Buses also head to Mumbai's Dadar TT Circle station (₹300 to ₹520, four hours, every 15 minutes, 5.30am to 10.30pm), all of which can drop you in Lonavla (₹70).

From the **Shivaji Nagar Bus Stand** (☑ 020-25536970; Shivajinagar Railway Station Rd), buses go to Aurangabad (non-AC/AC from ₹400/800, five to six hours, every 30 minutes, 5am to 11pm) and Nashik (non-AC/AC from ₹250/410, every 30 minutes, 3.30pm to 11pm). A few semiluxury AC buses also go to Mahabaleshwar (₹265, four hours, 6.15am, 7.45am and 9.30am).

From **Swargate Bus Stand** (☑ 020-24441591; Satara Rd), government buses head to Kolhapur (₹300 to ₹450, six hours, every 30 minutes, 4.30am to 11.30pm) and Mahabaleshwar (₹175 to ₹250, four hours, hourly, 5.40am to 7.20pm). To Donje (Golewadi), for access to Sinhagad Fort, bus 50 or 52 runs frequently from a bus stop (p114) on Shankar Sheth Rd just outside Swargate (₹30, 45 minutes, every 30 minutes, 5.20am to 9.30pm).

Ticket agents selling private long-distance bus tickets are across the street from Shivaji Nagar station – try **Sana Travels** (☑ 8888808984; www.sanakonduskarbus.com; 2 Sita Park, Shivajinagar). Destinations (all AC sleepers) include Bengaluru (from ₹1200, 14 hours, 10 daily, 2.30pm to 10pm), Hyderabad (from ₹1000, 10 hours, 15 daily, 6.30pm to midnight), Goa (from ₹1600, 10 hours, 81 per day, 6.30pm to 1.45am), Mangalore (from ₹1700, 14 hours, 13 daily, 4pm to 11pm) and Nagpur (₹1000, 14 hours, 86 daily, 3.30pm to 10.30pm). Buses for Bengaluru, Goa and Mangalore leave from Swargate; those to Hyderabad from Pune Station; and to Nagpur from Shivaji Nagar.

TAXI
Shared taxis (up to four passengers) link Pune with Mumbai airport around the clock. They leave from the **taxi stand** (☑ 020-26121090; Sanjay Ghandi Rd) in front of Pune Station Bus Stand (per seat ₹400 to ₹475, 2½ hours). There is also an Uber pick-up point just outside the train station exit.

To rent a car and driver try **Simran Travels** (☑ 020-26153222; www.mumbaiairportcab.com; 1st fl, Madhuban Bldg, Lane No 5, Koregaon Park; ⊙24hr).

TRAIN
Pune Junction train station (Agarkar Nagar) is in the heart of the city on HH Prince Aga Khan Rd. There are very regular, roughly hourly services to Mumbai and good links to cities including Delhi, Chennai and Hyderabad.

Around Pune

Sinhagad

The ruined **Sinhagad** (Lion Fort; Sinhagad Ghat Rd; ⊙dawn-dusk) FREE, about 24km southwest of Pune, was wrested by Maratha leader Shivaji from the Bijapur kings in 1670. In the epic battle (where he lost his son Sambhaji), Shivaji is said to have used monitor lizards yoked with ropes to scale the fort's craggy walls.

MAJOR TRAINS FROM PUNE

DESTINATION	TRAIN NO & NAME	FARE (₹)	DURATION (HR)	DEPARTURE
Bengaluru	11301 Udyan Express	450/1775	20½	11.45am
Chennai	12163 Chennai Express	515/1970	19½	12.10am
Delhi	11077 Jhelum Express	620/2455	27¾	5.20pm
Hyderabad	17031 Hyderabad Express	330/1295	13½	4.35pm
Mumbai CST	12124 Deccan Queen	105/375	3¼	7.15am

Express fares are sleeper/2AC; Deccan Queen fares are 2nd class/AC chair.

Today, it's in a poor state, but worth visiting for the sweeping views and opportunity to hike in the hills.

Sinhagad is an easy day trip from Pune so there is little reason to eat or sleep here. That said, there are a good deal of hotels and resorts (with restaurants) in the surrounding areas and near Lake Khadakwasla, though the road to the fort itself is virtually empty.

Bus 50 or 52 (Shankar Sheth Rd) runs frequently to Donje (Golewadi) village from Shankar Sheth Rd near Swargate bus stand i9n Pune (₹30, 45 minutes, every 30 minutes, 5.20am to 9.30pm), from where it's a 4km hike if you want to walk or catch a shared 4WD (₹60) that can cart you 10km to the base of the summit.

Shivneri

Situated 90km northwest of Pune, above the village of Junnar, **Shivneri Fort** (Imam Raza Nagar, Junnar; ◷dawn-dusk) `FREE` holds the distinction of being the birthplace of Shivaji. Within the ramparts of this ruined fort are the old royal stables, a mosque dating back to the Mughal era and several rock-cut reservoirs. The most important structure is Shivkunj, the pavilion in which Shivaji was born.

About 8km from Shivneri, on the other side of Junnar, is an interesting group of Hinayana Buddhist caves called **Lenyadri** (Lenyadri Ganapati Rd, Junnar; Indian/foreigner ₹25/300; ◷8am-6pm). Of the 27 caves, cave 7 is the most impressive and, interestingly, houses an image of the Hindu god Ganesh.

Views from both monuments are spectacular. There are buses (₹130, two hours, 5am to 4pm) hourly or so connecting Pune's Shivaji Nagar bus stand with Junnar (an Ola outstation day cab from Pune starts from about ₹2026 return). From Junnar's bus stand, a return rickshaw including one hour's wait time runs ₹300 to Shivneri and ₹400 to Lenyadri.

Kolhapur

📞 0231 / POP 561,300 / ELEV 550M

A little-visited city, Kolhapur is the perfect place to get intimate with the flamboyant side of India. Only a few hours from Goa, this historic settlement has an intensely fascinating temple complex. In August Kolhapur is at its vibrant best when Naag Panchami (p84), a snake-worshipping festival, is held in tandem with one at Pune. Gastro-nomes take note: the town is also the birthplace of the famed, spicy Kolhapuri cuisine, especially chicken and mutton dishes.

◉ Sights

★ Shree Chhatrapati Shahu Museum
MUSEUM

(New Palace; Indian/foreigner ₹35/80; ◷9.15am-5.30pm) 'Bizarre' takes on a whole new meaning at this 'new' palace, an Indo-Saracenic behemoth designed by British architect 'Mad' Charles Mant for the Kolhapur kings in 1884. The madcap museum is a maze of countless trophies from the kings' trigger-happy jungle safaris, including walking sticks made from leopard vertebrae and ashtrays fashioned out of tiger skulls and rhino feet.

★ Mahalaxmi Mandir
HINDU TEMPLE

(Mahadwar Rd; ◷3am-11pm) One of Maharashtra's most important and vibrant places of worship, the Mahalaxmi Temple is dedicated to Amba Bai (Mother Goddess). The temple's origins date back to AD 10, but much of the present structure is from the 18th century. It draws an unceasing tide of humanity, as pilgrims press to enter the holy inner sanctuary and bands of musicians and worshippers chant devotions. Non-Hindus are welcome and it's a fantastic place for people-watching.

Motibag Talim Mandal
TRAINING CENTRE

(Guru Maharaj Gali, Mangalwar Peth, C Ward; ◷4am-4pm) Kolhapur is famed for the calibre of its Kushti wrestlers and at the Motibag Thalim you can watch young athletes train in an earthen pit. The *akhara* (training ground) is reached through a low doorway and passage to the left of the entrance to Bhavani Mandap (ask for directions). You are free to walk in and watch, as long as you don't mind the sight of sweaty, seminaked men and the stench of urine emanating from the loos.

🛏 Sleeping & Eating

Hotel K Tree
HOTEL $$

(📞0231-2526990; www.hotelktree.com; 517E, Plot 65, Shivaji Park; s/d incl breakfast from ₹3660/4010; ❄🗐) With high service standards and 26 very inviting modish rooms, this newer hotel is starting to show some age, but it's fine value and wildly popular with Indians for its good buffet breakfast (which includes the spicy curry *misal*). It's a toss up between the clandestine bathrooms in deluxe rooms or elevated Asian-style beds in executive rooms.

Hotel Pavillion
HOTEL $$

(☐0231-2652751; www.hotelpavillion.co.in; 392E Assembly Rd, Shaupuri; s/d incl breakfast ₹2130/2350, with AC from ₹2520/2740; ❈☎) Located at the far end of a leafy park-cum-office-area, this hotel guarantees a peaceful stay, occasionally uninspired bathrooms aside. Its large, well-equipped rooms are perhaps a little dated, but many have windows that open out to delightful views of seasonal blossoms.

★ Dehaati
INDIAN $$

(Ayodha Park, Old Pune-Bangalore Hwy, Nimbalkar Colony; thalis ₹220-530; ⊘12.30-3.30pm & 7.30-10.30pm) The city's Kolhapuri thali specialist. Meals come in a number of mutton variations as well as chicken and veg. The vibrant curries, the spiced-up dhal, the rich *aakkha masoor* (Kolhapuri-style whole lentil curry), the intricate *tambda rassa* (spicy red mutton curry), the perfectly flaky chapatis – it's all delicious.

❶ Information

MTDC Tourist Booth (☐0231-2652935; www.maharashtratourism.gov.in; Near Mahalaxmi Mandir)

MTDC Tourist Office (Maharashtra Tourism Development Corporation; ☐0231-2665816; www.maharashtratourism.gov.in; 254B Udyog Bhavan, Assembly Rd; ⊘10am-6pm Mon-Sat, closed 2nd & 4th Sat)

❶ Getting There & Away

BUS

From the **bus stand** (CBS; ☐0231-2650620; Benadikar Path, Shahupur), services head regularly to Pune (ShivShahi AC ₹420, five hours, every 30 minutes, 5am to 11.30pm), Ratnagiri (ordinary/ShivShahi ₹172/255, 4½ hours, every 30 minutes, 1am and 5.30am to 6.30pm), three ordinary buses to Malvan (₹210, five hours, 5.15am, 6.15am and 12.30pm) and 11 daily buses to Mumbai (ordinary express/ShivShahi ₹485/710, 10 hours, 6.30am to 10pm). There is a reservation counter for all buses.

The best private bus agents gather at the Royal Plaza building at Dabholkar Corner, 300m north of the bus stand. **Paulo Travels** (☐9326012763; www.paulotravels.com; B/22, Royal Plaza, Dhabolkar Cnr) heads to Goa (Volvo AC seat/sleeper from ₹1300/1600, eight hours, 10 per day, 2.30am to midnight). **Neeta Tours & Travels** (☐0231-3290061; www.neetabus.in; B/16, Royal Plaza, Dabholkar Cnr) is a good bet for overnight AC services heading to Mumbai (Volvo AC sleeper from ₹1200, nine hours, 9am, 3pm, 5pm and 10.45pm) and Pune (Volvo AC seat from ₹550,

five hours, 7am, 9am, 3pm, 4pm, 5pm, 8pm and 11.30pm).

TRAIN

The **train station** (KOP; Railway Colony, New Shahupuri), known as Chattrapati Shahu Maharaj Terminus, is 10 minutes' walk west of the bus stand. Three daily expresses, including the 10.50pm Sahyadri Express, go to Mumbai (sleeper/?AC ₹305/1180, 13 hours) via Pune (₹210/815, eight hours). The Rani Chennama Express makes the long journey to Bengaluru (₹400/1575, 16½ hours, 2.05pm). There are no direct trains to Goa.

Mahabaleshwar

☐ 02168 / POP 12,750 / ELEV 1372M

Once a summer capital under the British, today the best thing about the hill station of Mahabaleshwar (1327m) is the jaw-dropping mountain scenery on the road to get here. It's an overdeveloped mess, tainted by an ugly building boom and traffic chaos as tourists attempt a mad dash to tick off its viewpoints and falls. There's no compelling reason to visit – it's basically one big bustling bazaar surrounded by resorts and views – though the town can be used as a base to visit the impressive Pratapgad Fort (p116) or Kass Pleateau of Flowers, both nearby.

Forget about coming during the monsoon when the whole town virtually shuts down (and an unbelievable 6m of rain falls). If you have an hour or so to kill between buses, budget-friendly **Nature Care Spa** (☐9168816683; Hotel Shreyas, Main Rd; massages from ₹1500; ⊘9am-8pm), across the street from the bus stand at Hotel Shreyas, hits the spot.

🛏 Sleeping & Eating

Glenogle
BUNGALOW $$$

(☐8888999018; www.glenogle.in; Sasoon Rd; 5-bedroom bungalow ₹15,000-30,000; ❈☎) This 1840s tin-roof heritage bungalow sits just as it did when it was built by the British government for one of its captains. Nestled in its own forest just 1.3km from the main bazaar, it feels a world away from the town, with five beautifully appointed bedrooms teeming with arts and antiques.

★ Grapevine
MULTICUISINE $$$

(☐02168-261100; Masjid Rd; mains ₹170-950; ⊘9.30am-3pm & 5-10pm) Way too hip for Mahabaleshwar, this classy restaurant/wine bar is unmissable. Chef/owner Raio's

---

WORTH A TRIP

PRATAPGAD FORT

Pratapgad Fort (Poladpur-Mahabaleshwar Rd; ⊙9am-dusk), built by Shivaji in 1656 (and still owned by his descendants), straddles a high mountain ridge 24km northwest of the town of Mahabaleshwar. In 1659, Shivaji agreed to meet Bijapuri General Afzal Khan here in an attempt to end a stalemate. Despite a no-arms agreement, Shivaji, upon greeting Khan, disembowelled his enemy with a set of iron *baghnakh* (tiger's claws). Khan's tomb (out of bounds) marks the site of this painful encounter at the base of the fort.

Pratapgad is reached by a 500-step climb that affords brilliant views. Fresh fruit, juice, snacks and simple restaurants are scattered about the staircase to the fort.

From the bus stand in Mahabaleshwar, a state bus tour (₹150 return, one hour, 9.30am) does a daily shuttle to the fort, with a waiting time of around one hour. Taxi drivers in Mahabaleshwar charge a fixed ₹1000 for the return trip, including one hour's waiting time.

---

culinary pedigree includes Taj Hotels and his creative takes on Parsi and fresh seafood are divine. The monstrous Mediterranean lamb burger (with feta and harissa mayo) and the soft-shell crab burger are worth the trip here alone, but there's also spicy tiger prawns, lamb shanks and lobster.

❶ Getting There & Away

From **Mahabaleshwar bus stand** (Hwy 72), state buses leave regularly for Pune (non-AC/ShivShahi ₹190/210, four hours, every 30 minutes, 5.30am to 6.30pm), Kohlapur (non-AC/ShivShahi ₹365/475, 5½ hours, 6.30am, 8am and 12.30pm) and Satara (non-AC ₹75, two hours, every 30 minutes, 7am to 6.30pm), where you can more often connect to Kolhapur (non-AC ₹175, every 30 minutes). Four daily buses head

to Mumbai between 9am and 9.30pm (non-AC ₹450, seven hours) and one ordinary bus to Goa (non-AC ₹780, 12 hours, 8am).

RB Travels (📞9422405772, 02168-260251; 49 Dr Sabne Rd; ⊙8am-11pm), located on a corner between an alley shortcut to Masjid Rd and the bazaar (across from Meghdoot restaurant), books luxury coaches to Goa (non-AC seat/Volvo AC sleeper ₹1100/1400, 12 hours). You will depart from the bazaar in a car at 7.30pm to Surur Phata junction, 42km away, to wait for the bus on the way from Pune. Transport to Mumbai (Volvo AC sleeper ₹800, six hours, 9.30am, 10.30am, noon, 4pm and 9.30pm) is also available.

For the Pratapgad Fort, a state bus (₹150 return, one hour, 9.30am) does a daily round trip, with a waiting time of around one hour; taxi drivers charge a fixed ₹1000 return.

Goa

📞 0832 / POP 1.82 MILLION

Includes ➡

Panaji	120
Old Goa	126
Mapusa	127
Candolim	128
Calangute & Baga	131
Anjuna	135
Vagator & Chapora	140
Arambol (Harmal)	147
Margao	150
Colva	151
Agonda	153
Palolem	155

Best Places to Eat

➡ Black Sheep Bistro (p124)

➡ Go With the Flow (p134)

➡ Baba Au Rhum (p138)

➡ Bomra's (p129)

➡ Ourem 88 (p159)

Best Places to Stay

➡ Mandala (p146)

➡ Dreams Hostel (p141)

➡ Panjim Inn (p123)

➡ Ciarans (p158)

➡ Vaayu Waterman's Village (p145)

Why Go?

Pint-sized Goa is much more than beaches and trance parties. A kaleidoscopic blend of Indian and Portuguese cultures, sweetened with sun, sea, sand, seafood and spirituality, there's nowhere in India quite like it.

The central region is Goa's historic and cultural heart, home to capital Panaji, Old Goa's glorious churches, inland islands, bird sanctuaries, spice plantations and the wild Western Ghats. North Goa draws the crowds with busy beaches, upbeat nightlife, Goan trance, great food, hippie markets and yoga retreats. South Goa is the state's more serene half, with cleaner, whiter, quieter beaches ranging from village-feel Benaulim to beach-hut bliss at Palolem, Patnem and Agonda.

Goa's rapidly increasing popularity with domestic tourists has put a strain on this tiny state, but most travellers will still find a place and a space to chill out and unwind from the rest of India.

When to Go
Panaji

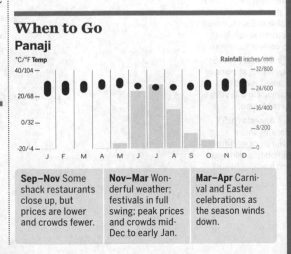

Sep–Nov Some shack restaurants close up, but prices are lower and crowds fewer.

Nov–Mar Wonderful weather; festivals in full swing; peak prices and crowds mid-Dec to early Jan.

Mar–Apr Carnival and Easter celebrations as the season winds down.

Goa Highlights

1 Panaji (p120)
Exploring the historic Latin Quarter, shopping and eating well in India's most laid-back state capital.

2 Assagao (p139)
Dropping in to a yoga or cooking class at Assagao, Anjuna, Arambol or Mandrem.

3 Anjuna Flea Market (p138)
Haggling for a bargain at this touristy but fun Wednesday market.

4 Old Goa (p77)
Standing in silence and taking in the extraordinary churches and cathedrals of Old Goa.

5 Cola Beach (p152) Trekking down to secluded Cola, one of Goa's prettiest beaches.

6 Mandrem (p146)
Sleeping in style and stretching out with a good book at this peaceful beach.

7 Palolem (p155)
Checking into a beach hut on beautiful Palolem Beach, where you can kayak, learn to cook or just relax.

8 Chandor (p148)
Marvelling at colonial mansions and palacios in this village near Margao.

9 Agonda (p153)
Booking into a luxurious beachfront hut on this wild beach and learning to surf.

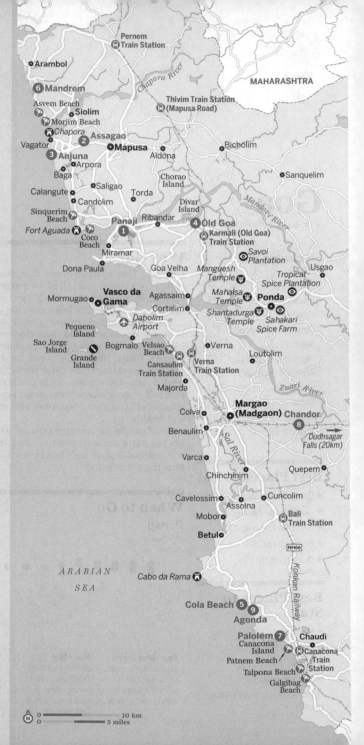

History

Goa went through a dizzying array of rulers from Ashoka's Mauryan empire in the 3rd century BC to the long-ruling Kadamba from the 3rd century AD. Subsequent conflict saw rival sultanates fighting the Hindu Vijayanagar empire for control, before the Adil Shahs of Bijapur created the capital we now call Old Goa in the 15th century.

The Portuguese arrived in 1510 and steadily extended their power from their grand capital at Old Goa out into the provinces, zealously converting the locals to Christianity. Their 400-year reign came to an end in 1961, when Goa was annexed to India after a three-day siege by the Indian Army, but the Portuguese legacy lives on in the state's colonial-era mansions, its cuisine, churches and even in its language.

Goa's hippie heyday began in the late 1960s and it has been a stalwart on the overland trail since, but these days the beaches are packed not so much with backpackers but with an increasing influx of interstate Indian tourists.

ℹ Information

Goa Tourism Development Corporation
(GTDC; ☑ 0832-2437132; www.goa-tourism. com; Paryatan Bhavan, Dr Alvaro Costa Rd, Panaji; ⊙ 9.30am-5.45pm Mon-Fri), usually called Goa Tourism these days, is the state government tourism body and it's a surprisingly progressive government organisation, acting more like a commercial business with numerous hotels and operating a host of tours and even a taxi smartphone app.

ℹ Getting There & Away

AIR

Goa's airport, **Dabolim** (Goa International Airport; ☑ 0832-2540806; NH566), is served directly by domestic flights, a handful of international flights from the Middle East, and seasonal package-holiday charters (mostly from Russia, Europe and the UK).

Unless you're on a charter, you'll generally have to fly into a major city such as Mumbai or Delhi and change to a domestic flight with Jet Airways, Air India, SpiceJet or IndiGo.

A new greenfield airport at Mopa in North Goa is expected to be completed by 2020.

LAND
Bus

Private and state-run long-distance buses run to and from Goa daily. Tickets can be booked in advance online, at ticket agents located near the bus stands or through travel agents or tourist accommodation. Note that travel into and out of Mumbai by road is interminably slow; the train is faster and more comfortable.

Kadamba (www.goakadamba.com), the state government bus company, operates across the state and to neighbouring regions. For private or state buses you can book online with www. redbus.in.

Train

The 760km-long Konkan Railway (www.konkan railway.com), completed in 1998, is the main train line running through the state, connecting Goa with Mumbai to the north and Mangalore to the south. The biggest station in Goa is Margao's Madgaon station (p151), and many trains also pass through Karmali station near Old Goa, 12km from Panaji. Smaller stations on the line include Pernem for Arambol, Thivim for Mapusa and the northern beaches, and Canacona for Palolem.

SEA

Cruise ships, mostly from UAE or travelling between Mumbai and the Maldives, call in at Goa's Mormugao cruise ship terminal as part of their itineraries.

In 2018 a Mumbai to Goa ferry began operating three times a week.

Angriya Cruises (☑ 8314810440; www. angriyacruises.com; Mormugao Cruise Terminal; ⊙ 4pm Tue, Thu, Sun Oct-May) is an overnight cruise. Onboard accommodation ranges from dormitory bunks (₹4300) and luxury single pods (₹4650) to spacious double rooms (₹8950 per person) and family rooms (₹5700 per person). Meals are an additional ₹2000/1000 adult/child.

ℹ Getting Around

Car & Motorcycle Many travellers hire a scooter or motorbike for their trip (₹250 to ₹500 per day). An international driving permit is required for foreigners. Self-drive cars are less common but car and driver services are affordable for groups.

GOA MILES

Ridesharing services such as Uber and Ola are currently banned in Goa, but Goa Tourism has started its own service called Goa Miles (www.goamiles.com), a taxi smartphone app that works much like Uber. The subsidised fares are roughly half what you would pay a taxi driver off the street (closer to the fares charged at the airport prepaid counter), though the success of the service will rely on how many drivers are on the road.

Taxi & autorickshaw Good for short hops around and between towns and beach resorts. Taxis will also take you on longer trips – agree on a fare beforehand.

Bus Extremely cheap, slow but fun local way of getting between towns and villages.

Train There are two rail lines in the state but it's not a particularly quick or convenient way of getting around.

PANAJI & CENTRAL GOA

Some travellers see Goa as one big beach resort, but the central region – with few beaches of note – is the state's historic and cultural heart and soul.

Panaji

☏ 0832 / POP 241,000

One of India's most relaxed state capitals, Panaji (Panjim) crowds around the peninsula overlooking the broad Mandovi River, where cruise boats and floating casinos ply the waters, and advertising signs cast neon reflections in the night.

But it's the tangle of narrow streets in the old Latin Quarter of Fontainhas that really steals the show. Nowhere is the Portuguese influence felt more openly than here, where the late afternoon sun lights up yellow houses with purple doors, and around each corner you'll find restored ochre-coloured mansions with terracotta-tiled roofs, wrought-iron balconies and arched oyster-shell windows.

A day or two in Panaji really is an essential part of the Goan experience.

⊙ Sights

Some of Panaji's great pleasures are leisurely strolls through the sleepy Portuguese-era Latin Quarter of Fontainhas and Sao Tomé and Altinho Hill. Riverside Campal Gardens, west of the centre, and Miramar Beach, 4km southwest of the city, are also popular spots.

★Church of Our Lady
of the Immaculate Conception   CHURCH
(cnr Emilio Gracia & Jose Falcao Rds; ⊙9am-12.30pm & 3-7.30pm Mon-Sat, 11am-12.30pm & 3.30-5pm Sun, English Mass 8am daily) Panaji's spiritual, as well as geographical, centre is this elevated, pearly white church, built in 1619 over an older, smaller 1540 chapel, and stacked like a fancy white wedding cake. When Panaji was little more than a sleepy fishing village, this church was the first port of call for sailors from Lisbon, who would give thanks for a safe crossing, before continuing to Ela (Old Goa) further east up the river. The church is beautifully illuminated at night.

Goa State Museum &
Secretariat Building   MUSEUM
(☏0832-2438006; www.goamuseum.gov.in; Avenida Dom Joao Castro; ⊙9.30am-5.30pm Mon-Fri) FREE Currently housed in the Secretariat, the oldest colonial building in Goa, the state museum features an eclectic, if not extensive, collection of items tracing aspects of Goan history. As well as some beautiful Hindu and Jain sculptures and bronzes, there are nice examples of Portuguese-era furniture, coins, an intricately carved chariot and a pair of quirky antique rotary lottery machines.

TOP STATE FESTIVALS

Feast of the Three Kings (⊙6 Jan) Boys re-enact the story of the three kings bearing gifts for Christ.

Shigmotsav of Holi (Shigmo; ⊙Feb/Mar) Goa's version of the Hindu festival Holi sees coloured powders thrown about and parades in most towns.

Sabado Gordo (Panaji; ⊙Feb/Mar) A procession of floats and street parties on the Saturday before Lent.

Carnival (⊙Mar) A four-day festival kicking off Lent; the party's particularly jubilant in Panaji.

Feast of the Menino Jesus (Colva; ⊙2nd Mon in Oct) Statue of the baby Jesus is paraded through the streets of Colva.

Feast of St Francis Xavier (Old Goa; ⊙3 Dec) A 10-day celebration of Goa's patron saint.

Feast of Our Lady of the Immaculate Conception (Margao, Panaji; ⊙8 Dec) Fairs and concerts around Panaji's famous church.

PONDA'S TEMPLES & SPICES

The Ponda region, around 30km southeast of Panaji, makes a worthwhile day trip for its Hindu temple complexes and nearby spice plantations.

For nearly 250 years after the arrival of the Portuguese in 1510, Ponda taluk (district) remained under the control of Muslim or Hindu rulers, and many of its temples came into existence when Hindus were forced to escape Portuguese persecution by fleeing across its district border, bringing their sacred temple deities with them as centuries-old edifices were destroyed by the new colonial regime. These 17th and 18th-century temples remain today. If you're short on time, the most appealing and accessible are Shri Manguesh and Shri Mahalsa near the village of Mardol. The Ponda region is also the centre of commercial spice farms in Goa and several have opened their doors as tourist operations, offering a guided tour of the plantation, buffet thali-style lunch and perhaps a cultural show. Farms include:

Pascoal Spice Farm (☎0832-2344268; farm tour & lunch ₹400; ⊙9am-4.30pm)

Sahakari Spice Farm (☎0832-2312394; www.sahakarifarms.com; admission & lunch ₹400; ⊙8am-4.30pm)

Savoi Plantation (☎9423888899, 0832-2340272; www.savoiplantations.com; adult/child ₹700/350; ⊙9am-4.30pm)

Tropical Spice Plantation (☎0832-2340329; www.tropicalspiceplantation.com; Keri; tour & lunch ₹400; ⊙9am-4pm)

Goa State Central Library LIBRARY
(Sanskruti Bhavan, Patto; ⊙9am-7.30pm Mon-Fri, 9.30am-5.45pm Sat & Sun) FREE Panaji's modern state library has six floors of reading material, a bookshop and gallery. The 2nd floor features a children's book section and internet browsing (free, but technically only for academic research). The 4th floor has Goan history books and the 6th a large collection of Portuguese books.

Mario Gallery GALLERY
(☎0832-2421776; www.mariodemiranda.com; Duarte Pacheco Rd; ⊙10am-5.30pm Mon-Fri, to 1pm Sat) FREE This gallery and shop showcases work by India's favourite cartoonist, Loutolim local Mario de Miranda, who died in 2011 at the age of 85. Along with prints, books and drawings, there are printed T-shirts, mugs and bags. His works are so popular that there are similar galleries in Calangute, Margao and Porvorim.

🏃 Activities

One-hour evening boat cruises run by Goa Tourism and private operators leave from the Tourism Jetty near Mandovi Bridge and are a popular way to see the river.

GTDC River Cruise CRUISE
(Avenida Dom Joao Castro, Tourism Jetty; sunset cruise ₹300; ⊙6pm) Goa Tourism operates an entertaining hour-long cruise along the Mandovi River aboard the *Santa Monica*, with a live band and/or performances of Goan folk songs and dances. There are also twice-weekly, two-hour dinner cruises. Departs from the Santa Monica Jetty next to the Mandovi Bridge.

Make It Happen WALKING
(www.makeithappen.co.in; 1/143 Dr Cunha Gonsalves Rd; walking tours from ₹700) For a local insight into Goan history and culture, this Panaji-based outfit of local tour guides leads a number of walks and tours, including Fontainhas and Old Goa heritage walks and tours of Divar Island, Chandor and Saligao. The Fontainhas walk includes access to heritage homes and a performance of *fado* (a melancholic form of Portuguese singing). Book online.

🛌 Sleeping

Panaji has its fair share of accommodation for all budgets but it's not saturated like the beach resorts.

★Old Quarter Hostel HOSTEL $
(☎7410069108; www.thehostelcrowd.com; 5/146 31st January Rd; dm ₹600-650, s/d with AC from ₹1100/1700; ❉⊛❖) In an old Portuguese house in historic Fontainhas, this flamboyant hostel is a beacon for budget travellers to Panaji. Slick four-bed dorms with lockers as well as private doubles in a separate building, along with the excellent Bombay Roasters Cafe, arty murals, good wi-fi and bikes for hire. Noon checkout.

Panaji

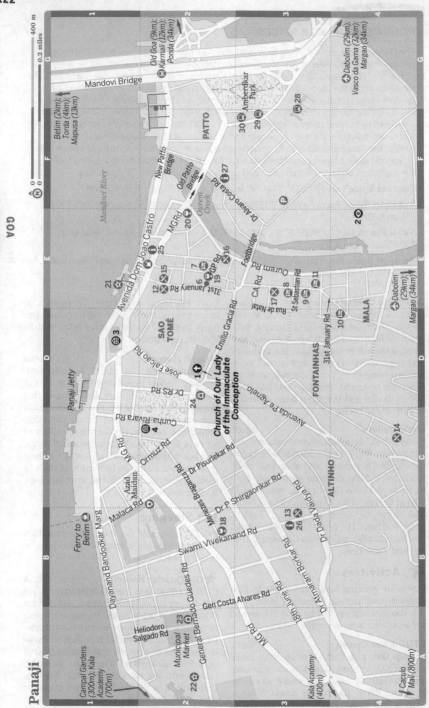

0 0 | 400 m
0 0 | 0.2 miles

Campal Gardens (300m); Kala Academy (700m)

Mandovi River

Betim (2km); Torda (4km); Mapusa (13km)

Mandovi Bridge

Old Goa (9km); Karmali (12km); Ponda (34km)

Ambedkar Park

Dabolim (29km); Vasco da Gama (32km); Margao (34km)

PATTO

30 | 29 | 28

New Patto Bridge

Old Patto Bridge

Dr Alvaro Costa Rd | 27

Ourem Creek

MGRd | 20

Avenida Dom João Castro

Footbridge

Ourem Rd

25 | 15 | 7 | GP Rd | 16
21 | 12 | 6 | 19
31st January Rd

CA Rd

St Sebastian Rd | 11
8
Rua de Natal | 17 | 9

SÃO TOMÉ

Emilio Gracia Rd

José Falcão Rd

2

Panaji Jetty

3

Dabolim (29km); Margao (34km)

MALA

31st January Rd

10

FONTAINHAS

Church of Our Lady of the Immaculate Conception | 1

Dr RS Rd | 24

Cunha-Rivara Rd

4

Avenida Pe Agnelo

Ormuz Rd

NJG Rd

Azad Maidan

Malaca Rd

Ferry to Betim

Dr Pisurlekar Rd

Menezes Braganza Rd

Dr P Shirgaonkar Rd

Dr Dada Vaidya Rd

ALTINHO

14

13 | 26

18

Swami Vivekanand Rd

Dayanand Bandodkar Marg

Gen Costa Alvares Rd

18th June Rd

Dr Atmaram Borkar Rd

MG Rd

Kala Academy (400m)

Caculo Mall (800m)

General Bernado Guedes Rd

Heliodoro Salgado Rd | 23

Municipal Market

22

Panaji

◎ Top Sights
1 Church of Our Lady of the
    Immaculate Conception D2

◎ Sights
2 Goa State Central Library E4
3 Goa State Museum & Secretariat
    Building D1
4 Mario Gallery C2

◎ Activities, Courses & Tours
5 GTDC River Cruise G2
6 Make It Happen E2

◎ Sleeping
7 A Pousada Guest House E2
8 Afonso Guesthouse E3
9 La Maison E3
10 Old Quarter Hostel D4
11 Panjim Inn E3

◎ Eating
12 Anandashram E2
13 Black Sheep Bistro B3
14 Cafe Bodega C4
15 Hotel Venite E2
16 Route 66 .... E2
17 Viva Panjim E3

◎ Drinking & Nightlife
18 Cafe Mojo B2
19 Joseph Bar E2
20 Riverfront & Down the Road E2

◎ Entertainment
21 Deltin Royale E1
22 INOX Cinema A2

◎ Shopping
23 Municipal Market A2
24 Singbal's Book House D2

◎ Information
25 Disability Rights Association of
    Goa E2
26 Forest Department B3
27 Goa Tourism F2
    Government of India
    Tourist Office .... (see 27)

◎ Transport
28 Kadamba Bus Stand G3
    Konkan Railway
    Reservation Office .... (see 28)
29 Paulo Travels F3
30 Private Bus Agents F3

GOA PANAJI

A Pousada Guest House   GUESTHOUSE $
(📞0832-2422618, 9850998213; sabrinateles@
yahoo.com; Luis de Menezes Rd; s/d from
₹950/1200, d with AC ₹1800; ❄🛜) The five
rooms in this bright-yellow place are simple but clean and come with comfy spring-
mattress beds and TV. Owner Sabrina is
friendly and no-nonsense, and it's one of the
better budget guesthouses in Fountainhas.

★**Panjim Inn**   HERITAGE HOTEL $$
(📞9823025748, 0832-2226523; www.panjiminn.
com; 31st January Rd; s/d from ₹5900/6500,
superior ₹8200/8700; ❄🛜) One of the origi-
nal heritage hotels in Fontainhas, the Pan-
jim Inn has been a long-standing favourite
for its character and charm. Run by the love-
ly Sukhija family and overseen by helpful
staff, this beautiful 19th-century mansion
has 12 charismatic rooms in the original
house, along with newer rooms with mod-
ern touches to complement four-poster
beds, colonial-era furniture and artworks.

Afonso Guesthouse   GUESTHOUSE $$
(📞0832-2222359, 9764300165; www.afonsoguest
house.com; St Sebastian Rd; d ₹2500-3250; ❄🛜)
Run by the friendly Jeanette, this pretty
Portuguese townhouse offers eight spacious, well-kept rooms with timber ceilings.
The little rooftop terrace makes for sunny

breakfasting (not included) with Fontainhas
views. It's a simple, serene stay in the heart
of the most atmospheric part of town. Checkout is 9am and bookings are accepted online
but not by phone.

La Maison   BOUTIQUE HOTEL $$
(📞0832-2235555; www.lamaisongoa.com; 31st
January Rd; r incl breakfast ₹4700-5300; ❄🛜)
One of the growing range of boutique her-
itage hotels in Fontainhas, La Maison is
historic on the outside but thoroughly mod-
ern and swanky within, with a Euro-meets-
Orient vibe. The eight rooms are deceptively
simple and homey but five-star comfortable
with soft beds, cloud-like pillows, writing
desks and flat-screen TVs. Breakfast is in-
cluded and attached is the French fusion
Desbue restaurant.

✗ Eating

You'll never go hungry in Panaji, where food
is enjoyed fully and frequently. The Latin
Quarter has a developing foodie scene, where
you can dine on traditional Goan specialities.

Anandashram   GOAN $
(31st January Rd; thalis ₹90-140, mains ₹100-350;
⏱noon-3.30pm & 7.30-10.30pm Mon-Sat, noon-
3pm Sun) This little place is renowned locally
for seafood, serving up simple but tasty fish

curries, as well as veg and nonveg thalis for lunch and dinner.

★ **Viva Panjim**   GOAN $$
(☑0832-2422405; 31st January Rd; mains ₹160-300; ⊙11.30am-3.30pm & 7-11pm Mon-Sat, 7-11pm Sun) Well-known to tourists, this little side-street eatery, in an old Portuguese house and with a few tables out on the laneway, delivers tasty Goan classics at reasonable prices. There's a whole page devoted to pork dishes, along with tasty *xacuti* (a spicy chicken or meat dish cooked in red coconut sauce) and *cafreal* (a marinated chicken dish) meals.

★ **Cafe Bodega**   CAFE $$
(☑0832-2421315; www.cafebodegagoa.in; Altinho; mains ₹170-340; ⊙10am-7pm Mon-Sat, to 4pm Sun; ☎) It's well worth a trip up to Altinho Hill to visit this serene inner courtyard cafe-gallery in an azure-and-white Portuguese mansion in the grounds of Sunaparanta Centre for the Arts. Enjoy good coffee, juices and freshly baked cakes around the inner courtyard or lunch on super pizzas and sandwiches.

★ **Hotel Venite**   GOAN $$$
(31st January Rd; mains ₹320-440; ⊙9am-10.30pm) With its cute rickety balcony tables overhanging the cobbled street, Venite has long been among the most atmospheric of Panaji's Goan restaurants. The menu is traditional, with spicy sausages, fish curry rice, pepper steak and *bebinca* (Goan 16-layer cake), but Venite is popular with tourists and prices are consequently inflated. Drop in for a beer or shot of feni (Goan liquor) before deciding.

★ **Black Sheep Bistro**   EUROPEAN $$$
(☑0832-2222901; www.blacksheepbistro.in; Swami Vivekanand Rd; tapas ₹250-400, mains ₹350-600; ⊙noon-4pm & 7pm-midnight) Among the best of Panaji's burgeoning boutique restaurants, Black Sheep's impressive pale-yellow facade gives way to a sexy dark-wood bar and loungy dining room. The tapas dishes are light, fresh and expertly prepared in keeping with their farm-to-table philosophy. Salads, pasta, seafood and dishes like lamb osso buco grace the menu, while an internationally trained sommelier matches food to wine.

Route 66   DINER $$$
(☑9623922796; Ourem Rd; mains ₹200-850; ⊙noon-11.30pm; ❂☎) Styled on an American diner, this roomy restaurant across from Ourem Creek specialises in burgers such as the SOB or Wolverine, but also excels at hot dogs, cheese chilli fries, hickory barbecue ribs and New York–style pizzas. For comfort fast food it's hard to beat and there's live music on Thursday, Friday and Saturday nights.

🍷 Drinking & Nightlife

★ **Cafe Mojo**   BAR
(☑0832-2431973; www.cafemojo.in; Menezes Braganza Rd; ⊙10am-5am Mon-Thu, to 6am Fri-Sun) The decor is a dark cosy English pub, the clientele young and up for a late party, and the novelty is the e-beer system. Each table has its own beer tap and LCD screen: you buy a card (₹500), swipe it at your table and start pouring – it automatically deducts what you drink (use the card for spirits, cocktails and food, too).

Joseph Bar   BAR
(Gomes Pereira Rd, Sao Tomé; ⊙6-11.30pm) This hole-in-the-wall bar is a place where locals and tourists gather streetside to chat and drink at tiny tables or perched on scooters. It's a warm and welcoming place with Goan craft beer available.

Riverfront & Down the Road   BAR
(cnr MG & Ourem Rds; ⊙11am-1am) The balcony of this restaurant-bar overlooking the creek and Old Patto Bridge makes for a cosy beer or cocktail spot with carved barrels for furniture. The ground-floor bar (from 6pm) is an old-school nightspot with occasional live music.

☆ Entertainment

Panaji's most visible form of entertainment are the casino boats anchored out in the Mandovi River.

Deltin Royale   CASINO
(☑9819698196; www.deltingroup.com/deltin-royale; Noah's Ark, RND Jetty, Dayanand Bandodkar Marg; weekday/weekend ₹2500/3500; ⊙24hr,

---

SLEEPING PRICE RANGES

The following price ranges refer to a double room with bathroom across the state:

$ less than ₹1500

$$ ₹1500–₹7500

$$$ more than ₹7500

Accommodation prices in Goa vary considerably depending on the season and demand.

entertainment 9pm-1am) Goa's biggest and best luxury floating casino, Deltin Royal has 123 tables, the Vegas Restaurant, a Whisky Bar and a creche. Entry includes gaming chips worth ₹1500/2000 (weekday/weekend). Unlimited food and drinks included.

INOX Cinema CINEMA
(🗹 0832-2420900; www.inoxmovies.com; Old GMC Heritage Precinct; tickets ₹210-240) This comfortable, plush multiplex cinema shows Hollywood and Bollywood blockbusters. Book online to choose your seats in advance.

Kala Academy PERFORMING ARTS
(🗹 0832-2420452; www.kalaacademygoa.co.in; Dayanand Bandodkar Marg) On the west side of the city, in Campal, is Goa's premier cultural centre, which features a program of dance, theatre, music and art exhibitions throughout the year. Many shows are in Konkani, but there are occasional English-language productions. The website usually has an up-to-date calendar of events.

🛍 Shopping

Municipal Market MARKET
(Heliogordo Salgado Rd; ⊘ from 7.30am) This atmospheric place, where narrow streets have been converted into covered markets, makes for a nice wander, offering fresh produce, clothing stalls and some tiny, enticing eateries. The fish market is a particularly interesting strip of activity.

Singbal's Book House BOOKS
(🗹 0832-2425747; Church Sq; ⊘ 9.30am-1pm & 3.30-7.30pm Mon-Sat) On the corner opposite Panaji's main church, Singbal's is a local landmark with an excellent selection of international magazines and newspapers, and lots of books on Goa and travel.

Caculo Mall MALL
(🗹 0832-2222068; www.caculomall.in; 16 Shanta, St Inez; ⊘ 10am-9pm) Goa's biggest mall is four levels of air-conditioned family shopping heaven with brand-name stores, food court, kids' toys, bowling alley and arcade games.

ℹ Information

MEDICAL SERVICES
Goa Medical College Hospital (🗹 0832-2458700; www.gmc.goa.gov.in; NH66, Bambolim; ⊘ 24hr) This 1000-bed hospital is 9km south of Panaji on NH66 in Bambolim.

TOURIST INFORMATION
Goa Tourism (p119) The GTDC office is in the large Paryatan Bhavan building across the Ourem Creek and near the bus stand. However, it's more marketing office than tourist office and is of little use to casual visitors, unless you want to book one of GTDC's host of tours.

Government of India Tourist Office (🗹 0832-2438812; www.incredibleindia.com; Paryatan Bhavan, Dr Alvaro Costa Rd; ⊘ 9.30am-1.30pm & 2.30-6pm Mon-Fri, 10am-1pm Sat) is in the same building, staff at this tourist office can be helpful, especially for information outside Goa.

ℹ Getting There & Away

AIR
Dabolim Airport (p119) is around 30km south of Panaji. A new airport bus (www.goakadamba.com) between Dabolim and Calangute stops at Panaji on request. Some higher-end hotels offer a minibus service, often included in the room tariff.

BOAT
Taking the rusty but free passenger/vehicle ferry across the Mandovi River to the fishing village of Betim makes a fun shortcut en route to the northern beaches. It departs the jetty on Dayanand Bandodkar Marg. From Betim there are regular buses onwards to Calangute and Candolim.

BUS
All local buses depart from Panaji's **Kadamba bus stand** (🗹 interstate 0832-2438035, local 0832-2438034; www.goakadamba.com; Patto Centre; ⊘ reservations 8am-8pm), with frequent local services (running to no apparent timetable) heading out every few minutes; major destinations are Mapusa (₹30, 30 minutes) in the north, Margao (₹40, one hour) to the south and Ponda (₹25, one hour) to the east. Most bus services run from 6am to 10pm. Ask at the bus stand to be directed to the right bus, or check the signs on the bus windscreens.

To get to the beaches in South Goa, take an express bus to Margao and change there; to get to beaches north of Baga, it's best to head to Mapusa and change there. There are direct buses to Candolim (₹20, 35 minutes), Calangute (₹25, 25 minutes) and Baga (₹30, 30 minutes).

State-run long-distance services also depart from the Kadamba bus stand, but prices offered by private operators are similar and they offer greater choice in type of bus and departure times. Many private operators have **booths** (Patto Place) outside the entrance to the bus stand (go there to compare prices and times). At the time of writing all interstate buses were operating from the Kadamba stand but there are plans to move them to a new stand on the Ponda bypass road.

TRAIN

The closest train station to Panaji is Karmali, 12km to the east near Old Goa. A number of long-distance services stop here, including services to and from Mumbai, and many trains coming from Margao also stop – but check in advance. Panaji's **Konkan Railway Reservation Office** (www.konkanrailway.com; Patto Place; ⊙8am-8pm Mon-Sat) is on the 1st floor of the Kadamba bus stand – not at the train station. You can also check times, prices and routes online at www.konkanrailway.com and www.indianrail.gov.in.

⊙ Getting Around

It's easy enough to get around central Panaji and Fontainhas on foot, which is just as well because taxis and autorickshaws charge extortionately for short trips (minimum ₹100). Autorickshaws and motorcycle taxis can also be found in front of the post office, on 18th June Rd, and just south of the church. A taxi from Panaji to the airport should cost ₹900 and takes about 45 minutes, but allow an hour for traffic.

Locals buses run to Miramar (₹5, 10 minutes), Dona Paula (₹8, 15 minutes) and to Old Goa (₹10, 20 minutes).

Goa Tourism's **Hop on Hop off bus** (☑7447473495; www.hohogoa.com; 1/2 route pass ₹400/700) plies a recurring route along the riverfront taking in the state museum, Kala Academy, Miramar Beach and Dona Paula, then returning and heading out to Old Goa and back.

Old Goa

From the 16th to the 18th centuries, when Old Goa's population exceeded that of Lisbon or London, Goa's former capital was considered the 'Rome of the East'. You can still sense that grandeur as you wander what's left of the city, with its towering churches and cathedrals and majestic convents. Its rise under the Portuguese, from 1510, was meteoric, but cholera and malaria outbreaks forced the abandonment of the city in the 17th century. In 1843 the capital was officially shifted to Panaji. Some of the most imposing churches and cathedrals are still in use and are remarkably well preserved, while other historical buildings have become museums or simply ruins. It's a fascinating day trip, but it can get crowded: consider visiting on a weekday morning.

⊙ Sights

★**Basilica de Bom Jesus**　　　CHURCH
(⊙7.30am-6.30pm) Famous throughout the Roman Catholic world, the imposing Basilica de Bom Jesus contains the tomb and mortal remains of St Francis Xavier, the so-called Apostle of the Indies. St Francis Xavier's missionary voyages throughout the East became legendary. His 'incorrupt' body is in the mausoleum to the right, in a glass-sided coffin amid a shower of gilt stars. Freelance guides at the entrance will show you around for ₹100.

★**Sé Cathedral**　　　CATHEDRAL
(⊙8am-6pm, Mass 7am & 6pm Mon-Sat, 7.15am, 10am & 4pm Sun) At over 76m long and 55m wide, the cavernous Sé Cathedral is the largest church in Asia. Building commenced in 1562, on the orders of King Dom Sebastiao of Portugal, and the finishing touches were finally made some 90 years later. The exterior is notable for its plain style, in the Tuscan tradition. Also of note is its rather lopsided look resulting from the loss of one of its bell

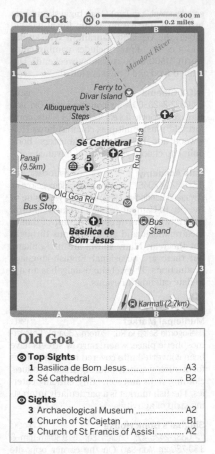

Old Goa

⊙ Top Sights
1 Basilica de Bom Jesus A3
2 Sé Cathedral B2

⊙ Sights
3 Archaeological Museum A2
4 Church of St Cajetan B1
5 Church of St Francis of Assisi A2

towers, which collapsed in 1776 after being struck by lightning.

Church of St Francis of Assisi   CHURCH
(⊙9am-5pm) West of the Sé Cathedral, the Church of St Francis of Assisi is no longer in use for worship, and consequently exudes a more mournful air than its neighbours.

Church of St Cajetan   CHURCH
(⊙9am-5.30pm) Modelled on the original design of St Peter's in Rome, the Church of St Cajetan was built by Italian friars of the Order of Theatines, who were sent by Pope Urban III to preach Christianity in the kingdom of Golconda (near Hyderabad). The friars were not permitted to work in Golconda, so settled at Old Goa in 1640. The construction of the church began in 1655.

Archaeological Museum   MUSEUM
(adult/child ₹10/free; ⊙9am-5pm) The archaeological museum houses some lovely fragments of sculpture from Hindu temple sites in Goa, and some sati stones, which once marked the spot where a Hindu widow committed suicide by flinging herself onto her husband's funeral pyre.

Other Sights
There are plenty of other monuments, churches and ruins in Old Goa to explore, including the Viceroy's Arch, Adil Shah Palace Gateway, the Chapel of St Anthony, the Chapel of St Catherine, the Church & Convent of St Monica (open from 8am to 5pm), the Convent & Church of St John, the Sisters' Convent, the Church of Our Lady of the Rosary (open from 8am to 5pm), the Monastery of St Augustine and, 2km east of the centre, the Church of Our Lady of the Mount.

ⓘ Getting There & Away
There are frequent buses to Old Goa (₹10, 20 minutes) from the Kadamba bus stand in Panaji to Old Goa's **bus stand** (Old Goa Rd) by the main roundabout. Buses to Panaji or Ponda from Old Goa leave when full (around every 10 minutes) from either the main roundabout bus stand or the bus stop (Old Goa Rd)/ATM at the western end of Old Goa Rd.

From the waterfront near the Viceroy's Arch, a free ferry runs to Divar Island. There's a petrol station near the main roundabout.

NORTH GOA

North Goa is the Goa you might have heard all about: crowded beaches, upbeat nightlife,

Goan trance, cosmopolitan cuisine, hippie markets and yoga retreats. If you like a fast pace and plenty of things to do, this is the place.

Mapusa
POP 40,500
Mapusa (pronounced 'Mapsa') is the largest town in northern Goa, and is most often visited for its busy Friday **market** (⊙8am-6.30pm Mon-Sat), which attracts scores of buyers and sellers from neighbouring towns and villages. It's a good place to pick up the usual range of embroidered bed sheets and the like, at prices far lower than in the beach resorts. Many travellers pass through Mapusa anyway as it's the major transport hub for northern Goa buses. Most amenities are arranged around the Municipal Gardens, just north of the Kadamba bus station and main market site.

The once budget **Hotel Vilena** (☑0832-2263115; hotelvilena@gmail.com; Feira Baixa Rd; d ₹1700-2000; ※🐝🎓) has had a refurb and all rooms are now air-conditioned with bathroom, but it's still good value and the rooms are well kept. There's a restaurant and bar on the 1st floor and a rooftop restaurant called Goan & Grills.

There are food stalls and cafes around the market area. For good people watching and a cold beer, head upstairs to the **Pub** (Market Rd; ⊙10am-4.30pm & 6.30-11pm Mon-Sat), opposite the market.

ⓘ Getting There & Away
BUS
If you're coming to Goa by bus from Mumbai, Mapusa's **Kadamba bus stand** (☑0832-2232161; Calangute-Mapusa Rd) is the jumping-off point for the northern beaches. Local bus services run every few minutes; just look for the correct destination on the sign in the bus windshield. For buses to the southern beaches, take one of the frequent buses to Panaji, then Margao, and change there.

Long-distance services are run by both government and private bus companies. Private operators have booking offices outside the bus stand (opposite the Municipal Gardens). You can check fares and timings for government buses at www.goakadamba.com.

Most long-distance buses depart in the late afternoon or evening. Sample fares include: Bengaluru (₹900, with AC ₹1200; 13 to 14 hours, Hampi (sleeper ₹1000; 9½ hours), Mumbai (₹850, with AC ₹900; 12 to 15 hours) and Pune (₹700, with AC ₹900, 11 to 13 hours).

TAXI

There's a prepaid taxi stand in the town square with a signboard of fixed prices. Cabs to Anjuna or Calangute cost ₹300; Candolim ₹400; Panaji ₹350; Arambol ₹700; Margao ₹1100; Dabolim Airport ₹1150. An autorickshaw to Anjuna or Calangute should cost ₹200.

TRAIN

Thivim, about 12km northeast of town, is the nearest train station on the Konkan Railway. An autorickshaw to or from Thivim station costs around ₹250.

Candolim

POP 8600

Candolim's long and languid beach, which curves to join smaller Sinquerim Beach to the south, is largely the preserve of charter tourists from the UK, Russia and, more than ever, elsewhere in India. It's fringed with a line of beach shacks, all offering sunbeds and shade in exchange for your custom.

⊙ Sights & Activities

Fort Aguada   FORT

(⊙8.30am-5.30pm) **FREE** Standing on the headland overlooking the mouth of the Mandovi River, Fort Aguada occupies a magnificent and successful position, confirmed by the fact it was never taken by force. A highly popular spot to watch the sunset, with uninterrupted views both north and south, the fort was built in 1612, following the increasing threat to Goa's Portuguese overlords by the Dutch, among others.

John's Boat Tours   TOURS

(☑9822182814, 0832-6520190; www.johnboattours.com; Fort Aguada Rd; ⊙10am-9pm) A respected and well-organised Candolim-based operator offering a wide variety of boat and jeep excursions, as well as overnight houseboat cruises (₹6500 per person including meals). The standard half-day dolphin-watching cruise is ₹1200 (no dolphins, no pay) or join the renowned 'Crocodile Dundee' river trip (₹1400), to catch a glimpse of the Mandovi's mugger crocodile. Boat to Anjuna market is ₹1000.

Sinquerim Dolphin Trips   BOATING

(per person ₹300; ⊙8.30am-5.30pm) The boat operators on the Nerul River below Fort Aguada have banded together, so trips are fixed price. A one-hour dolphin-spotting and sightseeing trip costs ₹300 per person with a minimum of 10 passengers. Trips pass Nerul (Coco) Beach, Fort Aguada Jail and the fort.

🛏 Sleeping

Backpacker Panda   HOSTEL $

(☑9172313995; www.backpackerpanda.com; 1116, Anna Vaddo; dm from ₹500; 🕸🛜) Down a winding lane and very close to the beach, this is Candolim's best bet for backpackers. Clean four- to eight-bed air-con dorms (some mixed, one female-only) have attached bathrooms and there's an open-sided cafe with loungy seating. Bike hire is available. Follow sign to Sonesta Inns and take the lane to the north.

Shanu's Seaside Inn   GUESTHOUSE $

(☑9823016187; www.shanu.in; Escrivao Vaddo; d ₹1000, with AC ₹1500-3400; 🕸🛜) Shanu is one of several large guesthouses in this little grove just behind the dunes of Candolim Beach and it's a fine choice. The 18 rooms vary from basic but comfortable to deluxe rooms with sea views, air-con, king-sized beds and fridge. The owners also run the popular Pete's Shack on the beach.

★ Bougainvillea Guest House   GUESTHOUSE $$

(☑9822151969, 0832-2479842; www.bougainvilleagoa.com; Sinquerim; r incl breakfast ₹4200-5400, penthouse ₹7800; 🕸🛜) A lush, plant-filled garden leads the way to this gorgeous family-run guesthouse, located off Fort Aguada Rd. The eight light-filled suite rooms are spacious and spotless, with fridge, flat-screen TV and either balcony or private sit-out; the top-floor penthouse has its own rooftop terrace. This is the kind of place guests come back to year after year. Book ahead.

★ Marbella Guest House   BOUTIQUE HOTEL $$

(☑0832-2479551, 9822100811; www.marbellagoa.com; Sinquerim; r ₹4200-4900, ste ₹6100-7800; 🕸🛜) This beautiful Portuguese villa, filled with antiques and enveloped in a peaceful courtyard garden, is a romantic and sophisticated old-world remnant. Rooms are individually themed, including Moghul, Rajasthani and Bougainvillea. The penthouse suite is a dream of polished tiles, four-poster bed with separate living room, dining room and terrace. The kitchen serves up some imaginative dishes. No kids under 12.

D'Hibiscus   BOUTIQUE HOTEL $$

(☑0832-2479842; www.dehibiscus.com; 83 Sinquerim; d ₹4200, penthouse ₹6600; 🕸🛜) Huge modern rooms with balconies are the draw at this Portuguese home off Sinquerim Beach. The top-floor penthouse rooms, with spa bath, big-screen TV and balcony sunbeds, are worth a splurge.

GREEN GOA

Goa's environment has suffered from an onslaught of tourism over the last 40 years, but also from the effects of logging, mining and local customs (rare turtle eggs have traditionally been considered a delicacy). Construction proceeds regardless of what the local infrastructure or ecosystem can sustain.

The **Goa Foundation** (📱0832-2256479; www.goafoundation.org; St Britto's Apartments, G-8 Feira Alta), based in Mapusa, is the state's main environmental pressure group. It has spearheaded a number of conservation projects, including pressure to stop illegal mining, and its website is a great place to learn more about Goan environmental issues. For environmental reading material, check out Mapusa's **Other India Bookstore** (📱0832-2263305; www.otherindiabook store.com; Mapusa Clinic Rd; ⊘9am-5pm Mon-Fri, to 1pm Sat).

D'Mello's Sea View Home
HOTEL **$$**

(📱0832-2489395; www.dmellos.com; Monteiro's Rd, Escrivao Vaddo; d with/without AC ₹3500/2500, sea view ₹4750/4150; 🌐🕿) D'Mello's has grown up from small beginnings, but is still family-run and occupies four buildings around a lovely garden just back from the beach. The front building has the premium sea-view rooms so check out a few, but all are clean and well maintained with balconies, four-poster beds and shuttered windows. Wifi is available in the central area.

✕ Eating

Newton's
SUPERMARKET **$**

(Fort Aguada Rd; ⊘9.30am-1am) If you're desperately missing Edam cheese or Marmite, or just want to do some self-catering, Newton's is Goa's biggest supermarket. There's a good line in toiletries, wines, children's toys and luxury food items. The downside is that it's often packed and security guards won't allow bags inside.

Viva Goa!
GOAN **$**

(Fort Aguada Rd; mains ₹100-210; ⊘11am-midnight) This inexpensive, locals-oriented little place, also popular with in-the-know tourists, serves fresh fish and Goan seafood specialities such as a spicy mussel fry. Check the market price of seafood before ordering.

★ Café Chocolatti
CAFE **$$**

(409A Fort Aguada Rd; sweets ₹50-200, mains ₹250-450; ⊘9am-5pm Mon-Sat; 🕿) The lovely garden tearoom at Café Chocolatti may be on the main Fort Aguada Rd, but it's a peaceful retreat where chocolate brownies, waffles and banoffee pie with a strong cup of coffee or organic green tea taste like heaven. Also has a great range of salads, paninis, crepes and quiches for lunch. Take away a bag of chocolate truffles, homemade by the in-house chocolatier.

Stone House
STEAK **$$**

(Fort Aguada Rd; mains ₹200-800; ⊘11am-3pm & 7pm-midnight) Surf 'n' turf's the thing at this venerable old Candolim venue, inhabiting a stone house and its leafy front courtyard, with the improbable-sounding 'Swedish Lobster' topping the list, along with some Goan dishes. It's also a popular blues bar with live music most nights of the week in season.

Fisherman's Cove
SEAFOOD **$$**

(📱9822143376; Fort Aguada Rd; mains ₹160-350; ⊘9am-4.30pm & 6-11.30pm) The corner streetside Fisherman's Cove is always busy thanks to a strong reputation for its seafood and Indian dishes. The food is good but this popularity can mean slow service or a wait for a table. Regular live music and a good bar area.

★ Bomra's
BURMESE **$$$**

(📱9767591056; www.bomras.com; 247 Fort Aguada Rd; mains ₹520-650; ⊘noon-2pm & 7-11pm) Wonderfully unusual food is on offer at this sleek little place serving interesting modern Burmese cuisine with a fusion twist. Aromatic dishes include Bomra's mussel curry, chicken pho or Burmese rice and noodle salad. Decor is palm-thatch style huts in a lovely courtyard garden.

🍷 Drinking & Nightlife

Bob's Inn
BAR

(Fort Aguada Rd; ⊘noon-4pm & 7pm-midnight) The African wall hangings, palm-thatch, communal tables and terracotta sculptures are a nice backdrop to the *rava* (semolina) fried mussels, but this Candolim institution is really just a great place to drop in for a drink.

LPK Waterfront
CLUB

(couples ₹1700; ⊘9.30pm-4am) The initials stand for Love, Peace and Karma: the whimsical, sculpted waterfront LPK across the Nerul River from Candolim is the biggest club in the area, attracting mainly Indian party-goers from all over with huge indoor

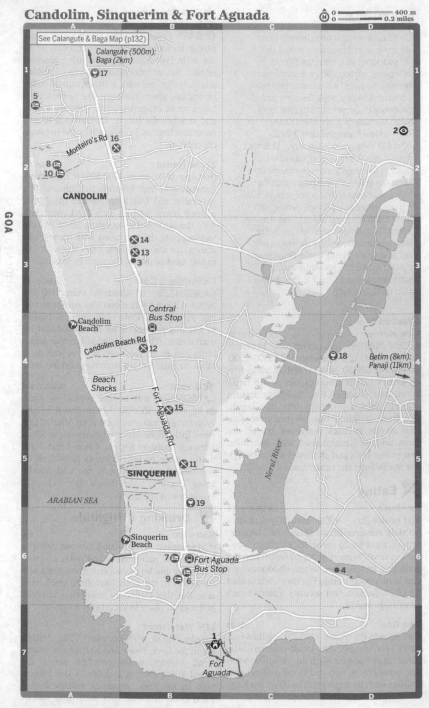

Candolim, Sinquerim & Fort Aguada

Candolim, Sinquerim & Fort Aguada

⊙ **Sights**
1 Fort Aguada B7
2 Museum of Goa D2

🔵 **Activities, Courses & Tours**
3 John's Boat Tours B3
4 Sinquerim Dolphin Trips D6

🛏 **Sleeping**
5 Backpacker Panda A1
6 Bougainvillea Guest House B6
7 D'Hibiscus B6
8 D'Mello's Sea View Home A2
9 Marbella Guest House B6

10 Shanu's Seaside Inn A2

🍴 **Eating**
11 Bomra's B5
12 Café Chocolatti B4
13 Fisherman's Cove B3
14 Newton's B3
15 Stone House B4
16 Viva Goa! A2

🍷 **Drinking & Nightlife**
17 Bob's Inn A1
18 LPK Waterfront D4
19 SinQ B5

and outdoor dance areas. Most popular on Thursday, Friday and Saturday nights, when cover prices vary and include drink coupons.

SinQ CLUB

(☑8308000080; www.sinq.co.in; Fort Aguada Rd; couples ₹1500, women ₹500; ☺10pm-3am) The SinQ entertainment scene, almost directly opposite Taj Holiday Village, is one for the cool people but it has expanded to include the Showbar gastropub as well as the beach lounge-bar with cabanas by the pool and a nightclub, so there's something for everyone. Events vary but Wednesday is usually ladies' night.

ℹ Getting There & Away

Buses run about every 10 minutes to and from Panaji (₹20, 35 minutes), and stop at the **central bus stop** (Fort Aguada Rd) near John's Boat Tours. Some continue south to the **Fort Aguada bus stop** (Fort Aguada Rd) at the bottom of Fort Aguada Rd, then head back to Panaji along the Mandovi River road, via the villages of Verem and Betim.

Frequent buses also run from Candolim to Calangute (₹10, 15 minutes) and can be flagged down on Fort Aguada Rd.

Calangute & Baga

POP 16,000

For many visitors, particularly cashed-up young Indian tourists from Bengaluru (Bangalore) and Mumbai plus Europeans on package holidays, this is Goa's party strip, where the raves and hippies have made way for modern thumping nightclubs and wall-to-wall drinking. The Calangute market area and the main Baga road can get very busy but everything you could ask for – from a Thai massage to a tattoo – is in close prox-

imity and the beach is lined with an excellent selection of increasingly sophisticated restaurant shacks with sunbeds, wi-fi and attentive service.

⊙ Sights & Activities

Yoga classes pop up around Calangute and Baga each season, though it's not as organised as it is in the resorts and retreats further north. Look out for up-to-date flyers and noticeboards for the latest.

You don't have to go far to find beach water sports along the Calangute–Baga strip.

Museum of Goa ARTS CENTRE

(☑7722089666; www.museumofgoa.com; 79, Pilerne Industrial Estate, Calangute; Indian/foreigner ₹100/300; ☺10am-6pm) Not so much a museum as a gallery for contemporary art, MOG features artworks, sculptures, exhibitions, workshops, courses, sitar concerts and an excellent cafe and shop. It's the brainchild of well-known local artist and sculptor Dr Subodh Kerkar, with the philosophy of making art accessible to all.

Benz Celebrity Wax Museum AMUSEMENT PARK

(Calangute-Anjuna Rd, Baga; ₹200) This quirky attraction features a wax museum with reasonably accurate figures of Hollywood and Bollywood celebrities, action heroes and sports stars. There's also a 9D cinema (₹200) and bumper cars (₹150). Good for kids or a rainy day.

Baga Snow Park SNOW SPORTS

(☑9595420781; www.snowparkgoa.com; Tito's Lane 2, Baga; ₹495; ☺11am-7pm; 🏂) This giant fridge is a mini wonderland of snowmen, igloos, slides and ice sculptures. You get kitted out with parka, pants and gloves (included) – it's novel being this cold in India! Good for kids.

GOA CALANGUTE & BAGA

Calangute & Baga

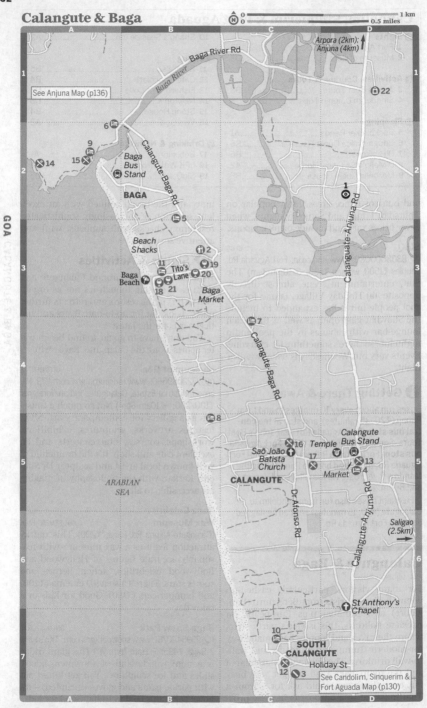

Calangute & Baga

⊙ Sights
1 Benz Celebrity Wax Museum D2

☺ Activities, Courses & Tours
2 Baga Snow Park B3
3 Goa Aquatics C7

⊜ Sleeping
4 Aerostel D5
5 Alidia Beach Cottages B2
6 Beach Box A2
7 Indian Kitchen C4
8 Johnny's Hotel B5
9 Melissa Guest House A2
10 Ospey's Shelter C7
11 Resort Fiesta B3

☒ Eating
12 A Reverie C7
13 Cafe Sussegado Souza D5
14 Cliff's Beach Restaurant A2
15 Go With the Flow A2
16 Infantaria C5
17 Plantain Leaf C5

☺ Drinking & Nightlife
18 Café Mambo B3
19 Cape Town Cafe B3
20 Keventers B3
21 Tito's B3

☺ Shopping
22 Saturday Night Market D1

Goa Aquatics　　　　　　　　　　DIVING
(☑ 9822685025; www.goaaquatics.com; 136/1 Gaura Vaddo, Calangute; dive trip/course from ₹5000/22,000) This professional dive resort offers a range of PADI courses and boat dives to Grande and Netrani Islands. An introductory dive for beginners is ₹5000 and a four-day PADI Open Water course is ₹22,000.

Barracuda Diving　　　　　　　　DIVING
(☑ 0832-2279409, 9822182402; www.barracuda diving.com; Sun Village Resort, Baga; dive trip/course from ₹5000/18,000) This long-standing school offers a range of PADI and SSI classes, dives and courses, including a 'Bubblemakers' introduction to scuba class of 1½ hours for children eight years and older (₹1500), Discover Scuba for ₹6500 and PADI Open Water for ₹22,000. For qualified divers a two-tank dive to Grande Island is ₹5000 (snorkellers ₹1500).

⊨ Sleeping

Calangute and Baga's sleeping options are broad and varied, though it's not a particularly budget-friendly destination, except in the off-season. Quite a few places here remain open year-round.

★ Indian Kitchen　　　　　GUESTHOUSE $
(☑ 0832-2277555, 9822149615; www.indiankitchen-goa.com; off Calangute-Baga Rd, Baga; s/d from ₹770/880, AC chalet/apt ₹2100/3500; ※ 🛜 🛏) Don't be fooled by the name – there's no longer a restaurant here but there is a great little budget guesthouse. Family-run Indian Kitchen has a range of rooms from basic to more spacious, comfy apartments and wooden chalets by the pool. There's a neat central courtyard and well-stocked library. Each room has its own terrace.

Johnny's Hotel　　　　　　　　HOTEL $
(☑ 0832-2277458; www.johnnyshotel.com; Khobra Vaddo, Calangute; s ₹800, d ₹1000-1500, with AC ₹1600-2000; ※ 🛜) The 12 simple rooms at this backpacker-popular place make for a sociable stay, with a downstairs restaurant-bar and regular yoga and reiki classes. A range of apartments and houses are available for longer stays. It's down a lane lined with unremarkable midrange hotels and is just a short walk to the beach.

Aerostel　　　　　　　　　　HOSTEL $
(☑ 9833345744; 2/201 Naikawaddo, Calangute; dm ₹500-750) This basic backpackers' hostel is a welcome budget addition to Calangute in a super-central location behind the main market (it's actually down a quiet lane opposite KFC). The six-/eight-/10-bed dorms are air-conditioned with en suite and there's a basic kitchen.

Ospey's Shelter　　　　　GUESTHOUSE $
(☑ 7798100981, 0832-2279505; ospeys.shelter@gmail.com; Calangute; d ₹1000) Tucked away between the beach and St Anthony's Chapel, in a quiet, lush little area full of palms and sandy paths, Ospey's is a traveller favourite and only a two-minute walk from the beach. Spotless upstairs rooms have fridges and balconies and the whole place has a cosy family feel. Take the road directly west of the chapel – but it's tough to find, so call ahead.

Melissa Guest House　　　GUESTHOUSE $
(☑ 9822180095; Baga River Rd, Baga; d ₹1000; 🛜) Across the Baga River, Melissa Guest House has just four neat little rooms, all with attached bathrooms and hot-water showers, in a tatty garden. Good value for the location.

★**Alidia Beach Cottages**   GUESTHOUSE **$$**
(✆9822876867, 0832-2279014; Calangute-Baga Rd, Saunta Waddo; d ₹2400, with AC from ₹3900; ❋🛜🏊) Set back behind a whitewashed chapel off busy Baga Rd, this convivial but quiet place has beautifully kept Mediterranean-style rooms orbiting a gorgeous pool. The cheaper non-AC rooms at the back are not as good, but all are in good condition, staff are eager to please, and there's a path leading directly to Baga Beach.

Beach Box   BOUTIQUE HOTEL **$$**
(✆9607473627; http://boxhotels.in; Baga River Rd, Baga; d ₹4200-5400; ❋🛜🏊) About time someone in Goa thought of recycling old shipping containers. The rooms here are pretty cosy but they're a bit of a novelty in fully equipped half or full-size shipping containers with en suite and air-con. The in-ground pool is also a shipping container and the restaurant-bar is made up of various recycled materials.

Resort Fiesta   BOUTIQUE HOTEL **$$$**
(✆9822104512; www.fiestagoa.com; Tito's Lane, Baga; d & ste incl breakfast ₹8000-10,200; ❋🛜🏊) Large, light-filled rooms are the signature at this beautifully designed boutique resort behind the beachfront restaurant of the same name. The labour of love by owner Yellow Mehta is stylishly appointed with a lovely garden and pool, large verandas and modern touches like TV, minibar and dual wash basins.

🍴 Eating

The beach shacks are an obvious go-to, but there are some interesting gems along the 'Strip' and a few excellent upmarket offerings on the north side of the Baga River.

Plantain Leaf   INDIAN **$**
(✆0832-2279860; Calangute Beach Rd, Calangute; veg thali ₹150, mains ₹130-270; ⊙11am-5pm & 7-11.45pm) In the heart of Calangute's busy market area, 1st-floor Plantain Leaf has consistently been the area's best pure veg restaurant for many years, with classic South Indian banana leaf thalis and dosas, along with more North Indian flavours. Most dishes sneak into the budget category.

Infantaria   ITALIAN **$$**
(Calangute-Baga Rd, Calangute; pastries ₹80-200, mains ₹200-780; ⊙7.30am-midnight; 🛜) Once Calangute's best bakery, Infantaria is still a popular Italian-Indian, fondue-meets-curry restaurant. The bakery roots are still there, though, with homemade cakes, croissants,

little flaky pastries and real coffee. Get in early for breakfast before the good stuff runs out. Regular live music in season and it's a popular bar in the evening.

Cliff's Beach Restaurant   INDIAN **$$**
(Baga; mains ₹180-400; ⊙9am-11pm; 🛜) The best way to get away from the Baga beach crowd is to walk around the cliff edge north of the Baga River to secluded Cliff's. The menu is typical beach shack but it's just a great location for a cold beer and a swim in the calm waters off the beach. After dark, staff will help walk you back around the cliff.

Cafe Sussegado Souza   GOAN **$$**
(✆09850141007; Calangute-Anjuna Rd, Calangute; mains ₹230-480; ⊙noon-11pm) In a little yellow Portuguese house just south of the Calangute market area, Cafe Sussegado is the place to come for Goan food such as fish curry rice, chicken *xacuti* and pork *sorpotel* (a vinegary stew made from liver, heart and kidneys), with a shot of feni to follow. Authentic, busy and good atmosphere.

★**Go With the Flow**   INTERNATIONAL **$$$**
(✆7507771556; www.gowiththeflowgoa.com; 614 Baga River Rd, Baga; small plates ₹180-420, mains ₹430-840; ⊙noon-10.30pm; 🛜) Stepping into the fantasy neon-lit garden of white-wicker furniture is impressive and the food is consistently good. With a global menu leaning towards European, African and Asian flavours, this remains one of Baga's best dining experiences. Try some of the small bites (ask about a tasting plate) or go straight for the signature pork belly or African inspired spicy prawn rice.

★**A Reverie**   INTERNATIONAL **$$$**
(✆8380095732; www.areverie.com; Holiday St, Calangute; mains ₹450-800; ⊙7pm-late; 🛜) A gorgeous lounge bar, all armchairs, cool jazz and whimsical outdoor space, this is the place to spoil yourself, with the likes of Spanish tapas, truffle bombs, grilled asparagus, French wines and Italian cheeses. A Reverie likes to style itself as 'fun dining' and doesn't take itself too seriously. Though it takes its cocktails seriously.

🍸 Drinking & Nightlife

★**Keventers**   MILKSHAKES
(Tito's Lane, Baga; milkshakes ₹80-230; ⊙11am-3am) Had enough of the Kingfisher? Keventers, the famous Delhi milkshake maker, has set up in Goa and on Tito's Lane no

SATURDAY NIGHT MARKETS

There are two well-established evening markets, **Saturday Night Market** (Calangute-Anjuna Rd; ⊙ from 6pm Sat late Nov-Mar) in Arpora and **Mackie's** (Baga River Rd; ⊙ from 6pm Sat Dec-Apr) in Baga, that make an interesting evening alternative to the Anjuna flea market.

The attractions here are as much about food stalls and entertainment as shopping, but there's a big range of so-so stalls, flashing jewellery, spices, clothing and textiles.

less. The hole-in-wall joint serves up classic milkshakes in its signature glass bottles, or sample the more exotic Oreo, bubblegum or salted caramel. It's the perfect antidote to a big night out.

Café Mambo   CLUB
(☑ 7507333003; Tito's Lane, Baga; cover charge couples ₹1000; ⊙ 6pm-3am) Part of the Tito's empire, Mambo is one of Baga's busiest clubs with an indoor/outdoor beachfront location and nightly DJs pumping out house, hip hop and Latino tunes. Couples or women only; Friday is the popular Bollywood night.

Tito's   CLUB
(☑ 9822765002; www.titos.in; Tito's Lane, Baga; cover charge varies; ⊙ 8pm-3am) The long-running titan of Goa's clubbing scene, Tito's has done its best to clean up its act and organises regular event nights that take on a distinctly Indian club scene. Saturday is Bollywood night. It's generally couples or ladies only – solo men (stags) get in on certain nights at an inflated cover charge, depending on the mood of door staff.

Cape Town Cafe   BAR
(www.capetowncafe.com; Tito's Lane, Baga; ⊙ 6pm-1am; 🛜) The most laid-back of the Tito's venues, Cape Town has a street-front lounge bar with wi-fi and live sports on big screens, while inside international DJs play until late. Goan food, bar snacks and hookah pipes available.

ⓘ Getting There & Away

Frequent buses go to Panaji (₹20, 45 minutes) and Mapusa (₹15, 30 minutes) from both the **Calangute** (Calangute Beach Rd) and Baga bus stands.

Kadamba runs a shuttle bus between Calangute bus stand and the airport four times a day (₹150, 1½ hours).

A taxi from Calangute or Baga to Panaji costs around ₹600 and takes about half an hour. A prepaid taxi from the airport to Calangute costs ₹1200.

ⓘ Getting Around

Motorcycle and scooter hire is easy to arrange in Calangute and Baga (ask at your accommodation). Prices are fairly steady at around ₹300 for a gearless Honda Kinetic and ₹350 to ₹400 for an Enfield, but high demand means you might have to pay much more in peak season. Definitely try bargaining in quieter times or for rentals of more than a week.

A local bus runs between the Calangute and Baga stands every few minutes (₹5); catch it anywhere along the way, though when traffic is bad it might be quicker to walk.

Taxis between Calangute and northern Baga beach charge an extortionate ₹100.

Anjuna

POP 9640

Anjuna has been a stalwart of the hippie scene since the 1960s and still drags out the sarongs and sandalwood each Wednesday (in season) for its famous flea market. Though it continues to pull in droves of backpackers, midrange and domestic tourists are increasingly making their way here for a dose of hippie-chic. Anjuna is continuing to evolve, with a heady beach party scene and a constant flowering of new restaurants, bars and backpacker hostels. If anything, Anjuna is having a renaissance.

The village itself is a bit ragged around the edges and is spread out over a wide area, but that's part of the charm. Do as most do: hire a scooter or motorbike and explore the back lanes and southern beach area and you'll find a place that suits. Anjuna will grow on you.

⊙ Sights & Activities

Anjuna's charismatic, narrow beach runs for almost 2km from the rocky, low-slung cliffs at the northern village area right down beyond the flea market in the south. In season there are water sports here, including jet skis, banana boats and parasailing.

Lots of yoga (p92), ayurveda and other alternative therapies and regimes are on offer in season; look out for noticeboards at popular cafes such as Artjuna Cafe (p138).

Brahmani Yoga   YOGA
(☑ 9545620578; www.brahmaniyoga.com; Tito's White House, Aguada-Siolim Rd; class ₹700, 10-class

Anjuna

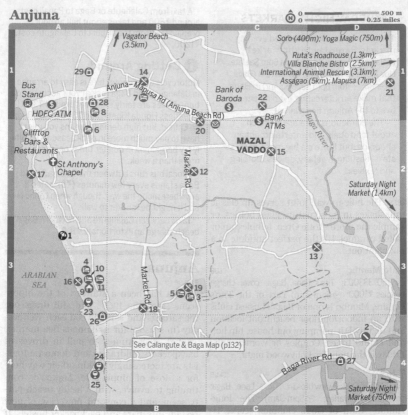

Anjuna

◎ Sights
1 Anjuna Beach...A3

◆ Activities, Courses & Tours
2 Barracuda Diving.....................................D4
Brahmani Yoga.................................(see 21)
Goa Muay Thai................................(see 21)

⛱ Sleeping
3 Banyan Soul...B3
4 Florinda's..A3
5 Headquarters..B3
6 Lazy Lama...A2
7 Paradise...B1
8 Red Door Hostel......................................A1
9 Sea Horse...A3
10 The Village..A3
11 Wonderland Hostel.................................A3

✖ Eating
12 Artjuna Cafe..B2

13 Baba Au Rhum...D3
14 Burger Factory...B1
15 Choco Cream Gelati...............................C2
16 Elephant Art Cafe....................................A3
17 Eva Cafe..A2
18 FlourPower Bakeria.................................B3
19 German Bakery..B3
20 Goa's Ark..B2
21 Lila Café..D1
22 Oltremarino...C1

◉ Drinking & Nightlife
23 Cafe Lilliput..A3
24 Curlies...A4
25 Shiva Valley..A4

⛒ Shopping
26 Anjuna Flea Market.................................A4
27 Mackie's Saturday Nite Bazaar.............D4
28 Manali Guest House................................A1
29 Oxford Arcade...A1

pass ₹5000; ☺classes 9.30am) This friendly drop-in centre offers daily classes from late November to April in ashtanga, vinyasa, hatha and dynamic yoga, as well as pranayama meditation. No need to book: just turn up 15 minutes before the beginning of class.

Goa Muay Thai   MARTIAL ARTS
(☑9767479486; www.goamuaythai.com; Tito's White House, Aguada-Siolim Rd; class ₹500, weekly pass ₹2000; ☺9-10.30am & 5-6.45pm Mon-Fri) These morning and afternoon classes are designed with fitness and technique in mind rather than full-on sparring, so are good for beginners. The boxing ring and gym at Tito's White House sets up in November.

🛌 Sleeping

Wonderland Hostel   HOSTEL $
(☑8692993770; www.wonderlandhostel.com; 69/6, Govekar Vaddo; dm ₹500-600, d ₹2000-2500, without bathroom ₹1200-1500; ✳🕓) Superchilled Wonderland, off the path behind Anjuna Beach near Lilliput, has a lineup of cabins comprising en-suite dorms and a few private rooms (some with AC), as well as a couple of old-school basic bamboo tree houses and space for tents. Owner Sandeep welcomes travellers into his loungy chill-out area with a small kitchen and cafe. Free yoga classes daily at 9am.

Red Door Hostel   HOSTEL $
(☑0832-2274423; reddoorhostels@gmail.com; dm with/without AC from ₹500/400, d with/without AC ₹2200/1900; ✳🕓) Red Door is a welcoming backpacker place close to Anjuna's central crossroads with clean four- and six-bed dorms plus a few private rooms. Facilities include lockers, free wi-fi, a garden, good communal areas – including a well-equipped kitchen – and a sociable cafe-bar.

Florinda's   GUESTHOUSE $
(☑9890216520; s/d ₹800/1000, with AC ₹1500; ✳🕓) One of the better budget places near the beach and a bit hidden next to Janet & John's, Florinda's has clean rooms, with 24-hour hot water, window screens and mosquito nets, set around a pretty garden. The few air-con rooms fill up fast.

Headquarters   HOSTEL $
(☑0832-2274510; dm with/without AC ₹500/400; ✳🕓) Near the German Bakery, Headquarters ticks all the budget boxes for cleanliness and comfort with upstairs dorms, kitchen and common areas downstairs and a garden with some potential out back.

Lazy Lama   HOSTEL $
(☑9717000955; lazylamagoa@gmail.com; dm ₹300-500) A laid-back hostel down a quiet lane in Anjuna village, Lazy Lama offers six- and 10-bed dorms in a partly converted Portuguese house. Attracts a chilled crowd.

Paradise   GUESTHOUSE $
(☑9922541714; janet_965@hotmail.com; Anjuna-Mapusa Rd; d ₹1000-1200, with AC ₹1500-2000; ✳@🕓) This friendly place is fronted by an old Portuguese home and offers neat, clean rooms with well-decorated options in the newer annex. The better rooms have TVs, fridges and hammocks on the balcony. Friendly owner Janet and family also run the pharmacy, general store, restaurant, internet cafe, Connexions travel agency and money exchange!

Banyan Soul   BOUTIQUE HOTEL $$
(☑9820707283; www.thebanyansoul.com; d ₹3000; ✳🕓) A slinky 12-room option, tucked down the lane off Market Rd, and lovingly conceived and run by Sumit, a young Mumbai escapee. Rooms are chic and well equipped with AC and TV, and there's a lovely library and shady seating area beneath a banyan tree.

Sea Horse   HUT $$
(☑9764465078; www.vistapraiaanjuna.com; ☺hut with/without AC ₹3500/2000; ✳🕓) A lineup of timber cabins behind the beach restaurant of the same name, Sea Horse offers a good location and decent value. The huts are small and get a little hot – ask for the air-con remote control if it's uncomfortably humid. Staff are friendly and accommodating. The same owners have a pricier beachfront setup nearby called Vista Praia Anjuna.

The Village   COTTAGE $$
(☑9988882021; d ₹3800-4500) The solid timber and rendered concrete cottages here are some of the best-designed on the beachfront. Set in a pleasant garden they feature large beds and bathrooms, and air-con to justify the price. It's behind Elephant Art Cafe (p138).

🍴 Eating

★**Choco Cream Gelati**   ICE CREAM $
(Mazal Vaddo; ice cream & gelato ₹120-180; ☺9am-midnight) This may well be the best Italian-style gelato and ice cream in Goa and regulars know it. Scoops in a cup or waffle cone, shakes, juices and espresso coffee are all available and there's a regular parade of flavours from lemon cheesecake to salted

ANJUNA FLEA MARKET

Anjuna's weekly Wednesday **flea market** (⊙8am-sunset Wed Nov-Apr) is as much part of the Goan experience as a day on the beach. More than three decades ago, it was conceived and created by hippies smoking jumbo joints, convening to compare experiences on the heady Indian circuit and selling pairs of Levi jeans or handmade jewellery to help fund the rest of their stay. These days it's almost entirely made up of traders from Kashmir, Gujurat, Karnataka and elsewhere selling a fairly standard line of spices, T-shirts, bejewelled bedspreads, saris and bags. It's still good fun, with live music in the afternoon and plenty of colour. The best time to visit is early (from 8am) or late afternoon (around 4pm till close just after sunset). The first market of the season is around mid-November, continuing until the end of April.

caramel and tiramisu. There's al fresco eating out front.

FlourPower Bakeria　　　　BAKERY $
(✎9867276541; Market Rd; bread & baked goods from ₹80; ⊙11am-8pm Wed, 7-11pm Fri-Sun) This artisanal bakery produces fresh sourdough bread loaves with loads of love, along with croissants, cakes, cookies and fabulous pizzas.

★ **Artjuna Cafe**　　　　CAFE $$
(✎0832-2274794; www.artjuna.com; Market Rd; mains ₹130-480; ⊙7.30am-10.30pm; 🛜) Artjuna is right up there with our favourite cafes in Anjuna. Along with all-day breakfast, outstanding espresso coffee, salads, smoothies, sandwiches and Middle Eastern surprises like baba ganoush, tahini and falafel, this sweet garden cafe has an excellent craft and lifestyle shop, yoga classes, movie nights and a useful noticeboard. Great meeting place.

German Bakery　　　　MULTICUISINE $$
(www.german-bakery.in; breakfast ₹60-240, mains ₹190-570; ⊙8.30am-11pm; 🛜✎) Leafy and adorned with lanterns, cushioned seating, occasional live music and garden lights, German Bakery is a long-standing favourite for hearty and healthy breakfasts, fresh-baked bread, organic food and tofu balls, but the menu also runs to Indian dishes, pasta, burgers and seafood. Has healthy juices (for

example wheatgrass and kombuchas) and espresso coffee.

Elephant Art Cafe　　　　CAFE $$
(✎9970668845; mains ₹250-450; ⊙8am-10pm; 🛜) A standout among the many restaurants lining Anjuna's beach, Elephant Art Cafe does a thoughtful range of tapas, sandwiches, fish and chips and pasta. Breakfasts are a highlight, with fruit bruschetta or shakshuka potato pesto eggs among the offerings.

Goa's Ark　　　　MIDDLE EASTERN $$
(✎9145050494; www.goas-ark.com; Anjuna Beach Rd; mains ₹150-670, meze from ₹50; ⊙10am-11pm; 🛜) Set in a pleasant garden, Goa's Ark breaks the mould of most same-same restaurants, specialising in Middle Eastern and Mediterranean cuisine with meze, barbecued meat and falafel. Chargrilled steaks and fish and chips contribute to a meat-heavy menu but vegetarians are not overlooked with baba ganoush, veg burgers and lentil salads.

Eva Cafe　　　　CAFE $$
(✎7350055717; Cliff Walk; mains ₹210-350; ⊙9am-8pm; 🛜) Oceanfront Eva Cafe is a small but cosy place for healthy sandwiches, salads and sublime breakfasts featuring fresh-baked bread and good coffee. The evening menu includes nachos and a cheese platter with wine. Great sunset spot.

Lila Café　　　　CAFE $$
(www.lilacafegoa.com; Tito's White House, Aguada-Siolim Rd; mains ₹100-290; ⊙8.30am-6pm) This German cafe has been a traveller favourite for many years, first in Baga and now at Tito's White House. It serves great home-baked breads, croissants, rösti and perfect frothy cappuccinos, and specialises in buffalo cheese and smoked ham.

★ **Baba Au Rhum**　　　　FRENCH $$$
(✎9657210468; Anjuna-Baga Rd; baguettes ₹210-300, mains ₹480-550) It's tucked away on the back road between Anjuna and Baga but Baba Au Rhum's reputation (it was previously in Arpora) means it's always busy. Part bakery, part French cafe, this is the place for filled baguettes, croissants, crostini or quiche, as well as creamy pastas or a filet mignon. Craft beer on tap and a relaxed, open garden–restaurant vibe.

Burger Factory　　　　BURGERS $$$
(Anjuna-Mapusa Rd; burgers ₹300-500; ⊙11.30am-3.30pm & 6.30-10.30pm Thu-Tue) There's no mistaking what's on offer at this little open-sided diner. The straightforward menu of burgers

isn't cheap, but the buns are big and they are interesting and well crafted. Choose between beef or chicken burgers and toppings such as blue cheese, bacon and avocado.

Oltremarino
ITALIAN $$$
(☑8412967105; Anjuna Beach Rd; mains ₹450-800; ☺1pm-midnight; ☏) It's high-end Italian dining but the homemade pasta and speciality wood-fired pizzas are worth the splurge at this sweet garden restaurant in the grounds of a fine Portuguese mansion. Helpful staff will walk you through the lengthy menu and will insist you finish your meal with a complimentary shot of homemade Baileys.

🍷 Drinking & Nightlife

Curlies
BAR
(www.curliesgoa.com; ☺9am-3am) Holding sway at South Anjuna Beach, Curlies mixes laid-back beach-bar vibe with sophisticated nightspot – the party nights here are notorious, legendary and loud. There's a rooftop lounge bar and an enclosed late-night dance club. Thursday and Saturday are big nights, as are full-moon nights.

Cafe Lilliput
CLUB
(☑0832-2274648; www.cafelilliput.com; ☺8am-1am, to 4am on party nights; ☏) Hovering over the beach near the flea-market site, Lilliput has built itself a reputation as one of the go-to nightspots, but it also has a good all-day restaurant and some interesting accommodation at the back.

Shiva Valley
CLUB
(☑9689628008; ☺8am-3am) At the very southern end of Anjuna Beach, past Curlies,

---

ℹ DRUGS & THEFT

Despite regular crackdowns and party restrictions, Anjuna and Vagator are still well-known places for procuring illicit substances, though they're not quite so freely available as in Goa's trance-party heyday. Participate at your peril – the police Anti-Narcotics Cell has been known to carry out checks on foreigners and Goa's central jail is not a place you want to spend a 10-year drug-related stretch. Even bribes might not get you out of trouble.

Take great care of your wallet, camera and the like on market day, when pickpocketing can be a problem.

Shiva Valley has grown from small beach shack to fully fledged trance club, with Tuesday the main party all-nighter.

🛍 Shopping

Oxford Arcade
SHOPPING CENTRE
(Anjuna-Vagator Rd; ☺9am-9pm) Oxford Arcade, 100m from the Starco crossroads on the road to Vagator, is a fully fledged two-storey supermarket, complete with trolleys and checkout scanners. It's an awesome place to stock up on toiletries, cheap booze and all those little international luxuries.

Manali Guest House
BOOKS
(☺9.30am-8.30pm) Long-running bookshop and travel agency.

ℹ Getting There & Away

Buses to Mapusa (₹15, 30 minutes) depart every half-hour or so from the main bus stand at the end of the Anjuna–Mapusa Rd near the beach; some buses coming from Mapusa continue on to Vagator and Chapora.

A couple of direct daily buses head south to Calangute; otherwise, take a bus to Mapusa and change there.

Plenty of motorcycle taxis and autorickshaws gather at the main crossroads and you can also easily hire scooters and motorcycles here from ₹250 to ₹400 – most Anjuna-based travellers get around on two wheels.

Assagao

Snuggled in the countryside between Mapusa and Anjuna or Vagator, Assagao is one of North Goa's prettiest villages, with almost traffic-free country lanes passing old Portuguese mansions and whitewashed churches. The area is inspiringly peaceful enough to be home to some of North Goa's best yoga retreats and a growing number of excellent restaurants.

Local organisation **El Shaddai** (☑0832-2461068, 0832-6513286; www.childrescue.net; El Shaddai House, Socol Vaddo), a child protection charity, has several schools based here.

🏃 Activities

Spicy Mama's
COOKING
(☑9623348958; www.spicymamasgoa.com; 517, Bouta Vaddo; 1-day course veg/nonveg ₹2000/3000, 3-day ₹5000/7000, 5-day ₹10,000/12,000) For cooking enthusiasts, Spicy Mama's specialises in spicy North Indian cuisine, from butter chicken to *aloo gobi* (cauliflower and potato

curry) and *palak paneer* (cheese in a puréed spinach gravy), prepared at the country home of Suchi. The standard one-day course is four hours; book online for in-depth multi-day masterclasses and for directions.

International
Animal Rescue   VOLUNTEERING
(AnimalTracks; ☑ 0832-2268272; www.international animalrescuegoa.org.in; Madungo Vaddo; ☺ 9am-4pm) The well-established International Animal Rescue collects and cares for stray dogs, cats and other four-legged animals in distress, carrying out sterilisations and vaccinations. Volunteers are welcome to help with dog walking and playing with puppies and kittens, but must have evidence of rabies vaccination.

🛏 Sleeping & Eating

Namaste Jungle Garden   GUESTHOUSE $$
(☑ 9850466105; 138/3 Bairo Alto; cottage & apt incl breakfast ₹3500; ❊ 🐾) There's a real feeling of communing with nature in these slick and spacious timber cottages set back in a jungly Assagao garden. It also has two apartment-style rooms with kitchen in the main building and massage and yoga available.

Gunpowder   MULTICUISINE $$
(mains ₹200-475; ☺ 8-10.30am, noon-3.30pm & 7-10.30pm Tue-Sun; 🐾) This garden restaurant behind the People Tree boutique exemplifies the Assagao trend in quality countryside dining, efficient service and wholesome, fresh food. Classic curries and stir-fries, both veg and nonveg, are the stars of the menu, along with tempting desserts (walnut, rum and raisin brownie) and cocktails.

Ruta's Roadhouse   INTERNATIONAL $$
(☑ 8380025757; www.rutas.in; Mapusa Rd; breakfast ₹300, small/big plates ₹200/300; ☺ 8.30am-6.30pm Mon-Sat) Ruta's has made a home in an old Portuguese house in Assagao, serving up excellent set breakfasts and global culinary offerings from jambalaya to spicy laksa.

★ Villa Blanche Bistro   CAFE $$$
(www.villablanche-goa.com; 283 Badem Church Rd; breakfast ₹100-380, mains ₹350-480; ☺ 9am-11pm Thu-Tue Nov-May; 🐾✍) This lovely, German-run chilled garden cafe draws diners to the back lanes of Assagao. Salads, sandwiches, filled bagels and cakes are specialities, but you'll also find Thai curry and German sausages, as well as lots of vegetarian and vegan options. For an indulgent breakfast or

brunch try the waffles and pancakes. Sunday brunch (from 10am) is legendary.

🍷 Drinking & Nightlife

Soro   PUB
(☑ 9881934440; Siolim Rd, Badem junction; ☺ 6pm-2am) The 'village pub' is a welcome addition to the back lanes of sleepy Assagao, with pumping live music on weekends, salsa dancing on Sunday and a fun atmosphere whenever there's a crowd. Decor is part English pub, part American bar, with exposed brick walls, barrel tables and a pool table. There's bar food but this is more for drinking and dancing.

ℹ Getting There & Away

Local buses between Mapusa and Anjuna (about 15 minutes from each) or Siolim pass through Assagao, but the village is best explored on a rented scooter or by taxi from your beach resort.

Vagator & Chapora

Dramatic red stone cliffs, thick palm groves and a crumbling 17th-century Portuguese fort give Vagator and its diminutive village neighbour Chapora one of the prettiest settings on the North Goan coast. Once known for their wild trance parties and heady, hippie lifestyles, things have slowed down considerably these days and upmarket restaurants are more the style, though Vagator has some of Goa's best clubs. Chapora – reminiscent of the Mos Eisley Cantina from *Star Wars* – remains a favourite for hippies and long-staying smokers, with the smell of charas (resin of the marijuana plant) clinging heavily to the light sea breeze.

◎ Sights & Activities

Chapora is a working fishing harbour nestled at the broad mouth of the Chapora River – the main sight here is the hilltop fort. Vagator has three small, charismatic beach coves below some dramatic cliffs.

Chapora Fort   FORT
FREE Chapora's old laterite fort, standing guard over the mouth of the Chapora River, was built by the Portuguese in 1617, to protect Bardez taluk (district), in Portuguese hands from 1543 onwards. Today it is a crumble of picturesque ruins with only the outer walls remaining, though you can still pick out the mouths of two escape tunnels. The main reason to make the climb up the hill is for the

INLAND YOGA RETREATS

The Anjuna/Vagator/Assagao area has a number of yoga retreats where you can immerse yourself in courses, classes and a Zen vibe during the October to March season.

Purple Valley Yoga Retreat (☑0832-2268363; www.yogagoa.com; 142 Bairo Alto; dm/s 1 week £770/850, 2 weeks £1150/1400) Popular yoga resort in Assagao.

Swan Yoga Retreat (☑8007360677, 0832-2268024; www.swan-yoga-goa.com; drop-in classes ₹500, 1 week s/d from ₹42,000/52,000) In a peaceful jungle corner of Assagao, Swan Retreat is a very Zen yoga experience.

Yoga Magic (☑0832-6523796; www.yogamagic.net; Mapusa-Chapora Rd; share/single ₹7700/11,600; 🖥🖨) 🍃 Solar lighting, vegetable farming and compost toilets are just some of the worthy initiatives practised in this luxurious yoga resort in Anjuna.

---

sensational views along the coast from atop the fort walls.

Mukti Kitchen
COOKING

(☑8007359170; www.muktikitchen.com; off Vagator Beach Rd, Vagator; veg/nonveg/Goan class ₹2000/2500/3000; ⏱11am-2pm & 6-9pm) Mukti shares her cooking skills twice daily at these recommended classes. Courses include around five dishes that can be tailored – veg or nonveg, Goan, Indian or ayurvedic. Minimum four people, maximum six; book one day ahead. You'll find Mukti's opposite Leoney Resort in Vagator.

🛏 Sleeping

Budget accommodation, much of it in private rooms, ranges along Ozran Beach Rd and Vagator Beach Rd; you'll see lots of signs for 'rooms to let'. Head down the road to the harbour at Chapora and you'll find lots of rooms – and whole homes – for rent, mainly for long-term stays from around ₹15,000 per month. Vagator also has a range of backpacker hostels and more upmarket accommodation.

★Dreams Hostel
HOSTEL $

(☑9920651760; www.dreams-hostel.goa-india-hotels-resorts.com; off Vagator Beach Rd, Vagator; dm ₹400-550, AC cabins ₹2400; 🖥🖨) With a philosophy of 'art, music, wellness', former backpacker and local DJ Ravi has established a great little creative space for like-minded travellers with a spacious garden, clean dorms, deluxe timber cabins and chilled common areas. The hostel also acts as an artistic residency – the murals and artworks are all done by guests.

★Jungle Hostel
HOSTEL $

(☑0832-2273006; www.thehostelcrowd.com; Vagator Beach Rd, Vagator; dm with/without AC ₹650/550, s/d from ₹1100/1800; 🖨🖥) One of the original backpacker hostels in North Goa, Jungle brought the dorm experience and an international vibe to Vagator and has expanded to three properties. It's still among the best around and offers cheap transfers to its other properties in Panaji and Palolem. There are clean and bright four- to six-bed dorms and private rooms. Lockers, wi-fi, breakfast and communal kitchen.

Pappi Chulo
HOSTEL $

(☑9075135343; pappichulohostel@gmail.com; Ozran Beach Rd, Vagator; dm with/without AC ₹550/450, d ₹2000) Unashamedly Vagator's party hostel, Pappi's has a bar in the garden, movie nights and an international vibe of travellers just hanging out. Themed dorms have lockers and bunk beds.

Baba Guesthouse & Villa
GUESTHOUSE $

(☑9822161142; babavilla11@yahoo.in; Main St, Chapora; d with/without AC ₹1000/700; 🖨) With its laid-back Chapora location, Baba is often full with long-stayers but you might be lucky as a walk-in. The 14 rooms are clean and simple but serviceable.

Casa de Olga
GUESTHOUSE $

(☑9822157145, 0832-2274355; eadsouza@yahoo.co.in; Harbour Rd, Chapora; r ₹800-1350, without bathroom from ₹500) This welcoming family-run homestay, set around a nice garden on the way to Chapora harbour, offers spotless rooms of varying sizes in a three-storey building. The best are the top-floor rooms with swanky bathrooms, TV and balcony.

Shalom
GUESTHOUSE $

(☑919881578459, 0832-2273166; www.shalomguesthousegoa.com; Ozran Beach Rd, Vagator; d ₹900-1500, with AC ₹2000; 🖨🖥) Arranged around a placid garden not far from the

Vagator & Chapora

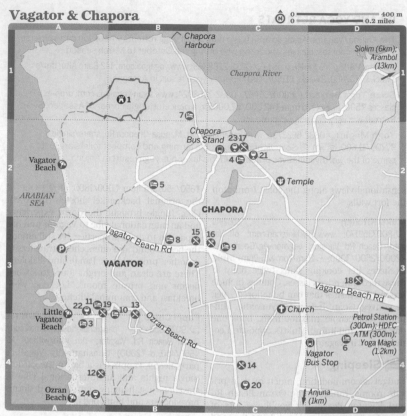

Vagator & Chapora

◎ Sights
1 Chapora Fort...B1

⊕ Activities, Courses & Tours
2 Mukti Kitchen...B3

🛏 Sleeping
3 Alcove Resort..A4
4 Baba Guesthouse & Villa.......................C2
5 Baba Place...B2
6 Bean Me Up Guest House.....................D4
7 Casa de Olga...B1
8 Dreams Hostel...B3
9 Jungle Hostel...C3
10 Pappi Chulo..B3
11 Shalom...A3

⊗ Eating
12 Antares..A4
Bean Me Up......................................(see 6)
13 Bluebird...B3
14 Food Chord...C4
15 Jaws..B3
16 Mango Tree Bar & Cafe.......................C3
17 Midnight Toker......................................C2
18 Piccolo Roma...D3
19 Yangkhor Moonlight............................A3

⊙ Drinking & Nightlife
20 Hilltop...C4
21 Jai Ganesh Fruit Juice
Centre..C2
22 Nine Bar..A3
23 Paulo's Antique Bar.............................C2
24 Waters Beach Lounge..........................A4

path down to Little Vagator Beach, this established place is run by a friendly family and offers a variety of extremely well-kept rooms and a two-bedroom apartment for long-stayers.

Bean Me Up Guest House   GUESTHOUSE $$
(☑ 7769095356; www.beanmeup.in; 1639/2 Deulvaddo, Vagator; d incl breakfast ₹1500-2500; ❊ 🛜) Set around a leafy, shaded courtyard that's home to Vagator's best vegan restaurant Bean Me Up, rooms here look simple but are themed with individual exotic decor, earthy shades, mosquito nets and shared verandahs. The mellow yoga-friendly vibe matches the clientele and the included breakfast is decadent. Morning yoga classes.

Baba Place   GUESTHOUSE $$
(☑ 9822156511; babaplace11@yahoo.com; Chapora Fort Rd, Chapora; d ₹2500; ❊ 🛜 ⛱) Baba Place, in the shadow of Chapora Fort, continues to improve with immaculate, decent-sized rooms with verandah, a small pool and a bar-restaurant.

Alcove Resort   HOTEL $$
(☑ 0832-2274491; www.alcovegoa.com; Little Vagator Beach; d ₹5400-8500; ❊ 🛜 ⛱) The location overlooking Little Vagator Beach is hard to beat at this price. Attractively furnished rooms, slightly larger cottages, and four suites surrounding a decent central pool, restaurant and bar, make this a good place for those who want a touch of affordable luxury near the beach. Add ₹500 for air-con.

✖ Eating

Jaws   INDIAN $
(Vagator Beach Rd, Vagator; mains ₹50-300; ⊙9am-9.30pm) With a bakery counter and inexpensive dosas and South Indian thalis, unassuming Jaws is an old-timer but one of the best-value eateries in Vagator. Good for a lazy breakfast or afternoon beer.

★ Bean Me Up   VEGAN $$
(www.beanmeup.in; 1639/2 Deulvaddo, Vagator; mains ₹200-400; ⊙8am-11pm; 🛜) Bean Me Up is vegan, but even nonveg travellers will be blown away by the taste, variety and filling plates on offer in this relaxed garden restaurant. The extensive menu includes vegan pizzas, ice creams, housemade tofu curry and innovative salads. Ingredients are as diverse as coconut, cashew milk and cashew cheese, quinoa, tempeh and lentil dhal.

Bluebird   GOAN $$
(www.bluebirdgoa.com; Ozran Beach Rd, Vagator; mains ₹280-480; ⊙8.30am-11pm; 🛜) Bluebird specialises in Goan cuisine, with genuine vindaloos, chicken *cafreal* (marinated in a sauce of chillies, garlic and ginger), fish curry rice and Goan sausages among the temptations, as well as some delicately spiced seafood dishes. Dine in the lovely open garden cafe.

Mango Tree Bar & Cafe   MULTICUISINE $$
(Vagator Beach Rd, Vagator; mains ₹190-510; ⊙24hr; 🛜) With loud reggae, crappy service, darkwood furniture, a sometimes rambunctious bar scene, ancient expats leaning over the bar, draught beer and an overall great vibe, the Mango Tree is a classic Vagator meeting place. It's open late (allegedly 24 hours if it's busy enough) with a menu from Goan to European, pizza and Mexican.

Piccolo Roma   ITALIAN $$
(☑ 7507806821; Anjuna-Chapora Rd, Vagator; pizza & pasta ₹210-520; ⊙10am-11pm; 🛜) With an Italian chef in the kitchen, some say the wood-fired pizzas and house-made pasta is the best in Vagator and there's an undeniably pleasant atmosphere in the garden cafe, with its cushions and fairy lights. Starters of antipasto, crostini, soups and salads also grace the menu.

Yangkhor Moonlight   TIBETAN $$
(Ozran Beach Rd, Vagator; mains ₹170-400; ⊙8am-11pm; 🛜) Well known locally for its fresh Tibetan food such as *momos* (Tibetan dumplings), *thukpa* (soup) and the rarely seen Tibetan thali (₹250), as well as pasta dishes and even sushi. The decor is simple but most travellers enjoy the food and the ambience.

Food Chord   DINER $$
(☑ 0832-6745000; 544/2, Ozran Beach Rd, Vagator; mains ₹175-550; ⊙7am-11.30pm; ❊ 🛜) At the crazy retro I Love Bellbottoms hotel, this American-style diner has booth seating, Arctic air-con and a menu of club sandwiches, burgers, hot dogs and pizzas. The inner window looks out to the violin-shaped pool (nonguests can swim for ₹1500, redeemable on food and drinks). Full bar with draught beer. Vagator or Vegas?

Midnight Toker   MULTICUISINE $$
(Main St, Chapora; mains ₹140-240; ⊙9am-1am; 🛜) The usual array of Indian, Chinese and Russian food is on the menu but this welcoming open-fronted restaurant is also a good place to watch the Chapora scene over a cold beer.

★ Thalassa   GREEK $$$
(☑ 9850033537; www.thalassaindia.com; Teso Waterfront; mains ₹300-750; ⊙4pm-midnight)

DUDHSAGAR FALLS

Goa's most impressive **waterfall** (entry/camera ₹50/300) splashes 603m down on the eastern border with Karnataka, in the far southeastern corner of the Bhagwan Mahavir Wildlife Sanctuary. The falls are best visited as soon after monsoon as possible (October is perfect), when water levels are highest. Get here via Colem village, 7km south of Molem, by car or by the scenic 8.15am local train from Margao (return train times vary seasonally). From Colem, pick up a shared jeep (₹500 per person for six people) for the bumpy remaining 45-minute journey. An easier option is a taxi or a full-day Goa Tourism Dudhsagar Special' tour (₹2300), starting at 6.30am from Calangute or Panaji.

North Goa's most famous Greek restaurant was forced out of its long-running Vagator location in 2018 but has found a new waterfront home at Teso in Siolim. Still authentic and awesomely good Greek food is served al fresco overlooking the Chapora River.

Antares INDIAN $$$
(☑ 7350011528; www.antaresgoa.com; Ozran Beach Rd, Vagator; mains ₹395-1295; ⊘ 11.30am-midnight) Perched on Vagator's southern clifftop, Antares is known as the project of Australian Masterchef contestant Sarah Todd. The atmosphere is beachfront chic meets nightclub and the food pricey Modern Australian meets Indian, with some Goan dishes such as crab *xacuti*.

Drinking & Nightlife

Hilltop CLUB
(www.hilltopgoa.in; Vagator; ⊘ sunset-3am) Hilltop is a long-serving Vagator trance and party venue that's deserted by day but comes alive from sunset. Its edge-of-town neon-lit coconut grove location allows it, on occasion, to bypass noise regulations to host indoor and outdoor concerts, parties and international DJs. Sunday sessions (5pm to 10pm) are legendary.

Nine Bar BAR
(Little Vagator Beach; ⊘ 5pm-4am) Once the hallowed epicentre of Goa's trance scene, the open-air Nine Bar terrace, on the clifftop overlooking Little Vagator Beach, is fading

but stills pumps out beats in its soundproof indoor space. It generally doesn't start until December; look out for flyers and local advice to see when the big party nights are on.

Paulo's Antique Bar BAR
(Main St, Chapora; ⊘ 3pm-11pm) In season this hole-in-the-wall bar on Chapora's main street overflows with good music and cold beer. In late afternoon the few tables on the veranda are a fine spot to watch the world in miniature go by.

Waters Beach Lounge CLUB
(☑ 9767200012; Ozran Beach, Vagator; ⊘ noon-4am) Terracing down the hillside on the Vagator cliffs, this restaurant, bar and club is known for its loud party nights, with open-air dance floors overlooking the Arabian Sea and a soundproof room for late at night – as late as 5am. Top DJs come to play.

Jai Ganesh Fruit Juice Centre JUICE BAR
(Main St, Chapora; ⊘ 8.30am-midnight) Thanks to its corner location, with views up and down Chapora's main street, this may be the most popular juice bar in Goa. It's a prime meeting spot and, once parked, most people are reluctant to give up their seat. Juices ₹60 to ₹80.

❶ Information

There's a **HDFC ATM** at the petrol station on the back road to Anjuna.

❶ Getting There & Away

Fairly frequent buses run to both Chapora and Vagator from Mapusa (₹15, 30 minutes) throughout the day, many via Anjuna. There are bus stops in **Chapora** (Main St, Chapora) and on Vagator Beach Rd and **Anjuna-Vagator Rd** (Anjuna-Vagator, Vagator). Practically anyone with legs will rent you a scooter/motorcycle from ₹300/500 per day.

Vagator has North Goa's most popular **petrol station** (Mapusa-Chapora Rd).

Morjim

Morjim Beach was once very low-key – almost deserted – and the southern end is still protected due to the presence of rare olive ridley marine turtles, which come to lay their annual clutches of eggs between November and February.

These days Morjim is super popular with Russian tourists – it's locally known as 'Little Russia' – and consequently there's a bit of a clubbing scene in season and a growing number of restaurants and beach shacks. Though there are lovely views down the headland to Chapora Fort, the southern beach is more black sand than golden due to river runoff.

Based at Marbela Beach Resort, **Banana Surf School** (📞7218063571; www.goasurf.com; Marbela Beach; 2-hour surf lesson US$70, 3-day course US$180, board hire per hour/day US$25/60) rents boards and offers beginner lessons, from two hours to five days.

🛏 Sleeping & Eating

★**Wanderers Hostel**　　　　HOSTEL $
(📞9619235302; www.wanderershostel.com; Morjim Beach Rd; dm with fan/AC ₹400/500, shared tents ₹300, luxury tents d ₹1500; ❄🔊🛜) About five minutes' walk back from Morjim Beach, Wanderers is a real find for budget travellers. The main building, decorated with original travellers' murals, has spotless dorms with lockers, bed lights and wi-fi, full kitchen, cosy communal areas and a pool table. In the garden next door is a tent village with swimming pool, yoga retreat centre and outdoor cinema.

Goan Café & Resort　　　　RESORT $
(📞0832-2244394; www.goancafe.com; apt & cottages from ₹1800, with AC ₹2200, tree houses ₹2200, without bathroom ₹1200; ❄🛜) Fronting Morjim Beach, this excellent family-run resort has a fine array of beachfront stilted 'tree house' huts and more solid rooms (some with AC) at the back. The beachfront restaurant is good and breakfast is included.

Bora Bora　　　　MULTICUISINE $$$
(📞8888558614; mains ₹270-550; ⏰24hr) Part restaurant, part club, part beach bar, Bora Bora is the only place in this area open 24 hours. Food runs to everything from pizza to Russian, Thai and Indian with seafood nights, but most people come here to chill out and enjoy a drink or one of the DJ nights. It's at the start of Morjim's little 'eat street'.

❶ Getting There & Away

Occasional local buses run between Siolim and Morjim village (₹10, 15 minutes), but most travellers taxi to their chosen accommodation, then either hire a scooter/motorbike or use taxis from there.

Asvem

Asven is a wide stretch of beach, growing busier each year but still a little overshadowed by Mandrem to the north. Beach-hut accommodation and beach-shack restaurants spring up each season on a very broad stretch of clean, white-sand with few hawkers. The main Morjim–Mandrem road is set some way back from the sands.

🏃 Activities

★**Vaayu Waterman's Village**　　SURFING
(📞9850050403; www.vaayuvision.com; surfboard hire per hour/day ₹500/1500, lessons ₹2500) Goa's premier surf shop is also an activity and art centre where you can arrange lessons and hire equipment for surfing, kiteboarding, stand-up paddleboarding (SUP), kayaking and wakeboarding. A highlight is the full-day SUP tour to Paradise Lagoon in Maharashtra. The enthusiastic young owners also run an art gallery, cafe and accommodation across the road from Asvem Beach.

Arti Spa　　　　AYURVEDA
(📞9049209597; www.artifabulousbodycare.com; massage & ayurvedic treatments ₹500-2000; ⏰8am-9pm) Arti and Dinesh run this well-regarded ayurvedic spa in Asvem (on the main road behind Sea View Resort). Treatments include Keralan massage, aromatherapy and *shirodhara* (an ayurvedic massage treatment where liquids are poured over the forehead).

🛏 Sleeping & Eating

Beachside by Bombay Backpackers　　HOSTEL $
(📞9781040244; Asvem Beach Rd; dm ₹400-450, d ₹1650; 🛜) Down a lane off the main road opposite the beach, this backpackers in a converted house makes a decent budget stay with four- to six-bed dorms with individual fans and lockers. There's a lack of traveller vibe compared with some of north Goa's hostels but the location and price are good.

Vaayu Waterman's Village　BOUTIQUE HOTEL $$
(📞9850050403; www.vaayuvision.com; hut ₹2500-4400, d with AC ₹4500; ❄🛜) The excellent boutique rooms at this water sports outfit are stylish with the sort of artistic and soulful vibe that goes with the attached gallery, wholefood Prana Cafe, yoga *shala* (studio) and surf shop. Across the road, facing the beach, are beautifully designed Keralan-style bamboo and thatch huts.

Wellness Inn　　　　　GUESTHOUSE $$

(☑ 9075006776; www.wellnessinn.in; d/f from ₹3200/4800; ❉🤫) This 13-room guesthouse will suit yoga practitioners with daily drop-in classes, yoga training on the rooftop terrace and a health-conscious veg restaurant. Rooms are spacious, airy and all have aircon. It's often busy with travellers on yoga retreats so book ahead.

Yab Yum　　　　　　　HUT $$$

(☑ 0832-6510392; www.yabyumresorts.com; hut/cottage from ₹10,600/12,050; ❉🤫) 🏄 This top-notch choice has unusual, stylish, dome-shaped huts – some look like giant hairy coconuts – made of a combination of all-natural local materials, including mud, stone and mango wood, as well as more traditional AC cottages. A host of yoga and massage options is available, and it's set in one of the most secluded beachfront jungle gardens you'll find in Goa.

ℹ️ Getting There & Away

Buses run between Siolim and Asvem, but it's easier to get a taxi straight to your chosen accommodation, then either hire a scooter/motorbike or use taxis from there.

Mandrem

Mellow Mandrem is something akin to beach bliss, with its miles of clean, white sand separated from the village by a shallow creek. The beach and village has developed in recent years from an in-the-know bolthole for those seeking respite from the relentless traveller scene of Arambol and Anjuna to a fairly mainstream but still very lovely beach hang-out. There's plenty of yoga, meditation and ayurveda on offer here, plus a growing dining scene and plenty of space to lay down with a good book. Many believe there's no better place in North Goa.

🏃 Activities

Kite Guru　　　　　WATER SPORTS

(☑ 8788314974; www.kiteguru.co.uk; 2/6/8hr course ₹7000/14,000/21,000, SUP lessons ₹2000) Based at Riverside in Mandrem, this is the best place in Goa to learn to kitesurf. Professional instructors offer group or solo IKO certified lessons and provide all the gear. Also stand-up paddleboard lessons and tours. Board hire for independent SUPers is ₹1000 an hour.

Shanti Ayurvedic Massage Centre　　　　　AYURVEDA

(☑ 8806205264; 1hr massage from ₹1000; ⏰ 9am-9pm) Ayurvedic massage is provided here by the delightful Shanti. Try the rejuvenating 75-minute massage and facial package, or go for an unusual 'Poulti' massage, using a poultice-like cloth bundle containing 12 herbal powders. You'll find her place on the right-hand side as you head down the beach road.

Ashiyana Retreat Centre　　　　　YOGA

(☑ 9850401714; www.ashiyana-yoga-goa.com; Junas Waddo; drop-in class ₹600) This 'tropical retreat centre' fronting Mandrem Beach and stretching back to the jungle has a long list of classes and courses available from October to April, from retreats and yoga holidays to spa, massage and 'massage camp'. Accommodation (includes free yoga) is in one of its gorgeous, heritage-styled rooms and huts.

Himalaya Yoga Valley　　　　　YOGA

(☑ 9960657852; www.yogagoaindia.com; Mandrem Beach) HYV specialises in hatha and ashtanga residential 200-hour teacher-training courses (€1475) in Goa, Dharamsala and Ireland.

🛏️ Sleeping & Eating

Riverside　　　　　HUT $

(☑ 9049503605; www.riversidemandrem.com; Junas Waddo; huts ₹800-1200; 🤫) At the southern end of Mandrem Beach, overlooking the creek, Riverside is an excellent two-level open-sided restaurant with a collection of well-designed but affordable palm-thatch and timber huts at the back and side. These are some of the best-value beachfront huts in Mandrem and there's a kitesurfing school here and stand-up paddleboards for rent.

★ **Dunes Holiday Village**　　　　　HUT $$

(☑ 0832-2247219; www.dunesgoa.com; huts ₹1500-1750, d with AC ₹2200; ❉🤫) The pretty huts here are peppered around a palm-filled lane leading to the beach; at night, lamps light up the place like a palm-tree dreamland. Huts range from basic to more sturdy 'tree houses' (huts on stilts) and there are some guesthouse rooms with air-con. It's a friendly, good-value place with a decent beach restaurant, yoga classes and a marked absence of trance.

★ **Mandala**　　　　　RESORT $$

(☑ 9158266093; www.themandalagoa.com; r & huts ₹1600-7000; ❉🤫) Mandala is a very peaceful and beautifully designed eco-village with a range of huts and a couple of quirky air-con rooms in the 'Art House'. Pride of place goes to the barn-sized two-storey villas inspired by the design of a Keralan houseboat. The location, overlooking the tidal lagoon, is serene, with a large garden, daily yoga sessions, an organic restaurant and juice bar.

Beach Street
RESORT $$

(Lazy Dog; ☑9403410679; Mandrem Beach; huts ₹4300-6900, chalets ₹8600-11,800; 🛜🏊) The beachfront huts are adorable at Beach Street, where the adjacent building encloses an inviting pool. Well-designed huts range from simple with bathroom and veranda to two-storey palm-thatch family 'chalets' sleeping five. The Lazy Dog beachfront restaurant here has five-star aspirations with waiters dressed in cruise uniforms.

Riva Beach Resort
RESORT $$

(☑0832-2247612; www.rivaresorts.com; d ₹5000-9500; ❄🛜🏊) This sprawling complex of seasonal cottages and hotel-style rooms tumbles down from the main road to the inlet, where bamboo bridges provide access to the beach. Spring mattresses, ocean-view balconies, a good restaurant and on-site yoga retreats. It's a bit of a party spot – Sunday is the pool party.

Karma Kitchen
MULTICUISINE $$

(☑8894204735; Junas Waddo; mains ₹220-650; ☺9am-10pm; 🛜) This cruisey courtyard cafe offers a bit of everything but specialises in thalis, tandoor kebabs and seafood, or a combination such as the seafood souvlaki kebab. It's also a good place to come for a drink, with wine by the glass and regular live music, including Sunday sessions.

Bed Rock
MULTICUISINE $$

(Junos Vaddo; mains ₹150-400; ☺8am-11pm; 🛜) Bed Rock is a welcome change from the beach shacks with a reliable menu of Indian and continental faves (pizza, pasta etc), a cosy chill-out lounge upstairs, welcoming staff and a loyal following of regulars. Look out for live music in season.

🛍 Shopping

Arambol Hammocks
HOMEWARES

(☑7798906816, 9619175722; www.arambol.com; 327, Junas Waddo) Now in Mandrem, Arambol Hammocks designs and sells hammocks, including their 'flying carpets' and 'flying chairs'.

ℹ Getting There & Around

Buses run between Siolim and Mandrem village (₹10, 20 minutes) hourly, but it's hard work trying to get anywhere in a hurry on public trans-port. Most travellers taxi to their chosen accommodation, then either hire a scooter/motorbike or use taxis from there.

Arambol (Harmal)
POP 5320

Arambol (also known as Harmal) is the most northerly of Goa's developed beach resorts and is still considered the beach of choice for many long-staying budget-minded travellers in the north.

Arambol first emerged in the 1960s as a mellow paradise for long-haired long-stayers escaping the scene at Calangute. Today things are still cheap and cheerful, with budget accommodation in little huts and rooms clinging to the cliffsides, though the main beach is now an uninterrupted string of beach shacks, many with accommodation operations stacked behind.

🏃 Activities

Arambol Paragliding
PARAGLIDING

(10min flight ₹2000; ☺11am-6pm) The headland above Kalacha Beach (Sweetwater Lake) is an ideal launching point for paragliding. There are a number of independent paragliders: ask around at the shack restaurants on the beach, arrange a pilot, then make the short hike to the top of the headland. Most flights are around 10 minutes, but if conditions are right you can stay up longer.

Himalayan Iyengar Yoga Centre
YOGA

(www.hiyogacentre.com; Madhlo Vaddo; 5-day yoga course ₹5500; ☺9am-6pm Nov-Mar) Arambol's reputable Himalayan Iyengar Yoga Centre, which runs five-day courses in hatha yoga from mid-November to mid-March, is the winter centre of the Iyengar yoga school in Dharamkot, near Dharamsala in north India. First-time students must take the introductory five-day course, and can then continue with more advanced five-day courses at a reduced rate.

Surf Wala
SURFING

(☑9011993147; www.surfwala.com; Arambol Beach; 1½hr lesson from ₹2500, 3-/5-day course ₹7000/11,500) If you're a beginner looking to get up on a board, join the international team of surfers based at Arambol's Surf Club. Prices include board hire, wax and rashie. Check the website for instructor contact details – between them they speak English, Russian, Hindi, Konkani and Japanese! Board-only rental is ₹500/1500 per hour/day.

🛏 Sleeping

Accommodation in Arambol has expanded from basic huts along the clifftop and guesthouses in the village to a mini-Palolem of beach huts along the main beach and a selection of backpacker hostels. Enter at the 'Glastonbury St' entrance and walk north to find plenty of places clinging to the headland between here and Kalacha Beach, or enter at the south end and ask at any of the beach shacks.

★ Happy Panda   HOSTEL $

(☑9619741681; www.happypanda.in; dm ₹500-650, tent from ₹400; ❇🛜) Traveller-painted murals cover the walls in this very chilled backpacker place near the main village. Young owners have worked hard making the dorms, neon common area, bar and garden a well-equipped and welcoming budget place to crash. Artists, cooks and other skilled travellers are encouraged to lend a hand. Bikes for hire and tent accommodation available.

Om Ganesh   GUESTHOUSE $

(☑9404313206; r ₹600-800; 🛜) Halfway along the cliff, Om Ganesh has been around for a while and has solid rooms in a building on the hillside, and seasonal huts-with-a-view on the rooftop.

Pitruchaya Cottages   COTTAGE $

(☑9404454596; r ₹700-800; 🛜) The sea-facing timber cottages here are among the best on the cliffs, with attached bathrooms, fans and verandahs.

Chilli's   HOTEL $

(☑9921882424; Glastonbury St; d ₹700, apt with AC ₹1200; ❇🛜) Near the beach entrance on Glastonbury St, this friendly canary-yellow place is one of Arambol's better nonbeach-front bargains. There are 10 decent, no-frills rooms, all with attached bathroom, fan and a hot-water shower. The top-floor apartment with AC and TV is good value. Motorbikes and scooters available for hire.

THE PORTUGUESE LEGACY

The Portuguese departed Goa in 1961 after more than 400 years of colonial rule but they left behind a rich legacy of culture, architecture, churches, schools and medical colleges.

Religion & Festivals

Around one quarter of the Goan population is Christian (largely Roman Catholic), mostly as a result of religious conversion during Portuguese rule. Today this legacy is most obvious in the many whitewashed parish churches across the state but also in the Christian festivals such as Christmas, Easter, Carnival and the Feast of St Francis Xavier.

Food

Goan cuisine is distinct from its South Indian neighbours with its liberal use of pork and uniquely spiced sauces such as *xacuti*, *cafreal* and *recheado*. *Vindaloo* is a Goan derivative of Portuguese port stew steeped in wine vinegar and garlic. Seafood is still king though and fish-curry-rice was a staple here long before colonisation. The Portuguese also introduced cashews to Goa, providing the basis for the national alcoholic drink, feni.

Architecture

You don't have to look far to see the fine architecture left behind by the Portuguese in residential mansions and palacios. Your first stop should be Panaji's Latin Quarter of Fontainhas and Sao Thome, where many Portuguese homes have been converted into boutique heritage hotels. In the countryside, South Goan villages such as Chandor, Loutolim and Quepem are awash with grand mansions but if you look past the tourist tat you'll see many well-preserved examples of Portuguese architecture in the backstreets of beach resorts such as Candolim and Calangute.

Susegad

This one is a little less tangible but you'll find it in everyday life during your time in Goa. Derived from the Portuguese *sossegado* ('quiet'), *susegad* is a uniquely Goan term that describes a laid-back attitude and contentment with life. Life might not look very relaxed during peak season in downtown Calangute but the concept of *susegad* lives on in the people of Goa.

Surf Club GUESTHOUSE **$**
(www.thesurfclubgoa.com; d ₹1000-1800; 🛜) In a quiet space at the end of a lane, on the southern end of Arambol Beach, the Surf Club is one of those cool little hang-outs that offer a bit of everything: simple but clean rooms, a fun bar with live music and surf lessons and board hire.

Lotus Sutra RESORT **$$**
(📞9146096940; www.lotussutragoa.com; d & cottages ₹4000-5500; ❋🛜) The fanciest place on Arambol's beachfront has a series of bright rooms in a quirky two-storey building and cute individual timber cottages facing a garden-lawn setting or towards the seafront. The Zen Oasis restaurant-bar is a popular spot and features live music.

✖️ Eating

Dylan's Toasted & Roasted CAFE **$**
(📞9604780316; www.dylanscoffee.com; coffee & desserts ₹80-200; ⊗9am-11pm late Nov-Apr; 🛜) The Goa (winter) incarnation of a Manali institution, Dylan's is a fine place for an espresso, chocolate chip cookies and old-school dessert. It's a nice hang-out, just back from the southern beach entrance, with occasional live music and open-mic nights.

German Bakery BAKERY **$**
(📞9822159699; Welcome Inn, Glastonbury St; pastries ₹30-100; ⊗8am-midnight) This popular little cafe bakes a good line in cakes and pastries, including lemon cheese pie and chocolate biscuit cake, as well as coffee and breakfast. It's a cool meeting spot close to the beach but away from the beach shacks.

★Shimon MIDDLE EASTERN **$$**
(📞9011113576; Glastonbury St; mains ₹160-250; ⊗9am-11pm; 🛜) Just back from the beach, and understandably popular with Israeli backpackers, Shimon is the place to fill up on exceptional falafel or *sabich* (crisp slices of eggplant stuffed into pita bread along with boiled egg, boiled potato and salad). The East-meets-Middle-East thali (₹450) comprises a little bit of almost everything on the menu. Follow up with a strong Turkish coffee or its signature iced coffee. No alcohol.

This Is It MULTICUISINE **$$**
(📞7775078620; mains ₹160-370; ⊗8am-11pm; 🛜) Many travellers rate this the coolest place on the northern beachfront. A big menu of well-prepared Indian staples, Goan dishes, Chinese, seafood, *momos* and pasta is complemented by a laid-back, traveller-friendly vibe, generous happy hours and regular live music. Popular Holy Cow Backpackers is behind.

Fellini ITALIAN **$$**
(📞9881461224; Glastonbury St; mains ₹200-450; ⊗from 6.30pm) On the left-hand side just before the beach, this long-standing evening-only Italian joint is perfect if you're craving a carbonara or calzone. More than 40 wood-fired, thin-crust pizza varieties are on the menu, but save space for a very decent rendition of tiramisu. Live music in season.

Double Dutch MULTICUISINE **$$**
(mains ₹120-450, steaks ₹420-500; ⊗8am-10pm) In a peaceful garden set back from the main road to the Glastonbury St beach entrance, Double Dutch has long been popular for its steaks, salads, Thai and Indonesian dishes, and famous apple pies. It's a relaxed meeting place with secondhand books, newspapers and a useful noticeboard for current Arambolic affairs.

Rice Bowl ASIAN **$$**
(📞9822748451; mains ₹110-290; ⊗8am-11pm; 🛜) Rice Bowl specialises in Chinese and Japanese cuisine and does it well. With a good view down to Arambol Beach, this is a great place to settle in with a plate of gyoza and a beer, or play a game of pool.

ℹ️ Information

There's an ATM on the main highway in Arambol's village, about 1.5km back from the beach. If it's not working there's another about 3km north in Paliyem or about the same distance south in Mandrem.

ℹ️ Getting There & Away

Frequent buses to and from Mapusa (₹40, one hour) stop on the main road at the 'backside' (as locals are fond of saying) of Arambol village, where there's a church, a school and a few local shops. From here, it's a 1.5km trek down through the village to the main beach drag (head straight for the southern beach entrance or bear right for the northern 'Glastonbury St' entrance another 500m further on). An autorickshaw will charge at least ₹50 for the trip. Plenty of places in the village advertise scooters and motorbikes for hire (per day scooter/motorbike ₹300/400).

A prepaid taxi from Mapusa to Arambol costs ₹700 but taxis on the street between Arambol and Mapusa or Anjuna/Vagator will ask closer to ₹1000. If you're heading north to Mumbai, travel agents can book bus tickets.

GOA ARAMBOL (HARMAL)

SOUTH GOA

South Goa is the more serene half of the state, and for many travellers that's the attraction. There are fewer activities and not as many bars, clubs or restaurants, but overall the beaches of the south are cleaner, whiter and not as crowded as those in the north.

Margao

POP 122,500

Margao (also known as Madgaon) is the capital of South Goa, a busy – at times traffic-clogged – market town of a manageable size for getting things done. As the major transport hub of the south, lots of travellers pass through Margao's train station or Kadamba bus stand; fewer choose to overnight here, but it's a useful place for market shopping, catching a local sporting event or simply enjoying the busy energy of big-city India in small-town form.

🛏️ Sleeping & Eating

Unlike Panaji, Margao doesn't have the range of accommodation that you'd expect in a town of this size. But with the beaches of the south so close, there's really no pressing reason to stay here.

Nanutel Margao HOTEL $$
(☑ 0832-6722222; www.nanuhotels.in; Padre Miranda Rd; s/d incl breakfast ₹5300/5900; ❈🔊☀) Margao's best business-class hotel by some margin, Nanutel is modern and slick with a lovely pool, good restaurant, bar and coffee shop, and clean air-con rooms. The location, between the Municipal Gardens and Largo de Igreja district, is convenient for everything.

Hotel Tanish HOTEL $$
(☑ 0832-2735858; www.hoteltanishgoa.com; Reliance Trade Centre, Valaulikar Rd; s/d ₹1200/1700, with AC ₹1500/2000; ❈🔊) Oddly situated inside a modern mall, this top-floor hotel offers good views of the surrounding countryside, with stylish, well-equipped rooms. Try for an outside-facing room, as some overlook the mall interior.

Café Tato INDIAN $
(Valaulikar Rd; thalis ₹100; ⊙ 7am-10pm Mon-Sat) A favourite local lunch spot: tasty vegetarian fare in a bustling backstreet canteen, and delicious all-you-can-eat thalis.

★Longhuino's GOAN $$
(☑ 0832-2739908; Luis Miranda Rd; mains ₹180-320; ⊙ 8.30am-10pm) A local institution since 1950, quaint old Longhuino's serves up tasty Indian, Goan and Chinese dishes, popular with locals and tourists alike. Go for a Goan dish like *ambot tik* (a slightly sour but fiery curry dish), and leave room for the retro desserts such as rum balls and tiramisu.

Chikoo Tree Project MULTICUISINE $$
(☑ 9920064597; 85 Dr Miranda Rd; mains ₹150-300; ⊙ 9am-10pm Tue-Sun) Breakfast on masala dosas and lunch on chicken *momos* or giant *kathi* wraps at this arty, eclectic but casual cafe that's made a welcome addition to Margao's dining scene. Good coffee and fresh-made juices.

Viva Goa GOAN $$
(mains ₹150-400; ⊙ 11am-3pm & 7-11pm) Upstairs in Clube Harmonia, South Goa's oldest cultural club venue, Viva Goa is a new iteration of the long-running Colva restaurant, serving genuine Goan cuisine, seafood and a full bar.

MAJOR TRAINS FROM MARGAO

DESTINATION	TRAIN NO & NAME	FARE (₹)	DURATION (HRS)	DEPARTURES
Bengaluru (Bangalore)	02779 Vasco da Gama-SBC Link (D)	380/1025	15	3.50pm
Chennai; via Yesvantpur	17312 Vasco da Gama-Chennai Express (C)	495/1325/1905	21	3.20pm Thu
Delhi	22633 Nizamuddin Exp (A)	2040/2965	30	8.25am
Ernakulam (Kochi)	12618 Lakshadweep Express (C)	465/1215/1715	15	7.40pm
Mangaluru (Mangalore)	12133 Mangalore Express (C)	310/785/1085	6	7.15am
Mumbai	10112 Konkan Kanya Express (C)	410/1105/1575	12	6pm
Pune	12779 Goa Express (C)	375/975/1365	12	3.50pm

Fares: (A) 3AC/2AC, (B) 2S/CC, (C) sleeper/3AC/2AC, (D) sleeper/3AC

🛍 Shopping

MMC New Market MARKET
(Rua F de Loiola; ⏱8.30am-9pm Mon-Sat) Margao's crowded, covered canopy of colourful stalls is a fun but busy place to wander around, sniffing spices, sampling soaps and browsing the household merchandise.

Golden Heart Emporium BOOKS
(Confidant House, Abade Faria Rd; ⏱10am-2pm & 4-7.30pm Mon-Sat) One of Goa's best bookshops, Golden Heart is crammed from floor to ceiling with fiction, nonfiction, children's books, and illustrated volumes on the state's food, architecture and history. It also stocks otherwise hard-to-get titles by local Goan authors. It's down a little lane off Abade Faria Rd.

ℹ Getting There & Away

BUS

Local and long-distance buses use the Kadamba bus stand, on the highway about 2km north of the Municipal Gardens. Buses to Palolem (₹40, one hour), Colva (₹15, 20 minutes), Benaulim (₹15, 20 minutes) and Betul (₹25, 40 minutes) stop both at the Kadamba bus stand and at informal bus stops on the east and west sides of the Municipal Gardens. For Panaji, take any local bus to the Kadamba bus stand and change to a frequent express bus (₹40, one hour). From there you can change for buses to Mapusa and the northern beaches.

Daily AC state-run buses go to Mumbai (₹900, 16 hours), Pune (₹735, 13 hours) and Bengaluru (₹660 to ₹1200, 12 hours), which can be booked online at www.goakadamba.com. Non-AC buses are about one-third cheaper but are becoming rare on long distance routes. For greater choice and flexibility but similar prices, private long-distance buses depart from the stand opposite Kadamba. You'll find booking offices all over town; **Paulo Travels** (📞0832-2702405; www.paulobus.com; NH66) is among the best, and also has the only buses to Hampi (seat/sleeper ₹900/1500, 11 hours), but the best booking site is Red Bus (www.redbus.in).

TAXI

Taxis are plentiful around the Municipal Gardens and Kadamba bus stand, and are a quick and comfortable way to reach any of Goa's beaches. Prepaid taxi stands are at the train station and main bus stand. Fares include the following: Panaji (₹1050), Palolem (₹1050), Calangute (₹1355), Anjuna (₹1500) and Arambol (₹2000), though you'll pay up to double these fares by hiring a taxi off the street.

For Colva and Benaulim, autorickshaws should do the trip for around ₹150 but taxis ask an inflated ₹500. Motorcycle taxis are still common in Margao and are good for short trips.

TRAIN

Margao's well-organised train station (known as Madgaon on train timetables), about 2km south of town, serves both the Konkan Railway and local South Central Railways routes, and is the main hub for trains from Mumbai to Goa and south to Kochi and beyond. Its **reservation hall** (📞0832-2712790; Train Station; ⏱8am-2pm & 2.15-8pm Mon-Sat, 8am-2pm Sun) is on the 1st floor and there's a foreign tourist quota counter upstairs.

Outside the station you'll find a useful prepaid taxi stand; use this to get to your beachside destination and you'll be assured of a fair price. Alternatively, a taxi or autorickshaw to or from the town centre to the station should cost around ₹100.

Colva

POP 3140
Once a sleepy fishing village, and in the sixties a hang-out for hippies escaping the scene up at Anjuna, Colva is still the main town-resort along this stretch of coast, but these days it has lost any semblance of the beach paradise vibe. Travel a little way north or south, though, and you'll find some of the peace missing in central Colva.

The **Goa Animal Welfare Trust shop** (📞0832-2653677; www.gawt.org; ⏱9.30am-1pm & 4-7pm Mon-Sat), next door to Leda Lounge, is a charity shop with secondhand books and souvenirs. All proceeds go toward helping out Goa's four-legged friends and the staff are happy to chat about the work of the GAWT, based in Curchorem.

🛏 Sleeping & Eating

Colva has a few budget guesthouses hidden in the wards north of the beach road, but overall good-value pickings are a little slim. Numerous beach shacks line the Colvan sands between November and April, offering the extensive standard range of fare and fresh seafood.

Sam's Guesthouse HOTEL $
(📞0832-2788753; r ₹800; 🛜) Away from the fray, north of Colva's main drag on the road running parallel to the beach, Sam's is a big, cheerful place with friendly owners and spacious rooms that are a steal at this price. Rooms are around a pleasant garden courtyard and there's a good restaurant and whacky 'cosy cave'. Wi-fi in the restaurant only.

⭐**Skylark Resort** HOTEL $$
(📞0832-2788052; www.skylarkresortgoa.com; d with AC ₹3350-4500, f ₹5000; ❄🛜🏊) A serious step up from the budget places, Skylark's

WORTH A TRIP

COLA BEACH

Cola Beach is one of those hidden gems of the south coast – a relatively hard-to-reach crescent of sand enclosed by forested cliffs and with a gorgeous emerald lagoon stretching back from the beach.

It has been discovered of course and between November and April several hut and tent villages such as **Blue Lagoon Resort** (☑9673277756; www.bluelagoon cola.com; cottages ₹3800-5400; 🅿) set up here, but it's still a beautiful, low-key place and popular with day trippers from Agonda and Palolem.

Further north around the headland is an even more remote beach known as Khancola Beach, or Kakolem, with one small resort reached via a steep set of jungly steps from the clifftop above.

clean, fresh rooms are graced with bits and pieces of locally made teak furniture and block-print bedspreads, while the lovely pool makes a pleasant place to lounge. The best (and more expensive) rooms are those facing the pool.

La Ben   HOTEL $$
(☑0832-2788040; www.laben.net; Colva Beach Rd; r with/without AC ₹1800/1650; ❄🅿🛜) Neat, clean and not entirely devoid of atmosphere, La Ben is a traveller hang-out in the middle of the action with decent, good-value rooms and has been around for ages. There's a rooftop bar and, at street level, the very good **Garden Restaurant** (mains ₹170-370; ⊙7.30am-11.30pm; 🛜).

Soul Vacation   HOTEL $$$
(☑0832-2788147; www.soulvacation.in; 4th Ward; d incl breakfast ₹6300-8300, f villas from ₹10,400; ❄🛜🏊) Thirty sleek, white rooms arranged around nice gardens and a neat pool are the trademarks of Soul Vacation, set 400m back from Colva Beach. This is central Colva's most upmarket choice and, though pricey, there's a nice air of exclusivity about it. There's an ayurvedic spa, garden cafe and bar.

Sagar Kinara   INDIAN $
(Colva Beach Rd; mains ₹70-190; ⊙7am-10.30pm) A pure-veg restaurant upstairs (nonveg is separate, downstairs) with tastes to please even committed carnivores, Sagar Kinara

is clean, efficient and offers cheap and delicious North and South Indian cuisine all day.

Leda Lounge & Restaurant   BAR
(⊙noon-3pm & 7-11pm) Part sports bar, part music venue, part cocktail bar, Leda is Colva's best nightspot, though it operates as much as a restaurant and even the bar closes in the afternoon. There's live music from Thursday to Sunday, fancy drinks (mojitos, Long Island iced teas) and good food at lunch and dinner.

❶ Getting There & Away

Buses from Colva to Margao run roughly every 15 minutes (₹15, 20 minutes) from 7.30am to about 7pm, departing from the **parking area** (Colva Beach Rd) at the end of the beach road. A taxi/autorickshaw to Margao is ₹500/150.

Scooters can be hired around the bus stand (with some difficulty) for ₹300 per day.

Benaulim

A long stretch of largely empty sand peppered with a few beach shacks and watersports enthusiasts, the beaches of Benaulim and nearby Sernabatim to the north are much quieter than Colva, partly because the village is a good kilometre back from the beach.

⊙ Sights

★**Goa Chitra**   MUSEUM
(☑0832-2772910; www.goachitra.com; St John the Baptist Rd, Mondo Vaddo; ₹300; ⊙9am-6pm Tue-Sun) Artist and restorer Victor Hugo Gomes first noticed the slow extinction of traditional objects – from farming tools to kitchen utensils to altarpieces – as a child in Benaulim. He created this ethnographic museum from the more than 4000 cast-off objects that he collected from across the state over 20 years. Admission is via a one-hour guided tour, held on the hour. Goa Chitra is 3km east of Maria Hall – ask locally for directions.

San Thome Museum   MUSEUM
(☑9822363917; www.goamuseum.com; Colva Rd; ₹200; ⊙9am-6pm) This quirky museum at the Varca (southern) end of Benaulim, dubbed 'Back in Time', has three floors of carefully presented technology through the ages, from old cameras and typewriters to gramophones, clocks and projectors. Highlights include a Scheidmayer grand piano,

Raleigh bicycle and an anchor cast from the same pattern as the *Titanic*'s.

🛏 Sleeping & Eating

★Blue Corner HUT $
(☑9850455770; www.bluecornergoa.com; huts ₹1300; 🛜) It's rare to find good old-fashioned palm-thatch cocohuts on this stretch of beachfront but the 11 sturdy thatched huts at Blue Corner are the best in Benaulim. Each one has a veranda, fan and wi-fi. The beachfront restaurant at the front gets rave reviews from guests.

Anthy's Guesthouse GUESTHOUSE $
(☑0832-2771680,9922854566; www.anthysguest housegoa.com; Sernabatim Beach; d with/without AC ₹1900/1600; ❄🛜) One of a handful of places lining Sernabatim Beach, Anthy's is a standout favourite with travellers for its good restaurant, book exchange and well-kept cottage-style garden rooms, which stretch back from the beach, surrounded by a garden. There are also a few comfortable wooden cabins.

Rosario's Inn GUESTHOUSE $
(☑0832-2770636; rosarioinn@ymail.com; r with/without AC ₹900/600; ❄🛜) Across a football field flitting with young players and dragonflies, family-run Rosario's is a large establishment with very clean, simple rooms and a restaurant. Excellent value for long-stayers.

Palm Grove Cottages HOTEL $$
(☑0832-2770059; www.palmgrovegoa.com; Vaswado; d incl breakfast ₹3800-4250; ❄🛜) Old-fashioned, secluded charm and Benaulim's leafiest garden welcomes you at Palm Grove Cottages, a fine midrange choice. The quiet AC rooms, some with balcony, all have a nice feel but the best are the spacious deluxe rooms in a separate Portuguese-style building. The Palm Garden Restaurant here is exceptionally good.

Cafe Malibu INDIAN $
(mains ₹120-200; ⏲8am-11pm) This unpretentious little family-run cafe offers a nice dining experience in its roadside garden setting on a back lane a short walk back from the beach. It does a good job of Goan specialities as well as Indian and continental dishes.

Farm House GOAN $$
(☑9822130430, 0832-2770534; Ascona; mains ₹180-340; ⏲11.30am-3pm & 7.30pm-midnight Tue-Sun; 🛜) Beneath a large palapa-style shelter overlooking a well-stocked fish pond beside the Sal River, the Farm House is renowned locally for its Goan dishes, seafood and steaks. Weekends are enormously popular for live music and the opportunity for a spot of fishing (11am to 3pm). It's off the main road at the southern end of Benaulim village.

Johncy Restaurant MULTICUISINE $$
(Vasvaddo Beach Rd; mains ₹150-450; ⏲7am-midnight) Not so much a shack as a beachfront restaurant, Johncy has been around forever, dispensing standard Goan, Indian and Western favourites – and cold beer – from its location just back from the sand. Live music on weekends.

Pedro's Bar & Restaurant MULTICUISINE $$
(Vasvaddo Beach Rd; mains ₹120-500; ⏲7am-midnight; 🛜) Set amid a large, shady garden at the beachfront car park and popular with local and international travellers, long-running Pedro's offers standard Indian, Chinese and Italian dishes, as well as Goan choices and 'sizzlers'. Regular live music in season.

Goodfellas ITALIAN $$$
(☑9657531631; pizzas & pasta ₹400-650; ⏲6pm-midnight; 🛜) Authentic wood-fired pizza is the standout at this corner bistro where Italians run the kitchen with aplomb. Fresh pasta, lasagne and ravioli also grace the menu with imported cheeses, porcini mushrooms and deli meats. Occasional live music and Sunday lunch.

❶ Getting There & Away

Buses from Margao to Benaulim are frequent (₹15, 20 minutes); some continue on south to Varca and Cavelossim. Buses stop at the Maria Hall crossroads, or at the junctions to Sernabatim or Taj Exotica – just ask to be let off. From Maria Hall an autorickshaw should cost around ₹60 for the five-minute ride to the sea.

If you're staying in Benaulim you'll appreciate having your own transport: look out for 'bike for rent' signs in the village or down at the beach shacks. Rental costs around ₹300 per day.

Agonda
POP 3800

Travellers have been drifting to Agonda for years and seasonal hut villages – some very luxurious – now occupy almost all available beachfront space in season, but it's still more low-key than Palolem and a good choice if you're after some beachy relaxation. The coast road between Betul and Palolem passes through Agonda village, while the main traveller centre is a single lane running parallel to the beach.

Agonda's beach is wide, quiet and picturesque, though the surf can be rough and swimming treacherous. A forestry department–staffed turtle centre at the northern end protects precious olive ridley sea turtle eggs.

The first surf school in Goa's deep south, **Aloha Surf India** (☑8605476576; 1hr/2hr/full day board rental ₹400/700/1500, group/private lesson from ₹1500/2500; ⊙8am-6pm Oct-May) is run by a passionate local crew. Learn to surf on Agonda's gentle 'green' waves or hire a board. Also stand-up paddleboard lessons and surf tours.

🛏 Sleeping

Fatima Guesthouse   GUESTHOUSE $
(☑0832-2647477; www.fatimasguesthouse.com; d ₹1000-1500, with AC ₹1500-2500; ❀🛜) An ever-popular budget guesthouse set back from the beach, with clean rooms, a good restaurant and obliging staff. Rooftop yoga classes in season.

Abba's Gloryland   GUESTHOUSE $
(☑0832-2647822, 9423412795; www.abbasgloryland.com; Agonda Beach Rd; huts ₹1200, r with AC ₹1900; ❀🛜) Back from the beach, Abba's is a decent budget choice with timber cottages at the side and air-con rooms in a separate building, all in a pleasant garden.

★Agonda White Sand   HUT $$
(☑9823548277; www.agondawhitesand.com; Agonda Beach; huts from ₹4600-5200; ❀🛜) Beautifully designed and constructed cottages with open-air bathrooms and spring mattresses surround a central bar and beachfront restaurant. Some have air-con.

H2O Agonda   HUT $$
(☑9921836730; www.h2oagonda.com; Agonda Beach; d incl breakfast from ₹5700-9300; ❀🛜) With its purple and mauve muslin curtains and Arabian nights ambience, H2O is among the most impressive of Agonda's luxury cottage setups. From the hotel-style reception, walk through a leafy garden to the spacious cottages with air-con and enormous open-air bathrooms. The more expensive sea-facing cottages with king-size beds may be worth paying extra for.

🍴 Eating & Drinking

Mandala Cafe   CAFE $
(☑8554091819; Agonda Beach Rd; chai ₹15, dishes ₹100-250; ⊙8am-11pm; 🛜) Feeling like a glass of masala chai or a vegan pancake? Slip into a cushioned alcove at this shanti little travellers' cafe for a down-to-earth antithesis to Agonda's over-the-top beach bars.

Kopi Desa   EUROPEAN $$
(☑7767831487; small plates ₹150-295, mains ₹350-695; ⊙8am-11pm; 🛜) The name translates from Indonesian as 'coffee village' but this al fresco restaurant and cocktail bar has become firmly established for its imaginative Euro-centric menu, tapas-style plates from pork belly bites to crab and lobster tortellini, sourdough pizzas and burgers. Regular live music in season.

La Dolce Vita   ITALIAN $$
(☑90799911; mains ₹250-500; ⊙from 9am-10pm; 🛜) Excellent Italian food is dished out at Dolce Vita, with gingham tablecloths, a long, sprawling blackboard menu, and plenty of passionate yelling and gesturing when the place gets busy. Wood-fired pizzas are authentic.

Zest Cafe   VEGETARIAN $$
(☑8806607919; Agonda Beach Rd; mains ₹190-360; ⊙8am-10pm; 🛜) The Agonda branch of Zest has a lush and loungy garden setting to complement the vegan and vegetarian menu of Mexican or teriyaki bowls, pizza, Balinese tofu and raw-food desserts. Great breakfast spot.

Blue Planet Cafe   VEGETARIAN $$
(☑0832-2647448; mains ₹140-250; ⊙9am-3pm & 6-9.30pm; 🛜) Scrambled tofu and vegan pancakes grace the menu of soul food at mostly vegan Blue Planet, a welcoming detox removed from the beach scene. You'll find salads, smoothies and innovative veg dishes and a bucolic vibe. It's in an off-track jungle location about 2km from Agonda village (follow the signs off the main Agonda–Palolem road).

Riverside Bar & Restaurant   BAR
(☑7517634728; Agonda Beach Rd; ⊙9am-midnight; 🛜) Head on down to the north end of the beach, but on the river side of the road, for a friendly, rustic bamboo-bar hangout with regular live music, open mic nights and fire dances.

❶ Getting There & Away

Scooters and motorbikes can be rented from places on the beach road for around ₹300 to ₹400. Autorickshaws depart from the main T-junction near Agonda's church to Palolem (₹300) and Patnem (₹300). Taxis are around ₹50 more.

Local buses run from Chaudi sporadically throughout the day (₹15), but ask for Agonda Beach, otherwise you'll be let off in the village about 1km away.

Palolem

POP 12,440

Palolem is undoubtedly one of Goa's most postcard-perfect beaches: a gentle curve of palm-fringed sand facing a calm bay. But in season the beachfront is transformed into a toy town of colourful and increasingly sophisticated timber and bamboo huts fronted by palm-thatch restaurants. It's still a great place to be and is popular with backpackers, long-stayers and families. The protected bay is one of the safest swimming spots in Goa and you can comfortably kayak and paddleboard for hours here.

Just around the headland at the southern end of the beach, Colomb Bay – reached by foot or by road – is another little hideaway with several low-key resorts and restaurants.

Away from the beach you can learn to cook, drop in to yoga classes or hire a motorbike and cruise to surrounding beaches, waterfalls and wildlife parks.

🏃 Activities

Palolem offers no shortage of yoga, reiki and meditation classes in season. Locations and teachers change seasonally – ask around locally to see whose hands-on healing powers are hot this season.

Palolem's calm waters are perfect for kayaking and stand-up paddleboarding. Kayaks are available for hire for around ₹200 per hour, paddleboards for ₹500. Mountain bikes (₹150 per day) can be hired from **Seema Bike Hire** (Ourem Rd).

You'll find plenty of local fishers keen to take you out on dolphin-spotting and fishing expeditions on their outrigger boats. They generally charge a minimum ₹2000 for a one-hour trip but bargaining is possible. They also do trips to nearby Butterfly and Honeymoon Beaches, or up to Agonda and Cola Beaches.

★ **Goa Jungle Adventure**　　OUTDOORS
(📱9850485641; www.goajungle.com; trekking & canyoning trips ₹2390-3990; ⊘Oct-May) This adventure company, run by experienced French guide Manu, will take you out for thrilling trekking and canyoning trips in the Netravali area at the base of the Western Ghats, where you can climb, jump and abseil into remote water-filled plunges. Trips, including jungle survival and sea-cliff jumping, run from half-day to several days. Meeting and registration is in Palolem.

Shoes can be rented for ₹200 per day. Call to arrange a meeting with Manu.

★ **Tanshikar Spice Farm**　　FOOD & DRINK
(📱9421184114, 0832-2608358; www.tanshikarspicefarm.com; Netravali; tours incl lunch ₹500; ⊘10am-4pm) Tanshikar Spice Farm is a working, family-run organic spice farm with crops including vanilla, cashews, pepper, nutmeg and chillies, as well as beekeeping. There are no tour buses out here and the amiable young owner Chinmay gives a personalised tour of the plantation and nearby bubble lake. It can also offer cooking classes and guided jungle treks to nearby waterfalls.

If you really want to feel the serenity, book into one of the excellent mud-walled eco-cottages (₹2000) with bamboo sit-outs, a lovely elevated stilt tree house (₹3000) or a room in the Hindu-style house.

Anand Yoga Village　　YOGA
(📱7066454773; www.anandyogavillage.com; off Ourem Rd; drop-in classes ₹400, five-pass ₹1500) An international team of yoga instructors runs three daily drop-in classes in hatha, vinyasa and ashtanga disciplines at this inclusive new yoga village. Week-long yoga holidays (€330 per person) including accommodation in comfy timber cabins, breakfast and lunch and unlimited yoga and meditation. Teacher training courses (200 hours) also available.

Aranya Yoga　　YOGA
(www.aranyayogaashram.com; off Palolem Beach Rd; ₹400; ⊘drop-in classes 8am, 10am & 4pm Sep-Mar) Highly regarded daily drop-in yoga classes in hatha, ashtanga and beginners, as well as five-day intensive courses (₹7500) and teacher training courses.

Rahul's Cooking Class　　COOKING
(📱7875990647; www.rahulcookingclass.com; Palolem Beach Rd; per person ₹1500; ⊘11.30am-2.30pm & 6-9pm) Rahul's is one of the original

Palolem

GOA PALOLEM

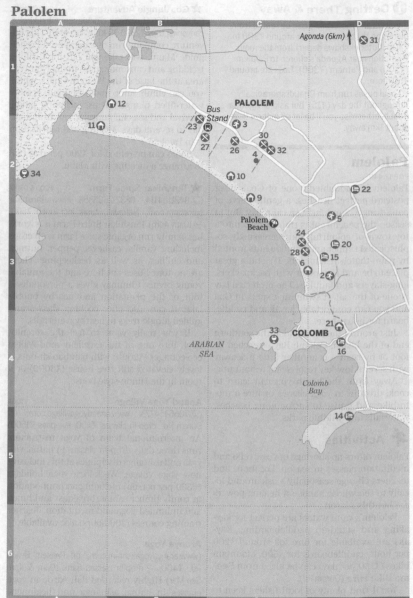

Agonda (6km)

31

PALOLEM

12

11

Bus
Stand

23

3

30

27

26

4

32

10

34

9

Palolem
Beach

22

5

24

28

20

15

6

2

ARABIAN
SEA

33

COLOMB

21

16

Colomb
Bay

14

cooking schools, with three-hour morning and afternoon classes each day. Prepare five dishes including chapati and coconut curry. Minimum two people; book at least one day in advance.

Masala Kitchen COOKING
(☏8390060421; www.aranyayogaashram.com/cooking-classes; Palolem Beach Rd; per person ₹1300) Established cooking classes at Aranya Yoga just off Palolem Beach Rd; book a day in advance. Includes South Indian thalis served on banana leaf and sattvic cooking.

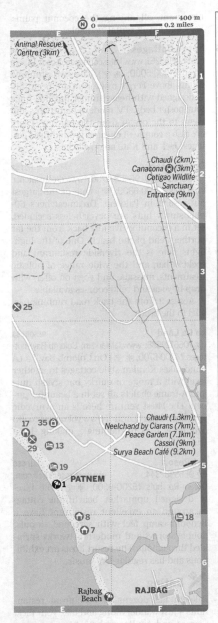

Palolem

◉ Sights
1 Patnem Beach	E5

⊕ Activities, Courses & Tours
2 Anand Yoga Village	D3
3 Aranya Yoga	C2
Humming Bird Spa	(see 10)
Masala Kitchen	(see 3)
4 Rahul's Cooking Class	C2
5 Seema Bike Hire	D3

🛏 Sleeping
6 Art Resort	C3
7 Bamboo Yoga Retreat	E6
8 Bougainvillea Patnem	E6
9 Camp San Francisco	C2
10 Ciarans	C2
11 Cozy Nook	A2
12 Dreamcatcher	B1
13 Home	E5
14 Kala Bahia	D5
15 Kate's Cottages	D3
16 La La Land	D4
17 Micky's	E5
18 Palm Trees Ayurvedic Heritage	F6
19 Papaya's	E5
20 Rainbow Lining	D3
21 Sevas	D4
22 Summer	D2

🍴 Eating
23 Café Inn	B2
Fern's By Kate's	(see 15)
24 German Bakery	C3
Jaali Cafe	(see 35)
25 Karma Cafe & Bakery	E3
26 Little World	C2
27 Magic Italy	B2
28 Ourem 88	C3
29 Salida del Sol	E5
30 Shiv Sai	C2
31 Space Goa	D1
32 Zest Cafe	C2

🍸 Drinking & Nightlife
33 Neptunes	C4
34 Sundowner	A2

🛍 Shopping
35 Jaali	E5

🛏 Sleeping

Most of Palolem's accommodation is of the seasonal beach-hut variety, though there are plenty of old-fashioned guesthouses or family homes with rooms to rent back from the beach.

Rainbow Lining HOSTEL $

(☎8390248102; 76 Ourem Rd; dm ₹450-600, d ₹2500; ❄️📶) This refurbished house is a good deal for backpackers with four- to 10-bed air-con dorms (bunks are curtained off) and a few private rooms. Friendly owners, rooftop yoga and breakfast available. At the time of writing, a new restaurant-bar MOG (Mad Over Goa) was about to open.

Camp San Francisco
HUT $

(☑ 9158057201; www.campsanfrancisco.com; huts & r ₹800-3500) This hut village and associated guesthouse (Casa San Francisco) runs all the way from the beach to Palolem Beach Rd, offering a room or hut to suit most travellers. It's a good deal in mid-season as it has some of the cheaper huts along this stretch of beach. Naturally, there's a restaurant at the front.

Summer
HOSTEL $

(☑ 0832-2643406; www.thehostelcrowd.com/summerhostel; 99/1 Ourem Rd; dm with/without AC ₹550/450, d ₹1500-1900; ☀ 🛜) The latest offering from the Hostel Crowd is minimalist in design but all the facilities are there, with free breakfast, lockers, communal kitchen and lounge, and the popular Bombay Roasters cafe.

Sevas
HUT $

(☑ 9422065437; www.sevaspalolemgoa.com; Colomb Bay; d huts ₹800-1500; 🛜) Hidden in the jungle on the Colomb Bay side of Palolem, Sevas has some of the more basic palm-thatch huts around, reflected in the price. But it's a very peaceful place set in a lovely shaded garden area.

★ Ciarans
HUT $$

(☑ 0832-2643477; www.ciarans.com; huts incl breakfast ₹4200-6300, r with AC ₹5500; ☀ 🛜) 🖋 Ciarans has some of the most impressive huts on the beachfront. Affable owner John has worked hard over two decades to maintain a high standard and his beautifully designed cottages around a plant-filled garden are top-notch. There's a popular multicuisine restaurant with nightly live music, tapas restaurant and quality massage and **spa centre** (1hr massage from ₹1900; ⊙ 9am-8pm).

Eco-credentials are also good here. Ciarans has a sewerage treatment plant, solar hot water and solar lighting. Ciarans also has fine hut resorts at Talpona and Galgibag beaches.

★ Cozy Nook
HUT $$

(☑ 9822584760, 9822382799; www.cozynookgoa.com; huts ₹2500-4000) At the northern end of the beach, long-running Cozy Nook is one of Palolem's originals and still builds well-designed cottages including two-storey bamboo pads with Rajasthani touches, chill-out decks, more pedestrian rooms and a bar and

restaurant, all among the coconut palms. Yoga and kayak rental available.

Kate's Cottages
GUESTHOUSE $$

(☑ 9822165261; www.katescottagesgoa.com; Ourem Rd; d ₹4000-5000; ☀ 🛜) The two stunning rooms above Fern's restaurant are beautifully designed with heavy timber finishes, huge four-poster beds, TV, modern bathrooms and views to the ocean from the balcony. There are also a couple of cheaper ground-floor cottages. Jack and Kate are lovely hosts.

Dreamcatcher
HUT $$

(☑ 9878550550, 9646872700; www.dreamcatcher.in; d huts ₹2500-6800; 🛜) One of the largest hut resorts in Palolem, Dreamcatcher's 60-plus sturdy huts are nevertheless secluded, set in a coconut grove just back from the far northern end of the beach. One of the highlights here is the riverside restaurant and cocktail bar, and the wide range of holistic treatments, massage and yoga on offer, with drop-in yoga and reiki courses available.

Access it from the back road running parallel to the beach.

La La Land
RESORT $$

(☑ 7066129588; www.lalaland.in; Colomb Bay; cottages ₹4200-8700; ☀ 🛜) On Colomb Bay, La La Land takes Keralan-style cottages to another level with a range of quirky but stylish huts and A-frame chalets all set in a beautiful garden. The latest venture here is an ayurvedic spa and Yoga Land (www.yokoyoga.co.uk) *shalas* set back in the jungle, making this a true retreat.

Art Resort
HUT $$$

(☑ 9665982344; www.art-resort-goa.com; Ourem Rd; huts ₹6200-9500; ☀ 🛜) The nicely designed upmarket beachfront cottages around an excellent restaurant have a Bedouin camp feel with screened sit-outs, double storeys and modern artworks sprinkled throughout. The resort hosts art exhibitions and has regular live music.

🍴 Eating

Palolem has dozens of beachfront restaurants – just wander along and take your pick. Ciarans and Art Resort both have good restaurants with regular live music.

Shiv Sai
INDIAN $

(thalis ₹100, mains ₹100-200; ⊙ 9am-11pm) A thoroughly local lunch joint on the parallel beach road, Shiv Sai serves tasty thalis of the veggie, fish and Gujarati kinds, as well as Goan dishes.

★ Magic Italy ITALIAN $$

(☑ 8805767705; 260 Palolem Beach Rd; mains ₹260-500; ☺ 1-11pm; 🖥) On the main beach road, Magic Italy has been around since 1999 and the quality of its pizza and pasta remains high, with imported Italian ingredients like ham, salami, cheese and olive oil, imaginative 13-inch wood-fired pizzas and homemade pasta. Sit at tables, or Arabian-style on floor cushions. The atmosphere is busy but chilled.

German Bakery BAKERY $$

(Ourem Rd; pastries ₹30-80, mains ₹100-300; ☺ 7am-10pm; 🖥) Tasty baked treats are the stars at the established Nepali-run German Bakery, but there is also an excellent range of set breakfasts and yummy stuff like yak-cheese croissants, along with Israeli, Chinese, Italian and Indian options. It's set in a peaceful garden festooned with flags.

Fern's By Kate's GOAN $$

(☑ 9822165261; Ourem Rd; mains ₹250-450; ☺ 8.30am-10.30pm; 🖥) On the road running behind the southern beach entrance, this solid timber family-run place serves up excellent authentic Goan food such as local sausages, fish curry rice and shark *amok tik*, along with a wide range of Indian, continental and sizzler dishes. Pizzas are a new addition – one features Goan sausage.

Little World VEGETARIAN $$

(☑ 9887956810; Palolem Beach Rd; mains ₹200-400; ☺ 8am-11pm; 🖥) Little World is a sweet little vegetarian and vegan cafe with a wholefood philosophy, quirky decor and an inventive menu. Buckwheat pancakes, waffles and scrambled tofu for breakfast, homemade bread and filling salad bowls.

Space Goa CAFE $$

(☑ 7066067642; www.thespacegoa.com; 261 Devabag; mains ₹180-350; ☺ 8.30am-5.30pm; 🖥) On the Agonda road, the Space Goa combines an excellent organic whole-food cafe with a gourmet deli, craft shop and a wellness centre offering meditation, acupuncture and other healing treatments. The food is fresh and delicious and the desserts – such as chocolate-beetroot cake – are divine. Drop-in morning yoga classes are ₹500.

Zest Cafe VEGETARIAN $$

(☑ 8806607919; www.zestgoa.com; Palolem Beach Rd; mains ₹190-360; ☺ 8am-9pm; 🖥 ☑)

Bowls of pad Thai, plates of meze, vegan platters, raw food cakes and soy or almond milkshakes, all freshly prepared, make Zest a popular hang-out among the vegan, health-conscious crowd. There's an almost identical branch in Agonda.

Café Inn CAFE $$

(☑ 7507322799; Palolem Beach Rd; mains ₹100-450; ☺ 8am-11pm; 🖥) If you're craving a strong latte or a rum-infused slushie, Café Inn, which grinds its own blend of coffee beans, is one of Palolem's more popular hang-outs off the beach. Breakfasts are filling, and comfort-food burgers and panini sandwiches hit the spot. Regular live music and party nights.

★ Ourem 88 EUROPEAN $$$

(☑ 8698827679; mains ₹550-800; ☺ 6-10pm Tue-Sun) British-run Ourem 88 is a gastronomic sensation. It has just a handful of tables and a small but masterful menu, with changing specials chalked up on the blackboard. Try baked brie, tender calamari stuffed with Goan sausage, braised lamb shank or fluffy soufflé. English roast dinner on Sunday. Worth a splurge.

🍷 Drinking & Nightlife

Palolem doesn't party like the northern beaches but it's certainly not devoid of nightlife. Some of the beach bars stay open 24 hours in season, there are silent headphone parties at least once a week and other DJ club nights are organised seasonally. Several beach bars such as Ciarans have live music so you'll find someone playing every night of the week in season.

Leopard Valley CLUB

(www.facebook.com/leopardvalley; Palolem-Agonda Rd; entry from ₹600; ☺ 9pm-4am Fri) South Goa's biggest outdoor dance club is a sight (and sound) to behold, with 3D laser light shows, pyrotechnics and state-of-the-art sound systems blasting local and international DJs on Friday nights. It's in an isolated but easily reached (by taxi) location between Palolem and Agonda. Check the Facebook page to see what's on.

Neptunes CLUB

(www.facebook.com/neptunesgoa; Neptune Point, Colomb Bay; ₹800; ☺ 9pm-4am Sat Nov-Apr) On a rocky headland just south of Palolem Beach, this was Palolem's only remaining silent disco at the time of writing. Don your

GALGIBAG & TALPONA

Galgibag and Talpona form another of South Goa's beach gems – a broad stretch of barely touched sand framed by the Talpona River in the north and the Galgibag River to the south, all backed by swaying pines and palms. The only disruption to this peace is the construction of the new highway bypass, though it's far enough back from the beach to be ignored. Near the southern end, 'Turtle Beach' is where rare, long-lived olive ridley sea turtles come to nest on the beach between November and March. This is a protected area: a Forest Department information hut here should be staffed during nesting season. Food and accommodation options include:

Neelchand by Ciarans (☑ 7796783663, 0832-2632082; www.neelchand.com; cottages ₹4000; ❄ 🛜) Absolute beachfront location on near-deserted Talpona Beach. Just seven lovely timber cottages in a sweet little garden.

Peace Garden (☑ 9168350727; www.peacegardengoa.com; huts ₹2100-4800; 🛜) Well-constructed hut village on Talpona Beach with a focus on yoga, wellness and relaxation.

Cassoi (☑ 7796456453; www.cassoibyciarans.com; huts & tents ₹3000-5000; ❄ 🛜) Woven into the palms on peaceful Galgibag Beach, this hut village has something for everyone.

Surya Beach Café (☑ 9923155396; Galgibag Beach; mains ₹200-350; ◷ 9am-10pm) Specialises in fresh oysters, clams, mussels and crabs caught from the Galgibag River.

headphones and tune into three DJ channels. No entry unless you're dancing.

Sundowner BAR
(www.sundowner-palolem.com; ◷ 9am-midnight; 🛜) At the far northern end of the beach, across the narrow estuary (easy to cross at low tide), Sundowner is indeed a cool place to watch the sunset. The seasonal bar is nicely isolated with views across the rocks to forested (and inaccessible) Canacona (Monkey) Island. Also serves pizzas and has a few cottages.

🛈 Getting There & Away

Frequent buses run to nearby Chaudi (₹8) from the **bus stand** (Palolem Beach Rd) on the corner of the road down to the beach. Hourly buses to Margao (₹40, one hour) depart from the same place, though these usually go via Chaudi anyway. From Chaudi you can pick up regular buses to Margao, from where you can change for Panaji, or south to Polem Beach and Karwar in Karnataka.

The closest train station is Canacona, 2km from Palolem's beach entrance.

An autorickshaw from Palolem to Patnem should cost ₹100, or ₹150 to Chaudi. A taxi to Dabolim Airport is around ₹2500, or ₹2000 to Margao.

Patnem

Smaller and less crowded than neighbouring Palolem, pretty Patnem makes a much quieter and more family-friendly alternative. The waters aren't as calm and protected as at Palolem, but Patnem Beach is patrolled by lifeguards and it's safe for paddling.

The beach is, naturally, lined with shack restaurants and beach-hut operations in season but it has an altogether relaxed vibe where lazing on the sand or sipping a cocktail is the order of the day. It's easy enough to walk around the northern headland to Colomb Bay and on to Palolem.

🛏 Sleeping & Eating

Patnem has a fairly consistent range of a dozen or so seasonal beach huts and a few hotels back from the beach. Long-stayers will revel in Patnem's choice of village homes and apartments available for rent from ₹15,000 to ₹50,000 per month.

Micky's HUT $$
(☑ 9850484884; www.mickyhuts.com; d ₹1500-2000; 🛜) Micky's is an old-timer at the north end of Patnem Beach with a range of simple budget huts and rooms. It's run by a friendly family and open most of the year. There's a cruisey beachfront bar and cafe in the palms.

Kala Bahia   GUESTHOUSE **$$**
(☑9764863073; www.kalabahia.com; r ₹3100-
4300; ⊙restaurant 8am-10pm Mon-Sat, to 4pm
Sun; ☎) At the northern end of Patnem
Beach (reached by road via Colomb), Kala
Bahia is a sweet guesthouse, veg restaurant
and something of an event centre, with
yoga, music and movie nights. Cocktails and
sunset views looking back down on Patnem
Beach are fabulous. Rooms are secure and
comfortable and there are a few cabins.

Papaya's   COTTAGE **$$**
(☑9923079447; www.papayasgoa.com; huts
₹2000-3000, cottages with AC ₹4500; ✹☎) Solid huts constructed with natural materials
head back into the palm grove from Papaya's
popular restaurant. These are easily some
of the best cabins and rooms on Patnem
Beach: each hut is lovingly built, with lots
of wood, four-poster beds and floating muslin, while the one and two-bedroom air-con
brick cottages are fitted out like apartments.

Palm Trees
Ayurvedic Heritage   RESORT **$$**
(☑9673178731; www.thepalmtreesayurvedagoa.
com; huts ₹5300-6800; ☎) This ayurvedic resort
has an exquisite riverside location in a thick
palm grove at the southern end of Patnem
village (access from Patnem–Rajbag road).

Home   GUESTHOUSE **$$**
(☑9923944670; www.homebeachresort.com;
r ₹2000-3500; ⊙8am-10pm; ☎) Home is a
lovely family-owned guesthouse-style resort
with a popular beachfront restaurant serving awesome dessert – chocolate brownies,
apple tarts and cheesecake. No beach huts
here but eight neatly decorated, light-filled
rooms behind the restaurant and some larger family rooms around the garden at the
street entrance. Minimum two-night stay.

Bougainvillea Patnem   HUT **$$**
(☑9822189913; www.bougainvilleapatnem.com;
huts ₹2000-3500; ☎) Simple but clean and
good value rooms behind the restaurant as
well as the few premium sea-facing huts at
the front. Yoga retreats and drop-in classes
and ayurvedic treatments available.

Bamboo Yoga Retreat   HUT **$$$**
(☑9637567730; www.bamboo-yoga-retreat.com;
cottages per person €82-92; ☎) This laid-back

yoga retreat, exclusive to guests, has a wonderful open-sided *shala* facing the ocean
at the southern end of Patnem Beach, and
three more *shalas* among the village of
beautifully designed timber and thatched
huts. Yoga holiday rates include brunch,
meditation and two daily yoga classes, but
there are also training courses and ayurvedic treatments.

★**Karma Cafe & Bakery**   CAFE **$**
(☑9764504253; Patnem Rd, Colomb; baked goods
from ₹60, mains ₹120-230; ⊙6.30am-9.30pm;
☎) Pull up a cushion at this chilled cafe and
bakery opposite the Colomb road and delve
into a superb range of freshly baked breads,
croissants and pastries as well as coffee and
smoothies. Delve further for *momos*, Nepali
thalis and even Vietnamese rice paper rolls.

★**Jaali Cafe**   CAFE **$$**
(☑8007712248; small plates ₹180-220; ⊙9am-
6pm Tue, to 11pm Wed-Sun) The menu at this
lovely garden cafe is something special
with a delicious range of tapas-style Middle
Eastern and Mediterranean plates – choose
two or three dishes each and share. Sunday
brunch is a stellar event popular with local
expats. There's also an excellent **boutique**
(☑8007712248;   ⊙9.30am-6.30pm Nov-Apr)
and a highly regarded massage therapist on
hand.

Salida del Sol   MULTICUISINE **$$**
(☑7507404102; www.salida-patnembeach.com;
mains ₹180-390; ⊙8am-11pm; ☎) Patnem's
beachfront restaurants all have their own
qualities and followings and Salida del Sol
works on many fronts, from the friendly
and attentive staff to fresh food and Arabian Nights atmosphere. A standouts are the
momos and Nepali set meals but of course
there's Indian and Western food including
pizza and pasta. Nice huts in the garden at
the back, too.

❶ Getting There & Away

The main entrance to Patnem Beach is reached
from the country lane running south from
Palolem, then turning right at the Hotel Sea
View. Alternatively, walk about 20 minutes along
the path from Palolem via Colomb Bay, or catch
a bus heading south (₹5). An autorickshaw
charges around ₹80 from Palolem.

GOA PATNEM

Ancient & Historic Sites

South India has a remarkable assortment of monuments and ruins testifying to the splendour of the many varied cultures that have paraded and battled it out across its broad canvas. From serene places of worship to remnants of grandiose empires, the opportunities to marvel at the genius of long-gone civilisations are manifold here. Temples all over the region are awash with colourful South Indian life, while wondrous hilltop forts, opulent palaces and serene tombs recall the lofty aspirations of long-gone leaders.

Contents

➤ **Palaces & Tombs**
➤ **Hindu Sacred Sites**
➤ **Forts**
➤ **Buddhist, Hindu & Jain Caves**

Above Mysuru Palace (p188), Mysuru (Mysore), Karnataka

Qutb Shahi Tombs (p235), Hyderabad, Telangana

Palaces & Tombs

The rulers of South India's bygone kingdoms and sultanates not only proclaimed their pomp by building impossibly splendid palaces, but many of them were also buried in opulent tombs – some of which rank among the region's most exquisite architecture.

Southern Palaces

First prize among South India's flamboyant royal residences goes to fabulous Mysuru Palace (p188), but Mysuru's (Mysore's) rival princely state of Hyderabad puts up a stern challenge with the shimmering, chandelier-laden Chowmahalla Palace (p231) and the hilltop Falaknuma Palace (p238), a splendiferous neoclassical construction now reincarnated as an ultraluxurious Taj-group hotel. In deepest south Tamil Nadu, teaktastic Padmanabhapuram Palace (p267) is India's finest surviving example of traditional Keralan architecture.

Vijapura's Tombs

Vijapura (Bijapur) ruled one of the five Deccan sultanates that dominated the plateau lands in the 16th and 17th centuries. Its delicately graceful Ibrahim Rouza (p224) is believed to have inspired the Taj Mahal with its minarets; it was built by a sultan as a mausoleum for his wife. Vijapura's massive Golgumbaz (p224), another royal mausoleum, has what is said to be the world's second-largest dome (with incredible acoustics).

Qutb Shahi Tombs

The final resting place of the builders of spectacular Golconda Fort and their kin, the magnificent domed Qutb Shahi Tombs (p235) stand within sight of the fort on the edge of Hyderabad, and have been jointly nominated for World Heritage status. The domes are mounted on cubical bases with beautiful colonnades and delicate stucco ornamentation.

Hindu Sacred Sites

South India is home to some of the most spectacular devotional architecture in this Hindu-majority country: soaring *gopurams* (gateway towers), exquisite *mandapas* (pavilions) and some of the world's most intricately chiselled deity sculptures.

Madurai

Madurai's Meenakshi Amman Temple (p385), abode of the triple-breasted goddess Meenakshi, is considered the pinnacle of classic South Indian temple architecture. This Tamil temple, with its 12 sky-reaching *gopurams,* predominantly dates from the 17th century, but its origins reach back 2000 years to when Madurai, one of India's most ancient cities, was a Pandyan capital.

Hampi

Now a sleepy Karnataka hamlet, from 1336 to 1565 Hampi was the thriving centre of the mighty Vijayanagar empire. Its World Heritage–listed ruins are strewn amid boulders of all shapes and sizes, the result of hundreds of millions of years of volcanic activity and erosion. Especially fine examples of temple art can be seen at the 15th-century, still-active Virupaksha Temple (p214) and the 16th-century Vittala Temple (p214).

Thanjavur

The multitiered *vimana* (tower) soaring above the Brihadishwara Temple (p379) in Tamil Nadu's Thanjavur (Tanjore) is the ultimate expression of the power and creativity of the medieval Chola dynasty.

1. Meenakshi Amman Temple (p389), Madurai, Tamil Nadu **2.** Virupaksha Temple (p214), Hampi, Karnataka **3.** Shore Temple (p355), Mamallapuram (Mahabalipuram), Tamil Nadu

This 11th-century honey-coloured granite temple, still very much a living place of worship, is adorned with glorious graceful sculptures of Hindu deities and elaborately carved *gopurams*.

Mamallapuram

The exquisite sculptures dotted around the seaside Tamil Nadu town of Mamallapuram (Mahabalipuram) were carved by artisans of the Pallava dynasty in the 7th and 8th centuries. They range from the beautifully sculpted free-standing Shore Temple (p355) to the Five Rathas (p355) – temples carved from the living rock, including several wonderful animal figures – and the giant Arjuna's Penance (p355) relief carving, exploding with episodes of Hindu myth.

ART DECO & VICTORIAN GOTHIC ARCHITECTURE

Beyond the Bollywood glitz and urban frenzy, Mumbai is famous for hosting the world's second-largest collection of art deco buildings (after Miami), which rubs shoulders with some superb 19th-century, British-built Victorian Gothic architecture. In mid-2018 the Victorian Gothic and Art Deco Ensembles of Mumbai were inscribed on Unesco's World Heritage list. Seek out especially the High Court (p59), University of Mumbai (p50), Rajabai Clock Tower (p50), Chhatrapati Shivaji Maharaj Terminus (p49) and Marine Drive (p50).

Forts

Battleground of many a rival empire in centuries gone by, South India is dotted with fantastical forts that have survived the vagaries of time – many of them sprawled across strategic hilltops and wrapped within sturdy walls protecting a treasure trove of monuments.

Golconda Fort

Hyderabad's 16th-century Qutb Shahs transformed Golconda Fort (p234), on a 120m-high granite hill, into a fortified city with two rings of ramparts, one 11km in circumference. Mughal ruler Aurangzeb had to resort to bribing a defending general to conquer the fort in 1687, after a fruitless year-long siege. Golconda is a feast of crenellated walls, cannon-mounted bastions, Deccan views, and imposing gates studded with iron spikes to repel raiding war elephants.

Daulatabad Fort

The central bastion of Maharashtra's crumbling Daulatabad Fort (p92) is reached by an hour's climb via spiked gates, multiple doorways and a pitch-black spiralling tunnel. Eccentric Delhi sultan Mohammed Tughlaq marched Delhi's entire population 1100km here in 1328 to make Daulatabad his capital. His dream was swiftly cut short, however, when Daulatabad proved strategically unviable as a capital.

1. Golconda Fort (p234), Hyderabad, Telangana 2. Bidar Fort (p227), Karnataka 3. Gingee Fort (p363), Tamil Nadu

Bidar Fort

South India's now-neglected largest fort, Bidar (p227), was once the bustling capital of much of the region. Although mostly in a state of deteriorating disrepair, this Karnataka fortress still retains noteworthy remnants of its glory days, including the Rangin Mahal (Painted Palace) and Solah Khamba Mosque (Sixteen-Pillared Mosque).

Janjira

The brooding fortress of Janjira (p101) looms sheer out of the sea 500m off the Konkan Coast. Built in the 16th century by descendants of African slaves, Janjira was never conquered by enemies. Only nature, finally, is succeeding in reclaiming the now-abandoned fort.

Gingee Fort

An arresting example of South Indian fort architecture, Tamil Nadu's abandoned Gingee Fort (p363) encompasses three hilltop citadels within a 6km perimeter of sheer cliffs and chunky walls. It was built mostly by the Vijayanagars in the 16th century, before being taken over by the Marathas, Mughals, French and British.

1. Kailasa Temple (p93), Ellora Caves, Maharashtra 2. Ajanta Caves (p95), Maharashtra 3. Ajanta Caves (p95), Maharashtra

Buddhist, Hindu & Jain Caves

Maharashtra's World Heritage–listed caves of Ajanta and Ellora, within 150km of each other, are stunning galleries of ancient cave art replete with historical sculptures, rock-cut shrines and natural-dye paintings. These are just the most glorious of the many cave or rock-cut shrines recalling the time before South India started building freestanding stone structures.

Ajanta

The 30 Buddhist caves of Ajanta (p95), with origins in the 2nd century BC, are clustered along a horseshoe-shaped gorge above the Waghore River. One of their most renowned features is the natural-dye tempera paintings (similar to frescoes) decorating many of the caves' interiors. Some of these murals are even coloured with crushed semiprecious stones such as lapis lazuli from Afghanistan. Don't miss Cave 1 (p96), with particularly superb artwork including a wonderful rendition of Buddhism's Bodhisattva Padmapani, or Cave 16 (p97), whose especially fine paintings include the famous 'dying' (actually fainting) princess.

Ellora

The Ellora Cave Temples (p92) – a collection of Hindu, Jain and Buddhist shrines constructed between AD 600 and 1000 – flank a 2km-long escarpment. There are 34 in all: 17 Hindu, 12 Buddhist and five Jain. Most famed is the Hindu Shiva-dedicated Kailasa Temple (p93), the world's biggest monolithic sculpture, which was skilfully carved into the cliff face by thousands of labourers over more than 150 years.

Guntupalli

One of more than 100 ancient Buddhist sites in rural Andhra Pradesh, the 2nd-century-BC monastery at Guntupalli (p252) sits high on a hilltop gazing out on forest and rice fields. Monks' dwellings line the cliffside, with lovely arched stone facades sculpted to look like wood.

Karnataka

POP 68.3 MILLION

Includes ➡

Bengaluru
(Bangalore).........172
Mysuru (Mysore) 187
Nagarhole
National Park 200
Karnataka Coast.... 206
Mangaluru
(Mangalore)........ 206
Gokarna........... 209
Hampi.............213
Hosapete (Hospet) ..221
Hubballi (Hubli) 221
Vijapura (Bijapur)... 224

Best Places to Eat

➡ Karavalli (p181)

➡ Mavalli Tiffin Rooms (p179)

➡ Girimanja's (p207)

➡ SodaBottleOpenerWala (p181)

➡ Raintree (p202)

Best Places to Stay

➡ Dhole's Den (p200)

➡ Electric Cats B&B (p178)

➡ Uramma Cottage (p220)

➡ Heritage Resort (p223)

➡ Waterwoods Lodge (p200)

Why Go?

A stunning introduction to southern India, Karnataka is a prosperous, compelling state loaded with a winning blend of urban cool, glittering palaces, national parks, ancient ruins, beaches, yoga centres and legendary travellers' hang-outs.

At its nerve centre is the capital, Bengaluru (Bangalore), a progressive cybercity famous for its craft-beer and restaurant scene. Heading out of town you'll encounter the evergreen rolling hills of Kodagu, dotted with spice and coffee plantations, the regal splendour of Mysuru (Mysore), and jungles teeming with monkeys, tigers and Asia's biggest population of elephants.

If that all sounds too mainstream, head to the counter-cultural enclave of tranquil Hampi, with hammocks, psychedelic sunsets and boulder-strewn ruins. Or the blissful, virtually untouched coastline around Gokarna, blessed with beautiful coves and empty sands.

When to Go
Bengaluru

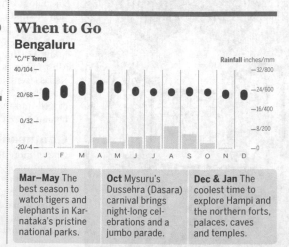

Mar–May The best season to watch tigers and elephants in Karnataka's pristine national parks.

Oct Mysuru's Dussehra (Dasara) carnival brings night-long celebrations and a jumbo parade.

Dec & Jan The coolest time to explore Hampi and the northern forts, palaces, caves and temples.

Karnataka Highlights

1 **Hampi** (p213) Soaking up the surreal landscapes, sociable travellers' scene and epic ruins in this magical destination.

2 **Mysuru** (Mysore; p187) Touring this civilised city's remarkable palace, then exploring its famous bazaar district.

3 **Gokarna** (p209) Searching for the perfect beach cove in a low-key coastal hideaway, then touring its atmospheric temples.

4 **Bengaluru** (Bangalore; p172) Sampling craft beers or sipping coffee, and enjoying the museums and sights of Karnataka's most cosmopolitan city.

5 **Badami** (p221) Exploring stunning cave temples, rich in sculpture and carvings, that overlook a lovely lake.

6 **Kodagu Region** (p201) Hiking lonely trails past spice plantations in these temperate, evergreen highlands.

7 **Nagarhole National Park** (p200) Spying on lazy tuskers in the forests bordering serene Kabini Lake.

8 **Vijapura** (Bijapur; p224) Strolling the peaceful, manicured grounds of exquisite 16th-century Islamic monuments.

History

A playing field of religions, cultures and kingdoms, the Karnataka region has had a string of charismatic rulers. India's first great emperor, Chandragupta Maurya, made the Karnataka area his retreat when he embraced Jainism at Sravanabelagola in the 3rd century BC. From the 6th to the 14th centuries the land was under a series of dynasties, such as the Chalukyas, Cholas, Gangas and Hoysalas, who left a lasting mark in the form of stunning cave shrines and temples across the state.

In 1327 Mohammed Tughlaq's army sacked Halebid. In 1347 Hasan Gangu, a Persian general in Tughlaq's army, led a rebellion to establish the Bahmani kingdom, which was later subdivided into five Deccan sultanates. Meanwhile, the Hindu kingdom of Vijayanagar, with its capital in Hampi, rose to prominence. Having peaked in the early 1550s, it fell in 1565 to a combined effort of the sultanates.

In subsequent years the Hindu Wodeyars of Mysuru grew in stature and extended their rule over a large part of southern India. They remained largely unchallenged until 1761, when Hyder Ali (one of their generals) deposed them. Backed by the French, Hyder Ali and his son Tipu Sultan set up capital in Srirangapatna and consolidated their rule. However, in 1799 the British defeated Tipu Sultan and reinstated the Wodeyars. Historically, this battle consolidated British territorial expansion in southern India.

Mysuru remained under the Wodeyars until Independence – post-1947, the reigning maharaja became the first governor. The state boundaries were redrawn along linguistic lines in 1956 and the extended Kannada-speaking state of Mysore was born. It was renamed Karnataka in 1972, with Bangalore (now Bengaluru) as the capital.

BENGALURU (BANGALORE)

🖉 080 / POP 11.7 MILLION / ELEV 920M

Cosmopolitan Bengaluru (formerly Bangalore) is one of India's most progressive and developed cities, blessed with a benevolent climate, a modern metro system, and a burgeoning drinking, dining and shopping scene. Its creature comforts are a godsend to the weary traveller who has done the hard yards, and it's a great city for mixing with locals in craft-beer joints or quirky independent cafes. Though there are no world-class sights, you'll find lovely parks and striking Victorian-era architecture.

The past decade or so has seen a mad surge of development, coupled with traffic

---

TOP STATE FESTIVALS

Udupi Paryaya (⊘ Jan/Feb) Held in even-numbered years, with a procession and ritual marking the handover of swamis at Udupi's Krishna Temple.

Classical Dance Festival (⊘ Jan/Feb) Some of India's best classical-dance performances take place in Pattadakal.

Vijaya Utsav (p216) A three-day extravaganza of culture, heritage and the arts in Hampi.

Tibetan New Year (⊘ Jan/Feb) Lamas in Tibetan refugee settlements in Bylakuppe take shifts leading nonstop prayers that span the week-long celebrations.

Vairamudi Festival (⊘ Mar/Apr) At Melkote's Cheluvanarayana Temple, Lord Vishnu is adorned with jewels, including a diamond-studded crown belonging to Mysuru's former maharajas, in a festival attracting 400,000 pilgrims.

Bengaluru Poetry Festival (p178) Draws a roster of international and local poets and writers.

Ganesh Chaturthi (⊘ Sep) Families march their Ganesh idols to the sea in Gokarna at sunset.

Dussehra (p193) Mysuru Palace is lit up in the evenings and a vibrant procession hits town, to the delight of thousands.

Lakshadeepotsava (⊘ Nov) Thousands and thousands of lamps light up the Jain pilgrimage town of Dharmasthala, offering spectacular photo ops.

Huthri (Nov/Dec) The Kodava community in Madikeri celebrates the start of the harvesting season with ceremony, music, traditional dances and much feasting for a week.

congestion and rising pollution levels. But the central district (dating back to the British Raj years) remains little changed, and the landmark corporate headquarters and business parks of the city's booming IT industry are mostly in the outer suburbs.

History

Literally meaning 'Town of Boiled Beans', Bengaluru supposedly derived its name from an ancient incident involving an old village woman who served cooked pulses to a lost and hungry Hoysala king. Kempegowda, a feudal lord, was the first person to mark out Bengaluru's extents, by building a mud fort in 1537. The town remained obscure until 1759, when it was gifted to Hyder Ali by the Mysuru maharaja. The British arrived in 1809 and made the city their regional administrative base in 1831, renaming it Bangalore. During the Raj era the city played host to many a British officer, including Winston Churchill, who enjoyed life here during his greener years and famously left a debt (still on the books) of ₹13 at the Bangalore Club.

Now home to countless software, electronics and business-outsourcing firms, Bengaluru's knack for technology developed early. In 1905 it was the first Indian city to have electric street lighting. Since the 1940s it has been home to Hindustan Aeronautics Ltd (HAL), India's largest aerospace company. The city's name was changed back to Bengaluru in November 2006, though few use it in practice.

⦿ Sights

★ National Gallery of Modern Art GALLERY

(NGMA; ☑ 080-22342338; www.ngmaindia.gov.in/ngma_bangaluru.asp; 49 Palace Rd; Indian/foreigner ₹20/500; ⊙ 11am-6.30pm Tue-Sun) Housed in a century-old mansion – the former vacation home of the raja of Mysuru – this world-class art museum showcases an impressive permanent collection (and exhibitions). The Old Wing exhibits works from pre-Independence, including paintings by Raja Ravi Varma and Abanindranath Tagore. Connected by a pedestrian bridge, the sleek New Wing focuses on contemporary post-Independence works by artists including Sudhir Patwardhan and Vivan Sundaram. Guided walks (11.30am Wednesday, 3pm Saturday) are a great way to learn about the museum's highlights.

There's a great art-reference library, a cafe and a museum shop here, too.

★ Cubbon Park GARDENS

(www.horticulture.kar.nic.in/cubbon.htm; Kasturba Rd; Ⓜ Cubbon Park) In the heart of Bengaluru's business district is Cubbon Park, a well-maintained 120-hectare garden where Bengaluru's residents converge to steal a moment from the rat race that rages outside. The gardens encompass the red-painted Gothic-style State Central Library. Unfortunately, Cubbon is not completely closed to traffic, except on Sundays, when there are concerts, fun runs, yoga and even a small farmers market.

Other wonderful colonial-era architecture around the park includes the colossal neo-Dravidian-style Vidhana Soudha (Dr Ambedkar Rd; Ⓜ Vidhana Soudha), built in 1954, which serves as the legislative chambers of the state government, and neoclassical Attara Kacheri, built in 1864 and housing the High Court. The latter two are closed to the public.

Opera House HISTORIC BUILDING

(☑ 9513899866; 57 Brigade Rd; ⊙ 11am-10pm; Ⓜ MG Rd) FREE Recently restored to its former glory thanks to the financial might of Samsung, the British-era Opera House has been transformed into a temple of tech, complete with virtual-reality experiences and gleaming displays of smartphones and notebooks. Commendably, the original structure has been sensitively renovated, its beautiful interior combining twin colonnades, an elegant curved balcony and a stage framed by classical columns. There's a cafe, and you can book the home-theatre zone to watch a film.

HAL Aerospace Museum & Heritage Centre MUSEUM

(www.hal-india.com; Airport-Varthur Rd; admission ₹50, mobile/camera/video ₹20/50/75; ⊙ 9am-5pm Tue-Sun) For a peek into India's aeronautical history, visit this wonderful museum past the old airport, where you can see some of the indigenous aircraft models designed by HAL. Interesting exhibits include a MIG-21, home-grown models such as the Marut and Kiran, and a vintage Canberra bomber.

Karnataka Chitrakala Parishath GALLERY

(www.karnatakachitrakalaparishath.com; Kumarakrupa Rd; ₹50; ⊙ 10am-5.30pm Mon-Sat; Ⓜ Mantri Sq Sampige Rd) A superb gallery with a wide range of Indian and international contemporary art, as well as permanent displays of Mysuru-style paintings and folk and tribal pieces from across Asia. A section is devoted to the works of Russian master Nicholas Roerich, known for his vivid paintings of the Himalaya. The Pan Indian Panorama

Bengaluru (Bangalore)

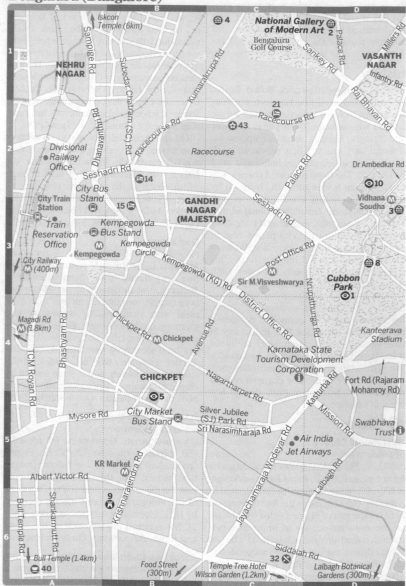

collection includes progressive art from SG Vasudev and Yusuf Arakkal.

Krishnarajendra Market
MARKET

(City Market; Silver Jubilee Park Rd; ⊘6am-10pm; MChickpet) For a taste of traditional urban India, dive into the bustling, gritty Krishnarajendra Market and the dense grid of streets that surround it. Weave your way around the lively, colourful stalls, past fresh produce, piles of vibrant dyes, spices and copper ware. The vibrant flower market is a highlight.

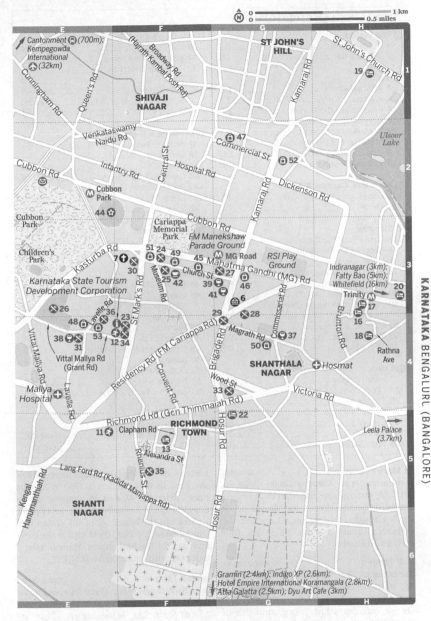

1 km
0.5 miles

ST JOHN'S HILL

Cantonment (700m); Kempegowda International (32km)

SHIVAJI NAGAR

Ulsoor Lake

Cubbon Park

Cubbon Park

Children's Park

Karnataka State Tourism Development Corporation

Cariappa Memorial Park

FM Manekshaw Parade Ground

MG Road

RSI Play Ground

Indiranagar (3km); Fatty Bao (5km); Whitefield (16km)

Trinity

SHANTHALA NAGAR

Hosmat

Rathna Ave

Mallya Hospital

Vittal Mallya Rd (Grant Rd)

RICHMOND TOWN

Leela Palace (3.7km)

SHANTI NAGAR

Gramin (2.4km); Indigo XP (2.6km); Hotel Empire International Koramangala (2.8km); Atta Galatta (2.9km); Dyu Art Cafe (3km)

KARNATAKA BENGALURU (BANGALORE)

Wonderla
AMUSEMENT PARK

(☏ 080-22010333; www.wonderla.com; Mysuru-Bengaluru Rd; adult/child Mon-Fri ₹908/725, Sat & Sun ₹1168/932; ⊙ 11am-6pm Mon-Fri, to 7pm Sat & Sun) Adrenaline seekers should look no further than this huge amusement park, which has more than 60 well-maintained rides, a wave pool, water slides and a 'rain disco'. It's just off the Mysuru–Bengaluru highway, 28km from the centre of Bengaluru, and connected by BMTC buses.

Bengaluru (Bangalore)

◎ **Top Sights**
1 Cubbon Park.................................D3
2 National Gallery of Modern Art.............D1

◎ **Sights**
3 Attara Kacheri...........................D3
4 Karnataka Chitrakala Parishath............C1
5 Krishnarajendra Market.....................B5
6 Opera House..............................G3
7 St Mark's Cathedral.......................F3
8 State Central Library......................D3
9 Tipu Sultan's Palace......................B6
10 Vidhana Soudha.........................D2

🟢 **Activities, Courses & Tours**
11 Body Raaga Wellness Spa....................E5
12 Meraki..................................F4

🛏 **Sleeping**
13 Casa Piccola Cottage.......................F5
14 Hotel ABM International....................B2
15 Hotel Adora.............................B3
16 Hotel Ajantha...........................H3
17 JüSTa MG Road..........................H3
18 Laika Boutique Stay......................H4
19 Lemon Tree Premier Ulsoor
   Lake..................................H1
20 Oberoi.................................H3
21 Taj West End...........................C2
22 Tom's Hotel............................G5

✖ **Eating**
23 Anna Kuteera...........................F4
24 Church Street Social.......................F3
25 Empire.................................F3
26 Fava...................................E3
27 Funjabi................................G3
28 Karavalli...............................G3
29 Khan Saheb............................G4

30 Koshy's Bar & Restaurant....................F3
31 Lady Baga..............................E4
32 Mavalli Tiffin Rooms......................C6
33 Olive Bar & Kitchen.......................G4
34 Open Box...............................F4
35 Plan B Loaded...........................F5
   SodaBottleOpenerWala................(see 31)
36 Sunny's................................E4

🟢 **Drinking & Nightlife**
37 Arbor Brewing Company....................G4
38 Biere Club.............................E4
39 blueFROG..............................G3
40 Brahmin's Coffee Bar.......................A6
41 Pecos Classic...........................G3
   Shiro................................(see 26)
42 Tata Cha...............................F3

🟢 **Entertainment**
43 Bangalore Turf Club.......................C2
44 M Chinnaswamy Stadium..................E2

🟢 **Shopping**
45 Blossom Book House......................F3
46 Cauvery Arts & Crafts
   Emporium..............................G3
   Fabindia.............................(see 50)
47 Fabindia...............................G2
48 Forest Essentials........................E4
49 Gangarams Book Bureau...................F3
50 Garuda Mall............................G4
51 Goobe's Book Republic....................F3
52 Mysore Saree Udyog......................G2
53 San-Cha Tea Boutique.....................E4

🟢 **Information**
Government of India
   Tourist Office.........................(see 49)
Skyway..............................(see 12)

St Mark's Cathedral   CATHEDRAL
(www.saintmarks.in; Mahatma Gandhi (MG) Rd; Ⓜ MG Rd) Atmospheric cathedral built in 1812 with a distinctive domed roof based on St Paul's Cathedral in London. Check out the entrance's ornate carvings. There are four services on Sunday.

Bull Temple   HINDU TEMPLE
(Basavanagudi; Bull Temple Rd,; ⊙ 7am-8.30pm; 🐾; Ⓜ National College) Built by Kempegowda in the 16th-century Dravidian style, the Bull Temple contains a huge stone monolith of Nandi (Shiva's bull), which is always embellished with lavish flower garlands. This is one of Bengaluru's most atmospheric temples, set in a small park and accessed via a shady path.

Lalbagh Botanical Gardens   GARDENS
(www.horticulture.kar.nic.in/lalbagh.htm; Lalbagh Rd; ₹20; ⊙ 6am-7pm; Ⓜ Lalbagh) Spread over 98 hectares of landscaped terrain, these expansive gardens were laid out in 1760 by famous ruler Hyder Ali. As well as amazing centuries-old trees, it has a diverse species of plant – check out the bonsai, giant silk-cotton tree and Japanese gardens. Try to visit in the early morning for the bird chorus. You can take a tour here with Bangalore Walks (p177).

Iskcon Temple   HINDU TEMPLE
(www.iskconbangalore.org; Chord Rd, Hare Krishna Hill; ⊙ 7.15am-1pm & 4.15-8.20pm Mon-Fri, 7.15am-8.30pm Sat & Sun; Ⓜ Mahalakshmi) Built by the Hare Krishnas, this impressive hilltop temple, inaugurated in 1997, is lavishly decorated in a mix of ultra-contemporary and traditional styles. There are many food stalls here, so bring an appetite, and concerts and lectures are regularly held. It's around 8km northwest of the centre of town.

Tipu Sultan's Palace PALACE
(Albert Victor Rd; Indian/foreigner ₹25/300, video ₹25; ⊙8.30am-5.30pm) The elegant Indo-Islamic summer residence of ruler Tipu Sultan is notable for its teak pillars and ornamental frescos.

🏃 Activities

Meraki SPA
(☑7619613118; www.merakispa.in; 8 Papanna St; 1hr massage from ₹3000; ⊙11.30am-9.30pm) Upmarket spa and wellness centre offering fine massages and treatments, body scrubs and reflexology. During happy hour (11.30am to 1.30pm) a full-body massage is a reasonable ₹2500. It's off St Marks Rd. Also has a **branch** (777,100 Feet Rd; ⊙11am-10pm) in Indiranagar.

Bangalore Mountaineering Club TREKKING
(☑7406319666; www.bmcadventures.com; 778 9th A Main Rd, Indiranagar; 3-day treks from ₹5666; ⊙10am-6pm Mon-Thu & Sat, to 10pm Fri; Ⓜ Indiranagar) Organises guided treks throughout southern India, including to Pushpagiri in the Western Ghats of Karnataka, and the hills of Kodagu. Trips to Himachal Pradesh (from ₹8900) and the Himalayas are also offered.

Equilibrium CLIMBING
(☑8861684444; http://equilibriumclimbing.com; 3rd fl, 546 Chinmaya Mission Hospital Rd, Indiranagar; day pass ₹399; ⊙6.30am-10pm Mon-Fri, 8am-10pm Sat & Sun; Ⓜ Indiranagar) A premier climbing centre offering excellent facilities, and instruction including lead climbing and speed climbing. Also arranges weekend and multiday climbing excursions to Badami and Hampi.

Soukya YOGA
(☑080-28017000; www.soukya.com; Soukya Rd, Samethanahalli, Whitefield; per day incl treatments, meals & accommodation from ₹10,500; ⊙6am-8.30pm) Very upmarket, internationally renowned retreat on a picture-perfect 12-hectare organic farm running programs in ayurvedic therapy and yoga, as well as medical and therapeutic skin treatments.

Body Raaga Wellness Spa SPA
(☑7829995050; www.bodyraaga.com; 93 Richmond Rd; 45min massage from ₹1250) Centrally located spa with professional masseurs and therapists; rates are moderate. Try a deep-tissue massage, which is perfect if you've just endured a long journey. Also has a branch in **Indiranagar** (☑080-50002828; www.bodyraaga.com; 1096 12th A Main Rd, Indirangar; 45min massage from ₹1250).

Total Yoga Oneness Centre YOGA
(☑9740980200; http://total-yoga.org; 872/A 80 Feet Rd, Indiranagar; ⊙7am-9pm Mon-Sat; Ⓜ Indiranagar) A large, professional studio offering vinyasa flow, classic hatha and power yoga. Classes include 15 minutes of pranayama and meditation.

Ayurvedagram AYURVEDA
(☑080-65651090; www.ayurvedagram.com; Hemmandanhalli, Whitefield; day packages from ₹4000) Set over 3 hectares of tranquil gardens, with heritage homes transplanted from Kerala, this retreat has tailored ayurvedic treatments, yoga and rejuvenation programs. It's in the outer suburb of Whitefield, around 25km from central Bengaluru.

🧭 Tours

⭐Unhurried Tours WALKING
(☑919880565446; www.unhurried.in; half-day tours ₹2500) Led by Poornima Dasharathi, an author and history enthusiast, these excellent walking tours explore backstreets, temples, street life and local cuisine. Tour duration is two to three hours. Monthly 'open walks' (you join others), cycling and walking tours, and trips to Mysuru are also offered.

⭐Bangalore Walks WALKING
(☑9845523660; www.bangalorewalks.com; walks ₹600-900; ⊙7-10am Sat & Sun) Runs highly recommended tours, including guided walks through Cubbon Park, a medieval old-city history walk and a 19th-century Victorian walk. Most walks include a delicious breakfast. Customised tours are also possible.

Bus Tours BUS
(https://kstdc.co; city day tour ₹485) The government's tourism department runs city bus tours that are worth considering (though they do cover a lot of places in a short space of time).

Day trips around Bengaluru are also offered, including a daily departure to Srirangapatna and Mysuru (₹950) that takes in several temples, palaces and gardens.

KARNATAKA BENGALURU (BANGALORE)

SLEEPING PRICE RANGES

The following price ranges are for a double room with bathroom and include tax within the state:

$ less than ₹1750
$$ ₹1750–₹5000
$$$ more than ₹5000

★✿ Festivals & Events

Bengaluru Poetry Festival LITERATURE
(☏080-41600677; www.facebook.com/bengaluru
poetryfestival; ⊙early Aug) This annual poetry
festival features local and international writers and musicians. In 2018 it was held over
two days at the Leela Palace hotel (p179).

🛏 Sleeping

Decent budget rooms are in short supply.
Most hostels are not centrally located, but
you'll find a stack of dive lodges on Subedar
Chatram (SC) Rd, east of the bus stands and
around the train station.

★ Electric Cats B&B HOSTEL $
(☏080-41104143; www.facebook.com/electric
catshostel; 1794 6th Cross Rd; ⊙dm ₹500-600;
❀ᐧ; Ⓜ Indiranagar) Well-organised, sociable
Electric Cats, close to the buzzing Indiranagar area, has good dorms (including one
female-only dorm) with a shared bathroom.
All beds have quality linen, private reading
lamps and charging facilities. Drinking water and wi-fi are free, there's no curfew, and
staff members are very switched on to travellers' needs, even organising Christmas dinners, pub crawls, barbecues and (free) yoga.

Cuckoo Hostel HOSTEL $
(☏7204156880; www.facebook.com/cuckoohostel;
561 17th A Main Rd, Koramangala; dm/s ₹399/1100;
❀@ᐧ) Run by and attracting a creative
crowd, the Cuckoo has regular craft, art and
music sessions and occasional debates about
the environment and global issues. There are
bicycles for hire, laundry facilities and clean,
well-presented dorms. It's about 6km southwest of the centre.

Hotel Adora HOTEL $$
(☏080-22200024; www.facebook.com/hoteladora;
47 Subedar Chatram Rd; s/d ₹650/890, with AC
₹1150/1780; ❀ᐧ; Ⓜ Kempegowda) A seven-
story budget option (there's a lift) with
decent, if functional, rooms near the train
station and Kempegowda bus stand. Staff
members are friendly and helpful, and there's
a good veg restaurant on the ground floor.

★ Casa Piccola Cottage HERITAGE HOTEL $$
(☏080-22990337; www.casacottage.com; 2
Clapham Rd; r incl breakfast from ₹4500; ❀ᐧ)
Tastefully renovated, Casa Piccola has a personalised brand of hospitality that has gar-
nered it a solid reputation. Its atmospheric
rooms, with tiled floors and traditional
bedspreads, offer a tranquil sanctuary. The

garden features papaya and avocado trees.
Book via the website for the best rates.

Laika Boutique Stay B&B $$
(☏9482806630; www.laikabangalore.in; Rathna
Rd; r from ₹4235; ❀ᐧ; Ⓜ Trinity) Hidden down
a leafy side street, this welcoming guest-
house is a wonderful choice for those seek-
ing a more local experience combined with
style and comfort. Extra touches, including
thoughtful service and home-cooked break-
fasts, make it a great choice.

JüSTa MG Road BOUTIQUE HOTEL $$
(☏080-41135555; www.justahotels.com/mg-
road-bangalore; 21/14 Craig Park Layout, MG Rd; r/
ste incl breakfast ₹3810/5120; ❀ᐧ; Ⓜ Trinity)
This intimate, arty hotel has slick and spacious rooms with Japanese-inspired motifs
throughout. It's very well located, with a
metro station and shopping malls close by.
The helpful, professional staff members are
eager to please.

Tom's Hotel HOTEL $$
(☏080-25575875; http://tomshotelbangalore.
com; 1/5 Hosur Rd; s/d incl breakfast with fan
₹2300/2500, with AC ₹2480/2610; ❀ᐧ❋) An
excellent place with high cleanliness stand-
ards and bright, cheerful rooms, Tom's al-
lows you to stay in a central location – it's a
15-minute walk from Mahatma Gandhi (MG)
Rd – and has a friendly staff and free wi-fi.
There's a fine Mangaluru restaurant here,
too, serving well-priced seafood dishes.

Purple Cloud Hotel HOTEL $$
(☏080-48091100; www.purplecloudhotels.com;
Down Town Park 2, Sadahalli Gate; r from ₹3850;
❀ᐧ) A smart hotel that's well worth considering as an affordable base handy for Kempegowda airport (15km away). Rooms are
modern and contemporary, and the in-house
Fiery Indian Kitchen is recommended for
North and South Indian food.

Hotel ABM International HOTEL $$
(☏080-41742030; www.hotelabminternational.
com; 232 Subedar Chatram Rd; r with fan from
₹1650, with AC ₹1900-2650; ❀ᐧ; Ⓜ Kempegow-
da) This well-run modern hotel, near Anand
Rao Circle, has neat, simple, well-presented
accommodation, room service and fast wi-fi.
There's a popular juice bar and restaurant
downstairs, and it's walking distance from
the Kempegowda Bus Stand and metro.

Temple Tree Hotel Wilson Garden HOTEL $$
(☏080-46622000; http://templetreehotel.com;
9th Cross Rd, Mavalli; r ₹3860-4600; ❀ᐧ) A short

stroll from Lalbagh Botanical Gardens (p176), this hip hotel has sleek bathrooms and modish design touches. Garden-view rooms have great balconies, and the rooftop restaurant is superb for breakfast.

Mass Residency
GUESTHOUSE $$

(☑ 9945091735; massresidency@yahoo.com; 18 2nd Main Rd, 11th Cross, JP Nagar; r incl breakfast with fan/AC ₹1600/2000; ✿ ☎) Run by very hospitable brothers (who are world travellers themselves), this guesthouse has comfortable-enough rooms and a great roof terrace ideal for socialising. It's in a relatively quiet location, 8km south of the centre.

Hotel Empire International Koramangala
HOTEL $$

(☑ 080-40222777; www.hotelempire.in; 103 Industrial Area, Koramangala; s/d ₹2160/2620; ✿ @ ☎) Located in the trendy Koramangala area, this hotel is a good choice for party people as the area's thick with bars and restaurants. Rooms are decent value, though bathrooms are small, and there's room service from the good in-house restaurant.

Hotel Ajantha
HOTEL $$

(☑ 080-25584321; www.hotelajantha.com; 22A MG Rd; s/d incl breakfast with fan ₹1450/1950, with AC from ₹2370; ✿ ☎; Ⓜ Trinity) Dependable, affordable budget favourite Ajantha is very close to Trinity metro station and has decent, well-maintained rooms with cable TV. There's a well-regarded restaurant in the compound and the complimentary breakfast is generous.

★ Oberoi
HOTEL $$$

(☑ 080-41358222; www.oberoihotels.com; 39 MG Rd; s/d from ₹12,900/13,800; ✿ @ ☎ ⊠; Ⓜ Trinity) The uber-opulent Oberoi is set in lush gardens around an enchanting 120-year-old tree, yet its central location could not be more convenient. It mixes colonial-era ambience with modern touches like tablet-controlled in-room devices and TVs in the bathrooms. Rooms all have balconies with garden views, and the spa and restaurants are superb.

★ Taj West End
HERITAGE HOTEL $$$

(☑ 080-66605660; www.tajhotels.com; Racecourse Rd; s/d incl breakfast from ₹13,400/14,500; ✿ ☎ ⊠) Expect superb service at this very fine hotel, spread over 8 hectares of stunning tropical gardens. The West End dates to 1887, when it was established as a base for British officers, and it still oozes colonial-era class.

Some of the city's best dining options lie within, include the Blue Ginger (Vietnamese cuisine) and the Masala Klub (Indian).

Lemon Tree Premier Ulsoor Lake
HOTEL $$$

(☑ 080-44802000; www.lemontreehotels.com; 2/1 St Johns Rd; s/d incl breakfast ₹6340/6620; ✿ ☎ ⊠) This well-run hotel is 2km north of MG Rd, so it's close to the city's main shopping and entertainment district. Rooms are equipped with all mod cons, and there's an elegant restaurant where guests can tuck into a lavish breakfast buffet.

Leela Palace
HOTEL $$$

(☑ 080-25211234; www.theleela.com; 23 HAL Airport Rd; s/d from ₹12,700/13,600; ✿ @ ☎ ⊠) Swanky Leela isn't actually a palace (it was built in 2003), but in terms of comfort it's fit for royalty, and golfers (it's next to a course). Gleaming marble, lush carpets, regal balconies and period features are done superbly, as are its beautiful gardens, restaurants, bars and boutiques. Located within the Leela Galleria complex, 5km east of MG Rd.

✕ Eating

Bengaluru's adventurous food scene includes high-end dining, gastropubs and cheap local favourites. Key areas in the centre are around MG Rd and neighbouring Lavelle Rd, while the more distant districts of Indiranagar and Koramangala also have a wide choice of restaurants and cafes.

★ Food Street
STREET FOOD $

(Dev Sagar; Sajjan Rao Circle, VV Puram; meals from ₹100; ⊙ from 5.30pm) For a local eating experience, head to VV Puram, aka Food Street, with its strip of hole-in-the-wall eateries cooking up classic street-food dishes from across India. It's quite a spectacle, with rotis being handmade and spun in the air and *bhajia* (vegetable fritters) dunked into hot oil before packed crowds.

★ Mavalli Tiffin Rooms
SOUTH INDIAN $

(MTR; ☑ 080-22220022; www.mavallitiffinrooms.com; 14 Lalbagh Rd, Mavalli; snacks from ₹52, meals from ₹90; ⊙ 6.30-11am & 12.30-9pm Tue-Sun) A legendary name in South Indian comfort food, this eatery has had Bengaluru eating out of its hand since 1924. Head to the dining room upstairs, queue for a table, and then enjoy as waiters bring you delicious *idli* (fermented rice cakes) and dosa (savoury crepes), capped by frothing filter coffee served in silverware.

Samosa Party INDIAN $
(www.samosaparty.co.in; 11 10th Main Rd, Indiranagar; samosas ₹25-70; ☺8am-9pm) This inexpensive samosa hotspot is perfect for a quick bite on the southwestern side of the Indiranagar area. There's a wide range of trad (and twisted) samosas – mac and cheese, anyone? Wash it all down with a delicious *adrak* (ginger) chai.

Khan Saheb INDIAN $
(www.khansaheb.co; 9A Block, Brigade Rd; rolls from ₹50; ☺noon-11.30pm; Ⓜ MG Rd) Famous for its terrific rolls (wholewheat chapatis), filled with anything from charcoal-grilled meats and tandoori prawns to paneer and sweet-corn tikka.

Gramin INDIAN $
(☎080-41104104; 20, 7th Block, Raheja Arcade, Koramangala; mains ₹136-180; ☺noon-3.30pm & 7-11pm Mon-Thu, to 11pm Fri-Sun) Gramin offers an affordable, wide choice of flavourful, rural, all-veg North Indian fare in cosy surrounds. Try the excellent range of lentils and curries with oven-fresh rotis, accompanied by sweet rose-flavoured lassi served in a copper vessel. The lunchtime thali (₹155) is always a good bet and includes two veg dishes, roti and some dhal (curry made from pulses).

Funjabi NORTH INDIAN $
(6A Church St; mains ₹95-250; ☺11am-11pm) Accessed via a side alley and a dingy rear staircase, this simple place doesn't have a great location or much atmosphere, but the tasty North Indian *dhaba* (roadside) style grub is satisfyingly rich and authentic. Try the tandoori roti and a butter murg (rich chicken curry) or *malai kofta* (creamy curry with paneer cheese).

Anna Kuteera SOUTH INDIAN $$
(14 St Marks Rd; snacks from ₹35, mains ₹160-220) For a quick bite that's easy on the pocket, join the throngs at this pure-veg eatery; it's very busy indeed at lunchtimes, when there's usually standing room only. Snacks include flavoursome *ravi dosa* (crispy semolina crepes) and good *idli* (spongy, round, fermented rice cakes) and *vada* (doughnut-shaped, deep-fried lentil savouries). North Indian and Chinese dishes are also on the menu.

Smoor Chocolates Signature Lounge CAFE $$
(www.smoorchocolates.com; 1131, 100 Feet Rd; snacks & mains ₹190-625; ☺8am-11pm Sun-Thu, to 1am Fri & Sat; 🛜) The city's finest *chocolaterie* has a lovely, air-conditioned and spacious interior where you can indulge in exquisite gateaux and cakes, and of course a chocolate or two. Also offers good breakfasts, wraps, sandwiches, burgers, tea and espresso coffee.

SlimSins Cafe INTERNATIONAL $$
(☎9535582766; www.facebook.com/slimsins; 34/1 36th Cross Rd, 4th Block, Jayanagar; mains ₹190-450; ☺11am-9.30pm Mon-Sat, 9am-9.45pm Sun; Ⓜ Rashtreeya Vidyalaya Rd) SlimSins lives up to its name, with an interesting menu of sinful-looking food actually made with wholesome ingredients. The open kitchen offers a peek into the culinary action: *ragi* (millet) buns being prepped for burgers, ketogenic-diet favourites like eggplant parmesan, and sweet-potato fries with fresh, healthy dips. It's the perfect place to binge after a workout.

Chinita Real Mexican Food MEXICAN $$
(www.chinita.in; 218 Double Rd, Indiranagar II Stage, Hoysala Nagar; mains ₹275-325; ☺12.30am-3.30pm & 7.30-11pm; Ⓜ Indiranagar) For authentic Mexican flavours in South India, look no further. The tempting menu features tasty tostadas (crispy tortillas with toppings), braised-pork burritos, and chicken or tofu smeared with a fine *mole* (rich, spicy very Mexican sauce). *Olé!* No tequila, mescal (or even cerveza), though.

Lady Baga GOAN $$
(☎080-49652751; www.facebook.com/ladybagablr; 24/5 Lavelle Rd; mains from ₹200; ☺noon-midnight Mon-Thu, to 1am Fri-Sun; 🛜) Hot out of the oven, Lady Baga brings its seafood specialities, Goan delicacies and chilled-out vibe to Bengaluru. The food is divine (try the mud crab in garlic sauce) and the retro hippie branding ('Baga' is a nod to a beach in Goa). Right on, maaan.

Koshy's Bar & Restaurant INDIAN $$
(39 St Mark's Rd; mains ₹95-400; ☺9am-11.30pm; Ⓜ MG Rd) This decidedly old-school resto-pub is an institution for the city's chattering classes: here you can put away tasty North Indian dishes in between mugs of beer and fervent discussions. The decor is all creaky ceiling fans, dusty wooden shuttered windows and lashings of nostalgia. Between lunch and dinner it's 'short eats' only (British-style snacks like baked beans on toast).

Enerjuvate Studio & Café INTERNATIONAL $$
(www.facebook.com/enerjuvatestudio; 82 7th Main Rd, 4th B Block, Koramangala; mains ₹190-450; ☺11.30am-10pm Mon-Fri, 8.30am-10pm Sat & Sun; 🛜) How do you appeal to Bengaluru's young

and hip? Healthy food plus a healthy dose of fast wi-fi is the winning formula at Enerju-vate. The bright dining spaces, partly alfresco, are ideal to work in, with a constant supply of juices and light eats such as millet and red-rice dosa (thin lentil-flour pancakes; ₹180) and great platters (₹150 to ₹350).

Tippler – On the Roof RUSSIAN $$
(276, 100 Feet Rd, HAL 2nd Stage, Indiranagar; mains from ₹165; ⊙noon-12.30am; 🕙) Thinking of a big night out? Now there's more than just vodka in Bengaluru. Tippler dishes up a full menu of Russian-inspired food and drinks. Order the platter and you can gorge on Sibe-rian fried potatoes and pickled cabbage with a beaker of rocket-fuel-strong vodka to share. On 'Molotov Mondays' there are all kinds of bar and food specials.

Carrots VEGAN $$
(☑080-41172812; www.carrots-india.com; 607, 80 Feet Rd, 6th Block, Koramangala; dishes & mains ₹150-375; ⊙noon-3.30pm & 7-10.30pm Mon, 11am-4pm & 7-10.30pm Wed-Fri, 11.30am-11pm Sat & Sun; 🕙) This 100% vegan restaurant offers or-ganic, gluten-free, largely sugar-free dishes cooked with minimal oil. Savour the veg en-chiladas (₹220), lentil pancakes (₹150), Thai peanut salad and desserts such as vegan ice cream. The premises are light and spacious, with rattan seating and a relaxed vibe.

Empire NORTH INDIAN $$
(www.facebook.com/hotelempire; 36 Church St; mains ₹120-250; ⊙11am-11pm; Ⓜ MG Rd) Empire is all about authentic, inexpensive tandoori and meat dishes in unpretentious surrounds (plastic banquette seating and fake wood); try the butter chicken, the kebabs or a mut-ton biryani. It's busy day and night, and its street-side kitchen dishes out tasty *shawar-ma* (spit-roasted kebabs) to time-pushed peeps on the go. There are numerous other branches around the city.

★ SodaBottleOpenerWala INDIAN $$$
(☑7022255299; www.sodabottleopenerwala.in; 25/4 Lavelle Rd; snacks from ₹55, meals ₹300-500; ⊙8.30am-midnight; 🕙) This terrific new place, with its brilliant comfort-food menu of Per-sian soups and Parsi specials like *salli boti* (mutton served with matchstick potatoes), is a kooky spin on a Bombay Irani cafe. The de-cor is semi-wacky, with mismatched seating, clashing colours and quirky ornaments. Defi-nitely order a rich, creamy and foamy Phateli coffee or Irani chai to finish your meal.

★ Sly Granny INTERNATIONAL $$$
(☑080-48536712; www.facebook.com/slygranny; 618 12th Main Rd, Indiranagar; mains from ₹369; ⊙noon-11.30pm Mon-Thu, to 1am Fri, 9am-1am Sat, 9am-11.30pm Sun; 🕙) Sly Granny is a fresh breath of flavours, serving up Europe-an-meets-Asian cuisine. Tables are on two levels, with a formal restaurant zone and a more casual roof terrace. Try the udon noo-dles, quinoa salad, walnut tart and massa-man curry, and stay for the live gigs.

★ Fatty Bao ASIAN $$$
(☑080-44114499; www.facebook.com/thefatty-bao; 610 12th Main Rd, Indiranagar; mains ₹380-650; ⊙noon-3pm & 7-10.30pm Sun-Thu, to 11.30pm Fri & Sat; 🕙; Ⓜ Indiranagar) This hip rooftop restau-rant serves up Asian hawker food to a crowd of fashionable young foodies in a vibrant setting with colourful chairs and wooden bench tables. There's sushi, dim sum, Thai curries and Malaysian street food, as well as Asian-inspired cocktails such as lemongrass mojitos. Presentation of both food and drink is superb.

★ Karavalli SEAFOOD $$$
(☑080-66604545; Gateway Hotel, 66 Residency Rd; mains ₹525-1575; ⊙12.30-3pm & 6.30-11.30pm; Ⓜ MG Rd) Superior seafood restaurant with a wonderfully atmospheric interior that takes in a traditional thatched roof, vintage wood-work and beaten brassware – though the garden seating is equally appealing. Choose from fiery Mangalorean fish dishes, prawns cooked with coriander and saffron (₹1100) or crab Milagu in a pepper masala (₹1575). Meat and veg dishes are also available.

★ Olive Bar & Kitchen MEDITERRANEAN $$$
(☑080-41128400; www.olivebarandkitchen.com; 16 Wood St, Ashoknagar; mains ₹525-795; ⊙noon-3.30pm & 7-11pm; 🕙) A whitewashed villa straight from the coast of Santorini, Olive Beach has a menu that evokes wistful mem-ories of sunny Mediterranean getaways. Things change seasonally, but expect Thes-saloniki salad, prawns *pil pil* (with garlic and hot peppers) and plenty of veg choices. Round things off with a dessert (all ₹390) like hazelnut chocolate cake or *tres leches* (sponge cake soaked in milk and cream).

Church Street Social GASTROPUB $$$
(http://socialoffline.in; 46/1 Church St; mains ₹195-700; ⊙9am-1am; 🕙; Ⓜ MG Rd) This warehouse-style bar-resto, drawing a cool urban crowd, serves cocktails in beakers and

KARNATAKA BENGALURU (BANGALORE)

offers napkins toilet-paper style (on a roll). The menu takes in fine breakfasts, meze platters, ghee roast chicken (₹500) and tikka tacos (₹250).

Fava
MEDITERRANEAN $$$

(www.fava.in; UB City, 24 Vittal Mallya Rd; mains ₹325-850; ⊙11am-11pm; �; MCubbon Park) Dine alfresco on Fava's canopy-covered decking, feasting on large plates of delectable dishes like Middle Eastern meze, minced-lamb kebabs or black-sesame deep-sea tiger prawns. There's a good happy hour (5pm to 8pm) when cocktails are discounted, too.

Ciclo Cafe
CAFE $$$

(12th Main Rd, Indiranagar; mains ₹250-550; ⊙11am-midnight Mon-Thu, to 1pm Fri, 7.30am-1am Sat & Sun; �) This cycle shop and cafe offers a great pit stop in the throbbing Indiranagar area. With food, alcohol, vintage cycles to ogle, and cycle parts and accessories to buy, Ciclo's quite a venue for a meal: try the kaffir-lime chicken tikka (₹350) or Goa pork sausage (₹450).

Siam Trading Company
THAI $$$

(☑7619415931; www.facebook.com/siambangalore; 1079 12th Main Rd, HAL 2nd Stage, Indiranagar; mains ₹258-438; ⊙noon-1am Wed-Sat, to 11pm Sun-Tue) An extension of the popular One Night in Bangkok pub, pub-like Siam Trading Company has deliberately dingy lighting but fresh and excellent Thai food. The chicken with young peppercorns and basil takes you to the streets of the Thai capital with the first bite.

Open Box
INTERNATIONAL $$$

(☑080-41290055; www.facebook.com/theopen boxblr; 4th fl, Halcyon Complex, St Mark's Rd; mains ₹250-425; ⊙noon-11.30pm Sun-Thu, to 1am Fri & Sat; �) For a place to unwind, good food and unlimited-drinks deals, look no further than Open Box. (The special that includes three hours of unlimited sangria and beer is particularly popular.) A lot of effort has been put into the menu, which is full of puns and cheesy tag lines.

Plan B Loaded
GASTROPUB $$$

(https://holycowhospitality.com; 13 Rhenius St, Richmond Town; mains ₹275-475; ⊙noon-1am; �",) Industrial-chic gastropub that's great for Indian-style pub-grub classics like Coorg pork, really meaty burgers and spinach-and-corn bake, as well as all-day breakfasts. Pitchers of beer are ₹345.

Sunny's
ITALIAN $$$

(☑080-41329366; 50 Lavelle Rd; mains ₹350-750; ⊙12.30-11.30pm; �",) A fixture on Bengaluru's restaurant scene, classy Sunny's has a lovely terrace for alfresco dining. On the menu you'll find authentic thin-crust pizza, Greek salad, homemade pasta, imported cheese and some of the best desserts in the city.

Drinking & Nightlife

Bengaluru's rock-steady reputation and wide choice of chic watering holes make it the place to indulge in a spirited session of pub-hopping in what is the original Indian beer town. Many microbreweries produce quality ales; all serve food, too.

The trendiest nightclubs typically charge a cover of around ₹1000 per couple, often it's redeemable against drinks or food.

★Third Wave Coffee Roasters
CAFE

(https://thirdwavecoffee.in; 984, 80 Feet Rd, Koramangala; ⊙9am-11pm; �",) A mecca for hardcore java heads, this temple to the arabica bean has a multitude of gourmet-coffee combos, including espresso classics, quirky cold brews like coffee colada (with coconut water and the sweetener jaggery) and seasonal specials. Coffee culture is a serious business here. The Third Wave scene is young freelancers on Macbooks, polished-concrete floors and acoustic tunes on the stereo.

★Brahmin's Coffee Bar
CAFE, SOUTH INDIAN

(Ranga Rao Rd, Basavanagudi; snacks ₹16-22; ⊙6am-noon & 3-7pm Mon-Sat; MNational College) This terrific *darshini* (South Indian cafe) is famous for its filter coffee (₹16). There are only four food items on the menu: *idli* (fermented rice cakes), *vada* (deep-fried lentil savouries), *khara bath* (semolina and cashew snack) and *kesari bath* (sweet made with ghee). It makes a good pit stop between the centre of town and the Bull Temple.

Tata Cha
TEAHOUSE

(www.tatacha.com; 2985 12th Main Rd, HAL 2nd Stage, Indiranagar; ⊙10am-11pm; �",) Classic and new flavours of tea, along with tasty food combos like butter chicken and *khichdi* (pureed lentils), make Tata Cha a big hit with Bengaluru tea-lovers. Great energy and atmosphere make this place better than more expensive options close by. There are other branches in the city, including one on **Church St**. (www.tatacha.com; 28 Church St; ⊙10am-11pm; �", ; MMG Rd)

COFFEE CULTURE

Tea may be the national drink, and Bengaluru is considered the birthplace of India's craft-brewing revolution, but the city also has the nation's most ingrained coffee culture. Arabica and robusta beans have been cultivated in Karnataka's evergreen hills for centuries and filter coffee consumed in Bengaluru *darshini* (South Indian cafes) for decades. In the best of these traditional places, like Brahmin's Coffee Bar customers often eat and drink breakfast standing up, munching on *idli* (South Indian spongy, round, fermented rice cakes) and *vada* (South Indian doughnut-shaped, deep-fried lentil savouries) and slugging filter coffee from glass or stainless-steel beakers.

In 1996 the city was the site of India's very first Café Coffee Day (on Brigade Rd), the founding stone of an espresso empire that now numbers more than 1500 branches across the subcontinent and beyond – though its HQ remains in Bengaluru.

In recent years young guns like Third Wave Coffee Roasters have introduced a fresh (even boffinish) approach to coffee making by offering syphon, chemex and cold-brew coffee to the city. Want the richest, most luxurious coffee in town? Head to SodaBottleOpenerWala (p181) and order a Phateli coffee.

blueFROG
CLUB

(http://bengalurubluefrog.club; 3 Church St; ⊙noon-11.30pm Sun-Thu, to 1am Fri & Sat; M MG Rd) Upmarket club and live-music venue that draws a hip, lively crowd with its fine roster of house, techno and trance DJs, and bands (everything from jazz to hip hop). Entrance is free to ₹500 depending on the night.

Atta Galatta
CAFE

(☑080-41600677; www.attagalatta.com; 134 KHB Colony, 5th Block, Koramangala; ⊙11am-8.30pm; 🛜) This fine cafe and bakery offers good sandwiches on nutritious bread, cookies and snacks (₹40 to ₹80), and doubles as a bookshop and art venue, hosting readings and performances.

Straight Up Pub
PUB

(www.straightuppub.com; 37 Hennur Bagalur Rd, Kuvempu Layout, Kothanur; ⊙11.30am-1am; 🛜) This octopus-themed pub (yes, you read that right) offers a fun, freewheeling night out, with Jocose Juleps (a cocktail of Bourbon and crème de menthe) on the menu and plenty of octopus-related quotes and trivia. Tree trunks for stools and suspended tables add to the vibe. The pub hosts a Ladies Night on Wednesday, live bands on Saturday and DJs.

Barebones
BAR

(www.barebonesbar.com; 303 Ashok Terrace, 100 Feet Rd, Indiranagar; ⊙11.30-1am; 🛜; M Indiranagar) Sometimes value for money trumps swanky ambience. Barebones lies in the belly of the nightlife area of Bengaluru and the cafe-like interior is a great place to drink and dine. There's plenty on the menu for veg and non-veg folks, but regulars swear by the ghee roast, a much-loved Bengaluru classic.

Bartin's Restobar
BAR

(1211 Milestone, 100 Feet Rd, Indiranagar; ⊙11-1am) Nothing beats the combination of spicy Andhra chilli chicken, cold beer and Bengaluru's evening breezes at this rooftop bar in the buzzy Indiranagar district. Weekends are all about notching up the volume and getting people on their feet.

What's in a Name?
BAR

(☑9591941003; www.facebook.com/whatsina nameblr; 146 5th Block, Koramangala; ⊙11am-1am; 🛜) Located above 1st Cross Rd, and adding to the clutch of bars that are tilting the balance of nightlife towards Koramangala, this is a great place to relax. The cocktails don't burn a hole in the pocket and there's good food, from pub-grub combos to specials such as the 'All Day and Night Breakfast'.

Dyu Art Cafe
CAFE

(www.dyuartcafe.yolasite.com; 23 MIG, KHB Colony, Koramangala; ⊙10am-10.30pm Tue-Sun, noon-10.30pm Mon; 🛜) Popular cafe-gallery in a leafy neighbourhood with a peaceful courtyard reminiscent of a Zen temple. It has coffee beans from Kerala and does good French press, espresso and iced coffee, along with breakfasts (₹120 to ₹320), homemade cakes, sandwiches and mains.

Pecos Classic
BAR

(www.pecospub.com; Rest House Rd; ⊙10.30am-11.30pm; M MG Rd) A kind of non-corporate, locally owned Hard Rock Cafe that's all about classic rock – Hendrix, Grateful Dead and Frank Zappa posters adorn the walls – though it also mixes in some jazz, blues and reggae from time to time. Beer costs from ₹105 a glass, or ₹525 a pitcher.

KARNATAKA BENGALURU (BANGALORE)

Shiro   BAR

(www.facebook.com/experienceshiro; UB City, 24 Vittal Mallya Rd; 12.30pm-midnight Sun-Thu, to 1am Fri & Sat;) Shiro is a hip lounge bar with elegant interiors complemented by monumental Buddha busts and *apsara* (celestial nymph) figurines. There's also outdoor deck seating. Has good Japanese and Southeast Asian food, and its 'Special Shiro' cocktails are the bomb.

Microbreweries

⭐**Biere Club**   PUB

(www.facebook.com/thebiereclub; 20/2 Vittal Mallya Rd; 11am-11pm Sun-Thu, to midnight Fri & Sat;) There's a continual buzz about this multistorey temple to craft beer, which always has a guest beer or two on the blackboard. You'll find plenty on the menu (platters, burgers) to nibble while you sup.

Prost   MICROBREWERY

(www.prost.in; 811 5th Cross Rd, Koramangala; noon-11.30pm Sun-Thu, to 1am Fri & Sat;) Prost has eclectic industrial decor, a rooftop with several quality craft beers on tap and a tempting food menu. There's live magic on Wednesday, comedy on Thursday, and weekend evenings go off with house DJs and dancing.

Brewsky   MICROBREWERY

(4th & 5th fl, Goenka Chambers, 19th Main Rd, JP Nagar; noon-12.30am;) With sweeping city views from its fine roof terrace, a mezzanine zone and a funky restaurant with vintage decor, Brewsky is a fine night out. It brews six beers on site, including a golden ale, a wheat beer and a stout. Tasty 'small bites' and substantial sharing platters are good value.

Barleyz   MICROBREWERY

(www.barleyz.com; 80 Feet Rd, Koramangala; 11am-11.30pm Sun-Thu, to 1am Fri & Sat;) A suave rooftop beer garden with potted plants, artificial grass and tables with built-in BBQ grills. Offers free tastings of its six beers, as well as rotating seasonal brews. There's also excellent wood-fired pizza, Indian snacks and Western food. Happy hour is 5pm to 7pm daily.

Vapour   BAR

(www.vapour.in; 773, 100 Feet Rd, Indiranagar; noon-1am;) Multilevel complex divided into several bars and restaurants, though the highlight is the rooftop with big screen, where you can sample its six microbrews, including a rice beer and a guest ale. Weekend nights are very lively, with DJs and dancing.

Toit Brewpub   MICROBREWERY

(www.toit.in; 298, 100 Feet Rd, Indiranagar; noon-11.30pm Mon & Tue, to 12.30am Wed, Thu & Sun, to 1am Fri & Sat; ; Indiranagar) A brick-walled gastropub split over three levels where you can sample quality beers brewed on site, including two seasonals and a wheat beer on tap. Try a glass of Bittersweet Symphony, a delicious, citrusy IPA.

Arbor Brewing Company   MICROBREWERY

(www.arborbrewing.in; 8 Magrath Rd; noon-12.30am; ; Trinity) This classic brewpub was one of the first microbreweries to get the craft-beer barrel rolling in Bengaluru. Choose from stout, porter, IPA, Belgian beers, spiced, sour and fruit beers. It also serves pub grub (pizza, tacos), artisan coffee and gourmet teas.

☆ Entertainment

Humming Tree   LIVE MUSIC

(9945532828; www.facebook.com/thehumming tree; 12th Main Rd, Indiranagar; 11am-11.30pm Sun-Thu, to 1am Fri & Sat; ; Indiranagar) This popular warehouse-style venue has bands (starting around 9pm), DJs and a rooftop terrace. The cover charge is anything from zero to ₹300. There's a good finger-food menu and happy hour until 7pm.

M Chinnaswamy Stadium   CRICKET

(www.ksca.cricket; MG Rd; Cubbon Park) A mecca for cricket-lovers, hosting many matches per year. Check online for the schedule of tests, one-dayers and Twenty20s.

Indigo XP   LIVE MUSIC

(080-25535330; www.facebook.com/indigo xpblr; 5/6th fl, Elite Bldg, Jyoti Nivas College Rd, Koramangala; 4pm-1am;) Always buzzing, this huge venue hosts bands, DJs, acoustic musicians and stand-up comedy. On the upper floor there's a large terrace for dining and lounging. Also a good place to catch the cricket or footy.

B Flat   LIVE MUSIC

(9591126639; www.facebook.com/bflatindira nagar; 776, 100 Feet Rd, Indiranagar; entry ₹300-500; noon-midnight; ; Indiranagar) Popular pub and performance venue that features some of India's best blues and jazz acts, alternative and indie bands, comedy, and even experimental theatre.

Ranga Shankara   THEATRE

(080-26592777; www.rangashankara.org; 36/2 8th Cross, JP Nagar) All kinds of interesting theatre (in a variety of languages and spanning various genres) and dance are staged at this cultural centre. Hosts an annual mini-festival in late October/early November.

Bangalore Turf Club HORSE RACING
(☑ 080-22262391; www.bangaloreraces.com; Race-course Rd) Horse racing is big in Bengaluru. Races are generally held on Friday and Saturday afternoons.

🛍 Shopping

Bengaluru's shopping options are abundant, ranging from teeming bazaars to glitzy malls. Some good shopping areas include Commercial St, Vittal Mallya Rd and the MG Rd area.

★**Goobe's Book Republic** BOOKS
(www.goobes.wordpress.com; 11 Church St; ⊙10.30am-9pm Mon-Sat, noon-9pm Sun; Ⓜ MG Rd) Great little bookshop selling new and secondhand, cult and mainstream books and comics. Good for titles on southern India and run by informed, helpful staff.

★**Mysore Saree Udyog** CLOTHING
(www.mysoresareeudyog.com; 1st fl, 316 Kamaraj Rd; ⊙10.30am-8.30pm) A great choice for top-quality silk saris, blouses, fabrics and men's shirts, this fine store has been in business for over 70 years and has something to suit all budgets. Most garments are made with Mysuru silk. Also stocks 100% *pashmina* (fine cashmere) shawls.

San-Cha Tea Boutique TEA
(☑ 080-22272028; www.sanchatea.com; 54 Lavelle Rd; ⊙11.30am-8.30pm) Tea-lovers, rejoice: this wonderful store has more than 70 varieties of tea, from grand crus to humble teabags, many personally curated by master tea taster Sanjay Kapur. Prices start at ₹240.

Forest Essentials COSMETICS
(www.forestessentialsindia.com; 4/1 Lavelle Junction Bldg, Vittal Mallya Rd; ⊙10am-9pm) High-end natural beauty products, including potions and lotions for hair, face and body as well as all-organic ayurvedic essential oils.

Gangarams Book Bureau BOOKS
(www.facebook.com/gangaramsbookbureau; 3rd fl, 48 Church St; ⊙10am-8pm Mon-Sat; Ⓜ MG Rd) Excellent selection of Indian titles, guidebooks and Penguin classics. Has a knowledgeable staff and author-signing sessions.

Fabindia CLOTHING, HOMEWARES
(www.fabindia.com; Garuda Mall, Magrath Rd; ⊙10am-8pm) Hugely successful chain with a range of stylish traditional clothing, home-

wares and accessories in traditional cotton prints and silks. Quality skincare products, too. Branches on **Commercial St** (152 Commercial St; ⊙10am-8.30pm), in **Koramangala** (54 17th Main Rd; ⊙10am-8pm) and at the **Lido Mall** (1 MG Rd-Lido Mall, Kensington Rd; ⊙10.30am-9pm; Ⓜ Trinity).

Cauvery Arts &
Crafts Emporium GIFTS & SOUVENIRS
(45 MG Rd; ⊙10am-8pm; Ⓜ MG Rd) Government-run store famous for its expansive collection of quality sandalwood and rosewood products as well as handmade weavings, silks and *bidriware* (metallic handicrafts). Fixed prices.

Blossom Book House BOOKS
(84/6 Church St; ⊙10.30am-9.30pm; Ⓜ MG Rd) Great deals on new and secondhand books.

Garuda Mall MALL
(www.garudamall.in; Magrath Rd; ⊙10am-10pm Sun-Thu, to 10.30pm Fri & Sat; Ⓜ Trinity) Modern mall in central Bengaluru with a wide selection of clothing chains and an Inox multiplex cinema.

ℹ Information

Explocity (https://bangalore.explocity.com) has the latest on restaurant openings, cultural events, nightlife and shopping in the city.

MEDICAL SERVICES
Hosmat (☑ 080-25593796; https://hosmat hospitals.com; 45 Magrath Rd; ⊙24hr) Hospital for critical injuries and general illnesses.
Mallya Hospital (☑ 080-22277979; www. mallyahospital.net; 2 Vittal Mallya Rd) Emergency services and 24-hour pharmacy.

POST
Main Post Office (Cubbon Rd; ⊙10am-7pm Mon-Sat, to 1pm Sun; Ⓜ Cubbon Park) On the north side of Cubbon Park.

TOURIST INFORMATION
These well-informed offices offer useful tourist information:
Government of India Tourist Office (GITO; ☑ 080-25583030; indiatourismbengaluru@gmail.com; 2nd fl, Triumph Towers, 48 Church St; ⊙9.30am-5.30pm Mon-Fri, to noon Sat; Ⓜ MG Rd)
Karnataka State Tourism Development Corporation (KSTDC; ☑ 080-41329211; www.kstdc. co; Karnataka Tourism House, 8 Papanna Lane, St Mark's Rd; ⊙10am-7pm Mon-Sat; Ⓜ MG Rd)
Karnataka State Tourism Development Corporation (KSTDC; ☑ 080-43344334; https://

kstdc.co; Badami House, Kasturba Rd; ⊙10am-7pm Mon-Sat)

TRAVEL AGENCIES

Skyway (☑080-22111401; www.skywaytour.com; 8 Papanna Lane, St Mark's Rd; ⊙9am-6pm Mon-Sat) is a professional and reliable outfit for booking long-distance taxis, air tickets and tours.

ⓘ Getting There & Away

AIR

International and domestic flights arrive at and depart from Bengaluru's **Kempegowda International Airport** (☑1800 4254425; www.bengaluruairport.com), about 35km north of the MG Rd area. There are connections to more than 25 Indian cities. Sample fares include ₹3350 to Mumbai, ₹4000 to Delhi and ₹4800 to Kolkata. Carriers include the following:

Air India (☑080-22978427; www.airindia.com; Unity Bldg, JC Rd; ⊙10am-5pm Mon-Sat)

GoAir (☑080-47406091; www.goair.in; Bengaluru airport)

IndiGo (☑9910383838; www.goindigo.in)

Jet Airways (☑080-39893333; www.jetairways.com; Unity Bldg, JC Rd; ⊙9.30am-6pm Mon-Sat)

BUS

Bengaluru's huge, well-organised **Kempegowda bus stand** (Majestic; Gubbi Thotadappa Rd; ⓜKempegowda), also commonly known as both Majestic and Central, is directly in front of the City train station. Karnataka State Road Transport Corporation (KSRTC; www.ksrtc.in) buses run to destinations in Karnataka and neighbouring states. **Mysuru Road Satellite Bus Stand** (Mysuru Rd), 8km southwest of the centre, is another important terminal: most KSRTC buses

to Mysuru, Mangaluru and other destinations southwest of Bengaluru leave from here, as does the Flybus to Bengaluru airport.

The KSRTC website lists current schedules and fares. Booking online isn't always possible using international credit cards, but travel agents can assist here. It's wise to book long-distance journeys in advance.

Private bus operators line the street facing Kempegowda bus stand.

TRAIN

Bengaluru's **City train station** (Gubbi Thotadappa Rd; ⓜKempegowda) is the main train hub. There's also **Cantonment train station** (Station Rd), a sensible spot to disembark if you're arriving and headed for the MG Rd area. **Yeshvantpur train station** (Rahman Khan Rd), 8km northwest of downtown, is the starting point for trains to Goa.

The computerised **reservation office** (☑139; City Train Station; ⊙8am-8pm Mon-Sat, to 2pm Sun; ⓜKempegowda) has separate counters for credit-card purchases, for women and for foreigners. Head to the **Divisional Railway Office** (Gubbi Thotadappa Rd) for last-minute reservations. Luggage can be left at the 24-hour cloakroom on Platform 1 at the City train station.

ⓘ Getting Around

TO/FROM THE AIRPORT

Metered AC taxis from the airport to the centre cost between ₹750 and ₹1000, while Uber/Ola cab rates are usually around ₹550 to ₹650; these rates include the ₹120 airport toll. Air-conditioned **Vayu Vajra** (☑1800 4251663; www.mybmtc.com) buses run regularly from the airport to destinations around the city and cost ₹170 to ₹260. Flybus (www.ksrtc.in) offers very regular service from the airport to Mysuru and other destinations including Tirupati.

MAJOR BUS SERVICES FROM BENGALURU

DESTINATION	FARE (₹)	DURATION (HR)	DEPARTURES
Chennai	549-955	6½-8	47 daily; 5.30am-11.45pm
Ernakulam	703-1265	10-11	7 daily; 4.10-10pm
Hampi	650-779	7½	11pm, 11.30pm
Hosapete (Hospet)	338-751	6-9	17 daily; 8.45am-11.45pm
Hyderabad	686-1210	8-11	28 daily; 7.15am-11.45pm
Mangaluru (Mangalore)	366-908	6½-9	32 daily; 6.05am-11.50pm
Mumbai	1575	18	3.05pm, 5.05pm, 8pm
Mysuru* (Mysore)	129-326	2½-4	33 daily; 1.30am-10.30pm
Ooty (Udhagamandalam)*	600-840	7-9½	8 daily; 6.15am-11.15pm
Panaji (Panjim)	619-1050	11-13½	3 daily; 7-8.30pm
Gokarna	518-843	9-12	3 daily; 8.30-10.15pm

*Also services from Mysuru Road Satellite Bus Stand

MAJOR TRAINS FROM BENGALURU

DESTINATION	TRAIN NO & NAME	FARE (₹)	DURATION (HR)	DEPARTURES
Chennai	12658 Chennai Mail	260/930	6	10.40pm
Chennai	12028 Shatabdi	790/1050	5	6am & 4.25pm Wed-Mon
Hosapete (Hospet)	16592 Hampi Exp	240/935	9	10.05pm
Hubballi (Hubli)	16589 Rani Chennamma Exp	270/1050	8½	9.15pm
Margao (Madgaon; Goa)	17311 Mas Vasco Exp	360/1420	16	8.10pm Fri
Mysuru (Mysore)	12007 Shatabdi	295/835	2	11am Thu-Tue
Mysuru (Mysore)	12614 Tippu Exp	90/315	2½	3.15pm
Thiruvanantha-puram (Trivandrum)	16526 Kanyakumari Exp	410/1620	16½	8pm

Shatabdi fares are AC chair/AC executive chair; express (Exp/Mail) fares are 2nd class/AC chair for day trains and sleeper/2AC for night trains.

AUTORICKSHAW
Very few autorickshaw drivers use meters, but if yours does 50% is added to the metered rate after 10pm.

BUS
Bengaluru has a comprehensive local bus network, operated by the Bangalore Metropolitan Transport Corporation (BMTC; www.mybmtc. com), with a useful website for timetables and fares. However, very few travellers use them these days, preferring the speed of the metro and the convenience of Uber/Ola.

Nevertheless, red AC Vajra buses criss-cross the city, while green Big10 deluxe buses connect the suburbs. Ordinary buses run from the **City bus stand** (Sayyali Rao Rd), next to Kempegowda bus stand; a few operate from the **City Market bus stand** (Ⓜ Chickpet) further south.

METRO
Bengaluru's shiny new AC metro service, known as **Namma Metro** (🖉 toll-free 1800-42512345; http://english.bmrc.co.in), now has two lines operating, connecting at Kempegowda/Majestic (for the bus terminal). It's by far the cheapest and quickest way to get between, say, the central MG Rd area and the nightlife hub of Indiranagar, using the Purple Line. Trains run about every 15 minutes from 6am to 10pm, and fares are ₹10 to ₹22 for most journeys. Travel cards (₹50) and single-journey tokens are available. See the website for the latest updates.

TAXI
There are thousands of Uber and Ola drivers in Bengaluru. To hire a conventional cab for a day, reckon on around ₹2000 for eight hours.

Olacabs (🖉 080-33553355; www.olacabs.com) Professional, efficient company with modern air-con cars. Online and phone bookings.

Meru Cabs (🖉 080-44224422; www.meru.in) Another good operator.

SOUTHERN KARNATAKA

Hesaraghatta
🖉 080 / POP 9250

Located 30km northwest of Bengaluru (Bangalore), the small town of Hesaraghatta is home to **Nrityagram** (🖉 080-28466313; www. nrityagram.org; self guided tour ₹100, children under 12yr free; ⊘ 10am-2pm Tue-Sun), a leading dance academy established in 1990 to revive and popularise Indian classical dance. The brainchild and living legacy of celebrated dancer Protima Gauri Bedi (1948–98), the complex was designed like a village by Goa-based architect Gerard da Cunha. Long-term courses in classical dance are offered to deserving students, while local children are taught for free on Sunday. Check the website for upcoming performances (₹1000 per person).

From Bengaluru's City Market, buses 266, 253 and 253E run to Hesaraghatta (₹30, one hour), with bus 266 continuing to Nrityagram. From Hesaraghatta an autorickshaw will cost around ₹80 to Nrityagram.

Mysuru (Mysore)
🖉 0821 / POP 1,036,000 / ELEV 707M

The historic settlement of Mysuru (which changed its name from Mysore in 2014) is one of South India's most enchanting cities, famed for its glittering royal heritage and magnificent monuments and buildings. Its

WINE & WHISKY IN NANDI HILLS

In a country not known for fine wines and liquors, Bengaluru is very much an exception to the rule. It has not only developed a thirst for craft beer but has on its doorstep one of India's premier wine-growing regions in the **Nandi Hills** (per person/car ₹10/150; ◷ 6am-6pm). While wine making is an emerging industry, it's fast gaining a reputation internationally, with many wineries in the area. A few clicks out of town is India's first single-malt whisky distillery.

Grover Wineries (☑ 080-27622826; www.groverzampa.in; 1½hr tour Mon-Fri ₹850, Sat & Sun ₹1000) At an altitude of 920m, this winery produces quality white and red varietals. Tours include tastings of five wines in the cellar rooms accompanied by cheese and crackers, followed by lunch. From February to May you'll also see grape crushing and can visit the vineyards. It's located on the approach to the Nandi Hills, around 40km north of Bengaluru.

Amrut (☑ 080-23100402; www.amrutdistilleries.com; Mysuru Rd; tours ₹750) Established in 1948, Amrut, India's first producer of single-malt whisky, offers free distillery tours run by knowledgeable guides. You'll be taken through the entire process before tasting the world-class single malts and blends. It's 20km outside Bengaluru on the road to Mysuru (Mysore); prebookings essential.

Buses head to the Nandi Hills (₹70, two hours) from Bengaluru's Kempegowda (Majestic/Central) bus stand.

World Heritage–listed palace brings most travellers here, but Mysuru is also rich in tradition, with a deeply atmospheric bazaar district replete with spice stores and incense stalls. Ashtanga yoga (p194) is another drawcard and there are several acclaimed schools that attract visitors from across the globe.

History

Mysuru owes its name to the mythical Mahisuru, a place where the demon Mahishasura was slain by the goddess Chamundi. Its regal history began in 1399, when the Wodeyar dynasty of Mysuru was founded, though it remained in service of the Vijayanagar empire until the mid-16th century. With the fall of Vijayanagar in 1565, the Wodeyars declared their sovereignty, which – save for a brief period of Hyder Ali and Tipu Sultan's supremacy in the late 18th century – remained unscathed until Independence in 1947. A new maharaja, Yaduveera Krishnadatta Chamaraja Wadiyar, was crowned in 2015, at the age of 23. He presided over his first Dussehra festival in September of that year.

◉ Sights

Mysuru isn't known as the City of Palaces for nothing: it's home to a total of seven, as well as an abundance of majestic heritage architecture (p189) dating from the Wodeyar dynasty and British rule. The majority of grand buildings are owned by the state and used as anything from hospitals, colleges and government buildings to heritage hotels. Visit www.karnatakatourism.org/mysore/en for a list of notable buildings.

★ Mysuru Palace   PALACE

(Maharaja's Palace; http://mysorepalace.gov.in; Purandara Dasa Rd; adult/child ₹50/free; ◷ 10am-5.30pm) The second-most-visited sight in India (after the Taj Mahal), this palace is among the very grandest of India's royal buildings and was the seat of the Wodeyar maharajas. The original palace was gutted by fire in 1897; today's structure was completed in 1912. The lavish Indo-Saracenic interior – a kaleidoscope of stained glass, mirrors and gaudy colours – is undoubtedly over the top. It's further embellished by carved wooden doors, mosaic floors and a series of paintings depicting life here during the Raj.

English architect Henry Irwin designed the palace and construction cost ₹4.5 million. On the way in you'll pass a fine collection of sculptures and artefacts. Don't forget to check out the armoury, with an intriguing collection of 700-plus weapons. From 7pm to 8pm every Sunday and national holiday, the palace is illuminated by nearly 100,000 light bulbs that accentuate its majestic profile against the night. Entrance to the grounds is at the South Gate ticket office. While you're allowed to snap the palace's exterior, photography within is strictly prohibited. Note that many visitors have been unable to download the palace-information app (promoted at the ticket office).

Devaraja Market
MARKET

(Sayyaji Rao Rd; ⏰6am-8.30pm) Dating from Tipu Sultan's reign, this huge and very lively bazaar has local traders selling traditional items such as flower garlands, incense, spices and conical piles of *kumkum* (coloured powder used for bindi dots), all of which makes for some great photo ops. There's a large fruit and veg section on the western side, too. Gully Tours (p193) offers good guided walks here.

Jaganmohan Palace
PALACE

(Jaganmohan Palace Rd) Built in 1861 as the royal auditorium, this stunning palace just west of Mysuru Palace houses the Jayachamarajendra Art Gallery. Set over three floors, it has a huge collection of Indian paintings, including works by noted artist Raja Ravi Varma, traditional Japanese art and some rare musical instruments. At the time of research it was closed for long-overdue renovations.

Chamundi Hill
VIEWPOINT

This 1062m hill is crowned with the **Sri Chamundeswari Temple** (⏰7am-2pm, 3.30-6pm & 7.30-9pm). It's a fine half-day excursion, offering spectacular views of the city below. Queues are long at weekends, so visit during the week. From Central bus stand take bus 201 (₹28; AC); a return autorickshaw/Uber trip is around ₹450/700.

Rail Museum
MUSEUM

(KRS Rd; Indian adult/child ₹20/10, foreigner adult/child ₹80/40, camera/video ₹20/30; ⏰9.30am-6pm Thu-Tue) This open-air museum's main exhibit is the Mysuru maharani's saloon, an 1899 wood-panelled beauty with gilded ceilings and chandeliers that provides an insight into the stylish way the royals once rode the rails. There are also steam engines, locomotives and carriages to investigate, many of which were manufactured in the UK. A toy train rides the track around the museum 16 times daily.

Indira Gandhi Rashtriya Manav Sangrahalaya
MUSEUM

(National Museum of Mankind; http://igrms.gov.in; Wellington Lodge, Irwin Rd; ⏰9.30am-5.30pm Tue-Sun) FREE This unassuming colonial building, known as Wellington Lodge, was the residence of Colonel Arthur Wellesley from 1799 to 1801. He later become the duke of Wellington, and defeated Napoleon at Waterloo. Today the building houses ageing exhibits, including textiles and handicrafts and some impressive terracotta sculptures from Rajasthan.

🏃 Activities & Courses

Turiya Wellness
SPA

(☎0821-2971123; http://turiya-wellness.com; 354/B 4th Main Rd, Gokulam; 45min massage from ₹1500; ⏰6am-8pm) A fine ayurvedic spa offering treatments and therapies. Ayurvedic cooking classes and massage courses are also recommended, and there's daily hatha and Ashtanga yoga.

Emerge Spa
SPA

(☎0821-2522500; www.thewindflowor.com; Wind flower Spa & Resort, Maharanapratap Rd, Nazarbad; massages from ₹2350; ⏰7am-9pm) Wonderful resort spa offering dozens of ayurvedic treatments, including hot-stone massages and pampering rituals. Day packages include access to the hotel's natural pool. Located 3km southeast of Mysuru Palace.

KARNATAKA MYSURU (MYSORE)

COLONIAL-ERA ARCHITECTURE

Mysuru's colonial heritage is considerable, with numerous grand edifices and quirky reminders of the past to investigate. Dating from 1805, **Government House** (Irwin Rd), formerly the British Residency, is a Tuscan Doric building set in 20 hectares of gardens. Facing the north gate of Mysuru Palace is the 1927 **Silver Jubilee Clock Tower** (Dodda Gadiara; Ashoka Rd). The beauty of towering **St Philomena's Cathedral** (St Philomena St; ⏰8am-5pm), built between 1933 and 1941 in neo-Gothic style, is emphasised by its elegant stained-glass windows. Wellington Lodge is an early colonial-era landmark that once housed Colonel Arthur Wellesley (later known as the duke of Wellington); today it's a museum: Indira Gandhi Rashtriya Manav Sangrahalaya. Other notable colonial-era structures include the neoclassical **Lalitha Mahal Palace** (☎0821-2526100; www.lalithamahalpalace.co.in; r incl breakfast ₹3170-6420, ste from ₹13,680; ❀@🛜❄), designed by British architect EW Fritchley, its white dome perhaps a nod to London's St Paul's Cathedral; it's now a heritage hotel.

Mysuru Palace

A HALF-DAY TOUR

The interior of Mysuru Palace houses opulent halls, royal paintings, intricate decorative details, as well as sculptures and ceremonial objects.

There is a lot of hidden detail and much to take in, so be sure to allow yourself at least a few hours for the experience. A guide can also be invaluable.

After entering the palace the first exhibit is the **① Dolls' Pavilion**, which showcases the maharaja's fine collection of traditional dolls and sculptures acquired from around the world. Opposite the **② Elephant Gate** you'll see the seven cannons that were used for special occasions, such as the birthdays of the maharajas. Today the cannons are still fired as part of Dussehra festivities.

At the end of the Dolls' Pavilion you'll find the **③ Golden Howdah**. Note the fly whisks on

Private Durbar Hall
Rosewood doors lead into this hall, which is richly decorated with stained-glass ceilings, steel grill work and chandeliers. It houses the Golden Throne, only on display to the public during Dussehra.

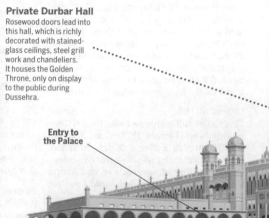

Entry to the Palace

Public Durbar Hall
The open-air hall contains a priceless collection of paintings by Raja Ravi Varma and opens onto an expansive balcony supported by massive pillars with an ornate painted ceiling of 10 incarnations of Vishnu.

ROBERT WYATT/ALAMY STOCK PHOTO ©

PJPHPIX/SHUTTERSTOCK ©

either side; the bristles are made from fine ivory.

Make sure you check out the paintings depicting the Dussehra procession in the halls on your way to the **④ Marriage Pavilion** and look into the courtyard to see what was once the wrestling arena. It's now used during Dussehra only. In the Marriage Pavilion, take a few minutes to scan the entire space. You can see the influence of three religions in the design of the hall: the glass ceiling represents Christianity, stone carvings along the hallway ceilings are Hindu design and the top-floor balcony roof (the traditional women's gallery) has Islamic-style arches.

When you move through to the **⑤ Private Durbar Hall**, take note of the intricate ivory-inlay motifs depicting Krishna in the rosewood doors. The **⑥ Public Durbar Hall** is usually the last stop, where you can admire the panoramic views of the gardens through the Islamic arches.

Dolls' Pavilion
The first exhibit, the Dolls' Pavilion, displays the gift collection of 19th- and early-20th-century dolls, statues and Hindu idols that were given to the maharaja by dignitaries from around the world.

Elephant Gate
Next to the Dolls' Pavilion, this brass gate has four bronze elephants inlaid at the bottom, an intricate double-headed eagle up the top and a hybrid lion-elephant creature (the state emblem of Karnataka) in the centre.

Marriage Pavilion
This lavish hall used for royal weddings features themes of Christianity, Hinduism and Islam in its design. The highlights are the octagonal painted-glass ceiling featuring peacock motifs, the bronze chandelier and the colonnaded turquoise pillars.

Golden Howdah
At the far end of the Dolls' Pavilion, a wooden elephant howdah decorated with 80kg of gold was used to carry the maharaja in the Dussehra festival. It now carries an idol of goddess Chamundeshwari.

Mysuru (Mysore)

Mysuru (Mysore)

◎ **Top Sights**
1 Mysuru Palace D4

◎ **Sights**
2 Devaraja Market C2
3 Government House F1
4 Indira Gandhi Rashtriya Manav
   Sangrahalaya E1
5 Jaganmohan Palace B3
6 Rail Museum A1
7 Silver Jubilee Clock Tower D2
8 South Gate Ticket Office D4

☉ **Activities, Courses & Tours**
9 Shruthi Musical Works C1

☐ **Sleeping**
10 Hotel Maurya C2

11 Mansion 1907 .... F2
12 Parklane Hotel E3
13 Royal Orchid Metropole A2
14 Southern Star A2

☒ **Eating**
15 Cafe Aramane C3
16 Dosa Point A2
17 Hotel RRR D2
18 Madhushahi Samosa Centre C2
   Parklane Hotel .... (see 12)
   Tiger Trail .... (see 13)

☉ **Drinking & Nightlife**
19 Infinit Doora E3

☐ **Shopping**
20 Sumangali Silks D2

Indus Valley Ayurvedic Centre   AYURVEDA
(☑ 0821-2473263; www.ayurindus.com; Lalithadri-

pura) Set in 10 hectares of gardens and 6km
from the city centre, this classy retreat de-

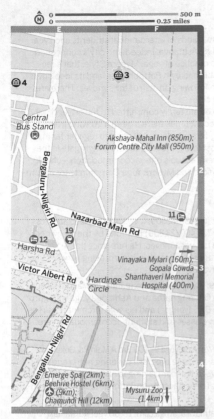

rives its therapies from ancient scriptures and prescriptions. Aromatherapy, *basti* detox treatments and all manner of ayurvedic treats are offered. The overnight package including full board, ayurveda treatment, yoga session and beauty therapy starts at US$212.

Shruthi Musical Works   MUSIC
(📞9845249518; 1189 3rd Cross, Irwin Rd; per hour ₹450; ⊙10.30am-9pm Mon-Sat, to 2pm Sun) Music teacher Jayashankar gets good reviews for his tabla (drum) instruction.

☞ Tours

★Gully Tours   WALKING
(📞9632044188; https://gully.tours; walks from ₹1100) Formerly Royal Mysore Walks, these excellent guided tours are the perfect way to familiarise yourself with Mysuru's epic history and heritage. Offers a range of walks (themes include royal history and food) as well as cycle and jeep tours.

KSTDC Transport Office   BUS
(📞0821-2423652; www.kstdc.co; city tour ₹400) KSTDC runs a daily Mysuru tour, taking in city sights (excluding the palace), Chamundi Hill, Srirangapatna and Brindavan Gardens. It starts at 8.30am, ends at 8.30pm and is likely to leave you breathless! Other tours go to Belur, Halebid and Sravanabelagola and the Kodagu region (₹890).

★★ Festivals & Events

Dussehra   CULTURAL
(Dasara; ⊙Sep/Oct) Mysuru is at its carnivalesque best during the 10-day Dussehra (locally spelt 'Dasara') festival. During this time Mysuru Palace (p188) is dramatically lit up every evening, while the town is transformed into a gigantic fairground, with concerts, dance performances, sporting demonstrations and cultural events running to packed houses. An Open Street Festival is also held, featuring festive food stalls and live music.

⌴ Sleeping

Mysuru has a decent selection of hotels and guesthouses. The city attracts tourists throughout the year and can fill up very quickly during Dussehra (when booking early is highly recommended).

★Beehive Hostel   HOSTEL $
(📞9916967853; https://beehivemysore.business.site; 12th Main Rd, JP Nagar; dm/r ₹600/1300; 🅿☏) A near-scenic location in huge lawned grounds makes this great new hostel a very tranquil base for travellers weary of urban India. The grand yellow villa has excellent facilities, with four private rooms, three dorms, a small library, a guests' kitchen and ample space to socialise. Located 6km south of the city centre.

★Mansion 1907   HOSTEL $
(📞9886523472; www.facebook.com/themansion1907; 36 Shalivahana Rd; dm with fan/AC ₹500/600, r with fan/AC ₹1400/1800; ❄☏) Excellent hostel in a historic house that shows Indian and British architectural influences. It's very well set up, with spacious dorms and private rooms, cool communal areas decorated with murals and LP covers, a kitchen and speedy wi-fi. There's (free) rooftop yoga for guests, too.

Sonder   HOSTEL $
(📞8971793193; www.sonderhostel.com; 6, Vivekananda Rd; dm incl breakfast ₹500; ❄☏) Fine backpackers' hostel in a tranquil, leafy

YOGA IN MYSURU

This world-famous centre for yoga attracts thousands of international students each year to learn, practise or become certified in teaching Ashtanga. Indeed, the city's connection with yoga is so profound that it is linked with a practice of yoga, Mysore Style, that's recognised around the world. This style was established by K Pattabhi Jois, and its ideology is more about developing Ashtanga asanas than following an instructor's moves. There are more than 20 established yoga schools in the city.

For the most part, students are required to be austerely committed to the art, and will need to stay at least a month. While in more recent times there's been a growing trend for drop-in classes or week-long courses, long-term students will need to register far in advance, as courses are often booked out. Most foreign yoga students congregate in the upmarket residential suburb of Gokulam. Several schools offer accommodation – check Facebook groups Ashtanga Community in Mysore and Mysore Yoga Community for accommodation rentals.

Yoga Centres

Ashtanga Yoga Research Institute (AYRI; ☎ 9880185500; www.kpjayi.org; 235 8th Cross Rd, 3rd Stage, Gokulam; 1st/2nd month excl taxes ₹35,400/23,800) Founded by the renowned teacher K Pattabhi Jois, who taught Madonna her yoga moves. He has since passed away and the reins have been handed over to his grandson Sharath, who is proving very popular. You need to register at least two months in advance.

IndeaYoga (Ananda Yoga India; ☎ 0821-2416779; www.indeayoga.com; 144E 7th Main Rd, Gokulam; 1 month classes incl food & lodging ₹25,000) Offering hatha and Ashtanga yoga with guru Bharath Shetty (who practised under the late BKS Iyengar) and his wife, Archana. Courses include anatomy and yoga philosophy. Drop-in classes and student accommodation are also offered.

Nirvana Yoga Shala (☎ 0821-4288490; http://mysoreyoga.in; 100 3rd A Main Rd, Gokulam; drop-in/1-month yoga classes ₹500/7500) Offers a diverse program covering hatha and Asthanga, meditation and lectures. Suspension-yoga teacher training is also available. Suitable for short- and long-term students at all levels. There's accommodation (studios with kitchenettes), a sauna, a plunge pool and a cafe.

Atmavikasa Centre (☎ 0821-2341978; www.atmavikasayoga.com; 18, 80 Feet Rd, Ramakrishnanagar; 1 month intensive course ₹42,500) Classical hatha yoga school set up by Acharya Venkatesh and Acharye Hema offering training, therapy and workshops. Enjoys a garden setting in a peaceful suburb 5km southwest of the palace.

Ramesh Shetty's Yoga Shala (☎ 7795977565; http://mysoreashtanga.net; 451/4 Vanivilas Double Rd, Chamarajapura) The Ashtanga vinyasa and hatha yoga teacher training here gets good feedback; courses are linked to Yoga Alliance for accreditation.

Yogadarshanam (☎ 9901760846; http://yogadarshanam.org; 77/A 4th Main Rd, 3rd Stage, Gokulam; courses ₹6200-30,500) Classical Indian yoga centre offering classes, teacher training, workshops and retreats. The one-month foundation course covers yoga fundamentals and is perfect for beginners. Meditation classes are also offered.

Yoga Bharata (☎ 0821-4242342; www.yogabharata.com; 1st fl, 810 Contour Rd, Gokulam; daily class for 1/4 weeks ₹2000/10,000) Ashtanga vinyasa and hatha yoga classes with experienced teachers. Linked to IndeaYoga. Drop-in classes (₹300) are available.

suburb close to many yoga schools. It's a well-designed space with comfy dorms, lockers, board games and books, a kitchen and a friendly vibe. There are regular events such as movie nights and cooking classes.

Hotel Maurya HOTEL $
(☎ 0821-2426677; www.hotelmauryamysore.com; 9/5 Hanumantha Rao St; s/d/tr from ₹200/375/500; ✳🛜) A good choice, with helpful management who are eager to help you make the most of Mysuru. There's a wide range of large, unremarkable but inexpensive rooms; you pay extra for AC. It's in the thick of things in the city centre, so expect some traffic noise, and hustle and bustle.

Anokhi Garden Guest House   GUESTHOUSE **$$**
(☑ 0821-4288923; www.anokhigarden.com; 408 Contour Rd, 3rd Stage, Gokulam; s/d from ₹2200/3200; ☎) Very popular with yoga students and young travellers, this cosy French-run guesthouse offers tidy rooms in a property that boasts a lovely garden cafe. Rooms are spacious, with a splash of colour from throws and local textiles.

Parklane Hotel   HOTEL **$$**
(☑ 0821-4003500; www.parklanemysore.com; 2720 Harsha Rd; r ₹1680-3190; ❊ @ ☎ ⊠) Right in the heart of the city, with most attractions within walking distance, this hotel represents fine value. Decor is over-the-top kitsch, but with its spacious, clean rooms the place is hard to dislike – though the bathrooms need upgrading. The lively open-air restaurant is always buzzing, and there's a small rooftop pool.

Southern Star   HOTEL **$$**
(☑ 0821-2426426; www.hotelsouthernstar.com; Vinoba Rd; r incl breakfast from ₹4880; ❊ ☎ ⊠) Offering good value, this large hotel has many advantages, including a very inviting pool, lovely leafy grounds and a handy location less than a kilometre from the train station. Rooms are quite elegant, with wooden floors, art on the walls and generously sized bathrooms.

Akshaya Mahal Inn   HOTEL **$$**
(☑ 0821-2447675; www.akshayamahalinn.com; 5/A Hydarali Rd; r incl breakfast from ₹2460; ❊ ☎) A couple of kilometres from the heart of town, this well-run hotel enjoys a convenient location, with a large mall on its doorstep. Rooms are spacious and represent fine value; all have flatscreen TVs (with cable) and tea- and coffee-making facilities.

Green Hotel   GUESTHOUSE **$$**
(☑ 0821-4255000; www.greenhotelindia.com; 2270 Vinoba Rd, Jayalakshmipuram; s/d incl breakfast from ₹3820/4460; ☎) The maharaja built the Green Hotel in the 1920s as a palace for his daughters. Today it's a heritage hotel set among charming gardens. Rooms in the old wing have plenty of period character, though some fixtures are looking a tad tired and there's no AC. There's a good **cafe** (cakes from ₹40, snacks from ₹70; ⊙ 10am-7pm; ☎) ✐, a restaurant and a travel agent.

★**Grand Mercure Mysore**   HOTEL **$$$**
(☑ 0821-4021212; www.accorhotels.com; Nelson Mandela Circle, New Sayyaji Rao Rd; r from ₹5160; ❊ @ ☎ ⊠) The Mercure is a very well-run hotel, with attentive, friendly staff members and sleek, well-equipped rooms. There's a large rooftop swimming pool (big enough for laps), a gym with city views, a small spa and a choice of restaurants. Located 4km north of the city centre.

Royal Orchid Metropole   HERITAGE HOTEL **$$$**
(☑ 0821-4255566; www.royalorchidhotels.com; 5 Jhansi Lakshmi Bai Rd; s/d incl breakfast from ₹6880/7250; ❊ ☎ ⊠) Recently renovated, this heritage property once served as the residence for the maharaja's British guests. It has spectacular grounds and a choice of atmospheric dining areas, including a sheltered courtyard. Rooms ooze character and boast all mod cons; there are four comfort levels to choose from. The fitness centre and very classy bar round things off in style.

Georgia Sunshine Village   BUNGALOW **$$$**
(☑ 0821-247646; https://georgiasunshine.com; Shimshapura Rd, Hebbani; d/ste incl full board ₹7780/9250; ❊ ☎ ⊠) The affable Hatherell couple runs this relaxing place, a fine family getaway with a sparkling swimming pool, delicious homemade food and accommodation in cosy bungalows. Treks (guides ₹300), birding walks and fishing trips can be arranged. It's 64km east of Mysuru.

✖ Eating

Mysuru has a good number of Indian restaurants and casual places for snacking. There are several healthy-eating cafes thanks to the sheer number of yogis in town.

★**Vinayaka Mylari**   SOUTH INDIAN **$**
(769 Nazarbad Main Rd; dosa ₹30-50; ⊙ 6am-1.30pm & 3-8.30pm) This tiny, no-nonsense place is one of the best spots in town to try the South Indian classic masala dosa (a large savoury crepe stuffed with spiced potatoes). Here they're beautifully light and fluffy and served on banana leaves. Locals eat them with coconut chutney and a coffee.

Madhushahi
Samosa Centre   STREET FOOD **$**
(1518 Vinoba Rd; samosas ₹15-30; ⊙ 4-9pm Mon-Sat) This hole-in-the-wall takeaway samosa place is only open limited hours, but it's well worth checking out. There's always a queue, such is its popularity, and of course the samosas are delicious.

Dosa Point   SOUTH INDIAN **$**
(1350 Devaraj Urs Rd; dosa ₹40-70; ⊙ 8am-10pm) This wildly popular dosa joint is so popular that people munch them on the street

outside when the cramped interior is full. Try a rava onion dosa or ghee dosa.

Cafe Aramane
SOUTH INDIAN $

(Sayyaji Rao Rd; mains ₹90-120; ⊘8am-10pm) 🖉 This atmospheric and authentic South Indian eatery rolls out steaming breakfast platters for Mysuru's office-goers, serves up thalis for lunch (from ₹80), and welcomes everyone back in the evenings with aromatic filter coffee and a convoy of delicious snacks. There are speciality dosa each day of the week.

Depth 'n' Green
VEGETARIAN $

(www.facebook.com/depthngreen; 228/3 1st Main Rd, Gokulam; mains ₹120-200; ⊘8.30am-9.30pm; 🖘) A small, simple but ever-popular all-veg cafe offering a menu of all-day breakfasts (try the 'hearty oats') and satisfying Indian and Western dishes, including great salads. The green smoothies and lassis are also superb. Occasionally hosts evening musical events.

Hotel RRR
SOUTH INDIAN $

(Gandhi Sq; mains ₹125-175; ⊘noon-4.30pm & 7-11pm) Classic Andhra-style food is ladled out at this ever-busy eatery, and you may need to queue for a table during lunch. Try its famous chicken or mutton biryanis (served on a banana leaf), too. There's a small AC section.

Anu's Bamboo Hut
HEALTH FOOD $$

(☑9900909428; www.facebook.com/cafeingo kulam; 367 2nd Main Rd, 3rd Stage, Gokulam; lunch buffet ₹250; ⊘1-3pm & 5-7pm Mon-Sat; 🖘) Rooftop cafe reminiscent of a shack that caters mainly to yoga students, with healthy vegetarian lunch buffets (at 1pm sharp; don't arrive at 2pm or many dishes many be gone) and evening smoothies. Chef-owner Anu is a great source of info and offers cooking classes (₹700, lunch included).

Parklane Hotel
MULTICUISINE $$

(Parklane Hotel, 2720 Harsha Rd; mains ₹110-175; 🖘) Mysuru's most social restaurant, with outdoor tables moodily lit by countless lanterns. There's often live traditional music, too. The menu offers delicious regional dishes from across India, as well as Chinese and Continental options and cold beers.

Rasa Dhatu
HEALTH FOOD $$

(www.dhatuorganics.com; 2826 10th Cross Rd, Gokulam; snacks/meals from ₹120/140; ⊘10am-10pm Mon-Fri, 8am-10pm Sat & Sun; 🖘) Organic cafe off Adipampa Rd serving up healthy specials such as dosa and roti made from millet grains, and salads, curries and North

or South Indian lunchtime thalis (₹199 to ₹299). Service can be a tad slow at times.

Old House
ITALIAN $$

(☑0821-2333255; 451 Jhansi Lakshmi Bai Rd; mains from ₹215; ⊘7.30am-9.45pm; 🖘) Classy Italian place with a delightful terrace where you can enjoy tasty salads, pasta, risotto and pizzas (baked in a wood-fired oven). Also a good bet for breakfast (with everything from croissants to Spanish omelettes). It serves a full range of mocktails and coffees but no alcohol.

Tiger Trail
INDIAN $$$

(☑0821-4255566; Royal Orchid Metropole, 5 Jhansi Lakshmi Bai Rd; mains ₹249-799; ⊘7.30-10am, 12.30-3.30pm & 7.30-11pm; 🖘) This hotel's grand dining room (with portraits, chandeliers and Murano-glass mirrors) makes quite a setting for delectable Indian cuisine, or opt for the courtyard, which twinkles with fairy lights at night. Try a Peshwari boti kebab (₹475), a Malabar fish curry (₹399) or any of the excellent North Indian dishes and be sure to have a tipple in the adjacent bar.

🍷 Drinking & Nightlife

★ Frosting
CAFE

(www.frosting.in; 2649 2nd Main Rd, Gokulam; mains ₹185-395; ⊘11am-11.30pm; 🖘) One of the city's most attractive cafes, occupying an elegant villa in an upmarket corner of town. It's a relaxing spot for an espresso or a glass of wine, with an attractive AC interior, a garden and a menu of Italian classics.

Infinit Doora
BAR

(www.facebook.com/Infinitmysore; Hotel Roopa, 2724/C Bengaluru-Nilgiri Rd; ⊘noon-11pm; 🖘) The nearest thing to a lounge in Mysuru, this rooftop bar has a classy ambience, a comprehensive drinks selection, smoking and nonsmoking zones and fine city views. Cocktails start at ₹250, and there's a full menu of North and South Indian grub.

Pelican Pub
PUB

(25 Hunsur Rd; mains ₹95-245; ⊘11am-11pm; 🖘) A venerable, still-popular watering hole located at the fringes of upmarket Gokulam. Serves draught beer (pitchers are ₹450) and food (try the chilli pork) at bargain-basement rates in the classic pub interior or the alfresco-style garden setting out the back. There's live music some nights.

🛍 Shopping

The bazaar area around Devaraja Market (p189) is a real highlight for those in search of spices, sandalwood products, incense and essential oils (and photographs).

Silk saris are another good buy. Look for the butterfly-esque 'Silk Mark' on your purchase; it's an endorsement indicating quality silk.

Dhatu Organics & Naturals
HEALTH & WELLNESS

(www.dhatuorganics.com; 2826 10th Cross Rd; ⊙8am-9.30pm) Simply outstanding selection of natural products (priced from ₹80), many of them organic, including essential oils and natural cosmetics, fruit and veg, pulses and seeds. Check out its cafe next door while you're here. Located off Adipampa Rd.

Government Silk-Weaving Factory
CLOTHING

(☑8025586550; www.ksicsilk.com; Mananthody Rd, Ashokapuram; ⊙8.30am-4pm Mon-Sat, outlet 10.30am-7pm daily) Given that Mysuru's prized silk is made under its very sheds, this government-run outlet, set up in 1912, is the best and cheapest place to shop for the exclusive textile. Behind the showroom is the factory, where you can drop by to see how the fabric is made. It's around 2km south of town.

Forum Centre City Mall
MALL

(http://forummalls.in/forum-centre-city; Hyder Ali Rd; ⊙10am-10pm) When you need a dose of aircon and some retail time, this mall fits the bill. Offers a wide range of clothing stores (including H&M and Levi's), cafes and restaurants.

Sumangali Silks
CLOTHING

(⊙10am-9pm) Exceptionally popular with Indian women, and usually very crowded, this multilevel store sells fine silk saris, with quality of varying degrees depending on how much you want to spend (prices start at ₹150). It's off Gandhi Sq.

Sandalwood Oil Factory
GIFTS & SOUVENIRS

(Mananthody Rd, Ashokapuram; ⊙outlet 9.30am-6.30pm, factory closed Sun) A quality-assured place for sandalwood products including incense, soap, cosmetics and the prohibitively expensive pure sandalwood oil (if in stock). Guided tours are available to show you around the factory.

ℹ️ Information

MEDICAL SERVICES

Government Hospital (☑0821-4269806; Dhanvanthri Rd; ⊙24hr) Centrally located and has a 24-hour pharmacy.

Gopala Gowda Shanthaveri Memorial Hospital (☑0821-4001600; www.gopalagowda hospital.com; T Narasipura Main Rd; ⊙24hr) Best intensive care in Mysuru.

POST

Main Post Office (cnr Irwin & Ashoka Rds; ⊙10am-6pm Mon-Sat)

TOURIST INFORMATION

Karnataka Tourism (☑0821-2422096; www.karnatakatourism.org; 1st fl, Hotel Mayura Hoysala, 2 Jhansi Lakshmi Bai Rd; ⊙10am-5pm Mon-Sat) Helpful and has plenty of brochures.

KSTDC Transport Office (☑0821-2423652; https://kstdc.co; Yatri Navas Bldg, 2 Jhansi Lakshmi Bai Rd; ⊙8.30am-8.30pm) Main office; provides a useful map.

ℹ️ Getting There & Away

AIR

Mysuru's airport only has one daily connection: Trujet flies to/from Chennai. During Dussehra (p193) there are special Air India flights to Bengaluru.

TRAINS FROM MYSURU

Train tickets can be bought from Mysuru's **railway reservation office** (☑131; ⊙8am-8pm Mon-Sat, to 2pm Sun).

DESTINATION	TRAIN NO & NAME	FARE (₹)	DURATION (HR)	DEPARTURES
Bengaluru (Bangalore)	12613 Tippu Exp	2nd class/AC chair 90/305	2½	11.30am
Bengaluru	12008 Shatabdi Exp	AC chair/AC executive chair 305/775	2	2.15pm Thu-Tue
Chennai	12008 Shatabdi Exp	AC chair/AC executive chair 1140/1840	7½	2.15pm Thu-Tue
Hosapete (Hospet)	16592 Hampi Exp	3AC/2AC sleeper 845/1210	12	7pm
Hubballi (Hubli)	17301 Mysuru Dharwad Exp	sleeper/2AC 275/1070	8½	10.30pm

BUS

The **Central bus stand** (Bengaluru-Nilgiri Rd) handles all KSRTC long-distance buses. The **City bus stand** (Sayyaji Rao Rd) is for city, Srirangapatna and Chamundi Hill buses. The **private bus stand** (Sayyaji Rao Rd) services Hubballi, Vijapura (Bijapur), Mangaluru, Ooty and Ernakulam. You'll find several ticketing agents around the stand.

🛈 Getting Around

Uber and Ola cabs are everywhere in Mysuru. Agencies at hotels can organise drivers for around ₹2000 per day in town, or from ₹2500 per day for out-of-town trips.

Count on around ₹1000 for a day's sightseeing in an autorickshaw.

Mysuru airport is 9km south of the centre. It's not served by public transport; taxis charge around ₹350.

Around Mysuru

Consider a KSTDC tour (p193) for visiting sights around Mysuru.

Venugopala Swamy Temple HINDU TEMPLE
(☉8am-6pm) Back from the dead, this stunning 12th-century Hoysala temple was submerged when the Kaveri River was dammed in 1930. However, villagers had tantalising glimpses of the ancient structure during drought years when the reservoir waters dropped. Liquor baron and philanthropist Sri Hari Khoday vowed to rebuilt the temple in 2003, and architects photographed and numbered each slab and stone, which were removed block by block and reconstructed by 200 workers at a cost of ₹25,000,000. The project took eight years.

It's 28km northwest of Mysuru, near Hosa Kannambadi village.

Brindavan Gardens GARDENS
(adult/child ₹40/20, camera/video ₹50/100; ☉6.30am-9pm) If you're familiar with Bollywood, these ornamental gardens might just give you a sense of déjà vu – they've been the backdrop to many a shimmying musical number. The best time to visit is in the evening, when the fountains are illuminated (at 6.30pm) and made to dance to the accompaniment of popular film tunes.

The gardens are 19km northwest of Mysuru. One of the KSTDC tours (p193) stops here, and bus 301 departs from Mysuru's City bus stand hourly (₹23, 45 minutes).

Srirangapatna (Srirangapatnam)

📲 08236 / POP 27,100
Steeped in bloody history, the fort town of Srirangapatna (Srirangapatnam), 16km from Mysuru, is built on an island straddling the Cauvery River. The seat of Hyder Ali and Tipu Sultan's power, this town was the de facto capital of much of southern India during the 18th century. The ramparts, battlements and some of the gates of the fort still stand, as do a clutch of monuments.

⊙ Sights

★**Daria Daulat Bagh** PALACE
(Summer Palace; Indian/foreigner ₹25/300; ☉8.30am-5.30pm) Set within lovely manicured grounds 1km east of the fort, Tipu's summer palace is Srirangapatna's star attraction. Built from teak and rosewood, it has impressively lavish decoration covering

BUSES FROM MYSURU

DESTINATION	FARE (₹)	DURATION (HR)	DEPARTURES
Bandipur	79	2	10 daily via Ooty
Bengaluru (Bangalore)	129-326	2½-4	33 daily midnight to 10pm
Bengaluru airport	800	3½-4	21 daily
Channarayapatna	88-175	2	17 daily
Chennai	674-1020	9-12½	6 daily from 4pm
Ernakulam	735-846	8½-10	3 daily from 6.05pm
Gokarna	504	12	1 daily at 6.05am
Hassan	118	2½-3	18 daily
Hospete (Hospet)	362-782	9-12½	9 daily
Mangaluru (Mangalore)	256-676	6-7	20 daily
Ooty (Udhagamandalam)	157-567	4-5	12 daily

Fares: (O) Ordinary, (R) Rajahamsa Semideluxe, (V) Airavath AC Volvo

every inch of its interiors. The ceilings are embellished with floral designs, while the walls bear murals depicting courtly life and Tipu's campaigns against the British. A small museum within displays artefacts and interesting paintings. Audio guides are available.

Colonel Bailey's Dungeon HISTORIC SITE
FREE North of the island, on the banks of the Cauvery, is this well-preserved 18th-century white-walled dungeon used to hold British prisoners of war, including Colonel Bailey, who died here in 1780. Jutting out from the walls are stone fixtures used to chain the naked prisoners, who were immersed in water up to their necks.

Gumbaz MAUSOLEUM
(⊘ 8am-6.30pm) **FREE** In a serene garden, the historically significant Persian-style Gumbaz is the resting place of the legendary Tipu Sultan, his equally famed father, Hyder Ali and his mother Fakr-Un-Nisa. Many other relatives of the sultan are buried in the mausoleum's grounds. The interior of the onion-domed mausoleum is impressive, painted in a tiger-like motif as a tribute to the sultan.

**Ranganathittu
Bird Sanctuary** BIRD SANCTUARY
(Indian/foreigner incl 15min boat ride ₹70/140, long-lens camera or video ₹500; ⊘ 8.30am-5.45pm) The sanctuary includes six islets and the banks of the Cauvery River. Storks, ibises, egrets, spoonbills and cormorants are best seen in the early morning or late afternoon on an extended boat ride (₹1500 per hour). There are also plenty of crocodiles, which are quite easy to spot. There's a restaurant on-site.

ℹ️ Getting There & Away

Hourly buses (₹22 to ₹32, 45 minutes) depart from Mysuru's City bus stand. Passenger trains travelling from Mysuru to Bengaluru also stop here. Bus 301 (₹18, 30 minutes) heading from Mysuru to Brindavan Gardens stops just across from Srirangapatna's main bus stand. A return autorickshaw from Mysuru is about ₹700, and a taxi around ₹1100.

Melukote

Life in the devout Hindu town of Melukote (also called Melkote), 51km north of Mysuru, revolves around the atmospheric 12th-century **Cheluvanarayana Temple** (Raja St; ⊘ 8am-1pm & 5-8pm), with its rose-coloured *gopuram* (gateway tower) and ornately carved pillars. Get a workout on the hike up

to the hilltop Yoganarasimha Temple, which offers fine views of the surrounding hills.

Three KSRTC buses shuttle daily between Mysuru and Melukote (₹108, 1½ hours).

Somnathpur

Small in scale but masterly in detail, the astonishingly beautiful **Keshava Temple** (Indian/foreigner ₹25/300; ⊘ 8.30am-5.30pm) is one of the finest examples of Hoysala architecture, on par with the masterpieces of Belur and Halebid. Built in 1268, this star-shaped temple, 33km from Mysuru, is adorned with superb stone sculptures depicting various scenes from the Ramayana and Mahabharata, and the life and times of the Hoysala kings.

Somnathpur is 8km south of Bannur. Take one of the half-hourly buses from Mysuru to Bannur (₹55, 50 minutes) and catch an autorickshaw (around ₹130 one way) from there. A half-day return trip by car from Mysuru should cost around ₹1200.

Bandipur National Park

📋 08229
Part of the Nilgiri Biosphere Reserve, **Bandipur National Park** (http://bandipurtigerreserve.in; Indian/foreigner ₹75/1000, video ₹1000; ⊘ 6am-9.30am & 4-6pm) is one of South India's most famous wilderness areas. Covering 880 sq km, it was once the Mysuru maharajas' private wildlife reserve, and is now a protected zone for more than 100 species of mammal, including tigers, elephants, leopards, gaurs (Indian bison), chitals (spotted deer), sambars, sloth bears, dholes, mongooses and langurs. It's also home to an impressive 350 bird species. It's only 72km south of Mysuru on the Ooty road.

The **forest department** (📋 08229-236043; https://bandipurtigerreserve.in; 1½hr safari per person bus/Gypsy ₹350/3250; ⊘ 6.30-9.30am & 3.30-6.30pm) has rushed drives on buses (capacity 20) and gypsy jeeps (capacity six), arranged at park headquarters. **Bandipur Safari Lodge** (📋 08229-233001; www.junglelodges.com; 2hr safari per person ₹2800; ⊘ 6am & 4pm) has open-air 4WDs and minibuses, accompanied by knowledgeable guides.

🛏️ Sleeping & Eating

Tiger Ranch LODGE **$$**
(📋 8095408505; http://tigerranch.net; Mangala Village; per person incl full board ₹1670) The very rustic Tiger Ranch has basic cottages, a thatched-roof dining hall and fine

home-cooked food. There's good walking in the surrounding forest, and you're sure to encounter wildlife. Evenings can be enjoyed around a bonfire (extra charge). It's located 10km from the park entrance; call ahead to arrange pick-up (₹300). Note that the access road is very rough.

Dhole's Den LODGE $$$
(☏9444468376; www.dholesden.com; Kaniyanapura Village; camping/s/d incl full board from ₹3000/12,900/14,300; ☎) ✿ Dhole's Den offers contemporary design in lovely pastoral surrounds. Stylish rooms and bungalows are decked out with art and colourful fabrics, plus couches and deckchairs. It's environmentally conscious, with solar power, tank water and organic vegies. Camping is available for those on a budget. Located a 20-minute drive from park headquarters; rates include a guided nature walk.

Serai RESORT $$$
(☏08229-236075; www.theserai.in; Kaniyanapura Village; r incl full board from ₹21,700; ❋☎❋) Set in a coffee plantation that backs onto the park, this luxurious resort has gorgeous Mediterranean-inspired villas (some with private pool) that are in harmony with the natural surroundings. Thatched-roof rooms feature elegant touches such as copper bathroom fixtures, stone-wall showers and wildlife photography on the walls. Its glassed-in restaurant and infinity pool both maximise outlooks to the Nilgiri Hills.

MC Resort HOTEL $$$
(☏9019954162; www.mcresorts.in; Bengaluru-Ooty Rd, Melukamanahally; s/d incl full board from ₹5310/6490; ☎❋) Decent, resort-style MC has 23 spacious, well-equipped rooms, a large swimming pool, a kids' pool, a multi-cuisine restaurant and a convenient location near the park. Rates include meals. Jungle safaris cost ₹1600 per person and are a step up in quality from the Forest Department's.

ℹ Getting There & Away

Buses between Mysuru and Ooty can drop you at Bandipur (₹92, 2½ hours). A taxi from Mysuru costs about ₹2200.

Nagarhole National Park

Rich in jungle and boasting a scenic lake, this **national park** (Rajiv Gandhi National Park; Indian/foreigner ₹200/1000, video ₹1000; ☉6am-6pm) is one of Karnataka's best wildlife getaways. It's home to good numbers of animals, including tigers and elephants. Flanking the Kabini River, it forms an important protected region that includes the neighbouring Bandipur National Park and several other reserves.

The Kabini River empties into the Kabini Reservoir, creating a vast watering hole for Nagarhole's wildlife. Herds of wild elephants and other animals gather on the banks to drink, and the high concentration of wildlife has made this one of the best spotting locations in Karnataka. The traditional inhabitants of the land, the hunter-gatherer Jenu Kuruba people, still live in the park, despite government efforts to relocate them.

Kabini was once a private hunting reserve for the maharaja of Mysuru, and today it hosts some of the top wildlife lodges in southern India. The best time to view wildlife is during summer (April to May), though winter (November to February) is more comfortable.

Government-run safaris (Kabini River Lodge; Indian/foreigner 4WD safari ₹350/1300, bus safari ₹100/300, camera ₹200-400; ☉6am-6pm) in both jeeps (capacity nine) and safari buses (capacity 25) leave at 7am and 3pm when conditions allow in the dry season. Organised by the Kabini River Lodge, **20-seater motorboat** (Kabini River Lodge; per person ₹2000) rides allow for relaxed wildlife viewing and are excellent for birders.

🛏 Sleeping & Eating

Kabini Lake makes a wonderful base and is home to most lodges, but there are no real budget hotels here. For inexpensive places, head to the park HQ.

Karapur Hotel GUESTHOUSE $
(☏9945904840; Karapura; r ₹1250) The only budget option close to Kabini is this simple lodge with a few rooms above a shop in the township of Karapura, 3km from the park.

★Waterwoods Lodge GUESTHOUSE $$$
(☏082-28264421; www.waterwoods.in; d incl full board from ₹15,300; ❋☎❋) On a grassy embankment overlooking scenic Kabini Lake, Waterwoods is a stunning lodge. Most rooms have balconies with wonderful lake views, swing chairs, hardwood floors and designer flair. It's kid friendly, with a trampoline, an infinity pool, free canoe hire and wood-fired pizzas. Pamper yourself in the spa, which has massage rooms, a Jacuzzi and a steam bath.

KAAV Safari Lodge LODGE $$$
(☏08228-264492; www.kaav.com; Mallali Cross, Kabini; r or luxury tents incl full board from ₹17,800;

✳🛈⛱) KAAV has open-plan rooms with polished-concrete floors, hip bathrooms and spacious balconies that open directly to the national park. The attention to detail is superb. Head up to the viewing tower to lounge on plush day beds, or take a dip in the infinity pool. No children under 10.

Bison Resort
LODGE $$$

(📞080-41278708; www.thebisonresort.com; Gundathur Village; camping per person from ₹2650, s/d incl full board from US$335/390; 🛈⛱) Inspired by luxury safari lodges in Africa, Bison succeeds in replicating the classic wilderness experience with a stunning waterfront location and a choice between canvas-walled cottages, stilted bungalows or bush camping. It offers a wide selection of activities, including treks to local tribal villages and sunset boat rides. Service standards are top notch and there are expert naturalists on hand.

Kabini River Lodge
LODGE $$$

(📞08228-264405; www.junglelodges.com/kabini-river-lodge; per person incl full board & activities dm ₹5900, r from ₹11,200; ✳) These attractive bungalows have a prime location beside the lake with a choice between large tented cottages and bungalows. You can enjoy a sundowner in the atmospheric colonial-style bar. Those in the dorm only get a boat (not jeep) safari included.

❶ Getting There & Away

Buses between Mysuru and Ooty can drop you at Bandipur (₹92, 2½ hours). A taxi from Mysuru costs about ₹2200.

Kodagu (Coorg) Region

Nestled amid evergreen hills that line the southernmost edge of Karnataka is the luscious Kodagu (Coorg) region, gifted with emerald landscapes and hectares of plantations. A major centre for coffee and spice production, this rural expanse is also home to the Kodava people, who are divided into 1000 clans. The uneven terrain and cool climate make it a fantastic area for trekking, birdwatching or lazily ambling down little-trodden paths winding around carpeted hills. All in all, Kodagu is rejuvenation guaranteed.

Kodagu was a state in its own right until 1956, when it merged with Karnataka. The region's chief town and transport hub is Madikeri, but for an authentic Kodagu experience you have to venture into the countryside. Avoid weekends if you can, when plac-es can quickly get filled up by weekenders from Bengaluru.

Exploring the region on foot is a highlight for many visitors. Treks are part cultural experience, part nature encounter, involving hill climbs, plantation visits, forest walks and homestays. Several local and Bengaluru-based tour operators offer walks. Popular peaks to trek to include Tadiyendamol (1745m), Pushpagiri (1712m) and Kotebetta (1620m). Plenty of day hikes are possible; a trekking guide is essential for navigating the labyrinth of forest tracks.

Madikeri (Mercara)

📞 08272 / POP 35,700 / ELEV 1525M

Madikeri (also known as Mercara) is a congested market town spread out along a series of ridges. The only reason for coming here is to organise treks or sort out the practicalities of travel.

◉ Sights & Activities

Popular local sights include Abbi Falls, the viewpoint at **Raja's Seat** (Mahatma Gandhi Rd; ₹5; ⊙5.30am-7pm) and **Raja's Tombs** (Gaddige) FREE, 7km from Madikeri.

Madikeri Fort
HISTORIC SITE

There are good views from this hilltop fort, built by Tipu Sultan in the 16th century, though today it's the less glamorous site of the municipal headquarters. You can walk a short section of ramparts, and within the fort's walls are the hexagonal palace (now the dusty district-commissioner's office) and a colonial-era church, which houses a quirky **museum** (free entry; ⊙10am-5.30pm Sun-Fri).

Ayurjeevan
AYURVEDA

(📞944974779; Kohinoor Rd; 1hr from ₹1400; ⊙7am-7pm) An ayurvedic 'hospital' that offers a whole range of intriguing and rejuvenating techniques, including rice-ball massages and oil baths. It's a short walk from the State Bank of India.

🛏 Sleeping & Eating

With fantastic guesthouses in the surrounding plantations, there's no real reason to stay in Madikeri, unless you arrive very late.

Hotel Chitra
HOTEL $

(📞08272-225372; www.hotelchitra.co.in; School Rd; d ₹950-1500; ✳) A dependable hotel close to Madikeri's main intersection (so expect some background traffic noise). Provides low-cost, no-frills rooms with cable TV and reliable hot water.

KARNATAKA KODAGU (COORG) REGION

Hotel Mayura Valley View
HOTEL $$

(☑ 08272-228387; www.kstdc.co/hotels/hotel-mayura-valley-view-madikeri; Stuart Hill; d/ste incl breakfast from ₹2400/3300; ❉ ☎) This government hotel is one of Madikeri's best, with large, bright rooms, a peaceful ambience and fantastic valley views. You pay extra for AC. Its restaurant-bar with a terrace overlooking the valley is a great spot for a tipple.

Coorg Cuisine
INDIAN $

(Main Rd; mains ₹100-195; ⊙ noon-4pm & 7-10pm) Specialising in Kodagu specialities such as *pandhi barthadh* (pork dry fry) and *koli nallamolu barthad* (chicken-pepper fry), this restaurant is well worth trying. It's not exactly atmospheric, located above a shop on the main road, but the seating is comfy and prices reasonable.

★ Raintree
INDIAN $$

(www.raintree.in; 13-14 Pension Lane; meals ₹160-300; ⊙ 11.30am-10pm) This cute converted bungalow makes a cosy place for a delicious meal, with solid wooden furniture and tribal art. The food doesn't disappoint, either, with local specialities and dishes from the coast. It also sells wine and great Kodagu coffee. Located just behind Madikeri Town Hall.

🍷 Drinking & Nightlife

Beans 'n' Brews Cafe
CAFE

(Bus Stand Rd; drinks ₹60-150; ⊙ 9am-10pm; ☎) A welcoming sight on a cool Coorg morning, this cafe offers a terrific range of steaming gourmet teas (try the Darjeeling Orange Summer tips) and great coffee, including Vietnamese drip.

🛍 Shopping

Choci Coorg
CHOCOLATE

(www.facebook.com/chocicoorgmadikeri; Bus Stand Rd; ⊙ 9am-9pm) Opposite the bus stand, Choci Coorg does many varieties of chocolate, lots of fruity and nut combos and a unique betel-nut flavour.

ℹ Getting There & Away

Madikeri is the main transport hub of the region, with very regular connections to Mysuru, Bengaluru and Mangaluru. There's near-zero public transport to the rural lodges and homestays, but autorickshaws are freely available in Madikeri.

Around Madikeri

The highlands around Madikeri offer some of Kodagu's most enchanting countryside with spice and coffee plantations and excellent accommodation.

🏃 Activities

★ Jiva Spa
SPA

(☑ 08272-2665900; jivaspa.coorg@tajhotels.com; 1st Monnangeri, Galibeedu Post; treatments from ₹2700; ⊙ 9am-9pm) Based at the stunning Taj Madikeri Resort & Spa (p203), this is an excellent place to indulge in a rejuvenating ayurvedic treatment. With soak tubs, a relaxation lounge, a beauty salon and a yoga-and-meditation zone, it's one of the best spas in South India. Appointments essential.

Swaasthya Ayurveda Retreat Village
AYURVEDA

(www.swaasthya.com; Bekkesodlur Village; per person per day incl full board & yoga class from ₹7200) For an exceptionally peaceful and refreshing ayurvedic vacation, head to south Coorg to soothe your soul among the lush greenery on 1.6 hectares of coffee and spice plantations. Prices include treatments.

🛏 Sleeping & Eating

★ Rainforest Retreat
GUESTHOUSE $$

(☑ 08272-265639, 08272-265638; www.rainforestours.com; Galibeedu; s/d tent ₹1500/2000, cottages from ₹2000/3000; ☎) 🌱 A great place to socialise with eco-minded Indians, this nature-soaked refuge is immersed within forest and plantations, and has an organic, sustainable set-up. Accommodation is lazy camping (prepitched tents with beds) or cottages with solar power. Rates include plantation tours and treks. Check the website for volunteering opportunities. An autorickshaw from Madikeri is ₹250.

Golden Mist
HOMESTAY $$

(☑ 9448903670, 08272-265629; Galibeedu; s/d incl full board ₹2500/4000) An incredibly peaceful, very rustic Indian-German-managed tea-, coffee- and rice-growing farm. The cottages have character, though they're basic and best suited to outdoor types rather than those who prize their creature comforts. Meals are tasty local dishes made from the farm's organic produce. Staff members are very hospitable. It's tricky to find and not signposted; an autorickshaw from Madikeri costs ₹250.

River Edge Valley Homestay
HOMESTAY $$

(☑ 9481759099, 9482422739; www.facebook.com/riveredgevalley; Mukkodlur; per person incl breakfast & dinner weekday/weekend ₹1500/1750) Owned by a hospitable couple, this rustic homestay boasts a hillside location and stunning valley views. It's just the spot to enjoy nature and perhaps do some birdwatching. Rooms are well presented and the home-cooked food is delicious. Located 21km north of Madikeri; the access road can be tough to tackle after heavy rain.

Victorian Verandaz
B&B $$

(📞9448059850; http://victorianverandaz.com; Modur Estate, Kadagadal Village; d self-catering ₹2500-6000, B&B ₹2950; 🛜) Fine family-owned lodgings on a huge estate that grows coffee, pepper, cardamom and rice. There's a choice of accommodation: two rental cottages with kitchens that are available on a self-catering basis, and two rooms in a cottage that operate on a B&B basis. There's good birding and trail walking on the estate.

★Taj Madikeri Resort & Spa
LUXURY HOTEL $$$

(Vivanta; 📞08272-265900; www.tajhotels.com; 1st Monnangeri, Galibeedu Post; r from ₹19,200; @🛜🏊) Nestling in misty rainforest, this supremely stylish hotel incorporates principles of space and minimalism, and effectively blends into its environment. Old cattle tracks lead to rooms, with pricier ones featuring private indoor pools, fireplaces and butlers. There are astonishing highland views from the lobby and infinity pool, and a top-class ayurvedic spa.

Kakkabe
📞 08272 / POP 588

Surrounded by forested hills, this tranquil village and hiking hotspot is an ideal base for an assault on Kodagu's highest peak, Tadiyendamol (1745m), or just for enjoying a wander along scenic highland trails.

🛏 Sleeping & Eating

Most hotels operate on a full-board basis. There are very few other eating options in the area.

★Honey Valley Estate
GUESTHOUSE $

(📞08272-238339; www.honeyvalleyindia.in; d ₹600-1900, f from ₹2400; 🛜) The friendly owners market their delightful homestay as 'perfect for the pleasure of doing nothing at all', but if you do want to shake a leg you'll find 18 local trekking routes. The lodge is at 1250m, so expect cool, fresh mornings. There are 10 accommodation options; meals are ₹150 to ₹200. Accessible by 4WD only (₹200; book via hotel) from Kakkabe.

Chingaara
GUESTHOUSE $$

(📞08272-238633; www.chingaara.com; Kabbinakad; r incl half board ₹1750-2700; 🛜) This delightful farmhouse is surrounded by verdant coffee plantations, with good birding in the vicinity. Its nine rooms are spacious, and most have good views. Good home-style cooking is served and staff members will light a bonfire at night. It's 2.5km up a rocky steep hill (4WD only); call ahead and Chingaara's 4WD will pick you up from Kabbinakad junction.

Palace Estate Home Stay
HOMESTAY $$

(http://palaceestate.co.in; s/d from ₹1400/3600; 🛜) In the foothills of the Western Ghats, 4.5km southwest of Kakkabe, this lodge is located on a farm where coffee, cardamom, fruit and avocado are cultivated. There's good trekking and a guests' library, and you can take a natural shower in the estate's waterfall if the climate is agreeable. Cash only.

Misty Woods
LODGE $$$

(📞08272-238561; www.coorgmisty.com; cottages ₹7000-12,000; 🛜🏊) The name Misty Woods aptly sums up the landscape that surrounds this mountain lodge. The *vastu shastra* (ancient science similar to feng shui) style cottages are both comfortable and stylish, and the games room (with pool table, ping pong, table football and chessboard) is great for rainy days.

ℹ Getting There & Away

Regular buses run to Kakkabe from Madikeri (₹52, 1½ hours). Most lodges will pick you up from either Kakkabe or Kabbinakad, 3km beyond Kakkabe.

Hassan
📞 08172 / POP 142,000

This sprawling, congested city has minimal appeal for the traveller other than as a base for visiting nearby Belur, Halebid or Sravanabelagola. It's something of a transport hub, with good bus and train connections, and has a decent range of accommodation.

The helpful **tourist office** (📞08172-268862; AVK College Rd; ⊙10am-5.30pm Mon-Fri) can advise on transport options.

🛏 Sleeping & Eating

Jewel Rock Hotel
HOTEL $

(📞08172-261048; www.jewelrockhotels.com; BM Rd; d from ₹1000, with air-con ₹1700; ✳🛜) This place is good value, with 36 spacious if somewhat dated rooms. There's a decent

WORTH A TRIP

BYLAKUPPE – TIBETAN VILLAGE

Tiny Bylakuppe was among the first refugee camps set up in South India to house thousands of Tibetans who fled from Tibet following the 1959 Chinese invasion. Over 10,000 Tibetans (including some 3300 monks) live around the town, forming South India's largest Tibetan community, but foreigners need a permit to stop overnight.

The area's highlight is the atmospheric **Namdroling Monastery** (www.namdroling.org; ☺7am-6pm), home to the spectacular **Golden Temple** (Padmasambhava Buddhist Vihara; ☺7am-6pm), presided over by three 18m-high gold-plated Buddha statues. The temple is at its dramatic best when prayers are in session and it rings out with gongs, drums and the drone of hundreds of young monks chanting. You're welcome to sit and meditate. The **Zangdogpalri Temple** (☺7am-6pm), a similarly ornate affair, is next door.

While day-trippers are welcome to visit, foreigners are not allowed to stay overnight in Bylakuppe without a Protected Area Permit (PAP) from the Ministry of Home Affairs in Delhi, which can take months to process. Contact the Tibet Bueau Office (www.tibet bureau.in) for details. If you have a permit, the simple **Paljor Dhargey Ling Guest House** (☏08223-258686; pdguesthouse@yahoo.com; r ₹300-500) is opposite the Golden Temple. For delicious *momos* (Tibetan dumplings) or *thukpa* (noodle soup), pop into the Tibetan-run **Malaya Restaurant** (momos ₹60-90; ☺7am-9pm). Otherwise there are many hotels in nearby Kushalnagar and in the countryside around the village.

Autorickshaws (shared/solo ₹15/30) run to Bylakuppe from Kushalnagar, 5km away. Buses frequently do the 34km run to Kushalnagar from Madikeri (₹40, 45 minutes) and Hassan (₹82, 2½ hours). Most buses on the Mysuru–Madikeri route stop at Kushalnagar.

in-house vegetarian restaurant and bar, plus 24-hour room service. It's 700m west of the train station, just off the busy highway to Bengaluru.

Mallige Residency
HOTEL $$
(☏08172-260333; www.malligeresidency.com; 266 High School Field Rd; r incl breakfast ₹1600-2400, ste ₹2600; ❄🛜) Almost a boutique hotel, the fine Malige offers rooms (there are four classes) that are spotless, contemporary and comfortable. It's also home to one of the best restaurants in town, Parijata Restaurant.

Hoysala Village
HOTEL $$$
(☏9591077400; http://hoysalavillageresorts.com; Belur Rd; cottages incl full board from ₹11,130; ❄🛜🏊) A fine upmarket lodge in leafy grounds with pretty cottages and suites, and a good ayurvedic spa. Lots of activities are offered, from guided birding walks to volleyball, and guests can enjoy traditional dance and music performances. Very relaxing and family friendly.

Parijata Restaurant
VEGETARIAN $$
(Mallige Residency, High School Field Rd; mains ₹80-220; ☺11am-10pm; 🛜) This popular, pure-veg hotel restaurant with inviting modern decor serves both North and South Indian cuisine, but it's the latter that stands out. Prices are moderate.

Swaad
INDIAN $$
(Hotel Raama, BM Rd; mains ₹120-240; ☺8am-10pm) This inviting air-conditioned all-veg hotel restaurant makes a relaxed place for a meal, serving tasty North and South Indian classics.

❶ Getting There & Away

From the **New Bus Stand** (Hwy 71), 500m south of the town centre, buses depart to Mysuru (₹120, three hours), Bengaluru (₹198 to ₹484, 3½ to 4½ hours) and Mangaluru (₹166 to ₹380, 3½ to 4½ hours). A day tour of Belur and Halebid or Sravanabelagola in a car will cost you about ₹2000.

From Hassan's well-organised train station there's a daily service at 7.45pm to Mysuru (AC chair class ₹260, 2½ hours) and another in the dead of night. For Bengaluru there are three to four daily trains, including the 11312 Solapur Express (sleeper/2AC ₹170/745, five hours).

Belur

☏08177 / POP 9580 / ELEV 968M

The 12th-century Hoysala temples at Belur (also called Beluru) are the apex of one of the most artistically exuberant periods of ancient Hindu cultural development. The main temple, dedicated to Vishnu, has been a place of worship for over 900 years.

Commissioned in 1116 to commemorate the Hoysalas' victory over the neighbouring

Cholas, **Channakeshava Temple** (Temple Rd; guide ₹250; ⊙7am-7.30pm) took more than a century to build, and is currently the only one of the three major Hoysala sites still in daily use – try to be there for one of the *puja* (offering or prayer) ceremonies, held at 9am, 3pm and 7.30pm.

Inviting, renovated, state-run **Mayura Velapuri** (☑0817-7222209, 8970650026; www.kstdc.co/hotels; Temple Rd; d with fan/AC from ₹1350/1460, ste ₹2240; ❋🐾), 700m from Channakeshava Temple, has comfortable, spacious rooms dotted around shady grounds. It's set back from the road and has a good restaurant-bar serving a variety of Indian dishes (from ₹80) to go with beer.

There are frequent buses to/from Hassan (₹42 to ₹92, 45 minutes), 38km away, and Halebid (₹25, 30 minutes). Tours taking in Belur and nearby Halebid can be easily set up in Hassan.

Halebid

☑08177 / POP 9450

Halebid (also called Halibidu or Halebeedu) is a small town that's home to a stunning Hoysala temple and some other minor Jain sites. Most travellers visit on a day trip from Belur or Hassan.

Construction of the **Hoysaleswara Temple** (⊙dawn-dusk), Halebid's claim to fame, began around 1121 and went on for more than 80 years. It was never completed but nonetheless stands today as a masterpiece of Hoysala architecture. The interior of its inner sanctum, chiselled out of black stone, is marvellous. On the outside, the temple's richly sculpted walls are covered with a flurry of Hindu deities, sages, stylised animals, and friezes depicting the life of the Hoysala rulers.

Set in a leafy garden right opposite the temple complex, **Hotel Mayura Shanthala** (☑08177-273224; www.kstdc.co/hotels; r/q incl breakfast from ₹1450/1680; ❋🐾) is the town's best sleeping option.

Regular buses depart for Hassan (₹38, one hour); buses to Belur (15km, ₹25) are also quite frequent.

Sravanabelagola

☑08176 / POP 5660

Atop the bare, rocky summit of Vindhyagiri Hill, the 17.5m-high statue of the Jain deity Gomateshvara (Bahubali) is visible long before you reach the pilgrimage town of Sravanabelagola (also spelt Shravanabelagola).

Viewing the statue close up is the main reason for heading to this sedate town, whose name means 'Monk of the White Pond'.

◉ Sights

Apart from the Gomateshvara statue, there are several interesting Jain temples in town. The **Chandragupta Basti** (Chandragupta Community; ⊙6am-6pm), on Chandragiri Hill opposite Vindhyagiri, is believed to have been built by Emperor Ashoka. The **Bhandari Basti** (Bhandari Community; ⊙6am-6pm), in the southeastern corner of town, is Sravanabelagola's largest temple. Nearby, **Chandranatha Basti** (Chandranatha Community; ⊙6am-6pm) has well-preserved paintings depicting Jain tales.

Gomateshvara Statue   JAIN SITE
(Bahubali; ⊙6.30am-6.30pm) A steep climb up 614 steps takes you to the top of Vindhyagiri Hill, the summit of which is lorded over by a towering naked statue of Jain deity Gomateshvara (Bahubali). Commissioned by a military commander in the service of the Ganga king Rachamalla and carved out of a single piece of granite by sculptor Aristenemi in AD 98, it is said to be the world's tallest monolithic statue. Leave your shoes at the foot of the hill.

Bahubali was the son of emperor Vrishabhadeva, who later became the first Jain *tirthankar* (revered teacher), Adinath. Embroiled in fierce competition with his brother Bharatha to succeed his father, Bahubali realised the futility of material gains and renounced his kingdom. As a recluse, he meditated in complete stillness in the forest until he attained enlightenment. His lengthy meditative spell is denoted by vines curling around his legs and an anthill at his feet.

Every 12 years, millions flock here to attend the **Mastakabhisheka** (⊙Feb) ceremony, when the statue is doused in holy water, pastes, powders, precious metals and stones. The next ceremony is slated for 2030.

🛏 Sleeping & Eating

The local Jain organisation **SDJMI** (☑08176-257258; d/tr ₹260/330) handles bookings for its 15 guesthouses. Otherwise, options are few.

Hotel Raghu   HOTEL $
(☑08176-257238; s/d from ₹500/600, d with AC ₹1000; ❋) Offers very basic rooms that are something of a last resort. However, the vegetarian restaurant downstairs serves an awesome thali (₹90).

ⓘ Getting There & Away

There are no direct buses from Sravanabelagola to Hassan or Belur – you must go to Channarayapatna (₹28, 25 minutes) and catch an onward connection there. One daily bus runs direct to Mysuru (₹110, two hours).

KARNATAKA COAST

Mangaluru (Mangalore)

☐ 0824 / POP 498,600

Alternating between relaxed coastal town and hectic nightmare, Mangaluru (more commonly known as Mangalore) has a Jekyll-and-Hyde thing going, but it's a useful gateway for the Konkan coast and the inland Kodagu region. While there's not a lot to do here, it has an appealing off-the-beaten-path feel, and the spicy seafood dishes are sensational. Mangaluru sits at the estuaries of the picturesque Netravathi and Gurupur

Rivers on the Arabian Sea and has been a major port on international trade routes since the 6th century.

◉ Sights

Sights are thin on the ground in Mangaluru, though there are some curious old Catholic structures that show a distinct European architectural influence.

Pilikula Nisarga Dhama THEME PARK
(☐ 0824-2263565; www.pilikula.com; adult/child ₹120/60, camera ₹150; ⊙ 9am-5.30pm) A kind of eco-educational theme park, Pilikula is spread over 149 hectares and includes a tropical forest, an arboretum, a herb garden full of rare medicinal plants, an artisan village with craft-making demonstrations, a zoo, a science centre and a lake. The 3D Planetarium (films in English at noon and 4pm daily) is certainly worth taking in. It's 8km east of central Mangaluru. Buses 3A, 3B and 3C head here from Mangaluru, or an Ola/Uber is around ₹200.

Mangaluru (Mangalore)

St Aloysius College Chapel   CHURCH
(Lighthouse Hill; ⊙9am-6pm) Catholicism's roots in Mangaluru date back to the arrival of the Portuguese in the early 1500s. One impressive legacy is the 1880 Sistine Chapel–like St Aloysius chapel, its walls and ceilings painted with brilliant frescos. No photography is permitted.

🛏 Sleeping & Eating

Hotel Manorama   HOTEL $
(☑0824-2440306; www.hotelmanorama.in; KS Rao Rd; r from ₹990; ❀🢅) Offering fine value, the Manorama has clean rooms and a lobby that provides a memorable first impression with its display of Hindu statues and artefacts. It's close to the City Center mall, which has a food court.

Phalguni River Lodge   LODGE $$
(☑0821-2444444; www.phalguniriverlodge.in; Moodushedde Rd; r incl breakfast from ₹3000; ❀🢅) Next to the Pilikula Nisarga Dhama park, with views of the Gurupur River and coconut groves, this lodge offers a tranquil natural environment for those stressed by Indian city life. Rooms are spacious and there's good grub, including local seafood, available in the restaurant. Managed by the Jungle Lodge chain. Around 8km west of the centre of town.

Hotel Roopa   HOTEL $$
(☑0824-2421272; www.roopahotel.com; Balmatta Rd; r incl breakfast from ₹1600; ❀🢅) Close to the KSRTC bus stand, this hotel is professionally managed and has well-presented, spacious rooms. Its restaurant serves authentic Mangalorean cuisine, and there's a bar.

Gateway Hotel   HOTEL $$$
(☑0824-6660420; www.tajhotels.com; Old Port Rd; s/d incl breakfast from ₹5720/6280; ❀@🢅⚊) At this well-managed hotel (part of the Taj group) in the heart of the city the spacious rooms have a touch of class, though some retain very dated bathrooms. The lovely 20m swimming pool at the rear is surrounded by lawn and loungers, and there's a small spa and a fine restaurant. Rates are a tad steep, however.

★Girimanja's   MANGALOREAN $$
(GKT Rd; meals ₹150-280; ⊙11.30am-3.30pm) Terrific, authentic Mangalorean food in very simple, no-nonsense surrounds and very fairly priced. Try the fish fry or prawn fry; sauces are incredibly rich and loaded with local chilli. Lunch only, and be prepared to wait.

Kadal   SOUTH INDIAN $$
(Nalapad Residency, Lighthouse Hill Rd; mains ₹120-300; ⊙11am-3.30pm & 6.30-11pm; 🢅) This high-rise restaurant has wonderful city views and elegant, warmly lit interiors. Try the fish thali. Prices are moderate for the quality and experience.

Gajalee   SEAFOOD $$$
(☑0824-2221900; Circuit House, Kadri Hills; mains ₹170-1280; ⊙10am-11pm; 🢅) One of Mangaluru's premier seafood restaurants, with a hillside location, sweeping views and a choice of indoor or outdoor seating. Try the clam *koshimbir,* cooked in a rich green masala, or a crab dish. Wine and beer are available, and vegetarians will also dine happily.

🍷 Drinking & Nightlife

★Spindrift   MICROBREWERY
(https://spindrift.in; 5th fl, Bharath Mall, Lalbagh; ⊙11am-11pm; 🢅) The city's premier microbrewery is a big space with indoor and outdoor seating; the acoustic artists, indie bands and DJs create quite a vibe on weekend nights. Beers on tap (from ₹230) include wheat beer, pilsner and IPA, and there's good finger food, too.

Liquid Lounge   PUB
(Balmatta Rd; ⊙10am-11.30pm; 🢅) Much more pub than lounge, this long-running place is your best bet for a beer and a chat. Expect loud rock music on the stereo. Popular with young locals and serves good comfort grub.

KARNATAKA MANGALURU (MANGALORE)

Mangaluru (Mangalore)

⊙ **Sights**
  1 St Aloysius College Chapel....................C3

🛏 **Sleeping**
  2 Gateway Hotel...B4
  3 Hotel Manorama....................................C3
  4 Hotel Roopa..D3

🍴 **Eating**
  5 Gajalee...D1
  6 Girimanja's...B3
  7 Kadal..C3

🍷 **Drinking & Nightlife**
  8 Liquid Lounge..D3
  9 Spindrift...C1

TRAINS FROM MANGALURU (MANGALORE)

The main train station, Mangaluru Central, is south of the city centre.

DESTINATION	TRAIN NO & NAME	FARE (₹)	DURATION (HR)	DEPARTURS
Bengaluru (Bangalore)	16512 & 16514 Bangalore Express	sleeper/2AC 255/985	10½	8.55pm
Chennai	12686 Chennai Express	sleeper/2AC 460/1735	16	4.15pm
Gokarna	16523 Karwar Express	sleeper/2AC 205/780	5	8.35pm
Gokarna	12620 Matsyaganda Express	sleeper/2AC 235/830	4	2.25pm
Thiruvanan-thapuram (Trivandrum)	16630 Malabar Express	sleeper/2AC 345/1355	15	6.15pm

❶ Getting There & Away

AIR
Mangaluru International Airport (☑ 0824-2254252; www.mangaloreairport.com) is about 15km northeast of town. There are daily flights to Mumbai, Delhi, Bengaluru, Hubballi, Hyderabad and Chennai, and international connections to Gulf locations including Abu Dhabi, Bahrain, Doha, Dubai and Muscat.

BUS
The **KSRTC bus stand** (☑ 0824-2211243; Bejai Main Rd) is 3km from the city centre. Deluxe buses depart half-hourly to Bengaluru (₹410 to ₹835, seven to nine hours) via Mysuru (₹250 to ₹520, five to six hours).

Dharmasthala

☑ 08256 / POP 10,560

Inland from Mangaluru is a string of Jain-temple towns, such as Venur, Mudabidri and Karkal. The most interesting among them is Dharmasthala village, by the Netravathi River. Tens of thousands of pilgrims pass through this tiny settlement every day. During holidays and major festivals, such as the five-day pilgrim festival of Lakshadeepotsava (p172), the footfall can go up tenfold.

⊙ Sights

Manjunatha Temple   HINDU TEMPLE
(⊙ 6.30am-2.30pm & 5-8.45pm) A striking Kerala-style temple with meticulously renovated woodcarvings and a pyramidal roof of gold-plated copper plates. Three elephants trunk out blessings to pilgrims outside; men have to enter bare-chested, with legs covered. You can fast-track the queue if you pay ₹200.

Car Museum   MUSEUM
(₹5; ⊙ 8.30am-1pm & 2-7pm) The fantastic Car Museum is home to 48 vintage autos, including a 1903 Renault and 1920s Studebaker

President used by Mahatma Gandhi, plus classic Mercedes Benz, Chevrolet and Rolls-Royce models. No photos are allowed.

Manjusha Museum   MUSEUM
(₹5; ⊙ 10am-1pm & 4.30-9pm) Houses an eclectic collection of Indian stone and metal sculptures, jewellery, local craft products, cameras and stamps. It's opposite the Manjunatha temple.

🛏 Sleeping & Eating

The **temple office** (☑ 08256-277121; www.shridharmasthala.org; r from ₹500) can help you find lodging.

Rajathadri Guest House   LODGE $
(www.shridharmasthala.org/accomodation; r with fan/AC ₹500/990) About 700m north of the main temple, this clean guesthouse is used by pilgrims and can be booked online. Rooms sleep up to three.

Manjunatha Temple Kitchen   INDIAN
(⊙ 11.30am-2.15pm & 7.30-10pm) FREE Attached to a hall that can seat up to 3000, this place offers simple free meals. It's very efficiently managed.

❶ Getting There & Away

There are frequent buses to Dharmasthala from Mangaluru (₹88, 2½ hours).

Udupi

☑ 0820 / POP 184,300

Udupi is home to the atmospheric 13th-century **Krishna Temple** (www.udupisrikrishna matha.org; Car St; ⊙ 3.30am-10pm), which draws thousands of Hindu pilgrims through the year. Surrounded by eight maths (monasteries), it's a hive of activity, with musicians playing at the entrance, elephants on hand for *puja* and pilgrims constantly coming and going. Non-Hindus are welcome inside the temple; men must enter bare-chested. Elaborate rituals are also performed in the temple during the Udupi Paryaya festival (p172).

Sleeping & Eating

Shri Vidyasamuda Choultry HOTEL $
(0820-2520820; Car St; r ₹180-380) This simple place has views looking over the ghat.

Hotel Sriram Residency HOTEL $
(0820-2530761; www.hotelsriramresidency.in; Head Post Office Rd; r with fan/AC from ₹1600/2400;) A well-run place with good choice of rooms; some on the upper floors overlook the Krishna Temple. There are two bars and a good seafood restaurant here.

Samanvay Boutique Hotel HOTEL $$
(0820-6600300; www.samanvayudupi.com; s/d from ₹2000/2500;) 'Boutique' is pushing it a tad, but this likeable hotel certainly has a modern feel, with elegant rooms and quality furnishings, including desks and flatscreen TVs. There's a cafe and two restaurants. It's fine value considering the pretty modest rates asked. It's 150m south of the town's Mahatma Gandhi stadium.

Woodlands INDIAN $
(Dr UR Rao Complex; dosa from ₹60, meals from ₹110; 8am-3.15pm & 5.30-10.30pm) Woodlands is regarded as the best vegetarian place in town and has an air-con dining room where you can escape the heat. Serves both South and North Indian food. It's a short walk south of Krishna Temple.

Mitra Samaja INDIAN $
(Car St; meals from ₹80; 8am-9pm) A famous old establishment that serves delicious snacks, dosa (lentil-flour pancakes) and coffee. Can get crowded. It's just south of the Krishna temple.

Getting There & Away

Udupi is 58km north of Mangaluru along the coast; very regular buses ply the route (₹42 to ₹68, 1½ hours). There's a daily bus to Gokarna (₹184, four hours) at 2pm and many services (mostly at night) to Bengaluru (₹440 to ₹890, eight to 10 hours). Regular buses head to Malpe (₹11, 30 minutes).

Malpe
0820 / POP 2100

A laid-back fishing harbour on the west coast 4km from Udupi, Malpe has nice beaches ideal for splashing about in the surf. During weekends and holidays jet skis, banana boats and quad bikes taint the scene, however.

From Malpe pier you can take a ferry to tiny St Mary's Island, where Portuguese explorer Vasco da Gama supposedly landed in 1498. Locals sell coconuts (its nickname is Coconut Island), but otherwise there's little to eat or drink. You can take a ferry (₹250 return, 45 minutes, departing from 9am when demand is sufficient) from Malpe pier or charter a private boat from nearby Malpe Beach.

Beachfront **Paradise Isle Beach Resort** (0820-2538777; http://udupibeaches.com; r ₹3700-6700;) has comfortable rooms, many with sea views. **Houseboat** (per couple ₹4000; Oct-Mar) trips around the backwaters of Hoode nearby can also be organised.

Gokarna
08386 / POP 29,200

A regular nominee among travellers' favourite beaches in India, Gokarna attracts a low-key, chilled-out beach holiday crowd, not for party people. Most accommodation is in thatched bamboo huts along the town's several stretches of blissful coast.

SURFING SWAMIS

While there's always been a spiritual bond between surfer and Mother Ocean, the **Surfing Ashram** (Mantra Surf Club; 9663141146; www.surfingindia.net; 6-64 Kolachikambla; board hire/3-day course ₹700/6600) at Mulki, 30km north of Mangaluru, takes things to a whole new plane. At this Hare Krishna ashram – established by its American guru, who's been surfing since 1963 – devotees follow a daily ritual of *puja* (prayers), chanting, meditation and vegetarian food in between catching barrels. There's surf year-round, but the best waves are May to June and September to October. If there are no waves there are SUP boards for the river or ocean, sea kayaks, and a jet ski for wakeboarding. Snorkelling trips to offshore islands are also possible. The swamis can also assist with information on surfing across India.

In fact there are two Gokarnas. For most Indian visitors Gokarna is a sacred pilgrimage town of ancient temples that are the focus of important festivals such as **Shivaratri** (⊙ Feb/Mar) and Ganesh Chaturthi (p172). International travellers flock to the 'other' Gokarna: a succession of ravishing sandy beaches south of town.

⊙ Sights

Temples

This is a deeply holy town and foreigners should be respectful in and around its many temples: do not try to enter their inner sanctums, which are reserved for Hindus only. It's customary for pilgrims to bathe in the sea and fast, and many shave their heads, before entering Gokarna's holy places.

★**Mahaganapati Temple**   HINDU TEMPLE
(Car St; ⊙6am-8.30pm) **FREE** Deeply atmospheric temple complex, encircled by lanes but peaceful inside. Here there's a (rare) stone statue of an upright, standing Ganesh, said to be over 1500 years old, who is depicted with a flat head – said to mark the spot where the demon Ravana struck him. This is the second most holy site in Gokarna and it's customary for pilgrims to visit here first before heading to the neighbouring Mahabaleshwara Temple. Foreigners are not allowed inside the inner sanctum.

★**Mahabaleshwara Temple**   HINDU TEMPLE
(Car St; ⊙6am-8.30pm) This is a profoundly spiritual temple, built of granite by Mayurasharma of the Kadamba dynasty and said to date to the 4th century. It's dedicated to Lord Shiva. Hindus believe it brings blessings to pilgrims who even glimpse it, and rituals are performed for the deceased. A *gopuram* (gateway tower) dominates the complex, while inside a stone statue of Nandi (Shiva's bull) faces the inner chamber, home to Shiva's lingam. Foreigners may enter the complex but not the inner sanctum.

Beaches

The best beaches are due south of Gokarna town: first, Kudle Beach (5km by road from Gokarna), then Om Beach (6km by road). Well hidden away south of Om Beach lie the small, sandy coves of Half Moon Bay and Paradise Beach, which don't have road access. A lovely coastal trail links all the beaches, but as there have been (very occasional) reports of muggings, it's probably best not to walk it alone.

Kudle Beach   BEACH
This lovely wide cove, backed by wooded headlands, offers plenty of room to stretch out on along its attractive sands. Restaurants, guesthouses and yoga camps are dotted around the rear of the beach, but they're well spaced and development remains peaceful and attractive.

★**Om Beach**   BEACH
One of Karnataka's best beaches, Gokarna has a famous stretch of sand that twists and turns over several kilometres to resemble the outline of an Om symbol. The beach comprises several gorgeous coves, with wide stretches interspersed with smaller patches of sand, perfect for sunbathing and swimming. There's fine swimming most of the season when the sea's not choppy, though signs officially ban it (local tourists have drowned here in rough seas). It's 6km from Gokarna town; autorickshaws cost ₹130.

Paradise Beach   BEACH
Lovely, isolated Paradise Beach is a mix of sand and rocks, and a haven for the long-term 'turn on, tune in, drop out' crowd. It's around a 45-minute walk from the southern end of Om Beach (the coastal path here passes Half Moon Bay on the way); there's no road

---

FORMULA BUFFALO

Call it an indigenous take on the Grand Prix: Kambla (traditional buffalo racing) is a hugely popular pastime for villagers along the southern Karnataka coast. Popularised in the early 20th century and born out of local farmers habitually racing their buffaloes home after a day in the fields, the races have now hit the big time. Thousands of spectators attend each edition, and racing buffaloes are pampered and prepared like thoroughbreds.

Kambla events are held between November and March, usually at weekends. Parallel tracks are laid out in a paddy field, and buffaloes hurtle along them towards the finish line. In most cases the rider travels on a board fixed to a ploughshare, literally surfing his way down the track behind the beasts. The faster creatures can cover the 120m-odd distance through water and mud in around 14 seconds!

access. Every season local entrepreneurs rig up huts (around ₹300), but the local government routinely tears them down, so it's pot luck whether you'll find a place to stay.

🏃 Activities

Cocopelli Surf School SURFING
(📱8105764969; www.cocopelli.org; Gokarna Beach; lessons per person ₹2000, board rental per 2hr ₹750; ⊙mid-Oct–May) This reputable surf school offers lessons by internationally certified instructors. It also rents boards and kayaks.

Shankar Prasad YOGA
(📱08386-256971; www.shankarprasad.org.in; Bankikodla Village) A beautiful ashram in a century-old heritage house, set in huge grounds dotted with coconut palms. Weekly and monthly yoga courses are well structured and good value; teacher training (200 hours costs from ₹59,000 including full board) is offered. Accommodation is in dorms or private rooms. It's 5km north of Gokarna town.

Shree Hari Yoga YOGA
(📱8351068174; www.shreehariyoga.in; Kudle Beach; 90min classes ₹300; ⊙6am-6.30pm Mon-Fri, to 1pm Sat Nov-May) Inland from the beach, this well-regarded yoga school offers excellent classes (hatha, Ashtanga vinyasa and occasionally Mysore style) and teacher training. Drop-ins are available four times a day, and there's evening meditation.

🛌 Sleeping

For most foreigners Gokarna means sleeping right on the beach in a simple shack. However, there's a growing number of more upmarket lodges and hotels, so if you don't want to rough it you don't have to. Note that most places are only open from November to April and prices are very flexible depending on demand.

Zostel Gokarna HOSTEL $
(📱in Dehli 011-39589002; www.zostel.com; Kudle Beach Rd; dm/cottages ₹800/2600; 🌬🛜) Some of the best dorms in Karnataka, with AC, lockers and sea views, await at this efficiently managed hostel. The cottages are also very inviting, perfect for couples, and there are cool common rooms and a restaurant. Located a 10-minute walk from Gokarna town, or a bit further away from Kudle Beach.

Nirvana Café GUESTHOUSE $
(📱9742466481, 8386257401; suresh.nirvana@gmail.com; Om Beach; cottages ₹750-1200; 🛜) These attractive cottages, towards the eastern

MURUDESHWAR

A worthwhile stopover for those taking the coastal route from Gokarna to Mangaluru, Murudeshwar is a beachside pilgrimage town. It's most notable for its colossal seashore statue of Lord Shiva, which sits directly on the shore overlooking the Arabian Sea, making for spectacular photo ops. For the best views, take the lift 18 storeys to the top of the skyscraper-like **Shri Murudeshwar temple** (lift ₹10; ⊙lift 7.45am-12.30pm & 3.15-6.45pm).

Around 500m from Murudeshwar beach, **Hotel Kawari's Palm Grove** (📱08385-260178; r with fan/AC from ₹700/1250; 🌬) has basic but clean and spacious rooms. **Mavalli Beach Heritage Home** (📱9901767993; http://mavallibeachheritage.com; r incl breakfast ₹4300; 🌬🛜) is a beachfront homestay with four stylish rooms and a warm ambience courtesy of the genial owners.

Murudeshwar is 3km off the main highway. It's accessed by trains and buses passing up and down the coast.

end of the beach, are some of Om's best, all with front porches that face a slim central garden. You'll find a good beachfront restaurant, a laundry and a travel agency

Half Moon Garden Cafe BUNGALOW $
(📱9743615820; Half Moon Bay; huts from ₹400; ⊙Nov-Apr) 🌿 A throwback to the hippie days, this hideaway has a blissful beach and pretty decent, well-kept huts in a coconut grove. It runs on solar power.

Strawberry Farmhouse GUESTHOUSE $
(📱7829367584; Kudle Beach; r ₹800-1300; 🌬🛜) Right on the sands at the northern section of Kudle, these spacious cottages (some with AC) all have verandahs, 24-hour hot water and prime water views.

Greenland Guesthouse GUESTHOUSE $
(📱9019651420; r from ₹500; 🛜) Hidden down a jungle path at the edge of town, this mellow, family-run guesthouse has clean rooms in vibrant colours and a lovely verdant garden to enjoy.

White Elephant GUESTHOUSE $$
(Arnav Cottages; 📱7090332555; http://whiteelephanthampi.com; cottages ₹2000-3000; 🌬🛜) Well-constructed, spacious cottages and fine

RANI ABBAKKA

The legendary exploits of Rani Abbakka, one of India's first freedom fighters, get little attention outside the Mangaluru region. Her inspiring story is just waiting to be picked up by a Bollywood/Hollywood screenwriter.

As the Portuguese consolidated power along India's western coastline in the 16th century, seizing towns across Goa and down to Mangalore, their attempts to take Ullal proved less successful. This was thanks to its queen, who proved to be a major thorn in their grand plans to control the lucrative spice trade. Her continual efforts to repel their advances is the stuff of local legend.

Well trained in the art of war, in both strategy and combat, Rani Abbakka knew how to brandish a sword. And while she was eventually defeated, this wasn't from a loss on the battlefield but due to her treacherous ex-husband, who conspired against her by leaking intelligence to the enemy.

Her efforts to rally her people to defeat the powerful Portuguese is not forgotten by locals: Rani Abbakka is immortalised in a bronze statue on horseback at the roundabout on the road to Ullal beach, and an annual festival is dedicated to her.

The shore temple that looks over the beautiful Someshwara beach a few kilometres south of Ullal marks the site of her fort, but only sections of its wall remain intact.

sea views are the main draws at this established place (previously called Arnav) above Kudle Beach. It's run by hospitable folk and there's an elevated deck perfect for yoga.

Arya Ayurvedic Panchakarma Centre
SPA HOTEL $$

(☑9611062468; www.ayurvedainindien.com; Kudle Beach; r from ₹1900; ❀🛜) At the southern end of Kudle (p210), this ayurvedic centre has some of the best rooms on the beach. It offers simple yet elegant accommodation with quality furnishings a few steps from the shore. Priority is given to those booking ayurvedic packages. There's a fine in-house cafe (p213).

Kudle Beach View Resort & Spa
HOTEL $$

(☑8130967666; http://kudlebeachview.com; r ₹4500-6000; ❀🛜🏊) There are mesmerising views of the ocean from this hotel's restaurant, high above Kudle Beach. Rooms, all modern and well equipped, are located well below, accessed by numerous steps. A new accommodation block was nearing completion at the time of research.

★ SwaSwara
HOTEL $$$

(☑08386-257132; www.swaswara.com; s/d 5 nights from €1780/2390; ❀@🛜🏊) 'Journeying into the self' is the mantra at SwaSwara and you certainly have the infrastructure to achieve that here, as this is one of South India's finest retreats. Yoga, ayurvedic treatments, a meditation dome, and elegant private villas with open-sky showers and lovely sitting areas await. No short stays are possible. It's inland from Om Beach.

Namaste Yoga Farm
BUNGALOW $$$

(☑9739600407; www.spiritualland.com; Kudle Beach; incl breakfast & 2 yoga classes r €69-88; 🛜) Cottages and rooms are scattered around a shady hillside plot in this Kudle institution, located above the beach and owned by a very amiable German yoga instructor. The accommodation is a little prosaic and perhaps a tad overpriced, but the yoga and breakfast (cooked to order) are exceptional and the vibe is very welcoming.

🍴 Eating

★ Prema
INDIAN $

(Gokarna Beach Rd; mains ₹100-200; ⊙8am-10pm) Always packed, this humble-looking place has a prime location just before the town beach. It offers Western food, but it's best to stick to the South or North Indian classics. Finish your meal with a rose or coconut ice cream (₹15).

Sunset Point
INDIAN $

(Om Beach; mains ₹120-200; ⊙7.30am-10pm) Family-run place at the eastern end of Om Beach with a great perch overlooking the waves. The long menu takes in breakfasts, sandwiches, and Indian and Chinese dishes; grilled prawns are around ₹200.

Chez Christophe
FRENCH $$

(☑9901459736; www.facebook.com/chezchristoff; Gokarna Town Beach; mains from ₹150; ⊙Nov-May; 🛜) For a very different vibe, stroll up the shore to this chilled French place, a 10-minute walk north from the main section of beach. You'll find authentic salads, fresh pasta, French desserts and wine by the glass.

There's low seating, beach swings, and live music some nights.

Arya Ayurvedic
Panchakarma Centre INDIAN $$
(www.ayurvedainindien.com; Kudle Beach; mains ₹130-220; ⊙8am-10pm; 🐾) Modish beachfront restaurant that boasts an open kitchen and a fine menu of vegetarian dishes freshly prepared using ayurvedic principles.

Namaste Cafe MULTICUISINE $$
(Om Beach; mains ₹115-450; ⊙8.30am-4pm & 6-11pm; 🐾) This attractive double-deck affair on Om Beach has dreamy, romantic ocean views (you can watch sea eagles soaring over the waves from your table), cold beer, and good seafood, pasta and Indian dishes.

🛍 Shopping

Organic & Herbals HEALTH & WELLNESS
(Car St; ⊙10am-9pm) A fine selection of natural beauty products, including handmade soaps, health foods, tea and spices. Prices are very fair.

Shree Radhakrishna Bookstore BOOKS
(Car St; ⊙10am-8pm) Postcards, maps and secondhand novels.

ℹ Information

MONEY
There are several ATMs in Gokarna town, including a **SBI ATM** (Main St).

POST
Post Office (Main St; ⊙10am-4.30pm Mon-Sat)

ℹ Getting There & Away

BUS
Local and private buses depart daily to Bengaluru (₹510 to ₹724, 12 hours) and Mysuru (from ₹578, 12 hours), as well as Mangaluru (from ₹266, 6½ hours) and Hubballi (₹198, four hours).

For Hampi, Paulo Travels (p221) is a popular choice (November to April only); its buses head via Hosapete (fan/AC ₹1400/1650, nine hours). Note that if you're coming from Hampi, you'll be dropped at Ankola, from where there's a free transfer for the 26km journey to Gokarna.

There are also regular buses to Panaji (Panjim; ₹135, three hours) and Mumbai (₹768 to ₹1035, 12 hours).

TRAIN
Many express trains stop at Gokarna Rd station, 9km from town. There are other options from Ankola, 26km away. Hotels and travel agencies in Gokarna can book tickets.

Of the three daily trains to Mangaluru the 3.12pm Bengaluru Express (sleeper/2AC ₹235/780, 5½ hours) is the most convenient. Heading to Margoa (Madgaon) there are three daily trains; the 8.42am (sleeper/2AC ₹170/745, 2½ hours) continues on to Mumbai (sleeper/2AC ₹460/1750, 12 hours).

Autorickshaws charge ₹230 to go to Gokarna Rd station (₹450 to Ankola); a bus from Gokarna town charges ₹30 and leaves every 30 minutes.

CENTRAL KARNATAKA

Hampi

📞 08394 / POP 3600
The magnificent ruins of Hampi dot an unearthly landscape that has captivated travellers for centuries. Heaps of giant boulders perch precariously over kilometres of undulating terrain, the rusty hues offset by jade-green palm groves, banana plantations and paddy fields. While it's possible to see this World Heritage Site in a day or two, plan on lingering for a while.

The main travellers' ghetto has traditionally been Hampi Bazaar, a village crammed with budget lodges, shops and restaurants, and towered over by the majestic Virupaksha Temple. Tranquil Virupapur Gaddi, across the river, has become a popular hang-out. However, recent demolitions (p214) in both areas have seen businesses closed.

Direct daily flights to Jindal Vijaynagar Airport, 35km south of the ruins, mean that Hampi has never been more accessible.

History

Hampi and its neighbouring areas are mentioned in the Hindu epic Ramayana as Kishkinda, the realm of the monkey gods. In 1336 Telugu prince Harihararaya chose Hampi as the site for his new capital Vijayanagar, which – over the next couple of centuries – grew into one of the largest Hindu empires in Indian history. By the 16th century it was a thriving metropolis of about 500,000 people, its busy bazaars dabbling in international commerce and brimming with precious

---

> ## ℹ HAMPI RUINS TICKET
>
> Your ticket for Vittala Temple entitles you to same-day admission to most of the paid sites across the ruins (including around the Royal Centre and the Archaeological Museum), so don't lose it.

stones and merchants from faraway lands. All this, however, ended at a stroke in 1565, when a confederacy of Deccan sultanates razed Vijayanagar to the ground, striking it a blow from which it never recovered.

⊙ Sights

Set over 36 sq km, the Hampi area has some 3700 monuments to explore – it would take months if you were to do it all justice. The ruins are divided into two main areas: the Sacred Centre around Hampi Bazaar with its temples, and the Royal Centre towards Kamalapuram, where the Vijayanagara royalty lived and governed.

⊙ Sacred Centre

★ Vittala Temple
HINDU TEMPLE

(Map p218; Indian/foreigner/child under 15yr ₹40/500/free; ⊙8.30am-5.30pm) Hampi's most exquisite structure, the 16th-century Vittala Temple stands amid boulders 2.5km from Hampi Bazaar. Work possibly started here during the reign of Krishnadevaraya (r 1509–29). The structure was never finished or consecrated, yet its incredible sculptural work remains the pinnacle of Vijayanagar

art. The courtyard's ornate stone chariot (illustrated on the ₹50 note) is the temple's showpiece and represents Vishnu's vehicle with an image of Garuda within. Its wheels were once capable of turning.

The outer 'musical' pillars, supposedly designed to replicate 81 different Indian instruments, reverberate when tapped. To protect them, authorities have placed them out of bounds. As well as the main temple, whose sanctum was illuminated using a design of reflective waters, you'll find the marriage hall and the prayer hall, to the left and right, respectively, as you enter.

★ Virupaksha Temple
HINDU TEMPLE

(Map p216; ₹2, camera/video ₹50/500; ⊙dawn-dusk) The focal point of Hampi Bazaar is this temple, one of the city's oldest structures, and Hampi's only remaining working temple. The main *gopuram* (gateway), almost 50m high, was built in 1442; a smaller one was added in 1510. The main shrine is dedicated to Virupaksha, an incarnation of Shiva.

An elephant called Lakshmi blesses devotees as they enter, in exchange for donations; she gets time off for a morning bath down by the river **ghats** (Map p216).

HAMPI BAZAAR DEMOLITIONS

While in 1865 it was the Deccan sultanates who levelled Vijayanagar, today a different battle rages in Hampi, between conservationists bent on protecting Hampi's architectural heritage and the locals who have settled there.

In 1999 Unesco placed Hampi on its list of World Heritage Sites in danger because of 'haphazard informal urbanisation' around the temples, particularly the ancient bazaar area near Virupaksha Temple. The government consequently produced a master plan that aimed to classify all of Hampi's ruins as protected monuments. After years of inaction this plan was dramatically and forcefully executed in July 2011. Shops, hotels and homes in the ancient bazaar were bulldozed overnight, reducing the atmospheric main strip to rubble in hours; 1500 villagers who'd made the site a living monument were evicted.

Business owners were compensated with small plots of land, some as far away as the village of Kaddirampur, 18km from the bazaar. There was talk of new guesthouses opening up there, but due to its distance from Hampi few bothered to build. Meanwhile, the displaced still await their payouts.

Then in May 2016 history repeated itself: homes, guesthouses and shops in the old village of Virupapur Gaddi were demolished. Larger establishments avoided the clearance by contesting eviction orders in court. Angry locals blame the Hampi World Heritage Area Management Authority (HWHAMA) and the Archaeological Survey of India (ASI) for the demolitions and argue that the master plan is causing a lifeless 'museumification' of what was a vibrant cultural monument.

The main temple road today is devoid of buildings and bustle, and legendary hang-outs like the (original) Mango Tree have been knocked down. By late 2018 things seemed to have stabilised: Hampi Bazaar still exists as an enclave of guesthouses and restaurants north of Virupaksha Temple and businesses were also open over the river in Virupapur Gaddi. But the future for both areas remains uncertain.

Lakshimi Narasmiha   HINDU TEMPLE
(Map p218) An interesting stop along the road to Virupaksha Temple is the 6.7m monolithic statue of the bulging-eyed Lakshimi Narasmiha in a cross-legged lotus position and topped by a hood of seven snakes.

Sule Bazaar   HISTORIC SITE
(Map p218) Halfway along the path from Hampi Bazaar to Vittala Temple, a track to the right leads over the rocks to deserted Sule Bazaar, one of ancient Hampi's principal centres of commerce and reputedly its red-light district. A near-kilometre-long stone colonnade flanking its eastern side is very well preserved. At the southern end of this area is the beautiful 16th-century Achyutaraya Temple.

★**Achyutaraya Temple**   HINDU TEMPLE
(Tiruvengalanatha Temple; Map p218) At the southern end of Sule Bazaar is the beautiful Achyutaraya Temple, dating from 1534, one of the last great monuments constructed before the fall of Hampi. You approach the temple via two partly ruined *gopuram* (gateways). The central hall boasts elaborately carved pillars and sculptures, including Krishna dancing with a snake. Its isolated location at the foot of Matanga Hill makes it quietly atmospheric – doubly so since it's rarely visited.

Hemakuta Hill   HISTORIC SITE
(Map p218) To the south, overlooking Virupaksha Temple, Hemakuta Hill has a scattering of early ruins, including monolithic sculptures of Narasimha (Vishnu in his man-lion incarnation) and Ganesh. It's worth the short walk up for the view.

Nandi Statue   STATUE
(Map p218) At the eastern end of Hampi Bazaar is a Nandi statue, around which stand some of the colonnaded blocks of the ancient marketplace. This is the main location for Vijaya Utsav (p216), the Hampi arts festival.

◉ Royal Centre & Around

While it can be accessed by a 2km foot trail from the Achyutaraya Temple, the Royal Centre is best reached via the Hampi–Kamalapuram road. A number of Hampi's major sites stand here.

Zenana Enclosure   RUINS
(Map p218; Indian/foreigner ₹40/500; ⊙8.30am-5.30pm) Northeast of the Royal Centre, within the walled ladies' quarters, is the Zenana Enclosure. Its peaceful grounds and manicured lawns feel like an oasis in the arid surrounds. The Lotus Mahal and Elephant Stables are found here.

Queen's Bath   RUINS
(Map p218; ⊙8.30am-5.30pm) South of the Royal Centre you'll find various temples and waterworks, including the Queen's Bath, deceptively plain on the outside but amazing within, featuring Indo-Islamic architecture.

Archaeological Museum   MUSEUM
(Map p218; Kamalapuram; ⊙10am-5pm Sat-Thu) Boasts a fine collection of sculpture from local sites, plus neolithic tools, 16th-century weaponry and a large floor model of the Vijayanagar ruins. Don't miss the information panels: one details the king's daily rituals, which included drinking 400ml of sesame oil, followed by a wrestling match and then a horse ride, all before daybreak!

Hazarama Temple   HINDU TEMPLE
(Map p218) Features exquisite carvings that depict scenes from the Ramayana, and polished black-granite pillars.

Mahanavami-diiba   RUINS
(Map p218) The Mahanavami-diiba is a 12m-high, three-tiered platform with intricate carvings and panoramic vistas of the walled complex of ruined temples, stepped tanks and the king's audience hall. The platform was used as a royal viewing area for festivities, allowing the Vijayanagar royals (and visiting nobility from other regions) to preside over military parades, sporting contests and musical performances in a show of power, tradition and celebration.

🏃 Activities

Hampi Waterfalls   WATERFALL
About a 2km walk west of Hampi Bazaar, past shady banana plantations, you can scramble over the boulders to reach the attractive Hampi 'waterfalls', a series of small whirlpools among the rocks amid superb scenery.

Bouldering
Hampi is the undisputed bouldering capital of India. The entire landscape is a climber's adventure playground made of granite crags and boulders, some bearing the marks of ancient stonemasons. *Golden Boulders* (2013), by Gerald Krug and Christiane Hupe, has a tonne of info on bouldering in Hampi.

Hampi Bazaar

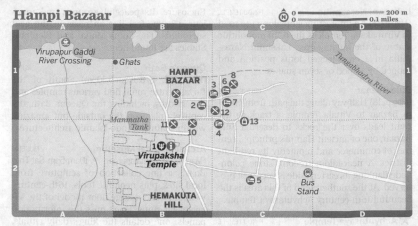

Thimmaclimb CLIMBING
(Map p218; ☑ 8762776498; www.thimmaclimb.
com/hampi-bouldering; Virupapur Gaddi; classes
from ₹500) Established operation run by local pro Thimma, who guides, runs lessons
and stocks professional equipment for
hire and sale. He also runs three-day trips
(₹5000) to Badami for sandstone climbing.

Tom & Jerry CLIMBING
(Map p218; ☑ 8277792588, 9482746697; http://
climbingshop.hampivillage.com; Virupapur Gaddi;
2½hr classes ₹600) Two local lads who are
doing great work in catering to climbers'
needs, providing quality mats, shoes and
regional knowledge, and running climbing
sessions. They also offer rappelling and
slacklining classes (each ₹500).

Birdwatching
Get in touch with the Kishkinda Trust
(p220) in Anegundi for info on birdwatching in the area, which has over 230 species,
including the greater flamingo. *The Birds of
Hampi* (2014), by Samad Kottur, is the definitive guide.

🎎 Festivals & Events

Golden Boulders SPORTS
(☑ 9482746697; http://goldenbouldersfestival.
hampivillage.com; ☺ Jan) Golden Boulders is
a non-competitive 10-day outdoor climbing
festival. Organised by local climbers Tom &
Jerry, it also features yoga, bouldering on
new routes and slacklining.

Vijaya Utsav CULTURAL
(Hampi Festival; ☺ Jan) Hampi's three-day extravaganza of culture, heritage and the arts.

Virupaksha Car Festival RELIGIOUS
(☺ Mar/Apr) This big event features a colourful procession characterised by a giant
wooden chariot (the temple car from Virupaksha Temple) being pulled along the main
strip of Hampi Bazaar.

🛏 Sleeping

Most guesthouses are cosy, family-run digs,
perfect for the budget traveller. Walk-in rates
are usually much better than those found
online. More upmarket places are located
further from the centre. Some tour operators
base their clients in Hosapete, a grim town
that's a world away from Hampi in terms of
ambience. Nearby Anegundi (p220) also has
good accommodation.

🛏 Hampi Bazaar

This little enclave is a classic travellers' ghetto. However, its existence is under threat as
there are plans to demolish it.

★ Manash Guesthouse GUESTHOUSE $
(Map p216; ☑ 9448877420; manashhampi@gmail.
com; r with fan/AC ₹1350/1600; ❄ 🛜) This place
consists of just two rooms set off a little yard,
but they're the best in Hampi Bazaar, each
with quality mattresses, attractive decorative
touches and free, fast wi-fi. It's owned by the
Mango Tree (p219) people just along the lane,
so if no one is around ask in the restaurant.

Thilak Homestay GUESTHOUSE $
(Map p216; ☑ 9449900964; www.facebook.com/
thilak.homestay; r with fan/AC ₹1300/2000; ❄ 🛜)
A step up from most places in the bazaar,
this clean, orderly place has eight well-
presented rooms (and more in another

Hampi Bazaar

⊙ Top Sights
1 Virupaksha Temple B2

⊜ Sleeping
2 Ganesh Guesthouse............................ B1
3 Gopi Guest House................................ C1
4 Manash Guesthouse C2
5 Padma Guest House............................ C2
6 Pushpa Guest House........................... C1
7 Thilak Homestay................................. C1

⊗ Eating
8 Chill Out... C1
9 Gopi Roof Restaurant........................... B1
10 Mango Tree.. B2
11 Moonlight... B2
12 Ravi's Rose.. C1

⊛ Shopping
13 Akash Art Gallery &
      Bookstore.......................................C2

---

block) that have spring mattresses and hot water. Owner Kish is very helpful and can arrange a reliable autorickshaw driver or make other transport arrangements.

Pushpa Guest House GUESTHOUSE $
(Map p216; ☑9448795120; pushpaguesthouse99@yahoo.in; d from ₹1000, with AC from ₹1700; ❋ 🛜) A decent all-rounder with comfortable, attractive and well-presented rooms that have mosquito nets. It has a lovely roof terrace and a reliable travel agency.

Ganesh Guesthouse GUESTHOUSE $
(Map p216; vishnuhampi@gmail.com; r ₹600-900, with AC from ₹1500; ❋ 🛜) The small, welcoming, family-run Ganesh has been around for over 20 years and has four tidy rooms. Also has a nice rooftop restaurant.

Padma Guest House GUESTHOUSE $
(Map p216; ☑08394-241331; padmaguesthouse@gmail.com; d ₹900-2000; ❋ 🛜) Slightly more upmarket than many guesthouses in the bazaar area, this place has a choice of basic, decent rooms, many with views of Virupaksha Temple, though facilities and bathrooms could do with an upgrade. Still, the owners are helpful and can arrange autorickshaw drivers, bikes and onward transport.

Gopi Guest House GUESTHOUSE $$
(Map p216; ☑08394-241695; www.facebook.com/gopiguesthouse; r with fan/AC ₹2000/2500; ❋@🛜) A dependable, welcoming place split over two properties on the same street. Gopi offers friendly service and has good-quality rooms that are almost upscale by Hampi standards. There are fine views from its rooftop cafe.

🛏 Virupapur Gaddi & Around

The rural tranquillity of village-like Virupapur Gaddi, across the river from Hampi Bazaar, has real appeal for long-term travellers. Its many nicknames include 'The Island',

'Hippy Island', and 'Little Jerusalem' as it's particularly popular with Israelis.

Sunny Guesthouse GUESTHOUSE $
(Map p218; ☑9448566368; www.sunnyguesthouse.com; Virupapur Gaddi; r ₹600-1500; @🛜) Sunny both in name and disposition, this popular guesthouse is a hit among backpackers for its characterful huts, very well-maintained tropical garden, hammocks and chilled-out restaurant.

Shanthi GUESTHOUSE $
(Map p218; ☑8533287038; http://shanthihampi.com; Virupapur Gaddi; cottages ₹1300-1850; 🛜) Shanthi offers attractive, earth-themed thatched cottages with couch swings dangling in their front porches. The location is stunning, with a row of cottages directly overlooking rice fields. The only drawback is that the restaurant's food is below par, but with many alternatives on your doorstep that's not a huge concern.

Hampi's Boulders LODGE $$$
(☑9448034202, 9480904202; www.hampisboulders.com; Narayanpet; r incl full board from ₹7100; ❋🛜) This 'eco-wilderness' resort is 10km west of Virupapur Gaddi by the Tungabhadra River. It's an isolated but supremely relaxed place to escape, with a choice of cottages that have elegant furnishings and river views. There's a stunning natural pool for chlorine-free swims. Rates include a guided walk, and the restaurant's food uses ingredients from its organic farm. Limited wi-fi.

🛏 Kamalapuram & Around

★ Shankar Homestay HOMESTAY $$
(Map p218; ☑9482169619; hanumayana@gmail.com; Ballari; r incl breakfast with fan/AC ₹2000/2300; ❋🛜) Lovely family-run homestay in a tranquil rural location around 2km west of the Royal Centre (bikes are available). The five spacious rooms are

Hampi & Anegundi

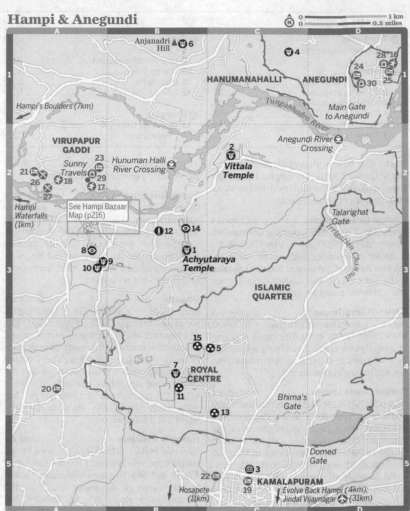

KARNATAKA HAMPI

furnished with handmade textiles and crafts, and the ever-helpful, welcoming hosts' cooking is superb: be sure to try dinner here.

Clarks Inn
HOTEL **$$**

(Map p218; ☑08394-241245; www.clarksinn.in; HCP Rd, Kamalapuram; r ₹3300-4500; 🕸🛜🏊) A tempting new option in Kamalapuram, this modern hotel has inviting, very clean rooms with contemporary decor and flatscreen TVs. The pool is a small indoor affair. It's right opposite the Archaeological Museum (p215).

Sri Sai Baba Lodge
GUESTHOUSE **$$**

(Map p218; ☑8050144139; www.facebook.com/sri-sai-baba-lodgehomestay-209949712953731; Kamalapuram; r ₹1800-2400; 🕸🛜) A new lodge with neat, clean and orderly rooms, some with four beds, and a welcoming staff. Located on the south side of the ruins in Kamalapuram, close to the museum.

Evolve Back Hampi
LUXURY HOTEL **$$$**

(www.evolveback.com/hampi; Hallikeri Village; ste from ₹23,000; 🕸🛜🏊) Seriously stylish new place with stunning accommodation. Book a terrace suite for maharaja-size space, in-

Hampi & Anegundi

◉ Top Sights
1 Achyutaraya Temple.............................B3
2 Vittala Temple....................................C2

◉ Sights
3 Archaeological Museum.......................C5
4 Durga Temple.....................................C1
5 Elephant Stables.................................C4
6 Hanuman Temple................................B1
7 Hazarama Temple...............................B4
8 Hemakuta Hill.....................................A3
9 Krishna Temple...................................A3
10 Lakshimi Narasmiha...........................A3
Lotus Mahal...............................(see 15)
11 Mahanavami-diiba...............................B4
12 Nandi Statue.......................................B3
13 Queen's Bath......................................C4
14 Sule Bazaar..B3
15 Zenana Enclosure...............................B4

◇ Activities, Courses & Tours
16 Kishkinda Trust...................................D1

17 Thimmaclimb......................................A2
18 Tom & Jerry..A2

◎ Sleeping
19 Clark Inn...C5
Peshegaar Guest House..............(see 28)
20 Shankar Homestay..............................A4
21 Shanthi...A2
22 Sri Sai Baba Lodge.............................C5
23 Sunny Guesthouse..............................A2
24 Uramma Cottage.................................D1
25 Uramma House....................................D1

⊗ Eating
26 Gouthami..A2
27 Laughing Buddha................................A2

⊕ Shopping
28 Banana Fibre Craft Workshop..............D1
29 Gali Djembe Music Shop......................A2
30 Kishkinda...D1

cluding your own hot tub. The grounds are gorgeous, the staff kindly and efficient, and the facilities good. As it's isolated, around 6km from the Royal Centre, consider a half-board package. Book via the resort's website for the best deal.

✗ Eating

Gouthami MULTICUISINE $
(Map p218; mains ₹80-250; ⊘8am-11pm) A well-run place with cushion seating (or dining tables) and an excess of psychedelic wall hangings. Serves tasty Indian, Israeli and Western classics. There's an espresso machine (cappuccinos ₹120), and it also offers good Turkish coffee and cardamom tea.

Moonlight MULTICUISINE $
(Map p216; mains ₹80-160; ⊘7.30am-10pm) A family-owned place right behind Virupaksha Temple that serves good breakfasts, pancakes, curries and espresso coffee.

Chill Out MULTICUISINE $
(Map p216; mains ₹90-300; ⊘8am-10.30pm; 🖣) Atmospheric rooftop restaurant with cushion seating and lantern lighting, and a menu of curries and Western favourites, including good pizza.

Laughing Buddha MULTICUISINE $
(Map p218; Virupapur Gaddi; mains from ₹80; ⊘8am-10pm; 🖣) Down a lane off the main drag in Virupapur Gaddi, this well-regarded place has serene river views that stretch over to Hampi's temples. Its menu includes

curries, burgers and pizzas; you dine on low tables and cushions. Cash only.

Ravi's Rose MULTICUISINE $
(Map p216; mains from ₹100; ⊘8am-10.30pm; 🖣) A social hang-out, with a good selection of dosa and thalis, but most folks are here for the, erm, special lassis (cough).

★ Mango Tree MULTICUISINE $$
(Map p216; mains ₹130-310; ⊘7.30am-9.30pm) Hampi's most famous restaurant has relocated to an atmospheric tented restaurant in the bazaar but is still run by three generations of the same local family. It's an efficiently managed place with good service and delicious Indian cuisines served on banana leaves. Try a thali.

Gopi Roof Restaurant MULTICUISINE $$
(Map p216; www.facebook.com/gopiguesthouse; mains ₹130-300; ⊘8am-10pm; 🖣) Serves up flavoursome Indian, Chinese and Israeli food, and even the Mexican grub (try the veg enchiladas) is quite tasty. Sip a lassi (₹60) or masala chai (₹30) while you're waiting for your meal.

🔒 Shopping

Gali Djembe Music Shop MUSICAL INSTRUMENTS
(Map p218; ☑9449982586; www.facebook.com/pg/galidurugappa; Virupapur Gaddi; ⊘10am-7pm) Run by an amiable musician who teaches djembe (drums) and didgeridoo, this store sells Indian and Western musical instruments at fair prices.

Akash Art Gallery & Bookstore BOOKS

(Map p216; ⏰7am-9pm) Excellent selection of books on Hampi and India, plus secondhand fiction. The owner offers a free Hampi map and sells postcards, too.

ℹ Information

DANGERS & ANNOYANCES

Hampi is generally a safe, peaceful place. However, exercise standard precautions and don't wander around the ruins after dark. Women should avoid being alone in the more remote parts of the site. Note that alcohol and narcotics are illegal in Hampi, and possession can get you into trouble.

MONEY

There's no ATM in Hampi or Virupapur Gaddi, but both have moneychangers. You'll find three ATMs in Kamalapuram (3km away) and one in Anegundi, on the other side of the river.

ℹ Getting There & Around

Hosapete is the gateway to Hampi. There's only one daily direct (very slow) bus from Hampi Bazaar to Goa (₹725, 11 hours, 7pm). Travel agents can book bus tickets to Bengaluru (from ₹600, seven hours, several at 11pm), Hyderabad (from ₹820, nine hours, four nightly), Mumbai (from ₹950, 14 hours, many nightly), Mysuru (₹750, 12 hours, 9.30pm) and other destinations; many of these include a minibus transfer from Hampi to Hosapete.

Local buses departing from the **stand** (Map p216) connect Hampi with Hosapete (₹18, 30 minutes, half-hourly) between 5.45am and 7.30pm. An autorickshaw costs around ₹180. For Badami, travel via Hosapete.

Hosapete is Hampi's nearest train station. **Sunny Travels** (Map p218; ☎9448969809; hampisunnytravels@gmail.com; ⏰9.30am-7pm) can help with bookings.

Jindal Vijaynagar Airport, 35km south of Hampi, has recently been upgraded and has daily TruJet flights to Bengaluru and Hyderabad.

Anegundi

☎08394 / POP 5300

Anegundi is an ancient fortified village that's part of the Hampi World Heritage Site, but it predates Hampi by way of human habitation. The settlement has been spared the blight of commercialisation, and retains a delightfully rustic feel: the seasons dictate the cycle of change and craft traditions endure. It's accessed by a river crossing or via a long loop from Virupapur Gaddi.

◎ Sights & Activities

Hanuman Temple HINDU TEMPLE

(Anjaneya Hill Temple; Map p218; ⏰dawn-dusk) Whitewashed Hanuman Temple, accessible by a 570-step climb up Anjanadri Hill, has fine views of the surrounding rugged terrain. Many believe that this is the birthplace of Hanuman, the Hindu monkey god who was Rama's devotee and helped him in his mission against Ravana. The hike up is pleasant, though you'll be courted by impish monkeys. At the temple you may encounter chillum-puffing sadhus (ascetics). It's a very popular sunset spot, with panoramic views over the Hampi region.

Durga Temple HINDU TEMPLE

(Map p218; ⏰dawn-dusk) An ancient shrine close to Anegundi village that's worth a visit. The journey from Anegundi is very beautiful, through classic Hampi terrain of ochre boulders and rice paddies.

Kishkinda Trust VOLUNTEERING

(TKT; Map p218; ☎08533-267777; http://tkt kishkinda.org; Main Rd) 🏵 For cultural events, activities and volunteering opportunities, get in touch with Kishkinda Trust, an NGO based in Anegundi that works with local people.

⌂ Sleeping

Peshegaar Guest House GUESTHOUSE $

(Map p218; ☎9449972230; www.uramma heritagehomes.com; Hanumanahalli; d ₹1344; ✆) This heritage house has five simple yet stylish rooms decorated with tribal textiles around a pleasant common area with a courtyard garden. Bathrooms are shared, but there are four.

★**Uramma Cottage** COTTAGE $$$

(Map p218; ☎9448284658; www.uramma heritagehomes.com; s/d incl breakfast ₹2688/5310; ✆) A wonderfully atmospheric lodge with rustic-chic cottages scattered around a large, grassy plot. The attention to detail is evident in the chunky wooden furniture, lovely bed linen and handmade textiles that add a splash of colour. Staff members couldn't be more helpful, and the restaurant serves very fine food (meals ₹400) and beer. Rates drop in low season.

Uramma House GUESTHOUSE $$$

(Map p218; ☎9449972230; www.uramma heritagehomes.com; s/d per person ₹2688/5310; ✆) This 4th-century heritage house is a gem, with traditional-style rooms featuring exposed beams and boutique touches. It has two bedrooms and a dining room, and is ideal for a family or small group.

🛍 Shopping

Kishkinda   ARTS & CRAFTS
(Map p218; http://tktkishkinda.org; Uramma Cottage; ⊙9am-5pm) Fair-trade shop selling handwoven textiles, banana-fibre products and other crafts made in and around Anegundi village.

**Banana Fibre
Craft Workshop**   ARTS & CRAFTS
(Map p218; ⊙10am-1pm & 2-5pm Mon-Sat) Look on at this small workshop as artisans make a range of handicrafts and accessories using the bark of a banana tree and recycled materials. It's all for sale, too.

ℹ Getting There & Away

Anegundi is 7km from Hampi, and reached by crossing the river on a boat (₹10) from the pier east of the Vittala Temple (p214). From Hampi, get here by moped or bicycle (if you're feeling energetic). An autorickshaw to the Anegundi crossing costs ₹100 from Hampi.

Hosapete (Hospet)

📞 08394 / POP 171,200

A hectic, dusty regional city, Hosapete (still called Hospet by many) is a transport hub for Hampi. There's no reason to stay here but if you get stuck try **Hotel Malligi** (📞 08394-228101; www.malligihotels.com; Jabunatha Rd; r ₹2400-4200, ste from ₹5000; ❉ 🛜 🏊).

ℹ Getting There & Away

Hosapete's bus stand has services to Hampi every half-hour (₹15, 30 minutes). Overnight private sleeper buses run to/from Goa (₹1000 to ₹1450, eight to 10 hours), Gokarna (₹700, 8½ hours), Bengaluru (₹540 to ₹740, seven hours), Mysuru (₹410 to ₹655, 8½ hours) and Hyderabad (₹880 to ₹1210, eight hours). Overnight buses run by **Paulo Travels** (📞 08394-225867; www.paulobus.com) go to Gokarna and Goa.

Hosapete's train station is a ₹30 autorickshaw ride from the town centre. The 18047 Amaravathi Express heads to Margao (Madgaon), Goa (sleeper/2AC ₹225/865, 7½ hours), four times a week at 6.20am. The 16591 Hampi Express departs nightly at 9.15pm for Bengaluru (2AC/1AC ₹935/1570, nine hours) and Mysuru (₹1210/2025, 12 hours). For Hyderabad there are two to three trains per day; the 7pm service is daily (sleeper/2AC ₹305/1195, 12 hours).

Hubballi (Hubli)

📞 0836 / POP 1,051,000

Industrial Hubballi (still called by its old name, Hubli, by many) is a hub for rail routes for Mumbai, Bengaluru, Goa and northern Karnataka. The airport also has good connections. There's no other reason to visit.

If you need to stay overnight, try the budget **Hotel Ajanta** (📞 0836-2362216; Koppikar Rd; s/d from ₹475/600; 🏱) or the more upmarket **Hotel Metropolis** (📞 0836-4266666; www.hotelmetropolishubli.com; Koppikar Rd; r with fan/AC from ₹1500/2500; ❉ 🏱), both near the train station.

ℹ Getting There & Away

The recently upgraded airport is 6km west of the centre of town. Four airlines offer daily flights to Ahmedabad, Bengaluru, Chennai, Goa, Kochi and Mumbai. NWKRTC air-conditioned buses connect the airport with the city's train station. A taxi is ₹230.

There are very regular services to Bengaluru, most overnight (₹430 to ₹680, seven to 8½ hours). Plenty of buses travel daily to Vijapura (₹200 to ₹276, five to six hours) and mainly night-time buses go to Hosapete (₹142 to ₹210, four hours). There are also regular connections to Mangaluru (₹480 to ₹654, seven to eight hours), Mumbai (₹725 to ₹1400, 11 to 14 hours), Mysuru (₹439 to ₹835, nine hours) and Panaji (Goa; ₹180 to ₹364, five to six hours).

From the train station, plenty of services head to Hosapete (sleeper/2AC ₹140/700, 2½ hours, six to eight daily), Bengaluru (sleeper/2AC ₹270/1050, eight to nine hours, eight daily), Mumbai (sleeper/2AC ₹380/1485, 15½ hours, one to two daily) and Goa (sleeper/3AC ₹160/700, five to six hours, one to three daily).

NORTHERN KARNATAKA

Badami

📞 08357 / POP 32,200

Once the capital of the mighty Chalukya empire, today Badami is famous for its magnificent rock-cut cave temples, and red-sandstone cliffs that resemble the American Wild West. The scenery is stunning, once you're away from the horrible, dusty, traffic-plagued main road that cuts through town.

Badami's backstreets are fascinating to explore, with old houses, carved wooden doorways and even the occasional Chalukyan ruin.

DANDELI

Located in the jungles of the Western Ghats about 100km from Goa, emerging Dandeli is a wildlife getaway that promises close encounters with diverse exotic animals such as elephants, leopards, sloth bears, gaur, wild dogs and flying squirrels. It's a chosen birding destination, too, with resident hornbills, golden-backed woodpeckers, serpent eagles and white-breasted kingfishers. Also on offer are a slew of adventure activities ranging from kayaking to bowel-churning white-water rafting on the swirling Kali River.

Kali Adventure camp (☑08284-230266; www.junglelodges.com/kali-adventure-camp; Dandeli; per person incl full board dm/tent/r from ₹2006/4142/4994; ☎) is a forest lodge adhering to ecofriendly principles with good accommodation in rooms or tented cottages. The camp organises white-water rafting on the Kali (possible for most of the year), guided canoe adventures, canyoning and mountain-biking trips. Rates include a jeep safari into Dandeli Wildlife Sanctuary, a coracle trip, a guided walk and all meals.

Frequent buses connect Dandeli to both Hubballi (₹60, two hours) and Dharwad (₹46, 1½ hours), with onward connections to Goa, Gokarna, Hosapete and Bengaluru.

◉ Sights

★**Cave Temples**   CAVE
(Indian/foreigner incl North Fort ₹25/300, child under 15yr free, camera ₹25, tour guide ₹300; ☺9am-5.30pm) Badami's highlights are its beautiful cave temples, three Hindu and one Jain, which display exquisite sculptures and intricate carvings. They're a magnificent example of Chalukya architecture and date to the 6th century. All have a columned verandah, an interior hall and a shrine at the rear.

Cave one, just above the entrance to the complex, is dedicated to Shiva. It's the oldest of the four caves, probably carved in the latter half of the 6th century. On the wall to the right of the porch is a captivating image of Nataraja striking 18 dance moves in the one pose, backed by a cobra head. On the right of the porch area is a huge figure of Ardhanarishvara. On the opposite wall is a large image of Harihara, half Shiva and half Vishnu.

Dedicated to Vishnu, cave two is simpler in design. As with caves one and three, the front edge of the platform is decorated with images of pot-bellied dwarfs in various poses. Four pillars support the verandah, their tops carved with a bracket in the shape of a yali (mythical lion creature). On the left wall of the porch is the bull-headed figure of Varaha, the emblem of the Chalukya empire. To his left is Naga, a snake with a human face. On the right wall is a large sculpture of Trivikrama, another incarnation of Vishnu.

Cave three, carved in 578, is the largest and most impressive. On the left wall is a carving of Vishnu, to whom the cave is dedicated, sitting on a snake. Nearby is an image of Varaha with four hands. The pillars have carved brackets in the shape of yalis. The ceiling panels contain images including Indra riding an elephant, Shiva on a bull and Brahma on a swan. Keep an eye out for the image of drunken revellers, in particular one woman being propped up by her husband. There's also original colour on the ceiling; the divots on the floor at the cave's entrance were used as paint palettes. There's a sublime view from cave three over the Agastyatirtha Tank far below, and you can often hear the echoes of women thrashing clothes on its steps reverberating around the hills.

Dedicated to Jainism, cave four is the smallest of the set and dates to between the 7th and 8th centuries. The right wall has an image of Suparshvanatha, the seventh Jain *tirthankar* (teacher), surrounded by 24 Jain *tirthankars*. The inner sanctum contains an image of Adinath, the first Jain *tirthankar*.

North Fort   RUINS
(with cave temples free; ☺9am-5.30pm) High above Badami and Agastyatirtha Tank, the ruins of the North Fort are worth exploring. Only the foundations remain of most of the site, but there are fortifications to investigate and restored granary towers. Of the three temples, the well-preserved 7th-century Malegitti Shivalaya temple is thought to be one of the earliest surviving examples of the Dravidian style in early Chalukya architecture. Entry included with cave-temple admission.

Archaeological Museum   MUSEUM
(₹5; ☺9am-5pm Sat-Thu) The archaeological museum houses superb examples of local sculpture, including a tremendous 12th-century *makara tokarna* (entrance deco-

ration) that has detailed carvings on both sides and a remarkably explicit Lajja-Gauri image of a fertility cult that once flourished in the area. There are many sculptures of Shiva in different forms and there's a diorama of the Shidlaphadi cave. No photography permitted.

🏃 Activities

The bluffs and horseshoe-shaped red-sandstone cliff of Badami offer some great low-altitude climbing. **Climbing Badami** (📲 8494809253; http://climbingbadami.in; climbing from ₹1000) organises climbs and treks in the region, as do operators in Hampi (p215).

🛏 Sleeping & Eating

Mookambika Deluxe HOTEL $
(📲 08357-220067; hotelmookambika@yahoo.com; Station Rd; d with fan/AC from ₹1300/1800; ❋ 🗺) For 'deluxe' read 'decent' – this hotel offers fair value, with rooms done up in matte orange and green. Staff members are a good source of travel info. It's opposite the bus stand. There's an adjoining bar-restaurant.

★ Heritage Resort HOTEL $$
(http://theheritage.co.in; Station Rd; incl breakfast r with fan/AC ₹2400/3000, cottages ₹3900; ❋ 🗺) Set back from the highway, the wonderfully peaceful Heritage Resort has 14 tasteful, airy and spacious rooms and cottages with all mod cons (kettle, flatscreen TV, minibar), attractive wooden furniture and a dash of contemporary style. Management is courteous and helpful, the grounds are leafy and the **restaurant** (Heritage Resort, Station Rd; mains from ₹110; 🗺) food is very tasty. It's 2km north of the centre.

Golden Caves Cuisine MULTICUISINE $
(Station Rd; mains ₹80-170; ⊘ 8.30am-11pm) Worth trying for North and South Indian food, though service can be a bit distracted. There's a pleasant outdoor yard at the back that's perfect for enjoying a beer.

Bridge Restaurant MULTICUISINE $$
(Clarks Inn, Veerpulakeshi Circle; mains ₹195-595; ⊘ 6.30am-10.30pm; 🗺) Just the place when you need some AC relief, this business hotel's restaurant takes a good stab at Western dishes such as pasta and pizza, as well as Chinese and North Indian fare. South Indian breakfast items like *idli* (spongy, round, fermented rice cakes) and *vada* (doughnut-shaped deep-fried lentil savouries) with chutney and sambal are tasty, too.

ℹ Getting There & Away

Badami doesn't have many direct bus services. From the bus stand on Station Rd there's one direct bus to both Vijapura (₹162, four hours, 5pm) and Hubballi (₹195, five hours, 3.15pm). Three daily buses run to Bengaluru (₹388 to ₹435, 10 hours, 7am, 7.30am and 7pm); both morning services go via Hospete (₹156, four hours). Otherwise, take one of the regular buses to Kerur (₹28, 45 minutes), 23km away, which has many more connections.

Around Badami

Pattadakal

📲 08357 / POP 1680
A secondary capital of the Badami Chalukyas, Pattadakal is known for its finely carved Hindu and Jain temples, which are collectively a World Heritage Site. The surrounding village of Pattadakal is tiny; most travellers visit the site from nearby Badami.

Barring a few that date to the 3rd century, most of Pattadakal's World Heritage-listed temples were built during the 7th and 8th centuries. The main **Virupaksha temple** (⊘ 6am-6pm) is a massive structure, its columns covered with intricate carvings depicting episodes from the Ramayana and Mahabharata. A giant stone sculpture of Nandi (Shiva's bull) sits to the temple's east. The Mallikarjuna temple, next to the Virupaksha temple, is almost identical in design.

Pattadakal is 20km from Badami, with buses (₹26, 45 minutes) departing every 30 minutes until about 5pm. There's a morning and an afternoon bus to Aihole (₹20), 13km away.

Aihole

📲 08351 / POP 3200
Some 100 temples, built between the 4th and 6th centuries AD, speck the ancient Chalukyan regional capital of Aihole (*ay*-ho-leh). Most, however, are either in ruins or engulfed by the modern village. Aihole documents the embryonic stage of South Indian Hindu architecture, from the earliest simple shrines, such as the most ancient Ladkhan Temple, to later and more complex buildings, such as the Meguti Temple.

Aihole is 35km from Badami and 13km from Pattadakal.

The impressive 7th-century **Durga Temple** (Indian/foreigner ₹30/200, camera ₹25; ⊘ 6am-6pm) is notable for its semicircular apse (inspired by Buddhist architecture) and the remains of the curvilinear *sikhara* (temple spire). It's said to be the inspiration for the Parliament of India building in New Delhi. The interiors house intricate stone carvings.

Vijapura (Bijapur)

📞 08352 / POP 343,800 / ELEV 593M

A historic city epitomising the Deccan's Islamic era, Vijapura (renamed in 2014 but still widely called Bijapur) tells a glorious tale dating back some 600 years. Blessed with a heap of mosques, mausoleums, palaces and fortifications, it was the capital of the Adil Shahi kings from 1489 to 1686, and one of the five splinter states formed after the Islamic Bahmani kingdom broke up in 1482. Despite its strong Islamic character, Vijapura is also a centre for the Lingayat brand of Shaivism, which emphasises a single personalised god. The **Lingayat Siddeshwara Festival** (◉ Jan/Feb) runs for eight days.

Until recently the city was somewhat lacking in tourist facilities and perhaps consequently few travellers dropped by. But new hotels have recently opened and there's now a decent selection of places to stay.

◉ Sights

★ Golgumbaz
MONUMENT

(Indian/foreigner ₹25/300; ◉ 6am-6pm) Set in tranquil gardens, the magnificent Golgumbaz houses the tombs of emperor Mohammed Adil Shah (r 1627–56), his two wives, his mistress (Rambha), one of his daughters and a grandson. Octagonal seven-storey towers stand at each corner of the monument, which is capped by an enormous dome. Once you're inside the sheer scale of the structure becomes apparent: its cavernous interior has a powerful, austere beauty. Climb the steep, narrow steps up one of the towers to reach the 'whispering gallery'.

Archaeological Museum
MUSEUM

(₹5; ◉ 9am-5pm Sat-Thu) A well-presented archaeological museum set in the Golgumbaz lawns. Skip the ground floor and head upstairs; there you'll find an excellent collection of artefacts, such as oriental carpets, china crockery, weapons, armour and scrolls.

★ Ibrahim Rouza
MONUMENT

(Indian/foreigner ₹15/200; ◉ 6am-6pm) The beautiful Ibrahim Rouza is among the most elegant and finely proportioned Islamic monuments in India. Its 24m-high minarets are said to have inspired those of the Taj Mahal, and its tale is similarly poignant: built by emperor Ibrahim Adil Shah II (r 1580–1627) as a future mausoleum for his queen, Taj Sultana. Ironically, he died before her and was thus the first person to be laid to rest here. Also interred are the emperor's queen, children and mother.

Citadel
FORT

FREE Surrounded by fortified walls and a moat, the citadel once contained the palaces, pleasure gardens and durbar (royal court) of the Adil Shahi kings. Now mainly in ruins, its remaining structures are in need of urgent maintenance. The most impressive of the remaining fragments are the colossal arches of the Gagan Mahal, built by Ali Adil Shah I around 1561. The gates here are locked, but someone will be on hand to let you in.

Vijapura (Bijapur)

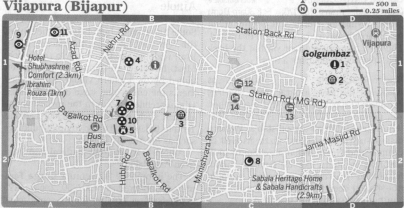

The ruins of Mohammed Adil Shah's seven-storey palace, the Sat Manzil, are nearby. Across the road stands the delicate Jala Manzil, once a water pavilion surrounded by secluded courts and gardens. On the other side of Station Rd (MG Rd) are the graceful arches of Bara Kaman, the ruined mausoleum of Ali Adil Shah II (Ali Roza).

Malik-e-Maidan   HISTORIC SITE

(Monarch of the Plains) Perched upon a platform is this beast of a cannon – over 4m long, almost 1.5m in diameter and estimated to weigh 55 tonnes. Cast in 1549, it was supposedly brought to Vijapura as a war trophy thanks to the efforts of 10 elephants, 400 oxen and hundreds of men!

Asar Mahal   HISTORIC BUILDING

(⊙6am-8.30pm) FREE Built by Mohammed Adil Shah in about 1646 to serve as a hall of justice, the graceful Asar Mahal once housed two hairs from Prophet Mohammed's beard. The rooms on the upper storey are decorated with frescoes and a square tank graces the front. It's out of bounds for women.

Jama Masjid   MOSQUE

(Jama Masjid Rd; ⊙9am-5.30pm) Constructed by Ali Adil Shah I (r 1557–80), the finely proportioned Jama Masjid has graceful arches, a fine dome and a vast inner courtyard with room for thousands of more worshippers. It is a sign of respect for women to cover their hair and men and women should wear modest clothing, preferably with long sleeves.

Upli Buruj   HISTORIC SITE

FREE Upli Buruj is a 16th-century, 24m-high watchtower near the western walls of the city. An external flight of stairs leads to the top, where you'll find two hefty cannons and good views of other monuments around town.

🛏 Sleeping & Eating

Hotel Madhuvan International   HOTEL $

(✉08352-255571; Station Rd; r with fan/AC from ₹1300/1800; ❄🅐) Located on a quiet side street, this excellent hotel has smart rooms with cable TV, marble floors and attractive furnishings (most with desk and wardrobe). There's a courtyard garden at the front and a good restaurant.

Hotel Shubhashree Comfort   HOTEL $

(✉08352-260505; Solapur Rd; r with fan/AC from ₹1000/1300; ❄🅐) On the north side of the city, this hotel offers a comfortable and affordable base. Its well-kept rooms have beds with deep mattresses and good linen. There's a decent all-veg restaurant, too.

★Kyriad Hotel   HOTEL $$

(✉08352-254242; www.kyriadindia.com; Station Rd; incl breakfast r ₹2400-2800, ste from ₹4800; ❄🅐) This fine business hotel has modern rooms equipped with flat-screen TVs (with cable) and modish furniture. Staff members are very helpful and attentive, and there's a lift and 24-hour room service. You'll enjoy the two restaurants; a bar and a gym are planned.

★Sabala Heritage Home   HERITAGE HOTEL $$

(✉9448118204; www.sabalaheritagehome.org; Bijapur Bypass, NH-13; r incl breakfast & dinner ₹1500, with AC from ₹2500; ❄🅐) 🍴 At the edge of the city, this hotel has attractive, artistically decorated rooms overlooking farmland. Food is home cooked, flavoursome and inventive. The hotel is linked to an NGO that empowers women and trades fine handicrafts (there's a store here, too). It's 4.5km southeast of the centre.

Hotel Madhuvan International   INDIAN $

(Station Rd; mains ₹80-220; ⊙9-11am, noon-4pm & 7-11pm; 🅐) There's a choice of indoor or

KARNATAKA VIJAPURA (BIJAPUR)

Vijapura (Bijapur)

◉ **Top Sights**
 1 Golgumbaz D1

◎ **Sights**
 2 Archaeological Museum D1
 3 Asar Mahal B2
 4 Bara Kaman B1
 5 Citadel B2
 6 Gagan Mahal B1
 7 Jala Manzil B1
 8 Jama Masjid C2
 9 Malik-e-Maidan A1

 10 Sat Manzil B2
 11 Upli Buruj A1

🛏 **Sleeping**
 12 Hotel Madhuvan International C1
 13 Hotel Pearl C1
 14 Kyriad Hotel C1

🍴 **Eating**
    Haritam .... (see 14)
    Hotel Madhuvan International ...... (see 12)
    Qaswa Hills .... (see 13)

TRAINS FROM VIJAPURA (BIJAPUR)

The following services depart from Vijapura station.

DESTINATION	TRAIN NO & NAME	FARE (₹)	DURATION (HR)	DEPARTURES
Badami	17320 Hubli-Secunderabad Exp	sleeper/2AC 140/700	2½	1.10am & 2 other daily trains
Bengaluru (Bangalore)	16536 Golgumbaz Exp	sleeper/2AC 375/1470	15	4.55pm & 1 other daily train
Hyderabad	17319 Secunderabad Exp	sleeper/2AC 250/965	12	2.10am
Mumbai	1140 Gadag-Mumbai Exp	sleeper/2AC 350/1300	11½	6 weekly at 5.45pm, via Pune

outdoor garden seating at this fine hotel restaurant, which does fantastic vegetarian dishes, including 13 kinds of dosa (thin lentil-flour pancakes) and lots of paneer and korma dishes. Sandwiches and burgers are also available. No booze.

Haritam　　　　　　　　　VEGETARIAN $$
(www.kyriadindia.com; Kyriad Hotel, Station Rd; mains ₹149-199; ⊙7am-10pm; 🕸🛜) Excellent South and North Indian dishes are on offer here at very fair rates; try a *paneer kadai* (cottage cheese cooked in thick tomato gravy). The premises are modern and air-conditioned, and there's an espresso machine and very warm service.

Qaswa Hills　　　　　　MULTICUISINE $$
(Hotel Pearl, Station Rd; mains ₹85-390; ⊙7am-4pm & 7-10pm; 🛜) This basement hotel restaurant buzzes day and night with contented diners. It's renowned for its meat dishes; try a chicken or mutton biryani.

🛍 Shopping

Sabala Handicrafts　　　　ARTS & CRAFTS
(http://sabalahandicrafts.com; Bijapur Bypass, NH13; ⊙8am-5.30pm) Fair-trade store selling beautiful handmade textiles, bags, saris, kurtas and accessories. Prices start at ₹800. Profits benefit an NGO that empowers village women. It's 4km southeast of the centre.

ℹ Information

Tourist Office (☎08352-250359; Hotel Mayura Adil Shahi Annexe, Station Rd; ⊙10am-5.30pm Mon-Sat) With friendly staff.

ℹ Getting There & Away

There are many additional services from private-bus-company offices to Bengaluru, Hyderabad and Mumbai.

ℹ Getting Around

Given the amount to see and the distances to cover, ₹800 is a fair price to hire an autorickshaw for a full day of sightseeing. Short hops around town cost ₹50.

BUSES FROM VIJAPURA (BIJAPUR)

The following services leave from the **bus stand** (☎08352-0251344; Meenakshi Chowk Rd; ⊙24hr):

DESTINATION	FARE (₹)	DURATION (HR)	FREQUENCY
Bengaluru (Bangalore)	ordinary/sleeper 530/795	9½-11	6 daily
Bidar	270	6	5 daily
Kalaburgi (Gulbarga)	168	4	3 daily
Hosapete (Hospet)	248	5	6 daily
Hubballi (Hubli)	198-242	5	3 daily
Hyderabad	388-740	8-10	5 daily
Mumbai	660	11-13	5 daily
Panaji (Panjim)	335-455	9	2 daily

The service to Mumbai runs via Pune (₹438, eight hours).

Bidar

08482 / POP 223,800 / ELEV 664M

Despite being home to amazing ruins and monuments, Bidar, hidden away in Karnataka's far-northeastern corner, gets very little tourist traffic. Drenched in Islamic Indian history, this old-walled town was first the capital of the Bahmani kingdom (1428–87) and later the capital of the Barid Shahi dynasty. This is one of the least Westernised parts of Karnataka, with many niqab-wearing women and turbaned Sikh pilgrims, and though locals are welcoming to visitors, conservative values predominate.

Sights

Bidar Fort   FORT

(⊙6am-6pm) FREE The remnants of this magnificent 15th-century fort, the largest in South India – and once the administrative capital of much of the region – constitute Bidar's most famous historic site. Surrounded by a triple moat hewn out of solid red rock and many kilometres of defensive walls, the fort has a fairy-tale entrance that twists in an elaborate chicane through three gateways. Bidar Fort once had 37 bastions, several wells and a vast magazine. Reckon on a couple of hours to explore it properly.

Bahmani Tombs   HISTORIC SITE

(⊙dawn-dusk) FREE The huge domed tombs of the Bahmani kings in Ashtur, 3km east of Bidar, were built to house the remains of the sultans, of which the stunning painted interior of 15th-century Ahmad Shah al Wali's tomb is the most impressive. Sadly, the paintings are in a very poor state today, with years of bird and bat excrement smearing the walls and virtually no internal lighting. A caretaker will likely appear and use a mirror to illuminate the art.

Khwaja Mahmud Gawan Madrasa   RUIN

(⊙dawn-dusk) FREE Dominating the heart of the old town are the ruins of Khwaja Mahmud Gawan Madrasa, a college for advanced learning built in 1472. To get an idea of its former grandeur, check out the remnants of exquisite coloured tiles on the front gate and one of the minarets, which still stands intact. Tens of thousands of scholars from across the Islamic world once studied here.

Guru Nanak Jhira Sahib   SIKH TEMPLE

(Shiva Nagar; ⊙24hr) This large Sikh temple on the northwestern side of town is dedicated to the Guru Nanak and was built in 1948. It's centred on the Amrit Kund (a water tank), where pilgrims cleanse their souls.

Sleeping & Eating

Hotel Sapna Continental   HOTEL $

(08482-22081; www.hotelsapnacontinental.com; Udgir Rd; r from ₹1100; ❉ ⊙) Offers good value, with spacious rooms and helpful staff. There's no restaurant, but it's right above the popular Kamat Hotel, and under the same management.

Kamat Hotel   SOUTH INDIAN $

(Udgir Rd; meals ₹60-160; ⊙7.30am-10pm) Scores highly for Indian staples at very affordable rates – a dhal fry is just ₹68. It's busy through the day. There's an AC room upstairs.

Getting There & Away

From the bus stand, frequent buses run to Kalaburgi (Gulbarga; ₹128, three hours) and there are two evening buses to Vijapura (₹320, seven hours). There are also regular buses to Hyderabad (₹148, four hours, seven daily) and Bengaluru (semideluxe/AC ₹760/925, 13 hours, five daily).

Four daily trains head to Hyderabad, though times are not convenient; the 7.25pm service is your best bet (sleeper/2AC ₹170/745, three hours). For Bengaluru there's a daily train at 12.15pm (sleeper/1AC ₹385/2560, 17 hours).

KARNATAKA BIDAR

Telangana & Andhra Pradesh

POP 89.4 MILLION

Includes ➜

Hyderabad	230
Bhongir	248
Warangal	248
Palampet	248
Vijayawada	249
Amaravathi	251
Nagarjunakonda	251
Visakhapatnam	252
Tirumala & Tirupati	256

Best Places to Eat

➜ Firdaus (p241)

➜ SO – The Sky Kitchen (p241)

➜ Hotel Mayura (p258)

➜ Dhaba By Claridges (p241)

➜ TFL (p250)

Best Places to Stay

➜ Taj Falaknuma Palace (p238)

➜ Hotel Marasa Sarovar Premiere Tirupati (p257)

➜ Novotel Visakhapatnam Varun Beach (p253)

➜ Ruby Pride Luxury Hotel (p237)

➜ Taj Krishna (p238)

Why Go?

Hyderabad, one of Islamic India's greatest cities, is reason enough on its own to visit this region. Its skyline is a sight to behold, defined by the great domes and minarets of ancient mosques, mausoleums and palaces of once-mighty dynasties. Delve inside the city's fabled old quarter for fascinating street markets, Sufi shrines, teahouses and biryani restaurants. Meanwhile, Hyderabad's newer districts are awash with the upmarket restaurants of IT-fuelled economic advancement.

The other attractions of these two states (which were one entity until 2014) are less brazen, but there are hidden gems like the wonderful temple sculptures of Ramappa and ancient Buddhist sites at Sankaram and Guntupalli. Coastal Visakhapatnam has a cheery vibe, while joining the pilgrim crowds on the hike up to Tirumala's temple is an unforgettable experience.

When to Go
Hyderabad

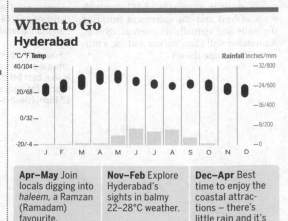

Apr–May Join locals digging into *haleem*, a Ramzan (Ramadam) favourite.

Nov–Feb Explore Hyderabad's sights in balmy 22–28°C weather.

Dec–Apr Best time to enjoy the coastal attractions – there's little rain and it's not *too* hot.

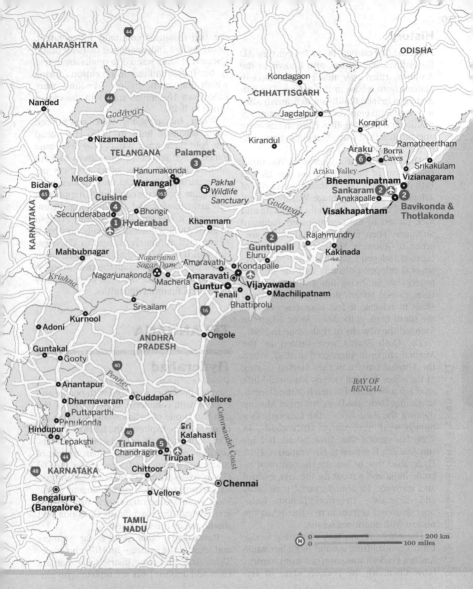

Telangana & Andhra Pradesh Highlights

1 Hyderabad (p230)
Exploring the Old City and its unique markets, architectural marvels and hidden shrines.

2 Monastic trail (p255)
Absorbing the meditative ambience at beautiful Sankaram, as well as Bavikonda, Thotlakonda and Guntupalli, all destinations on this 2300-year-old trail.

3 Palampet (p248)
Revelling in the genius of Kakatiya sculptors at the temple near this village.

4 Cuisine (p240) Feasting on fiery Andhra curries and indulging in memorable biryanis and street snacks.

5 Tirumala (p256) Going with the crowd and finding a spiritual calling with Hindu pilgrims.

6 Araku (p255) Enjoying the delightful train ride here through the lush forests and wide green valleys of the Eastern Ghats.

History

From the 3rd century BC to 3rd century AD the Satavahana empire, also known as the Andhras, ruled over much of the Deccan plateau from a base in this region. The Satavahanas helped Buddhism to flourish after it arrived with emperor Ashoka's missionary monks, and today Andhra Pradesh has more ancient Buddhist sites than almost any other Indian state.

The Hindu Kakatiyas, based at Warangal, ruled most of the region from the 12th to 14th centuries, a period that saw the rise of Telugu culture and language. Warangal eventually fell to the Muslim Delhi Sultanate and then passed to the Deccan-based Bahmani Sultanate. Then, in 1518, the Bahmanis' governor at Golconda, Sultan Quli Qutb Shah, claimed independence. His Qutb Shahi dynasty developed Golconda into the massive fortress we see today. But a water shortage there caused Sultan Mohammed Quli Qutb Shah to relocate a few kilometres east to the south bank of the Musi River, where he founded the new city of Hyderabad in 1591.

The Qutb Shahis were ousted by the Mughal emperor Aurangzeb in 1687. When the Mughal empire in turn started fraying at the edges, its local viceroy Nizam ul-Mulk Asaf Jah took control of much of the Deccan, launching Hyderabad's second great Muslim dynasty, the Asaf Jahis – the famously fabulously wealthy nizams of Hyderabad – in 1724. His capital was Aurangabad, but his son Asaf Jah II moved to Hyderabad in 1763. Hyderabad rose to become the centre of Islamic India and a focus for the arts, culture and learning. Its abundance of rare gems and minerals – the world-famous Kohinoor diamond is from here – furnished the nizams with enormous wealth.

The whole region was effectively under British control from around 1800, but while Andhra Pradesh was governed from Madras (now Chennai), the princely state of Hyderabad remained nominally independent. Come Indian Independence in 1947, nizam Osman Ali Khan wanted to retain sovereignty, but Indian military intervention (during which thousands, mainly Muslims, were killed) saw Hyderabad state join the Indian union in 1948.

When Indian states were reorganised along linguistic lines in 1956, Hyderabad was split three ways. What's now Telangana joined other Telugu-speaking areas to form Andhra Pradesh state; other districts became parts of Karnataka and Maharashtra. Telangana was never completely happy with this arrangement, and after prolonged campaigning, it was split from Andhra Pradesh in 2014. Andhra Pradesh officially now has a new capital at Amaravati (next to Vijayawada), which should eventually be smart, green and ultramodern – though the vast project is way behind schedule and has been beset by delays and financial difficulties.

TELANGANA

Hyderabad

📞 040 / POP 11.5 MILLION / ELEV 600M

Steeped in history, thronged with people and buzzing with commerce, the Old City of Hyderabad is one of India's most evocative ancient quarters. Exploring the lanes of this district, with its chai shops and spice merchants, you'll encounter a teeming urban masala of colour and commerce. Looming over the Old City is some of Islamic India's most impressive architecture, in varying states of repair. Most visitors concentrate their time in this area, though the magnificent Golconda Fort should not be missed either.

Hyderabad's other pole is far younger and west of the centre – its Hi-Tech City, or 'Cyberabad', and other districts like Banjara Hills and Jubilee Hills are replete with glit-

---

TOP STATE FESTIVALS

Sankranti (☉ Jan) This important regionwide Telugu festival marks the end of harvest season. Kite-flying abounds, doorsteps are decorated with colourful *kolams* (rice-flour designs) and men adorn cattle with bells and fresh horn paint.

Brahmotsavam (☉ Sep/Oct) This nine-day festival sees the Venkateshwara Temple at Tirumala awash in vast crowds of worshippers. Special *pujas* (offerings) and chariot processions are held, and it's an auspicious time for *darshan* (deity-viewing).

Muharram (☉ Aug/Sep) Commemorates the martyrdom of Mohammed's grandson Hussain. A huge procession throngs the Old City in Hyderabad.

Hyderabad

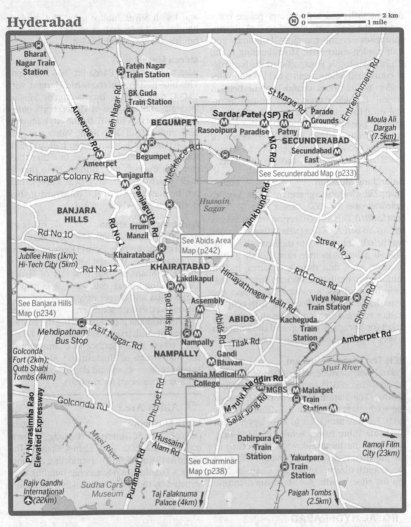

See Secunderabad Map (p233)

See Abids Area Map (p242)

See Banjara Hills Map (p234)

See Charminar Map (p238)

TELANGANA & ANDHRA PRADESH HYDERABAD

tery malls, multiplexes, clubs, pubs and sleek restaurants.

Hyderabad traffic is appalling, though with the opening of a new metro rail rapid-transit system things should ease somewhat in the coming years.

◉ Sights

◉ Old City

★**Charminar** MONUMENT
(Map p238; Charminar Rd; Indian/foreigner ₹5/100; ⊙9am-5.30pm) Hyderabad's principal landmark and city symbol was built by Mohammed Quli Qutb Shah in 1591 to commemorate the founding of Hyderabad and the end of epidemics caused by Golconda's water shortage. The gargantuan four-column, 56m-high structure has four arches facing the cardinal points, with minarets atop each column (hence the name Charminar, 'four minarets'). It's certainly an impressive sight, though the relentless traffic that swirls around the structure, crowds and queues make it somewhat less rewarding to visit.

★**Chowmahalla Palace** PALACE
(Map p238; off Charimar Rd; Indian/foreigner ₹50/200, camera ₹50; ⊙10am-5pm Sat-Thu) This

opulent 18th- and 19th-century palace compound, the main residence of several nizams, comprises several grandiose buildings and four garden courtyards. Most dazzling is the Khilwat Mubarak, a magnificent durbar (royal court) hall where nizams held ceremonies under 19 enormous chandeliers of Belgian crystal. Its side rooms today house historical exhibits, arts and crafts, and exhibits of nizams' personal possessions. In the southernmost courtyard is a priceless collection of carriages and vintage cars including a 1911 yellow Rolls-Royce and 1937 Buick convertible.

Salar Jung Museum   MUSEUM
(Map p238; www.salarjungmuseum.in; Salar Jung Rd; Indian/foreigner ₹20/500, camera ₹50; ⊘10am-5pm Sat-Thu) This vast collection was amassed by Mir Yousuf Ali Khan (Salar Jung III), who was briefly grand vizier to the seventh nizam. The 39 galleries include early South Indian bronzes, wood and stone sculptures, Indian miniature paintings, European fine art, historic manuscripts, a room of jade and the remarkable *Veiled Rebecca* by 19th-century Italian sculptor Benzoni. Note the entrance ticket for foreigners is steep and the museum is very popular (near bedlam on Sundays).

HEH The Nizam's Museum   MUSEUM
(Purani Haveli; Map p238; off Dur-e-Sharwah Hospital Rd; adult/child ₹80/15, camera ₹150; ⊘10am-5pm Sat-Thu) The Purani Haveli was a home of the sixth nizam, Mahbub Ali Khan (r 1869–1911). He was rumoured to have never worn the same thing twice: hence the 54m-long, two-storey Burmese teak wardrobe. Much of the museum is devoted to personal effects of the seventh nizam, Osman Ali Khan, including his silver cradle, gold-burnished throne

and lavish Silver Jubilee gifts. The displays, lighting and information could be improved, but it's still a worthwhile visit.

Mecca Masjid   MOSQUE
(Map p238; Shah Ali Banda Rd; ⊘4.30am-9pm) This mosque is one of the world's largest, with 10,000 men praying here at major Muslim festivals, and also one of Hyderabad's oldest buildings, begun in 1617 by the city's founder Mohammed Quli Qutb Shah. Women are not allowed inside the main prayer hall, and male tourists are unlikely to be let in either (they can look through the railings). Note that female tourists, even with headscarves, may not be permitted into the courtyard if their clothing is judged inappropriate.

Badshahi Ashurkhana   ISLAMIC SITE
(Map p238; High Court Rd) The 1594 Badshahi Ashurkhana (literally Royal House of Mourning) was one of the first structures built by the Qutb Shahs in their new city of Hyderabad. Facing a huge courtyard, it is in poor shape today and desperately in need of renovation but there are some terrific tile mosaics. The Ashurkhana is packed during the Islamic festival of Muharram, as well as on Thursdays, when Shiites gather to commemorate the martyrdom of Hussain Ibn Ali. Visitors should remove shoes and dress modestly (including a headscarf for women).

⊙ Abids Area

State Museum   MUSEUM
(Map p242; Public Gardens Rd, Nampally; ₹10, camera/video ₹100/500; ⊘10.30am-4.30pm Sat-Thu, closed 2nd Sat of month) This sprawling museum is in a fanciful Indo-Saracenic building constructed by the seventh nizam as a playhouse

---

ROYAL HYDERABAD

Founded by the Qutb Shahi dynasty in the late sixteenth century, the city of Hyderabad boasts a unique royal heritage of palaces and tombs, monuments and mosques. With fabulous wealth generated from nearby diamond mines and pearl trading, the city's rulers amassed an astonishing collection of art and antiques, and many pieces are showcased in former royal residences.

Palaces such as the spectacular Chowmahalla Palace (p231) and Purani Haveli, now HEH The Nizam's Museum, harbour priceless objects gathered from across the globe. South of the city centre, the former home of the last nizam of the princely state of Hyderabad Deccan has been expertly restored to become the Taj Falaknuma Palace (p238). It's well worth dropping by for 'high tea' or dinner so you can take in the splendour of its staterooms, halls and grounds.

On the western fringes of the city lies the greatest of all royal residences, Golconda Fort (p234), which predates Hyderabad by centuries. One of India's most impressive fortified monuments, it's in ruins today, though its scale is tremendous.

Secunderabad

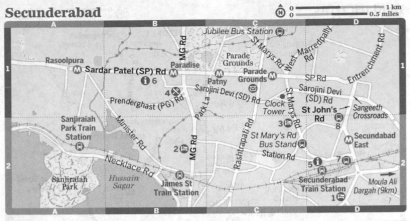

Secunderabad

Sleeping
1 OYO 984 GN International D2
2 Raj Classic Inn B2
3 Ruby Pride Luxury Hotel C2

Eating
4 Paradise B1

Information
5 Telangana Tourism D2
6 Telangana Tourism B1

Transport
7 Rathifile Bus Stand D2
8 Secunderabad Bus Stop
(Pushpak) D2
Secunderabad Junction
Bus Stop .... (see 5)
Secunderabad Reservation
Complex .... (see 7)

for one of his daughters. It hosts a collection of important archaeological finds as well as an exhibit on the region's Buddhist history. There's an interesting decorative arts gallery, where you can learn about the art of *bidriware,* or inlaid metalwork, and *kalamkari* textile painting, plus a bronze-sculpture gallery and a 4500-year-old Egyptian mummy.

British Residency   HISTORIC BUILDING
(Koti Women's College; Map p242; Koti Main Rd) This palatial Palladian residence, built in 1803–06 by James Achilles Kirkpatrick, the British Resident (official East India Company representative) in Hyderabad, features in William Dalrymple's brilliant love story *White Mughals.* Work is ongoing to restore the building to its former glory, a project that will take many years to accomplish. There's no official access but Detours (p236) can usually gain entry for those booking one of its fascinating White Mughal tours.

Birla Mandir   HINDU TEMPLE
(Map p234; Hill Fort Rd; ⊘7am-noon & 2-9pm) The ethereal Birla Mandir, constructed of white

Rajasthani marble in 1976, graces Kalapahad (Black Mountain), one of two rocky hills overlooking the lake of Hussain Sagar. Dedicated to Venkateshwara, it's a popular Hindu worship centre, with a relaxed atmosphere, and affords magnificent views over the city, especially at sunset. There are several imposing statues including a huge granite image of Venkateshwara. Disabled access is good: there's a lift in the curious clock tower.

Banjara Hills

★Lamakaan   CULTURAL CENTRE
(Map p234; ☑9642731329; www.lamakaan.com; next to JVR Park, Banjara Hills; ⊘10am-10pm Tue-Sun) This noncommercial 'inclusive cultural space' is an open centre that hosts plays, films, musical events, exhibitions, organic markets and lectures; some events are free. It also has a great Irani cafe, with cheap tea and snacks and free wi-fi. On a lane off Rd No 1.

Kalakriti Art Gallery   GALLERY
(Map p234; www.kalakritiartgallery.com; Rd No 10, Banjara Hills; ⊘11am-7pm) FREE One of the city's

Banjara Hills

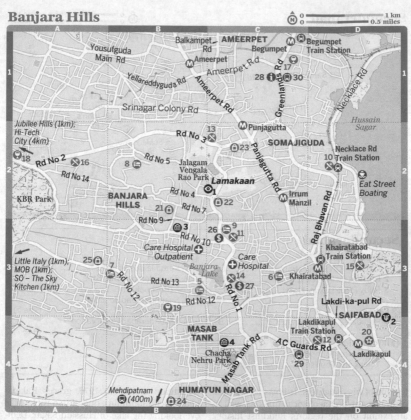

best contemporary galleries, Kalakriti hosts excellent exhibitions by some of India's leading artists, and collaborative programme's with the Alliance Française and Goethe Zentrum. There's a good cafe here too.

Other Areas

★ **Golconda Fort**   FORT
(Indian/foreigner ₹20/200, 1hr sound-and-light show ₹140; ⏱ 9am-5.30pm, English-language sound-and-light show 6.30pm Nov-Feb, 7pm Mar-Oct) Hyderabad's most impressive sight, this monumental fort lies on the western edge of town. In the 16th century the Qutb Shahs made Golconda a fortified citadel, built atop a 120m-high granite hill surrounded by mighty ramparts, all ringed by further necklaces of crenellated fortifications, 11km in perimeter. From the summit there are stunning vistas across dusty Deccan foothills and the crumbling outer ramparts, over the domed

tombs of Qutb Shahs, past distant shanty towns to the horizon haze of the inner city.

By the time of the Qutb Shahs, Golconda Fort had already existed for at least three centuries under the Kakatiyas and Bahmani sultanate, and was already famed for its diamonds, which were mostly mined in the Krishna River valley, but cut and traded here. The Qutb Shahs moved to their new city of Hyderabad in 1591, but maintained Golconda as a citadel until the Mughal emperor Aurangzeb took it in 1687 after a year-long siege, ending Qutb Shahi rule.

Golconda's massive gates were studded with iron spikes to obstruct war elephants. Within the fort, a series of concealed glazed earthenware pipes ensured a reliable water supply, while the ingenious acoustics guaranteed that even the smallest sound from the entrance would echo across the fort complex.

Allow at least a couple of hours to explore the site. Guides charge around ₹600 per

Banjara Hills

◉ Top Sights
1 Lamakaan...C2

◉ Sights
2 Birla Mandir..D4
3 Kalakriti Art Gallery...............................B3
4 Nehru Centenary Tribal Museum C4

◎ Sleeping
5 Beehive Hostel......................................B3
6 Elysium Inn Backpackers Hostel C3
7 Fortune Park Vallabha.........................B3
8 Golden Glory Guesthouse...................B2
9 Taj Krishna..C3

◉ Eating
10 Aish...D2
11 Barbeque Nation.................................C3
12 Chicha's...D4
13 Chutneys...C2
   Firdaus... (see 9)
14 Karachi Bakery C3
15 Paradise...D3
16 Roastery..A2

◉ Drinking & Nightlife
17 10 Downing Street...............................C1

18 Coco's Bar & Grill................................A2
   Kismet...(see 10)
19 Vertigo.. B3

◉ Entertainment
20 Ravindra Bharathi Theatre...................D4

◉ Shopping
21 Fabindia.. B2
22 GVK One...C2
23 Himalaya Book World...........................C2
24 Malkha..B4
25 Suvasa...A3

❶ Information
26 Citibank ATM.......................................C3
27 Citibank ATM.......................................C3
   Citibank ATM..............................(see 22)
   Indiatourism.................................(see 28)
28 Telangana Tourism...............................C1

❶ Transport
29 AC Guards Bus Stop (Pushpak)...........C4
30 Paryatak Bhavan Bus Stop
   (Pushpak)...C1

90-minute tour. Small ₹20 guide booklets are also available. Inside the citadel gate, an anticlockwise circuit leads through gardens and up past mostly minor buildings to the top of the hill, where you'll find the functioning Hindu Jagadamba Mahakali Temple and the three-storey durbar hall, with fine panoramas. You then descend to the old palace buildings in the southeastern part of the fort and return to the entrance, passing the elegant three-arched Taramati Mosque.

Golconda is about 10km west from Abids or Charminar: an Uber cab or auto is around ₹270 one way. Buses 65G and 66G run from Charminar to Golconda via GPO Abids hourly; the journey takes about an hour.

★ Qutb Shahi Tombs   HISTORIC SITE
(Tolichowki; Indian/foreigner ₹15/100, camera or smartphone/video ₹50/100; ⊙9.30am-5pm Sat-Thu) The subject of one of India's most ambitious heritage projects, these magnificent domed granite tombs form part of a huge archaeological park that is steadily being renovated by the Aga Khan Development Network. All in all there are 40 mausoleums, 23 mosques, a hammam and several pavilions located in landscaped gardens. Seven of the eight Qutb Shahi rulers were buried here under great domes mounted on cubical bas-

es, many of which have beautiful colonnades and delicate lime stucco ornamentation.

★ Paigah Tombs   HISTORIC SITE
(Santoshnagar; ⊙ Sat-Thu 10am-5pm) FREE The aristocratic Paigah family, purportedly descendants of the second Caliph of Islam, were fierce loyalists of the nizams, serving as statespeople, philanthropists and generals. The Paigahs' necropolis, in a quiet neighbourhood 4km southeast of Charminar, is a small compound of exquisite mausoleums made of marble and lime stucco. It's signposted down a small lane opposite Owaisi Hospital on the Inner Ring Rd.

Moula Ali Dargah   ISLAMIC SITE
Out on the city's northeastern fringes, the dramatic rock mound of Moula Ali hill has long-distance views, cool breezes and at the top, up 500 steps, a dargah (shrine to a Sufi saint) containing what's believed to be a handprint of Ali, the son-in-law of the Prophet Mohammed. The dargah's reputed healing properties make it a pilgrimage site for the sick.

Buddha Statue
& Hussain Sagar   BUDDHIST MONUMENT
(Map p242; boats adult/child ₹55/35; ⊙ boats 9am-9pm) Set magnificently on a plinth in the

Hussain Sagar, a lake created by the Qutb Shahs, is a colossal stone statue of the Buddha (18m tall). The Dalai Lama consecrated the monument in 2006, which is evocatively illuminated at night. Frequent boats make the 30-minute return trip to the statue from both Eat Street (p247) and popular Lumbini Park (p247). The Tankbund Rd promenade, on the eastern shore of Hussain Sagar, has great views of the statue.

Nehru Centenary Tribal Museum
MUSEUM

(Map p234; DSS Bhavan, Owaisipura Rd, Masab Tank; Indian/foreigner ₹10/100; ⊙ Mon-Sat 10.30am-5pm) This museum exhibits photographs, dioramas of village life, musical instruments and some exquisite Naikpod masks. It's basic, but you'll get a glimpse into tribal cultures (there are 33 tribal groups in the region, comprising several million people). No photos permitted.

🏃 Activities

Travelling Spoon
FOOD

(www.travelingspoon.com; from US$22) Ever wanted to eat real home cooking in India? Travelling Spoon hooks you up with a Hyderabadi family so you can eat their food in their home. Cooking lessons and market visits are also offered.

Vipassana International Meditation Centre
HEALTH & WELLBEING

(Dhamma Khetta; ☑ 040-24240290; www.khetta. dhamma.org; Nagarjuna Sagar Rd, Km12.6) Silent meditation (two-, three-,and 10-day courses) in peaceful grounds 20km outside the city. Apply online. There's no official charge; you donate according to your means.

🧭 Tours

★ Detours
TOURS

(☑ 9000850505; www.detoursindia.com; per 3hr walk ₹2500) Outstanding cultural tours led by the enthusiastic, knowledgeable Jonty Rajagopalan and her small team. Options cover off-the-beaten-track corners of Hyderabad plus markets, food (including cooking lessons and eating) and religion. The crafts tour educates about the use of wood and coconut shells in toy making, as well as tribal art.

★ Heritage Walks
WALKING

(Map p238; ☑ 9849728841; www.telanganatourism. gov.in/heritagewalks; per person ₹50; ⊙ 7.30-9am Sun & every 2nd Sat) Starting at Charminar and ending at the Chowmahalla Palace, these highly informative (and incredibly inexpensive) walks were designed, and are sometimes led, by architect and historian Madhu Vottery. The price includes breakfast.

SIA Photo Walks
WALKING

(☑ 8008633354; http://siaphotography.in/tours; group walks from ₹300) Excellent street-photography tours of the city curated by Saurabh Chatterjee, who is a knowledgable guide and experienced photographer. Smartphone users will also benefit from his expertise.

Telangana Tourism
TOURS

(☑ 1800 42546464; www.telanganatourism.gov.in) Offers fine weekend tours, such as a 'Nizam Palace' trip that includes the Chowmahalla Palace, Falaknuma Palace and the Golconda Fort (for the sound-and-light show) for ₹3100/2000 with/without high tea at Falaknuma. Also has daily bus tours of city sights (from ₹250 plus admission tickets) and evening Golconda sound-and-light trips. Book at any Telangana Tourism office.

🎉 Festivals & Events

Hyderabad Literary Festival
LITERATURE

(www.hydlitfest.org; ⊙ lateJan) A well-established three-day annual event that celebrates literature and the local tradition of *mushaira* (poetry recital). Held at locations including Lamakaan (p233).

Pandit Motiram– Maniram Sangeet Samaroh
MUSIC

(⊙ Nov/Dec) This four-day music festival, named for two renowned classical musicians, celebrates Hindustani music. It's held in the Chowmahalla Palace.

Mahankali Jatra
RELIGIOUS

(⊙ Jun/Jul) A statewide festival honouring Kali, with colourful processions in which devotees convey *bonalu* (pots of food offerings) to the deity. Secunderabad's Mahankali Temple goes wild.

Deccan Festival
MUSIC

(⊙ Feb/Mar) Held in Hyderabad, this five-day festival pays tribute to Deccan culture. Urdu *mushairas* (poetry readings) are held, along with *qawwali* (Sufi devotional music) and other local music and dance performances.

🛌 Sleeping

The inner-city Abids area is convenient for Nampally station and the Old City, though it is congested and polluted. For more space

KITSCHABAD

Mixed in with Hyderabad's world-class sights are some attractions on the quirkier side.

Ramoji Film City (www.ramojifilmcity.com; adult/child from ₹1150/950; ⊙9am-5.30pm) The Telangana/Andhra Pradesh film industry, 'Tollywood', is massive, and so is the 6.7-sq-km Film City, where films and TV shows in Telugu, Tamil and Hindi, among others, are made. The day visit ticket includes a bus tour, funfair rides and shows. Telangana Tourism (p236) runs tours here.

Sudha Cars Museum (19-5-15/1/D, Bahadurpura; Indian/foreigner ₹50/200, camera ₹50; ⊙9.30am-6pm) The eccentric creations of auto-enthusiast K Sudhakar include cars and bikes in the shape of a snooker table, golf ball and lipstick, among other wacky designs. And they all work. The museum is 3km west of Charminar.

National Fisheries Development Board (PV Narasimha Rao Expressway) You'll pass this curious fish-shaped building on your way to or from the city's airport. Its eyes are two circular windows, and it boasts impressive fins.

and greenery head to middle-class Banjara Hills, about 4km northwest of Abids.

Elysium Inn Backpackers Hostel HOSTEL $
(Map p234; ☑8897751857; www.facebook.com/elysiumInnbackpackershostel; 6-3-609/147/A, Anand Nagar Colony, Khairatabad; dm ₹500-585, r ₹1300; ❄✸☞; ⓂKhairatabad) A small hostel in a quiet location with helpful management, a guests' lounge and small kitchen. There are two dorms (one female-only) and a private room: note only the mixed dorm has air-con. It's an 800m walk west of Khairatabad Metro station.

Beehive Hostel HOSTEL $
(Map p234; ☑951995858; https://beehive-hostel.business.site; Rd No.12, Banjara Hills; dm ₹650; ❄✸☞) This bright new hostel is a great choice with its kitchen-diner and spacious lounge. Dorms (mixed and female-only) are well-presented with good bunks, lockers and en-suites. Cleanliness is very good throughout the property.

OYO 984 GN International HOTEL $
(Map p233; ☑070-65067406; www.oyorooms.com; Bhoiguda Road, Railway Officer Colony, Secunderabad; s/d from ₹1380/1480; ✸☞) Rooms here give more than a nod to contemporary style, and wi-fi is reliable. There's no in-house restaurant facility but lots close by as the location is near Secunderabad station. Breakfast is available for ₹50, but it's very basic.

Golden Glory Guesthouse GUESTHOUSE $
(Map p234; ☑040-23554765; www.goldenglory guesthouse.com; off Rd No 3, Banjara Hills; s/d incl breakfast ₹1100/1300, with AC ₹1300/1700; ✸☞) Offering fine value for the upmarket Banjara Hills location, with ample cafes and eateries

close by, this modestly priced place has clean simple rooms, some with balconies. There's free wi-fi throughout and staff are eager to please.

★**Ruby Pride Luxury Hotel** HOTEL $$
(Map p233; ☑040-49527844; www.rubypride.com; 167-169 Turner Street, Secunderabad; r incl breakfast ₹2800; ✸☞; ⓂParade Grounds) A well-managed mid-range hotel with modern furnishings; rooms are all air-conditioned and have attractive furniture, minifridge and flatscreen TV. Staff are very switched on and helpful. It's a short walk from Secunderabad station and a kilometre from a metro stop.

Raj Classic Inn HOTEL $$
(Map p233; ☑040-27815291; rajclassicinn@gmail.com; 50 MG Rd, Secunderabad; s/d incl breakfast from ₹1792/2128; ✸☞; ⓂParadise) A pocket-friendly hotel that has been recently renovated, with well-maintained and spacious rooms and friendly, courteous staff. Expect some traffic noise due to its busy location. In-house Chilly's restaurant is recommended for veg food.

Royalton Hotel HOTEL $$
(Map p242; ☑040-67122000; www.royaltonhotel.in; Fateh Sultan Lane, Abids; s/d incl breakfast from ₹2875/3150; ✸☞; ⓂNampally) In a relatively quiet part of Abids, Royalton's gargantuan black lobby chandelier and mirrored lifts give off a slight Manhattan vibe. Rooms have tasteful textiles, glass showers and tea/coffee makers. The hotel is vegetarian and alcohol-free.

Taj Mahal Hotel Abids HOTEL $$
(Map p242; ☑040-24758250; www.hoteltaj mahalindia.com; Abids Rd, Abids; incl breakfast s/d

TELANGANA & ANDHRA PRADESH HYDERABAD

Charminar

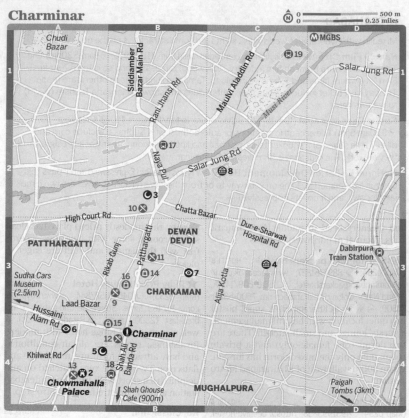

from ₹3066/4210; 🏃🏼♪) Not part of the up-market Taj group, this 1924 building nevertheless has a classy, if slightly faded colonial ambience. 'Heritage' rooms have character, but most rooms are modern and located in a functional modern block to the side. It's very convenient for sightseeing and the in-house restaurant is excellent for vegetarian food.

★ **Taj Falaknuma Palace** HERITAGE HOTEL $$$

(📞 040-66298585; www.tajhotels.com; Engine Bowli, Falaknuma; s/d from ₹39,850/42,600; 🏃🏼@♪) The former residence of the sixth nizam, this 1884 neoclassical palace now run by the Taj group oozes class and grandeur with its embossed-leather wallpaper and 24-karat-gold ceiling trim. The rooms are stunning, facilities marvellous and you'll love the views over the city from its hilltop location. In-house restaurants (Adaa for Indian cuisine and Celeste for international) are exceptional too.

★ **Taj Krishna** HOTEL $$$

(Map p234; 📞 040-66662323; www.tajhotels.com; Rd No 1, Banjara Hills; s/d from ₹8680/9450; 🏃🏼@♪🏊) On the fringe of the Banjara Hills district this landmark hotel has exceptionally lush tropical gardens and one of the nation's nicest hotel pools, 40m in length. Its commodious rooms are being steadily upgraded – those at the rear are quieter. Staff here really go the extra mile to make guests feel at home, and restaurants are superb for authentic Hyderabadi cuisine.

Fortune Park Vallabha HOTEL $$$

(Map p234; 📞 040-39884444; www.fortunehotels.in; Rd No 12, Banjara Hills; s/d incl breakfast from ₹5230/6520; 🏃🏼@♪🏊) Enjoys a good location and has large contemporary rooms with stained-glass panels, many with balconies. Room service is available at reasonable prices and the South Indian food and breakfast buffet are excellent.

Charminar

◉ Top Sights
1 Charminar B4
2 Chowmahalla Palace A4

◉ Sights
3 Badshahi Ashurkhana B2
4 HEH The Nizam's Museum C3
5 Mecca Masjid A4
6 Mehboob Chowk A4
7 Mir Alam Mandi B3
8 Salar Jung Museum C2

◉ Activities, Courses & Tours
Heritage Walks .... (see 1)

◎ Eating
9 Govind Dosa B3
10 Hotel Shadab B2
11 Meerut Hotel B3
12 Nimrah B4
13 Taj Restaurant A4

◎ Shopping
14 Hyderabad Perfumers B3
15 Laad Bazar B4
16 Patel Market B3

◉ Transport
17 Afzalgunj Bus Stop B2
18 Charminar Bus Stop B4
19 Mahatma Gandhi Bus Station C1

🍴 Eating

The one dish you must try is biryani, which Hyderabadis claim as their own.

In the early evenings, look out for *mirchi bhajji* (chilli fritters), served at street stalls with tea. The Hyderabadi style is famous: chillis are stripped of their seeds, stuffed with tamarind, sesame and spices, dipped in chickpea batter and fried.

Local usage refers to 'thalis' as 'meals'.

Nimrah
CAFE $

(Map p238; Charminar; baked goods ₹3-12; ⊙5.30am-11pm) This classic Irani cafe, always packed to the rafters, Is located almost un derneath the Charminar's arches. It offers a particularly tasty range of Irani baked goods to accompany your chai pick-me-up. The classic dunk is Osmania biscuits (melt-in-the-mouth shortbreads) but there are many other options including sponge breads and plum slices.

Karachi Bakery
BAKERY $

(Map p234; www.karachibakery.com; Rd Number 1, Banjara Hills; snacks from ₹25; ⊙10am-10pm) Established in 1953 and famous for its cakes, biscuits and bread. Try the traditional *dilkhush* (a pie stuffed with grated coconut, nuts and dry fruit). Has over 20 branches across the city. They also serve meals, including sandwiches and pizza.

Meerut Hotel
INDIAN $

(Map p238; Mir Alam Mandi Rd; mains ₹50-55; ⊙8am-10pm) Offers filling meat and veg curries, delicious tandoor roti (which is baked on the street in front of you) and a mean mutton korma.

Govind Dosa
STREET FOOD $

(Map p238; Charkaman; snacks ₹40-100; ⊙6am-noon) A famous breakfast spot, cheery Govind's street-corner stand is permanently surrounded by happy Hyderabadis savouring his delicious dosa (South Indian savoury crepe; try the butter masala) and *idli* (South Indian spongy, round, fermented rice cakes); the *tawa idli* topped with chilli powder and spices is a great way to kick-start the day.

Kamat Hotel
SOUTH INDIAN $

(Map p242; Nampally Station Rd, Nampally; meals ₹130-270; ⊙7am-10pm; Ⓜ Nampally) Cheap and reliably good for tasty South Indian fare. It's a good option for breakfast or a speedy lunch – try their *idli* or *masala vada* (spicy, deep-fried lentil savoury). There's also a larger AC branch in Saifabad, and two in Secunderabad.

★ Shah Ghouse Cafe
HYDERABADI $$

(Shah Ali Banda Rd; mains ₹80-310; ⊙5am-1am) During Ramadan, Hyderabadis line up for Shah Ghouse's famous *haleem* (a thick soup of pounded spiced wheat, with goat, chicken or beef, and lentils) and at any time of year the mutton biryani is near-perfect. Don't expect ambience: just good traditional food, in a no-frills upstairs dining hall. Wash it down with a delicious lassi (₹60).

Cafe Bahar
HYDERABADI $$

(Map p242; 3-5-815/A, Avanti Nagar, Basheer Bagh; biryanis ₹90-?90; ⊙11am-1am) Consistently recommended by locals for authentic Hyderabadi cuisine, this AC place serves generous portions of flavoursome biryanis at modest prices (veg is just ₹90, while a mutton biryani costs ₹150). Kebabs are also good. It's usually crowded so be prepared for a wait.

TELANGANA & ANDHRA PRADESH HYDERABAD

Chutneys

SOUTH INDIAN $$

(Map p234; ✆040-66778484; Shilpa Arcade, Rd No 3, Banjara Hills; meals ₹260-340; ☺7am-11pm; 🛜; Ⓜ Panjagutta) Chutneys is famous for its South Indian meals and all-day dosa, *idli* and *uttapams* (thick, savoury rice pancake with finely chopped onions, green chillies, coriander and coconut). Try a *pesarattu* (dosa made with green mung beans). Its dishes are moderate on chilli, and Chinese food and North Indian thalis are also available. No booze served.

Paradise

HYDERABADI $$

(Persis; Map p233; www.paradisefoodcourt.in; cnr SD & MG Rds; biryani ₹239-319; ☺11.30am-11pm; Ⓜ Paradise) Paradise is synonymous with biryani in these parts. The main Secunderabad location has five different dining areas: head to the attractive 'roof garden', complete with whirring fans, or pay an AC surcharge to eat inside. Also serves lots of (less pleasing) Chinese dishes. There are over a dozen Paradise restaurants across the city including a large, modern branch at **Khairatabad** (Map p234; ✆040-67408400; NTR Gardens,

Khairatabad; mains ₹211-377; ☺11am-11pm; Ⓜ Khairatabad) close to Abids and Banjara Hills.

Roastery

CAFE $$

(Map p234; 418 Rd 14, Banjara Hills; mains ₹188-388; ☺8am-11.30pm) Located in a converted villa, this is one of west Hyderabad's most popular cafes. Banjara Hills' bright young things flock here for the Western food: salads (try the grilled chicken), bruschettas, burgers, pasta dishes and sandwiches. As the name indicates, Roastery is also famous for its coffee, including nitro cold brew, French press and hot black options.

Chicha's

HYDERABADI $$

(Map p234; ✆9959911100; www.facebook.com/chichashyderabad; AC Guards Rd, Lakdikapul; mains ₹219-349; ☺noon-1.45am; Ⓜ Lakdikapul) Hip hang-out where you can feast on delicious, authentic Hyderabadi dishes and street food in quirky, air-conditioned surrounds. Price are moderate with biryanis starting at ₹219 and every Friday there's a special mutton *haleem* (₹179). Curries are also excellent. No booze.

HYDERABADI CUISINE

Hyderabad has a food culture all of its own and Hyderabadis take great pride and pleasure in it. It was the Mughals who brought the tasty biryanis, skewer kebabs and special Ramadan dishes like *haleem*, so many dishes have a hint of Persia about them.

Biryani is the definitive local meal. In Hyderabad it's often prepared in layers, with uncooked meat at the bottom of the pan (the highest temperature), topped with rice, then another layer of half-cooked spiced meat so that the ingredients are ready at the same time. Hyderabadi biryanis are spicy, but not fancy or fragrant like the biryanis of Lucknow, another town synonymous with the dish. Biryanis in Hyderabad are always served with *mirchi ka slan* (a richly spiced gravy) and *dahi ki* (raita, often called chutney locally). Mutton (goat or lamb) is the classic biryani base, though chicken, egg, fish and vegetable biryanis are plentiful too. Biryanis come in vast quantities and one serve may satisfy two people. Good places to order a biryani include Hotel Shadab in the Old City, Cafe Bahar (p239), Shah Ghouse Cafe (p239) and Paradise, which has several branches across Hyderabad.

To experience the other classic Hyderabadi dish, *haleem* (a thick soup of pounded, spiced wheat with goat, chicken or beef, and lentils) you really need to be in the city during Ramadan (known locally as Ramzan). Come nightfall at this time, the serious business of eating begins, as thousands of stalls are set up across the city and locals go *haleem*-hopping to assess the best. Look out for the clay ovens called *bhattis;* you'll probably hear them before you see them. Men gather around, taking turns to vigorously pound *haleem* and the crowds are quite something. Outside Ramzan, *haleem* is rare on local menus. Chicha's serves up the dish each Friday, while hotel restaurants Firdaus and Aish offer fine versions of the dish all year round.

Look out too for *pesarattu* (a pancake-like dosa made with green mung beans), which are stuffed with *upma* (semolina seasoned with cumin, onion, ginger and green chilli) and served with chutney. It's a popular breakfast dish, which you can find at Chutneys.

Taj Restaurant   HYDERABADI **$$**
(Map p238; Khilwat Rd; mains ₹100-210; ⊙10am-9pm) A bustling, no-nonsense place that specialises in biryani and delicious chicken and mutton curries, located just around the corner from the Chowmahalla Palace. There's an AC room on the upper floor.

Hotel Shadab   HYDERABADI **$$**
(Map p238; High Court Rd, north of Charminar; mains ₹180-340; ⊙noon-11.30pm) The time-warp decor looks like it's been based on a 1970s disco but the cuisine is great at this hopping Hyderabadi restaurant. Great for biryanis (veg/non-veg starting at ₹190/270), kebabs and mutton in all configurations and, during Ramadan, *haleem*. Downstairs it's very solo-male; head upstairs to the AC room for more of a family vibe.

Dakshina Mandapa   SOUTH INDIAN **$$$**
(Map p242; Taj Mahal Hotel, Abids Rd, Abids; meals ₹330-425; ⊙7am-10.30pm) Highly regarded spot for South Indian vegetarian food. You may have to wait for a lunch table, but order the South Indian thali and you'll be brought heap after heap of rice and refills of authentic dishes. The AC room upstairs does a superb lunch buffet (noon to 3.30pm).

★Olive Bistro   MEDITERRANEAN **$$$**
(☑9248912347; www.olivebarandkitchen.com; Rd No 46, Jubilee Hills, Durgam Cheruvu; mains ₹540-815; ⊙Mon-Fri 7-11pm, Sat & Sun noon-3.30pm & 7pm-1am; 🖤) Located in a secluded leafy location with lake views from its terrace, this atmospheric restaurant is one of the hottest places in town for Italian and Mediterranean food. Choose from pasta, risottos, meat (like lamb ribs with roasted cous cous) or great seafood; try the *gambas pil pil* (prawns cooked in a garlic and hot pepper sauce).

★Dhaba By Claridges   MODERN INDIAN **$$$**
(☑040-29706704; www.dhababyclaridges.com; Western Pearl Bldg, Survey 13, Kondapur; mains ₹265-445; ⊙noon-11.30pm; 🖤) A good reason to head out west to Hi-Tech City, this hip hang-out offers a contemporary take on North Indian street food (minus the fumes and traffic of course). Dhaba's decor is kooky, with Bollywood-style murals and bold colours to the fore. House cocktails and mocktails are wonderful too.

★Firdaus   INDIAN **$$$**
(Map p234; ☑040-66662323; Taj Krishna hotel, Rd No 1, Banjara Hills; mains ₹550-1650; ⊙Sun-Thu 7.30-11.45pm, Fri & Sat noon-2:45pm & 7.30-11.45pm;

🖤) A classy hotel restaurant, Firdaus offers great Hyderabadi (and also North Indian) dishes to the strains of live *ghazals* (classical Urdu love songs, accompanied by harmonium and tabla). They even serve *haleem* outside Ramadan and superb meat dishes – try the *raan-e-firdaus* (pot roasted lamb).

★SO – The Sky Kitchen   MULTICUISINE **$$$**
(☑040-23558004; www.notjustso.com; Rd No 92, near Apollo Hospital, Jubilee Hills; mains ₹340-530; ⊙noon-midnight; 🖤) Jubilee Hills rooftop restaurant, with candles and loungey playlists, which makes a highly atmospheric eating spot. The superb menu has been crafted carefully, mixing pan-Asian and Mediterranean dishes, with a nod to healthy eating: most dishes are grilled, baked or stir-fried. Indian dishes are also excellent, try the *nizami takari biryani* (rice and vegetables cooked in a terracotta pot).

Aish   HYDERABADI **$$$**
(Map p234; www.theparkhotels.com; The Park, 22 Raj Bhavan Rd; mains ₹485-1225; ⊙12.30-2.45pm, 7-11.30pm; 🖤; Ⓜ Irrum Manzil) Renowned for its Hyderabadi dishes, this elegant hotel restaurant serves fine biryanis, kebabs and wonderful *haleem*, including a veg version (₹675) of this classic dish.

Southern Spice   SOUTH INDIAN **$$$**
(Rd No 10, Jubilee Hills; meals ₹180-479; ⊙noon-3.30pm & 7-10.30pm) Southern Spice offers sublime Andhra-style cooking and specialities from across the South. Try a special veg thali (₹299), which features an unlimited flow of delectable dishes, or the *royala eguru* (prawns in rich gravy). The premises are spacious and air-conditioned, but always busy; book ahead.

Barbeque Nation   INDIAN **$$$**
(Map p234; ☑040-64806060; www.barbeque nation.com; ANR Centre, Rd No 1, Banjara Hills; veg/non-veg buffet from ₹640/765, dinner from ₹970/1140; ⊙noon-11.30pm; 🖤) All-you-can-eat kebabs, curries, salads and desserts, with many veg and non-veg options. A great-value place to come when you're hungry! Prices fluctuate a little depending on the day and time. Slurp on one of their excellent Indian wines while you dine.

🍸 Drinking & Nightlife

Hyderabad does not have a big drinking scene, and due to local licensing laws many of the liveliest lounges serve nothing stronger than mocktails. Some of the hottest new

Abids Area

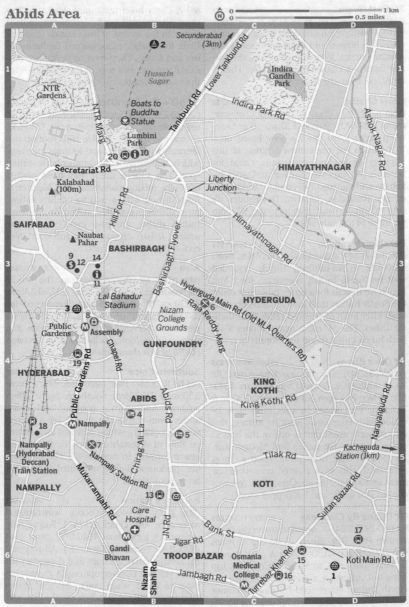

places are west of the centre in leafy Banjara Hills and Jubilee Hills, where you'll find a slew of good rooftop venues.

★ **Prost Brewpub**　　　MICROBREWERY
(☑040-33194195; www.prost.in; 882/A Rd No 45, Jubilee Hills; bites from ₹260; ☺noon-midnight;

☎) A highly popular, cavernous brewhouse with five tap beers, including an English ale and a stout, plus cider. There are several zones, all stylishly lit, including ample outdoor space and an extensive East-meets-West pub-grub menu (egg fritters, Cajun potatoes, Jeera coriander prawns). Also

Abids Area

⊙ Sights
1 British Residency D6
2 Buddha Statue & Hussain Sagar B1
3 State Museum A3

🛏 Sleeping
4 Royalton Hotel B5
5 Taj Mahal Hotel Abids B5

✕ Eating
6 Cafe Bahar C3
  Dakshina Mandapa .... (see 5)
7 Kamat Hotel A5

🛍 Shopping
8 Fabindia A4

ℹ Information
9 State Bank of India A3
10 Telangana Tourism B2
11 Telangana Tourism A3

ℹ Transport
12 Air India A3
13 GPO Abids Bus Stop B5
14 Jet Airways A3
15 Koti Bus Stand C6
16 Koti Bus Stop C6
17 Koti Women's College Bus Stand D6
18 Nampally Reservation Complex A5
19 Public Gardens Bus Stop A4
20 Secretariat Bus Stop (Pushpak) B2

hosts comedy (every Thursday), DJs and live music.

★ **Coffee Cup** CAFE
(☑ 040-40037571; www.facebook.com/the coffeecupp; E 89, off 5th Crescent Rd, Sainikpuri, Secunderabad; ⊗ 9am-11.30pm; 🛜) Excellent neighbourhood cafe and creative hub that's a magnet for East Hyderabad's arty crew. Offers a fine selection of interesting coffees, teas, snacks and meals (try a loaded jacket potato). There's stand-up comedy here most Fridays. It's above Canara Bank.

★ **MOB** BAR
(www.facebook.com/itismob; Aryan's, Rd No 92, near Apollo Hospital, Jubilee Hills; ⊗ noon-midnight; 🛜) A stylish, sociable Belgium beer house that draws a refreshingly mixed-gender, mixed-age crowd. Try a 'beer platter' for a sample of four choice brews, while on the menu you'll find good fish satay (₹350), fiery prawns (₹445) and other pan-Asian bites. There's live music on Saturday nights. It's 4km west of Banjara Hills' Rd No 1.

Vapour MICROBREWERY
(☑ 040-33165132; www.facebook.com/Vapour Hyderabad; 753 Rd 36, Jubilee Hills; ⊗ 11am-1am; 🛜) Buzzing most nights, Vapour is one of the most happening pubs in Hyderabad; book a table ahead on weekends. Brews include apple cider beer, lager, stout and wheat beers. There's a stunning terrace framed by tropical foliage, live music and regular DJ events – check their Facebook page for regular drink and menu promos.

Autumn Leaf Cafe CAFE
(www.facebook.com/autumnleafcafe; 823, Rd No 41, Jubilee Hills; ⊗ Mon-Fri noon-10.30pm, Sat & Sun from 9am; 🛜) Tucked away on a quiet side street, this green oasis has a superb garden where you can nurse a latte or enjoy a juice or milkshake. The menu (dishes ₹200-350) features all-day breakfasts, pasta, pancakes, salads and soups. Look out for 'Chill and Grill' evenings with mellow electronic vibes.

Kismet CLUB
(Map p234; ☑ 040-23456789; www.thepark hotels.com; The Park, Raj Bhavan Rd, Somajiguda; admission per couple ₹700-2000; ⊗ 8pm-midnight or later Wed-Sun; Ⓜ Irrum Manzi) A sleek, upmarket nightclub, with loungey booth seating and a pumping bass-driven sound system. Men won't get past the ranks of bouncers without female companions. Drinks are pricey (cocktails around ₹600), not that the wealthy crowd are too bothered. Musically things range from EDM to Bollywood.

Vertigo BAR
(Map p234; www.facebook.com/vertigothehigh life; 5th fl, Shiv Shakti Tower, Rd No 12, Banjara Hills; ⊗ 11am-midnight) A rooftop bar that boasts a great terrace, with elegant seating and interior rooms for live music and DJs. The eating 'zone' serves North Indian, Chinese and Western food while cocktails start at ₹375. It's opposite Ratnadeep supermarket.

10 Downing Street BAR
(Map p234; http://10ds.in; Lifestyle Bldg, Greenlands Rd, My Home Tycoon department store rear yard; ⊗ 11am-11pm; 🛜; Ⓜ Begumpet) With its classic decor of wood panelling and leather sofas, this place is just the ticket for a relaxed drinking session (check out the terrific daytime cocktail prices) and some pub grub. Things rev up as the evening progresses,

TELANGANA & ANDHRA PRADESH HYDERABAD

CHARMINAR MARKETS

Hyderabadis and visitors of every stripe flock to the Charminar area's labyrinthine lanes to browse, buy and wander. Patthargatti, the broad avenue leading in from the Musi River, is lined with shops selling clothes (especially wedding outfits), perfumes and Hyderabad's famous pearls. **Laad Bazar** (Map p238; ⊙10am-8.30pm), running west from the Charminar, is famed for its sparkling bangle shops: lac bangles, made from a resinous insect secretion and encrusted with colourful beads or stones, are a Hyderabad speciality. In Laad Bazar you'll also find perfumers, wedding goods and fabrics.

Laad Bazar opens into **Mehboob Chowk** (Map p238), a square with shops selling antiquarian books and antiques, a livestock market on its south side, and a market in exotic birds, Chiddi Bazar, just southwest. A short distance north, the **Patel Market** (Map p238; ⊙approximately 11am-8pm) sells cloth fabrics and cranks into action from around 11am in the back lanes between Patthargatti and Rikab Gunj. Further north again and on the other side of Patthargatti, the wholesale vegetable market **Mir Alam Mandi** (Map p238; Patthargatti Rd; ⊙5am-6.30pm) trades in all kinds of fresh stuff from 6.30am to 6.30pm daily.

with different music nightly – club Saturday, Bollywood Sunday and so on.

Coco's Bar & Grill BAR
(Map p234; ☏040-65542730; 217 Rd No 2, Jubilee Hills; ⊙noon-midnight; 🐾) The rooftop setting, with rustic bamboo couches and thatch roofs, makes Coco's perfect for a cold drink on a balmy evening (beer/mocktails from ₹175/170). There's live blues and soft rock nightly, and decent Indian and Continental food. Happy hour runs between noon and 6pm. Enter down a lane beside Café Coffee Day.

☆ Entertainment

Ravindra Bharathi Theatre THEATRE
(Map p234; ☏040-23233672; www.ravindra bharathi.org; Ladki-ka-pul Rd, Saifabad; Ⓜ Lakdika-pul) Well-curated music, dance and drama performances, and cinema.

🔒 Shopping

Charminar is the most exciting place to shop: you'll find exquisite pearls, slippers, gold and fabrics alongside billions of bangles. Upmarket boutiques and malls are scattered around Banjara Hills and the western suburbs. Patthargatti has dozens of pearl vendors.

GVK One MALL
(Map p234; www.gvkone.com; Rd No 1, Banjara Hills; ⊙11am-11pm) An upmarket mall with a good selection of clothes shops including M&S and Levi's, ATMs, a small food court, cafes and a cinema.

Kalanjali CLOTHING
(www.kalanjali.com; 237 Rd No 16, Jubilee Hills; ⊙10.30am-8pm) Fine quality saris, kurtas

(long collarless shirts), *salwar kameez* (dresslike tunic and loose, long pants for women) sets (from ₹2545) and other traditional clothing. They also sell exquisite silver, stone and wooden handicrafts.

Malkha CLOTHING
(Map p234; www.malkha.in; 4th Floor, 10-3-76, Mehdipatnam, Humayun Nagar; ⊙10am-7pm Mon-Sat) 🌿 Malkha cloth is made near the cotton fields, by hand and with natural dyes, reducing strain on the environment and putting primary producers in control. The result is gorgeous; here you can pick up fabric, saris, dupattas (long scarves; from ₹1200) and kurtas at fair prices.

Suvasa CLOTHING
(Map p234; www.suvasa.in; Rd No 12, Banjara Hills; ⊙11am-7.30pm) Suvasa's block-printed kurtas are priced from around ₹1200 in cotton, and they also have high-quality *salwar* and dupattas. Homeware, including gorgeous bed and table linen, is worth looking at too.

Hyderabad Perfumers PERFUME
(Map p238; Patthargatti; ⊙10am-8.30pm Mon-Sat) This fourth-generation family business can conjure something aromatic up for you on the spot. They specialise in *ittar,* natural perfume oils from flowers and herbs; prices start as low as ₹200 and rise to over ₹7000 per bottle.

Fabindia CLOTHING
(Map p234; www.fabindia.com; Rd No 9, Banjara Hills; ⊙11am-9.30pm) 🌿 Lovely women's (and some men's) clothes in artisanal fabrics with contemporary prints and colours. It also sells homeware including bed linen, cushions and *dhurries* (rugs). Prices are fair. Or visit its

other branch at **Fateh Maidan** (Map p242; ⊗10.30am-8.30pm; Ⓜ Assembly).

Himalaya Book World   BOOKS
(Map p234; Panjagutta Circle, Banjara Hills; ⊗10.30am-10.30pm) A fine selection of English-language fiction and nonfiction by Indian and international authors. It has several other branches in town.

❶ Information

MEDICAL SERVICES

Reputable Care Hospitals are on **Mukarramjahi Road** (Map p242; ⟋040-30417777; www.carehospitals.com; Mukarramjahi Rd; Ⓜ Gandhi Bhavan) and **Road No 1** (Map p234; ⟋040-30418888; www.carehospitals.com; Rd No 1, Banjara Hills). There's also an outpatient hospital on **Road No 10** (Map p234; ⟋040-39310444; 4th Lane, Rd No 10, Banjara Hills).

MONEY

ATMs are everywhere. Citibank ATMs allow large withdrawals: these are at **Banjara Hills** (Map p234; Prashanthi Mansion, Rd No 1, Banjara Hills), **City Center Mall** (Map p234; City Center Mall, Rd No 1, Banjara Hills) and **GVK One Mall** (Map p234; GVK One Mall, Rd No 1, Banjara Hills).

State Bank of India (Map p242; HACA Bhavan, Saifabad; ⊗10.30am-4pm Mon-Fri;

Ⓜ Assembly) Has currency exchange; banks generally offer the best rates.

POST

General Post Office (Map p242; Abids Circle, Troop Bazar; ⊗8am-7pm Mon-Sat, 10am-1pm Sun; Ⓜ Gandhi Bhavan)

Secunderabad Post Office (Map p233; Rashtrapati Rd, Secunderabad; ⊗8am-7pm Mon-Sat; Ⓜ Parade Grounds)

TOURIST INFORMATION

Indiatourism (Map p234; ⟋040-23409199; www.incredibleindia.org; Tourism Plaza, Greenlands Rd; ⊗9am-6pm Mon-Fri, 9.30am-1pm Sat; Ⓜ Begumpet) A useful office, with good information on Hyderabad, Telangana and beyond.

Telangana Tourism (www.telanganatourism.gov.in) Has information offices with bookings desks for state-government-run tours, heritage walks and hotels in Telangana. Branches at **Shakar Bhavan** (Map p242; ⟋040-66745986; ⊗9.30am-6pm Mon-Fri 9am-noon Sat; Ⓜ Assembly), **Tank Bund Road** (Map p242; ⟋040-65581555; ⊗9.30am-6pm Mon-Fri, 9am-noon Sat), **Greenlands Road** (Map p234; ⟋040-23414334; Tourism Plaza; ⊗9.30am-6pm Mon-Fri, 9am-noon Sat; Ⓜ Begumpet), **Rajiv Gandhi International Airport** (⟋040-24253215; ⊗7am-8pm), **Secunderabad** (Map p233; ⟋040-27893100; Yatri Nivas Hotel, SP Rd; ⊗9.30am-6pm Mon-Fri, 9am-noon Sat; Ⓜ Paradise) and **Secunderabad train station**

QAWWALI AND SUFISM IN HYDERABAD

Emerging in the subcontinent in the 13th century, Qawwali music is closely linked with Sufism. Hyderabad is a hotbed of Qawwali singing, and it's not uncommon to hear people softly practicing on trains and buses as they ride about the city. The music of mystical Islam, Qawwali performances usually last for many hours, with the aim of achieving a state of spiritual ecstasy. Improvisation is key, with a lead vocalist alternating with supporting singers. To the untrained ear the singing almost sounds erotic, though the songs are purely religious in their devotion. Musicians accompany the singers with tablas and instruments.

Qawwali is frequently performed at the hundreds of *dargahs* (Sufi shrines) in Hyderabad, including two famous *dargahs* in the Nampally area. There's no formal timetable for events, but performances at **Dargah Yousufain Sharifain** (Nampally Dargah; Nampally Darga Rd; ⊗ singing 10pm-1am Thu & Fri; Ⓜ Nampally), the resting place of two Sufi saints, are almost always held on Thursdays and Fridays (10pm-1am). **Dargah Hazrat Shah Khamosh** (Darussalam Rd; Ⓜ Nampally) is another shrine close by where Qawwali sessions are regularly performed. It's the resting place of Sufi saint Hazrat Shah Khamosh, who legend has it, took a vow of silence for 25 years. This large *dargah* dates from the late 19th century and is an unusual blend of Islamic and Gothic styles. Diners at the Taj Falaknuma Palace (p238) are accompanied by Qawwali singing on Sundays. Look out too for festive *urs* (the veneration of the anniversary of death of a Sufi saint; 'urs' means 'marriage' in Arabic and symbolises the union of the saint with God). These are held at shrines across the city, which always feature Qawwalli music.

Perhaps the most famous Qawwali singer of recent times was Nusrat Fateh Ali Khan who released six albums on Real World records (the English band Massive Attack once unofficially remixed a track of his). Leading female Qawwali singers today include the Nooran Sisters from Jalandhar.

(Map p233; ☎040-27801614; ◷10am-8pm; Ⓜ Secunderabad East).

❶ Getting There & Away

AIR

Hyderabad's massive, modern, efficient **Rajiv Gandhi International Airport** (☎040-66546370; http://hyderabad.aero; Shamshabad) is 25km southwest of the city centre. It has direct daily flights, including with **Air India** (Map p242; ☎040-23389711; www.airindia.com; HACA Bhavan, Saifabad; ◷9.30am-6pm Mon-Sat; Ⓜ Assembly) and **Jet Airways** (Map p242; ☎020-39893333; www.jetairways.com; Summit Apartments, Hill Fort Rd; ◷10am-6pm Mon-Sat; Ⓜ Assembly), to over 25 Indian cities plus international cities including Chicago, London, Hong Kong and many Southeast Asian and Gulf destinations.

BUS

The main terminal is the vast **Mahatma Gandhi Bus Station** (MGBS; Imlibun Bus Station; Map p238; ☎040-24614406; off Salar Jung Rd; ◷advance booking offices 8am-10.30pm) near Abids. Air-con services by the **Telangana State Road Transport Corporation** (Telangana State Road Transport Corporation; ☎1800 2004599; http://tsrtcbus.in) are quite good. Buses run to many destinations in Madhya Pradesh, Maharashtra and Tamil Nadu too. Nearly all long-distance services depart in the evening. When booking ahead, women should request seats up front as these are reserved for female passengers.

Secunderabad's **Jubilee bus station** (JBS; Map p233; ☎040-27802203; Gandhi Nagar, Secunderabad; Ⓜ Parade Grounds) is smaller, with buses to cities including Chennai, Mumbai and these routes:

Bengaluru (Bangalore) ordinary/Volvo AC/sleeper ₹655/from 844/1280, eight to 11 hours, 20 daily

Vijayawada non-AC/AC ₹326/448, four to six hours, 18 daily

Other useful bus stops include the **bus stand** (Map p233; St Mary's Rd, Secunderabad) on St Mary's Rd, the **Charminar bus stop** (Map p238; Shah Ali Banda Rd) for the Old City, **Koti bus stand** (Map p242; Turrebaz Khan Rd), **Koti Women's College bus stand** (Map p242; Koti Main Rd) and **Rathifile bus stand** (Map p233; Station Rd, Secunderabad) for Secunderabad.

There are also many other private bus companies offering long-distance services. These tend to use their own terminals; check www.makemytrip.com for information and bookings.

TRAIN

Secunderabad, Nampally (officially called Hyderabad Deccan) and Kacheguda are Hyderabad's three major train stations. Most through trains stop at Kacheguda.

The reservation complexes at **Nampally** (Map p242; ☎040-27829999; Public Gardens Rd; ◷8am-8pm Mon-Sat, to 2pm Sun; Ⓜ Nampally) and **Secunderabad** (Rathifile; Map p233; St John's Rd; ◷8am-8pm Mon-Sat, 8am-2pm Sun), both in separate buildings away from the stations, have foreign-tourist-quota counters (bring your passport and visa photocopies, along with originals).

❶ Getting Around

TO/FROM THE AIRPORT

The airport is about a 45-minute drive from town.

Bus

The TSRTC's Pushpak air-conditioned bus service runs between 4am, or 5am and 11pm to/from various stops in the city including:

AC Guards (Map p234; AC Guards Rd; ₹212, two or three hourly) About 1.5km from Abids.

Paryatak Bhavan (Map p234; Greenlands Rd; ₹265, about hourly)

Secretariat (Map p242; NTR Marg) (₹265, about hourly) About 1.5km from Abids.

Secunderabad (Map p233; Rail Nilayam Rd, Secunderabad; ₹265, twice hourly)

BUSES FROM HYDERABAD

DESTINATION	FARE (₹)	DURATION (HR)	FREQUENCY
Bengaluru (Bangalore)	680-1210	8-11	29 buses 5.45am-11.40pm
Chennai	688-1191	11-14	18 buses 6-10.20pm
Hosapete (Hospet)	760-1000	8-10	5 buses daily
Mumbai	999-2235	12-16	49 buses 4.30am-11.50pm
Mysuru (Mysore)	1050-1733	11-13	10 buses 5.30-9pm
Tirupati	652-1991	9-13	36 buses 8am-10pm
Vijayawada	317-497	4-5	every 15-30min 3am-11.59pm
Visakhapatnam	676-1630	11-13	8 buses 4-11pm
Warangal	147-230	2-4	half-hourly

MAJOR TRAINS FROM HYDERABAD & SECUNDERABAD

DESTINATION	TRAIN NO & NAME	FARE (₹)	DURATION (HR)	DEPARTURE TIME & STATION
Bengaluru (Bangalore)	Rajdhani (Nos 22692/4), 12785 Bangalore Exp	1785/2630(B), 370/1390(A)	12, 11½	6.40pm Secunderabad, 7.05pm Kacheguda
Chennai	12604 Chennai Express, 12760 Charminar Exp	405/1520(A), 425/1610(A)	13, 14	4.50pm Nampally, 6.30pm Nampally
Delhi	12723 Telangana Exp, Rajdhani (Nos 22691/3)	670/2575(A), 3110/4645(B)	27, 22	6.25am Nampally, 7.50am Secunderabad
Hosapete (for Hampi)	17603 Exp	275/1070(A)	9	9.05pm Kacheguda
Kolkata	18646 East Coast Exp	615/2430(A)	30	9.50am Nampally
Mumbai	12702 Hussainsagar Exp	425/1610(A)	14	2.45pm Nampally
Tirupati	12734 Narayanadri Exp	395/1475(A	12	6.05pm Nampally
Visakhapatnam	12728 Godavari Exp	400/1505(A)	12½	5.15pm Nampally

Fares: (A) – sleeper/2AC; (B) – 3AC/2AC

The trip takes around one hour. Contact TSRTC or check http://hyderabad.aero for exact timings.

Taxi

The prepaid taxi booth is on the lowest level of the terminal. Fares to Abids or Banjara Hills are ₹600 to ₹750. **Meru Cabs** (☏ 040-44224422) and **Sky Cabs** (☏ 040-49494949) charge similar rates. Uber and Ola are cheaper, around ₹400 to ₹550, and they both have designated pick-up points in Parking Zone C.

AUTORICKSHAW

Expect to pay ₹30 to ₹50 for a short ride, and around ₹120 for 4km. Few drivers use meters.

BOAT

Frequent boats make the 30-minute return trip to the Buddha Statue from both **Eat Street** (Map p234; child/adult ₹35/55; ☒ 3-8pm) and popular **Lumbini Park** (Map p242; off NTR Marg; child/adult ₹35/55; ☒ 10.30am-8pm).

BUS

Few travellers bother with local buses (₹6 to ₹12 for most rides) but there are some useful routes. Try www.hyderabadcitybus.com (although it can be inaccurate).

City stops include **Afzalgunj** (Map p238; Afzalgunj), **GPO Abids** (Map p242; JN Rd, Abids), **Koti** (Map p242; Turrebaz Khan Rd), **Mehdipatnam** (Mehdipatnam Rd), **Public Gardens** (Map p242; Public Gardens Rd) and **Secunderabad Junction** (Map p233; Station Rd, Secunderabad).

CAR

The going rate for a small AC car with a driver is from ₹1600 per day for city sightseeing,

and ₹2800 to ₹3700 per day for out-of-town trips (including fuel, tolls and driver expenses). **Golkonda Tours** (☏ 9441294987; www.golkondatours.com) are recommended.

METRO RAIL

Hyderabad modern air-conditioned **Metro Rail** (☏ 040-23332555; www.ltmetro.com) runs on elevated tracks above Hyderabad's streets. Lines 1 and 3 commenced service in 2018. The metro stop at MG Bus Station provides a useful link for travellers, and will be a major interchange when future lines are completed. Eventually five lines are planned, covering over 100km, and including links to the airport and Hi-Tec City.

Passengers can choose a smart card (complicated registration necessary and a ₹20 charge) or a token for travelling. Single trips cost ₹10 to ₹60. You can check routes and project updates on the website.

TAXI

There are thousands of Uber and Ola drivers in Hyderabad and fares are very fair indeed (often cheaper than those quoted by autorickshaw drivers). A 3km ride will be around ₹80 to ₹120. Reliable taxi companies include Meru Cabs and Sky Cabs.

TRAIN

The suburban **MMTS trains** (Multi-Modal Transport System; www.mmtstraintimings.in; fares ₹5-10) are not very useful for travellers, but infrequent trains (every 30 to 45 minutes) run between Hyderabad (Nampally) and Lingampalli via Necklace Rd, Begumpet and Hi-Tech City. There's also a route between Falaknuma (south of Old City) and Lingampalli via Kacheguda and Secunderabad stations.

TELANGANA & ANDHRA PRADESH HYDERABAD

Bhongir

Most Hyderabad–Warangal buses and trains stop at the town of Bhongir, 60km from Hyderabad. It's worth stopping to climb the impressive **Chalukyan hill fort** (off DVK Rd; Indian/foreigner ₹5/100, camera ₹10; ⊙9am-5pm) on the eastern side of town. You can leave backpacks at the ticket office.

The ramparts and ruined remains of this fantastical-looking 12th-century fort sit on what resembles a gargantuan stone egg on the eastern side of town. Access is via many hundreds of steps that have been cut into the rocky hillside; the climb takes around 40 minutes. Sadly there's a fair bit of trash to guide your way.

Warangal

📞 0870 / POP 637,000

Warangal was the capital of the Kakatiya kingdom, which ruled most of present-day Telangana and Andhra Pradesh from the 12th to early 14th centuries. The city merges with the town of Hanumakonda, which has many temples.

⊙ Sights

Ancient temples in Hanumakonda include the lakeside **Bhadrakali Temple** (Bhadrakali Temple Rd), 2km southeast of the 1000-Pillared Temple, whose idol of the mother goddess Kali sits with a weapon in each of her eight hands, and the small **Siddeshwara Temple** (Hanumakonda Hill) on the south side of Hanumakonda Hill.

Fort
FORT

(Fort Rd) Warangal's fort, on the southern edge of town, was a massive construction with three circles of walls (the outermost 7km in circumference). Most of it now is either fields or buildings, but at the centre is a huge, partly reassembled Shaivite **Svayambhu Temple** (off Fort Rd; Indian/foreigner ₹25/200, camera ₹25; ⊙9am-8pm), with handsome, large *torana* (architrave) gateways at its cardinal points. An autorickshaw from Warangal station costs around ₹300 return.

1000-Pillared Temple
HINDU TEMPLE

(south of NH163, Hanumakonda; ⊙6am-6pm) The 1000-Pillared Temple, constructed in the 12th century, is in a leafy setting and is a fine example of Kakatiya architecture and sculpture. Unusually, the cross-shaped building has shrines to the sun god Surya (to the right as you enter), Vishnu (centre) and Shiva (left). Despite the name, it certainly does not have 1000 pillars. Behind rises Hanumakonda Hill, site of the original Kakatiya capital.

⏢ Sleeping & Eating

Hotel Shreya
HOTEL $

(📞 0870-2547788; www.hotelshreyawarangal. com; New Bus Stand Rd, Hanumakonda; r incl breakfast ₹1600-2200, ste ₹3200; ❄🔊) Great value, with well-presented rooms that have flatscreen TVs and minifridges. Book a suite for extra space. There's a restaurant for tasty veg dishes and room service. It's steps from Hanumakonda bus stand.

Oyo Hotel Ashoka 3420
HOTEL $$

(📞 0870-2578491; www.oyorooms.com; Main Rd, Hanumakonda; r incl breakfast ₹1710-2850; ❄🔊) Near the Hanumakonda bus stand and 1000-Pillared Temple, this large hotel is now managed by Oyo and has a selection of AC rooms in several price categories. Also here is the good veg restaurant **Kanishka** (mains ₹135-260; ⊙6.30am-10.30pm), plus a non-veg restaurant, and a bar and small gym.

Sri Geetha Bhavan
ANDHRA $

(Market Rd, Hanumakonda; mains ₹90-130; ⊙6am-11pm) Good South Indian meals in pleasant AC surroundings. Follow the Supreme Hotels sign.

ⓘ Information

Telangana Tourism (📞 0870-2571339; www. telanganatourism.gov.in; opposite Indian Oil, Nakkalagutta, Hanumakonda; ⊙10.30am-5pm Mon-Sat) Helpful staff.

ⓘ Getting There & Away

Buses to Hyderabad (₹138 to ₹280, four hours) leave about three times hourly from **Hanumakonda bus stand** (New Bus Stand Rd), and seven times daily (express/deluxe ₹135/196) from **Warangal bus stand** (📞 0870-2565595; Station Rd) opposite the train station.

From Warangal several trains run daily to Hyderabad (sleeper/2AC ₹170/700, three hours), Vijayawada (₹190/745, three hours) and Chennai (₹375/1400, 10½ to 12 hours).

Shared autorickshaws (₹15) ply fixed routes around Warangal and Hanumakonda.

Palampet

About 70km northeast of Warangal, the stunning **Ramappa Temple** (camera ₹25; ⊙6am-6pm) is near the village of Palampet. Built in the early 13th century, it's the outstanding gem of Kakatiya architecture, covered in wonderfully detailed carvings of animals, lovers, wrestlers, musicians, dancers, deities and Hindu legends. Brackets on its external pillars support superb black-basalt carvings of mythical creatures and sinuous women twined with snakes. The large temple tank, Ramappa Cheruvu, 1km south, is popular with migrating birds.

There is one government-run **lodge** (0871-5200200, 9848036622; www.telangana tourism.gov.in; Ramappa Cheruvu; cottage ₹1750-3100;) nearby but nothing else. Many travellers base themselves in nearby Warangal.

The easiest way to get here is by chartered taxi (around ₹2200 return from Warangal), but buses also run half-hourly from Hanumakonda (sister town of Warangal) to Mulugu (₹34, one hour), then a further 13km to Palampet (₹18), or ₹200 in an auto.

ANDHRA PRADESH

The state of Andhra Pradesh stretches 972km along the Bay of Bengal between Tamil Nadu and Odisha (Orissa), and inland up into the picturesque Eastern Ghats. Its epicentre of Telugu language and culture. Explorers will discover one of India's most visited temples (at Tirumala), some fascinating and remote ancient sites from the earliest days of Buddhism and one of the nicest stretches of India's east coast, north of Visakhapatnam – plus you'll be able to enjoy the spicily delicious Andhra cuisine everywhere.

Andhra's tourism website is www.ap tourism.gov.in.

Vijayawada

 0866 / POP 1.19 MILLION

This commercial and industrial city, on the north bank of the Krishna River, forms Andhra's new state capital, with its emerging sister settlement of Amaravati, a showpiece capital complex located on the south bank. Politicians have declared Vijayawada-Amaravati will eventually have 2.5 million inhabitants.

Though the construction of Amaravati has been delayed, there are big changes afoot in and around Vijayawada. Work on new highways continues apace and the city's airport has now been designated international status. Right now there's not much of interest for travellers in the city itself, and nothing at all to see in Amaravati, but Vijayawada makes a logical base for visiting some fascinating historic sites in the lush and green surrounding area.

⊙ Sights

★**Undavalli Cave Temples** HINDU TEMPLE (Indian/foreigner ₹25/300; 9am-5.30pm) This stunning four-storey cave temple was probably originally carved out of the hillside for Buddhist monks in the 2nd century AD, then converted to Hindu use in the 7th century. The shrines are now largely empty, except those on the third level, one of which houses a huge reclining Vishnu. A row of gnomelike stone Vaishnavaite gurus/preachers gaze out over the rice paddies from the terrace. It's 9km southwest of downtown Vijayawada: autorickshaws or Ola/Uber cabs here cost ₹150 one way.

Kanaka Durga Temple HINDU TEMPLE (www.kanakadurgatemple.org; Durga Temple Ghat Rd, Indrakeeladri Hill; 4am-9pm) Dating back to the 12th century, this important temple is located on Indrakeeladri Hill, close to the Krishna River, and draws many pilgrims.

Kondapalli Fort FORT (₹10, camera Indian/foreigner ₹20/100; 10am-5pm) This ruined fortress, 25km northwest of Vijayawada, was built around 1360 by the Reddy kings, and passed through a succession of later rulers, including the Qutb Shahis of Golconda in the 16th century, before becoming a British military camp in 1767. You can wander round several half-ruined halls and courtyards and step into the old royal prison. The structure is currently the subject of a renovation program.

🛏 Sleeping & Eating

Hotel Sripada HOTEL $ (0866-2579641; hotelsripada@rediffmail.com; Gandhi Nagar; s ₹900-1460, d ₹1010-1690;) A short walk from the train station, this is one of the few decent budget hotels in Vijayawada. Offers small AC rooms in reasonable condition, and helpful staff. However, there's no in-house restaurant.

★**Minerva Hotel** HOTEL $$ (0866-6678888; www.minervahotels.in; MG Rd; s/d ₹3500/4000, ste ₹7500;) This hotel has rooms with a pleasing contemporary touch, large flatscreen TVs, wooden floors, safe and minibar. The Blue Fox restaurant here is good, there's a coffee shop, and you'll find a cinema and ample shopping close by.

Hotel Southern Grand HOTEL **$$**
(☑0866-6677777; www.hotelsoutherngrand.com; Papaiah St, Gandhi Nagar; incl breakfast s/d from ₹2200/2600; ❇🛜) Offers inviting, contemporary rooms and located just 600m from the train station. The hotel also has an excellent veg restaurant, Arya Bhavan, and a useful travel desk, **Southern Travels** (☑0866-6677777). Book in advance for the best deals.

⭐**Minerva Coffee Shop** INDIAN **$$**
(Museum Rd; mains ₹160-280; ☺7am-11pm) Great North and South Indian veg cuisine in bright, spotless AC premises. Meals (thalis) are only available from 11.30am to 3.30pm but top-notch dosa, *idli* and *uttapam* (₹35 to ₹75) are served all day and the biryanis are also good. There's another **branch** (Minerva Hotel, mains ₹160-280; ☺7am-11pm) in airy, sophisticated surrounds on MG Rd.

Avista INDIAN **$$**
(Hotel Aria, 40 Benz Circle; mains ₹170-350; ☺7.30am-10.30pm; 🛜) Offering comfortable AC surrounds, this hotel restaurant has an eclectic menu, including Western and Chinese dishes, but it's the North Indian food that stands out; try the *malai kofta* (cottage cheese in cardamom gravy, ₹200) or *murgh makhani* (chicken tikka in tomato sauce, ₹300)

Arya Bhavan INDIAN **$$**
(Hotel Southern Grand, Papaiah St, Gandhi Nagar; mains ₹130-170, thalis ₹120-180; ☺7am-11pm) Pure-veg food in a bright, clean, busy environment, with dosa and other South Indian breakfast items available all day. Good ice cream too!

⭐**TFL** MULTICUISINE **$$$**
(www.facebook.com/tflvijayawada; Santhi Nagar First Lane; mains ₹180-360; ☺10am-11.45pm; 🛜) A stylish cafe-resto in a converted suburban bungalow with a great covered terrace. Offers Italian, Mexican, American, European and East Asian dishes, including risotto, good pizza and excellent Western breakfasts.

Don't skip on their desserts, which are perfect for chocoholics.

ℹ️ Information

Department of Tourism (☑0866-2578880; Vijayawada Junction station; ☺10am-5pm) Has helpful staff and can assist with travel planning.

ℹ️ Getting There & Away

AIR
Vijayawada Airport (http://vijayawadaairport.in) is 17km northeast of the city centre. There are daily flights to Indian cities including Bengaluru, Chennai, Delhi, Hyderabad, Mumbai, Tirupati and Visakhapatnam. Airlines include Air India, Alliance Air, IndiGo, SpiceJet and TruJet.

An IndiGo international connection started flying to Singapore in 2018.

There are 14 daily buses (non-AC/AC ₹50/100, 30 minutes) between the airport and **Pandit Nehru bus station** (Arjuna St; ☺24hr). Taxis from the official airport rank charge a steep ₹700 to central Vijayawada.

BUS
Services from the large Pandit Nehru bus station (p250) include the following:

Chennai non-AC/AC/semi-sleeper ₹518/777/1170, eight to ten hours, nine daily

Eluru non-AC/AC ₹72/122, 1½ hours, half-hourly

Hyderabad non-AC/AC ₹317/467, four to six hours, half-hourly

Tirupati non-AC/AC ₹474/812, nine hours, half-hourly

Visakhapatnam non-AC/AC ₹430/737, eight to nine hours, half-hourly

Many private bus companies depart from stops around Benz Circle, 4km east of the centre.

TRAIN
Vijayawada Junction station is on the main Chennai–Kolkata and Chennai–Delhi railway lines. The 12841/12842 Coromandel Express between Chennai and Kolkata is quick for journeys up and down the coast. Typical journey times and frequencies, for sleeper/2AC fares:

Bengaluru (Bangalore) ₹780/2750, 12 to 15 hours, five to six daily

Chennai ₹290/1050, 6 to 8 hours, 13 daily

Hyderabad ₹240/800, 5½ to 7 hours, 15 daily

Kolkata ₹555/2125, 18 to 21 hours, five to six daily

Tirupati ₹265/965, six to eight hours, 11-13 daily

Warangal ₹190/745, three hours, 15 daily

Amaravathi

☑ 08645 / POP 4800

The historic Buddhist site of Amaravathi (not to be confused with the new state capital, Amaravati) is 43km west of Vijayawada. This was the earliest centre of Buddhism in the southern half of India, with the nation's biggest **stupa** (Indian/foreigner ₹25/300; ☺9am-5.30pm, to 6pm Apr-Nov), 27m high and 49m across, constructed here from the 3rd century BC. Amaravathi flourished as a capital of the Satavahana kingdom, which ruled from Andhra across the Deccan for four or five centuries, becoming a fountainhead of Buddhist art. All that remains onsite of the stupa ruins now are its circular base and a few parts of the surrounding stone railing. (Museums worldwide hold pieces from the ruin, including the British Museum with a collection of 120 marble sculptures and inscriptions.) The great hemispherical dome is gone – but the neighbouring **museum** (₹5; ☺9am-5pm Sat-Thu) has a model of the stupa and some of the intricate marble carvings, depicting the Buddha's life, with which the Satavahanas covered and surrounded it. The giant modern **Dhyana Buddha statue** (₹20; ☺8am-8pm) of a seated Buddha overlooks the Krishna River nearby.

Bus 301 from Vijayawada bus station runs to Amaravathi (₹56, 1½ hours) every 20 minutes, via Unduvalli. Drivers charge around ₹1800 for a half-day excursion from Vijayawada.

Nagarjunakonda

☑ 08680

The unique island of Nagarjunakonda is peppered with ancient Buddhist structures. The Ikshvaku dynasty had its capital here in the 3rd and 4th centuries AD, when the area was probably the most important Buddhist centre in South India. There's a huge dam here that is a tourist attraction for domestic tourists.

⊙ Sights

Nagarjuna Sagar Dam   DAM

This vast structure, which dams the river Krishna, is 180m in height from its deepest foundation and 1.6km long. The adjacent hydroelectric plant has a power generation capacity of 815.6 MW.

Sri Parvata Arama   BUDDHIST SITE

(Buddhavanam; ☺9.30am-6pm) FREE This Buddhism heritage park, featuring a recre-

ation of the huge Amaravathi stupa, is 8km north of the dam. It's been under construction by the state tourism authorities for many years and is still far from complete. The 9m replica of the Avukana Buddha statue was donated by Sri Lanka. There's also an attractive meditation area, Dhyanavanam, with fine lake views. Alight at Buddha Park when coming by bus from Hyderabad.

Nagarjunakonda Museum   MUSEUM

(Indian/foreigner incl monuments ₹20/120; ☺9am-4pm Sat-Thu) The thoughtfully laid-out Nagarjunakonda Museum has Buddha statues and some superbly detailed carvings depicting local contemporary life and the Buddha's lives. The reassembled remains of several buildings, including stupa bases, walls of monastery complexes and pits for horse sacrifice, are arranged on a 1km path running along the island. The largest stupa, in the Chamtasri Chaitya Griha group, contained a bone fragment thought to be from the Buddha himself.

🍴 Courses

Dhamma Nagajjuna   HEALTH & WELLBEING

(☑ 9440139329, 9348456780; www.nagajjuna. dhamma.org; Hill Colony) Keeping the Buddha's teachings alive in the region, this centre offers 10-day silent meditation courses in charming flower-filled grounds overlooking Nagarjuna Sagar. Apply in advance; payment is by donation. Alight at Buddha Park when coming by bus from Hyderabad.

🛏 Sleeping & Eating

Nagarjuna Resort   HOTEL $

(☑ 08642-242471; Vijayapuri South; r without/with AC ₹900/1600; ❄) Offers spacious though drab rooms, while the balconies enjoy good views. It's conveniently located across the road from the boat launch.

Haritha Vijaya Vihar   HOTEL $$

(☑ 08680-277362; www.telanganatourism.gov.in; r with AC incl breakfast Mon-Thu ₹1400-1870, Fri-Sun ₹2400-2970; ❄🔊❄) This government hotel is 6km north of the dam, with decent rooms, nice gardens, a good pool (nonguests ₹50) and lovely lake views. It's a little overpriced, but the location is exceptional, the restaurant is quite decent and there's a bar.

Hotel Siddhartha   INDIAN $$

(Buddhavanam, Hill Colony; mains ₹125-260; ☺6am-11pm) Beside Sri Parvata Arama, with

GUNTUPALLI

Well off the beaten path, the Buddhist site of **Guntupalli** (Indian/foreigner ₹5/200; ⊙10am-5pm) makes a very scenic adventure. This former hilltop monastery is especially noteworthy for its caves, carvings and *chaitya-griha* (prayer hall). Guntupalli was active from the 2nd century BC to the 3rd century AD.

The cave's domed ceiling is carved with 'wooden beams' designed to look like those in a hut. The *chaitya-griha* has a well-preserved stupa and, like the monks' dwellings that line the same cliff, a gorgeous arched facade also designed to look like wood.

From Eluru, on the Vijayawada–Visakhapatnam road and railway, take a bus 35km north to Kamavarapukota (₹44, 1½ hours, half-hourly), then an autorickshaw 10km west to Guntupalli. A taxi from Eluru costs around ₹1800 return.

tasty curries, biryanis, fish dishes and lots of snacks served in a pleasant, airy pavilion.

ℹ Getting There & Away

The easiest way to visit Nagarjunakonda, other than with a private vehicle, is on a bus tour (₹550) from Hyderabad with Telangana Tourism (p236), running on weekends only. It's a very long (15 hours!) day trip, however, on a non-AC bus.

Public buses from Hyderabad's Mahatma Gandhi Bus Station run hourly to Hill Colony/Nagarjuna Sagar (₹230, four hours): alight at Pylon and catch an autorickshaw (shared/private ₹20/120) 8km to Vijayapuri South.

Boats (₹150 return) depart for the island from Vijayapuri South, 7km south of the dam, theoretically at 9.30am, 11.30am and 1.30pm (but they invariably leave late), and stay for one to two hours. The first two boats may not go if not enough people turn up, but the 1.30pm boat goes every day (barring high winds) and starts back from the island around 4.30pm.

Visakhapatnam

📞 0891 / POP 1.79 MILLION

Visakhapatnam – also called Vizag (*vie*-zag) – is Andhra Pradesh's largest city, famous for steel and its big port, but also doubling as a beach resort for sea-breeze-seeking domestic tourists. During the main December–February holiday season there's a distinctly kitschy vibe, with camel rides and thousands of bathers (though no swimmers).

The pedestrian promenade along **Ramakrishna Beach** (Beach Rd) is pleasant for a stroll, and nearby Rushikonda Beach is perhaps Andhra's best. Every year the city hosts **Visakha Utsav** (⊙mid-Jan), a festival with food stalls on Ramakrishna Beach, exhibitions and cultural events.

With international connections to the Far East from its increasingly busy airport, more international travellers are passing through now.

◉ Sights

★**Submarine Museum**   MUSEUM
(Beach Rd; adult/child ₹40/20, camera ₹50; ⊙2pm-8.30pm Tue-Sat, 10am-12.30pm & 2pm-8.30pm Sun) A fantastic attraction located towards the north end of Ramakrishna Beach, the 91m-long, Soviet-built, Indian navy submarine *Kursura* is now a fascinating museum. You're given about 15 minutes to explore the incredibly confined quarters and check out the torpedoes, kitchens and sleeping areas. Some staff speak a little English.

★**Aircraft Museum**   MUSEUM
(Beach Rd; adult/child ₹70/40; ⊙2pm-8.30pm Mon-Fri, 10am-8.30pm Sat & Sun) Opened in 2017, this museum showcases a Soviet-era TU-142M aircraft that was used by the Indian military for 29 years (and 30,000 hours of accident-free flying). There's excellent information about the history of the plane and Indian aviation. You can enter the aircraft (though access to the cockpit may not be possible due to crowds) and your ticket includes an audio guide. You'll also find a VR gaming zone and cafe here.

Simhachalam Temple   HINDU TEMPLE
(http://simhachalamdevasthanam.net; ⊙4am-10pm) Andhra's second-most visited temple (after Tirumala) is a 16km drive northwest of town. It's dedicated to Varahalakshmi Narasimha, a combination of Vishnu's boar and lion-man avatars, and can get crowded. A ₹100 ticket will get you to the deity (and a sip of holy water) much quicker than a ₹20

one. Buses 6A and 28 go here from the RTC Complex and train station.

🏃 Activities

Andhra Pradesh Tourism (Andhra Pradesh Tourism Development Corporation; ☑ 0891-2788820; http://aptdc.gov.in; RTC Complex; ☺ 8am-8pm Mon-Fri, 9am-1pm Sat) does all-day city tours (₹475 to ₹650), temple visits and trips to Araku Valley, from its RTC Complex (p254) and train station (p254) offices.

Surfers and kayakers can rent decent boards and kayaks from local surf pioneer **Melville Smythe** (☑ 9848561052; melsmythe@gmail.com; per hr surfboard ₹400-600, 2-person kayak ₹300, surf tuition ₹300), by the jet-ski hut at the south end of Rushikonda Beach.

🛏 Sleeping

Hotels are scattered around town. Beach Rd is the best place to stay, but it's low on inexpensive hotels. There were no hostels in town at the time of research.

Hotel Morya   HOTEL $
(☑ 0891-2731112; www.hotelmorya.com; Bowdara Rd; r ₹990, r with AC from ₹1490; ❋ 🛜) A good choice, the Morya's standard rooms are small and lack ventilation, but their better AC options are quite spacious, bright and relatively smart. There's a lift, but no restaurant.

SKML Beach Guest House   GUESTHOUSE $
(☑ 9848355131; ramkisg.1074@gmail.com; Beach Rd, Varun Beach; r ₹1200-1300, with AC ₹1850-2300; ❋ 🛜) SKML is towards the less select southern end of Ramakrishna Beach, but its 12 rooms are clean and decent. Best are the two top-floor 'suites' with sea views, a terrace and a bit of art.

Ambica Sea Green   HOTEL $$
(☑ 0891-2821818; www.ambicaseagreen.com; Beach Rd; r incl breakfast from ₹4680; ❋ 🛜) A good choice, the contemporary, well-equipped rooms here all have sea views. Breakfast is an excellent buffet spread and staff go the extra mile to help.

Dolphin Hotel   HOTEL $$
(☑ 0891-2567000; http://dolphinhotelsvizag.com; Dabagardens; r/ste incl breakfast from ₹3510/6340; ❋ 🛜🛝) A large concrete hotel in the centre with quite spacious rooms and an attractive restaurant. Its trump card is the 20m pool, and there's also an excellent gym, one of the best in the city.

Haritha Beach Resort   HOTEL $$
(☑ 0891-2788826; http://aptdc.gov.in; Rushikonda Beach; r with AC incl breakfast ₹2100-3200; ❋ 🛜) This government-run place has a fine hillside location facing Rushikonda Beach. Rooms are a little old-fashioned, but the executive and luxury categories are large; all have views overlooking the ocean. Just below, and with beach access, **Vihar** (Rushikonda; ☺ 11am-10.30pm; 🛜) is great for a beer or meal.

⭐ **Novotel Visakhapatnam Varun Beach**   HOTEL $$$
(☑ 0891-2822222; www.accorhotels.com; Beach Rd; r incl breakfast ₹9620; ❋ @🛜🛝) A modernist landmark that boasts a commanding position on Beach Rd facing the Bay of Bengal. Rooms are very well-appointed and immaculately presented, all with direct sea views. Dining options are first class, the bar is great for a tipple, the spa is excellent and the pool big enough for laps.

🍴 Eating

The snack stalls on Ramakrishna Beach are hopping at night.

Hotel V Parlour   INDIAN $
(https://v-parlour.business.site; Rama Talkies Rd; mains ₹90-270; ☺ noon-10:30pm) A pure-veg place with simple surrounds and generous portions that's always popular. Choose from North or South Indian, or Chinese-style dishes. The stall at the front sells Irani chai too.

⭐ **Sea Inn**   ANDHRA $$
(Raju Ka Dhaba; ☑ 9989012102; http://seainn.info; Beach Rd, Rushikonda; mains ₹100-240; ☺ noon-4pm Tue-Sun) Chef Devi cooks Andhra-style curries the way her mum did. Biryanis are spicy-delicious and filling, and you'll also find a short menu of local fish, seafood, chicken and veg dishes. All are served up in a simple, semi-open-air dining room with bench seating, 300m north of the Haritha Beach Resort turn-off. Be prepared to wait for a table; cash only.

⭐ **Dharani**   INDIAN $$
(Daspalla Hotel, off Town Main Rd, Suryabagh; thalis & mains ₹100-240; ☺ 6am-10.30pm) One of the city's best-regarded restaurants, with simply superb veg thalis – order a 'Special' for an authentic taste of the South (₹240). The hotel has several other restaurants too, including Andhra non-veg and North Indian veg options.

WORTH A TRIP

BHEEMUNIPATNAM

This former Dutch settlement, 25km north of Vizag, is the oldest municipality in mainland India, with bizarre sculptures on the beach, an 1861 lighthouse, an interesting Dutch cemetery, and Bheemli Beach, where local grommets surf not-very-clean waters on crude homemade boards. Buses (₹32,one hour, every 30min) trundle up the coast road from Vizag beach, or a one-way Uber/Ola is around ₹375.

Little Italy　　　　　　　ITALIAN $$
(http://littleitaly.in; 1st fl, South Wing, ATR Towers, Vutagedda Rd, Paandurangapuram; mains ₹240-450; ☺11.30am-11pm; 🛜) This Italian restaurant does fine thin-crust pizza, pasta and reasonable salads in stylish surrounds. No alcohol, but good fruit mocktails. It's behind Ramakrishna Beach.

Bamboo Bay　　　　　　ANDHRA $$$
(The Park, Beach Rd; mains ₹485-990; ☺7.30-11pm; 🛜) Excellent Andhra, Chettinad and Mughlai food in the Park hotel's beachside gardens, including lots of seafood. There's a good choice for vegetarians and you can dine on the terrace by candlelight in the evening.

🍸 Drinking & Nightlife

★**Moksha Restocafe**　　　　　CAFE
(www.facebook.com/moksha.restocafe; Ootagadda Rd, Daspalla Hills; ☺8am-midnight; 🛜) Community cafe popular with a hip young Vizag crowd, with distant sea views from its terrace. There's fine coffee, including espresso options, and good juices (try the minty lemon). On the menu you'll find Western, Thai, Tibetan and Indian dishes (plus treats like Nutella crepes). Also hosts talks and events.

Tribe　　　　　　　　　　CLUB
(www.facebook.com/tribevizag; The Park, Beach Rd; ☺Fri & Sat 8pm-1am or later) One of Vizag's busiest and most fashionable clubs, with DJs playing house, R'n'B and Bollywood to a lively crowd; there are also live bands. It opens some Sundays for chill-out sessions. Smart dress required.

ⓘ Getting There & Away

AIR

Vizag airport has direct daily flights to over 20 Indian cities including Bengaluru, Bhubaneswar, Chennai, Delhi, Hyderabad, Kolkata, Mumbai, Port Blair and Vijayawada. There are also international connections to Bangkok, Dubai, Kuala Lumpur and Singapore.

BOAT

Boats depart roughly once a month for Port Blair in the Andaman Islands. Call or email for schedules, or check www.andamanbeacon.com. Book for the 56-hour journey (bunk ₹2500, cabin berth from ₹4960) at **AV Bhanoji Rao, Garuda Pattabhiramayya & Co** (📞0891-2562661, 0891-2565597; ops@avbgpr.com; Harbour Approach Rd, next to NMDC, port area; ☺9am-5pm Mon-Sat). Tickets go on sale around a week before departure. Bring your passport, two photocopies of its data page, and two passport photos.

BUS

Services from Vizag's well-organised **RTC Complex** (📞0891-2746400; RTC Complex Inner Rd) include the following:

Hyderabad non-AC/AC ₹746/1352, 12-15 hours, 12 daily

Jagdalpur non-AC ₹342, nine hours, one daily

Vijayawada general/superluxury/AC ₹408/430/593-808, seven to nine hours, every 30min

CAR

English-speaking **Srinivasa 'Srinu' Rao** (📞7382468137) is a reliable, friendly driver for out-of-town trips. He charges around ₹3300 for an Araku Valley day trip and ₹1700 to Sankaram and back.

TRAIN

Visakhapatnam station (Station Rd), on the western edge of town, is on the main Kolkata-Chennai line. Destinations travelling sleeper/2AC include the following:

Bhubaneswar ₹290/1065, seven hours, 11 daily

Chennai ₹425/1600, 13-16 hours, three to four daily

Hyderabad ₹380/1485, 12-15 hours, eight daily

Kolkata ₹460/1735, 13-16 hours, six to seven daily

Vijayawada ₹255/850, six hours, 16 to 18 daily

The **railway reservation centre** (Station Approach Rd; ☺8am-10pm Mon-Sat, to 2pm Sun) is 300m south of the main station building.

❶ Getting Around

There are over 2000 Uber (and a similar number of Ola) drivers in Visakhapatnam, so you won't have to wait long for a ride.

For the airport, 12km west of downtown, app-cabs or autorickshaws charge about ₹260. Or take bus 38 from the RTC Complex (₹20, 30 minutes). The airport's arrivals hall has a prepaid taxi booth.

The train station has a prepaid autorickshaw booth. Shared autorickshaws run along Beach Rd from the port at the south end of town to Rushikonda, 10km north of Vizag, charging ₹10 for a short hop.

Around Visakhapatnam

Sankaram

Located 40km west of Vizag, the stunning seldom-visited Buddhist complex of **Sankaram** (⊙8am-6pm) is also known by the names of its two parts, Bojjannakonda and Lingalakonda. Bojjannakonda, the eastern part, has a pair of rock-cut shrines with several gorgeous carvings of the Buddha inside and outside. Above sit the ruins of a huge stupa and a monastery. Lingalakonda, at the western end, is piled with tiers of rock-cut stupas, some of them enormous.

A car from Vizag costs around ₹1700. Or take a bus (₹46, 1½ hours, every half-hour from the RTC Complex) or train (₹38, one hour) to Anakapalle, 3km away, and then an autorickshaw (around ₹140 return including waiting).

Bavikonda & Thotlakonda

Bavikonda (⊙9am-5pm) and **Thotlakonda** (car ₹30; ⊙8am-5.30pm) were Buddhist monasteries on scenic hilltop sites north of Vizag that each hosted up to 150 monks, with the help of massive rainwater tanks. Their remains were unearthed in the 1980s and 1990s.

The monasteries flourished from around the 3rd century BC to the 3rd century AD, and had votive stupas, congregation halls, *chaitya-grihas* (prayer halls), *viharas* (refuges for monks) and refectories. Thotlakonda has sea views, and Bavikonda has special importance because a relic vessel found in its Mahachaitya stupa contained a piece of bone believed to be from the Buddha himself.

Bavikonda and Thotlakonda are reached from turn-offs 14km and 15km, respectively, from Vizag on the Bheemunipatnam road:

Bavikonda is 3km off the main road and Thotlakonda 1.25km. Vizag autorickshaw or Ola/Uber drivers charge around ₹700 return to see both.

Araku Valley

☑ 08936 / ELEV 975M

Andhra's best train ride is through the beautiful, lushly forested Eastern Ghats to the Araku Valley, centred on Araku town, 115km north of Visakhapatnam. The area is home to isolated tribal communities and known for its tasty organic coffee and lovely green countryside. En route you can visit the impressive Borra Caves.

◉ Sights

Borra Caves   CAVE
(adult/child ₹60/45, camera/mobile camera ₹100/25; ⊙10am-1pm & 2-5pm) Illuminated with fancy lighting, the huge million-year-old limestone Borra Caves are 38km before Araku town and can be combined with a visit to the Araku Valley. Stairways penetrate the caves, but they can get very crowded, especially on Sundays. Watch out for monkeys. You'll find snack stands close to the entrance; try the bamboo chicken.

Museum of Habitat   MUSEUM
(₹40; ⊙8am-1.30pm & 2.30-8pm) This museum has extensive exhibits on the tribal peoples of eastern Andhra Pradesh, including full-scale mock-ups of hunting, ceremonial and other scenes, and a few craft stalls. Worthwhile, but displays and information could be better. Located next to the bus station and 2km east of the train station.

🛏 Sleeping & Eating

The main drag in Araku has several eateries. The local speciality is *bongulo* chicken, which is spiced chicken cooked in a section of bamboo cane. Do try the local coffee while you're here.

Dream Valley Residency   GUESTHOUSE $
(☑ 9398803229; https://dream-valley-residency. business.site; r ₹1300; 📶) A pocket-friendly motel-style place on the south side of the railway tracks. Rooms are in decent shape and have cable TV and en-suites with reliable hot water. The management are helpful and can advise travellers about local attractions.

Hotel Rajadhani   HOTEL $
(☑ 08936-249580; r without/with AC ₹900/1400; ❉📶) Reasonable budget hotel with over

30 rooms. They could all be better presented, and service can be lacking, but rooms on
the upper floor enjoy valley views from their
balconies. There's an **in-house restaurant**
(mains ₹120-260; ⊙7am-10pm).

Haritha Valley Resort
HOTEL $$

(☑08936-249202; http://aptdc.gov.in/aptdc; r incl
breakfast ₹1900, with AC from ₹2260; ✳❋✉)
The best place to stay in Araku, with a pool
and landscaped grounds. It's a government-
run hotel and rooms are maintained
quite well, though service is very leisurely.
Favoured by Tollywood film crews.

Star Annapurna
INDIAN $

(mains ₹110-250; ⊙7.30am-10pm) Offers a wide
choice of flavoursome dishes including a
good chicken biryani, fish dishes and lots of
well-spiced vegetable curries.

Araku Valley Coffee House
CAFE $

(coffee ₹25-100; ⊙8.30am-9pm) You can
sample and buy local coffee and all kinds
of chocolatey goods (brownies, chocolate-
covered coffee beans) at Araku Valley Coffee
House, which also has a tiny **coffee muse-
um** (₹25; ⊙8.30am-9pm). A trampoline will
keep the kids entertained and there are of-
ten tribal dancing performances too.

ⓘ Getting There & Away

From Visakhapatnam a train (₹100, four hours)
leaves daily at 6.50am, returning from Araku at
3.40pm. Get to Visakhapatnam early to secure
a seat and be aware that the return train often
leaves late. A special AC 'vistadome' (glass
roof) carriage has been added to this service;
you need to book 'Executive Chair' class on the
IRCTC website (www.irctc.co.in) and tickets cost
₹665.

Buses (roughly hourly) from Visakhapatnam
(from ₹130) take 4½ hours. A taxi day trip costs
₹3300 to ₹4000. The APTDC (Andhra Pradesh
Tourism Development Corporation; http://aptdc.
gov.in) runs tours that all include the Borra
Caves; however its day trips are very rushed.

Tirumala & Tirupati

☑0877 / POP 7900 (TIRUMALA) / 296,000 (TIRUPATI)
One of the globe's largest pilgrimage des-
tinations, the holy hill of Tirumala is, on
any given day, thronged with thousands of
devotees who've journeyed to venerate Lord
Venkateshwara here, at his home. Around
60,000 pilgrims come each day, and *dar-
shan* runs 24/7. The **Tirumala Tirupathi
Devasthanams** (TTD; ☑0877-2277777, 0877-

2233333; www.tirumala.org; KT Rd; ⊙9am-5.30pm
Mon-Fri, to 1pm Sat) efficiently administers the
multitudes, employing 20,000 people to do
so. Despite the crowds, a sense of order, se-
renity and ease mostly prevails, and a trip to
the Holy Hill can be fulfilling even if you're
not a pilgrim. Queues during the annual
nine-day Brahmotsavam festival (p230) can
stretch for kilometres.

Tirupati, the humdrum town at the bot-
tom of the hill, is the functional gateway to
Tirumala.

⊙ Sights & Activities

Venkateshwara Temple
HINDU TEMPLE

(www.tirumala.org; ⊙24hr) Legends about the
hill itself and the surrounding area appear
in the Puranas, and the temple's history
may date back 2000 years. Devotees flock to
Tirumala to see Venkateshwara, an avatar of
Vishnu. Among the many powers attribut-
ed to Venkateshwara is the granting of any
wish made at this holy site. Foreigners (with
passport) are able to gain fast-entry (₹300)
at the Supatham Gate and avoid the worst of
the scrum, though expect jostling.

The main temple is an atmospheric place,
though you'll be pressed between hundreds
of devotees when you see it. Venkateshwara
inspires bliss and love among his visitors
from the back of the dark and magical inner
sanctum; it smells of incense and resonates
with chanting. You'll have a moment to say
a prayer and then you'll be shoved out again.
Don't forget to collect your delicious *ladoo*
from the counter: Tirumala *ladoos* (sweet
balls made with chickpea flour, cardamom
and dried fruits) are famous across India.

Many pilgrims donate their hair to the de-
ity – in gratitude for a wish fulfilled, or to re-
nounce ego – so hundreds of barbers attend
to devotees. Tirumala and Tirupati are filled
with tonsured men, women and children.

Upon entry, you'll have to sign a form de-
claring your faith in Lord Venkateshwara.

Pity the locals queuing for 'ordinary
darshan', a wait of anywhere from three to
eight hours in claustrophobic metal cages
ringing the temple. Special-entry darshan
ticketsare also bookable online and allow
quicker access.

🛏 Sleeping

Avoid weekends if you can, when Tirupati
is uber-rammed. There's a fair selection of
hotels in town, though standards are not
that high.

HIKING THE HOLY HILL

There are two pilgrims' paths from Tirupati to Tirumala's temple. The shorter (9km) Srivari Metlu heads straight up the mountain, taking a relentlessly steep route up. The second option, the 12km Alipiri Metlu, is an ancient pilgrims' path that begins at Alipiri, some 3.5km northwest of the centre of Tirupati, and is the preferred walk for most. Chartered buses from distant Deccan villages line the road leading to the start of the hike, disgorging hundreds of barefoot pilgrims intent on darshan (deity-viewing).

If you want to walk with the pilgrims, try to get as early a start as possible to avoid the heat of the day (the paths and temple are open 24 hours). You don't need to take supplies as there are ample food stalls and drink vendors (and WCs) en route. Most of the hike consists of concrete stairways (each individual step smeared with scarlet and orange dyes, blessings left by the faithful) and paved paths. The route is (mostly) covered with protective roofing, so the pilgrimage is possible no matter what the weather, rain or shine.

Villagers and urbanites, sadhus and techies, children and grannies march together up the holy hill. Cries of encouragement – 'Ola!' – ring across the valley to aid progress. The first, distinctly tough, half of the trek is not particularly scenic as concrete roofing and dense forest hides views back down the mountain. After 2100 or so incredibly steep steps there's the Gali Goporum (temple gateway), the ideal spot for a break. Then the forest clears to reveal a statue of Hanuman, a medical centre and a clutch of food stalls.

The next section is easier, a steady incline along a covered path for 3km or so, passing a deer reserve, before the route then follows a road for around 2km, that enjoys fine mountain vistas. You then reach the Mokala Parvatham temple from where many pilgrims ascend a final flight of steps on their knees, in an act of extreme devotion. The summit is not far from here, some 3550 steps from the starting point, and 980m above sea level. It represents a return to the realities of India complete with honking traffic, hustle and bustle, with the main temple a short walk beyond. Shouts of 'Jai Shri Ram' ('Hail Lord Rama') ensue, as the faithful approach their final destination.

Virtually all Hindu pilgrims perform the entire hike barefoot (though you won't be chastised for wearing footwear). Foreigners (with passport) are able to gain fast-entry (₹300) at the Supatham Gate for entry to Venkateshwara Temple (p256) and darshan.

The Tirumala Tirupathi Devasthanams runs vast **dormitories** (Tirumala; beds free) and **guesthouses** (Tirumala; r ₹50-3000; ❄) near the temple in Tirumala, intended for pilgrims. To stay here, check in at the Central Reception Office.

Athidhi Residency   HOTEL $
(✆0877-2281222; Peddakapu Layout, Tirupati; r ₹1000-1600; ❄🛜) Keenly priced, this is a deservedly popular place with well-presented rooms that have flat-screen TVs, ceiling fans and attractive en suites. It's a short drive from the train station or walkable from the bus stand.

★**Hotel Marasa**
Sarovar Premiere Tirupati   BOUTIQUE HOTEL $$
(✆0877-6660000; www.sarovarhotels.com; 12th Cross Karakambadi Rd, Tirupati; r incl breakfast from ₹3300; ❄🛜🏊) Really raising the bar in terms of quality in Tirupati, this sleek contemporary hotel is the best in town by

some distance and represents fine value. It's beautifully styled, with modish furnishings throughout and boasts a lovely pool area, two fine **restaurants** (mains ₹250-500; ⊙7.30-10am, noon-3.30pm & 7-11pm; 🛜), cafe-bar and spa. Rooms are supremely comfortable, and the location on the edge of town is very tranquil.

Hotel Regalia   HOTEL $$
(✆0877-2238699; www.regaliahotels.com; Ramanuja Circle, Tirupati; r/ste incl breakfast ₹2999/4999; ❄🛜) The Regalia provides inviting, contemporary rooms with sleek en suites. There's a pure veg restaurant for Indian cuisine while Flavours scores for global grub and meat dishes. On the east side of town, 1.5km from the train station.

Minerva Grand   HOTEL $$
(✆0877-6688888; http://minervahotels.in; Renigunta Rd, Tirupati; s/d with AC from ₹2900/3500; ❄🛜) In the heart of town, this well-run

establishment has business-style rooms equipped with desks, plump pillows and good mattresses. Its two restaurants, both with icy AC, are great too and there's a bar and small gym.

Eating & Drinking

Tirupati is well-endowed with restaurants. Huge **dining halls** (Tirumala; meals free; ⊙hours vary) on the hill feed thousands of pilgrims daily; veg restaurants also serve meals for ₹25.

Kafe Tirumala   SOUTH INDIAN $
(Lakshmipuram Circle, Tirupati; light meals ₹80-130; ⊙8am-10pm) A kind of modern take on a traditional *darshini* (South Indian breakfast joint) this small likeable place serves up snacks like *idli* and dosa at very reasonable rates. It's standing room only.

★**Hotel Mayura**   INDIAN $$
(209 TP Area, Tirupati; meals ₹99-280; ⊙7am-10pm) One of the best places in town for South Indian thalis (₹220), with delicious dishes and lots of chutneys neatly arranged on a banana leaf. Ten kinds of dosa (from ₹99) are available and North Indian dishes are also offered. It's opposite the bus station.

★**Minerva Coffee Shop**   INDIAN $$
(Minerva Grand, Renigunta Rd, Tirupati; thalis ₹185-240; ⊙7am-11.30pm; 🛜) The veg-only Minerva does superb Andhra and North Indian thalis (with free refills) and fine filter coffee. Staff are efficient and the ambience is family orientated. It's also a good choice for a local breakfast buffet (₹195).

Maya   INDIAN $$
(Bhimas Deluxe Hotel, 34-38 G Car St, Tirupati; mains ₹120-220; ⊙6am-10pm; 🛜) Great veg meals in the basement of the Bhimas Deluxe, near the train station. Don't confuse it with the Bhimas Hotel next door.

ⓘ Getting There & Away

From Visakhapatnam a train (₹100, four hours) leaves daily at 6.50am, returning from Araku at 3.40pm. Get to Visakhapatnam early to secure a seat and be aware that the return train often leaves late. A special AC 'vistadome' (glass roof) carriage has been added to this service; you need to book 'Executive Chair' class on the IRCTC website (www.irctc.co.in) and tickets cost ₹665.

Buses (roughly hourly) from Visakhapatnam (from ₹130) take 4½ hours. A taxi day trip costs ₹3300 to ₹4000. The APTDC (Andhra Pradesh Tourism Development Corporation; http://aptdc.gov.in) runs tours that all include the Borra Caves; however its day trips are very rushed.

Around Tirumala & Tirupati

Chandragiri Fort

This fort complex, 15km west of Tirupati, dates back 1000 years but its heyday came in the late 16th century when the rulers of the declining Vijayanagar empire, having fled from Hampi, made it their capital. The upper fort on the hillside is (frustratingly) out of bounds.

The **palace area** (Chandragiri Fort; Indian/foreigner ₹25/200; ⊙9am-5pm Sat-Thu) contains nice gardens and the Raja Mahal, a heavily restored Vijayanagar palace reminiscent of Hampi buildings. It's at the heart of a 1.5km-long stout-walled enclosure at the foot of a rocky hill.

There's a reasonably interesting museum of bronze and stone sculptures here, which is worth a visit even though it's somewhat lacking in information and context.

Buses for Chandragiri (₹12) leave Tirupati hourly. Cabs charge around ₹600 return.

Kerala

Includes ➡

Thiruvananthapuram
(Trivandrum) 261
Kollam (Quilon) 276
Alappuzha
(Alleppey) 278
Kottayam 284
Periyar Tiger
Reserve 287
Munnar 292
Kochi (Cochin) 297
Kozhikode (Calicut) . . 314
Lakshadweep 323

Best Places to Eat

➡ Kashi Art Cafe (p305)

➡ Villa Maya (p265)

➡ Malabar Junction (p306)

➡ Bait (p270)

➡ Paragon
Restaurant (p316)

Best Places to Stay

➡ Neeleshwar Hermitage
(p323)

➡ Varnam Homestay (p318)

➡ Rosegardens (p294)

➡ Old Harbour Hotel (p301)

➡ Reds Residency (p301)

➡ Marari Villas (p284)

Why Go?

For many travellers, Kerala is South India's most serenely beautiful state. This slender coastal strip is defined by its landscape: almost 600km of glorious Arabian Sea coast and beaches; a languid network of glistening backwaters; and the spice- and tea-covered hills of the Western Ghats, dotted with protected wildlife reserves and cool hill stations. Just setting foot on this swathe of soul-soothing, palm-shaded green will slow your subcontinental stride to a blissed-out amble. Kerala is a world away from the frenzy of the rest of India, its long, fascinating backstory illuminated by historically evocative cities like Kochi (Cochin) and Thiruvananthapuram (Trivandrum).

Besides the backwaters, elegant houseboats, ayurvedic treatments and delicately spiced, taste-bud-tingling cuisine, Kerala is home to wild elephants, exotic birds and the odd tiger, while vibrant traditions such as Kathakali, *theyyam* (a trance-induced ritual), festivals and snake-boat races frequently bring even the smallest villages to life.

When to Go
Thiruvananthapuram

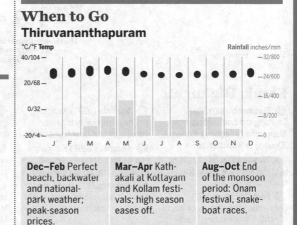

Dec–Feb Perfect beach, backwater and national-park weather; peak-season prices.

Mar–Apr Kathakali at Kottayam and Kollam festivals; high season eases off.

Aug–Oct End of the monsoon period: Onam festival, snake-boat races.

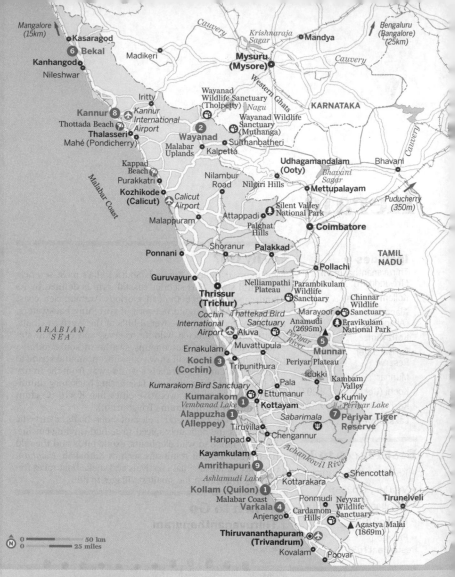

Kerala Highlights

1 Backwaters (p286)
Cruising the backwaters from Alappuzha (Alleppey), Kollam (Quilon) or Kumarakom.

2 Wayanad (p317) Spotting wild elephants, walking the spice-carpeted hills.

3 Fort Cochin (p297) Unravelling the history of Kochi (Cochin), while lazing in art-filled cafes.

4 Varkala (p271) Watching the days slip away between yoga, surf and beach sessions.

5 Munnar (p292) Sleeping in a secluded homestay and trekking through tea plantations.

6 Bekal (p322) Wandering Kerala's unexplored, white-gold northernmost beaches.

7 Periyar Tiger Reserve (p287) Hiking, rafting or boating this protected space.

8 Kannur (p320) Seeking unspoilt beaches and *theyyam* (a trance-induced ritual).

9 Amrithapuri (p278) Experiencing ashram life at Matha Amrithanandamayi Mission.

History

Traders have been drawn to Kerala's spices for more than 3000 years. The coast was known to the Phoenicians, the Romans, the Arabs and the Chinese, and was a transit point for spices from the Moluccas (eastern Indonesia).

The Cheras ruled much of Kerala until the early Middle Ages, competing with kingdoms and small fiefdoms for territory and trade, but were defeated by the Cholas in the 12th century. St Thomas the Apostle is said to have landed in Kerala in AD 52, bringing Christianity to the subcontinent. Vasco da Gama's arrival at Kappad, just north of Kozhikode (Calicut), in 1498 opened the floodgates to European colonialism as Portuguese, Dutch and English interests fought Arab traders, and then each other, for control of the lucrative spice trade.

The present-day state of Kerala was created in 1956 from the former states of Travancore, Cochin and Malabar (the first two remained independent during British rule). A tradition of valuing the arts and education resulted in a post-Independence state that is one of the most progressive in India, with the nation's highest literacy rate.

In 1957 Kerala voted in the first freely elected communist government in the world, which has gone on to hold power regularly since; the Congress-led United Democratic Front (UDF) governed from 2006 to 2011, but was replaced by the Communist Party of India-led Left Democratic Front in 2016. Many Malayalis (speakers of Malayalam, the state's official language) work in the Middle East and their remittances play a significant part in the economy. A big hope for the state's future is the relatively recent boom in tourism, with Kerala emerging in the past two decades as one of India's most popular tourist hot spots.

SOUTHERN KERALA

Thiruvananthapuram (Trivandrum)

☑ 0471 / POP 743,690

Thiruvananthapuram, Kerala's capital – still usually referred to by its colonial-era name, Trivandrum – is a relatively compact but energetic city spread across low-lying hills and is an easy-going introduction to urban life down south. Most travellers merely springboard from here to the nearby beaches of Kovalam and Varkala, but Trivandrum (once capital of the princely state of Travancore) has enough good food and intriguing sights to justify a stay.

The ancient core of the city, home to the Shri Padmanabhaswamy Temple (closed to non-Hindus), is the southern Fort area, 1km southwest of the main bus and train stations. Around 3km north of Fort along Mahatma Gandhi (MG Rd) lie the museums and Zoological Gardens.

◉ Sights

★ **Museum of History & Heritage**   MUSEUM
(KeralaM; www.museumkeralam.org; Park View, Museum Rd; adult/child Indian ₹20/10, foreigner

---

TOP STATE FESTIVALS

As well as the major state festivals, Kerala has hundreds of annual temple festivals, *theyyam* (a trance-induced ritual), boat-race regattas and street parades.

Ernakulathappan Utsavam (p300; Kochi; ☺ Jan/Feb) Eight days of festivities that peak with music and fireworks; features elephant parades.

Thrissur Pooram (p312; Thrissur; ☺ Apr/May) Kerala's biggest and most vibrant festival; features elephant processions.

Nehru Trophy Boat Race (p279; Alleppey; ☺ Aug) The most celebrated of Kerala's boat races.

Onam (statewide; ☺ Aug/Sep) The entire state celebrates the golden age of mythical King Mahabali for 10 days.

Cochin Carnival (p300; Kochi; ☺ Dec) Ten days of parades, costumes and the arts in Fort Cochin.

Kochi–Muziris Biennale (p300; Kochi; ☺ Dec–Mar) One of Asia's major biennial contemporary-art festivals sweeps through Fort Cochin.

Thiruvananthapuram (Trivandrum)

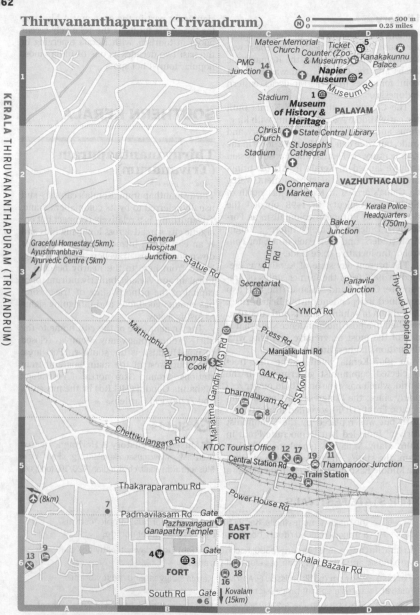

₹200/50, camera ₹25; ⊙10am-5.30pm Tue-Sun) Occupying a handsome 120-year-old heritage building within the Kerala Tourism complex, this intelligently presented museum traces Kerala's history and culture through superb static and multimedia displays. Exhibits range from Iron Age implements to bronze, wood and terracotta sculptures, murals, *dhulichitra* (floor paintings), Roman-era coins, re-creations of traditional Keralite homes and replicas of engravings at Wayanad's Edakkal Caves (p318).

Thiruvananthapuram (Trivandrum)

◎ **Top Sights**
1 Museum of History & Heritage D1
2 Napier Museum D1

◎ **Sights**
3 Puthe Maliga Palace Museum B6
4 Shri Padmanabhaswamy Temple B6
5 Zoological Gardens...............................D1

◉ **Activities, Courses & Tours**
6 CVN Kalari Sangham...........................B6
KTDC Tours .... (see 14)
7 Margi Kathakali School A5

◎ **Sleeping**
8 Hotel Regency.......................................C4
9 Padmavilasom Palace A6
10 Princess Inn...C4

◆ **Eating**
11 Ariya Nivaas... D5
12 Indian Coffee House............................ C5
Padmavilasom Palace................... (see 9)
13 Villa Maya... A6

ⓘ **Information**
14 KTDC Central Reservation Centre.......C1
15 SBI ATM C3
Tourist Office ....(see 1)

ⓘ **Transport**
16 East Fort Bus Stand C6
17 KSRTC Bus Station Complex C5
18 Municipal Bus Stand C6
Pre-Paid Autorickshaw Stand .....(see 17)
19 Pre-Paid Autorickshaw Stand C5
20 Train Station Reservation Office.........C5

★ **Napier Museum**   MUSEUM
(Art Museum; off Museum Rd; adult/child Indian ₹20/10, foreigner ₹200/100; ◷10am-4.45pm Tue & Thu-Sun, 1-4.45pm Wed) Housed in an 1880 wooden building designed by Robert Chisholm (a British architect whose Fair Isle–style version of the Keralite vernacular shows his enthusiasm for local craft), this museum holds an eclectic display of bronzes, Buddhist sculptures, temple carts, ivory carvings and a wood-carved model of Kerala's famous Guruvayur temple. The architectural style fuses neo-Gothic and Keralan elements, and the carnivalesque interior is worth a look in its own right.

Zoological Gardens   ZOO
(off Museum Rd; adult/child Indian ₹30/10, foreigner ₹200/100, camera/video ₹50/200; ◷9am-5.15pm Tue-Sun) Yann Martel famously based the animals in his novel *Life of Pi* on those he observed in Trivandrum's Zoological Gardens. Shaded paths meander through woodland, lakes and native forest, where tigers, macaques, hippos, peacocks, deer, leopards and other creatures gather, though some live in small, not very open enclosures.

Shri Padmanabhaswamy Temple   HINDU TEMPLE
(Fort; ◷3.30am-7.30pm) Trivandrum's spiritual heart is this 18th-century temple (closed to non-Hindus) in the Fort area, which fuses Keralan and Dravidian architecture and whose origins go back to at least the 8th century. The main entrance is through the 30m-tall, seven-tier eastern *gopuram* (gateway tower), in Tamil Nadu style.

Puthe Maliga Palace Museum   MUSEUM
(Fort; adult/child Indian ₹70/25, foreigner ₹200/70, phone camera ₹20; ◷9am-12.45pm & 2-4.45pm Tue-Sun) Overlooking the Shri Padmanabhaswamy Temple tank, the opulent 18th-century palace of the Travancore maharajas is a classically Keralan world of beautifully carved wooden ceilings, tiled roofs, marble sculptures and imported Belgian glass. Inside you'll find Kathakali images, an armoury, portraits of maharajas, ornate thrones and other artefacts. Admission is by informative one-hour tour, though you can just visit the outside of the palace grounds (free).

🏃 **Activities**

An excellent way to get under the skin of the city is with a **Storytrails** (☑9061222267; www.storytrails.in; tour per person ₹1100) walking tour. The KTDC runs several bus day **tours** (☑0471-2316736; www.ktdc.com; Mascot Hotel, Mascot Sq), including a Glorious Thiruvananthapuram itinerary (₹680) and a Mesmerising Kanyakumari trip (₹990), from its office (p265) at Mascot Hotel (600m west of the Zoological Gardens).

Margi Kathakali School   CULTURAL PROGRAM
(☑0471-2478806; www.margitheatre.org; Fort; admission by donation) Conducts courses in Kathakali and Kootiattam (traditional Sanskrit drama) for beginner and advanced students (enquire directly for rates), and occasionally puts on Kathakali performances. Visitors can peek at uncostumed practise sessions, usually held from 10am to noon Monday

THE INDIAN COFFEE HOUSE STORY

Founded by the Coffee Board in the 1940s, under British rule, the Indian Coffee House is a place stuck in time. Its 400-odd India-wide branches feature old-India prices and waiters dressed in starched white with peacock-style head-dresses. In the 1950s the Board began to close down cafes across India, making employees redundant. At this point, Kerala-born communist leader Ayillyath Kuttiari Gopalan Nambiar began to support the workers and founded with them the India Coffee Board Workers' Co-operative Society. The Coffee House has remained ever since, always atmospheric, and still run by its employees, all of whom share ownership.

to Friday. It's behind the Fort School, 200m west of the fort.

CVN Kalari Sangham   MARTIAL ARTS

(☑0471-2474182; www.cvnkalari.in; South Rd; 15-day/1-month course ₹1000/2000) Three- to six-month courses in *kalarippayat* for serious students (aged under 30) with some experience in martial arts. Visitors are welcome to watch training sessions from 6.30am to 7.30am Monday to Saturday.

🛏 Sleeping

There are decent-value budget and mid-range hotels along Manjalikulam Rd, north of the main train and bus stations.

Princess Inn   HOTEL $

(☑0471-2339150; princess_inn@yahoo.com; Manjalikulam Rd; with AC s ₹990-1450, d ₹1290-1620, without AC s ₹580-900, d ₹780-1400; ❈❋) In a glass-fronted building, the Princess Inn promises a relatively quiet no-frills sleep in a central side-street location. It's comfortable, with TVs, immaculate bathrooms, 24-hour checkout and friendly staff. Worth paying slightly extra for the more spacious 'deluxe' rooms.

Hotel Regency   HOTEL $

(☑0471-2330377; www.hotelregency.com; Manjalikulam Cross Rd; with AC s ₹1080-1300, d ₹1550-1700, without AC s ₹750-950, d ₹1080-1150; ❈❋) Around 600m northwest of the bus and train stations, this tidy, popular place

offers small but spotless rooms with TV; the deluxe rooms are more spacious and there's wi-fi in the lobby, as well as a rooftop garden.

★ Graceful Homestay   HOMESTAY $$

(☑9847249556, 0471-2444358; www.gracefulhomestay.com; Pothujanam Rd, Philip's Hill; downstairs s/d ₹1800/2000, upstairs & ste s/d ₹2750/3000, all incl breakfast; ❋) In the leafy western suburbs of Trivandrum, this lovely, serene family house amid sprawling gardens has four fan-cooled rooms, neatly furnished with individual character and access to kitchen, living areas and balconies. The top-floor double comes with a covered terrace overlooking a sea of palms. Call ahead for directions from the attentive hosts, who prepare fresh Keralan breakfasts.

★ Padmavilasom Palace   HOMESTAY $$$

(☑8086080286, 7902203111; http://padmavilasompalace.com; TC29/1769 Perumthanni, Airport Rd, Injakkal; r incl breakfast ₹5000-10,000; ❈❋) The brainchild (and former family home) of local entrepreneur Archana Mohan, Padmavilasom tactfully reimagines a 150-year-old royal palace into a luxury homestay with a tangible old-Travancore atmosphere. The two upper-floor suites have chequered floors, four-poster beds, desks and sweeping bathrooms. Victorian-era tiles carpet the lobby, beyond which the fabulous **restaurant** (breakfast ₹370, lunch ₹530; ⏱7.30-10.30am & 12.30-3pm; ❋) serves Keralan-style vegetarian meals around a traditional *naalukettu* (homestead courtyard).

🍴 Eating

★ Ariya Nivaas   SOUTH INDIAN $

(Manorama Rd; mains ₹40-150, thalis ₹120; ⏱7am-10pm) Trivandrum's best all-you-can-eat South Indian veg thalis mean long-running Ariya Nivaas is always busy (especially at lunchtime), but service is snappy and the food fresh. There's an air-con dining room upstairs.

Indian Coffee House   INDIAN $

(Maveli Cafe; http://indiancoffeehouse.com; Central Station Rd; snacks ₹15-70; ⏱6.30am-10pm) Right beside Trivandrum's main bus stand, this branch of the famous Indian Coffee House serves its strong coffee and wallet-friendly snacks (biryanis, omelettes, masala dosa; savoury crepe stuffed with spiced potatoes) in a red-brick tower that looks like a cross between a lighthouse and a pigeon coop, and has a spiralling interior lined with concrete benches and tables.

⭐Villa Maya   KERALAN $$$
(🖉0471-2578901; www.villamaya.in; 120 Airport Rd, Injakkal; mains ₹600-1600; ⏲noon-11pm; 🔊) Villa Maya is more an experience than a mere restaurant. Dining is either in the magnificent 18th-century Dutch-built mansion or in private curtained niches in the tranquil courtyard garden. The Keralan cuisine is expertly crafted, delicately spiced and beautifully presented. Seafood is a speciality, with dishes like stuffed crab with lobster butter, though there are some tantalising vegetarian offerings, too.

🛈 Information

KIMS (Kerala Institute of Medical Sciences; 🖉0471-2941144, emergency 0471-2941400; http://trivandrum.kimsglobal.com; Anayara; ⏲24hr) Hospital around 6km northwest of Trivandrum Central train station.

KTDC Central Reservation Centre (🖉0471-2316736; www.ktdc.com; Mascot Hotel, Mascot Sq; ⏲10.15am-1.15pm & 2-5.15pm)

KTDC Tourist Office (www.ktdc.com; KTDC Hotel Chaithram, Central Station Rd; ⏲9.30am-7pm)

Tourist Office (🖉0471-2321132; Museum Rd; ⏲24hr)

🛈 Getting There & Away

AIR

Trivandrum International Airport (www. trivandrumairport.com), 4km west of the city centre, has direct flights to/from Colombo in Sri Lanka, Malé in the Maldives, and Gulf destinations.

Within India, Air India (p522), Jet Airways (p522), IndiGo (p522) and/or SpiceJet (p522) fly to/from Mumbai, Kochi (Cochin), Calicut, Bengaluru (Bangalore), Chennai, Delhi, Goa and Hyderabad.

BUS

State-run and private buses use Trivandrum's giant but orderly enough **KSRTC Bus Station Complex** (🖉0471-2462290; www.keralartc. com; Central Station Rd, Thampanoor), opposite Trivandrum Central train station.

Buses leave for Kovalam (₹17, 30 minutes) every 20 minutes between 6am and 6.30pm from the southern end of the **East Fort bus stand** (MG Rd), next to the **Municipal bus stand** (Chalai Bazaar Rd). For Varkala, it's easier to take the train.

TRAIN

Trains are often heavily booked; reserve ahead online or visit the upstairs **reservation office** (1st fl, Trivandrum Central; ⏲8am-2pm & 2.15-5.30pm) just north of Platform 1 on the north side of Trivandrum Central train station. While most major trains arrive into Trivandrum Central in the city centre, some express services

BUSES FROM TRIVANDRUM KSRTC BUS STATION COMPLEX

DESTINATION	FARE (₹)	DURATION (HR)	FREQUENCY
Alleppey	150-240	3½	every 10min
Bengaluru	920-1450	16	2pm, 2.30pm, 3.15pm, 5pm, 7.30pm
Chennai	830	12-16	8 daily 9.45am-7.30pm
Ernakulam (Kochi)	230-390	5½	every 20min (AC hourly)
Kanyakumari	80	3	2.30am, 4.30am, 5.30am
Kollam	80-150	2	every 15min (AC hourly)
Kumily (for Periyar)	250	8	8.15pm
Madurai	370	8	13 daily 8am-9.30pm
Munnar	400	8	6.45am, 1pm, 10.30pm, 11.15pm, 11.45pm
Mysuru	1050	14	5pm, 7.30pm, 8pm
Neyyar Dam	40	1½	every 30-60min 5.05am-7.50pm, 10.55pm
Ooty	695	15	3pm
Puducherry	720	14	1.15pm
Thrissur	350-400	7½	every 20min

MAJOR INTERSTATE TRAINS FROM TRIVANDRUM CENTRAL

DESTINATION	TRAIN NAME & NO	FARE (₹; SLEEP-ER/3AC/2AC)	DURATION (HR)	DEPAR-TURES (DAILY)
Bengaluru	16525 Bangalore Exp	420/1145/1650	18¾	12.45pm
Chennai	12696 Chennai Exp	470/1245/1785	16¾	5.15pm
Coimbatore	17229 Sabari Exp	255/685/985	9½	7.15am
Mangaluru	16604 Maveli Exp	370/980/1325	13¾	6.45pm
Mumbai	16346 Netravathi Exp	670/1805/2655	31	9.30am

terminate at Kochuveli train station, 7km north-west of the centre – check in advance.

Within Kerala there are frequent express trains to Varkala (2nd class/sleeper/3AC ₹45/140/495, one hour), Kollam (Quilon; ₹55/170/540, 50 minutes to two hours) and Ernakulam (Kochi; ₹95/165/495, 3¾ to five hours), via Alleppey (₹80/140/495, 2¼ to 3¼ hours) or Kottayam (₹80/140/495, three hours). There are also numerous daily services to Kanyakumari (2nd class/sleeper/3AC ₹60/140/490, 1½ to three hours).

ⓘ Getting Around

Buses run between Trivandrum's East Fort bus stand (p265) and the airport (₹12, 10 minutes) every 20 minutes from 6am to 8.30pm, including several daily orange FlyBus air-con services. Prepaid taxis from the airport cost ₹350 to the city and ₹500 to Kovalam.

Taxi apps Ola Cabs and Uber are the easiest way to get around town. Autorickshaw drivers will *sometimes* use their meters; short hops cost ₹20 to ₹50. There are prepaid autorickshaw stands outside the bus (Central Station Rd) and train (Thampanoor Junction) stations.

Around Trivandrum

On the western fringes of Neyyar Dam, 30km east of Trivandrum, the superbly located 1978 **Sivananda Yoga Vedanta Dhanwantari Ashram** (⌨9495630951, 9446580764; www.sivananda.org.in/neyyardam; Neyyar Dam; dm & tents ₹830, tw with AC ₹1940, without AC ₹1050-1310) is renowned for its hatha yoga courses, starting on the 1st and 16th of each month. Courses run for a minimum of two weeks and include accommodation and vegetarian meals; one-month yoga-teacher training is also offered. Bookings essential.

From Neyyar Dam, buses run to Trivandrum's KSRTC Bus Station Complex (p265; ₹35, one to two hours) every 30 minutes from 4.30am to 8.15pm, returning every 30 to 60 minutes from 5.05am to 7.50pm, then 10.55pm.

Kovalam

⌨0471 / POP 25,700

Once a calm fishing village clustered around its crescent beaches and backed by a sea of cascading palms, Kovalam now competes with Varkala as Kerala's most developed resort. The touristed main stretch, Lighthouse Beach, is flanked by hotels and restaurants stretching back into the hillside from the shore; just north, Hawa Beach is usually crowded with day trippers. Neither beach could be described as pristine, but at under 15km southeast from Trivandrum, Kovalam remains an immensely popular place for fun by the sea; there are promising waves (and a surf club), as well as charming guesthouses and a flourishing ayurveda and yoga scene.

About 2km further north, more peaceful Samudra Beach hosts several upmarket resorts.

⊙ Sights & Activities

Vizhinjam Lighthouse LIGHTHOUSE
(Lighthouse Rd; Indian/foreigner ₹20/50, camera ₹10; ⊙10am-1pm & 2-6pm Tue-Sun) Kovalam's most distinguishing feature is the working candy-striped lighthouse at the southern end of Lighthouse Beach. Climb the spiral staircase – or zip up in the lift – for vertigo-inducing, palm-drenched views sweeping up and down the coast.

Rock-Cut Temple HINDU TEMPLE
(Vinzhinjam; ⊙dawn-dusk) Amid neatly tended, banyan-shaded grounds 500m north of Vizhinjam harbour, this small shrine is one of Kerala's most ancient rock-cut temples. A sculpture of Dakshinamurthy is flanked by unfinished reliefs of Shiva as Nataraja (with Parvati) and Tripurantaka (carrying a bow

and arrow), all believed to date from the 8th century.

Padmakarma
YOGA

(☑ 9895882915; www.padmakarma.com; Lighthouse Beach; classes ₹500; ⊙ classes 8.15am & 4pm) Has twice-daily drop-in yoga and meditation sessions (morning Iyengar-based, afternoon hatha) with a Sivananda-trained teacher, in a leafy setting tucked back from the southern end of Lighthouse Beach (near Hotel Peacock). Also does 200-hour teacher training.

Kovalam Surf Club
SURFING

(☑ 9847347367; www.kovalamsurfclub.com; Lighthouse Beach; 1½hr group lesson ₹1000) ✎ This established, multilingual surf shop and club with a community focus, just back from Lighthouse Beach, offers introductory lessons (group or private), board rental (three hours ₹600) and customised surfing tours. The team runs free weekend surf classes for disadvantaged local kids and encourages education.

Cool Divers & Bond Safari
DIVING

(☑ 9946550073, 7560906575; www.bondsafari kovalam.com; Suseela Tower, Kovalam Beach Rd; introductory dive ₹6000; ⊙ 8.30am-5.30pm) An efficient dive outfit providing state-of-the-art equipment, PADI courses (four-day Open Water Diver ₹25,000) and guided trips to local dive sites.

🛏 Sleeping

Look for smaller, better-value picks behind Lighthouse Beach. There are few true budget places, especially during the December-to-January peak season (when advance bookings are essential). Expect excellent discounts outside high season.

Lost Hostel
HOSTEL $

(www.thelosthostels.com; near Avaduthura Temple; dm ₹500-600, r ₹1100-1700; 🖭) A fresh budget-traveller bolthole hidden in a yellow house 500m inland from Lighthouse Beach,

> **DON'T MISS**
>
> ## PADMANABHAPURAM PALACE
>
> Around 50km southeast of Kovalam, just over the border in Tamil Nadu, beautiful Padmanabhapuram Palace (p395) is considered India's finest surviving example of traditional Keralan architecture. This feast of polished and carved wood is accessible by bus or taxi from Kovalam, Thiruvananthapuram (Trivandrum) or Kanyakumari, via the village of Thuckalay. Kovalam taxis charge ₹3500 for a return trip including waiting time.

providing neat, simple six-bed dorms with fans, personal lockers and modern bathrooms, plus plain en suite twin rooms, communal areas and a shared kitchen.

Paradesh Inn
GUESTHOUSE $$

(☑ 9995362952; inn.paradesh@yahoo.com; Avaduthura; incl breakfast s ₹2600-3500, d ₹2900-3800; ⊙ mid-Oct–Mar; 🖭) Overlooking palms from its hillside perch, a five-minute climb inland from Lighthouse Beach, tranquil, Italian-operated, adults-only Paradesh Inn resembles a Greek-island home, with its whitewashed walls, sky-blue accents and Mediterranean charm. Each of the six fan-cooled rooms has a hanging chair outside and there are rooftop views, tasty breakfasts and vegetarian *satya* cooking ('yoga food').

Beach Hotel II
HOTEL $$

(www.thebeachhotel-kovalam.com; Lighthouse Beach; r ₹5310-5900, with AC ₹6490-7080; ❄🖭🖵) Tucked into the southern curl of Lighthouse Beach, the 14 elegant and refreshingly spacious rooms at this stylish pad gaze out on the beach from private balconies beyond sliding French doors. Wooden furniture, terracotta-tiled floors and earthy patterned textiles create a simple-chic look, while the terrace hosts the excellent restaurant Fusion (p269) and there's a brand-new pool.

Treetops
GUESTHOUSE $$

(☑ 9847912398; treetopsofkovalam@yahoo.in; r ₹2000; 🖭) Indeed amid palms and colourful gardens high above Lighthouse Beach (but only a five-minute walk away), British-run Treetops is a warm, calming and easy-going escape from the action below. The four bright, impeccable rooms come with colour and character, plus incense sticks

KERALA

Kovalam

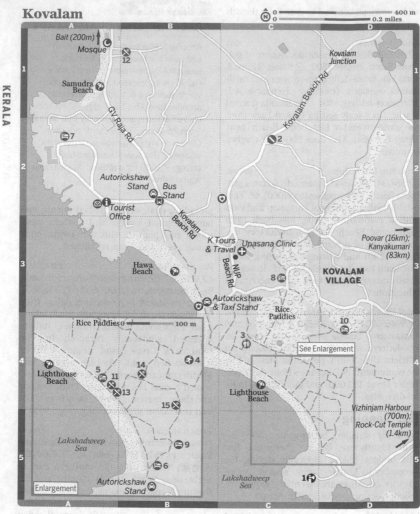

Kovalam

◎ Sights
1 Vizhinjam Lighthouse C5

✈ Activities, Courses & Tours
2 Cool Divers & Bond Safari...................C2
3 Kovalam Surf Club................................C4
4 Padmakarma..B4

🛏 Sleeping
5 Beach Hotel..A4
6 Beach Hotel II..B5
7 Leela..A2
8 Lost Hostel...C3
9 Maharaju Palace B5

10 Paradesh Inn...D4
   Treetops...(see 10)

🍽 Eating
11 A Beach Cafe A4
12 Curry Leaf...B1
   Fusion...(see 6)
13 Malabar Cafe..A4
14 Suprabhatham..B4
   Terrace Restaurant.....................(see 7)
15 Varsha...B4
   Waves Restaurant &
   German Bakery.............................(see 5)

and their own balconies, and there's a roof-top terrace with sweeping views. Call ahead for bookings and directions.

Beach Hotel HOTEL $$
(www.thebeachhotel-kovalam.com; Lighthouse Beach; r ₹2800; ☎) All calming ochre tones, terracotta tiling and minimalist flair, this intimate German-owned seafront pick has eight ground-floor rooms finished with printed throws, modern bathrooms and smart, arty touches, topped by the forever popular Waves Restaurant & Germany Bakery. Each room has its own terrace and staff are helpful and welcoming.

Maharaju Palace GUESTHOUSE $$
(☎9946854270; www.maharajupalace.com; Lighthouse Beach; incl breakfast r ₹2500, with AC ₹2850, cottage room ₹2500-3500; ✳☎) More peaceful retreat than palace, long-running Dutch-owned Maharaju lies pocketed away down a lane at the southern end of Lighthouse Beach. Timber furnishings, vibrant linens and the odd mural and four-poster mean it's styled with more character than its competition. There's a sweet wood-walled two-room cottage in the garden and chintzy chandeliers adorn the breezy breakfast terrace.

Ganesh House Homestay HOMESTAY $$
(☎9995012627, 0471-2584212; www.theganeshhouse.com; TC 64/2048 Nedumom, Country Spa Rd, Samudra Beach; incl breakfast r ₹1500, with AC ₹2300-2500, ✳☎) Seek out a family-style stay at this peach-orange, efficiently run modern home surrounded by greenery, down a dirt path just five minutes' walk inland from quiet Samudra Beach. 'Budget' fan rooms dot the ground floor, while larger air-con rooms sit upstairs beside a small terrace – all bright, clean and comfortable. Days begin with traditional Keralan breakfasts.

Leela LUXURY HOTEL $$$
(☎0471-3051234; www.theleela.com; Samudra Beach; r from ₹13,800, ste from ₹40,880; ✳@☎▨) Scented by frangipanis, the sumptuous Leela sprawls across the headland separating Hawa and Samudra beaches. Spacious, smartly designed rooms have colourful textiles, Keralan artwork and sea or garden views. The sophisticated Terrace Restaurant (p271) sits beside the show-stealing clifftop infinity pool, and there's an ayurvedic spa as well as a gym, a 'private' beach, yoga and dance performances.

Taj Green Cove LUXURY HOTEL $$$
(☎0471-6613000; https://taj.tajhotels.com; GV Raja Vattapara Rd, Samudra Beach; r/ste incl breakfast from ₹14,200/21,890; ✳☎▨) The Kovalam branch of this glitzy Indian group is nuzzled into lush grounds with direct seafront access. Individual thatched cottages come tastefully adorned, some with private gardens, others with primo sea views. Top-end dining offerings include poolside breakfasts and the magical, seafood-focused waterfront Bait (p270). The signature Jiva Spa (☎0471-6613048; massage or treatment ₹2100-4000; ☺8am-9pm) delivers yoga, ayurveda and massage in a luxe setting.

🍴 Eating & Drinking

Each evening the restaurants along the Lighthouse Beach promenade display the catch of the day; costs are around ₹90 per 100g of snapper. There are good restaurants in the tangle of lanes behind, and on quieter Samudra Beach.

★Varsha SOUTH INDIAN $$
(☎9995100301; dishes ₹150-225; ☺8am-10pm; ☎) In the lanes behind southern Lighthouse Beach, this little restaurant plates up some of Kovalam's best vegetarian food at reasonable prices, in a simple garden-like space with sandy floors, plastic chairs and a few potted plants. Dishes are fresh and carefully prepared, including spicy masala dosa and a deliciously light off-menu pumpkin-and-spinach curry.

Fusion MULTICUISINE $$
(www.thebeachhotel-kovalam.com; Beach Hotel II, Lighthouse Beach; mains ₹220-550; ☺7.30am-10.30pm; ☎) With its imaginative East-meets-West menu and stylish terrace vibe, the restaurant at Beach Hotel II (p267) is one of Lighthouse Beach's top dining experiences, rustling up Continental favourites, Asian fusion such as chilli-pesto pasta, and interesting seafood numbers like lobster steamed in vodka. It's also good for breakfast: French-press coffee, herbal teas and muesli-and-fruit bowls overlooking beachfront palms.

Waves Restaurant & German Bakery INTERNATIONAL $$
(www.thebeachhotel-kovalam.com; Beach Hotel, Lighthouse Beach; mains ₹220-550; ☺7.30am-11pm; ☎) The burnt-orange balcony, ambient soundtrack, sea views and a wide-roaming, well-executed menu keep Waves – atop

WORTH A TRIP

AYURVEDIC RESORTS NEAR KOVALAM

Between Kovalam and Poovar, amid seemingly endless swaying palms, laid-back village life and some empty golden-sand beaches, are a string of upmarket ayurvedic resorts designed for those serious about fully immersing themselves in ayurveda. They're all 6km to 10km southeast of Kovalam; taxis cost ₹250 to ₹450.

Niraamaya Retreats Surya Samudra (☎0471-2267333, 8045104510; www.niraamaya. in; Pulinkudi; r incl breakfast ₹18,990-40,700; ❄☎☲) Built into natural groves of mango, banana and banyan trees and offering A-list-style seclusion, glammed-up traditional Keralan homes, a beachside infinity pool and a renowned ayurvedic spa.

Dr Franklin's Panchakarma Institute (☎0471-2480870; www.dr-franklin.com; Chowara; incl meals & treatments with AC s ₹9620-10,260, d ₹17,230-17,630, without AC s ₹8330-9620, d ₹14,660-17,230; ☎☲) A friendly, reputable, more affordable alternative, with yoga, personalised ayurveda packages and tidy rooms and cottages.

Bethsaida Hermitage (☎0471-2267554; www.bethsaidahermitage.com; Mulloor, Pulinkudi; s/d incl meals with AC from ₹10,280/11,310, without AC from ₹6240/7580; ❄☎☲) Charitable Bethsaida is a smart beachside escape with sculpted gardens, hammocks, two sea-view pools, yoga and professional ayurvedic treatments.

Somatheeram (☎0471-2268101; https://somatheeram.in; Chowara; with AC s ₹17,900-20,550, d ₹19,900-22,950, without AC s ₹6820-15,330, d ₹7540-17,000; ❄☎☲) 🌿 One of the area's original retreats, award-winning Somatheeram provides ayurveda, yoga, and comfortable red-brick or wooden rooms and cottages.

Beach Hotel (p269) – busy with foreigners. It doubles as the German Bakery, a great spot for breakfast with fresh bread, croissants, pastries and French-press coffee, while dinner turns up Thai curries, German sausages, Indian snacks, pizza, pasta and seafood. There's a small bookshop attached.

Suprabhatham   KERALAN $$
(☎9947209756; meals ₹120-250; ⊙7am-11pm; ☎) It doesn't look like much, but this rustic pure-veg courtyard restaurant hidden back from Lighthouse Beach dishes up excellent Keralan-style cooking, vegetarian thalis and fresh fruit juices. It's all fresh and full of flavour, and local breakfasts of masala dosa, *puttu* and coconut *uttapam* (rice pancake) are available too.

Malabar Cafe   INDIAN $$
(Lighthouse Beach; mains ₹110-450; ⊙7.30am-11pm; ☎) The busy red-cloth tables tell a story: attentive service, candlelight at night and views through pot plants to the crashing waves set the tone for Malabar's tasty India-wide cooking, including nightly fresh-seafood displays and tandoori faves such as paneer tikka. One of the more popular spots along the Lighthouse Beach strip.

Curry Leaf   MULTICUISINE $$
(☎9746430087; Samudra Beach; mains ₹100-600; ⊙8am-11pm) On a gently sloping hillside above Samudra Beach, this two-storey restaurant boasts enviable ocean and sunset views beyond slender palms, while keen staff deliver fresh seafood, Continental dishes and tandoori deliciousness. It's well signposted from the beach, up a few stairs, and the uncrowded location is part of the charm.

A Beach Cafe   INTERNATIONAL $$
(Lighthouse Beach; mains ₹150-450; ⊙8am-10pm; ☎) An easy-going balcony restaurant overlooking Lighthouse Beach, the Indian-Swedish-operated ABC does a wide-ranging global menu of omelettes, soups, veg curries, fresh seafood and coconut-pomegranate pancakes, using local organic produce wherever possible, as well as good coffee infused with Kerala-sourced beans.

★ Bait   SEAFOOD $$$
(☎0471-6613000; https://taj.tajhotels.com; Taj Green Cove, GV Raja Vattapara Rd, Samudra Beach; mains ₹360-990; ⊙12.30-10.30pm) Designed as an upmarket alfresco beach shack, the fabulous seafood restaurant at the Taj Green Cove (p269) fronts the sea, with waves and palms on one side and chefs in a semi-open kitchen on the other. Seafood and spicy preparations are as glorious as the blazing sunsets, including delicious fresh fish or tofu steak soaked in 'Kerala coast' spices, with Maharashtrian Sula wines.

Terrace Restaurant
INTERNATIONAL $$$

(📞0471-3051234; www.theleela.com; Leela, Samudra Beach; mains ₹550-850; ⊙7-10.30am, 12.30-3pm & 7-11pm) One of Kovalam's most scenic (and expensive) restaurants, overlooking the turquoise-tinted infinity pool at the top-end clifftop Leela (p269). The elegant menu plays with Indian and international flavours; tempting bites range from chilli-infused pasta to Keralan specialities like Malabar prawn curry or coconut-laced *pachakkari* (vegetable stew). Or just drop in for a spiced cocktail (₹450 to ₹800) as the sun sets.

❶ Information

ATMs cluster along Kovalam Beach Rd.
Tourist office (📞0471-2480085; Kovalam Beach Rd; ⊙9.30am-5pm Mon-Sat)
Upasana Clinic (📞0471-2480632)

❶ Getting There & Around

BUS

Buses use the unofficial bus stand outside the entrance to the Leela resort; all buses pass through Kovalam Junction, 2km north of Lighthouse Beach. Buses run to Trivandrum (₹16, 30 minutes) every 15 minutes from 6am to 9pm, with air-con buses (₹40) hourly.

For northbound onward travel, including to Varkala, and (illogically) for Kanyakumari, change in Trivandrum.

MOTORCYCLE, TAXI & AUTORICKSHAW

Taxis between Trivandrum and Kovalam cost ₹500; autorickshaws charge ₹350. Taxis to Kanyakumari are ₹4000 and to Varkala ₹2800. Short autorickshaw hops cost ₹50.

K Tours & Travel (📞8089493376; peter sheeba@yahoo.com; NUP Beach Rd; per day scooters/Enfields from ₹400/600; ⊙9am-late Mon-Sat, reduced hours Sun) rents out scooters and Enfields.

Varkala

📞0470 / POP 40,050

Perched almost perilously along the edge of majestic 15m-high red laterite cliffs, 50km northwest of Trivandrum, Varkala has a naturally beautiful setting that has allowed it to steadily grow into Kerala's most popular backpacker hang-out. A small strand of golden beach nuzzles Varkala's North Cliff area, where restaurants play innocuous world music and shops sell elephant-stamped trousers, silver jewellery and cotton yoga-mat bags. While it's certainly on the beaten track and the sales pitch can

be tiring, it's still a great place to watch days slowly turn into weeks, and it's easy to escape the crowds further north or south where beaches are cleaner and quieter.

And despite its traveller vibe, Varkala remains essentially an important temple town: the main Papanasham Beach is a holy Hindu spot, overlooked by the ancient Janardhana Temple. About 2km east of here is busy Varkala town.

◉ Sights

Janardhana Temple
HINDU TEMPLE

(Temple Junction; ⊙4am-noon & 5-8pm) Varkala is a temple town and the Janardhana Temple, dedicated to Vishnu, is the main event – with its roots dating back to the 13th century, this technicolour Hindu spectacle hovers above Beach Rd, reached by steep stone staircases. Though the main shrine is closed to non-Hindus, visitors are welcome to wander the grounds, home to a huge banyan tree, a Tamil-style *mandapa* (pillared pavilion) with granite columns, and shrines to Ayyappan, Hanuman and other Hindu deities.

Papanasham Beach
BEACH

Ringed by rust-red cliffs, Varkala's main beach is a holy spot for Hindus, who for centuries have made offerings for passed loves ones and washed away worldly sins (assisted by priests) near the junction with Beach Rd. Swimmers and sunbathers congregate towards its northern end.

Black Beach
BEACH

(Thiruvambady Beach) A sandy little blonde-and-black beach just north of Varkala's North Cliff.

Odayam Beach
BEACH

This gold-hued stretch of sand, around 1km north of the North Cliff, makes a peaceful alternative to Varkala's main beach.

Kappil Beach
BEACH

About 8km north of Varkala, this long, beautiful and (so far) undeveloped stretch of golden sand is the beginning of a mini network of backwaters. A two-hour seaside walk leads here along a gently undulating path from Varkala's North Cliff, passing a subtly changing beach landscape, including Odayam Beach and the fishing village of Edava.

Sivagiri Mutt
ASHRAM

(📞0470-2602807; ⊙dawn-dusk) Just east of central Varkala, Sivagiri Mutt is the headquarters of the Shri Narayana Dharma

Varkala

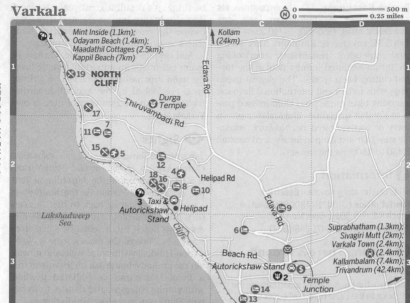

Varkala

◉ Sights
1 Black Beach...A1
2 Janardhana Temple...........................C3
3 Papanasham Beach...........................B2

✦ Activities, Courses & Tours
4 AyurSoul..B2
5 Haridas Yoga.......................................B2
  Soul & Surf ....(see 13)

🛏 Sleeping
6 Gateway Hotel Janardhanapuram.......C3
7 InDa Hotel..A2
8 Jicky's Nest...B2

9 Kaiya House...C2
10 Lost Hostel..B2
11 Mad About Coco................................A2
12 Mango Villa...B2
13 Soul & Surf...C3
14 Villa Jacaranda..................................C3

✖ Eating
15 ABBA...A2
16 Coffee Temple...................................B2
17 Darjeeling Cafe..................................A1
18 God's Own Country Kitchen................B2
  Soul Food Cafe ....(see 13)
19 Trattorias..A1

Sanghom Trust, devoted to Shri Narayana Guru (1855–1928), Kerala's most prominent guru and a leading social reformer. It's a major pilgrimage site, with devotees recognisable by their distinctive yellow clothing.

Ponnumthuruthu (Golden) Island
ISLAND
(boat ride 2/3/4 people ₹600/700/800, island admission per person ₹50; ⊙6am-6pm) Around 10km south of Varkala, this acacia-filled island in the middle of a backwater lake conceals a Shiva-Parvati Hindu temple also known as the Golden Temple. The vibrantly coloured, century-old shrine is usually

closed to non-Hindus, but the main reason to venture here is the scenic punt-powered boat ride to and around the island. Allow 1½ hours round trip; autorickshaws from Varkala cost ₹600 with waiting time.

🏃 Activities

Yoga (₹350 to ₹550) is offered *everywhere;* reliable options include **Haridas Yoga** (☑ 9846374231; www.pranayogavidya.com; Hotel Green Palace, North Cliff; classes ₹350; ⊙8am & 4.30pm late Aug–mid-May), Soul & Surf and Mad About Coco.

Surfboards (from ₹250) and boogie boards (₹300) can be hired along the beach and cliffs; be wary of strong currents. Surfing, kayaking, stand-up paddleboarding and SUP yoga sessions are also popular.

Soul & Surf
SURFING, YOGA

(☑9961711099; www.soulandsurf.com; South Cliff; surf lessons ₹2500, board rental half/full day ₹900/1700, yoga ₹550-1000; ☺Oct-Apr) 🍴 This UK-based outfit organises surfing trips and yoga retreats in season, with stylish accommodation (p274) and a wonderful, laid-back garden cafe (p275) gracing its South Cliff grounds. The on-the-ball international team also offers 1½-hour surf lessons (though nonguest spaces are limited) and board rental, while drop-in rooftop yoga sessions range from vinyasa to candlelight yin meditation.

AyurSoul
MASSAGE

(☑9946645599; www.ayursoulindia.com; Helipad Rd, North Cliff; massage ₹1000-3000; ☺7.30am-7.30pm) A professional, in-demand ayurveda centre, 300m inland from the helipad. Following a doctor consultation, choose from ayurvedic classics or Western-style spa treatments, all using oils made in-house. Also offers extended packages and accommodation.

Can Fly
PARAGLIDING, WATERSPORTS

(☑9048795781; www.canflyadventure.com; 20min flight ₹3800) This experienced adventure operator offers tandem paragliding from the North Cliff helipad, as well as stand-up paddleboarding and kayaking trips (₹1900 to ₹2200). Activities run from October to May, though you may be able to rent kayaks and paddleboards (₹600) throughout the low season.

🛏 Sleeping

Most places to stay are along and just back from Varkala's North Cliff, around the southern cliffs and on tranquil, less-developed Odayam Beach. Prices skyrocket from mid-December to mid-January, when you'll want to book ahead.

Jicky's Nest
GUESTHOUSE $

(☑0470-2606994, 9846179325; jickys2002@ yahoo.co.in; off Helipad Rd; r ₹750-1500, AC cottage ₹2500-3000; ❄🌐) In the palm groves just back from the cliffs, friendly family-run Jicky's has blossomed into several buildings offering plenty of choice for travellers. Rooms in the main whitewashed building are fresh, with sit-out spaces; nearby are a few charming octagonal cottages and some larger air-con rooms. The most char-

acterful rooms are adorned with colourful hand-painted murals of birds and flowers.

Lost Hostel
HOSTEL $

(☑7012416343; www.thelosthostels.com; off Helipad Rd; dm with AC ₹600-900, without AC ₹500-700, r ₹1100-2200; ❄🌐) Six-person, locker-equipped en suite dorms (some are air-conditioned) and smartish private doubles with simple murals are the draw at this social budget hang-out hidden (but well signposted!) down a lane just inland from the helipad. Hammocks dot the front garden, there's a communal kitchen plus a lounge with books and games, and enthusiastic staff provide local information and rent out bikes (₹100).

★Kaiya House
GUESTHOUSE $$

(☑9746126909; www.kaiyahouse.com; Edava Rd; incl breakfast r with/without AC ₹3300/2800; ❄🌐) 🍴 Not your typical Varkala address, this gorgeously original hideaway is packed with art and antiques and topped by a breezy roof terrace. The five rooms are thoughtfully themed (African, Indian, Chinese, Japanese, English): four-poster beds, wooden carvings, embroidered wall hangings. American owner Debra organises beach clean-ups and welcomes guests with tea, tips, water refills, yoga mats and free walking tours.

InDa Hotel
GUESTHOUSE $$

(☑7025029861; https://inda-in.book.direct; North Cliff, Kurakkanni; incl breakfast s ₹2070-4810, d ₹2130-5020; 🌐) Tucked away behind the North Cliff, this warm, highly regarded guesthouse throws boutique style into its impeccably kept gleaming-white rooms and six individual cottages, scattered across a garden with a leafy lounge area. Open-brick walls meet rattan chairs, floral-print sheets and the odd mural, and the health-oriented cafe specialises in salads, wraps and Buddha bowls (dishes ₹180 to ₹350).

Mad About Coco
GUESTHOUSE $$

(☑9061932651; www.madaboutcocovarkala.com; North Cliff; r with AC ₹3000-5000, without AC

SLEEPING PRICE RANGES

The following price ranges refer to a double room with bathroom in Kerala:

$ less than ₹1200

$$ ₹1200–₹5000

$$$ more than ₹5000

₹2000-3000; ❋🛜) 🍃 Comprising two revamped houses huddled back from the North Cliff, German-run MAC fuses a sociable traveller/yogi vibe with uncluttered rooms jazzed up by colour feature walls and terraces with lounge corners or swing chairs. The boutique-inspired cafe serves healthy bites (overnight oats, fruit bowls, wholemeal French toast) and free water refills, and there's twice-daily rooftop yoga in season.

Mango Villa
GUESTHOUSE $$
(📞9995040610; www.facebook.com/mangovilla varkala; North Cliff; r with AC ₹3000, without AC ₹900-1200; ❋🛜) Hidden just inland from the southern end of the North Cliff, the Belgian-Indian-run Mango Villa lives up to its alluring name with six airy, spotless, contemporary rooms decked out with bamboo furniture, smart desks, original artwork and, for some, private balconies. There's also a handful of comfy, similarly styled, coldwater 'budget' rooms.

Maadathil Cottages
COTTAGE $$
(📞9746113495; www.maadathilcottages.com; Manthara Temple Rd, Odayam Beach; r incl breakfast ₹1900-5000; ❋🛜) With an excellent location on tranquil Odayam Beach, this cluster of delightful beachfront cottages is designed in traditional Kerala style, flaunting heritage furniture, tiled roofs and wood-carved doors alongside large beds and modern bathrooms. All rooms enjoy sea views from spacious private balconies and some are enlivened by vibrant hand-painted exterior murals.

Villa Jacaranda
GUESTHOUSE $$$
(📞0470-2610296; www.villa-jacaranda.biz; Temple Rd West; r incl breakfast ₹7900-10,000; ❋🛜) This intimate, romantic and elegantly understated boutiquey retreat just inland from southern Papanasham Beach revolves around four bright, spacious rooms in a beautiful two-storey house wrapped in greenery. Each room has a terrace (where delicious homecooked breakfasts are served) and is styled with a chic blend of minimalist modern design and antique touches.

Soul & Surf
GUESTHOUSE $$$
(📞9961711099; www.soulandsurf.com; South Cliff; incl breakfast s ₹4320-6760, d ₹7320-12,200; ⊙Oct-Apr; ❋🛜) 🍃 Bold pink and turquoise design meets a homely, social feel at this boutiqueified British-run yoga and surf retreat (p273) spread across lush gardens atop the South Cliff, where rooms, yoga class-

es and the wonderful cafe are open to all. Along with the main guesthouse (which has contemporary top-tier rooms with sea-view terraces), there are smaller rooms in a traditional 150-year-old house opposite.

Mint Inside
GUESTHOUSE $$$
(📞Whatsapp 7356979929; www.mint-inside. com; Odayam Beach; incl breakfast s ₹800-1600, d ₹2450-5500; ❋🛜) Chicly stripped-back rooms and cottages, sharp service and hanging chairs and hammocks greet you at this fresh and welcome arrival on Varkala's growing boutique-guesthouse scene. Expect tasteful grey-and-white styling, concrete bed frames, polished bathrooms, touches of bamboo and a roof terrace. The four seafacing rooms have air-con and private terraces, and Odayam Beach is a few minutes' walk away.

Gateway Hotel Janardhanapuram
HOTEL $$$
(📞0470-6673300; https://gateway.tajhotels.com; r incl breakfast from ₹11,520; ❋🛜🏊) Varkala's flashiest hotel, the hillside Taj-Group Gateway is all gleaming linen and mocha cushions in smart contemporary rooms overlooking manicured gardens; the best boudoirs have sea views and private balconies. There's a fantastic pool overlooking the beach beyond a sea of palms, along with a bar and a restaurant (though overall it feels a little tired).

🍴 Eating & Drinking

Some of the clifftop 'shacks' are now impressive multilevel hang-outs with a growing health and environmental awareness.

Suprabhatham
SOUTH INDIAN $
(📞0470-2606697; www.suprabhathamrestaurant. com; Maithanam, Varkala Town; dishes ₹30-95; ⊙7am-9.30pm) Keralan-style meals, masala dosa and *uttapam* topped with onion, coconut or tomato are the expertly spiced stars at this bustling pure-veg South Indian eatery squirrelled away in Varkala town.

Darjeeling Cafe
INTERNATIONAL $$
(www.facebook.com/darjeelingcafevarkala; North Cliff; mains ₹140-450; ⊙7am-11pm) With giant dreamcatchers and tiered candlelit tables strewn with flower petals, Darjeeling is always packed with travellers. Snappy, cheerful service complements cocktails (₹250; with metallic straws), fresh juices, good coffee and an alluring global menu: chapati rolls, smoothie bowls, masala dosa,

KERALA'S DRY EXPERIMENT

In 2017 Kerala's left-wing coalition government reversed the controversial 2014 alcohol ban implemented by the then Congress-led government, which was at the time the first step in a 10-year move towards total prohibition. The 2014 ruling saw more than 700 bars promptly shut down (though most eventually reopened as beer and wine parlours); only five-star hotels could have bars and spirits were only available from government liquor shops.

At the time of writing, however, bars can now stay open until 11pm, three- and four-star hotels can serve liquor, two-star hotels can have beer parlours and new bars are able to apply for liquor licenses, though the first day of each month remains a dry day across the state.

Kerala's per capita alcohol consumption is estimated at 8.3L – double the national average, and the highest in the country.

pan-Indian curries, banana-leaf fish, and enormous platters of paneer or fish tikka with chips and salad.

Coffee Temple
INTERNATIONAL $$

(North Cliff; mains ₹100-450; ⊘6.30am-10pm; 🕿) 🖉 At the southern end of the North Cliff trail, this leafy terrace cafe-restaurant remains a firm favourite for your morning coffee fix. Freshly ground beans accompany free water refills and breakfasts of muesli bowls, French toast, smashed avocado, just-squeezed juices and fresh brown bread. The globetrotting menu also features crepes, pastas and Mexican burritos, plus an excellent vegan selection.

ABBA
INTERNATIONAL $$

(www.abbarestaurant.tk; Hotel Green Palace, North Cliff; mains ₹150-400; ⊘7am-11pm; 🕿) Halfway along the North Cliff, this relaxed and welcoming terrace spot with a handy book exchange remains firmly popular for its inventive salads (perhaps carrot, beetroot and mint, or with lashings of halloumi) and world-roaming breakfasts centred on just-baked bread from the attached bakery, but also whips up pastas, pizzas, *momos* (Tibetan dumplings), burgers, curries, fresh seafood and cocktails (₹220 to ₹300).

God's Own Country Kitchen
MULTICUISINE $$

(North Cliff; mains ₹150-450; ⊘8am-11pm; 🕿) This fun place doesn't really need to play on the Kerala Tourism tagline – the Indian-international food is good (including spiced fish wrapped in banana leaf), there's a great little upper-floor deck and live music sometimes happens in season.

Trattorias
MULTICUISINE $$

(North Cliff; mains ₹130-450; ⊘7am-10.30pm; 🕿) Trattorias sounds Italian and does indeed rustle up decent pastas, pizzas and European breakfasts, but the menu is equally pan-Asian and Indian (with seafood platters and Keralan fish dishes) and the food consistently good. This was one of the original places in Varkala with an Italian coffee machine; the sea-facing terrace is cosy and the team attentive.

★Soul Food Cafe
INTERNATIONAL $$$

(📞9961711099; www.soulandsurf.com; Soul & Surf, South Cliff; mains ₹300-480; ⊘9-11am, 1-4pm & 6.30-9pm Mon-Sat, 9-11am & 1-4pm Sun Oct-Apr; 🕿) 🖉 Fresh local ingredients fuel inspired, artfully prepared dishes at the beautifully located clifftop garden cafe at Soul & Surf (p273). Here zingy mezze platters arrive with mini pappadams and slithers of chapati, coffee is sourced from South India's Western Ghats, and Kerala favourites on the short-but-sweet menu include *meen pollichathu* (steamed banana-leaf fish). It's usually busy with yogis and surfers. Free water refills.

❶ Information

DANGERS & ANNOYANCES

Varkala's beaches have strong currents; during the monsoon the beach all but disappears, and the cliffs are slowly being eroded. Take care walking on the cliff path, especially at night – some of it is unfenced and slippery.

The commission racket is alive and well – ensure your driver takes you to the accommodation you've asked for.

Many female travellers wear bikinis and swimsuits on the beaches here, though bear in mind that you may feel uncomfortably exposed to stares. Wearing a sarong when out of the water helps avoid offending local sensibilities. Dress conservatively if going into Varkala town or to the Janardhana Temple.

ℹ️ Getting There & Away

Varkala's main bus stand is buried in Varkala town, opposite the train station; a handful of daily buses run to/from Trivandrum (₹65, 1½ to two hours) and Kollam (₹45, one hour), a few of them via Temple Junction. Schedules are erratic, so it's usually easier to take the train.

Taxis go to Kollam (₹1200), Trivandrum (₹1500) and Kovalam (₹1900); autorickshaws charge ₹800, ₹1100 and ₹1400 respectively.

There are frequent local and express trains to Trivandrum (2nd class/sleeper/3AC ₹45/140/495, one to 1½ hours) and Kollam (₹45/140/495, 25 minutes to 1¼ hours), plus six daily services to Alleppey (₹65/140/495, two hours).

ℹ️ Getting Around

Varkala beach is 3km west of Varkala Sivagiri train station; autorickshaws run to/from Temple Junction for ₹80 and North Cliff for ₹100. Local buses travel regularly between the train station and Temple Junction (₹8 to ₹10) from 6am to 7.30pm.

A few places along the cliff hire out scooters and motorbikes for ₹300 to ₹450 per day.

Kollam (Quilon)

📞 0474 / POP 348,660

One of the oldest ports in the Arabian Sea, Kollam was once a major commercial hub that saw Roman, Arab, Chinese and later Portuguese, Dutch and British traders jostle into town – eager to get their hands on spices and the region's cashew crops. Today the town marks the southern approach to Kerala's backwaters and one end of the popular backwater ferry trip to Alleppey. Its centre and bazaar are hectic, but surrounding them are the calm waterways of Ashtamudi Lake, fringed with coconut palms, cashew plantations and traditional villages – making Kollam a great place to get a feel for the backwaters (with fewer crowds than Alleppey) and, along with nearby Munroe Island, an increasingly popular overnight stop for travellers.

👁 Sights & Activities

Kollam Beach is 2km south of town but there are better stretches of sand further south at Eravipuram and Mayyanad. There's a rowdy fish market and harbour north of Kollam's beach.

Thangassery AREA

Flanking the north end of the harbour, west of Kollam centre, Thangassery was once an important Portuguese, then Dutch and finally British trading post. You can still see the remains of the 1519 Portuguese-era Fort Thomas, next to the early-20th-century lighthouse (Indian/foreigner ₹20/50, camera ₹10; ⊙10am-1pm & 2-6pm Tue-Sun).

★ **Munroe Island Cruise** BOATING

(tours per person ₹600-750) Excellent tours through the canals of quiet Munroe Island are organised by Kollam's DTPC (p278) and a number of private local operators, including Ashtamudi Villas and Munroe Island Backwaters Homestay. Usually starting at 9am or 2pm, the popular trips begin 15km north of Kollam, from where you take a leisurely three-hour punted canoe ride through a network of canals.

On the canals you can observe daily village life, see *kettuvallam* (rice barge) construction, toddy (palm beer) tapping, coir-making and prawn and fish farming, and do some birdwatching on spice-garden visits. Development and tourism have increased on Munroe Island in recent years, but it's still a pleasant place to explore.

Houseboat Cruises BOATING

(day/overnight cruise from ₹6490/7090) Kollam has far fewer houseboats than Alleppey, which means its surrounding waters remain slightly less touristed. The DTPC (p278) organises various houseboat day-cruise packages, along with overnight stays and trips from Kollam to Alleppey (from ₹32,000). A couple of private operators, also based at the jetty, offer similar itineraries.

🎉 Festivals & Events

Kollam Pooram CULTURAL

(Asramam Shri Krishna Swami Temple; ⊙Apr) A 10-day Kollam festival with nightly Kathakali performances and a procession of 30 to 40 ornamented elephants.

President's Trophy Boat Race SPORTS

(⊙1 Nov) The most prestigious boat regatta in the Kollam region, on Ashtamudi Lake.

🛏 Sleeping & Eating

Munroe Island Backwaters Homestay HOMESTAY $

(📞9048176186; www.facebook.com/Munroel slandBackwatersHomestay; Chittamula Rd, Munroe

Kollam (Quilon)

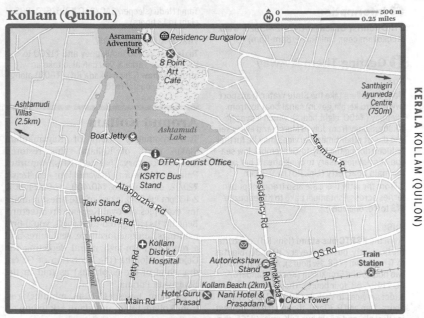

Asramam Adventure Park

Residency Bungalow

8 Point Art Cafe

Ashtamudi Villas (2.5km)

Boat Jetty

Ashtamudi Lake

Santhigiri Ayurveda Centre (750m)

Asramam Rd

DTPC Tourist Office

KSRTC Bus Stand

Alappuzha Rd

Taxi Stand

Hospital Rd

Residency Rd

Kollam Canal

Kollam District Hospital

Jetty Rd

Autorickshaw Stand

Chinnakkada Rd

QS Rd

Train Station

Kollam Beach (2km)

Hotel Guru Prasad

Main Rd

Nani Hotel & Prasadam

Clock Tower

500 m
0.25 miles

Island; r incl breakfast ₹1200-1500; 🛜) Hidden away in the backwaters of Munroe Island, 16km north of Kollam, this cheery hammock-strewn homestay is popular with travellers for its low-key village setting and warm family feel. There are three colourful cottages in Kerala style, plus three contemporary rooms upstairs overlooking a loungey terrace. Owner Vijeesh runs canoe tours (₹450 to ₹500) and has kayaks and bicycles to borrow.

★ **Ashtamudi Villas** GUESTHOUSE $$
(📞9847132449, 0474-2706090; www.ashtamudi villas.com; near Kadavoor Church, Mathilil; r ₹1000-3000; 🛜) 🅿 These charming lakeside cottages are easily the best choice for a relaxing, affordable stay in Kollam. Host Prabhath Joseph offers a warm welcome, with ecofriendly architectural design (solar power, rainwater harvesting), colourful decor, gleaming bathrooms, hammocks swinging between palms, a library of Kerala books, tasty meals, and free kayaks and yoga mats. Munroe Island tours are also available.

Nani Hotel BUSINESS HOTEL $$
(📞9207736707; www.hotelnani.com; Chinnakkada Rd; incl breakfast r ₹2520-3840, ste ₹4480; ✳@🛜) Built by a cashew magnate and with on-the-ball staff, this boutique-inspired busi-

ness hotel is a welcome surprise in Kollam's chaotic centre. The sleek architecture mixes traditional Keralan elements and modern lines. Even the standard rooms come with TV, feathery pillows and sumptuous bathrooms, and there's an elegant multicuisine restaurant, **Prasadam** (📞920773670; mains ₹160-280; ⊙7-10am, noon-3pm & 7-10pm).

8 Point Art Cafe CAFE $
(📞0474-2970256; www.facebook.com/8pointart cafe; Asramam; mains ₹90-130; ⊙11am-9.30pm) On the fun side of Ashtamudi Lake, 1km north of the jetty, this creative cafe in a restored heritage building with a breezy verandah and a leafy garden is part local art gallery, part fashionable hang-out. Come for the changing free exhibitions, good coffee, small library, and short but thoughtfully prepped menu of sandwiches, burgers and cakes.

Hotel Guru Prasad SOUTH INDIAN $
(Main Rd; dishes ₹12-45; ⊙7am-9pm) Tucked into a neatly repurposed red-and-white colonial-style building, in the heart of town, this busy all-veg spot draws the crowds with its cheap thalis, dosa (savoury crepe), *vada* (doughnut-shaped deep-fried lentil savoury), *idli* (spongy, round, fermented rice cake) and other snacks.

ℹ Information

DTPC Tourist Office (☑ 0474-2745625; www.
dtpckollam.com; Link Rd; ☺8am-5pm)

ℹ Getting There & Away

BOAT

Many travellers take the State Water Transport
(www.swtd.kerala.gov.in) canal boat to/from
Alleppey (₹400, eight hours), which leaves at
10.30am daily from July to March and every second day at other times. Services may be further
reduced during the May-to-September low season. It's not necessary to book ahead, but be at
the **main boat jetty** (Link Rd) by 9.30am.

From the jetty there are also frequent public
ferries across Ashtamudi Lake to Kureepuzha
(₹3 to ₹6, one hour).

BUS

From the **KSRTC bus stand** (Link Rd), opposite
the boat jetty, buses run every 20 or 30 minutes
to Trivandrum (₹68, 1½ hours), Alleppey (₹80,
two hours) and Ernakulam (Kochi; standard/
AC ₹140/258, four hours). There are two daily
direct services to Varkala (₹90 to ₹130, 1½
hours, 7am and 9.30am), though trains are best
for Varkala, and a 5am bus to Kumily (₹165, five
hours).

TRAIN

There are frequent express trains to Ernakulam
(sleeper/3AC ₹140/495, 2½ to 3½ hours, 23 daily), some via Alleppey (₹140/495, 1½ hours), and
Trivandrum (₹140/495, 1½ to 2½ hours, 25 daily), via Varkala (₹140/495, 30 minutes). Trains
also run four times daily to/from Madurai in

Tamil Nadu (sleeper/3AC/2AC ₹315/620/885,
eight to 13 hours).

TAXI & AUTORICKSHAW

Taxis cost ₹2200 to Alleppey and ₹1200 to
Varkala. For Varkala, you can also take an
autorickshaw (Chinnakkada Rd) (₹800) along
the scenic coastal road.

Around Kollam

Two kilometres south of Kayamkulam
(35km north of Kollam), this restored
mid-18th-century palace, **Krishnapuram
Palace Museum** (Kayamkulam; adult/child
₹20/12, camera/video ₹40/400; ☺9am-1pm &
2-4.30pm Tue-Sun), is one of the finest remaining examples of royal Keralan architecture.
Beneath its gabled red-tiled roofs, you'll find
paintings, antique furniture, sculptures and
a renowned 3m-high mural depicting the
Gajendra Moksha (the liberation of Gajendra, chief of the elephants) as told in the
Bhagavata Puraṇa.

Frequent buses (₹50, 45 minutes) run
from Kollam to Kayamkulam; ask to hop off
on the main road near the palace.

Alappuzha (Alleppey)

☑ 0477 / POP 174,180

Alappuzha – most still call it Alleppey – is
the hub of Kerala's backwaters, home to a
vast network of waterways, over a thousand
houseboats and an important coir industry.

MATHA AMRITHANANDAMAYI MISSION

The incongruously salmon-pink **Matha Amrithanandamayi Mission** (☑ 0476-2897578,
9072580923; www.amritapuri.org; Amrithapuri), 30km northwest of Kollam (Quilon), is the
famous ashram of one of India's few female gurus, Amrithanandamayi, also known as
Amma (Mother) or 'The Hugging Mother' because of the *darshan* (audience) she offers,
often hugging thousands of people in marathon all-night sessions. The ashram runs official tours at 5pm daily (check details online or download the Amma app).

It's a huge complex, with about 3500 people living here permanently – monks, nuns,
students and families, both Indian and foreign. It offers food, ayurvedic treatments, and
a daily schedule of yoga, meditation and *darshan*. Amma herself travels for much of the
year (her schedule is online); a busy time of year at the ashram is around Amma's birthday on 27 September.

Visitors should dress conservatively and there is a strict code of behaviour. With prior
arrangement – register online – you can stay at the ashram in a triple room for ₹250 per
person or a single for ₹500 (including simple vegetarian meals).

Since the ashram is on the main canal between Kollam and Alappuzha (Alleppey),
many travellers break the popular ferry ride (p286) by getting off here, staying a day or
two, then picking up another cruise. Alternatively, cross the canal via pedestrian bridge to
Vallickavu and grab a rickshaw 10km south to Karunagappally or 12km north to Kayamkulam (around ₹200), from where you can catch onward buses or trains.

Wandering around the small but chaotic city centre, with its modest grid of canals, you'd be hard-pressed to agree with the 'Venice of the East' tag, and, sadly, at research time a hulking new highway flyover was marring the beauty of Alleppey's popular beach. But head out towards the backwaters and Alleppey becomes graceful and greenery-fringed, disappearing into a watery world of villages, punted canoes, toddy shops and, of course, houseboats. Floating along and gazing over paddy fields of succulent green, curvaceous rice barges and village life along the banks is one of Kerala's most mesmerisingly beautiful and relaxing experiences.

Kerala's main backwaters stretch north, east and south of Alleppey, while Vembanad Lake, Kerala's largest, reaches all the way north to Kochi.

◉ Sights & Activities

RKK Memorial Museum   MUSEUM
(☑0477-2242923; www.rkkmuseum.com; NH47; Indian/foreigner ₹150/350; ⊙9am-5pm Tue-Sun) In a grand building fronted by Greco-Roman columns, this intriguing museum houses a priceless, astonishing collection of crystal, porcelain, South Indian antiques, furniture, artworks and (sadly) ivory from the personal family collection of wealthy local businessman Revi Karuna Karan. It was created by his wife Betty as a memorial after he passed away in 2003.

Alleppey Beach   BEACH
Alleppey's main beach is 2km west of the city centre; swimming is fraught due to strong currents, but the sunsets are good and there are a few places for a drink or a snack. Unfortunately, at research time, the setting was being slightly ruined by the construction of an enormous flyover road right by the beach.

Alleppey Lighthouse   LIGHTHOUSE
(Indian/foreigner ₹20/50, camera ₹10; ⊙9-11.45am & 2-5.30pm Tue-Sun) A few blocks back from the beach, the candy-striped 1862 lighthouse contains a small museum with an original oil lamp, but is best visited for the 360-degree views of a surprisingly green Alleppey from the top of its spiralling staircase.

Kerala Kayaking   KAYAKING
(☑9846585674, 8547487701; www.keralakayaking.com; Vazhicherry Bridge, VCNB Rd; per person 4/7/10hr ₹1500/3000/4500) Alleppey's original and best kayaking outfit. The young crew offers excellent guided kayaking trips through narrow backwater canals. Paddles in single or double kayaks include a support boat and motorboat transport to your starting point. There are four-hour morning and afternoon trips and seven- or 10-hour day trips, as well as multiday village tours (from ₹13,000 per two people).

Houseboat Dock   BOATING
(☑9400051796; dtpcalpy@yahoo.com; off Punnamada Rd; ⊙prepaid counter 9.30am-4.30pm) Dozens of houseboats gather at Alleppey's main dock. There's a government-run prepaid counter with 'official' posted prices, starting at ₹7000 for two people and up to ₹34,000 for a seven-berth boat (reduced rates June to October), though even these fluctuate with demand. Note that some houseboats dock elsewhere and the most reputable ones often get booked up in advance.

☞ Tours

Any guesthouse, hotel or travel agent, plus the DTPC (p283), can and will arrange canoe or houseboat tours of the backwaters.

Kashmiri-style *shikaras* (covered boats) gather along the North Canal on the road to the houseboat dock; they charge around ₹400 per hour for motorised canal and backwater trips. Punt-powered dugout canoes are slower but more ecofriendly; most tours require four to five hours, with village visits, walks and a stop at a toddy bar; full-day tours cost around ₹700 to ₹900.

✵ Festivals & Events

Nehru Trophy Boat Race   SPORTS
(www.nehrutrophy.nic.in; tickets ₹100-3000; ⊙Aug) The most renowned and fiercely contested of Kerala's boat-race regattas, held annually on the second Saturday of August since 1954. Thousands of people, many aboard houseboats, gather around the starting and finishing points on Alleppey's Punnamada Lake to watch snake boats with up to 100 rowers battle it out.

🛏 Sleeping

Alleppey has some of Kerala's most charming and best-value accommodation, particularly when it comes to homestays and backpacker hostels. Homestays are also mushrooming along the coast north of Alleppey and around the remote backwaters.

Alappuzha (Alleppey)

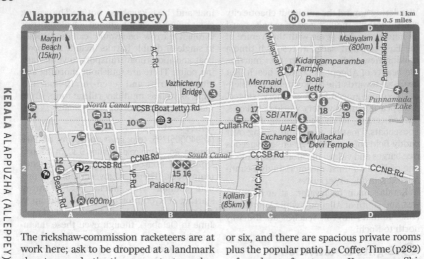

The rickshaw-commission racketeers are at work here; ask to be dropped at a landmark close to your destination, or contact your hotel for a pickup.

Zostel   HOSTEL $
(☑011-39589008; www.zostel.com; Beach Rd; dm ₹500-550, r ₹1200-2220; ☀☜) ✦ Just steps from the sand, Alleppey's lively, contemporary-style branch of India's favourite hostel chain is adorned with colourful shutters and murals – including Indiana Jones on the wall in one of the spacious upper-floor, sea-glimpse private rooms. Six-bunk en suite air-con dorms (mixed or women-only) come with individual lockers, and there's a laid-back lounge. Free water refills.

Artpackers.Life   HOSTEL $
(☑8281486865; www.artpackers.life; incl breakfast dm with/without AC ₹600/490, r ₹1570-1790; ☀☜) Overlooking leafy gardens, 400m from the beach, this beautiful old whitewashed building with sky-blue shutters – once a radio station – now doubles as a creative hostel and a resident-artist studio. The two eight-bed dorms have personal lockers, lights and plugs, private bathrooms, soaring ceilings, polished-concrete decor and bunks at mismatched levels; the two private rooms are comfily stylish (though with ceilingless bathrooms).

Nanni Backpackers Hostel   HOSTEL $
(☑9895039767; www.nannitours.com; Cullan Rd; dm ₹300, r with/without AC ₹1400/700) A very good deal, this easy-going, homely and colourful backpacker hang-out sits 500m inland from the beach and 2km north of the train station. The two neat dorms sleep four

or six, and there are spacious private rooms plus the popular patio Le Coffee Time (p282) cafe and a rooftop terrace. Keen owner Shibu is an excellent source of local information and offers scooter hire (p283).

Dream Nest   GUESTHOUSE $
(☑9895860716; http://thedreamnest.com; Cullan Rd; dm ₹250, d ₹500-900, r with AC ₹1400-1600; ☀☜) The colourfully themed modern rooms and three-bed dorm set back from the road are a good-value find at this budget town-centre guesthouse, with a social communal lounge, a shared kitchen, a book exchange and a youthful traveller vibe. Houseboats, canoe tours and kayaking trips available.

Malayalam   GUESTHOUSE $$
(☑0477-2234591, 9496829424; www.facebook. com/MalayalamLakeResorts; East Thottathodu Bridge, Punnamada; r ₹1500-2500; ☜) Fringed by gardens of orchids, family-run Malayalam revolves around a pair of spacious two-storey four-room houses facing the lake near the Nehru Trophy Boat Race starting point. Views are sweet and the style is charmingly traditional yet comfortable, with deck chairs on verandahs and glossy woods. It's 2.5km north of town on the canal bank, signposted off Punnamada Rd.

Cherukara Nest   GUESTHOUSE $$
(☑0477-2251509, 9947059628; www.cherukara nest.com; incl breakfast r with/without AC ₹1800/1400; ☀☜) Set in well-tended gardens, this lovely heritage home reveals four large, character-filled rooms with high ceilings, lots of polished-wood touches, and antediluvian doors with ornate locks. There's also a more modern cottage attached. Own-

Alappuzha (Alleppey)

◉ **Sights**
1 Alleppey Beach A2
2 Alleppey Lighthouse A2
3 RKK Memorial Museum B1

⊕ **Activities, Courses & Tours**
4 Houseboat Dock D1
5 Kerala Kayaking B1

⊜ **Sleeping**
6 Alasr Heritage A2
7 Artpackers.Life A2
8 Cherukara Nest D1
9 Dream Nest C1
10 Johnson's B2
11 Nanni Backpackers Hostel A2
12 Raheem Residency A2
13 Tharavad A1

14 Zostel A1

⊗ **Eating**
Cafe Katamaran .... (see 14)
Chakara .... (see 12)
15 Halais B2
Harbour Restaurant .... (see 12)
Le Coffee Time .... (see 11)
16 Mushroom D2
17 Royale Chimney C1

❶ **Information**
18 DTPC Tourist Office D1
Tourist Police .... (see 4)

❶ **Transport**
19 KSRTC Bus Stand D1
Nanni Tours & Travel .... (see 11)

er Tony has a good-value houseboat (two/four people ₹6000/8000) and organises full-day canoe or village tours (₹900). It's just east of the bus stand.

Alasr Heritage HOMESTAY $$
(☎9947066699; www.facebook.com/alasr-heritage-home-1050461414981804; CCNB Rd; r incl breakfast with/without AC ₹2300/1500; �) A beautiful family house with its roots in the 17th century, canalside Alasr is strung riad-style around a wood-banistered patio. There are seven impeccable rooms with tall ceilings, antique furniture, heritage touches, colourful bedding and modern bathrooms, and the charming family owners rustle up home-cooked breakfasts and organise houseboats, canoe trips and bike hire.

Canoe Ville COTTAGE $$
(☎9895213162, 0477-2232535; www.facebook.com/CanoeVilleResort; Choolakkadav Rd, Punnamada; incl breakfast tent per person ₹500, r ₹2000, cottages ₹3000; ☀�) In a peaceful lakefront setting 4km north of Alleppey, this welcoming, creative operation amid natural canals sleeps guests on a floating mini houseboat cottage for a 'houseboat on land' experience (complete with air-con, private bathroom and a large verandah). Owner Jijo also has two lakeside rooms and some budget safari tents, and books kayak, canoe and bike jaunts.

The same family runs the nearby heritage-style **Punnamada Homestay** (☎Whatsapp 9895213162; Kayaloram Resort Rd, Punnamada; r incl breakfast ₹1500; �) with two comfortable rooms and delicious home cooking.

Tharavad GUESTHOUSE $$
(☎9349440406, 0477-2244599; alleppeytharavad@gmail.com; west of North Police Station; r incl breakfast ₹2500-3500; ☀☀) Glossy teak and antiques, shuttered windows, five characterful rooms, cordial service and well-maintained gardens set the tone at charming, 118-year-old ancestral home Tharavad. It's in a fairly hushed canalside location between Alleppey's town centre and beach, a little back from the road. Premium rooms are most spacious.

Johnson's GUESTHOUSE $$
(☎0477-2245825, 9846466399; http://johnsonskerala.com; Cullan Rd; incl breakfast r with/without AC ₹2500/1300; ☀☀) This quirky longtime favourite, run by the gregarious Johnson Gilbert, is a rambling two-storey family residence with themed rooms, old-school furniture, hanging chairs, outdoor bathtubs and hydromassage showers, overlooking a garden with an open-air barbecue and a pet horse. Johnson also has an excellent 'eco-houseboat' (http://ecohouseboat.com; for two people ₹9000 to ₹14,000).

Raheem Residency HERITAGE HOTEL $$$
(☎0477-2239767; www.raheemresidency.com; Beach Rd; s ₹9220-11,980, d ₹10,240-13,310; ☀☀☀) Across the road from the beach, this thoughtfully renovated 1860s heritage home offers Alleppey's most character-filled accommodation. The 10 rooms have been restored to their former glory by Irish personality Bibi Baskin and have bathtubs, antique furniture and period fixtures. Common areas include indoor courtyards, a private pool and two excellent restaurants,

Chakara and Harbour, and there's yoga and ayurveda.

Unfortunately, the new flyover on Alleppey Beach detracts from the otherwise charming setting.

Purity
LUXURY HOTEL $$$

(☑0478-2862862; www.purityresort.com; east of Muhamma; r incl breakfast €210-340; ✳🤙) Fronting Vembanad Lake, 16km north of Alleppey, this Spanish-German-run jewel blends heritage style and Indian antiques with bold contemporary design and a soothing position. Hot pinks, reds and aquamarines wash the 14 boutique-chic rooms with statement bathrooms; some have in-room tubs, others jazzy Tamil Nadu tiles. There's a professional ayurvedic spa, plus yoga, boat rides and a sleek Kerala-inspired restaurant.

🍴 Eating & Drinking

Mushroom
ARABIC, INDIAN $

(☑9633085702; www.facebook.com/Mushroom Restaurant; CCSB Rd; mains ₹90-170; ⏰noon-midnight) A breezy open-air town-centre restaurant embellished with fairy lights and greenery, specialising in cheap, spicy halal meals like chicken *kali mirch*, fish tandoori and chilli mushrooms, plus peppery noodle and rice stir-fries. Lots of locals and travellers give it a fun, relaxed vibe. Also does takeaway.

Le Coffee Time
CAFE $

(☑9895039767; www.nannitours.com; Nanni Backpackers Hostel, Cullan Rd; snacks ₹70-150; ⏰8am-9pm; 🤙) A friendly, tucked-away courtyard cafe at Nanni Backpackers Hostel (p280), 500m west of the beach, with a genuine Ital-

ian espresso machine, where you can tuck into pancakes, masala omelettes and other lovingly prepared breakfasts amid hot-pink walls and a stack of books for borrowing.

Cafe Katamaran
INTERNATIONAL $$

(☑9746402340; www.facebook.com/cafecatama ran; Beach Rd; mains ₹180-350; ⏰8am-midnight) Loved by both visitors and locals, mellow, welcoming Katamaran brings a traveller-style menu to its elevated, low-seating deck looking right out on the beach – *momos,* grilled sandwiches, pastas, curries and seafood specials like grilled garlic-butter fish. There are deliciously fresh juices, lassis and smoothies (including vegan versions), along with breakfasts of pancakes, omelettes or granola, and regular live music.

Halais
INDIAN, ARABIC $$

(☑9446053338; www.facebook.com/haneefsaithal ais; CCSB Rd; mains ₹60-400; ⏰9.30am-11.30pm) Locally famous for its chicken and mutton biryanis, busy Halais is a clean restaurant hidden behind a street-front sweet shop. It's also popular for Arabian and Yemeni dishes such as shawarma, and does a few dosa, masalas and thalis too.

Royale Chimney
INDIAN $$

(☑0477-2237828; www.hotelroyalepark.com; Hotel Royale Park, YMCA Rd; mains ₹160-350; ⏰7am-10pm, bar noon-10pm; 🤙) There's an extensive menu at this always-busy air-con hotel restaurant, and the food – including biryanis, tandoori, Keralan fish curry and veg and fish thalis – is consistently delicious. You can order from the same menu in the surprisingly smart upstairs beer parlour and wash down

---

KERALA'S 2018 FLOODS

The worst in a century, the devastating floods that swept through Kerala in July and August 2018 killed more than 400 people, displaced over a million more and caused an estimated US$2.5 billion of damage. The exceptionally high rainfall and flooding also had serious knock-on effects, including fatal landslides (which some claim were worsened by deforestation) and a huge drop in tourism (which accounts for 10% of Kerala's GDP).

As a result of climate change, severe flooding is becoming increasingly common across South India; Kerala is one of the country's most vulnerable-to-flooding states, but also, says a 2018 government report, one of its least adept at water management. Many experts claim that the Kerala government should have been better prepared for a natural disaster of this kind.

Idukki district (including Munnar) was one of worst affected areas; others included Alappuzha (Alleppey), Wayanad, Thrissur, Kozhikode (Calicut), Kannur, Chennamangalam (p311) and Kochi (Cochin; though not Fort Cochin), where the airport was closed for two weeks. At the time of writing, Kerala is open, working hard to get back on its feet and in need of strong support from the tourism industry, and tourism services are expected to be back on track by late 2019.

your meal with a cold Kingfisher, while breakfasts wander from omelettes to dosa.

Chakara   MULTICUISINE $$$
(☑0477-2239767; www.raheemresidency.com; Beach Rd; mains ₹350-550; ◷7.30-10am, 12.30-3pm & 7-10pm) Opposite the beach, this elegant restaurant at the 1860s heritage-style Raheem Residency hotel (p281) is Alleppey's finest. It has seating on a bijou open-sided terrace reached via a spiral staircase (though the sea views are now mostly blocked by a flyover). The menu creatively combines Keralan and European cuisine, specialising in local seafood; try the Alleppey fish curry or paneer-cashew curry.

Indian wines, Goan port and beer are all served, too, as are mini Keralan meals (₹350). In the fairy-lit garden below is the equally popular **Harbour Restaurant** (☑0477-2239767; mains ₹170-500; ◷11am-10pm), with a similar menu and deliciously cool beers.

ℹ Information

DTPC Tourist Office (☑9400051796, 0477-2251796; www.dtpcalappuzha.com; Boat Jetty Rd; ◷9.30am-5.30pm)

ℹ Getting There & Away

BOAT

From Alleppey's **boat jetty** (VCSB Rd), State Water Transport (www.swtd.gov.in) ferries are *scheduled* for Kottayam (₹15, 2½ hours) at 7.30am, 9.30am, 11.30am, 2.30pm and 5.15pm, returning at 6.45am, 11.30am, 1pm, 3.30pm and 5.15pm; at the time of writing, ongoing renovation works meant only the 11.30am ferry (returning at 1pm) was operating. Ferries leave for Kollam (₹400, eight hours) daily at 10.30am (every other day April to June).

BUS

From the **KSRTC bus stand** (VCSB Rd), buses head every 30 minutes to Trivandrum (₹150, four hours), Kollam (₹90, 2½ hours) and Ernakulam (Kochi; ₹100, 1½ hours). Buses to Kottayam (₹50, 1½ hours, every 30 minutes 5.40am to 7.30pm) are faster than the ferry. Buses leave for Kumily (Periyar; ₹150, six hours) at 6.40am, 7.50am and 1.10pm; for Munnar (₹150, six hours) at 2am, 4.30am, 8.45am (AC) and 2pm; and for Varkala (₹90, three hours) at 8am, 8.50am and 5.30pm.

TRAIN

Alleppey's train station is 4km southwest of the town centre, with numerous daily trains to Ernakulam (2nd class/sleeper/3AC ₹50/140/495, 1½ hours) and Trivandrum (₹80/140/495, three

WORTH A TRIP

GREEN PALM HOMES

Around 12km southeast of Alappuzha (Alleppey), long-running **Green Palm Homes** (☑9496956665, 0477-2725865; www.greenpalmhomes.com; Chennamkary; incl full board r ₹2800-5000, cottages ₹6000-8000; ❀) is a series of homestays in a picturesque village on a backwater island, where you sleep in simple rooms in villagers' homes among rice paddies (though 'premium' rooms with bathroom and air-con are available). Take a guided walk (₹500), hire bicycles or kayaks (from ₹300), or join a cooking class (₹250).

The cheapest rooms have shared bathroom; some others have an air-con option (₹500 extra). There's a 30% discount for solo guests.

to four hours) via Kollam (₹60/140/495, 1½ to 2½ hours). Six daily trains go to Varkala (2nd class/AC chair ₹65/315, two to three hours).

ℹ Getting Around

Autorickshaws from the town centre or bus stand to the beach cost around ₹60. Guesthouses hire out scooters for ₹300 to ₹400 per day, including reliable **Nanni Tours & Travel** (☑9895039767; www.nannitours.com; Cullan Rd; ◷8am-9pm).

Marari & Kattoor
☑0478

The increasingly popular white-gold beaches at Kattoor and Marari, 10km and 14km north of Alleppey respectively, are gorgeous beachside alternatives to the region's backwaters. Marari, the flashier of the two, is transforming into a fully fledged (yet still naturally beautiful) beach resort, with some exclusive five-star seafront accommodation. Kattoor, sometimes known as 'Secret Beach', is more of a fishing village, where development remains at a minimum and sandy back lanes lead down to near-deserted sands.

🛏 Sleeping & Eating

★**Secret Beach Yoga Homestay**   HOMESTAY $$
(☑9447786931; www.secretbeach.in; Kattoor; r ₹1000-2500; ❀🡡) The location is sublime at this peaceful three-room homestay, separated from a quiet piece of Kattoor Beach by a small lagoon (cross in a borrowed canoe!).

WORTH A TRIP

CHURCHES IN NORTHWESTERN KOTTAYAM

Next to the Meenachil River, 2km northwest of Kottayam's centre, lie a couple of ancient churches well worth exploring. The whitewashed, hilltop St Mary's Syrian Knanaya Church (Valiyapally; off River Bank Rd; ⊙ hours vary) was founded in 1550 by Syrian Knanaya Christians, though the existing building is from 1588; it's decorated with two granite-carved crosses dated to least as far back as the 7th century with Pahalavi inscriptions. Just 200m south, the elegant, Portuguese-built 1579 St Mary's Orthodox Church (Cheriapally; off Kottayam–Kumarakom Rd; ⊙ dawn-dusk) is famous for its blend of European baroque and Keralan temple architecture, as well as for the Portuguese-style vegetable-dye paintings that festoon its altar.

Talented, welcoming young owner Vimal is an accredited yoga and *kalari* instructor (classes ₹300) and, with his family, also offers free bikes and home-cooked meals. Ask locally for 'Akkichen's house'.

★ **Marari Villas** LUXURY HOTEL $$$
(☑ 9947948868; www.mararivillas.com; Kattoor; incl breakfast r ₹14,000-19,500, 1-room villa ₹18,500-22,000; ❉ ⓐ ⓢ) ✐ Marari stays don't get better than this: four intimate, independent boutique villas dotted along or near the beachfront, washed in dusty reds, whites and turquoises, serving wonderful Keralan cooking and with honey-coloured sand gracing front gardens. Two-room Lotus shares its back-garden pool, yoga deck and ayurvedic massage rooms with Palm (three rooms) and one-room, private-pool Hibiscus and Orchid. Book ahead.

A Beach Symphony COTTAGE $$$
(☑ 9947107150; www.abeachsymphony.com; Marari; cottage ₹9900-22,960; ⊙ Sep-May; ❉ ⓐ ⓢ) These four individually designed cottages at the main beach entrance shine as one of Marari's most exclusive seafront resorts. Amid breezy gardens, the Keralan-inspired cottages are plush and private, with a luxurious, earthy feel. Khombu and Nagaswaram enjoy beach views; Violin has its own plunge pool. Yoga, bicycle tours, boat trips and meals on your verandah can all be arranged.

ⓘ Getting There & Away

Frequent buses head north from Alleppey's KSRTC bus stand (p283) towards Cherthala from 5am to 9pm, stopping along the main NH66 2km inland from Marari beach. Taxis to/ from Alleppey cost around ₹700.

Kottayam

📞 0481 / POP 357,300

Poised between the backwaters and the Western Ghats, 60km southeast of Kochi, Kottayam is renowned for being the centre of Kerala's spice and rubber trade, rather than for its aesthetic appeal. It was also the first town in India to achieve 100% literacy, in 1989. For most travellers it's a hub town, well connected to the mountains and the backwaters, with many travellers taking the public canal cruise to or from Alleppey before heading east to Kumily, west to Kumarakom or north to Kochi. The city has a traffic-clogged centre, but there are a couple of intriguing sights in its northwestern suburbs.

🛏 Sleeping & Eating

Homestead Hotel HOTEL $
(☑ 0481-2560467; KK Rd; s ₹600, d ₹990-1400, r with AC ₹2010; ❉ ⓐ) In a handy little compound tucked back from busy KK Rd, super-central Homestead has a variety of well-maintained budget rooms, the best of them with prettily patterned sheets and the odd feature wall (ask to view a few). Air-con rooms come with hot water; for others, it's by the bucket.

Windsor Castle & Lake Village Resort HOTEL $$
(☑ 0481-2363637; www.thewindsorcastle.co.in; MC Rd, Kodimatha; s ₹3540-4720, d ₹4130-5310, cottages ₹8790; ❉ ⓐ ⓢ) Some of Kottayam's comfiest rooms inhabit this grandiose white box, 3km south of the town centre, though the more impressive accommodation is in the Lake Village behind. Smart deluxe cottages, some with a houseboat-like atmosphere, are strewn between private backwaters, manicured gardens and two pools, and there's an upmarket multi-cuisine restaurant.

Thali SOUTH INDIAN $
(KK Rd; dishes ₹30-200; ⊙ 8am-8.30pm) This lovely, spotlessly kept 1st-floor dining room with slatted blinds is a swankier version of Kerala's typical set-meals restaurants. The South Indian food here is great, including Malabar fish curry, thalis, masala dosa and

lightly spiced *pachakkari* mopped up with fluffy *appam* (rice pancakes).

Upstairs is equally popular **Meenachil** (dishes ₹60-180; ⊘noon-3pm & 6-9.30pm), turning out tasty Chinese and Indian cooking in a warm family setting.

ⓘ Information

DTPC Tourist Office (☑0481-2560479; www. dtpckottayam.com; Kodimatha; ⊘10am-5pm Mon-Sat) At the boat jetty.

ⓘ Getting There & Around

Autorickshaws charge ₹40 from the bus stand to the jetty or the train station.

BOAT

State Water Transport (www.swtd.gov.in) ferries *usually* leave Kottayam's **boat jetty** (Kodimatha), 1.5km south of the town centre, for Alleppey (₹15, 2½ hours) at 6.45am, 11.30am, 1pm, 3.30pm and 5.15pm, returning at 7.30am, 9.30am, 11.30am, 2.30pm and 5.15pm. At research time, only the 1pm (returning 11.30am) service was operating due to ongoing restoration work; full services may well have resumed by the time you read this.

BUS

The **KSRTC bus stand** (NH183) is 600m south of the town centre.

TRAIN

Kottayam's train station, 1.5km northeast of the town centre, is served by frequent trains running between Trivandrum (2nd class/sleeper/3AC ₹80/140/495, 3½ to 4½ hours) and Ernakulam (Kochi, ₹50/140/495, 1½ hours).

Kumarakom

☑0481

Kumarakom, 15km west of Kottayam on the shores of vast, beautiful Vembanad Lake – Kerala's largest lake – is an unhurried backwater village with a smattering of dazzling top-end resorts, a renowned bird sanctuary and less-crowded canals than Alleppey.

Arundhati Roy, author of the 1997 Booker Prize–winning *The God of Small Things,* was raised in the nearby village of Aymanam.

⊙ Sights

Kumarakom Bird
Sanctuary   NATURE RESERVE
(☑0481-2525864, 9400008620; Kumarakom; Indian/foreigner ₹50/150; ⊘6am-5pm) This reserve on the 5-hectare site of a former rubber plantation on Vembanad Lake is the haunt of a variety of domestic and migratory birds. October to February is the time for travelling birds like the garganey teal, osprey, marsh harrier and steppey eagle; May to July is the breeding season for local species such as the Indian shag, pond herons, egrets and darters. Guides cost ₹300 for a two-hour tour; there are also motorboat (₹650) and speedboat trips (₹1200).

🛏 Sleeping

Cruise 'N Lake   GUESTHOUSE $$
(☑9447126784, 9846036375; puthenpurajose@ gmail.com; Puthenpura Tourist Enclave, Cheerpunkal; r with/without AC ₹2000/1500; ❋🛈) Surrounded by backwaters on one side and a lawn of rice paddies on the other, this is the affordable Kumarakom getaway. The eight rooms are plain but modern, with verandahs facing the water, and there's a low-key on-site restaurant gazing out on the lake. It's 3km northwest of Kumarakom Bird Sanctuary; the final 1.5km is down a rugged dirt road.

Kumarakom
Lake Resort   RESORT $$$
(☑0481-2524900; www.kumarakomlakeresort. in; Kumarakom North; r/ste incl breakfast from

BUSES FROM KOTTAYAM

DESTINATION	FARE (₹)	DURATION (HR)	FREQUENCY
Alleppey	47	1½	every 20-40min 6am-5.40pm
Ernakulam (Kochi)	76-236	1-2	every 15min 4.20am-12.30am
Kollam	100	3½	4.30am, 6.45am, 7.30am, 9.40am, 2.20pm
Kumarakom	30	30min	5.30am, every 20min 6.40am-9.30pm
Kumily (for Periyar)	100	3½	3am, 3.40am, 4.40am, every 20min 6am-7pm, hourly 7pm-midnight
Munnar	100	4	3am, 7.50am, 9am, 10.30am, 12.40pm, 2pm, 5pm
Trivandrum	186	4	every 20-30min
Varkala	150	4	6.45am

BOATING KERALA'S BACKWATERS

The undisputed highlight of a trip to Kerala is travelling through the 900km network of waterways that fringe the coast and trickle inland. Long before the advent of roads, these waters were the slippery highways of Kerala, and many villagers still use paddle power as their main form of transport. Trips through the backwaters traverse palm-fringed lakes studded with cantilevered Chinese fishing nets, and wind their way along narrow, shady canals where coir (coconut fibre), copra (dried coconut kernels) and cashews are loaded onto boats. Along the way are remote villages where farming life continues as it has for aeons.

Tourist Cruises

The popular State Water Transport (www.swtd.kerala.gov.in) tourist cruise between Kollam (Quilon) and Alappuzha (Alleppey; ₹400) departs from either end at 10.30am, arriving at 6.30pm, usually daily from July to March and every second day at other times, though it may start running later in the season. Generally, there's a 1pm lunch stop and a brief afternoon chai stop. It's a scenic and leisurely eight-hour journey, though the boat travels along only the major canals, so you won't get many close-up views of the village life that makes the backwaters so special. Some travellers take the trip halfway (₹140 to ₹270) and hop off at the Matha Amrithanandamayi Mission (p278).

Houseboats

If the stars align, renting a houseboat designed like a *kettuvallam* (rice barge) could well be one of the highlights of your trip to India. It can be an expensive experience (depending on your budget) but for a couple on a romantic overnight jaunt or split between a group of travellers, it's usually worth every rupee.

Houseboats cater for couples (one or two double bedrooms) and groups (up to seven bedrooms!). Food (and an onboard chef) is generally included in the quoted cost, as is a driver/captain. Houseboats can be chartered through a multitude of private operators in Alleppey, Kollam, Kottayam and, to a lesser extent, the Valiyaparamba area (p322) in northern Kerala. The quality of boats varies widely, from ageing boats to floating palaces.

Travel-agency reps will be pushing you to book a boat as soon as you set foot in Kerala, though many travellers prefer to wait until they reach a backwaters hub. The choice is greatest in Alleppey; you're more likely to be able to bargain down a price if you turn up and see what's on offer. That said, many of the most professionally run houseboats now take online bookings and can get snapped up in advance (and may not even dock at the main jetties). Talk to other travellers and choose a houseboat based on a strong local recommendation (whether that's from a friend, a locally based contact or a reputable guesthouse) and book directly with the owner (online or by phone) or through your guesthouse.

In the busy high season or during domestic holidays (such as Pooja, Onam or Diwali) when prices peak, you're likely to get caught in backwater-gridlock – some travellers are disappointed by the number of boats on the water. Expect a boat for two people for 24

₹19,350/60,300; ❄☎❄) The queen of Kumarakom's luxury accommodation is this 67-room Keralan-inspired beauty fronting Vembanad Lake, complete with ayurvedic spa, yoga, two restaurants, its own houseboats and idyllic tropical gardens. Most rooms open onto interconnecting palm-fringed pools or have their own plunge pools. Even the standard rooms are spacious, stylish and gloriously comfortable, with hot tubs in the bathroom.

❶ Getting There & Away

Kumarakom is served by buses from Kottayam (₹30, 30 minutes) at 5.30am then every 20 minutes from 6.40am to 9.30pm.

KERALA'S WESTERN GHATS

The Unesco-listed Western Ghats – one of the world's key biodiversity hotspots – are thick with wildlife sanctuaries, outstanding trekking, and fragrant spice, coffee and tea plantations. Kerala's far northern Ghats are hours to cost ₹6000 to ₹8000 at the budget level; for four people ₹10,000 to ₹12,000; for larger boats or for air-conditioning expect to pay ₹15,000 to ₹35,000. Prices triple from around 20 December to 5 January.

Village Tours, Canoe Boats & Kayaks

Village tours are an excellent way to see the backwaters by day at a slow pace, and usually involve small groups of five to six visitors, a knowledgeable guide and an open canoe or covered *kettuvallam*. The tours (from Kochi, Kollam or Alleppey) last three to 10 hours and cost around ₹500 to ₹1000 per person. They include visits to watch coir-making, boat-building, toddy (palm beer) tapping and fish farming. The Munroe Island trip (p276) from Kollam is a particularly scenic tour of this type; Kochi's Tourist Desk (p308) also organises recommended tours. Kayaking backwaters trips, making similar village stops at similar prices, are becoming a popular alternative.

Public Ferries

For the local backwater transport experience at just a few rupees, there are State Water Transport (www.swtd.gov.in) boats from Alleppey to Kottayam (₹15, 2½ hours) at 7.30am, 9.30am, 11.30am, 2.30pm and 5.15pm, returning at 6.45am, 11.30am, 1pm, 3.30pm and 5.15pm (though only the 11.30am service, returning at 1pm, was operating at research time). The trip crosses Vembanad Lake and has a more varied landscape than the Kollam–Alleppey cruise. Other ageing boats operate from the jetties at Alleppey and Kollam, ferrying locals to backwater villages.

Environmental Issues

Pollution from houseboats is becoming a major problem as boat numbers continue to rise. They were only introduced in the 1990s, and there are now thought to be 1200 to 1400 houseboats plying Kerala's inland waterways – with around 400 to 500 of them believed to be unregistered. Sadly, the backwaters are facing increasing contamination from spilled houseboat fuel, as well as plastic, food and even human waste from houseboats (despite the existence of designated sewage-treatment plants for cleaning houseboat bio-toilets). This translates into water shortages and potential health hazards for local villagers, as well as declining bird populations and fish stocks (which in turn impacts the livelihoods of local fishers). Noise pollution from some of the larger 'party-style' houseboats that have become popular in recent years is also a growing concern. That said, most houseboats do now have bio-toilets, and India's first solar-powered ferry was even successfully introduced on Lake Vembanad in 2017.

Consider choosing one of the few remaining punting, rather than motorised, boats if possible, though these only operate in shallow water – or explore the backwaters with an environmentally responsible kayaking operator instead.

home to the serene Wayanad region (p317), usually accessed from Calicut.

Periyar Tiger Reserve

☎ 04869 / POP 30,300 (KUMILY) / ELEV 880M (KUMILY)

South India's most popular wildlife reserve, **Periyar** (Thekkady Tiger Reserve; ☎ 04869-224571, 8547603066; www.periyartigerreserve. org; Indian ₹40, adult/child foreigner ₹475/170; ☻ 6.30am-5.30pm, last entry 4.30pm), encompasses 777 sq km, including a 26-sq-km 1895 artificial lake created by the British. This vast expanse – which became Kerala's first tiger reserve in 1978 (though founded as a sanctuary in 1934) – shelters wild boar, sambar, bison, langur, 2000 elephants and 35 to 40 hard-to-spot tigers. It's firmly established on both the Indian and foreigner tourist trails and known for its scenic lake cruise (p288). But if you dig deeper, perhaps on a trek with a tribal villager or former poacher, Periyar's hilly jungle scenery takes on a wild, magical feel. Bring warm, waterproof clothing.

Kumily is the closest town, and has hotels, restaurants and Kashmiri emporiums. Thekkady, 4km south of Kumily, is the park centre, with the KTDC hotels and boat jetty.

Confusingly, when people refer to the reserve they use Thekkady, Kumily and Periyar interchangeably. The best wildlife-spotting months are December to April.

◉ Sights & Activities

The Forest Department's Ecotourism Centre (p291) handles all trips accessing the reserve. For the November-to-March high season, book well ahead (online or through your guesthouse). Reservations are *theoretically* via www.periyarfoundation.online, though it wasn't accepting foreign cards at research time. Last resort: try for tickets in person after 7.30pm the day before.

The main way to tour the reserve without taking a guided walk is by 1½-hour KTDC boat trips with the **Periyar Lake Cruise** (Periyar Lake; adult/child ₹240/80; ⊘ departures 7.30am, 9.30am, 11.15am, 1.45pm & 3.30pm). You might see deer, boar, otters and birdlife, but it's generally more cruise than wildlife-spotting experience. If you haven't prebooked (at www.periyarfoundation.online), buy tickets from the office above the boat jetty or the boating counter at Kumily's shuttle-bus (p292) car park.

Hiking & Rafting

The Ecotourism Centre (p291) arranges full-day border hikes (₹1800 per person), 2½-hour nature walks (₹350 per person), bamboo rafting (half/full day ₹1800/2400 per person) and three-hour night 'jungle scouts' (₹1200 per person), accompanied by trained tribal guides, as well as overnight 'tiger trail' camping treks (one-night trail ₹6000 per person; minimum charge ₹9000), covering 20km to 30km and led by former poachers retrained as guides. Trips usually require a minimum of two or four people; solo travellers may be able to join other groups. Children must be 12 years or over for most hikes.

Jeep Safaris

The Forest Department runs 40km **jeep safaris** (☑ 8289821306, 8547123776; per jeep ₹2200, incl boating, trekking & lunch adult/child ₹1500/750) in the reserve's Gavi buffer zone, with the first 20km along main roads. Jeeps depart at 6am, returning at 3pm or 4pm, and kids can join. Book through your guesthouse (admission costs extra).

Cooking Classes

Many local homestays, including Green View (p289) and El-Paradiso (p290), offer cooking classes (₹300 to ₹600 per person). There are also recommended two-hour classes (followed by a feast) at well-established **Bar-B-Que** (☑ 9895613036; KK Rd; class per person veg/nonveg ₹400/500; ⊘ 6.30pm), 1km west of the bazaar.

Spice & Tea Plantation Tours

These hills are known for their production of spices (cardamom, vanilla, pepper, cinnamon) and ayurvedic herbs. Several local spice plantations offer guided tours (₹100), including the long-established **Abraham's Spice Garden** (☑ 9746129050; www.abrahamspice.com; NH183, Spring Valley; tours ₹100; ⊘ 6am-6pm), 3km west of Kumily. The four-decade-old working **Connemara Tea Factory** (☑ 8075715496; NH183, Vandiperiyar; tours ₹150; ⊘ tours hourly 9am-4pm Mon-Sat), 14km southwest of Kumily, runs one-hour guided tours; buses run from Kumily to Vandiperiyar (₹25) every 30 minutes.

🛏 Sleeping

🛏 Inside the Park

The KTDC runs Periyar House, Aranya Nivas and the grand Lake Palace, all inside the reserve. Note that there's effectively a curfew at these hotels – guests are not permitted to roam the reserve after 6pm.

The Ecotourism Centre (p291) arranges tented accommodation within the reserve's buffer zone at the **Jungle Camp** (☑ 8547603066, 04869-22457; www.periyartigerreserve.org; d incl meals ₹5000), and has basic cottages at **Bamboo Grove** (r incl breakfast ₹1800) on the southwest edge of Kumily.

Lake Palace   HOTEL $$$
(☑ 9400008589, 04869-223887; www.ktdc.com/lake-palace; Thekkady; r incl meals ₹16,000-32,000) There's a faint whiff of royalty at this restored KTDC-operated Travancore summer palace on Periyar Lake, accessible only by 20-minute boat ride. The six charismatic rooms are decorated with flair and antique furnishings. Though there's a 6pm curfew, staying inside the reserve gives you a good chance of seeing wildlife from your private terrace. Rates include a boat trip.

🛏 Kumily

Mickey Homestay   HOMESTAY $
(☑ 04869-223196, 9447284160; www.mickeyhomestay.com; Bypass Rd; r ₹750-1000; 🕾) A genuine homestay with just five intimate,

Kumily & Periyar Tiger Reserve

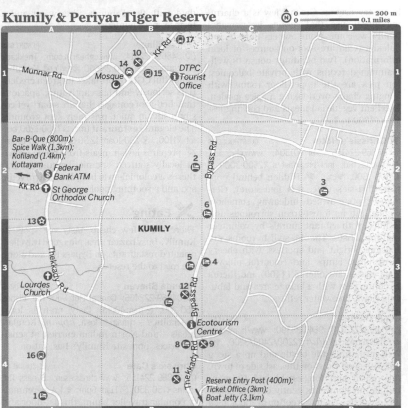

KERALA PERIYAR TIGER RESERVE

Kumily & Periyar Tiger Reserve

Sleeping
1 Bamboo Grove...A4
2 Chrissie's Hotel...B2
3 Claus Garden...D2
4 El-Paradiso..C3
5 Green View...B3
6 Mickey Homestay...C2
7 Spice Village..B3
8 Thekkady Homestay.......................................B4

Eating
9 Ambadi...C4
10 Ananda Bhavan..B1
Chrissie's Cafe..(see 2)

11 French Restaurant & Bakery.........................B4
12 Grandma's Cafe..B3
Spice Village...(see 7)

Entertainment
13 Mudra Cultural Centre..................................A3

Transport
14 Autorickshaw Stand.......................................B1
15 Kumily Bus Stand...B1
16 Park Shuttle Bus Stop...................................A4
17 Tamil Nadu Bus Stand....................................B1
Taxi & Jeep Stand..................................(see 15)

fan-cooled rooms in a welcoming family house, with homely touches making them some of Kumily's cosiest budget picks. Balconies have rattan furniture and hanging bamboo seats and the whole place is fringed by greenery. The two cheapest rooms, with separate bathroom, can interconnect, and

home-cooked breakfasts are available (₹300 for two).

★ **Green View** GUESTHOUSE $$
(☏9447432008, 04869-224617; www.suresh greenview.com; Bypass Rd; r incl breakfast ₹750-2000; ☏) ✿ Grown from its humble

homestay origins, Green View is a charming guesthouse that retains its personal family welcome from owners Suresh and Sulekha (who are spot-on sources of local information). Two buildings house 18 well-maintained rooms with private balconies; top pick are the upper-floor rooms with hanging chairs overlooking a spice garden. Excellent vegetarian meals and cooking lessons (₹300 to ₹500).

★ Chrissie's Hotel   GUESTHOUSE $$

(☑ 04869-224155, 9447601304; www.chrissies.in; Bypass Rd; incl breakfast s ₹2500-3000, d ₹2800-3300; 🛜🖾) 🏊 Hidden behind popular Chrissie's Cafe, this four-storey, German-Egyptian-owned hideaway somehow blends into its forest-green surrounds and is filled with vibrant murals by volunteer visiting artists. The 15 stylish rooms are spacious, bright and spotless, with cheery furnishings, lamps and colourful pillows. Yoga classes are offered (₹400) and there's a rooftop pool with a lounge area and fabulous views. Free water refills.

Claus Garden   HOMESTAY $$

(☑ 04869-222320, 9645138390; www.homestay.in; Thekkumkadu; d/tr/f ₹2200/2400/3200; 🛜) Well away from the bustle and up a steep hill with good views on the east side of town, this warm and long-established German-Indian-run home has gently curving balconies, swinging chairs, a rooftop overlooking a lush garden, and spotless tile-floored rooms with attractive wooden furniture and splashes of art. Organic breakfasts include fresh-baked bread and homemade jams (₹300).

El-Paradiso   HOMESTAY $$

(☑ 7034337350, 04869-222350; www.elparadiso.in; Bypass Rd; r ₹1800; 🛜) An immaculate and friendly family homestay with fresh, modern rooms, most opening onto a terrace overlooking greenery and featuring fun touches like elephants on wooden bedheads. The best four have balconies and hanging chairs. Cooking classes (₹600) are a speciality here, as is the coffee straight from the owners' farm.

Thekkady Homestay   HOMESTAY $$

(☑ 9446205008, 04869-224006; www.thekkadyhomestay.com; Puthenparambil House, Thekkady Rd; r ₹1500-1900; 🛜) Murals of leopards, jungle landscapes and Periyar Lake line the stairs to this genial, characterful homestay, where a handful of rooms unfolds across the top floor above the family home on the road to the reserve. Rooms are spotless and up to

date, with floral murals, filter water and a terrace space outdoors.

Spice Village   RESORT $$$

(☑ 04869-222314; www.cghearth.com; Thekkady Rd; cottages ₹20,600-28,600; 🛜🖾) 🏊 Kumily's delightful CGH resort takes its green credentials seriously and has captivating, spacious thatched-roof cottages that are smart yet cosily rustic, in quiet, pristinely kept grounds. The elegant **restaurant** (mains ₹350-1200, buffet ₹1100; ⊙ 7.30-10am,12.30-3pm & 7.30-10pm) 🍴 prepares lavish meals from home-grown or locally sourced organic ingredients, and there's a colonial-style bar plus an ayurvedic spa and a soothing pool.

✖ Eating

There are a few cheap, tasty veg spots in Kumily's busy bazaar area, plus good traveller-oriented restaurants on Bypass Rd and along the road to the reserve.

Ananda Bhavan   INDIAN $

(☑ 04869-222466; Central Hotel, KK Rd; dishes ₹50-200; ⊙ 8am-10pm) Tasty, no-frills local specialities – masala dosa, *appam*, Keralan meals – and North Indian curries, at sensible prices, opposite Kumily's bus station.

Chrissie's Cafe   MULTICUISINE $$

(☑ 04869-222155; www.chrissies.in; Bypass Rd; mains ₹150-350; ⊙ 11am-6pm; 🛜) A perennially popular traveller haunt, this 1st-floor and rooftop cafe delivers with cakes and snacks, excellent coffee, free water refills, well-prepared Continental faves like pastas and salads, and fabulous signature Middle Eastern meze platters and falafel wraps, served amid scattered pot plants.

Ambadi   INDIAN $$

(☑ 04869-222193; http://hotelambadi.com; Thekkady Rd; mains ₹100-300; ⊙ 7am-9.30pm; 🛜) At the English-manor-style hotel of the same name, Ambadi feels more formal than most Kumily eateries, with an almost churchlike decor of carved wood and tiled floors. It's popular with locals and visitors alike for its well-executed, reasonably priced and extensive selection of North and South Indian favourites.

Grandma's Cafe   MULTICUISINE $$

(☑ 9995317261; Bypass Rd; mains ₹180-300; ⊙ 7am-11pm Nov-Mar, from noon Apr-Oct; 🛜) Hidden down a few steps, this lively indoor-outdoor cafe-restaurant is all bamboo tables, good vibes and bright yellow walls scrawled

AYURVEDA

With its roots in Sanskrit, the word ayurveda comes from *ayu* (life) and *veda* (knowledge): the knowledge or science of life. Principles of ayurvedic medicine were first documented in the Vedas some 2000 years ago, but may have been practised centuries earlier, making this the most ancient known medical discipline.

Ayurveda sees the world as having an intrinsic order and balance. It argues that we possess three *doshas* (humours): *vata* (wind or air), *pitta* (fire) and *kapha* (water/earth), known together as the *tridoshas*. Most people have one or two dominant *doshas*, but deficiency or excess in any of them can lead to disease. An excess of *vata* may result in dizziness and debility; an increase in *pitta* may cause fever, inflammation and infection; *kapha* is essential for hydration.

Ayurvedic treatment, under the watch of university-trained doctors, aims to restore the balance, and hence good health, principally through two methods: *panchakarma* (internal purification) and herbal massage. *Panchakarma* is used to treat serious ailments, and is an intense detox regime, a combination of five types of different therapies to rid the body of built-up endotoxins. These include *vaman* (therapeutic vomiting), *virechan* (purgation), *vasti* (enemas), *nasya* (elimination of toxins through the nose) and *raktamoksha* (detoxification of the blood). Before *panchakarma* begins, the body is first prepared over several days with a special diet, oil massages *(snehana)* and herbal steambaths *(swedana)*. Although it may sound pretty grim, *panchakarma* purification might only use a few of these treatments at a time, with therapies like bloodletting and leeches only used in rare cases. But while yoga, meditation and ayurveda are all intertwined, this is still no spa holiday.

The herbs used in ayurveda grow in abundance in Kerala's humid climate – the monsoon is thought to be the best time of year for treatment, when there is less dust in the air and the pores are open – and every village has its own ayurvedic pharmacy.

with messages from past diners. Breakfasts wander the globe from French toast to Keralan veg curry with *appam,* while South Indian signatures (such as Chettinadu curries and masala-fried fish) mingle with noodles, biryanis and salads.

French Restaurant & Bakery   CAFE, BAKERY **$$**
(☑9961213107; Thekkady Rd; meals ₹100-280; ☺8.30am-8pm) A shack-like, yellow-walled family operation just back from the park access road that's particularly good for breakfast or lunch – mainly for the fluffy tuna, veg or cheese baguettes baked on-site, but also for pasta, pizza, omelettes and noodle dishes.

☆ Entertainment

Mudra Cultural Centre   LIVE PERFORMANCE
(☑9061263382; www.mudraculturalcentre.com; Thekkady Rd; tickets ₹200; ☺Kathakali 5pm & 7pm, kalarippayat 6pm & 7.15pm) Kathakali shows at this cultural centre are highly entertaining. Make-up and costume starts 30 minutes before each show. Arrive early for a good seat; use of cameras is free and welcome. There also two *kalarippayat* performances nightly. Schedules are usually reduced during the low season.

ⓘ Information

DTPC Tourist Office (☑04869-222620; www.dtpcidukki.com; off KK Rd; ☺10am-5pm Mon-Sat)

Ecotourism Centre (☑04869-224571, 8547603066; www.periyartigerreserve.org; Thekkady Rd; ☺6.30am-9pm)

ⓘ Getting There & Away

Kumily's **bus stand** (☑04869224242; KK Rd) is at the northeastern edge of town, with both private and KSRTC services:

Alleppey ₹140, 5½ hours, 5.15am, 7.40am, 10am, 1pm, 1.45pm

Bengaluru (Bangalore) ₹800 to ₹1050, 10 to 12 hours, 6pm, 7.15pm, 8pm, 9pm

Ernakulam (Kochi) ₹150 to ₹160, six hours, at least 20 daily

Kollam ₹150, 6½ hours, 10.50am, 11.45am

Kottayam ₹96 to ₹120, four hours, every 30 minutes

Munnar ₹120, five hours, 7am, 7.30am, 9.45am, noon

Trivandrum ₹200, six to eight hours, 3am, 8.45am, 10.15am, 3.40pm

Buses leave at 7.45pm and 9pm for Chennai (Madras; ₹900 to ₹1000, 10 hours) and every 30 minutes for Madurai (₹90, four hours) from the

SABARIMALA

Deep in the Western Ghats, 20km west of Gavi (which is 40km south of Kumily) and 50km east of Erumeli, Sabarimala is home to the Ayyappan Temple. It's said to be one of the world's most visited pilgrimage centres, with 40 to 60 million Hindu devotees trekking here each year. Followers believe the god Ayyappan (son of Shiva and Vishnu as his female incarnation Mohini) meditated at this spot.

Women aged 10 to 50 (ie of 'menstruating age') have traditionally only been allowed as far as the Pamba checkpoint, but, in September 2018, India's Supreme Court overturned the ban in a historic ruling, for the first time allowing women of any age to visit the temple. This led to large-scale, international-headline-hitting protests and some violent clashes between mobs of protesters (who disagreed with the Supreme Court's ruling, which they said, among other things, disregarded the wishes of the celibate god Ayyappan) and the police, media and several young women attempting the pilgrimage. Among the protesters were many women, though a countermovement in favour of the Supreme Court's verdict also emerged. Several thousand people were arrested for their roles in the 'protests' (which saw female journalists attacked). Two women of 'forbidden' age finally managed to access the temple in early January 2019, protected by a police escort, but, at the time of writing, the Supreme Court had agreed to reconsider its verdict and some of the few women who attempted the pilgrimage after the ban was lifted had been discriminated against upon returning home.

Tamil Nadu bus stand (KK Rd) just north over the border.

ℹ Getting Around

It's 1.5km southeast from Kumily bus stand (p291) to the **main reserve entrance** (Thekkady Rd), and another 3km south from there to Periyar Lake. Private vehicles are no longer allowed on the main access road; you *can* still walk it, or hop on one of the frequent **official shuttle buses** (off Thekkady Rd) (₹20 return) from the car park on the southwest edge of Kumily.

Kumily town is small enough to explore on foot, though you can hire bicycles (₹200). **Autorickshaws** (KK Rd) charge ₹30 for short hops.

Munnar

📞 04865 / POP 38,500 / ELEV 1524M

The rolling hills around Munnar, South India's largest tea-growing region, are carpeted in emerald-green tea plantations, and the low Western Ghats scenery here is magnificent – you're often up above the clouds watching veils of mist clinging to mountaintops. Munnar itself is a scruffy, traffic-clogged administration hub, not unlike a North Indian hill station, but wander just a few kilometres out and you'll be engulfed in a thousand shades of green.

Once known as the High Range of Travancore, Munnar flourished as a tea-producing area from 1880 onwards. Today it's the commercial centre of some of the world's highest tea-growing estates, most operated by the corporate giant Tata, with some overseen by local cooperative Kannan Devan Hills Plantation Company (KDHP); Harrisons Malayalam also owns a share.

Munnar and the surrounding Idukki district were badly hit by the 2018 floods (p282); tourism services were expected to be mostly back to normal by late 2019.

◉ Sights & Activities

Most travellers visit Munnar to explore the lush, tea-filled hillocks that surround it. Day trips to Top Station (p296), Eravikulam National Park (p297) and Chinnar Wildlife Sanctuary (p297) are especially popular, as are treks through the hills.

CSI Christ Church   CHURCH
(off AM Rd/NH85; ⊙9am-5pm) Constructed in neo-Gothic style in 1911, with granite imported from the UK, Munnar's oldest church contains a series of plaques commemorating prominent foreign tea planters laid to rest here.

Tea Museum   MUSEUM
(adult/child ₹125/40, camera ₹20; ⊙9am-5pm Tue-Sun) Around 1.5km northwest of town, this KDHP-owned museum is a demo model of a working tea factory, but still shows the basic process, along with a collection of relics from the British era including photographs and a 1905 tea-roller (skip the disappointingly bizarre factory demonstration). The walk to/from Munnar follows a busy

road with views across tea plantations; autorickshaws charge ₹25 from the bazaar.

★**Nimi's Lip Smacking Classes** COOKING
(🖀9447330773; http://nimisrecipes.com; AM Rd/ NH85; class per person ₹3000; ⏱3pm Mon-Fri, 2pm Sat & Sun) Award-winning food writer and cook Nimi Sunilkumar has earned a solid reputation for her Keralan cuisine, publishing her own cookbooks, website and blog, and offering popular hands-on classes in her home (next to Munnar's DTPC). You'll learn traditional Keralan recipes and take home a copy of her book *Lip Smacking Dishes of Kerala*.

Trekking

The best way to experience Munnar's beautiful hills is on a guided trek. Options range from half-day 'soft treks' around tea plantations (₹500 to ₹1000) to more arduous full-day mountain treks (from ₹1000), which open up stupendous views when the mist clears. Trekking guides are easily organised through your accommodation or the DTPC Tourist Office (p296). **Munnar Trekking** (🖉04865-230940, 9447825447; www.munnartrek king.com; trek per person ₹650-1000) is a reputable operation run by Green View Inn, while Green Valley Vista (p294) offers excellent trekking, too.

At the time of writing, the DTPC is also arranging overnight trekking trips (per person ₹3000) with camping in the Top Station area (p296).

Which areas are open for treks depends on current Forest Department regulations, which change roughly yearly. There are walks that you can do independently, but bear in mind that tea plantations are private property and trekking around them without a licensed guide is trespassing.

☞ Tours

Taxis, jeeps and guesthouses charge ₹1200 to ₹1500 for a spin around the main local sights. The DTPC (p296) runs several fairly rushed but inexpensive full-day tours to points around Munnar. The **Sandal Valley Tour** (🖉04865-231516; www.dtpcidukki.com; per person ₹400; ⏱tour 9am-5pm) visits Eravikulam National Park (p297), several viewpoints, waterfalls, tea plantations and a sandalwood forest; the **Village Tour** (🖉04865-231516; www. dtpcidukki.com; per person ₹400; ⏱9am-5pm) covers a spice farm, Ponmudi Dam, and a few waterfalls and viewpoints. Note that the Tea Valley Tour includes elephant riding, which

Munnar

☻ Eating

| 1 | Rapsy Restaurant | A1 |
| 2 | Sree Mahaveer Bhojanalaya | B1 |

🛈 Transport

3	Autorickshaw & Jeep Stand	B2
	Autorickshaw Stand	(see 7)
4	Buses to Coimbatore & Chinnar Wildlife Sanctuary	A2
5	Buses to Ernakulam & Trivandrum	A2
6	Buses to Kumily & Madurai	B2
7	Buses to Top Station	A2
8	Jeep Stand	B1
	Taxi Stand	(see 5)

Lonely Planet does not recommend due to the serious animal-welfare concerns involved.

🛌 Sleeping

Munnar town has good budget options just south of the centre near the bus station. That said, the views and peace are out in the hills and valleys, where homestays and upmarket resorts make scenic bases; it can be quite a hike into town from some of these.

🛌 Munnar Town

Green View Inn GUESTHOUSE $
(🖉04865-230940, 9447825447; www.greenview munnar.com; r ₹600-900; 🛜) Handily located near the main bus station, this popular guesthouse has fresh, clean budget rooms (the best on the upper floor), a friendly welcome, and reliable tours and treks. Young owner Deepak also runs Munnar Trekking and cosy nearby cafe Taste the Brews (p295), as well

as comfy, good-value **Greenwoods Cottage** (☑ 9447825447, 04865-230189; www.greenview munnar.com; Anachal; s/d ₹750/900; ☜), 12km southwest of town.

JJ Cottage
GUESTHOUSE $

(☑ 04865-230104, 9447228599; jjcottagemnr@ gmail.com; r ₹500-1000; ☜) The charming family at this long-standing pink-walled spot 1.5km south of central Munnar (tucked into a lane just far enough from the main bus station) offers a varied and uncomplicated set of clean, bright and colourful great-value rooms with hot water. The top-floor deluxe has a separate sitting room and views across town.

Zina Cottage
GUESTHOUSE $

(☑ 09496822163, 04865-230349; r ₹800-1200; ☜) If you want to be immersed in lush tea plantations but still close to town, Zina is the budget choice. While it looks slightly run-down, this fading, rose-pink, 50-year-old bungalow offers five clean, simple rooms, in a scenic location with rippling views and good hikes on its doorstep. It's 1km south of the main bus station (call for directions).

🏕 Munnar Hills

★ Rosegardens
HOMESTAY $$

(☑ 04864-278243, 9447378524; www.munnar homestays.com; NH85, Karadipara; r incl breakfast ₹5000; ☜) 🍃 An award-winning, totally charming family homestay, peacefully located 12km southwest of Munnar, overlooking owner Tomy's exquisite nursery and organic spice and fruit plantation (complete with biogas plant!). The five spacious rooms are immaculate, with tea/coffee trays, so-lar-heated water and greenery-fringed balconies. Fuelled by own-grown ingredients, the home-cooked meals are a treat, from coconut-stuffed pancakes to delicately spiced Keralan dinners (₹300).

It's on the main road to Kochi, linked by regular buses, and also does free garden tours for guests and cooking classes (₹2000).

★ Green Valley Vista
GUESTHOUSE $$

(☑ 04865-263261, 940004311; www.green valleyvista.com; Chithirapuram; r incl breakfast ₹2250-3850; ☜) 🍃 Green Valley's views are superb, its rooms smartly up to date, and its welcome warm. Rooms sprawl across three floors, all facing the valley, and have TVs, modern bathrooms, natural light, and private balconies with dreamy panoramas. There's an outdoor terrace, plus yoga mats, a restaurant and water refills, and staff organ-

ise trekking. It's 11km south of Munnar, with good bus connections.

Shade
HOMESTAY $$

(☑ 9539103538, 9447825984; www.theshade. in; Chithirapuram; r incl breakfast ₹3000) Folded into a verdant valley, 13km south of Munnar, Santhosh and Maya's tranquil family home is encircled by palms, betel-nut trees and their own cardamom and fruit plantations. The four unfussy rooms are kept comfy and spotless; go for the corner room gazing out across the valley. Trekking and home-cooked dinners (₹200) are available.

Anna Homestay
GUESTHOUSE $$

(☑ 8129980088, 8156980088; www.annahome stay.com; Chithirapuram; r incl breakfast with/ without AC ₹4500/2500; ❇) Near Anachal village, 12km southwest of Munnar, Anna is more of a cosy guesthouse than a homestay, with 11 very tidy modern rooms, spacious rooftop common areas, Keralan cooking and yoga classes on offer. Best are the colourful corner pads with balconies, such as room A, and there are two large air-con rooms.

Windermere Estate
RESORT $$$

(☑ 0484-2425237; www.windermere-retreats. com; Bison Valley Rd, Pothamedu; r incl break-fast ₹13,440-27,520; ❇☜☽) 🍃 An elegant boutique-meets-country retreat, 4km south-east of Munnar, where 18 supremely spa-cious garden- and valley-view rooms are sprinkled around serene grounds flanking an infinity pool with tea-garden panoramas. Top choice are the two suite-like 'Plantation Villas', surrounded by cardamom and coffee plantations and spectacular vistas. There's a cosy library above the country-inspired res-taurant, which delivers Indian cuisine root-ed in homegrown produce.

Tall Trees
RESORT $$$

(☑ 04865-230641; www.ttr.in; Bison Valley Rd; r incl breakfast ₹11,500-17,000; ☜) The 26 smart, lemon-scented, contemporary-meets-classic-Keralan cottages at this shaded hillside re-sort are hidden away under a luxuriant *shola* (virgin forest) canopy, 6km southeast from Munnar, and come with balconies, kettle kits and filtered water. Activities on offer include tea tastings, campfires, ayurvedic massages and guided walks, while meals are served alfresco or in the glass-ceilinged restaurant.

🍴 Eating

Early-morning food stalls in the bazaar serve breakfast snacks and cheap meals and there

OFF THE BEATEN TRACK

PARAMBIKULAM TIGER RESERVE

Possibly the most protected environment in South India (nestled behind three dams in a valley at 300m to 1440m, surrounded by Kerala and Tamil Nadu sanctuaries), **Parambikulam** (✆8300014873, 9442201691, 9442201690; https://parambikulam.org; Indian/foreigner ₹30/300; ⏰7am-6pm, last entry 3pm) constitutes 644 sq km of Kipling-storybook scenery and wildlife-spotting goodness, designated a tiger reserve in 2009. Far less touristed than Kerala's Periyar Tiger Reserve, it's home to elephants, leopards, sloths and around 26 tigers, though its gaur, sambar, chital and crocodiles, plus some of the largest and oldest teak trees in Asia, are more easily sighted.

Bookings for access to the park's buffer zones and Forest Department accommodation are *theoretically* done online up to six months ahead (though there were technical issues with this at the time of writing). Otherwise, contact the **reserve office** (✆9442201691, 9442201690; https://parambikulam.org; Anappady; ⏰7am-6pm), which *may* also have spots and accommodation available on the day. Activities include minibus safaris (₹200) and treks (Indian ₹1200 to ₹3600, foreigner ₹2400 to ₹6100).

Accommodation is in tented niches (Indian ₹6100 to ₹7300, foreigner ₹9700 to ₹12,100), treetop huts (Indian ₹3000 to ₹6100, foreigner ₹3600 to ₹9700) and an air-conditioned colonial-era bungalow (Indian ₹5000 to ₹6100, foreigner ₹7300 to ₹8500); rates are per room and cover meals plus trekking, rafting and wildlife-spotting minibus safaris.

Access to the reserve is via Pollachi (44km south of Coimbatore and 46km southeast of Palakkad) in Tamil Nadu, also the access point for Anamalai Tiger Reserve (p415). There are three daily buses from Pollachi to Parambikulam (₹85, three hours) via Anamalai at 6am, 9.30am or 10am and 3.15pm. Taxis from Pollachi cost around ₹1700. The reserve sometimes closes due to fire risk in March and April, and is best avoided during the monsoon (June to August).

are some good affordable restaurants in Munnar town, but the region's best food is served at its homestays and resorts.

Rapsy Restaurant INDIAN $
(✆04865-230456; Bazaar; dishes ₹50-200; ⏰7am-10pm) This spotless glass-fronted sanctuary in the bazaar is packed at lunchtime, with locals lining up for Rapsy's famous *paratha* (Indian-style flaky bread) or biryani. It's equally popular with travellers and makes a decent stab at North Indian curries and fancy international dishes like Spanish omelette and Israeli shakshuka (eggs with tomatoes and spices).

Taste the Brews CAFE $
(dishes ₹20-90; ⏰hours vary) An easy-going traveller-oriented cafe, opposite the bus station, for Continental-style breakfasts (omelettes, fruit salads), fresh juices, carrot cake and tastings of local tea and coffee.

Sree Mahaveer Bhojanalaya NORTH INDIAN $$
(✆9633906581; Hotel SN Annex, Government Guesthouse Rd; thalis ₹90-320; ⏰7am-10pm) Friendly and well-dressed, this all-veg hit at the northern end of Munnar keeps busy with families for its great range of thalis: pick from Rajasthani, Gujarati, Punjabi and more, plus a dazzling array of vegetarian rices and curries

Ali Baba & 41 Dishes MULTICUISINE $$
(✆8078801666, 04865-233303; www.alibaba 41dishes.com; Mulakkada Jn, Lakshmi Rd; mains ₹130-300; ⏰11.30am-10.30pm; 🛜) A sizzling Indian-international menu of red-hot noodles, spiced seafood platters, paneer/chicken tikka, northern gravies and southern thalis draws locals and travellers to this halal restaurant with Munnar-themed murals on the walls, located near the bus station at the southern end of town.

☆ Entertainment

Punarjani Traditional Village LIVE PERFORMANCE
(✆9895999701, 04865-263888; http://punarjani munnar.com; 2nd Mile, NH85, Pallivasal; ₹200-300; ⏰Kathakali 5pm, kalarippayat 6pm) Entertaining (though aimed at tourists) daily performances of Kathakali and *kalarippayat*, 7km southwest of Munnar. Same-day

THATTEKKAD BIRD SANCTUARY

A serene 25-sq-km park in the foothills of the Western Ghats, cut through by two rivers and two streams, **Thattekkad Bird Sanctuary** (☑04862-232271, 8547603194; www. thattekadbirdsanctuary.org; adult/child Indian ₹45/40, foreigner ₹190/40, camera/video ₹40/240; ⊙7am-5pm) shelters around 300 fluttering species – unusual in that they are mostly forest rather than water birds – including Malabar grey hornbills, Jerdon's nightjars, grey drongos, darters, kingfishers, flycatchers, warblers, sunbirds, tiny 4g flowerpeckers and rarer species like the Sri Lankan frogmouth.

River boating (₹150 per person) and guided birdwatching trips (rates vary) are organised by the efficient reception office at the sanctuary's entrance; accommodation places also offer birdwatching. Local homestays make excellent bases; we recommend two-room **Bird Song Homestay** (☑8943894087, 9746248274; http://thattekadhomestay. com; Thattekkad Bird Sanctuary; r incl meals with/without AC ₹3500/3000; ▣ 🅥), run by welcoming naturalist Vinod, and blue-walled **Jungle Bird Homestay** (☑9947506188, 0485-2588143; http://junglebirdhomestay.blogspot.com; Thattekkad Bird Sanctuary; r incl meals per person ₹1500, with AC d ₹3300-4000; ▣ 🅥), both just inside the sanctuary. **Windermere Riverhouse** (☑0484-2425237; www.windermere-retreats.com; Neriamangalam Rd, Inchathotty; r incl breakfast & dinner ₹19,520; ▣ 🅥 🅢) is a graceful, cream-coloured riverside bungalow in colonial-era tea-planter style, a 20km drive southeast of the sanctuary.

Thattekkad is on the Ernakulam–Munnar road. Buses from Ernakulam (₹40, two hours) and Munnar (₹60, two to three hours) run to Kothamangalam, from where you can catch an autorickshaw (₹150) or a bus (₹12, 25 minutes) for the final 12km northeast to Thattekkad.

tickets are usually available but for the best seats consider booking ahead.

ℹ Information

DTPC Tourist Office (☑04865-231516; www. dtpcidukki.com; AM Rd/NH85; ⊙8.30am-6.30pm)

Forest Information Centre (☑8547382391; ⊙10am-5pm)

ℹ Getting There & Away

Roads around Munnar are winding and often in poor condition following monsoon rains, so travel times may vary.

The main **KSRTC bus station** (AM Rd/NH85) is 1.5km south of the town centre, though all government buses also stop at one of several stands in Munnar town (from where private buses depart).

There are at least 18 daily buses to Ernakulam (Kochi; ₹115, five hours, 5.40am to 9.45pm); the 3pm is an air-con service. Government buses also run to Trivandrum (₹270 to ₹600, eight to nine hours, seven daily 4.50am to 9pm), Alleppey (₹150, five hours, four daily 6.20am to 4.30pm), Kumily (₹100, four to five hours, 6.30am) and Bengaluru (Bangalore; ₹800, 16 hours, 3.30pm) via Wayanad (₹500, 10 hours) and Mysuru (Mysore; ₹680, 13½ hours). Private buses go to Kumily (₹115, four to five hours) at 12.15pm and Madurai (₹110, five hours) at

12.30pm, 2.20pm and 5.30pm. There are separate stands for buses to Top Station (₹60, one hour, 8am, 9am and 9.30am) and Coimbatore (₹140, six hours, 3.30pm) via Chinnar Wildlife Sanctuary (₹60, one hour).

Taxis cost ₹2800 to Ernakulam, ₹3800 to Alleppey and ₹2400 to Kumily.

ℹ Getting Around

Autorickshaws ply the hills around Munnar with bone-shuddering efficiency; short hops cost ₹20 to ₹50.

Gokulam Bike Hire (☑9447237165; per day ₹400-500; ⊙9am-6pm) rents out motorbikes and scooters; call ahead.

Around Munnar

Top Station

High above Kerala's border with Tamil Nadu, Top Station (elevation 1880m) is popular for its spectacular views over the Western Ghats. From Munnar, three daily buses (₹60, 8am, 9am and 9.30am) make the 32km climb northeast past tea estates in around an hour, or take a return taxi or jeep (₹1200). You may see wild elephants on the way up.

Eravikulam National Park

Around 11km north of Munnar, the 97 sq km of grasslands and *shola* of **Eravikulam National Park** (☑04865-231587; www.eravikulam.org; Indian/foreigner ₹120/400, camera/video ₹40/400; ☻8am-4pm Apr-Jan) conceal the world's largest population (700 to 800) of endangered, but almost tame, Nilgiri tahr. Safari buses take you into the Rajamala tourist zone where the likelihood of sightings is high. The park also hosts Anamudi, South India's highest peak (2695m), though it was closed to climbers at the time of research, as were all Eravikulam treks (these may reopen). From Munnar, taxis cost ₹800 return.

CENTRAL KERALA

Kochi (Cochin)

☑0484 / POP 602,050

Set on a magnificent estuary, serene Kochi has been drawing traders, explorers and travellers to its shores for over 600 years. Nowhere else in India could you find such an intriguing mix: giant Chinese fishing nets, a 450-year-old synagogue, ancient mosques, Portuguese- and Dutch-era houses and the crumbling remains of the British Raj. The result is an unlikely blend of medieval Portugal and Holland and an English village grafted onto the tropical Malabar Coast. It's a delightful place to explore, laze in arty cafes and relax at some of India's finest homestays and heritage hotels. It's also an important centre for Keralan arts (traditional and contemporary) and a standout place to see Kathakali and *kalarippayat*.

Mainland Ernakulam is Kochi's hectic transport and cosmopolitan hub, while the historical towns of Fort Cochin and Mattancherry, though well touristed, remain wonderfully atmospheric.

◉ Sights

◉ Fort Cochin

The historical European part of the city, Fort Cochin has a couple of small, sandy beaches, which are only really good for people-watching in the evening and gazing out at the incoming tankers. A popular promenade meanders from west-coast Mahatma Gandhi Beach to the Chinese fishing nets and fish market (p305).

Keep an eye out along the shore for the scant remains of Fort Immanuel, the 16th-century Portuguese fort from which the area takes its name.

Chinese Fishing Nets LANDMARK
(Map p304) The unofficial emblems of the backwaters, and perhaps the most photographed, are the half-dozen giant cantilevered Chinese fishing nets on Fort Cochin's northeastern shore, known locally as *cheena vala*. A legacy of traders from the AD 1400 court of Kublai Khan, these spiderlike, 10m-tall contraptions rest on teak or bamboo poles and require five or six people to operate their counterweights at high tide.

St Francis Church CHURCH
(Map p304; Church Rd; ☻8.30am-5pm) Constructed in 1503 by Portuguese Franciscan friars, this is believed to be India's oldest European-built church. The faded-yellow edifice that stands here today was built in the mid-16th century to replace the original wooden chapel, though it was later altered by both the Dutch and British. Explorer Vasco da Gama, who died in Cochin in 1524, was buried in this spot for 14 years before his remains were taken to Lisbon – you can still visit his tombstone in the church.

> ### WORTH A TRIP
>
> ### CHINNAR WILDLIFE SANCTUARY
>
> This 90-sq-km **sanctuary** (☑04865-231587; www.chinnar.org; entry with 3hr trek Indian/foreigner ₹250/600; ☻8am-3pm), 50km northeast of Munnar, protects deer, leopards, elephants, gaur, langurs and endangered Nilgiri tahr and grizzled giant squirrels. Entry is by three-hour trek with tribal guides (two tribal groups live here). Tree-house (₹4000), mud-hut (₹5000) and log-house (₹4000) accommodation within the sanctuary are available; rates are per couple, including breakfast and dinner. For details contact Munnar's Forest Information Centre or DTPC.
>
> Coimbatore- and Udumalpet-bound buses from Munnar stop at Chinnar (₹60, 1½ hours); return taxis cost ₹2000.

Kochi (Cochin)

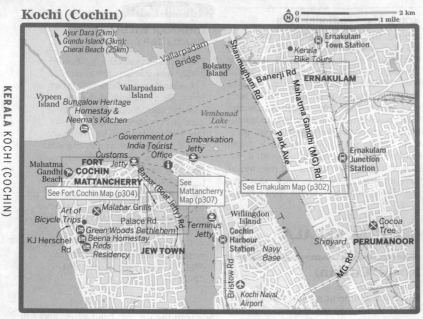

David Hall
GALLERY

(Map p304; www.davidhall.in; Church Rd; ⊙11am-9pm Tue-Sun, hours vary) Opposite the parade ground, this beautiful restored bungalow is all that remains of three 17th-century Dutch-era houses built using materials from demolished Portuguese churches. It's now an arts-and-culture centre, showcasing up-and-coming artists with performances and changing exhibitions.

Dutch Cemetery
CEMETERY

(Map p304; Beach Rd) Consecrated in 1724, this cemetery near Kochi's beach contains the worn and dilapidated graves of Dutch traders and soldiers. Its gates are normally locked but a caretaker might let you in, or ask at nearby St Francis Church (p297).

Santa Cruz Basilica
BASILICA

(Map p304; cnr Bastion St & KB Jacob Rd; ⊙9am-1pm & 2.30-5.30pm Mon-Sat, 10.30am-1pm Sun) Built on the site of an early-16th-century Portuguese church (demolished during the British Raj), Fort Cochin's imposing neoclassical Catholic basilica dates to 1902. In the striking pastel-coloured interior you'll find artefacts from the different historical eras in Kochi.

Kashi Art Gallery
GALLERY

(Map p304; ☑ 0484-2215769; www.kashiartgallery. com; Burgher St; ⊙8.30am-10pm) The pioneer of Fort Cochin's art revival, Kashi displays changing exhibitions of local artists in a creatively restored Dutch heritage house, attached to one of Kerala's most fabulous cafes (p305).

Indo-Portuguese Museum
MUSEUM

(Map p304; ☑0484-2215400; Bishop Kureethara Rd; adult/child ₹40/20; ⊙9am-1pm & 2-6pm Tue-Sun) The heritage of one of India's earliest Catholic communities – including vestments, silver processional crosses, altarpieces from the Kochi diocese and 19th-century sketches of Santa Cruz Basilica – is on show at this thoughtfully presented museum hidden in the tranquil garden of the Bishop's House. The basement contains remnants of the 16th-century Portuguese-built Fort Immanuel.

⊙ Mattancherry & Jew Town

About 2.5km southeast of Fort Cochin, Mattancherry is the old bazaar district and centre of the spice trade. These days it's packed with spice shops and pricey Kashmiri-run emporiums that autorickshaw drivers will fall over backwards to take you to for a healthy commission – any offer of a cheap tour of the district will inevitably lead to a few shops. In the midst of this, Jew Town is a bustling port area with a fine synagogue. Scores of small firms huddle together in dilapidated old buildings and the air is filled with the biting aromas of ginger, cardamom, cumin, turmeric and cloves, though the lanes around Mattancherry Palace and the synagogue are packed with antique and tourist-curio shops rather than spices. Just south is Kochi's old Muslim quarter.

★**Mattancherry Palace**   MUSEUM
(Dutch Palace; Map p307; Palace Rd, Mattancherry; adult/child ₹5/free; ⊙9am-5pm Sat-Thu) Mattancherry Palace was a generous gift presented to the Raja of Kochi, Veera Kerala Varma (1537–65), as a gesture of goodwill by the Portuguese in 1555. The Dutch renovated it in 1663, hence the alternative name, the Dutch Palace. The building combines European and Keralan styles, but the star attractions are the royal bedchamber's astonishingly preserved Hindu murals from the 17th to 19th centuries, which depict scenes from the Ramayana, Mahabharata and Puranic legends in intricate, colourful detail.

★**Pardesi Synagogue**   SYNAGOGUE
(Map p307; Synagogue Lane, Mattancherry; ₹5; ⊙10am-1pm & 3-5pm Sun-Thu, 10am-1pm Fri, closed Sat & Jewish holidays) Originally built in 1568, Mattancherry's synagogue was partially destroyed by the Portuguese in 1662, and rebuilt two years later when the Dutch took Kochi. It features an ornate brass bema, elegant wooden benches, and elaborate hand-painted, willow-pattern floor tiles from Canton, China, added in 1762 during major remodelling under Ezekial Rahabi. It's magnificently illuminated by Belgian chandeliers and coloured-glass lamps. The graceful clock tower dates from 1760, with inscriptions in Malayalam, Hebrew, Roman and Arabic script.

The majority of Kochi's Pardesi Jews have emigrated, but the synagogue remains excellently preserved.

Jewish Cemetery   CEMETERY
(Map p307; AB Salem Rd, Mattancherry) Just southwest of Mattancherry's synagogue, the undisturbed Jewish Cemetery contains ancient tombstones marked with Hebrew script.

◎ **Ernakulam & Around**

Kerala Folklore Museum   MUSEUM
(0484-2665452; www.keralafolkloremuseum. org; Folklore Junction, Thevara; Indian/foreigner ₹100/200, camera ₹100; ⊙9am-6pm) Created in Kerala style from ancient temples and beautiful old houses collected by its owner, an antique dealer, the family-run folklore museum houses a priceless collection of over 5000 artefacts and covers three architectural styles: Malabar on the ground floor; Kochi/Portuguese on the 1st; and Travancore on the 2nd (top). The fine top-floor theatre has an 18th-century wood-carved ceiling depicting Hindu gods, as well as colourful Ramayana and Mahabharata murals. It's 4.5km south of Ernakulam Junction.

🏃 **Activities**

Popular South Indian cooking classes are held at **Neema's Kitchen** (9539300010; https:// neemaskitchen.co.in; Bungalow Heritage Homestay, Vypeen Island; classes per person ₹2000-2500; ⊙10.30am-1.30pm & 3.30-6.30pm) on Vypeen Island (just north of the jetty) and in Fort Cochin at Mrs Leelu Roy's **Cook & Eat** (Map p304; 0484-2215377, 9846055377; www.leelu homestay.com; 1/629 Quiros St, Fort Cochin; classes per person ₹1000; ⊙11am-1pm & 4-6pm Mon-Sat) and Green Woods Bethlehem (p301).

Ayurdara   AYURVEDA, YOGA
(9447721041; https://ayurdara.com; Murikkumpadam, Vypeen Island; per day ₹1650; ⊙9am-5.30pm) Run by third-generation ayurvedic practitioner Dr Subhash, this delightful, appointment-only waterside treatment centre specialises in personalised therapies of one to three weeks and also offers yoga (₹200). It's on Vypeen Island, 3km north of the Fort Cochin ferry jetty.

Loving Earth Yoga   YOGA
(Map p304; www.lovingearthyogacafe.com; 1/839 Quiros St, Fort Cochin; yoga ₹500; ⊙cafe 8am-8pm Tue-Sun) Drop-in daily vinyasa, ashtanga, hatha and/or yin yoga classes on a breezy rooftop attached to an all-vegan cafe serving mezze platters, Buddha bowls and creative salads (₹200 to ₹300); see the website for current schedules.

🗨 **Courses**

The Kerala Kathakali Centre (p307) has short- and long-term courses in classical Kathakali dance, music and make-up as well as *kalarippayat* (from ₹650 per hour).

For a crash course in the martial art of *kalarippayat,* head to famed training centre Ens Kalari (p308), 6.5km southeast of Ernakulam, which offers intensive courses from one week to one month.

👉 Tours

Ernakulam's knowledgeable Tourist Desk (p308) runs the popular full-day Great Water Valley Tour (₹1250, departs 8am, returns 6pm), by *shikara* and canoe, through backwater canals, villages and lagoons and vast Vembanad Lake; rates include lunch and some sections are by bus.

Art of Bicycle Trips CYCLING, WALKING
(☎8129945707; https://artofbicycletrips.com; KB Jacob Rd; 3hr/half-day tours ₹2250/4200; ⊙9am-6pm Mon-Sat) Guided bicycle tours on quality mountain bikes with this India-wide operator include the three-hour Vasco Safari morning tour of the historic Fort area and a half-day ride around the backwaters. There are also evening walking food tours of Fort Cochin and Mattancherry (₹950).

Kerala Bike Tours TOURS
(☎9446492382, 9388476817; www.keralabike tours.com; 42/2252B St Benedict Road North, Kacheripady, Ernakulam) Organises multilingual Enfield Bullet tours around Kerala and the Western Ghats (six-day full-board trip per person including accommodation ₹109,000) and hires out touring-quality Enfields (from ₹12,000 per week) for serious riders with unlimited mileage, full insurance and free recovery/maintenance options.

🎎 Festivals & Events

Ernakulathappan Utsavam RELIGIOUS
(Shiva Temple, Ernakulam; ⊙Jan/Feb) Eight days of festivities culminating in fireworks, music and a parade of 15 splendidly decorated elephants (which won't please everyone).

Kochi–Muziris Biennale ART
(☎0484-2215287; http://kochimuzirisbiennale. org; ₹100, free Mon; ⊙Dec-Mar) Into its fourth edition (2018), this major contemporary biennial arts festival is one of the largest of its kind in Asia. Over 90 Indian and international artists bring their creativity to workshops, talks and exhibitions across Kochi, with heritage properties as venues.

Cochin Carnival CARNIVAL
(www.cochincarnival.org; ⊙21 Dec) Fort Cochin's biggest bash, a 10-day festival culminating on New Year's Eve. Street parades, colourful costumes, embellished elephants (which won't appeal to all), music, folk dancing and lots of fun.

🛏 Sleeping

Fort Cochin is the homestay capital of India – around 200! It's also home to some of Kerala's finest heritage accommodation, as well as contemporary-style hostels.

Ernakulam is cheaper and more convenient for onward travel, but the ambience and accommodation choices are less inspiring than in Fort Cochin.

Book ahead during the November-to-March high season, especially December and January.

🏠 Fort Cochin

Happy Camper HOSTEL $
(Map p304; ☎9742725668; www.facebook.com/ happycamperkochi; KB Jacob Rd; dm ₹500-600; ❄️🛜) 🅿 Billing itself as a boutique hostel, Happy Camper is a relaxed place with three en suite, air-con dorms (for four or eight; lockers provided), a small kitchen, free water refills, vibrant wall art, an excellent little cafe and rooftop area, and friendly staff. Good location just south of the main tourist hub.

Zostel HOSTEL $
(Map p304; ☎011-39589007; www.zostel.com; 1/751A Njaliparambu Junction; dm ₹450, r ₹1270-1500; ❄️🛜) Zipped away down a small lane, Kochi's popular and sociable Zostel ticks all the right backpacker boxes. There are personal plugs, lights and lockers in the updated air-con dorms, which sleep four (mixed) or six (women only), along with three polished private doubles, and communal spaces adorned with lively cushions and murals.

Maritime HOSTEL $
(Map p304; ☎0484-2214785; https://thehostel crowd.com; 2/227 Calvathy Rd; dm ₹500, r ₹1200-1600; ❄️🛜) Behind a red-and-white facade, this branch of the Goan Hostel Crowd chain is just west of the Customs jetty. The nautical theme is a characterful touch; the en suite air-con dorms for four to six people have individual lockers and plugs; double rooms (with fan or air-con) are clean, compact and well kept; and there's a small kitchen plus a laundry and a library.

★ **Reds Residency** HOMESTAY $$
(☎ 9847030342, 9388643747; www.redsresidency.
in; 11/372 A KJ Herschel Rd; r incl breakfast with
AC from ₹1200, without AC ₹900-1200, AC rooftop
cottage ₹1800; ❄ 🔊) *✦* Hotel-quality rooms
come with solar-powered showers and a
true family welcome from knowledgable
hosts Philip and Maryann at this delight-
ful homestay. The five rooms – including
a four-bed family room – are modern and
immaculate, and there's a self-contained
rooftop 'penthouse' cottage with a kitchen.
Days begin with fabulous, lovingly prepared
breakfasts. It's in a peaceful spot 1km south
of central Fort Cochin.

★ **Green Woods Bethlehem** HOMESTAY $$
(☎ 0484-2216069, 9846014924; www.greenwoods
bethlehem.com; Kurisingal House; r incl breakfast
with AC ₹1700-2000, without AC ₹1000-1500;
❄ 🔊) With a smile that brightens weary
travellers, welcoming owner Sheeba looks
ready to sign your adoption papers the minute you walk through the door. Down a quiet
laneway, amid walled gardens thick with
palms, this is one of Kochi's most serene
homestays. The 10 humble but cosy rooms
are scattered up rambling staircases; breakfast is served on the leafy rooftop.

Cooking classes/demonstrations (₹1000)
happen daily. It's 1km south of central Fort
Cochin.

Raintree Lodge HERITAGE HOTEL $$
(Map p304; ☎ 9747721091; www.fortcochin.
com; 1/618 Peter Celli St; r incl breakfast ₹3300;
❄ 🔊) The five intimate, graceful and
good-value rooms at this cheerful convert-
ed 18th-century house flirt with boutique-
hotel status. Each mixes contemporary style
with heritage carved-wood furniture; the
two front upstairs rooms have gorgeous
vine-covered Romeo-and-Juliet balconies.
Breakfast is served at the wonderful Kashi
Art Cafe (p305), run by the same team.

Beena Homestay HOMESTAY $$
(☎ 9447574579, 0484-2215458; www.
homestaykochi.com; 11/359B Kadathanad; r incl
breakfast & dinner with/without AC ₹3000/2500;
❄ 🔊) *✦* Beena has been feeding and shel-
tering travellers for years in the family
homestay, just off Ponnoonjal Rd 1km south
of central Fort Cochin, and maintains high
standards with six spotless rooms, solar
power, and home-cooked meals taken in the
dining room.

Delight Home Stay HOMESTAY $$
(Map p304; ☎ 98461121421, 0484-2217658; www.
delightfulhomestay.com; Post Office Rd; r incl break-
fast ₹3000-4000; ❄ 🔊) One of Fort Cochin's
original homestays, this charming white-
washed house is adorned with elaborate
woodwork and dangling terracotta plant
pots, while the six custom-designed rooms
are spacious and polished with heritage
character. Good home-cooked food is served
and there's a colourful garden.

Travellers Inn GUESTHOUSE $$
(Map p304; ☎ 9446332662, 0484-2215551; www.
travelsinmind.com; 1/326B Princess St; r ₹1500-
2500) In the heart of Fort Cochin, with a
handy travel desk, this welcoming, efficiently operated Indian-Italian-run guesthouse
has six unpretentious modern rooms, decorated with a single custom-made mono-
chrome drawing of Kochi by a local artist.
The two upper-floor front rooms come with
small balconies.

★ **Old Harbour Hotel** HERITAGE HOTEL $$$
(Map p304; ☎ 0484-2218006; www.oldharbour
hotel.com; 1/328 Tower Rd; r ₹15,000-27,000;
❄ ❄) Overlooking a lush garden with lily
ponds and a pool, the stylish Old Har-
bour is housed in a 300-year-old Dutch/
Portuguese heritage building. The elegant
mix of period and modern design lends it
a more intimate feel than some of the more
grandiose competition. The four garden-view
rooms with balcony are divine; others have
freestanding tubs or plant-filled, open air
bathrooms.

Brunton Boatyard LUXURY HOTEL $$$
(Map p304; ☎ 0484-2846500; www.cghearth.com;
River Rd; r ₹28,160-56,320; ❄ 🔊 ❄) *✦* On the
site of a Victorian-era shipyard, this grand
CGH creation faithfully reproduces 16th-,
17th- and 18th-century Dutch, British and
Portuguese architecture for an updated
heritage look. Most rooms gaze out over the
harbour, and have bathtubs and balconies
with refreshing sea breezes. There are three
excellent restaurants, complimentary yoga
and bicycles, and a waterfront pool shaded
by tangles of bougainvillea.

Malabar House BOUTIQUE HOTEL $$$
(Map p304; ☎ 0484-2216666; www.malabar
house.com; 1/269 Parade Ground Rd; r incl break-
fast €220-360; ❄ ❄) What may just be one of
the most romantic boutique hotels in Ker-
ala, Malabar flaunts its chic blend of con-
temporary design and original 18th-century

Ernakulam

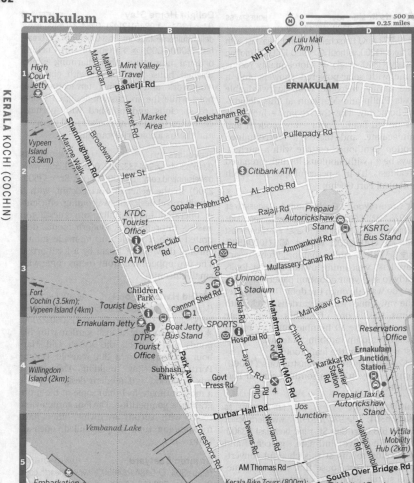

architecture like it's not even trying. Rooms are strung around a small pool; while suites are huge and lavishly appointed, standard rooms feel more snug. The award-winning Malabar Junction restaurant (p306) and Di-Vine wine bar (p306) are top-notch.

Forte Kochi HERITAGE HOTEL $$$
(Map p304; ☎0484-2704800; www.fortekochi. in; Princess St; r incl breakfast ₹9600-22,400; ❊❡❀❀) A chicly remodelled mango-yellow 1800s home with its origins dating back to the Portuguese-rule era, Forte Kochi is a welcome 2018 luxe arrival. Tiled floors and design-led bathrooms breathe fresh contem-

Ernakulam

🛏 Sleeping
1 Boat Jetty Bungalow B3
2 Grand Hotel C4
3 John's Residency B3

🍴 Eating
4 Chillies C4
5 Frys Village Restaurant C1
   Grand Pavilion .... (see 2)

🍷 Drinking & Nightlife
   Couchyn .... (see 2)

porary style into the 27 heritage-inspired rooms, which orbit an enticing pool, and there's an enormous suite with a freestanding claw-foot bath. Excellent location, good restaurant, charming staff.

Fort House Hotel HOTEL $$$
(Map p304; ☑0484-2217103, 9539375431; www.hotelforthouse.com; 2/6A Calvathy Rd; r incl breakfast ₹7/500; ❄❓) Around 200m west of Fort Cochin's Customs jetty, this family-owned hideaway is one of the old core's few truly waterfront hotels, though the 16 smart, contemporary-Keralan rooms and well-regarded ayurvedic centre are tucked back in a lush garden, with the excellent restaurant (p306) taking prime lakeside position.

Mattancherry & Jew Town

**Ginger House
Museum Hotel** HERITAGE HOTEL $$$
(Map p307; ☑0484-2213400; http://museumhotel.in; Ginger House Bldg, Mattancherry; r incl breakfast US$300-750; ❄❓❄) Above an astonishing private antiques collection, each of these eight exquisitely and individually themed design-meets-heritage rooms – with glossy contemporary bathrooms, personal coffee trays and beautiful period furnishings – feels like its own sumptuous little world. Expect a feast of carved teakwood, mirrored ceilings and baroque chandeliers. The rooftop has a small lake-view infinity pool, and there's an excellent waterfront restaurant (p307).

Ernakulam

John's Residency HOTEL $
(Map p302; ☑9995070834, 8281321395; TD Rd; r with AC ₹1600, s/d without AC ₹650/850; ❄@❓) A genuine backpacker place, efficiently run John's is your best budget bet for an overnight stop in Ernakulam, especially if John himself is in residence. It's 600m east of the boat jetty. Rooms are small (deluxes are bigger) but clean and decorated with flashes of colour and, for some, balconies, providing a welcoming feel for this price bracket.

Boat Jetty Bungalow HOTEL $$
(Map p302; ☑9746013198, 0484-2373211; www.boatjettybungalow.com; Cannon Shed Rd; s/d with AC ₹1350/1900, without AC ₹560/850; ❄) An 1891 former jetty-manager's house and ancestral home has been thoughtfully refurbished into budget-to-midrange accommodation, its palette of greys and compact,

impeccably kept rooms with bottled water offset by original wooden ceilings. It's 300m east of Ernakulam's jetty for Fort Cochin.

Grand Hotel HOTEL $$
(Map p302; ☑0484-2382061, 9895721014; https://grandhotelkerala.com; MG Rd; s ₹3780-4100, d ₹4740-6260, all incl breakfast; ❄❓) This 1960s hotel, with its polished original art deco fittings, exudes the sort of retro glamour that contemporary hotels would love to re-create. The smart, spacious rooms have gleaming parquet floors, tea/coffee trays and large modern bathrooms with hairdryers. Also here are good global-cuisine restaurant **Grand Pavilion** (☑0484-2382061, 9895721014; mains ₹245-480; ☻7.30-10.30am, noon-3.30pm & 7-10pm) and Ernakulam's most sophisticated bar, **Couchyn** (☻11am-11pm).

Around Kochi

Bungalow Heritage Homestay HOMESTAY $$
(☑9846302347; https://thebungalow.co.in; Vypeen Island; r incl breakfast with AC ₹5100-6600, without AC ₹4500-6000; ❄❓) Just 300m north from Vypeen Island's ferry dock, this beautiful 1930 Keralan heritage house is a delight, with two large connecting rooms featuring quaint furnishings and grand wooden flooring on its Dutch-inspired upper floor. Owner Neema runs excellent cooking classes (p299) on the Portuguese-styled lower level. Minimum two-night stay.

Kallanchery Retreat HOMESTAY $$
(☑9847446683, 0484-2240564; www.kallancheryretreat.com; Panakkal House, Kumbalanghi; r & cottage incl breakfast ₹2000-3000; ❄❓) Escape the Kochi crowds at this peaceful waterside homestay and expansive garden in the village of Kumbalanghi, 13km south of Fort Cochin. Tidy rooms are either in the family home or in a lakefront cottage. Chinese fishing nets are on your doorstep, and boat trips, village tours, and home-cooked meals (₹350) courtesy of chef-owner Rockey are available.

Eating & Drinking

Fort Cochin

Some of Kochi's best cooking is served in Fort Cochin's homestays; also here are some of Kerala's finest cafes. Several top-end

Fort Cochin

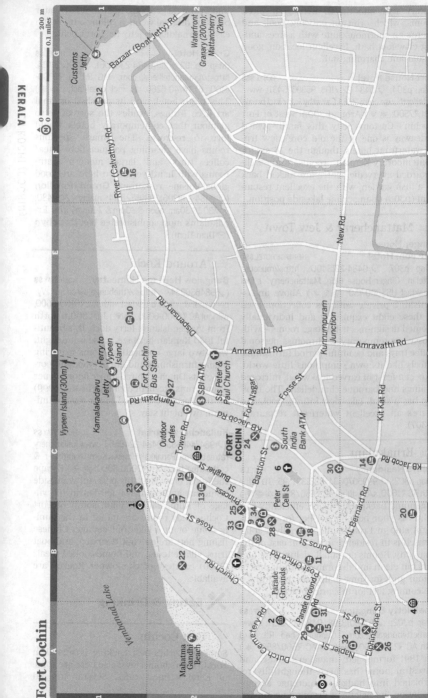

Fort Cochin

◉ Sights
1 Chinese Fishing Nets	B1
2 David Hall	A3
3 Dutch Cemetery	A3
4 Indo-Portuguese Museum	A4
5 Kashi Art Gallery	C2
6 Santa Cruz Basilica	C3
7 St Francis Church	B2

✪ Activities, Courses & Tours
8 Cook & Eat	B3
9 Loving Earth Yoga	B3

🛏 Sleeping
10 Brunton Boatyard	D1
11 Delight Home Stay	B3
12 Fort House Hotel	G1
13 Forte Kochi	C2
14 Happy Camper	C4
15 Malabar House	A3
16 Maritime	F1
17 Old Harbour Hotel	C2
18 Raintree Lodge	B3
19 Travellers Inn	C2
20 Zostel	B4

⊗ Eating
21 Dal Roti	A4
22 Drawing Room	B2
23 Fishmongers	C1
Fort House Restaurant	(see 12)
24 Fusion Bay	C3
Kashi Art Cafe	(see 5)
25 Loafers Corner	B2
Malabar Junction	(see 15)
26 Oceanos	A4
27 Qissa Cafe	D2
28 Teapot	B3

◗ Drinking & Nightlife
Clubb18	(see 27)
29 DiVine	A3

◉ Entertainment
30 Kerala Kathakali Centre	C3

🛍 Shopping
31 Anokhi	A3
32 Fabindia	A4
33 Idiom Bookshop	B2
34 Niraamaya	B3

hotels have excellent restaurants, too. Only a few places serve alcohol with meals.

Behind the Chinese fishing nets are a handful of **fishmongers** (Map p304; River Rd; ⊙restaurants 8am-9pm), from whom you can buy the day's catch then have it cooked at one of the simple restaurants on nearby Tower Rd (for an additional charge); a fillet of kingfish costs around ₹400.

★Kashi Art Cafe CAFE $$
(Map p304; Burgher St; dishes ₹150-350; ⊙8.30am-10pm; 🛜) 🍴 Fort Cochin's original (and best) art cafe, this fashionable, light-filled space has a Zen vibe, a creeping vertical garden and stylish wood tables spreading out into a courtyard dotted with contemporary artwork. The coffee is strong, organic ingredients are used wherever possible, and the luscious breakfasts and lunches are excellent (French toast, home-baked cakes, creative salads).

★Dal Roti INDIAN $$
(Map p304; ☑9746459244; 1/293 Lily St; mains ₹170-350; ⊙noon-3pm & 6.30-10pm Wed-Mon) Always-busy Dal Roti is one of Fort Cochin's most-loved restaurants. The knowledgeable owner Ramesh will hold your hand through his expansive North Indian menu and help you dive into a delicious world of vegetarian, eggetarian and nonveg options. From *kati* rolls (filled *paratha* fried with a coating of

egg) and stuffed *paratha* to seven thali types, you won't go hungry. At the time of research there were rumours of the pending closure of Dal Roti. Check before heading there.

Fusion Bay SEAFOOD $$
(Map p304; ☑9995105110; KB Jacob Rd; mains ₹150-450; ⊙12.30-11pm) This unassuming little family restaurant in central Fort Cochin is renowned locally for its imaginative Kerala Syrian fish delicacies cooked in the *pollichathu* style (masala spiced and grilled in a banana leaf), and assorted seafood dishes such as spicy fish *pappas,* coconut-fried prawns and fish in mango curry. There are a few veg choices too.

Loafers Corner CAFE $$
(Map p304; ☑0484-2215351; www.facebook.com/loaferscornercafe; 1/351 Princess St; dishes ₹170-200; ⊙9am-10pm; 🛜) A stylishly restored 200-year-old Dutch-Portuguese-style building, Loafers is all reclaimed wood, minimalist design, cosy window booths and delicate murals. It's a good, relaxed spot for a coffee, a fresh juice, breakfast or a light meal, with a bistro-style menu of sandwiches, wraps, pancakes, pastas and homemade cakes.

Drawing Room INTERNATIONAL, INDIAN $$
(Map p304; www.facebook.com/thedrawingroom kochi; Church Rd; mains ₹150-450; ⊙11am-11pm) Set in the grand Cochin Club, this stylish

cafe-restaurant enjoys a wonderful garden location with large windows facing out to the water, and is jazzed up by freehand murals that weave together classic Kerala scenes with musical elements. The lightly creative menu, based on family recipes, features salads, pastas, soups and fish or prawn curries. There's regular live music in season.

Fort House Restaurant
SEAFOOD, INDIAN $$
(Map p304; ☑ 9539375431, 0484-2217103; www.hotelforthouse.com; 2/6A Calvathy Rd; mains ₹170-900; ☉ 7.30am-10.30pm) The waterside restaurant at the family-owned Fort House Hotel (p302) is a prime choice for a leisurely lunch, fringed by hot-pink bougainvillea and plants overflowing from earthy-red pots. The signatures are the seafood dishes (including Keralan-style fish curry), though the flavoursome veg dishes pack a punch too. Dine at tables overlooking the water or in the calm covered garden.

Qissa Cafe
CAFE $$
(Map p304; ☑ 0484-2215769; www.facebook.com/QissaCafe; No 18 Hotel, Rampath Rd; dishes ₹180-300; ☉ 7.30am-10pm; 🛜) Usually packed with fashionable Kochiites, Qissa channels a cosmopolitan scene with its mismatched pastel-painted chairs, outdoor garden and buzzy atmosphere. Come for the homemade cakes, brunch-type snacks (avocado toast has arrived!), stuffed omelettes, heartier creations like lemon-pesto pasta, and chilled fresh juices and lemonades presented in jam jars. Good coffee and tea too.

Teapot
CAFE $$
(Map p304; Peter Celli St; dishes ₹180-300; ☉ 8.30am-9pm) Behind an ivy-covered facade, this atmospheric cafe is perfect for 'high tea', with an impressive choice of brews, sandwiches and cakes turned out in airy, heritage-style rooms amid canary yellow walls and wood-beamed ceilings. Witty tea-themed accents include antique teapots, tea chests for tables and a gnarled, tea-tree-based glass table. Snacks include omelettes, grilled sandwiches and a veggie stew with *appam*.

Oceanos
SEAFOOD $$
(Map p304; ☑ 9633713653; Elphinstone St; mains ₹180-600; ☉ 12.30-10pm) Gloriously fresh seafood is the thing at this smart, locally popular restaurant with turquoise table runners and touches of greenery. Fish is served in spicy *pollichathu* style, in mango curry or

perhaps grilled with a coconut sauce. There are also Goan-Portuguese seafood classics like *peixe recheado* (grilled spice-stuffed fish) and some South and North Indian veg and nonveg favourites.

Malabar Grills
INDIAN $$
(☑ 9061800042; www.facebook.com/malabargrillskochi; Kokers Junction, Amaravathi Rd; mains ₹110-350; ☉ 9am-11pm; 🛜) Join feasting Indian families at this sprawling modern restaurant fronted by a barbecue just southeast of Fort Cochin's tourist centre. Breakfasts (₹30 to ₹80) are classic South India: *puttu*, *iddiyappam* (a rice noodle dish), dosa, *idli* with *sambar* (soupy lentil dish with vegetables). Later, the focus turns to thalis (₹90 to ₹140), biryanis and, especially, grilled meats and seafood.

★ Malabar Junction
INTERNATIONAL $$$
(Map p304; ☑ 0484-2216666; www.malabarhouse.com; Parade Ground Rd; mains ₹450-800, tasting menus ₹2500; ☉ 7am-11pm) Set in an open-sided pavilion or at candlelit poolside tables, this outstanding restaurant at Malabar House (p301) is (almost) Bollywood-star glam. The ambitious East-meets-West menu creatively fuses local and European flavours – the signature dish is the seafood platter (₹3200), or try an elegant 'trilogy' of Indian curries. An impressive choice of Indian wines (Sula, Fratelli, Grover Zampa) accompanies meals.

Upstairs, the **DiVine wine bar** (☉ 11am-11pm) serves upmarket tapas-style snacks and wines by the glass.

Clubb18
CLUB, BAR
(Map p304; www.no18.co.in; No 18 Hotel, Rampath Rd; ☉ 11.30am-midnight) Hands down Fort Cochin's liveliest after-dark hang-out, this moodily lit muralled club-bar spills out onto a poolside terrace, serving cool Kingfishers (₹200), cocktails (₹500) and Indian wines (₹400 to ₹800) to a trendy local crowd. Busy from 9pm, with DJs Friday to Sunday.

✖ Mattancherry & Jew Town

Kayees Ramathula Hotel
INDIAN $
(Map p307; Kayees Junction, Mattancherry; biryani ₹130-170; ☉ noon-2pm) This no-frills spot is legendary among Kochi locals for its lunchtime chicken, mutton and seafood biryanis – get here early or miss out. Don't confuse it with the lime-green biryani place on the corner – Kayees is next door.

Mattancherry

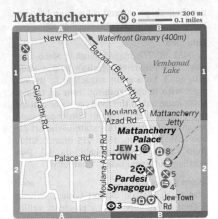

Mattancherry

◎ **Top Sights**
1 Mattancherry Palace B2
2 Pardesi Synagogue B2

◎ **Sights**
3 Jewish Cemetery B2

🛏 **Sleeping**
4 Ginger House Museum Hotel B2

🍴 **Eating**
5 Ginger House B2
6 Kayees Ramathula Hotel A1
7 Mocha Art Cafe B2

🛍 **Shopping**
8 Idiom Bookshop B2
9 Niraamaya B2

Mocha Art Cafe CAFE $$
(Map p307; ☑ 0484-2224357; www.facebook.com/themochaartcafe; Synagogue Lane, Mattancherry; dishes ₹150-450; ⊙ 9am-9pm) This gorgeous, multiroom, 300-year-old spice warehouse, built in Dutch style, was once lived in by the rabbis of Mattancherry's synagogue, which you can admire from a snug original window booth. Open-brick walls, vertical gardens and local art add a contemporary touch. Cooking here is a skilful blend of Keralan curries, omelettes and wholewheat sandwiches, and cakes from the on-site bakery.

Ginger House INDIAN $$$
(Map p307; ☑ 0484-2213400; http://museumhotel.in; Jew Town Rd, Mattancherry; mains ₹230-800; ⊙ 8am-8pm May-Oct, to midnight Nov-Apr) Hidden behind a massive antique-filled godown (warehouse) is this wonderful waterfront restaurant, where you can relax over fresh juices and punchy Indian dishes and snacks (including a deliciously creamy cashew-paneer curry). Walk through the priceless Heritage Arts showroom (check out the giant antique snake-boat canoe) to reach it.

✗ Ernakulam

Ernakulam's mega shopping malls provide food-court dining, and there are some reliable South Indian restaurants. Leafy Panampilly Nagar Ave, in a residential area 1.5km south of Ernakulam Junction train station, is lined with modern restaurants and cafes.

Frys Village Restaurant KERALAN $
(Map p302; Chittoor Rd; mains ₹90-180; ⊙ noon-3.30pm & 7-10.30pm) This brightly decorated and breezy place with an arched ceiling is a great family restaurant with authentic Keralan food, especially seafood like *pollichathu* or crab roast. Fish and veg thalis are available for lunch.

Cocoa Tree CAFE $$
(☑ 0484-4119529; www.facebook.com/cocoatree cafe; MG Rd, Panampilly Nagar, Avenue Regent; dishes ₹270-500; ⊙ 11am-11pm; 🛜) With trailing plants, gleaming fresh-cake displays and newspapers to flick through, this bright cafe makes a sophisticated, rustic-chic retreat from busy Ernakulam. Salads, sandwiches, burgers, omelettes and pastas fill the global-inspired menu, or just pop in for a coffee, a hot chocolate or a fresh juice. It's 1.5km south of Ernakulam Junction.

Chillies ANDHRA $$
(Map p302; ☑ 0484-2354938; Layam Rd; mains ₹100-300; ⊙ 11.30am-4pm & 7-11pm) A dark, buzzing 1st-floor restaurant, serving Kochi's best spicy Andhra cuisine on banana leaves, from biryanis to fish curry. Try a thali (₹170 to ₹190) for all-you-can-eat joy. Downstairs is a tandoori sister venture.

☆ Entertainment

There are several centres in Kochi where you can view Kathakali, the fast-paced traditional martial art of *kalarippayat* and performances of classical music and traditional *bharatanatyam* dance.

Kerala Kathakali Centre LIVE PERFORMANCE
(Map p304; ☑ 9895534939, 0484-2217552; www.kathakalicentre.com; KB Jacob Rd, Fort Cochin; shows ₹300-350; ⊙ shows from 4pm) In an intimate, wood-lined theatre, this

recommended long-running arts centre provides a useful introduction to Kathakali. It also hosts performances of *kalarippayat* (4pm), classical music (8pm to 9pm Sunday to Friday) and traditional dance (8pm Saturday), plus early-morning yoga (₹400) and meditation (₹250) sessions and a range of short- and long-term courses, including Kathakali (from ₹650 per hour).

Ens Kalari   LIVE PERFORMANCE
(📞0484-2700810; www.enskalari.org.in; Nettoor; entry by donation) To see real professionals practising *kalarippayat*, seek out this renowned 65-year-old training school 6.5km southeast of central Ernakulam. There are daily one-hour demonstrations (7.15pm; one day's notice required) or you can watch training sessions from 5.30pm daily except Sunday. The centre also runs intensive courses from one week (₹5000) to one month (₹19,500).

🔒 Shopping

Anokhi   FASHION & ACCESSORIES
(Map p304; 📞0484-2216275; www.anokhi.com; Lily St, Fort Cochin) Fabulous hand-block printed dresses, kurtas, skirts, bags and shirts in floaty fabrics blend Indian and European design at Anokhi, a Jaipur brand famous for its traditional-meets-contemporary fashion. You'll also find bedspreads, tablecloths and other home accessories in an alluring rainbow of colours.

Niraamaya   FASHION & ACCESSORIES
(Map p304; 📞0484-2217778; https://niraamaya.org; 1/605 Peter Celli St, Fort Cochin; ⊙10am-5.30pm Mon-Sat) A world of soothing pinks, greys and oranges, Niraamaya sells 'ayurvedic' clothing, accessories, homewares and yoga mats – all made of organic cotton, coloured with natural herb dyes, or infused with ayurvedic oils, based on the ancient concept of *ayurvastra* (healthy fabrics). There's another **branch** (Map p307; 6/217 AB Salem Rd; ⊙10am-5.30pm) in Mattancherry.

Fabindia   CLOTHING, HOMEWARES
(Map p304; 📞0484-2217077; www.fabindia.com; 1/281 Napier St, Fort Cochin; ⊙9.30am-9pm) 🌿
This renowned fair-trade Indian brand has fine Indian textiles, fabrics, clothes, homewares, ceramics and natural beauty products, created using traditional techniques by village craftspeople across the country. The style is modern Indian, with silks and cottons in lively prints and colours, and the line works to encourage rural employment.

Lulu Mall   MALL
(📞0484-2727777; http://lulumall.in; NH66, Edappally; ⊙9am-11pm; 📶) India's largest shopping mall, Lulu is an attraction in its own right with people coming from all over to shop, hang out in the food courts or cinema, or go ice skating or tenpin bowling. Sprawling over 7 hectares, this state-of-the-art aircon mall has more than 215 brand outlets from Calvin Klein to Fabindia. It's 9km northeast of Ernakulam's boat jetty.

Idiom Bookshop   BOOKS
(Map p304; Bastion St, Fort Cochin; ⊙10am-6.30pm) Originally just a pushcart selling books on Kochi's beaches, Idiom has a huge range of quality new and used tomes, including India-focused literature. There's another **branch** (Map p307; Bazaar Rd; ⊙10am-5pm) in Mattancherry.

ℹ Information

MEDICAL SERVICES
Lakeshore Hospital (📞emergency 9961630000; www.vpslakeshorehospital.com; NH Bypass, Marudu) Modern hospital 8km southeast of central Ernakulam.
Medical Trust (Map p302; 📞0484-2358001; www.medicaltrusthospital.com; MG Rd, Ernakulam; ⊙24hr)

MONEY
ATMs in Fort Cochin cluster around Kunnumpuram Junction.
   Unimoni (UAE Exchange; Map p302; 📞0484-4392416; www.unimoni.com; Chettupuzha Towers, PT Usha Rd, Ernakulam; ⊙9.30am-6pm Mon-Fri, to 2pm Sat) has a foreign exchange.

TOURIST INFORMATION
DTPC Tourist Office (Map p302; 📞0484-2350300; Ernakulam Jetty, Ernakulam; ⊙10am-5pm Mon-Sat)
Government of India Tourist Office (📞0484-2669125; www.incredibleindia.org; Willingdon Island; ⊙9am-6pm Mon-Fri)
KTDC Tourist Office (Map p302; 📞0484-2353234; www.ktdc.com; Shanmugham Rd, Ernakulam; ⊙8am-6.30pm) Just north of Ernakulam's main jetty.
Tourist Desk (Map p302; 📞9847044688, 0484-2371761; touristdesk1990@gmail.com; Ferry Jetty, Ernakulam; ⊙8am-6pm) This private tour agency is extremely knowledgeable and helpful about Kochi and beyond, and runs a good backwaters tour. It also provides maps,

ferry schedules and self-guided walking tours entitled *Historical Places in Fort Cochin*.

ⓘ Getting There & Away

AIR

Cochin International Airport (☑ 0484-2610115; http://cial.aero; Nedumbassery), 30km northeast of Ernakulam, is a popular hub, with international flights to/from the Gulf States, Sri Lanka, the Maldives, Malaysia, Bangkok and Singapore.

On domestic routes, Jet Airways (p522), Air India (p522), IndiGo (p522), SpiceJet (p522), Vistara (p522) and/or GoAir (p522) fly direct to Chennai, Mumbai, Bengaluru (Bangalore), Hyderabad, Delhi, Goa and Trivandrum. Air India flies daily to Agatti in Lakshadweep.

BUS

All long-distance services operate from Ernakulam's **KSRTC bus stand** (Map p302; ☑ 0484-2372033; Ernakulam; ⏰ reservations 6am-10pm) or the massive **Vyttila Mobility Hub** (☑ 0484-2306611; www.vyttilamobility hub.com; Vyttila), a state-of-the-art transport terminal 4km east of Ernakulam Junction train station. Numerous private bus companies have superdeluxe, air-con, video and Volvo buses to long-distance destinations, such as Bengaluru

(Bangalore), Chennai, Mangaluru (Mangalore), Trivandrum and Coimbatore; prices vary depending on the standard. Agents in Ernakulam and Fort Cochin sell tickets. Private buses use Vyttila as well as **Kaloor bus stand** (Kaloor), 3km north of Ernakulam Junction.

TRAIN

Ernakulam has two train stations, Ernakulam Junction and Ernakulam Town. There's a **reservations office** (Map p302; Ernakulam Junction, Ernakulam; ⏰ 8am-8pm Mon-Sat, to 1pm Sun) for both at Ernakulam Junction, but it's easier to book online or through a travel agent.

There are frequent local and express trains to Trivandrum (2nd class/sleeper/3AC ₹95/165/490, four to five hours), via Alleppey (₹50/140/495, 1½ hours) or Kottayam (₹50/140/495, one to two hours), and to Thrissur (2nd class/AC chair ₹60/260, 1½ hours). There are also 10 daily trains to Calicut (2nd class/sleeper/3AC ₹90/140/495, four to five hours) and Kannur (₹115/190/495, five to 6½ hours).

ⓘ Getting Around

TO/FROM THE AIRPORT

Bright-orange AC buses run between the airport and Fort Cochin (₹88, 1¾ hours, at least 16

MAJOR BUSES FROM ERNAKULAM

Buses to the following destinations operate from the KSRTC Bus Stand and/or Vyttila Mobility Hub. In addition, private buses operate on long-haul routes.

DESTINATION	FARE (₹)	DURATION (HR)	FREQUENCY
Alleppey	60-110	1½	every 10-30min
Bengaluru	790-1270	12	11 daily
Calicut	360	5	hourly
Chennai*	1533	16-18	4.30pm
Coimbatore	185-200	5	14 daily
Kalpetta (for Wayanad)	300	7	5 daily
Kannur	300-385	8	5 daily
Kanyakumari*	280	8	2.30pm
Kollam	135-250	4	every 10-20min
Kottayam	70-135	2	every 10min 3.45am-10pm
Kumily (for Periyar)	220	5	15 daily
Madurai*	450	10	8pm, 8.15pm, 8.30pm
Mangaluru*	400	11	6.30pm, 8.35pm, 10.30pm
Munnar*	125	4½	10 daily
Mysuru*	740-850	10	6pm, 7pm, 8pm, 10.50pm
Puducherry*	675	18	4pm
Thrissur	70	2	every 10-20min
Trivandrum	185-380	5-7	every 20-30min

* Departs only from KSRTC bus stand

daily) via Ernakulam's MG Rd or the Vyttila Mobility Hub. There are 24-hour prepaid taxi stands at the domestic and international terminals: ₹880 to Ernakulam, ₹1250 to Fort Cochin. Uber and Ola taxis charge around ₹700 and ₹1000 respectively.

AUTORICKSHAW & TAXI

Autorickshaw trips shouldn't cost more than ₹30 around Fort Cochin, ₹50 around Ernakulam or ₹80 from Fort Cochin to Mattancherry.

Prepaid autorickshaws from Vyttila cost ₹86 to Ernakulam Jetty, ₹110 to Ernakulam Junction and ₹214 to Fort Cochin; from prepaid autorickshaw stands at the **KSRTC bus stand** (Map p302; KSRTC bus stand, Ernakulam; ⊘ 6.30am-11pm) or Ernakulam Junction it's ₹30 to the jetty and ₹180 to Fort Cochin. To get from Ernakulam to Fort Cochin after ferries (and buses) stop running you'll need a taxi or an autorickshaw.

Uber (www.uber.com) and Ola Cabs (www.olacabs.com) drivers are a popular alternative to **taxis** (Map p304; River Rd, Fort Cochin) for trips around Kochi; short hops cost around ₹60. In Ernakulam, there's a **prepaid taxi stand** (Map p302; Ernakulam Junction, Ernakulam; ⊘24hr) at Ernakulam Junction.

BOAT

Ferries are the fastest and most enjoyable form of transport between Fort Cochin and the mainland. The main stop at Fort Cochin is **Customs Jetty** (Map p304; Bazaar Rd, Fort Cochin); some ferries also use Fort Cochin's **Kamalakadavu Jetty** (Map p304; River Rd, Fort Cochin). **Mattancherry Jetty** (Map p307; Bazaar Rd, Mattancherry), near the palace and synagogue, was closed indefinitely at research time, but may resume services to Willingdon Island. The jetty on the eastern side of Willingdon Island is **Embarkation** (Map p302; Willingdon Island); the west one, opposite Mattancherry, is **Terminus** (Willingdon Island). One-way fares are ₹3 or ₹4.

Ferries run to Vypeen Island from **Ernakulam Jetty** (Map p302; Park Ave, Ernakulam) and **Fort Cochin** (Map p304; River Rd, Fort Cochin). Ferries to Bolgatty Island depart from **High Court Jetty** (Map p302; Shanmugham Rd, Ernakulam).

Fort Cochin

Ferries go from Fort Cochin's Customs Jetty to Ernakulam Jetty (20 minutes) every 10 to 25 minutes from 5.55am to 9.50pm. There's also a new high-speed ferry from Kamalakadavu Jetty to Ernakulam (with/without air-con ₹20/10, 12 minutes, six daily). Ferries also hop between Customs and Willingdon Island 24 times a day.

Roll-on, roll-off car and passenger ferries go every 20 minutes from Fort Cochin to Vypeen Island between 6.40am and 9.30pm (five minutes).

Ernakulam

Ferries run from Ernakulam Jetty to Fort Cochin's Customs Jetty (20 minutes) every 15 to 20 minutes from 4.40am to 9.10pm, some via Willingdon Island (10 minutes). Ernakulam Jetty has ferries to Vypeen Island (25 minutes) every 25 to 35 minutes from 6am to 9.30pm, also via Willingdon; return ferries run from 6.25am to 10pm.

BUS

Airport buses and local buses from Ernakulam use the central **Fort Cochin bus stand** (Map p304; River Rd, Fort Cochin). There are no regular buses between Fort Cochin and Mattancherry Palace, but it's an enjoyable 2km (30-minute) walk (or a quick cycle) through the busy warehouse area along Bazaar Rd.

BICYCLE & MOTORCYCLE

Bicycles (from ₹150) and scooters (₹400 per day) or Enfields (from ₹1300 per day) can be hired from agents in Fort Cochin.

METRO

Partly inaugurated in mid-2017, Kochi's elevated metro (https://kochimetro.org) will eventually connect Kochi's bus and train stations, additional suburbs and the airport, though at the time of writing wasn't yet very useful to travellers.

MAJOR LONG-DISTANCE TRAINS FROM ERNAKULAM

DESTINATION	TRAIN NO & NAME	FARES (₹; SLEEPER/ 3AC/2AC)	DURATION (HR)	DEPARTURE (DAILY)
Bengaluru	16525 Bangalore Exp (A)	345/945/1355	11½	6.05pm
Chennai	12624 Chennai Mail (A)	395/1050/1490	12	7.30pm
Delhi	12625 Kerala Exp (B)	885/2300/3415	46	3.50pm
Goa (Madgaon)	16346 Netravathi Exp (A)	415/1135/1640	14½	2.05pm
Mumbai	16346 Netravathi Exp (A)	615/1655/2430	27	2.05pm

Trains: (A) departs from Ernakulam Junction; (B) departs from Ernakulam Town

Around Kochi

Cherai Beach

On Vypeen Island, 25km north of Fort Cochin, golden 3km-long Cherai Beach makes a fun day trip or getaway from Kochi, especially if you hire a scooter or a motorbike in Fort Cochin. The main beach entrance can get busy, but with kilometres of lazy backwaters just a few hundred metres from the seafront and a smattering of quiet fishing villages to explore, this unhurried area is becoming increasingly appealing for travellers.

🛏 Sleeping & Eating

Les 3 Elephants RESORT $$$
(☑0484-2480005, 9946012040; www.3elephants. in; Convent St, Cherai Beach; cottages incl breakfast with AC ₹8020-13,770, without AC ₹5070-8850; ❂🛜❄) Hidden from the beach but with the backwaters on your doorstep, Les 3 Elephants is a soothing French-Indian-owned resort with boutique flair. The beautifully and uniquely designed cottages have private sit-outs and lovely backwater views across gardens to Chinese fishing nets. There's yoga and meditation plus an ayurvedic spa (massage ₹1500), and the restaurant serves excellent home-cooked French-Indian fare (mains ₹200 to ₹500). Guests can use the pool at a neighbouring property, while nearby Mini Elephant rooms offer a more budget-friendly experience (₹1000).

La Dame Rouge HERITAGE HOTEL $$$
(☑0484-2481062, 9496016599; www.ladame rouge.com; Manapilly, Ayyampally; r incl breakfast & dinner €80-180; 🛜) Wrapped in greenery, 4.5km southeast of Cherai Beach, this blue-washed 250-year-old house makes an intimate, character-filled escape. French owner Marco has five thoughtfully styled, all-different heritage-chic rooms; one is a massive split-level suite with its own massage room. The food, served at a communal table, is a tasty fusion of French, Indian and fresh seafood. Ask locally for 'Marco's house'.

Chilliout Cafe CAFE $$
(☑9744138387; www.facebook.com/chillioutcafe; Cherai Beach; mains ₹180-550; ⏱noon-9pm Thu-Tue; 🛜) A breezy, open-sided, French-Portuguese-Indian-run hang-out for sea views, relaxed vibes and authentically good European-style comfort food right by the

beach. Delicious burgers, pizzas, pastas, crepes, fresh juices, home-cooked fries and barbecue dishes are all carefully prepared by a charming team.

❶ Getting There & Away

To get here from Fort Cochin, catch the roll-on roll-off vehicle ferry to Vypeen Island (per person ₹3, two-wheeler ₹9, car ₹50), then either take an autorickshaw from the jetty (₹500 to ₹600) or catch one of the frequent northbound buses (₹20, one hour) to Cherai village, 1.5km east of the beach. Buses also run every 10 minutes from Ernakulam's **Boat Jetty bus stand** (Map p302; Ernakulam Boat Jetty, Ernakulam) to North Paravur (₹20, one hour; 6km east of Cherai Beach).

North Paravur & Chennamangalam

Nowhere is the tightly woven religious cloth that is India more apparent than in North Paravur and Chennamangalam, 30km north of Kochi, home to one of the oldest synagogues (p312) in Kerala. Also here are a Jesuit church and the ruins of a Jesuit college (the Jesuits first arrived in Chennamangalam in 1577), a Hindu temple on a hill overlooking the Periyar River, a 16th-century mosque, and Muslim and Jewish burial grounds. In North Paravur town, you'll find the *agraharam* (place of Brahmins), a small street of closely packed and brightly coloured houses originally settled by Tamil Brahmins.

Travel agencies in Fort Cochin organise tours to both places.

CHENNAMANGALAM'S HANDLOOM WEAVERS

The Chennamangalam area is known for its traditional handloom weaving industry, which was devastated by the 2018 Kerala floods, with the livelihoods of its 600 weavers (mostly women) suddenly at immense risk. The flood damage to the five handloom cooperative societies here is estimated to have hit a staggering 150 million rupees. A high-profile campaign spearheaded by Kochi designers has since been working to get this female-powered industry back on its feet – its *chekkutty* dolls, made using ruined saris, have become a symbol of the weavers' (and Kerala's) resilience.

Buses serve North Paravur every 10 minutes from Ernakulam's Boat Jetty bus stand (p311; ₹20, one hour). The area is also easily reached by local bus from Cherai Beach (only 6km west).

Around 5km northeast of North Paravur, the beautifully restored **Chennamangalam Synagogue** (admission ₹2, camera ₹10; ☺10am-4.30pm Tue-Sun) is one of Kerala's most ancient, established in 1420 (though rebuilt in 1614 following a fire). The interior is awash with door and ceiling wood-reliefs in dazzling colours, while just outside lies one of the oldest tombstones in India – inscribed with the Hebrew date corresponding to 1269.

Thrissur (Trichur)

☑0487 / POP 315,960

While the rest of Kerala has its fair share of celebrations, untouristed, slightly chaotic Thrissur is the cultural cherry on the festival cake, with a seemingly endless list of energetic festivities. Centred around a large park (known as the 'Round') and a Hindu temple complex, Thrissur worked as a second capital for the Cochin royal family during the 16th century, and is also home to a Nestorian Christian community whose denomination dates to the 3rd century AD.

⊙ Sights

Thrissur is renowned for its central temple, as well as for its impressive churches, including the massive whitewashed **Our Lady of Lourdes Cathedral** (St Thomas College Rd; ☺dawn-dusk), the splendid neo-Gothic 1925 **Basilica of Our Lady of Dolours** (Puttanpalli Church, New Church; High Rd; ☺dawn-dusk), and the 1814 **Marth Mariam Church** (Chaldean Church, Nestorian Church; www.churchoftheeast india.org; High Rd; ☺dawn-dusk), headquarters of India's Chaldean Syrian community.

Archaeology Museum   MUSEUM
(☑0487-2333056; Thrissur-Shornur Rd; adult/child ₹20/5; ☺9.30am-1pm & 2-4.30pm Tue-Sun) The refurbished Archaeology Museum is housed in the wonderful 200-year-old Sakthan Thampuran Palace, built in Keralan-Dutch style. Its mix of artefacts includes 12th-century Keralan bronze sculptures and giant earthenware pots, weaponry, coins and a lovely carved chessboard. To the side is a shady heritage garden.

Vadakkunathan Kshetram Temple   HINDU TEMPLE
(Round; ☺5-10am & 5-8pm) Finished in classic Keralan architecture, one of the oldest Hindu temples in the state crowns the low hill at the heart of Thrissur. It's dedicated to Shiva and though its present form dates from the 16th to 17th centuries, it has its roots in the 9th century. Only Hindus are allowed inside, though the intricate wood carvings on the main gate are worth admiring and the surrounding park is a popular spot to linger.

✯ Festivals & Events

Thrissur Pooram   RELIGIOUS
(www.thrissurpooramfestival.com; ☺Apr/May) The largest and most colourful of Kerala's temple festivals, with huge processions of caparisoned elephants around the Vadakkunathan Kshetram Temple. Animal-rights campaigns against Thrissur Pooram have started to gain momentum in recent years, as concerns have grown over the welfare of the captive temple elephants.

⊨ Sleeping & Eating

Gurukripa Heritage   HERITAGE HOTEL $
(☑0487-2421895; http://gurukripaheritage.in; Chembottil Lane; r with AC ₹1600-1900, without AC ₹900; ▣ ⊚) Almost a century old but now neatly refurbished, Gurukripa is a fine budget heritage hotel with more charm than most, in a quietish spot set back from the road just south of the Round. Simple rooms are unpretentious but clean, with heavy wooden doors, though some of the cheapest air-con ones are a tad musty.

Hotel Luciya Palace   HOTEL $$
(☑0487-2424731; www.hotelluciyapalace.com; Marar Rd; s ₹3250-3780, d ₹4070-7670; ▣ ⊚) In a cream-coloured, colonial-style building, this is Thrissur's most characterful midranger, and its spacious, modern rooms are great value (desks, hairdryers, tea/coffee trays, even shower curtains!). It's tucked into a quiet cul-de-sac just 200m southwest of the Round, and has a good all-day multicuisine restaurant (mains ₹150 to ₹360).

Clayfingers Pottery   GUESTHOUSE $$
(☑0480-2792234; www.clayfingerspottery.com; Kadalassery; r incl breakfast ₹4750; ▣ ⊚) For something uniquely creative, seek out these four palm-fringed 'art cottages' attached to an artisan pottery warehouse, which occupies a reincarnated 1950s brick-and-tile factory 13km south of Thrissur. Terracot-

Thrissur (Trichur)

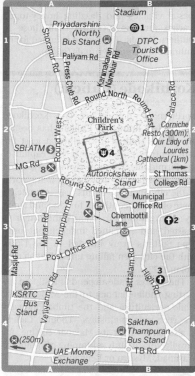

◉ Sights
1 Archaeology Museum B1
2 Basilica of Our Lady of Dolours B3
3 Marth Mariam Church B4
4 Vadakkunathan Kshetram Temple ... B2

⊜ Sleeping
5 Gurukripa Heritage A3
6 Hotel Luciya Palace A3

⊗ Eating
7 Hotel Bharath A3
8 Navaratna Restaurant A2

laced omelettes, and there are freshly squeezed juices. It's 500m east of the Round.

Navaratna Restaurant   MULTICUISINE **$$**
(☑ 0484-7241994; Round West; mains ₹130-210; ⊙ 10am-11pm) Dark, intimate and air-con-cooled, this is one of the classier dining experiences in the city centre, with marble-effect floors and seating at check-cloth tables on raised platforms. Downstairs is veg and upstairs is nonveg, highlighting lots of North Indian specialities and a few Chinese and Keralan dishes.

ⓘ Getting There & Around

Hundreds of **autorickshaws** (Round South) gather at the Round and usually use the meter; short trips cost ₹20.

BUS

From Thrissur's **KSRTC bus stand** (☑ 0487-2421150; RS Rd) buses leave every 20 to 30 minutes for Trivandrum (₹250, seven hours), Ernakulam (Kochi; ₹72, 3½ hours), Calicut (₹102, four hours), Palakkad (₹60, three hours) and Kottayam (₹124, four hours). Hourly buses go to Kannur (₹130, six hours). There's a noon bus to Coimbatore (₹100, three hours); otherwise change at Palakkad. Buses also serve Mysuru (Mysore; ₹600, eight hours, 2.30pm, 9pm and 10pm) and Bengaluru (Bangalore; ₹700 to ₹1000, nine hours, 8pm and 9pm).

Frequent local services chug along to Guruvayur (₹35, one hour), Irinjalakuda (₹32, 50 minutes) and Cheruthuruthy (₹40, 1½ hours). Two private bus stands – **Sakthan Thampuran** (Pattalam Rd) and **Priyadarshini (North)** (Thrissur-Shornur Rd) – have more buses to these destinations, though the chaos involved in navigating the two hardly makes using them worthwhile.

TRAIN

The train station is 1.5km southwest of the Round, with regular services to Ernakulam (2nd class/

ta floors, stylish bathrooms, wooden bed frames and subtle wall art embellish the rooms, and the on-the-ball team also runs a terrace cafe. Guests can join resident artists for clay-pottery workshops.

★ Hotel Bharath   SOUTH INDIAN **$**
(☑ 0487-2421720; hotelbharathtcr@gmail.com; Chembottil Lane; mains ₹90-150; ⊙ 6.30am-10pm) Spotless, air-conditioned Bharath is widely regarded as the best veg restaurant in town and *the* place for a lunchtime thali (₹86 to ₹165), a Keralan breakfast or a spicy curry.

Corniche Resto   INTERNATIONAL **$$**
(☑ 819733448; www.facebook.com/cornicheresto; 1st fl, PIK Tower, St Thomas College Rd; dishes ₹90-360; ⊙ 11.30am-11pm; ☎) Indian flavours infuse the global-inspired menu at this fashionable hang-out furnished with cosy booths, suspended lamps and coffee paraphernalia. Spicy-pumpkin pastas and paneer-masala wraps meet chicken-tikka burgers and spice-

MAHÉ

On the Malabar Coast about 10km south of Thalasseri (formerly Tellicherry), riverside Mahé is surrounded by, but not actually part of, Kerala – it's part of the Union Territory of Puducherry (Pondicherry), formerly under French India. It was occupied by the French in 1721, and finally returned to India in 1954 (though some inhabitants opted for French citizenship). Apart from the riverfront promenade with its Parisian-style street lamps, the province is similar to other towns along Kerala's coast, and Malayalam and English are the main languages. The other obvious difference is that there is no restriction on the sale of alcohol here (unlike in Kerala) and sales tax is low.

sleeper/3AC ₹60/140/495, 1½ to 2½ hours), Calicut (₹70/140/495, three hours), Coimbatore (₹90/140/495, three hours) and Trivandrum (₹110/195/495, six to 7½ hours).

Around Thrissur

The Thrissur region supports several institutions that are nursing the dying classical Keralan performing arts back to health, while Guruvayur, 25km northwest of Thrissur, is home to the celebrated **Shri Krishna Temple** (Guruvayur; ☺3am-1pm & 4.30-10pm), closed to non-Hindus.

Frequent local buses from Thrissur's KSRTC bus stand (p313) serve Guruvayur (₹35, one hour), Irinjalakuda (₹32, 50 minutes) and Cheruthuruthy (₹40, 1½ hours), or take a taxi.

Kerala Kalamandalam CULTURAL PROGRAMS
(☑0488-4262418; www.kalamandalam.org; Cheruthuruthy; courses per month ₹600; ☺Jun-Mar) Using an ancient Gurukula system of learning, students undergo intensive study in Kathakali, *mohiniyattam* (dance of the enchantress), Kootiattam, percussion, voice and violin. A Day with the Masters (Indian/foreigner ₹1000/1400) is a morning program allowing visitors to tour the theatre and classes and see various art and cultural presentations; book ahead by email. It's 30km north of Thrissur.

NORTHERN KERALA

The Malabar Coast from Calicut north to the Karnataka border features a string of coastal villages and dazzling honey-toned beaches far less touristed than those in southern Kerala. The region is famed for its enthralling *theyyam* rituals (p330).

Kozhikode (Calicut)

☑0495 / POP 431,560

Northern Kerala's largest city, Kozhikode (still widely known as Calicut) has been a prosperous trading town since at least the 14th century and was once the capital of the formidable Zamorin dynasty. Vasco da Gama first landed at Kappad, 15km north of the city, in 1498, on his way to snatch a share of the subcontinent for king and country (Portugal that is) – though the Zamorins resisted and remained independent until Tipu Sultan's army invaded in the 1760s, with the city then falling under British control in 1792.

These days trade depends mostly on exporting Indian labour to the Middle East, while agriculture and the timber industry are economic mainstays. Though Calicut is also famous for its Malabar cuisine, for travellers it's mainly a jumping-off point for Wayanad, Mysuru or Bengaluru.

◉ Sights

At the heart of the city, Mananchira Sq, the former courtyard of the Zamorins, preserves its original spring-fed tank and a leafy park. The central **Church of South India** (Bank Rd; ☺dawn-dusk), with its unique European-Keralan architecture and three-tiered tower, was established in 1842 by Swiss missionaries. About 1km west of Mananchira Sq is Calicut Beach – not much for swimming but good enough for a sunset stroll along the promenade.

Around 2km southwest of the city centre sits the 14th-century wooden **Miskhal Masjid** (Kuttichira Mosque; Kuttichira; ☺dawn-dusk), an attractive, four-storey aquamarine mosque supported by impressive wooden pillars and with traditional sloping tiled roofs.

Kozhikode (Calicut)

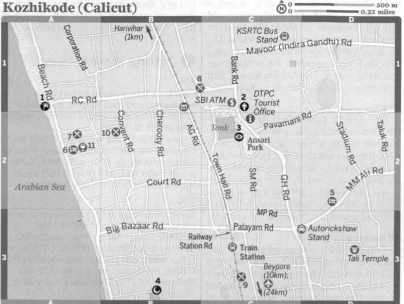

🛏 Sleeping & Eating

Famous for its Malabar cuisine, Calicut is regarded as the food capital of northern Kerala. With its large student population, it's also easily northern Kerala's liveliest nightlife spot (mostly within five-star hotels).

Beach Hotel   HERITAGE HOTEL **$$**
(☑ 9745062055, 0495-2762055; www.beachheritage.com; Beach Rd; r incl breakfast ₹4130-4720; ✿ 🛜) Built in 1890 to house the Malabar British Club, this slightly worn but quite charming six-room hotel has more character than most other Calicut accommodation (though the service underwhelms). Upstairs rooms come with indoor lounges, soaring ceilings, sea views and original polished-wood floors; those on the ground floor have tucked-away garden-facing terraces and tiled flooring.

On-site **Salkaram** (☑ 9745062055, 0495-2762055; mains ₹150-300; ⊘ 7am-10.30pm) turns out tasty pan-Indian cooking, while the bamboo **Hut** (⊘ 11am-11pm) bar-restaurant is popular for beers and snacks.

Alakapuri   HOTEL **$$**
(☑ 0495-2723451; www.hotelalakapuri.com; MM Ali Rd; with AC s ₹1300, d ₹1850-3150, without AC s

Kozhikode (Calicut)

◉ Sights
1	Calicut Beach	A1
2	Church of South India	C1
3	Mananchira Square	C2
4	Miskhal Masjid	B3

🛏 Sleeping
5	Alakapuri	D2
6	Beach Hotel	A2

✕ Eating
7	Adam's Teashop	A2
8	Paragon Restaurant	B1
9	Salkara	C3
	Salkaram	(see 6)
10	Zains	B2

🍷 Drinking & Nightlife
11	Hut	A2

₹600-800, d ₹1750-3050; ✿ 🛜) Set back from a busy market area, friendly in-demand Alakapuri is built motel-style around a green lawn (complete with fountain!). Various rooms are a little scuffed, but reasonable value, and there's a restaurant plus bar.

★ Harivihar
HOMESTAY **$$$**
(☑ 0495-2765865, 9847072203; www.harivihar.com; Bilathikulam; s/d incl meals €100/125; 🛜) In northern Calicut, the restored 1850 home of

the Kadathanadu royal family is as serene as it gets – a traditional family compound with pristine lawns, constructed around the architectural principles of Kerala Vastu. The six large rooms are beautifully furnished with dark-wood antiques. It's primarily an ayurvedic, yoga and meditation retreat, with vegetarian meals and various packages.

Zains SOUTH INDIAN $
($ 0495-2366311; Convent Cross Rd; dishes ₹40-180; ⊙ noon-10pm) A local favourite for its Malabar dishes, biryanis and snacks, with a small terrace out the front, three-decades-old Zains is run by the entrepreneurial Zainabi Noor and is usually busy in the afternoons and evenings. It's also known for its *meen pathiri* (rice-based bread with fried fish) and *unnakai* (a boiled-banana sweet).

★Paragon Restaurant INDIAN $$
($ 0495-2767020; www.paragonrestaurant.net; Kannur Rd; dishes ₹170-370; ⊙ 6am-midnight) Join the inevitably long queue out the door at this always-packed restaurant, founded in 1939. The overwhelming menu is famous for its legendary chicken biryani and fish dishes – such as *pollichathu* or *molee* (fish pieces in coconut sauce). Also has an aircon room (from noon only).

The team also runs busy-busy **Salkara** ($ 0495-2300042; http://salkara.com; Platform 1, dishes ₹45-180; ⊙ 5.30am-2.30pm & 3.30-11pm) at the train station.

Adam's Teashop SOUTH INDIAN $$
(Adaminde Chayakkada; $ 0495-2365800; www.ackd.in; Beach Rd; mains ₹80-400; ⊙ noon-midnight) Distressed-wood shutters, vibrant paintwork and old-school radios create a retro-style scene at this wildly popular restaurant near the beach, where classic Malabari dishes are given a creative makeover.

Biryanis come wrapped in banana leaves; there are jazzed-up chicken, beef or prawn tiffin boxes; or try the *pachakkari* or fish *pollichathu*.

⊙ Getting There & Away

AIR
Kozhikode International Airport (www.kozhikodeairport.com; Karipur), 25km southeast of the city, serves major domestic destinations as well as the Gulf.

SpiceJet (p522) and IndiGo (p522) have the best domestic connections, with direct flights to Bengaluru (Bangalore), Chennai, Delhi, Mumbai and/or Hyderabad. Jet Airways (p522) flies to Mumbai and Air India (p521) to Trivandrum.

BUS
Government buses operate from the enormous but orderly **KSRTC bus stand** ($ 0495-2723796; Mavoor Rd). For Wayanad district, buses go to Sultanbatheri (₹80 to ₹200, three to four hours, every 15 minutes), Kalpetta (₹60 to ₹160, three hours, every 10 minutes) and Mananthavadi (₹90, three hours, every 20 to 30 minutes).

TRAIN
The train station is 1km south of Mananchira Sq, with frequent trains to Kannur (2nd class/sleeper/3AC ₹60/140/495, two hours), Mangaluru (sleeper/3AC/2AC ₹165/495/700, 3¾ to five hours), Ernakulam (₹170/495/745, 3½ to five hours) and Trivandrum (₹240/710/1000, 10 hours).

Heading southeast, eight daily trains go to Coimbatore (sleeper/3AC/2AC ₹140/495/700, four to five hours), via Palakkad (₹140/495/700, 2½ hours).

⊙ Getting Around
Calicut has a glut of **autorickshaws** (MM Ali Rd) and most use the meter, with short hops costing ₹20 to ₹40; it's around ₹40 from the city centre

BUSES FROM CALICUT'S KSRTC BUS STAND

DESTINATION	FARE (₹)	DURATION (HR)	FREQUENCY
Bengaluru	336-1000	9	7 daily
Ernakulam (Kochi)	370	6	hourly 5am-10pm, midnight, 12.25am, 1.15am, 1.30am
Kannur	90	3	every 30min
Mangaluru	430	6-7	11.58pm
Mysuru	204-370	5	11 daily
Ooty	380	5½	hourly 4am-10pm
Thrissur	121	3½	every 10min
Trivandrum	389-693	10	16 daily

to the train station. Taxis charge around ₹800 to the airport, which has a prepaid-taxi counter.

Wayanad Region

☏ 04935 & 04936 / POP 817,420 / ELEV 760M (MANANTHAVADI)

Many Keralites rate the northern elevated Wayanad region, which rises to between 700m and 2100m northeast from Calicut, as the most beautiful part of their state. Encompassing part of the Western Ghats' Nilgiri Biopshere Reserve (p286), which spills into Tamil Nadu and Karnataka, Wayanad's landscape combines mountain scenery, rice paddies of ludicrous green, skinny betel nut trees, bamboo, red earth, spiky ginger fields, slender eucalyptuses, and rubber, cardamom and coffee plantations. It's an excellent place to spot wild elephants. Foreign travellers stop here between Mysuru (Mysore), Bengaluru (Bangalore) or Ooty (Udhagamandalam) and Kerala, and Wayanad is a popular escape for city-based Indians – yet it remains fantastically unspoilt and satisfyingly secluded.

The 345-sq-km sanctuary has two pockets: Muthanga (east) bordering Tamil Nadu, Tholpetty (north) bordering Karnataka. The district's three main towns make good transport hubs – Kalpetta (south), Sultanbatheri (Sultan Battery; east) and Mananthavadi (northwest) – but the best accommodation is scattered across Wayanad.

◉ Sights & Activities

Rafting, kayaking, zip-lining and other adventure activities have sprung up in recent years.

★ Wayanad
Wildlife Sanctuary   NATURE RESERVE
(☏ 04936-271013, 04935-250853; www.wayanad sanctuary.org; entry to each part Indian/foreigner ₹115/310, camera/video ₹40/240; ⊙ 7-10am & 3-5pm mid-Apr–mid-Mar) Wayanad's ethereal 345-sq-km sanctuary is accessible only by two-hour jeep safari (₹680), on which you might spot langurs, chital deer, sambar, peacocks, wild boar or wild elephants; the odd tiger and leopard wanders through, though you'd be incredibly lucky to spot one. Jeeps are arranged at either of the sanctuary's two entrances, **Tholpetty** (Tholpetty–Coorg Rd; Indian/foreigner ₹115/310, camera/video ₹40/240, jeep ₹680; ⊙ 7-10am & 3-5pm mid-Apr–mid-Mar) and **Muthanga** (NH766; Indian/foreigner ₹115/310, camera/video ₹40/240, jeep ₹680; ⊙ 7-10am & 3-5pm mid-Apr–mid-Mar); during the November-to-March high season, arrive

Wayanad Region

WORTH A TRIP

NAGARHOLE NATIONAL PARK

South India's much-loved Nagarhole National Park (p200), in neighbouring Karnataka, is within day-tripping reach from northern Wayanad (just 18km north of Tholpetty).

at least an hour before the morning or afternoon openings to register and secure a vehicle.

Whether you go to Tholpetty or Muthanga essentially depends on whether you're staying in the north or south of Wayanad, as there's no difference in the chances of spotting wildlife or the visiting arrangements. Both Tholpetty and Muthanga close from mid-March to mid-April, but remain open during the monsoon. There are a limited number of guides and jeeps permitted in the park at one time, and trekking is not permitted.

Thirunelly Temple   HINDU TEMPLE
(http://thirunellitemple.com; ⊘5.30am-noon & 5.30-8pm) Thought to be one of the oldest temples on the subcontinent, Thirunelly Temple huddles beneath the Brahmagiri Hills 15km southwest of Tholpetty. Non-Hindus cannot enter the temple itself, but it's worth visiting for the otherworldly mix of ancient and intricate pillars backed by mountain views. Follow the path uphill behind the temple to the stream known as Papanasini, where Hindus believe you can wash away all your sins; a trail branches off halfway up to an ancient Shiva shrine. Buses run to Thirunelly from Mananthavadi (₹35, 1½ hours).

Jain Temple   JAIN TEMPLE
(NH766, Sultanbatheri; ⊘8am-noon & 2-6pm) The 13th-century Jain temple on the western edge of Sultanbatheri has splendid stone carvings and is an important monument to the region's strong historical Jain presence.

Edakkal Caves   CAVE
(adult/child ₹30/20, camera/video ₹50/200; ⊘8am-4pm Tue-Sun) These remote hilltop 'caves' – more accurately a small series of caverns – are celebrated for the ancient collection of petroglyphs in their top chamber, thought to date back over 3000 years. From the car park near Ambalavayal (12km southwest of Sultanbatheri) it's a steep 20-minute

walk up a winding road to the ticket window, then another steep climb up to the light-filled top cave.

Wayanad Heritage Museum   MUSEUM
(Ambalavayal; adult/child ₹20/10, camera/video ₹20/150; ⊘9am-5.30pm) In the village of Ambalavayal, 12km southwest from Sultanbatheri near the Edakkal Caves, this small but fascinating museum exhibits tools, weapons, pottery, carvings and other artefacts dating back to the 9th century, shedding light on Wayanad's significant Adivasi population. Displays of note include Neolithic axes, 13th-to 14th-century hero stones and a fine stone-carved Rama from the Vijayanagar era.

Trekking
There's some good trekking around the district (though not in the wildlife sanctuary itself), but it's tightly controlled by the Forest Department and various trekking areas open and close depending on current environmental concerns. Kalpetta's DTPC Tourist Office (p320) can advise on which treks are available. At the time of research, three treks were open: Chembra Peak (2100m; but only to the midway point); Banasura Hills in the south; and Brahmagiri Hills in the north. Permits and guides are mandatory and can be arranged at forest offices in south or north Wayanad or, more easily, through your accommodation. A permit and guide for up to five people costs around ₹1500 for Chembra, ₹2950 for Banasura and ₹2000 for Brahmagiri. Weather permitting, trekking is available year-round, though beware the rainy-season leeches.

🛏 Sleeping & Eating

🛏 Mananthavadi & Around

★Varnam Homestay   HOMESTAY $$
(☑9745745860, 9400055873; www.varnam homestay.com; Kurukanmoola, Kattikulam; s/d incl breakfast & dinner ₹1500/2500, villa ₹2000/3000; ✴🔊🏊) Surrounded by jungle and spice plantations, lovely Varnam is an oasis of calm 3km south of Katikulam in northern Wayanad. Varghese and Beena will look after you with Wayanad stories, local information and delicious home cooking using organic farm-fresh ingredients. Rooms are in the traditional 50-year-old family home or an elevated 'tree-house' villa, and there's a pool on the way.

Jungle Retreat Wayanad   GUESTHOUSE $$
(✆9742565333; www.jungleretreatwayanad.com; Thirunelly; per person incl meals from ₹3250; 🛜) The handful of rooms at this welcoming jungle guesthouse are comfortably appealing, but the standout factor is the fabulous location on the sanctuary boundary (13km southwest of Tholpetty). Best are the rustic cottages with terraces facing the reserve, beyond a watering hole frequented by local wildlife. Rates include a wildlife-spotting walk, and a host of activities can be arranged (₹350).

Ente Veedu   HOMESTAY $$
(✆9446834834, 9847511437; www.enteveedu. co.in; Panamaram–Sultanbatheri Rd, Panamaram; r incl breakfast with AC ₹3500-4500, without AC ₹2500-3000; ❄🛜) Secluded and on an 80-year-old estate overlooking banana plantations, ginger crops and rice paddies, this charming homestay (which translates as My Own Home) 15km southeast of Mananthavadi is definitely worth seeking out. Large, simply styled rooms – some interconnecting – are split between a modern house and a bamboo block (with details crafted by local artisans), and there's a colourful wicker-strewn lounge.

🛏 Kalpetta & Around

Hibernest Chembra   HOSTEL $
(✆9846642171; www.hibernest.com; APJLP School Rd, Kunnambetta; dm ₹1000; ❄🛜) Chembra Peak looms high above this peacefully positioned, red-brick, colonial-era bungalow turned boutiqueish hostel, set in leafy gardens 6km south of Kalpetta. Four-person en suite dorms (mixed or women-only) are equipped with personal lockers, plugs, lights and curtained bunks, while facilities include a communal kitchen. There's another branch just west of Kalpetta.

Greenex Farms   RESORT $$
(✆8606818555, 9645091512; http://greenexfarms.com; Chundale Estate Rd, Moovatty; incl breakfast dm ₹1460, r ₹3070-5780; 🛜🍽) A beautifully remote-feeling resort fringed by spice, coffee and tea plantations, 8km southwest of Kalpetta. Each of the private cottages is individually designed, most with a separate lounge, bathroom, balcony and superb views; there's also tree-house accommodation, as well as a bunker-style 12-bed dorm. There are also restaurants, a campfire, walks, activities and a swimming pond.

🛏 Sultanbatheri & Around

Mint Flower Residency   HOTEL $$
(✆04936-222206, 9745222206; www.mintflower residency.com; Chungam, Sultanbatheri; s/d with AC from ₹1230/1790, without AC ₹850/1570) Immediately north of central Sultanbatheri, the efficiently operated budget annexe of Mint Flower Hotel is in great condition. It's no frills, but the surprisingly contemporary rooms are spotless and come with colour feature walls (though no hot showers).

★ Tranquil   RESORT $$$
(✆04936-220244; www.tranquilresort.com; Kuppamudi Coffee Estate, Kolagapara; r incl breakfast ₹11,770-17,600, tree house ₹18,430-23,000; ⊘closed Easter; 🛜🍽) With a warm family welcome, this wonderfully peaceful and exclusive resort is pocketed away on an incredibly lush 1.5 sq km of working pepper, coffee, vanilla and cardamom plantations. The elegant eight-room house has sweeping verandahs filled with plants and handsome furniture, and there are also two custom-designed tree houses that may be Kerala's finest (complete with French-press coffee grown on-site).

A network of 11 marked walking trails meanders around the plantation, and you'll also enjoy a bar, a lounge area and a pool. It's 7km southwest of Sultanbatheri, but feels a world away.

Amaryllis   HOMESTAY $$$
(✆9847865824, 9847180244; http://amarylliskerala.com; Narikund; r incl meals ₹13,340-32,000; 🛜🍽) Amid coffee, fruit and spice plantations with sweeping reservoir panoramas, Amaryllis elevates the humble Kerala homestay into a luxury-boutique affair. Personally designed by welcoming, well-travelled owners Victor and Jini, the nine inviting rooms include a wood-walled cottage, a suite with a lake-view bath, and two stylish polished-bamboo tree houses with terraces and glassed-in showers. Breakfast happens on the verandah overlooking the pool.

ℹ **BOOKING BUSES**

Some Kerala buses can be prebooked online via www.keralartc.in or www.kurtcbooking.com (though foreign cards aren't always accepted).

ⓘ Information

DTPC Tourist Office (☑ 04936-202134, 9446072134; http://wayanadtourism.org; Kalpetta; ⊙ 9.30am-5pm Mon-Sat) Also has offices at Kalpetta's new bus stand and seasonally at Lakkidi (southern Wayanad) and Katikulam (northern Wayanad).

ⓘ Getting There & Away

WITHIN KERALA

Buses brave the winding roads – including a series of nine spectacular hairpin bends – between Calicut and Kalpetta (₹60 to ₹160, three hours) every 10 minutes; Calicut buses also run to/from Sultanbatheri (Pulpally Rd, Sultanbatheri; ₹80 to ₹200, three to four hours, every 15 minutes) and Mananthavadi (Kozhikode Rd; 73 to ₹90, three hours, every 20 to 30 minutes). Buses operate roughly hourly during daylight hours between Kannur and Mananthavadi (₹73, three hours). Kalpetta also has eight daily buses to Trivandrum (₹490, 23 hours) via Ernakulam (Kochi; ₹300, six hours). All Kalpetta buses stop at its **New bus stand** (Main Rd, Kalpetta).

TO/FROM TAMIL NADU & KARNATAKA

From Sultanbatheri's KSRTC bus stand, buses go to Ooty (Udhagamandalam; ₹200, three hours) at 8am and 12.45pm. From Mananthavadi's Municipal bus stand, there are buses to Ooty (₹150, 4½ hours) at 11am and midnight.

Buses run from Kalpetta to Bengaluru (Bangalore; ₹390, 6½ hours) via Mysuru (Mysore; ₹167, 3½ hours) every 30 minutes, most of them stopping in Sultanbatheri; note that the border gate here on the NH766 is closed between 9pm and 6am.

There are buses from Mananthavadi to Mysuru (₹85, three hours) at 9.30am, 11.30am, 12.30pm, 2pm and 4.30pm, via the alternative northern (Kutta–Gonikoppal) route, whose border is open 24 hours.

ⓘ Getting Around

The Wayanad district is quite spread out but buses link Mananthavadi, Kalpetta and Sultanbatheri every 10 to 30 minutes during daylight hours (₹22 to ₹35, one to two hours). From Mananthavadi, buses head to Tholpetty (₹28, one hour) every 30 minutes from 6.30am to 9.30pm. From Sultanbatheri, private buses serve Muthanga (₹20 minutes, one hour) every 10 minutes from 6am to 7pm.

Taxis tour the region for ₹1500 to ₹2000 per day.

Kannur & Around

☑ 0497 / POP 56.820

Under the Kolathiri rajas, Kannur (formerly Cannanore) was a major port bristling with international trade. Since then, the usual colonial suspects, including the Portuguese, Dutch and British, have had a go at exerting their influence on the region, leaving behind the odd fort. Today Kannur, 80km north of Calicut, is an unexciting, though agreeable, town known mostly for its weaving industry and cashew trade. For travellers, this area's appeal lies in its entrancing *theyyam* rituals and untouristed golden beaches.

This is a predominantly Muslim part of Kerala, so local sensibilities should be kept in mind: wear a sarong over your bikini on the beach.

◉ Sights & Activities

The Kannur region is the best place in Kerala to see the spirit-possession ritual called *theyyam* (p330); on most nights of the year between November and April there should be a *theyyam* ritual on at a village temple somewhere in the vicinity. Ask at your hotel/guesthouse or contact Kurien at Costa Malabari.

Fort St Angelo   FORT
(Fort Rd; ⊙ 9am-6pm) 𝗙𝗥𝗘𝗘 One of the earliest Portuguese settlements in India (constructed with permission from Kannur's rulers), the 1505 St Angelo Fort looms tall on a promontory 3km south of town, displaying a fusion of Portuguese, Dutch and British architecture. Wander the well-preserved walls and gardens within.

Arakkal Museum   MUSEUM
(Ayikkara Hospital Rd; adult/child ₹20/10, camera ₹25; ⊙ 10am-5pm Tue-Sun) Housed in part of the royal palace of the Arakkal family, a powerful Kannur dynasty with its roots dating to the 12th century, this harbourfront museum features antiques, furniture, weapons, silver and portraits, between tiled roofs, white walls and shuttered windows. It's a fascinating look into the life of Kerala's only Muslim royal family.

Thottada Beach   BEACH
Framed by low palm-sprinkled headlands and a shallow lagoon, this beautiful powdery gold-sand expanse, 8km southeast of Kannur centre, is home to the area's most

charming homestays. It's wonderfully secluded, though the sea can get rough.

🛏 Sleeping & Eating

Although there are plenty of hotels in Kannur town, the best places to stay are the homestays dotted around near the beach at Thottada (8km southeast).

Blue Mermaid Homestay   HOMESTAY $$

(📱9497300234; www.bluemermaid.in; Thottada Beach; r incl breakfast & dinner with/without AC ₹4000/3000, cottage ₹4000; 🕸🛜) 🏄 In a prime spot among palms, frangipanis and oleanders, facing northern Thottada Beach, charming Blue Mermaid has two immaculate rooms in a traditional home, eight bright air-con rooms occupying a modern mint-green building, and a whimsical stilted 'honeymoon cottage'. Friendly owners Indu and Parveen serve fine Kerala meals using garden-fresh ingredients and home-grown Wayanad coffee (plus free water refills).

Waves Beach Resort   GUESTHOUSE $$

(📱9447173889, 9495050850; www.wavesbeachresort.co.in; Thottada Beach, Adikadalayi; r incl meals ₹3000-3500; 🛜) Crashing waves will lull you to sleep at these four simply styled, very cute hexagonal laterite huts and adjacent four-room cottage above a semiprivate little cove, just north of Thottada Beach. The welcoming owners, Seema and Arun, have extra high-season rooms at another neighbouring property.

Costa Malabari   GUESTHOUSE $$

(📱9447775691; ps_kurian@rediffmail.com; Thottada Beach, Adikadalayi; r incl meals ₹3000-4000; 🕸🛜) Costa Malabari pioneered tourism in this area and consists of three lovely homestay-style properties just back from Thottada Beach. Costa Malabari 1 has spotless, spacious rooms in an old hand-loom factory; there are more rooms in two other nearby bungalows, and all serve home-cooked Keralan food on banana leaves. Manager Kurien is an expert on *theyyam* and arranges visits.

Kannur Beach House   HOMESTAY $$

(📱9847186330; www.kannurbeachhouse.com; Thottada Beach; s/d incl breakfast & dinner ₹2600/3600; 😊Sep-Apr) A century-old traditional Keralan building with handsome wooden shutters, hidden beneath coconut palms and separated from Thottada Beach by a small lagoon – this is an original seafront homestay. The five rooms are simply done, but you can enjoy sensational ocean sunsets from your porch or balcony and dig into home-cooked Malabar meals. Yoga and trips to see *theyyam* are offered.

Ezhara Beach House   HOMESTAY $$

(📱9846424723, 0497-2835022; www.ezharabeachhouse.com; Ezhara Kadappuram; r from ₹950; 🛜) Under the watch of welcoming Hyacinth, this character-filled heritage home fronts unspoilt, palm-fringed Ezhara Beach, 9.5km southeast of Kannur. Rooms are simple but functional, a world of activities can be arranged (from market visits to trekking), and guests rave about the homemade Keralan and Continental meals.

KK Heritage Home   HOMESTAY $$

(📱9446677254, 9447486020; www.kkheritage.com; Thottada Beach; r incl meals ₹2600-3100; 😊Sep-May; 🕸🛜) Slightly back from Thottada Beach in the palm groves, this long-established two-storey home pleases with its six spotless rooms, good food, deckchair-laden terraces and cheerful welcome. There's a ₹500 aircon surcharge, and owner Sreeranj can advise on *theyyam* performances.

Hotel Odhen's   INDIAN $

(Onden Rd; mains ₹30-100; 😊noon-4pm) Kannur's must-try restaurant, in the market area, is usually packed at lunchtime. The speciality is Malabar cuisine, specifically the banana-leaf thalis with a dazzling range of spicy extras including masala-fried fish.

ℹ Getting There & Away

AIR

The much-anticipated **Kannur International Airport** (www.kannurairport.in; Mattannur), 27km east of Kannur, opened in December 2018. At the time of writing, GoAir (p522) flies to Bengaluru (Bangalore) and Hyderabad; IndiGo (p522) to Bengaluru, Chennai, Goa and Hyderabad; and Air India (p521) to Gulf destinations including Abu Dhabi and Doha.

BUS

Kannur's enormous (one of the largest in Kerala) but orderly **Central bus stand** (New bus stand; Thavakkara), 1km southeast of the town-centre train station, is used by private and some government buses, but most long-distance state buses still operate from the **KSRTC bus stand** (Caltex Junction), 1.5km northeast of the train station.

VALIYAPARAMBA BACKWATERS & THEJASWINI RIVER

Unfolding just inland from the coast halfway between Kannur and Kasaragod, Kerala's 'northern backwaters' offer a more peaceful alternative to the better-known waterways down south. Valiyaparamba's large body of water is fed by five rivers, including the Thejaswini, and fringed by ludicrously green groves of nodding palms.

Houseboat trips in this region tend to be day cruises, popular with domestic tourists. Based near the mouth of the Thejaswini, **Bekal Ripples** (☑ 7025488222; www.bekal ripples.com; Thejaswini River) is one of a few local operators offering houseboat trips here, with options from 5½-hour daytime jaunts (₹1500 per person) to overnight stays for two (₹14,000); book ahead. Neeleshwar Hermitage (p323), meanwhile, offers overnight trips aboard one of Kerala's most luxurious houseboats, the two-room Lotus (from ₹22,500; www.thelotuskerala.com).

Alternatively, with advance planning, it's possible to explore the northern backwaters using the region's public State Water Transport Department ferries (www.swtd.kerala. gov.in). From Kotti (500m west of the train station at Payyanur, which is 38km northwest of Kannur and 45km southeast of Bekal), ferries run at 6.30am to Ori (17km northwest; ₹20, 2¾ hours), via surrounding islands. You can hop off along the way at, take a later ferry to or start from Ayitti Jetty (9km northwest of Kotti), which has at least three daily ferries to/from Kotti (₹10, 1½ hours).

For accommodation on land, stay at **V Retreat** (☑ 9845022056; www.vretreat.in; Kadapuram Rd, Valiyaparamba; r incl breakfast ₹3500; ☀ ☎), a secluded homestay with three simple rooms and local-style meals (₹250 to ₹300), perched between the backwaters and an almost-deserted golden beach; it's 10km northwest of Payyanur and 5km southwest of Ayitti Jetty.

The KSRTC bus stand has buses to Mananthavadi in Wayanad (₹90, three hours, every 30 minutes 5am to 10pm); Ooty (Udhagamandalam; via Wayanad; ₹220, nine hours, 7.30am and 10pm); Ernakulam (Kochi; ₹300 to ₹350, seven hours, 11 daily) via Thrissur (₹200, six hours); Calicut (₹90, two to three hours, every 10 minutes); Kasaragod (for Bekal; ₹75, 2½ hours, every 10 minutes); and Bengaluru (Bangalore; ₹450, nine hours, six daily) via Mysuru (Mysore; ₹250, six hours).

There are also buses to Mananthavadi (₹90, three hours, eight daily 8.20am to 2.45pm) from the Central bus stand.

TRAIN

There are frequent trains to Thalasseri (2nd class/sleeper ₹60/140, 20 minutes, 21 daily), Calicut (sleeper/3AC/2AC ₹140/495/700, 1½ hours, 20 daily), Thrissur (₹190/540/745, four hours, 10 daily), Ernakulam (₹190/495/700, five to 6½ hours, eight daily) and Alleppey (₹245/630/880, five daily).

Heading north, trains run to Mangaluru (Mangalore; sleeper/3AC/2AC ₹140/495/700, three hours, 14 daily) via Bekal Fort (₹140/495/700, 1½ hours, four daily), and up to Goa (₹320/870/1300, eight hours, three daily).

ⓘ Getting Around

For Thottada Beach, take bus 29 (₹10, 20 minutes) from Plaza Junction opposite the train station and get off at Adikadalayi village temple, 1km north of the beach. Autorickshaws charge ₹200.

Bekal & Around

☑ 0467 / POP 54,170 (KASARAGOD)

Bordering Karnataka in Kerala's far north, Kasaragod district is known for the long, unspoilt, honey-gold beaches at Bekal and nearby Palakunnu and Udma (just north) and Nileshwar (just southeast), as well as for the enormous 17th-century Bekal Fort – all of which are begging for DIY exploration.

Kannur lies 76km southeast of Bekal while Mangaluru (Karnataka) sits 70km north, and you'll probably hear Kannada and Tulu just as much as Malayalam on the streets here. This area is gradually being colonised by glitzy five-star resorts, but it's still worth the trip for off-the-beaten-track adventurers. Bearing in mind the sensibilities of the local Hindu and Muslim population, it's best to cover up with a sarong on the beach.

◉ Sights & Activities

Bekal Fort
FORT
(Bekal; Indian/foreigner ₹25/300; ☺8am-5pm)
The huge laterite-brick Bekal Fort, built between 1645 and 1660, is the largest in Kerala and sits on Bekal's rocky headland with fine views. It passed into British hands in 1792, having originally been seized from the Ikkeri Nayaks by Hyder Ali in 1763.

Kappil Beach
BEACH
Isolated Kappil Beach, 6km north of Bekal, is a beautiful, lonely stretch of fine gold-hued sand with calm water, but beware of shifting sandbars. Autorickshaws from Bekal cost around ₹100.

Nileshwar Beach
BEACH
Around 18km southeast of Bekal, Nileshwar's gorgeous beach is a tranquil, palm-bordered expanse of blonde sand that fades into the hazy distance; there are a couple of lovely resorts here.

⌂ Sleeping & Eating

The five-star hotels are the most popular places to stay in the Bekal area, but there are also a couple of homestays and cheap, average-quality hotels between Kanhangad (10km south) and Kasaragod (16km north).

★Neeleshwar Hermitage
RESORT $$$
(☑0467-2287510; www.neeleshwarhermitage.com; Ozhinhavalappu, Nileshwar; s ₹16,910-33,540, d ₹19,590-40,070; ☺closed Jul; ❈�☀) ♨ This fabulous, plastic-free beachfront ecoresort consists of 18 sleekly designed thatch-roof cottages inspired by Kerala fishers' huts, with voguish touches like pre-loaded iPods and stylish indoor-outdoor bathrooms (two with plunge pools). Built according to Kerala Vastu, the Hermitage has a beachfront infinity pool, lush gardens fragrant with frangipani, superb organic food, a luxurious houseboat (www.thelotuskerala.com), and yoga, meditation and ayurveda.

Taj Bekal Resort & Spa
RESORT $$$
(☑0467-6616612; www.tajhotels.com; Kappil Beach, Udma West; r ₹12,160-30,340; ❈ল☀) An elegant blend of Balinese and Keralan architecture infuses Bekal's opulent Taj, on secluded southern Kappil Beach 6km north of town. The pool overlooks the backwaters (go kayaking or rafting), and there are three restaurants, a bar and a stunning 2-hectare spa. All 66 rooms are sumptuously styled, with tubs and hanging outdoor beds; the stars are the exquisite private-pool villas.

Kanan Beach Resort
RESORT $$$
(☑0467-2288880, 8606208880; http://kanan beachresort.com; Nileshwar; cottages incl breakfast ₹12,800-15,360; ❈ল☀) Comfortable whitewashed cottages with terraces and traditional Mangaluru-tile roofs surround a pool amid shady grounds of palms and hibiscus at this warm, French-founded resort fronting Nileshwar's beautiful beach (18km southeast of Bekal). The friendly team organises yoga, kayaking, ayurvedic treatments and other activities.

❶ Getting There & Away

AIR
Bekal is easily accessible from both Kannur's new airport (p321) in Kerala and Karnataka's Mangaluru International Airport (p208).

BUS
Frequent buses run from the main NH66 through Bekal to both Kanhangad (₹12, 20 minutes) and Kasaragod (₹15, 20 minutes), from where you can pick up trains to Mangaluru, Goa or Kochi.

TRAIN
Kanhangad, 10km south of Bekal, and Kasaragod, 16km north of Bekal, are major train hubs. Tiny Bekal Fort station, right on Bekal's beach, has trains to/from Mangaluru (Mangalore; sleeper/3AC/2AC ₹140/495/700, two hours, five daily), Kannur (₹140/495/700, two hours, four daily), Calicut (₹140/495/700, three hours, three daily) and Ernakulam (Kochi; ₹220/595/880, eight hours, one daily).

LAKSHADWEEP
POP 64,470
Comprising a string of 36 palm-covered, white-sand-skirted coral islands 300km off the Kerala coast, Lakshadweep (India's smallest Union Territory) is as stunning as it is isolated. Only 10 of these islands are inhabited, mostly by Sunni Muslim fishers. With fishing and coir production the main sources of income, local life here remains highly traditional, and a caste system divides islanders between Koya (land owners), Malmi (sailors) and Melachery (farmers). The archipelago's administrative centre is Kavaratti island, and most islanders speak a dialect of Malayalam.

At the time of writing, foreigners were only allowed to stay on a few islands: Kadmat, Kavaratti, Bangaram, Thinnakara, Agatti and Minicoy, effectively from mid-September to mid-May. During monsoon months, while most resorts remain open, transport can be difficult.

Lakshadweep's real attraction lies underwater: the 4200 sq km of pristine archipelago lagoons, unspoilt coral reefs and warm waters are a magnet for scuba divers and snorkellers.

Lakshadweep can only be visited on a prearranged package trip. At the time of research, resorts on Kadmat, Minicoy, Kavaratti, Agatti and Bangaram islands were open to tourists – though some trips are boat-based packages that include a cruise from Kochi, island visits, water sports, diving and nights on board the boat. At research time foreigners were permitted to stay on Agatti Island, but most people just fly to Agatti airport and take a boat transfer to other islands. Packages include permits and in some cases meals, and can be arranged though Kochi-based **SPORTS** (Society for the Promotion of Recreational Tourism & Sports; Map p302; ✆ 0484-2355387, 9495984001; http://lakshadweeptourism.com; Anzaz Arcade, Hospital Rd, Ernakulam; ⊙ 10am-5pm Mon-Fri).

🛏 Sleeping & Eating

Accommodation in Lakshadweep is limited; it's best to book this before arranging flights and permits, via Kochi-based SPORTS or an authorised private tour operator (SPORTS has a list of these).

There are some basic **cottages** (✆ 0484-2355387; http://lakshadweeptourism.com; s/d ₹10,000/15,000) and the more upmarket **Bangaram Island Resort** (✆ 8547703595; http://bangaramislandresort.in; s/d ₹10,700/15,960) on otherwise uninhabited Bangaram Island, reached by one-hour boat from Agatti. On nearby Thinnakara Island, also an hour away from Agatti by boat, you can sleep in tents (single/double ₹8000/10,000).

Kavaratti Island has beachfront huts (single/double ₹5250/9450) accessed by boat from Agatti (two hours); these are available as part of the four- to five-day SPORTS Taratashi package.

Kadmat Island Resort (✆ 0484-4011134, 0484-2397550; www.kadmat.com; Kadmat; 2 night s/d incl meals with AC ₹13,450/20,210, without AC ₹11,450/16,030; ❄) on Kadmat offers 28 modern cottages overlooking the beach, some air-conditioned; get here by overnight boat from Kochi or boat transfer from Agatti (two hours).

On the remote island of Minicoy, Lakshadweep's second-largest and southernmost island, you can stay in beachside rooms and cottages at **Minicoy Island Resort** (✆ 0484-2355387; http://lakshadweeptourism.com; Minicoy; s ₹5250-6330, d ₹7350-9450; ❄); bookings are through the six- or seven-day SPORTS Swaying Palms cruise package (₹5250 to ₹10,500).

ℹ Information

PERMITS
All visits require a special permit, which can be organised by tour operators or SPORTS in Kochi and is readily available for travellers who have confirmed accommodation bookings in Lakshadweep.

TOURIST INFORMATION
Mint Valley Travel (Map p302; ✆ 0484-2397550; www.mintvalley.com/travel; 5th fl, Metro Plaza Bdg, Market Road Junction, Ernakulam; ⊙ 10am-5pm Mon-Fri, to 2pm Sat) Reliable private tour operator.

SPORTS is the main organisation for tourist information and package tours, based in Kochi.

ℹ Getting There & Away

Air India (p521) flies between Kochi and Agatti Island daily; flights must be booked independently from tour packages. Boat transfers from Agatti airport to Bangaram, Thinnakara, Kadmat and Kavaratti cost ₹1000 to ₹4000 per person, though are often included in packages. During monsoon season, boats to Kavaratti, Bangaram and Kadmat may be replaced by helicopters.

Six passenger ships travel between Kochi and Lakshadweep, taking 14 to 18 hours, though obtaining tickets for these can be tricky; contact SPORTS. Cruise packages include the five-day, three-island Samudram trip (adult/child ₹32,030/23,100). See the tour packages section of https://lakshadweeptourism.com for details.

VJVERMA_111 / SHUTTERSTOCK ©

Kerala

Serene Kerala is a state shaped by its wonderful natural landscape: a long, luxurious coastline; wandering backwaters; lush palms and spice plantations; and cool, sky-reaching mountainscapes. Add the kaleidoscope of culture best experienced in the unique performing arts and you'll understand why Kerala is a destination not to be missed.

Contents
➡ Beaches
➡ Backwaters
➡ Performing Arts
➡ Hill Stations & Sanctuaries

Above Chinese fishing nets (p297), Kochi (Cochin)

Beaches

Goa might pull in the beach-holiday crowds, but Kerala's coastline – almost 600km of it – features a stunning string of golden-sand beaches, fringed by palms and washed by the Arabian Sea. The southern beaches are the most popular, while wilder, less-discovered choices await in the north.

Southern Beaches

The most established of the resorts along Kerala's southern coast is Kovalam (p266), just a short hop from the capital Thiruvananthapuram (Trivandrum). Once a quiet fishing village, Kovalam has two sheltered crescents of beach perfect for paddling or novice surfing, overlooked by low-rise hotels, ayurvedic centres and restaurants. Some lovely beaches and ayurvedic resorts cluster southeast of Kovalam in less-busy Pulinkudi and Chowara. North of Trivandrum is Varkala (p271), which straggles along dramatic, russet-and-gold-streaked cliffs. Although a holy town popular with Hindu pilgrims, Varkala has also developed into Kerala's favourite backpacker bolthole and the cliffs are lined with guesthouses, open-front cafes and bars all moving to a reggae, rock and trance soundtrack. Travellers looking for a quieter scene are drifting north to Odayam Beach (p271).

Even further north, Alappuzha (Alleppey; p278) is best known for its backwaters, but also has a pretty coastline stretching up to increasingly popular Marari (p283), with its golden sands and intimate resorts. Just north of Kochi (Cochin) on Vypeen Island lies Cherai Beach (p311), a lovely stretch of dusty-blonde sand, with kilometres of lazy lagoons and backwaters only a few hundred metres inland.

1. Lighthouse Beach, Kovalam (p266)
2. Lakshadweep (p323)
3. Yoga practiticnor, Varkala (p271)

Far North & Islands

Fewer travellers make it to Kerala's far north, which means there are some deserted pockets of powdery beach, where resorts are replaced by more traditional village life. Among the best are the peaceful gold sands just south of Kannur (p320), or a little further north around the Valiyaparamba backwaters, Nileshwar and Bekal (p322). Kannur's mellow homestays and Bekal's luxury hotels add to the appeal.

Even more far flung are Lakshadweep's islands (p323), a palm-fringed archipelago 300km west of Kerala. As well as pristine bleach-blonde beaches, these islands have some of India's best scuba diving and snorkelling.

Best Beach Towns

The beautiful cliff-edged coastline of Varkala (p271) is an important Hindu holy place as well as a lively backpacker-focused beach hang-out. Great base for yoga, surfing and traveller vibes.

Kovalam (p266) is Kerala's most commercial beach resort, but still fun and easily accessible with good waves, yoga and surfing. Resorts here and further southeast have a strong ayurvedic focus.

The blissfully quiet gold-tinted beaches of Bekal (p322), strung along Kerala's northernmost coast, are a world away from the busy resorts in the south.

While Kannur (p320) itself is not particularly exciting for visitors, head 8km southeast to Thottada for gorgeous beaches and family-owned homestays.

Just north of Alleppey, Marari (p283) is growing into a favourite seafront getaway for its honey-coloured beaches and luxury accommodation.

Backwaters

Kerala's 900km of waterways weave watery tendrils through a lusciously green landscape. Palm-shaded, winding canals are lined by back-in-time villages, many of which are accessible only by boat. It's an environment unique to Kerala – and an unforgettable South India experience.

Houseboats

To glide along the canals in a punted canoe, or sleep under a firmament of stars in a traditional houseboat, is pure enchantment. The distinctive house-boats that cluster around the main hubs of Alappuzha (Alleppey) and Kollam (Quilon) are designed like traditional rice barges or *kettuvallam* ('boats with knots', so-called because the curvaceous structure is held together by knotted coir).

There are several ways to explore the backwaters. The most popular is to rent a houseboat for a night or two; these sleep anywhere from two to 14 or more people, and vary wildly in luxury and amenities. The hire includes staff (at least a driver and cook, but often additional kitchen staff and crew), so catering is included, and you'll eat traditional Keralan meals of fish and vegetables cooked in coconut milk. The popularity of these tours can mean that the main waterways get very busy – even gridlocked – in peak season. A one-night houseboat trip won't get you far through the backwaters.

Talk to returning travellers or guest-house owners, and search online to gauge costs, quality and recommendations; note that some of the best houseboats get booked up in advance.

1. Traditional houseboat, Alappuzha (Alleppey; p278) **2.** Canoeing the backwaters of Munroe Island (p276)

Ferries, Canoes & Kayaks

The cheapest means of seeing the waterways is to take a public ferry. You can take trips from town to town, though you won't travel much of the smaller canals. Two of the most popular trips are the all-day tourist cruise (p278) between Kollam and Alleppey, a scenic but slow eight-hour trip, and the 2½-hour ferry (p283) from Alleppey to Kottayam.

A better way to venture deep into the network and escape the bigger boats is on a canoe tour (p287), which allows you to travel along the narrower canals and see village life in a way that's impossible on a houseboat or ferry. Village tours with a knowledgeable guide are another tranquil way to explore the region and understand some of the local culture.

Kayaking the canals is gaining popularity; operators such as Kerala Kayaking (p279) will take you far into the backwaters where you can paddle through villages.

Ecofriendly Backwaters Tourism

The choice of houseboats – especially at Alleppey's houseboat dock – is mind-boggling, and your selection of boat and operator can make or break the experience in a variety of ways. Meanwhile, houseboat tourism is taking its toll on the local environment (p287). Look for houseboats that take steps to minimise their environmental impact (such as by using solar panels), and avoid peak season (mid-December to mid-January) and domestic holidays when prices peak and the waterways are clogged. Or consider exploring by punt-powered canoe, kayak or public ferry instead.

Performing Arts

Kerala has an intensely rich culture of performing arts – living art forms are passed on to new generations in specialised schools and arts centres. Many of these arts are performed in tourist destinations.

Kathakali

Kathakali – with its elaborate ritualised gestures, heavy masklike make-up, and dramatic stories of love, lust and power struggles based on the Ramayana, the Mahabharata and the Puranas – stems in part from 2nd-century temple rituals, though its current form developed around the 16th century. The actors tell stories through precise facial expressions and *mudras* (hand gestures). Traditionally, the male-led performances start in temple grounds at around 8pm and go on all night, though condensed versions for those with shorter attention spans are performed in many tourist centres.

Kalarippayat

Taking its moves from both Kathakali and *theyyam* is the martial art of *kalarippayat*, an ancient, ritualistic discipline practised across Kerala. It's taught and displayed in an arena called a *kalari*, which combines a gymnasium, school and a temple.

Theyyam

Theyyam is believed to be older than Hinduism, having developed from harvest folk dances. It's performed in *kavus* (sacred groves) in northern Kerala. The word refers to the ritual itself, and to the shape of the deity or hero portrayed, of which there are around 450. The costumes are

1. Kathakali actors at the new year's carnival in Kochi
2. Practising the martial art of *kalarippayat*
3. *Theyyam* performer during the Onam festival

magnificent, with face paint, armour, garlands and huge headdresses. Performances consist of frenzied dancing to a wild drumbeat, creating a trance-like atmosphere, and are primarily religious rituals rather than demonstrations for audiences.

Places to See Performing Arts

The easiest places for travellers to see performances are at cultural centres such as the Kerala Kathakali Centre (p307) in Kochi; Mudra Cultural Centre (p291) in Kumily; and Punarjani Traditional Village (p295) in Munnar. In Kovalam and Varkala there are often short versions of Kathakali shows in season. In spring, numerous festivals offer the chance to see Kathakali, including Kollam's Pooram festival (p276) in April.

If you're interested in learning more about the art of Kathakali, Kerala Kala-

mandalam (p314) near Thrissur and Margi Kathakali School (p263) in Trivandrum offer courses for serious students, or you can attend these schools to see performances and practise sessions. Kochi's Kerala Kathakali Centre also runs classes.

The Kochi, Munnar and Kumily centres have demonstrations of *kalarippayat,* or you can visit the martial art training centres of CVN Kalari Sangham (p263) in Trivandrum and Ens Kalari (p308) in Nettoor, close to Ernakulam.

The best areas to see *theyyam* performances are around Kannur, Payyanur and Valiyaparamba, in the northern backwaters area, where there are more than 500 *kavus*. The season is from October to May. For advice on finding performances, contact the Tourist Desk (p308) in Kochi or homestays at Thottada Beach, especially Costa Malabari (p321).

MAZUR TRAVEL / SHUTTERSTOCK ©

Tea plantations, Munnar (p292)

Hill Stations & Sanctuaries

Extending through the World Heritage–listed Western Ghats, Kerala's hill country is a sumptuous natural spectacle of narrow roads meandering up through thick jungle vegetation and providing dizzying views over peacock-green tea plantations. A cooling altitude makes its upland towns soothing places to escape from the sultry coast, while wildlife sanctuaries here are largely unspoilt wildernesses offering the chance to spot wild animals and birdlife.

Munnar

Best known of Kerala's hill stations is Munnar (p292), with contoured green tea fields and plantations carpeting the hills as far as the eye can see. This is South India's tea-growing heartland, but also a great place to trek to viewpoints across fine mountain scenery. Some wonderfully remote lodgings are hidden in the hills, tucked deep into spice and flower gardens or cardamom and coffee plantations.

Wayanad & Periyar

The northern area around Wayanad Wildlife Sanctuary (p317) has shimmering green paddy fields, peaks rising to 2100m and plantations of coffee, cardamom, ginger and pepper, and its rolling hills are fragrant with wild herbs and punctuated by mammoth clumps of bamboo. This is one of South India's best places to spot wild elephants, and there's some good trekking.

At Periyar Tiger Reserve (p287), Kerala's most-visited wildlife park, you can cruise on Periyar Lake, hang out in the laid-back hill town of Kumily, paddle on a bamboo raft or embark on a jungle trek with a trained tribal guide.

Tamil Nadu

POP 80.8 MILLION

Includes ➡

Chennai (Madras) . . 335

Mamallapuram
(Mahabalipuram) . . . 355

Puducherry
(Pondicherry) 364

Trichy
(Tiruchirappalli) 382

Madurai 389

Kanyakumari
(Cape Comorin) 395

Ooty (Udhaga-
mandalam) 409

Anamalai Tiger
Reserve 415

Best Places to Eat

➡ Villa Shanti (p371)

➡ Dreaming Tree (p363)

➡ Bangala (p388)

➡ Murugan Idli Shop (p392)

➡ La Belle Vie (p407)

➡ Annalakshmi (p346)

Best Places to Stay

➡ Saratha Vilas (p388)

➡ La Maison (p408)

➡ Jungle Hut (p415)

➡ Villa Shanti (p369)

➡ Svatma (p381)

➡ Surf Turf (p354)

Why Go?

Tamil Nadu is the homeland of one of humanity's living classical civilisations, stretching back uninterrupted for two millennia and very much alive today in the Tamils' language, dance, poetry and forms of Hinduism.

Some of the temples here are among India's finest, from the sculpted stonework at Thanjavur (Tanjore) to the sprawling halls at Madurai. Across the state, pulsing urban centres rise like concrete islands amid a landscape of palm and banana plantations, rice fields and rugged sandstone scarps. Among them you'll find yoga and meditation retreats, ancient forts and bohemian B&Bs.

When the hot chaos of Tamil temple towns overwhelms, escape to the southernmost tip of India where three seas mingle; to the splendid mansions sprinkled across arid Chettinadu; or to the cool, forest-clad, wildlife-prowled Western Ghats. Tamil Nadu is welcoming but remains proudly distinct from the rest of India.

When to Go
Chennai

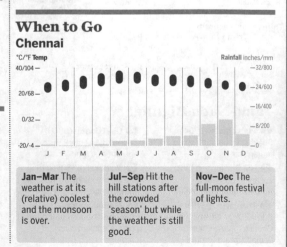

Jan–Mar The weather is at its (relative) coolest and the monsoon is over.

Jul–Sep Hit the hill stations after the crowded 'season' but while the weather is still good.

Nov–Dec The full-moon festival of lights.

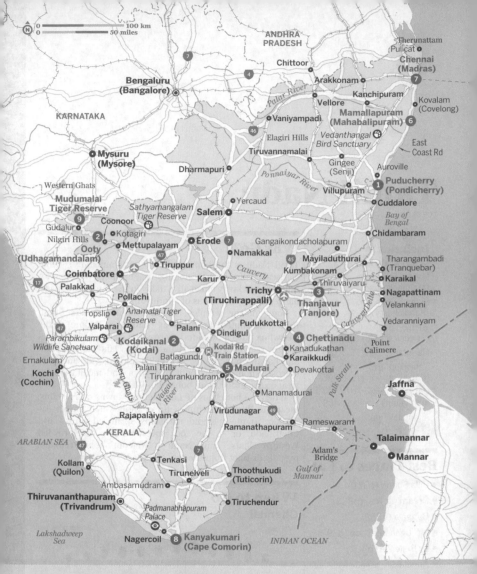

Tamil Nadu Highlights

1 Puducherry (p364) Soaking up unique Franco-Indian flair.

2 Hill Stations (p398) Escaping the heat at Kodaikanal or Ooty.

3 Thanjavur (p379) Admiring the crowning glory of Chola temple architecture, the Brihadishwara Temple.

4 Chettinadu (p386) Spending the night in an opulent mansion.

5 Madurai (p389) Getting lost in the colourful chaos of Tamil temple life.

6 Mamallapuram (p355) Enjoying a beachy vibe amid remarkable temples and carvings.

7 Chennai (p335) Exploring Tamil Nadu's traditional but cosmopolitan capital.

8 Kanyakumari (p395) Standing on the wave-swept tip of the subcontinent.

9 Mudumalai Tiger Reserve (p414) Tracking down rare exotic wildlife in majestic mountains.

History

While some would have you believe that the uniting feature among South Indian states is a preference for rice over roti, their ancient cultural connection is perhaps most profoundly rooted in language. Tamil (of Tamil Nadu), Malayalam (of Kerala), Telugu (Telangana and Andhra Pradesh) and Kannada (Karnataka) are all Dravidian tongues and their speakers trace their cultural and religious identity back in an unbroken line to classical antiquity, long before the Aryan people arrived on the subcontinent from the north. Tamils consider themselves the standard bearers of Dravidian civilisation, with a considerable amount of pride.

The Tamil language was well established in Tamil Nadu by the 3rd century BC, the approximate start of the Sangam Age, when Tamil poets produced the body of classical literature known as Sangam literature. The Sangam period lasted until about AD 300, with three main Tamil dynasties arising in different parts of Tamil Nadu ('Tamil Country'): the early Cholas in the centre, the Cheras in the west and the Pandyas in the south.

By the 7th century the Pallavas, also Tamil, established an empire based at Kanchipuram, extending from Tamil Nadu north into Andhra Pradesh. They take credit for the great stone carvings of Mamallapuram (Mahabalipuram) and constructed the region's first free-standing temples.

Next in power were the medieval Cholas (whose connection with the early Cholas is hazy). Based in the Cauvery Valley of central Tamil Nadu, at their peak the Cholas ruled Sri Lanka and the Maldives plus much of South India, and extended their influence to Southeast Asia, spreading Tamil ideas of reincarnation, karma and yogic practice.

The Cholas raised Dravidian architecture to new heights with the magnificent towered temples at Thanjavur and Gangaikondacholapuram, and carried the art of bronze image casting to its peak, especially in their images of Shiva as Nataraja, the cosmic dancer. *Gopurams,* the tall temple gate towers characteristic of Tamil Nadu, made their appearance in late Chola times.

By the late 14th century much of Tamil Nadu was under the sway of the Vijayanagar empire based at Hampi (Karnataka). As the Vijayanagar state weakened in the 16th century, some of their local governors, the Nayaks, set up strong independent kingdoms, notably at Madurai and Thanjavur. Vijayanagar and Nayak sculptors carved wonderfully detailed temple statues and reliefs.

Europeans first landed on Tamil shores in the 16th century, when the Portuguese settled at San Thome. The Dutch, British, French and Danes followed in the 17th century, striking deals with local rulers to set up coastal trading colonies. Eventually it came down to the British, based at Chennai (then Madras), against the French, based at Puducherry (then Pondicherry). The British won out in the three Carnatic Wars, fought between 1744 and 1763. By the end of the 18th century British dominance over most Tamil lands was assured.

The area governed by the British from Madras, the Madras Presidency, included parts of Andhra Pradesh, Kerala and Karnataka, an arrangement that continued as Madras State after Indian Independence in 1947, until Kerala, Karnataka, Andhra Pradesh and present-day Tamil Nadu (130,058 sq km) were created on linguistic lines in the 1950s. It wasn't until 1968 that the current state (population 80 million) was officially named Tamil Nadu.

Tamil Nadu's political parties are often headed up by former film stars, most prominent among them controversial former chief minister and AIADMK (All India Anna Dravida Munnetra Kazhagam) leader Jayalalithaa Jayaram. Known as Amma (Mother), Jayalalithaa was worshipped with almost deitylike status across the state until her death on 5 December 2016. You're sure to see her face round and benevolent – on posters and billboards throughout the state, conferring blessings from beyond on current political candidates.

CHENNAI (MADRAS)

♪044 / POP 10.4 MILLION

If you have time to explore Chennai (formerly Madras), this 400-sq-km conglomerate of urban villages and diverse neighbourhoods making up Tamil Nadu's capital will pleasantly surprise you. Its role is as keeper of South Indian artistic, religious and culinary traditions.

With its sweltering southern heat, roaring traffic and lack of outstanding sights, Chennai has often been seen as the dowdier sibling among India's four biggest cities. But it's well worth poking around its museums and temples, savouring deliciously authentic

TOP STATE FESTIVALS

International Yoga Festival (Puducherry/Pondicherry; ⊙4-7 Jan) Workshops, demonstrations and competitions, attracting experts from across India and beyond.

Pongal (statewide; ⊙mid-Jan) Marks the end of the harvest season and is one of Tamil Nadu's most important festivals.

Thyagaraja Aradhana (Thiruvaiyaru; www.thiruvaiyaruthyagarajaaradhana.org; ⊙Jan) This important five-day Carnatic music festival honours the saint and composer Thyagaraja.

Teppam Festival (Float Festival; Madurai; ⊙Jan/Feb) Meenakshi Amman Temple deities are paraded around town in elaborate procession and floated in a brightly lit 'minitemple'.

Natyanjali Dance Festival (Chidambaram ; www.natyanjalichidambaram.com; ⊙Feb) This five-day dance festival attracts 300 to 400 classical dancers from all over India.

Chithirai Festival (Madurai; ⊙Apr/May) A two-week celebration/reenactment of the marriage of Meenakshi to Sundareswarar (Shiva).

Karthikai Deepam Festival (statewide; ⊙Nov/Dec) Festival of lights, best seen at Tiruvannamalai, where the legend began.

Chennai Festival of Music & Dance (Madras Music & Dance Season; Chennai; ⊙mid-Dec–mid-Jan) One of the largest of its type in the world, this festival celebrates South Indian music and dance.

Mamallapuram Dance Festival (Mamallapuram; ⊙Dec-Jan) Showcasing classical and folk dances from all over India, with many performances on an open-air stage.

Covelong Point Surf, Music & Yoga Festival (Covelong/Kovalam; www.covelongpoint. com; ⊙Aug) Expect kayak races, volleyball tournaments, group yoga and plenty of surfing.

South Indian delicacies or taking a sunset saunter along Marina Beach – the world's second-longest urban beach.

Among Chennai's greatest assets are its people, infectiously enthusiastic about their home town; they won't hit you with a lot of hustle and hassle. Recent years have thrown in a new layer of cosmopolitan glamour: luxe hotels, sparkling boutiques, quirky cafes, and smart contemporary restaurants – but the best of Chennai remains its old soul.

History

The southern neighbourhood of Mylapore is Chennai's Ur-settlement; in ancient times it traded with Roman, Chinese and Greek merchants. In 1523 the Portuguese established their nearby coastal enclave, San Thome. Another century passed before Francis Day and the British East India Company rocked up in 1639, searching for a good southeast-Indian trading base, and struck a deal with the local Vijayanagar ruler to set up a fort-cum-trading-post at Madraspatnam fishing village. This was Fort St George, built from 1640 to 1653.

The three Carnatic Wars between 1744 and 1763 saw Britain and its colonialist rival France allying with competing South Indi-

an princes in their efforts to get the upper hand over local rulers – and each other. The French occupied Fort St George from 1746 to 1749 but the British eventually triumphed, and the French withdrew to Pondicherry (today Puducherry).

As capital of the Madras Presidency, one of the four major divisions of British-era India, Madras grew into an important naval and commercial centre. After Independence, it became capital of Madras State and then of its successor, Tamil Nadu. The city was renamed Chennai in 1996. Today it's a major IT hub and is often called 'the Detroit of India' for its booming motor-vehicle industry.

⊙ Sights

★**Government Museum**   MUSEUM
(Map p344; www.chennaimuseum.org; Pantheon Rd, Egmore; Indian/foreigner ₹15/250, camera/video ₹200/500; ⊙9.30am-5pm Sat-Thu) Housed across from the striking British-built Pantheon Complex, this excellent museum is Chennai's best. The big highlight is building 3, the Bronze Gallery, with a superb collection of South Indian bronzes from the 7th-century Pallava era through to modern times (and English-language explanatory material).

It was from the 9th to 11th centuries, in the Chola period, that bronze sculpture peaked. Among the Bronze Gallery's impressive pieces are many of Shiva as Nataraja, the cosmic dancer, and an outstanding Chola bronze of Ardhanarishvara, the androgynous incarnation of Shiva and Parvati.

The main Archaeological Galleries (building 1) represent all the major South Indian periods from 2nd-century BC Buddhist sculptures to 16th-century Vijayanagar work, with rooms devoted to Hindu, Buddhist and Jain sculpture. Building 2, the Anthropology Galleries, traces South Indian human history back to prehistoric times, displaying tribal artefacts from across the region; outside it is a tiger-head cannon captured from Tipu Sultan's army in 1799 upon his defeat at Srirangapatnam.

The museum also includes the National Art Gallery, Contemporary Art Gallery and Children's Museum, on the same ticket. Some sections may be closed for renovation.

★ **Kapaleeshwarar Temple** HINDU TEMPLE
(Map p338; Ponnambala Vathiar St, Mylapore; ⊙6am-noon & 4-9.30pm) Mylapore is one of Chennai's most charactertul and traditional neighbourhoods; it predated colonial Madras by several centuries. Its Kapaleeshwarar Temple is Chennai's most active and impressive, and is believed to have been built after the Portuguese destroyed the seaside original in 1566. It displays the main architectural elements of many a Tamil Nadu temple – a rainbow-coloured *gopuram*, pillared *mandapas* (pavilions) and a huge tank – and is dedicated to the state's most popular deity, Shiva.

Legend tells that in an angry fit Shiva turned his consort Parvati into a peacock, and commanded her to worship him here to regain her normal form. Parvati supposedly did so at a spot just outside the northeast corner of the temple's central block, where a shrine commemorates the event. Hence the name Mylapore, 'town of peacocks'. The story is depicted at the west end of the inner courtyard, on the exterior of the main sanctum.

The temple's colourful **Brahmotsavam festival** (⊙Mar/Apr) sees the deities paraded around Mylapore's streets.

St Thomas Mount RELIGIOUS SITE
(Parangi Malai; off Lawrence Rd, Guindy; ⊙6am-8pm) FREE The reputed site of St Thomas' martyrdom in AD 72 rises in the southwest of Chennai, 2.5km north of St Thomas Mount train station. The Church of Our Lady of Expectation, built atop the 'mount' by the Portuguese in 1523, contains what are supposedly a fragment of Thomas' finger bone and the 'Bleeding Cross' he carved. The city and airport views are wonderful. Take the metro to the Nanganullar Rd stop and catch an autorickshaw there.

Tara Books GALLERY
(☑044-24426696; www.tarabooks.com; ⊙10am-7pm) Producers of beautiful hand-printed books, this publishing company is based in southern Chennai. Visit its **Book Building** (☑044-24426696; www.tarabooks.com; Plot 9, CGE Colony, Kuppam Beach Rd, Thiruvanmiyur; ⊙10am-7.30pm Mon-Sat) FREE showroom, where you can browse, buy and maybe catch a talk by an author or artist. You can also check out the printing shop, **AMM Screens** (☑9962525740; 1 Elim Nagar, Perungudi; ⊙10am-1pm & 2-6pm), and watch pages being silk-screened and hand-bound into finished volumes. The Book Building is conveniently visited together with the nearby Kalakshetra Foundation (p341), just 700m north. The print shop is about a 10-minute autorickshaw ride southwest.

Vivekananda House MUSEUM
(Vivekanandar Illam, Ice House; Map p338; www.vivekanandahouse.org; Kamarajar Salai; adult/child ₹20/10; ⊙10am-12.30pm & 3-7.15pm Tue-Sat) The marshmallow-pink Vivekananda House is interesting not only for its displays on the famous 'wandering monk', Swami Vivekananda, but also for its semicircular form, built in 1842 to store ice imported from the USA. Vivekananda stayed here briefly in 1897, preaching his ascetic Hindu philosophy to adoring crowds. Displays include a photo exhibition on the swami's life, a 3D reproduction of Vivekananda's celebrated 1893 Chicago World's Parliament of Religions speech, and the room where he stayed, now used for meditation.

San Thome Cathedral CATHEDRAL
(Map p338; Santhome High Rd, Mylapore; ⊙5.30am-8.30pm) This soaring Roman Catholic cathedral, a stone's throw from the beach, was founded by the Portuguese in 1523, then rebuilt by the British in neo-Gothic style in 1896, and is said to mark the final resting place of St Thomas the Apostle. It's believed 'Doubting Thomas' brought Christianity to the subcontinent in AD 52 and was killed at St Thomas Mount, Chennai, in AD 72. Behind the cathedral is the **tomb of St**

Chennai (Madras)

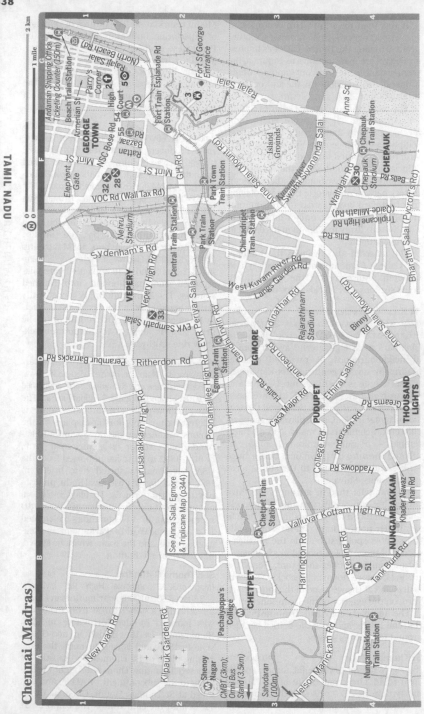

See Anna Salai, Egmore
& Triplicane Map (p344)

GEORGE TOWN

CHEPAUK

VEPERY

EGMORE

PUDUPET

CHETPET

THOUSAND
LIGHTS

NUNGAMBAKKAM

Andaman Shipping Office
Ticketing Counter (350m)

Beach Train Station

Rajaji Salai (North Beach Rd)

Parry's
Corner

Fort St George
Entrance

Fort St Esplanade Rd

Rajaji Salai

High Court

Armenian St

Mint St

NSC Bose Rd

Rattan Bazaar Rd

54 Court

55

Fort Train
Station

Island
Grounds

Anna Sq

Chepauk
Train Station

Bells Rd

Chepauk
Stadium

Wallajah Rd

Elephant
Gate

Mint St

GH Rd

VOC Rd (Wall Tax Rd)

Nehru
Stadium

Park Town
Train Station

Anna Salai (Mount Rd)

Swami Sivananda Salai

Sydenham's Rd

Central Train Station

Park Train
Station

Chintadripet
Train Station

Triplicane High Rd
(Quaide-Millath Rd)

Ellis Rd

Bharath Salai (Pycroft's Rd)

Vepery High Rd

EVK Sampath Salai

Poonamallee High Rd (EVR Periyar Salai)

West Kuvam River Rd

Langs Garden Rd

Adinathar Rd

Anna Salai (Mount Rd)

Perambur Barracks Rd

Ritherdon Rd

Purusavakkam High Rd

Egmore Train
Station

Gandhi Irwin Rd

Halls Rd

Pantheon Rd

Casa Major Rd

Rajarathinam
Stadium

Binny
Rd

Greams Rd

Anderson Rd

Ethiraj Salai

College Rd

Haddows Rd

New Avadi Rd

Kilpauk Garden Rd

Pachaiyappa's
College

Shenoy
Nagar

CMBT (3km);
Omni Bus
Stand (3.5km)

Sahodaran
(100m)

Nelson Manickam Rd

Harrington Rd

Chetpet Train
Station

Valluvar Kottam High Rd

Sterling Rd

Tank Bund Rd

Khader Nawaz
Khan Rd

Nungambakkam
Train Station

2

3

5

28

32

33

51

N

0   1 mile
0   2 km

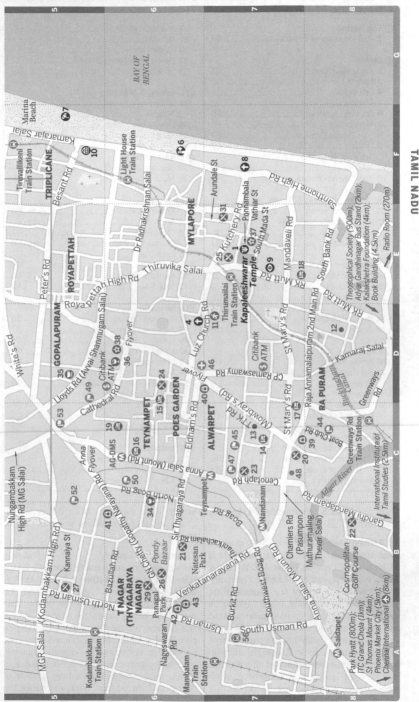

Chennai (Madras)

◎ Top Sights
1 Kapaleeshwarar Temple........................E7

◎ Sights
2 Armenian Church................................G1
3 Fort St George.................................G2
4 Luz Church D6
5 Madras High Court G1
6 Madras Lighthouse..............................F6
7 Marina Beach F5
8 San Thome Cathedral...........................F7
9 Sri Ramakrishna Math E7
   Tomb of St Thomas the
   Apostle..(see 8)
10 Vivekananda House..............................F5

◎ Activities, Courses & Tours
11 Isha Yoga Center............................... D7
12 Krishnamacharya Yoga
   Mandiram..D8
13 Storytrails..C7

◎ Sleeping
14 Footprint B&B C7
15 Hanu Reddy Residences.......................D6
16 Hyatt Regency..................................C6
17 Raintree... C7
18 Red Lollipop Hostel E7
19 Zostel..C6

◎ Eating
20 Amma Naana C7
21 Big Bazaar..B6
   Chamiers.................................. (see 39)
   Chap Chay .... (see 17)
22 Ciclo Cafe....................................... B8
   Copper Chimney.......................... (see 36)
23 Double Roti C7
24 Enté Keralam....................................D6
25 Hotel Saravana Bhavan E7
26 Hotel Saravana Bhavan B6
27 Junior Kuppanna.................................B5
28 Mehta Brothers................................. F1

29 Murugan Idli Shop...............................B6
30 Nair Mess..F4
31 Rayars Mess..................................... E7
32 Seena Bhai Tiffin Centre F1
33 Spencer's..D2

◎ Drinking & Nightlife
34 10 Downing Street..............................C6
   365 AS ....(see 16)
35 Lloyds Tea House...............................D5
36 Sera the Tapas Bar D6

◎ Entertainment
37 Bharatiya Vidya Bhavan...................... E7
38 Music Academy D6

◎ Shopping
   Amethyst Room...........................(see 39)
   Anokhi.......................................(see 39)
39 Chamiers...C7
   Chamiers for Men.......................(see 39)
40 Fabindia D7
41 Fabindia B6
42 Kumaran Silks..................................A6
43 Nalli Silks.......................................A6

◎ Information
44 German Consulate..............................C8
45 Japanese Consulate...........................C7
46 Kauvery Hospital................................D6
47 Malaysian Consulate...........................C7
48 Milesworth Travel...............................C7
49 New Zealand Honorary Consul..............D5
50 Singaporean Consulate........................C6
51 Sri Lankan Deputy High
   Commission...................................B4
52 Thai Consulate..................................C5
53 US Consulate....................................C5

◎ Transport
54 Broadway Bus Terminus.......................F1
55 Rattan Bazaar Road Bus Stop...............F1
56 T Nagar Bus Terminus..........................A7

Thomas (Map p338; Santhome High Rd, Mylapore; ⊙9am-8pm) FREE.

Sri Ramakrishna Math   RELIGIOUS SITE
(Map p338; www.chennaimath.org; 31 RK Mutt Rd, Mylapore; ⊙Universal Temple 4.30-11.45am & 3-9pm, evening prayers 6.30-7.30pm) The tranquil, flowery grounds of the Ramakrishna Math are a world away from Mylapore's chaos. Orange-robed monks glide around and there's a reverential feel. The Math is a monastic order following the teachings of the 19th-century sage Sri Ramakrishna, who preached the essential unity of all religions. Its Universal Temple is a handsome, modern, salmon-pink building incorporating

architectural elements from different religions, and is open to all, to worship, pray or meditate.

Theosophical Society   GARDENS
(www.ts-adyar.org; south end of Thiru Vi Ka Bridge, Adyar; ⊙grounds 8.30-10am & 2-4pm Mon-Sat) FREE Between the Adyar River and the coast, the 100-hectare grounds of the Theosophical Society provide a peaceful, green, vehicle-free retreat from the city. Despite restricted opening hours, it's a lovely spot to wander, containing a church, mosque, Buddhist shrine, Zoroastrian temple and Hindu temple as well as a huge variety of native and introduced flora, including the

offshoots of a 450-year-old banyan tree severely damaged by a storm in the 1980s.

Marina Beach
BEACH

(Map p338) Take an early morning or evening stroll (you don't want to roast here at any other time) along the 3km-long main stretch of Marina Beach and you'll pass cricket matches, flying kites, fortune-tellers, fish markets, corn-roasters and families enjoying the sea breeze. But don't swim: strong rips make it dangerous. At the southern end, the ridiculously popular **Madras Lighthouse** (Map p338; Indian/foreigner ₹20/50, camera ₹25; ⊗10am-1pm & 3-6pm Tue-Sun) is India's only lighthouse with a lift; the panoramic city and beach views are fabulous.

Kalakshetra Foundation
ARTS CENTRE

(⟳044-24521169; www.kalakshetra.in; Muthulakshmi St, Thiruvanmiyur; ⊗campus 8.30-11.30am Mon-Fri Jul-Feb, craft centre 9am-1pm & 2-5pm Mon-Sat, all closed 2nd & 4th Sat of month) Founded in 1936, Kalakshetra is a leading serious school of Tamil classical dance and music (sponsoring many students from disadvantaged backgrounds), set in beautiful, shady grounds in south Chennai. During morning class times visitors can (quietly) wander the complex. Across the road is the **Kalakshetra Craft Centre** (Indian/foreigner ₹100/500), where you can see Kanchipuram-style handloom weaving, textile block-printing and the fascinating, rare art of *kalamkari* (hand-painting on textiles with vegetable dyes), if you're feeling inspired, there are courses too. For upcoming performances, check the website.

Madras High Court
NOTABLE BUILDING

(Map p338; Parry's Corner, George Town) Completed in 1892, this imposing red Indo-Saracenic structure is said to be the world's largest judicial building after the Courts of London. The central tower was added in 1912. At research time, visitors were not permitted to wander the grounds, but if you fancy trying, take your passport.

Fort St George
FORT

(Map p338; Rajaji Salai; ⊗10am-5pm) FREE Finished in 1653 by the British East India Company, the fort has undergone many facelifts. Inside the vast perimeter walls (the ramparts are 18th-century replacements) is now a precinct housing Tamil Nadu's Legislative Assembly & Secretariat, and a smattering of older buildings.

Valluvar Kottam
MONUMENT

(Map p344; Valluvar Kottam High Rd, Nungambakkam; adult/child ₹3/2; ⊗8am-6pm) This 1976 memorial honours the Tamil poet Thiruvalluvar and his classic work, the 133-chapter *Thirukural*. Its most striking element is a 31m-high stone replica of Tamil Nadu's largest temple chariot (from Thiruvarur), pulled by two stone elephants and with giant wheels. In the adjacent auditorium, the Thirukural's 1330 couplets are inscribed on granite tablets. From the auditorium's step-accessed roof, you can walk to the foot of the shrine below the chariot's dome, which holds a life-size seated Thiruvalluvar.

🏃 Activities

Isha Yoga Center
YOGA

(Map p338; ⟳044-24981185; www.ishayoga.org; 117 Luz Church Rd, Mylapore; ⊗7am-9pm) Offers a variety of well-regarded yoga programs, covering a range of mastery levels. Course lengths vary.

Krishnamacharya Yoga Mandiram
YOGA, MEDITATION

(KYM; Map p338; ⟳044-24937998; www.kym.org; 31 4th Cross St, RK Nagar; prices vary; ⊗8am-7pm) Highly regarded, serious two-week and month-long yoga courses, yoga therapy and intensive teacher training. See the KYM website for schedule and prices.

🐚 Courses

Kalakshetra Foundation
ART

(⟳044-24525423; www.kalakshetra.in; Muthulakshmi St, Thiruvanmiyur; per day ₹500) Kalakshetra's craft centre offers one- to two-month courses in the intricate old art of *kalamkari* – hand-painting fabrics with natural vegetable dyes – which survives in only a handful of places. Courses run 10am to 1pm Monday to Friday.

International Institute of Tamil Studies
LANGUAGE

(⟳9952448862; www.ulakaththamizh.org; CIT Campus, 2nd Main Rd, Tharamani; 3-/6-month course ₹5000/10,000) Intensive three-month and six-month Tamil-language courses.

👉 Tours

★ Storytrails
WALKING

(Map p338; ⟳9940040215, 044-45010202; www.storytrails.in; 21/2 1st Cross St, TTK Rd, Alwarpet; from ₹1500) An excellent way to get a feel for Chennai, these neighbourhood walking

CHENNAI'S OTHER CHURCHES

Armenian Church (Map p338; Armenian St, George Town; ⊘ 9.30am-2.30pm, hours vary) A leafy, frangipani-scented haven in the midst of the George Town mayhem, the 18th-century Armenian Church is testament to the city's once-flourishing Armenian merchant community.

St Andrew's Church (St Andrew's Kirk; Map p344; www.thekirk.in; 37 Poonamallee High Rd, Egmore; ⊘ 10am-5.30pm) This 1821 neoclassical Scottish Presbyterian church is one of India's most exquisite churches, rising up in leafy grounds in the middle of frenzied Egmore. Inspired by London's St Martin-in-the-Fields church, it has a grand columned portico.

Luz Church (Shrine of our Lady of Light; Map p338; www.luzchurch.org; off Luz Church Rd, Mylapore; ⊘ dawn-dusk) Styled with blue-and-white baroque elegance, pretty little palm-fringed Luz Church is Chennai's oldest European building, dating to 1516 – which also makes it one of India's oldest churches.

tours highlight themes like dance, temples, jewellery and bazaars. There are also popular food-tasting tours through George Town and in-house cooking classes. Most tours last 2½ hours. Calling is the best way to book; prices may vary depending on group size.

Royal Enfield Factory TOURS
(☑ 044-42230400; www.royalenfield.com; Tiruvottiyur High Rd, Tiruvottiyur; per person ₹600) The classic Enfield Bullet 350 motorcycle has been manufactured since 1955 in far northern Chennai. Two-hour tours run on the second and fourth Saturdays of each month at 10am. Bookings essential.

🛏 Sleeping

Hotels in Chennai are pricier than elsewhere in Tamil Nadu and not particularly good value. The Triplicane area is known for budget accommodation, but much of it is pretty gritty. Better cheapies are found in Egmore, and there are a couple of good hostels in other neighbourhoods. You'll find upper-midrange B&Bs in Nungambakkam, Poes Garden and Alwarpet. Top-end hotels are plentiful. Many hotels fill up by noon – book ahead!

Red Lollipop Hostel HOSTEL $
(Map p338; ☑ 044-24629822; www.redlollipop.in; 129/68 RK Mutt Rd, Mandavelli; dm/s/d ₹650/1400/1680; ❈ 🛜) A boon for Chennai's budget travellers, Red Lollipop is a genuine, sociable hostel, 700m south of Mylapore's temple. Boldly colourful walls are scrawled with inspirational messages. Each of the spotless, locker-equipped six- to 10-bed dorms (one women-only) has its own bathroom. There's one private room, a rooftop

terrace, a shared kitchen, a lounge and very helpful staff.

Zostel HOSTEL $
(Map p338; ☑ 011-39589002; www.zostel.com; 120/61 Ellaiamman Colony, 5th St, Teynampet; dm/r ₹600/1680; ❈ 🛜) Fresh on the Chennai scene, this branch of India's popular hostel chain is a success, with eight-bed dorms, a straightforward private room, a couple of spacious common areas, a shared kitchen and a washing machine. It's a five-minute walk from a metro stop in a quiet residential neighbourhood.

Paradise Guest House GUESTHOUSE $
(Map p344; ☑ 044-28594252; www.paradiseguesthouse.co.in; 17/1 Vallabha Agraharam St, Triplicane; s/d ₹500/700, with AC ₹1000/1200; ❈ 🛜) Welcoming Paradise offers some of Triplicane's best-value digs: simple rooms with clean tiles, a breezy rooftop, friendly staff and hot water by the steaming bucket. It's basic, but unlike some other hotels in the neighborhood, it's not gritty and there are no dark vibes.

⭐ **Footprint B&B** B&B $$
(Map p338; ☑ 9840037483; www.footprint.in; Gayatri Apts, 16 South St, Alwarpet; r incl breakfast ₹3400; ❈ 🛜) A beautifully comfortable, relaxed base on a quiet street in a leafy south Chennai neighbourhood. Three immaculate private rooms with king-size or wide twin beds share a thoughtfully arranged common area decorated with bowls of wild roses and old-Madras photos. Home-cooked breakfasts are generous, service is excellent, and the welcoming owners are full of Tamil Nadu tips. Book ahead.

Hanu Reddy Residences GUESTHOUSE **$$**
(Map p344; 044-43084563, 9176869926; www.
hanureddyresidences.com; 6A/24 3rd St, Wallace
Garden, Nungambakkam; incl breakfast s ₹3540-
4130, d ₹4130-4720; ❄🛜) Perfectly located
on a quiet street just a block away from
an international mix of restaurants, cafes
and upscale shops. The 13 unpretentious
rooms come with air-con, free wi-fi, tea/
coffee sets, splashes of colourful artwork
– and antimosquito racquets! Terraces
have bamboo lounging chairs. Service hits
that ideal personal-yet-professional bal-
ance. There's another **branch** (Map p338;
044-24661021; 41/19 Poes Garden; r/ste incl
breakfast ₹5900/10,240; ❄🛜) in exclusive
Poes Garden.

YWCA International
Guest House GUESTHOUSE **$$**
(Map p344; 044-25324234; http://ywca
madras.org/international-guest-house; 1086 Poonamallee High Rd; incl breakfast s ₹2065-2700, d
₹2600-3590, without AC s/d ₹1475/1890; ❄@🛜)
Chennai's YWCA guesthouse, set in shady
grounds just north of Egmore station, offers a meticulously run property in a calm
atmosphere. It has good-sized, brilliantly
clean rooms, spacious common areas and
solid-value meals (veg/nonveg ₹225/330).
Lobby-only wi-fi costs ₹150 per day. In all, it's
a fair value.

Hotel Victoria HOTEL **$$**
(Map p344; 044-28193638; www.empeehotels.
com; 3 Kennet Lane, Egmore; incl breakfast s ₹2800-
5075, d ₹3300-5550; ❄🛜) Easily your smartest
choice on hectic Kennet Lane. Rooms are
clean and inviting, with kettles and flat-
screen TVs, though not as exciting as the
shiny lobby and cordial service suggest.

La Woods HOTEL **$$**
(Map p344; 044-28608040; www.lawoodshotel.
com; 1 Woods Rd, Anna Salai; r incl breakfast ₹3540;
❄🛜) Wonderfully erratic colour schemes
throw fresh whites against lime greens
and bright turquoises at this friendly, well-
managed modern hotel. The shiny, spotless,
contemporary rooms are perfectly comfy,
with mountains of pillows, kettles, hairdryers and 'global' plug sockets. You can
even plug your laptop or phone into the TV!
On-site restaurant and futuristic-looking bar.

Hotel Chandra Park HOTEL **$$**
(Map p344; 044-40506060; www.hotelchandra
park.com; 9 Gandhi Irwin Rd, Egmore; incl breakfast
s ₹1450-2900, d ₹1680-3540; ❄🛜) Chandra

Park's prices remain mysteriously lower than
those at most similar establishments. 'Stand-
ard' rooms are smallish and a bit dated but
have air-con, clean towels and tight, white
sheets. Throw in polite service, 24-hour
checkout and free wi-fi, and this is one of the
best values in Chennai.

⭐**ITC Grand Chola** HOTEL **$$$**
(044-22200000; www.itchotels.in; 63 Mount Rd,
Guindy; r from ₹15,050; ❄🛜♨) ✿ Chennai's
most talked-about hotel is this ultraluxurious, 600-room, temple-inspired beauty in
the city's southwest. A maze of sumptuous
iPad-operated rooms, complete with soaking
tubs and French press coffee kits, unfolds
beyond the sweeping lantern-lit marble lobby. One corridor caters exclusively to women
travellers. Also here are seven swish restaurants, two glitzy bars, three gyms, a spa and
five pools. The hotel runs mostly on wind
and solar power, and incorporates sustainable materials.

⭐**Ikhaya** BOUTIQUE HOTEL **$$$**
(Map p344; 7550120885; www.ikhaya.in; 6
Nawab Habibulah Ave, 1st St, Nungambakkam; r
incl breakfast ₹4950-5900) A new iteration
of a favourite old B&B, Ikhaya brilliantly
brings together the best of heritage ambi-
ence and contemporary amenities. Rooms
have carved wooden beds, throw rugs and
modern bathrooms; some have balconies.
The indoor dining area is a charming tur-
quoise-and-white space, and there's an
inner courtyard with tables, all part of the
everything-made-from-scratch Mediterrane-
an restaurant.

⭐**Raintree** HOTEL **$$$**
(Map p338; 044-42252525; www.raintree
hotels.com; 120 St Mary's Rd, Alwarpet; r from
₹8730; ❄@🛜♨) ✿ At this 'eco-sensitive'
business-style hotel, floors are bamboo or
rubber, water and electricity conservation
hold pride of place, and AC-generated heat
warms the bathroom water. Sleek, fresh,
minimalist rooms are bright, comfy and
stylish, with wonderful city vistas. A sea-
view infinity pool (doubling as insulation)
and an open-air bar-restaurant grace the
rooftop. Downstairs is excellent pan-Asian
restaurant **Chap Chay** (mains ₹450-800, set
menu ₹1900; ⏲noon-3pm & 7-11pm).

Taj Coromandel HOTEL **$$$**
(Map p344; 044-66002827; www.tajhotels.com;
37 Nungambakkam High Rd, Nungambakkam; r
from ₹12,000; ❄🛜♨) Luxurious without

Anna Salai, Egmore & Triplicane

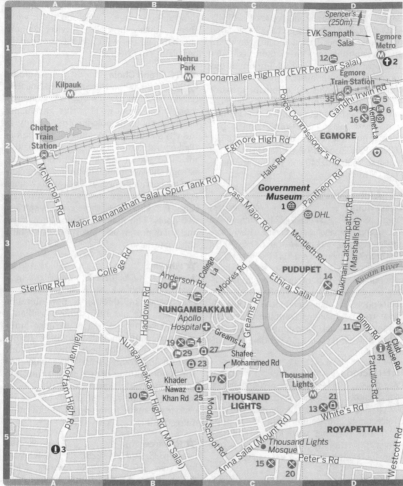

being overly ostentatious, the glittering Coromandel offers a sensibly central top-end retreat from the city. Rooms flaunt a smart stripped-back style – with surround-sound speakers – and there's a lovely palm-shaded pool.

The marble-effect lobby hosts fine-dining South Indian restaurant **Southern Spice** (Map p344; ☑044-66002827; mains ₹750-2100, thalis ₹1800-2200; ⊙12.30-2.45pm & 7-11pm), along with a busy cocktail bar.

Hyatt Regency HOTEL **$$$**
(Map p338; ☑044-61001234; http://chennai. regency.hyatt.com; 365 Anna Salai, Teynampet; r ₹10,000-11,950; ❋@☎☒) Smart, swish and bang up to date, this towering, triangular hotel is the most central of Chennai's newer top-end offerings. Contemporary art surrounds the sun-flooded atrium, local chefs head up three good restaurants and an insanely popular bar (p348), and glossy rooms have walk-through bathrooms and fabulous sea/city panoramas through massive picture windows. Flowers fringe the pool and there's a luxury spa.

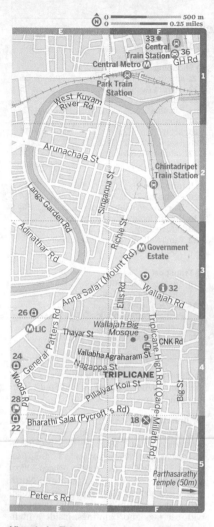

✕ Eating

Chennai is packed with inexpensive 'meals' joints ('messes') serving lunch and dinner thalis (all-you-can-eat meals) and tiffin (snacks) like *idli* (spongy, round fermented rice cakes), *vada* (doughnut-shaped deep-fried lentil savouries) and dosa (savoury crepes). Hotel Saravana Bhavan is always a quality veg choice. In the Muslim Triplicane High Rd area, you'll find great biryanis (fragrant, spiced steamed rice with meat and vegetables).

There's plenty of upmarket dining: classier Indian restaurants and international cuisines are on the rise.

Useful, well-stocked supermarkets include **Spencer's** (Map p338; 15 EVK Sampath Salai, Vepery; ☺7.45am-10pm), near Egmore and Central stations; Big Bazaar at **T Nagar** (Map p338; 34 Sir Thyagaraya Rd, Pondy Bazaar, T Nagar; ☺10.30am-9.30pm) and **Express Avenue mall** (Map p344; Express Avenue, White's Rd; ☺10am-9.30pm Mon-Fri, to 10pm Sat & Sun); **Nilgiri's** (Map p344; 25 Shafee Mohammed Rd, Nungambakkam; ☺9am-9.30pm) off Nungambakkam's Khader Nawaz Khan Rd; and **Amma Naana** (Map p338; www.ammanaana. com; 82/100 Chamiers Rd; ☺9am-9pm Mon-Sat) in Alwarpet.

Rayars Mess   SOUTH INDIAN $
(Map p338; off Arundale St, Mylapore; dishes ₹10-45; ☺7-10.30am & 3.30-6.30pm, hours vary) Down a dusty narrow alley off Arundale St, shoebox-sized Rayars has been pulling in ravenous crowds for over 70 years with its crispy evening *bonda* (mashed potato patties), *vada* and dosa. Breakfast at this family-run spot revolves around feathery *idli* and South Indian filter coffee.

Nair Mess   SOUTH INDIAN $
(Map p338; 22 Mohammed Abdullah Sahib, 2nd St, Chepauk; meals ₹70; ☺11.30am-3.30pm & 7-10pm) Big flavours are rustled up in a starkly simple setting at this no-nonsense, forever-busy spot, pocketed away in a lane opposite the Chepauk cricket stadium since 1961. Loaded banana-leaf thalis complemented by fish-fry dishes are the speciality.

Hotel Saravana Bhavan   INDIAN $
(Map p344; ☎044-28192055; www.saravana bhavan.com; 21 Kennet Lane, Egmore; mains ₹125-250, thalis ₹125-155; ☺6am-10.30pm) Dependably delish, Chennai's famous vegetarian chain doles out epically good South Indian thalis and breakfasts (*idli* and *vada* ₹45 to

Vivanta by Taj – Connemara   HERITAGE HOTEL $$$
(Map p344; ☎044-66000000; www.vivantabytaj. com; Binny Rd, Anna Salai; r incl breakfast ₹11,990-14,390; ❉@☎❉) The top-end Taj Group has five hotels in and around Chennai, but this is the only one with historical ambience, built in the 1850s as the British governor's residence. Recently renovated throughout, tasteful luxury has been achieved in every detail. There's a beautiful pool in tropical gardens and the Chettinadu Raintree (p347) restaurant is regarded as one of Chennai's best.

Anna Salai, Egmore & Triplicane

◉ Top Sights
1 Government Museum C3

◉ Sights
2 St Andrew's Church D1
3 Valluvar Kottam A5

⊟ Sleeping
4 Hanu Reddy Residences B4
5 Hotel Chandra Park D2
6 Hotel Victoria D2
7 Ikhaya B4
8 La Woods D4
9 Paradise Guest House F4
10 Taj Coromandel B5
11 Vivanta by Taj – Connemara D4
12 YWCA International Guest House D1

✖ Eating
13 Amethyst D5
14 Annalakshmi D3
   Big Bazaar .... (see 22)
15 Hotel Saravana Bhavan C5
16 Hotel Saravana Bhavan D2
17 Nilgiri's C4
   Raintree .... (see 11)
18 Ratna Café F5
   Southern Spice .... (see 10)
19 Tuscana Pizzeria B4

20 Writer's Cafe C5

🛍 Shopping
21 Amethyst D5
22 Express Avenue E5
23 Fabindia B4
   Fabindia .... (see 22)
24 Fabindia E4
25 Good Earth B4
26 Higginbothams E3
27 Naturally Auroville C4
   Starmark .... (see 22)

ℹ Information
28 Australian Consulate E4
29 Belgian Consulate B4
30 British Deputy High Commission B3
31 Indiatourism D4
32 Tamil Nadu Tourism Development
   Corporation F3

ℹ Transport
33 Advanced Computerised
   Reservation Office F1
34 Parveen Travels D2
   Passenger Reservation Office ..... (see 35)
35 Prepaid Taxi Stand D1
36 Prepaid Taxi Stand F1

₹70, dosa ₹70 to ₹160), other Indian vegetarian fare and filter coffee. This branch is handy for Egmore station. Others include **Mylapore** (Map p338; ☎044-24611177; 70 North Mada St; mains ₹125-250, thalis ₹125-155; ⊙6am-10.30pm), **Pondy Bazaar** (Map p338; ☎044-281576677; 102 Sir Thyagaraya Rd, T Nagar; mains ₹125-250, thalis ₹125-155; ⊙6am-11pm) and, more upscale with a ₹320 buffet, **Thousand Lights** (Map p344; ☎044-28353377; 293 Peter's Rd; mains ₹125-250, thalis ₹125-155; ⊙8am-10.30pm), plus London, Paris and New York!

Ratna Café   SOUTH INDIAN $
(Map p344; 255 Triplicane High Rd, Triplicane; dishes ₹35-85; ⊙6am-11pm) Often crowded and cramped, Ratna is famous for its scrumptious *idli* accompanied by hearty doses of its signature *sambar* (soupy lentil dish with cubed vegetables). People have been gathering here since 1948. There are also North Indian mains, and an air-con room out the back.

Murugan Idli Shop   SOUTH INDIAN $
(Map p338; http://muruganidlishop.com; 77 GN Chetty Rd, T Nagar; dishes ₹20-100; ⊙7am-11.30pm) Those in the know generally agree that this particular branch of the small

Madurai-born Murugan chain serves some of the best *idli*, dosa, *uttapam* and South Indian meals in town.

★ Annalakshmi   INDIAN $$
(Map p344; ☎044-28525109; www.annalakshmichennai.co.in; 1st fl, Sigapi Achi Bldg, 18/3 Rukmani Lakshmipathy Rd, Egmore; mains ₹825-1300, set menus ₹220-320, buffet ₹525; ⊙noon-2.15pm & 7-9pm Tue-Sun) Very fine South and North Indian vegetarian fare, plus glorious fresh juices, in a beautiful dining room decorated with carvings and paintings, inside a high-rise behind the Air India building. Buffet lunches and dinners are served in another part of the same block. Annalakshmi is run by devotees of Swami Shanthanand Saraswathi; proceeds support medical programs for the poor.

Writer's Cafe   CAFE $$
(Map p344; 127 Peter's Rd, Thousand Lights; mains ₹150-220; ⊙9.15am-10pm) Half Higginbotham's bookshop, half casual cafe/restaurant, this is one of the best spots in Chennai for inexpensively priced, finely prepared, international food – from pastas to Thai curries and chicken with gravy and mash. There are plenty of tasty snacks, salads and pastries

too. Profits go to help victims of domestic violence.

Double Roti
BURGERS $$
(Map p338; ☑044-30853732; http://doubleroti.in; 4/27 1st St, Cenotaph Rd, Teynampet; mains ₹215-650; ☻11am-11pm; ☎) 'Double roti' refers to burger buns – the semi-open kitchen at this always-packed, super-casual, industrial-chic cafe plates them up with fun, flair and buckets of flavour. Lemonades and milkshakes are served in jars; burgers arrive in mini-frying pans; buckets come filled with masala fries; and witty slogans are chalked up on boards. There's plenty for vegetarians too, including fantastic spicy-falafel burgers.

Junior Kuppanna
SOUTH INDIAN $$
(Map p338; ☑044-28340071; 4 Kannaiya St, North Usman Rd, T Nagar; mains ₹110-250, thalis ₹220; ☻noon-4pm & 6.30-11.30pm) From an impeccably clean kitchen (which you're welcome to tour) come limitless, flavour-packed lunchtime thalis, dished up traditional-style on banana leaves. This typical, frenzied Chennai 'mess' also has a full menu. Carnivores tiring of the pure-veg lifestyle can seek solace in specialities like mutton brains and pan-fried seer fish. Arrive early: it's incredibly popular. Branches across Chennai.

★Peshawri
NORTH INDIAN $$$
(☑044-22200000; www.itchotels.in; ITC Grand Chola, 63 Mount Rd, Guindy; mains ₹895-2450, set meals ₹3240-4140; ☻noon-3pm & 7-11.30pm) Perfect for a five-star splash-out, the ITC's signature Northwest Frontier restaurant serves inventive, flavour-popping creations at intimate booths alongside a glassed-in kitchen that gets you right in on the culinary action. Try huge hunks of pillowy chilli-grilled paneer, expertly spiced kebabs, or the deliciously rich house-special *dhal bukhara*, simmered overnight. There's an astounding international wine/cocktail list.

★Copper Chimney
NORTH INDIAN $$$
(Map p338; ☑044-28115770; 74 Cathedral Rd, Gopalapuram; mains ₹265-750; ☻noon-3pm & 7-11.30pm) Meat-eaters will drool over the yummy North Indian tandoori dishes served in well-lit, stylishly minimalist surroundings, but the veg food here is fantastic too. Jain specialities mingle with biryanis, chicken kebabs, chargrilled prawns and fluffy-fresh naan. The *machchi* tikka – skewers of tandoori-baked fish – is superb, as is the spiced paneer kebab and grilled lamb.

★Amethyst
MULTICUISINE, CAFE $$$
(Wild Garden Cafe; Map p344; ☑044-45991633; www.amethystchennai.com; White's Rd, Royapettah; mains ₹300-500; ☻10am-11pm; ☎) Set in an exquisitely converted warehouse with a wraparound veranda from which tables spill out into lush gardens, Amethyst is a nostalgically posh haven that's outrageously popular with expats and well-off Chennaiites. Well-executed European-flavoured dishes range over quiches, pastas, sandwiches, crepes, creative salads, all-day breakfasts and afternoon teas. Fight for your table, then check out the stunning Indian couture boutique (p349).

Enté Keralam
KERALAN $$$
(Map p338; ☑7604915091; http://entekeralam.in; 1 Kasturi Estate, 1st St, Poes Garden; mains ₹290-575; ☻noon-3pm & 7-11pm) A calm ambience seeps through the four orange-toned, three-to four-table rooms of this elegant Keralan restaurant. Lightly spiced *pachakkari* vegetable stew is served with light, fluffy *appam* (rice pancake), the Alleppey curry is rich with mango, and there are plenty of fish dishes. Wind up with tender coconut ice cream. Set meals (veg/nonveg ₹945/1450) give a multidish miniformat taster.

Raintree
CHETTINADU $$$
(Map p344; www.vivantabytaj.com; Vivanta by Taj – Connemara, Binny Rd, Anna Salai; mains ₹450-1000; ☻12.30-2.45pm & 7.30pm-midnight) This refined, wood-ceilinged restaurant is arguably Chennai's best place to savour the flavours of Tamil Nadu's Chettinadu region. Chettinadu cuisine is famously meat-heavy and superbly spicy without being chilli-laden, but veg dishes are good too. Dine outside in the leafy garden with water lilies.

Chamiers
MULTICUISINE, CAFE $$$
(Map p338; ☑044-42030734; www.chamiershop.com; 106 Chamiers Rd, RA Puram; mains ₹300-500; ☻8.30am-11pm; ☎) This bubbly 1st-floor cafe feels a continent away from Chennai, except that Chennaiites love it too. Flowery wallpaper, printed cushions, wicker chairs, wi-fi (per hour ₹100), wonderful carrot cake, croissants and cappuccino, English breakfasts, American pancakes, pastas, quiches, quesadillas, salads...

Ciclo Cafe
CAFE $$$
(Map p338; ☑044-42048666; www.facebook.com/theciclocafe; 33/47 Gandhi Mandapam Rd, Kotturpuram; drinks ₹100-250, dishes ₹250-550; ☻11am-11pm daily, 7-10.30am Sat & Sun) Cycle-mad decor includes wheels on lamps,

DON'T MISS

CHENNAI STREET FOOD

Chennai may not have the same killer street-food reputation as Delhi or Mumbai, but there are some sensational South Indian street-side delicacies around, especially in Mylapore, George Town, Egmore and T Nagar, and along Marina Beach. If you'd like some guidance, Storytrails (p341) runs fun story-themed food-tasting tours through George Town.

Mehta Brothers (Map p338; 325 Mint St, George Town; dishes ₹20-40; ⏱ 4-9pm Mon-Sat) Pulls in the crowds with the deep-fried delights of its signature Maharashtrian *vada pav* – spiced potato fritters in buns, doused in garlicky chutney.

Seena Bhai Tiffin Centre (Map p338; 15/105 NSC Bose Rd, George Town; idlis & uttapams ₹40; ⏱ 7-11pm) Deliciously griddled, ghee-coated *idli* and *uttapam*.

Jannal Kadai (Ponnambala Vathiar St, Mylapore; items ₹20-30; ⏱ 8-10am & 5-9.30pm Mon-Sat) Fast-and-furious hole-in-the-wall place famous for its hot crispy *bhajia* (vegetable fritters), *bonda* (battered potato balls) and *vada*.

chandeliers made from chains and bikes dangling in the window. But this place is more than just a gimmick: there's an extensive international menu, from Thai green curry to grilled Scottish salmon, plus a long list of sandwiches, burgers, and salads, all gigantic and delicious. Coffees, fresh juices and smoothies are also good.

Tuscana Pizzeria ITALIAN $$$
(Map p344; ☎044-45038008; www.tuscana pizzeria.com; 19, 3rd St, Wallace Garden, Nungambakkam; mains ₹425-775; ⏱noon-11.30pm) Tuscana turns out authentic thin-crust pizzas with toppings like prosciutto, mozzarella and sun-dried tomatoes, as well as more creative takes such as paneer tikka pizza, and tasty pastas, salads and topped breads. It even has whole-wheat and gluten-free pizzas. Eat in or takeaway.

🍷 Drinking & Nightlife

Chennai nightlife is on the up, with a smattering of lively new openings, but you'll need a full wallet for a night out here. Continental-style cafes are growing in number, and, yes, Starbucks has arrived.

Bars and clubs in five-star hotels serve alcohol 24 hours a day, seven days a week, so that's where most of the after-dark fun happens. Solo guys ('stags') are often turned away, and there's usually a hefty admission charge for couples and men. Dress codes are strict: no shorts or sandals.

Other hotel bars, mostly male-dominated, generally close by midnight. If you're buying your own alcohol, look for 'premium' or 'elite' government-run TASMAC liquor shops inside malls.

Radio Room BAR
(☎8500005672; www.radioroom.in; Somerset Greenways, 94 Sathyadev Ave, MRC Nagar, RA Puram; cocktails ₹450-600, dishes ₹200-300; ⏱6-11.30pm Mon-Fri, 4-11.30pm Sat & Sun) From a keen young team comes this incredibly popular radio-themed bar in southeast Chennai. It's all about mismatched furniture, a bar made of speakers and carefully mixed, inspired cocktails and pitchers – some full of local flavour, like chai punch. Creative twists on Chennai's culinary favourites include mozzarella-stuffed *bhajias* (vegetable fritters) delivered in bicycle-shaped baskets.

365 AS LOUNGE, CLUB
(Map p338; ☎044-61001234; https://chennai. regency.hyatt.com; Hyatt Regency, 365 Anna Salai, Teynampet; drinks ₹700; ⏱3pm-2am) In the glamorous Hyatt Regency (p344), Chennai's hottest party spot bursts into life on weekends, when wild DJ sets kick off on the terrace, playing pop music on Fridays and techno on Saturdays. Otherwise, it's a swish, sultry lounge serving carefully crafted cocktails alongside Indian and international wines, beers and spirits. Dress code is smart casual (for guys, trousers and closed shoes).

Flying Elephant BAR
(☎044-71771234; https://chennai.park.hyatt.com; Park Hyatt, 39 Velachery Rd, Guindy; drinks ₹300-575; ⏱6pm-1am) Slickly contemporary and favoured by the elite, the high-energy, multi-level restaurant at the **Park Hyatt** (☎044-71771234; s/d incl breakfast from ₹14,880/15,520; ❄🛜🏊) morphs into a busy party spot from 11pm on Saturday. It's all very glam, with a sunken bar and garden-fresh herbs infusing

cocktails. The world-fusion food (₹650 to ₹2500), whipped up in five live kitchens, is good.

Sera the Tapas Bar
BAR

(Map p338; ☑044-28111462; www.facebook.com/serathetapasbar; 71 Cathedral Rd, Gopalapuram; cocktails ₹275-500, tapas ₹235-325; ☺12.30pm-midnight) Where else in the world can you find DJs playing club music beneath bullfight posters next to TVs showing cricket? Sera is packed most nights with a young, fashionable crowd sipping sangria and cocktails. It's a good idea to book. Tapas include garlic prawns, fried calamari and aubergine dips; the *tortilla española* (potato omelette) is authentically good.

Lloyds Tea House
TEAHOUSE

(Map p338; 179 Lloyds Rd, Gopalapuram; teas ₹70-180, dishes ₹150-320; ☺11am-11pm Mon-Fri, 8am-11pm Sat & Sun) Teas from across the globe collide in fabulously refreshing hot or iced concoctions at this soothing, contemporary teahouse. Pick from green teas, herbal infusions, Indian chais, Darjeeling offerings and Chinese Pu-erh teas. The Vietnamese 'Zen Garden' (iced, in a jar) is a fruity delight. Also does coffee, light meals and cakes.

10 Downing Street
PUB

(10D; Map p338; www.10ds.in; 50 North Boag Rd, T Nagar; drinks ₹245-520, food ₹215-500; ☺11am-midnight) Casual British-themed pub (Big Ben on the wall, fish fingers on the menu, the Beatles and the Who on the sound system) with a small dance floor. It's popular with men and women, and the bar food is surprisingly good – try the Andhra 65 chicken.

☆ Entertainment

Classical Music & Dance

There's *bharatanatyam* (Tamil classical dance) and/or a Carnatic music concert going on in Chennai almost every evening. Check listings in the *Hindu* or *Times of India*.

The **Music Academy** (Map p338; ☑044-28112231; www.musicacademymadras.in; 168/306 TTK Rd, Royapettah) is the most popular venue. The Kalakshetra Foundation (p341) and **Bharatiya Vidya Bhavan** (Map p338; ☑044-24643420; www.bhavanschennai.org; East Mada St, Mylapore) also stage many events, often free.

Cinema

Chennai has more than 100 cinemas, a reflection of the vibrant Tamil film industry ('Kollywood'). Most screen Tamil films, but the Phoenix Market City and Express Avenue (p350) mall cinemas, among others, have regular English-language screenings. Tickets cost around ₹185.

🔒 Shopping

★ Nalli Silks
TEXTILES

(Map p338; www.nallisilks.com; 9 Nageswaran Rd, I Nagar; ☺9am-9pm) Set up in 1928, the enormous, supercolourful granddaddy of Chennai silk shops sparkles with wedding saris and rainbows of Kanchipuram silks, as well as silk dhotis (long loincloths) for men.

★ Higginbothams
BOOKS

(Map p344; higginbothams@vsnl.com; 116 Anna Salai, Anna Salai; ☺9am-8pm Mon-Sat, 10.30am-7.30pm Sun) Open since 1844, this grand white building is reckoned to be India's oldest bookshop. It has a brilliant English-language selection, including travel and fiction books, and a good range of maps.

Fabindia
CLOTHING, HANDICRAFTS

(Map p338; www.fabindia.com; 390 TTK Rd, Alwarpet; ☺10.30am-8.30pm) 🍃 This fair-trade, nationwide chain sells stylishly contemporary village-made clothes and crafts. Perfect for picking up a kurta (long shirt with short/no collar) to throw over trousers. This branch is the brand new, two-storey flagship shop (opposite Kauvery Hospital), which has a top-floor cafe. Other branches are at **Woods Rd** (Map p344; 3 Woods Rd, Anna Salai; ☺10.30am-8.30pm), **Express Ave** (Map p344; 1st fl, Express Avenue Mall, White's Rd, Royapettah; ☺11.30am-9pm), **Nungambakkam** (Map p344; 2nd fl, 9/15 Khader Nawaz Khan Rd; ☺10.30am-8.30pm), T Nagar (Map p338; 44 GN Chetty Rd; ☺10.30am-8.30pm) 🍃 and Besant Nagar (T-25, 7th Ave, ☺10.30am-8.30pm).

Amethyst
FASHION & ACCESSORIES

(Map p344; www.amethystchennai.com; White's Rd, Royapettah; ☺11am-7.30pm) Hidden away in a revamped warehouse surrounded by tropical greenery, Amethyst stocks luxury Indian fashion with ultracolourful contemporary flair. Downstairs, there's a dreamy flower shop and an insanely popular cafe (p347).

Phoenix Market City
SHOPPING CENTRE

(www.phoenixmarketcity.com; 142 Velachery Main Rd, Velachery; ☺11am-10pm) Chennai's newest, most luxurious shopping mall hosts all the big-name Indian and international brands and chains, from Chanel and Zara to Bata, Lifestyle, and Global Desi (plus the city's original Starbucks). The multiplex cinema shows new release Tamil and Hollywood movies and has one IMAX screen.

Chamiers CLOTHING, HANDICRAFTS
(Map p338; www.chamiershop.com; 106 Chamiers Rd, RA Puram; ☺10.30am-7.30pm) On the ground floor of this popular cafe-and-boutique-complex, **Anokhi** (Map p338; www.anokhi. com; 106 Chamiers Rd, RA Puram; ☺10.30am-7.30pm) has wonderful, East-meets-West, hand-block-printed clothes, bedding, bags and accessories in floaty fabrics, at good prices. Elegant **Amethyst Room** (Map p338; www.amethystchennai.com; 106 Chamiers Rd, RA Puram; ☺10.30am-7pm) next door takes things upmarket with beautiful Indian-design couture. Upstairs is **Chamiers for Men** (Map p338; ☺10.30am-7.30pm).

Naturally Auroville ARTS & CRAFTS
(Map p344; www.naturallyaurovillechennai. com; 8 Khader Nawaz Khan Rd, Nungambakkam; ☺10.15am-9pm) Colourful handicrafts and home-decor trinkets, including bedspreads, cushions, incense, scented candles and hand-made-paper notebooks, all from Auroville, near Puducherry.

Good Earth HOMEWARES
(Map p344; www.goodearth.in; 3 Rutland Gate 4th St, Nungambakkam; ☺11am-8pm) For the ultimate in India-chic interior design, glitzy Good Earth has everything from scented candles, gorgeously embroidered bedspreads and floral-stamped cushion covers to swanky teacups and delicately perfumed soaps. There's an air-conditioned cafe with cakes and pastries that are well worth your attention.

Starmark BOOKS
(www.starmark.in; 2nd fl, Phoenix Market City, Velachery; ☺11am-9.30pm Mon-Fri, 10am-10pm Sat & Sun) Reliable modern bookshop stocking English-, Indian- and Tamil-language fiction and nonfiction, kids' books, magazines, Lonely Planet guides and other travel books. Also at **Express Avenue** (Map p344; 2nd fl, Express Avenue, White's Rd, Royapettah; ☺10.30am-9.30pm Mon-Fri, 10am-10pm Sat & Sun) mall.

Express Avenue MALL
(Map p344; www.expressavenue.in; White's Rd, Royapettah; ☺10am-10pm) This is one of Chennai's best and most central shopping malls, full of major international and Indian apparel chains. The top-floor food court is good for a quick bite.

Kumaran Silks TEXTILES
(Map p338; www.kumaransilksonline.com; 12 Nageswaran Rd, T Nagar; ☺9am-10pm) Housed in a beautiful building with an art deco facade and an interior of old-school wooden shelves, this is a classy place to browse saris (including 'budget saris') and plenty of Kanchipuram silk.

ⓘ Information

MEDICAL SERVICES
Apollo Hospital (Map p344; ☎044-28290200, emergency 044-28293333; www.apollo hospitals.com; 21 Greams Lane, Nungambakkam; ☺24hr) State-of-the-art, expensive hospital, popular with 'medical tourists'.
Kauvery Hospital (Map p338; ☎044-40006000; www.kauveryhospital.com; 199 Luz Church Rd, Mylapore; ☺24hr) Good, private, general hospital.

MONEY
ATMs are everywhere, including at Central train station, the airport and the CMBT bus station.
Citibank (Map p338; 50 CP Ramaswamy Rd, Alwarpet)
Citibank (Map p338; Cathedral Rd, Teynampet)

POST
DHL (Map p344; ☎044-42148886; www.dhl. com; 85 VVV Sq, Pantheon Rd, Egmore; ☺9am-9pm) Secure international parcel delivery; branches around town.
Main Post Office (Map p338; Rajaji Salai, George Town; ☺8am-9pm Mon-Sat, 10am-4pm Sun)
Post Office (Map p344; Kennet Lane, Egmore; ☺10am-6pm Mon-Sat)

TOURIST INFORMATION
Indiatourism (Map p344; ☎044-28460285, 044-28461459; www.incredibleindia.org; 154 Anna Salai, Anna Salai; ☺9.15am-5.45pm Mon-Fri) Helpful on Chennai, plus other India destinations.
Tamil Nadu Tourism Development Corporation (TTDC; Map p344; ☎044-25333333; www. tamilnadutourism.org; Tamil Nadu Tourism Complex, 2 Wallajah Rd, Triplicane; ☺24hr) The state tourism body's main office takes bookings for its bus tours and answers questions. In the same building are state tourist offices from across India, mostly open 10am to 6pm. The TTDC also has a branch at Egmore train station.

TRAVEL AGENCIES
Milesworth Travel (Map p338; ☎044-24338664; www.milesworth.com; RM Towers, 1st fl, 108 Chamiers Rd, Alwarpet; ☺10am-6pm Mon-Fri, to 1.30pm Sat) Very professional,

welcoming agency that will help with all your travel needs.

ⓘ Getting There & Away

AIR

Chennai International Airport (☏044-22560551; Tirusulam) is in the far southwest of the city. The international terminal is 500m west of the domestic terminal; walkways link the two terminals.

BOAT

Passenger ships sail from George Town harbour direct to Port Blair in the Andaman Islands once or twice a month. There's no set schedule, so call for departure dates. The **Andaman Shipping Office Ticketing Counter** (☏044-25226873; www.andaman.gov.in; 2nd fl, Shipping Corporation of India, Jawahar Bldg, 17 Rajaji Salai, George Town; ⊙10am-4pm Mon-Fri, to noon Sat) sells tickets – from ₹2825 for a bunk in an 80-bed dorm to ₹10,815 for a bed in a semiprivate room, with several categories in between – for the five-day trip. Book several days ahead, and take four copies each of your passport data page and Indian visa along with the originals. It can be a long process.

BUS
Government Buses

Most government buses operate from the large but surprisingly orderly **CMBT** (Chennai Mofussil Bus Terminus; Jawaharlal Nehru Rd, Koyambedu), 6km west of the centre. The most comfortable and expensive are the air-con buses (best of these are Volvo AC services), followed by the UD ('Ultra Deluxe'); these can generally be reserved in advance. You can book up to 60 days ahead at the computerised reservation centre at the left end of the main hall, or online (www.tnstc.in).

The **Adyar Gandhinagar Bus Stand** (2nd Cross St, Adyar) is handy for bus 588 to Mamallapuram (₹40, 1½ hours, hourly 5am to 7.30pm).

Private Buses

Private buses generally offer greater comfort than non-AC government buses, at up to double the price. Their main terminal is the **Omni Bus Stand** (off Kaliamman Koil St, Koyambedu), 500m west of the CMBT, but some companies also pick up and drop off elsewhere in the city. Service information is at www.redbus.in; tickets can be booked through travel agencies.

Parveen Travels (Map p344; ☏044-28192577; www.parveentravels.com; 11/5 Kennet Lane, Egmore) services to Bengaluru, Ernakulam (Kochi; Cochin), Kodaikanal, Madurai, Ooty (Udhagamandalam), Puducherry, Trichy and Thiruvananthapuram (Trivandrum) depart from its Egmore office.

TRAIN

Interstate trains and those heading west generally depart from Central station, while trains heading south mostly leave from Egmore. The **Advanced Reservation Office** (Map p344; 1st fl, Chennai Central suburban station, Periyamet; ⊙8am-2pm & 2.15-8pm Mon-Sat, 8am-2pm Sun), with its incredibly helpful Foreign Tourist Cell, is on the 1st floor in a separate 11-storey building just west of the main Central station building; go to counter 22. Bring photocopies of your passport visa and photo pages. Egmore station has its own **Passenger Reservation Office** (Map p344; 1st fl, Egmore station; ⊙8am-2pm & 2.15-8pm Mon-Sat, 8am-2pm Sun).

BUSES FROM CHENNAI CMBT

DESTINATION	FARE (₹)	TIME (HR)	DEPARTURES
Bengaluru (Bangalore)	585-700	7-8	at least 50 daily
Coimbatore	570-600	11	15 daily
Ernakulam (Kochi)	1300	12-16	4.30pm
Hyderabad	845-1480	14	6.30pm, 7.30pm, 8.30pm
Kodaikanal	580	10-13	5pm
Madurai	500-1000	9-10	30 daily
Mamallapuram	40	2-2½	every 10min
Mysuru (Mysore)	670-1020	10	7pm, 7.45pm, 8.40pm, 10.05pm, 11.30pm
Ooty	600	12	4.30pm, 5pm, 7.15pm
Puducherry (Pondicherry)	250	4	every 15min
Thanjavur	380	8½	every 30min
Tirupati	200-350	4	every 15min
Trichy (Tiruchirappalli)	370	6½-7	every 30min
Trivandrum	1000	14	6 daily

ℹ Getting Around

TO/FROM THE AIRPORT
Bus

From the CMBT (p351), city buses 70 and 170 to Tambaram stop on the highway across from the airport (₹12 to ₹15, 30 to 40 minutes).

Chennai Metro Rail

The Chennai Metro Rail system provides cheap, easy transport between the airport and some useful parts of the city, though its reach is limited. If you need to go somewhere along its route, it's worth taking (₹70 or less). The metro station is between the two airport terminals.

Taxi

Prepaid taxi kiosks outside the airport's international terminal charge ₹550/600 for a non-AC/AC cab to Egmore, and ₹450/500 to T Nagar. Rates are slightly lower at prepaid taxi kiosks outside the domestic terminal, and can be much lower by using Ola or Uber. Both terminals have Fast Track taxi booking counters, which can be good for long-distance trips.

Train

The cheapest airport transport option is suburban trains to/from Tirusulam station, opposite the domestic terminal parking areas, accessed via a signposted pedestrian subway under the highway. Trains run roughly every 15 minutes from 4.13am to midnight to/from Chennai Beach station (₹10, 40 minutes); stops include Nungambakkam, Egmore, Chennai Park and Chennai Fort.

AUTORICKSHAW

Most autorickshaw drivers refuse to use their meters and quote astronomical fares that come down quickly with some firm haggling. Avoid paying upfront, and always establish the price before getting into a rickshaw. Rates rise by up to 50% from 11pm to 5am.

There are prepaid autorickshaw booths outside the CMBT and 24-hour prepaid stands on the south side of Central station and outside the north and south exits of Egmore station.

Tempting offers of ₹50 autorickshaw 'city tours' sound too good to be true. They are. You'll spend the day being dragged from one shop to another.

MAJOR TRAINS FROM CHENNAI

DESTINATION	TRAIN NO & NAME	FARE (₹)	TIME (HR)	DEPARTURE
Agra	12615 Grand Trunk Express	745/1970/2880 (C)	31½	7.15pm CC
Bengaluru (Banglaore)	12007 Shatabdi Express*	775/1435 (A)	5	6am CC
	12609 Bangalore Express	150/545 (B)	6½	1.35pm CC
Coimbatore	12675 Kovai Express	180/665 (B)	7½	6.10am CC
	12671 Nilgiri Express	315/815/1150 (C)	7¾	8.55pm CC
Delhi	12621 Tamil Nadu Express	780/2050/3005 (C)	33	10pm CC
Goa	17311 Vasco Express (Friday only)	480/1310/1900 (C)	22	3pm CC
Hyderabad	12603 Hyderabad Express	405/1070/1520 (C)	13	4.45pm CC
Kochi	22639 Alleppey Express	400/1060/1505 (C)	11½	8.45pm CC
Kolkata	12842 Coromandel Express	665/1755/2555 (C)	27	8.45am CC
Madurai	12635 Vaigai Express	180/665 (B)	7¾	1.40pm CE
	12637 Pandian Express	315/815/1150 (C)	8	9.40pm CE
Mumbai	11042 Mumbai Express	540/1460/2125 (C)	25¼	12.20pm CC
Mysuru (Mysore)	12007 Shatabdi Express*	910/1815 (A)	7	6am CC
	16021 Kaveri Express	315/765/1100 (C)	9½	9.15pm CC
Tirupati	16053 Tirupathi Express	80/290 (B)	3½	2.15pm CC
Trichy (Tiruchirappalli)	12635 Vaigai Express	145/520 (B)	5	1.40pm CE
Trivandrum	12695 Trivandrum Express	470/1245/1785 (C)	16½	3.25pm CC

Departure Codes: CC – Chennai Central, CE – Chennai Egmore
*Daily except Wednesday
Fares: (A) chair/executive; (B) 2nd class/chair; (C) sleeper/3AC/2AC

CHENNAI BUS ROUTES

BUS NO	ROUTE
A1	Central–Anna Salai–RK Mutt Rd (Mylapore) –Theosophical Society–Thiruvanmiyur
1B	Parry's–Central–Anna Salai–Airport
10A	Parry's–Central–Egmore (S)–Pantheon Rd–T Nagar
11	Rattan–Central–Anna Salai–T Nagar
12	T Nagar–Pondy Bazaar–Eldham's Rd–Dr Radhakrishnan Salai–Vivekananda House
13	T Nagar–Royapettah–Triplicane
15B & 15F	Broadway–Central–CMBT
M27	CMBT–T Nagar
27B	CMBT–Egmore (S)–Bharathi Salai (Triplicane)
27D	Egmore (S)–Anna Salai–Cathedral Rd–Dr Radhakrishnan Salai–San Thome Cathedral
32A	Central–Vivekananda House
102	Broadway–Fort St George–Kamarajar Salai–San Thome Cathedral–Theosophical Society

Routes operate in both directions.
Broadway – **Broadway Bus Terminus** (Map p338; George Town)
Central – Central Station
Egmore (S) – Egmore station (south side)
Parry's – Parry's Corner
Rattan – **Rattan Bazaar Rd Bus Stop** (Map p338; Rattan Bazaar Rd, George Town)
T Nagar – **T Nagar Bus Terminus** (Map p338; South Usman Rd, T Nagar)

BUS

Chennai's city bus system is worth getting to know, although buses get packed to overflowing at busy times.

Fares are between ₹5 and ₹15 (up to double for express and deluxe services, and multiplied by five for Volvo AC services).

Route information is on www.mtcbus.org.

CHENNAI METRO RAIL

Chennai Metro Rail is an incredibly efficient way to get around the limited areas it serves – fortunately, stops include major transport hubs such as the airport, CMBT, and Egmore and Central railway stations. At the time of research, the system was nearly complete and travel was easy and uncrowded (but the Delhi metro was once like this too!). If you plan on using it more than once, get a metro card (₹50 refundable deposit) that you can preload with credit. Trains run from 5am to 10pm; trips cost ₹10 to ₹70.

TRAIN

Efficient, cheap suburban trains run from Beach station to Fort, Park (near Central station), Egmore, Chetpet, Nungambakkam, Kodambakkam, Mambalam, Saidapet, Guindy, St Thomas Mount, Tirusulam (for the airport), and on south to Tambaram. At Egmore station, the suburban platforms (10 and 11) and ticket office are on the station's north side. A second line branches south after Fort to Park Town, Chepauk, Tiruvallikeni (for Marina Beach), Light House and Thirumailai (near the Kapaleeshwarar Temple). Trains run several times hourly from 4am to midnight, costing ₹10.

NORTHERN TAMIL NADU

East Coast Road

Chennai's sprawl peters out after an hour or so heading south on the East Coast Rd (ECR), at which point Tamil Nadu becomes red dirt, blue skies, palm trees and green fields, sprinkled with towns and villages (or, if you take the 'IT Expressway' inland, enormous new buildings).

There are several very worthwhile ECR stops if you're travelling between Chennai and Mamallapuram, 50km south. Among these is the low-key fishing-turned-surfing village of Kovalam (Covelong). Swimming along the coast is dangerous due to strong currents.

☉ Sights

★**Cholamandal Artists' Village**   MUSEUM
(☑044-24490092; www.cholamandalartistvillage.com; Injambakkam; museum Indian/foreigner ₹30/50; ☺museum 9.30am-6.30pm) There's a

tropical bohemian groove floating around Injambakkam village, site of the Cholamandal Artists' Village, 10km south of Chennai's Adyar River. This 4-hectare artists' cooperative – founded in 1966 by artists of the Madras Movement, pioneers of modern art in South India – is a serene haven away from the world. Its fantastic art gallery features paintings and sculptures that blend tradition and postmodernity into provocative and moving expressions of imagination; it's one of the most worthwhile museums in Tamil Nadu.

DakshinaChitra   ARTS CENTRE

(☑044-27472603; www.dakshinachitra.net; East Coast Rd, Muttukadu; adult/student Indian ₹110/50, foreign ₹250/70; ◷10am-6pm Wed-Mon) DakshinaChitra, 22km south of Chennai's Adyar River, offers a fantastic insight into South India's traditional arts and crafts. Like a treasure chest of local art and architecture, this jumble of open-air museum, preserved village, artisan workshops (pottery, silk-weaving, basket-making) and galleries is strewn among an exquisite collection of real-deal traditional South Indian homes. You can see silk-weavers in action, have *mehndi* (ornate henna designs) applied and enjoy an array of shows.

Madras Crocodile Bank   ZOO

(☑044-27472447; www.madrascrocodilebank.org; Vadanemmeli; adult/child ₹40/20; ◷9am-5pm Tue-Sun) 🌿 Just 6km south of Kovalam, this incredible conservation and research trust is a fascinating peek into the reptile world. Founded by croc/snake-expert Romulus

---

SURFING TAMIL NADU

The Tamil Nadu coast has become an increasingly popular destination for learning how to surf, windsurf, sea kayak and scuba dive. If you'd like to get on – or under – the water, check out these places (listed from north to south), some of which have great activity-and-accommodation packages:

➡ Kovalam: Covelong Point

➡ Mamallapuram: Mumu Surf School (p357)

➡ Puducherry: Kallialay Surf School (p366)

➡ Rameswaram: Quest Academy (p394)

Whitaker, the bank has thousands of reptiles, including 17 of the world's 23 species of crocodilian (crocodiles and similar creatures), and does crucial work in maintaining genetic reserves of these animals, several of which are endangered. There's also a snake venom extraction centre (open 10am to 1pm and 2pm to 5pm), where you can watch scary serpents being milked.

Tiger Cave   HINDU SITE

(Saluvankuppam; ◷6am-6pm) FREE The Tiger Cave, 5km north of Mamallapuram, is an unfinished but impressive rock-cut shrine, dedicated to Durga (a form of Devi, Shiva's wife), probably dating from the 7th century. What's special is the 'necklace' of 11 monstrous tigerlike heads framing its central shrine-cavity, next to two carved elephant heads. At the north end of the parklike complex is a same-era rock-cut Shiva shrine. Beyond the fence lies the Subrahmanya Temple: an 8th-century granite shrine built over a brick, Sangam-era Murugan temple.

Kovalam (Covelong)

☑044 / POP 8120

This low-key fishing village, 30km south of Chennai and 20km north of Mamallapuram, has sprung into the spotlight for having probably the best surfing waves on the Tamil Nadu coast. It's now an increasingly popular travellers' hang-out, hosting a high-profile surfing/yoga festival and offering all kinds of water sports – everything from surfing and kayaking to blissful beachfront yoga.

Covelong Point Surf, Music & Yoga Festival (p336) is a popular event in August.

For surf classes or surfing friends, head to 'social surfing school' **Covelong Point** (☑9840975916; www.covelongpoint.com; 10 Pearl Beach, Ansari Nagar; per hour board rental/surf classes ₹300/500; ◷hours vary), under the watch of Kovalam's original local surf pioneer Murthy. There are options for all levels, or try kayaking, diving, windsurfing and stand-up paddleboarding (SUP). The team also runs a lovely, relaxed **Surf Turf** (☑9884272572; www.surfturf.in; 10 Pearl Beach, Ansari Nagar; r incl breakfast ₹2065-5190, 2-person 'surf & stay' packages from ₹7000; ❋⚏), a surf-mad B&B guesthouse with an unbelievably beautiful beachfront location.

Most buses travelling between Chennai and Mamallapuram will drop you at the ECR's Kovalam turnoff. Taxis to/from Mamallapuram or Chennai cost around ₹1000.

Mamallapuram (Mahabalipuram)

☎044 / POP 15,170

Mamallapuram, 50km south of Chennai, was the major seaport of the ancient Pallava kingdom based at Kanchipuram. A wander around the town's magnificent, World Heritage–listed temples and carvings inflames the imagination, especially at sunset.

In addition to ancient archaeological wonders, salty air and coastal beauty, there's also the traveller hub of Othavadai and Othavadai Cross Sts, where restaurants serve pasta, pizza and pancakes, and shops sell Tibetan trinkets. The town's buzzing, growing surf scene is another attraction.

'Mahabs', as most call it, is less than two hours by bus from Chennai, and many travellers make a beeline straight here. It's small and laid-back, and sights can be explored on foot or by bicycle.

⊙ Sights

You can easily spend the better part of a day exploring Mamallapuram's marvellous temples, caves and rock carvings. Most were carved from the rock during the 7th-century reign of Pallava king Narasimhavarman I, whose nickname Mamalla (Great Wrestler) gave the town its name. Official Archaeological Survey of India guides can be hired at sites.

★ Arjuna's Penance   HINDU MONUMENT

(West Raja St; ⊙24hr) FREE The crowning masterpiece of Mamallapuram's stonework, this giant relief carving is one of India's greatest ancient artworks. Inscribed on two huge, adjacent boulders, the Penance bursts with scenes of Hindu myth and everyday South Indian life. In the centre, *nagas* (snake-beings) descend a once water-filled cleft, representing the Ganges. To the left Arjuna (hero of the Mahabharata) performs self-mortification (fasting on one leg), so that the four-armed Shiva will grant him his most powerful weapon, the god-slaying Pasupata.

Some scholars believe the carving actually shows the sage Bagiratha, who did severe penance to obtain Shiva's help in bringing the Ganges to earth. Shiva is attended by dwarves, and celestial beings fly across the carving's upper sections. Below Arjuna/Bagiratha is a temple to Vishnu (mythical ancestor of the Pallava kings), with sages, deer and

a lion. The many wonderfully carved animals include a herd of elephants and – humour amid the holy – a cat mimicking Arjuna's penance to a crowd of mice.

South along the road from Arjuna's Penance are the unfinished **Panch Pandava Mandapa** (West Raja St; ⊙6am-6pm) FREE cave temple; the **Krishna Mandapa** (West Raja St; ⊙6am-6pm) FREE, which famously depicts Krishna lifting Govardhana Hill to protect cows and villagers from a storm sent by Indra; an **unfinished relief carving** (West Raja St; ⊙24hr) FREE of similar size to Arjuna's Penance; and the empty **Dharmaraja Cave Temple** (Five Rathas Rd; ⊙6am-6pm) FREE.

★ Trimurti Cave Temple   HINDU TEMPLE

(Mamallapuram Hill; ⊙6am-6pm) FREE At the northern end of the Mamallapuram Hill compound, the Trimurti Cave Temple depicts the Hindu 'trinity' amid guardian figures: Brahma (left), Shiva (centre) and Vishnu (right). A fine carving of elephants adorns the back side of the rock.

Shore Temple   HINDU TEMPLE

(Beach Rd; combined 1-day ticket with Five Rathas Indian/foreigner ₹30/500, video ₹25; ⊙6am-6pm) Standing like a magnificent fist of rock-cut elegance overlooking the sea, surrounded by gardens and ruined courts, the two-towered Shore Temple symbolises the heights of Pallava architecture and the maritime ambitions of the Pallava kings. Its small size belies its excellent proportion and the supreme quality of the carvings, many now eroded into vaguely Impressionist embellishments. Built under Narasimhavarman II in the 8th century, it's the earliest significant free-standing stone temple in Tamil Nadu.

Five Rathas   HINDU TEMPLE

(Pancha Ratha; Five Rathas Rd; combined 1-day ticket with Shore Temple Indian/foreigner ₹30/500, video ₹25; ⊙6am-6pm) Huddled together at the southern end of Mamallapuram, the Five Rathas were, astonishingly, all carved from single large rocks. Each of these fine 7th-century temples was dedicated to a Hindu god and is now named after one or more of the Pandavas, the five hero-brothers of the epic Mahabharata, or their common wife, Draupadi. The *rathas* were hidden in the sand until excavated by the British 200 years ago.

Ratha is Sanskrit for 'chariot', and may refer to the temples' form or to their function as vehicles for the gods. It's thought that

Mamallapuram (Mahabalipuram)

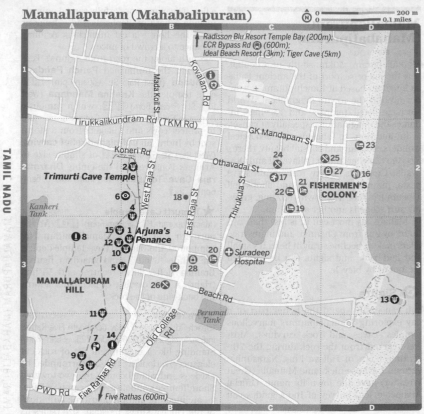

Radisson Blu Resort Temple Bay (200m);
ECR Bypass Rd (600m);
Ideal Beach Resort (3km); Tiger Cave (5km)

Mamallapuram (Mahabalipuram)

Top Sights
1 Arjuna's Penance	B3
2 Trimurti Cave Temple	B2

Sights
3 Dharmaraja Cave Temple	A4
4 Ganesh Ratha	B2
5 Krishna Mandapa	B3
6 Krishna's Butterball	B2
7 Lighthouse	A4
8 Lion Throne	A3
9 Mahishamardini Mandapa	A4
10 Panch Pandava Mandapa	B3
11 Ramanuja Mandapa	A3
12 Raya Gopura	A3
13 Shore Temple	D3
14 Unfinished Relief Carving	A4
15 Varaha Mandapa	A3

Activities, Courses & Tours
16 Mumu Surf School	D2

| | |
|---|---|
| 17 Sri Durga | C2 |
| 18 Travel XS | B2 |

Sleeping
19 Hotel Daphne	C2
20 Hotel Mahabs	B3
21 Rajalakshmi Guesthouse	C2
22 Silver Moon	C2
23 Sri Harul Guest House	D2

Eating
24 Gecko Restaurant	C2
Joe's Cafe	(see 22)
25 Le Yogi	D2
26 Mamalla Bhavan	B3

Shopping
27 Apollo Books	D2
28 Southern Arts & Crafts	B3

they didn't originally serve as places of worship, but as architectural models.

The first *ratha* on the left after you enter is the Draupadi Ratha, in the form of a stylised South Indian hut. It's dedicated to the demon-fighting goddess Durga, who looks out from inside, standing on a lotus, and is depicted on the outside walls. Female guardians flank the entrance; a huge sculpted lion, Durga's mount, stands outside.

Next, on the same plinth, is the 'chariot' of the most important Pandava, the Arjuna Ratha, dedicated to Shiva. Its pilasters, miniature roof shrines and small octagonal dome make it a precursor of many later South Indian temples. A huge Nandi sits behind. Shiva (leaning on Nandi, south side) and other gods are depicted on the temple's outer walls.

The barrel-roofed Bhima Ratha was never completed, as evidenced by the missing north-side colonnade; inside is a shrine to Vishnu. The Dharmaraja Ratha, tallest of the temples, is similar to the Arjuna Ratha but one storey higher, with lion pillars. The carvings on its outer walls mostly represent gods, including the androgynous Ardhanarishvara (half Shiva, half Parvati) on the east side. King Narasimhavarman I appears at the west end of the south side.

The Nakula-Sahadeva Ratha (named after twin Pandavas) stands aside from the other four and is dedicated to Indra. The life-size stone elephant beside it is one of India's most famous sculpted elephants. Approaching from the gate to the north you see its back end first, hence its nickname Gajaprishthakara (elephant's backside).

Tour groups tend to arrive around 10am, so do yourself a favour and arrive earlier!

🏃 Activities

Numerous places in town offer massage (₹750 to ₹1500), yoga (per hour ₹300) and ayurvedic treatments, at similar rates. Ask fellow travellers, question therapists carefully and, if you have any misgivings, don't proceed.

Mumu Surf School SURFING
(☎9789844191; www.mumusurfindia.com; Othavadai St; 90min group/private classes ₹1100/1300; ⊙8am-6pm) Popular, well-organised school for all levels and board rental (per hour/day ₹250/1000); also runs beach clean-ups and the relaxed Sandy Bottom cafe.

Sri Durga AYURVEDA
(☎9840288280; sridurgaayurclinic@gmail.com; 35 Othavadai St; massages ₹750-1500, yoga per hour ₹300; ⊙7am-10pm) Massages and ayurvedic treatments (male therapists for men, female for women).

👆 Tours

Travel XS CYCLING, BIRDWATCHING
(☎9840244326U; www.travel-xs.com; 123 East Raja St; bicycle tours per person ₹800; ⊙9.30am-8pm Mon-Sat year-round, to 1pm Sun Nov-Mar) Runs half-day bicycle tours (minimum two people) to nearby villages, visiting local potters and observing *kolam* drawing (elaborate chalk, rice-paste or coloured powder designs, also called *rangoli*), and organises day trips, including to Kanchipuram and (seasonally) **Vedanthangal Bird Sanctuary** (☎044-22351471; adult/child ₹20/5, camera/video ₹25/150; ⊙6am-6pm Nov-Mar).

🛏 Sleeping

Budget-friendly backpacker guesthouses and a few midrange hotels are strung along Othavadai and Othavadai Cross Sts and the narrow village lanes off them. There are several top-end resorts on the northern edge of town. Prices rise on busy weekends and holidays.

Rajalakshmi Guesthouse GUESTHOUSE $
(☎9840545858; www.rajalakshmiguesthouse.in; 5 Othavadai Cross St; r ₹600-700, with AC ₹1200; ❄🛜) This friendly ochre-walled guesthouse has some of the best budget rooms in town. Those without AC are simple but well kept, while AC rooms are newer and perfectly comfortable. Hammocks hang on both floors and the in-house restaurant makes good food. Online discounts can bring AC room prices below ₹1000.

Silver Moon GUESTHOUSE $
(☎9952009952; silvermoonmahabs@gmail.com; 11 Othavadai Cross St; r ₹800-1500, with AC ₹1500-2000; ❄🛜) Conveniently attached to Joe's Cafe (p358), the standard rooms here feel stylistically dated but are clean and in good shape. Deluxe rooms are spacious, with artistic wall murals and plenty of character for this price range. One of the better budget options in town.

Sri Harul Guest House GUESTHOUSE $
(☎9384620137; sriharul@gmail.com; 181 Bajanai Koil St, Fishermen's Colony; r ₹800, with AC

₹1000-1200; ❁) The beach sits right below your balcony when you land one of the half-dozen sea-view rooms at Sri Harul, one of Mamallapuram's better seafront budget deals. Rooms are basic, medium-sized and quite clean.

Hotel Daphne
HOTEL $

(✆9894282876; www.moonrakersrestaurants.com; 24 Othavadai Cross St; r with/without AC ₹1700/900; ❁⊛) Non-AC rooms are perfectly acceptable and clean if nothing fancy, but the Daphne's seven air-con rooms are great value (especially top-floor rooms 13 and 14), most with four-poster beds, balconies and cane swing-chairs. The shaded, immaculate, fairy-lit courtyard, cordial staff and free wi-fi are other drawcards. Singles may get discounts if it's slow.

Hotel Mahabs
HOTEL $$

(✆044-27442645; www.hotelmahabs.com; 68 East Raja St; incl breakfast r ₹1625, with AC ₹2460-3775; ❁⊛⊛) Friendly Mahabs is centred on a pretty mural-lined pool surrounded by lush gardens. Boring brown is the room theme, but they're very clean and comfy, with individual sit-out spaces. There's a decent in-house restaurant.

Radisson Blu Resort Temple Bay
RESORT $$$

(✆044-27443636; http://radissonblu.com/hotel-mamallapuram; 57 Kovalam Rd; r incl breakfast from ₹11,100; ❁@⊛⊛) The Radisson's luxurious chalets, villas and bungalows are strewn across manicured gardens stretching 500m to the beach. Somewhere in the middle is India's longest swimming pool (220m). Rooms range from large to enormous; the most expensive have private pools. The Radisson also offers Mamallapuram's finest (priciest) dining and a top-notch ayurvedic spa (massage ₹2500). It's ridiculously popular. Best rates online.

✗ Eating

Joe's Cafe
CAFE $

(Othavadai Cross St; snacks ₹45-130; ⊘7.30am-8.30pm) A relaxed cafe with some 'sidewalk' seating, Joe's serves up crêpes, burgers and other snacks, along with good lassis, juices and coffee drinks. The iced cappuccino is perfect!

Mamalla Bhavan
SOUTH INDIAN $

(South Mada St; mains ₹55-90, meals ₹80-105; ⊘7am-9.30pm) For an authentically good, wallet-friendly South Indian fill-up, swing by this simple, packed-out veg restaurant pumping out morning *idli*, *vada* and dosa, ₹20 filter coffee and banana-leaf lunchtime thalis. It's right beside the bus stand.

Gecko Restaurant
MULTICUISINE $$

(www.gecko-web.com; 37 Othavadai St; mains ₹180-380; ⊘9am-10pm; ⊛) Two friendly brothers run this cute blue-and-yellow-walled spot sprinkled with colourful artwork and wood carvings, and with daily seafood specials chalked up on boards. The offerings and prices aren't that different from other tourist-oriented restaurants, but the personalised service and excellent cooking makes it worth a visit.

Le Yogi
MULTICUISINE $$

(✆8870944267, 9840706340; 19 Othavadai St; mains ₹190-450; ⊘7.30am-11pm; ⊛) Some of Mamallapuram's best continental food. The pasta, pizza, sizzlers, crepes and *momos* (Tibetan dumplings) are genuine and tasty, service is exuberant, and the chilled-out setting, with bamboo posts, floor cushions and lamps dangling from a thatched roof, has a classic backpacker vibe.

Water's Edge Cafe
MULTICUISINE $$$

(✆044-27443636; www.radissonblu.com/hotel-mamallapuram; Radisson Blu Resort Temple Bay, 57 Kovalam Rd; mains ₹625-1150; ⊘24hr) The Radisson's pool-side 'cafe' offers everything from American pancakes to grilled tofu, Indian veg dishes, pan-Asian cuisine and a fantastic breakfast buffet (₹1190). It's expensive, but smart and popular.

⌂ Shopping

The roar of electric stone-grinders has just about replaced the tink-tink of chisels in Mamallapuram's stone-carving workshops, enabling sculptors to turn out ever more granite sculptures (of varying quality), from

MAMALLAPURAM HILL

Many interesting monuments, mostly dating from the late 7th and early 8th centuries, are scattered across the rock-strewn hill on the west side of town. It takes about an hour to walk around the main ones. The hill is open from 6am to 6pm and has entrances on West Raja St and just off Five Rathas Rd.

Straight ahead inside the northernmost West Raja St entrance stands a huge, impossible-to-miss boulder with the inspired name of **Krishna's Butterball** (☉6am-6pm) FREE, immovable but apparently balancing precariously. Beyond the rocks north of here is the Trimurti Cave Temple (p355), honouring the Hindu 'trinity': Brahma (left), Shiva (centre) and Vishnu (right), flanked by guardians. On the back of this rock is a beautiful group of carved elephants.

South of Krishna's Butterball you reach the **Ganesh Ratha** (☉6am-6pm) FREE, carved from a single rock, with lion-shaped pillar bases. Once a Shiva temple, it became a shrine to Ganesh (Shiva's elephant-headed son) after the original lingam was removed. Southwest of here, the **Varaha Mandapa** (☉6am-6pm) FREE houses some of Mamallapuram's finest carvings, including columns with seated lions. The left panel shows Vishnu's boar avatar, Varaha, lifting the earth out of the oceans. The outward-facing panels show Vishnu's consort Lakshmi (washed by elephants) and Durga, while the right-hand panel has Vishnu in his eight-armed giant form, Trivikrama, overcoming the demon king Bali.

A little further south, then east (up to the left), is the 16th-century **Raya Gopura** (Olakkanatha Temple; ☉6am-6pm) FREE, probably an unfinished *gopuram* (gateway tower). West just up the hill is the finely carved **Lion Throne** (☉6am-6pm) FREE, depicted roaring. The main path continues south to the **Ramanuja Mandapa** (☉6am-6pm) FREE and up to Mamallapuram's **lighthouse** (Indian/foreigner ₹10/25, camera/video ₹20/25; ☉10am-5pm). Southwest of the lighthouse is the rock-carved **Mahishamardini Mandapa** (☉6am-6pm) FREE, with excellent scenes from the Puranas (Sanskrit stories from the 5th century AD). The left-side panel shows Vishnu sleeping on the coils of a snake; on the right, Durga bestrides her lion vehicle while killing the demon-buffalo Mahisha. Inside the central shrine, Murugan sits between his parents, Shiva and Parvati.

₹100 pendants to person-sized Ganeshas (good luck getting one home!). There are also some decent art galleries, tailors and antique shops.

Apollo Books   BOOKS
(150 Fishermen's Colony; ☉9.30am-9.30pm) Good collection of books in several languages, to sell and swap.

Southern Arts & Crafts   ANTIQUES, HANDICRAFTS
(☏044-27443675; 72 East Raja St; ☉10.30am-10.30pm) Expensive but beautiful furniture, paintings, sculpture and carvings acquired from local homes, along with new quality sculpture.

❶ Information

Suradeep Hospital (☏044-27442448; 15 Thirukula St; ☉24hr) Recommended by travellers.
Mamallapuram's **tourist office** (☏044-27442232; Kovalam Rd; ☉10am-5.30pm Mon-Fri) is one of the most helpful in the entire state.

❶ Getting There & Away

From the **bus stand** (East Raja St), bus 599 heads to Chennai's Adyar/Gandhinagar Bus Terminus (₹45, 1½ hours) every 30 minutes from 6.50am to 8.30pm. Buses to Kanchipuram (₹50, two hours) leave at 8am, noon, and 5.30pm.

Virtually all other useful buses to and from Mamallapuram stop at the ECR Bypass Rd Bus Stop, about 1km north of the town centre, including bus 118 to Chennai's CMBT (₹45, two hours) half-hourly, 4am to 8pm. (From there, the Chennai Metro connects to the airport, plus Central and Egmore railway stations.) Buses to Puducherry (₹150, two hours) stop roughly every 15 minutes.

Kanchipuram

☏044 / POP 165,000

Kanchipuram, 80km southwest of Chennai, was capital of the Pallava dynasty during the 6th to 8th centuries, when the Pallavas created the great stone monuments of Mamallapuram. Today a typically hectic modern

Kanchipuram

Kanchipuram

◎ Sights
1 Ekambareshwara Temple................A1
2 Kamakshi Amman Temple.............A1
3 Vaikunta Perumal Temple.............B2

🛏 Sleeping
4 GRT Regency.................................B3
5 SSK Grand....................................B2

✕ Eating
   Dakshin..(see 4)
   Hotel Saravana Bhavan..............(see 4)
6 Hotel Saravana Bhavan...................A2

Indian town, it's famous for its numerous important and vibrant temples (and their colourful festivals), some dating from Pallava, Chola or Vijayanagar times. It's also known for its high-quality silk saris, woven on hand looms by thousands of families in the town and nearby villages. Silk and sari shops are strung along Gandhi Rd, southeast of the centre, though their wares are generally no cheaper than at Chennai silk shops.

Kanchipuram is easily visited in a day trip from Mamallapuram or Chennai, but it's worth seeing some of the temples after dark.

◎ Sights

All temples have free admission, though you may have to pay small amounts for shoe-keeping and/or cameras. Ignore claims that there's an entrance fee for non-Hindus.

Ekambareshwara Temple
HINDU TEMPLE

(Ekambaranathar Temple; Ekambaranathar Sannidhi St; phone-camera/camera/video ₹10/20/100; ☺6am-12.30pm & 4-8.30pm) Of South India's five Shiva temples associated with each of the five elements, this 12-hectare precinct is the shrine of earth. You enter beneath the 59m-high, unpainted south *gopuram,* whose lively carvings were chiselled in 1509 under Vijayanagar rule. Inside, a columned hall leads left into the central compound,

which Nandi faces from the right. The inner sanctum (Hindus only) contains a lingam made of earth and a mirror chamber where the central Shiva image is reflected in endless repetition.

Kamakshi Amman Temple
HINDU TEMPLE

(Kamakshi Amman Sannidhi St; ☺5.30am-noon & 4-8pm) This imposing temple, dedicated to Kamakshi/Parvati, is one of India's most important places of *shakti* (female energy/deities) worship, said to mark the spot where Parvati's midriff fell to earth. It's thought to have been founded by the Pallavas. The entire main building, with its gold-topped sanctuary, is off limits to non-Hindus, but the compound itself is beautiful, including a square tank with a shrine in the middle. It's wonderfully lit at night, making that the best time to visit.

Vaikunta Perumal Temple
HINDU TEMPLE

(Vaikundaperumal Koil St; ☺6am-noon & 4-8pm) This 1200-year-old Vishnu temple is a Pallava creation. The passage around the central shrine has lion pillars and a wealth of weathered but extremely detailed wall panels, some depicting historical events. The main shrine, uniquely spread over three levels and with jumping *yalis* (mythical lion creatures) on the exterior, contains images of Vishnu standing, sitting, reclining and riding his preferred mount, Garuda (half-eagle, half-man). It's well worth seeing.

Varadaraja
Perumal Temple
HINDU TEMPLE

(Devarajaswami Temple; off Kanchipuram-Chengalpattu Rd, Little Kanchipuram; 100-pillared hall ₹1, camera/video ₹5/100; ☺7.30am-12.30pm & 3.30-8pm) This enormous 11th-century Chola-built temple in southeast Kanchipuram is dedicated to Vishnu. Non-Hindus cannot enter the central compound, but the artistic highlight is the 16th-century '100-pillared' marriage hall, just inside the (main) western entrance. Its pillars (actually 96) are superbly carved with animals, monsters, warriors and several erotic sculptures. *Yalis* frame its inner southern steps and at its corners hang four stone chains, each carved from a single rock.

Every 40 years the temple tank is drained, revealing a huge wooden statue of Vishnu that is worshipped for 48 days. After 2019's showing, the next is due in 2059.

Kailasanatha Temple　　HINDU TEMPLE
(SVN Pillai St; ⊘6am-6.30pm, inner sanctum 6am-noon & 4-6.30pm) Kanchipuram's oldest temple is small, interesting mainly for its stonework. Dedicated to Shiva, it was built in the 8th century by Pallava king Narasimhavarman II (Rajasimha), who also created Mamallapuram's Shore Temple. Quieter than other temples in town, it has – sadly – been heavily restored, as the remaining older, eroded reliefs are much more evocative than the repaired ones.

🏃 Tours

RIDE　　CULTURAL
(Rural Institute for Development Education; ☑044-27268223; www.rideindia.org; 48 Periyar Nagar, Little Kanchipuram; half-day tours incl lunch ₹1000) Kanchipuram's famous silk-weaving industry has traditionally depended heavily on child labour. This long-standing NGO helps reduce the industry's child-labour numbers, from over 40,000 in 1997 to under 4000 by 2007 (its own estimates), and empower the rural poor, especially women. It also runs some interesting tours that provide insights into the lives of people working in the industry.

🛏️ Sleeping & Eating

RIDE　　GUESTHOUSE $
(Rural Institute for Development Education; ☑044-27268223; www.rideindia.org; 48 Periyar Nagar,

Little Kanchipuram; per person ₹1000; ✴) This NGO offers simple, clean rooms at its base in a residential area, 5km southeast of central Kanchipuram. If things are quiet, the friendly owners put you up in their own colourful home next door. Home-cooked breakfast (₹150), lunch (₹250) and dinner (₹250) available. Book a day ahead. It's signposted 1km east of the Varadaraja Perumal Temple.

GRT Regency　　HOTEL $$
(☑044-27225250; www.grthotels.com; 487 Gandhi Rd; r incl breakfast ₹2800; ✴🛜) The cleanest, comfiest and most stylish rooms in Kanchi, with marble floors, tea/coffee makers and glass-partitioned showers. The GRT's smart-ish **Dakshin** (mains ₹260-660; ⊘7am-11pm; 🛜) restaurant is overpriced, but offers a lengthy multicuisine menu of breakfast omelettes, South Indian favourites and tasty tandoori. Book online for discounts.

SSK Grand　　HOTEL $$
(☑9443221774; www.hotelsskgrand.com; 70 Nellukara St; d incl breakfast ₹2230; ✴🛜) This brand new hotel has good-sized rooms with thick mattresses, couches, tea kettles and glassed-in showers. With online discounts that can knock ₹700 off the price, it's the best value in town.

Hotel Saravana Bhavan　　SOUTH INDIAN $
(☑044-27226877; www.saravanabhavan.com; 66 Nellukara St; mains ₹80-250, meals ₹100-160; ⊘6am-10.30pm) A reliably good pure-veg restaurant with delicious dosa, a few North Indian surprises, a welcome air-con hall and thalis on the 1st floor. There's another (scruffier) **branch** (☑044-27222505; 504 Gandhi Rd; mains ₹80-250, meals ₹100-160; ⊘6am-10.30pm) just west of Gandhi Rd.

ℹ️ Getting There & Away
Suburban trains to Kanchipuram (₹25, 2½ hours) leave Chennai's Egmore station (platform 10 or 11) roughly hourly from 4.30am to 8.30pm.

BUSES FROM KANCHIPURAM

DESTINATION	FARE (₹)	TIME (HR)	DEPARTURES
Chennai	65-80	2	every 10min 3.30am-10.30pm
Mamallapuram	56	2	5.30am, 9.30am, 10.50am, 2.55pm, 4pm, 8pm
Puducherry (Pondicherry)	72	3	hourly 5.45am-9.20pm
Tiruvannamalai	110	3	every 30min 5.10am-9.30pm
Vellore	50	2	every 30min 3.30am-11pm

ℹ️ Getting Around

➥ Bicycle hire is available at **stalls** (Kamarajar St; per day ₹50; ⊙7.30am-8pm) outside the bus stand .

➥ An autorickshaw for a half-day tour of the five main temples (around ₹500) will inevitably involve stopping at a silk shop.

Tiruvannamalai

📞04175 / POP 145,280

There are temple towns, there are mountain towns, and then there are temple-mountain towns where God appears as a phallus of fire. Welcome to Tiruvannamalai, one of Tamil Nadu's holiest destinations.

Set below boulder-strewn Mt Arunachala, this is one of South India's five 'elemental' cities of Shiva; here the god is worshipped in his fire incarnation as Arunachaleshwar. At every full moon, 'Tiru' swells with thousands of pilgrims who circumnavigate Arunachala's base in a purifying ritual known as Girivalam; at any time you'll see Shaivite priests, sadhus (spiritual men) and devotees gathered around the Arunachaleshwar Temple.

Tiru's reputation for strong spiritual energies has produced numerous ashrams, and the town now attracts ever-growing numbers of spiritual-minded travellers.

◎ Sights

★**Arunachaleshwar Temple**   HINDU TEMPLE
(Annamalaiyar Temple; www.arunachaleswarar temple.tnhrce.in; ⊙5.30am-12.30pm & 3.30-9.30pm) This 10-hectare temple is one of India's largest. Its oldest parts date to the 9th century, but the site was a place of worship long before that. Four huge, unpainted white *gopurams* mark the entrances; the main, 17th-century eastern one rises 13 storeys (an astonishing 66m), its sculpted passageway depicting dancers, dwarves and elephants. During festivals the Arunachaleshwar is awash with golden flames and the scent of burning ghee, as befits the fire incarnation of Shiva, Destroyer of the Universe.

Mt Arunachala   MOUNTAIN

This 800m-high extinct volcano dominates Tiruvannamalai – and local conceptions of the element of fire, which supposedly finds its sacred abode in Arunachala's heart. Devout barefoot pilgrims make the 14km (four-hour) circumambulation of the mountain, stopping at eight famous linga, especially on

full-moon and festival days. The inner path is closed for the foreseeable future, but it's possible to circle around on the main road, or climb the hill past two caves where Sri Ramana Maharshi lived and meditated (1899–1922).

The hot ascent to the top opens up superb views of Tiruvannamalai, and takes five or six hours round trip: start early and take water. An unsigned path across the road from the northwest corner of the Arunachaleshwar Temple leads the way up past homes and the two caves, Virupaksha (about 20 minutes up) and Skandasramam (30 minutes). Women are advised not to hike alone, and it's suggested that no one go up after dark due to 'too many drunk boys'. Note that the trail to the top closes a month or two before the Deepam festival (p336), but the caves remain accessible.

If you aren't that devoted, buy a Giri-pradakshina map (₹15) from the bookshop at Sri Ramana Ashram, hire a bicycle from a shop on the roadside 200m east of the ashram (per day ₹40) and ride around. Or make an autorickshaw circuit for about ₹400 (up to double at busy times).

🏃 Activities

Yoga, meditation and ayurveda sessions are advertised everywhere in the main ashram area.

Sri Ramana Ashram   MEDITATION
(Sri Ramanasramam; 📞04175-237200; www.sri ramanamaharshi.org; Chengam Rd; ⊙5am-9pm) This tranquil ashram, 2km southwest of Tiruvannamalai centre amid green, peacock-filled grounds, draws devotees of Sri Ramana Maharshi, one of the first Hindu gurus to gain an international following; he died here in 1950 after half a century in contemplation. Visitors can meditate and attend daily *pujas* (prayers) and chantings, mostly in the samadhi hall (closed 12.30pm to 2pm), where the guru's body is enshrined.

Arunachala Animal Sanctuary   VOLUNTEERING
(📞9442246108; www.arunachalasanctuary.com; Chengam Rd; ⊙9am-5.30pm) 🐾 Aimed at sterilisation, castration, rabies control, rehoming and affordable treatments, this nonprofit sanctuary, at the western end of Tiruvannamalai's ashram area, provides shelter to over 200 homeless and/or injured dogs, plus a few cats. Travellers may be able to help with bathing, feeding, applying creams or

simply playing with the animals – it's best to show up after 10.30am. Prepare to be deeply moved.

🛏 Sleeping & Eating

Rainbow Guest House   GUESTHOUSE $
(📞04175-236408, 9443886408; rainbowguest housetiru@gmail.com; 27/28 Lakshmanan Nagar, Perumbakkam Rd; s/d ₹600/1250; 🕾) A great-value, spick-and-span spot 800m southwest off Chengam Rd. Beyond the psychedelic exterior, wood-carved doors reveal simple, immaculate, fan-cooled rooms with hot water and tiled floors. Doubles are almost like suites: huge, some with small kitchens. Staff are gracious, cane chairs dangle along corridors and there are fantastic Mt Arunachala views from the spartan rooftop terrace.

Arunaalaya Residency   HOTEL $
(📞8098083062; www.arunaalaya.com; 120 Seshatri Mada St; r ₹800, with AC ₹1960-3080; 🕸) Though slightly overpriced if you want AC, Arunaalaya offers large, cool, clean-ish marble-floored rooms with colourful walls around two small garden patios, up a lane north off Chengam Rd. The non-AC rooms are good value. '

Sunshine Guest House   GUESTHOUSE $$
(📞04175-235335; www.sunshineguesthouseindia. com; 5 Annamalai Nagar, Perumbakkam Rd; s/d ₹1625/2350; 🕸🕾) In a blissfully quiet spot 1km southwest of the main ashram area, this colourful guesthouse is fronted by gardens. Singles feel flimsy, like cheap mobile homes. Doubles are huge with plenty of character,

each styled after a Hindu god; they have printed sheets, sequinned fabrics, cane swing-chairs and in-room water filters. Book way ahead for November-to-March dates.

Hotel Arunachala   HOTEL $$
(Arunachala Inn; 📞04175-228300; www.hotel arunachala.com; 5 Vada Sannathi St; r ₹950, with AC s ₹1500, d ₹1680-2750; 🕸) Right next to the Arunachaleshwar Temple's east entrance, Hotel Arunachala is clean and decent with pretensions to luxury in the marblesque floors, ugly furniture, keen management and lobby fish pond. Standard rooms feel halfway conceived; deluxe rooms are much better. Downstairs, pure-veg **Hotel Sri Arul Jothi** (dishes ₹40-80; ⏰5.30am-10.30pm) provides good South Indian dishes (thalis ₹80 to ₹120).

Shanti Café   CAFE $
(www.facebook.com/shanticafetiru; 115A Chengam Rd; dishes ₹60-200, drinks ₹30-90; ⏰8.30am-8.30pm; 🕾) This popular and relaxed cafe with floor-cushion seating, up a lane off Chengam Rd, serves wonderful croissants, cakes, baguettes, pancakes, juices, coffees, teas, breakfasts and Indian meals with an extra-healthy twist. Omelettes are a good choice. It's run by a delightful team and there's an **internet cafe** (www.shantionline. com; per hour ₹25; ⏰8.30am-1.30pm & 3-7pm Mon-Sat) downstairs.

⭐ Dreaming Tree   CAFE $$
(📞8870057753; www.dreamingtree.in; Ramana Nagar; mains ₹250-290; ⏰8.30am-10pm) 🌿 Super-chilled Dreaming Tree dishes out

---

GINGEE FORT

With three separate hilltop citadels and a 6km perimeter of cliffs and thick walls, the ruins of enormous **Gingee Fort** (📞04145-222072; Gingee; Indian/foreigner ₹25/300; ⏰8am-5pm) rise out of the Tamil plain, 37km east of Tiruvannamalai, like castles misplaced by the Lord of the Rings. It was constructed mainly in the 16th century by the Vijayanagars and was later occupied by the Marathas, Mughals, French and British, then abandoned in the 19th century. The fort's sheer scale, dramatic beauty and peaceful setting make it a very worthwhile stop.

Today, few foreigners make it here, but Gingee is popular with domestic tourists for its starring role in various films. The main road linking Tiruvannamalai and Puducherry cuts between the fortified hills, just west of Gingee town. Of the three citadels, the easiest to reach, Krishnagiri, rises north of the road. To the south are the highest of the three, Rajagiri, and the most distant and least interesting, Chakklidurg (which you can't climb). Ticket offices (with maps) are at the foot of Krishnagiri and Rajagiri.

Gingee is on the Tiruvannamalai–Puducherry bus route, with buses from Tiruvannamalai (₹37, one hour) every 10 minutes. Hop off at the fort to save a trip back out from Gingee town. A taxi between Tiruvannamalai and Puducherry with a two- to three-hour stop at Gingee costs around ₹3000.

BUSES FROM TIRUVANNAMALAI

DESTINATION	FARE (₹)	TIME (HR)	DEPARTURES
Chennai	120-140	5	every 10min
Kanchipuram	63	3	hourly
Puducherry (Pondicherry)	63	3	hourly
Trichy (Tiruchirappalli)	123	5	every 45min
Vellore	37-50	2½	every 10min

huge portions of exquisite, health-focused veg fare, prepped with mostly organic ingredients, on a breezy thatched rooftop loaded with low-slung purple-cushioned booths. Expect fabulous 'hippie salads' and tofu stir-fries, luscious breakfasts, and all kinds of cakes, juices, lassis, lemonades and organic coffees. Signs lead the way (500m) across the road from Sri Ramana Ashram.

Tasty Café CAFE $$
(Lakshmanan Nagar, Perumbakkam Rd; mains ₹100-240; ☺7am-10pm) In a peaceful, shady courtyard of plastic chairs and wooden tables, friendly Tasty Café does well-prepared Indian and continental food, including pizza, pasta, pancakes and salads. It's 700m southwest off Chengam Rd. Try the daily specials.

🛍 Shopping

**Shantimalai Handicrafts
Development Society** ARTS & CRAFTS
(www.smhds.org; 83/1 Chengam Rd; ☺9am-7pm Mon-Sat) Beautiful bedspreads, bags, incense, candles, oils, bangles, scarves and cards, all made by local village women.

❶ Getting There & Away

The **bus stand** (Polur Rd) is 800m north of the Arunachaleshwar Temple, and a ₹50 to ₹60 autorickshaw ride from the main ashram area. For Chennai, the best options are the hourly Ultra Deluxe services.

❶ Getting Around

Bike hire (per hour/day ₹10/40) is available opposite Sri Ramana Ashram (p362), in the southwest part of town.

Puducherry (Pondicherry)

☑0413 / POP 1.3 MILLION
The union territory of Puducherry (formerly Pondicherry; generally known as 'Pondy') was under French rule until 1954. Some people here still speak French (and English with

French accents). Hotels, restaurants and 'lifestyle' shops sell a seductive vision of the French-subcontinental aesthetic, enhanced by Gallic creative types and Indian artists and designers. The internationally famous Sri Aurobindo Ashram and its offshoot just north of town, Auroville, draw large numbers of spiritually minded visitors. Thus Pondy's vibe: less faded colonial-era *ville*, more bohemian-chic, New Age–meets–Old World hang-out on the international travel trail.

The older 'French' part of town (where you'll probably spend most of your time) is full of quiet, clean streets, lined with bougainvillea-draped colonial-style townhouses numbered in an almost logical manner. Newer Pondy is typically, hectically South Indian.

Enjoy fabulous shopping, French food (*bonjour* steak!), beer (*au revoir* Tamil Nadu alcohol taxes), and plenty of yoga and meditation.

◉ Sights

Seafront WATERFRONT
(Goubert Ave) Pondy is a seaside town, but that doesn't make it a beach destination; the city's sand is a thin strip of dirty brown that slurps into a seawall of jagged rocks. But Goubert Ave (Beach Rd) is a killer stroll, especially at dawn and dusk when half the town takes a romantic wander. In a stroke of genius, authorities have banned traffic here from 6pm to 7.30am.

Sri Aurobindo Ashram ASHRAM
(☑0413-2233649; www.sriaurobindoashram.org; Marine St; ☺8am-noon & 2-6pm) FREE Founded in 1926 by Sri Aurobindo and a French-born woman, 'the Mother', this famous spiritual community has about 2000 members in its many departments. Aurobindo's teachings focus on 'integral yoga' that sees devotees work in the world, rather than retreat from it. Visits to the main, grey-walled ashram building are cursory: you see the flower-festooned samadhi of Aurobindo and the Mother, then the bookshop. Ashram-

accommodation guests can access other areas and activities. Evening meditation around the samadhi is for everyone.

There are daily weekday ashram tours (per person ₹50), which begin at 8.30am with a film about Sri Aurobindo and the Mother and include visits to various ashram workshops where you can see batik work, hand-printing on saris, handloom weaving and more; enquire online (www.sri aurobindoautocare.com) or at the ashram's Bureau Central (p372).

Puducherry Museum   MUSEUM
(http://art.puducherry.gov.in/museum.html; St Louis St; Indian/foreigner ₹10/50; ⊙9am-6.30pm Tue-Sun) Goodness knows how this convert-ed late-18th-century villa keeps its artefacts from disintegrating, considering there's a whole floor of French-era furniture sitting in the South Indian humidity. On the ground floor look especially for Chola, Vijayanagar and Nayak bronzes, and pieces of ancient Greek and Spanish pottery and amphorae (storage vessels) excavated from Arikamedu, a once-major trading port just south of Puducherry. Upstairs is Governor Dupleix' bed.

**Institut Français
de Pondichéry**   LIBRARY
(☑0413-2231616; www.ifpindia.org; 11 St Louis St; ₹100; ⊙9am-6pm Mon-Fri) This grand 19th-century neoclassical building is also a flourishing research institution devoted to

---

TAMIL NADU TEMPLES

Tamil Nadu is home to some of India's most spectacular temple architecture and sculpture, and few parts of the country are as fervent in their worship of the Hindu gods. Its 5000-odd shrines are constantly abuzz with worshippers flocking in for *puja* (offering or prayer), and colourful temple festivals abound. More Tamil temples are dedicated to the various forms of Shiva than to any other deity, including his depiction as Nataraja, the cosmic dancer, who dances in a ring of fire with two of his four hands holding the flame of destruction and the drum of creation. Tamils also have a soft spot for Shiva's peacock-riding son Murugan (also Kartikeya or Skanda), who is intricately associated with their cultural identity.

The special significance of many Tamil temples makes them goals of countless Hindu pilgrims from all over India. The Pancha Sabhai Sthalangal are the five temples where Shiva is believed to have performed his cosmic dance (chief among them Chidambaram). Then there's the Pancha Bootha Sthalangal, the five temples where Shiva is worshipped as one of the five elements: Tiruvannamalai's Arunachaleshwar Temple (p362), fire; Kanchipuram's Ekambareshwara Temple (p360), earth; Chidambaram's Nataraja Temple (p374), space; Trichy's Sri Jambukeshwara Temple (p382), water; and, in Andhra Pradesh, **Sri Kalahasteeswara Temple** (www.srikalahasthitemple.com; off Sannidhi Rd; ⊙5.30am-9pm), air. Each of Kumbakonam's nine Navagraha temples is the abode of one of the nine celestial bodies of Hindu astronomy – key sites given the importance of astrology in Hindu faith. Architecturally, Brihadishwara Temple (p379) in Thanjavur is a priceless gem.

Typical Tamil temple design features tall layered entrance towers (*gopurams*), encrusted with often colourfully painted sculptures of gods and demons; halls of richly carved columns (*mandapas*); a sacred water tank; and a series of compounds (*prakarams*), one within the next, with the innermost containing the central sanctum where the temple's main deity resides. The earliest Tamil temples were small rock-cut shrines; the first free-standing temples were built in the 8th century AD; *gopurams* first appeared around the 12th century.

Admission to most temples is free, but non-Hindus are often not allowed inside inner sanctums. At other temples priests may invite you in and in no time you are doing *puja*, having an auspicious *tilak* mark daubed on your forehead and being hassled for a donation.

Temple touts can be a nuisance, but there are also many excellent guides; use your judgment and be on the lookout for badge-wearing official guides.

A South Indian Journey by Michael Wood and *Southern India: A Guide to Monuments, Sites & Museums* by George Michell are great reads if you're interested in Tamil temple culture. TempleNet (www.templenet.com) is one of the best online resources.

PUDUCHERRY'S CATHEDRALS

Pondy hosts one of India's best collections of over-the-top cathedrals. *Merci, French missionaries.* **Our Lady of Immaculate Conception Cathedral** (Mission St; ◉6am-noon & 3-7pm), completed in 1791, is a sky-blue, hot-yellow and cloud-white typically Jesuit edifice in a Goa-like Portuguese style. The brown-and-white grandiosity of the **Sacred Heart Basilica** (Subbaiah Salai; ◉5.30am-1pm & 6-8pm) is set off by beautifully restored stained glass and a Gothic sense of proportion. The twin towers and dome of the mellow-pink-and-yellow Notre Dame des Anges, built in the 1850s, look sublime in the late-afternoon light. Its smooth limestone interior was made using eggshell plaster; in the square opposite, there's a Joan of Arc statue.

Indian culture, history and ecology. Visitors can browse books in the beach-facing library.

Sri Manakula Vinayagar Temple
HINDU TEMPLE

(www.manakulavinayagartemple.com; Manakula Vinayagar Koil St; ◉5.45am-12.30pm & 4-9.30pm) Pondy may have more churches than most Indian towns, but the Hindu faith still reigns supreme. Pilgrims, tourists and the curious get a head pat from the temple elephant at this centuries-old temple dedicated to Ganesh, which contains around 40 skilfully painted friezes.

◉ French Quarter

Pocketed away just behind the seafront is a series of cobbled bougainvillea-wrapped streets and white-and-mustard buildings in various states of romantic *déshabillé*, otherwise known as Puducherry's French Quarter. A do-it-yourself heritage walk could start at the French consulate (p512), near the north end of Goubert Ave, the seafront promenade (p364). Head south, passing the 1836 **lighthouse** (Goubert Ave), then turn inland to shady, landscaped **Bharathi Park** (Compagnie St; ◉6am-7pm) FREE. The neoclassical governor's residence, **Raj Nivas** (Rangapillai St), faces the park's north side. Return to the seafront at the **Gandhi Memorial** (Goubert Ave), wander south past **Notre Dame des Anges** (Dumas St; ◉6-10am & 4-7pm) church,

and then potter south through the 'white town' – Dumas, Romain Rolland, Suffren and Labourdonnais Sts. Towards the southern end of Dumas St, pop in to the beautiful **École Française d'Extrême-Orient** (www.efeo.fr; 16-19 Dumas St; ◉8.30am-noon & 2-5.30pm Mon-Fri) FREE, with its extensive library of Indology.

A lot of restoration has been happening in this area: if you're interested in Pondy's architectural heritage, check out INTACH Pondicherry (www.intachpondicherry.org). The tourist office website (www.pondytourism.in) details heritage walks.

🏃 Activities

Yoganjali Natyalayam
YOGA

(☎0413-2241561; www.icyer.com; 25 II Cross, Iyyanar Nagar; ◉9am-6pm) One-on-one, 10-lesson introductory yoga courses (₹7000) at the central-Pondy branch of the renowned International Centre for Yoga Education & Research. Contact the office at least a day before you'd like to begin.

Kallialay Surf School
SURFING

(☎9442992874; www.surfschoolindia.com; Serenity Beach, Tandriankuppam; 1hr private classes ₹1800, board rental per 90min ₹400; ◉hours vary) Surfing continues to soar in popularity along Tamil Nadu's coast, and this long-standing, well-equipped, Spanish-run school, 5km north of Puducherry, offers everything from beginner sessions to intensive two-week courses.

La Casita
CULTURAL PROGRAMS

(www.lacasitaindia.com; 147 Eshwaran Koil St; classes ₹250-350; ◉11am-3.30pm & 5.30-9pm Tue-Sun) A fun-filled Latino-inspired arts centre offering drop-in (and longer-term) yoga and Bollywood classes, along with tango, salsa, capoeira and Zumba. There's also a cosy rooftop travellers' cafe.

🐾 Courses

Sita
CULTURAL PROGRAMS

(☎0413-4200718; www.pondicherry-arts.com; 22 Candappa Moudaliar St; classes ₹300-1200; ◉9am-1pm & 3-7pm Mon-Sat) This energetic Franco-Indian cultural centre runs a host of activities, open to visitors (even for a single session): Indian cooking, *bharatanatyam* or Bollywood dance, *kolam* making, *mehndi* (henna 'tattoos'), yoga, pilates, ayurveda and sari 'workshops', plus brilliant cycling and photography tours.

**International Centre for
Yoga Education
& Research** YOGA
(Ananda Ashram; ☑0413-2622902; www.icyer.
com; 16A Mettu St, Chinnamudaliarchavady, Kot-
tukuppam; ☺10am-2pm) Rigorous six-month
yoga-teacher-trainings are offered at Ananda Ashram, north of town, from October to
March; fill out the application on the website
and submit it well in advance.

👣 Tours

Storytrails WALKING
(☑7339147770; www.storytrails.in; 551 Kamaraj
Salai, 1st fl; tours per person ₹1100-6000; ☺7am-
6.30pm) Chennai-born Storytrails runs terrific story-themed jaunts through the French
Quarter – the perfect walking introduction to Pondy's historical and architectural
delights.

🛏 Sleeping

If you've been saving for a splurge, this is the
place: Puducherry's lodgings are as good as
South India gets. Local heritage houses combine colonial-era romanticism with modern
comfort and chic French-inspired styling,
and there are some beautifully updated
properties. Most of these rooms would cost
five times as much in Europe. Book ahead
for weekends, when some places raise prices.

Park Guest House ASHRAM GUESTHOUSE $
(☑0413-2233644; parkgh@sriaurobindoashram.
org; 1 Goubert Ave; r with/without AC ₹1500/950;
☀) Pondy's most sought-after ashram guesthouse, thanks to its wonderful seafront
position, with the best-value air-con rooms
around but no advance bookings. All front
rooms face the sea and have a porch or balcony. There's a garden for yoga or meditation,
plus vegetarian buffet lunches (₹150) and bicycle hire (per day ₹60).

**International
Guest House** ASHRAM GUESTHOUSE $
(INGH; ☑0413-233669; ingh@aurosociety.org;
47 NSC Bose St; s ₹450, d ₹550-700, s/d with AC
₹750/1680; ☀) The sparse, spotless rooms
here, adorned with a single photo of the
Mother, make for good-value ashram lodgings. It's very popular: book three weeks
ahead.

Kailash Guest House GUESTHOUSE $
(☑0413-2224485; http://kailashguesthouse.in; 43
Vysial St; s/d ₹1100/1500; with AC ₹1250/1750; ☀)

Good-value Kailash has simple, superclean
rooms with well-mosquito-proofed windows,
friendly management and a covered top-
floor terrace. The lobby is a comfy but classy
communal area. One of the best budget options in town.

★ Les Hibiscus GUESTHOUSE $$
(☑0413-2227480, 9442066763; www.leshibiscus.
in; 49 Suffren St; incl breakfast s ₹2000 2750, d
₹2250-3300; ☀@⏅) Mango-yellow Les Hi-
biscus has just a handful of fabulous high-
ceilinged rooms with antique beds, coffee
makers and a mix of quaint Indian art and
old Pondy photos, at astoundingly reason-
able prices. (The top-floor single room is a
great deal.) The whole place is immaculate-
ly styled, fresh breakfasts are fantastic and
management is genuinely friendly and help-
ful. Book well ahead.

Patricia Guest House GUESTHOUSE $$
(☑0413-2335130; http://patriciaguesthouse.word
press.com; 20/28 Francois Martin St; r ₹3300-4500;
☀⏅) A hot-orange (unsigned) heritage home
has been lovingly transformed into a unique,
relaxed, colour-bursting retreat in the northern French Quarter. Each of the seven rooms
(some with separate bathrooms) surprises
with individual character, and all are packed
with South Indian art, printed fabrics and
vibrant paintwork. The upper-floor 'cottage'
opens on to its own thatched-roof terrace.
Breakfast available (₹200).

Gratitude GUESTHOUSE $$
(☑0413-2226029; www.gratitudeheritage.in; 52 Ro-
main Rolland St; r incl breakfast ₹3540-7080; ☀⏅)
A wonderfully tranquil 19th-century house
(no shoes, no TVs, no children), sun-yellow
Gratitude has been delightfully restored.
Nine individually styled rooms sprawl across
two floors around a tropically shaded court-
yard; a couple of them could use another
dose of refurbishment, so look at a few if you
can. There's a roof terrace for yoga and mas-
sages. Breakfast is delicious.

**Coloniale Heritage
Guest House** GUESTHOUSE $$
(☑0413-2224720; http://colonialeheritage.com;
54 Romain Rolland St; r incl breakfast ₹2950-
4700; ☀⏅) This leafy colonial-era hav-
en with six comfy rooms (some up steep
stairs) is crammed with character thanks
to the owner's impressive collection of gem-
studded Thanjavur paintings, Ravi Varma
lithographs and other 19th- and 20th-century

Puducherry (Pondicherry)

South Indian art. One room has a swing, another its own balcony. Breakfast is laid out in the sunken garden-side patio.

Hotel de Pondichéry HERITAGE HOTEL $$
(☎0413-2227409; www.hoteldepondichery.com; 38 Dumas St; incl breakfast s ₹2500, d ₹3000-5000; ❄☞) A colourful heritage spot with 14 comfy, quiet and spacious rooms, some sporting semi-open bathrooms, most with splashes of original modern art. A few are beginning to show some wear and tear, but most are in great shape. The excellent restaurant, Le Club (p371), takes up the charming front courtyard and staff are lovely.

Red Lotus BOUTIQUE HOTEL $$
(☎8870344334; www.redlotuspondicherry.com; 48-58 Nehru St; r ₹2465; ❄☞) Behind the flaming-red doors of a revamped merchant house, this glossy oriental-inspired guesthouse overlooks a busy street in the thick of Pondy's bazaar area. Cheery staff lead you to modish rooms decorated with witty wall slogans, floral murals, varnished wood and tea/coffee kits. The roof-terrace cafe-bar is full of aqua-cushioned sofas.

Nila Home Stay GUESTHOUSE $$
(☎9443537209; www.nilahomestay.com; 18 Labourdonnais St; r ₹2800; ❄☞) A simple but

Puducherry (Pondicherry)

⊙ **Sights**
1 Bharathi Park D2
2 École Française d'Extrême-Orient D5
3 Gandhi Memorial D3
4 Institut Français de Pondichéry D1
5 Notre Dame des Anges D3
6 Old Lighthouse D2
7 Our Lady of the Immaculate
  Conception Cathedral B2
8 Puducherry Museum D2
9 Raj Nivas D2
10 Sacred Heart Basilica A5
11 Seafront D4
12 Sri Aurobindo Ashram D1
13 Sri Manakula Vinayagar Temple C2

⊙ **Activities, Courses & Tours**
14 Sita B3

⊜ **Sleeping**
15 Coloniale Heritage Guest House C5
16 Dune Mansion Calvé B1
17 Gratitude C4
18 Hotel de L'Orient C4
19 Hotel de Pondichéry C5
20 International Guest House C2
21 Kailash Guest House C1
22 La Villa C4
23 Les Hibiscus C5
24 Nila Home Stay C4
25 Palais de Mahé D4
26 Park Guest House D5
27 Patricia Guest House D1
28 Promenade D2
29 Red Lotus C1

30 Villa Helena C4
31 Villa Shanti C4

⊗ **Eating**
32 Baker Street B4
33 Café des Arts C3
  Chez Francis .... (see 18)
34 Gelateria Montecatini Terme C5
35 Kasha Ki Aasha C3
36 La Pasta World C1
37 Le Café D3
  Le Club .... (see 19)
  Palais de Mahé .... (see 25)
38 Surguru C2
39 Surguru Spot D2
  Villa Helena .... (see 30)
  Villa Shanti .... (see 31)

⊖ **Drinking & Nightlife**
40 L'e-Space C4

⊕ **Shopping**
41 Anokhi D3
42 Auroshikha C1
43 Fabindia C2
44 Focus B2
45 Geethanjali C4
46 Hidesign C2
47 Kalki C1
48 La Boutique d'Auroville C1
49 LivingArt Lifestyles C4

ⓘ **Information**
50 Bureau Central C2
51 French Consulate D1

brilliantly characterful and well-kept French Quarter guesthouse run by welcoming hosts, with a range of fresh, colourful rooms (some with kitchens and/or terraces), handy communal kitchens and a low-key lounge area.

★ **La Villa**   BOUTIQUE HOTEL $$$
(☏0413-2338555; www.lavillapondicherry.com; 11 Surcouf St; r incl breakfast ₹13,300-20,500; ❈⊜⊠) Queen of local boutique hotels is this intimate, six-room 19th-century beauty, sleekly updated by one of Pondy's top French-architect teams. From curved wooden bedheads to cocoonlike swing-chairs and abstract artwork, rooms blend white-on-white luxury with bold, contemporary design. It's impeccably styled, there's an upmarket patio restaurant, and you can breakfast overlooking the turquoise rooftop pool.

★ **Villa Shanti**   HERITAGE HOTEL $$$
(☏0413-4200028; www.lavillashanti.com; 14 Suffren St; r incl breakfast ₹8100-14,000; ❈⊜) Oc-

cupying a 100-year-old building revamped by two French architects, Villa Shanti puts an exquisitely contemporary twist on the French Quarter heritage hotel. Beautiful modern rooms combine superchic design with typically Tamil materials and colonial-style elegance: four-poster beds, Chettinadu tiles, walk-through bathrooms, Tamil-language murals. The sunken courtyard houses a hugely popular restaurant (p371) and bar.

Villa Helena   HERITAGE HOTEL $$$
(☏0413-2226789; www.villa-helena-pondicherry.com; 13 Rue Bussy; incl breakfast s ₹2500-4500, d ₹4000-8000; ❈⊜) This gorgeous 19th-century French-run mansion is infused with contemporary character. Spread along plant-dotted galleries, immaculate, soft-toned rooms are done up in tasteful minimalist style, with stripy bedding, printed cushions, vintage furniture and stylish modern bathrooms. There's wonderful continental

cooking in the romantic courtyard restaurant.

Palais de Mahé
HERITAGE HOTEL $$$

(☏0413-2345611; www.cghearth.com; 4 Rue Bussy; r incl breakfast ₹23,000-28,100; ❋🌐🏊) Three colonnaded floors of swish, soaring-ceilinged rooms with colonial-style wood furnishings and varnished-concrete floors rise around a seductive turquoise pool at this imposing heritage hotel. The first-rate rooftop restaurant serves impressive, creative fusion cuisine, including cooked-to-order breakfasts. From May through September rates drop by 30%.

Maison Perumal
HERITAGE HOTEL $$$

(☏0413-2227519; www.cghearth.com; 44 Perumal Koil St; r incl breakfast ₹13,300-14,850; ❋🌐) Secluded rooms with colourful flourishes, antique beds and photos of the original owners surround two pillared patios at this renovated 130-year-old home, pocketed away in Pondy's less touristic Tamil Quarter. The excellent Tamil/French **restaurant** (☏0413-2227519; www.cghearth.com; 44 Perumal Koil St; lunch mains ₹350-550, dinner ₹1200; ⊙12.30-3pm & 7.30-9.30pm) cooks everything from market-fresh ingredients and gives culinary demonstrations. Heritage walking tours are offered and guests can use the pool at sister property Palais de Mahé.

Hotel de L'Orient
HERITAGE HOTEL $$$

(☏0413-2226111; www.dunewellnessgroup.com; 17 Romain Rolland St; r incl breakfast ₹7700-12,800; ❋🌐) This grand restored 18th-century mansion has breezy verandas, keen staff and antique-filled old-world rooms in all shapes and sizes: some are cosy attics, others palatial, many have four-poster beds. A place to get that old Pondy feel while enjoying polished service and French, creole (French Indian) or South Indian food in the courtyard restaurant, Chez Francis (p371).

Dune Mansion Calvé
HERITAGE HOTEL $$$

(☏0413-2970500; www.dunewellnessgroup.com; 36 Vysial St; r incl breakfast ₹6500-8850; ❋🌐) 🌿 The old Tamil Quarter has almost as many mansions as the French Quarter but is off most tourists' radars. Reincarnated under environmentally friendly management, this 150-year-old heritage choice, on a quiet, tree-shaded street, mixes a soaring sense of space with a teak-columned atrium, Chettinadu-tiled floors, and 10 elegantly styled rooms featuring free-standing bathtubs and solar-powered hot-water systems.

Promenade
BOUTIQUE HOTEL $$$

(☏0413-2227750; www.sarovarhotels.com; 23 Goubert Ave; r incl breakfast ₹7670-9600; ❋🌐) The Promenade is a flashy boutiquelike beachfront spot owned by the swish Hidesign group, with upscale, oriental-themed, (mostly) sea-facing rooms. If you're looking for modern and stylish, this is your hotel. The elegant rooftop restaurant serves good, pricey pan-Asian dishes and cocktails in a breezy, leafy, lantern-lit setting – you're forking out more for the location.

🍴 Eating

Puducherry is a culinary highlight of Tamil Nadu. You can get great South Indian cooking, well-prepped French and Italian cuisine, and delicious fusion food. If you've been missing cheese or have a craving for croissants, you're in luck, and *everyone* in the French Quarter does good brewed coffee and crêpes. There are some fabulous arty cafes too.

It's also worth exploring some of the options around nearby Auroville (p373), especially in Kuilapalayam village.

Surguru Spot
SOUTH INDIAN $

(☏0413-4308084; www.hotelsurguru.com; 12 Nehru St; mains ₹115-140, thalis ₹150-220; ⊙6.30am-11pm) Fill up on crispy dosa and *vada,* pillowy *idli* and spicy lunchtime thalis in a smarter-than-average AC dining hall with yellow-washed pillars, just a couple of blocks from Sri Aurobindo Ashram. There's another **branch** (☏0413-4308083; 235 Mission St; mains ₹70-140, thalis ₹135-190; ⊙7am-10.40pm) in the Tamil Quarter.

Gelateria Montecatini Terme
ICE CREAM $

(GMT; Goubert Ave; ice creams ₹50-80; ⊙11am-11.30pm) Join the seafront crowds for creamy, authentic Italian gelato in tropical-tastic flavours like mango, watermelon and guava – or try something more exotic, like Himalaya salted caramel or Dubai Cream, with milk, chocolate, almonds and dates.

Baker Street
CAFE $

(123 Rue Bussy; dishes ₹40-200; ⊙7am-9pm; 🌐) A popular upmarket French-style bakery that does impressively delectable cakes, sandwiches, croissants and biscuits. The baguettes, brownies and quiches hold their own too. Eat in or takeaway.

★ **Café des Arts**   CAFE $$
(www.facebook.com/café-des-arts-155637583166;
10 Suffren St; dishes ₹140-370; ☺8.30am-6.30pm
Wed-Mon; 🐟) This bohemian cafe would look
perfectly at home in Europe, but this is Pon-
dy, so there's a cycle rickshaw in the garden.
Perfectly prepared dishes range from salads
to crêpes, baguettes, omelettes and toasties.
Coffees and fresh juices are great. The old
town house setting is casual yet refined, with
low tables and lounge chairs arranged across
several rooms and an outdoor terrace.

Kasha Ki Aasha   CAFE $$
(www.kkapondy.com; 23 Surcouf St; mains ₹150-
295; ☺10am-8pm Thu-Tue; 🐟) A friendly all-
female team whips up great pancake breakfasts, lunches and cakes on the thatched
rooftop of this colonial-era-house-turned-
craft-shop-and-cafe, where the all-veg fusion
food includes 'European thalis' and 'Indian
enchiladas' (which feel a little overpriced for
what you get). The floaty fabrics and leather
sandals for sale downstairs come direct from
their makers. Live music Saturday night.

Le Café   CAFE $$
(☎0413-2334949; Goubert Ave; dishes ₹115-260;
☺24hr) Pondy's only seafront cafe is good for
croissants, cakes, salads, baguettes, break-
fasts and organic South Indian coffee (hot or
iced), plus welcome fresh breezes from the
Bay of Bengal. It's popular, so you often have
to wait for, or share, a table. But hey, it's all
about the location.

★ **Villa Helena**   CONTINENTAL, INDIAN $$$
(☎0413-4210806;   www.villa-helena-pondicherry.
com; 13 Rue Bussy; mains ₹340-720; ☺noon-3pm
& 7-10pm) One of Pondy's favourite culinary
teams heads up this fashionable continental-
Indian eatery, launched in 2016 in a dreamy,
lantern-lit patio engulfed by tropical gardens
and lined with white-columned corridors.
The menu leaps around the globe, delivering
luscious creative salads alongside beef fillets,
pastas, cheese boards, Indian classics and
the odd fusion invention.

★ **Villa Shanti**   CONTINENTAL, INDIAN $$$
(☎0413-4200028;   www.lavillashanti.com;   14
Suffren St; mains ₹250-780; ☺noon-2.30pm &
7.30-10.30pm) Smart candlelit tables in a
palm-dotted, pillared courtyard attached
to a colourful cocktail bar create a casually
fancy vibe at this packed-out hotel restau-
rant, one of Pondy's hottest dining spots.

The building's contemporary Franco-Indian
flair runs right through the North Indian/
European menu. While portions are small,
flavours are exquisite, and there are some
deliciously creative veg dishes. Open all day
for snacks and drinks.

Chez Francis   CREOLE, FRENCH $$$
(☎9159550341; 17 Romain Rolland St; mains ₹260-
590; ☺7.30-10am, 12.30-2.30pm & 7.30-10.30pm)
Fabulous French and creole cooking – such
as the fantastic prawn curry – is the order
of the day at this atmospheric courtyard restaurant at the heart of the Hotel de L'Orient.

Palais de Mahé   FUSION $$$
(☎0413-2345611; www.cghearth.com; 4 Rue Bussy;
mains ₹350-600; ☺12.30-3pm & 7-10.30pm) On a
magical roof terrace just back from Pondy's
seafront promenade, the Palais de Mahé's
superb restaurant specialises in ambitious,
beautifully presented fusion dishes, best
enjoyed alongside a signature Prohibition-
inspired cocktail. Seafood and steaks are per-
fectly prepared.

La Pasta World   ITALIAN $$$
(☎9994670282; www.facebook.com/lapastaworld;
55 Vysial St; mains ₹310-500; ☺5-10pm) Pasta lovers should make a pilgrimage to this
casual little Tamil Quarter spot with just a
few check-cloth tables. Run by Italians, sauces are authentically yummy and served over
perfect pasta in an open-plan kitchen as big
as the dining area. No alcohol: it's all about
the food.

Le Club   CONTINENTAL, INDIAN $$$
(☎0413-2227409;   www.leclubraj.com;   38 Dumas
St; mains ₹370-550; ☺11.30am-3pm & 6.30-10pm)
The steaks (with sauces like blue cheese or
Béarnaise), pizzas, pastas and crêpes are all
top-class at this romantically lit garden res-
taurant. Tempting local-themed options in-
clude creole prawn curry, veg-paneer kebabs
and Malabar-style fish. Servings are large,
and there are plenty of wines, mojitos and
margaritas to wash it all down.

🍸 **Drinking & Nightlife**

Although Pondy is one of the better places
in Tamil Nadu to knock back beers, closing
time is a strictly enforced 11pm. Despite low
alcohol taxes, you'll only really find cheap
beer in 'liquor shops' and their darkened
bars. Hotel restaurants and bars make good
drinking spots.

TAMIL NADU PUDUCHERRY (PONDICHERRY)

L'e-Space
BAR

(2 Labourdonnais St; cocktails ₹200, dishes ₹250-350; ⊙5-11pm daily & 10am-3pm Sat & Sun) A quirky little semi-open-air rooftop bar/cafe lounge that's friendly, laid-back and sociable, and which does good cocktails (assuming the bartender hasn't disappeared) and food.

🔒 Shopping

With all the yogis congregating here, Pondy specialises in boutique-chic-meets-Indian-bazaar fashion and souvenirs. There's some beautiful and original stuff, a lot of it produced by Sri Aurobindo Ashram or Auroville. Nehru St and MG Rd are the shopping hot spots; boutiques line the French Quarter.

★ Kalki
FASHION & ACCESSORIES

(134 Mission St; ⊙9.30am-8.30pm) Dazzling, jewel-coloured silk and cotton fashion, as well as accessories, incense, oils, scented candles, handmade-paper trinkets and more, mostly made at Auroville, where there's another branch (visitor centre; ⊙9.30am-6.30pm).

LivingArt Lifestyles
FASHION & ACCESSORIES

(14 Rue Bazar St Laurent; ⊙10am-2pm & 3-8pm Tue-Sat) Breezy, boho-chic, block-printed dresses, skirts, trousers and crop-tops in fun-but-fashionable geometric patterns (all handmade at Auroville) sit side-by-side with beautifully crafted saris from across India.

Anokhi
FASHION & ACCESSORIES

(www.anokhi.com; 1 Caserne St; ⊙10am-7.30pm) A sophisticated Jaipur-born boutique popular for its beautiful, bold block-printed garments with a traditional-turns-modern twist, and gorgeous colourful bedspreads, tablecloths, scarves, bags, homewares and accessories.

Auroshikha
INCENSE

(www.auroshikha.com; 28 Marine St; ⊙9am-1pm & 3-7pm Tue-Sun) An endless array of incense, perfumed candles, essential oils and other scented trinkets, made by Sri Aurobindo Ashram.

Geethanjali
ANTIQUES

(www.geethanjaliartifacts.com; 20 Rue Bussy; ⊙10am-8.30pm Mon-Sat, to 7.30pm Sun) The kind of place where Indiana Jones gets the sweats, this antique shop sells sculptures, carved doors, wooden chests, paintings and furniture sourced from Puducherry's colonial and even precolonial history. It ships to Europe for ₹20,000 per cu metre (check that your purchases aren't subject to export restrictions).

Fabindia
CLOTHING, TEXTILES

(www.fabindia.com; 223 Mission St; ⊙10.30am-8.30pm) 🌐 Going strong since 1960, the Fabindia chain stocks stunning handmade, fair-trade products made by villagers using traditional craft techniques, and promotes rural employment. This branch has wonderful cotton and silk contemporary Indian clothing, along with high-quality fabrics, tablecloths, beauty products and furniture.

La Boutique d'Auroville
FASHION & ACCESSORIES

(www.auroville.com; 38 Nehru St; ⊙9.30am-1pm & 2.30-8pm) Perfect for browsing through Auroville-made crafts: jewellery, pottery, clothing, shawls, handmade cards and herbal toiletries.

Hidesign
FASHION & ACCESSORIES

(www.hidesign.com; 69 Nehru St; ⊙9am-9.30pm) Established in Pondy in 1978, Hidesign sells elegantly made designer leather bags, briefcases, purses, wallets and belts, at reasonable prices, and has outlets across the world.

Focus
BOOKS

(204 Mission St; ⊙9.30am-1.30pm & 3-9pm Mon-Sat) Good collection of India-related and other English-language books (including Lonely Planet guides).

ℹ Information

MEDICAL SERVICES

New Medical Centre (☑0413-2261200; www.nmcpondy.com; 470 Mahatma Gandhi Rd; ⊙24hr) Recommended private clinic and hospital.

TOURIST INFORMATION

Bureau Central (☑0413-2233604; bureau central@sriaurobindoashram.org; Ambour Salai; ⊙6am-noon & 4-6pm) Information on ashram-run accommodation, plus exhibitions on Sri Aurobindo and the Mother.

Tourist office (☑0413-2339497; www.pondy tourism.in; 40 Goubert Ave; ⊙9am-5pm) Has tours on its website. The office itself is pretty useless.

TRAVEL AGENCIES

Parveen Travels (☑0413-2201919; www.parveentravels.com; 288 Maraimalai Adigal Salai; ⊙24hr), near the bus stand, is a reliable option for private buses.

ℹ Getting There & Away

AIR

Puducherry's airport is 6km northwest of the town centre. At the time of research, it was only

BUSES FROM PUDUCHERRY

The **bus stand** (Maraimalai Adigal Salai) is 2km west of the French Quarter, though buses to many major destinations run from Villupuram (₹35, one hour, every 15 minutes), 38km west of Puducherry.

Private bus companies, operating mostly overnight to various destinations, have offices along Maraimalai Adigal Salai west of the bus stand. Parveen Travels is reliable.

DESTINATION	FARE (₹)	TIME (HR)	DEPARTURES
Bengaluru	270	8	10.30am, 7.30pm
Chennai	160 (Volvo AC 300)	4	every 10min; Volvo AC 6 daily
Chidambaram	80	2	every 30min
Kumbakonam	80	3	6.30am, 7.30am, 9.30am
Mamallapuram	72	2	every 10min
Tiruvannamalai	88	3	every 30min

being served by SpiceJet, with one daily flight to/from Bengaluru and another to/from Hyderabad.

TRAIN

Puducherry train station has just a few services. One daily train goes to Chennai Egmore at 5.35am, 2nd class only (₹90, four hours). Leave from Villupuram for many more services. The station has a computerised booking office for trains throughout India.

❶ Getting Around

➡ Pondy's flat streets are great for getting around by foot.

➡ Autorickshaws are plentiful, but drivers often quote absurdly high rates, so prepare to haggle before you get in. A trip from the bus stand to the French Quarter costs ₹100. From Pondy to Auroville costs ₹300.

➡ A good way to explore Pondy and Auroville is by rented bicycle or motorbike from **outlets** (Mission St; per day bicycle ₹100, scooter or motorbike ₹250-400) on northern Mission St, between Nehru and Vysial Sts.

Auroville

☎0413 / POP 2953

Auroville, 'the City of Dawn', is a place that anyone with idealistic leanings will find compelling. It's an international community dedicated to peace, sustainability and 'divine consciousness', where people from across the globe, ignoring creed, colour and nationality, work together to build a universal, cash-free, nonreligious township. Some 12km northwest of Puducherry, Auroville was founded in 1968 by 'the Mother', cofounder of Puducherry's Sri Aurobindo Ashram (p364).

Tucked into the jungle are more than 100 scattered settlements, with about 2500 residents of 52 nationalities – some 60% of Auro-villians are foreign. Visiting offers a glimpse into this self-styled utopia, where you can bliss out on the peaceful setting, the oddly beautiful Matrimandir (p374) and the easygoing friendliness. What's more, you'll find some excellent restaurants and cafes within Auroville and surrounding villages. The community benefits the area with a variety of projects, from schools and IT to organic farming, renewable energy and handicrafts production, employing 4000 to 5000 local villagers – but like most idealistic endeavours, it has a shadow, too, and some outsiders accuse Auroville's inhabitants of self-indulgent escapism.

◉ Sights

Auroville isn't directly geared for tourism – most inhabitants are just busy getting on with their lives – but it does have a good **visitor centre** (☎0413-2622239; www.auroville. org; ⊙9.30am-1pm & 1.30-5pm) with information desks, exhibitions and Auroville products. You can buy a handbook and map (₹20), and watch a 10-minute video. Free passes for external viewing of the Matrimandir (p374), Auroville's 'soul', a 1km woodland walk away, are handed out here.

Visitors are free to wander Auroville's 10-sq-km network of roads and tracks. With two million trees planted since Auroville's foundation, it's a lovely shaded space. It's best explored by bicycle, with rentals available behind the visitor centre for ₹30 per half-day (with a ₹500 deposit).

If you're interested in getting to know Auroville, authorities recommend you stay at least 10 days and join an introduction and orientation program. To get properly involved, you'll need to come as a volunteer for six to 12 months. Contact the **Auroville**

Guest Service (☑0413-2622675; http://guest-service.auroville.org; Solar Kitchen Bldg; ☺9.30am-12.30pm & 2-4pm Mon-Fri, 9.30am-12.30pm Sat) for advice on active participation.

Matrimandir   NOTABLE BUILDING
(☺passes issued 9.30am-1pm & 1.30-4.45pm Mon-Sat, to 1pm Sun) FREE To some, the large, golden, almost spherical Matrimandir (Auroville's focal point), set amid red (cement) lotus petals and surrounded by pristine green parkland, evokes divine consciousness. To others, it looks like a giant golf ball or an alien spaceship. The main inner chamber, lined with white marble, houses a large glass crystal orb that suffuses a beam of sunlight around the space, conducive to deep meditation. To view it from outside, get a free pass from the visitor centre (p373).

If you want to meditate inside, you must reserve one to six days ahead, in person, at Auroville's **Matrimandir Access Office** (☑0413-2622204; mmconcentration@auroville.org. in; visitor centre; ☺10-11am & 2-3pm Wed-Mon).

🛏 Sleeping & Eating

Auroville has more than 80 guesthouses and homestays of hugely varied comfort levels and budgets, from ₹200 dorm beds to ₹5400 two-person cottages with pools.

Guest Accommodation Service (☑0413-2622704; http://guesthouses.auroville.org; visitor centre; ☺9.30am-12.30pm & 2-5pm) offers advice on guesthouses in Auroville, but bookings are direct with each property. It's best to research and book through the website.

Dreamers Cafe   CAFE $
(visitor centre; snacks ₹80-150; ☺8am-8pm) An open-air cafe featuring delicious pastries, sandwiches and other quick bites, along with top-notch coffee.

❶ Getting There & Away

➔ The main turning to Auroville from the East Coast Rd is at Periyar Mudaliarchavadi village,
6km north of Puducherry. From there it's 6km west to the visitor centre.

➔ A one-way autorickshaw to or from Puducherry costs ₹300. Otherwise, rent a bicycle or motorcycle from outlets (p373) on northern Mission St in Puducherry.

CENTRAL TAMIL NADU

Chidambaram

☑04144 / POP 62,150

There's one reason to visit Chidambaram: the great temple complex of Nataraja, Shiva as the Dancer of the Universe. One of the holiest of all Shiva sites, this also happens to be a Dravidian architectural highlight. It's easily visited on a day trip from Puducherry, or en route between Puducherry and Tharangambadi or Kumbakonam.

Most accommodation is near the temple or the bus stand (500m southeast of the temple). The train station is 1km further southeast.

Opposite the bus stand, the busy, friendly **Saradharam** (☑04144-221336; 19 VGP St; r incl breakfast ₹1150, with AC ₹2000-2300; ❄@⊚) is as good as it gets. It's a bit worn but comfortable enough, and a welcome respite from the town-centre frenzy.

◉ Sights

Nataraja Temple   HINDU TEMPLE
(East Car St; ☺inner compound 6am-noon & 4.30-10pm) According to legend, Shiva and Kali got into a dance-off judged by Vishnu. Shiva dropped an earring and picked it up with his foot, a move that Kali could not duplicate, so Shiva won the title Nataraja (Lord of the Dance). It's in this form that endless streams of people come to worship him at this great temple. It was built during Chola times (Chidambaram was a Chola capital), but the main shrines date to at least the 6th century.

BUSES FROM CHIDAMBARAM

DESTINATION	FARE (₹)	TIME (HR)	DEPARTURES
Chennai	300	6	every 30min
Kumbakonam	60	3	hourly
Puducherry	75	2	every 30min
Thanjavur	120	3-4	hourly
Tharangambadi	40	2-3	every 30min

TRAINS FROM CHIDAMBARAM

DESTINATION	FARE (₹)	TIME (HR)	DEPARTURES
Chennai	300	6	every 30min
Kumbakonam	60	3	hourly
Puducherry	75	2	every 30min
Thanjavur	120	3-4	hourly
Tharangambadi	40	2-3	every 30min

The high-walled 22-hectare complex has four towering 12th-century *gopurams* decked out in ornate Dravidian stone and stucco work. The main entrance is through the east (oldest) *gopuram;* the 108 sacred positions of classical Tamil dance are carved in its passageway. To your right through the gopuram are the 1000-pillared 12th-century Raja Sabha (King's Hall; open only festival days), with carved elephants, and the large Sivaganga tank.

You enter the central compound (no cameras) from the east. In its southern part (left from the entrance) is the 13th-century Nritta Sabha (Dance Hall), shaped like a chariot with 56 finely carved pillars. Some say this is the spot where Shiva out-danced Kali.

North of the Nritta Sabha, through a door, you enter the inner courtyard, where most temple rituals are performed. Right in front are the attached hutlike, golden-roofed Kanaka Sabha and Chit Sabha (Wisdom Hall). The Chit Sabha, the innermost sanctum, holds the temple's central bronze image of Nataraja – Shiva the cosmic dancer, ending one cycle of creation, beginning another and uniting all opposites. Shiva's invisible 'space' form is also worshipped here.

At *puja* times devotees crowd into the encircling pavilion to witness rites performed by the temple's hereditary Brahmin priests, the Dikshithars, who shave off some of their hair but grow the rest of it long (thus representing both Shiva and Parvati) and tie it into topknots.

On the south side of the two inner shrines is the Govindaraja Shrine with a reclining Vishnu. Overlooking the tank from the west, the Shivakamasundari Shrine displays fine ochre-and-white 17th-century Nayak ceiling murals.

Priests may offer to guide you around the temple for ₹200 to ₹300. Unusually for Tamil Nadu, this magnificent temple is privately funded and managed, so you may wish to support it by hiring one, but there are no official guides.

❶ Getting There & Away

Government buses depart from the **bus stand** (VGP St). **Universal Travels** (☏044-9842440926; VGP St; ⊙9am-10pm), opposite the bus stand, runs Volvo AC buses to Chennai (₹500, five hours) at 8am and 4.30pm.

Destinations include those listed opposite.

Tharangambadi (Tranquebar)

☏04364 / POP 22,500

South of Chidambaram, the Cauvery River's many-armed delta stretches 180km along the coast and into the hinterland. The Cauvery is the beating heart of Tamil agriculture and its valley was the heartland of the Chola empire. Today the delta is one of Tamil Nadu's prettiest, poorest and most traditional areas.

The tiny seaside town of Tharangambadi, still known as Tranquebar, is easily the most appealing base. A great place to recharge from the crowded towns inland, this quiet former Danish colony is set right on a long sandy beach with delicious sea breezes and fishing boats. Denmark sold it to the British East India Company in 1845.

With its colonial-era buildings, the old part of town inside the 1792 Landporten Gate makes a brilliantly peaceful stroll, and has been significantly restored since the 2004 tsunami, which killed about 800 people here. INTACH Pondicherry (www.intachpondicherry.org) has a good downloadable map.

Notable buildings in town include the 1884 **post office** (Post Office St; ⊙8.30am-6pm Mon-Sat), the 1718 **New Jerusalem Church** (Tamil Evangelical Lutheran Church; King's St; ⊙dawn-dusk) and the tiny **Maritime Museum** (Queen's St; Indian/foreigner ₹5/50; ⊙9.30am-2pm & 2.30-5pm, hours vary), with a display on the 2004 tsunami. The peach-hued seafront **Dansborg fort** (Parade Ground, King's St; Indian/foreigner ₹5/50, camera/video

₹30/100; ◷10am-5.45pm Sat-Thu) dates from 1624 and was occupied by the British in 1801. In its prime, it was the world's second-largest Danish castle.

🛏 Sleeping & Eating

Nippon Palace　　　　　　　　HOTEL $
(📞9344440088; East Coast Rd; d ₹980-1200, with AC₹1500-1700; @🛜) This newcomer is efficiently run by a manager fluent in English and helpful staff. Rooms are spacious and clean, delivering solid value. It's on the main road, about 300m from the bus stand.

★Bungalow on the Beach　　　　HERITAGE HOTEL $$$
(📞04364-289036; www.neemranahotels.com; 24 King's St; r incl breakfast ₹8260-11,520; ❋🛜❋) Most Tranquebar accommodation is run by the sea-front Bungalow on the Beach, in the exquisitely restored 17th-century former residence of the British administrator. There are 17 beautiful old-world rooms in the main building and two other heritage locations in town. The main block has a cute multi-cuisine **restaurant** (📞04364-289036; mains ₹250-550; ◷7.30-9.30am, 12-3pm & 7.30-9.30pm), a dreamy swimming pool and a fantastic wraparound terrace. Book ahead.

❶ Getting There & Away

Buses in this region get incredibly crowded. Tharangambadi has regular connections with Chidambaram (₹75, two hours, hourly) and Karaikal (₹16, 30 minutes, half-hourly). From Karaikal buses go to Kumbakonam (₹55, two hours, half-hourly), Thanjavur (₹75, three hours, every hour) and Puducherry (₹115, four hours, half-hourly).

Kumbakonam

📞0435 / POP 170,000

At first glance Kumbakonam is just another chaotic Indian junction town, but then you notice the dozens of colourful *gopurams* pointing skyward from its 18 temples – a reminder that this was once a seat of medieval South Indian power. With another two magnificent World Heritage–listed Chola temples nearby, it's worth staying the night.

◉ Sights

Nageshwara Temple　　　　HINDU TEMPLE
(Nageswaran Koil St; ◷6.30am-12.30pm & 4-8.30pm) Founded by the Cholas in 886, this is Kumbakonam's oldest temple, dedicated to

Shiva as Nagaraja, the serpent king. On three days of the year (in April or May) the sun's rays fall on the lingam. The elevated Nataraja shrine on the right in front of the inner sanctum is fashioned, in typical Chola style, like a horse-drawn chariot; colourful modern elephants stand beside it.

Kumbeshwara Temple　　　　HINDU TEMPLE
(off Kumbeswarar East St; ◷6.30am-12.30pm & 4-8.30pm) Kumbeshwara Temple, entered via a nine-storey *gopuram*, a small bazaar and a long porticoed *mandapa*, is Kumbakonam's biggest Shiva temple. It dates from the 17th and 18th centuries and contains a lingam said to have been made by Shiva himself when he mixed the nectar of immortality with sand.

Mahamaham Tank　　　　RELIGIOUS SITE
(LBS Rd) Surrounded by 16 pavilions, the huge Mahamaham Tank is one of Kumbakonam's most sacred sites. It's believed that every 12 years the waters of India's holiest rivers, including the Ganges, flow into it, and at this time a festival is held (next due: 2028). On the tank's north side, the **Kashivishvanatha Temple** (LBS Rd; ◷6.30am-12.30pm & 4-8.30pm) contains an intriguing trio of river goddesses, the central of which embodies the Cauvery River.

Sarangapani Temple　　　　HINDU TEMPLE
(Sarangapani Koil Sannadhi St; ◷6.30am-12.30pm & 4-8.30pm) Sarangapani is Kumbakonam's largest Vishnu temple, with a 45m-high eastern *gopuram* embellished with low-level dancing panels as its main entrance. Past the temple cowshed (Krishna the cowherd is one of Vishnu's forms), another *gopuram* and a pillared hall, you reach the inner sanctuary, a 12th-century Chola creation styled like a chariot with big carved elephants, horses and wheels. Photography is not permitted inside.

Ramaswami Temple　　　　HINDU TEMPLE
(Sarangapani 5th St; ◷6.30am-12.30pm & 4-8.30pm) Dating back to 1620, this temple at the southernmost end of Kumbakonam's main bazaar street has beautiful Nayak horse and *yali* carvings and fine frescoes.

🛏 Sleeping & Eating

Hotel Metro　　　　HOTEL $
(📞0435-2403377; www.thehotelmetro.com; 19/11 Sarangapani Koil Sannadhi St; r ₹1300-1900; ❋🛜🛜) Comfortable modern rooms with good beds make this the best value in Kumbakonam,

CHOLA TEMPLES NEAR KUMBAKONAM

Two of the three great monuments of Chola civilisation stand in villages just outside Kumbakonam: Darasuram's Airavatesvara Temple and the Gangaikondacholapuram Temple. Unlike the also World Heritage–listed Brihadishwara Temple (p379) at Thanjavur, today these two temples receive relatively few worshippers (and visitors). They are wonderful both for their overall form (with pyramidal towers rising at the heart of rectangular walled compounds) and for the exquisite detail of their carved, unpainted stone.

Three kilometres west of Kumbakonam, the late-Chola Shiva **Airavatesvara Temple** (Darasuram; ⊘6am-8pm, inner shrine 6am-1pm & 4-8pm) was constructed by Raja Raja II (1146–73). The steps of Rajagambhira Hall are carved with vivid elephants and horses pulling chariots. This pavilion's 108 pillars, each unique, have marvellously detailed carvings, including dancers, acrobats and the five-in-one beast *yali* (elephant's head, lion's body, goat's horns, pig's ears and cow's backside). Inside the **main shrine** (flanked by guardians), you can honour the central lingam and get a *tilak* (auspicious forehead mark) for ₹10. On the outside of the shrine are several fine carved images of Shiva. Four *mandapas* frame the corners of the courtyardlike complex.

The temple at **Gangaikondacholapuram** (Brihadishwara Temple; ⊘6am-noon & 4-8pm) – 'City of the Chola who Conquered the Ganges' – 35km north of Kumbakonam, is dedicated to Shiva. It was built by Rajendra I in the 11th century when he moved the Chola capital here from Thanjavur, and has many similarities to Thanjavur's earlier Brihadishwara Temple. Its beautiful 49m-tall tower, however, has a slightly concave curve, making it the 'feminine' counterpart to the mildly convex Thanjavur one. Artistic highlights are the wonderfully graceful sculptures around the tower's exterior.

A massive Nandi (Shiva's vehicle) faces the temple from the tranquil surrounding gardens; a lion stands guard nearby. The main shrine, beneath the tower, contains a huge lingam and is approached through a long 17th-century hall. The fine carvings on the tower's exterior include: Shiva as the beggar Bhikshatana, immediately left of the southern steps; Ardhanarishvara (Shiva as half-man, half-woman) and Shiva as Nataraja, on the south side; Shiva with Ganga, Shiva emerging from the lingam, and Vishnu with Lakshmi and Bhudevi (the southernmost three images on the west side); and Shiva with Parvati (the northernmost image on the west side). Most famous is the masterful panel of Shiva garlanding the head of his follower, Chandesvara, beside the northern steps.

Most travellers visit the temples as a day trip from Kumbakonam. From Kumbakonam bus stand (p378), buses to Gangaikondacholapuram (₹20, 1½ hours) run every 30 minutes. Returning, it can be quicker to catch a bus to Jayamkondan and transfer to Kumbakonam there. A half-day car trip to both temples, through Kumbakonam's reliable Hotel Raya's, costs ₹2400 (₹2700 with AC).

especially since discounts are offered if it isn't fully booked.

Hotel Raya's HOTEL $$
(☏0435-2423170; www.hotelrayas.com; 18 Head Post Office Rd; r ₹1290, with AC ₹1515-1960; ❄) The Swiss-army knife of Kumbakonam hotels, Raya's has something for almost everyone, and can be busy. Service is friendly, but the lower-class rooms feel like they've been too neglected for too long. The **Hotel Raya's Annexe** (☏0435-2423270; 19 Head Post Office Rd; r ₹1850; ❄🛜) has the best, brightest rooms, but look at a few before settling on one if you can. The hotel's restaurant

Sathars Restaurant (☏0435-2423170; mains ₹140-240; ⊘11.30am-11.30pm) is popular for its veg and nonveg fare.

★**Mantra Koodam** RESORT $$$
(☏0435-2462621; www.cghearth.com; 1 Bagavathapuram Main Rd Extension, Srisailapathipuram Village; incl breakfast s ₹8500-9720, d ₹9720-10,940; ❄🛜⊠) 🌱 Lost in the riverside jungle, 10km northeast of Kumbakonam, this is a wonderful retreat from temple town chaos. Comfy modern-rustic, Chettiar-style cottages are fronted by porches with rocking chairs, and have open-air showers and carved-teak doors. Cooking classes and trips

Kumbakonam

Kumbakonam

◎ Sights
1 Kashivishvanatha Temple C2
2 Kumbeshwara Temple.........................A2
3 Mahamaham Tank.................................C2
4 Nageshwara Temple B1
5 Ramaswami Temple..............................B2
6 Sarangapani Temple B1

🛏 Sleeping
7 Hotel Metro..B1
8 Hotel Raya's..C2
9 Hotel Raya's Annexe C2

🍴 Eating
Sathars Restaurant ....(see 8)

to local silk weavers, traditional fabric painters and wax-casting sculptors are offered. The exquisite restaurant is Indian gourmet.

ⓘ Getting There & Away

BUS
Government buses depart from the **bus stand** (60 Feet Rd).

TRAIN
Five daily trains head to Thanjavur (2nd class/3AC/2AC ₹45/495/700, 30 minutes to one hour) and four to Trichy (₹60/495/700, 1½ to 2½ hours). Five daily trains to/from Chennai Egmore include the overnight Chennai Express/Train 16852 (sleeper/3AC/2AC/1AC ₹210/560/800/1335, 6½ hours) and the daytime Chennai Express/Train 16796 (₹210/555/795/1325, six to seven hours).

Thanjavur (Tanjore)
☎ 04362 / POP 500,000

Here are the ochre foundation blocks of perhaps the most remarkable civilisation of Dravidian history, one of the few kingdoms to expand Hinduism beyond India, a bedrock for aesthetic styles that spread from Madurai to the Mekong. A dizzying historical legacy was forged from Thanjavur, capital of the great Chola empire during its heyday. Today Thanjavur is a crowded, hectic, modern Indian town – but the past is still very much present. Every day thousands of people worship at the Cholas' grand Brihadishwara Temple, and the city's labyrinthine royal palace preserves memories of other, later powerful dynasties.

BUSES FROM KUMBAKONAM

DESTINATION	FARE (₹)	TIME (HR)	DEPARTURES
Chennai (AC)	300	8	1.50pm
Chidambaram	50	2½-3	every 30min
Karaikal	40	2¼	every 15min
Thanjavur (Tanjore)	30	2	every 5min
Trichy (Tiruchirappalli)	60	4	every 5min

⊙ Sights

★ **Brihadishwara Temple**   HINDU TEMPLE
(Big Temple; Big Temple St; ⊙6am-8.30pm, central shrine 8.30am-12.30pm & 4-8.30pm) Come here twice: in the morning, when the honey-hued granite begins to assert its dominance over the white dawn sunshine, and in the evening, when the rocks capture a hot palette of reds, oranges, yellows and pinks on the crowning glory of Chola temple architecture. The World Heritage–listed Brihadishwara Temple was built between 1003 and 1010 by Raja Raja I ('king of kings'). The outer fortifications were put up by Thanjavur's later Nayak and British regimes.

You enter through a Maratha-era gate, followed by two original *gopurams* with elaborate stucco sculptures. You might find the temple elephant under one of the *gopurams*. Several shrines are dotted around the extensive grassy areas of the walled temple compound, including one of India's largest statues of Nandi (Shiva's sacred bull), facing the main temple building. Cut from a single rock and framed by slim pillars, this 16th-century Nayak creation is 6m long. Don't miss the sublime sculptures at the shrine dedicated to Lakshmi, to the right of Nandi when entering the complex.

A long, columned assembly hall leads to the central shrine with its 4m-high Shiva lingam, beneath the superb 61m-high *vimana* (tower). The assembly hall's southern steps are flanked by two huge *dwarpals* (temple guardians). Many graceful deity images stand in niches around the *vimana's* lower outer levels, including Shiva emerging from the lingam (beside the southern steps); Shiva as the beggar Bhikshatana (first image, south side); Shiva as Nataraja, the cosmic dancer (west end of south wall); Harihara (half Shiva, half Vishnu) on the west wall; and Ardhanarishvara (Shiva as half-man, half-woman), leaning on Nandi, on the north side. Between the deity images are panels showing classical dance poses. On the *vimana's* upper east side is a later Maratha-period Shiva within three arches.

The compound also contains an interpretation centre along the south wall and, in the colonnade along the west and north walls, hundreds more linga. Both west and north walls are lined with exquisite lime-plaster Chola frescoes, for years buried under later Nayak-era murals. North of the temple compound, but still within the outer fortifications, are the 18th-century neoclassical

Schwartz's Church (off Big Temple St; ⊙dawn-dusk) and a park containing the **Sivaganga tank** (off Big Temple St; ₹5, camera/video ₹10/25; ⊙dawn-dusk).

Official guides can be hired at the tourist information booth just outside the temple for 90-minute tours (₹500).

★ **Royal Palace**   PALACE
(East Main St; Indian/foreigner ₹50/200, camera ₹30/100; ⊙9am-1pm & 1.30-5.30pm, art gallery 9.30am-1pm & 2-5pm) Thanjavur's royal palace is a mixed bag of ruin and renovation, superb art and random royal paraphernalia. The mazelike complex was constructed partly by the Nayaks who took over Thanjavur in 1535, and partly by a local Maratha dynasty that ruled from 1676 to 1855. The two don't-miss sections are the Saraswati Mahal Library Museum and the Art Gallery.

Seven different sections of the palace can be visited. 'Full' tickets include the Art Gallery and Saraswati Mahal Library Museum, along with the Mahratta Dharbar Hall, bell tower and Saarjah Madi; other sections require extra tickets. The main entrance is from the north, off East Main St. On the way in you'll come to the main ticket office, followed by the Maratha Palace complex.

Past the ticket office, a passage to the left leads to: first, the **Royal Palace Museum** (₹2), a small miscellany of sculptures, weaponry, elephant bells and rajas' headgear; second, the **Maharaja Serfoji Memorial Hall** (₹4), commemorating the enlightened Maratha scholar-king Serfoji II (1798–1832), with a better collection overlooking a once-splendid, now crumbling courtyard; and third, the **Mahratta Dharbar Hall** (⊙10am-5pm), where Maratha rulers gave audience in a grand but faded pavilion adorned with colourful murals (including their own portraits behind the dais) and sturdy pillars topped by arches filled with gods.

Exiting the passage, the fabulous Saraswati Mahal Library Museum is on your left, through a vibrant entranceway. Perhaps Serfoji II's greatest contribution to posterity, this is testimony both to the 19th-century obsession with knowledge accumulation and to an eclectic mind that collected prints of Chinese torture methods, Audubon-style paintings of Indian flora and fauna, world atlases, dictionaries and rare medieval books. Serfoji amassed more than 65,000 books and 50,000 palm-leaf paper manuscripts in Indian and European languages, though most aren't displayed. Hourly **audiovisual**

Thanjavur (Tanjore)

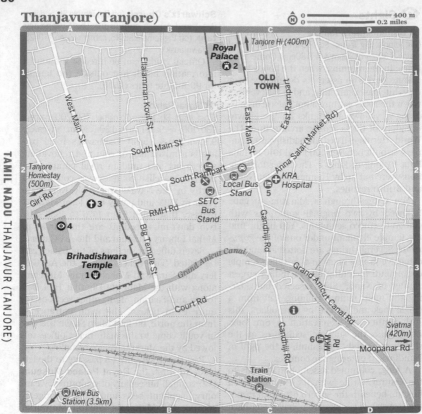

displays (⊙10.30am-4.30pm), highlight Thanjavur's sights, history and traditions in the attached cinema room.

Leaving the library, turn left for the Art Gallery, set around the Nayak Palace courtyard behind the bell tower. It contains a collection of stone carvings and superb, mainly Chola, bronzes, including some fabulous Natarajas in the New Visitors Hall; its main room, the 1600 Nayak Durbar Hall, has a statue of Serfoji II. From the courtyard, steps lead part of the way up a large *gopuram*-like tower to a whale skeleton that washed up in Tharangambadi.

The renovated Saarjah Madi is best admired from East Main Rd for its ornate balconies.

🛏 Sleeping

It's well worth staying in Thanjavur to see the 'Big' Temple at sunset. Central Thanjavur has a bunch of nondescript, cheap lodges opposite the SETC and local bus stands, a couple of decent midrange hotels, and a fabulous heritage option.

Kasi Inn   HOTEL $
(☎04362-231908; 1493 South Rampart Rd; s ₹1000, d₹1120-1650) Thanjavur's best value in the town centre has smallish but well-kept rooms with good mattresses and (sometimes) wi-fi. Plus, it's kitty-corner to an ice-cream shop!

Hotel Valli   HOTEL $
(☎04362-231584; 2948 MKM Rd; s/d ₹610/770, r with AC from ₹1090; ❄🛜) Near the train station, green-painted Valli offers no-frills, spick-and-span rooms, friendly staff and a basic restaurant. It's in a reasonably peaceful leafy spot beyond a bunch of greasy backstreet workshops and a booze shop.

Tanjore Homestay   HOMESTAY $$
(☎9443157667; www.tanjorehomestay.blogspot.in; 64A Giri Rd, Srinivasa Puram; s/d incl breakfast ₹1800/2300; @🛜) Under the watch of a wel-

Thanjavur (Tanjore)

◎ **Top Sights**
1 Brihadishwara Temple........................A3
2 Royal Palace C1

◎ **Sights**
3 Schwartz's Church A2
4 Sivaganga Tank....................................A3

🛏 **Sleeping**
5 Hotel Gnanam C2
6 Hotel Valli..D4
7 Kasi Inn...B2

✕ **Eating**
Diana..(see 5)
8 Jigarthanda..B2
Sahana..(see 5)

coming Indian couple who serve tasty home-cooked meals, this low-key homestay offers four simple rooms with splashes of art. Breakfast is served in the pretty back garden and there's a rooftop terrace, plus hot water, air-con and wi-fi. It's in a residential area, 1.5km west of Thanjavur's main temple; no sign.

Hotel Gnanam HOTEL $$
(✆04362-278501; www.hotelgnanam.com; Anna Salai; s/d incl breakfast ₹2700/3200; ❇🛜) One of the better values in town, the Gnanam has comfy, stylish rooms (some with balconies), with marble floors and polka-dot curtains. It's perfect for anyone needing modern amenities in Thanjavur's geographical centre. Its **Diana** (✆04362-278501; mains ₹125-350; ⊙11.30am-3.30pm & 6.30-10.30pm) and **Sahana** (✆04362-278501; mains ₹120-185; ⊙7am-10.30pm) restaurants are both good. Book ahead.

★ **Svatma** HERITAGE HOTEL $$$
(✆04362-273222; www.svatma.in; 4/1116 Blake Higher Secondary School Rd, Maharnonbu Chavadi; r incl breakfast ₹13,440-22,400; ❇🛜🏊) This gorgeous boutique-heritage hotel has an elegant, uncluttered look inspired by and incorporating traditional local arts and crafts. Of the 38 rooms, those in the revamped heritage wing have the most character. Enjoy the dance shows, cooking classes, bronze-casting demonstrations – plus a spa and heavenly pool. It's 1.5km southeast of central Thanjavur.

Tanjore Hi BOUTIQUE HOTEL $$$
(✆9487810301, 04362-252111; www.dunewellness group.com; 464 East Main St; r ₹4720; ❇🛜) ✏ Just north of Thanjavur's palace, Tanjore Hi is a century-old, ecofriendly house refurbished with strikingly contemporary flair. Bold modern decor is all about deep blues, fresh whites, warm woods, wall murals and wildly illuminated ceilings. A staircase spirals up to the good, organic-fuelled, Indian-international rooftop restaurant.

✕ **Eating**

Jigarthanda ICE CREAM $
(South Rampart Rd; scoops ₹30; ⊙9.30am-10.30pm) Cool off here with the best ice cream in town – it's 'homemade in a factory', according to the workers.

Tanjore Hi MULTICUISINE $$
(✆04362-252111; www.duneecogroup.com; 464 East Main St; mains ₹210-325; ⊙7.30-10am, 12.30-2.30pm & 7.30-10pm) ✏ On a boutique-hotel rooftop, this industrial-chic restaurant is a welcome surprise in traditional Thanjavur. The world-wandering menu is fuelled by fresh, organic ingredients grown at the hotel's sister property in Kodaikanal. Dine at terrace tables outside or in the glassed-in air-con room.

Ideal River View Resort MULTICUISINE $$
(✆04362-250533; www.idealresort.com; Vennar Bank, Palliagraharam; mains ₹200-450; ⊙7-9.30am, 12.30-2.30pm & 7.30-9.30pm) The good, semi-open-air Indian/Sri Lankan/Chinese restaurant at the jungle-fringed **Ideal River View Resort** (✆04362-250533; s/d incl breakfast ₹6500/7080; ❇🛜🏊) overlooks the river.

ℹ **Information**

Tourist office (✆04362-230984; Hotel Tamil Nadu, Gandhiji Rd; ⊙10am-5.45pm Mon-Fri) One of Tamil Nadu's more helpful offices.

ℹ **Getting There & Away**

BUS
The downtown **SETC Bus Stand** (RMH Rd) has hourly express buses to Chennai (₹420, 8¼ hours) from 7.30am to 12.30pm and 8pm to 11pm. Buses for most other cities leave from the **New Bus Station** (Trichy Main Rd), 5km southwest of the centre. Many arriving buses will drop you off in the city centre on the way out there. Services from the New Bus Station include: Chidambaram (₹100, four hours, hourly), Kumbakonam (₹40, 1½ hours, every five minutes),

TAMIL NADU THANJAVUR (TANJORE)

Madurai (₹130, four hours, every 15 minutes) and Trichy (Tiruchirappalli; ₹43, 1½ hours, every five minutes)

TRAIN
The train station is at the southern end of Gandhiji Rd.

Chennai Four daily trains head to Chennai Egmore (seven hours) including the 11.20pm Chennai Express – train 16852 (sleeper/3AC/2AC/1AC ₹225/605/865/1450).

Kumbakonam Twelve daily trains – five with reserved seating (sleeper/3AC/2AC ₹45/495/700, 30 minutes to 1¼ hours).

Madurai Seventeen services per day (sleeper/3AC/2AC ₹160/495/700, four to five hours).

Trichy Nineteen daily trains – six have reserved seating (2nd class/3AC/2AC ₹45/495/700, 1½ hours), 13 are unreserved (₹15).

ⓘ Getting Around

Bus 74 (₹10) shuttles between the New Bus Station and the central **local bus stand** (South Rampart); autorickshaws cost ₹120.

Trichy (Tiruchirappalli)

📞 0431 / POP 847,390

Welcome to (more or less) the geographical centre of Tamil Nadu. Tiruchirappalli, universally called Trichy or Tiruchi, isn't just a travel junction: it also mixes up a heaving bazaar with some major temples. It's a huge, crowded, busy city, and the fact that most hotels are clumped together around the big bus station isn't exactly a plus point. But Trichy has a strong character and long history, and a way of overturning first impressions.

Trichy may have been a capital of the early Cholas in the 3rd century BC. It passed through the hands of the Pallavas, medieval Cholas, Pandyas, Delhi Sultanate and Vijayanagars before the Madurai Nayaks brought it to prominence, making it a capital in the 17th century and building its famous Rock Fort Temple (p383). Under British control, it became an important railway hub known as Trichinopoly.

⊙ Sights

★ Sri Ranganathaswamy Temple

HINDU TEMPLE

(Map p383; Srirangam; camera/video ₹50/100; ⊙6am-9.30pm) So large it feels like a self-enclosed city, Sri Ranganathaswamy is quite possibly India's biggest temple. It has 49 separate Vishnu shrines, and reaching the inner sanctum from the south, as most worshippers do, requires passing through seven *gopurams*. The first (southernmost), the **Rajagopuram** (Map p383), was added in 1987, and is one of Asia's tallest temple towers at 73m high. Non-Hindus cannot pass the sixth *gopuram* so won't see the innermost sanctum, where Vishnu as Ranganatha reclines on a five-headed snake.

You pass through streets with shops, restaurants, motorbikes and cars until you reach the temple proper at the fourth *gopuram*. Inside on the left is an information counter selling tickets for the **roof viewpoint** (₹20), which affords semipanoramic views. Take no notice of would-be guides who spin stories to get hired. Also here, in the southwest corner, is the beautiful 16th-century Venugopal Shrine, adorned with superbly detailed Nayak-era carvings of preening *gopis* (milkmaids) and the flute-playing Krishna (Vishnu's eighth incarnation).

Turn right just before the fifth *gopuram* for the small **Art Museum** (Map p383; ₹5; ⊙9am-1pm & 2-6pm), displaying fine bronzes, tusks of bygone temple elephants, and a collection of exquisite 17th-century Nayak ivory figurines depicting gods, demons, and kings and queens (some in erotic poses). Continue left past the museum to the Sesha Mandapa, a 16th-century pillared hall with magnificently detailed monolithic Vijayanagar carvings of rearing battle horses and Vishnu's 10 incarnations sculpted on pillars. Immediately north is the 1000-pillared hall, whose recently unearthed lower base is carved into dance positions.

Inside the fifth gopuram is the Garuda Mandapa, containing an enormous shrine to Vishnu's man-eagle assistant, posed in semiseated position to show that he's ever-ready to leap up and go to Vishnu the moment he is called to fly the god somewhere. Note, too, four remarkable sculptures of Nayak donors (with daggers on the hip).

Take bus 1 to/from the Central Bus Station or the Rock Fort stops just south of the Rajagopuram.

Sri Jambukeshwara Temple

HINDU TEMPLE

(Tiruvanakoil, Srirangam; ⊙5am-8pm) Of Tamil Nadu's five Shiva elemental temples, Sri Jambukeshwara is dedicated to Shiva, Parvati and the medium of water. The liquid theme is realised in the central shrine (closed to non-Hindus), whose Shiva lingam reputedly issues a nonstop trickle of water. In the north part of the complex is a shrine dedicated to Akilandeswari, Jambukeshwara's consort. A

Trichy (Tiruchirappalli)

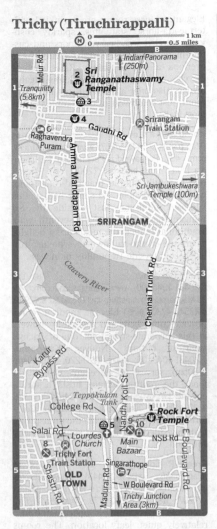

Trichy (Tiruchirappalli)

⊙ **Top Sights**
1 Rock Fort Temple B4
2 Sri Ranganathaswamy Temple A1

⊙ **Sights**
3 Art Museum.. A1
4 Rajagopuram.. A1
5 St Joseph's College Museum..............A5

🛏 **Sleeping**
6 Home with a View A2
7 Hotel Royal Sathyam..........................B5

🍴 **Eating**
8 DiMora..A5
9 Vasanta Bhavan B5

🛍 **Shopping**
10 Saratha's..B5

strategic use of the naturally fortified position. Reaching the top requires climbing over 400 stone-cut steps.

From NSB Rd on the south side, you pass between small shops and cross a street before entering the temple precinct itself, where there's a shoe stand. You might meet the temple elephant here. Then it's 180 steps up to the Thayumanaswamy Temple, the rock's biggest temple, on the left (closed to non-Hindus); a gold-topped tower rises over its sanctum. Further up, you pass the 6th-century Pallava upper cave temple on the left (usually railed off); on the left inside is a famous Gangadhara panel showing Shiva restraining the Ganges with a single strand of his hair. From here it's another 183 steps to the summit's small Uchipillaiyar Temple, dedicated to Ganesh. The views are wonderful, with eagles wheeling beneath and Trichy sprawling all around.

Back at the bottom, check out the 8th-century Pandya lower rock-cut cave temple, with particularly fine pillars (turn right as you exit the temple precinct, past five or six houses, then right again down a small lane).

The stone steps get scorching-hot in the midday sun and it's a barefoot climb, so time your visit carefully.

good time to visit is around noon, when the temple elephant is involved in a procession between the two shrines.

If you're taking bus 1, ask for 'Tiruvanakoil'; the temple is 350m east of the main road.

⭐ **Rock Fort Temple**   HINDU TEMPLE
(Map p383; NSB Rd; camera/video ₹5/20; ⊙6am-8pm) The Rock Fort Temple, perched 83m high on a massive outcrop, lords over Trichy with stony arrogance. The ancient rock was first hewn by the Pallavas and Pandyas, who cut small cave temples on its south side, but it was the war-savvy Nayaks who later made

Railway Museum   MUSEUM
(Map p386; Bharatiyar Salai; adult/child ₹10/5, camera/video ₹20/40; ⊙9.30am-5.30pm Tue-Sun) Trichy's Railway Museum is a fascinating jumble of disused train-related equipment (phones, clocks, control boards), British-era railway construction photos, old train-line

maps (including a 1935 pre-Independence Indian Railway map) – and even modern-day London Underground tickets. It's 500m east of Trichy Junction.

St Joseph's College Museum
MUSEUM

(Map p383; College Rd; ☺10am-noon & 2-4pm Mon-Sat) FREE In the cool, green campus next to Lourdes Church, this dusty museum contains the creepy natural history collections of the Jesuit priests' Western Ghats excursions of the 1870s. Ask for access at reception on the left as you approach the museum. It was being renovated at the time of research.

St John's Church
CHURCH

(Map p386; off Rockins Rd; ☺dawn-dusk, hours vary) Adorned with original-period shuttered doors, elegant – and very white – St John's Church dates from the early 19th century.

Lourdes Church
CHURCH

(Map p383; College Rd; ☺6am-8.30pm) The hush of this 19th-century neo-Gothic church makes an interesting contrast to Trichy's frenetic Hindu temples. Note the cakelike pink-accented arches and the rose window at the eastern end.

🛏 Sleeping

Hotel Abbirami
HOTEL $

(Map p386; ☎0431-2415001; 10 McDonald's Rd; r ₹750-850, with AC ₹1345-2360; ❈❞) Despite the ground-floor bustle, this is the best deal in town. Even the cheapest AC rooms are appealing, with light wood, colourful glass panels and decent mattresses. Non-AC rooms are a bit worn, but still well kept.

Ashby Hotel
HOTEL $

(Map p386; ☎0431-2460652; 17A Rockins Rd; s ₹650-900, d ₹750-950, with AC s ₹1120-1350, d ₹1680-1900; ❈) On the street between the train station and the Central Bus Station, this long-running budget spot greets you with elephant murals on its facade. Rooms are clearly due for some upgrades but are clean enough, though those with AC are overpriced. All are set around a shady, surprisingly quiet courtyard that manages to be almost charming.

Tranquility
GUESTHOUSE $$

(☎9443157667; www.tranquilitytrichy.com; Anakkarai, Melur, Srirangam; s/d incl breakfast ₹3200/4000; ❈❞) This charming rustic-chic guesthouse sits in a gloriously rural setting 6km west of Sri Ranganathaswamy Temple.

Elegant, unfussy rooms are sprinkled with terracotta-horse statuettes, sparkly cushions, recycled wood-carved doors and custom-made furniture. Terrace swing-chairs overlook a sea of palms. Rates include bicycles and transfers. The knowledgable owners also offer a thatched-roof homestay room just southwest of the temple's outermost wall.

Home with a View
HOMESTAY $$

(Map p383; ☎9443157667; www.tranquilitytrichy.com; 43C Raghavendra Puram, opp Raghavendra Mutt; r incl breakfast ₹2000; ❞) There's one tastefully simple thatched-roof room, with both a double and single bed, at this laid-back homestay just outside the Sri Ranganathaswamy Temple's seventh wall. Traditional homemade meals are a delight, as are the on-the-ball owners, who also run lovely countryside Tranquility, 6km west.

Grand Gardenia
HOTEL $$

(☎0431-4045000; www.grandgardenia.com; 22-25 Mannarpuram Junction; incl breakfast s ₹2950, d ₹3540-4720; ❈❞) Elegant, modern rooms provide comfy beds and glassed-in showers at this corporate-style hotel, one of Trichy's smartest options. Nonveg **Kannappa** (☎0431-4045000; mains ₹120-220; ☺11.30am-11.30pm) serves up excellent Chettinadu food; the rooftop terrace hosts a multicuisine **restaurant** (☎0431-4045000; mains ₹120-240; ☺11.30am-3.30pm & 7-11pm). Comfort and amenities outweigh the uninspiring highway-side location, 1km south of Trichy Junction.

Breeze Residency
HOTEL $$

(Map p386; ☎0431-2414414; www.breezeresidency.com; 3/14 McDonald's Rd; incl breakfast s ₹2075-3185, d ₹2250-3775; ❈@❞❈) The Breeze is huge, aiming at upscale and in a relatively quiet, leafy location. The rooms are clean and comfortable, but feel institutional, with nothing special about them. Facilities include a gym, the buffet-only **Madras Restaurant** (Map p386; ☎0431-4045333; lunch/dinner buffet from ₹350/450; ☺noon-3pm & 7.30-11pm; ❈), a 24-hour coffee shop and a bizarre American Wild West–themed bar.

Ramyas Hotel
HOTEL $$

(Map p386; ☎0431-2414646; www.ramyas.com; 13D/2 Williams Rd; incl breakfast s ₹2100-3250, d ₹2575-3850; ❈@❞) Good service and facilities, plus comfortable rooms in shades of white, brown and copper, make this business-oriented hotel excellent value, though 'business-class' rooms are ironically small. Turquoise-clad **Meridian** (Map p386; 0431-2414646; mains ₹130-250; ⊙noon-3.30pm & 7-11.30pm) does tasty multicuisine fare, breakfast is a nice buffet and the breezy **Thendral** (Map p386; 0431-2414646; mains ₹140-250; ⊙7-10.30pm) roof-garden restaurant is brilliant.

Hotel Royal Sathyam   HOTEL $$
(Map p383; 0431-4011414; www.sathyamgroup hotels.in; 42A Singarathope; incl breakfast s/d ₹1700/2000; ❄❀❀) The best option if you want to be close to the temple and market action. Rooms are small but smart enough, with a fresh wood-and-whitewash theme, and service is friendly.

✗ Eating

Shri Sangeetas   INDIAN $
(Map p386; www.shrisangeetas.com; 2 VOC Rd; mains ₹95-130, thalis ₹85-150; ⊙6am-12.30am) Don't let the behind-the-bus-station address put you off. Super-popular Sangeetas has tables in a buzzing, fairy-lit courtyard (or inside in air-con comfort) and a tantalising menu of pure-veg North and South Indian favourites – everything from *idli* and dosa to samosas, thalis and paneer tikka.

Vasanta Bhavan   INDIAN $
(Map p383; 3 NSB Rd; mains ₹95-125, thalis ₹80-150; ⊙6am-11pm) A great spot for a meal with views, near the Rock Fort. Tables on the outer gallery overlook the Teppakulam Tank, or there's an air-con hall. It's good for both North Indian veg food (of the paneer and naan genre) and South Indian. People

crowd in for lunchtime thalis. There's another **branch** (Map p386; Rockins Rd; mains ₹95-125, thalis ₹80-150; ⊙6am-11pm) in the Cantonment.

DiMora   MULTICUISINE $$
(Map p383; 0431-4040056; www.dimora.co.in; 4th fl, Ambigai City Center, B29-30 Shastri Rd; mains ₹165-455; ⊙noon-3.30pm & 7-11pm; ❀) Waiters in all-black take orders on mobile phones to a chart-toppers soundtrack that makes this smart, busy top-floor restaurant feel more Chennai than Trichy. The menu roams all over the world, but it's good for pastas, wood-fired pizzas, stir-fries and fresh juices, as well as tandoori and other Indian dishes.

🛍 Shopping

Saratha's   CLOTHING
(Map p383; 45 NSB Rd; ⊙9am-9.30pm) Bursting with clothing of every conceivable kind and colour, Saratha's claims to be (and might well be) the 'largest textile showroom in India'.

ℹ Information

Indian Panorama (0431-4226122; www.indianpanorama.in; 5 Annai Ave, Srirangam; ⊙10am-6pm) Trichy-based and covering all of India, this professional, reliable travel agency/tour operator is run by an Indian–New Zealander couple.

Tourist Office (Map p386; 0431-2460136; Williams Rd; ⊙10am-5.45pm Mon-Fri)

ℹ Getting There & Away

Trichy is virtually in the geographical centre of Tamil Nadu and is well connected by air, bus and train.

GOVERNMENT BUSES FROM TRICHY

DESTINATION	FARE (₹)	TIME (HR)	DEPARTURES
Bengaluru (Bangalore)	450 (A)	8	20 UD daily
Chennai	245/340/460 (B)	6-7	15 UD, 2 AC daily
Coimbatore	215 (C)	4½-6	every 10min
Kodaikanal	400 (C)	5½	midnight
Madurai	120 (C)	2½	every 15min
Ooty	430 (A)	8½	UD 10.15pm
Rameswaram	185 (C)	6	hourly
Thanjavur (Tanjore)	45 (C)	1½	every 5min
Trivandrum	485 (A)	8	UD 8am, 7.30pm, 9.30pm, 10.30pm

Fares: (A) Ultra Deluxe (UD), (B) regular/UD/AC, (C) regular

For Kodaikanal, you can also take a bus to Dindigul (₹70, two hours, every 15 minutes) and change there.

TAMIL NADU TRICHY (TIRUCHIRAPPALLI)

Trichy Junction Area

Trichy Junction Area

⊙ **Sights**
1 Railway Museum	B2
2 St John's Church	A3

🛏 **Sleeping**
3 Ashby Hotel	A3
4 Breeze Residency	B2
5 Hotel Abbirami	A2
6 Ramyas Hotel	A2

✗ **Eating**
Madras Restaurant	(see 4)
Meridian	(see 6)
7 Shri Sangeetas	A3
Thendral	(see 6)
8 Vasanta Bhavan	A2

ⓘ **Transport**
9 Parveen Travels	A3

AIR

Trichy's airport is 6km southeast of Trichy Junction and the Central Bus Station.

BUS

Government buses use the busy but orderly **Central Bus Station** (Map p386; Rockins Rd). The best services for longer trips are the UD ('Ultra Deluxe') buses; there's a booking office for these in the southwest corner of the station.

Private Buses

Private bus companies have offices near the Central Bus Station.

Parveen Travels (Map p386; ☎9840962198; www.parveentravels.com; 12B Ashby Complex, Rockins Rd; ⊕24hr) AC buses to Chennai (₹720, six hours, 12 daily), Trivandrum (₹1300, seven hours, 10pm and 11.30pm), and Kodaikanal (₹850, 4½ hours, 1.30am) plus non-AC semisleeper buses to Puducherry (₹550, four hours, 11.50pm) and Kodaikanal (₹550, 4½ hours, 2.15am).

TRAIN

Trichy Junction station is on the main Chennai–Madurai line. Of the 16 daily express services to Chennai, the best daytime option is the 9.05am Vaigai Express (2nd/chair class ₹145/520, 5½ hours). The overnight Pandian Express (sleeper/3AC/2AC/1AC ₹245/630/880/1470, 6¼ hours) leaves at 11.10pm.

Eleven daily trains to Madurai include the 7.05am Tirunelveli Express (2nd class/chair class ₹95/345, 2¼ hours) and the 1.35pm Guruvayur Express (2nd class/sleeper/3AC/2AC ₹80/140/495/700, 2¾ hours).

At least six daily trains head to Thanjavur (2nd class/sleeper/3AC ₹45/140/495, 40 minutes to 1½ hours).

TAXI

➡ Travel agencies and hotels provide cars with drivers.

➡ Reasonably priced **Femina Travels** (Map p386; ☎0431-2418532; www.feminahotel.net; 109 Williams Rd; ⊕6.30am-10pm) charges ₹2000 for up to eight hours and 100km (AC car).

➡ There's an **Ola kiosk** (Map p386; ⊕24hr) outside the railway station.

ⓘ Getting Around

➡ Bus 1 from Rockins Rd outside the Central Bus Station goes every few minutes to the Sri Ranganathaswamy Temple (₹10) and back, stopping near the Rock Fort Temple and Sri Jambukeshwara Temple en route.

➡ Autorickshaws from the Central Bus Station cost ₹200 to the Sri Ranganathaswamy Temple and ₹150 to the Rock Fort Temple.

SOUTHERN TAMIL NADU

Chettinadu

The Chettiars, a community of traders based around Karaikkudi (95km south of Trichy), hit the big time in the 19th century as financiers and entrepreneurs in colonial-era Sri Lanka and Southeast Asia. They lavished their fortunes on building 10,000 (maybe even 30,000) ridiculously opulent mansions in the 75 towns and villages of their arid rural homeland, Chettinadu. No expense was spared on finding the finest materials for these palatial homes: Burmese teak, Italian marble, Indian rosewood, English steel, and art and sculpture from everywhere.

After WWII, the Chettiars' businesses crashed. Many families left Chettinadu, and disused mansions decayed and were demolished or sold. Awareness of their value started to revive around the turn of the 21st century, with Chettinadu making it on to Unesco's tentative World Heritage list in 2014. Several mansions have now been converted into gorgeous heritage hotels that are some of Tamil Nadu's best.

⊙ Sights & Activities

While there are a number of worthwhile sights scattered among Chettinadu's numerous villages, just being here is enough to make a stop rewarding. Aside from the main hubs of Pudukkottai and Karaikkudi, most towns are rural and peaceful, offering a unique combination of simple country life and impressive mansion architecture. The village of Kanadukathan is a great base from which to explore, and has a variety of accommodation and attractions – though nearby Kothamangalam, with the remarkable Saratha Vilas hotel, is also a choice place to stay. Other places worth visiting include Athangudi, with its famed mansion and tile makers, and Namunasamudram, with a unique religious shrine. To see the various sights in the area, it's easiest to hire a car or a rickshaw for full or half-day tours.

Vijayalaya Cholisvaram   HINDU TEMPLE
(Narthamalai; ⊙dawn-dusk) This small but stunning temple stands on a dramatically deserted rock slope 1km southwest of Narthamalai village (16km north of Pudukkottai). Reminiscent of the Shore Temple at Mamallapuram, without the crowds, it was probably built in the 8th or 9th century AD. Two (often locked) rock-cut shrines adorn the rock face behind, one with 12 impressively large reliefs of Vishnu. The Narthamalai turnoff is 7km south of Keeranur on the Trichy–Pudukkottai road; it's 2km west to Narthamalai itself.

Sittannavasal   JAIN TEMPLE
(Sittannavasal; Indian/foreigner ₹25/300, car ₹40; ⊙dawn-dusk) About 16km northwest of Pudukkottai, this small Jain cave temple conceals magnificent vegetable-oil frescoes, which you'll probably get to appreciate all by yourself. Note the Edenic garden paradise painted on the main ceiling, which includes fish, mythical sea monsters and beautiful water maidens. Or try making your 'Om' echo across an acoustic masterpiece of a meditation chamber, where statues of Jain saints sit cross-legged.

Pudukkottai Museum   MUSEUM
(Thirukokarnam, Pudukkottai; Indian/foreigner ₹5/100, camera/video ₹20/100; ⊙9.30am-5pm Sat-Thu) The relics of Chettinadu's bygone days are on display at this wonderful museum, 4km north of Pudukkottai train station. Its eclectic collection includes musical instruments, stamps, jewellery, megalithic burial artefacts, and some remarkable paintings, sculptures and miniatures.

Athangudi Palace Tiles   WORKSHOP
(☑9442229331; www.athangudipalacetiles.com; Athangudi Rd, Athangudi; ₹100; ⊙8am-6pm) Lusting after those exquisite handmade Chettinadu-mansion tiles? Then swing by this long-standing Athangudi workshop, where you can watch expert tile-makers displaying their technique. And of course, there are tiles for sale. Tile production starts each morning around 11am.

Sri Mahalakshmi Handloom Weaving Centre   WORKSHOP
(19/6 KM St, Kanadukathan; ⊙9.30am-5.30pm) FREE Chettinadu is known for its handwoven, contrasting-colour silk-and-cotton Kandaangi saris (now increasingly hard to find). At this small weaving complex, you can watch weavers at work and browse racks of beautiful textiles.

🛏 Sleeping & Eating
To get a feel for the palatial life, book into one of Chettinadu's top-end hotels; they're pricey, but the experience is unique.

Chettinad Packer   HOSTEL $
(☑9786396414; www.facebook.com/Chettinad Packer; 30 AR St, Kanadukathan; per person ₹900; ❄🌐) Chettinadu's only backpacker-oriented accommodation features dorm rooms with bunk beds, plus one private room with four single beds. Simple but clean and well cared for, it's run by the same family that owns

CHETTINADU'S MANSIONS

Chettiar mansions are deeply traditional, privately owned family homes, with very limited visitor information. Several are open to the public, but opening hours can be erratic.

Athangudi Palace (Lakshmi House; Athangudi Rd, Athangudi; ₹100; ⊙9am-5pm) With perhaps the most exquisitely painted wood-carved ceilings in Chettinadu, Athangudi Palace is a popular film set. Take in the especially fine materials (Belgian marble, English iron), Chettiar history panels, chequered floors, and curious statues of British colonials and Hindu gods looming above the entrance.

CVCT and CVR House (CVRMCT St, Kanadukathan; ₹50; ⊙9am-5pm) Backed by the typical succession of pillar-lined courtyards, the impressive reception hall of this 'twin house' is shared by two branches of the same family. Don't miss the fabulous views over neighbouring mansions from the rooftop terrace.

VVR House (CVRMCT St, Kanadukathan; ⊙9am-5pm, hours vary) One of Chettinadu's oldest mansions, built in 1870 with distinctive egg-plaster walls, Burmese-teak columns, patterned tiled floors and intricate wood carvings. A ₹50 group 'donation' is expected.

Chettinadu Mansion. There's a shared kitchen and a pleasant, shaded outdoor garden space. If you're on a budget, stay here.

★**Saratha Vilas**   BOUTIQUE HOTEL $$$
(☏9884936158, 9884203175; www.sarathavilas.com; 832 Main Rd, Kothamangalam; r incl breakfast ₹7200-12,100; ✳@☎☀) A different Chettiar charm inhabits this gorgeously renovated, French-run mansion from 1910, 6km east of Kanadukathan. Rooms combine the traditional and the contemporary with distinct French panache; the food is an exquisite mix of Chettiar and French; and there's a chic saltwater pool.

Most furnishings were personally designed by the knowledgable architect owners, hugely active players in the preservation of Chettinadu heritage.

They're also founders of local conservation NGO ArcHeS.

★**Bangala**   HERITAGE HOTEL $$$
(☏04565-220221; www.thebangala.com; Devakottai Rd, Karaikkudi; r incl breakfast ₹7640-8860; ✳☎☀) Chettinadu's original heritage hotel, this lovingly revamped, efficiently managed whitewashed 'bungalow' isn't a typical mansion but has all the requisite charm: colourcrammed rooms, antique furniture, old family photos and a beautiful tile-fringed pool. It's famous for its food: banana-leaf 'meals' (veg/nonveg ₹900/1000) are actually Chettiar wedding feasts (12.30pm to 2.30pm and 8pm to 10pm; book two hours ahead).

There are cooking 'masterclasses', yoga retreats, massage, and exclusive-access visits to local mansions.

★**Visalam**   HERITAGE HOTEL $$$
(☏04565-273301; www.cghearth.com; Local Fund Rd, Kanadukathan; r incl breakfast from ₹8140; ✳@☎☀) Stunningly restored and professionally run by a Malayali hotel chain, Visalam is a relatively young Chettiar mansion, done in a fashionable 1930s art deco style. It's still decorated with the original owners' photos, furniture and paintings. The garden is exquisite, the 15 large rooms full of character, and the pool setting magical, with overflowing bougainvillea and a low-key restaurant alongside.

Chettinadu Court   HOTEL $$$
(☏9585594087; www.chettinadcourt.com; Raja's St, Kanadukathan; r incl breakfast from ₹4490; ✳☎☀) For a (relatively) economical Chettinadu sojourn, welcoming Chettinadu Court offers eight pleasant rooms sporting Athangudi tiles and a few heritage touches, along with a casual dining room that's really Kanadukathan's main tourist restaurant. The hotel shares an off-site pool with its nearby sister property Chettinadu Mansion.

Chettinadu Mansion   HERITAGE HOTEL $$$
(☏04565-273080; www.chettinadmansion.com; SARM House, 11 AR St, Kanadukathan; r incl breakfast from ₹6850; ✳☎☀) Friendly, well run and packed with character, this colourful century-old mansion is still owned (and lived in) by the original family. Of its 126 rooms, 12 are open to guests – all sizeable, with wacky colour schemes and private balconies gazing out over other mansions. The owners also run nearby Chettinadu Court, which has eight heritage-inspired rooms. The two share an off-site pool.

ⓘ Getting There & Away

Car is the best way to get to and around Chettinadu. Renting one with a driver from Trichy, Thanjavur or Madurai for two days costs around ₹7500. Or take a bus to whichever town you'd like to stay in – or as close to it as you can get – and hire a car there for day trips, for about ₹2500 per day.

From Trichy, buses run every five or 10 minutes to Pudukkottai (₹44, 1½ hours) and Karaikkudi (₹90, two hours); you can hop off and on along the way. From Madurai, buses run to Karaikkudi (₹95, two hours) every 30 minutes. There are also buses from Thanjavur and Rameswaram.

Three daily trains connect Chennai Egmore with Pudukkottai (sleeper/2AC/3AC ₹265/720/1035, six to eight hours) and Karaikkudi (₹280/775/1085, 6½ to 9½ hours). One train connects Chennai with Chettinad Station, for Kanadukathan (₹275/745/1070, nine hours).

Madurai

📞 0452 / POP 1.6 MILLION

Chennai may be the capital of Tamil Nadu, but Madurai claims its soul. Madurai is Tamil-born and Tamil-rooted, one of the oldest cities in India, a metropolis that traded with ancient Rome and was a great capital long before Chennai was even dreamed of.

Tourists, Indian and foreign, come here for the celebrated Meenakshi Amman Temple, a dazzling mazelike structure ranking among India's greatest temples. Otherwise, Madurai, perhaps appropriately given its age, captures many of India's glaring dichotomies: a centre dominated by a medieval temple and an economy increasingly driven by IT, all overlaid with the hustle, energy and excitement of a big Indian city and slotted into a much more manageable package than Chennai's sprawl.

History

Legend has it that Shiva showered drops of nectar *(madhuram)* from his locks on to the city, giving rise to the name Madurai – 'the City of Nectar'.

Ancient documents record the existence of Madurai from the 3rd century BC. It was a trading town, especially in spices, and according to legend was home to the third *sangam* (gathering of Tamil scholars and poets). Over the centuries Madurai came under the sway of the Cholas, Pandyas, local Muslim sultans, Hindu Vijayanagar kings and the Nayaks, who ruled until 1736 and set out the old city's lotus shape. The bulk of the Meenakshi Amman Temple was built under Tirumalai Nayak (1623–59), and Madurai became the hub of Tamil culture, playing an important role in the development of the Tamil language.

In 1840 the British East India Company razed Madurai's fort and filled in its moat. The four broad Veli streets were constructed on top and to this day define the old city's limits.

⊙ Sights

★ Meenakshi
Amman Temple   HINDU TEMPLE
(East Chitrai St; Indian/foreigner ₹5/50; ⊙5am-12.30pm & 3.30-10pm) The colourful abode of the triple-breasted warrior goddess Meenakshi ('fish-eyed' – an epithet for perfect eyes in classical Tamil poetry) is generally considered to be the peak of South Indian temple architecture, as vital to this region's aesthetic heritage as the Taj Mahal to North India. It's not so much a 17th-century temple as a 6-hectare complex with 12 tall *gopurams,* encrusted with a staggering array of gods, goddesses, demons and heroes (1511 on the 55m-high south *gopuram* alone).

According to legend, the beautiful Meenakshi (a version of Parvati) was born with three breasts and this prophecy: her superfluous breast would melt away when she met her husband. This happened when she met Shiva and took her place as his consort. The existing temple was mostly built during the 17th-century reign of Tirumalai Nayak, but its origins go back 2000 years to when Madurai was a Pandyan capital.

The four streets surrounding the temple are pedestrian-only. Temple dress codes and security are airport-strict: no shoulders or legs (of either gender) may be exposed, and no bags or cameras are allowed inside. Despite this, the temple has a happier atmosphere than some of Tamil Nadu's more solemn shrines, and is adorned with especially vibrant ceiling and wall paintings. Every evening at 9pm, a frenetic, incense-clouded procession carries an icon of Sundareswarar (Shiva) to Meenakshi's shrine to spend the night; visitors can follow along.

Before or after entering the temple, look around the **Pudhu Mandapa** (⊙dawn-dusk) **FREE**. The main temple entrance is through the eastern (oldest) *gopuram.* First, on the right, you'll come to the Thousand Pillared Hall, now housing the fascinating **Temple Art Museum** (Indian/foreigner ₹5/50, phone

Madurai

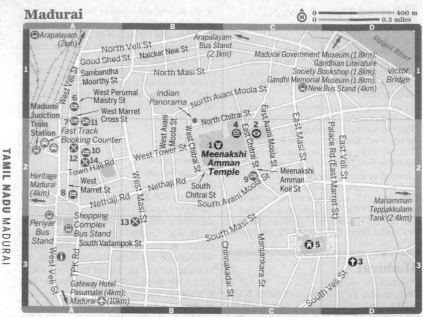

camera ₹50; ⊙6am-2pm & 3-9pm). Moving on into the temple, you'll reach a Nandi shrine surrounded by more beautifully carved columns. Ahead is the main Shiva shrine, flanked on each side by massive *dwarpals*, and further ahead to the left in a separate enclosure is the main Meenakshi shrine, both off limits to non-Hindus. Anyone can, however, wander round the Golden Lotus Tank, where a small pavilion jutting out at the western end has ceiling murals depicting Sundareswarar and Meenakshi's marriage. Leave the temple via a hall of flower sellers and the arch-ceilinged Ashta Shakti Mandapa – lined with relief carvings of the goddess' eight attributes and displaying the loveliest of all the temple's elaborately painted ceilings; this is actually the temple entrance for most worshippers.

Gandhi Memorial Museum   MUSEUM
(www.gandhimmm.org; Gandhi Museum Rd; camera ₹50; ⊙10am-1pm & 2-5.45pm) FREE Housed in a 17th-century Nayak queen's palace, this impressive museum contains a moving, comprehensive account of Gandhi's life and India's struggle for independence from 1757 to 1947; the English-language displays spare no detail about British rule. They include the blood-stained dhoti that Gandhi was wearing when he was assassinated in Delhi in 1948; it was here in Madurai, in 1921, that he first took up wearing the dhoti as a sign of native pride.

The small **Madurai Government Museum** (Gandhi Museum Rd; Indian/foreigner ₹5/100, camera ₹20; ⊙9.30am-5pm Sat-Thu) is next door, and the Gandhian Literature Society Bookshop behind. Buses 3, 66, 75 and 700 from the **Periyar Bus Stand** (West Veli St) go to the Tamukkam bus stop on Alagarkoil Rd, 600m west of the museum.

Tirumalai Nayak Palace   PALACE
(Palace Rd; Indian/foreigner ₹10/50, camera/video ₹30/100; ⊙9am-1pm & 1.30-5pm) What Madurai's Meenakshi Amman Temple is to Nayak religious architecture, Tirumalai Nayak's crumbling palace is to the secular. It's said to be only a quarter of its original size, but its massive scale and hybrid Dravidian Islamic style still testify to the lofty aspirations of its creator. From the east-side entrance, a large courtyard surrounded by tall, thick columns topped with fancy stucco work leads to the grand throne chamber with its 25m-high dome; two stone-carved horses frame the steps up.

Off the chamber's northwest corner is the Natakasala (Dance Hall), with a small archaeological collection.

Madurai

◎ Top Sights
1 Meenakshi Amman Temple	B2

◎ Sights
2 Pudhu Mandapa	C2
3 St Mary's Cathedral	D3
4 Temple Art Museum	C2
5 Tirumalai Nayak Palace	C3

⊜ Sleeping
6 Hotel Park Plaza	A1
7 Hotel Supreme	A2
8 Madurai Residency	A2
9 Simap Residency	C2
10 TM Lodge	A2
11 Treebo Berrys Boutique	A2

⊗ Eating
12 Kumar Mess	A2
13 Murugan Idli Shop	B3
14 Sri Sabareesh	A2
Surya	(see 7)

St Mary's Cathedral   CHURCH
(East Veli St; ⊘6am-6pm) This 20th-century neo-Gothic construction's simple stained-glass windows and bold-orange vaulting are offset by a magnificent blue-and-white exterior with twirling spires.

It's just around the corner from the Tirumalai Nayak Palace.

🏃 Activities

Sivananda Vedanta Yoga Centre   YOGA
(☑0452-2521170, http://sivananda.org.in; 444 KK Nagar, East 9th St; classes ₹400; ⊘6am-8.30pm Mon-Sat, 6.30am-5.30pm Sun) Offers daily drop-in yoga classes (book a day ahead) and 10-day programs (₹6000). Also runs rigorous extended courses at its ashram, 22km north of Madurai.

👉 Tours

Storytrails   WALKING
(☑7373675756; www.storytrails.in; 23 Park Ave, Old Natham Rd; tours per person ₹1600-6000) This Chennai-born organisation runs highly rated story-based neighbourhood walking tours. Prices depend on group size.

Foodies Day Out   FOOD & DRINK
(☑9840992340; www.foodiesdayout.com; 2nd fl, 393 Anna Nagar Main Rd; per person from ₹2500) The best way to delve into Madurai's famous foodie culture is on a fantastic evening tour with these local culinary enthusiasts. Vegetarian and vegan options available.

🛌 Sleeping

TM Lodge   HOTEL $
(☑0452-2341651; 50 West Perumal Maistry St; s/d ₹680/980, with AC ₹1350-1570; ▣) The walls are a bit scuffed, but the rooms are clean, mattresses are good, and TM is efficiently run. Not bad at all for the price.

Treebo Berrys Boutique   HOTEL $$
(☑0452 2340250; www.berrysboutique.in; 25 West Perumal Maistry St; incl breakfast s/d from ₹1600/1900; ▣⟡) Berrys' 15 smart, contemporary, minimalist fruit-named rooms are the most stylish on this hotel-packed street. There's a soothing atmosphere, plus a friendly welcome and an in-house restaurant. One of the best values in town – check for online discounts.

Simap Residency   HOTEL $$
(☑0452-2350088; www.simapresidency.com; 12A/1 Meenakshi Amman Koil St; r incl breakfast ₹2500-2880; ▣⟡) Billing itself as a pilgrim hotel open to all, the Simap is right in on the temple action (and noise). Bare but good-sized, modern rooms with tight white sheets, AC and solar-heated water hide behind shiny wooden doors.

Madurai Residency   HOTEL $$
(☑0452-4380000; www.madurairesidency.com; 15 West Marret St; incl breakfast s ₹2950-3420, d ₹3300-3800; ▣⟡) The service is stellar and the rooms are comfy and fresh at this winner, which has a handy transport desk and one of the the highest rooftop restaurants in town. It's very popular, particularly with Indian businessmen: book at least a day ahead.

Hotel Park Plaza   HOTEL $$
(☑0452-4511111; www.hotelparkplaza.in; 114 West Perumal Maistry St; s ₹2240-4800, d ₹2700-4800; ▣⟡) The Plaza's rooms are comfortable and simply but smartly done up, with marble floors, blue accent lighting and chunky mattresses; four have temple views. The (inappropriately named) Sky High Bar graces the 1st floor.

Hotel Supreme   HOTEL $$
(☑0452-2343151; www.hotelsupreme.in; 110 West Perumal Maistry St; incl breakfast s ₹2450-3060, d ₹2700-3300; ▣⟡) A well-presented, slightly faded hotel with friendly service; it's very popular with domestic tourists. There's good all-veg food at the rooftop Surya restaurant (p392).

★ **Heritage Madurai**   HERITAGE HOTEL **$$$**
(☎9003043205; www.heritagemadurai.com; 11 Melakkal Main Rd, Kochadai; r ₹6500-9600; ❋⊛⊛) This leafy haven, 4km northwest of central Madurai, originally housed the old Madurai Club. It's been impeccably tarted up, with intricate Kerala-style woodwork, a sultry sunken pool and airy, terracotta-floored 'deluxe' rooms. Best are the 'villas' featuring private plunge pools. There's a good upscale North and South Indian restaurant, along with a spa, bar and 24-hour cafe.

Gateway Hotel
Pasumalai   HERITAGE HOTEL **$$$**
(☎0452-6633000; www.gateway.tajhotels.com; 40 TPK Rd, Pasumalai; r incl breakfast ₹8100-12,800; ⊛⊛⊛) A refreshing escape from the city scramble, the Taj-group Gateway sprawls across hilltop gardens 6km southwest of Madurai centre. The views, outdoor pool and 60 resident peacocks are wonderful, and rooms are comfy and well equipped, with glassed-in showers and do-it-yourself yoga kits. The **Garden All Day** (☎0452-6633000; www.gateway.tajhotels.com; mains ₹300-700; ⊗6.30am-11pm) restaurant is excellent.

✗ Eating

★ **Murugan Idli Shop**   SOUTH INDIAN **$**
(http://muruganidlishop.com; 196 West Masi St; dishes ₹15-75; ⊗7am-10.30pm) Though it now has multiple Chennai branches, Murugan is Madurai born and bred. Here you can put the fluffy signature *idli* and chutneys to the test, and feast on South Indian favourites like dosa, *vada* and *uttapam*.

★ **Sri Sabareesh**   INDIAN **$**
(49A West Perumal Maistry St; mains ₹65-90; ⊗6am-11.30pm) Decked with old-Madurai photos, Sri Sabareesh is a popular pure-veg cheapie that rustles up good South Indian thalis (₹90), dosa, *idli, uttapam* and *vada*, plus sturdy mains.

Surya   MULTICUISINE **$**
(www.hotelsupreme.in; Hotel Supreme, 110 West Perumal Maistry St; mains ₹80-160; ⊗4pm-midnight) The Hotel Supreme's rooftop restaurant offers excellent service, good pure-veg food and superb city and temple views. The iced coffee might have been brewed by the gods when you sip it on a hot, dusty day. The downstairs AC restaurant is open from 7am.

Kumar Mess   SOUTH INDIAN **$$**
(96A West Perumal Maistry St; mains ₹140-280; ⊗noon-4pm & 6.30-11pm) The nondescript facade leads into a casual dining space with impeccable service, where a long list of meat dishes is the main attraction. The chicken dosa is fluffy and delicious!

Banyan Restaurant   INDIAN **$$$**
(☎0452-3244187; www.heritagemadurai.com; Heritage Madurai, 11 Melakkal Main Rd, Kochadai; mains ₹200-450; ⊗7am-10.30pm) Set in the green-clad Kerala-inspired grounds of the top-end Heritage Madurai hotel, this elegant eatery does beautifully spiced pan-Indian dishes, along with popular lunchtime buffets. It's 4km northwest of central Madurai.

🛍 Shopping

Madurai teems with cloth stalls and tailors' shops, as you might notice upon being approached by tailor touts. Drivers, guides and touts will also be keen to lead you to the craft shops in North and West Chitrai Sts, offering to show you the rooftop temple view – the views are good, and so is the inevitable sales pitch.

A great place for getting clothes made up is the Pudhu Mandapa (p389). Here you'll find rows of tailors busily treadling away and capable of whipping up a good replica of whatever you're wearing in an hour or two. A cotton top or shirt can cost ₹350.

ℹ Information

Indian Panorama (☎0452-2525821; www.indianpanorama.in; North Chitrai St; ⊗10am-7pm Mon-Sat) Reliable South India–based agency covering all of India.
Tourist office (☎0452-2334757; www.tamilnadutourism.org; 1 West Veli St; ⊗10am-6pm Mon-Fri) Also has branches at the airport and train station.

ℹ Getting There & Away

AIR
➜ Madurai Airport is 12km south of town.
➜ SpiceJet (www.spicejet.com) flies once daily to Colombo, Dubai and Hyderabad, and three times daily to Chennai.
➜ Indigo (www.goindigo.in) flies five times a day to Chennai and twice to Bengaluru and Hyderabad.
➜ Jet Airways (www.jetairways.com) flies daily to Chennai and Mumbai.

BUS

Most government buses arrive at and depart from the **New Bus Stand** (Melur Rd), 4km northeast of the centre. Services to Coimbatore, Kodaikanal, Ooty and Munnar go from the **Arapalayam Bus Stand** (Puttuthoppu Main Rd), 2km northwest of the old city. For Kanyakumari, take the bus to Nagercoil and change there. Tickets for more expensive (and more comfortable) private buses are sold by agencies on the south side of the **Shopping Complex Bus Stand** (btwn West Veli St & TPK Rd); most travel overnight.

TRAIN

From Madurai Junction station, 12 daily trains head to Trichy and 10 to Chennai; fastest is the 7am Vaigai Express (Trichy 2nd/chair class ₹95/345, two hours; Chennai ₹180/665, 7¾ hours). A good overnight Chennai train is the 8.40pm Pandian Express (sleeper/3AC/2AC/1AC ₹315/815/1150/1940, nine hours). To Kanyakumari the only daily train departs at 1.30am (sleeper/3AC/2AC/1AC ₹210/540/745/1245, five hours), but there are six daily trains to Nagercoil, near Kanyakumari.

Other destinations include the following (prices are for sleeper/3AC/2AC):

Bengaluru (two daily, ₹260/700/1000, 9½ hours)

Coimbatore (two daily, ₹235/595/830, 5½ hours)

Mumbai (Monday, Tuesday, Wednesday and Friday, ₹645/1705/2505, 34 hours)

Trivandrum (five daily, ₹205/550/780, seven hours)

ⓘ Getting Around

TO/FROM THE AIRPORT

Taxis cost ₹550 between the centre and the airport; Ola cars are closer to ₹400. Alterna-tively, bus 10 (₹15) runs to/from the Shopping Complex Bus Stand.

BUS

➡ From the New Bus Stand, buses 3, 48 and 700 shuttle into the city; an autorickshaw is ₹150.

➡ From Arapalayam Bus Stand, take a rickshaw to the centre for ₹100.

➡ Buses 3, 66, 75 and 700 from the central Periyar Bus Stand (p390) run to the Gandhi Museum area.

TAXI

➡ There's a fixed-rate **taxi stand** (Madurai Junction) outside Madurai Junction train station, with fare boards (one day around Madurai ₹1400 to ₹1800).

➡ Fast Track also has a **taxi booking counter** (☑0452-2888999; Madurai Junction; ⊙24hr) here; rates are ₹90 for the first 3km, then ₹16 per kilometre.

Rameswaram

☑04573 / POP 45,000

Rameswaram was once the southernmost point of sacred India; leaving its boundaries meant abandoning caste and falling below the status of the lowliest skinner of sacred cows. Then Rama (incarnation of Vishnu, hero of the Ramayana) led a monkey-and-bear army across a monkey-built bridge to (Sri) Lanka, defeating the demon Ravana and rescuing his wife, Sita. Afterwards, prince and princess offered thanks to Shiva here. Today, millions of Hindus flock to the Ramanathaswamy Temple (p394) to worship where a god worshipped a god.

GOVERNMENT BUSES FROM MADURAI

DESTINATION	FARE (₹)	TIME (HR)	DEPARTURES
Bengaluru (Bangalore)	515-700	9-10	8 buses 7pm-9.35pm
Chennai	635-975	9-10	every 30min, 5 AC buses 4pm-10pm
Kodaikanal	100	4	13 buses 1.30am-2.50pm, 5.50pm, 8.30pm
Coimbatore	170	5	every 10min
Ernakulam (Kochi)	325	9½	9am, 8pm, 9pm
Nagercoil	240	6	every 30min
Munnar	180	5	5.55am, 8am, 10.40am
Mysuru (Mysore)	375-490	9-12	4.35pm, 6pm, 8pm, 9pm
Ooty	300	8	7.15am, 9.15pm
Puducherry (Pondicherry)	240-260	7½	9.05pm, 9.30pm
Rameswaram	140	4-5	every 15min
Trichy (Tiruchirappalli)	90	2¼-3	every 5min

DHANUSHKODI

Pamban Island's promontory stretches 22km southeast from Rameswaram, narrowing to a thin strip of silky sand dunes halfway along. Near the southeastern-most tip stands the ghost town of Dhanushkodi. Once a thriving port, Dhanushkodi was washed away by a monster cyclone in 1964. The shells of its train station, church, post office and other ruins stand among a scattering of fishers' shacks; Adam's Bridge (Rama's Bridge), the chain of reefs, sandbanks and islets that almost connects India with Sri Lanka, stretches away to the east. For many, this is the final stop of a long pilgrimage. The atmosphere is at its most magical at sunrise, with pilgrims performing *pujas*.

In years past, reaching Dhanushkodi required an adventurous drive or walk across several kilometres of dunes. But a new tarmac road has made the trip a snap – and much more popular. The best way to go is by car (₹1200 round trip), which can be arranged by the reliable **Pavan Tours & Travels** (9952556605; www.pavantoursand travels.com; East Car St, Rameswaram). You can explore the ruins, watch teams of fishers pulling in their nets, and get as close as possible to Sri Lanka from the Indian mainland – with the sea on both sides of you.

Otherwise, Rameswaram is a small, scruffy fishing town on conch-shaped Pamban Island, connected to the mainland by 2km-long bridges. If you aren't a pilgrim, the temple alone barely merits the journey here. But the island's eastern tip, Dhanushkodi, only 30km from Sri Lanka, has a magical natural beauty that adds to Rameswaram's appeal. And for activity-loving travellers, the island's western edge is buzzing as a low-key water-sports destination.

Sights & Activities

Ramanathaswamy Temple   HINDU TEMPLE
(East Car St; 6am-1pm & 3-8.30pm) Housing the world's most sacred sand mound (a lingam said to have been created by Rama's wife Sita, so he could worship Shiva), this temple is one of India's holiest shrines. Dating mainly from the 16th to 18th centuries, it's notable for its lengthy 1000-pillar halls and 22 *theertham* (temple tanks), in which pilgrims bathe before visiting the deity. Attendants tip pails of water over the (often fully dressed) faithful, who rush from *theertham* to *theertham*.

Quest Academy   WATER SPORTS
(9820367412; www.quest-asia.com; Pirappan Valasai, off Madurai-Rameswaram Hwy) Run by a team of Mumbaikar adventure-activity experts, this laid-back, ecofriendly water-sports centre offers kitesurfing, kayaking, windsurfing, snorkelling, SUP, sailing, camping, beach clean-ups and after-dark wildlife walks. See the website for prices. It's based on the mainland, 18km west of the Pamban Island bridge.

Sleeping & Eating

Kathadi South   HUT $$
(9820367412; www.quest-asia.com; off Old Dhanushkodhi Rd, Pamban Island; s/d incl breakfast ₹2000/2750) In calm palm-shaded grounds, Quest Academy offers three fuss-free thatched huts with shared bathrooms, along with a clutch of tents (single/double ₹1250/2200). There's solar power, home-cooked meals (₹350) and a shimmering white stretch of seafront sand just metres away. At the time of research, the camp was closed, and it was unknown whether it would reopen.

Kathadi North   COTTAGE $$
(9820367412; www.quest-asia.com; Pirappan Valasai, off Madurai-Rameswaram Hwy; s/d incl breakfast ₹3500/4000;) Part of the wonderful Quest Academy water-sports centre, these four fan-cooled, beach-chic concrete huts with thatched roofs and open-air bathrooms huddle just inland from bleach-blond sands, on the mainland 18km west of Pamban Island. Rainwater is harvested, power is solar, doors are recycled and palm fences use on-site materials. The open kitchen dishes out communal meals (₹450 to ₹550).

Hotel Saara   HOTEL $$
(9442700601; www.hotelsaara.com; 25 Mandi St; r ₹1680;) This new hotel is probably the best bang for your buck in Rameswaram. Fresh rooms have tiled walls (no scuffed and hand-smudged paint!), in-room wi-fi and helpful management. It's on a relatively quiet side street near the temple.

Jiwan Residency HOTEL **$$**

(☑04573-222207; www.jiwanresidency.com; Sangumal, Olaikuda Rd; r incl breakfast ₹3420-4110, ste ₹5400-5900; ❋☎) Towards the northeastern end of Rameswaram's seafront road, Jiwan is one of your best options: a fresh, neat business-styled hotel with bright, modern rooms in creams and beiges. Spacious 'superior' rooms have balconies; the two 'suites' enjoy ocean panoramas.

Daiwik Hotel HOTEL **$$**

(☑04573-223222; www.daiwikhotels.com; Madurai–Rameswaram Hwy; r ₹4150-5000; ❋☎) Gleaming, comfy and welcoming, 'India's first four-star pilgrim hotel', 200m west of the bus station, is your classiest choice in Rameswaram. Airy rooms come smartly decked out with huge mirrors and local-life photos, there's a spa, and the pure-veg **Ahaan** (mains ₹160-270; ☺7am-10pm) restaurant is good.

Hotel Sri Saravana HOTEL **$$**

(☑04573-223367; www.srisaravanahotel.com; 1/9A South Car St; r ₹1500-4500; ❋☎) The most popular of the town-centre hotels, Sri Saravana is friendly and clean enough, with decent service and spacious, erratically styled rooms. Higher-rated, huge rooms towards the top have sea views.

Hotel Annapoorna INDIAN **$**

(West Car St; mains ₹70-120; ☺7am-10pm) A busy joint for south Indian breakfasts and thalis.

❶ Getting There & Away

Rameswaram's **bus stand** (Madurai-Rameswaram Hwy) is 2.5km west of town. Buses run to Madurai (₹150, four hours) every 10 minutes and to Trichy (₹250, seven hours) every 30 minutes. 'Ultra Deluxe' (UD) services are scheduled to Chennai (₹630, 13 hours) at 4.30pm and 5pm, plus one AC bus at 4pm (₹900). Other routes include Kanyakumari (₹300, eight hours) at 1.30pm and 5.55pm, and Bengaluru (₹7400, 12 hours) at 4.30pm, but these don't always run.

The train station is 1.5km southwest of the temple. Six daily trains to/from Madurai (₹35, four hours) have unreserved seating only. The Rameswaram–Chennai Express departs daily at 8.15pm (sleeper/3AC/2AC ₹360/950/1340, 11 hours) via Trichy (₹215/540/745, five hours). The Rameswaram–Kanyakumari Express leaves at 8.50pm Monday, Thursday and Saturday, reaching Kanyakumari (sleeper/3AC ₹275/710) at 4.10am.

Kanyakumari (Cape Comorin)

☑04652 / POP 22,450

This is it, the end of India. There's a sense of accomplishment on making it to the tip of the subcontinent's 'V', past the final dramatic flourish of the Western Ghats and the green fields, glinting rice paddies and slow-looping wind turbines of India's deep south. Kanyakumari can feel surreal; at certain times of year you'll see the sun set and the moon rise over three seas (Bay of Bengal, Arabian Sea, Indian Ocean) simultaneously. The Temple of the Virgin Sea Goddess, Swami Vivekananda's legacy and the 'Land's End' symbolism draw crowds of pilgrims and tourists to Kanyakumari, but it remains a small-scale, refreshing respite from the hectic Indian road.

◉ Sights

★**Padmanabhapuram Palace** PALACE

(☑04651-250255; Padmanabhapuram; Indian/foreigner ₹35/300, camera/video ₹50/2000; ☺9am-12.30pm & 2-4.30pm Tue-Sun) With a forest's worth of intricately carved rosewood ceilings and polished-teak beams, this labyrinthine palace, 35km northwest of Kanyakumari, near the Kerala border, is considered the finest example of traditional Keralan architecture today. Asia's largest wooden palace complex, it was once capital of Travancore, an unstable princely state taking in parts of both Tamil Nadu and Kerala. Under successive rulers it expanded into a magnificent conglomeration of corridors, courtyards, gabled roofs and 14 palaces. The oldest sections date to 1550.

Buses run every 20 minutes from Kanyakumari to Thuckalay (₹33, 1½ hours), from where it's an autorickshaw ride or 15-minute walk to the palace. Return taxis from Kanyakumari cost ₹1200.

From Thiruvananthapurum, take any bus towards Kanyakumari (₹80, three hours, four daily) and get off at Thuckalay. The Kerala Tourist Development Corporation (p265) runs full-day Kanyakumari tours from Thiruvananthapurum covering Padmanabhapuram (₹990, minimum four people, Tuesday to Sunday).

Vivekananda Memorial MONUMENT

(₹20; ☺7.45am-4pm) Four hundred metres offshore is the rock where famous Hindu apostle Swami Vivekananda meditated from 25 to 27 December 1892, and decided to take his moral message beyond India's shores. A two-*mandapa* 1970 memorial to Vivekananda reflects temple architectural styles from across India. The lower *mandapa* contains what's believed to be goddess Kumari's footprint. With the constant tourist crowds this brings, Vivekananda would no doubt choose somewhere else to meditate today. Ferries shuttle out to the rock (₹50 return).

Vivekanandapuram   ASHRAM

(☑04652-247012; www.vrmvk.org; Vivekanandapuram; ⊙9am-8pm) Just 1km north of Kanyakumari, this peaceful ashram (offering a variety of yoga retreats) is the headquarters of spiritual organisation Vivekananda Kendra, devoted to carrying out Vivekananda's teachings. Its Vivekananda-focused **'Arise! Awake!'** (₹10; ⊙9am-1pm & 4-8pm Wed-Mon, 9am-1pm Tue) exhibition is worth a visit, as is the **Ramayana Darshanam** (₹30; ⊙10am-1pm & 4-9pm), and you can stroll to the sea past a beautiful lotus-pool-lined memorial to the swami.

Thiruvalluvar Statue   MONUMENT

(⊙7.45am-4pm) FREE Looking like an Indian Colossus of Rhodes, the towering statue on the smaller island next to the Vivekananda Memorial (p395) is of the ancient Tamil poet Thiruvalluvar. The work of more than 5000 sculptors, it was erected in 2000 and honours the poet's 133-chapter work *Thirukural* – hence its height of exactly 133ft (40.5m). Tides permitting, Vivekananda Memorial ferries (₹50 return) continue to Thiruvalluvar.

Kumari Amman Temple   HINDU TEMPLE

(Sannathi St; ⊙4.30am-noon & 4-8.30pm) The legends say the *kanya* (virgin) goddess Kumari, a manifestation of the Great Goddess Devi, single-handedly conquered demons and secured freedom for the world. At this temple on the tip of the subcontinent, pilgrims give her thanks in an intimately spaced, beautifully decorated temple, where the crash of waves from three seas can be heard beyond the twilight glow of oil fires clutched in vulva-shaped votive candles (referencing the sacred femininity of the goddess).

It's said that the temple's east-facing door stays locked to prevent the shimmer of the goddess' diamond nose-stud leading ships astray. From the main north-side gate, you'll be asked for a ₹20 donation to enter the 18th-century inner precinct, where men must remove their shirts, and cameras are forbidden.

The shoreline around the temple has a couple of tiny beaches, and bathing ghats where worshippers immerse themselves before visiting the temple. The *mandapa* just south of the temple is popular for sunset-watching and daytime shade.

Swami Vivekananda Wandering Monk Exhibition   MUSEUM

(Beach Rd; ₹10; ⊙8am-noon & 4-8pm) In lovely leafy grounds, this excellent exhibition details Swami Vivekananda's wisdom, sayings, and encounters with the mighty and the lowly during his five years as a wandering monk around India from 1888 to 1893. Tickets also cover the Vivekananda-inspired 'Arise! Awake!' exhibition in Vivekanandapuram, 1km north of town.

🛏 Sleeping

Hotel Narmadha   HOTEL $

(☑04652-246365; Kovalam Rd; r ₹500-1000, with AC ₹1500; ❄☎) This long, colourful concrete block conceals friendly staff, a back-up generator and a range of budget rooms, with big steps up in quality the more you pay. The cheapest are bucket-water only, but the ₹1000 sea-view doubles with turquoise walls are good value.

Hotel Ocean Heritage   HOTEL $$

(☑04652-247557; www.hoteloceanheritage.in; East Car St; s/d ₹1600/1800) Rupee for rupee perhaps the best value in Kanyakumari, this friendly hotel has comfortable beds, in-room wi-fi and 24-hour hot water. The best rooms have balconies with ocean glimpses, and the top floor restaurant makes a killer cold coffee.

Temple Citi   HOTEL $$

(☑04652-246083; www.hoteltempleciti.com; West Car St; d from ₹1800; ❄☎) Plain, gleaming, cream-clad rooms for two to six people, with AC, 24-hour hot water and spotless bathrooms, make this new-build block a popular choice and good value. Breakfast is included.

Hotel Sivamurugan   HOTEL $$

(☑04652-246862; www.hotelsivamurugan.com; 2/93 North Car St; r ₹2600-3300; ❄☎) A welcoming, well-appointed hotel, with spacious, spotless, marble-floored rooms and lobby-only wi-fi. 'Super-deluxes' have sea glimpses past a couple of buildings. Rates stay fixed year-round (a novelty for Kanyakumari) and there's 24-hour hot water.

Kanyakumari (Cape Comorin)

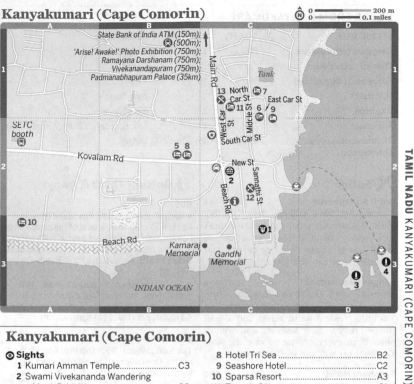

Kanyakumari (Cape Comorin)

◉ Sights
1 Kumari Amman Temple........................C3
2 Swami Vivekananda Wandering
Monk Exhibition C2
3 Thiruvalluvar Statue.............................D3
4 Vivekananda Memorial D3

⌂ Sleeping
5 Hotel Narmadha.....................................B2
6 Hotel Ocean Heritage...........................C1
7 Hotel Sivamurugan................................C1

8 Hotel Tri Sea B2
9 Seashore Hotel.......................................C2
10 Sparsa Resort...A3
11 Temple Citi C1

✕ Eating
Auroma..(see 10)
12 Hotel Annapoorna..................................C2
13 Sangam Restaurant................................C1
Seashore Hotel ....(see 9)

Hotel Tri Sea　　　　　　　　HOTEL **$$**
(☎04652-246586; www.hoteltrisea.in; Kovalam Rd; r ₹1000, with AC ₹1680-3200; ✳🛜☒) You can't miss the high-rise Tri Sea, whose sea-view rooms are spacious, spotless and airy, with particularly hectic colour schemes. Cheaper rooms are smaller, but sometimes nicer, than pricier ones. Sunrise/sunset-viewing platforms and free in-room wi-fi are welcome bonuses, but the rooftop pool costs extra (₹200 per hour).

Sparsa Resort　　　　　　RESORT **$$$**
(☎04652-247041; www.sparsaresorts.com; 6/112B Beach Rd; r incl breakfast ₹5300-7100; ✳🛜☒) Away from the temple frenzy, on the west edge of town, elegant Sparsa is several notch-es above Kanyakumari's other hotels. Fresh, orange-walled rooms with low dark-wood beds, lounge chairs and mood-lighting make for a contemporary-oriental vibe, and there's a lovely pool surrounded by palms, as well as good Indian cooking at Auroma (p398).

Seashore Hotel　　　　　　HOTEL **$$$**
(☎04652-246704; www.theseashorehotel.com; East Car St; r ₹4100-7700; ✳🛜) The fanciest town-centre hotel has shiny, roomy chambers with golden curtains and cushions, glassed-in showers and kettles. It's lost its original sparkle, but all rooms except the cheapest offer panoramic sea views, and the 7th-floor restaurant (p398) is one of Kanyakumari's best.

BUSES FROM KANYAKUMARI

DESTINATION	FARE (₹)	TIME (HR)	DEPARTURES
Bengaluru (ultra deluxe)	866	12-14	4.30pm, 5pm
Chennai (ultra deluxe)	775	12-14	5 daily
Kodaikanal (ultra deluxe)	360	10	8.15pm
Madurai	250	8	2pm, 3pm
Nagercoil	22	1	every 10min
Rameswaram	250-375	8	7am, 6pm daily, 7.30am, 7.30pm Fri-Sun
Thiruvananthapuram (Trivandrum)	90	2½	10 daily

✖ Eating

Hotel Annapoorna   INDIAN $
(Sannathi St; mains ₹110-150, thalis ₹120-180; ⊙6am-9.30pm) A popular pan-Indian budget spot serving breakfast *idli*, filter coffee and South Indian thalis alongside curries and biryanis, in a clean, friendly setting.

Sangam Restaurant   INDIAN $
(Main Rd; mains ₹110-300, thalis ₹100-150; ⊙7am-10.30pm) It's as if the Sangam started in Kashmir, trekked south across India, and stopped here to offer tasty veg and nonveg picks from every province along the way. The seats are soft and the food is good.

Seashore Hotel   MULTICUISINE $$
(www.theseashorehotel.com; East Car St; mains ₹190-360; ⊙7-10am & 12.30-10.30pm; ⊛) Amazingly, this spruced-up 7th-floor hotel (p397) restaurant is the only one in Kanyakumari with a proper sea view. There are plenty of Indian veg and nonveg choices, plus the odd continental creation. The Irani fish tikka is fantastic. Service is spot on, and it's a good breakfast bet (buffet ₹270).

Auroma   MULTICUISINE $$$
(www.sparsaresorts.com; Sparsa Resort, 6/112B Beach Rd; mains ₹200-700; ⊙7-10am, noon-3pm, 7-11pm) Tucked away inside the stylish Sparsa Resort (p397), 1km west of Kanyakumari's centre, lime-themed Auroma turns out tasty, refined tandoori and South Indian fare, plenty of seafood and decent breakfasts in fancy surrounds.

ℹ Information

Tourist Office (☎04652-246276; Beach Rd; ⊙10am-5.30pm Mon-Fri) Friendly but essentially useless.

ℹ Getting There & Away

BUS
➜ Kanyakumari's sedate **bus stand** (Kovalam Rd) is a 10-minute walk west of the centre. Most comfortable are the 'Ultra Deluxe' (UD) buses. Advance reservations can be made at the **SETC ticket booth** (Kanyakumari Bus Stand; ⊙noon-7.45pm).

➜ There are many more buses to many more destinations, including frequent services to Madurai, from the bus stand at Nagercoil, about 45 minutes northwest of Kanyakumari.

TRAIN
The train station is 800m north of Kanyakumari's centre. One daily northbound train, the Kanyakumari Express, departs at 5.20pm for Chennai (sleeper/3AC/2AC/1AC ₹415/1100/1565/2640, 13 hours) via Madurai (₹210/540/745/1245, 4½ hours) and Trichy (₹275/710/1000/1675, seven hours). Two daily express trains depart at 6.40am and 10am for Thiruvananthapuram (Trivandrum; sleeper/3AC/2AC ₹140/495/700, 2¼ hours), continuing to Kollam (Quilon; ₹140/495/700, 3½ hours) and Ernakulam (Kochi; ₹205/550/780, seven hours). More trains go from Nagercoil Junction, 20km northwest of Kanyakumari.

For real train buffs, the Vivek Express runs to Dibrugarh (Assam), 4236km and 80 hours away – India's longest single train ride. It departs Kanyakumari at 11pm Thursday (₹1085/2830/4265).

THE WESTERN GHATS

Welcome to the lush Western Ghats, some of the most precious heat relief in India. Rising like an impassable bulwark of evergreen and deciduous tangle, from north of Mumbai to the tip of Tamil Nadu, the World Heritage–listed Ghats (with an average elevation of 915m) contain 27% of India's flowering plant species and an incredible array of endemic wildlife. In Tamil Nadu they rise to over 2000m in the Palani Hills around Kodaikanal and the Nilgiris around Ooty. British influence lingers a little stronger up in these hills, where colonialists built 'hill stations' to escape the sweltering plains and covered slopes in neatly trimmed tea plantations. It's not just the air and (relative) lack of pollution that's refreshing – there's a certain acceptance of quirkiness and eccentricity here. Expect organic farms, handlebar-moustached trekking guides and leopard-print earmuffs.

Kodaikanal (Kodai)

☎ 04542 / POP 36,500 / ELEV 2100M

There are few more refreshing Tamil Nadu moments than leaving the heat-soaked plains for the sharp pinch of a Kodaikanal night or morning. This misty hill station, 120km northwest of Madurai in the protected Palani Hills, is more relaxed and intimate than its big sister Ooty (Kodai is the 'Princess of Hill Stations', Ooty the Queen). It's not all cold either; days feel more like deep spring than early winter.

Centred on a beautiful star-shaped lake, Kodai rambles up and down hillsides with patches of *shola* (virgin forest), unique to South India's Western Ghats, and evergreen broadleaf trees like magnolia, mahogany, myrtle and rhododendron. Another plant speciality is the *kurinji* shrub, whose lilac-blue blossoms appear every 12 years (next due 2030).

Kodai is popular with honeymooners and groups, who flock to its spectacular viewpoints and waterfalls. The renowned Kodaikanal International School provides some cosmopolitan flair. Visit midweek for peace and quiet.

⊙ Sights

Berijam Lake
LAKE

(⊘9am-3pm) FREE Visiting forest-fringed Berijam Lake, 21km southwest of Kodaikanal, requires a Forest Department permit (₹250). Taxi drivers will organise this, if asked the day before, and do half-day 'forest tours' to Berijam, via other lookouts, for ₹2000.

Sacred Heart Natural
Science Museum
MUSEUM

(Kodaikanal Museum; Sacred Heart College, Law's Ghat Rd; adult/child ₹20/10, camera ₹20; ⊘9am-6pm) In the grounds of a former Jesuit

seminary 4km downhill east of town, this museum has a ghoulishly intriguing miscellany of flora and fauna put together over more than 100 years by priests and trainees. Displays range over bottled snakes, human embryos (!), giant moths and stuffed animal carcasses. You can also see pressed famous *kurinji* flowers *(Strobilanthes kunthiana)*.

Parks, Viewpoints & Waterfalls
Several natural beauty spots around Kodai (crowded with souvenir and snack stalls) are very popular with Indian tourists. They're best visited by taxi; drivers offer three-hour 12-stop tours for ₹1600 to ₹2000. On clear days, **Green Valley View** (⊘dawn-dusk) FREE, 6km from the centre, **Pillar Rocks** (₹5, camera ₹20; ⊘9am-4pm) FREE, 7km from the centre, and less-visited **Moir's Point** (₹10; ⊘10am-5pm), 13km from the centre, all along the same road west of town, have spectacular views to the plains below.

Other popular beauty spots include **Bryant Park** (off Lake Rd; adult/child ₹30/15, camera/video ₹50/100; ⊘9am-6pm), **Bear Shola Falls** and **Coaker's Walk** (₹10; ⊘7am-7pm).

🏃 Activities

The 5km Kodaikanal Lake circuit is lovely in the early morning before the crowds roll in. A walk along Lower Shola Rd takes you through the Bombay Shola, the nearest surviving patch of shola to central Kodai.

At the time of research, all hiking and trekking in the forests around Kodai was banned, following a forest fire in March 2018 in which 23 people died. To see if the situation has changed, contact the **District Forest Office** (☎04542-241287; Muthaliarpuram; ⊘10am-5.45pm Mon-Fri); at the time of research they would not even offer a guess as to if or when the forests would reopen. Trails & Tracks (p400) is your best local hiking resource, and Greenlands Youth Hostel (p401) can also put you in touch with local guides (₹600 to ₹1000 per half-day) who can take you to places that are open.

Dolphin's Nose Walk
WALKING

This is a lovely walk of 4.5km (each way) from central Kodai, passing through budget-traveller hang-out Vattakanal to reach the Dolphin's Nose, a narrow rock lookout overhanging a precipitous drop. You might spot gaur (bison) or giant squirrels in the forested bits.

Kodaikanal (Kodai)

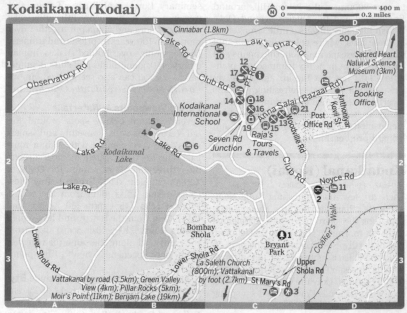

Trails & Tracks

TREKKING

(☎7598472791, 9965524279; thenaturetrails@gmail.com; day walks per person per hour ₹100-500) A reliable, well-established trekking outfit run by very experienced local guide Vijay Kumar, offering day walks and overnight treks. With the restrictions on hiking and camping around Kodaikanal, he knows the best places that are still open, and operates multiday trips overnighting in guesthouses. Book by phone or email. Per-person price depends on group size.

Boating & Cycling

If you're sappy in love like a bad Bollywood song, the thing to do in Kodai is rent a pedal boat, rowing boat or Kashmiri *shikara* (honeymoon boat) from the **Kodaikanal Boat & Rowing Club** (Lake Rd; per 30min pedal boat ₹100, shikara incl boater ₹490; ☺9am-6pm) or **TTDC Boat House** (Lake Rd; per 30min pedal boat ₹100, rowing boat/shikara incl boater ₹330/495; ☺9am-5.30pm).

Bicycle-rental (per hour ₹100) stands are dotted around the lake.

🛏 Sleeping

Some hotels hike prices by up to 100% during the 'season' (April to June). There are some gorgeous heritage places, and good-value midrange options if you can live with-

out colonial-era ambience. Most hotels have a 9am or 10am checkout April to June.

Sri Vignesh Guest House

GUESTHOUSE $

(☎9094972524; umaarkrishnan@gmail.com; Lake Rd; r from ₹800; 🐾) Up a steep driveway, surrounded by neat flowery gardens with a swing, this simple but characterful Raj-era home is run by the kindly and interesting Uma and Krishnan, who spent years in Africa for Krishnan's work as a humanitarian doctor. Rooms are clean and very basic; you have to schedule hot water as needed.

Snooze Inn

HOTEL $

(☎04542-240837; www.jayarajgroup.com; Anna Salai; r ₹1000-1400; 🐾) Rooms don't have quite as much character as the exterior suggests, but this is a decent-value budget choice sporting clean bathrooms, plenty of blankets and friendly staff.

★ Kodai Heaven

GUESTHOUSE $$

(☎8754707207, 9994116207; www.kodaiheaven. com; 6 Dolphin's Nose Rd, Vattakanal; d ₹2800-3800; 🐾) This multilevel hillside guesthouse will blow your mind with jaw-dropping views that are far better than those offered by any hotels in Kodaikanal proper. Rooms are fun – some with wild murals inside and out, others more subdued but still unique. Most front on to terraces where you can sit

Kodaikanal (Kodai)

◉ **Sights**
1 Bryant Park.................................C3
2 Coaker's Walk..............................D2

✦ **Activities, Courses & Tours**
3 Dolphin's Nose Walk.......................C3
4 Kodaikanal Boat & Rowing Club.........B2
5 TTDC Boat House...........................B2

◉ **Sleeping**
6 Carlton.......................................B2
7 Greenlands Youth Hostel..................C3
8 Hilltop Towers..............................C1
9 Snooze Inn..................................D1
10 Sri Vignesh Guest House.................C1
11 Villa Retreat...............................D2

✖ **Eating**
Carlton....................................(see 6)
12 Cloud Street...............................C1
13 Hotel Astoria..............................C1
14 Muncheez..................................C1
15 Pastry Corner..............................C2
16 Tava...C1
Ten Degrees.............................(see 8)

◉ **Drinking & Nightlife**
17 Cafe Cariappa.............................C1

◉ **Shopping**
18 Potter's Shed..............................C1
19 Re Shop.....................................C2

ⓘ **Information**
20 District Forest Office.....................D1

ⓘ **Transport**
21 Bus Stand..................................C1
Taxi Stand..............................(see 21)

and gaze to your heart's content. Discounts are often available.

Altaf's Cafe GUESTHOUSE $$
(☏9487120846; www.altafscafe.com; Vattakanal; r ₹1500-3500) Popular little Middle Eastern–Italian Altaf's Cafe (p403) runs a few sizeable doubles and three-bed rooms for six people (sometimes more!) with private bathroom, scattered across Vattakanal's hillside.

Mount Pleasant HOTEL $$
(☏9655126023, 04542-242023; www.kodaikanal-heritage.com; 19/12-20 Observatory Rd; d incl breakfast ₹2250-2600; ☎) Despite being out on the fringes of Kodai's spaghetti-like street map, 2km west of the centre, Mount Pleasant is worth finding for its quiet setting, tasty food, and the welcoming Keralan owner's quirky

style (colourful wall weavings, coconut-wood beds, coir matting) – though the rooms feel a bit dowdy. Book ahead.

Greenlands Youth Hostel HOSTEL $$
(☏04542-240899; www.greenlandskodaikanal.com; St Mary's Rd; dm ₹600, d ₹1900-3000; ☎) This long-running, sociable budget favourite has moved into the midrange category, though many of its rooms don't reflect this. There's a pretty garden and wonderful views but the cheaper digs are basic. Hot water runs only from 8am to 10am. Dorms *may* be available, but are aimed at groups. Newer, comfier 'superdeluxes' are more modern, with colourful decor and balconies.

Hilltop Towers HOTEL $$
(☏04542-240413; www.hilltopgroup.in; Club Rd; incl breakfast d ₹2775-3150, ste ₹3600; ☎) Although it's bland on the outside, rustic flourishes like polished-teak floors, plus keen staff, in-room tea/coffee sets and a central location make the Hilltop a good-value midranger.

★**Carlton** HERITAGE HOTEL $$$
(☏04542-248555; www.carlton-kodaikanal.com; Lake Rd; r incl breakfast weekday/weekend from ₹8820/11,780; ☎) The cream of Kodai's hotels is a magnificent five-star colonial-era mansion overlooking the lake. Rooms are spacious with extra-comfy beds and, for some, huge private balconies. The grounds and common areas get the old hill-station ambience spot on: open-stone walls, billiards, evening bingo, fireplaces, a hot tub and a bar that immediately makes you want to demand a Scotch.

The good, buffet-focused restaurant (p403) is Kodai's classiest.

Cinnabar HOMESTAY $$$
(☏9842145220; www.cinnabar.in; Chettiar Rd; r incl half-board ₹6000; ☎) ✎ Cinnabar's two elegant yet homey rooms offer a blissful escape, with 24-hour hot water, tea/coffee kits, glassed-in showers and lovely wooden floors and ceilings. Homemade cheese, bread, granola, jams and 'world' cuisine come courtesy of the clued-up owners, who recommend local hikes and source all ingredients from their organic fruit-and-veg garden out front. It's 2km north of town.

Elephant Valley FARMSTAY $$$
(☏9655439879; www.duneecogroup.com; Ganesh Puram, Pethupari; r incl breakfast with/without AC ₹9500/6500, ste from ₹15,350; ☎) ✎ Deep in

THE NILGIRIS & THEIR TRIBES

The forest-clothed, waterfall-threaded Nilgiris (Blue Mountains) rise abruptly from the surrounding plains between the lowland towns of Mettupalayam (southeast) and Gudalur (northwest). The upland territory, a jumble of valleys and hills with more than 20 peaks above 2000m, is a botanist's dream, with over 2300 flowering plant species, although much of the native *shola* forest and grasslands have been displaced by tea, coffee, eucalyptus and cattle.

Parts of the range are included in the Unesco-designated Nilgiri Biosphere Reserve, a 5520-sq-km area that arcs through Kerala, Tamil Nadu and Karnataka. One of the world's biodiversity hot spots, it contains several important tiger reserves, national parks and wildlife sanctuaries.

The Nilgiris' tribal inhabitants were left pretty much to themselves in this isolated homeland until the British arrived two centuries ago. Today, colonialism, migration, and Forest Department policies have reduced many tribal cultures to the point of collapse, and some have assimilated to the point of invisibility. Others, however, continue at least a semitraditional lifestyle.

Best known in Tamil Nadu's Western Ghats, thanks to their proximity to Ooty, are the Toda (around 1500). Some still inhabit tiny villages *(munds)* of traditional barrel-shaped huts made of bamboo, cane and grass. Toda women style their hair in long, shoulder-length ringlets, and are skilled embroiderers; both sexes wear distinctive black-and-red-embroidered shawls. Central to Toda life is the water buffalo, which provides milk and ghee. Traditionally, it is only at funerals that the strictly vegetarian Toda kill a buffalo, to accompany the deceased.

Other tribes include the Kota (from around Kotagiri), Badaga, Irula, and Kurumba.

If you're interested in learning more about these communities, don't miss the Tribal Research Centre Museum (p409), 10km southwest of Ooty. Organisations such as the Kotagiri-based Keystone Foundation (p408) work to promote traditional crafts and activities.

the valley 22km northeast of Kodaikanal, off the Kodaikanal–Palani Rd, this ecofriendly French-run retreat sprawls across 48 hectares of mountain jungle and organic farm. Elephants, peacocks and bison wander through, and comfy local-material cottages, including a tree house, sit either side of a river. The French-Indian restaurant does wonderful meals packed with garden-fresh veg, and home-grown coffee. Wildlife spotting peaks April to July.

Cardamom House HOTEL $$$
(☏9360691793, 0451-2556765; www.cardamom house.com; near Athoor Village; r ₹4130-5550, with AC ₹5200-6500; ❄️🛜🐕) 🏊 A beautiful hill-fringed hideaway, three hours' drive below Kodaikanal, seven-room Cardamom House overlooks bird-rich Lake Kamarajar (which you can admire from the pool). It's run with love by a retired Brit and local staff, and delicious meals (₹400 to ₹700) are made from locally sourced ingredients. Book well ahead. It's 5km west of Athoor Village, off the Dindigul–Batlagundu Rd.

Villa Retreat HOTEL $$$
(☏04542-240940; www.villaretreat.com; Club Rd; r incl breakfast ₹4250-7660; 🛜) Take in the fantastic Coaker's Walk views from your garden breakfast table at this lovely old stone-built hotel, right next to the walk's northern end. It's a friendly place with comfy, good-sized rooms and, when it's cold, a roaring fire in the dining room. Prices are steep, but service is attentive. Morning nature walks are offered.

🍽 Eating

⭐ **Hotel Astoria** INDIAN $
(Anna Salai; mains ₹110-150, thalis ₹115-155; ⏰7am-10pm) This pure-veg restaurant is always packed with locals and tourists, especially at lunchtime when it serves fantastic all-you-can-eat thalis.

Pastry Corner BAKERY $
(3 Maratta Shopping Complex, Anna Salai; pastries from ₹80; ⏰10.30am-2pm & 3-6.30pm) Pick up oven-fresh muffins, croissants, cakes, cinnamon swirls and sandwiches at this popular bakery, or squeeze on to the benches with a cuppa.

Tava   INDIAN $
(PT Rd; mains ₹70-140; ☺11.30am-8.45pm Thu-Tue) Cheap, fast and clean, pure-veg Tava has a wide all-Indian menu; try the spicy, cauliflower-stuffed *gobi paratha* or *sev puri* (crisp, puffy fried bread with potato and chutney).

Ten Degrees   MULTICUISINE $$
(PT Rd; mains ₹260-480; ☺noon-10pm) Honey-coloured wood and monochrome Kodai photos set the tone for tasty, elegantly prepared Indian and continental food. It does mouth-meltingly spicy wraps, homemade-bread sandwiches, burgers, salads, sizzlers, egg-based breakfasts and drinks served in jars.

Altaf's Cafe   MULTICUISINE $$
(☑9487120846; www.altafscafe.com; Vattakanal; dishes ₹70-200; ☺8am-8.30pm) This open-sided cafe whips up soulful Italian, Indian and Middle Eastern dishes including breakfasts and *sabich* (Israeli aubergine-and-egg pita sandwiches), plus teas, coffees, juices and lassis, for hungry travellers in Vattakanal.

Muncheez   CONTINENTAL $$
(www.facebook.com/kodaimuncheez; PT Rd; mains ₹80-450; ☺noon-9pm Fri-Wed) An always-busy hole-in-the-wall turned contemporary lounge with a signature-plastered bar, Muncheez is all about a short, simple menu of wraps, burgers, sandwiches and pizzas. Some fillings have delicious Indian twists, like *aloo jeera* (cumin potato) or red-hot paneer.

Carlton   MULTICUISINE $$$
(Lake Rd; buffet ₹950; ☺7.30-10.30am, 1-3pm & 7.30-10pm) Definitely the place to come for a splash-out buffet-dinner fill-up: a huge variety of excellent Indian and continental dishes in limitless quantity. Lunch is à la carte.

Cloud Street   MULTICUISINE $$$
(www.cloudstreetcafe.com; PT Rd; mains ₹290-600; ☺9-11am, 12.30-4pm & 6-9pm; ☏) Why yes,

that is a real Italian-style wood-fire pizza oven. And yes, that's hummus and falafel on the menu, along with oven-baked pasta and homemade cakes. It's all great food in a simple, relaxed, family-run setting with scattered candles and a crackling fire on cold nights. Live music every other Saturday.

🍷 Drinking & Nightlife

★**Cafe Cariappa**   CAFE
(www.facebook.com/cafecariappa; PT Rd; coffees ₹80-100; ☺11am-6.30pm Tue-Sun; ☏) A caffeine addict's dream, this rustic-chic wood-panelled shoebox of a cafe crafts fantastic brews from its own locally grown organic coffee. It also does homemade carrot cake, crêpes, sandwiches and fresh juices, and sells Kodai-made cheeses.

🛍 Shopping

Re Shop   ARTS & CRAFTS
(www.facebook.com/bluemangotrust; Seven Rd Junction; ☺10am-1pm & 2-7pm Mon-Sat) ✄ Stylish jewellery, fabrics, cards and more, at reasonable prices, made by and benefiting marginalised village women around Tamil Nadu.

Potter's Shed   CERAMICS
(PT Rd; ☺11am-1pm & 2-6pm Mon-Sat) Perfect for pretty locally made mugs, bowls, plates and other pottery.

ⓘ Information

Tourist office (☑04542-241675; PT Rd; ☺10am-5.30pm Mon-Sat, to 2pm Sun) Doesn't look too promising at first glance but it's helpful enough.

ⓘ Getting There & Away

BUS
For most destinations, it's quickest and easiest to take a bus from Kodai's **bus stand** (Anna Salai).

Private Buses
Raja's Tours & Travels (☑9842142851; http://rajastours.com; Anna Salai; ☺8am-9pm) runs 20-seat minibuses with push-back seats to Ooty

TAMIL NADU KODAIKANAL (KODAI)

GOVERNMENT BUSES FROM KODAIKANAL

DESTINATION	FARE (₹)	TIME (HR)	DEPARTURES
Bengaluru (Bangalore)	650	12	5.30pm
Chennai	600	12	6.30pm
Coimbatore	175	6	8.20am, 4.15pm
Madurai	120	4	15 daily
Trichy (Tiruchirappalli)	190	6	1.45pm, 3.30pm, 5.40pm, 6pm, 7pm

(₹500, eight hours, 7.30pm), plus overnight AC sleeper and semisleeper buses to Chennai (₹800 to ₹1200, 12 hours, 6.30pm) and Bengaluru (₹700 to ₹1000, 12 hours, 6.30pm). There are many other tour companies based at the bus stand.

TRAIN

The nearest train station is Kodai Rd, down in the plains 80km east of Kodaikanal. There are four daily trains to/from Chennai Egmore including the overnight Pandian Express (sleeper/3AC/2AC/1AC ₹295/765/1075/1815, 7½ hours), departing Chennai at 9.20pm and departing Kodai Rd northbound at 9.10pm. Kodai's post office has a **train booking office** (Post Office, Post Office Rd; ◷9am-4pm Mon-Fri, to 2pm Sat).

Direct buses from Kodaikanal to Kodai Rd leave daily at 10.20am and 4.25pm (₹55, three hours); there are also plenty of buses between the train station and Batlagundu, on the Kodai–Madurai bus route. Taxis to/from the station cost ₹1200.

ⓘ Getting Around

Central Kodaikanal is compact and easily walkable. There are no autorickshaws (believe it or not), but plenty of taxis. The minimum charge is ₹150 for up to 3km; to/from Vattakanal costs ₹400.

Bike rental is available around the lake (per hour ₹100).

Coimbatore

☏0422 / POP 1.6 MILLION

This big business and junction city – Tamil Nadu's second largest, often known as the Manchester of India for its textile industry – is friendly enough and increasingly cosmopolitan, but the lack of interesting sights means that for most travellers it's just a stepping stone towards Ooty or Kerala. There are plenty of accommodation and eating options if you're staying overnight.

🏃 Activities

Isha Yoga Center
YOGA, MEDITATION

(☏8300083111; www.ishafoundation.org; Poondi) This well-known ashram is 30km west of Coimbatore. Outside, there's a massive black sculpture of Shiva – claimed as the world's biggest bust-statue; inside are a series of artistically designed temples, including one housing the Dhyanalinga, believed to embody all seven chakras. Visitors are welcome for meditations; if you want to stay or take yoga courses, book ahead.

Direct buses to the ashram leave from Coimbatore's Town Bus Stand (Gandhipu-

ram) – go to the website and click on Travel Information for timings and bus numbers.

🛏 Sleeping & Eating

iStay
HOTEL $$

(www.hotelistay.com; Devi & Co Lane; s/d incl breakfast ₹2100/2600; ❄️🛜) More modern, more comfortable and less noisy than some of its neighbours, iStay offers some of the best-value AC rooms across from the railway station – and in all of Coimbatore.

Corner Stay
GUESTHOUSE $$

(☏9842220742; www.cornerstay.in; 4/1 Abdul Rahim Rd, opp DIG office; r ₹2000-3000; ❄️🛜) On a quiet Racecourse-area lane, this homey guesthouse offers three impeccable, tastefully styled rooms with a communal lounge and balcony. Two share a kitchen, the other has its own, and there are home-cooked meals. It's 2km northeast of the train station.

Hotel ESS Grande
HOTEL $$

(☏0422-2230271; www.hotelessgrande.com; 358-360 Nehru St; incl breakfast s/d from ₹2450/2900; ❄️@) Handy for a few of Coimbatore's bus stands, friendly ESS has small but very clean, fresh rooms. Steep discounts are available on slow days. There are several other midrange and budget hotels on this street.

Residency Towers
HOTEL $$$

(☏0422-2241414; www.theresidency.com; 1076 Avinashi Rd; s/d from ₹5200/5750; ❄️@🛜🏊) Opening through a soaring lobby, the Residency is a top choice for its professional staff, well-equipped rooms, swimming pool, and excellent eating and drinking options, including great-value buffet meals at the **Pavilion** (buffet breakfast/lunch/dinner ₹650/1215/1330; ◷7-10am, 12.30-3pm & 7-11pm). Check discounts online.

Junior Kuppanna
SOUTH INDIAN $$

(☏0422-235773; www.hoteljuniorkuppanna.com; 177 Sarojini Rd, Ram Nagar; mains ₹140-200, thalis ₹140-180; ◷noon-4pm & 6.30-11pm) Your favourite South Indian thalis come piled on to banana leaves with traditional flourish, and hungry carnivores will love the long menu of famously nonveg southern specialities, all from a perfectly spotless kitchen. Three branches across town.

Bird On Tree
MULTICUISINE $$$

(☏9865831000; www.birdontree.com; 23 Kamaraj Rd; mains ₹275-550; ◷noon-3pm & 7-10.30pm) With a tiny terrace up in the trees and several indoor spaces, this fashionable restaurant plates up well-prepared dishes covering everything from Southeast Asian sizzlers and stir-fries to Indian clay-pot curries and continental pastas and salads. It's 3km northeast of Coimbatore Junction.

On The Go MULTICUISINE $$$

(☏0422-4520116; www.onthegocbe.com; 167 Racecourse Rd; mains ₹275-560; ⊙12.30-2.45pm & 7.30-10.30pm) Colourful, contemporary, and filled with cartoons and turquoise sofas, this is a great place for tasty (if pricey) global fare, from Italian and Middle Eastern to Sri Lankan and North Indian.

⊙ Getting There & Away

AIR

The airport is 10km east of town. Direct daily flights to domestic destinations include Bengaluru, Chennai, Delhi, Hyderabad and Mumbai on Air India (www.airindia.in), IndiGo (www.goindigo.in) and Jet Airways (www.jetairways.com). SilkAir (www.silkair.com) flies four times weekly to/from Singapore.

BUS
SETC Bus Stand

Express or superfast AC and Volvo government buses go from the **SETC Bus Stand** (Thiruvalluvar Bus Stand; Bharathiyar Rd), which is across the street from the **Town Bus Stand** (Gandhipuram Bus Stand; cnr Dr Nanjappa & Bharathiyar Rds).

Bengaluru non-AC/AC ₹460/740, nine hours, 12 daily

Chennai non-AC ₹510, AC ₹663-1020, 11 hours, eight buses 5.30pm to 10.30pm

Ernakulam non-AC ₹182, 5½ hours, eight daily

Mysuru non-AC/AC ₹190/420, six hours, 27 daily

Trivandrum non-AC/AC ₹355/725, 10½ hours, seven daily

Ooty Bus Stand

The **Ooty Bus Stand** (New Bus Stand; Mettupalayam Rd), 5km northwest of the train station, has services to Ooty (₹60, four hours) via Mettupalayam (₹20, one hour) and Coonoor (₹45, three hours) every 10 minutes, plus half-hourly buses to Kotagiri (₹34, three hours), 28 buses daily to Mysuru (₹188 to ₹420, six hours) and 11 to Bengaluru (₹460 to ₹740, nine hours). At busy times, you may wait up to two hours to board buses to Ooty/Coonoor.

Singanallur Bus Stand

From **Singanallur Bus Stand** (Kamaraj Rd), 6km east of the centre, buses go to Trichy (₹160, five

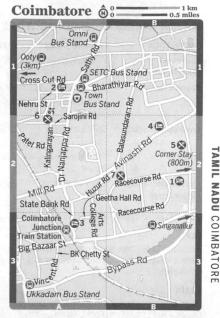

Coimbatore

⊙ Sleeping
1 Corner Stay	B2
2 Hotel ESS Grande	A1
3 iStay	A3
4 Residency Towers	B2

⊗ Eating
5 Bird On Tree	B2
6 Junior Kuppanna	A2
7 On The Go	B2
Pavilion	(see 4)

hours), Thanjavur (₹200, 7¼ hours) and Madurai (₹170, five hours) every 10 minutes. Bus 140 (₹14) shuttles between here and the Town Bus Stand.

Ukkadam

Ukkadam Bus Stand (NH Rd), 1.5km southwest of the train station, has buses to southern destinations including Pollachi (₹33, 1¼ hours, every five minutes), Kodaikanal (₹144, six hours, 10am) and Munnar (₹157, 6½ hours, 8.15am).

Private Buses

Private buses to destinations such as Bengaluru, Chennai, Ernakulam, Puducherry, Trichy and Trivandrum start from the **Omni Bus Stand** (Sathy Rd), 500m north of the Town Bus Stand, or from ticket-selling agencies on Sathy Rd.

MAJOR TRAINS FROM COIMBATORE

DESTINATION	TRAIN NO & NAME	FARE (₹)	DURATION (HR)	DEPARTURES
Bengaluru (Bangalore)	16525 Bangalore Express	260/700/1000 (B)	8½	10.55pm
Chennai Central	12676 Kovai Express	180/665 (A)	7½	3.20pm
	22640 Chennai Express	315/815/1150 (B)	7½	10.10pm
Ernakulam (Kochi)	12677 Ernakulam Express	105/390 (A)	3¾	12.55pm
Madurai	16610 Nagercoil Express	235/595 (C)	5½	7.20pm
Thiruvananthapuram (Trivandrum)	12695 Trivandrum Express	285/735/1030 (B)	9	11.10pm

Fares: (A) 2nd class/AC chair; (B) sleeper/3AC/2AC; (C) sleeper/3AC

TAXI

Taxis up to Ooty (three hours) cost ₹2500; Ooty buses often get so crowded that a taxi is worth considering.

TRAIN

Coimbatore Junction is on the main line between Chennai and Ernakulam (Kochi, Kerala), with at least 13 daily trains in each direction. The 5.15am Nilgiri Express to Mettupalayam (sleeper/3AC/2AC ₹170/540/745, one hour) connects with the miniature railway departure from Mettupalayam to Ooty at 7.10am. The whole trip to Ooty takes seven hours.

🛈 Getting Around

Many buses run between the train station and the Town Bus Stand (p405).

Autorickshaws charge ₹80 from the train station to the Ukkadam Bus Station (p405), ₹100 to the SETC (p405) or Town Bus Stand (p405) and ₹180 to the Ooty Bus Stand (p405).

Coonoor

📍0423 / POP 46,000 / ELEV 1720M

Coonoor is one of the three Nilgiri hill stations – Ooty, Kotagiri and Coonoor – that sit high above the southern plains. Smaller and quieter than Ooty (20km northwest), it has some fantastic heritage hotels and guesthouses, from which you can do exactly the same things (hike, visit tea plantations, marvel at mountain views) you would do from bigger, busier Ooty. From upper Coonoor, 1km to 3km northeast (uphill) from the town centre, you can look down over a sea of red-tile rooftops to the slopes beyond and soak up the cool climate, quiet environment

and beautiful scenery. But you get none of the above in lower (central) Coonoor, which is a bustling, honking mess.

⊙ Sights

Highfield Tea Estate   PLANTATION

(Walker's Hill Rd; ⊙9am-6pm) FREE Over 50 years old, this estate (2km northeast of upper Coonoor) is one of the few working Nilgiri tea factories open to visitors. Guides jump in quickly, but you're perfectly welcome to watch the full tea-making process independently. You can also, of course, taste and buy. The factory is closed Mondays, but the tea fields remain open.

Lamb's Rock   VIEWPOINT

(Dolphin's Nose Rd; ₹10, camera/video ₹20/50; ⊙8.30am-6pm) A favourite picnic spot in a patch of monkey-patrolled forest, Lamb's Rock has incredible views past glimmering tea and coffee plantations to the hazy plains below. It's 6km east of upper Coonoor – walkable, if you like.

Dolphin's Nose   VIEWPOINT

(Dolphin's Nose Rd; ₹10, camera/video ₹20/50; ⊙8.30am-6.30pm) About 10km west of town, this popular viewpoint exposes vast panoramas encompassing Catherine Falls (p408) across the valley.

Sim's Park   PARK

(Upper Coonoor; adult/child ₹30/15, camera/video ₹50/100; ⊙9am-5pm) Upper Coonoor's 12-hectare Sim's Park, established in 1874, is a peaceful oasis of sloping manicured lawns with more than 1000 plant species from several continents, including magnolia, tree ferns, roses and camellia. Kotagiri-bound buses drop you here.

🛏 Sleeping & Eating

Acres Wild FARMSTAY **$$**
(📞9443232621; www.acres-wild.com; 571 Upper Meanjee Estate, Kanni Mariamman Kovil St; r incl breakfast ₹3775-4360; 🛜) 🍴 This beautifully positioned farm on Coonoor's southeast edge is sustainably run with solar heating, rainwater harvesting and fresh cheeses from the milk of its own cows. Five large, stylish rooms, in three cottages, include kitchens and fireplaces. Your friendly host, Mansoor, is a great conversationalist and full of ideas for things to do away from the tourist crowds. Book ahead.

It also offers guests-only cheesemaking courses (from ₹8000).

YWCA Wyoming Guesthouse GUESTHOUSE **$$**
(📞0423-2234426;http://ywcaagooty.com;Bedford; s/d ₹1200/1900) A ramshackle, 150-year-old gem, the good-value Wyoming is draughty and creaky but oozes colonial character, with wooden terraces and serene town views through trees. Rooms are good and clean, with geysers, and simple meals are available on request.

★180° McIver HERITAGE HOTEL **$$$**
(📞0423-2233323; http://serendipityo.com; Orange Grove Rd, Upper Coonoor; r incl breakfast ₹4720-7080; 🛜) A classic 1900s British bungalow at the top of town has been transformed into something special. The six handsome, airy rooms sport antique furniture, working fireplaces and big fresh bathrooms. Panoramas from the wraparound lawn (where you can dine) of the on-site restaurant La Belle Vie are fabulous.

Gateway HERITAGE HOTEL **$$$**
(📞0423-2225400; www.tajhotels.com; Church Rd, Upper Coonoor; incl breakfast s from ₹6780, d/ste from ₹7375/13,400; 🛜) A colonial-era priory turned gorgeous heritage hotel, the Taj-group Gateway has homey cream-coloured rooms immersed in greenery, most graced by working fireplaces. Garden view rooms open onto a grassy terrace with views. Evening bonfires are lit on the lawn, the good Gateway All Day restaurant overlooks the gardens, and there's free yoga along with Keralan ayurvedic massages.

Nilgiri's Supermarket SUPERMARKET **$**
(Upper Coonoor; 🕤9am-9pm) Well-organised shelves are stocked with all of your self-

catering needs, from fresh veggies to candy bars, plus tonnes of toiletries.

★La Belle Vie MULTICUISINE **$$$**
(📞0423-2233323; http://serendipityo.com; 180° McIver, Orange Grove Rd, Upper Coonoor; mains ₹320-580; 🕤12.30-3.30pm & 7.30-10.30pm) With tables on the veranda of a beautifully revamped 19th-century bungalow, La Belle Vie has guests driving miles for its flavour-popping European-Indian food. Gazing out over the Nilgiris beyond a lovely lawn full of flower gardens, it's arguably Coonoor's most perfectly positioned restaurant.

Gateway All Day MULTICUISINE **$$$**
(📞0423-2225400; www.tajhotels.com; Gateway Hotel, Church Rd, Upper Coonoor; mains ₹400-600, dinner buffet ₹1060; 🕤7.30-10.30am, 12.30-2.45pm & 7.30-10.30pm) Tucked between manicured gardens, this signature heritage-hotel restaurant is a lovely place for splurging on polished global cuisine and brilliant breakfast buffets. You'll feel like a Raj-era VIP, sipping Nilgiri-grown tea in the suitably characterful colonial-style setting of a 160-year-old converted priory.

🛍 Shopping

Green Shop HANDICRAFTS, FOOD
(www.lastforest.in; Jograj Bldg, Bedford Circle; 🕤9.30am-7.30pm Mon-Sat) 🍴 Beautiful fair-trade local tribal crafts, clothes, fabrics and notebooks, plus organic wild honey, nuts, chocolates, soaps and teas.

ℹ Getting There & Away

Coonoor's **bus stand** (Lower Coonor) has frequent services to/from Ooty (₹16, one hour) and Kotagiri (₹20, 50 minutes).

Pick up buses to Coimbatore (₹45, three hours) at the **bus stop** (Coonoor Rd Roundabout) at the roundabout at the entrance to town, every 30 minutes.

Coonoor is on the miniature train line between Mettupalayam (1st/2nd class ₹185/25, 2¼ to 3¼ hours) and Ooty (₹150/25, 1¼ hours), with three daily trains just to/from Ooty, as well as the daily Mettupalayam–Ooty–Mettupalayam service.

Kotagiri
📞04266 / POP 28,200 / ELEV 1800M

The oldest and smallest of the three Nilgiri hill stations, Kotagiri is set in the most beautiful location of them all – 30km east of Ooty, beyond one of Tamil Nadu's highest passes. The forgettable town centre is surrounded

Nilgiri Hills

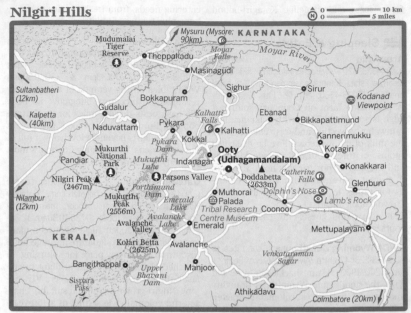

by plunging ridges sculpted with tea estates and dotted with pastel villages, framed by the high green walls of the Nilgiris.

Sights & Activities

A half-day taxi tour encompassing **Catherine Falls** (Kotagiri-Mettupalayam Rd) and **Kodanad Viewpoint** (Kodanad; ☻dawn-dusk) costs around ₹1200.

Sullivan Memorial   MUSEUM
(☎9488771571; Kannerimukku; adult/child ₹10/5; ☻10am-5pm Thu-Tue) Just 2km north of Kotagiri centre, the house built in 1819 by Ooty founder John Sullivan has been refurbished in bright red and filled with fascinating photos, newspaper cuttings and artefacts related to local tribal groups, European settlement and icons like the miniature train. Also here is the Nilgiri Documentation Centre (www.nilgiridocumentation.com), dedicated to preserving the region's beauty and heritage.

Keystone Foundation   VOLUNTEERING
(☎04266-272277; http://keystone-foundation.org; Groves Hill Rd) ☙ This Kotagiri-based NGO works to improve environmental conditions in the Nilgiris while involving, and improving living standards for, indigenous communities. Occasional openings for volunteers who are willing to stay at least one month.

Sleeping

★La Maison   HERITAGE HOTEL $$$
(☎9585857732; www.lamaison.in; Hadatharai; s/d from ₹5625/6750; ☎) Flower-draped, French-owned La Maison is a beautifully renovated 1890s Scottish bungalow superbly situated on a hilltop surrounded by tea plantations, 5km southwest of Kotagiri. Casual yet stylish, here you'll find antique furniture, tribal handicrafts, old-Ooty paintings and two friendly dogs. Hike to waterfalls, visit tribal villages, savour home-cooked meals (₹900) or laze in the valley-facing hot tub. A special place!

Shopping

Green Shop   FOOD, HANDICRAFTS
(http://lastforest.in; Johnstone Sq; ☻9.30am-7pm) ☙ The ecofriendly Keystone Foundation's shop has goodies for picnics (local chocolates, wild honey) plus lovely tribal crafts.

Getting There & Away

Buses run half-hourly to/from Ooty (₹26, 1½ hours) and every 15 minutes to/from Coonoor (₹16, one hour) and Mettupalayam (₹25, 1½ hours). Buses to Coimbatore (₹60, 2½ hours) leave every 45 minutes.

Taxis to/from Ooty cost ₹1500.

Ooty (Udhagamandalam)

⚹0423 / POP 90,000 / ELEV 2240M

Ooty, 'Queen of Hill Stations', mixes Indian bustle and Hindu temples with beautiful gardens, an international school and charming Raj-era bungalows (which provide its most atmospheric accommodation). It may be a bit hectic, especially its messy centre, but it doesn't take long to escape into quieter, greener areas where tall pines rise above what could almost be English country lanes.

Memorably nicknamed 'Snooty Ooty', it was established by the British in the early 19th century as the summer headquarters of the Madras government. Development ploughed through a few decades ago, but old Ooty survives in patches – you just have to walk further out to find it.

The journey up here on the celebrated miniature train is romantic and the scenery stunning. Even the road up is impressive. During the April-to-June 'season', Ooty is a welcome relief from the steaming plains. Between October and March, overnight temperatures occasionally drop to 0°C.

⊙ Sights

Tribal Research Centre Museum   MUSEUM
(Muthorai Palada; Indian/foreigner ₹5/100; ☺10am-1pm & 2-5pm Mon-Fri, hours vary) If you're interested in the Nilgiris' tribal communities you'll love this slightly scruffy, erratically open museum, with its fascinating exhibits on Nilgiri and other Tamil Nadu tribal groups (including model huts) and its fantastic artefacts (like the skulls of buffalo sacrificed at Toda funerals). Detailed English-language descriptions are good. It's just southwest of Muthorai Palada (M Palada), 10km southwest of Ooty en route to Avalanche and served by frequent buses.

Botanical Gardens   GARDENS
(www.ootygardens.com; Garden Rd; adult/child ₹30/15, camera/video ₹50/100; ☺7am-6.30pm) Established in 1848, these pretty 22-hectare gardens are a living gallery of the Nilgiris' natural flora. Keep an eye out for a typical Toda *mund* (village), a fossilised tree trunk believed to be 20 million years old and, on busy days, around 20 million tourists.

St Thomas' Church   CHURCH
(St Thomas Rd; ☺dawn-dusk) Set between trees at the eastern end of Ooty Lake, simple St Thomas' dates back to 1870.

Doddabetta   VIEWPOINT
(Ooty-Kotagiri Rd; ₹10, camera/video ₹10/50; ☺8am-5pm) About 7km east of Ooty, Doddabetta is the highest point (2633m) in the Nilgiris. On clear days, it's one of the best viewpoints around; go early for a better chance of mist-free views. Kotagiri buses will drop you at the Doddabetta junction, then it's a steep 3km walk or a quick jeep ride. Taxis do return trips from Charring Cross (₹700).

Rose Garden   GARDENS
(Selbourne Rd; adult/child ₹30/15, camera/video ₹50/100; ☺7.30am-6.30pm) With terraced lawns and over 20,000 rose bushes of more than 2000 varieties – best between May and July – the Rose Garden is a sweet place for a stroll, and has good Ooty views from its hillside location.

Nilgiri Library   LIBRARY
(⚹0423-2441699; Hospital Rd; ☺9.30am-1.30pm & 2.30-5.30pm) This quaint little haven in a crumbling, earthy-red 1867 building houses more than 30,000 books, including rare titles on the Nilgiris and hill tribes, and 19th-century British journals. Visitors can consult books in the reading room with a temporary one-month membership (₹500). Upstairs is a portrait of Queen Victoria presented to Ooty on her 1887 Golden Jubilee.

The library hosts the Ooty Literary Festival (www.ootylitfest.com) each September.

St Stephen's Church   CHURCH
(Church Hill Rd; ☺9.30am-4.30pm Mon-Sat, 6.30am-1.30pm Sun) Perched above Ooty's centre, immaculate pale-yellow St Stephen's, built in 1829, is the Nilgiris' oldest church. It has lovely stained glass, huge wooden beams hauled by elephant from the palace of Tipu Sultan 120km away, and slabs and plaques donated by colonial-era churchgoers. In the overgrown cemetery you'll find headstones commemorating many an Ooty Brit, including Ooty founder John Sullivan's wife and daughter.

🏃 Activities

The best of Ooty is out in the beautiful Nilgiri Hills. Most hotels can put you in touch with local guides who do half-day hikes for around ₹600 per person. You'll normally drive out of town and walk through hills, tribal villages and tea plantations. The **Tourist Office** (⚹0423-2443977; www.tamilnadu tourism.org; Wenlock Rd; ☺10am-5pm) can also

Ooty (Udhagamandalam)

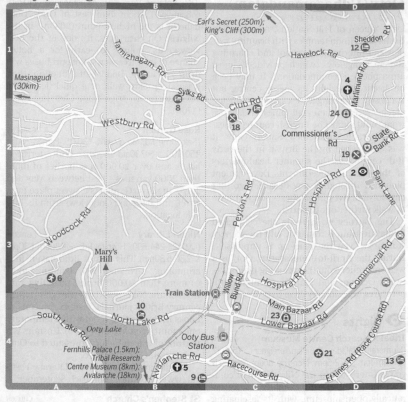

suggest some nice routes for do-it-yourself 'rural walks' between villages south of Ooty.

Overnight trekking in the forests around Ooty has been banned due to rising human–animal conflict in the region; a couple of foreigners have been trampled to death by elephants, and multiple tiger attacks on local villagers (some fatal) have occurred.

There are also concerns that unruly tourists are too disruptive in the forest at night. If you're interested in finding out if the policy has changed, contact the **Office of the Field Director** (☎0423-2445971; fdmtr@ tn.nic.in; Mt Stuart Hill; ⊙10am-5.45pm Mon-Fri) for info.

Boathouse
BOATING

(North Lake Rd; ₹13, camera/video ₹25/150; ⊙9am-6pm) Rowing boats and pedal boats can be rented from the boathouse by Ooty Lake. Prices start from ₹85 per person (with a ₹180 deposit) for a two-seater pedal boat (30 minutes).

🛏 Sleeping

Ooty has some gorgeous colonial-era homes at the high end and some decent backpacker crashpads, but there isn't much in the lower midrange. During the 'season' (1 April to 15 June) hotels hike rates and checkout time is often 9am. Book well ahead for public holidays.

YWCA Anandagiri
GUESTHOUSE **$**

(☎0423-2444262; www.ywcaagooty.com; Ettines Rd; dm ₹250, s ₹500-3300, d ₹1200-3300) This former brewery and sprawling complex of cottages is dotted with flower gardens. With clean, character-filled and freshly painted rooms, helpful staff, spacious common areas and a good restaurant (book ahead), you've got some excellent-value budget accommodation. The cheapest rooms have private bathrooms across the corridor. High ceilings can mean cold nights, but you can ask for extra blankets.

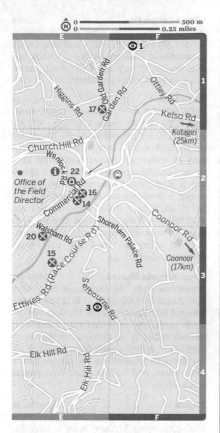

Ooty (Udhagamandalam)

◉ Sights
1 Botanical Gardens F1
2 Nilgiri Library......................................D2
3 Rose Garden..E3
4 St Stephen's Church D1
5 St Thomas' Church..............................B4

◎ Activities, Courses & Tours
6 Boathouse...A3

◎ Sleeping
7 Hotel Welbeck Residency...................C2
8 Lymond House.....................................B2
9 Mount View Hotel B4
10 Reflections Guest House B4
11 Savoy...B1
12 Wyoming..D1
13 YWCA Anandagiri D4

◎ Eating
14 Adyar Ananda Bhavan E2
15 Angaara..E3
16 Junior Kuppana....................................E2
17 Modern Stores......................................E1
18 Place to Bee...C2
   Savoy..(see 11)
19 Shinkow's Chinese Restaurant...........D2
20 Willy's Coffee Pub................................E3

◎ Entertainment
21 Ooty Racecourse D4

◎ Shopping
   Green Shop...................................(see 18)
22 Higginbothams......................................E2
23 K Mahaveer Chand C4
24 Mohan's..D2

Reflections Guest House
GUESTHOUSE $

(☑9843637974; reflectionsin@yahoo.co.in; 1B North Lake Rd; r ₹600-1600; ☎) A long-standing budget haunt, Reflections sits across the road from Ooty Lake. Most of its 12 spotless, good-value rooms have lake views; the best come with freshly updated bathrooms and open on to a grassy terrace. The super attentive owners serve snacks on request and can organise guided treks. Hot water is available anytime when requested.

Wyoming
HERITAGE HOTEL $$

(☑0423-2452008; www.wyoming.in; 46 Sheddon Rd; r incl breakfast ₹3200-3800; ☎) Six simple, wonderfully spacious colonial-feel rooms open up to classic Nilgiri panoramas at this delightful sun-yellow heritage house high above Ooty. All have kettles, bottled water and pretty wood-panelled floors. It's well run by friendly hosts and you can enjoy breakfast in the table-dotted garden.

Lymond House
HERITAGE HOTEL $$

(☑9843149490; www.serendipityo.com; Sylks Rd; r incl breakfast ₹4200-5470; ☎) This 1855 British bungalow has an edge over many of its peers. The cosy cottage features garden-fresh flowers, four-poster beds, working fireplaces and antique-lined lounges. The more expensive rooms are spacious and dramatic, while cheaper ones have less character and are perhaps showing wear around the edges. The cute restaurant serves good multicuisine food. Management is informal yet efficient.

Hotel Welbeck Residency
HOTEL $$

(☑0423-2223300; www.welbeck.in; Welbeck Circle, Club Rd; r from ₹3650; ☎) An attractive older building that's been thoroughly spruced up with comfortable rooms, a touch of colonial-era class (a 1920 Austin saloon car at the front door!), a decent restaurant and very keen staff.

Mount View Hotel
HOTEL **$$**

(☎9566410117; www.mountviewheritage.com; Ettines Rd; r ₹1770-4130; ☜) Perched on a quiet (bumpy) driveway handy for the bus and train stations, the nine enormous, high-ceilinged, wood-lined rooms in this old bungalow have been done up comfortably enough. The best have private terraces. Hot water is available in the morning and evening, and management is attentive. Look at a few rooms, as each is different.

Savoy
HERITAGE HOTEL **$$$**

(☎0423-2225500; www.gateway.tajhotels.com; 77 Sylks Rd; r incl breakfast from ₹6400; ☜) The Savoy is one of Ooty's oldest hotels, with parts dating back to 1829. Cottages and swing-chairs are set around a charming lawn and garden. Colonial-style rooms have huge marble-clad bathrooms, log fires and bay windows. Welcome touches include a cocktail bar, an ayurveda centre and an excellent multicuisine dining room. Suites are much nicer than standard rooms.

King's Cliff
HERITAGE HOTEL **$$$**

(☎0423-2244000; www.littlearth.in; Havelock Rd; r incl breakfast ₹3275-9410; ☜) Hidden away above Ooty on Strawberry Hill is this classic colonial-era house with wood panelling, antique furnishings, a snug lounge and good Indian/continental cooking at Earl's Secret, partly in a glassed-in conservatory. It's refined and comfortable. Cheaper rooms don't have the same old-world charm as the most expensive ones.

Fernhills Palace
HERITAGE HOTEL **$$$**

(☎0423-2443910; www.welcomheritagehotels.in; Fern Hill; r incl breakfast ₹12,160-38,400; ☜) The Maharaja of Mysore's exquisite Anglo-Indian summer palace is full of totally over-the-top princely colonial style. All 19 rooms are gigantic suites, with antique furnishings, teak flourishes, tiled floors, fireplaces and hot tubs. Some are pristine, others need a paint job. You can play billiards, stroll the forest-fringed grounds and dine beneath wood-carved ceilings. The Maharaja himself stays here sometimes.

 Eating

Modern Stores
SUPERMARKET **$**

(144 Garden Rd; ☺9.30am-8.30pm Wed-Mon, 11am-8.30pm Tue) Stocks all kinds of international foods, from muesli to marmalade, along with particularly good Western Ghats produce, such as breads, cheeses and chocolates.

Willy's Coffee Pub
CAFE **$**

(KCR Arcade, Walsham Rd; dishes ₹60-120; ☺10am-9.30pm; ☜) Climb the stairs and join Ooty's international students for board games, wifi, a lending library and well-priced pizzas, chips, toasties, cakes and biscuits.

Place to Bee
ITALIAN **$$**

(☎0423-2449464; www.facebook.com/placetObee; 176A Club Rd; mains ₹260-400; ☺12.30-3pm & 6.30-9.30pm Wed-Mon) 🍃 Brush up on Nilgiri-bee facts over meals at this arty, fairy-lit restaurant tucked inside the Keystone Foundation's (p408) little Bee Museum. It might sound bizarre, but the concept works, ingredients are locally sourced, and the divinely fresh dishes – many involving wild honey – don't disappoint. Choose from expertly executed pastas, Mediterranean-inspired salads and real-deal, build-your-own wood-fired pizzas.

Adyar Ananda Bhavan
INDIAN **$$**

(www.aabsweets.in; 58 Commercial Rd; mains ₹130-200, thalis ₹100-200; ☺7.30-11.30am, noon-3.30pm & 6-10.30pm) This sparkly Ooty favourite is constantly crammed with locals and tourists filling up on delicious, swiftly delivered South Indian staples (dosa, *vada, idli*), North Indian classics (try the paneer tikka), fresh juices, and thalis heaped onto plastic yellow trays.

Angaara
INDIAN **$$**

(www.angaaraooty.com; 420 Ettines Rd; mains ₹200-450; ☺noon-10.30pm) With a long list of nonveg tandoori and curry dishes, this is Ooty's best place to satisfy your meat craving. There's indoor/outdoor seating, and the decor is a weird mash-up of vintage and modern. There's also plenty here for vegetarians.

Junior Kuppana
SOUTH INDIAN **$$**

(www.hoteljuniorkuppanna.com; Commercial Rd; mains ₹150-220, thalis ₹160; ☺8.30am-4.30pm & 6.30-10pm) Ooty's branch of the much-loved Tamil Nadu chain – known for its pristine kitchens and brilliantly fresh ingredients – delivers the South Indian goods with *idli,* dosa, *sambar,* chutneys, limitless thalis and plenty of meaty extras for carnivores.

Shinkow's Chinese Restaurant
CHINESE **$$**

(38/83 Commissioner's Rd; mains ₹180-350; ☺noon-4pm & 6.30-10pm) Shinkow's is an Ooty institution. The simple, tasty chicken, pork, beef, seafood, veg, noodle and rice dishes are reliably good and quick to arrive at your chequer-print table. You'll leave full!

| WORTH A TRIP |

AVALANCHE VALLEY

The serene, protected Avalanche Valley – which extends towards Kerala from around 20km southwest of Ooty – provides the perfect antidote to Ooty's crowds. Rolling farmlands and twinkling tea plantations give way to hushed hills thick with orchids and native *shola* (virgin forest), where wildlife includes leopards, sloth bears, deer, langurs and the odd tiger (though you'd be lucky to spot them).

Access is restricted, so the only way to explore this blissfully peaceful area is by official two-hour forest department minibus **'ecotours'** (www.ootyavalanche.com; per person ₹150; ⊙9.30am-3pm) or private-hire jeep trips (₹2000). There are several scenic stops along the way.

Minibuses depart from the southern side of Avalanche Lake – officially at 9.30am, 11.30am, 1.30pm and 3.30pm Monday to Friday, and about 30 minutes later on weekends. Timings, however, are inconsistent, as they leave when full, and if you miss a bus you may have to wait a long time for the next one.

Ooty taxi drivers charge ₹1600 for a return trip to the ecotour starting point, including waiting time.

Earl's Secret MULTICUISINE $$$
(☑0423-2452888; www.littlearth.in; King's Cliff, Havelock Rd; mains ₹350-550; ⊙8-10am, noon-3pm & 7-10pm; ☎) You get a taste of everything at this elegant heritage-hotel restaurant up above Ooty. Half glassed-in conservatory, half tables scattered across Raj-era lounges with roaring winter fires, it does beautifully prepared Indian (mostly northern), continental and Southeast Asian dishes, including deliciously hot soups that are a godsend for chilly Ooty nights.

Savoy MULTICUISINE $$$
(☑0423-2225500; www.gateway.tajhotels.com; 77 Sylks Rd; mains ₹275-650; ⊙7.30-10am, 12.30-3pm & 7.30-10.30pm) All wood walls, intimate lighting, live piano and plush orange velvets, the Savoy's candlelit dining room dishes up fabulous contemporary continental, Indian and pan-Asian cuisine – including all-day breakfasts, yummy salads, pastas and kebabs, and some unique tribal-inspired dishes.

☆ Entertainment

Ooty Racecourse HORSE RACING
(Ettines Rd; ₹100; ⊙mid-Apr–mid-Jun) Ooty's racecourse dominates the valley between Charring Cross and the lake. Racing season runs from mid-April to mid-June, and on the two or three race days held each week the town is a hive of activity. Racing usually happens between 10am and 1pm, though this varies depending on participant numbers.

🛍 Shopping

K Mahaveer Chand JEWELLERY
(291 Main Bazaar Rd; ⊙10am-8pm) K Mahaveer Chand has been selling particularly beautiful Toda tribal and silver jewellery for nearly 50 years.

Green Shop HANDICRAFTS, FOOD
(www.lastforest.in; Sargan Villa, off Club Rd; ⊙9.30am-8.45pm) 🌿 Run by Kotagiri's Keystone Foundation (p408), this fair-trade, organic-oriented shop sells gorgeous tribal crafts and clothes (including Toda embroidery), and wild honey harvested by local indigenous farmers.

Higginbothams BOOKS
(Commercial Rd; ⊙9am-1pm & 3.30-7.30pm) A well-known chain with a good stash of English-language books.

Mohan's CLOTHING, ANTIQUES
(Commissioner's Rd; ⊙10am-1.30pm & 3-8pm Fri-Wed) A curious assortment of antique telephones, radios and clocks, along with shawls, jewellery and warm clothes.

ℹ Getting There & Away

The fun way to arrive in Ooty is on the miniature train from Mettupalayam. Buses also run regularly up and down the mountain from across Tamil Nadu, from Kerala, and from Mysuru and Bengaluru in Karnataka.

BUS

The Tamil Nadu and Karnataka state bus companies have reservation offices at Ooty's busy **bus**

BUSES FROM OOTY (UDHAGAMANDALAM)

DESTINATION	FARE (₹)	TIME (HR)	DEPARTURES
Bengaluru (Bangalore)	520-660	8	Volvo 7 daily
Chennai	650	14	4.30pm, 5.45pm, 6.30pm
Coimbatore	80	4	every 20min 5.50am-8.40pm
Coonoor	20	1	every 10min 5.30am-10pm
Kotagiri	26	1½	every 30min 6.30am-7pm, 7.40pm, 8.20pm
Mysuru (Mysore)	157-380	5	Express/Volvo 12/6 daily

station. For Kochi take a bus to Palakkad (₹96, six hours, 7am, 8am and 2pm) and change.

TRAIN

The miniature ('toy') train from Mettupalayam to Ooty – one of the Mountain Railways of India given World Heritage status by Unesco – is the best way to get here. The Nilgiri Mountain Railway requires special cog wheels on the locomotive, meshing with a third, 'toothed' rail on the ground, to manage the exceptionally steep gradients. There are wonderful forest, waterfall, mountainside and tea-plantation views along the way. The section between Mettupalayam and Coonoor uses steam engines, which push, rather than pull, the train up the hill.

For high season, book several weeks ahead; at other times a few days ahead is advisable (though not always essential). The train departs Mettupalayam for Ooty at 7.10am daily (1st/2nd class ₹205/30, 4¾ hours). From Ooty to Mettupalayam the train leaves at 2pm (3½ hours). There are also three daily trains each way just between Ooty and Coonoor (₹150/25, 1¼ hours). Departures and arrivals at Mettupalayam connect with the Nilgiri Express to/from Chennai Central (sleeper/3AC/2AC ₹340/895/1255, 9¼ hours).

Ooty is often listed as Udhagamandalam in train timetables. Mettupalayam is listed as Metupalaiyam (MTP).

TAXI

Taxis cluster at stands around town. Fixed one-way fares to many destinations include Coonoor (₹1200), Kotagiri (₹1500), Coimbatore (₹3000) and Mudumalai Tiger Reserve (₹1700). There are taxi stands at Charring Cross, Lower Bazaar Rd and Commercial Rd.

ⓘ Getting Around

Autorickshaws and taxis are everywhere. You'll find taxi fare charts at Charring Cross and outside the bus station. Autorickshaw fare charts are posted outside the bus station and botanical gardens and elsewhere. An autorickshaw from the train or bus station to Charring Cross costs ₹60.

There are jeep taxi stands near the **bus station** (Avalanche Rd) and **municipal market** (Hobert Park Cross Rd); expect to pay about 1½ times the local taxi fares.

Mudumalai Tiger Reserve

☑0423

In the Nilgiris' foothills, the newly enlarged 765-sq-km **Mudumalai Tiger Reserve** (☑0423-2445971; www.mudumalaitigerreserve. com; ₹400; ⊙sometimes closed Apr, May or Jun) is like a classical Indian landscape painting given life: thin, spindly trees and light-slotted leaves conceal spotted chital deer and grunting wild boar. Also here are over 60 tigers, giving Mudumalai one of India's highest tiger population densities (though you'd be lucky to see one). Overall the reserve is Tamil Nadu's top wildlife-spotting place. You're most likely to see deer, peacocks, wild boar, langurs, jackals, Malabar giant squirrels, wild elephants (the park has several hundred) and gaur (Indian bison).

Mudumalai is one important link in an unbroken chain of wildlife sanctuaries known as the Nilgiri Biosphere Reserve, which spans parts of Kerala, Karnataka and Tamil Nadu, and is home to approximately 585 tigers – the world's single largest tiger population.

Mudumalai sometimes closes due to fire risk in April, May or June. Rainy July and August are the least favourable months for visiting.

◉ Sights & Activities

Hiking in the reserve is banned and private vehicles are only permitted on the main Ooty–Gudalur–Theppakadu–Mysuru road and the Theppakadu–Masinagudi and Masinagudi–Moyar River roads. The least expensive way to get inside the reserve is on an official **minibus safari** (☑0423-2445971; www.mudumalaitigerreserve.com; per person Indian/foreigner ₹340/2500, camera ₹53/500; ⊙hourly 6.30-10am & 3-5pm), but the **Gypsy/jeep safaris** (☑0423-2445971; www.mudumalaitiger

reserve.com; per vehicle ₹4200, plus per passenger Indian/foreigner ₹130/400, camera ₹53/500; ☺6.30-10am & 3-5pm) provide a much better experience. Some unlicensed operators offer hikes in the buffer zone but these are potentially dangerous with wild elephants wandering around.

Elephant Camp
STABLES

(₹300; ☺8.30-9am & 5.30-6pm) In mornings and evenings you can see the reserve's working elephants being fed at the elephant camp just east of the Mudumalai **reception centre** (☑0423-2526235; www.mudumalai tigerreserve.com; Theppakadu; ☺6.30am-6pm), where you'll need to buy tickets. Most elephants here are rescued from the timber trade and are unfit to return to the wild. (While Lonely Planet does not recommend or condone recreational elephant rides, the admission fee to elephant camp helps keep these animals fed.)

🛏 Sleeping & Eating

Sylvan Lodge
LODGE $$

(☑bookings 0423-2445971; www.mudumalai tigerreserve.com; Theppakadu; d ₹1700) Scruffy rooms straight out of a cheap hotel, but in a peaceful setting virtually right beside the Moyar River.

Theppakadu Log House
LODGE $$

(☑bookings 0423-2445971; www.mudumalai tigerreserve.com; Theppakadu; d ₹2600) The best of Theppakadu's reserve-owned accommodation: well-maintained wooden rooms with private bathrooms, but still pretty basic.

★ Jungle Hut
RESORT $$$

(☑0423-2526463; www.junglehut.in; Bokkapuram; full board r ₹7310-9730; 🅿🛜🏊) 🍴 Along with ecofriendly touches (solar power, rainwater harvesting), Jungle Hut has probably the best food in Bokkapuram (if you're visiting from another resort after dark, don't walk home alone!). Spacious, newly renovated rooms and luxury tents sprawl across large grounds at the foot of the soaring Nilgiris, where chital deer graze. Jeep safaris, treks and birdwatching can be arranged.

Bamboo Banks Farm
LODGE $$$

(☑9443373201; www.bamboobanks.com; Masinagudi; full board s/d ₹6570/7830; 🅿🛜🏊) This family-run operation has seven simple, comfy cottages tucked into its own patch of unkempt jungle, 2km south of Masinagudi. Geese waddle around; there's a peaceful pool area with hammocks, swing-chairs and

a treetop viewing platform; meals are good Indian buffets; and the efficient owners organise biking and horse riding.

ℹ Getting There & Away

Small buses that can handle the Sighur Ghat road run from Ooty to Masinagudi (₹30, 1½ hours, 12 daily), from where there are jeeps and a few buses to Theppakadu.

Taxi day trips to Mudumalai from Ooty cost ₹2000, usually via the alternative Sighur Ghat road with its spectacular 36-hairpin-bend hill. (One-way trips cost the same.)

ℹ Getting Around

Slow local buses run a few times daily between Masinagudi and Theppakadu (₹5). Shared jeeps also ply this route for ₹15 per person (or you can have one to yourself for ₹150). Costs are similar for jeeps between Masinagudi and Bokkapuram.

Anamalai Tiger Reserve (Indira Gandhi Wildlife Sanctuary & National Park)

Well off most tourists' radar, **Anamalai Tiger Reserve** (www.atrpollachi.com; Indian/foreigner adult ₹30/300, child ₹20/200, camera/video ₹300/500; ☺6am-4pm) is a pristine 958-sq-km reserve of tropical jungle, *shola* forest and grassland rising to 2400m and spilling over the Western Ghats into Kerala between Kodaikanal and Coimbatore. Declared a tiger reserve in 2007, it's home to all kinds of exotic endemic wildlife, much of it rare and endangered – including leopards and around 30 elusive tigers, though you're much more likely to see lion-tailed macaques, peacocks, langurs, spotted deer and elephants.

The reserve's bare-bones **Reception & Interpretation Centre** (☑04259-238360; Topslip; ☺7am-6pm), plus basic park accommodation, is at Topslip, 35km southwest of Pollachi (which is 40km south of Coimbatore). Questions are best referred to the **Pollachi Reception Office** (☑9443435583, accommodation bookings 04259-238360; www. atrpollachi.com; 365/1 Meenkarai Rd, Pollachi; ☺10am-5.45pm Mon-Fri), where you're more likely to reach an English speaker. Pollachi is also the nearest access point for Parambikulam Tiger Reserve (p295) in Kerala.

Tiny tea-plantation town Valparai, on the reserve's fringes 65km south from Pollachi and with one outstanding heritage hotel makes a more comfortable Anamalai base. Though it's surrounded by cultivated land, not jungle, you're just as likely to spot wildlife here.

From Topslip, there are 45-minute **minibus jungle 'safaris'** (⏰9443435583; www.atrpollachi.com; Topslip; Indian/foreigner adult ₹200/2000, child ₹50/500; ⏰7.30am-4.30pm), but rupee for rupee the **guided treks** (⏰9443435583; www.atrpollachi.com; Topslip; treks per person 2km/4km/over 4km ₹200/500/1000; ⏰7am-2pm) are much more worthwhile. The reserve also offers elephant rides; however, we recommend against riding elephants because of the harm that this causes to the animals.

🛏 Sleeping

Aditya Residency   HOTEL $
(⏰04259-233093;   adityaresidencypollachi@gmail.com; 27/1 S V V Naidu St; s/d ₹1000/1300; ❄🖥) Helpful staff, clean air-conditioned rooms, and a quick walk to the bus stand make this a good overnight choice in Pollachi.

**Forest Department
Accommodation**   GUESTHOUSE $$
(⏰bookings 9443435583; www.atrpollachi.com; Topslip; r ₹1500-4000) Most people visit on day trips, but for those staying overnight, Topslip has simple Forest Department accommodation of varying comfort and cleanliness levels. Book several days ahead via the park's website.

⭐**Sinna Dorai's
Bungalow**   HERITAGE HOTEL $$$
(⏰7094739309; www.sinnadorai.com; Valparai; incl full board s ₹7650-8650, d ₹9750-11,000; 🖥) Exquisitely located on a rambling tea estate, Sinna Dorai has just six huge rooms bursting with local early-20th-century history. A cosy library, wonderful homemade meals and charming service make you feel right at home. After-dark wildlife-spotting drives (you may see elephants, bison, lion-tailed macaques and leopards) run regularly, and experienced trekkers lead you out along local paths.

It's well signposted from central Valparai, 65km south of Pollachi.

ℹ Getting There & Away

The reserve's main access town is Pollachi. Buses connect Pollachi with Topslip (₹70, two hours, 6am, 10am, 11.15am and 3.15pm) and Valparai (₹65, three hours, half-hourly). Taxis cost ₹2000 to Topslip, ₹3000 to Valparai, whether you go one-way or return. From Coimbatore's Ukkadam Bus Stand (p405), buses to Pollachi (₹39, one hour) run every five minutes, and there's one daily service to Valparai (₹65, four hours, 3pm). From Kodaikanal, most buses head to Pollachi via Palani. If you have to stay overnight in Pollachi, the Aditya Residency, near the bus stand, is a good choice.

Andaman Islands

Includes ➡
Port Blair 421
Around Port Blair . . . 425
Havelock Island
(Swaraj Dweep) 426
Neil Island
(Shaheed Dweep). . . .431
Middle & North
Andaman 434
Little Andaman 436

Best Beaches
➡ Radhanagar (p427)

➡ Ross & Smith Islands (p435)

➡ Butler Bay (p436)

➡ Lalaji Bay (p435)

➡ Merk Bay (p435)

➡ Kalapathar (p427)

Best Places to Stay
➡ Jalakara (p429)

➡ Barefoot at Havelock (p429)

➡ Emerald Gecko (p433)

➡ Taj Exotica (p429)

➡ Ko Hee Homestay (p438)

Why Go?
With shimmering turquoise waters fringed by primeval jungle, fantastic diving, and sugar-white, sun-toasted beaches melting under flame-and-purple sunsets, the far-flung Andaman Islands are the perfect Indian escape.

The population is a friendly mix of South and Southeast Asian settlers, as well as Negrito ethnic groups whose arrival here has anthropologists baffled. Adding to the islands' intrigue is their remoteness, 1370km east of the Indian mainland – but only 200km from Indonesia and 300km from Myanmar (Burma).

Of the archipelago's 572 islands, only 36 are inhabited and a small selection is open to travellers. With splendid beaches and diving, Havelock (Swaraj) is by far the most popular.

Permit requirements for the Andamans were eased in 2018; the effects of this on the islands' unspoilt state, not to mention the survival of their indigenous peoples, remains to be seen. To the south, the Nicobar Islands have, so far, been strictly off limits to tourists.

When to Go
Port Blair

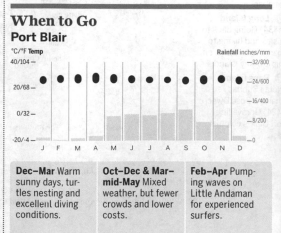

°C/°F Temp · Rainfall inches/mm

Dec–Mar Warm sunny days, turtles nesting and excellent diving conditions.

Oct–Dec & Mar–mid-May Mixed weather, but fewer crowds and lower costs.

Feb–Apr Pumping waves on Little Andaman for experienced surfers.

Andaman Islands Highlights

1 Havelock Island (Swaraj Dweep; p426) Diving, snorkelling, sun-soaking, socialising, and feasting on fresh seafood on this dreamy, jungle-cloaked island.

2 Neil Island (Shaheed Dweep; p431) Easing into a blissfully mellow pace of life and cycling between beaches and rice paddies.

3 Kalipur (p435) Experiencing the wilds of North Andaman and seeing nesting turtles while island-hopping to pristine sands and coral reefs.

4 Little Andaman (p436) Finding beautiful Butler Bay and a little piece of tropical paradise.

5 Smith & Ross Islands (p435) Meeting this dazzling duo of northern islands, linked by a bleach-blonde sandbar.

6 Long Island (p434) Going back to basics and hiking to sparkling beaches on this low-key island.

7 Ross Island (Netaji Subhas Chandra Bose Dweep; p424) Unravelling Port Blair's colonial past.

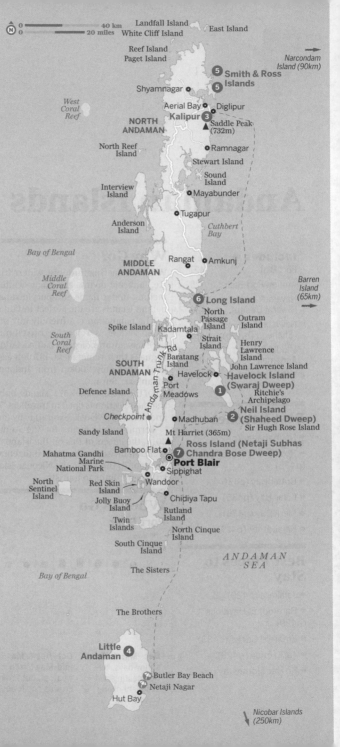

History

The date of initial human settlement on the Andamans and Nicobars is lost to history. Anthropologists say stone-tool crafters have lived here for around 2000 years, and scholars of human migration believe local indigenous tribes have roots in Negrito and Malay ethnic groups in Southeast Asia.

The Marathas started arriving in the late 17th century and, 200 years later, the British, used the Andamans as a penal colony for political dissidents following the 1857 First War of Independence (Indian Uprising). During WWII, some islanders greeted the invading Japanese as liberators, but the Japanese military proved to be harsh occupiers.

Following Indian Independence in 1947, the Andaman and Nicobar Islands were incorporated into the Indian Union, and became a Union Territory in 1956. With migration from the mainland (including Bengali refugees fleeing the chaos of partition), the population has grown from just a few thousand to more than 380,000. During the 20th-century influx, tribal land rights and environmental protection were often disregarded; while some conditions are now improving, indigenous tribes (p437) remain largely in decline.

The islands were devastated by the 2004 Indian Ocean earthquake and the resulting tsunami, which caused more than 1000 fatalities. The Nicobars were especially hard hit; some estimate a fifth of the population was killed, while others were relocated to Port Blair. But by and large normalcy has returned, and tourism (especially domestic) has boomed in recent years, mostly on Havelock (Swaraj) and Neil (Shaheed) Islands.

Geography & Environment

Incredibly, the Andaman and Nicobar Islands form the peaks of the Arakan Yoma, a mountain range that begins in western Myanmar (Burma) and extends south into the Bay of Bengal and Andaman Sea, running all the way to Sumatra in Indonesia.

The isolation of the islands, separated from each other by the 150km-wide Ten Degree Channel, has led to the evolution of many endemic species. Of 62 identified mammals, 32 are unique to the islands, including the Andaman wild pig, crab-eating macaque, masked palm civet, and species of tree shrews and bats. Of the islands' 270 bird species, 18 are endemic, including ground-dwelling megapodes, *hawabills* (swiftlets) and the emerald Nicobar pigeon.

Climate

Sea breezes keep temperatures within the 23°C to 31°C range and the humidity at around 80% all year. It's very wet during the southwest (wet) monsoon between roughly mid-May and early October, while the northeast (dry) monsoon between November and December also has its fair share of rainy days.

ⓘ Information

Even though they are 1370km east of mainland India, the Andamans still run on Indian time. This means that it can be dark by 5pm and light by 4am; people here tend to be very early risers.

DANGERS & ANNOYANCES

Crocodiles are part of life in many parts of the Andamans, particularly Little Andaman, Wandoor, Corbyn's Cove, Baratang and North Andaman. An American tourist was killed by a saltwater crocodile while snorkelling off Havelock (Swaraj; at Neil's Cove) in 2010, as was a young Indian at Wandoor Beach in 2017. Reports suggest that human-crocodile conflict is on the rise: officially there have been six crocodile attacks since 2014, though the media suggests it's around 15. A high level of vigilance remains in place and swimming is banned at some beaches. It's important you keep informed, heed any warnings by authorities and avoid being in the water at dawn or dusk.

PERMITS

In a bid to boost tourism, the Indian government has overturned the requirement for foreigners to have a Restricted Area Permit (RAP) to visit 29 inhabited and 11 uninhabited islands in the Andamans.

The new list of RAP-free islands includes Havelock Island (Swaraj Dweep), Neil Island (Shaheed Dweep), Baratang Island, Long Island, North Andaman, South and Middle Andaman (including Port Blair but excluding tribal areas), North Passage, Interview Island, Smith Island and Little Andaman (excluding tribal areas), as well as Great Nicobar, Kamorta and Little Nicobar.

ANDAMAN NAME CHANGES

At the end of 2018, the Indian government announced that the names of several Andaman islands would be changed as part of a nationwide policy of 'decolonialisation'. Ross Island will henceforth be known as Netaji Subhas Chandra Bose Dweep, Neil Island has been renamed as Shaheed Dweep and Havelock Island has become Swaraj Dweep. As with other government-imposed name changes, expect the old names to remain in use on the ground for some time.

ℹ SANDFLIES

Sandflies can be irksome, with these small biting insects sometimes causing havoc on the beach. Bring along hydrocortisone cream and calamine lotion for these bites. Seek medical assistance if it gets infected. To prevent bites, repellent containing DEET is your best bet, and avoid the beach at dawn and dusk.

Day visits without RAPs are now allowed to 11 uninhabited islands. At the time of writing, however, you still need additional permits for day trips to Jolly Buoy, Red Skin, North and South Cinque, Ross (north), Narcondam and Rutland Islands, as well as the Brothers and the Sisters. For most day permits, it's not the hassle that proves a barrier, but the cost; for Wandoor's Mahatma Gandhi Marine National Park, for example, permits cost ₹1000 for foreigners (₹75 for Indians).

The Nicobar Islands have long been off limits to all except Indian nationals engaged in approved research, government business or trade. With RAPs no longer required for Great Nicobar, Little Nicobar and Kamorta, what, if any, tourism impact will follow has yet to be seen.

ℹ Getting There & Away

Ferry and flight services are often cancelled if conditions are too rough; build in a few days' buffer to avoid being marooned or missing your flight. These days, most travellers fly (rather than sail) to/from Port Blair.

AIR

Port Blair's Veer Savarkar International Airport has daily flights to/from Bengaluru (Bangalore), Chennai, Kolkata, Mumbai, Hyderabad and Delhi with Air India (p521), IndiGo (p522), GoAir (p522), SpiceJet (p522) and Vistara (p522). At the time of writing, there were no international services, though direct flights to/from Southeast Asia were being talked about.

BOAT

Depending on who you ask, the infamous boat to Port Blair is either the only *real* way to get to the Andamans or a hassle and a half. The truth lies somewhere in between. Andaman Shipping Office (p351) has boats from Chennai (₹2825 to ₹10,815, one to two monthly); Shipping Corporation of India (www.shipindia.com) departs from Kolkata (₹2776 to ₹10,766, scheduled monthly dates); and AV Bhanoji Rao, Garuda Pattabhiramayya & Co (p254) leaves from Visakhapatnam (₹2500 to ₹10,000, monthly). All arrive at Port Blair's Haddo Jetty (p424).

Take sailing times with a large grain of salt. With hold-ups and variable weather and sea conditions, the trip can take a day or two more than the projected travel time.

You can organise your return ticket at the ferry booking office (p424) at Port Blair's Phoenix Bay Jetty (p424). Bring three passport photos, plus copies of your passport and visa. Updated schedules and fares can be found through the Shipping Corporation of India website (www.shipindia.com); otherwise enquire at Phoenix Bay's info office (p424).

Classes vary slightly between boats, but the cheapest is bunk (₹2500), followed by 2nd class (six beds, ₹5000 to ₹6500), 1st class (four beds, ₹8000) and deluxe cabins (two beds, ₹10,000). Higher-end tickets cost as much as, if not more than, a plane ticket. If you go bunk, prepare for little privacy and unpleasant toilets. Food (tiffin snack for breakfast, meal-on-a-plate thalis for lunch and dinner) costs around ₹150/200 per day for bunk/cabin class, though bring extras. Some bedding is supplied, but if you're travelling bunk class bring a sleeping sheet.

There is no ferry between Port Blair and Thailand, but private yachts can usually get clearance. You can't legally get from the Andamans to Myanmar (Burma) by sea.

ℹ Getting Around

AIR

At the time of writing, interisland sea planes were not operating and it was unlikely they would resume.

While the interisland helicopter service is generally reserved for islanders and VIPs, you

INTERNET ACCESS & MOBILE PHONES

Getting online in the Andamans continues to be a struggle. There are internet cafes in Port Blair and a few resorts with 'wi-fi' in Port Blair, and on Havelock (Swaraj) and Neil (Shaheed) Islands, but strong connections and smartphone data are rare. A new submarine optical fibre cable, which will link Chennai to Port Blair, Havelock, Little Andaman, Great Nicobar, Car Nicobar and Kamorta, is *scheduled* to be completed by the time you read this. Meanwhile, Jio, India's biggest 4G network, has been installing its services in the Port Blair area, with hopes of expanding across most popular islands in the near future.

All telephone numbers must include the ☏ 03192 area code, even when dialling locally. BSNL is the most reliable mobile-phone operator.

can chance your luck by applying one day before at the **Directorate of Civil Aviation office** (☑ 03192-233601; Port Blair Helipad, VIP Rd; ☺ 8.30am-5pm Mon-Fri) at the helipad by the airport. However, the 5kg baggage limit and soaring price tag (for example ₹19,000 from Port Blair to Diglipur) precludes most tourists from using this service.

BOAT

Most islands can only be reached by water. Ferry ticket offices can be chaotic: expect hot waits (queues start hours in advance), slow service, queue-jumping and a rugby scrum to the ticket window; ladies' queues are a godsend, but they really only apply in Port Blair. Have your passport (for photo ID) and, if required, your ticket form handy. You may be able to buy tickets the day you travel by arriving at the appropriate jetty an hour beforehand, but this is risky; government ferry tickets are released one to three days ahead, so buy them as soon as possible. Hotels and travel agents can usually book ferry tickets for you.

There are regular boat services to Havelock (Swaraj) and Neil (Shaheed) Islands, as well as Rangat, Long Island, Mayabunder, Diglipur and Little Andaman. Ferry schedules are not currently available online; ask locally or check with Port Blair's Phoenix Bay Jetty ferry information office (p424). All schedules are liable to change.

More comfortable (and more expensive) private ferry companies also run to Havelock and Neil Islands from Port Blair; tickets are usually available a month in advance online and in person, making these the easiest option for visitors. **Makruzz** (☑ 03192-236677; www.makruzz.com; 1st fl, TCI XPS Building, 100 JN Rd, Delaripur; ☺ 9am-5.30pm) and **Green Ocean** (☑ 03192-230777; http://greenoceanseaways.com; 1st fl, Island Arcade, Junglighat; ☺ 9am-1pm & 2-4pm Mon-Sat, 9am-1pm Sun) are the main operators.

BUS

The main island group – South, Middle and North Andaman – is connected by road, with ferry crossings and, increasingly, bridges. Buses run south from Port Blair to Wandoor and Chidiya Tapu, and north to Baratang, Rangat, Mayabunder and finally to Diglipur.

PRIVATE CAR

A car with driver costs ₹900 to ₹1100 per 35km, or around ₹11,250 for a return trip to Diglipur from Port Blair (including stopovers along the way). Due to restrictions in travel within tribal areas, foreigners are not permitted to drive their own vehicles to North and Middle Andaman.

Port Blair

POP 108,060

Surrounded by tropical forest and rugged coastline, the Andamans' lively provincial capital, Port Blair, is a vibrant mix of Indian Ocean inhabitants – Bengalis, Tamils, Telugus, Nicobarese and Myanmarese. Most travellers don't hang around any longer than necessary (usually one or two days while waiting to book onward travel in the islands, or returning for departure), but PB's fascinating history warrants exploration while you're in town. There are also some enticing day trips, such as to Mahatma Gandhi Marine National Park (p425) and Chidiya Tapu (p426).

◉ Sights

★ Cellular Jail National Memorial
HISTORIC BUILDING

(GB Pant Rd; Indian/foreigner ₹30/100, camera ₹200, sound-and-light show adult/child ₹50/25; ☺ 8.45am-12.30pm & 1.30-4.45pm) A former British prison, the Cellular Jail now serves as a shrine to the political dissidents it once imprisoned. Construction began in 1896 and was completed in 1906 – the original seven wings (several of which were destroyed by the Japanese during WWII; only three now remain) contained 698 cells radiating from a central tower. Like many political prisons, it became something of a university for freedom fighters, who exchanged books, ideas and debates despite the walls and wardens.

Controversial Hindu freedom fighter Vinayak Damodar Savarkar was held here from 1914 to 1921 and his former cell is open to visitors.

Anthropological Museum
MUSEUM

(MG Rd; Indian/foreigner ₹20/150; ☺ 9am-1pm & 1.30-4.30pm Tue-Sun) Port Blair's engaging anthropology museum provides a thorough and sympathetic portrait of the islands' indigenous tribal communities. The glass display cases may seem old school, but they don't feel anywhere near as ancient as the simple geometric patterns etched into a Jarawa chest guard, the skull left in a Sentinelese lean-to, the Andamanese shell waist girdle, or the totemic spirits represented by Nicobarese shamanic sculptures. No photography.

Samudrika Naval Marine Museum
MUSEUM

(Haddo Rd; adult/child ₹50/25; ☺ 9am-12.30pm & 2-5pm Tue-Sun) Run by the Indian Navy, this diverse museum provides helpful insight into the islands' ecosystems, tribal communities, flora and fauna (including a small aquarium). On display are hawksbill turtle shells recovered from poachers and, outside, the skeleton of a young blue whale washed ashore on Kamorta Island in the Nicobars.

ANDAMAN ISLANDS PORT BLAIR

Port Blair

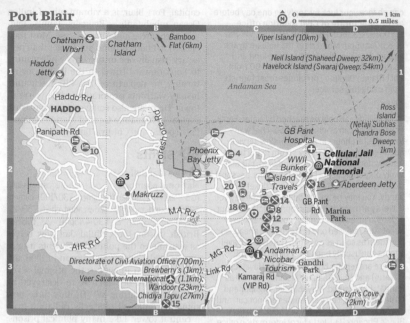

Port Blair

◉ Top Sights
1 Cellular Jail National Memorial D2

◉ Sights
Aberdeen Bazaar .... (see 5)
2 Anthropological Museum C3
Clock Tower .... (see 14)
Gandhi Statue .... (see 18)
3 Samudrika Naval Marine Museum B2

🛏 Sleeping
4 Aashiaanaa C2
5 Amina Lodge C2
6 Andaman Homestay............................ A2
7 Fortune Resort Bay Island C2
8 J Hotel C2
9 Lalaji Bay View C2
10 Port Vista....................................... A2
11 Sinclairs Bayview D3

✕ Eating
Amaya.. (see 7)
12 Ananda C2

13 Annapurna Cafeteria............................ C3
Bayview .... (see 11)
Excel Restaurant .... (see 9)
14 Gagan Restaurant C2
15 Icy Spicy B3
16 New Lighthouse Restaurant................ D2

◉ Drinking & Nightlife
Nico Bar... (see 7)

ℹ Information
E-Cafe...(see 14)

ℹ Transport
17 Directorate of Shipping
Information Office C2
Ferry Booking Office .... (see 17)
Green Ocean ....(see 15)
18 Mohanpura Bus Terminus C2
19 Private Bus Stand.............................. C2
20 Saro Tours & Travels C2
Taxi & Autorickshaw Stand ....(see 18)

🛏 Sleeping

The tourist office (p424) provides a list of approved homestays.

Aashiaanaa   GUESTHOUSE $
(☏ 03192-234123; Marine Hill; r with AC ₹1700, without AC ₹850-950; ❄ 🛜) A reliable budget choice

under efficient management, Aashiaanaa has homely, well-kept rooms just 800m uphill from Phoenix Bay Jetty. Pricier rooms get you a balcony and air-con. Wi-fi is ₹60 per hour.

Amina Lodge   GUESTHOUSE $
(☏ 9933258703, 9474275441; aminalodge@ymail.com; MA Rd, Aberdeen Bazaar; s ₹500, d ₹700-800;

🖰) Popular with budget travellers, friendly Amina offers four clean rooms with TV and an hour's free wi-fi, in a handy though somewhat-noisy location in the thick of Aberdeen Bazaar. Call ahead.

Lalaji Bay View GUESTHOUSE $
(🖰 9476005820, 03192-236333; www.lalajibay view.com; RP Rd, Dignabad; r ₹800-1000, with AC ₹1400; ❄🖰) This popular backpacker spot keeps busy for its basic, sprucely maintained rooms, but it's the sociable rooftop Excel restaurant-bar that makes the place tick. Wi-fi costs ₹60 per hour.

Port Vista GUESTHOUSE $$
(🖰 03192-241080, 8860427712; theportvista@ gmail.com; 10 DP St, Haddo; r incl breakfast ₹2800-4000) At this friendly little guesthouse, oleanders and bougainvillea line the stairs to a terrace with wraparound views and just two colourful, pristine rooms with a dash more charm than most Port Blair offerings.

Andaman Homestay HOMESTAY $$
(🖰 9474208233; www.andamanhomestay.com; Khushnaz Bungalow, 13 DP St, Haddo; r with AC ₹2500, s/d without AC ₹1000/1500, apt with/ without AC ₹4000/2700; ❄🖰) A collection of spotless rooms and a split-level four-person apartment in a warm, mandarin-orange family home, just over 1km south of Haddo Jetty. The helpful Nobles also run popular kayaking trips from Port Blair and on Havelock Island (Swaraj Dweep).

Fortune Resort Bay Island HOTEL $$$
(🖰 03192-234101; www.fortunehotels.in; Marine Hill; r incl breakfast from ₹12,800; ❄🖰❄) One of PB's finest hotels, with panoramic sea views, pretty hillside gardens and elegant contemporary rooms with polished-wood floors; ask for one that's sea-facing. Relax over cocktails in Nico bar (p424) and dine on refined global fare at the terrace restaurant.

J Hotel HOTEL $$$
(🖰 03192-243700; www.jhotel.in; Aberdeen Bazaar; r incl breakfast ₹5900-7080; ❄🖰) A sleek, modern, professionally run find in the heart of Aberdeen Bazaar, with up-to-date, wood-floored, gold-and-cream rooms and a rooftop restaurant turning out multicuisine fare.

Sinclairs Bayview HOTEL $$$
(🖰 03192-227824; www.sinclairshotels.com; South Point; incl breakfast d ₹12,800-17,920, q ₹17,920-25,600; ❄🖰❄) Recently revamped, Sinclairs delivers some of Port Blair's smartest accommodation, with spacious, current rooms

looking out on the bay and seaside gardens, 2km southeast of town. There's a reliably good on-site multicuisine **restaurant** (mains ₹230-600; ⊙7.30-10.30am, 12.30-3.30pm & 7.30-10.30pm), plus a bar and spa.

🍴 Eating & Drinking

⭐**New Lighthouse Restaurant** INDIAN $$
(Marina Park; mains ₹130-360; ⊙11am-10.30pm) Fresh seafood grilled, steamed or barbecued to taste is the speciality at this unadorned favourite, but there's also punchy veg or prawn biryani and an impressive globe-trotting menu. The upstairs beer terrace (from 5pm) gets busy.

Excel Restaurant INTERNATIONAL $$
(🖰 9476005820, 03192-236333; www.lalajibay view.com; RP Rd, Dignabad, Lalaji Bay View; mains ₹120-350; ⊙7.30am-10.30pm) The atmospheric bamboo restaurant atop Lalaji Bay View guesthouse brings a Havelock-style menu to the city, with grilled fish, burgers, *momos* (Tibetan dumplings) and more. A mellow, social place to chill out over a beer.

Annapurna Cafeteria INDIAN $$
(MG Rd; mains ₹170-250; ⊙6.30am-10.30pm) An excellent frills-free pure-veg option, reminiscent of a high-school cafeteria, that rustles up rich North Indian–style curries and delicious South Indian favourites, such as dosas (large savoury crêpe), *vadas* (doughnut-shaped deep-fried lentil savoury) and *uttapams* (thick, savoury South Indian rice pancake with finely chopped onions, green chillies, coriander and coconut).

Icy Spicy INDIAN $$
(🖰 03192-329304, 03192-232704; Basement, Island Arcade, Junglighat; mains ₹150-215; ⊙11am-11.30pm) It doesn't look much from the outside, but buried away in this small mall is a busy, smartish pure-veg restaurant. It's often packed with visiting Indians, here for the tasty thalis (₹180 to ₹220), biryanis, North Indian gravies, and sugar-free goodies from the upstairs bakery.

Gagan Restaurant INDIAN $$
(Clock Tower, Aberdeen Bazaar; mains ₹150-200; ⊙7.30am-10pm) This locally loved and low-key Bengali hole-in-the-wall serves great food at good prices, including Nicobari fish, crab curries and paneer in a world of versions.

There's a samosa stand out front and the owners also run nearby restaurant **Ananda** (🖰 03192-244041; Aberdeen Bazaar; mains ₹170-330; ⊙7am-10pm).

DON'T MISS

ROSS ISLAND (NETAJI SUBHAS CHANDRA BOSE DWEEP)

Renamed Netaji Subhas Chandra Bose Dweep in 2018 and just a 1.5km boat ride away from Port Blair, **Ross Island** (₹30; ☺8.30am-2pm Thu-Tue) feels like a jungle-clad lost city, à la Angkor Wat, except here the ruins are Victorian English rather than ancient Khmer. The former British administrative headquarters in the Andamans, the island lost its vibrant social scene with the double whammy of a 1941 earthquake and invasion by the Japanese, but its ruined colonial-era architecture is still standing. In its day, Ross (not to be confused with its namesake island in North Andaman) was fondly called the 'Paris of the East' (along with Pondicherry, Saigon etc etc...). Landscaped paths criss-cross to dilapidated buildings, most of which are labelled (a church, a printing press). There's a herd of resident spotted deer, plus a small museum with historical displays.

Boats (₹320, 20 minutes) to Ross Island depart roughly hourly from Port Blair's Aberdeen Jetty between 8.30am and 2pm. Good sound-and-light shows (₹335 per person including return ferry) are often staged on the island; tickets are sold at Port Blair's tourist office.

Brewberry's
CAFE $$

(☎9679596637; MG Rd, Lamba Line; dishes ₹130-260; ☺11am-10.30pm; ☎) Port Blair's only real contemporary, wi-fi-equipped hang-out cafe is opposite the airport, 2km south of the city centre. The chocolate-brown decor sets the tone for brownies, espresso, French-press coffee and well-executed wraps, pastas and other snacks.

Amaya
INTERNATIONAL $$$

(☎03192-242773; http://seashellhotels.net; Marine Hill, SeaShell Port Blair; mains ₹340-1000; ☺11am-10.30pm; ☎) Amid palmtops, the SeaShell hotel's breezy and sophisticated rooftop lounge appeals for its sleek bar (cocktails ₹415), open-plan kitchen, high-season live music and views of Ross Island (Netaji Subhas Chandra Bose Dweep). Elegantly prepared dishes wander from fish tikka to spicy paneer (soft, unfermented milk-curd cheese) satay.

Nico Bar
BAR

(☎03192-234101; www.fortunehotels.in; Marine Hill, Fortune Resort Bay Island; ☺11am-10.45pm) The closest you'll get to the Nicobars, the Fortune's bar is a classic for sea breezes and palm-spangled coastal views (the image on the old ₹20 note is based on this spot). A pleasant place to while away an afternoon or balmy evening with a frosty cocktail (₹300).

ℹ Information

Port Blair is the only place in the Andamans where you can reliably change cash and find enough ATMs, especially in Aberdeen Bazaar and MG Rd.

There are internet cafes with wi-fi and computer terminals in Aberdeen Bazaar near the clock tower, including **E-Cafe** (Ainternet & wi-fi per hour ₹40; ☺9am-9.30pm Mon-Sat).

Andaman & Nicobar Tourism (☎03192-232694; www.andamantourism.gov.in; Kamaraj Rd; ☺9am-1pm & 1.30-5pm Mon-Sat) The Andamans' main tourist office; books permits for restricted areas around Port Blair.

GB Pant Hospital (☎03192-233473, emergency 03192-232102; GB Pant Rd; ☺24hr) Offers medical services.

Island Travels (☎03192-233358; www.islandtravelsandaman.com; MA Rd, Aberdeen Bazaar; ☺9.30am-6.30pm Mon-Sat) Books hotels and transport.

ℹ Getting There & Away

BOAT

Most inter-island ferries depart from Phoenix Bay Jetty. Tickets can be purchased from its **ferry booking office** (☺9am-1pm & 2-4pm Mon-Fri, to 12.45pm Sat) one to three days in advance; if they are sold out, you can chance your luck with a same-day ticket issued an hour before departure. There's a **ferry information office** (☎03192-245555; ☺6am-7.30pm) inside the ticket office. New arrivals should make the jetty their first port of call to book tickets; hotels and travel agents can usually reserve ferries, too. Note that queues can start as early as 4am and tickets sell out fast, while ferry schedules may change.

Havelock (Swaraj) & Neil (Shaheed)

Given the challenges of securing government ferry tickets to reach Havelock Island (Swaraj Dweep) and Neil Island (Shaheed Dweep), most travellers use pricier private ferries from Haddo Jetty, which can be booked a month ahead.

Makruzz (p421) has daily departures to Havelock (₹1407 to ₹3118, 1½ hours) at 8am and 1.30pm, plus a high-season-only ferry to Neil (₹1289 to ₹2802, one hour). Green Ocean (p421) heads to Havelock (₹1050 to ₹1350, 2½ hours) at 6.30am, 7am and 12.30pm, returning at 9.30am and 3pm; from October to March, the 7am Havelock ferry continues to Neil (₹1850 to ₹2450, three hours).

Government ferries to Havelock (₹460 to ₹650, 2½ hours) depart daily at 6.20am and 2pm, returning at 9am and 4.30pm; ferries to Neil (₹460 to ₹650; two hours) leave at 6.30am and 11am, returning at 8.30am and 4pm. All these services book out fast.

Middle & North Andaman

There are at least two ferries a week to/from Diglipur (₹1050 to ₹1470, 17 hours) via Maya-bunder (₹840 to ₹1260, 10 hours), and three to four ferries a week to/from Long Island (₹630 to ₹1050, five hours) via Havelock and Neil.

Little Andaman

There are daily boats between Haddo Jetty and Little Andaman (₹500 to ₹1500, 5½ to eight hours), which regularly sell out.

BUS

Government buses run from the central **Mohanpura Bus Terminus** (MA Rd, Aberdeen Bazaar). Andaman Trunk Rd (p434) services can be booked up to nine days ahead.

Baratang ₹110, three hours, six daily 4am–12.15pm

Chidiya Tapu ₹24, one hour, nine daily 5.50am–8.10pm

Diglipur and Aerial Bay ₹280–₹290, 12 hours, 4am, 7am

Mayabunder ₹220, 10 hours, 4am, 9.45am

Rangat ₹160, seven hours, five daily 4am–12.15pm

Wandoor ₹24, one hour, hourly 6am–4.45pm

More comfortable, but pricier, private buses operate from a **bus stand** (off MA Rd) just north of the main bus station.

❶ Getting Around

TO/FROM THE AIRPORT
Taxis or autorickshaws from the airport to Aberdeen Bazaar cost around ₹150. Alternatively, jump on any bus (₹10 to ₹20) heading into Port Blair's main bus stand from the main road outside the airport.

SLEEPING PRICE RANGES

The following price ranges refer to a double room with bathroom during high season (November to March) in the Andamans.

$ less than ₹1200

$$ ₹1200–₹4000

$$$ more than ₹4000

AUTORICKSHAW & MOTORCYCLE

Autorickshaws from Aberdeen Bazaar cost around ₹40 to Phoenix Bay Jetty and ₹60 to Haddo Jetty.

You can hire motorcycles for ₹500 per day, with outlets including the reliable **Saro Tours & Travels** (☑ 9933291466; Marine Rd, Aberdeen Bazaar; ☉ 7am-7.30pm).

Around Port Blair

Wandoor

Wandoor, a tiny speck of a village with a pretty nearby beach 25km southwest of Port Blair, is a good spot to explore South Andaman's lush interior. It's mostly known as a jumping-off point for Mahatma Gandhi Marine National Park.

◉ Sights & Activities

Mahatma Gandhi Marine National Park NATIONAL PARK
(☉ Tue-Sun) 🏊 Comprising 15 islands of mangrove creeks, tropical rainforest and reefs supporting 50 types of coral and plenty of colourful fish, the 280-sq-km Mahatma Gandhi Marine National Park is ideal for snorkelling (gear rental ₹300). Three boats depart on half-day trips from Wandoor Jetty from 7.30am depending on demand, costing ₹885 in addition to the permit (Indian/foreigner ₹75/1000) you'll need to prearrange from Port Blair's tourist office up to three days ahead. No plastics allowed. The marine park's snorkelling sites alternate every six months between Jolly Buoy and Red Skin, allowing the other to regenerate.

Wandoor Beach BEACH
Wandoor has a lovely blonde beach, though at the time of writing swimming was prohibited due to a fatal crocodile attack in 2017.

ANET VOLUNTEERING
(Andaman & Nicobar Environmental Team; ☑ 03192-280081; www.anetindia.org; North Wandoor) 🏊 Led by an inspiring team of dynamic Indian ecologists, this energetic research and conservation centre, founded in 1990, has occasional openings for specialised volunteers; check directly.

🛏 Sleeping & Eating

Sea Princess Beach Resort RESORT **$$$**
(☑ 9609508000, 03192-280002; www.seaprincess andaman.com; Wandoor Beach; r incl breakfast ₹8260-12,800; ❄ 🛜 🏊) Overlooking Wandoor's

CINQUE ISLAND

Surrounded by coral reefs, the uninhabited islands of North and South Cinque are connected by a sparkling-white sand-bar beach that disappears at high tide. They're among the most beautiful in the Andamans, with great snorkelling and diving. Only day visits are allowed, however, and unless you're on one of the day trips occasionally organised by local travel agencies, you'll need to get permission in advance by purchasing the Mahatma Gandhi Marine National Park permit (p419) from Port Blair's tourist office (p424) – and potentially an additional permit. By boat, the islands are 20km south (two hours) from Chidiya Tapu or 30km southeast (3½ hours) from Wandoor.

silky (though unswimmable) beach, this palm-studded resort provides a bar, a restaurant (meals ₹880) and well-equipped, wood-walled rooms dotted around a pool, with the spacious suites being the pick of the bunch.

⊙ Getting There & Away

Buses from Port Blair run to Wandoor (₹24, one hour) hourly from 6am to 4.45pm; the latest return is at 8.15pm. Taxis charge ₹1000 to ₹1800 one way.

Chidiya Tapu

Chidiya Tapu, 25km south of Port Blair, is a tiny settlement fringed by beaches and mangroves, and famous for its celestial sunsets and silvery Munda Pahar Beach. It gets busy with day trippers from Port Blair.

⊙ Sights & Activities

Chidiya Tapu–based Lacadives and Infinity Scuba run dive trips to local sites including Corruption Rock and a WWII British minesweeper wreck. They may also be able to organise trips to Cinque Island and Rutland Island.

Munda Pahar Beach   BEACH
(⊙9am-5pm) Loved for its fiery sunsets and wonderfully natural setting, this powdery silver-sand beach is popular with day trippers, although swimming was prohibited at research time due to crocodiles. A signposted 1km, 20-minute hike leads to a viewpoint.

Lacadives   DIVING
(☑9531866304, 03192-281013; www.lacadives.com; single dive ₹3550, PADI Open Water course ₹29,500; ⊙Oct-May) ⊘ A long-established, environmentally responsible dive company that also offers nature walks (₹250 to ₹1000).

Infinity Scuba   DIVING
(☑03192-281183, 9474204508; www.infinityscub andamans.wordpress.com; Wild Grass Resort; 2-dive trip ₹4700, PADI Open Water course ₹25,960) Set up by ex-navy commander and expert Andamans diver Baath; offers diving and some snorkelling trips.

Reef Watch Marine Conservation   VOLUNTEERING
(☑9476073291; www.reefwatchindia.org; Lacadives) ⊘ This NGO with a focus on marine conservation accepts volunteers (minimum one week) to be involved in beach clean-ups, fish surveys and more. Contact the team to discuss opportunities that match your skills with their needs.

🛏 Sleeping & Eating

Wild Grass Resort   RESORT $$$
(☑9474204508; www.wildgrassresorts.in; r incl breakfast ₹4500-6500; ❄) Set against a verdant jungle backdrop, 1.5km northwest of Chidiya Tapu village, Wild Grass' smart, modern cottages have an easygoing ambience; best are the two-storey bungalows with elevated terraces. It also has a recommended dive school, Infinity Scuba, and an atmospheric bamboo restaurant for beers and meals.

⊙ Getting There & Away

Buses head from Port Blair to Chidiya Tapu (₹24, one hour) nine times daily from 5.50am to 8.10pm; the last return bus leaves at 6pm. Taxis charge ₹1250 to ₹1750 one way.

Havelock Island (Swaraj Dweep)

POP 5500

With sublime silken-blonde beaches, twinkling teal shallows and some of the best diving in South Asia, thickly forested Havelock (Swaraj) enjoys the well-deserved reputation of being a travellers' paradise. Indeed, for many, Havelock *is* the Andamans – it's what lures most visitors across the Bay of Bengal, many of them content to stay here for the entirety of their trip.

Havelock has been developing fast in recent years, with a rise in domestic tourism and concrete-clad resorts chasing away many of the original bamboo beach huts. But much of the island's 92 sq km (it's the largest in Ritchie's Archipelago) remains untouched, and the beaches and diving remain bewitching.

◉ Sights & Activities

Beaches

★ Radhanagar Beach   BEACH
(Beach 7) One of India's (and indeed Asia's) most fabulous and famous stretches of sand: a beautiful bleach-blonde curve of powdery sugar fronted by perfectly spiralled aqua waves, all fringed by lush native forest. It's on the northwest side of the island, 11km southwest of the jetty. Visit early morning to avoid the heat and crowds.

Beach 5   BEACH
On Havelock's eastern coast, palm-ringed Beach 5 has your classic tropical vibe with cream-coloured sand, cerulean sea, shady patches and few sandflies. Swimming can be difficult at low tide, when the water shallows out for kilometres.

Beach 3   BEACH
A slender strip of platinum east-coast beach, dotted with palms and a few fishing boats and overlooked by clumps of natural jungle. Beautiful, though not ideal for swimming as it's rocky. It's 3km southeast of the jetty.

Neil's Cove   BEACH
With its gorgeous teal 'lagoon', Neil's Cove is a gem of sheltered sand and crystalline water. Swimming is prohibited at dusk and dawn; take heed of warnings regarding crocodiles.

Kalapathar   BEACH
Pristine Kalapathar is a salt-white swathe of sand lapped by clear turquoise water. It's a favourite sunrise-gazing spot, and you may have to walk a bit to get away from the masses and souvenir shops.

Elephant Beach   BEACH
Along the island's northwest coastline, the alabaster sands of Elephant Beach, a popular snorkelling spot, are reached by a 40-minute, 1.8km walk through a muddy elephant logging trail. The path is well signposted off the cross-island road, 7.5km southwest of Havelock's jetty, but turns to bog if it's been raining. Head over around 6am for a better chance of having the place to yourself.

Diving & Snorkelling
With options for all levels, Havelock's diving scene is one of the Andamans' key attrac-

tions. Prices are around ₹6500 to ₹7500 for a two-tank dive, with options of Professional Association of Diving Instructors (PADI) or Scuba Schools International (SSI) introductory dives (₹4000 to ₹7000), open-water courses (four dives ₹26,000 to ₹31,000) and advanced courses (three to five dives ₹21,000 to ₹23,600).

Popular sites include Dixon's Pinnacle and Pilot Reef, with colourful soft coral; South Button for macro dives and rock formations; the Wall, for soft coral, pelagic fish and night dives; Jackson's Bar or Johnny's Gorge for deeper dives with schools of snapper, sharks, rays and turtles; and Minerva Ledge for a bit of everything. There are also wreck dives to SS *Incheket*, a 1950s cargo carrier, and MV *Mars*.

Snorkelling trips (₹2500 to ₹5000) can be booked through dive schools and hotels; most go to Elephant Beach.

Dive India   DIVING
(☑ 8001122205, 03192-214247; www.diveindia.com; Beach 3; 2-dive trip ₹7380, PADI Open Water course ₹30,680) The original PADI company on Havelock, and still one of the best, with basic beach-hut accommodation.

Barefoot Scuba   DIVING
(☑ 9474263120, 9566088560; www.barefoot scuba.in; Beach 3; 2-dive trip ₹6785, PADI Open Water course ₹29,740) Popular, long-established company with dive and accommodation packages (p430) and snorkelling trips (₹2500 to ₹5000).

Ocean Tribe   DIVING
(☑ 9476012783, 9474240746, 03192-282255; http://ocean-tribe.com; Beach 3; 2-dive trip ₹6490, SSI/PADI Open Water course ₹21,500/24,500) Run by legendary local Karen divers Dixon, Jackson and Johnny, all of whom have dive sites named after them.

Andaman Bubbles   DIVING
(☑ 03192-282140, 8900936494; www.andaman bubbles.com; Beach 5; 2-dive trip ₹6785, SSI/PADI Open Water course ₹26,550/28,320) Quality outfit with professional, personable staff.

Other Activities
Some resorts organise guided jungle treks for keen walkers or birdwatchers. The rainforest is a spectacular, emerald-coloured hinterland cavern, and the birdwatching – especially on the forest fringes – is rewarding; look out for the blue-black greater racket-tailed drongo or black-naped oriole.

Yoga lessons may be available during high season at Flying Elephant (p429).

ANDAMAN ISLANDS HAVELOCK ISLAND ('SWARAJ DWEEP)

Swaraj Dweep (Havelock Island)

Peel Island

No 1 Village

No 2 Village

Karmatang Bay

No 4 Village
Shyam Nagar

No 3 Village

No 5 Village
Vijay Nagar

Beach 5

No 7 Village

No 6 Village
Krishna Nagar

Radhanagar Beach

Kalapathar

Andaman Kayak Tours KAYAKING
(☎9476051158, 9933269653; www.andamanhome
stay.com; per person ₹3000-3500; ☺Sep-May)
A popular activity operator that explores
Havelock's mangroves by sea kayak, runs
snorkel-and-kayak excursions, and organises memorable night trips to glide among
bioluminescence. Trips last 2½ hours.

🛏 Sleeping

Green Imperial BUNGALOW $
(☎03192-282004, 9474206301; www.green
imperial.com; Beach 3; bungalows ₹800, r with AC
₹2500-4000; ❄️🖥️) A favourite backpacker
hang-out, sprinkled across lush gardens of
palms and betel nuts just a few minutes'
walk from the beach. There are fan-cooled
bamboo bungalows with beds (not floor
mattresses) and private bathrooms, and
plain, well-kept, air-conditioned concrete
cottages.

Coconut Grove Beach Resort GUESTHOUSE $
(☎9538191748; http://coconutgrovebeachresort.
com; Beach 5; huts ₹1000-2200) Low-key Coconut Grove has a relaxed communal vibe
with no-frills, slightly-rough-around-the-
edges bamboo huts (some featuring open-
air showers, others sharing bathrooms)
arranged in a circular, palm-studded cluster.

Sea View Beach Resort HUT $
(☎9531829129; http://ocean-tribe.com; Beach 3; r
₹1000-2000) Chilled-out thatched beach huts
with mosquito nets and concrete bathrooms,
plus slightly musty fan-cooled bungalows,
backing on to the Ocean Tribe (p427) dive
shop, a bit away from the crowds.

Orient Legend Resort GUESTHOUSE $
(☎9434291008, 03192-282389; www.havelock
beachresort.in; Beach 5; huts ₹500-600, r with AC
₹3000, without AC ₹1000-1500) This popular,
sprawling place covers most budgets, from
doghouse A-frame bamboo huts (the cheap-

Swaraj Dweep (Havelock Island)

◉ Top Sights
1 Radhanagar Beach B3

◎ Sights
2 Beach 3...C2
3 Beach 5...D2
4 Elephant Beach A2
5 Kalapathar..D3
6 Neil's Cove...A3

⊕ Activities, Courses & Tours
  Andaman Bubbles.........................(see 19)
  Barefoot Scuba ....(see 9)
7 Dive India...D2
  Ocean Tribe....................................(see 9)

⊟ Sleeping
8 Barefoot at Havelock.......................A3
9 Barefoot Scuba C1
10 Coconut Grove Beach Resort...............D2
11 Emerald Gecko D2
12 Flying Elephant D3
13 Green Imperial C2
14 Jalakara C2
15 Orient Legend Resort D2
  Sea View Beach Resort ....(see 9)
16 SeaShell Havelock C1
17 Silver Sand Beach Resort D2
18 Taj Exotica..B3

19 Wild Orchid.......................................D2

⊗ Eating
20 Anju-Coco Resto................................C2
21 B3 – Barefoot Bar & Brasserie C1
  Dakshin ....(see 21)
22 Fat Martin's.......................................D3
  Full Moon Cafe ....(see 7)
  Red Snapper...................................(see 19)
  Rony's Restaurant ....(see 15)

◎ Drinking & Nightlife
23 Cicada D2
  Emerald Gecko Bar.......................(see 19)

⊜ Shopping
24 Seven Heaven C2
  Wine Shop......................................(see 24)

ⓘ Information
  Havelock Tourist
  Information Centre...................(see 21)

ⓘ Transport
  Government Ferry Ticket
  Office ....(see 21)
  Green Ocean....................................(see 21)
  Havelock Jetty...............................(see 21)
  Makruzz ....(see 21)

est share bathrooms) to colourful concrete rooms offering a glimpse of the ocean.

Flying Elephant BUNGALOW $$
(☑ 8900920809, 9531861903; www.flying-elephant.in; Kalapathar; r incl breakfast ₹3980) Hidden away just inland from Kalapathar beach, among rice paddies, mango trees and betel palms, this serene and efficiently run retreat has a yoga *shala* and simple, earthy bamboo bungalows (some duplexes) with landscaped outdoor stone-garden bathrooms.

Emerald Gecko BUNGALOW $$
(☑ 9531860527, 03192-233358; www.emerald-gecko.com; Beach 5; huts/bungalows/lodges ₹1890/3110/₹3760) ✎ These double-storey, fan-cooled huts (with private shower but communal toilet) look to the water; the cosy bamboo bungalows have open-air bathrooms; and individual lodges, constructed from bamboo rafts that have drifted ashore from Myanmar (Burma), come with ambient lighting, private terraces and outdoor bathrooms. Free water refills.

★ Jalakara BOUTIQUE HOTEL $$$
(www.jalakara.info; No 4 Village; incl breakfast r ₹17,860-39,620, villas ₹35,800-63,950; ⊘ Oct-May;

❄ ❉) ✎ Easily the chicest place to stay in the Andamans, this ecoconscious British-owned luxe-boutique hideaway is built into a banana-and-betel-nut plantation, 3.5km south of the jetty. It wows with its rainforest-view infinity pool, organic cooking, small spa, daily yoga, open-air bathrooms and seven highly original, design-led, tropical-life rooms, styled with antiques, earthy tones, polished concrete, and curtains crafted from saris.

★ Barefoot at Havelock RESORT $$$
(☑ 9731557551, 9840238042; www.barefoot-andaman.com; Radhanagar; tented cottages ₹10,500-13,000 cottages ₹14,500-21,500; ❄ ❄) ✎ A thoughtfully designed, long-established, ecofriendly resort with elegantly comfortable timber, bamboo-thatched or tented cottages, just back from Radhanagar's sands. There's also a spa, a bar, a good restaurant, and seafood feasts served at private beach tables.

Taj Exotica LUXURY HOTEL $$$
(☑ 03192-283333; taj.tajhotels.com; Radhanagar; r incl breakfast ₹43,840-96,380; ❄ ❄ ❉) ✎ Respecting (and replanting) the local rainforest, this much-anticipated Taj Group property brings contemporary luxury to Radhanagar. Glossy villas, inspired by Jarawa

tribe huts, are graced by enormous walk-through bathrooms, canvases of local marine life and, in some cases, private pools. You'll glimpse the glittering sea from the excellent restaurant overlooking a jungle-shrouded infinity pool.

Barefoot Scuba
BUNGALOW $$$

(☑ 9474263120; www.barefootscuba.in; Beach 3; cottages incl breakfast ₹5310-8260; ✦) ✐ Smart, orange-walled, polished-wood cottages with terraces and a bit of style, in a knot of palms just steps from the beach. The most affordable 'cottages' are tentlike canvas constructions. Free water refills.

SeaShell Havelock
RESORT $$$

(☑ 9531907001, 03192-242773; www.seashellhotels.net; Beach 3; r incl breakfast ₹12,160-27,520; ✦ ⬛ ❄ ✦) One of Havelock's sleeker choices, featuring elegant all-wood cottages with tea-and-coffee kits, dotted around palm-shaded paths to an infinity pool with sea glimpses. There's beachfront yoga, a dive school and a smart cafe-pub for coffee and wi-fi.

Wild Orchid
RESORT $$$

(☑ 03192-282472; www.wildorchidandaman.com; Beach 5; r incl breakfast ₹8000-9000; ✦ ❄) Well-established Wild Orchid's contemporary, wooden Andamanese-style cottages are strung around a tropical garden, the best of them vibrantly coloured and sporting half-canopied beds.

✖ Eating & Drinking

There are *dhabas* (casual eateries, serving snacks and basic meals) near the jetty. The main bazaar (No 3 Village) has local meals, a market and a supermarket.

Alcohol is available from a **store** (⊘ 9am-noon & 3-8pm) near the ATMs at No 3 Village. Apart from a couple of bars and the wonderful jungle-shrouded club **Cicada** (Beach 5;

⊘ hours vary), due to reopen in 2019, Havelock nightlife is on the mellow beachy side.

Dakshin
SOUTH INDIAN $

(www.barefoot-andaman.com; No 1 Village; mains ₹80 270; ⊘ 6.30-10am & noon-3.30pm) Masala dosas, *uttapams* (thick, savoury rice pancake) and tasty thalis are swiftly served at this South Indian specialist, next to Havelock's jetty.

Fat Martin's
INDIAN $

(Beach 5; mains ₹70-140; ⊘ 11.30am-9pm) Popular open-air cafe with a good selection of Indian dishes and some particularly impressive dosas (paper-thin lentil-flour pancakes) including paneer tikka and Nutella.

★ Anju-Coco Resto
INTERNATIONAL $$

(www.facebook.com/pg/Anjucocoresto; Beach 5; mains ₹200-800; ⊘ 8am-10.30pm) One of Havelock's faves, down-to-earth roadside Anju-Coco offers a flavour-packed menu of zealously guarded Indian-international family recipes, with outstanding breakfasts, barbecue dishes, seafood and platters. Try a signature veg platter with charred paneer.

Rony's Restaurant
INDIAN $$

(Beach 5; mains ₹160-350; ⊘ 7am-10.30pm) A simple open-sided cafe with red plastic chairs and a few colourful murals, popular Rony's cooks up delish seafood curries, wood-fired pizzas, Israeli *sabich* (stuffed pita sandwich), breakfast pancakes and other backpacker favourites.

★ Full Moon Cafe
INTERNATIONAL $$$

(www.facebook.com/fullmoonandaman; Dive India, Beach 3; mains ₹140-550; ⊘ 7am-3.30pm & 6-10pm) ✐ Run by an Irish-Indian couple, this mellow thatched-roof restaurant shares a sandy floored site with Dive India (p427) and does fabulous seafood, salads, pastas, wraps, fresh juices, falafel platters, Indian

---

RAJAN: THE ANDAMANS' LAST SWIMMING ELEPHANT

In 2016 Havelock Island (Swaraj Dweep) lost one of its most celebrated, instantly recognisable and beloved residents: at the grand old age of 66, the Andamans' last swimming elephant, Rajan, passed away, and his 5-ton body was returned to the depths of the island.

Elephants were first brought to the Andaman Islands in the 1880s by the British to work in the logging industry fuelled by the lush local rainforests. The easiest way for them to travel between islands was by swimming, using their trunks as snorkels. But when logging was banned in 2000, the islands' 200 famous and often-spotted swimming elephants were mostly shipped off to mainland India. Rajan, however, fell into the care of the Barefoot at Havelock (p429) resort on Havelock's Radhanagar Beach, starring in photo shoots and films, including Hollywood flick *The Fall* (2006), until he 'retired' here in 2014.

bites, and French-press coffee from South Indian beans. Free water refills, plus a book exchange.

B3 – Barefoot Bar
& Brasserie MULTICUISINE $$$
(www.barefoot-andaman.com; No 1 Village; mains ₹350-600; ⊙noon-9.30pm) Right by the jetty, with sea views, B3's breezy wooden deck makes a great place to wait for the ferry. Come for the scrumptious homemade pasta, the fresh-seafood specials and the best pizza on Havelock.

Red Snapper INDIAN $$$
(☑ 03192-282472; www.wildorchidandaman.com; Beach 5, Wild Orchid; mains ₹250-800; ⊙8-10am, noon-2.30pm & 6-10.30pm) The thatched-roof, bamboo-clad Wild Orchid resort's restaurant exudes a romantic, candlelit island ambience, sizzling up lavish seafood platters, pepper-crust tuna, paneer or fish tikka (marinated in spices and dry-roasted) and other goodies. The mellow attached deck **bar** (⊙hours vary) is a good spot for a beer.

🛍 Shopping

Seven Heaven FASHION & ACCESSORIES
(☑ 9531835632; No 3 Village; ⊙hours vary) A beach-chic 'island lifestyle' boutique filled with breezy dresses, kaftans and pants, plus beachwear, tribal-inspired jewellery and a few books.

ℹ Information

There are a couple of ATMs in No 3 Village. A handful of places have wi-fi, but it's *sloooow*.
Havelock Tourist Information Centre (☑ 09474287741; Havelock Jetty, No 1 Village; ⊙8am-1pm & 2.30-5pm)

ℹ Getting There & Away

Government ferries run from **Havelock Jetty** (No 1 Village) in the island's north to Port Blair (₹650, 2½ hours) at 9am and 4.30pm, returning at 6.20am and 2pm. One ferry links Havelock (Swaraj Dweep) with Neil Island (Shaheed Dweep; ₹650, 1¼ hours) at 2.45pm, while three to four boats a week (9.30am on Monday, Wednesday, Friday and, sometimes, Saturday) head to Long Island (₹460, two hours) en route to Rangat, returning at 7am on Tuesday, Thursday and Sunday and 2pm on Friday. Tickets are available from the **ferry ticket office** (☑ 03192-245555; Havelock Jetty, No 1 Village; ⊙8am-1pm & 2-4pm Mon-Sat) one to three days in advance (most hotels arrange tickets for a fee). Schedules may change, and additional services might run during the November-to-April season.

Makruzz (☑ 03192-212355; www.makruzz.com; Havelock Jetty, No 1 Village; ⊙8am-4.30pm) runs at least once daily to Port Blair (₹1407 to ₹3118, 1½ hours) and Neil Island (₹1289 to ₹2882, one hour) and back. **Green Ocean** (☑ 03192-230777; http://greenocean seaways.com; Havelock Jetty, No 1 Village; ⊙8am-noon & 1-5pm) has two to three daily ferries to/from Port Blair (₹1171 to ₹1407, 2¼ hours) and one or two to Neil (₹876 to ₹994, 1¼ hours; returns may operate in high season). These can be booked online a month ahead.

At the time of writing, there were plans to introduce new express ferries between Port Blair and Havelock.

ℹ Getting Around

From 7am to 5.45pm, local buses run from the jetty to Kalapathar (₹12) via the east-coast villages every 1½ hours, and to Radhanagar hourly; the latest return buses are at 6.30pm. Autorickshaws from the jetty cost ₹50 to No 3 Village, ₹90 to No 5 and ₹500 to Radhanagar.

Otherwise, rent a scooter (per 24 hours ₹400 to ₹500) or bicycle (per day ₹100).

Neil Island (Shaheed Dweep)

Although its beaches are not as luxurious as those of its more famous island neighbour, Havelock (Swaraj Dweep), tranquil and wonderfully unhurried Neil (recently renamed Shaheed Dweep) has its own rustic charm, with a lusciously green landscape of rice paddies, fruit plantations and coconut palms. The main bazaar, at Neil Kendra in the centre of the island, has a mellow vibe; the jetty is 500m north of the bazaar.

Development has begun to creep in on Neil, however, and there's been a surge in domestic tourist activity near the jetty and along the north coast, especially on Beach 4.

◉ Sights & Activities
Beaches
Neil Island's five beaches all have their own personalities, though they aren't great for swimming due to shallow, rocky sea floors.

Beach 1 BEACH
(Lakshmanpur) A long sweep of sandy white coastline and mangroves wrapping around the northwest end of the island, 2km from the jetty, and gazing across to Havelock (Swaraj) Island's densely forested southern tip. There's a sunset viewpoint here, plus good snorkelling and snack stalls, and dugongs are sometimes spotted.

Beach 2
BEACH

On the southwest side of the island, sign-posted from Neil Kendra (1.5km), this rocky cove is famous for its striking Natural Bridge rock formation, accessible only at low tide.

Beach 3
BEACH

(Ramnagar Beach) This secluded rock-studded cove with powdery sand and good snorkelling sits on Neil's south coast and is one of the better beaches for lazing around.

Beach 4
BEACH

(Bharatpur) Neil Island's best swimming beach, though its proximity to the jetty (just west) is a turn-off, as is the rowdy day-trip scene packed with motorised boats, jet skis and banana-boat rides.

Beach 5
BEACH

On the far east of the island, 5km southeast of the jetty, Sitapur is a rugged sweep of silver-white sand, with small limestone caves accessible at low tide. It's popular for sunrise, and has some low-key accommodation.

Diving & Snorkelling

Neil offers some brilliant dive sites, with fish, large schools of jack, turtles, rays, reef sharks, soft and hard corals, and even the odd dugong. PADI Discover Scuba (₹7000 to ₹8000) and Open Water courses (₹28,300 to ₹30,700), among others, are available; two-dive trips cost around ₹6600 to ₹7400.

The island's best snorkelling is at the far (western) end of Beach 1 at high tide. Beach 3 also has good snorkelling. Gear hire costs around ₹200.

India Scuba Explorers
DIVING

(☑ 9933271450; www.indiascubaexplorers.com; Beach 1; 2-dive trip ₹6600, PADI Open Water course ₹28,320) Neil's original dive shop, set up in 2007 by a husband-and-wife team, is popular for its personalised service and offers simple, clean budget rooms (₹700).

Dive India
DIVING

(☑ 8001122205, 9679574266; www.diveindia.com; Neil Jetty; 2-dive trip ₹7380, PADI Open Water course ₹30,680) This professional and well-established Havelock Island (Swaraj Dweep) dive operator also has a Neil branch, just east of the jetty, with straightforward, modern accommodation (☑ 9476007249; r ₹3500-5500; ❋).

DIVING IN THE ANDAMAN ISLANDS

Havelock Island (Swaraj Dweep; p427) is the premier spot for diving in the Andamans, famed for its crystal-clear waters, deep-sea corals and kaleidoscopic marine life, including turtles, sharks and manta rays. There are also dive schools on Neil Island (Shaheed Dweep). The main dive season is November to April, with prime conditions from December, but trips run year-round, weather permitting. Diving is suitable for all levels.

While coral bleaching has been a major issue since 2010 (said to be linked to El Niño weather patterns) and an estimated 23% of corals off the coast of the Andaman and Nicobar Islands was lost to bleaching in 2016, diving remains world class. The shallows (where most of the bleaching happened) may not have particularly bright corals, but all the colourful fish are still here, and for depths beyond 16m, the corals remain as vivid as ever. The Andamans recovered from a similar bleaching in 1998, and today things are, likewise, slowly repairing themselves.

Keep an eye out for trips further afield such as to Barren Island, home to India's only active volcano, whose ash produces an eerie underwater spectacle for divers.

Protecting Marine Life

In general, you should only snorkel when it's high tide, as during low tide it's very easy to step on coral or sea sponges, which can irreparably damage them. In areas that have reefs with very shallow water, avoid wearing flippers – even the gentle sweep of a flipper-kick can damage decades' worth of growth. Divers need to be extra cautious about descents near reefs; colliding with the coral at a strong pace with full gear can be environmentally disastrous. Choose ecologically responsible dive operators and heed their advice.

Avoid touching marine life of any kind, including coral, as doing so may not only stress them and cause damage, but they could also be toxic. Finally, clear any rubbish you come across and refrain from taking souvenir shells or coral out of the ocean (it's ecologically detrimental but also potentially illegal).

🛏 Sleeping & Eating

There are cheap restaurants in the bazaar.

Kalapani BUNGALOW $
(📞9933225575; Beach 3; huts ₹200-600) Laid-back Kalapani has simple budget bungalows amid neat sandy gardens, the cheapest of which share communal bathrooms. Motorbikes, bicycles and snorkelling gear are available, and lovely owners Prakash and Bina are full of local tips.

Breakwater Beach Resort BUNGALOW $
(📞9933292654, 9531852332; neilbreakwater@gmail.com; Beach 3; huts ₹600-2000, bungalows with/without AC ₹4000/2800; 📶) An easy-going ambience, attractive gardens and a small restaurant (mains ₹140 to ₹250), with accommodation in basic thatched huts (some share bathrooms) and well-kept whitewashed concrete bungalows set back from Beach 3.

Sunrise Beach Resort BUNGALOW $
(📞9474202539; Beach 5; r ₹500-800) Simple turquoise-painted, fan-cooled concrete bungalows with hammocks sit 100m from Sitapur beach, and there's a cheerful welcome plus a sweet little restaurant among flowers. The cheapest rooms share bathrooms.

Sunset Garden HUT $
(📞9474220472, 9933294573; Beach 1; huts ₹300-800) Popular with foreign travellers, these basic sea-view bamboo huts (the most economical with communal bathrooms) enjoy a fairly secluded site, accessed via a 15-minute walk through rice fields (signposted) or round the back of Pearl Park Beach Resort.

★Emerald Gecko BUNGALOW $$
(📞9020064604, 9820023416; www.emerald-gecko.com; Beach 5; r incl breakfast ₹2700-3700) 🌿 Ecofriendly boho bungalows, with ceiling fans, concrete bathrooms, mosquito nets, filtered water and hand-painted murals of local birds, set in a coconut plantation behind rice fields. Some rooms are split-level and there's a mellow cafe.

Silver Sand Beach Resort RESORT $$$
(📞03192-244914, 9476019332; http://silversandhotels.com; Neil Kendra; r incl breakfast ₹7260-12,800; 🌀🍽) Arguably the island's most sophisticated resort: pool, restaurant, and cosy contemporary-style cottages done in earthy oranges and woods are dotted across a peaceful palm-shaded garden just a short wander from the water. It's 600m south of Neil Kendra.

SeaShell RESORT $$$
(📞9679587575; http://seashellhotels.net; Beach 1; r incl breakfast ₹8260-15,360; 🌀) One of Neil's swishest stays, with an on-site dive school and smart bar-restaurant (mains ₹250 to ₹600). The elegantly contemporary rooms, featuring TVs and tea-and-coffee trays, trickle down to a mangrove-lined beach.

Garden View Restaurant INDIAN $$
(dishes ₹80-300; ⏰6am-10pm, hours vary) Occupying a colourful garden pavilion, 1km west of Beach 5, this family-run operation is a relaxing little spot to knock back a Kingfisher or papaya lassi and tuck into thalis, biryanis, fish curries, prawn fried rice and much more.

Blue Sea INDIAN $$
(📞9476013330; Beach 3; mains ₹120-500; ⏰6am-10.30pm) A quirky shack-restaurant just back from Beach 3. Come for the unpretentious, chilled-out character, nearby beach and simple, well-prepared Indian and Continental fare, including fresh-seafood specials.

Chand Restaurant INDIAN $$
(Neil Kendra; mains ₹130-250; ⏰7.30am-9pm) A blue-washed facade marks out this simple home-style restaurant in Neil's bazaar, where bread omelettes, steaming coffee and *paratha* (hotplate-cooked flaky bread with ghee) are whipped up.

There's also a jetty-side branch, **Sea View Chand** (Neil Jetty; dishes ₹60-300; ⏰hours vary).

ℹ Information

There are two ATMs in the main bazaar, but it's best to bring extra cash. Some accommodation has slow, patchy wi-fi.

ℹ Getting There & Away

Government ferries (Neil Jetty; ⏰6.30-8am & 10.30am-1pm) go to Port Blair (₹460 to ₹640, two hours) at 8.30am and 4pm; to Havelock (Swaraj; ₹650, one hour) at 1pm; and to Long Island (₹700, five hours) at 8am on Monday, Wednesday and Saturday.

Makruzz (📞9679536651, 9933265867; www.makruzz.com; Neil Jetty; ⏰8am-1pm & 2.30-4.30pm) has at least one daily ferry to/from Port Blair (₹1000 to ₹2300, one hour) and Havelock (₹900 to ₹2000, one hour). **Green Ocean** (📞03192-230777; http://greenoceanseaways.com; Neil Jetty; ⏰8am-noon & 1-5pm) runs to Port Blair (₹1290 to ₹1640, two hours), then back via Havelock; there may be direct services to Havelock in high season. Schedules change seasonally.

❶ Getting Around

Roads are flat and distances short, so hiring a bicycle (per day ₹150) or scooter (per day ₹500) is the best way to get about; ask in the main bazaar or at your guesthouse. Autorickshaws charge ₹75 to ₹100 from the jetty to Beach 1 or 3.

Middle & North Andaman

Beyond the sun, sea and sand, the Andamans unfold into dense jungle that feels as primeval as the Jurassic, a green tangle of ancient forest that could have been birthed in Mother Nature's subconscious. This wild, antediluvian side of the islands can be seen on a long journey north from Port Blair to Middle and North Andaman. The loping, controversial Andaman Trunk Rd travels northwards, slicing through the homeland of the Jarawa tribe (p437) and crossing tannin-red rivers prowled by saltwater crocodiles. The roll-on, roll-off ferries en route are slowly being replaced by bridges.

The first main stop of interest as you travel north is Baratang's limestone **caves** (Baratang; ☉ trips 7.30am & 11am Tue-Sun), 90km north of Port Blair. After crossing from South Andaman to Baratang Island by vehicle ferry, it's a scenic 45-minute boat trip (return per person ₹700) from the jetty to the caves through mangrove forest. Free permits are required, organised at the jetty.

Rangat

Travelling north on the Andaman Trunk Rd (ATR), inland Rangat is the first main town in Middle Andaman after Baratang Island. It's primarily a transport hub, and most travellers just pass through en route to/from Long Island, Mayabunder or Diglipur.

❶ Getting There & Away

BOAT

Rangat Bay, 7.5km southeast of town, has ferries to Port Blair (₹630 to ₹1050, six hours) via Havelock (Swaraj), Neil (Shaheed) and Long Islands at 6.15am on Tuesday, Thursday and Sunday, returning at 6.15am on Monday, Wednesday and Saturday.

Ferries for Long Island (₹20, one hour) also depart from Yeratta Jetty, 12km southeast of Rangat (and accessed by local bus), at 9am and 3.30pm, returning at 7am and 2pm.

BUS

From Rangat's main bazaar, buses go to Port Blair (₹160 to ₹190, seven hours) at 4.30am, 5.45am, 9.15am and noon, and Diglipur (₹50 to ₹100, four hours) at 4.30am and 11.30am. Additional 'express' services to/from Port Blair and Diglipur pass through town. There are also hourly buses to Yeratta Jetty (₹10 to ₹20), for boats to Long Island.

Long Island

With its friendly island community, wooden homes left over from the logging industry and deliciously slow pace of life, Long Island is perfect for those seeking to dial life down a few more notches. Other than the odd motorcycle, there are no motorised vehicles on the island, and at certain times you'll be one of just a few tourists here. Long Island is off Middle Andaman, 10km south of Rangat.

Though there was no diving available at research time, there's good offshore snorkelling at Lalaji Bay and the beach near Blue

---

THE CONTROVERSIAL ANDAMAN TRUNK ROAD

Built in the 1970s, the Andaman Trunk Rd (ATR; NH4) from Port Blair to Diglipur cuts through the homeland of the Jarawa (p437) and has brought the tribe into incessant contact with the outside world. Modern India and tribal life do not seem able to coexist – every time Jarawa and settlers interact, misunderstandings have led to friction, confusion and, at worst, violent attacks and death. Indian anthropologists and indigenous rights groups such as Survival International have called for the ATR to be closed; India's Supreme Court ordered it closed in 2002, but the closure was never implemented and its status continues to be under review.

At the time of writing, vehicles were permitted to travel only in convoys at set times from 6am to 3pm (though queues start from 4.30am). Photography is strictly prohibited, as is stopping or any other interaction with the Jarawa people, who are becoming increasingly reliant on handouts from passing traffic.

A ferry service, called the Alternate Sea Route, from Port Blair to Baratang was launched in 2017. An attempt to reduce traffic through South Andaman's Jarawa tribal reserve, it has so far failed to attract tourists.

Planet. You can also take a boat to North Passage Island for swimming and snorkelling at stunning Merk Bay (₹5000 to ₹6000 per small group), with its blinding-white sand and translucent waters. Blue Planet hires out snorkelling gear (around ₹150).

A 10km, 1½-hour trek through the jungle leads to secluded Lalaji Bay, a beautiful white-sand east-coast beach with good swimming and snorkelling; follow the arrows from the jetty, or arrange a guide (₹1000) through Blue Planet. Hiring a boat (₹5000 per small group) is also an option. You'll need a permit (free) from the Forest Office near the jetty.

Blue Planet (📱9474212180; www.blueplanet andamans.com; r ₹1680-2800, without bathroom ₹500) is a favourite place to stay, with its thatched bamboo rooms set around a Padauk tree, and is a 15-minute, 1.5km walk east from the jetty. There's good home-cooked food plus free filtered water, a low-key vibe, hammocks, and bamboo cottages (₹2200 to ₹3360) at a nearby location.

❶ Getting There & Away

There are three to four ferries a week from Port Blair (₹630 to ₹1050, five hours) to Long Island via Havelock (Swaraj) and Neil (Shaheed). Boats leave Port Blair at 6.15am on Monday, Wednesday, Friday and, usually, Saturday, returning at 7am on Tuesday, Thursday and Sunday and 2pm on Friday. From Yeratta Jetty, 12km southeast of Rangat, boats (₹20, one hour) cross to Long Island at 9am and 3.30pm, then back at 7am and 2pm. Hourly buses (₹10 to ₹20) go to Yeratta from Rangat.

Diglipur & Around

Those who make it as far as sparsely populated North Andaman are rewarded with some impressive natural attractions. The Diglipur area is a giant outdoor adventure playground, home to a world-famous turtle-nesting site, the Andamans' highest peak and a network of limestone caves, not to mention glorious snow-white beaches and some of the best snorkelling in the Andamans.

However, don't expect much of the sprawling, gritty bazaar town Diglipur itself (population 43,200), the Andamans' second-largest urban settlement, 80km north of Mayabunder. Instead, head straight for the tranquil coastal village of Kalipur, a 17km drive east of Diglipur.

There are rumblings of impending tourism development, with a bridge now linking North and Middle Andaman and plans for a public airport near Kalipur. But for now, the area remains satisfyingly remote.

◉ Sights & Activities

★ Ross & Smith Islands   BEACH

Like lovely tropical counterweights, the twin islands of Smith and Ross are connected by a slender, dazzlingly white sandbar, and are up there with the best in the Andamans for both swimming and snorkelling.

No permits are required for Smith, which is accessed by boat (₹5000 per boat, fits five people) from Aerial Bay, 4km southwest. Theoretically you need a permit for Ross (Indian/foreigner ₹75/1000) once you're on Smith, but as it's walkable from Smith, permits sometimes aren't checked.

Kalipur Beach   BEACH

Fringed by lush jungle and sparkling cerulean waves, the brown-sand beach at Kalipur, 17km east of Diglipur by road, is famous for its turtle nesting (p436) from mid-December to April.

Craggy Island   ISLAND

A speck of an island off Kalipur Beach, Craggy is a good spot for snorkelling. Very strong swimmers can make it across, in good conditions only (flippers recommended); otherwise, a small motorised boat (₹3000 return) runs here from Aerial Bay, on the road from Diglipur to Kalipur.

Excelsior Island   ISLAND

North from Aerial Bay, Excelsior has beautiful, creamy white beaches, good snorkelling and resident spotted deer. Six-person boats from Aerial Bay cost ₹5000 to ₹6000, and you'll need a (free) permit; visiting arrangements may change, however, so it's best to ask locally.

Saddle Peak   TREKKING

(📱Forest Office checkpoint 9679505917; permits Indian/foreigner ₹50/500) At 732m, Saddle Peak is the Andamans' highest point, opening up astounding archipelago views. You can trek through subtropical forest to the top and back (14km) from Lamiya Bay (just south of Kalipur) in six to seven hours. Permits must be procured on the day from the Forest Office checkpoint at the trailhead from 6.30am to noon; bring your passport.

It's a demanding trek, so start first thing and bring plenty of water (around 4L). For a local guide (₹500), contact the checkpoint after 2pm the day before. Otherwise, follow the blue arrows marked on the trees.

TURTLE NESTING AT KALIPUR

Reputedly the only beach in the world where leatherback, hawksbill, green and olive ridley marine turtles all nest along the same coastline, Kalipur is a fantastic place to observe this evening show from mid-December to March or April. Turtles can be seen most nights, and you may be able to assist with collecting eggs, or with the release of hatchlings. Ask locally.

🛏 Sleeping & Eating

Saddle Peak View Resort   RESORT $$
(☑ 9434271731; www.facebook.com/saddlepeak viewresort; Kalipur Beach; r with/without AC ₹2500/2000; ❄) A small, simple, palm-dotted resort offering five well-kept, colour-walled rooms and home-cooked meals, just back from Kalipur Beach.

Pristine Beach Resort   GUESTHOUSE $$$
(☑ 9474286787, 03192-271793; www.andaman pristineresorts.com; Kalipur Beach; r incl breakfast ₹2400-5900; ❄🛜🏊) Huddled among palms between paddy fields and the beach, this relaxing resort sleeps travellers in a range of immaculate wood or concrete rooms with kettles, air-con and hot water. There's a good multicuisine restaurant serving delicious fish Nicobari, and a pool may be in place by the time you read this.

ⓘ Getting There & Away

From Diglipur's bazaar, buses run to Port Blair (₹250 to ₹410, 12 hours) via Rangat (₹65 to ₹150, 4½ hours) at 5am, 7am and 10pm or 10.30pm; some of these stop in Mayabunder (₹55 to ₹70, two hours). There are additional buses to Rangat via Mayabunder at 6.30am, 8.30am, 8.45am, 10am, 1.30pm and 5pm, and a 4.30am bus from Aerial Bay all the way south to Port Blair.

Ferries to Port Blair (₹1050 to ₹1470, 17 hours) via Mayabunder depart from Aerial Bay at 2pm on Tuesday and Sunday, returning at 9pm on Monday and Saturday.

ⓘ Getting Around

Ferries arrive into Aerial Bay, 9km northeast of Diglipur and 9km northwest of Kalipur. Buses run every 30 to 45 minutes from Diglipur's bazaar to Kalipur (₹20, 45 minutes) via Aerial Bay (₹20, 25 minutes).

Little Andaman

As far south as you can go (for now) in the islands, Little Andaman, 130km south of Port Blair, has an appealing end-of-the-world feel. It's a gorgeous fist of mangroves, jungle and teal, ringed by fresh, sandy white beaches with fantastic surf. It rates highly as many travellers' favourite spot in the Andamans.

Badly hit by the 2004 tsunami, Little Andaman has slowly rebuilt itself. Much of the island is an off-limits 25-sq-km Onge tribal reserve. The main settlement is small, pleasant, southeast-coast Indira Bazaar, 2km west of Hut Bay Jetty. There are ATMs in Indira Bazaar and the village at Km16.

⊙ Sights & Activities

Little Andaman Lighthouse   LIGHTHOUSE
Little Andaman's 41m-tall lighthouse makes for a worthwhile excursion, around 10km south of Hut Bay. Its 200 steps spiral up to magnificent views over the coastline and forest. The easiest way to get here is by jeep, motorcycle or a sweaty bicycle journey.

Beaches

Come prepared for sandflies (p419); seek local advice as to where crocs may be currently congregating.

★Butler Bay   BEACH
(Km14) Little Andaman's best beach: a spectacular, powder-soft golden-white sweep of sand, famed for having some of India's best surfing waves.

Kalapathar   BEACH
Kalapathar lagoon is a popular enclosed swimming area with shady patches of sand, around 12km north of Hut Bay. Look for the cave in the cliff face that you can scramble through for stunning ocean views.

Netaji Nagar   BEACH
The sprawling, rugged and blonde Netaji Nagar, stretching 8km to 12km north of Hut Bay, is the beach where most accommodation is located.

Surfing

Intrepid surfer travellers have been whispering about Little Andaman since it first opened to foreigners some years back. The reef breaks are legendary, but best suited to experienced surfers. The most accessible is Jarawa Point, a left reef break at the northern point of Butler Bay. Beginners should stick to beach breaks along Km8 to Km11. February to April generally bring the best waves. Some guesthouses rent surfboards for around ₹500/1000 per half-/full day and may be able to arrange classes (₹1500).

ISLAND INDIGENES

The Andaman and Nicobar Islands' indigenous peoples constitute 7.5% of the population and, in most cases, their numbers are decreasing. The Onge, Sentinelese, Andamanese and Jarawa are all of Negrito ethnicity, and share a strong resemblance to people from Africa. Tragically, numerous groups have become extinct over the past century. In 2010 the last speaker of the Great Andamanese Bo language passed away, bringing an end to a culture and language that originated 65,000 years ago. It's important to note that these tribal groups live in areas strictly off limits to foreigners – for their protection and dignity – and people have been arrested for trying to visit these regions.

Sentinelese

The self-sufficient hunter-gatherer Sentinelese, unlike the other tribes on these islands, have consistently repelled outside contact. For years, contact parties arrived on the beaches of North Sentinel Island, the last redoubt of the Sentinelese, with gifts of coconuts, bananas, pigs and plastic buckets, only to be showered with arrows, though some encounters have been a little less hostile. An estimated 150 Sentinelese remain. In late 2018 an American tourist/missionary was killed by arrows fired by the Sentinelese while attempting (illegally) to approach North Sentinel Island.

Jarawa

The 270 or so remaining Jarawa occupy a 1000-sq-km reserve on South and Middle Andaman Islands. In 1953 the chief commissioner requested that an armed seaplane bomb Jarawa settlements, and their territory has been consistently disrupted by the much-disputed Andaman Trunk Rd (p434), forest clearance, and settler and tourist encroachment. In 2012 a video went viral showing an exchange between Jarawa and tourists, whereby a policeman orders them to dance in exchange for food. This resulted in a government inquest that saw the end of the so-called 'human safari' tours, but tourist traffic through their homeland continues to be a problem.

Onge

Two thirds of Little Andaman's Onge Island was taken over by the Forest Department and 'settled' in 1977. The 100 or so remaining members of the Onge tribe, traditionally hunters but now dependent on government handouts, live in a 25-sq-km reserve covering Dugong Creek and South Bay. When the 2004 tsunami struck, the Onge were able to interpret natural wind, sea and wildlife signs and survived by fleeing to higher, forested ground.

Andamanese

There were 7000 to 8000 Andamanese in the mid-19th century, living across South and Middle Andaman, but friendliness to colonisers was their undoing. By 1971, all but 19 of the population had been wiped out by measles, syphilis and influenza epidemics. Their population, on the brink of extinction, now numbers only 43 and has been resettled on tiny Strait Island – controversially, this is one of the islands now theoretically accessible for tourism without Restricted Area Permits (p419).

Shompen

Only about 300 Shompen remain in the forests on Great Nicobar. Seminomadic hunter-gatherers who live along the riverbanks, they have resisted integration and avoid areas occupied by Indian immigrants.

Nicobarese

The 30,000 Nicobarese are the only indigenous people whose numbers are not decreasing. The majority have converted to Christianity and partly assimilated into contemporary Indian society. Mostly living in village units led by a headman, they probably descended from people of Malaysia and Myanmar (Burma), and inhabit a number of islands in the Nicobar group, centred on Car Nicobar, the region worst affected by the 2004 tsunami.

Waterfalls

Around 1km inland from Km5, the White Surf waterfalls offer a pleasant jungle experience for when you're done lazing on the beach. Meanwhile, the Whisper Wave waterfalls (inland from Kalapathar) involve a 4km forest trek, for which a guide is highly recommended; ask locally. You may be

ANDAMAN ISLANDS LITTLE ANDAMAN

MAYABUNDER & AROUND

In 'upper' Middle Andaman, 70km north of Rangat, the Mayabunder area is best known for its villages inhabited by Karen, members of a Burmese hill tribe who were relocated here during the British colonial period. It's a low-key destination that appeals to travellers looking for an experience away from the crowds. Seaside Mayabunder is the main hub, while a homestay scene is blossoming in Webi, the Andamans' original Karen settlement, founded in 1925, 7km southwest of town.

The highlight of this area's day trips is creepy Interview Island, inhabited by 35 wild elephants released after a logging company closed for business in the 1950s. Though closed to visitors at the time of writing, it's expected to reopen for day trips and was one of the islands for which Restricted Area Permits were removed (p419) in 2018; ask locally. Other trips include to Rangat's **Dhaninallah Mangrove** (off NH4; ☉ 6am-5pm) and to **Avis Island** (permit ₹250, boat hire ₹1000) for its snorkelling and cream-coloured beach.

Karen conservationist couple Saw John and Naw Doris have opened their traditional wood-and-palm home **Ko Hee Homestay** (☑ 9476090117, 9474215682; www.kohhee. wordpress.com; Webi; r without bathroom incl meals ₹1500) ✎ to guests. It offers organic home-produce meals and three no-frills but comfy fan-cooled rooms and a cottage, all featuring Andaman redwood furniture, filtered water and shared bathroom. The setting, among Webi's electric-green rice fields, is beautifully serene.

The best place to stay in Mayabunder town is **Sea'n'Sand** (☑ 9531877578; NH4; r with AC ₹1200-1400, without AC ₹750; ❄). This pastel-pink guesthouse provides tasty meals, spick-and-span rooms with hot water by bucket, and tips from Karen hosts Titus and Elizabeth.

Mayabunder has daily buses (₹80 to ₹100, two hours) to Rangat and Diglipur at 5am, 9am, 1pm and 5pm. Buses trundle south to Port Blair at 4.30am, 6.30am and 7am (₹250 to ₹300, 10 hours). Port Blair–Diglipur ferries stop in Mayabunder (from Port Blair ₹840 to ₹1260, 10 hours), departing Port Blair at 9pm on Monday and Saturday and returning from Mayabunder at 9pm on Sunday and Tuesday.

tempted to swim in the rock pools, but beware of crocodiles.

🛏 Sleeping & Eating

Some accommodation closes outside the October-to-April high season. There are cheap and tasty thali places in Indira Bazaar.

Hawva Beach Resort　　　BUNGALOW $
(☑9775181290, Whatsapp 9474206130; Km8, Netaji Nagar; r ₹800) This laid-back family-run lodging has a handful of simple yellow-walled concrete cottages. It rents surfboards (₹500 for three hours) and cooks up flavoursome homemade meals (₹550 per day).

Rainbow Resort　　　BUNGALOW $
(☑9775274587, 9474204862; rainbowresort10km@gmail.com; Km10, Netaji Nagar; r ₹300-600) A warm, family-run guesthouse with nine bungalows amid the palms. Rooms are unfussy, with the cheapest sharing bathrooms. Fresh Indian meals, surfboards and motorcycles can all be arranged.

Ieshika Resort　　　BUNGALOW $
(☑9531861060, Whatsapp 9474222951; Km8, Netaji Nagar; d/tr ₹800/1500) No-frills tin-roof

concrete-and-bamboo cottages for two to three (some bunk-style), plus surfboard hire (₹1000 per day) and home-cooked meals (₹180).

❶ Getting There & Away

Boats sail to/from Port Blair daily, alternating between afternoon and evening departures on vessels ranging from big ferries with four- or two-bed rooms (six to 8½ hours) to faster 5½-hour government boats; all have air-con. Rates vary according to the class booked: seat (₹500), bunk (₹900), first class (₹1100), semideluxe (₹1300) or deluxe (₹1500). Ferries dock at Hut Bay Jetty; its ferry office is closed on Sunday.

Taxis/autorickshaws charge ₹700/100 between the jetty and Netaji Nagar.

❶ Getting Around

Frequent buses (₹17) to Netaji Nagar usually coincide with ferry arrivals; pricier shared jeeps (per person ₹140) are an alternative.

Motorbikes (₹500 per 24 hours) and bicycles (₹200) are popular for getting around. Otherwise, shared jeeps (₹20 to ₹30) and buses (₹17 to ₹30) are very handy.

Understand
South India

SOUTH INDIA TODAY....................440
Key facts, figures and issues in contemporary South India.

HISTORY 443
From ancient empires to independent India to the modern-day
south: a fantastic parade of cultures and change.

THE WAY OF LIFE...........................458
Life in the south: weddings, pilgrimages, sporting obsessions,
the caste system, the status of women and more.

SPIRITUAL INDIA............................465
Hindus, Muslims, Sikhs, Buddhists, Christians, Zoroastrians,
Jains, Jews and followers of tribal religions.

DELICIOUS INDIA...........................472
South Indian cuisine: a feast for all the senses.

THE GREAT INDIAN BAZAAR.................483
Sparkling silks, seductive spices, tribal art, the key to haggling...

THE ARTS 490
The essence of South Indian dance, music, art, film and
literature.

ARCHITECTURAL SPLENDOUR...............494
Cave shrines, towering temples, resplendent royal tombs,
formidable forts, serene churches and opulent palaces.

WILDLIFE & LANDSCAPE....................497
Scout for big cats, wild elephants, sloth bears, primates, deer
and other South Indian signature species.

South India Today

While South India is very much part of the Indian nation, subject to Delhi-based decisions, there is a sense that, with its locally focused politics, the south is different – some would say more progressive – with booming IT, tourism, film and automotive industries, and above-average employment, literacy and life expectancy. However, South India also faces major issues. Violence against women and alcoholism frequently hit the headlines, and there is ever-growing concern about pollution, dwindling water resources and dramatically worsening weather patterns linked to climate change.

Best in Print

Midnight's Children (Salman Rushdie; 1981) Allegory on Independence and Partition.

White Tiger (Aravind Adiga; 2008) Page-turner about class injustice.

Shantaram (Gregory David Roberts; 2003) Vivid tale of Roberts' life in India.

A Fine Balance (Rohinton Mistry; 1995) Tragic, heart-warming tale of Mumbai survival.

The God of Small Things (Arundhati Roy; 1997) Magically written Kerala-based novel of passion and caste.

White Mughals (William Dalrymple; 2002) Fascinating Hyderabad historical investigation.

The Nehrus and the Gandhis (Tariq Ali; 1985) Astute portrait-history.

The House of Blue Mangoes (David Davidar; 2002) Pre-Independence southern family saga.

Best on Film

Fire (1996), **Earth** (1998) and **Water** (2005) The Deepa Mehta–directed trilogy on social issues; popular abroad, controversial in India.

The Lunchbox (2013) A romantic Mumbai tale directed by Ritesh Batra.

Dhobi Ghat (2011) Understated, absorbing story directed by Kiran Rao; life in Mumbai and India.

Gandhi (1982) The classic, directed by Richard Attenborough and starring Ben Kingsley.

The Balance Tilts Southward

In the decades after Independence in 1947, many South Indians headed north for work. Today, the trend is in the opposite direction. Some argue that better, more stable governance in southern states (despite deep-seated corruption) and a less rigid caste system have contributed to the south's upswing. Nearly all South Indian states now have above-average literacy, employment, life expectancy, income per head and female-to-male population ratio. Kerala has India's highest literacy rate.

Mumbai remains India's financial, commercial and industrial powerhouse, as well as its film and fashion capital. Chennai makes one-third of India's cars. Goa and Kerala are huge tourism success stories. But the biggest story is the technology boom, sparked by India's 1991 economic liberalisation and globalisation. Bengaluru (Bangalore) is India's 'Silicon Valley', and together with Hyderabad and Pune forms the 'Deccan Triangle' at the heart of India's thriving IT industry, fuelled by well-educated, English-speaking young professionals.

Problems intertwined with the south's economic progress include the growth of city slums (60% of Mumbai's population lives in slums) and ever-more dreadful traffic and pollution – though new metro systems in Mumbai, Bengaluru, Chennai, Kochi (Cochin) and Hyderabad are slowly modernising transport. Kerala, despite its educational successes, has high unemployment and India's highest alcohol-consumption rates, while Chennai and Bengaluru often top 'suicide capital' lists.

The Political Landscape

South Indian politics continues to be dominated by regional parties, appealing to the Dravidian linguistic majorities in their states, and focused on local issues and personalities – often charismatic leaders who started out in the movie industry, then masterfully used their fame to transition into politics. National parties have to strike alliances with local parties to gain a foothold in southern regions.

Tamil Nadu may be entering a new political era following the deaths of its two dominant figures from rival Dravidian parties, ex-film star Jayalalithaa Jayaram in 2016, and ex-scriptwriter Muthuvel Karunanidhi in 2018. Some things don't change, however: two major new challengers with their own new parties, Rajinikanth and Kamal Haasan, are film stars themselves.

Chandrababu Naidu, chief minister of Andhra Pradesh (whose career was helped along by his marriage to a movie director's daughter), takes most of the credit for the transformation of Hyderabad into an IT hub, but he now faces the challenge of leading a Hyderabad-less Andhra Pradesh following the splitting off of Telangana as a separate state in 2014.

Maharashtra shows more support for a national party – the Hindu-nationalist-oriented Bharatiya Janata Party (BJP) – than any state further south, but the BJP has long had to ally with the regional rightwing, pro-Marathi Shiv Sena.

Having voted in the world's first freely elected communist government in 1957, highly educated Kerala has been dominated by two main coalitions since the 1980s. The communist-led Left Democratic Front (LDF), elected in 2016, regularly alternates power with the United Democratic Front (UDF), led by the Congress Party.

In Karnataka yet another regional party, Janata Dal-Secular (JDS), rules in coalition with Congress. The BJP won more seats than either of them in the 2018 state elections, but failed to gain an overall majority.

Violence Against Women

Following the brutal 2012 gang rape and murder of 23-year-old physiotherapy student Jyoti Singh (known as Nirbhaya) in Delhi, India passed new, stronger laws aimed at deterring violence against women. These were again toughened in 2018 amid rising reports of child rape (19,000 cases in 2016) and national outrage over the gang rape and murder in Jammu and Kashmir of eight-year-old Muslim Asifa Bano by (allegedly) Hindu assailants. Rape now carries a 10-year minimum sentence (20 years for the rape of girls under 12), or the death penalty if the victim dies; the penalty for the gang rape of a child under 12 is life imprisonment or death. New fast-track courts deal exclusively with rape prosecutions. Meanwhile, in 2018, India's Supreme Court outlawed the ancient practice of triple *talaq* (by which Muslim men could instantly divorce their wives).

Sadly, reports of sexual assaults against women and girls, including tourists, are on the increase all over India, including the south. Reported rapes rose to 38,947 in 2016, according to India's National Crime Records Bureau (NCRB), yet conviction rates remain

POPULATION: **393.7 MILLION**

AREA: **956,000 SQ KM**

GDP: **US$3300 PER CAPITA**

LITERACY RATE: **80.6%**

GENDER RATIO:
FEMALE/MALE 976/1000

FERTILITY RATE: **BIRTHS PER WOMAN: 1.56**

if India were 100 people

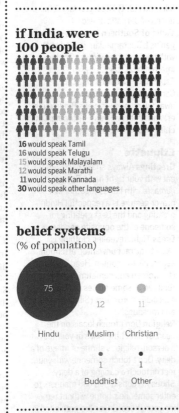

16 would speak Tamil
16 would speak Telugu
15 would speak Malayalam
12 would speak Marathi
11 would speak Kannada
30 would speak other languages

belief systems
(% of population)

75 Hindu 12 Muslim 11 Christian
1 Buddhist 1 Other

population per sq km

SOUTH INDIA UK USA

= 35 people

Sairat (2016) Anti-Bollywood Marathi-language hit about doomed intercaste love; by Dalit director Nagraj Manjule.

Lion (2016) Touching biographic drama, directed by Garth Davis.

Best in Music

Gems of Carnatic Music: TM Krishna (Live in Concert 2006) Innovative Chennai-born Carnatic vocalist and socio-political activist.

Popular Melodies of MS Subbulakshmi (1971) The legendary Tamil queen of Carnatic music.

Violin of Southern India (1996) Violin genius L Subramaniam is credited with taking Carnatic music to the international stage.

Esperanza (SubraMania; 2016) Carnatic-flamenco fusion by award-winning musicians Bindu (singer) and Ambi (violinist) Subramaniam, children of L Subramaniam.

Etiquette

Greetings Always shake hands and eat with your right hand. Saying *namaste* with hands together in a prayer gesture is a respectful Hindu greeting and the best greeting for someone of the opposite gender.

Dress Tight/revealing clothing is likely to attract unwanted attention, especially for women. Head cover (for women and sometimes men) is required at some places of worship – especially gurdwaras (Sikh temples) and mosques.

Religion Don't touch locals on the head, or direct the soles of your feet at a person, religious shrine or image of a deity. Don't touch someone with your feet or touch a carving of a deity.

Shoes It's considered bad manners to enter someone's home without removing your shoes. Shoes are prohibited in many temples and shrines.

Photography Photography inside religious shrines is generally prohibited; photography of funerals or processions of the dead is likely to cause offence. Ask before photographing people, ceremonies or sacred sites.

worryingly low (18.9% in 2016). The saving grace is that, now in the spotlight, India's gender-based violence is finally being fiercely debated. The government of Prime Minister Narendra Modi, re-elected in 2019, actively tried to change the national psyche regarding gender equality, but came under fire for not tackling this successfully enough. Many Indians are also now reflecting on other abuses of women (20 women per day die in dowry-related violence), widespread police and judicial mishandling of cases, and wider gender-equality problems.

Climate Change

Despite the Modi government's pledges to increase India's use of solar power and end water issues (involving a controversial countrywide river-linking scheme), climate change is a rapidly growing concern in South India. Devastating heatwaves, cyclones, floods and droughts, plus sky-rocketing pollution levels, are wreaking havoc with increasing frequency. In 2015 deadly heatwaves and floods killed, officially, around 3000 people (but probably more). All the southern states have seen severe flooding in recent years; in 2018 the worst floods in a century hit Kerala, where 400 people were killed and at least a million displaced. There is growing conflict over limited water resources, especially between Tamil Nadu and Karnataka, while Lakshadweep's islands are at risk from rising sea levels.

Sustainably motivated moves such as the 2018–19 ban on single-use plastics in Maharashtra, Telangana and Tamil Nadu, or clean-ups organised by local inhabitants, are *slowly* starting to tackle some pressing environmental issues – but there is a very long way to go.

The Sabarimala Question

In a historic move, in September 2018 the Supreme Court lifted a long-established ban on women aged 10 to 50 (ie of 'menstruating age') entering the Ayyappan Temple at Sabarimala (Kerala), one of India's most important Hindu pilgrimage sites. Protests, strikes and violent clashes between demonstrators, police and the media ensued. It wasn't until January 2019 that two women of 'forbidden' age – Bindu Ammini and Kanakadurga – finally managed to reach the temple, with a police escort. At the time of writing, however, the Supreme Court had agreed to reconsider its verdict, and the women who had succeeded in entering the temple reported discrimination and, in Kanakadurga's case, physically violent clashes with her mother-in-law upon returning home; several other women who had attempted the pilgrimage also reported being discriminated against once home.

The Sabarimala conflict spotlights many of South India's glaring points of tension: it's a question of women's rights, the rule of law, politics (Kerala's communist-led government supports the Supreme Court's decision, Prime Minister Modi opposes it), and the growing contradictions between perceived tradition and social progress.

History

South India has always laid claim to its own unique history, largely resulting from its insulation, by distance, from political developments up north. The cradle of Dravidian culture, it has a long and colourful historical tapestry of wrangling dynasties and empires, interwoven with an influx of traders and conquerors arriving by sea, all of which have richly contributed to a remarkable mix of southern traditions that persists to the present day.

Indus Valley Civilisation

India's first major civilisation flourished between around 3000 and 1700 BC in the Indus Valley, much of which lies within present-day Pakistan. Known as the Harappan culture, it appears to have been the culmination of thousands of years of settlement. Some historians attribute its eventual demise to floods or decreased rainfall, which threatened the Harappans' agricultural base. A more enduring theory, though with little archaeological proof or evidence from ancient Indian texts, is that an invasion from the northwest by Aryans (peoples speaking languages of the Indo-Iranian branch of the Indo-European language family) put paid to the Harappans. Others say that the arrival of the Aryans was more of a gentle migration that gradually subsumed Harappan culture, rather than an invasion. Some nationalist historians argue that the Aryans (the term comes from a Sanskrit word meaning 'noble') were in fact the original inhabitants of India and that the invasion theory was invented by later, self-serving foreign conquerors. Invasion theorists believe that from around 1500 BC Aryan tribes from Afghanistan and Central Asia began to gradually filter into northwest India, eventually controlling northern India as far south as the Vindhya Range (just north of central India's Narmada River), and that, as a consequence, many of the original inhabitants, the Dravidians, were pushed south.

Influences from the North

Aryan culture had a gradual but profound effect on the social order and ethos of South India as well as the north – among other things in

To learn more about the ancient Indus Valley civilisation, ramble around Harappa (www. harappa.com), which presents an illustrated yet scholarly overview.

India: A History, by John Keay, is an astute, readable account of subcontinental history, spanning the Harappan civilisation to post-Independence India.

TIMELINE	2600–1700 BC	1500 BC	1500–1200 BC
	The heyday of the Indus Valley civilisation, spanning parts of Rajasthan, Gujarat and the Sindh province in present-day Pakistan, and including cities such as Harappa and Moenjodaro.	The Indo-Aryan civilisation takes root in the fertile Indo-Gangetic basin. Settlers speak an early form of Sanskrit, from which several Indian vernaculars, including Hindi, later evolve.	The Rig-Veda, the first and longest of Hinduism's canonical texts, the Vedas, is written; three more books follow. Earliest forms of priestly Brahmanic Hinduism emerge.

George Michell's *Southern India: A Guide to Monuments, Sites & Museums* looks at South India's history from an architectural perspective, providing plenty of insightful regional detail.

Best Buddhist Sites in South India

Ajanta (Maharashtra)

Ellora (Maharashtra)

Amaravathi (Andhra Pradesh)

Nagarjunakonda (Andhra Pradesh)

Guntupalli (Andhra Pradesh)

Karla & Bhaga Caves (Maharashtra)

Aurangabad Caves (Maharashtra)

literature (the four Vedas, a collection of sacred Hindu hymns), religion (gods such as Agni, Varuna, Shiva and Vishnu), language (Sanskrit) and a social structure that organised people into castes, with Brahmins at the top.

Over the centuries other influences flowed from north to south, including Buddhism and Jainism. Sravanabelagola, in modern-day Karnataka (to this day an auspicious place of pilgrimage), is where, tradition says, the northern ruler Chandragupta Maurya, who had embraced Jainism and renounced his kingdom, arrived with his guru around 300 BC. Jainism was then adopted by the trading community (its tenet of ahimsa – nonviolence – disqualified occupations tainted by the taking of life), who spread it across South India.

Emperor Ashoka (p445), a successor of Chandragupta who ruled for 40 years from about 272 BC, was a major force behind Buddhism's inroads into the south. Once a campaigning king, his epiphany came in 260 BC when, overcome by the horrific carnage and suffering caused by his campaign against the powerful Kalinga kingdom of Odisha, he renounced violence and embraced Buddhism. He sent Buddhist missionaries far and wide, and his edicts (carved into rock and incised into specially erected pillars) have been found in Andhra Pradesh and Karnataka. Stupas were also built in South India under Ashoka's patronage, mostly in Andhra Pradesh, although at least one was constructed as far south as Kanchipuram in Tamil Nadu.

The appeal of Jainism and Buddhism was that they rejected the Vedas and condemned the caste system. Buddhism, however, gradually lost favour with its devotees, and was replaced with a new brand of Hinduism, which emphasised devotion to a personal god. This bhakti (surrendering to the gods) order developed in South India around AD 500. Bhakti adherents opposed Jainism and Buddhism, and the movement hastened the decline of both in South India.

Mauryan Empire & Southern Kingdoms

Chandragupta Maurya was the first in a line of Mauryan kings who ruled what was effectively the first Indian empire. The empire's capital was in present-day Patna in Bihar. Chandragupta's son, Bindusara, who came to the throne around 300 BC, extended the empire as far as Karnataka. He seems to have stopped there, possibly because the Mauryan empire was on cordial terms with the southern chieftains of the day.

The identity and customs of these southern chiefdoms have been gleaned from various sources, including archaeological remains and ancient Tamil literature. These literary records describe a land known as the 'abode of the Tamils', within which resided three major ruling families: the Pandyas (centred on Madurai), the Cheras (in what is now

599–528 BC	563–483 BC	321–185 BC	300 BC–AD 300
The life of Mahavir, the 24th and last *tirthankar* (enlightened teacher), who established Jainism. Like the Buddha, he preaches compassion and a path to enlightenment for all castes.	The life of Siddhartha Gautama. The prince is born in modern-day Nepal and attains enlightenment beneath the Bodhi Tree in Bodhgaya (Bihar), transforming into Buddha (Awakened One).	Rule of the Mauryan kings. Founded by Chandragupta Maurya, this pan-Indian empire is ruled from Pataliputra (present-day Patna), briefly adopting Buddhism during the reign of Emperor Ashoka.	Sangam Age, during which Tamil poets produce a body of classical Tamil literature and the Tamil area is dominated by three dynasties: the Pandyas, Cheras and early Cholas.

Kerala and western Tamil Nadu) and the Cholas (Thanjavur [Tanjore] and the Cauvery Valley). The region described in classical Sangam literature (written between 300 BC and AD 300) was still relatively insulated from Sanskrit culture, but the literature indicates that Sanskrit traditions were starting to take root in South India around 200 BC.

A degree of rivalry characterised relations between the main chiefdoms and the numerous minor chiefdoms, and there were occasional clashes with Sri Lankan rulers. Ultimately, the southern powers all suffered at the hands of the Kalabhras, about whom little is known except that they appear to have originated from somewhere north of the Tamil region.

By around 180 BC the Mauryan empire, which had started to disintegrate soon after the death of Emperor Ashoka in 232 BC, had been overtaken by a series of rival kingdoms that were subjected to repeated invasions from the northwest by the Bactrian Greeks and others. The post-Ashokan era did, however, produce at least one line of royalty whose patronage of the arts and ability to maintain a relatively high degree of social cohesion have left an enduring legacy. This was the Satavahanas, who eventually controlled all of modern-day Maharashtra, Madhya Pradesh, Chhattisgarh, Karnataka, Telangana and Andhra Pradesh.

The concepts of zero and infinity are widely believed to have been devised by eminent Indian mathematicians during the reign of the North Indian Guptas.

HISTORY MAURYAN EMPIRE & SOUTHERN KINGDOMS

ASHOKA: AN ENLIGHTENED EMPEROR

Apart from the Mughals and, many centuries later, the British, no other power controlled more Indian territory than the Mauryan empire. It also provided India with one of its most significant historical figures: Emperor Ashoka, grandson of Chandragupta Maurya.

Emperor Ashoka's rule was characterised by flourishing art and sculpture, while his reputation as a philosopher-king was enhanced by the rock-hewn edicts he used both to instruct his people and to delineate the enormous span of his territory (they are found from Afghanistan to Nepal to Andhra Pradesh).

Ashoka's reign also represented an undoubted historical high point for Buddhism: he embraced the religion in 260 BC, declaring it the state religion and cutting a radical swathe through the spiritual and social body of Hinduism. The emperor also built thousands of stupas and monasteries across the region. Ashoka sent missions to Thailand, Greece, the Middle East and North Africa, and is revered in Sri Lanka because his son and daughter carried Buddhism to the island.

The long shadow this 3rd-century-BC emperor still casts over India is evident in the fact that the central motif of the Indian national flag is the Ashoka Chakra, a wheel with 24 spokes. Ashoka's standard (four lions sitting back to back atop an abacus decorated with a frieze and the inscription 'truth alone triumphs'), which topped many pillars, is also the seal of modern-day India and its national emblem.

200 BC–AD 200	AD 52	319–467	6th–8th Centuries
The Satavahana empire, of Andhra origin, rules over much of the Deccan plateau. Buddhism flourishes and literature, sculpture and philosophy blossom.	Possible arrival of St Thomas the Apostle on the coast of Kerala. Christianity is believed to have been introduced to India with his preaching in Kerala and Tamil Nadu.	The golden era of the North India–based Gupta dynasty, the second of India's great empires after the Mauryas. This era is marked by a creative surge in literature and the arts.	The heyday of the Pallava dynasty, which dominates Andhra Pradesh and northern Tamil Nadu from its southern capital, Kanchipuram, and creates marvellous carvings at Mamallapuram.

Pallava Architecture in Tamil Nadu

Shore Temple (Mamallapuram)

Arjuna's Penance (Mamallapuram)

Five Rathas (Mamallapuram)

Kailasanatha Temple (Kanchipuram)

Chalukya Sites in South India

Ellora Cave Temples (Maharashtra)

Badami Cave Temples (Karnataka)

Pattadakal (Karnataka)

Aihole (Karnataka)

Bhongir Fort (Telangana)

Under their rule, between about 200 BC and AD 200, the arts blossomed, especially literature, sculpture and philosophy. Buddhism reached a peak in Maharashtra under the Satavahanas, although the greatest of the Buddhist cave temples at Ajanta and Ellora were built later by the Chalukya and Rashtrakuta dynasties. Most of all, the subcontinent enjoyed a period of considerable prosperity. South India may have lacked North India's vast and fertile agricultural plains, but it compensated by building strategic trade links via the Indian Ocean.

The Chalukyas & Pallavas

Following the suppression of the Tamil chiefdoms by the Kalabhras, South India split into numerous warring kingdoms. The Cholas virtually disappeared and the Cheras on the west coast seem to have prospered through trading, although little is known about them. It wasn't until the late 6th century AD, when the Kalabhras were overthrown, that the political uncertainty in the region ceased. For the next 300 years the history of South India was dominated by the fortunes of the Chalukyas of Badami in northern Karnataka, the Pallavas of Kanchi (Kanchipuram) and the Pandyas of Madurai (these last two in modern-day Tamil Nadu).

The Badami Chalukyas controlled most of the Deccan at their peak under King Pulakesi II in the early 7th century. A related clan, known as the eastern Chalukyas, ruled Andhra Pradesh from Vengi near Eluru. It's unclear where the Pallavas originated, but it's thought they may have emigrated to Kanchi from Andhra Pradesh. After their successful defeat of the Kalabhras, the Pallavas extended their territory as far south as the Cauvery River, and in the 7th and 8th centuries were at the height of their power, building major monuments such as the Shore Temple and Arjuna's Penance at Mamallapuram (Mahabalipuram). They engaged in long-running clashes with the Pandyas, who extended their control into Kerala and, in the 8th century, allied themselves with the Gangas of Mysore (now Mysuru). By the 9th century significant Pallava power had been snuffed out by the Pandyas and the Rashtrakutas, a dynasty based in Gulbarga (Kalaburagi), Karnataka, who replaced the Chalukyas as the dominant force on the Deccan from the 8th to 10th centuries.

The Chola Empire

As the Pallava dynasty came to an end, a new Chola dynasty was laying the foundations for what would come to be one of the subcontinent's most significant empires. From their Tamil capitals at Thanjavur and, briefly, Gangaikondacholapuram, the Cholas spread north, absorbing what was left of the Pallavas' territory, and made inroads southward. Under Raja Raja Chola I (r 985–1014) the Chola kingdom really started to emerge as a great empire. Raja Raja Chola I successfully waged war

10th–12th Centuries	13th Century	1290s	1336
The Chola empire, based in and around Thanjavur, spreads its influence over much of South India and Southeast Asia, leaving a superb legacy in the arts including sculpture and architecture.	The Pandyas, a Tamil dynasty dating back to the 6th century BC, assume control of Chola territory, expanding into Andhra Pradesh, Kalinga (Odisha) and Sri Lanka from their Tamil capital, Madurai.	The Delhi sultanate starts its southward expansion, bringing parts of the Deccan under northern Muslim rule for the first time and reaching Madurai by 1323.	The mighty Vijayanagar empire (Hindu), named after its capital city, is founded. Its ruins can be seen today in the vicinity of Hampi (in modern-day Karnataka).

against the Pandyas in the south, the Gangas of Mysore (now Mysuru) and the Eastern Chalukyas. He also launched a series of naval campaigns that captured the Maldives, the Malabar Coast (coasts of Kerala and Karnataka) and northern Sri Lanka, which became a province of the Chola empire. These conquests gave the Cholas control over critical ports and trading links between India, Southeast Asia, Arabia and East Africa. They were therefore in a position to grab a share of the huge profits made from selling spices to Europe.

Raja Raja Chola's son, Rajendra Chola I (r 1014–44), continued to expand Chola territory, conquering the remainder of Sri Lanka and campaigning up the east coast as far as Bengal and the Ganges River. Rajendra also launched a campaign in Southeast Asia against the Sumatra-based Srivijaya kingdom, and sent trade missions as far as China. Furthermore, the arts blossomed brilliantly under the Chola empire, whose legacy includes three magnificent Shiva temples at Thanjavur and near Kumbakonam. Bronze sculpture reached astonishing heights of aesthetic and technical refinement. Music, dance and literature flourished and developed a distinctly Tamil flavour, enduring in South India long after the Cholas had faded from the picture. The Cholas also took their culture to Southeast Asia, where it lives on in Myanmar (Burma), Thailand, Bali and Cambodia in dance, religion and mythology.

But the Cholas, weakened by constant campaigning, eventually succumbed to expansionist pressure from the Hoysalas of Halebid (Karnataka) and the resurgent Pandyas of Madurai; by the 13th century they were finally supplanted by the Pandyas. The Hoysalas were themselves eclipsed by the Vijayanagar empire, which arose in the 14th century. The Pandyas prospered and were much admired by Marco Polo when he visited in 1288 and 1293. But their glory was short-lived, as they were unable to fend off Muslim rivals from the north. Meanwhile, the Rashtrakutas were replaced by the Yadavas based at Devagiri (Daulatabad) in Maharashtra.

Muslim Expansion & the Vijayanagar Empire

Muslim raiders from the northwest began incursions into northern India in the 11th century and the powerful Delhi sultanate was established in 1206. The sultanate's expansion towards South India began in the 1290s, and by 1323 it was established at Madurai.

In 1328 Sultan Mohammed Tughlaq, in pursuit of his dream of conquering the whole of India, moved his capital 1100km south to Devagiri in Maharashtra, renaming it Daulatabad and forcing the entire Delhi population to move with him, but had to revert to Delhi after two years

Chola Bronzes
....
Government Museum (Chennai)

Royal Palace (Thanjavur)

Puducherry Museum

HISTORY MUSLIM EXPANSION & THE VIJAYANAGAR EMPIRE

1345	1480s	1498	1510
Bahmani sultanate (Muslim) is established in the Deccan following a revolt against the Tughlaqs of Delhi. The capital is set up at Gulbarga, in today's northern Karnataka, later shifting to Bidar.	Bahmani sultanate begins to break up. By 1528 there are five Deccan sultanates: Berar, Ahmadnagar, Bidar, Bijapur and Golconda.	Vasco da Gama, a Portuguese voyager, finds the sea route from Europe to India via East Africa. He arrives in present-day Kerala and engages in trade with the local nobility.	Portuguese forces capture Goa under the command of Alfonso de Albuquerque, whose initial attempt was thwarted by then-ruler Sultan Adil Shah of Bijapur. He succeeds following Shah's death.

A History of South India: from Prehistoric Times to the Fall of Vijayanagar, by KA Nilakanta Sastri, is arguably the most thorough history of this region (especially recommended if you're heading for Hampi).

because of a water shortage. Though Mohammed Tughlaq controlled a very large part of the subcontinent by 1330, his forces became overstretched and scattered revolts had begun by 1327. From 1335 his empire started shrinking. Not only did local Muslim rulers in places such as Madurai and Daulatabad declare independence, but the foundations of what was to become one of South India's greatest empires, Vijayanagar, were being laid by Hindu chiefs at Hampi.

The Vijayanagar empire is said to have been founded by two brothers who, having been captured and taken to Delhi, converted to Islam and were sent back south to serve as governors for the sultanate. The brothers, however, reconverted to Hinduism and around 1336 established a kingdom that eventually encompassed most of Karnataka and Andhra Pradesh, and all of Tamil Nadu and Kerala. More than seven centuries later the centre of this kingdom – the ruins and temples of Hampi – is one of South India's biggest tourist drawcards.

The Muslim Bahmani sultanate, initially based at Daulatabad, established its capital at Gulbarga in Karnataka, relocating to Bidar in the 15th century. Its territory eventually included Maharashtra, Telangana and northern Karnataka – and the sultanate took pains to protect it.

Ongoing rivalry characterised the relationship between Vijayanagar and the Bahmani sultanate. Much of the conflict centred on control of trading ports and the fertile agricultural land between the Krishna and Tungabhadra Rivers; at one stage the Bahmanis wrested the important port of Goa from their rivals, but the Vijayanagars seized it back in 1378. The Bahmani empire was eventually torn apart by factional fighting and, between 1490 and 1528, broke into five separate sultanates: Bidar, Bijapur, Berar, Ahmadnagar and Golconda. In 1565 the combined forces of the five sultanates laid waste to Vijayanagar's vibrant capital at Hampi, terminating Vijayanagar power.

The Vijayanagar empire is notable for its prosperity, which was the result of a deliberate policy of giving every encouragement to traders from afar, combined with the development of an efficient administrative system and access to important trading links, including west-coast ports. Hampi became quite cosmopolitan, with people from various parts of India as well as from abroad mingling in the bazaars.

Portuguese chronicler Domingo Paez arrived in Vijayanagar during the reign of one of its greatest kings, Krishnadevaraya (r 1509–29), under whom Vijayanagar enjoyed a period of unparalleled prosperity and power. Paez recorded the achievements of the Vijayanagars and described how they had constructed large water tanks and irrigated their fields. He also described how human and animal sacrifices were carried out to propitiate the gods after one of the water tanks had burst repeatedly. He included detail about the fine houses of wealthy merchants and the

Architecture of the Deccan Sultanates

Hyderabad *(Telangana)* Golconda Fort, Qutb Shahi Tombs, Charminar, Mecca Masjid

Vijapura *(Bijapur; Karnataka)* Citadel, Golgumbaz, Ibrahim Rouza, Jama Masjid

Bidar *(Karnataka)* Bidar Fort, Bahmani Tombs

1526	1542–45	1565	1560–1812
The central Asian conqueror Babur becomes the first Mughal emperor after conquering Delhi. Within a century the Mughal empire extends from Afghanistan to Bengal and into the northern Deccan.	St Francis Xavier's first mission to India. He preaches Catholicism in Goa, Tamil Nadu and Sri Lanka, returning in 1548–49 and 1552 in between travels in the Far East.	The great Vijayanagar empire collapses and its vibrant capital, Hampi, is destroyed at the hands of the five combined Deccan sultanates of Berar, Ahmadnagar, Bidar, Bijapur and Golconda.	Portuguese Inquisition in Goa. Trials focus on converted Hindus and Muslims thought to have 'relapsed'. Thousands are tried and tortured, and several dozen executed, before it is abolished.

bazaars full of precious stones (rubies, diamonds, emeralds, pearls) and textiles (including silk).

Like the Bahmanis, the Vijayanagar kings invested heavily in protecting their territory and trading links. Krishnadevaraya employed Portuguese and Muslim mercenaries to guard the forts and protect his domains. He also fostered good relations with the Portuguese, upon whom he depended for access to trade goods, especially Arab horses for his cavalry.

As a result of the weakening of Vijayanagar, Nayak governors at Gingee, Thanjavur and Madurai in Tamil Nadu began to proclaim their independence from the second half of the 16th century. The Nayaks ruled until the early 18th century, with Madurai's Tirumalai Nayak being their most important leader, responsible for such architectural gems as Madurai's Meenakshi Amman Temple.

Arrival of the Europeans & Christianity

Vasco da Gama's arrival in Kerala (p449) in 1498 ushered in a new era of European contact. He was followed by Francisco de Ameida and Alfonso de Albuquerque, who established an eastern Portuguese empire that included Goa (first taken in 1510). Albuquerque waged a constant battle against the local Muslims in Goa, finally defeating them. But perhaps his greatest achievement was in playing off two deadly threats

Between approximately the 12th and 19th centuries, African slaves were brought to South India's Konkan Coast as part of trade with the Persian Gulf. Known as Siddis or Habshis, they became servants, dock workers and soldiers, and famously built Maharashtra's Janjira Fort (p101).

ENTER THE PORTUGUESE

On 20 May 1498 Vasco da Gama dropped anchor off the southwest Indian coast near the town of Calicut (now Kozhikode, in modern-day Kerala). It had taken him 23 days to sail from the east coast of Africa, guided by a pilot named Ibn Majid, sent by the ruler of Malindi in Gujarat – the first time Europeans had made the voyage across the Indian Ocean from Africa to India. The Portuguese sought a sea route between Europe and the east so they could trade directly in spices. They also hoped they might find Christians cut off from Europe by the Muslim dominance of the Middle East, including the legendary kingdom of Prester John, a supposedly powerful Christian ruler with whom they could unite against the Middle East's Muslim rulers. In India they found spices and the Syrian Orthodox community, but no Prester John.

Vasco da Gama was well received by the ruler of Calicut. The Portuguese engaged in a limited amount of trading, but became increasingly suspicious that Muslim traders were turning the Calicut ruler against them. They resolved to leave Calicut, in August 1498. Within a few years other Portuguese expeditions began arriving on India's west coast not just to trade but also to conquer, resulting in an empire of scattered Portuguese possessions around India's coasts which lasted until 1961 when India invaded Goa, Daman and Diu.

1639	1661	1673	1674
Francis Day and the British East India Company strike a deal to set up a fort-cum-trading-post at Madraspatnam fishing village, which goes on to become Madras (now Chennai).	Britain acquires Bombay (now Mumbai) from Portugal in the marriage settlement between King Charles II and Catherine of Braganza. The East India Company moves its headquarters to Bombay in 1687.	The French East India Company establishes a post at Pondicherry (now Puducherry), which the French, Dutch and British fight over repeatedly in the following century.	Shivaji establishes the Maratha kingdom in modern Maharashtra, assuming the imperial title Chhatrapati. Within half a century the Marathas dominate much of northern and central India.

HISTORY ARRIVAL OF THE EUROPEANS & CHRISTIANITY

Vasco da Gama died in Kochi in 1524. He was originally buried at Kochi's St Francis Church, where you can still visit his tombstone. His remains were transferred to Portugal 14 years later and entombed at Lisbon's Mosteiro dos Jerónimos.

against each other: the Vijayanagar empire (for whom access to Goa's ports was extremely important) and the Bijapur sultanate (which controlled part of Goa).

The Bijapuris and Vijayanagars were sworn enemies, and Albuquerque skilfully exploited this by supplying both sides with Arab horses for their warring cavalries. The horses died in alarming numbers once on Indian soil, so a constant supply had to be imported, keeping Portugal's Goan ports busy and profitable.

The Portuguese also introduced and forcefully spread Catholicism, and the arrival of the Inquisition in 1560 marked the beginning of 250 years of religious suppression in the Portuguese-controlled areas on the west coast of India.

Today the Portuguese influence is most obvious in Goa, with its chalk-white Catholic churches, Christian festivals and unique cuisine, though the Portuguese also had influence in Kerala in towns such as Cochin (now Kochi), and landed at what was to become Madras (now Chennai) in the 16th century, before the British. By the mid-16th century Old Goa had grown into a thriving city said to rival Lisbon in magnificence: now only a ruined shadow of that time, its churches and buildings still recall Portuguese rule.

In 1580 Spain annexed Portugal and, until Portugal regained its independence in 1640, its interests were subservient to Spain's. After the English defeat of the Spanish Armada in 1588, the sea route to the east lay open to the English and the Dutch.

The Dutch were more interested in trade than in religion and empire. Indonesia was their main source of spices; trade with South India was primarily for pepper and cardamom. The Dutch East India Company set up a string of trading posts (called factories), which allowed them to maintain a complicated trading structure all the way from the Persian Gulf to Japan. They set up trading posts at Surat (Gujarat) and on southeast India's Coromandel Coast, and entered into a treaty with the ruler of Calicut (now Kozhikode). In 1660 they captured the Portuguese forts at Cochin and Kodungallor.

The Career and Legend of Vasco da Gama, by Sanjay Subrahmanyam, is one of the better investigations of the explorer credited with finding the sea route from Europe to India.

The English also set up a trading venture, the British East India Company, to which in 1600 Queen Elizabeth I granted a monopoly on trade east of Africa's Cape of Good Hope. Like the Dutch, the English were initially mainly interested in Indonesian spices. But the Dutch proved too strong there and the English turned instead to India, setting up a trading post at Madras in 1639. The Danes traded at Tranquebar (Tharangambadi; on Tamil Nadu's Coromandel Coast) from 1616, and the French acquired Pondicherry (now Puducherry) in 1673.

1707	1757	1775–1818	1857
Death of Aurangzeb, the last of the Mughal greats. His demise triggers the gradual collapse of the Mughal empire, as anarchy and rebellion erupt across its territory.	The East India Company registers its first military victory on Indian soil. Siraj-ud-daula, Nawab of Bengal, is defeated by Robert Clive in the Battle of Plassey.	The three Anglo-Maratha Wars (1775–82, 1803–05 and 1817–18) between the East India Company and the Marathas. The third war terminates the Maratha empire, leaving most of India under British control.	The First War of Independence (Indian Uprising) against the British. In the absence of a national leader, freedom fighters coerce the Mughal king to proclaim himself emperor of India.

The Mughals & their Legacy

During the 17th century the Delhi-based Mughal empire made inroads into South India, especially under Emperor Aurangzeb (r 1658–1707), gaining the sultanates of Ahmadnagar, Bijapur and Golconda (including Hyderabad) before moving into Tamil Nadu. Among the rivals the Mughals came up against were the Marathas – Hindu warriors originating from near Pune in Maharashtra, who controlled much of the Deccan by 1680, the year their first emperor, Shivaji (p451), died. Pressing on southward in a series of guerrillalike raids, the Marathas captured Thanjavur and in the 1690s set up a capital at Gingee near Madras. The Mughal-Maratha wars (1680 to 1707) ended with the Marathas very much on top. By the mid-18th century the Marathas controlled a huge swathe of territory extending from the Punjab and Gujarat in the northwest to Odisha (formerly Orissa) in the east and Karnataka in the south; Mughal power barely extended beyond Delhi.

In the Deccan and the south the Marathas had plenty of rivals. One was the Asaf Jahi dynasty (later the nizams of Hyderabad), which broke

MIGHTY SHIVAJI

The name Chhatrapati Shivaji is revered in Maharashtra, with statues of the great warrior astride his horse gracing towns, and many streets and monuments being named – or renamed, as in the case of Mumbai's (Bombay's) Victoria Terminus – after him.

Shivaji founded the powerful Hindu Maratha kingdom, which controlled much of the Deccan region and beyond from the late 17th to early 19th centuries, and which played a big part in the decline of the mighty Delhi-based Mughal empire in the early 18th century. A courageous warrior and charismatic leader, Shivaji was born in 1627 to a prominent Maratha family at Shivneri. With a very small army, Shivaji seized his first fort at the age of 20 and over the next three decades continued to expand Maratha power around his base in Pune, holding out against Muslim rivals from the north (the Mughal empire) and the south (the sultanate of Bijapur), and eventually ruling much of the Deccan. He was shrewd enough to play his enemies (among them Mughal emperor Aurangzeb) off against each other. In a famous 1659 incident, he killed Bijapuri general Afzal Khan in a face-to-face encounter at Pratapgad Fort.

In 1674 Shivaji was crowned Chhatrapati (Emperor or Great Protector) of the Marathas at Raigad Fort. He died six years later. His son and successor, Sambhaji, suffered serious reversals at the hands of the Mughals, but the resilient Marathas bounced back and by the mid-18th century controlled a large proportion of the subcontinent.

Shivaji is an icon to the modern Maharashtrian-nationalist and Hindu-nationalist political party Shiv Sena (Shivaji's Army) which, among other things, opposes immigration into Maharashtra by non-Maharashtrians. For this reason the widespread use of his name is not wholly welcomed by everybody in Maharashtra.

1858	2 October 1869	1885	1891
British government assumes control over India, with power officially transferred from the East India Company to the Crown – beginning the period known as the British Raj.	The birth of Mohandas Karamchand Gandhi in Porbandar (Gujarat) – the man who would later become popularly known as Mahatma Gandhi, 'Father of the Nation'.	The Indian National Congress, India's first home-grown political organisation, is set up. It brings educated Indians together and plays a key role in India's enduring freedom struggle.	BR Ambedkar, activist, economist, lawyer and writer, is born to a poor outcast family. He earns several advanced degrees, becomes a Buddhist and advocates forcefully for Dalit rights.

away from the Mughal empire in 1724 to control much of the Deccan, with its capital initially at Aurangabad (Maharashtra) and then, from 1763, at Hyderabad. Another was Mysore, a landlocked kingdom until a cavalry officer, Hyder Ali, assumed power in 1761 and set about acquiring coastal territory. Hyder Ali and his son Tipu Sultan eventually ruled a kingdom that included southern Karnataka and northern Kerala. Tipu conducted trade directly with the Middle East through the west-coast ports he controlled. The other important players were the British East India Company, based at Madras, and the French, at Pondicherry. The 18th century saw a constantly shifting succession of alliances and conflicts between these five rivals. The British won out over the French in the three Carnatic Wars fought between 1744 and 1763, and their control over the eastern seaboard denied both Hyderabad and Mysore access to trading ports there. Meanwhile, the Portuguese retained control of Goa.

Down in the far south, the kingdom of Travancore (occupying what is now the southern half of Kerala and a bit of Tamil Nadu) was also trying to consolidate its power by gaining control of strategic trade links. Ruler Martanda Varma (r 1729–58) created his own army and tried to keep the local Syrian Orthodox trading community onside by limiting the activities of European traders. Trade in many goods, with the exception of pepper, became a royal monopoly, especially under Martanda's son Rama Varma (r 1758–98).

The British Take Hold

Initially the British East India Company was supposedly interested only in trade, not conquest. But Mysore's rulers proved something of a vexation. In 1780 Hyder Ali formed an alliance with the nizam of Hyderabad and the Marathas to attack all three British bases in India (Bombay, Madras and Bengal). It came to nothing but left the British keen to quash the Mysore menace. This time the Marathas and Hyderabad allied with the British against Mysore, now led by Tipu Sultan, whose river-island citadel, Seringapatam (now Srirangapatnam), surrendered in 1793 after a year-long siege.

Within the East India Company there was a growing feeling that only total control of India would satisfy British trading interests. This was reinforced by fears of a renewed French bid for land in India following Napoleon's Egyptian expedition of 1798–99. The company's governor-general, Lord Richard Wellesley, ordered a new strike against Mysore, with an ally in the nizam of Hyderabad (who was required to disband his French-trained troops in return for British protection). Tipu Sultan, who may have counted on support from the French, was killed when the British again stormed Seringapatam in 1799. He was stripped of his arms

Several dozen people were burned at the stake during the Goa Inquisition, which lasted more than 250 years. The judgment ceremonies took place outside the Sé Cathedral in Old Goa and targeted converted Hindus and Muslims accused of 'relapsing'.

13 April 1919	1940	1942	1947
The massacre of unarmed Indian protesters at Jallianwala Bagh in Amritsar (Punjab). Gandhi responds with a program of civil (nonviolent) disobedience against British rule.	The Muslim League adopts its Lahore Resolution, which champions greater Muslim autonomy in India. Campaigns for the creation of a separate Islamic nation follow.	Mahatma Gandhi launches the nonviolent Quit India campaign, demanding that the British leave India without delay and allow the country to get on with self-governance.	India gains independence on 15 August; Pakistan is formed a day earlier. Partition brings a mass cross-border exodus and massacres, as Hindus and Sikhs migrate to India, and Muslims to Pakistan.

and armour, which ended up in British museums such as London's V&A via colonial-era administration or from revolutionary sales following the French revolution.

Wellesley restored the old ruling family, the Wodeyars, to half of Tipu's kingdom; the rest went to Hyderabad and the East India Company. Thanjavur and Karnataka were also absorbed by the British, who, when the rulers of the day died, pensioned off their successors. By 1818 the Marathas, racked by internal strife, had collapsed and most of India was under British influence. In the south, the East India Company had direct control over the Madras Presidency, which stretched from present-day Andhra Pradesh to the southern tip of the subcontinent, and across to northern parts of the Kerala coast. Travancore, Hyderabad, Mysore and other, smaller, chunks of the interior kept their nominal independence as 'princely states', but they were closely watched by their British Residents (de facto governors). Similarly, much of Maharashtra was part of the Bombay Presidency, but there were a dozen or so small princely states scattered around, including Kolhapur, Sawantwadi, Aundh and Janjira.

The First War of Independence (Indian Uprising)

In 1857, half a century after establishing firm control over India, the British suffered a serious setback. To this day, the causes of the Uprising (known at the time as the Indian Mutiny and subsequently labelled by nationalist historians as a War of Independence) are the subject of debate. Key factors included the influx of cheap goods, such as textiles, from Britain that destroyed many livelihoods; the dispossession of territories from many rulers; and taxes imposed on landowners.

The incident that's popularly held to have sparked the Uprising, however, took place at an army barracks in Meerut in Uttar Pradesh on 10 May 1857. A rumour leaked that a new type of bullet was greased with what Hindus claimed was cow fat, while Muslims maintained that it came from pigs; pigs are considered unclean to Muslims, and cows are sacred to Hindus. Since loading a rifle involved biting the end off the waxed cartridge, these rumours provoked considerable unrest.

The commanding officer in Meerut lined up his soldiers and ordered them to bite off the ends of their issued bullets. Those who refused were marched off to prison. The following morning, the garrison's soldiers rebelled, shot their officers and marched to Delhi. Of the 74 Indian battalions of the Bengal army, seven (one of them Gurkhas) remained loyal, 20 were disarmed and the other 47 mutinied. The soldiers and peasants rallied around the ageing, reluctant Mughal emperor Bahadur Shah Zafar in Delhi. They held Delhi for some months and besieged the

Best Goan Churches

Basilica de Bom Jesus (Old Goa)

Church of Our Lady of the Immaculate Conception (Panaji; Panjim)

Church & Convent of St Cajetan (Old Goa)

Church of Our Lady of the Rosary (Old Goa)

Church of the Holy Spirit (Margao)

HISTORY THE FIRST WAR OF INDEPENDENCE (INDIAN UPRISING)

1947–48	30 January 1948	17 September 1948	November 1949
First war between India and Pakistan takes place after the Maharaja of Kashmir signs the Instrument of Accession that cedes his state to India. Pakistan challenges the document's legality.	Mahatma Gandhi is assassinated by Nathuram Godse in New Delhi. Godse and his co-conspirator Narayan Apte are later tried, convicted and executed (by hanging).	Asaf Jah VII, the last nizam of Hyderabad, surrenders to the Indian government. His Muslim dynasty was receiving support from Pakistan but had refused to join either new nation.	The Constitution of India, drafted over two years by a 308-member Constituent Assembly, is adopted. The Assembly includes dozens of members from the Scheduled Castes (Dalits).

The British never actually attempted to annex Goa, but, in 1839, the British government offered to buy Goa from the Portuguese for half a million pounds. The offer was swiftly rejected.

British Residency in Lucknow for five months before they were finally suppressed. The incident left festering sores on both sides.

Almost immediately the East India Company was wound up, and direct control of the country was assumed by the British government, which announced its support for the existing rulers of the princely states, claiming they would not interfere in local matters as long as the states remained loyal to the British. Though not felt as strongly in the south as in the north, the First War of Independence kicked off calls for self-rule all over India.

The Road to Independence & the Partition of India

The desire of many Indians to be free from foreign rule remained. Opposition to the British began to increase at the turn of the 20th century, spearheaded by the Indian National Congress (Congress Party), the nation's oldest political party, formed in 1885. The fight for independence gained momentum when, in April 1919, following riots in Amritsar (Punjab), a British army contingent was sent to quell the unrest. The army ruthlessly fired into a crowd of unarmed protesters attending a meeting, killing an estimated 1500 people. News of the massacre spread rapidly throughout India, turning huge numbers of otherwise apolitical Indians into Congress supporters. The Congress movement found a new leader in Mohandas Gandhi, better known as Mahatma Gandhi (p455).

After three decades of intense nonviolent campaigning for an independent India, Gandhi's dream finally materialised. However, despite his plea for a united India, the Muslim League's leader, Mohammed Ali Jinnah, demanded a separate state for India's sizeable Muslim population. The decision was made to split the country: India as it had been was divided into India and newly created Pakistan.

The Partition of India in 1947 contained all the ingredients for an epic disaster, but the resulting bloodshed was far worse than anticipated. Massive population exchanges took place. Trains of Muslims, fleeing westward into Pakistan, were held up and slaughtered by Hindu and Sikh mobs. Hindus and Sikhs fleeing eastwards into India suffered the same fate at Muslim hands. By the time the chaos had run its course, more than 10 million people had relocated and at least 500,000 had been killed.

India and Pakistan became sovereign nations within the British Commonwealth in August 1947, but the violence, migrations and uncertainty over a few states, especially Kashmir, continued. The violence over Kashmir – then a predominantly Muslim-populated state with a Hindu maharaja, which officially became part of India in October 1947 –

26 January 1950	1956–60	1961	1965
India becomes a republic. This date commemorates the Purna Swaraj Declaration (Declaration of Independence) put forth by the Indian National Congress in 1930.	Indian states are reorganised on linguistic lines, giving birth to modern Maharashtra, Andhra Pradesh, Kerala, Mysore (Karnataka) and Madras (Tamil Nadu) states.	In a military action code-named 'Operation Vijay' the Indian government sends armed troops into Goa and – with little resistance – ends more than four centuries of Portuguese colonial rule there.	Skirmishes in Kashmir and Gujarat flare into the Second India–Pakistan War, said to have involved the biggest tank battles since WWII. The war ends with a UN-mandated ceasefire.

continues today, and is estimated to have killed around 47,000 people so far. Many of the terrorist attacks that have hit tourist spots in India have a Kashmiri link, including the 2008 Mumbai terror attacks.

The Constitution of India was at last adopted in November 1949 and went into effect on 26 January 1950 when, after untold struggle, independent India officially became a republic.

Mahatma Gandhi

One of the great figures of the 20th century, Mohandas Karamchand Gandhi was born on 2 October 1869 in Porbandar, Gujarat. After studying in London (1888–91), he worked as a barrister in South Africa. Here, the young Gandhi became politicised, railing against the racial discrimination he encountered. He soon became the spokesperson for South Africa's Indian community, championing equality for all.

Gandhi returned to India in 1915 with the doctrine of ahimsa (nonviolence) central to his political plans, and committed to a simple and disciplined lifestyle. He set up the Sabarmati Ashram in Ahmedabad, which was innovative for its admission of Untouchables (now known as Dalits).

Within a year, Gandhi had won his first victory, defending farmers in Bihar from exploitation. It's said that this was when he first received the title 'Mahatma' (Great Soul) from an admirer. The passage of the discriminatory Rowlatt Acts (which allowed certain political cases to be tried without juries) in 1919 spurred him to further action and he organised a national protest. In the days following this hartal (strike), feelings ran high throughout the country. After the massacre of unarmed protesters in Amritsar (Punjab), a deeply shocked Gandhi immediately called off the movement.

By 1920 Gandhi was a key figure in the Indian National Congress, and he coordinated a national campaign of satyagraha (passive resistance) to British rule, with the effect of raising nationalist feeling while earning the lasting enmity of the British. In early 1930 Gandhi captured the imagination of the country, and the world, when he led a march of several thousand followers from Ahmedabad to Dandi on the coast of Gujarat. On arrival, Gandhi ceremoniously made salt by evaporating seawater, thus publicly defying the much-hated British-imposed salt tax; not for the first time, he was imprisoned. Released in 1931 to represent the Indian National Congress at the second Round Table Conference in London, he won the hearts of many British people but failed to gain any real concessions from the government.

Disillusioned with politics, Gandhi resigned from the Congress Party in 1934. He returned spectacularly to the fray in 1942 with the Quit India

Amar Chitra Katha, a popular publisher of comic books about Indian folklore, mythology and history, has several books about Shivaji, including *Shivaji: The Great Maratha*, *Tales of Shivaji* and *Tanaji, the Maratha Lion*, about Shivaji's close friend and fellow warrior.

1966	1971	1984	1991
Indira Gandhi, daughter of independent India's first prime minister, Jawaharlal Nehru, becomes prime minister of India. She has so far been India's only female prime minister.	East Pakistan seeks independence from West Pakistan. India gets involved, sparking the Third India–Pakistan War. West Pakistan surrenders, losing sovereignty of East Pakistan, which becomes Bangladesh.	Prime Minister Indira Gandhi is assassinated by two of her Sikh bodyguards after her highly controversial decision to have Indian troops storm Amritsar's Golden Temple, the Sikhs' holiest shrine.	Former prime minister Rajiv Gandhi, son of Indira Gandhi, is assassinated by a suicide bomber believed to belong to Sri Lanka's Tamil Tigers, at Sriperumbudur near Chennai (formerly Madras).

campaign, in which he urged the British to leave India immediately. His actions were deemed subversive and he and most of the Congress leadership were imprisoned.

In the frantic Independence bargaining that followed the end of WWII, Gandhi was largely excluded and watched helplessly as plans were made to partition the country – a dire tragedy in his eyes. Gandhi stood almost alone in urging tolerance and the preservation of a single India, and his work on behalf of members of all communities drew resentment from some Hindu hardliners. On his way to a prayer meeting in Delhi on 30 January 1948, he was assassinated by a Hindu zealot, Nathuram Godse.

In 21st-century India, including the south, Mahatma Gandhi continues to be an iconic figure, still widely revered as the 'Father of the Nation'.

Carving up the South

While the chaos of Partition was mostly felt in the north – mainly in Punjab, Kashmir and Bengal – the south faced its own problems. Though most of the princely states acceded to India peacefully, an exception was Hyderabad state, where the Indian army moved in and forcibly took control in 1948. Tens of thousands of Muslims were massacred by Hindus during and after this so-called 'police action' (p230).

In the 1950s the princely states and British-delineated provinces were dismantled and South India was reorganised into states along linguistic lines. Mysore state was extended in 1956 into the Kannada-speaking state of Greater Mysore, which was renamed Karnataka in 1972.

Malayalam-speaking Kerala was created in 1956 from Travancore (except for its Tamil-speaking far south), Cochin (now Kochi) and Malabar (formerly part of the Madras Presidency). The maharajas in both Travancore and Cochin had been especially attentive to the provision of basic services and education, and their legacy today is India's most literate state. Kerala also blazed a trail in post-Independence India by becoming the first state in the world to freely elect a communist government in 1957.

Andhra Pradesh was created in 1956 by combining the Telugu-speaking Andhra state (the northern parts of the old Madras Presidency) with Telugu-speaking areas of the old Hyderabad state. In 2014 the latter were separated off as the new state of Telangana (with Hyderabad as its capital), after years of complaints that they were neglected and exploited within Andhra Pradesh. However, the brand-new Andhra Pradesh capital, Amaravati, remains decades from completion.

Tamil Nadu was the name given in 1968 to the former Madras state, which since 1956 had comprised the Tamil-speaking areas of the old Madras Presidency plus the southernmost areas of the former Travancore kingdom (also Tamil-speaking).

2004	2008	May 2014	June 2014
A tsunami batters coastal parts of eastern and South India as well as the Andaman and Nicobar Islands, killing over 10,000 people and leaving hundreds of thousands homeless.	On 26 November a series of coordinated bombing and shooting attacks on landmark Mumbai sites begins; the terrorist attacks last three days and kill at least 163 people.	Narendra Modi, born to a Gujarati grocery family, becomes prime minister after achieving a historic landslide victory for the Hindu-nationalist-oriented Bharatiya Janata Party (BJP), routing the Congress Party.	The northern part of Andhra Pradesh splits off to become India's 29th state, Telangana, following years of agitation and allegations of neglect and unfair treatment.

The creation of Maharashtra was one of the most contested issues of the language-based demarcation of states. After Independence, western Maharashtra and Gujarat were joined to form Bombay state, to which Marathi-speaking parts of Hyderabad and Madhya Pradesh states were added in 1956. In 1960, after agitation by both Marathis and Gujaratis, Bombay state was divided into the existing states of Maharashtra and Gujarat.

The French relinquished Pondicherry (now Puducherry) in 1954 – 140 years after reclaiming it from the British. It's a Union Territory (controlled by the government in Delhi), though largely self-governing. Lakshadweep was granted Union Territory status in 1956, as were the Andaman and Nicobar Islands.

Throughout most of this carve-up, Goa was still under Portuguese rule. Although a rumbling independence movement had existed in Goa since the early 20th century, the Indian government was reluctant to take Goa by force, hoping the Portuguese would leave of their own volition. The Portuguese refused, so in December 1961 Indian troops crossed the border and liberated the state with surprisingly little resistance. It became a Union Territory of India, but after splitting from Daman and Diu (Gujarat) in 1987, it was officially recognised as the 25th state of the Indian Union.

South India in the Modern Age

The reorganisation of states along linguistic lines has encouraged South Indians' sense of being distinct from the north, with the main languages of Andhra Pradesh, Karnataka, Kerala, Telangana and Tamil Nadu (respectively Telugu, Kannada, Malayalam, Telugu and Tamil) all being in the (non-Indo-European) Dravidian family. The main national political parties, Congress and the Bharatiya Janata Party (BJP), have relatively little support down south, where local state-based political parties (often led by film stars) have come to the fore, many of them with populist platforms that have helped alleviate some of the worst of rural and urban poverty. All seven main southern states are now in the top half of India's income-per-person table. Mumbai has long been the nation's commercial capital, and cities like Hyderabad, Pune, Chennai and, especially, Bengaluru (Bangalore) have been powerhouses of India's IT boom since the 1990s.

5 December 2016	July & August 2018	7 August 2018	September 2018
Tamil Nadu's adored former Chief Minister Jayalalithaa Jayaram – one of India's most popular and controversial politicians – passes away in Chennai, following several months of illness.	The worst floods in a century batter Kerala, causing 400 deaths and an estimated US$2.5 billion of damage, mostly in the central and northern parts of the state.	Another Tamil Nadu political giant and great rival of Jayalalithaa, former movie scriptwriter and five-time state chief minister Muthuvel Karunanidhi, dies.	Historic decisions by India's Supreme Court overturns the ban on women aged 10 to 50 entering Kerala's Ayyappan Temple at Sabarimala; and in another landmark ruling decriminalises homosexuality.

The Way of Life

Spirituality is the common thread in the richly diverse tapestry that is India. Along with family, it lies at the heart of society, and these two tenets intertwine in ceremonies to celebrate life's milestones. Despite the rising number of nuclear families – primarily in the more cosmopolitan cities such as Mumbai, Bengaluru (Bangalore) and Delhi – the extended family remains a cornerstone in both urban and rural India, with males – usually the breadwinners – considered the head of the household.

Marriage, Birth & Death

Matchmaking is now, inevitably, online, with popular sites including www.shaadi.com, www.bharat matrimony.com and, in a sign of the times, www. secondshaadi. com – for those seeking a partner again.

South India's different religions practise different traditions, but for all communities, marriage, birth and death are important and marked with traditional ceremonies according to faith. Hindus are the 80% majority in India; only 14.2% of the population is Muslim (though at 176 million, Indian Muslims roughly equal the population of Pakistan) and 2.3% Christian (still India's third most practised religion, with 28 million followers).

Marriage is an exceptionally auspicious event for Indians – for most Indians, the idea of being unmarried by their mid-30s is unpalatable. Although 'love marriages' have spiralled upward in recent times (mainly in urban hubs), most Indian marriages are still arranged, be the family Hindu, Muslim, Sikh or Buddhist. Discreet enquiries are made within the community. If a suitable match is not found, the help of professional matchmakers may be sought, or advertisements placed in newspapers and/or online. In Hindu families, the horoscopes of both potential partners are checked and, if propitious, there's a meeting between the two families.

Dowries (p461), although illegal since 1961, are still a key issue in many arranged marriages (mostly in conservative communities), with some families plunging into debt to raise the required cash and merchandise (from cars and computers to refrigerators, TVs and apartments). Muslim grooms have to pay what is called a *mehr* to the bride.

The Hindu wedding ceremony is officiated over by a priest and the marriage is formalised when the couple walk around a sacred fire seven times. Muslim ceremonies involve the reading of the Quran; traditionally the husband and wife view each other via mirrors. Despite the existence of nuclear families, it's still the norm for a wife to live with her husband's family once married and assume the household duties outlined by her mother-in-law. Not surprisingly, the mother–daughter-in-law relationship can be a tricky one, often portrayed in Indian TV soap operas.

India has one of the world's largest diasporas – over 25 million people – with Indian banks holding an estimated US$70 billion in Non-Resident Indian (NRI) accounts.

Divorce and remarriage is becoming more common (primarily in bigger cities), but divorce is still not granted by courts as a matter of routine and is not looked upon very favourably by society. Among the higher castes, in more traditional areas, widows are traditionally expected not to remarry and to wear white and live pious, celibate lives. In late 2018, among mounting pressure from women's rights groups, India criminalised the centuries-old instant-divorce practice of triple *talaq*, which had until then allowed Muslim men to obtain oral divorce according to sharia law (by uttering, emailing or texting the word *talaq* [divorce] three times).

The birth of a child is a momentous occasion, with its own set of special ceremonies which take place at various auspicious times during the early years of childhood. For Hindus these include the casting of the child's first horoscope, name-giving, feeding the first solid food and the first hair cutting.

Hindus cremate their dead, and funeral ceremonies are designed to purify and console both the living and the deceased. An important aspect of the proceedings is the *sharadda*, paying respect to one's ancestors by offering water and rice cakes, an observance that's repeated at each anniversary of the death. After the cremation, the ashes are collected and, 13 days after the death (when blood relatives are deemed ritually pure), a member of the family usually scatters them in a holy river such as the Ganges or in the ocean. Sikhs similarly wash then cremate their dead. Muslims also prepare their dead carefully, but bury them. The minority Zoroastrian Parsi community place their dead in 'Towers of Silence' (stone towers) to be devoured by vultures.

The Caste System

Although the Indian constitution does not recognise the caste system, caste still wields a powerful influence, especially in rural India, where the caste you are born into largely determines your social standing in the community. It can also influence your vocational and marriage prospects. Castes are further divided into thousands of *jati*, groups of 'families' or social communities, which are sometimes but not always linked to occupation. Conservative Hindus will only marry someone of the same *jati*, and you'll often see caste as a criteria in matrimonial adverts. In some traditional areas, young people who fall in love outside their caste have been murdered; while still rare, intercaste marriages are slowly on the rise in urban areas.

According to tradition, caste is the basic social structure of Hindu society. Living a righteous life and fulfilling your dharma (moral duty) raises your chances of being reborn into a higher caste and thus into better circumstances. Hindus are born into one of four varnas (castes): Brahmin (priests and scholars), Kshatriya (soldiers and administrators), Vaishya (merchants) and Shudra (labourers). The Brahmins were said to have emerged from the mouth of Lord Brahma at the moment of creation, Kshatriyas were said to have come from his arms, Vaishyas from his thighs and Shudras from his feet.

Beneath the four main castes are the Dalits (formerly known as Untouchables), who hold menial jobs such as sweepers and latrine cleaners and account for around a sixth of the population. Many of India's complex codes of ritual purity were devised to prevent physical contact between people of higher castes and Dalits. A less rigid system exists in Islamic communities in India, with society divided into *ashraf* (high born), *ajlaf* (low born) and *arzal* (equivalent to the Dalits). The word 'pariah' is derived from the name of a Tamil Dalit group, the Paraiyars. Some Dalit leaders, such as the renowned Dr BR Ambedkar (1891–1956), architect of India's constitution, sought to change their status by adopting another faith – in his case, Buddhism.

At the bottom of the social heap are the Denotified Tribes. They were known as the Criminal Tribes until 1952, when a reforming law officially recognised 198 tribes and castes. Many are nomadic or seminomadic tribes, forced by the wider community to eke out a living on society's fringes.

To improve the Dalits' position, the government reserves a considerable number of public-sector jobs, parliamentary seats and university places for them. Today these quotas account for almost 25% of government

The Wonder that was India, by AL Basham, proffers descriptions of Indian civilisations, major religions and social customs – a good thematic approach to weave the disparate strands together.

If you want to learn more about India's caste system, read *Interrogating Caste*, by Dipankar Gupta, and *Translating Caste*, edited by Tapan Basu.

THE WAY OF LIFE THE CASTE SYSTEM

Read more about India's tribal communities at www.tribal.nic.in, an insightful website maintained by the Indian government's Ministry of Tribal Affairs.

jobs and university (student) positions. The situation varies regionally, as different political leaders chase caste vote-banks by promising to include them in reservations. The reservation system, while generally regarded in a favourable light, has also been criticised for unfairly blocking tertiary and employment opportunities for those who would have otherwise got positions on merit, and for excluding other poor communities. On the other hand, there is still regular discrimination against Dalits in daily life, such as higher castes denying them entry into certain temples, and extending to beatings and even murder. In 2017, in a landmark ruling by the Travancore Devaswom (Temple) Board (TDB), six Dalits became the first of their caste to serve as priests at a Keralan Hindu temple.

Pilgrimage

Devout Hindus are expected to go on a *yatra* (pilgrimage) at least once a year. Pilgrimages are undertaken to implore the gods or goddesses to grant a wish, to take the ashes of a cremated relative to a holy river, or to gain spiritual merit. India has thousands of holy sites to which pilgrims travel. The elderly often make Varanasi their final one, as it's believed that dying in this sacred city releases a person from the cycle of rebirth. The pilgrimage to Sabarimala (p292) in Kerala is one of India's largest Hindu pilgrimages; traditionally women aged 10 to 50 (of 'menstruating age') have been banned from the temple, but this was overturned in a historic ruling by India's Supreme Court in 2018, leading to widespread, violent protests across the state.

Sufi shrines in India attract thousands of Muslims to commemorate holy days, such as the birthday of a Sufi saint; many Muslims also make the hajj to Mecca in Saudi Arabia.

Most festivals in India are spiritual occasions, rooted in religion (even those that have a carnivalesque sheen), and are thus a magnet for throngs of pilgrims. Remember to behave respectfully, and be aware that there are deaths at festivals every year because of stampedes, so be cautious in large crowds.

ADIVASIS

India's Adivasis (tribal communities; Adivasi translates to 'original inhabitant' in Sanskrit) have origins that precede the Vedic Aryans and the Dravidians of the south. These groups range from the Gondi of the central plains to the animist tribes of the Northeast States to Tamil Nadu's Todas. Today, they constitute approximately 8.6% of the population and are comprised of more than 400 different tribal groups. Around 95% of India's Adivasis live in rural areas, mostly in mountain regions in the Northeastern States; there are some Adivasi communities living in South India's hills, as well as in the Andaman Islands (where their survival is under serious threat). The literacy rate for Adivasis is significantly below the national average.

Historically, contact between Adivasis and villagers on the plains rarely led to friction as there was little or no competition for resources and land. However, in recent decades an increasing number of Adivasis have been dispossessed of their ancestral land and turned into impoverished labourers. Although they still have political representation thanks to a parliamentary quota system, the dispossession and exploitation of Adivasis has reportedly sometimes been with the connivance of officialdom – an accusation the government denies. The creation of wildlife reserves in South India, meanwhile, has also forced some forest-dwelling Adivasis to resettle, with conservationists arguing that the only way to save India's tigers is to completely ban humans from the animals' natural environment. Unless more is done, the Adivasis' future is an uncertain one.

Read more about Adivasis in *Tribes of India: The Struggle for Survival* by Christoph von Fürer-Haimendorf.

INDIAN ATTIRE

Widely worn by Indian women, the beautiful, elegant sari comes in a single piece (between 5m and 9m long and 1m wide), ingeniously tucked and pleated into place without pins or buttons. Worn with the sari is the choli (tight-fitting blouse) and a drawstring petticoat. The *palloo* is the part of the sari draped over the shoulder. Also commonly worn is the *salwar kameez*, a traditional dresslike tunic and trouser combination for women, accompanied by a dupatta (long scarf).

Traditional attire for men includes the dhoti, and in the south the lungi and the *mundu*. The dhoti is a loose, long loincloth pulled up between the legs. The lungi is more like a sarong, with its end usually sewn up like a tube. The *mundu* is like a lungi but always white. A kurta is a long tunic or shirt worn mainly by men (but also women), usually with no collar. Kurta pyjama is a cotton shirt and trousers set worn for relaxing or sleeping. *Churidar* are close-fitting trousers often worn under a kurta, by both men and women. A *sherwani* is a long coatlike men's garment, originally a fusion of the *salwar kameez* with the British frock coat.

There are regional and religious variations in costume; for example, you may see Muslim women wearing the all-enveloping burka.

In South India's bigger cities, like Mumbai, and touristed areas such as Goa and Kerala, Western-style clothing is increasingly common, particularly among younger-generation Indians, and there's also a colourfully stylish world of contemporary Indian fashion.

Women in South India

Despite the highly sexualised images of women churned out by Bollywood, India remains an extremely prudish and conservative society, and many traditionally minded people consider a woman wanton if she so much as goes out after dark.

According to the 2011 census, India's population includes 586 million women, with an estimated 68% of these working in the agricultural sector, mostly as labourers. Women in India are entitled to vote and own property. While the percentage of women in politics has risen over the past decade, they're still notably underrepresented in the national parliament, accounting for just 11% of parliamentary members.

Although the professions are male dominated, women are steadily making inroads, especially in urban centres. Kerala was India's first state to break societal norms by recruiting female police officers (1938) and establishing an all-female police station (1973, in Kozhikode [Calicut]); there are now around 500 all-female police stations across the country. For village women it's much more difficult to get ahead, but groups such as Gujarat's Self-Employed Women's Association (SEWA; www.sewa.org) have shown what's possible, organising socially disadvantaged women into unions and offering microfinance loans.

In low-income families especially, girls can be regarded as a financial liability because a marriage dowry must often be supplied. Figures from India's National Crime Records Bureau (NCRB) show that 7634 women died in 2015 (that's 20 a day) due to dowry harassment. Some feel compelled to take their own lives, others are murdered; the majority are young, new brides. Health workers claim that India's high rate of abortion of female foetuses is predominantly due to the financial burden of providing a daughter's dowry. Prenatal sex identification has been banned in India since 1984; however, tests still occur clandestinely, and health officials warn that some wealthier Indian couples may now be seeking tests and abortions abroad to sidestep local laws. An estimated 300,000 to 600,000 female foetuses are illegally aborted each year, which, according to BBC reporting, has resulted in a skewed sex ratio of 112 boys for every 100 girls.

The urban middle-class woman, broadly speaking, is far more likely to receive a tertiary education, but once married she is still usually

The distressing, important BBC documentary *India's Daughter*, directed by Leslee Udwin, details the events of the much-publicised 2012 Delhi gang rape and murder of Jyoti Singh. The documentary was banned in India (after it emerged that the film-makers had interviewed one of the jailed rapists), but widely circulated online.

MEHNDI

Mehndi is the traditional art of painting a woman's hands (and sometimes feet, legs and forearms) with intricate henna designs for auspicious ceremonies, especially marriage, for which elaborate *mehndi* ceremonies take place. Indian *mehndi* designs are known for their fine lines and floral and paisley patterns. Some believe the practice was introduced to India in the 12th century by the Mughals.

In touristed areas, *mehndi*-wallahs are adept at applying henna tattoo 'bands' on the arms, hands, legs and lower back. Allow at least a few hours for the design process and required drying time. If quality henna is used, the orange-brown designs can last up to one month. It's wise to request that the artist do a test spot on your arm before proceeding: some dyes contain chemicals that can cause allergies. Avoid 'black henna', which is mixed with chemicals that may be harmful.

expected to 'fit in' with her in-laws and be a homemaker. As for her village counterpart, if she fails to live up to expectations – even if it's just not being able to produce a son – the consequences can sometimes be dire, as demonstrated by the extreme practice of 'bride burning': a wife is doused with flammable liquid and set alight, typically by her husband or mother-in-law. In 2013 the NCRB figures reported 8083 such incidences, around one every hour; it's thought that actual numbers are even higher, while conviction rates remain shockingly low. Acid attacks by would-be suitors on women who have rejected them are also common. A 2012 Unicef study revealed that almost 60% of Indian adolescent males believe it's justifiable to beat a wife, and some reports suggest around a third of the country's married women have suffered domestic violence.

Although the constitution allows for divorcees (and widows) to remarry, relatively few reportedly do so: divorcees are traditionally considered outcasts from society, most evidently so beyond big cities. Divorce rates in India are among the worlds' lowest, though rising. Most divorces happen in urban centres and are deemed less socially unacceptable among the upper levels of society.

In October 2006, following women's civil rights campaigns, the Indian parliament passed a landmark bill (on top of existing legislation) which gives women suffering domestic violence increased protection and rights. Prior to this legislation, although women could lodge police complaints against abusive spouses, they weren't automatically entitled to a share of the marital property or to ongoing financial support. Critics claim that many women, especially those outside India's larger cities, are still reluctant to seek legal protection because of the social stigma involved. Despite legal reforms, conviction rates remain low enough for perpetrators to feel a sense of impunity.

Following the highly publicised gang rape and murder of 23-year-old Indian physiotherapy student Jyoti Singh (Nirbhaya, 'Fearless One') in Delhi in 2012, it took a further year before legal amendments were made to existing laws to address the problem of sexual violence, including stiffer punishments such as life imprisonment and the death penalty. There is still limited recognition of marital rape (a horrifically common phenomenon).

Sati: A Study of Widow Burning in India, by Sakuntala Narasimhan, explores the history of *sati* (a widow's ritual suicide on her husband's funeral pyre; now banned) on the subcontinent.

Despite the action taken, shocking cases are regular occurrences. According to the NCRB, reported incidences of rape have gone up over 50% in the last 10 years (38,947 cases reported in 2016), but it's thought that the vast majority of sexual assaults still go unreported, due to family pressure and/or shame. Women themselves continue to be blamed for rapes, and the conviction rate for rape was just 18.9% in 2016. It's undeniable that sexual and gender-based violence is a pervasive social problem in India and, despite government efforts, including Modi's Beti Bachao, Beti Padhao (Save the Daughter, Teach the Daughter) campaign and harsher sentences, that it remains rampant, fuelled, many believe, by patriarchy and the country's gender ratio imbalance. A 2018 Thompson Reuters Foundation report ranked India as the most dangerous country in the world for women (though there has been much dispute over this).

Many Indian women are fighting back against gender-based violence; India's first women's crisis centre, Gauravi (www.actionaid.org. uk), opened in Bhopal (Madhya Pradesh) in 2014, while in 2018 India's Supreme Court ruled that Kerala's Sabarimala temple (p292) should be open to all women, a decision that led, sadly, to violent protests.

Most female visitors' Indian travels progress safely, but it is important to be careful and alert (p506).

Sport

Cricket has long been engraved on the Indian nation's heart, with the first recorded match in 1721, and India's first test match victory in 1952 in Chennai (then Madras) against England. It's not only a national sporting obsession, but a matter of enormous patriotism, especially evident whenever India plays against Pakistan. Matches between these South Asian neighbours – who have had rocky relations since Independence – attract especially passionate support, and the players of both sides are under immense pressure to do their respective countries proud. The most celebrated Indian cricketer of recent years is Sachin Tendulkar (the 'Little Master'), who, in 2012, became the first ever player to score 100 international centuries, retiring on a high the following year. Cricket – especially the Twenty20 format (www.cricket20.com) – is big business in India, attracting lucrative sponsorship deals and celebrity status for its players. In 2016 India hosted the ICC World Twenty20, into its sixth edition. The sport has not been without its murky side though, with Indian cricketers among those embroiled in match-fixing scandals. International games are played at various centres – see Indian newspapers or check online for details. Keep your finger on the cricketing pulse at www.espncricinfo.com (rated most highly by many cricket aficionados) and www.cricbuzz.com.

The 2013 launch of the Indian Super League (ISL; www.indiansuper league.com) has achieved its aim of promoting football as a big-time, big-money sport. With games attracting huge crowds, celebrity funding and international players, such as legendary Juventus footballer Alessandro del Piero (who was signed for the Delhi Dynamos in 2014, then

HIJRAS

India's most visible nonheterosexual group are the *hijras*, an ancient caste of transvestites and eunuchs who dress in sparkling saris and exuberant makeup. Some are gay, some are intersex and some were sadly kidnapped and castrated. *Hijras* have been part of the subcontinent's culture for thousands of years, are intimately intertwined with Hindu mythology and were traditionally subject to a certain amount of respect – until the arrival of conservative British colonists, who criminalised the community in 1897. In 2014, however, the Indian Supreme Court officially recognised trans people, including *hijras*, as a third gender; *hijras* are now entitled to quotas in education and government jobs. Homosexuality, meanwhile, was decriminalised in 2018.

Within the modern-day Indian LGBT community, *hijras* occupy something of their own subculture, working mainly as uninvited entertainers at weddings and celebrations of the birth of male children, and also as prostitutes and beggars, especially in larger cities. In 2014 Tamil Nadu's Padmini Prakash became India's first transgender daily television news-show anchor, indicating a new level of acceptance.

A growing collection of writing about India's *hijra* community includes *The Invisibles* by Zia Jaffrey, *Ardhanarishvara the Androgyne* by Dr Alka Pande, *The Truth About Me: A Hijra Life Story* by A Revathi and *Me Hijra, Me Laxmi* by Laxmi Tripathi.

RANGOLIS

Rangolis, the breathtakingly intricate chalk, rice-paste or coloured powder designs (also called *kolams*) that adorn Indian thresholds, are both auspicious and symbolic. *Rangolis* are traditionally drawn at sunrise and are sometimes made of rice-flour paste, which may be eaten by little creatures – symbolising reverence for even the smallest living things. Deities are deemed to be attracted to a beautiful *rangoli*, which may also signal to sadhus (ascetics) that they will be offered food at a particular house. *Rangolis* are often drawn in public spaces at festival times, too, and some people believe they protect against the evil eye.

Cricket lovers are likely to be bowled over by *The Illustrated History of Indian Cricket*, by Boria Majumdar, and *The States of Indian Cricket*, by Ramachandra Guha.

retired a year later) or Marco Materazzi (of World Cup headbutt fame) as ex-trainer of Chennai, the ISL has become an international talking point. The I-League is the longer-running domestic league, but it has never attracted such media attention or funding.

India is also known for its historical links to horse polo, which intermittently thrived on the subcontinent (especially among nobility) until Independence, after which patronage steeply declined due to dwindling funds. Today there's a renewed interest in polo thanks to beefed-up sponsorship and, although it remains an elite sport, it's attracting more attention from the country's burgeoning upper middle class. Believed to have its roots in Persia and China around 2000 years ago, polo is thought to have first been played on the subcontinent in Baltistan (in present-day Pakistan). Some say that Emperor Akbar (who reigned in India from 1556 to 1605) first introduced rules to the game, but that polo, as it's played today, was largely influenced by a British cavalry regiment stationed in India during the 1870s. A set of international rules was implemented after WWI. The world's oldest surviving polo club, established in 1862, is Kolkata's Calcutta Polo Club (http://calcuttapolo.com). Polo takes place during the cooler winter months in major cities, including Delhi, Jaipur, Mumbai, Kolkata and Hyderabad, and occasionally in Ladakh and Manipur.

Although officially the national sport, field hockey no longer enjoys the same fervent following it once did, though, as of 2018, India's national men's/women's hockey world rankings are fifth and ninth, respectively. During its golden era, between 1928 and 1956, India won six consecutive Olympic gold medals in hockey; it later bagged two further Olympic gold medals, one in 1964 and the other in 1980. Recent initiatives to ignite renewed interest in the game have had mixed results. Tap into India's hockey scene at Hockey India (http://hockeyindia.org) and Indian Field Hockey (www.bharatiyahockey.org).

Kabaddi is another competitive sport popular across India and especially in Tamil Nadu. Two teams each occupy one side of a court. A raider runs into the opposing side, taking a breath and trying to tag one or more members of the opposite team. The raider chants '*kabaddi*' repeatedly to show that they have not taken a breath, returning to the home half before exhaling.

Aamir Khan's untraditional wrestling drama *Dangal* (2016) – based on the true story of Indian female wrestling champions Geeta and Babita Phogat – became, at the time, Bollywood's highest-grossing film in its first three weeks.

Other sports which are gaining ground in India include tennis (the country's star performers are Sania Mirza, Leander Paes and Mahesh Bhupathi; delve deeper at www.aitatennis.com) and horse racing, which is reasonably popular in larger cities such as Mumbai, Delhi, Kolkata, Hyderabad and Bengaluru, and in Tamil hill station Ooty (Udhagamandalam).

A record 118 athletes competed at the 2016 Rio Olympics, but India scored just two medals – both by women. PV Sindhu became the first Indian woman to win a silver medal (for badminton), while Sakshi Malik set a record as India's first female wrestler to win an Olympic medal (bronze).

If you're interested in catching a sports match during your time in India, check online or consult local newspapers or tourist offices for current details about dates and venues.

Spiritual India

From elaborate urban shrines to humble village temples, spirituality suffuses almost every facet of life in India. The nation's major faith, Hinduism, is practised by around 80% of the population (slightly less in the south) and is one of the world's oldest extant religions, with roots extending beyond 1000 BC. Buddhism and Jainism are also among the oldest religions, dating back to the 6th century BC.

Hinduism

Hinduism has no founder or central authority and it isn't a proselytising religion. Hindus believe in Brahman, who is eternal, uncreated and infinite. Everything that exists emanates from Brahman and will ultimately return to it. The multitude of gods and goddesses are merely manifestations – knowable aspects of this formless phenomenon.

Hindus believe that earthly life is cyclical: you are born again and again (a process known as 'samsara'), the quality of these rebirths depending upon your karma (conduct or action) in previous lives. Living a righteous life and fulfilling your dharma (moral code of behaviour; social duty) will enhance your chances of being born into a higher caste and better circumstances. Alternatively, if enough bad karma has accumulated, rebirth may take animal form. But it's only as a human that you can gain sufficient self-knowledge to escape the cycle of reincarnation and achieve moksha (liberation).

> The Hindu pantheon is said to have around 330 million deities; those worshipped are a matter of personal choice or local tradition.

Gods & Godesses

All Hindu deities are regarded as manifestations of Brahman, who is often described as having three main representations, the Trimurti: Brahma, Vishnu and Shiva.

Brahman

The One; the ultimate reality. Brahman is formless, eternal, the source of all existence. Brahman is *nirguna* (without attributes), as opposed to all the other gods and goddesses, which are manifestations of Brahman and therefore *saguna* (with attributes).

Brahma

Only during the creation of the universe does Brahma play an active role. At other times he is in meditation. His consort is Saraswati, goddess of learning, and his vehicle is a swan. He is sometimes shown sitting on a lotus that rises from Vishnu's navel, symbolising the interdependence of the gods. Brahma is generally depicted with four (crowned and bearded) heads, and today is the least worshipped of the Trimurti gods.

Vishnu

The preserver or sustainer, Vishnu is associated with 'right action'. He protects and sustains all that is good, and has 10 avatars. He is usually depicted with four arms, holding a lotus, a conch shell (it can be blown like a trumpet and so symbolises the cosmic vibration from which existence emanates), a discus *(chakra)* and a mace. His consort is Lakshmi, goddess of wealth, and his vehicle is Garuda, the man-bird creature.

> Unravelling the basic tenets of Hinduism are two books both called *Hinduism: An Introduction* – one by Shakunthala Jagannathan, the other by Dharam Vir Singh.

OM

One of Hinduism's most venerated symbols is 'Om'. Pronounced 'aum', it's a highly propitious mantra (sacred word or syllable). The 'three' shape symbolises the creation, maintenance and destruction of the universe (and thus the holy Trimurti). The inverted *chandra* (crescent or half moon) represents the discursive mind and the *bindu* (dot) within it, Brahman. Buddhists believe that, if intoned often enough with complete concentration, it will lead to a state of blissful emptiness.

Said to emanate from the causal ocean, from which all physical things are created, the sacred River Ganges (Ganga) flows into the material world from Vishnu's feet, but is held back by the matted hair of Lord Shiva to prevent it destroying the earth.

Shiva is sometimes characterised as the lord of yoga – a Himalaya-dwelling, marijuana-smoking ascetic with matted hair, an ash-smeared body and a third eye symbolising wisdom.

Shiva

Shiva is the destroyer – destroying to deliver salvation at the end of each cycle of the universe – without whom creation of the new cycle couldn't occur. Shiva's creative role is phallically symbolised by his representation as the frequently worshipped lingam. With 1008 names, Shiva takes many forms, including Nataraja, lord of the *tandava* (cosmic victory dance), who paces out the creation and destruction of the cosmos.

Sometimes Shiva has snakes draped around his neck and is shown holding a trident (representative of the Trimurti) as a weapon while riding Nandi, his bull. Nandi symbolises power and potency, justice and moral order. Shiva's consort, Parvati, takes many forms.

Ganesh

Elephant-headed Ganesh is the god of good fortune, remover of obstacles and patron of scribes (the broken tusk he holds was used to write sections of the Mahabharata). His animal vehicle is Mooshak (a ratlike creature). How Ganesh came to have an elephant's head is a story with several variations. One legend says that Ganesh was born to Parvati in the absence of his father Shiva. One day, as Ganesh stood guard while his mother bathed, Shiva returned and asked to be let into Parvati's presence. Ganesh, who didn't recognise Shiva, refused. Enraged, Shiva lopped off Ganesh's head, only to later discover that he had slaughtered his own son. He vowed to replace Ganesh's head with that of the first creature he came across: an elephant. The Ganesh Chaturthi festival is particularly popular in South India.

Krishna

Krishna is the eighth incarnation of Vishnu, sent to earth to fight for good and combat evil. His dalliances with the *gopis* (milkmaids) and his love for Radha (a favourite mistress when he lived as a cowherd) have inspired countless paintings and songs. Depicted with blue skin, Krishna is often seen playing the flute.

Did you know that blood-drinking Kali is another form of milk-giving Gauri? *Myth = Mithya: A Handbook of Hindu Mythology*, by Devdutt Pattanaik, sheds light on this and other fascinating Hindu folklore.

Hanuman

Hanuman is the hero of the Ramayana and loyal ally of Rama (the seventh incarnation of Vishnu). He embodies the concept of bhakti (devotion). He is the king of the monkeys, but capable of taking on other forms.

Shakti & Female Goddesses

Among Shaivites (followers of Shiva), Shakti, the universe's divine feminine creative force, is worshipped in her own right. The concept of *shakti* is embodied in the ancient goddess Devi (divine mother), who is also manifested as Durga and Amman, and in a fiercer, evil-destroying incarnation, Kali. Other widely worshipped goddesses include Lakshmi, goddess of wealth, and Saraswati, goddess of learning.

Murugan

Murugan, one of Shiva's sons, is a popular deity in South India, especially in Tamil Nadu. He is sometimes identified with another of Shiva's sons, Skanda (also Kartikiya), who enjoys a strong following in North India. Murugan's main role is that of protector; he is depicted young and victorious.

Ayyappan

A son of Shiva who, like Murugan, is identified with the role of protector is Ayyappan, whose temple at Sabarimala (p292) in Kerala attracts 40 to 60 million pilgrims a year. It's said that he was born from the union of Shiva and Vishnu, both male. Vishnu is said to have assumed female form (Mohini) to give birth. The celibate Ayyappan is often depicted riding a tiger and accompanied by leopards, symbols of his victory over dark forces. The Ayyappan following has become something of a men's movement (though this was challenged by the 2018 Supreme Court ruling that women of all ages should be able to join the pilgrimage). Devotees are required to avoid alcohol, drugs, cigarettes and misbehaviour before making the pilgrimage.

Sacred Texts

Hindu sacred texts fall into two categories: those believed to be the word of god (*shruti*, meaning 'heard') and those produced by people (*smriti*, meaning 'remembered'). The Vedas are regarded as *shruti* knowledge and considered the authoritative basis for Hinduism. The oldest and longest of the Vedic texts, the Rig-Veda, was compiled over 3000 years ago. Within its 1028 verses are prayers for prosperity and longevity, as well as an explanation of the universe's origins. The Upanishads, the last parts of the Vedas, reflect on the mystery of death and emphasise the oneness of the universe. The oldest of the Vedic texts were written in Vedic Sanskrit (related to Old Persian). Later texts were composed in classical Sanskrit, but many have been translated into the vernacular.

The *smriti* texts comprise a collection of literature spanning centuries and include expositions on the proper performance of domestic ceremonies, as well as the proper pursuit of government, economics and religious law. Among well-known works are the Ramayana and Mahabharata, as well as the Puranas, which expand on the Ramayana and Mahabharata and promote the notion of the Trimurti. Unlike with the Vedas, reading the Puranas is not restricted to initiated higher-caste males.

The Mahabharata

Thought to have been composed around 1000 BC, the Mahabharata focuses on the exploits of Krishna. By about 500 BC the Mahabharata had evolved into a far more complex creation with substantial additions, including the Bhagavad Gita (where Krishna proffers advice to Arjuna before a battle).

The story centres on conflict between the heroic gods (Pandavas) and the demons (Kauravas). Krishna acts as charioteer for the Pandava hero Arjuna, who eventually triumphs in a great battle against the Kauravas.

The Ramayana

Composed around the 3rd or 2nd century BC, the Ramayana is believed to be largely the work of the poet Valmiki. Like the Mahabharata, it centres on conflict between the gods and the demons.

The story goes that Dasharatha, the childless king of Ayodhya, called upon the gods to provide him with a son. His wife duly gave birth to a boy. But this child, named Rama, was in fact an incarnation of Vishnu, who had assumed human form to overthrow the demon king of (Sri) Lanka, Ravana.

As an adult, Rama, who won the hand of the princess Sita in a competition, was chosen by his father to inherit his kingdom. At the last minute

Two recommended publications containing English translations of holy Hindu texts are The Bhagavad Gita by S Radhakrishnan and The Valmiki Ramayana by Romesh Dutt.

SPIRITUAL INDIA HINDUISM

THE SACRED SEVEN

The number seven has special significance in Hinduism. There are seven sacred rivers: the Ganges (Ganga), Saraswati (thought to be underground), Yamuna, Indus, Narmada, Godavari and Cauvery (Kaveri). There are also seven sacred Indian cities, all major pilgrimage centres:

Varanasi Associated with Shiva

Haridwar Where the Ganges enters the plains from the Himalaya

Ayodhya Birthplace of Rama

Dwarka An older city, said to have been Krishna's capital, is believed to be beneath the sea nearby

Mathura Birthplace of Krishna

Kanchipuram Site of historic Shiva temples

Ujjain Venue of the Kumbh Mela every 12 years

Rama's stepmother intervened and demanded her son, Barathan, take Rama's place. Rama, Sita and Rama's brother, Lakshmana, were exiled and went off to the forests, where Rama and Lakshmana battled demons and dark forces. Ravana captured Sita and spirited her away to his palace in Lanka.

Rama, assisted by an army of monkeys led by the loyal monkey god Hanuman, eventually found the palace, killed Ravana and rescued Sita. All returned victorious to Ayodhya, where Rama was welcomed by Barathan and crowned king. It is this legend that is celebrated in Tamil Nadu at Rameswaram's Ramanathaswamy Temple (p394).

Naturally Sacred

Animals, particularly snakes and cows, have long been worshipped on the subcontinent. For Hindus, cows represent fertility and nurturing; snakes (especially cobras) are associated with fertility and welfare. Naga stones (snake stones) serve the dual purpose of protecting humans from snakes and appeasing snake gods.

Plants can also have sacred associations. Banyan trees represent the Trimurti, and mango trees are symbolic of love – Shiva married Parvati under one. Meanwhile, the lotus flower is said to have emerged from the primeval waters and is connected to the mythical centre of the earth through its stem. Often found in the most polluted of waters, the fragile yet resolute lotus has the remarkable ability to blossom above murky depths. The centre of the lotus corresponds to the centre of the universe, the navel of the earth: all is held together by the stem and the eternal waters. Embodying beauty and strength, the lotus is a reminder to Hindus of how their own lives should be. So revered has the lotus become that today it's India's national flower.

Worship

Worship and ritual play a paramount role in Hinduism. In most Hindu homes you'll find a dedicated worship area, where members of the family pray to the deities of their choice. Beyond the home, Hindus worship at temples. *Puja* is a focal point of worship, ranging from silent prayer to elaborate ceremonies; it usually involves *darshan* (auspicious viewing of the deity). Devotees leave the temple with a handful of *prasad* (temple-blessed food), which is shared among others. Other forms of worship include *aarti* (auspicious lighting of lamps or candles) and the playing of bhajans (devotional songs).

A sadhu is someone who has surrendered all material possessions in pursuit of spirituality through meditation, the study of sacred texts, self-mortification and pilgrimage. Read more in *Sadhus: India's Mystic Holy Men* by Dolf Hartsuiker.

Islam

Islam is India's largest minority religion, followed by approximately 14.2% of the population. It's believed that Islam was introduced to northern India by Muslim rulers (parts of the north first came under Muslim rule in the 12th century) and to the south by Arab traders.

Islam was founded in Arabia by the Prophet Mohammed in the 7th century AD. The Arabic term islam means 'to surrender', and believers (Muslims) undertake to surrender to the will of Allah (God), revealed in the scriptures, the Quran. In this monotheistic religion, God's word is conveyed through prophets (messengers), of whom Mohammed was the most recent. Following Mohammed's death, a succession dispute split the movement; the legacy today is the Sunnis and the Shiites. The Sunnis emphasise the 'well-trodden' path or the orthodox way. Shiites believe that only imams (exemplary leaders) can reveal the Quran's true meaning. Most Indian Muslims are Sunnis.

All Muslims, however, share a belief in the Five Pillars of Islam: the shahada (declaration of faith: 'There is no God but Allah; Mohammed is his prophet'); prayer (ideally five times a day); the zakat (tax), in the form of a charitable donation; fasting (during Ramadan) for all except the sick, young children, pregnant women, the elderly and those undertaking arduous journeys; and the hajj (pilgrimage) to Mecca, which every Muslim aspires to do at least once.

Muslims form more than a quarter of the population of Kerala; more than 10% in Maharashtra and Karnataka; around 9% in Goa, Andhra Pradesh and the Andaman Islands; and around 6% in Tamil Nadu.

Christianity

There are various theories circulating about Christ's link to the Indian subcontinent. Some, for instance, believe that Jesus spent his 'lost years' in India, while others say that Christianity came to South India with St Thomas the Apostle through Kerala in AD 52. However, many scholars attest it's more likely Christianity is traced to around the 4th century with a Syrian merchant, Thomas Cana, who set out for Kerala with around 400 families. India's Christian community today stands at about 2.3% of the population, with the bulk residing in South India, particularly Kerala.

Catholicism established a strong presence in South India in the wake of Portuguese explorer Vasco da Gama's visit in 1498, and orders that have been active – not always welcomed – in the region include the Dominicans, Franciscans and Jesuits. Protestant missionaries are believed to have begun arriving – with a conversion agenda – from around the 18th century.

Sikhism

Sikhism, founded in Punjab by Guru Nanak in the 15th century, began as a reaction against the caste system and Brahmin domination of ritual. Sikhs believe in one god and, although they reject the worship of idols, some keep pictures of the 10 Sikh gurus as a focal point. The Sikhs' holy book, the Guru Granth Sahib, contains the teachings of the 10 gurus. Like Hindus and Buddhists, Sikhs believe in rebirth and karma. In Sikhism, there's no ascetic or monastic tradition ending the cycles of rebirth.

Born in present-day Pakistan, Guru Nanak (1469–1539) was dissatisfied with both Muslim and Hindu religious practices. He believed in family life and the value of hard work. He is said to have performed miracles and he encouraged meditation on God's name as a prime path to enlightenment. Nanak believed in equality centuries before it became socially fashionable and campaigned against the caste system. He was a practical guru, and appointed his most talented disciple to be his successor, not one of his sons. Almost 2% of India's citizens are Sikhs; 75% of them live in Punjab.

Few parts of India worship the Hindu gods as passionately as Tamil Nadu, the state in which South India's splendid temple architecture reaches its peak. Tamil Nadu's most worshipped deity is Shiva, in widely varied forms including dancing Nataraja. Shiva's peacock-riding son Murugan is also immensely popular.

Christians make up 18.3% of the population in Kerala, 25% in Goa and 21.3% in the Andaman Islands, compared to just 1% in Maharashtra and 1.9% in Karnataka.

To grasp the intricacies of Sikhism read *Volume One (1469–1839)* or *Volume Two (1839–2004)* of *A History of the Sikhs*, by Khushwant Singh.

SPIRITUAL INDIA ISLAM

There are very few Sikhs in South India; Maharashtra is home to the highest percentage, but even here Sikhs only account for 0.2% of the population.

Buddhism

Buddhism arose in the 6th century BC as a reaction against the strictures of Brahminical Hinduism. The Buddha (Awakened One) is believed to have lived from about 563 to 483 BC. Formerly a prince (Siddhartha Gautama), the Buddha, at 29, embarked on a quest for emancipation from the world of suffering. He achieved nirvana (the state of full awareness) at Bodhgaya, in the northern state of Bihar, aged 35. Critical of the caste system and the unthinking worship of gods, the Buddha urged his disciples to seek truth within their own experiences. About 0.8% of India's population is Buddhist.

The Buddha taught that existence is based on Four Noble Truths: that life is rooted in suffering, that suffering is caused by craving, that one can find release from suffering by eliminating craving, and that the way to eliminate craving is by following the Noble Eightfold Path. This path consists of right understanding, right intention, right speech, right action, right livelihood, right effort, right awareness and right concentration. By successfully complying with these one can attain nirvana.

Buddhism was spread widely around India by the Mauryan emperor Ashoka in the 3rd century BC. Buddhist communities were quite influential in Andhra Pradesh between the 3rd century BC and 5th century AD; missionaries from Andhra helped establish monasteries and temples in countries such as Thailand. But Buddhism had ceased to play a major role in India by the 12th century AD. It saw a revival in the 1950s among intellectuals and Dalits, disillusioned with the caste system, with nearly half a million people converting under the guidance of Dalit leader, BR Ambedkar.

About three-quarters of Indian Buddhists today live in Maharashtra, making up 5.8% of the state's population. The number of Buddhists has further increased with the influx of Tibetan refugees into India. Both the current Dalai Lama and the lama (monk) widely accepted as the 17th Karmapa reside in the northern state of Himachal Pradesh. There are several Tibetan refugee communities in South India, the biggest being Bylakuppe in Karnataka, a state in which Buddhists comprise 0.2% of the population.

Jainism

Jainism arose in the 6th century BC as a reaction against the caste restraints and rituals of Hinduism. It was popularised by Mahavira, a contemporary of the Buddha. Jains believe that liberation is attained by achieving complete purity of the soul. Purity means shedding all *karman* (matter generated by one's actions that binds itself to the soul). By following various austerities (fasting, meditation) one can shed *karman* and purify the soul. Right conduct is essential, and fundamental to this is ahimsa (nonviolence) in thought and deed towards any living thing. The religious disciplines of followers are less severe than those for monks (some Jain monks go naked). The slightly less ascetic maintain a bare minimum of possessions, including a broom to sweep the path before them to avoid stepping on any living creature, and a piece of cloth tied over their mouth to prevent accidental inhalation of insects.

Today, around 0.4% of India's population is Jain, the majority in Gujarat, Rajasthan, Maharashtra and Mumbai. Notable Jain holy sites in South India include Sravanabelagola in Karnataka.

Zoroastrianism

Zoroastrianism appears in recorded history in the mid-5th-century BC, and is based on the concept of dualism, whereby good and evil are locked in a continuous battle. Zoroastrianism isn't quite monotheistic: good and

For an insight into the depth, breadth and quirks of Tamils' Hindu beliefs, as well as absorbing travel writing, read Michael Wood's *A South Indian Journey*.

The Zoroastrian funerary ritual involves 'Towers of Silence' (seen, for example, in Mumbai and Hyderabad), where the corpse is laid out and exposed to vultures that pick the bones clean.

RELIGIOUS ETIQUETTE

➡ When visiting a sacred site, dress and behave respectfully. Don't wear shorts or sleeveless tops (this applies to men and women), and refrain from smoking. Loud and intrusive behaviour isn't appreciated, nor are public displays of affection.

➡ Before entering a holy place, remove your shoes (tip the shoe-minder a few rupees when retrieving them) and check if photography is allowed. You're permitted to wear socks in most places of worship – often necessary during warmer months, when floors can be uncomfortably hot.

➡ Head cover (for women and sometimes men) is required at some places of worship – especially gurdwaras (Sikh temples) and mosques – so carry a scarf.

➡ There are some religious sites that don't admit women and some that deny entry to nonadherents of their faith; enquire in advance. Women may be required to sit apart from men and some sites ask that menstruating women do not enter. Jain temples request the removal of leather items you may be wearing or carrying. Non-Hindus are often not allowed into the inner sanctums of Hindu temples.

➡ When walking around any Buddhist sacred site (chortens, stupas, temples, gompas) go clockwise. Don't touch them with your left hand. Turn prayer wheels clockwise, with your right hand.

➡ Taking photos inside a shrine, at a funeral, at a religious ceremony or of people taking a holy dip can be offensive – ask first. Flash photography may be prohibited in certain areas of a shrine, or may not be permitted at all.

evil entities coexist, although believers are urged to honour only the good and a pleasant afterlife does depend on one's deeds, words and thoughts during earthly existence. Some historians believe the prophet Zoroaster was a reformer of the polytheistic Iranian religion who lived in the 10th century BC, though others date him to the 6th century BC.

Zoroastrianism was eclipsed in Persia by the rise of Islam in the 7th century. Over the ensuing centuries some followers emigrated to India, where they became known as Parsis. Historically, Parsis settled in Gujarat and became farmers; during British rule they moved into commerce, forming a prosperous community in Bombay (Mumbai). There are now believed to be around 61,000 Parsis left in India, including 40,000 to 45,000 in Mumbai.

Set in Kerala against the backdrop of caste conflict and India's struggle for independence, *The House of Blue Mangoes*, by David Davidar, spans three generations of a Christian family.

Judaism

There are fewer than 4500 Jews left in India, mostly in Mumbai and scattered pockets of South India. South India's Jews first settled in the region from the Middle East as far back as the 1st century. They became established at Kochi (Cochin; Kerala) and their legacy continues in the city's still-standing trading houses and synagogue.

Tribal Religions

Tribal religions have merged with Hinduism and other mainstream religions so that very few are now clearly identifiable. It's believed that some basic tenets of Hinduism may have originated in ancient tribal culture.

Village and tribal people in South India have their own belief systems, which are less accessible or obvious than the temples, rituals and other outward manifestations of the mainstream religions. The village deity may be represented by a stone pillar in a field, a platform under a tree or an iron spear in the ground. Village deities are seen as less remote and more concerned with the community's immediate happiness and prosperity. There are also beliefs about ancestral spirits, including those who died violently.

Delicious India

India's culinary terrain is a feast for all the senses. Its multifaceted vegetarian cuisine is especially impressive – and South India is particularly famous for it. You'll delight in everything from sensational street food to work-of-art thalis, from contemporary fusion masterpieces to 50-year-old family-run stalls serving up one speciality, all using fresh local ingredients. Regional variations add extra flair. There's plenty for carnivores and seafood-lovers, too. Indeed, it's this sheer diversity that makes eating your way around South India so deliciously rewarding.

A Culinary Carnival

Containing handy tips, including how to best store spices, Monisha Bharadwaj's *The Indian Spice Kitchen* is a slick cookbook with more than 200 traditional recipes.

India's culinary story is an ancient one: the food you'll find in South India today reflects millenniums of regional and global influences, with distinct (and delicious!) local variations.

Land of Spices

Christopher Columbus was actually searching for the black pepper of Kerala's Malabar Coast when he stumbled upon America. The region still grows the finest quality of the world's favourite spice, integral to most savoury Indian dishes. Andhra Pradesh, meanwhile, is India's largest producer of chilli, followed by Maharashtra and Karnataka.

Turmeric is the essence of the majority of Indian curries, but coriander seeds are the most widely used spice and lend flavour and body to just about every savoury dish. Indian 'wet' dishes ('curries' in the West) usually begin with the crackle of cumin seeds in hot oil. Tamarind is

---

THE GREAT SOUTH INDIAN THALI

In South India, the thali is a favourite all-you-can-eat lunchtime meal, often called just a 'meal'. Inexpensive, satiating, wholesome and incredibly tasty, this is Indian food at its simple best. The name 'thali' refers to the stainless-steel plate on which the meal is served. In North India the plate usually has indentations for the various side dishes, but in South India a thali is traditionally served on a flat steel plate often covered with a fresh banana leaf, or straight on a banana leaf itself.

In a restaurant, when the steel plate is placed in front of you, you can follow local custom and pour some bottled or filtered water on the leaf then spread it around with your right hand. A waiter will pile rotis (breads) on to your plate, followed by servings of dhal, *sambar* (soupy lentils), *rasam* (dhal-based broth flavoured with tamarind), vegetable dishes, chutneys, pickles and *dahi* (curd/yoghurt). When you're done with the rotis, waiters will materialise with large pots of rice and top-ups of side dishes. Using the fingers of your right hand, mix the side dishes with the rice, kneading and scraping it into mouth-sized balls, then scoop it into your mouth using your thumb to push the food. It's considered poor form to stick your hand right into your mouth or to lick your fingers. Observing fellow diners will help you master your thali technique. If it's all getting a bit messy, there's usually a finger bowl of water available. Waiters will continue refilling your plate until you wave your hand over one or all of the offerings, or fold over your banana leaf, to indicate you have had enough. If a thali alone isn't enough, there are often extra side dishes you can order to accompany it, such as fried fish in coastal regions.

FEASTING: INDIAN-STYLE

Most people in India eat with their right hand. In the south, they use as much of the hand as is necessary; elsewhere they use the tips of the fingers. The left hand is reserved for unsanitary actions such as removing shoes. You can use your left hand for holding drinks and serving yourself from a communal bowl, but it shouldn't be used for bringing food to your mouth. Before and after a meal, wash your hands.

Once your meal is served, mix the food with your fingers. If you are having dhal and *sabzi* (vegetables), only mix the dhal into your rice and have the *sabzi* in small scoops with each mouthful. If you are having fish or meat curry, mix the gravy into your rice. Scoop up lumps of the mix and, with your knuckles facing the dish, use your thumb to shovel the food into your mouth.

sometimes known as the 'Indian date' and is a popular souring agent in South India. The green cardamom of Kerala's Western Ghats is regarded as the world's best; you'll find it in savouries, desserts and warming chai (tea). Saffron, the dried stigmas of crocus flowers grown in Kashmir, is so light it takes more than 1500 hand-plucked flowers to yield just one gram. Coconut, often shaved, is also worked into many southern dishes, as is locally grown ginger.

Bilkul Lathif's *Essential Andhra Cookbook* opens the door on the little-known cuisine of Andhra Pradesh, and also covers Hyderabadi recipes.

Rice Paradise

Rice is a staple throughout India, and especially in South India. Long-grain white-rice varieties are most popular, served hot with every thali and just about any 'wet' cooked dish. From Kerala's red grains to the black rice of Tamil Nadu's arid Chettinadu region, you'll find countless regional varieties, even just between southern states. The title of best rice in India is usually conceded to basmati, a fragrant long-grain variety grown in northern and central India and widely exported around the world.

Rice is typically served after you have finished with the rotis, accompanied by enriching curd. It's also turned into tasty pilau and biryani, the latter particularly famous in Hyderabad and on Kerala's Malabar Coast.

Flippin' Fantastic Bread

Although rice is South India's mainstay, traditional breads are also widely eaten. Roti, the generic term for Indian-style bread, is a name used interchangeably with chapati to describe the most common variety, the irresistible unleavened round bread made with whole-wheat flour and cooked on a *tawa* (hotplate). It may be smothered with ghee (clarified butter) or oil. In some places, rotis are bigger and thicker than chapatis, and sometimes cooked in a tandoor. *Paratha* is a layered pan-fried flat bread that may also be stuffed and which makes a popular breakfast; South India's *parotta* is similar. Naan is a larger, thicker, tandoor-cooked bread, usually eaten with northern-style meaty sauces or kebabs. *Puri* is an unleavened bread that puffs up like a balloon when deep-fried, served with accompaniments such as *bhajia* (vegetable fritters).

Dhal-icious!

The whole of India is united in its love for dhal (curried lentils or pulses). You may encounter up to 60 different pulses: the most common are *channa* (chickpeas); tiny yellow or green ovals called *moong* (mung beans); salmon-coloured *masoor* (red lentils); the ochre-coloured southern favourite *tuvar* (yellow lentils; also known as *arhar*); *rajma* (kidney beans); *urad* (black gram or lentils); and *lobhia* (black-eyed peas).

Complete Indian Cooking, by Mridula Baljekar, Rafi Fernandez, Shehzad Husain and Manisha Kanani, contains over 400 favourite southern recipes, from chicken with green mango to Goan prawn curry.

Meaty Matters

Although India probably has more vegetarians than the rest of the world combined, it still has an extensive repertoire of carnivorous fare. Chicken,

In coastal areas, especially Goa and Kerala, it's hard to beat the basic beach shacks for fresh, inexpensive seafood, from fried mussels, prawns and calamari to steamed fish, crab and lobster.

lamb and mutton (sometimes actually goat) are the staples; religious taboos make beef forbidden to devout Hindus, and pork to Muslims.

In South India, meaty Chettinadu cuisine from Tamil Nadu is beautifully spiced without being too fiery. In some southern restaurants you'll find meat-dominated Mughlai cuisine, which includes rich curries, kebabs, koftas and biryanis – the last is a particular speciality of Hyderabad, a city that traces the history of its spicy meat-heavy cuisine back to the (Islamic) Mughal empire that once reigned supreme over much of India. *Haleem* is Hyderabad's other most famous meaty dish: a thick soup of pounded, spiced wheat with goat, chicken or beef, and lentils, available only during Ramadan. Tandoori meat dishes are another North Indian favourite also found in the south; the name is derived from the clay oven (tandoor) in which the marinated meat is cooked.

Beef has been banned in Maharashtra since 2015 (though technically beef imported from outside the state can still be legally consumed) and you'll often see 'buf' or 'b**f' on menus, which means it's buffalo meat. Kerala, meanwhile, is known for eating beef, especially beef fry. In the last few years there have been growing instances of 'cow vigilantism' mob attacks across India, carried out by Hindus mostly on Muslims, allegedly in the name of protecting cows.

Deep-Sea Delights

India has around 7500km of coastline, so it's no surprise that seafood is a key South Indian ingredient, especially on the west coast, from Mumbai down to Kerala. Kerala is the biggest fishing state (only a small percentage of its population is vegetarian), while Goa has particularly succulent prawns and fiery fish curries; the fishing communities of the Konkan Coast – between Mumbai and Goa – are renowned for their seafood. The far-flung Andaman Islands are a treat for seafood lovers, with fresh catches on all menus, while fresh seafood also abounds in coastal Tamil Nadu and Andhra Pradesh.

Dear Dairy

Fish is a staple of nonvegetarian Maharashtrian food; Maharashtra's signature fish dish is *bombil* (Bombay Duck; a misnomer for this slimy, pikelike fish), which is eaten fresh, sun-dried or deep-fried.

Milk and milk products make a staggering contribution to Indian cuisine. *Dahi* (curd/yoghurt) is commonly served with meals and is great for subduing heat; paneer (soft unfermented cheese) is a godsend for the vegetarian majority; lassi (a yoghurt drink) is one of a host of sweet and savoury beverages; ghee (clarified butter) is the traditional, pure cooking medium; and some of the finest *mithai* (Indian sweets) are made with milk.

The Fruits (& Vegetables) of Mother Nature

A visit to any South Indian market reveals a vast, vibrant assortment of fresh fruit and vegetables, overflowing from baskets or stacked in tidy

PAAN

Meals across India are often rounded off with *paan*, a fragrant mixture of betel nut (also called areca nut), lime paste, spices and condiments wrapped in an edible, silky *paan* leaf. Peddled by *paan*-wallahs, usually strategically positioned outside busy restaurants, *paan* is eaten as a digestive and mouth-freshener. The betel nut is mildly narcotic and some aficionados eat *paan* the same way heavy smokers consume cigarettes; over the years these people's teeth can become rotted red and black. Usually the gloopy red juice is spat out – not particularly sightly. There are two basic types of *paan*: *mitha* (sweet) and *saadha* (with tobacco). A parcel of *mitha paan* is a splendid way to finish a meal: pop the whole parcel in your mouth and chew slowly.

Note that some studies suggest that chewing *paan*, even without tobacco, can increase a person's risk of developing cancer.

COOKING COURSES & FOOD TOURS

You might find yourself so inspired by South Indian food that you want to take home a little Indian kitchen know-how. A growing number of recommended cooking courses is offered in Goa, Karnataka, Kerala, Tamil Nadu, Telangana and elsewhere. Some are professionally run, others informal; most require a few days' notice. Food tours are also an increasingly popular way to get under South India's skin.

Goa

➡ Masala Kitchen, Palolem (p156) Well-established cooking courses.

➡ Mukti Kitchen, Vagator (p141) Five-dish cooking classes (Goan, Indian, ayurvedic).

➡ Rahul's Cooking Class, Palolem (p155) One of Palolem's original culinary schools.

Mumbai

➡ Flavour Diaries (p55) Cooking classes with a renowned chef and food writer.

Kerala

➡ Nimi's Lip Smacking Classes, Munnar (p293) Expert-led Keralan cooking.

➡ Popular cookathons at Cook & Eat (p299), Neema's Kitchen (p299) and Green Woods Bethlehem (p301), plus good walking food tours with Art of Bicycle (p300) in Kerala.

Tamil Nadu

➡ Chettinadu (p386) Heritage hotels give cooking demos and classes.

➡ Sita, Puducherry (Pondicherry; p366) Tamil, French and North Indian cuisine.

➡ Storytrails, Chennai (p341), Puducherry (p367) and Madurai (p391) Fab food tours and cookery classes.

➡ Foodies Day Out, Madurai (p391) Culinary tours of a famously food-mad city.

➡ Svatma, Thanjavur (Tanjore; p381) Cooking classes in a heritage-style property.

Telangana

➡ Detours, Hyderabad (p236) Outstanding food tours incorporating cooking lessons.

---

pyramids. The south is especially well known for its abundance of tropical fruits such as papaya, pineapple (Kerala's Vazhakulam pineapple is famous) and avocado (this last grown almost exclusively on southern hillsides and often referred to as butter fruit). Mangoes abound during summer months (especially April and May); the pick of India's 500 luscious varieties is the sweet Maharashtrian Alphonso. Nashik, in Maharashtra, is the country's grape-producing capital, though these days its grapes end up in wines as much as in fruit baskets. You'll find fruit inventively fashioned into a *chatni* or pickle, and flavouring lassi, *kulfi* and other sweet treats.

Naturally in a region with so many vegetarians, *sabzi* (vegetables) make up a predominant part of the diet. Vegetables can be cooked *sukhi* (dry) or *tari* (in a sauce), and within these two categories they can be fried, roasted, curried, baked, mashed and stuffed into dosas, or dipped in chickpea-flour batter to make a deep-fried *pakora* (fritter). Potatoes are ubiquitous and popularly cooked with various masalas (spice mixes), with other vegetables, stuffed inside *masala dosas* or mashed and fried for the street snack *aloo tikki* (mashed-potato patties).

Onions are fried with other vegetables, ground into a paste for cooking with meats or served raw as relishes. Heads of cauliflower are cooked dry on their own, with potatoes as *aloo gobi* (potato-and-cauliflower curry), or with other vegetables such as carrots and beans. Fresh green peas turn up stir-fried with other vegetables in pilaus (rice cooked in spiced stock) and

Ghee is made by melting butter and removing the water and milk solids: ghee is the clear butter fat that remains. It's better for high-heat cooking than butter, and keeps for longer, and so is often used in Indian cooking.

GP Vijay's *101 Kerala Delicacies* is a detailed recipe book of vegetarian and nonvegetarian dishes and cooking tips from this coast-hugging state.

biryanis. *Baigan* (aubergine/eggplant) can be curried or sliced and deep-fried. Also popular is *saag* (leafy greens), which can include mustard, spinach and fenugreek. Something a little more unusual is the bumpy-skinned *karela* (bitter gourd), which, like the delectable *bhindi* (okra), is commonly prepared dry with spices. Tamil Nadu is known for growing the drumstick vegetable – a long, thin pod often used in *sambar*.

Pickles, Chutneys & Relishes

Pickles, chutneys and relishes are accompaniments that add zing to meals and appear alongside almost every South Indian *idli*, dosa or *uttapam*. A relish can be anything from a tiny pickled onion to a delicately crafted fusion of fruit, nuts and spices. One of the most popular side dishes is yoghurt-based raita, a tongue-cooling antidote to spicy food. *Chatnis* come in all kinds of varieties (sweet or savoury) and can be made from many different vegetables, fruits, herbs and spices.

Sweet at Heart

India has a colourful kaleidoscope of often sticky and squishy *mithai* (Indian sweets), most of them sinfully sugary. The main categories are *barfi* (a fudgelike milk-based sweet); soft *halwa* (made with vegetables, cereals, lentils, nuts or fruit); *ladoos* (sweet balls made of gram flour and semolina – Maharashtra's *til ladoos* come with sesame seeds); and sweet balls made from *chhana* (unpressed paneer), such as *rasgullas* (syrupy cream-cheese balls). There are also simpler – but equally scrumptious – offerings such as crunchy *jalebis* (orange-coloured coils of deep-fried batter dunked in sugar syrup; served hot) all over India.

Bulbul Sharma's *The Anger of Aubergines: Stories of Women and Food* is an amusing culinary analysis of social relationships interspersed with enticing recipes.

Payasam (*kheer* in the north) is one of South India's most popular desserts, often served at festival times. It's a creamy rice pudding with a light, delicate flavour, enhanced with cardamom, saffron, pistachios, flaked almonds, chopped cashews or slivered dried fruit. Other favourites include *kulfi* (flavoured firm-textured ice cream), *falooda* (a rose-flavoured dessert made with milk, cream, nuts and strands of vermicelli) and *gulab jamun* (deep-fried dough balls soaked in rose-flavoured syrup). Kerala's *unniyappam*, made from rice flour, banana, coconut, cardamom, jaggery, sesame seeds and ghee, is similar to *gulab jamun*.

In Maharashtra's hill areas you'll find *chikki* (a rock-hard, toffeelike confectionery for snacking). Madurai, in Tamil Nadu, is famous for its refreshing drink *jigarthanda* (boiled milk, almond essence, rose syrup and vanilla ice cream). Karnataka's Mysuru (Mysore) is known for Mysuru *pak*, which combines ghee, gram flour, sugar and cardamom into a sweet not unlike fudge.

Each year, an estimated 14 tonnes of pure silver is converted into the edible foil that decorates many Indian sweets, especially during Diwali.

Vegetarians & Vegans

Dakshin: Vegetarian Cuisine from South India, by Chandra Padmanabhan, is an easy-to-read, beautifully illustrated tome of southern recipes. *Southern Flavours: the Best of South Indian Cuisine* comes from the same author.

South India is king when it comes to vegetarian food in India, a nation where an estimated 23% to 37% of the population is vegetarian. There's little understanding of veganism ('pure vegetarian' means without eggs) and animal products such as milk, butter, ghee and curd are included in most Indian dishes. As a vegan, your first problem is likely to be getting the cook to understand your requirements, though big hotels and larger cities such as Bengaluru (Bangalore) are getting better at catering to vegans and you'll now find vegan menus in many southern traveller hubs. In the south, coconut milk is often used in curries instead of cream – great news for travelling vegans.

For further information, check out Happy Cow (www.happycow.net) and The Nomadic Vegan (www.thenomadicvegan.com).

Where to Fill Up?

You can eat well everywhere in South India, from ramshackle *dhabas* (simple streetside eateries) and frenzied lunchtime 'messes' (canteens) to other-worldly five-star hotels. Most midrange restaurants serve a few basic genres: South Indian (which usually means the vegetarian food of Tamil Nadu and Karnataka) and North Indian (which largely comprises Punjabi/Mughlai fare), plus, often, Indian interpretations of Chinese dishes (with varying levels of success). You'll also encounter the cuisines of neighbouring regions and states. Indians frequently migrate for work and these restaurants cater to large communities seeking familiar home tastes.

Not to be confused with burger joints and pizzerias, restaurants in the south advertising 'fast food' are some of India's best. They serve the whole gamut of tiffin (snack) items and often have separate sweet counters. Many upmarket hotels have outstanding restaurants, some with pan-Indian menus so you can explore various regional cuisines, others deliciously specialised. Meanwhile, the independent restaurant-dining scene continues to blossom across the larger southern cities, with every kind of cuisine available, from Mexican and Mediterranean to Japanese and Italian.

Dhabas are oases to millions of truck drivers, bus passengers and sundry travellers going anywhere by road. The original *dhabas* dot the North Indian landscape, but you'll find versions of them throughout the country. The rough-and-ready but satisfying food served in these happy-go-lucky shacks has become a genre of its own known as '*dhaba* food'.

Street Food

Whatever the time of day, street-food vendors are frying, boiling, griddling, roasting, peeling, simmering, mixing, juicing or baking different types of food and drink to lure peckish passers-by. Small operations usually have one special that they serve all day; other vendors have different dishes for breakfast, lunch and dinner. The fare varies as you venture between neighbourhoods, towns and regions; it can be as simple as puffed rice or peanuts

Food that is first offered to the gods at temples then shared among devotees is known as *prasad*. Note that it may not be hygienic to eat, however, and is best avoided by travellers.

Got the munchies? Grab *Street Foods of India*, by Vimla and Deb Kumar Mukerji, which has recipes for much-loved Indian snacks.

DELICIOUS INDIA WHERE TO FILL UP?

STREET FOOD TIPS

Tucking into street eats is one of the great joys of travelling in South India, here are some tips to help avoid tummy troubles.

➜ Give yourself a few days to adjust to the local cuisine, especially if you're not used to spicy food.

➜ If the locals are avoiding a particular vendor, you should too. Take notice of the profile of the customers: any place popular with families will probably be your safest bet.

➜ Check how and where the vendor is cleaning the utensils, and how and where the food is covered. If the vendor is cooking in oil, have a peek to check it's clean. If the pots or surfaces are dirty, there are food scraps about or too many buzzing flies, don't be shy about making a hasty retreat.

➜ Don't be put off when you order some deep-fried snack and the cook throws it back into the wok. It's common practice to partly cook the snacks first and then finish them off once they've been ordered. Frying them again kills germs.

➜ Unless a place is reputable (and busy), it's best to avoid eating meat from the street.

➜ The hygiene standards at juice stalls vary, so exercise caution. Have the vendor press the juice in front of you and steer clear of anything stored in a jug or served in a glass (unless you're absolutely convinced of the washing standards).

➜ Keep hands clean (a small tub of hand sanitiser can be a godsend).

➜ Don't be tempted by glistening presliced melon and other fruit, which keeps its luscious veneer with regular dousings of (often dubious) water.

Nimi Sunilku-mar's award-winning Keralan cookbooks *Lip Smacking Dishes of Kerala* and *4 O'Clock Tempta-tions of Kerala* offer a tantalising insight into local cuisine. Nimi shares more tips on her website (http://nimis recipes.com), and you can learn in person at her popular cooking classes in Munnar (p293).

roasted in hot sand, or as complex as the riot of different flavours known as *chaat* (a savoury snack). *Idli sambar* (rice patties served with lentil sauce and chutney) is a favourite in Chennai, along with *vadas* (doughnut-shaped deep-fried spiced lentil savouries) and *uttapams* (thick savoury South Indi-an rice pancakes with finely chopped onions, green chillies, coriander and coconut). Mumbai is famed for its *pav bhaji* (spiced veg and bread) and *bhelpuri* (fried rounds of dough with puffed rice, lentils, lemon juice, onion, herbs and chutney), while *misal pav* (spicy bean sprouts and pulses) is a Maharashtrian breakfast favourite. *Mirchi bhajji* (chilli fritters stuffed with tamarind, sesame and spices) are a Hyderabad delicacy, served with tea in the early evenings at street stalls. Samosas (deep-fried pastry triangles filled with spiced vegetables) and *golgappa/panipuri/gup chup* (puffed spheres of bread with spicy filling) are found all over India, while banana chips deep-fried in coconut oil are a classic southern snack.

Railway Snack Attack

One of the thrills of travelling by rail in India is the culinary circus that greets you at almost every station. Roving vendors accost arriving trains, yelling and scampering up and down carriages; fruit, *namkin* (savoury nibbles), omelettes, nuts and sweets are offered through the window grilles; and platform cooks try to lure you from the train with the sizzle of spicy goodies like fresh samosas. Frequent rail travellers know which station is famous for which food item: Maharashtra's Lonavla station is known for *chikki,* while Chennai Central is (predictably) famed for *idlis, vadas* and dosas. Even some trains have famous kitchens, such as the Gitanjali Express between Mumbai and Kolkata, with its celebrated chicken cutlets.

Daily Dining Habits

Three main meals a day is the norm in India. South Indians generally have a light, early breakfast, often *idlis* with *sambar.* Lunch can be sub-stantial (perhaps a thali) or lighter, especially for time-strapped office workers. Many people also have tiffin (between-meal snacks) throughout the day. Dinner is the main meal of the day: usually large serves of rice, rotis, vegetables, curd and spicy side dishes (maybe also meat or fish), all

SOUTHERN BELLES

Savoury dosas (also spelt dosai) – large, crispy, papery, rice-flour crêpes, usually served with a bowl of hot *sambar* (soupy lentil dish) and another of cooling coconut *chatni* (chut-ney) – are a South Indian breakfast speciality that can be eaten at any time of day, all over India. Most popular is the *masala dosa* (stuffed with spiced potatoes), but other fantastic dosa varieties include the *rava dosa* (batter made with semolina), the Mysuru *dosa* (like *masala dosa* but with more vegetables and chilli), and the *pessarettu dosa* (batter made with mung-bean dhal) from Telangana and Andhra Pradesh. Meanwhile, inventive contem-porary creations see dosas stuffed with everything from grilled paneer to chocolate sauce.

The humble *idli*, a traditional South Indian snack or breakfast, is a low-calorie alterna-tive to oil, spice and chilli. *Idlis* are spongy, round, white, fermented rice cakes that you dip in *sambar* and coconut and other *chatnis*. *Dahi idli* is an *idli* dunked in very lightly spiced yoghurt (brilliant for tender tummies). Other super southern favourites include *vadas* (doughnut-shaped deep-fried spiced lentil savouries), often served with coconut *chatni; uttapams* (thick, savoury rice pancakes with finely chopped onions, green chillies, coriander and coconut); *iddiyappams* (rice-flour string hoppers) eaten with spicy curry or coconut milk and sugar; and *appams* (light, thin, fluffy rice-flour pancakes) accompanied by coconut-infused stew. Keralan *puttu* is a popular breakfast dish of rice powder and coconut, steamed in a metal or bamboo holder and dished up with bananas or curry.

served at once. Desserts are optional and most prevalent during festivals or other special occasions. In many Indian homes, dinner can be a late affair (post 9pm) depending on personal preference and the season (eg later dinners during warmer months). Restaurants usually spring to life after 9pm in big cities, but get busy (and close) earlier in small towns.

Spiritual Sustenance

For many Indians, food is considered just as critical for fine-tuning the spirit as it is for sustaining the body. Broadly speaking, Hindus traditionally avoid foods that are thought to inhibit physical and spiritual development, although there are few hard-and-fast rules. The taboo on eating beef (the cow is holy to Hindus) is the most rigid restriction, with beef banned in Maharashtra. Jains avoid foods such as garlic, onions and potatoes, which, apart from harming insects on their extraction from the ground, are thought to heat the blood and arouse sexual desire. You may come across vegetarian restaurants that make it a point to advertise the absence of onion and garlic from their dishes for this reason. Devout Hindus may also avoid garlic and onions. These items are banned from many ashrams, too.

Some foods, such as dairy products, are considered innately pure and are eaten to cleanse the body, mind and spirit. Ayurveda, the ancient science of life, health and longevity, also influences food customs, especially in Kerala.

Pork is taboo for Muslims, and stimulants such as alcohol are avoided by the most devout. Halal is the term for all permitted foods, and haram for those prohibited. Fasting is considered an opportunity to earn the approval of Allah, wipe the sin-slate clean and understand the suffering of the poor.

Buddhists and Jains subscribe to the philosophy of ahimsa (non-violence) and are mostly vegetarian. Jainism's central tenet is ultra-vegetarianism, and rigid restrictions are in place to avoid injury to any living creature.

India's Sikh, Christian and Parsi communities have few or no restrictions on what they can eat.

Drinks, Anyone?

Alcoholic Beverages

Gujarat, Nagaland, Mizoram, Manipur and Bihar, all in the north, plus the Lakshadweep Islands off Kerala (excluding Bangaram), are India's only dry states, but there are drinking laws in place all over the country. Each state may have regular dry days when the sale of alcohol from liquor shops is banned. On Gandhi's birthday (2 October), you'll find it hard to get alcoholic drinks anywhere in India. Kerala, where alcohol consumption is estimated to be twice the national average, removed liquor licences from some 700 bars in 2014, but this controversial ban was reversed in 2017; now, three- and four-star hotels can serve liquor, two-star hotels are permitted to run beer parlours and new bars can apply for liquor licences, though the first day of each month remains a dry day. In Goa, alcohol taxes are lower and the drinking culture is less restricted.

You'll find excellent watering holes in most big cities, all at their liveliest on weekends, and Mumbai, of course, has the busiest drinking scene. Bengaluru is India's craft-beer capital, but Mumbai, Pune and, most recently, Goa have started creeping up behind with their own brew-pub scenes. More upmarket bars serve an impressive selection of domestic and imported alcohol plus draught beers. Many of South India's best bars are in flashy hotels and often turn into heaving nightclubs anytime after 8pm. In smaller towns, the bar scene is usually a seedy, male-dominated

Goan cuisine is a delicious blend of Portuguese and South Indian flavours, with lots of meats and fresh seafood. The famous, fiery vindaloo (curry in a marinade of vinegar and garlic) is a Goan favourite.

The Bangala Table: Flavors and Recipes from Chettinad, by Sumeet Nair, Meenakshi Meyyappan and Jill Donenfeld, is a gorgeous, photo-heavy recipe tome focused on southern Tamil Nadu's Chettinadu region.

New microbreweries such as Goa Brewing Co, Susegado Brewing and Bengaluru-born Arbour Brewing Co are bringing India's blossoming craft-beer scene to Goa's golden shores.

The Suriani Kitchen, by Lathika George, delves into the flavours and stories behind Kerala's Syrian Christian culinary traditions.

affair – not the kind of places thirsty female travellers will feel comfortable venturing into.

Despite India's domestic wine industry still being relatively new, wine-drinking is steadily on the rise. The favourable climate and soil conditions in certain areas – especially parts of Maharashtra and Karnataka – have spawned commendable Indian wineries like Nashik's Grover Zampa (p86) and Sula Vineyards (p86); Fratelli Wines, southeast of Pune, is another top Indian winery. Many of these Indian wines are gradually making their way onto menus across the south.

Stringent licensing laws discourage drinking in some restaurants, though places that depend on the tourist rupee may covertly serve you beer in teapots and disguised glasses – but don't assume anything, at the risk of causing offence. Very few vegetarian restaurants serve alcohol.

Home-Grown Brews

An estimated three-quarters of India's drinking population quaffs 'country liquor', such as the south's notorious arak (liquor distilled from coconut-palm sap, potatoes or rice). This is widely known as the poor-man's drink; millions are addicted to the stuff. Each year, many people are blinded, paralysed or even killed by the methyl alcohol in illegal arak.

An interesting local drink is *mahua*, a clear spirit with a heady pungent flavour, distilled from the flower of the *mahua* tree. It's brewed in makeshift village stalls all over central India during March and April, when the trees bloom. *Mahua* is safe to drink as long as it comes from a trustworthy source, but there have been plenty of cases of people being blinded after drinking *mahua* adulterated with methyl alcohol.

Toddy (sap from palm trees) is drunk in coastal areas, especially Kerala, while feni is the primo Indian spirit and the preserve of laid-back Goa. Coconut feni is light and unexceptional but the more popular cashew feni – made from cashew fruit – is worth a try.

Nonalcoholic Beverages

Peruse Mallika Badrinath's *200 South Indian Classic Vegetarian Lunch Recipes* for a taste of the south's many, deliciously varied cuisines.

Chai, the much-loved drink of the masses, is made with copious amounts of milk and sugar. A glass of steaming, frothy chai is the perfect antidote to the vicissitudes of life on the Indian road; the disembodied voice droning '*garam* chai, *garam* chai' (hot tea, hot tea) is likely to become one of the most familiar and welcome sounds of your trip. Masala chai adds cardamom, ginger and other spices.

While chai is most of India's traditional choice, South Indians have long shared their loyalty with coffee. The popular South Indian *kaapi* (filter coffee) is a combination of boiled milk, sugar and a strong decoction made from freshly ground coffee beans, often with a dash of chicory; it's poured from high up between two cups, before being presented in a stainless steel tumbler. In bigger cities, you'll find countless branches of modern coffee-house chains (Café Coffee Day, Starbucks), plus an ever-growing number of fashionable independent cafes, all serving standard international coffees. The third-wave coffee scene is particularly strong in Mumbai and Bengaluru, with cold brews, proper espresso and Chemex livening things up; Chennai and Bengaluru are also famed for their traditional South Indian brews.

Third-wave coffee has finally whirled into Mumbai with the creative, professional likes of Koinonia Coffee Roasters (www.koinoniacoffeeroasters.com) and Blue Tokai (www.bluetokaicoffee.com).

Masala soda is the quintessential Indian soft drink: a freshly opened bottle of fizzy soda, pepped up with lime, spices, salt and sugar. You can also try a plain lime soda, with fresh lime, served sweet (with sugar), salted or plain. Also refreshing is *jal jeera*, made of lime juice, cumin, mint and rock salt. Sweet and savoury lassi, a yoghurt-based drink, is another wonderfully cooling beverage, popular nationwide. *Sol kadhi*, a pink-coloured, slightly sour drink made from coconut milk, is a staple of South India's Konkan Coast (between Mumbai and Goa). *Badam* milk (hot or cold) is flavoured with almonds and saffron.

Menu Decoder

achar	pickle
aloo	potato; also *alu*
aloo gobi	potato-and-cauliflower curry
aloo tikki	mashed-potato patty
appam	South Indian rice pancake
arak	liquor distilled from coconut milk, potatoes or rice
baigan	aubergine/eggplant; also *brinjal*
barfi	fudgelike sweet made from milk
bebinca	Goan 16-layer cake
besan	chickpea flour
betel	nut of the betel tree; also areca nut
bhajia	vegetable fritters
bhang lassi	blend of lassi and bhang (a derivative of marijuana)
bhelpuri	thin, fried rounds of dough with rice, lentils, lemon juice, onion, herbs and chutney
bhindi	okra
biryani	fragrant, spiced steamed rice with meat or vegetables
bonda	mashed-potato patty
chaat	savoury snack, may be seasoned with *chaat masala*
chach	buttermilk beverage
chai	tea
channa	spiced chickpeas
chapati	round, unleavened Indian-style bread; also roti
chawal	rice
cheiku	small, sweet brown fruit
dahi	curd/yoghurt
dhal	spiced lentil dish
dhal makhani	black lentils and red kidney beans with cream and butter
dhansak	Parsi dish; meat, usually chicken or lamb, with curried lentils, pumpkin or gourd, and rice
dosa	large South Indian savoury crêpe
falooda	rose-flavoured drink made with milk, cream, nuts and vermicelli
faluda	long chickpea-flour noodles
feni	Goan liquor distilled from coconut milk or cashews
ghee	clarified butter
gobi	cauliflower
gulab jamun	deep-fried balls of dough soaked in rose-flavoured syrup
halwa	soft sweet made with vegetables, lentils, nuts or fruit
iddiyappam	rice-flour string hoppers
idli	South Indian spongy, round, fermented rice cake
imli	tamarind
jaggery	hard, brown, sugarlike sweetener made from palm sap
jalebi	orange-coloured coils of deep-fried batter dunked in sugar syrup; served hot
jigarthanda	drink made with boiled milk, almond essence, rose syrup and vanilla ice cream
karela	bitter gourd
keema	spiced minced meat
khichdi	blend of lightly spiced rice and lentils; also *khichri*

kofta	minced vegetables or meat; often ball-shaped
korma	currylike braised dish
kulcha	soft, leavened Indian-style bread
kulfi	flavoured (often with pistachio), firm-textured ice cream
ladoo	sweet ball made with gram flour and semolina; also *ladu*
lassi	yoghurt-and-iced-water drink
malai kofta	paneer cooked in a creamy sauce of cashews and tomato
masala dosa	large South Indian savoury crêpe *(dosa)* stuffed with spiced potatoes
mattar paneer	unfermented-cheese and pea curry
methi	fenugreek
mishti doi	Bengali sweet; curd sweetened with jaggery
mithai	Indian sweets
momo	savoury Tibetan dumpling
naan	tandoor-cooked flat bread
namak	salt
namkin	savoury nibbles
pakora	bite-sized vegetable pieces in batter
palak paneer	unfermented cheese chunks in a puréed spinach gravy
paneer	soft, unfermented cheese made from milk curd
pani	water
pappadam	thin, crispy lentil or chickpea-flour circle-shaped wafer; also *pappad*
paratha	(also parantha/parotta) flaky flat bread (thicker than chapati); often stuffed
pasayam	creamy rice pudding; *kheer* in nothern India
phulka	chapati that puffs up on an open flame
pilau	rice cooked in spiced stock; also *pulau, pilao* or *pilaf*
pudina	mint
puri	flat, savoury dough that puffs up when deep-fried; also *poori*
raita	mildly spiced yoghurt, often containing shredded cucumber or diced pineapple
rasam	dhal-based broth flavoured with tamarind
rasgulla	cream-cheese balls flavoured with rose water
rogan josh	rich, spicy lamb curry
saag	leafy greens
sabzi	vegetables
sambar	South Indian soupy lentil dish with cubed vegetables
samosa	deep-fried pastry triangles filled with spiced vegetables
sol kadhi	pink-coloured, slightly sour drink made from coconut milk
sonf	aniseed; used as a digestive and mouth-freshener; also *saunf*
tawa	flat hotplate/iron griddle
thukpa	Tibetan noodle soup
tiffin	snack; also refers to meal container often made of stainless steel
tikka	spiced, often marinated, chunks of chicken, paneer etc
toddy	alcoholic drink, tapped from palm trees
upma	*rava* (semolina) cooked with onions, spices, chilli peppers and coconut
uttapam	Savoury rice pancake with finely chopped onions, green chillies, coriander and coconut
vada	South Indian doughnut-shaped, deep-fried lentil savoury
vindaloo	Goan dish; fiery curry in a marinade of vinegar and garlic

The Great Indian Bazaar

South India's bazaars and shops sell a staggering range of goodies: from woodwork to shimmering silks, chunky tribal jewellery to finely embroidered shawls, sparkling gemstones to rustic village handicrafts. The array of arts and handicrafts is vast, with every area – sometimes every village – maintaining its own specialities and traditions, some of them going back centuries. Indeed, South India's shopping opportunities are as inspiring and multifarious as the region itself.

Bronze Figures, Pottery, Stone Carving & Terracotta

In southern India (and parts of the Himalaya), small bronze images of deities are created by the age-old lost-wax process. A wax figure is made, a mould is formed around it, then the wax is melted, poured out and replaced with molten metal; the mould is then broken open to reveal the figure inside. Figures of Shiva as dancing Nataraja (a tradition going back to medieval Chola times in Tamil Nadu) are the most popular, but you can also find images of numerous other Hindu gods, and images of the Buddha and Tantric deities. Don't confuse bronze (a copper-tin alloy) with brass (a cheaper copper-zinc alloy).

In Mamallapuram (Mahabalipuram) in Tamil Nadu, craftspeople using local granite and soapstone have revived the ancient artistry of Pallava sculptors, some of them using traditional hammer-and-chisel techniques; souvenirs range from tiny stone elephants to enormous half-a-tonne deity statues. Tamil Nadu is also known for bronzeware from Thanjavur (Tanjore) and Trichy (Tiruchirappalli).

A number of places produce attractive terracotta items, ranging from vases to images of deities and children's toys. In Chettinadu (southern Tamil Nadu), enormous terracotta horses and other beasts are crafted as offerings to the popular pre-Hindu deity Ayyanar.

Outside temples across India you can buy small clay or plaster effigies of Hindu deities.

State-government handicraft emporiums usually have reasonable fixed prices and good local crafts. Try Tamil Nadu's Poompuhar (http://tn poompuhar.org); Lepakshi (www. lepakshi handicrafts.gov. in) in Andhra Pradesh and Telangana; Kerala's SMSM Institute (www. keralahandicrafts. in); and Karnataka's Cauvery Handicrafts Emporium (www.cauvery handicrafts.net).

Carpets, Carpets, Carpets!

Carpet-making is a living craft in India. Workshops throughout the country produce fine wool and silkwork, though most of the finest carpets are made in the north. Most Tibetan refugee settlements have cooperative carpet workshops (there are several Tibetan refugee communities in South India, most famously at Bylakuppe, Karnataka). 'Antique' carpets usually aren't antique, unless you buy from an internationally reputable dealer; stick to 'new' carpets.

Coarsely woven woollen *namdas* (*numdas*) from Kashmir and Rajasthan are much cheaper than knotted carpets. Various regions manufacture flat-weave *dhurries* (kilim-like cotton rugs); Warangal in Telangana is one of the south's main centres. Puducherry (Pondicherry) and Bengaluru (Bangalore) are other South India carpet producers.

The glossy, vibrant tiles that adorn mansions and hotels in Tamil Nadu's dry Chettinadu region are a local speciality, particularly those made in the village of Athangudi.

Note that children have been employed as carpet weavers in the sub-continent for centuries. Child labour maintains a cycle of poverty, driving down adult wages, reducing adult work opportunities and depriving children of education. Carpets produced by Tibetan refugee cooperatives are almost always made by adults. Government emporiums and charitable cooperatives are usually best for buying.

Costs & Shipping

The price of a carpet is determined by the number and the size of the hand-tied knots, the range of dyes and colours, the intricacy of the design and the material. Silk carpets cost more and look more luxurious, but wool carpets usually last longer. Expect to pay upward of US$200 for a 90cm by 1.8m traditional wool carpet, and around US$2000 for a similar-sized silk carpet. A Tibetan carpet of the same size costs around ₹10,500.

Many places ship carpets home for you, although it may be safest to send them independently to avoid scams. Shipping for a 90cm by 1.8m carpet costs around ₹4000 to Europe and ₹4500 to the USA. You can also carry carpets as check-in baggage on a plane (allow 5kg to 10kg of your baggage allowance for the above carpet; check your airline allows oversize baggage).

Jewellery

Virtually every Indian town has at least one bangle shop with an extraordinary range, from colourful plastic and glass bracelets to brass, silver and gold creations. In Telangana, Hyderabad is a centre for bangles made from lac (a resinous insect secretion), encrusted with colourful beads or stones.

Heavy folk-art silver jewellery can be bought in various parts of India, as can chunky Tibetan jewellery made from silver (or white metal) and semiprecious stones. Many Tibetan pieces feature Buddhist motifs and text in Tibetan script, including the famous mantra *Om Mani Padme Hum* (Hail to the Jewel in the Lotus). However, there's a huge industry in India, Nepal and China making artificially aged Tibetan souvenirs. Loose beads of agate, turquoise, carnelian and silver are also widely available. In South India's Western Ghats, you might encounter rare jewellery crafted by local indigenous communities, such as the Todas near Ooty (Udhagamandalam).

Pearls are produced by most Indian seaside states, but they're a particular speciality of Hyderabad, home to 30,000 pearl dealers (though Hyderabadi pearls are usually imported, these days mostly from China). Prices vary depending on colour and shape: you pay more for pure white pearls or rare colours such as black, and perfectly round pearls are more expensive than misshapen or elongated pearls. A single strand of seeded pearls can cost as little as ₹500, but better-quality pearls cost upward of ₹1200 (the finest can fetch ₹30,000!).

Beware of scammers asking you to buy jewels and resell them overseas to a particular buyer – the jewels are often fake, or the buyer they were intended for never shows up.

South India's bazaars, the heart and soul of its commercial life, are usually a street lined with shops and/ or stalls, rather than a separate trading area.

Paintings

India has a sizeable contemporary-art scene, and major Southern cities such as Chennai, Bengaluru, Kochi (Cochin) and Hyderabad host many independent galleries and shops selling work by local artists.

Miniatures

Reproductions of Indian miniature paintings are widely available, but quality varies: the cheaper ones have less detail and are made with inferior materials. A bigger range of quality miniatures is generally found in northern India than in the south, but state-run craft emporiums and antique shops are always worth a browse.

In southern regions such as Kerala and Tamil Nadu, you'll come across miniature paintings on leaf skeletons that portray domestic life, rural scenes and deities.

Tanjore Paintings

Tamil Nadu's famous Thanjavur (Tanjore) paintings typically depict Hindu deities in bright colours with gold foil and glass beads, or occasionally gemstones. They may be done on canvas, wood or glass. Much of today's output is a somewhat kitschified version of a venerable tradition that goes back to at least the 17th century, but it's worth keeping an eye open for originals in local antique shops.

Folk Art & Kalamkari

Telangana's *cheriyal* scroll painting (in bright, primary colours and originally created for travelling storytellers) is a celebrated 500-year-old, though sadly disappearing, art. Nakashi masks are also made here, from decorated coconut shells or concrete.

The ancient textile-painting art of *kalamkari* is practised in Andhra Pradesh, where Sri Kalahasti is the best place to see artists at work and buy their art, and at Chennai's Kalakshetra Foundation (p341), which offers *kalamkari* courses. It involves priming cotton cloth with resin and cow's milk, then drawing and painting deities or legendary or historic events with a pointed bamboo stick *(kalam)* dipped in fermented jaggery and water; dyes are made from cow dung, ground seeds, plants and flowers. *Kalamkari* from Machilipatnam, also in Andhra Pradesh, employs block-printing in combination with freehand drawing.

Be cautious when buying items that include international delivery, and avoid being led to shops by smooth-talking touts, but don't worry about too much else – except your luggage allowance!

THE ART OF HAGGLING

Government emporiums, fair-trade cooperatives, department stores and modern shopping centres almost always charge fixed prices. Almost anywhere else you need to bargain. Shopkeepers in tourist hubs are accustomed to travellers who have lots of money and little time to spend it, so you may be charged double or triple the going rate.

The first 'rule' of haggling is to never show too much interest in the item you've got your heart set upon. Second, resist purchasing the first thing that takes your fancy. Wander around several shops and price items, but don't make it too obvious: if you return to the first shop, the vendor will know it's because they are the cheapest (resulting in less haggling leeway).

Decide how much you would be happy paying, then express a casual interest in buying. If you have absolutely no idea of the going rate, a common approach is to start by slashing the price by half. The vendor will, most likely, look aghast, but you can now work up and down respectively in small increments until you reach a mutually agreeable price. Many shopkeepers lower their 'final price' if you head out of the shop saying you'll 'think about it'.

Haggling is a way of life in India and usually taken in good spirit. It should never turn ugly. Always keep in mind how much a rupee is worth in your home currency, and how much you'd pay for the item back home, to put things in perspective. If you're not sure of the 'right' price for an item, think about how much it is worth to you; the idea is to reach a price you can agree on, not necessarily a bargain-basement rate. If a vendor seems to be charging an unreasonably high price, look elsewhere. You'll usually get a better rate if you buy multiple items at the same time.

Thangkas

Tibetan craft shops often sell beautiful *thangkas* (rectangular Tibetan cloth paintings) depicting Tantric Buddhist deities and ceremonial mandalas. Some re-create the glory of murals in India's medieval gompas (Tibetan Buddhist monasteries); others are simpler. Prices vary, but expect to pay at least ₹5000 for a decent-quality A3-size *thangka*, and a lot more (up to around ₹50,000) for large intricate *thangkas*.

Textiles

Textile production is India's major industry. Around 40% takes place at village level, where the cloth produced is known as *khadi* (homespun cloth, usually cotton) – hence the government-backed *khadi* emporiums around the country. These inexpensive superstores sell all sorts of items made from *khadi*, including the popular Nehru jackets and kurta pyjamas (long shirt and loose-fitting trousers), with sales benefiting rural communities. *Khadi* has recently become increasingly chic, with Indian designers such as Sandeep Khosla referencing and incorporating the fabrics in their collections.

In tourist centres such as Goa, Kerala, Rajasthan and Himachal Pradesh, patterned textiles are made into shoulder bags, wall hangings, cushion covers, bedspreads, clothes, yoga-mat bags and more. Items made by the Adivasi (tribal) peoples of Telangana, Gujarat and Rajasthan often have small pieces of mirrored glass embroidered on to them.

The Chennamangalam area (p311) in central Kerala is known for its traditional handloom weaving industry, which was seriously damaged by the devastating 2018 floods.

Shawls

Indian shawls are famously warm and lightweight. It's worth buying one to use as a blanket on cold night journeys. Shawls are made from all sorts of wool; many are embroidered with intricate designs. The best-known varieties all come from northern India but some make their way to outlets in the south, including Kashmiri *pashmina* (made from the downy hair of the pashmina goat and subtly embroidered and mirrored lambswool shawls from Gujarat's Kachchh (Kutch) region. Authentic *pashmina* shawls cost several thousand rupees, though many *'pashminas'* are actually a *pashmina*-silk blend, which means they're cheaper (around ₹1200) but still beautiful.

Saris

Saris are a very popular souvenir, especially as they can be easily adapted to other purposes (from cushion covers to skirts). Real silk saris are the most expensive; the silk usually needs to be washed before it becomes soft. India's 'silk capital' is Kanchipuram in Tamil Nadu (Kanchipuram silk is also widely available in Chennai), but you can also find fine silk saris (and cheaper scarves) in other centres including Mysuru (Mysore). You'll pay upward of ₹3000 for a quality embroidered silk sari.

Aurangabad, in Maharashtra, is the traditional producer of Himroo shawls, sheets and saris, made from a blend of cotton, silk and metallic thread. Silk and gold-thread saris produced at Paithan (near Aurangabad) are some of India's finest; prices range from around ₹8000 to a mind-blowing ₹300,000. Madhya Pradesh is famous for its cotton Maheshwari saris and silk Chanderi saris, while Chettinadu (Tamil Nadu) is known for its handwoven silk-and-cotton Kandaangi saris.

Patan in Gujarat is the centre for the ancient, laborious craft of Patolamaking: every thread in these splendid silk saris is individually hand-dyed before weaving, and patterned borders are woven with real gold.

Indian Textiles (John Gillow and Nicholas Barnard) explores the cultural background of India's many beautiful textile techniques, including weaving, block-printing, painting, tie-dye and embroidery, and details products by regions.

Ever bigger, brighter and flashier, modern malls are an integral part of the South Indian city shopping scene. They're full of Indian and international fashion, with prices similar to those in the Western world. Lulu Mall in Kochi, Kerala, is India's largest.

Appliqué & Block Print

Appliqué, where decorative motifs are sewn on to a larger cloth, is an ancient art in India, with most states producing their own version, often featuring abstract or anthropomorphic patterns. Traditional lampshades and *pandals* (marquees) used in weddings and festivals are usually produced using this technique.

Block-printed and woven textiles are made and sold by fabric shops all over India: each region has its own speciality. Block-printing involves stamping the design on the fabric with carved wooden blocks – a laborious, highly skilled process that produces beautiful results. India-wide retail chains Fabindia (www.fabindia.com) and Anokhi (www.anokhi. com) strive to preserve traditional patterns and fabrics, transforming them into home-decor items and Indian- and Western-style fashions.

Throughout South India you'll find finely crafted gold and silver rings, anklets, earrings, toe rings, necklaces and bangles; pieces can often be made to order.

THE GREAT INDIAN BAZAAR LEATHERWORK

Leatherwork

As cows are sacred in India, leatherwork is, in theory, made from the skin of buffaloes, camels, goats or other animals. Most large cities offer smart, modern leather footwear at reasonable prices, some stitched with zillions of sparkly sequins. Jootis (traditional, often pointy-toed, slip-in shoes) from the northern states of Punjab and Rajasthan can be found in South India.

Chappals, those curly-toed leather sandals, are sold throughout India, but the Maharashtrian cities of Kolhapur, Pune and Matheran are particularly famous for them. Tamil Nadu is a big leather producer, while Puducherry is known for its international-influenced leather creations.

Cow slaughter (for consumption, leatherwork or anything else) is illegal in most of India, and some states, such as Maharashtra, have also banned the killing of bulls and bullocks, but discerning travellers will want to be aware that India's leather industry is rife with reports of malpractice and involves complex, unsettling animal-welfare issues.

Metalware

You'll find copper and brassware throughout India. Candle holders, trays, bowls, tankards and ashtrays are popular buys.

In all Indian towns you can find *kadhai* (Indian woks, also known as *balti*) and other cookware for incredibly low prices. Beaten-brass pots are particularly attractive, while steel storage vessels, copper-bottomed cooking pans and steel thali trays are also popular souvenirs.

PUTTING YOUR MONEY WHERE IT COUNTS

Overall, a comparatively small proportion of the money brought to India by tourism reaches people in rural areas. Travellers can make a greater contribution by shopping at community cooperatives, set up to protect and promote traditional cottage industries, and to provide education, training and a sustainable livelihood at the grassroots level. Many of these projects focus on low-caste women, tribal people, refugees and others living on society's fringes.

The quality of products sold at cooperatives is high and prices are usually fixed, so you won't have to haggle. A share of the sales money is channelled directly into social projects such as schools, health care, training and other advocacy programmes for socially disadvantaged groups. Shopping at the national network of Khadi & Village Industries Commission emporiums (www.kvic.org.in), or the shops of Tribes India (http://tribes india.com), the profits of which help support tribal artisans, also contributes to rural communities. Popular fashion brand Fabindia (www.fabindia.com) is also known for working sustainably with villagers.

Wherever you travel, keep your eyes peeled for fair-trade cooperatives.

GANDHI'S CLOTH

A century ago, Mohandas Gandhi urged Indians to support the freedom movement by ditching their foreign-made clothing and turning to *khadi* (homespun cloth). *Khadi* became a symbol of Indian independence, and the fabric is still closely associated with politics. The government-run, nonprofit group Khadi & Village Industries Commission (www. kvic.org.in) serves to promote *khadi*, which is usually cotton, but can also be silk or wool.

Khadi outlets are simple, no-nonsense places where you can pick up genuine Indian clothing such as kurta pyjamas, headscarves, saris and, at some branches, assorted handicrafts – you'll find them all over India. Prices are reasonable and often discounted in the period around Gandhi's birthday (2 October). A number of outlets also have tailoring services.

Many Tibetan religious objects are created by inlaying silver in copper: prayer wheels and traditional document cases are inexpensive purchases.

The people of Bastar in Chhattisgarh use an iron-smelting technique similar to one discovered 35,000 years ago to create abstract sculptures of spindly animal and human figures. These are often also made into functional items such as lamp stands and coat racks, and are found in tribal-crafts shops around India.

Bidri, a damascening method where silver wire is inlaid in gunmetal (a zinc alloy) and rubbed with a paste incorporating soil from Bidar (Karnataka), is used for jewellery, boxes, bowls and ornaments, particularly in Bidar itself and Hyderabad; it's believed to date back to the 14th century.

Musical Instruments

Quality Indian musical instruments are mostly available in larger cities; prices vary according to quality and sound.

Decent tabla sets – a pair of hand drums comprising a wooden tabla (tuned treble drum) and a metal *dugi* or *bayan* (bass drum) – cost upward of ₹5000. Cheaper sets are generally heavier and often sound inferior.

Sitars range from ₹5000 to ₹35,000 (possibly even more). The sound of each sitar will vary with the wood used and the shape of the gourd, so try a few. Note that some cheaper sitars can warp in colder or hotter climates. On any sitar, make sure the strings ring clearly and check the gourd carefully for damage. Spare string sets, sitar plectrums and a screw-in 'amplifier' gourd are sensible additions.

Other popular instruments include the *shehnai* (Indian flute), the sarod (like an Indian lute), the harmonium and the *esraj* (similar to an upright violin). Conventional violins are great value, starting at around ₹3500.

India-Craft (www. india-crafts.com) is a handy online resource packed with detail about the subcontinent's many varied handicrafts, from textiles to terracotta.

Woodcarving

Woodcarving is an ancient art form throughout India. Sandalwood carvings of Hindu deities are one of Karnataka's specialities, with high prices to match: a 10cm-high Ganesh costs around ₹2500 in sandalwood (which releases fragrance for years), compared to roughly ₹300 in kadamb wood. Beautiful deity figures and decorative inlaid boxes and furniture are carved from rosewood in Andhra Pradesh, Karnataka and Kerala.

Buddhist woodcarvings are a speciality of Tibetan refugee areas – including wall plaques of the eight lucky signs, carved dragons and reproductions of *chaam* masks used for ritual dances.

On the Papier Mâché Trail

Artisans in Jammu and Kashmir have been producing lacquered papier mâché for centuries, and papier mâché–ware is now sold across India, making inexpensive yet beautiful gifts. The basic shape is made in a mould from layers of paper (often recycled newsprint), then painted with fine brushes and lacquered for protection. Prices depend on design complexity and quality and the amount of gold leaf used. Many pieces feature patterns of animals and flowers, or hunting scenes from Mughal miniature paintings. Products include papier mâché bowls, boxes, coasters, trays, lamps, puppets and Christmas decorations. Colourful Rajasthani puppets and Tamil Nadu dolls are other Indian papier mâché specialities.

Other Great Finds

Every South India town has shops and bazaars selling locally made spices at great prices. Karnataka, Kerala, Uttar Pradesh, Rajasthan and Tamil Nadu produce most of the spices that go into garam masala (the 'hot mix' used to flavour Indian dishes), while Keralan cardamom and black pepper are also prime buys. Note that some countries have stringent rules regarding the import of animal and plant products.

Attar (essential oil, mostly made from flowers) can be found around the country. Mysuru, in Karnataka, is famous for its sandalwood oil, while Mumbai is a major centre for the trade of traditional fragrances, including valuable *oud,* made from a rare mould that grows on the bark of the agarwood tree. In Tamil Nadu, Ooty and Kodaikanal (Kodai) produce aromatic and medicinal oils from herbs, flowers and eucalyptus.

Indian incense is exported worldwide, with Karnataka's Bengaluru and Mysuru being major producers. Incense, as well as clothing, essential oils and perfumed candles, from Auroville in Tamil Nadu and Sri Aurobindo Ashram (p364) in Puducherry is also renowned and easy to find locally.

A Goan speciality is feni: a head-spinning spirit distilled from coconut milk or cashews that often comes in decorative bottles.

Quality Indian tea and coffee is grown and sold in parts of South India, such as Munnar in Kerala and the Ooty area in Tamil Nadu's Western Ghats. There are also top tea retailers in urban hubs.

Thanjavur in Tamil Nadu is famed for its brightly painted bobble-head dolls, made from terracotta or wood.

Fine-quality handmade paper – often fashioned into cards, boxes and notebooks – is worth seeking out, especially in Puducherry and Mumbai.

South Indian cities have good, reasonably priced bookshops. Higginbothams (p349) in Chennai, in business since 1844, is India's oldest bookshop and still going strong; it also has a Bengaluru branch, plus the Writer's Cafe (p346) in Chennai. Kochi hosts two well-known age-old bookshops: Idiom (p308) and **Walton's** (☏9995955915; www.waltons homestay.com; Princess St, Fort Cochin; r incl breakfast ₹1700, with AC ₹2100; ✱☏).

Among the tribal communities of Tamil Nadu's Nilgiri Hills, the embroidery-skilled Todas make, wear and sell unique, beautiful black-and-red-embroidered shawls.

THE GREAT INDIAN BAZAAR ON THE PAPIER MÂCHÉ TRAIL

The Arts

Over the millenniums India's many ethnic groups have spawned a rich artistic heritage, and today you'll experience art both lofty and humble around every corner: from intricately painted trucks to harmonic chanting emanating from ancient temples and booming Bollywood blockbusters blasting on long-distance buses. The wealth of creative expression is a highlight of travelling in South India, and today's artists fuse ancient and modern influences to create works of art, dance, literature and music as evocative as they are beautiful.

Dance

Pioneers of modern dance forms in India include Uday Shankar (older brother of the sitar master, Ravi Shankar), who once partnered the Russian ballerina Anna Pavlova.

The ancient Indian art of dance is traditionally linked to mythology and classical literature. Dance can be divided into two main forms: classical and folk. The dance you'll most commonly see, though, is in films; dance has featured in Indian movies since the dawn of 'talkies' and often combines traditional, folk, modern and contemporary choreography.

Classical

Classical dance is based on well-defined traditional disciplines. Of India's eight schools of classical dance, these are the ones you're most likely to encounter in South India.

➤ *Bharatanatyam*, which originated in Tamil Nadu, has been embraced throughout India. Noted for its graceful movements, it was traditionally performed by solo women, but now often includes male dancers and/or group performances. Songs, poems, prayers and Carnatic (characteristic of South India) music are part of the performance.

➤ Kathakali, with its roots in Kerala (possibly around the 17th century), is a classical dance-drama with drum and vocal accompaniment, based on the Hindu epics. It usually stars an all-male cast, though there's now the odd female Kathakali artist.

➤ Kuchipudi is a 17th-century dance-drama that originated in the Andhra Pradesh village from which it takes its name. The story centres on the envious wife of Krishna.

➤ *Mohiniyattam*, the 'dance of the enchantress', is a graceful Keralan form performed by solo women.

Folk

Most big South Indian cities have venues staging regular classical dance or music performances, but Chennai and Mumbai have the most frequent performances (almost nightly). Kochi is the best place to catch Kathakali performances.

Indian folk dance is widespread and varied, ranging from the theatrical dummy-horse dances of Karnataka and Tamil Nadu to Punjab's high-spirited bhangra dance. Northern Kerala's *theyyam* rituals feature wild drumming and frenzied dancing by participants embodying deities or heroes, with bold make-up and headdresses sometimes several metres high.

Music

Indian classical music traces its roots back to Vedic times, when religious poems chanted by priests were first collated in the Rig-Veda. Over the millenniums classical music has been shaped by many influences, and

CLASSICAL DANCE & MUSIC FESTIVALS

➡ Mamallapuram Dance Festival (p336) Tamil Nadu; December/January

➡ Chennai Festival of Music & Dance (p336); December/January

➡ Mumbai Sanskruti (p47); January

➡ Thyagaraja Aradhana (p336) Thiruvaiyuru, Tamil Nadu; January

➡ Natyanjali Dance Festival (p336) Chidambaram, Tamil Nadu; February

➡ Elephanta Festival (p47) Mumbai; February

➡ Deccan Festival (p236) Hyderabad; February/March

the legacy today is Carnatic and Hindustani (the classical style of North India) music. With common origins, they share a number of features. Composition and improvisation are both based on the raga (the melodic shape of the music) and the *tala* (the rhythmic metre characterised by the number of beats); *tintal*, for example, has a *tala* of 16 beats. The audience follows the *tala* by clapping at the appropriate beat, which in *tintal* is at beats one, five and 13. The ninth beat is the *khali* (empty section), indicated by a wave of the hand.

Both Carnatic and Hindustani music are performed by small ensembles, generally comprising three to six musicians, and both have many instruments in common. The most obvious difference is Carnatic's greater use of voice. Hindustani has been more heavily influenced by Persian musical conventions (a result of Mughal rule); Carnatic music, as it developed in South India, cleaves more closely to theory.

One of the best-known Indian instruments is the sitar (a large stringed instrument), with which the soloist plays the raga. Ravi Shankar, master of the sitar, is generally praised as the 20th century's most influential Hindustani classical musician, bringing sitar-playing to the international stage in the 1960s. Other stringed instruments include the sarod (which is plucked) and the *sarangi* (played with a bow). Also popular is the tabla (twin drums), which provides the *tala*. The drone, which runs on two basic notes, is provided by the oboelike *shehnai* or the stringed *tampura* (also spelt tamboura). The hand-pumped keyboard harmonium is used as a secondary melody instrument for vocal music.

Indian regional folk music is widespread and varied. Wandering musicians, magicians, snake charmers and storytellers often use song to entertain their audiences; the storyteller usually sings the tales from the great epics.

You might also come across *qawwali* (Sufi devotional singing), typically performed over several hours in mosques or at musical concerts, especially in Hyderabad. Aimed at achieving a state of spiritual ecstasy, this art dates back to the 13th century and is centred on improvisation, with a lead singer supported by other vocalists and harmonium and tabla players, all sitting cross-legged on the floor.

A completely different genre altogether, filmi (music from films) includes modern, slower-paced love serenades along with hyperactive, impeccably choreographed dance songs, usually performed by lip-synching actors.

Painting

South India's earliest art was painted on cave walls, or etched on to rocky outcrops (as in the petroglyphs recently unearthed on Maharashtra's Konkan Coast), but painting reached its supreme expression around 1500 years ago when artists covered the walls and ceilings of the Ajanta Caves (p95), in Maharashtra, with scenes from the Buddha's past lives.

The prolific Bengali writer and artist Rabindranath Tagore won the Nobel Prize in Literature in 1913 for *Gitanjali*. For a taste of Tagore's work, read *Selected Short Stories*.

Kerala's increasingly popular and reputed Kochi–Muziris Biennale (http://kochi muzirisbiennale. org) sees a feast of contemporary art sweep across Kochi's heritage buildings.

Industry estimates show that India produces an astonishing 1500 to 2500 films a year – more than anywhere else on the planet. Apart from hundreds of millions of local Bolly-, Tolly- and Kollywood buffs, there are millions of Non-Resident Indian (NRI) fans, who have catapulted Indian cinema on to the international stage.

The figures are endowed with an unusual freedom and grace. Later, painters also decorated the walls of temples and palaces, though little of this mural art has survived from before the time of the Vijayanagar empire (14th to 16th centuries), which left fine frescoes at Hampi's Virupaksha Temple (p214).

The Indo-Persian painting style, coupling geometric design with flowing form, developed in Islamic royal courts, with some indigenous influences. Persian influence blossomed when artisans fled to India following the 1507 Uzbek attack on Herat (in present-day Afghanistan), and with trade and gift-swapping between Shiraz, a Persian centre for miniature production, and Indian provincial sultans. The most celebrated Indo-Persian art developed at the Mughal court in northern India from the mid-16th century, particularly under emperor Akbar (r 1556–1605). The Mughal style, often in colourful miniature form, largely depicts court life, architecture, battle and hunting scenes, as well as detailed portraits.

Miniature painting also flourished in the Deccan sultanates of the 16th and 17th centuries. The landscapes and floral backgrounds here reflect Persian influence, though Deccani in subject matter, while the elongated figures draw on Vijayanagar traditions. Colours are rich, with much use of gold and white.

Temple mural painting, on multifarious historical and mythological themes, continued to flourish in the south: there are fine Nayak-era frescoes at Thanjavur, (p378) Kumbakonam (p376) and Chidambaram (p374) in Tamil Nadu. Superb Hindu-myth murals were painted at Kochi's Mattancherry Palace (p299) in the 16th century.

A unique local South Indian art known as Thanjavur (Tanjore) painting took root in Thanjavur from the 17th century, typically depicting Krishna and other Hindu deities in bright colours, against a background of thrones, curtains and arches which, along with the deities' clothing, are picked out in gold leaf studded with gemstones or glass beads. This tradition lives on today, largely in a somewhat debased, kitsch form.

Kerala's Ravi Varma (1848–1906) popularised oil painting with colourful, European-style treatments of scenes from Indian mythology and literature, including depictions of Hindu goddesses modelled on South Indian women, and has had a huge influence on subsequent religious art and movie posters. Maharashtra's Maqbool Fida Husain (1915–2011), India's major post-Independence artist, was famed for his often controversial modified cubist works, among them representations of naked Hindu gods.

The Madras Movement, whose cooperative base you can visit at Cholamandal Artists' Village (p353) near Chennai, pioneered modern art in South India in the 1960s. In the 21st century, paintings by modern and contemporary Indian artists have been selling at record numbers (and prices) around the world. Delhi and Mumbai are India's contemporary-art centres, but most large cities have worthwhile galleries.

Cinema

India's film industry was born in the late 19th century – the first major Indian-made motion picture, *Panorama of Calcutta*, was screened in 1899. India's first real feature film, *Raja Harishchandra*, was made during the silent era in 1913 and it's ultimately from this film that Indian cinema traces its vibrant lineage.

Today, India's film industry is the biggest in the world. Mumbai, the Hindi-language film capital, aka 'Bollywood', is the biggest name, but India's other major film-producing cities – Chennai (Kollywood), Hyderabad (Tollywood) and Bengaluru (Sandalwood) – also have a huge output. In fact, South Indian audiences tend to prefer films in regional

Shot on a shoestring budget by Dalit director Nagraj Manjule, anti-Bollywood *Sairat* (2016) tells the heart-wrenchingly realistic story of doomed intercaste love between an upper-caste girl and a fisherman's son. To date, it is the highest-grossing film in Marathi cinema history.

languages, rather than Bollywood's Hindi. In recent years, there has also been a surge in the number of films produced in Goa. Big-budget films are often partly or entirely shot abroad, with some countries vigorously wooing Indian production companies because of the spin-off tourism these films can generate.

Broadly speaking, there are two categories of Indian films. Most prominent is the mainstream 'masala' movie, named for its 'spice mix' of elements for every member of the family – romance, action, slapstick humour and moral themes. Three hours and still running, these often tear-jerking blockbusters are packed with dramatic twists interspersed with numerous song-and-dance performances. There's no explicit sex in Indian films made for the local market; even kissing is rare. Instead, it's all about intense flirting and loaded innuendo; heroines are often seen in skimpy or body-hugging attire.

The second genre is art house, or parallel cinema, which adopts Indian 'reality' as its base and aims to be socially and politically relevant. Usually made on infinitely smaller budgets than their commercial cousins, these films are the ones that win kudos at global film festivals. The late Bengali director Satyajit Ray (1921–1992), most famous for his 1950s work, is considered the father of Indian art films.

Literature

India has a long tradition of Sanskrit literature, and works in the vernacular languages have also contributed to a particularly rich legacy. In fact, it's claimed that there are as many literary traditions in India as there are written languages. The Tamil poetic works known as the Sangams, written between the 3rd century BC and 3rd century AD, are the earliest known South Indian literature.

Bengal is traditionally credited with producing some of India's finest literature, and Rabindranath Tagore (1861–1941) was the first Indian writer to really propel India's cultural richness on to the world literary stage, through the fiction, plays and poetry he wrote in Bengali.

One of the earliest Indian authors to receive an international audience was RK Narayan, who wrote in English in the 1930s and whose deceptively simple writing about life in a fictional South Indian town called Malgudi is subtly hilarious. Keralan Kamala Das (Kamala Suraiyya) wrote poetry and memoirs in English; her frank approach to love and sexuality broke ground for women writers in the 1960s and '70s.

India has an ever-growing list of internationally acclaimed contemporary authors. Winners of the prestigious Man Booker Prize have included Chennai-bred Aravind Adiga (2008), for his debut novel *The White Tiger*, set between Bengaluru (Bangalore) and northern India, and Kiran Desai (2006) for *The Inheritance of Loss*. Desai's mother Anita Desai has thrice made the Booker shortlist, as has Rohinton Mistry, a Mumbai-bred Parsi, with three novels all set in Mumbai. Kolkata- (Calcutta-) born Amitav Ghosh's *Sea of Poppies* (the first in his *Ibis Trilogy*) was shortlisted for the 2008 Booker. In 1997 Keralan Arundhati Roy won the Booker for *The God of Small Things*, set in a small Keralan town, while Mumbai-born Salman Rushdie took this coveted award in 1981 for *Midnight's Children*, which also won the Booker of Bookers award in 1993. Roy's second novel, *The Ministry of Utmost Happiness*, published in 2017, made the Booker longlist.

THE ARTS LITERATURE

Bengaluru's annual Literature Festival draws Indian and international writers and musicians to the techie Karnataka capital each year.

A Telugu–Tamil Hyderabad-produced venture, fantasy epic *Baahubali 2: The Conclusion* smashed all box-office records in 2017, becoming the highest-grossing Indian film of all time (US$250 million). Shining the spotlight on southern film beyond Bollywood, it was written by KV Vijayendra Prasad and directed by his son SS Rajamouli.

Architectural Splendour

From lofty temple gateways adorned with rainbows of delicately carved deities to whitewashed cubelike village houses, South India has a fascinatingly rich architectural heritage. Traditional buildings often have a superb sense of placement within their local environment, whether perched on a boulder-strewn hill or hidden in the depths of a frenzied city. British bungalows with corrugated-iron roofs linger in most hill stations, but most memorable are the buildings that beautifully blend European and Indian architecture, such as Mysuru Palace (p188).

Sacred Creations

Temples

Discover more about India's diverse temple architecture (in addition to other temple-related information and recommendations) at insightful Temple Net (www.templenet.com).

Throughout India, most early large-scale architecture was not built but excavated. Buddhist, Hindu and Jain temples, shrines and monasteries were carved out of solid rock or developed from existing caves at various times between the 3rd century BC and 10th century AD. Outstanding rock-cut architecture in South India includes Maharashtra's awe-inspiring Ajanta (p95) and Ellora (p92) Caves, the World Heritage-listed temples and carvings (p355) of Mamallapuram (Mahabalipuram) in Tamil Nadu, Mumbai's (Bombay's) Elephanta Island cave temples (p54), Karnataka's Badami (p221) cave temples, and Andhra Pradesh's Buddhist complex Guntupalli (p252).

It was during the Gupta period in North India (4th to 6th century AD) that the first free-standing temples were built, to enshrine Hindu deities. The Badami Chalukyas of Karnataka took up the idea at Aihole and Pattadakal between the 4th and 8th centuries, as did the Pallavas of Tamil Nadu at Kanchipuram and Mamallapuram in the 8th century. Towers called *vimanas* on southern temples were equivalent to the *sikhara* towers of North Indian temples. The three great 11th- and 12th-century Chola temples at Thanjavur (Tanjore; p378) and outside Kumbakonam, with enormous *vimanas* rising above their central shrines, represent the apogee of early southern temple architecture. In many later southern temples, tall, sculpture-encrusted entrance towers called *gopurams* replaced *vimanas* as the main architectural feature. Madurai's Meenakshi Amman Temple (p389), in Tamil Nadu, with its 12 sky-reaching *gopurams*, is reckoned to be the peak of South Indian temple architecture. Also typical of what has become known as the Dravidian temple style is the *mandapa*, a pavilion of often richly carved columns that serves as a meeting hall or approach to the central shrine.

The Hoysala empire based in southern Karnataka in the 12th and 13th centuries developed a distinctive style of temples covered in elaborate, detailed carving, with relatively low *vimanas*, as seen at Belur, Halebid and Somnathpur. The mighty 14th-to-16th-century Vijayanagar empire took the *gopuram* and *mandapa* to some of their finest levels not only at the capital, Karnataka's Hampi, but also at Trichy's (Tiruchirappalli's) Sri Ranganathaswamy Temple (p382) in Tamil Nadu.

Holy Squares & Purifying Waters

For Hindus, the square is a perfect shape, and southern temples often take the form of several square (or rectangular) compounds of diminishing size nested one inside another. Complex rules govern the location, design and building of temples, based on numerology, astrology, astronomy and religious principles. Essentially, a temple represents a map of the universe. At the centre is the *garbhagriha* (inner sanctum), symbolic of the 'womb-cave' from which the universe is believed to have emerged. This provides a residence for the deity to which the temple is dedicated.

Commonly used for ritual bathing and religious ceremonies, as well as adding aesthetic appeal to places of worship, temple tanks have long been a focal point of temple activity. These often vast, angular, engineered reservoirs of water, sometimes fed by rain, sometimes fed by rivers (via complicated drainage systems), serve both sacred and secular purposes. The waters of some temple tanks are believed to have healing properties; others are said to wash away sins.

Islamic Monuments

Muslim rule over much of northern India from the late 12th century, extending later to the Deccan, saw typical Islamic forms such as domes, arches and minaret towers dominate monumental architecture. Karnataka's 15th-century Bahmani Tombs (p227) at Bidar are among the earliest major Islamic monuments on the Deccan. They were followed by the great 16th- and 17th-century Qutb Shahi monuments of Hyderabad and Golconda – magnificent big-domed royal tombs (p235), which are now being systematically restored and have been nominated for World Heritage Status, a huge mosque (p232) and a unique mosque-landmark, the Charminar (p231) – as well as Vijapura's (Bijapur's) wonderful 17th-century mausoleum, the Golgumbaz (p224). The latter was completed in Karnataka just a few years after Mughal architecture in northern India achieved its peak of perfection in the Taj Mahal. In Maharashtra, Aurangabad's Bibi-qa-Maqbara (p89), or the poor man's Taj, also dates from the 17th century.

Churches & Cathedrals

Most of India's estimated 27.8 million Christians reside in South India, and the extended presence of European colonialists here engendered a wealth of majestic churches. According to legend, Christianity was introduced to India through Kerala in AD 52 by St Thomas the Apostle, who was martyred at St Thomas Mount (p337), Chennai, and buried at what is now the city's 19th-century neo-Gothic San Thome Cathedral (p337). Chennai's Portuguese-built 1516 Luz Church (p342) is one of India's most ancient churches.

Thanks to the Portuguese (who controlled Goa from the 16th century until 1961), it is Goa that famously takes South Indian church architecture to its finest heights. Sporting sumptuous interiors, Goa's late-Renaissance- and baroque-inspired churches are typically made of whitewashed laterite. You'll find some of the best in Old Goa, including the celebrated 1605 Basilica de Bom Jesus (p126). Goa is also known for its Portuguese Manueline church architecture, exemplified by Old Goa's **Church of Our Lady of the Rosary** (⊗8am-5pm).

In Kerala (controlled variously by the Portuguese, Dutch and British), Kochi's (Cochin's) impressive collection of churches includes 19th-century Santa Cruz Basilica (p298) and 16th-century St Francis Church (p297), India's oldest European-built church – and the original burial spot of Portuguese voyager Vasco da Gama (his remains were later moved to Lisbon).

The basic elements of mosque layout are similar worldwide. A large hall is dedicated to communal prayer; within is the mihrab, a niche indicating the direction of Mecca. Outside is often a courtyard with a pool or fountain for ritual preprayer ablutions. The faithful are called to prayer from minarets.

Mumbai's elegant Mumbaikar-built art deco and fantastical British-era Victorian neo-Gothic architectural creations were inscribed on Unesco's World Heritage list in mid-2018.

ARCHITECTURAL SPLENDOUR SACRED CREATIONS

George Michell's *Southern India: A Guide to Monuments, Sites & Museums* shines a detailed light on the region's multi-faceted architectural treasures, from Tamil Nadu's psychedelic temples to Goa's elegant churches.

Former French colony Puducherry (Pondicherry) hosts some of India's most magnificent churches, including 19th-century Notre Dame des Anges (p366) and Goa-like 1791 Our Lady of the Immaculate Conception Cathedral (p366). British-built churches tend to be neoclassical or neo-Gothic; Chennai's St Andrew's Church (p342) is an exquisite example of the former. Most of South India's hill stations, including Ooty (Udhagamandalam) and Munnar, have moody colonial-era British-style churches.

Forts & Palaces

The frequent wars between old Indian kingdoms and empires, as well as the later involvement of colonial powers, naturally led to the construction of some highly imposing fortresses. A typical South Indian fort sits on a hill or rocky outcrop, with a ring or rings of moated battlements protecting the inner citadel. It usually has a town nestled at its base and often features spike-studded doors to ward off war elephants. Gingee (p363) in Tamil Nadu is a particularly good example. Bidar (p227) and Vijapura (p224) in Karnataka and Golconda (p234) in Hyderabad host great metropolitan forts.

Daulatabad (p292) in Maharashtra is another magnificent structure, with 5km of walls surrounding a hilltop fortress reached by passageways filled with ingenious defences like false tunnels. Maharashtra's many other impressive forts include several built or used by the 17th-century Maratha hero Shivaji, including Raigad (p102) and Pratapgad (p116) forts. The 16th-century Janjira Fort (p101), off Maharashtra's Konkan Coast, was built by descendants of African slaves and will blow you away with its 12m walls rising straight from the sea, brooding gateway and mighty bastions. Like Goa's almost as impressively situated 17th-century riverside Fort Aguada (p128), it was never conquered.

Few old palaces remain in South India: conquerors often targeted these for destruction. The remains of the Vijayanagar royal complex at Hampi indicate local engineers weren't averse to using the sound structural techniques and fashions (domes, arches) of their Muslim adversaries, the Bahmanis. In Tamil Nadu, the remarkable palace of the Travancore maharajas at Padmanabhapuram (p267) dates back to 1550 and is South India's finest example of traditional Keralan architecture. Other notable palaces include Mattancherry Palace (p299) in Kochi, Kerala; Thanjavur Royal Palace (p379), Tamil Nadu; Aga Khan Palace (p108) in Pune, Maharashtra, where Gandhi was once imprisoned; and Tipu Sultan's Summer Palace (Daria Daulat Bagh; p198) at Srirangapatnam.

Blue Guide India, by Sam Miller, is an excellent and thoughtful resource for anyone delving into the country's historical and architectural legacies, with detailed coverage of the south.

Indo-Saracenic, a conflation of European, Islamic and Hindu architectural styles that blossomed all over India in the late 19th century, produced not only grandiose functional edifices, such as Mumbai's Chhatrapati Shivaji Maharaj Terminus (p49) railway station and Chennai's Madras High Court (p341), but also numerous flamboyant Indian royal palaces. The opulent diamond of the south is marvellous Mysuru Palace (p188), its interior a kaleidoscope of stained glass, mirrors and mosaic floors.

Wildlife & Landscape

South India's wildlife is a fascinating melange of animals whose ancestors roamed Europe, Asia and the ancient southern supercontinent Gondwana, in a great mix of habitats from steamy mangrove forests to expansive plains, flower-filled hill-country meadows and coral-rich waters. The South Asian subcontinent is an ancient block of earth crust that arrived with a wealth of unique plants and animals when it collided with the Eurasian Plate 40 million years ago, after a 100-million-year journey from Gondwana.

Wildlife

Signature Species

It's fortunate that Asian elephants (p500) – a thoroughly different species to the larger African elephant – are revered in Hindu custom. Otherwise they may well have been hunted to extinction long ago, as in neighbouring China. Indian wild-elephant numbers were estimated to be 27,312 in 2017, down from 30,000 in 2012; at time of writing, Karnataka and Kerala, along with Assam, have the largest elephant populations, with 6049, 5719 and 3054 pachyderms respectively. These 3000kg animals migrate long distances in search of food and require huge parks, running into predictable conflict when herds attempt to follow ancestral paths now occupied by villages and farms. The purchase of ivory souvenirs supports the poaching of these magnificent creatures, and many countries have strict customs guidelines preventing ivory importation.

Online Wildlife Resources

Sanctuary Asia (www.sanctuary asia.com)

Wildlife Trust of India (www.wti. org.in)

Birding in India (www.birding.in)

PROJECT TIGER

When hunter-turned-naturalist Jim Corbett first raised the alarm in the 1930s, no one else believed that tigers would ever be threatened. At the time it was thought there were 40,000 tigers in India, although no one had ever counted them. Then came Independence, which put guns into the hands of villagers who pushed into formerly off-limits hunting reserves seeking profitable tiger skins. By the time an official census was conducted in 1972, there were only an estimated 1800 tigers left and international outcry prompted Indira Gandhi to set up Project Tiger.

The project has since established 50 tiger reserves totalling over 70,000 sq km (including buffer zones) that protect not only this top predator but all animals that live in the same habitats; at the time of writing, there were several new tiger reserves on the cards, too. After an initial round of successes, neglect, habitat loss, corruption and relentless poaching – spurred by the international skin trade and demand for tiger parts in Chinese traditional medicine – saw tiger numbers down to just 1411 in 2006, the first year a relatively reliable counting system based on camera traps was used. That year, Project Tiger was transformed into the National Tiger Conservation Authority (www.tigernet.nic.in), a statutory body with a bigger budget, more on-the-ground staff, and more teeth to fight poaching and the trade in tiger parts. Tiger numbers rose to 1706 in the 2010 census and 2226 in the 2014 census – encouraging statistics, but tigers continue to be poached, their habitat outside tiger reserves is shrinking and there's still doubt over the reliability of collected data. India's tigers account for 70% of the total world tiger population, living in just 25% of the globe's tiger habitat.

Despite India's seemingly encouraging tiger numbers, a shocking 95 tigers were documented to have died in 2018, according to the National Tiger Conservation Authority. Causes include poaching, infighting, loss of prey and habitat, vehicle accidents and human-wildlife conflict.

The tiger is fixed in the subcontinent's subconscious as the mythological mount of the powerful, demon-slaying goddess Durga, while prowling the West's image of India as Mowgli's jungle nemesis. This awesome, iconic animal is endangered, but its numbers in India seem to be on the rise, up from 1706 in 2010 to 2226 in 2014, according to India's latest official census (though there are some doubts about data accuracy). The tiger can be seen, if you're very lucky, at South India's tiger reserves (p500).

India is also home to 15 other species of cat. Leopards are quite widespread in different types of forest and in several parks and sanctuaries in the south – but elusive, nevertheless. In recent decades some leopards have increasingly been found close to (and even within) some of India's ever-expanding towns and cities, where they prey on dogs, cats, pigs and rodents (with the occasional human fatality, too).

Common Encounters

Easily the most abundant forms of wildlife you'll see in India are deer (nine species), antelope (six species), goats and sheep (10 species), and primates (15 species). The ones you're most likely to see in the parks and reserves of the south include chital (spotted deer), sambar (a large deer), nilgai or bluebull (a large antelope), the elegant grey (Hanuman) langur with its characteristic black face and ears, and the bonnet macaque which often loiters around temples and tourist sites. Also fairly often spotted are gaurs (Indian bison) and wild boars; you can also hope to see the occasional sloth bear (with its long white snout), golden jackal or giant squirrel.

Endangered Species

Get the inside track on Indian environmental issues at Down to Earth (www.downtoearth.org.in), an online magazine that delves into stories overlooked by mainstream media.

Despite its amazing biodiversity, India's environment faces an ever-growing challenge from the country's exploding human population. Wildlife is severely threatened by poaching, habitat loss and human-animal conflict. As of early 2019, the Red List of the International Union for Conservation of Nature listed 1092 threatened species in India. Of these, 175 are in the most at-risk category, 'critically endangered'; 384 are in the next most imperilled group, 'endangered'; and 551 are 'vulnerable'.

Even the massively resourced National Tiger Conservation Authority (p497) faces an uphill battle every day. The number of tiger reserves is growing, but the total amount of territory roamed by tigers is shrinking. And every encouraging tiger news story seems to be followed by another of poaching gangs or tiger or leopard attacks on villagers; the controversial 2018 killing of tigress T1, who had fatally attacked 13 villagers over two years in Maharashtra, is just the latest in a long line of human-animal conflict. The Wildlife Protection Society of India (www.wpsi-india.org) documented 1110 tigers and 4539 leopards killed by poachers between 1994 and 2017, but warns that total numbers may be far higher.

'Critically endangered' animals found in South India include the great Indian bustard, a large, heavy bird of which less than 250 survive in isolated pockets of South and North India; the Malabar large-spotted civet (less than 250 in the Western Ghats, possibly even extinct); and four species of vulture (p499).

India's national animal is the tiger, its national bird is the peacock and its national flower is the lotus. The national emblem of India is a column topped by three Asiatic lions.

Species of South India on the 'endangered' list include the tiger; elephant; dhole (wild dog; around 2000 surviving); the lion-tailed macaque, with its splendid silvery-white mane (3000 to 3500 remaining, in the Western Ghats); and the Nilgiri tahr, a wild sheep of the Nilgiri Hills (around 1800 remaining).

Birds

With over 1250 highly varied species (925 of which breed here), India is a birdwatcher's dream. Wherever critical habitat has been preserved in the midst of dense human activity, you might see phenomenal numbers of birds in one location. Winter (November to February) is a particular-

INDIA'S DISAPPEARING VULTURES

The story of India's vultures is perhaps the most devastating of all India's wildlife struggles – especially that of the white-rumped vulture, which in the 1980s numbered around 80 million and was the world's most abundant vulture. Today white-rumped vultures number no more than several thousand – a near-annihilation blamed on the veterinary chemical diclofenac, which causes kidney failure in birds that eat the carcasses of cattle that have been treated with it. The birds' population has ever-so-slightly stabilised since diclofenac was banned in India, Nepal and Pakistan in 2006 and Bangladesh in 2010, but the species remains critically endangered. The absence of vultures has led to a rise in the number of disease-spreading feral dogs, feeding on carcasses that would formerly have been picked clean by the birds.

ly good time, as wetlands host northern migrants arriving to kick back in the subtropical warmth of the Indian peninsula. Bird sanctuaries are generally the best places for intensive birdwatching (p500), but many other protected areas also have vast avian variety.

Around 2000 plant species are described in ayurveda (traditional Indian herbal medicine) texts.

Plants

India was once almost entirely covered in forest; now its total forest cover is around 20%. The 2016 Red List of the International Union for Conservation of Nature listed 77 'critically endangered' Indian plants, plus 172 'endangered'. But the country still has over 45,000 documented plant species, over 4000 of them endemic.

High-value trees such as Indian rosewood, Malabar kino and teak have been virtually cleared from the Western Ghats, and sandalwood is endangered across India due to illegal logging for the incense and wood-carving industries. A bigger threat on forested lands is firewood harvesting, often carried out by landless peasants squatting on government land. Many forests have also been cleared to make way for tea and coffee plantations.

Several Indian trees have significant religious value, including the huge silk-cotton tree, with its spiny bark and large red flowers under which Pitamaha (Brahma), the creator of the world, sat after his labours. Two well-known figs, the banyan and peepal, grow to immense size by dangling roots from their branches and fusing into massive jungles of trunks and stems. It is said that the Buddha achieved enlightenment while sitting under a peepal (also known as the Bodhi tree).

Parks, Sanctuaries & Reserves

Before 1972 India had only five national parks. That year, the Wildlife Protection Act was introduced to set aside national parks and stem the abuse of wildlife. The act was followed by a string of similar pieces of legislation with bold ambitions but often too few teeth with which to enforce them.

India now has over 100 national parks and 500 wildlife sanctuaries, covering around 5% of its territory. There are also 50 tiger reserves and 18 biosphere reserves (designed to protect ecosystems and biodiversity while permitting human activities), often overlapping with other protected areas. At research time there were plans to form three to five new tiger reserves. Many contiguous parks, reserves and sanctuaries in the highly biodiverse Western Ghats provide valuable migration corridors for wildlife.

One consequence of creating protected areas has been that about 1.6 million Adivasis (tribal people) and other forest-dwellers have had to leave their traditional lands. Many were resettled into villages and forced to abandon their age-old ways of life. The Forest Rights Act of 2006 forbids the displacement of forest-dwellers from national parks (except in so-called 'critical wildlife habitat'), and should protect the four million or so people who still live in them.

India harbours some of the world's richest biodiversity. There are around 400 mammal species, 1250 bird species, 500 reptile species, 340 amphibian species and 3000 fish species – nearly 7% of the earth's animal species on just 2.5% of its land, which is also inhabited by 18% of the planet's human population.

Visiting Protected Areas

Many parks, sanctuaries and reserves encourage visitors, and your visit adds momentum to efforts to protect India's natural resources. The experience of watching an elephant, sloth bear or even, if you're lucky, a leopard or tiger in the wild will stay with you. The best parks and reserves take time to reach, but usually have a range of accommodation – from comfortable lodges to tree huts – inside or just outside the park. In some parks, guided hikes and 4WD safaris are available; others may offer only cursory minibus tours. Independent operators offer 4WD safaris or guided treks on some parks' fringes, which can be just as wildlife-rich as the park itself. Free hiking within parks is generally banned for safety reasons.

The monsoon months (June to August in most places) are usually the least favourable for visits; during holiday periods, parks and their accommodation can overflow with visitors. A few parks close during the ultra-dry and hot couple of premonsoon months, though this can be the best time to view wildlife, as the cover is thinner and animals seek out scarce waterholes.

Some South Indian wildlife reserves continue to offer elephant rides, but Lonely Planet does not recommend them due to the significant animal-welfare concerns involved.

Founded by celebrated tiger champion Belinda Wright, the **Wildlife Protection Society of India** (www.wpsi-india.org) is a premier wildlife conservation organisation campaigning for animal welfare via education, lobbying and legal action against poachers.

The Lie of the Land

The Himalaya, the world's highest mountains, form an almost-impregnable barrier separating India from its northern neighbours (India's highest peak, Khangchendzonga, reaches 8598m). The Himalaya were formed when the Indian subcontinent, after a 100-million-year northward drift from Gondwana, slammed slowly into the Eurasian continent, buckling the ancient sea floor upward.

South of the Himalaya, the floodplains of the Indus and Ganges Rivers form the fertile heartland of North India. To their south, the elevated Deccan plateau forms the core of India's triangular southern peninsula. The Deccan is bounded by the hills of the Western and Eastern Ghats.

TOP PARKS FOR WILDLIFE

Tigers

Maharashtra's Tadoba-Andhari Tiger Reserve (p100) and Madhya Pradesh's Pench Tiger Reserve in North India (easily accessed from Nagpur in Maharashtra) are among India's top spots for tiger sightings. Chances are slimmer, but not negligible, in Karnataka's Nagarhole (p200) and Bandipur (p199) National Parks, Kerala's Periyar Tiger Reserve (p287) and Tamil Nadu's Mudumalai Tiger Reserve (p414).

Elephants

South India's best parks for spotting wild elephants include Nagarhole National Park (p200), Karnataka; Wayanad Wildlife Sanctuary (p317), Kerala; and Mudumalai Tiger Reserve (p414), Tamil Nadu.

Birds

Kerala's Kumarakom Bird Sanctuary (p285) and Tamil Nadu's Vedanthangal Bird Sanctuary (p357) are top spots for migratory waterbirds between November and February. Thattekkad Bird Sanctuary (p296) in Kerala is home to 300 mainly forest species.

Other Wildlife

Parambikulam Tiger Reserve (p295) Kerala; elephants, gaurs, teak forest

Anamalai Tiger Reserve (p415) Tamil Nadu; elephants, lion-tailed macaques, crocodiles

The Western Ghats, stretching from north of Mumbai almost to India's southern tip, drop sharply down to a narrow coastal lowland, forming a luxuriant slope of rainforest. Their highest peak is Anamudi (2695m), in Kerala. With many endemic species, they are one of the world's top biodiversity hot spots; 39 areas of the Western Ghats, spread over 7950 sq km, were inscribed on the World Heritage list in 2012 for their natural values. The lower Eastern Ghats stretch from West Bengal to south-central Tamil Nadu, and are cut by the four major rivers of peninsular India, flowing west-to-east across the Deccan: the Mahanadi, Godavari, Krishna and Cauvery.

Offshore are a series of island groups, politically part of India but geographically linked to the land masses of Southeast Asia and islands of the Indian Ocean. The 572 Andaman and Nicobar Islands, far east in the Andaman Sea, are the peaks of a submerged mountain range extending almost 1000km between Myanmar (Burma) and Sumatra. The coral atolls of Lakshadweep, 300km west of Kerala, are a northerly extension of the Maldives.

Environmental Issues

Given India's 2016 population of 1.37 billion (expected to reach 1.51 billion by 2030), ever-expanding industrial and urban centres, and growth in chemical-intensive farming, India's environment is under tremendous pressure. An estimated 65% of the land is degraded in some way. Many current problems are a direct result of the Green Revolution of the 1960s, when chemical fertilisers and pesticides enabled huge growth in agricultural output, at enormous cost to the environment.

Despite numerous environmental laws, corruption has exacerbated environmental degradation – exemplified by flagrant flouting of laws by companies involved in hydroelectricity and mining. Usually, the people most affected are low-caste rural farmers and Adivasis (tribal people). Agricultural production has been reduced by soil degradation from overfarming, rising soil salinity, loss of tree cover and, increasingly, lack of water resources. The human cost is heart-rending, and India constantly grapples with the dilemma of how to develop economically without destroying what's left of its environment. Air and noise pollution have also become major problems across the country.

Prime Minister Narendra Modi, in power since 2014, continues to offer mixed signals about his priorities. On one hand, Modi famously instigated plans to clean 80% of the appallingly polluted Ganges River by March 2019; launched the much-publicised Swachh Bharat (Clean India) Mission to reduce trash pollution nationwide; supports large-scale solar-power generation; pledged to reduce air pollution by 20% to 30% by 2024 in 102 cities (including Delhi, Mumbai, Bengaluru [Bangalore] and Pune); and, by ratifying the UN's Paris Agreement, committed to producing 40% of India's electricity from non-fossil-fuel sources by 2030. But his government also vowed to increase domestic coal mining and double coal use, adding significantly to India's greenhouse gas emissions (which account for about 4.5% of global greenhouse gas emissions), and there are doubts as to whether projects such as the Ganges clean-up will be completed (as of April 2019, only 63 of 236 planned Ganges clean-up jobs had been finished).

In March 2018, Maharashtra became the first state in India to ban single-use plastics; it was followed by Telangana and Himachal Pradesh in 2018, then Tamil Nadu in 2019. At the time of writing, almost all Indian states have banned plastic bags. While these are, of course, promising steps, concerns abound regarding the physical implementation of the ban and whether authorities are offering suitable alternatives to meet the population's needs.

Wildlife Books

Indian Mammals: A Field Guide, by Vivek Menon

Birds of Southern India, by Richard Grimmett and Tim Inskipp

Treasures of Indian Wildlife, by Ashok Kothari and BS Chhapgar

India has 238 species of snake, of which about 50 are poisonous. Of the various species of cobra, the king cobra is the world's largest venomous snake, attaining a length of 5m!

Veerappan: Chasing the Brigand, by K Vijay Kumar, tackles the topic of notoriously murderous ivory smuggler Koose Muniswamy Veerappan, who ruled the forests around the Tamil Nadu–Karnataka border as India's most feared man for 17 years before he was killed in a 2004 gun battle with police.

As anywhere, tourists tread a fine line between providing an incentive for change and making the problem worse. Many of Goa's environmental problems, for example, are the direct result of irresponsible development for tourism, while overtourism is starting to chip away at the pristine beauty and limited resources of the Andaman Islands (where tourists have been left stranded due to cyclones).

Climate Change

Changing climate patterns, linked to carbon emissions, have been creating dangerous extremes of weather in India. While India's per capita carbon emissions still rank far behind those of the West and China, the sheer size of its population makes it the world's third-largest CO2 emitter. It has been estimated that by 2030 India will see a 30% increase in the severity of its floods and droughts. Islands in the Lakshadweep group, as well as the low-lying Ganges delta, are being inundated by rising sea levels.

Evidenced by deadly heatwaves, cyclones, drinking-water shortages, disputes over dwindling water resources and other disasters, climate change is a major issue in the south, while soaring air and noise pollution is also a rapidly growing concern. A 2015 heatwave is thought to have caused the death of at least 2500 people, with Telangana and Andhra Pradesh worst affected. In 2018 the worst floods in a century devastated Kerala, with over 400 people killed, a million displaced and approximately US$2.5 billion of damage left behind. Sadly, severe flooding is increasingly a normal situation for South India, with Goa, Mumbai, Tamil Nadu, Kerala and Karnataka also hit in recent years.

Deforestation

In the last three decades, over 14,000 sq km of India's forests have been cleared for logging and farming, or destroyed by urban expansion, mining, industrialisation and river dams. Forests now cover only 21.3% of the country. The number of mangrove forests has halved since the early 1990s, reducing the nursery grounds for the fish that stock the Indian Ocean and Bay of Bengal.

India's first Five Year Plan in 1951 recognised the importance of forests for soil conservation, and various policies have been introduced to increase forest cover. Almost all have been flouted by officials or criminals – including the notorious bandit, Veerappan, who funded his exploits in Karnataka, Kerala and Tamil Nadu partly through poaching and smuggling illegally harvested sandalwood – and by ordinary people clearing forests for firewood and grazing.

Water Resources

Arguably the biggest threat to public health in India is inadequate access to clean drinking water and proper sanitation. With the population continuing to grow, agricultural, industrial and domestic water usage are all expected to spiral. Sewage treatment facilities can handle only about a quarter of waste water produced. Many cities dump untreated sewage and partially cremated bodies directly into rivers. Open defecation is a simple fact of life for much of the rural population, though Modi's Swachh Bharat Mission is working to end it in 2019; at time of writing, reports suggest that the number of people practising open defecation has been reduced by 50% between 2014 and 2018.

Rivers are also affected by run-off, industrial pollution and sewage contamination. At least 70% of the freshwater sources in India are now polluted in some way, affecting three in four Indians.

In addition, there is South India's growing strife over the sharing of water resources – most recently highlighted in the bitter (and at times violent) Cauvery dispute, over the splitting of the Cauvery River's waters between the drought-hit states of Karnataka and Tamil Nadu.

Spanning Karnataka, Kerala and Tamil Nadu, the contiguous Bandipur, Nagarhole, Wayanad, Sathyamangalam, Mudumalai and several other protected areas in South India's Western Ghats are home to 585 tigers – the world's single largest tiger population.

The World Health Organization reports that 14 of the world's most polluted cities are in India. In 2017 Delhi declared a public health emergency when pollution levels reached 70 times the recommended safe limit.

Since 1947 an estimated 35 million Indians have been displaced by major dams, mostly built to provide hydroelectricity. Valleys across India are being sacrificed to create new power plants, and displaced people rarely receive adequate compensation.

Survival Guide

SCAMS 504

Contaminated
Food & Drink 504
Credit-Card Cons 504
Druggings 504
Gem Scams 505
Overpricing 505
Photography 505
Theft 505
Touts & Commission
Agents 505
Transport Scams 505

WOMEN & SOLO TRAVELLERS 506

Women Travellers 506
Solo Travellers 507

DIRECTORY A-Z ... 508

Accessible Travel 508
Accommodation 508
Customs
Regulations 511
Electricity 511
Embassies & Consulates . 511
Food 512

Insurance 513
Internet Access 513
Legal Matters 513
LGBT+ Travellers 514
Maps 514
Money 514
Opening Hours 516
Photography 516
Post 516
Public Holidays 517
Safe Travel 517
Telephone 518
Time 519
Toilets 519
Tourist
Information 519
Visas 519

TRANSPORT 521

GETTING THERE
& AWAY 521
GETTING AROUND 522

HEALTH 530

LANGUAGE 535

Scams

India has an unfortunately deserved reputation for scams, both classic and new-fangled. Of course, most can be avoided with some common sense and an appropriate amount of caution. They tend to be more of a problem in the major gateway cities (such as Delhi or Mumbai), or very touristy spots (such as Rajasthan). Chat with fellow travellers and check the India branch of Lonely Planet's Thorn Tree forum (www.lonelyplanet.com/thorntree) to keep abreast of the latest cons.

Contaminated Food & Drink

➜ Most bottled water is legit, but ensure that the seal is intact and the bottom of the bottle hasn't been tampered with.

➜ While in transit, try to carry packed food if possible, and politely decline offers of food or drink from locals on buses or trains; hygiene can be an issue and people have been drugged in the past.

➜ Though there have been no recent reports, the late 1990s saw a scam where travellers died after consuming food laced with dangerous bacteria from restaurants linked to dodgy medical clinics. In unrelated incidents, some clinics have given more treatment than necessary to procure larger payments from insurance companies.

OTHER TOP SCAMS

➜ Gunk (dirt, paint, poo) suddenly appears on your shoes, only for a shoe cleaner to magically appear and offer to clean it off – for a price.

➜ Some shops are selling overpriced SIMs and not activating them; it's best to buy your SIM from an official outlet such as Airtel, Vodafone etc and check it works before leaving the area.

➜ Shops, restaurants or tour guides 'borrow' the name of their more successful and popular competitor.

➜ Touts claim to be 'government-approved' guides or agents, and sting you for large sums of cash. Enquire at the local tourist office about licensed guides and ask to see identification from guides themselves.

➜ 'Tourist offices' turn out to be dodgy travel agencies whose aim is to sell you overpriced tours, tickets and tourist services.

Credit-Card Cons

Be careful when paying for souvenirs with a credit card. While government shops are usually legitimate, private souvenir shops have been known to surreptitiously run off extra copies of the credit-card imprint slip and use them for phoney transactions later.

Ask the trader to process the transaction in front of you. Memorising the CVV/CVC2 number and scratching it off the card is also a good idea, to avoid misuse. If anyone asks for your PIN with the intention of taking your credit card to the machine, insist on using the machine in person.

Druggings

Be extremely wary of accepting food or drink from strangers, even if you feel you're being rude. Women should be particularly circumspect. Occasionally, tourists (especially those travelling solo) have been drugged and robbed or even attacked. A spiked drink is the most common method, but snacks and even homemade meals have also been used.

Gem Scams

Don't be fooled by smooth-talking con artists who promise foolproof 'get rich quick' schemes. In this scam, travellers are asked to carry or mail gems home and then sell them to the trader's (nonexistent) overseas representatives at a profit. Without exception, the goods – if they arrive at all – are worth a fraction of what you paid, and the 'representatives' never materialise.

Travellers have reported this con happening in Agra, Delhi and Jaisalmer, but it's particularly prevalent in Jaipur. Carpets, curios and *pashmina* woollens are other favourites for this con.

Overpricing

Always agree on prices beforehand while using services that don't have regulated tariffs. This particularly applies to friendly neighbourhood guides, snack bars at touristy places, and autorickshaws and taxis without meters.

Photography

Ask for permission where possible while photographing people. If you don't have permission, you may be asked to pay a fee.

Theft

➡ Theft is a risk in India, as anywhere else. Keep your eye on your luggage at all times on public transport, and consider locking it, or even chaining it on overnight buses and trains. Remember that snatchings often occur when a train is pulling out of the station, as it's too late for you to give chase.

➡ Take extra care in dormitories and never leave your valuables unattended. Use safe deposit boxes where possible.

➡ Remember to lock your door at night; it is not unknown for thieves to take things from hotel rooms while occupants are sleeping.

Touts & Commission Agents

➡ Cabbies and autorickshaw drivers will often try to coerce you into staying at a hotel of their choice, only to collect a commission (added to your room tariff) afterward. Where possible, prearrange hotel bookings and request a hotel pick-up.

➡ You'll often hear stories about hotels of your choice being 'full' or 'closed' – check things out yourself and reconfirm and double-check your booking the day before you arrive.

➡ Be very sceptical of phrases like 'my brother's shop' and 'special deal at my friend's place'. Many fraudsters operate in collusion with souvenir stalls.

➡ Avoid friendly people and 'officials' in train and bus stations who offer unsolicited help, only to guide you to a commission-paying travel agent. Look confident, and if anyone asks if this is your first trip to India, say you've been here several times and that your onward travel is already booked.

Transport Scams

➡ Upon arriving at train stations and airports, if you haven't prearranged a pick-up, use public transport, or call an Uber or equivalent, or go to the prepaid taxi or airport shuttle-bus counters. Never choose a loitering cabbie who offers you a cheap ride into town, especially at night.

➡ While booking multiday sightseeing tours, research your own itinerary, and be extremely wary of anyone in Delhi offering houseboat tours to Kashmir – we've received many complaints over the years about dodgy deals.

➡ When buying a bus, train or plane ticket anywhere other than the registered office of the transport company, make sure you're getting the ticket class you paid for. Use official online booking facilities where possible.

➡ Train-station touts (even in uniform or with 'official' badges) may tell you that your intended train is cancelled/flooded/broken down or that your ticket is invalid or that you must pay to have your e-ticket validated on the platform. Do not respond to any approaches at train stations.

KEEPING SAFE

➡ A good travel-insurance policy is essential.

➡ Email copies of your passport identity page, visa and airline tickets to yourself, and keep copies on you.

➡ Keep your money and passport in a concealed money belt or a secure place under your shirt.

➡ Store at least US$100 separately from your main stash.

➡ Don't publicly display large wads of cash when paying.

➡ Consider using your own padlock at cheaper hotels.

➡ If you can't lock your hotel room securely from inside, stay elsewhere.

Women & Solo Travellers

Women Travellers

Although Bollywood might suggest otherwise, India remains a conservative society. Female travellers should be aware that their behaviour and choice of attire are likely to be under constant scrutiny. Unfortunately, reports of sexual assaults against women are on the increase, despite tougher punishments being established following the 2012 gang rape and murder of a Delhi woman. There have been numerous instances of female tourists being attacked in recent years.

Unwanted Attention

Unwanted attention from men is a common problem.

➡ Be prepared to be stared at.

➡ Refrain from returning male stares; this can be considered encouragement.

➡ Dark glasses, phones, books, tablets and headphones are useful for averting unwanted conversations.

➡ Wearing a pseudo wedding ring and saying early on that you're married (perhaps meeting your 'husband' shortly), is another way to ward off unwanted interest.

Clothing

More touristy regions (such as Goa) and bigger, cosmopolitan cities (like Mumbai and Kochi [Cochin]) are less conservative in terms of what to wear, especially if you're hitting bars, hotels or restaurants popular with younger Indian women (who may well dress in skinny jeans, shorts and minidresses here). Elsewhere, women dress conservatively and traditionally, and avoiding culturally inappropriate clothing will help avert undesirable attention. If in doubt, keep things conservative.

➡ Generally speaking, dress modestly and avoid strappy tops, shorts, short skirts (ankle- or, at least, midi-length skirts are recommended) and anything else that's skimpy, see-through or tight-fitting.

➡ Wearing Indian-style clothes is viewed favourably.

➡ Draping a dupatta (long scarf) over T-shirts is good for avoiding stares – it's shorthand for modesty, and also handy for shrines that require covering your head.

➡ Wearing a salwar kameez (traditional dresslike tunic and trousers) will help you blend in; a smart alternative is a kurta (long shirt) over jeans or trousers.

➡ Avoid going out in public wearing a choli (sari blouse) or a sari petticoat (which some foreign women mistake for a skirt); it's like strutting around half-dressed.

➡ Many Indian women wear long shorts and a T-shirt when swimming in public; it's wise to wear a sarong from beach to hotel.

➡ Avoid wearing yoga pants/leggings out in public without covering your bum with an oversize shirt, kurta or similar.

Health & Hygiene

Sanitary pads are widely available but tampons are usually restricted to pharmacies in big cities and tourist towns (even then, choice is limited). Carry additional stocks for travel off the beaten track.

Sexual Harassment

Sexual harassment, known locally as 'Eve-teasing', is widespread in India and many female travellers experience some form of sexual harassment, such as lewd comments, invasion of privacy, provocative gestures, jeering, getting 'accidentally' bumped into and even groping and being followed. Follow similar safety precautions as you would at home.

➡ Incidents are particularly common at crowded public events (such as the Holi festival) and busy transport hubs or markets. If a crowd is gathering, find a safer place.

➡ Women travelling with a male partner will receive far less hassle, but this is not a guarantee of safety.

Staying Safe

➡ Always be aware of your surroundings. If it feels wrong, trust your instincts. Don't be scared, but don't be reckless either.

➡ When travelling after dark, use recommended, registered, ideally prebooked taxi services.

➡ Organise travel so that you arrive in towns before dark.

➡ Keep conversations with unknown men short.

➡ If you feel that a guy is encroaching on your space, he probably is. A firm request to keep away usually does the trick. Don't be afraid to be impolite when required.

➡ Follow local women's cues and instead of shaking hands say *namaste* (the traditional, respectful Hindu greeting).

➡ Check the reputation of any teacher or therapist before going to a solo session, and request female therapists. Some women have reported being molested by male therapists.

➡ Lone women may want to invest in good-quality hotels in better neighbourhoods and carry a pepper spray.

➡ At hotels, keep your door locked, as staff (particularly at budget and midrange places) can knock and walk in without permission.

➡ Avoid wandering alone in isolated areas, even during daylight. Steer clear of *galis* (narrow lanes) and deserted roads.

➡ When taking rickshaws or taxis alone (especially at night), call/text someone, or pretend to, to indicate someone knows where you are.

➡ Act confidently in public; to avoid looking lost (and vulnerable) consult maps at your hotel (or at a restaurant) rather than on the street.

➡ Smartphone users can use maps to track where they are to avoid getting lost and to tell if a taxi/rickshaw is taking the wrong road.

➡ Never get into a taxi or autorickshaw containing anyone other than the driver.

➡ There are now women-only dorms in many hostels.

➡ In some big cities and tourist spots, take advantage of police squads dedicated to female safety, such as Kerala's **Pink Police Patrol** (☑15150).

Transport

Being female has advantages. Women can usually queue-jump for buses and trains. On trains there are special ladies-only carriages; there are also women-only waiting rooms at some stations.

➡ Prearrange airport taxi pickups with your hotel, especially if your flight arrives after dark.

➡ Some cities have licensed prepaid radio cab services; they're more expensive than regular prepaid taxis, but promote themselves as safe, with vetted drivers.

➡ Uber and Ola Cabs taxi apps are very useful, as rates are fixed and you'll have the driver's licence plate in advance, so you can ensure you get into the correct taxi. In Goa, use Goa Tourism's Goa Miles (p119) or **Women's Taxi Service** (☑0832-2437437). There are a few other female-only taxi services in big southern cities.

➡ Avoid taking taxis alone late at night and never agree to have more than one man (the driver) in the car; ignore claims that this is 'just my brother' etc.

➡ Solo women have reported less hassle when taking more expensive classes on trains, though others believe the busiest carriages are in fact safest.

➡ When travelling overnight in a two- or three-tier carriage, the uppermost berth gives you more privacy (and distance from potential gropers); travelling in 2AC or 3AC prevents the possibility of you being boxed into a 1AC compartment, potentially only with men.

➡ On public transport, don't hesitate to return any errant limbs, be vocal (attracting public attention, thus shaming the pest), or simply find a new spot.

➡ Sit next to other women or families on transport and, for long-distance buses, book seats towards the front.

Solo Travellers

One of the joys of travelling solo in India is that you're more likely to be 'adopted' by families. If you're keen to link up with fellow travellers, southern tourist hubs such as Goa and Kerala are popular. You may also find travel companions through digital platforms.

Cost

➡ Single-room accommodation rates are sometimes not much lower than double rates, though it's always worth trying to negotiate.

➡ Some tours and packages are aimed at two people sharing, and lone travellers may need to pay a surcharge.

Safety

Most solo travellers experience no major problems in India but, like anywhere else, it's wise to stay on your toes in unfamiliar surroundings.

➡ Some less honourable souls (locals and travellers alike) view lone tourists as easy targets for theft and sexual assault.

➡ Single men wandering around isolated areas have been mugged or attacked, even during the day, including in Goa.

➡ It's best not to trek solo (hiring a guide can solve this).

➡ It's also a good idea to let someone know if you're heading off the beaten track.

Transport

➡ You'll save money if you find others to share taxis, autorickshaws and tours. The Uber and Ola Cabs taxi apps also offer shared services.

➡ Solo travellers may be able to grab the 'copilot' (near the driver) seat on buses (handy for big bags).

Directory A-Z

Accessible Travel

India's crowded public transport, crush of humanity and often-lacking infrastructure test even the hardiest traveller. If you have a physical disability or are vision-impaired, these can pose even more of a challenge, as can variable societal attitudes. If your mobility is considerably restricted, you may like to ease the stress by travelling with a companion.

Over the last few years operators such as Planet Abled (http://planetabled.com) and Cox & Kings' Enable Travel (www.enabletravel.com) have been working hard to enable and increase accessible travel across India.

Accommodation Wheelchair-friendly hotels are almost exclusively top-end. Make pretrip enquiries and book ground-floor rooms at hotels that lack adequate facilities.

Accessibility Some restaurants and offices have ramps but most tend to have at least one step. Staircases are often steep; lifts frequently stop at mezzanines between floors.

Footpaths Where footpaths exist, they can be riddled with holes, littered with debris and packed with pedestrians and stalls. If using crutches, bring along spare rubber caps.

Transport Hiring a car with driver will make moving around a lot easier; if you use a wheelchair, make sure the car-hire company can provide an appropriate vehicle to carry it.

For further advice pertaining to your specific requirements, consult your doctor before heading to India.

Download Lonely Planet's free Accessible Travel guide from http://lptravel.to/AccessibleTravel.

The following provide further information and/or help book trips:

Accessible Journeys (www.accessiblejourneys.com)

Curb Free with Cory Lee (www.curbfreewithcorylee.com)

Enable Travel (www.enabletravel.com)

Mobility International USA (MIUSA; www.miusa.org)

Planet Abled (http://planetabled.com)

Accommodation

Accommodation in South India varies wildly in quality, character and cost. It's usually advisable to book ahead (online or by phone) and essential during high seasons.

Categories

As a general rule, budget ($) covers everything from basic hostels, hotels and guesthouses in urban areas to traditional homestays in villages. Midrange hotels ($$) tend to have larger, cleaner rooms, usually with air-con, and are more likely to have restaurants; homestays often fall in this price range, too. Top-end accommodation ($$$) varies from luxurious chain hotels to gorgeous, one-of-a-kind heritage palaces and sleek boutique boltholes.

Costs

Costs vary widely: highest in large cities (especially Mumbai; Bombay) or, often, by the beach; lowest in small cities and rural areas. Costs are also highly seasonal; hotel prices can drop by 20% to 50% outside peak season. Most establishments raise tariffs annually, so prices may have risen since this edition was last researched.

Reservations

➜ It's a good idea to book ahead, online or by phone, especially for more popular destinations. Some hotels require a credit-card deposit for bookings.

➜ Some budget places won't take reservations as they don't know when people are

---

BOOK YOUR STAY ONLINE

For more accommodation reviews by Lonely Planet writers, check out http://lonelyplanet.com/hotels/. You'll find independent reviews, as well as recommendations on the best places to stay. Best of all, you can book online.

going to check out; call ahead or just turn up around check-in time.

→ A deposit or full payment may be requested at check in; ask for a receipt and be wary of any request for you to sign a blank impression of your credit card. If the hotel insists, pay cash.

→ Verify the check-out time when you arrive – some hotels have a fixed check-out time (usually 10am or noon, but can be earlier), while others offer 24-hour check out (you have the room for 24 hours from check in). Sometimes you can request to check in early or check out late, and hotels will oblige if the room is empty (though some charge for this).

→ Booking online can reap major discounts, often bringing very good midrange options almost into the budget price range or making top-end hotels significantly more affordable.

Seasons

→ High season usually coincides with the best weather for the area's sights and activities – normally spring in the hills (April to June), and the cooler months in the lowlands (November to February).

→ In areas popular with tourists, there's an additional peak period over Christmas and New Year; make reservations well in advance.

→ At other times you may find significant discounts; if the hotel seems quiet, it's worth asking, or checking for deals online.

→ Some hotels in places such as Goa close during the monsoon period.

→ Many temple towns have additional peak seasons around major festivals and pilgrimages; book ahead.

Taxes & Service Charges

→ Hotels usually quote rates excluding taxes; it's best

to check. Rates we quote include taxes unless noted.

→ India's Goods & Service Tax (GST), introduced in 2017, levies fixed charges per price range. Hotels with tariffs up to ₹999 are not subject to tax. For others, it's 12% for hotels charging ₹1000 to ₹2499 per night, 18% for ₹2500 to ₹7499 per night, and 28% for ₹7500-plus per night.

Accommodation Types
BEACH HUTS

→ Goa's quintessential accommodation is the humble beach hut, also sometimes referred to as 'coco-huts' or 'treehouses' (on stilts). They're typically made of palm-leaf and bamboo, with a balcony, toilet and cold-water shower, though some have seriously upped their game and prices.

→ Goan beach huts set up between mid-October and mid-November, and are packed away in late-April or May. The widest choice and best deals are available in November, March and April.

→ Beach huts are also common in the Andaman Islands.

BUDGET & MIDRANGE HOTELS

→ Sometimes you'll find budget and midrange hotels in atmospheric old houses or heritage buildings, but most are in modern-style blocks with varying degrees of comfort and cleanliness. Some are charming, spotless and good value; others less so.

→ Room quality can vary considerably within a hotel, so inspect a few rooms before settling on one. Many places have a range of prices for rooms of different quality. Avoid carpeted rooms at cheaper hotels (unless you like the smell of mouldy socks).

→ Shared bathrooms (often with squat toilets) are usually found only at the cheapest lodgings.

→ Most rooms have ceiling fans and better rooms have mosquito-screened windows; cheaper rooms may lack windows altogether.

→ If you're mostly staying in budget places, bring your own sheet or sleeping-bag liner (or even a sarong/shawl). Sheets at cheap hotels can be stained, worn and dirty. You may also have to provide a towel, toilet paper and soap.

→ Insect repellent and a torch (flashlight) are recommended for budget hotels.

→ Noise can be irksome (particularly in urban hubs); pack good-quality earplugs and request a room that doesn't face a busy road.

→ Keep your door locked, as staff (especially in budget hotels) may knock and walk in without awaiting permission.

→ Blackouts are common (especially during the monsoon), so double-check that the hotel has a backup generator if you're paying for electric 'extras' (air-con, TV, wi-fi).

→ Some hotels lock their doors at night. Staff might sleep in the lobby, but waking them up can be a challenge. Let the hotel know in advance if you'll be arriving late at night or leaving early.

→ Wall cleanliness often leaves something to be desired (even in more expensive hotels!).

→ Away from tourist areas, cheaper hotels may not have the required foreigner-registration forms, and so may be unable to accommodate foreigners.

CAMPING

→ There are very few public campgrounds. The only places where you're likely to find yourself sleeping in a tent are a few coastal resorts and lodges in and around wildlife sanctuaries, where tents are usually permanently sited and often as large and comfortable as hotel rooms, with bathrooms, too.

GET TO KNOW YOUR BATHROOM

Most of South India's midrange hotels and all top-end ones have sit-down toilets with toilet paper and soap. Bathrooms in this category are generally improving and increasingly modern; the best have amenities like rainhead showers, designer baths and a range of toiletries.

In ultracheap hotels, bus and train stations and places off the tourist trail, squat toilets are the norm and toilet paper is often not provided. Squat toilets are described as 'Indian-style', 'Indian' or 'floor' toilets; the sit-down variety may be called 'Western' or 'commode' toilets.

Not all rooms have hot water. 'Running' or '24-hour' water means that hot water is available round-the-clock (though this is not always the case in reality). 'Bucket' hot water is only available in buckets (sometimes for a small charge). Glassed-in showers are rare in lower price brackets, and even shower curtains aren't very common.

GOVERNMENT-RUN ACCOMMODATION

➜ The Indian federal and state governments maintain networks of guesthouses for travelling officials and public workers, known variously as rest houses, dak bungalows, circuit houses, PWD (Public Works Department) bungalows and forest rest houses. These places may accept travellers if no government employees need the rooms, but permission is often required from local officials and in practice it's usually very difficult to gain access to them.

➜ Most state governments run chains of budget and midrange hotels aimed primarily at domestic tourists. They include a few lovely heritage properties, but most fall in the functional-but-painfully-bland category. State tourism offices normally provide details.

HOMESTAYS

➜ Available only in some areas, these family-run guesthouses will appeal to travellers seeking a small-scale, uncommercial, intimate setting, with home-cooked meals and, usually, sensible prices.

➜ Options range from mud-and-stone village huts with hole-in-the-floor toilets to very comfortable, middle-class urban homes.

➜ Particularly popular in Kerala, where Fort Cochin is the homestay capital of India, with Alappuzha (Alleppey), Munnar, Wayanad, Kumily and Kannur following behind.

➜ Local tourist offices often provide lists of participating families.

HOSTELS

➜ South India (particularly Goa and Kerala, but also Karnataka, Tamil Nadu and Mumbai) has an ever-growing number of contemporary-style backpacker hostels with clean dorms (some women-only), free wi-fi, lockers, communal kitchens, shared lounges and the odd private room. Some are independent, others chain run.

➜ Most popular tourist spots now have good hostel offerings, from Goa, Mumbai, Mysuru, Bengaluru (Bangalore), Chennai, Kochi (Cochin) and Alleppey to less-obvious spots such as Wayanad and Chettinadu.

➜ At the time of writing, popular chains include Zostel (www.zostel.com), Lost Hostels (www.thelosthostels. com), Hostel Crowd (https:// thehostelcrowd.com) and Backpacker Panda (www. backpackerpanda.com),

though it's a fast-changing scene.

➜ The YWCA, YMCA and Salvation Army run a few hostels, sometimes called 'guesthouses'. These usually have clean, comfy rooms (some with AC) as well as (or instead of) dorms, at high-budget or low-midrange prices.

RAILWAY RETIRING ROOMS

➜ Most large train stations (listed at www.irctctourism. com) have basic rooms for travellers holding an ongoing train ticket. Some are grim; others are surprisingly pleasant, but can suffer from the noise of passengers and trains.

➜ They're useful for early-morning train departures and there's usually a choice of dormitories or private rooms (24-hour check out) depending on the class you're travelling in.

➜ Some smaller stations only have waiting rooms, with different rooms for passengers in different classes and for men and women.

TEMPLES & PILGRIMS' REST HOUSES

➜ Accommodation is available at some ashrams (spiritual communities), gurdwaras (Sikh temples) and dharamsalas (pilgrims' rest houses) for a donation or fee.

➜ These have been established for genuine pilgrims so please exercise judgement about the appropriateness of your staying in one.

➜ Always abide by any protocols. Smoking and drinking are complete no-nos; there's usually a curfew.

TOP-END & HERITAGE HOTELS

➜ South India has a wealth of tempting top-end properties, from contemporary high-end chain hotels to glorious palaces, luxury beach resorts, boutique hideaways, heritage bungalows, and dreamy lodges in and around wildlife reserves.

➡ Heritage hotels give you the unique opportunity to stay in former (or sometimes still current) palaces, mansions and other abodes of Indian royalty and aristocracy.

Customs Regulations

➡ Technically on arrival you should declare any amount of cash over US$5000, or anything over US$10,000 in all forms of currency (including cash, drafts and travellers cheques).

➡ Indian rupees shouldn't be taken out of India; however, this is rarely policed.

➡ Officials may very occasionally ask tourists to enter expensive items such as video cameras and laptop computers on a 'Tourist Baggage Re-export' form to ensure they're taken out of India at the time of departure.

➡ The export of certain antiques is prohibited (p514); see the Archaeological Survey of India (ASI) website (http://asi.nic.in) for details.

Electricity

Type C
230V/50Hz

Type D
230V/50Hz

Type M
230V/50Hz

Embassies & Consulates

Most foreign diplomatic missions are based in Delhi, but several nations operate consulates in other Indian cities. Many missions have certain timings for visa applications, usually mornings; phone for details.

Australian Chennai (☏044-45921300; www.chennai. consulate.gov.au; 9th fl, Express Chambers, Express Avenue Estate, White's Rd, Royapettah; ◷9am-5pm Mon-Fri); Delhi (☏011-41399900; www.india. highcommission.gov.au; 1/50G Shantipath, Chanakyapuri; MLok Kalyan Marg); Mumbai (☏022-67574900; www. mumbai.consulate.gov.au; 10th fl, A Wing, Crescenzo Bldg, G Block, Plot C 38-39, Bandra Kurla Complex, Bandra East)

Bangladeshi Delhi (☏011-24121394; www.bdhcdelhi.org; EP39 Dr Radakrishnan Marg, Chanakyapuri; MChanakyapuri); Kolkata (☏033-40127500; 9 Circus Ave; ◷visas 9-11am Sat-Thu)

Belgian Chennai (☏044-40485500; http://india. diplomatie.belgium.be; Khader Nawaz Khan Rd, Nungambakkam; ◷9.30am-12.30pm & 2.30-4.30pm)

Bhutanese Delhi (☏011-26889230; www.mfa.gov.bt/ rbedelhi; Chandragupta Marg, Chanakyapuri; MChanakyapuri); Kolkata (Tivoli Court, Ballygunge Circular Rd; ◷10am-4pm Mon-Fri)

Canadian Delhi (☏011-41782000; www.india.gc.ca; 7/8 Shantipath, Chanakyapuri; ◷consular services 9am-noon Mon-Fri; MChanakyapuri); Mumbai (☏022-67494444; https://international.gc.ca/ world-monde/india-inde/ mumbai.aspx?lang=eng; 21st fl, Tower 2, Indiabulls Finance Centre, Senapati Bapat Marg, Elphinstone Rd West)

Chinese Delhi (☏consular 011-24677525, visas 011-30013601; http://in.china-embassy.org; 50-D Shantipath, Chanakyapuri; ◷9am-12.30pm & 3-5.30pm Mon-Fri; MChanakyapuri)

Dutch Delhi (☏011-24197600; www.netherlandsworldwide.nl/ countries/india; 6/50F Shantipath, Chanakyapuri; ◷9am-5pm Mon-Fri; MChanakyapuri); Mumbai (☏022-22194200; https://www.netherlands worldwide.nl/countries/india/ about-us/consulate-general-in-mumbai; 1st fl, Forbes Bldg, Charanjit Rai Marg, Fort)

French Delhi (☎011-24196100; www.ambafrance-in.org; 2/50E Shantipath, Chanakyapuri; Ⓜ022-66694000; www.amba france-in.org/-Consulate-in-Bombay-; Wockhardt Towers, East Wing, 5th fl, Bandra Kurla Complex, Bandra East); Puducherry (☎0413-2231000; www.ambafrance-in.org; 2 Marine St; ⊗8am-1pm & 2.30-5pm Mon-Thu, to 1pm Fri)

German Chennai (☎044-24301600; www.india.diplo.de; 9 Boat Club Rd, RA Puram; ⊗7.30am-3.30pm Mon-Thu, to 1.30pm Fri); Delhi (https://india.diplo.de; 6/50G Shantipath, Chanakyapuri; Ⓜ Chanakyapuri); Kolkata (☎033-24791141; 1 Hastings Park Rd, Alipore); Mumbai (☎022-22832422; https://india.diplo.de/in-en/vertretungen/gkmumbai; 10th fl, Hoechst House, Nariman Point)

Irish Delhi (☎011-24940 3200; www.dfa.ie/irish-embassy/india; C17 Malcha Marg, Chanakyapuri; ⊗9am-1.30pm & 2.30-5pm Mon-Fri; Ⓜ Chanakyapuri)

Israeli Delhi (☎011-30414500, visas 011-30414538; www.embassies.gov.il/delhi; 3 Dr APJ Abdul Kalam Rd; ⊗9.30am-1pm Mon-Fri; Ⓜ Khan Market); Mumbai (☎022-61600500; www.embassies.gov.il/mumbai; Marathon Futurex, 1301, A Wing, NM Joshi Marg, Lower Parel)

Japanese Chennai (☎044-24323860; www.chennai.in.emb-japan.go.jp; 12/1 1st St, Cenotaph Rd, Teynampet; ⊗9am-5.45pm Mon-Fri); Delhi (☎011-26876581; www.in.emb-japan.go.jp; 50G Shantipath, Chanakyapuri; ⊗9am-1pm & 2-5.30pm Mon-Fri; Ⓜ Chanakyapuri); Mumbai (☎022-23517101; www.mumbai.in.emb-japan.go.jp; 1 ML Dahanukar Marg, Cumballa Hill)

Malaysian Chennai (☎044-24334434; www.kln.gov.my; 7 Cenotaph Rd, 1st St, Teynampet; ⊗9am-5pm Mon-Fri); Delhi (☎011-24159300; http://mw.kln.gov.my/web/ind_new-delhi/home; 50M Satya Marg, Chanakyapuri; ⊗8.30am-4.30pm Mon-Fri; Ⓜ Chanakyapuri); Mumbai

(☎022-26455751; www.kln.gov.my/web/ind_mumbai/home; 5th fl, Notan Classic Bldg, off Turner Rd, Bandra West)

Maldivian Delhi (☎011-41435701; www.maldives embassy.in; C-3 Anand Niketan; Ⓜ Sir Vishvshwaraiah Moti Bagh)

Myanmar Delhi (☎011-24678822; www.myanmedelhi.com; 3/50F Nyaya Marg; ⊗9.30am-4.30pm Mon-Fri; Ⓜ Lok Kalyan Marg); Kolkata (☎033-24851658; 57K Ballygunge Circular Rd; ⊗visas 9am-noon Mon-Fri)

Nepali Delhi (☎011-23476200; http://in.nepalembassy.gov.np; Mandi House, Barakhamba Rd; ⊗visa services 9am-1pm Mon-Fri; Ⓜ Mandi House)

New Zealand Chennai (☎044-28112472; www.mfat.govt.nz; Rane Holdings Ltd, Maithri, 132 Cathedral Rd, Gopalapuram; ⊗8am-5.30pm Mon-Fri); Delhi (☎011-46883170; www.nzembassy.com/india; Sir Edmund Hillary Marg, Chanakyapuri; ⊗8.30am-5pm Mon-Fri; Ⓜ Sir Vishvshwaraiah Moti Bagh); Mumbai (☎022-61316666; www.mfat.govt.nz/en/countries-and-regions/south-asia/india/new-zealand-high-commission/new-zealand-consulate-general-mumbai-india; Level 2, Maker Maxity, 3 North Ave, Bandra Kurla Complex)

Singaporean Chennai (☎044-28158207; www.mfa.gov.sg; 17A North Boag Rd, T Nagar; ⊗9am-5pm Mon-Fri); Delhi (☎011-46000915; www.mfa.gov.sg/newdelhi; E6 Chandragupta Marg, Chanakyapuri; ⊗9am-1pm & 1.30-5pm Mon-Fri; Ⓜ Chanakyapuri); Mumbai (☎022-22043205; www.mfa.gov.sg/content/mfa/overseasmission/mumbai.html; Maker Chambers IV, 14th fl, 222 Jamnalal Bajaj Rd, Nariman Point)

Sri Lankan Chennai (☎044-28241896; www.sldhcchennai.org; 56 Sterling Rd, Nungambakkam; ⊗9am-5.15pm); Delhi (☎011-23010201; www.slhcindia.org; 27 Kautilya Marg, Chanakyapuri; ⊗8.45am-5pm Mon-Fri; Ⓜ Lok Kalyan Marg);

Mumbai (☎022-22045861; www.mumbai.mission.gov.lk; Mulla House, 34 Homi Modi St, Fort)

Thai Chennai (☎044-42300730; www.vfs-thailand.co.in; 3 1st Main Rd, Vidyodaya Colony, T Nagar; ⊗8am-noon & 1-3pm Mon-Fri); Delhi (☎011-49774100; http://newdelhi.thaiembassy.org; D-1/3 Vasant Vihar; ⊗9am-5pm Mon-Fri; Ⓜ Vasant Vihar); Kolkata (☎033-24407836; 18B Mandeville Gardens, Ballygunge); Mumbai (☎022-22823535; www.thaiembassy.org/mumbai; 12th fl, Express Towers, Barrister Rajni Patel Marg, Nariman Point)

UK Chennai (☎044-42192151; www.gov.uk; 20 Anderson Rd, Nungambakkam; ⊗8.30am-4.30pm Mon-Thu, to 1.30pm Fri); Delhi (☎011-24192100; Shantipath, Chanakyapuri; ⊗9am-5pm Mon-Fri; Ⓜ Lok Kalyan Marg); Kolkata (☎033-22885172; 1A Ho Chi Minh Sarani); Mumbai (☎022-66502222; www.gov.uk/government/world/organisations/british-deputy-high-commission-mumbai; Naman Chambers, C/32 G Block Bandra Kurla Complex, Bandra East)

USA Chennai (☎044-28574000; http://in.usembassy.gov; 220 Anna Salai, Gemini Circle; ⊗9am-5pm Mon-Fri); Delhi (☎011-24198000; https://in.usembassy.gov; Shantipath, Chanakyapuri; Ⓜ Lok Kalyan Marg); Kolkata (☎033-3984 2400; 5/1 Ho Chi Minh Sarani); Mumbai (☎022-26724000; https://in.usembassy.gov/embassy-consulates/mumbai; C49, G Block, Bandra Kurla Complex, Bandra East)

Food

Eating in restaurants is a big risk for contracting illnesses. Ways to avoid them include:

➡ eating only freshly cooked food

➡ avoiding shellfish and buffets

➡ peeling fruit

➡ cooking vegetables

EATING PRICE RANGES

The following price ranges refer to a standard main.

$ less than ₹150

$$ ₹150–₹300

$$$ more than ₹300

→ soaking salads in iodine water for at least 20 minutes

→ eating in busy restaurants with a high turnover of customers

→ washing hands thoroughly before and after eating and/ or using hand sanitiser

See Delicious India (p472) for information about food in South India.

Insurance

→ Comprehensive travel insurance to cover theft, loss and medical problems (as well as air evacuation) is strongly recommended.

→ Some policies specifically exclude potentially dangerous activities such as scuba diving, rock climbing, motorcycling and even trekking: read the fine print.

→ Some trekking agents may accept only customers who have cover for emergency helicopter evacuation.

→ If you plan to hire a motorcycle in India, make sure the rental policy includes at least third-party insurance.

→ Check in advance if your insurance policy will pay doctors and hospitals directly or reimburse you later for overseas health expenditures (keep all documentation for your claim).

→ It's crucial to get a police report in India if you've had anything stolen; insurance companies may refuse to reimburse you without one.

→ Worldwide travel insurance is available at www.lonelyplanet.com/ travel-insurance. You can buy, extend and claim online anytime – even if you're already on the road.

Internet Access

→ Wi-fi is available in most places to stay, and at many cafes, bars and restaurants in larger cities. Access is most often free but not always – you'll still come across the occasional holdout.

→ Free wi-fi is now offered at around 700 train stations across India.

→ Wi-fi signals everywhere are subject to temporary outages because of power cuts and the vagaries of servers.

→ With an Indian SIM (recommended) 3G/4G access is widely available at very reasonable prices, thanks to game-changing 2016 telecoms arrival Jio, the world's first mobile network to run entirely on 4G data technology. Jio charges around ₹149 for a one-month plan with 1GB of data per day, for example.

→ Portable data hot spots (used for both smartphones and laptops, and for up to 10 devices) are also available; Jio hot spots, for example, cost ₹999 to ₹1999, and you'll need a Jio SIM (free with a minimum recharge). As when procuring a local SIM, to organise a connection you have to submit your proof of identity and address in India, and activation can take up to 24 hours.

→ Internet cafes are a dwindling breed. Where found, connections are usually reasonably fast, except in more remote areas.

Legal Matters

If you're in a sticky legal situation, contact your embassy as quickly as possible. However, be aware that all your embassy may be able to do is monitor your treatment in custody and arrange a lawyer. In the Indian justice system, the burden of proof can often be on the accused and stints in prison before trial are not unheard of.

Antisocial Behaviour

→ Smoking in public places is illegal throughout India but this is very rarely enforced; fines are ₹200, though there are plans to raise this to ₹1000.

→ People can smoke inside their homes and in most open spaces such as streets (heed any signs stating otherwise).

→ Some Indian cities have banned spitting and littering, but this is also variably enforced.

Drugs

→ Indian law does not distinguish between 'hard' and 'soft' drugs; possession of any illegal drug is regarded as a criminal offence, which will result in a custodial sentence.

→ Sentences may be up to a year for possession of a small amount for personal use, to a minimum of 10 years if it's deemed the purpose was for sale or distribution. There's also usually a hefty fine on top of any sentence.

→ Cases can take months, even several years, to appear before a court, during which time the accused may have to wait in prison.

→ Be aware that travellers have been targeted in sting operations in Goa and other backpacker enclaves.

→ Police are getting particularly tough on foreigners who use drugs, so you should take this risk very seriously.

→ Marijuana grows wild in various parts of India, but consuming it is still an offence, except in towns where bhang is legally sold for religious rituals.

PROHIBITED EXPORTS

To protect India's cultural heritage, the export of certain antiques is prohibited, especially those which are verifiably more than 100 years old. Reputable antique dealers know the laws and can make arrangements for an export-clearance certificate for old items that are OK to export. Detailed information on prohibited items can be found on the Archaeological Survey of India (ASI) website (http://asi.nic.in). The rules may seem stringent, but the loss of ancient artworks and sculptures due to the international trade in antiques has been alarming. Look for quality reproductions instead.

The Indian Wildlife Protection Act bans any form of wildlife trade. Don't buy any product that endangers threatened species and habitats – doing so can result in heavy fines and even imprisonment. This includes ivory, shahtoosh shawls (made from the down of the rare chiru, the Tibetan antelope) and anything made from the fur, skin, horns or shell of any endangered species. Products made from certain rare plants are also banned.

➡ Pharmaceutical drugs that are restricted in other countries may be available in India over the counter or via prescription. Be aware that taking these without professional guidance can be dangerous.

Police

➡ You should always carry your passport; police are entitled to ask you for identification at any time.

➡ If you're arrested for an alleged offence and asked for a bribe, note: it is illegal to pay a bribe in India. Many people deal with an on-the-spot fine by just paying it to avoid trumped-up charges.

➡ Corruption is rife so the less you have to do with local police the better; try to avoid all potentially risky situations.

➡ Police in Goa have cracked down on all traffic (foreigners on scooters included) in recent years.

LGBT+ Travellers

➡ In September 2018 India's Supreme Court decriminalised homosexuality, which had been banned in 2013 after being decriminalised since 2009.

The Supreme Court gave legal recognition to transgender people as a third gender in a landmark 2014 ruling.

➡ Indian society remains conservative, however, especially outside of the big cities. LGBT travellers should be discreet, and public displays of affection are frowned upon for both homosexual and heterosexual couples.

➡ There are gay scenes (and Gay Pride marches) in a number of cities including Mumbai, Chennai, Bengaluru, Puducherry and Hyderabad, as well as in Delhi, and a holiday gay scene in Goa.

Resources

Bombay Dost (www.bombay dost.co.in) A reputable Mumbai-based LGBT+ publication.

Gay Bombay (https://gay bombay.org) Lists events and offers support and advice.

Gaylaxy (www.gaylaxymag.com) India's best gay e-zine, including news, blogs, articles, reviews and fashion.

Gaysi (http://gaysifamily.com) A pioneering, powerful website and magazine featuring LGBTQ writing and issues; also hosts events.

Indian Dost (https://indiandost. com) News and information including contact groups in India.

Indja Pink (www.indjapink.co.in) India's first gay boutique travel agency, founded by well-known Indian fashion designer Sanjay Malhotra.

LGBT Events India (www. lgbteventsindia.com) Nightlife and other events.

Nomadic Boys (https:// nomadicboys.com) Helpful gay travel blog, including India coverage.

Orinam (http://orinam.net) Chennai-based support group for advice and events. Handy on Twitter @chennaipride, too.

Queer Azaadi Mumbai (www. queerazaadi.wordpress.com) Mumbai's queer pride blog, with news.

Queer Ink (http://queer-ink. com) Develops, promotes and sells India-focused LGBTQ books and films.

Maps

Maps available inside India are of variable quality. Most state-government tourist offices stock basic local maps. These are some of the better map series, which should be available online or at good bookshops:

Eicher (www.eicher.in)

Nelles (www.nelles-verlag.de)

Survey of India (www.survey ofindia.gov.in) Many maps are downloadable for free.

TTK (www.ttkmaps.com)

Money

ATMs are widely available; credit/debit cards are accepted in midrange hotels, shops and restaurants, but much of India remains a cash-based economy.

Currency

The Indian rupee (₹) is divided into 100 paise (p), but only 50 paise coins are legal tender and these are rarely seen. Coins come in denominations of ₹1, ₹2, ₹5 and ₹10 (the ₹1s and ₹2s look almost identical); notes come in ₹5, ₹10, ₹20, ₹50, ₹100, and the newly introduced ₹500 and ₹2000 (this last is handy for paying large bills but can pose problems when getting change for small purchases). The Indian rupee is linked to a basket of currencies and has been subject to fluctuations in recent years.

ATMs

➤ ATMs are found in most urban centres.

➤ Visa, MasterCard, Cirrus, Maestro and Plus are the most commonly accepted cards.

➤ ATMs at Axis Bank, Citibank, HDFC, HSBC, ICICI and State Bank of India recognise foreign cards. Other banks' ATMs may accept major cards (Visa, MasterCard etc).

➤ Most ATMs have a limit of ₹10,000 per withdrawal. Citibank ATMs generally allow you to withdraw ₹20,000 in one transaction, reducing transaction charges, which are often in the region of ₹250.

➤ Before your trip, check whether your card can reliably access banking networks in India and find out details of charges.

➤ Notify your bank that you'll be using your card in India to avoid having it blocked; note your bank's phone number just in case.

➤ Away from major towns, always carry cash.

Black Market

➤ Black-market money changers exist, but legal money changers are so common there's no reason to use illegal services.

➤ If someone approaches you on the street and offers to change money, you're probably being set up for a scam.

Cash

➤ Major currencies such as US dollars, pounds sterling and euros are easy to change throughout India. Some banks also accept other currencies such as Australian and Canadian dollars, and Swiss francs.

➤ Private money changers deal with a wider range of currencies than banks, but Pakistani, Nepali and Bangladeshi currency can be harder to change away from the border.

➤ When travelling off the beaten track, always carry an adequate stock of rupees.

➤ When changing money, check every note. Don't accept any filthy, ripped or disintegrating notes, as these may be difficult to use.

➤ It can be tough getting change in India, so a stock of smaller currency is invaluable (especially ₹10, ₹20 and ₹50 notes).

➤ Officially you cannot take rupees out of India, but this is laxly enforced. You can change any leftover rupees back into foreign currency, most easily at the airport. You may have to present encashment certificates or credit-card/ATM receipts, and show your passport and airline ticket.

Credit Cards

➤ Credit cards are accepted at many shops, better restaurants and midrange and top-end hotels, and they can usually be used to pay for flights and train tickets.

➤ Cash advances on major credit cards are possible at some banks.

➤ MasterCard and Visa are the most widely accepted cards.

Digital Wallets

PayTM (www.paytm.com) is India's major digital wallet company. Local users pay for things through their smartphone, which is linked to their bank account. For now, at least, you cannot link a PayTM account to a foreign bank account, but do look into it as things may change.

Encashment Certificates

➤ Indian law states that all foreign currency must be changed at official money changers or banks.

➤ For every (official) foreign-exchange transaction, you'll

MEDIA

Magazines Current-affairs magazines include *Frontline* (www.frontline.in), *India Today* (www.indiatoday.in), the *Week* (www.theweek.in), *Tehelka* (http://tehelka.com) and *Outlook* (www.outlookindia.com).

Newpapers English-language dailies include the *Hindustan Times* (www.hindustan times.com), *Times of India* (https://timesofindia.indiatimes.com), *Indian Express* (https://indianexpress.com), the *Hindu* (www.thehindu.com), *Daily News & Analysis* (DNA; www.dnaindia.com) and *Economic Times* (www.economictimes.indiatimes.com).

Radio Government-controlled All India Radio (AIR; www.allindiaradio.gov.in) is India's national broadcaster, There are also private FM channels broadcasting music, current affairs, talkback and more.

TV The national TV broadcaster is Doordarshan (DD; http://doordarshan.gov.in).

TIPPING

Restaurants A service charge ranging from 4% to 10% is often added to your bill; tipping is optional.

Hotels Bellboys and helpful hotel staff appreciate ₹20 to ₹50.

Porters Train/airport porters appreciate anything around ₹50.

Taxis and Rickshaws Not normally tipped beyond rounding to nearest ₹10.

Hired Cars 10% is recommended for good service.

receive an encashment certificate (receipt), which will allow you to change rupees back into foreign currency when departing India.

➤ Encashment certificates should cover the amount of rupees you intend to change back to foreign currency.

➤ Printed receipts from ATMs are also accepted as evidence of an international transaction at most banks.

International Transfers

➤ If you run out of money, someone back home can wire you cash via money changers affiliated with Moneygram (www. moneygram.com) or Western Union (www. westernunion.com). A fee is added to the transaction.

➤ To collect cash, bring your passport and the name and reference number of the person who sent the funds.

Money Changers

➤ Private money changers are usually open longer hours than banks, and are found almost everywhere (many also double as internet cafes and travel agents).

➤ Upmarket hotels may also change money, but their rates are usually not as competitive.

Opening Hours

For typical opening hours, see Need to Know (p15).

Photography

➤ India is touchy about anyone taking photographs of military installations – these can include train stations, bridges, airports, military sites and sensitive border regions.

➤ Photography from the air is mostly OK, unless you're taking off from (or landing in) airports actively shared by defence forces.

➤ Many places of worship – such as monasteries, temples and mosques – prohibit photography. Taking photos inside shrines or at funerals or religious ceremonies, or of people publicly bathing (including in rivers) can be offensive – ask first.

➤ Flash photography may be prohibited in certain areas with shrines or historical monuments.

➤ Exercise sensitivity when photographing people, especially women and children – some may find it offensive, so obtain permission in advance.

➤ It is not uncommon for people in touristic areas to demand a posing fee in return for being photographed. Exercise your discretion in these situations. In any case, ask first to avoid misunderstandings later.

Post

➤ India Post (www.indiapost. gov.in) runs the most widely distributed postal service on earth. Mail and poste-restante services are generally good, though the speed of delivery depends on the efficiency of the office. Airmail is faster and more reliable than sea mail, although it's best to use courier services (such as DHL and TNT) to send and receive items of value. Expect to pay around ₹3500 per kilo for a parcel to Europe, Australia or the USA. Private couriers are often cheaper, but goods may be repacked into large packages to cut costs and things sometimes go missing.

Sending Mail

LETTERS

➤ Posting airmail letters/postcards overseas costs ₹25/12.

➤ Sending a letter overseas by registered post costs an extra ₹70.

➤ Stick the stamps on postcards before writing on them, as post offices can give you as many as four stamps per card.

PARCELS

➤ Posting parcels can be either relatively straightforward or involve multiple counters and lots of queuing; get to the post office in the morning.

➤ All parcels sent through the government postal service must be packed up in white linen and the seams sealed with wax – agents near post offices usually offer this service for a small fee.

➤ An unregistered airmail package up to 250g in weight costs around ₹600 to ₹1000 to any country, plus ₹50 to ₹270 per additional 250g.

➤ Parcel post has a maximum of 20kg to 30kg depending on the destination.

➤ Airmail takes one to three weeks, sea mail two to four months, and Surface Air-Lifted (SAL) – a curious hybrid where parcels travel by both air and sea – around one month.

➡ Express mail service (EMS; delivery within three days) costs around 30% more than the normal airmail price.

➡ Customs declaration forms, available from the post office, must be stitched or pasted to the parcel. No duty is payable by the recipient for gifts under the value of ₹1000

➡ Carry a permanent marker to write on the parcel any information requested by the desk.

➡ You can send printed matter via surface mail 'Bulk Bag' for ₹600 (maximum 5kg), plus ₹100 per additional kilo. The parcel has to be packed with an opening so it can be checked by customs – tailors can do this in such a way that nothing falls out.

➡ India Post has an online calculator for domestic and international postal tariffs.

Receiving Mail

➡ Ask senders to address letters to you with your surname in capital letters and underlined, followed by Poste Restante, GPO (main post office), and the city or town in question.

➡ To claim mail you'll need to show your passport.

➡ Letters sent via poste restante are generally held for around one to two months before being returned.

➡ Many 'lost' letters are simply misfiled under given/first names, so check under both your names and ask senders to provide a return address.

➡ It's best to have any parcels sent to you by registered post.

Public Holidays

There are three official national public holidays – Republic and Independence Days and Gandhi's birthday (Gandhi Jayanti) – plus a dizzying array of other holidays celebrat-ed nationally or locally, many of them marking important days in various religions and falling on variable dates. The most important are the 'gazetted holidays' (listed), which are observed by central-government offices throughout India – see https://www.india.gov.in/calendar for the latest dates. On these days most businesses (offices, shops etc), banks and tourist sites close, but transport is usually unaffected. It's wise to make transport and hotel reservations well in advance if you intend visiting during major festivals.

Republic Day 26 January

Maha Shivaratri February

Holi February/March

Mahavir Jayanti March/April

Good Friday March/April

Buddha Jayanti April/May

Eid al-Fitr May/June

Independence Day 15 August

Janmastami August

Eid al-Adha (Id ul-Zuha) July/August

Muharram August/September

Dussehra September/October

Gandhi Jayanti 2 October

Diwali October/November

Eid-Milad-un-Nabi October/November

Guru Nanak Jayanti November

Christmas Day 25 December

Safe Travel

➡ Travellers to South India may fall prey to petty and opportunistic crime, but most problems can be avoided with common sense and appropriate caution.

➡ Travellers often post timely warnings about problems they've encountered on Lonely Planet's Thorn Tree travel forum (www.lonelyplanet.com/thorntree/forums/asia-indian-subcontinent).

➡ Reports of sexual assault have increased in recent years; women should take extra precautions (p506).

➡ Scams and frauds (p504) change as often as the bed sheets.

➡ Always check your government's travel advisory warnings.

➡ Air and noise pollution (p501) are growing problems across India; consider earplugs and/or a mouth cover.

➡ Airport security is tight: you'll have to show your passport and ticket to enter.

Political Violence

India has a number of (sometimes armed) dissident groups fighting on behalf of various causes, which have employed the same tried and tested techniques as rebel groups everywhere: assassinations and bomb attacks on government infrastructure, public transport, religious centres, tourist sites and markets. Certain areas, mostly (but not exclusively) in the north of the country, are prone to insurgent violence: read the latest government travel advisories for recent reports on where is considered unsafe.

WARNING: BHANG LASSI

Although it's rarely printed on menus, some restaurants in tourist centres will clandestinely whip up bhang lassi, a yoghurt and iced-water beverage laced with cannabis (occasionally other narcotics). This often-potent concoction can cause varying degrees of ecstasy, drawn-out delirium, hallucination, nausea and paranoia. Some travellers have been ill for several days, robbed or hurt in accidents after drinking this fickle brew. A few towns have legal (controlled) bhang outlets.

International terrorism is as much of a risk in Europe or the USA, so this is no reason not to go to India, but check the local security situation carefully before travelling (especially in high-risk areas).

Strikes and political protests can close roads (as well as banks, shops etc) for days on end in any region.

Telephone

Local SIM cards are now readily available to tourists, at extremely low prices – and they make life significantly easier!

Call Booths

There are few payphones in South India (apart from in airports), but private STD/ISD/PCO call booths do the same job, offering inexpensive local, interstate and international calls, though they aren't as widespread as in the past. A digital meter displays how much the call is costing and usually provides a printed receipt when the call is finished.

Mobile Phones

Roaming connections are excellent in urban areas, poor in the countryside and hills. Local prepaid SIMs are widely available; the paperwork is fairly straightforward but you'll have to wait 24 hours for activation.

GETTING CONNECTED

➡ Indian mobile numbers usually have 10 digits, mostly beginning with 9 (but sometimes 6, 7 or 8), and operate on the GSM network at 900MHz, the world's most common, so mobile phones from most countries will work on the subcontinent.

➡ Mobiles bought in some countries may be locked to a particular network; you'll have to get the phone unlocked, or buy a local phone (available from around ₹1000) to use an Indian SIM card.

➡ Getting connected is inexpensive but requires a bit more hoop-jumping than in many other parts of the world, though it's getting much easier. It's easiest to obtain a local SIM card in large cities and tourist centres – or, better yet, directly at airport booths when you land. Some regions require fiddlier processes than others.

➡ Foreigners must supply between one and five passport photos, and photocopies of their passport identity and visa pages. Often mobile shops can arrange all this for you, or you can ask your hotel to help you.

➡ You must also provide a residential address, which can be the address of your hotel, as well as a local reference (your hotel is generally fine for this, too). Usually the phone company will call your hotel (warn the hotel a call will come through) any time up to 24 hours after your application to verify that you are staying there.

➡ It's a good idea to obtain the SIM card in a place that you're staying in for a day or two so that you can return to the vendor if there's any problem. To avoid scams, obtain your SIM card only from a reputable branded phone shop.

➡ SIMs are sold as regular size from some vendors, but most places have machines to cut them down to the required size if necessary; official stores usually have multifit SIMs.

➡ Another option is to get a friendly local to obtain a connection in their name.

➡ Prepaid mobile-phone packages are readily available for short-term visitors. SIMs often come free with a minimum data and call package. Game-changing Jio (www.jio.com), the first ever mobile network to run entirely on 4G data technology, which brought connectivity to 150 million users in its first 18 months from launching in 2016, has deals from ₹149 for 1.5GB of data per day to ₹509 for 4GB per day, both for 28 days. Airtel (www.airtel.in) offers, for example,1.5GB per day for 28 days (₹199). Most large data packages are good for 28 days and prices are fairly standardised.

➡ You can then purchase more data or a new prepaid package at stalls and shops all over (just look for phone-company logos). You pay the vendor and the package/credit is deposited straight into your account.

CHARGES, COVERAGE & OPERATORS

➡ Calls within India are often included in the prepaid package you purchase along with your local SIM. International calls start from around ₹1 a minute.

➡ International outgoing messages cost ₹5. Incoming calls and messages are less than ₹1 and free, respectively.

➡ Unreliable signals and problems with international texting (messages or replies not coming through or being delayed) are not uncommon.

➡ The leading service providers are Jio (part of Reliance), Airtel, Vodafone–Idea and BSNL. Coverage varies from region to region – Vodafone–Idea, Jio and Airtel have the widest coverage, while BSNL is best for the remote Andaman Islands.

Phone Codes

➡ Calling India from abroad, dial your country's international access code, then 91 (India's country code), then the area code (without the initial zero), then the local number. For mobile phones, the area code and initial zero are not required.

➡ Calling internationally from India, dial 00 (the international access code), then the country code of the country you're calling, then the area code (without the initial zero) and the local number.

➡ Indian landline phone numbers have an area code followed by up to eight digits.

➡ Toll-free numbers begin with 1800.

➡ To call a landline phone from a mobile phone, add the area code (with the initial zero).

Time

Indian Standard Time (IST) is 5½ hours ahead of GMT/UTC. The floating half-hour was added to maximise daylight hours over such a vast country.

CITY	TIME DIFFERENCE
London (UK)	+5½hr
Cape Town (South Africa)	+3½hr
Buenos Aires (Argentina)	+8½hr
Washington DC (USA)	+10½hr
Singapore	-2½hr
Canberra (Australia)	-5½hr

Toilets

➡ Public toilets are most easily found in major cities and tourist sites; the cleanest are usually at modern restaurants and hotels, shopping complexes and cinemas.

➡ Beyond urban centres, toilets are often of the squat variety and locals may use the 'hand-and-water' technique, which involves performing ablutions with a small jug of water and the left hand. It's always a good idea to carry toilet paper/baby wipes and hand sanitiser, just in case.

Tourist Information

In addition to Government of India tourist offices (known as 'Indiatourism'), each state maintains its own network of tourist offices. These vary in their efficiency and usefulness – some are run by enthusiastic souls who go out of their way to help, others are little more than a means of drumming up business for State Tourism Development Corporation tours.

The first stop for information should be the Government of India tourism website, Incredible India (www.incredibleindia.org). Official state tourism websites often contain helpful information, too. The government has also introduced a toll-free 24-hour tourist helpline: 1800 111363.

Handy Government of India tourism offices in South India:

Bengaluru (GITO; ☎080-25583030; indiatourism bengaluru@gmail.com; 2nd fl, Triumph Towers, 48 Church St; ⊗9.30am-5.30pm Mon-Fri, to noon Sat; ⓜMG Rd)

Chennai (☎044-28460285, 044-28461459; www.incredible india.org; 154 Anna Salai, Anna Salai; ⊗9.15am-5.45pm Mon-Fri)

Kochi (☎0484-2669125; www.incredibleindia.org; Willingdon Island; ⊗9am-6pm Mon-Fri)

Mumbai (Government of India Tourist Office;☎022-22074333; www.incredibleindia.com; ground fl, Air India Bldg, Vidhan Bhavan Marg, Nariman Point; ⊗8.30am-6pm Mon-Fri, to 2pm Sat)

Panaji (☎0832-2438812; www.incredibleindia.com; Paryatan Bhavan, Dr Alvaro Costa Rd; ⊗9.30am-1.30pm & 2.30-6pm Mon-Fri, 10am-1pm Sat)

Visas

Many nationalities can obtain 60-day visas through India's e-Visa scheme. For longer trips, most people get a six-month tourist visa, valid from the date of issue (not arrival).

E-Visa Scheme

➡ Citizens of more than 150 countries, including Argentina, Australia, Brazil, Canada, Chile, China, Colombia, Israel, Japan, Mexico, New Zealand, Republic of Korea, Singapore, Taiwan, Thailand and the USA, in addition to most European countries, must apply for an e-Visa at https://indianvisaonline.gov.in a minimum of four days and maximum of 120 days before they are due to arrive in India.

➡ The nonrefundable fee ranges from US$80 to US$100 for most countries, plus a 2.5% bank transaction charge.

➡ You have to upload a photograph as well as a copy of your passport.

➡ At the time of writing, the two-entry e-Visa is valid for entry through 26 designated airports including Bengaluru (Bangalore), Chennai, Kochi (Cochin), Kozhikode (Calicut), Delhi, Goa, Jaipur, Kolkata, Mumbai, Trichy (Tiruchirappalli), Thiruvananthapuram (Trivandrum) and Varanasi.

➡ The e-Visa is valid for 60 days from the date of your arrival; your passport must be valid for at least six months from the date of arrival and you must carry a copy of your Electronic Travel Authorization (ETA).

➡ You can exit India through any authorised immigration check-post.

➡ E-Visas can be requested a maximum of three times per calendar year.

Other Visas

If you want to stay longer than 60 days, or are not covered by the e-Visa scheme, you must get a visa before arriving in India (apart from Nepali or Bhutanese citizens, who do not need visas). Visas are available from Indian missions worldwide, though in many countries applications are processed by a separate private company. In some countries or where biometrics are required, you must apply in person at the designated office as well as filing an application online.

➡ Your passport must be valid for at least six months from the date of your visa application (or from the date of issue of your visa, or its date of expiry, or your date of arrival in India, depending on which arm of Indian bureaucracy is dealing with it), with at least two blank pages.

➡ Most people are issued a standard six-month tourist visa, which for most nationalities permits multiple entry.

➡ Tourist visas are valid from the date of issue, not from the date you arrive in India (unlike e-Visas).

➡ Student and business visas have strict conditions: journalist, missionary and research visas, among others, require biometric enrolment. Consult the Indian embassy for details.

➡ Five- and 10-year tourist visas are available to US citizens under a bilateral arrangement; however, you can still only stay in India for up to 180 days continuously.

➡ Currently visa applicants are required to submit two passport photographs with their application; these must be in colour and must be 5.08cm by 5.08cm (2in by 2in; larger than regular passport photos).

➡ An onward travel ticket is a requirement for some visas, but this isn't always enforced (check in advance).

➡ Additional restrictions apply to travellers from Bangladesh and Pakistan, as well as certain Eastern European, African and Central Asian countries. Check any special conditions for your nationality with the Indian embassy in your country.

➡ Visas are priced in the local currency and may have an added service fee.

➡ Extended visas are possible for people of Indian origin who hold a non-Indian passport and live abroad (excluding those in Pakistan and Bangladesh).

➡ For visas lasting more than six months, travellers no longer need to register at the Foreigners' Regional Registration Office in Delhi; instead, you register online through the e-FRRO scheme (https://indianfrro.gov.in), launched in 2018.

Re-Entry Requirements

Most tourists are permitted to transit freely between India and its neighbouring countries. However, citizens of China, Pakistan, Iraq, Iran, Afghanistan, Bangladesh and Sudan (and foreigners of Pakistani or Bangladeshi origin) are barred from reentry into India within two months of their last exit.

Travel Permits

Even with a visa, you're not permitted to travel everywhere in South India.

➡ Some national parks and forest reserves call for a permit.

➡ A special permit is required to visit Lakshadweep and for trekking in Kerala's Wayanad region.

➡ In 2018 the old requirement of a Restricted Area Permit (RAP) was removed for most tourist destinations in the Andaman Islands, though some places still require additional permits, and change is ongoing (p419).

Visa Extensions

➡ India has traditionally been very stringent with visa extensions. At the time of writing, the government was granting extensions only in circumstances such as medical emergencies or theft of passport just before the expiry of an applicant's visa.

➡ If you do need to extend your visa due to any such exigency, you can now apply to do so through the Foreigners' Regional Registration Office (FRRO) online portal (e-FRRO; https://indianfrro.gov.in). You must supply a passport photo; copies of your passport identity, visa and Indian immigration stamp pages; and various other supporting documents, usually including your onward-travel air ticket. At research time, the portal offered 27 visa-related services, including replacement visas and replacements of lost/stolen passports (required before you can leave the country). Otherwise, contact the FRRO office in Delhi; regional FRROs are even less likely to grant an extension.

➡ Assuming you meet the stringent criteria, the FRRO is permitted to issue an extension of 14 days (free for nationals of most countries). Note that this system is designed to get you out of the country promptly with the correct official stamps, not to give you two extra weeks of travel and leisure.

Transport

GETTING THERE & AWAY

Entering the Country/Region

South India is most easily accessed via its major international airports at Bengaluru (Bangalore), Chennai, Mumbai and Kochi (Cochin). Some countries also offer charter flights to Goa, where a new international airport at Mopa is expected by 2020. The south is also well served by India's extensive rail network as well as inexpensive (and often adventure-filled) buses from elsewhere in India. Flights, cars and tours can be booked online at lonelyplanet.com/bookings.

Passports

To enter India you need a valid passport, a visa and an onward/return ticket. Your passport needs to be valid for at least six months beyond your intended stay in India, with at least two blank pages. Keep photocopies/scans of the identity and visa pages of your passport.

Air

South India has four main gateways for international flights: **Bengaluru** (☑1800 4254425; www.bengaluruairport.com), **Chennai** (☑044-22560551; Tirusulam), **Mumbai** (☑022-66851010; www.csia.in; Santa Cruz East) and **Kochi** (☑0484-2610115; http://cial.aero; Nedumbassery), though a number of other cities also handle international flights, such as Thiruvananthapuram (Trivandrum), Hyderabad, Pune, Kannur and Kozhikode (Calicut). Direct charter flights from Russia, the UK and certain other parts of Europe land at Goa's **Dabolim Airport** (Goa International Airport; ☑0832-2540806; NH566); most noncharter flight passengers bound for Goa fly into Mumbai. A new greenfield international airport at Mopa, North Goa, is due for completion by 2020.

India's national carrier is **Air India** (☑1860-2331407, 011-24667473; www.airindia.com), which has had a relatively decent air-safety record in recent years; some recent studies have branded it one of the world's least safe airlines, but Air India has strongly disputed these claims and AirlineRatings (www.airlineratings.com) rates it six stars (out of seven).

Land

Although most visitors fly into South India, it's possible, of course, to get here overland via the long haul through North India. The classic hippie route from Europe to Goa involves travelling via Turkey, Iran and Pakistan, but politics makes this more tricky these days; other popular overland options are via Bangladesh or Nepal. If you enter India by bus or train you'll be required to disembark at the border for standard immigration and customs checks.

You *must* acquire a valid Indian visa in advance, as no visas are available at the border; e-Visas are only valid for travellers arriving by air.

CLIMATE CHANGE & TRAVEL

Every form of transport that relies on carbon-based fuel generates CO_2, the main cause of human-induced climate change. Modern travel is dependent on aeroplanes, which might use less fuel per kilometre per person than most cars but travel much greater distances. The altitude at which aircraft emit gases (including CO_2) and particles also contributes to their climate change impact. Many websites offer 'carbon calculators' that allow people to estimate the carbon emissions generated by their journey and, for those who wish to do so, to offset the impact of the greenhouse gases emitted with contributions to portfolios of climate-friendly initiatives throughout the world. Lonely Planet offsets the carbon footprint of all staff and author travel.

For detailed up-to-date information about crossing into India from neighbouring countries, consult Lonely Planet's *India* and/or Thorn-Tree forum (https://www.lonelyplanet.com/thorntree).

Car & Motorcycle

Drivers of cars and motorbikes will need the vehicle's registration papers, liability insurance and an international driving permit in addition to their domestic licence. You'll also need a *Carnet de passage en douane*, which acts as a temporary waiver of import duty; otherwise you have to leave a deposit with a local bank, which is predictably time-consuming and fiddly.

Sea

There are several sea routes between mainland India and surrounding islands, including the Andaman Islands, but none leave Indian sovereign territory. There has long been talk of a passenger ferry service between southern India and Colombo in Sri Lanka but this has yet to materialise; enquire locally to see if there has been any progress.

Tours

Ampersand Travel (www.ampersandtravel.com) Bespoke and small-group luxury/boutique tours.

Cox & Kings (www.coxandkings.com) Long-standing operator offering tours across South India, including houseboat options and a travel branch for mobility-impaired travellers, **Enable Travel** (www.enabletravel.com).

Dragoman (www.dragoman.com) One of several reputable overland tour companies.

Exodus (www.exodus.co.uk) A wide array of specialist trips, including Kerala tours with houseboats.

Greaves India (www.greaves india.co.uk) Family-owned UK-based operator with a sustainable focus.

India Wildlife Tours (www.india-wildlife-tours.com) All sorts of wildlife tours, plus jeep/horse safaris and birdwatching.

Indian Panorama (www.indian panorama.in) Itineraries include temples, wildlife and food.

Intrepid Travel (www.intrepidtravel.com) Endless possibilities, from wildlife tours to sacred rambles.

Kerala Connections (http://keralaconnections.co.uk) Tailor-made trips, including islands.

KOKOindia (www.kokoindia.com) UK- and Goa-based company for bespoke tours, retreats and safaris.

Martin Randall (www.martin randall.com) Cultural tours including Gastronomic Kerala.

Shanti Travel (www.shantitravel.com) A range of tours from a Franco-Indian team.

Village Ways (www.villageways.com) Walking- and village-based itineraries involving local communities.

World Expeditions (www.worldexpeditions.com) Options include trekking and cycling tours.

GETTING AROUND

Air

India has a very competitive, well-established domestic airline industry. Most of India's main carriers have a six-star (out of seven) safety record, according to AirlineRatings (www.airlineratings.com) – with the exception of SpiceJet (three stars) and Air India Express (five stars).

At the time of writing, the following airlines were the major players operating across South India:

Air India (☎1860-2331407, 011-24667473; www.airindia.com)

GoAir (☎18602-100999; www.goair.in)

IndiGo (☎011-43513200; www.goindigo.in)

Jet Airways (☎91-39893333; www.jetairways.com)

SpiceJet (☎0987-1803333; www.spicejet.com)

Vistara (☎9289-228888; www.airvistara.com)

The competitive nature of the aviation industry means that fares fluctuate dramatically. Holidays, festivals and seasons also have a serious effect on ticket prices.

Security at airports is generally stringent. You must present your passport and a valid ticket/boarding pass (print or digital) to enter airport terminals. All hold baggage must be X-rayed prior to check-in and every item of cabin baggage needs a label, which must be stamped as part of the security check (collect tags at the check-in counter).

Bicycle

South India offers loads of variety for cyclists, from pretty coastal routes to winding roads passing fragrant spice plantations. There are no restrictions on bringing a bicycle into the country. However, bicycles sent by sea can take a few weeks to clear customs in India, so it's better to fly bikes in. It may actually be cheaper – and less hassle – to hire or buy a bicycle in India itself.

Read up on bicycle touring before you travel – Rob Van Der Plas' *Bicycle Touring Manual* and Stephen Lord's *Adventure Cycle-Touring Handbook* are good places to start. Consult local cycling magazines and cycling clubs for useful information and advice.

Hire

➜ Tourist centres and traveller hang-outs are the easiest spots to hire bicycles; enquire locally.

➜ Prices vary: anywhere from around ₹100 to ₹200 per day for a roadworthy, Indian-made bicycle. Mountain bikes, where available, can run at around ₹200 to ₹700 per day (try Rentomo; www.rentomo.com).

➡ Hire places may require a cash security deposit (avoid leaving your airline ticket or passport).

➡ As of 2019 bike-sharing schemes have started to arrive in India, though the business is still its infancy and usually tricky for foreigners to access due to complex payment practicalities (though this may change).

➡ Guided bike tours are increasingly common and popular across South India; a half-day ride from Kochi to Alappuzha (Alleppey) in Kerala, for example, generally costs about ₹4900.

Purchase

➡ Mountain bikes from reputable brands, including Hero Cycles (https://herocycles.com) and Atlas (www.atlascycles.co.in), start at around ₹5000.

➡ Reselling is usually fairly easy – ask at local cycle or hire shops or put up an advert on travel noticeboards.

Practicalities

➡ Mountain bikes with off-road tyres give the best protection against India's puncture-prone roads.

➡ Roadside cycle mechanics abound but you should still bring spare tyres and brake cables, lubricating oil and a chain repair kit, plus plenty of puncture repair patches.

➡ Bikes can often be carried for free, or for a small luggage fee, on the roof of public buses – handy for uphill stretches.

➡ Contact your airline for information about transporting your bike and customs formalities in your home country.

Road Rules

➡ Vehicles drive on the left in India but otherwise road rules

are virtually nonexistent. Cities and national highways can be hazardous places to cycle so, where possible, stick to back roads.

➡ Be conservative about the distances you expect to cover – an experienced cyclist can manage around 60km to 100km a day on the plains, 40km to 60km on sealed mountain roads and 40km or less on dirt roads.

Boat

➡ Scheduled ships connect Kolkata, Chennai and Visakhapatnam in mainland India to Port Blair in the Andaman Islands, though services have been reduced in recent years with the advent of budget airlines.

➡ From mid-September to mid-May, ferries travel from Kochi to the Lakshadweep Islands, though tickets are almost exclusively available through package tours.

➡ A new luxury ship, Angriya Cruises (p119), was launched in late 2018, cruising between Mumbai and Goa.

Bus

➡ Buses go almost everywhere in South India and tend to be the cheapest way to travel. Services are fast and frequent.

➡ Buses are the only public transport option around many mountainous areas.

➡ Roads in mountainous terrain can be especially perilous: buses are often driven with willful abandon and accidents are always a risk.

➡ Avoid night buses unless there's no alternative. Driving conditions are more hazardous and drivers may also be suffering from lack of sleep.

➡ All buses make snack and toilet stops (some more frequently than others), providing a break but

possibly adding hours to journey times.

➡ Many long-distance buses travel overnight – bring earplugs if you want to block out the Bollywood films.

➡ Traffic jams can wreak havoc on bus schedules; always allow plenty of extra time.

Classes

➡ There are state-owned and private bus companies and both offer 'ordinary' buses and more expensive 'deluxe' and 'superdeluxe' buses. Many state tourist offices run their own reliable bus services.

➡ 'Ordinary' buses tend to be ageing rattletraps, while 'deluxe' buses range from less decrepit versions of ordinary buses to flashy Volvo buses with AC and reclining two-by-two seating.

➡ Buses run by the state government are usually the more reliable option (if there's a breakdown, another bus will be sent to pick up passengers), and seats can usually be booked up to a month in advance.

➡ Private buses are usually more expensive (and more comfortable) and can also be booked ahead, but some have kamikaze drivers and conductors who speed ahead and try to cram on as many passengers as possible to maximise profits.

➡ Travel agencies in many tourist towns offer relatively expensive private two-by-two buses, which tend to leave and terminate at conveniently central stops.

➡ Be warned that some agencies have been known to book people on to ordinary buses at superdeluxe prices – if possible, book directly with the bus company.

➡ Timetables and destinations may be displayed on signs or billboards at travel agencies and tourist offices, but don't count on it.

➜ Earplugs are a boon on all long-distance buses to muffle the often deafening music/films. Try to sit near the front to minimise the bumpy effect of potholes; never sit above the wheels.

Costs

➜ The cheapest buses are 'ordinary' government buses, but prices vary from state to state.

➜ Add around 50% to the ordinary fare for deluxe services, double the fare for AC, and triple or quadruple the fare for a two-by-two service.

Reservations

➜ Most deluxe buses can be booked in advance – usually up to a month in advance for government buses – at the bus station, at travel agencies or online. RedBus (www.redbus.in) is India's most comprehensive booking site/app; MakeMyTrip (www.makemytrip.com) also books buses. Some government buses can be booked online through the relevant state transport corporation. Websites have varying tolerance for foreign cards.

➜ Reservations are rarely possible on 'ordinary' buses and travellers often get left behind in the mad rush for a seat.

➜ To maximise your chances of securing a seat, either send a travelling companion ahead to grab some space, or pass a book or article of clothing through an open window and place it on an empty seat. This 'reservation' method rarely fails.

➜ If you board a bus midway through its journey, you'll often have to stand until a seat becomes free.

➜ Many buses only depart when full – you may find your bus suddenly empties as passengers move to another bus that's ready to leave before yours.

➜ At many bus stations there's a separate women's queue, though this isn't always obvious because signs are often not in English and men frequently join the melee. Women have an unspoken right to elbow their way to the front of any bus queue in India, so don't be shy, ladies!

Luggage

➜ Luggage is either stored in compartments underneath the bus (sometimes for a small fee) or carried on the roof.

➜ Arrive at least an hour ahead of the departure time – some buses cover the roof-stored bags with a large sheet of canvas, making last-minute additions inconvenient or impossible.

➜ If your bags go on the roof, make sure they're securely locked and tied to the metal baggage rack – some unlucky travellers have seen their belongings go bouncing off the roof on rough roads!

➜ Theft is a minor risk: keep an eye on your bags at snack and toilet stops and *never* leave day packs or valuables unattended inside the bus.

Car

Self-drive car hire is theoretically possible in South India's larger cities, but given the hair-raising driving conditions most travellers opt for a car with driver (an affordable option for many visitors, especially if several people share the cost). Seatbelts are either nonexistent or tucked so deep into the backseat they require a bulldozer to dig them out. For travellers who want to drive themselves, Hertz (www.hertz.com) is one of the few international companies with representatives in South India.

Hiring a Car & Driver

➜ Most towns have taxi stands or car-and-driver-hire companies where you can arrange short or long tours;

alternatively, book through your accommodation.

➜ Not all cars are licensed to travel beyond their home state. Those that are have to pay extra (often hefty) state taxes, added to the cost of hiring a car and driver.

➜ Ask for a driver who speaks some English and knows the region you intend to visit, and try to see the car and meet the driver before paying any money.

➜ Hindustan Ambassador cars look great but can be slow and uncomfortable when travelling long distances. In any event, these Indian classics are sadly disappearing – production of them ended in 2014.

➜ For multiday trips, charges cover the driver's meals and accommodation; drivers should make their own sleeping and eating arrangements.

➜ It is *essential* to set the ground rules from day one; politely but firmly let the driver know that you're boss in order to avoid anguish later.

Costs

➜ Prices depend on the distance, terrain and destination (driving on mountain roads uses more petrol, hence the higher cost), and the make and model of the car.

➜ One-way trips usually cost the same as return ones (to cover the petrol and driver charges for getting back).

➜ Hire charges vary from state to state. Some taxi unions set a time limit or a maximum kilometre distance for day trips – if you go over, you'll have to pay extra.

➜ To avoid potential misunderstandings, ensure you get *in writing* what you've been promised (quotes should include petrol, sightseeing stops, all your chosen destinations, and meals and accommodation for the driver). If drivers ask you for money to pay for petrol en route because they're short of cash, get receipts so it can be accounted for later. Avoid paying the full fee upfront.

➜ For sightseeing day trips within a single city, expect to pay anywhere upward of ₹1500 for an AC car with an eight-hour, 80km limit per day (extra charges apply beyond this). Non-AC options are slightly cheaper. For multiday journeys, charges hover at around ₹2400 to ₹4000 for an AC car with around 250km per day; parking and tolls are usually, but not always, included. With some operators, the maximum daily allowance is 100km; extra kilometres cost around ₹12 to ₹20 per kilometre.

➜ A tip is customary at the end of your journey; ₹200 per day is fair, ₹100 for a short trip (and more if you're really pleased with the driver's service).

Hitching

Hitching is not much of an option in South India; considering the inexpensive public transport options available, the concept of a 'free ride' is relatively unknown. Be aware that truck drivers have a reputation for driving under the influence of alcohol.

Hitching is never entirely safe, and we don't recommend it. Travellers who hitch should understand that they're taking a small but potentially serious risk. As anywhere, women are strongly advised against hitching alone or even as a pair. Always use your instincts.

Local Transport

Buses, cycle-rickshaws, autorickshaws, taxis, boats and urban trains provide transport around South India.

➜ On any form of transport without a fixed fare, agree on the price *before* you start your journey and make sure that it covers your luggage and every passenger.

➜ Even where local transport is metered, drivers may refuse to use the meter, demanding an elevated 'fixed' fare; bargain hard.

➜ Fares usually increase at night (by up to 100%) and some drivers charge a few rupees extra for luggage.

➜ Carry plenty of small bills for taxi and rickshaw fares as drivers rarely have change.

➜ Some taxi/autorickshaw drivers are involved in the commission racket (p505), wherein they may pressure you to switch to a hotel of their choice. Stand your ground and walk if necessary.

➜ Taxi apps (p526) such as Uber and Ola Cabs have transformed local transport, with easy smartphone access and electronically calculated rates.

Autorickshaw, Tempo & Vikram

➜ The Indian autorickshaw is basically a three-wheeled motorised contraption with a tin or canvas roof and sides, providing room for two passengers (although you'll often see many more bodies squeezed in) and limited luggage. They are also referred to as autos, scooters, riks or tuk-tuks.

➜ They are mostly cheaper than taxis and are usually metered, although getting drivers to turn on meters can be a challenge.

➜ You can arrange autos through the Ola Cabs app, (p526) which charges only around ₹10 more than the relevant meter price for your journey.

➜ Tempos and *vikrams* (large tempos) are outsize autorickshaws with room for more passengers, running on fixed routes for a fixed fare.

Boat

Various kinds of local boats offer transport across and down rivers in South India, from big car ferries to wooden canoes and wicker coracles.

Most larger boats carry bicycles and motorcycles for a fee. Kerala is especially renowned for its breathtaking backwater boat cruises, while ferries are the main mode of transport between islands in the Andamans.

Bus

Urban buses in South India range from fume-belching, human-stuffed mechanical monsters that hurtle along at breakneck speed to newer sanitised air-con vehicles with comfortable seating and smoother driving. It's usually far more convenient, fast and comfortable to opt for an autorickshaw or taxi, though there are some good airport bus services these days.

Cycle Rickshaw

A cycle-rickshaw is a pedal cycle with two rear wheels, supporting a bench seat for passengers.

➜ Many big cities have phased out (or hugely reduced the number of) cycle-rickshaws, but they are still a means of local transport in many smaller towns.

➜ Fares must be agreed upon in advance – speak to locals to get an idea of what is a fair price for the distance you intend travelling. Tips are always appreciated, given the slog involved.

Taxi

➜ Most towns have taxis with meters; however, getting drivers to use them can be a major hassle. Drivers often claim that the meter is broken and proceed to request a hugely elevated 'fixed' fare instead. Threatening to get another taxi will often miraculously fix the meter.

➜ To avoid fare-setting shenanigans, use prepaid taxis or, better still, taxi apps (p526).

➜ Most airports and many train stations have prepaid-taxi booths, normally just outside the terminal building. Here, you can book a taxi

TAXI APPS

➜ Taxi apps like Uber (www.uber.com), Ola Cabs (www.olacabs.com) and Goa Tourism's Goa Miles (https://goa-tourism.com) have completely changed the intracity transport game for travellers in India. At the time of writing, Uber was operating in 31 Indian cities. Ola, in 110 cities, is often available where Uber is not and includes an autorickshaw option.

➜ Ola Outstation, launched in 2016, offers one-way fares for long-distance trips, so you no longer have to pay for the return kilometres of your driver. At the time of writing, it was available in more than 80 Indian cities, including Mumbai, Bengaluru, Chennai, Hyderabad, Kochi and Pune. You can book anywhere between one hour and seven days ahead; rates start from ₹8 per kilometre.

for a fixed price (which will include baggage) and thus avoid commission scams. Hold on to the payment coupon until you reach your chosen destination. Smaller airports and train stations may have prepaid autorickshaw booths instead.

Train

Mumbai and Chennai, among other cities, have suburban trains that leave from ordinary train stations.

Motorcycle

Goa is the only place in South India where motorcycle taxis are a licensed form of transport. They take one person on the back and, though not as common as they used to be, are a quick, inexpensive way to cover short distances, costing half the price of a taxi.

Despite the traffic challenges, South India is an amazing region for long-distance motorcycle touring. Motorcycles generally handle the pitted roads better than four-wheeled vehicles, and you'll have the added bonus of being able to stop when and where you want. However, motorcycle touring can be quite an undertaking – there are some popular motorcycle tours for those who don't want the rigmarole of going

it alone. Weather is an important factor to consider – a monsoon-sprayed motorcycle tour is probably not on your to-do list.

To cross from neighbouring countries, check the latest regulations and paperwork requirements from the relevant diplomatic mission.

Driving Licence

To hire a motorcycle in India, technically you're required to have a valid international drivers' permit in addition to your domestic licence. In tourist areas, some places may rent out a motorcycle without asking for a driving permit/licence, but without a permit you won't be covered by insurance in the event of an accident, and may also face a fine.

Hire

➜ The classic way to motorcycle around India is on an Enfield Bullet, still built to the original 1940s specifications. As well as making a satisfying chugging sound, these bikes are fully manual, making them easy to repair (parts can be found almost everywhere in India). On the other hand, Enfields are often less reliable than many of the newer, Japanese-designed bikes, and production can struggle to keep up with demand,

creating a scarcity in the market and higher prices.

➜ Plenty of places rent out motorcycles for local trips and longer tours. Japanese- and Indian-made bikes in the 100cc to 220cc range are cheaper than the big 350cc to 500cc Enfields.

➜ For a week's hire, a 350cc Enfield can cost ₹10,000; prices usually include advice and an invaluable crash course in Enfield mechanics and repairs.

➜ In Goa, the Andaman Islands and other touristed areas, including parts of Kerala, scooter hire is easily available for around ₹250 to ₹400 per day.

➜ Touring bike outlets include **Kerala Bike Tours** (☏9446492382, 9388476817; www.keralabiketours.com; 42/2252B St Benedict Road North, Kacheripady, Ernakulam), Rent a Bike (www.rentabike.in) and Ziphop (www.ziphop.in).

➜ As a deposit, you'll need to leave a large cash lump sum (ensure you get a receipt that also stipulates the refundable amount), your passport or your air ticket. It's strongly advisable to avoid leaving your air ticket or passport; you'll need the latter to check in at hotels, and the police can demand to see it at any time.

➜ Take photos of any damage or scratches to the bike before setting off, to ensure you aren't held responsible for them and asked to pay repair costs.

Purchase

➜ If you're planning a longer tour, renting is the way to go, but purchasing a motorcycle is not impossible. Though nonresident foreigners cannot officially purchase a bike, loopholes vary by state and secondhand bikes are widely available (the paperwork is a lot easier for these than for a new machine). To find a secondhand motorcycle, check travellers' noticeboards and ask motorcycle mechanics and other bikers.

➡ A well-looked-after secondhand 350cc Enfield will cost anywhere from ₹60,000 to ₹120,000. The 500cc model costs anywhere from ₹90,000 to ₹120,000. You will also have to pay for insurance.

➡ It's advisable to get any secondhand bike serviced before you set off.

➡ When reselling your bike, expect to get between half and two-thirds of the price you paid, if the bike is still in reasonable condition.

➡ Helmets are available for ₹500 to ₹5000 and extras like panniers, luggage racks, protection bars, rear-view mirrors, lockable fuel caps, petrol filters and extra tools are easy to come by. One useful extra is a customised fuel tank, which will increase the range you can cover between fuel stops. An Enfield 500cc gives about 25km/L; the 350cc model gives slightly more.

Fuel, Spare Parts & Extras

➡ Petrol and engine oil are widely available on the plains, but petrol stations are widely spaced in the mountains. If you intend to travel to remote regions, ensure you carry enough extra fuel. At research time, petrol cost around ₹69 to ₹75 per litre in South India.

➡ If you're going to remote regions it's also important to carry basic spares (valves, fuel lines, piston rings etc). Spare parts for Indian and Japanese machines are widely available in cities and larger towns.

➡ Check the engine and gearbox oil level regularly (at least every 500km) and clean the oil filter every few thousand kilometres.

➡ Given the road conditions, chances are you'll make at least a couple of visits to a puncture-wallah – start your trip with new tyres and carry

spanners to remove your own wheels.

➡ It's a good idea to bring your own protective equipment (jackets, gloves etc).

Insurance

➡ Only hire a bike that has insurance – if you hit someone without insurance, the consequences can be very costly. Reputable companies will include third-party cover in their policies; those that don't probably aren't trustworthy.

➡ You must also arrange insurance if you buy a motorcycle (usually you can organise this through the person selling the bike).

➡ The minimum level of cover is third-party insurance – available for around ₹700 per year. This will cover repair and medical costs for any other vehicles, people or property you might hit, but no cover for your own machine. Comprehensive insurance (recommended) costs upward of ₹1400 to ₹1500 per year.

Organised Motorcycle Tours

Dozens of companies offer organised motorcycle tours around South India with a support vehicle, mechanic and guide:

Classic Bike Adventure (www.classic-bike-india.com; Assagao)

Enfield Riders (www.enfield riders.com)

Indiabikes (www.indiabikes.com)

Kerala Bike Tours (☑9446492382, 9388476817; www.keralabiketours.com; 42/2252B St Benedict Rd North, Kacheripady, Ernakulam)

Live India (☑0845-2241917; www.liveindia.co.uk)

Vintage Rides (www.vintagerides.travel)

Road Conditions

Given the varied road conditions, India can be challenging for novice riders. Hazards

range from cows and chickens crossing the carriageway to broken-down trucks, pedestrians on the road, perpetual potholes and unmarked speed humps. Rural roads sometimes have grain crops strewn across them to be threshed by passing vehicles – a serious sliding hazard for bikers.

Try not to cover too much territory in one day and avoid travelling after dark – many vehicles drive without lights, and dynamo-powered motorcycle headlamps are useless at low revs while negotiating potholes.

On busy national highways expect to average 40km/h to 50km/h without stops; on winding back roads and dirt tracks this can drop to 10km/h.

Tours

Tours are available all over South India, run by tourist offices, local transport companies, travel agencies and (usually better and more expensive) independent operators. Organised tours can be an inexpensive way to see several places on one trip, although they're often fast-paced. Tailor-made tours give you more freedom about where you go and how long you stay.

Drivers may double as guides or you can hire qualified local guides for a fee. In tourist towns, be wary of touts claiming to be professional guides.

Walking, cycling, food and other themed tours are becoming increasingly popular and available across South India.

Train

Travelling by train is a quintessential Indian experience. Trains offer a smoother ride than buses and are especially recommended for long journeys that include overnight travel. India's rail network is one of the largest and busiest in the world and Indian Railways is one of the largest employers on earth, with roughly 1.5 million workers. There are around 7170 train stations scattered across the country, used by an estimated 23 million passengers a day.

The best way of sourcing updated railway information is online, through sites such as Indian Railways (www.indianrailways.gov.in/railwayboard), Erail (https://erail.in) and the very useful Seat 61 (www.seat61.com/India).

Booking Tickets in India

You can book tickets online, through a travel agency or hotel (for a commission), or in person at the train station. Big stations often have English-speaking staff who can help with choosing the best train. At smaller stations, midlevel officials, such as the deputy station master, usually speak English. Note, however, that many trains get booked up far ahead online. The nationwide railways enquiries number is 139 (with SMS support).

To find out which trains travel between any two destinations, check the IRCTC (www.irctc.co.in), Cleartrip (www.cleartrip.com), Erail (http://erail.in), 12Go (www.12go.asia) or Make My Trip (www.makemytrip.com)

websites, all of which also provide fares and timings.

AT THE STATION

Chennai, Mumbai, Bengaluru (Bangalore) and Hyderabad have International Tourist Bureau counters, which allow you to book tickets in relative peace – check www.indianrail.gov.in/international_Tourist.html for details.

➡ Get a reservation slip from the information window, fill in the name of the departure station, the destination station, the class you want to travel and the name and number of the train. Join the long queue at the ticket window where your ticket will be printed. Women should use the separate women's queue – if there isn't one, go to the front of the regular queue.

➡ Indian Railways has been busy installing some 10,000 point-of-sale terminals within its nationwide network since 2016, allowing for cashless machine ticket buying, but these aren't yet much use to foreign travellers as they require local credit/debit cards.

Costs

➡ Fares are calculated by distance and class of travel; Rajdhani and Shatabdi trains are slightly more expensive, but prices include meals. Most air-conditioned carriages have a catering

service (meals are brought to your seat). In unreserved classes it's a good idea to carry portable snacks.

➡ Seniors discounts – 40% off for men over 60 and 50% off for women over 58, in all classes on all types of train – were discontinued for foreigners in 2016, and are now only available to resident Indians. Children below the age of five travel free; those aged between five and 12 are charged half price if they do not have their own berth, but full price if they do.

➡ Indian Rail introduced surge pricing on Rajdhani, Shatabdi and Duronto express trains in 2016, though it has since been dropped for some services. Fares increase 10% with every 10% of berths sold subject to a prescribed ceiling limit.

Reservations

Book well ahead for overnight journeys or travel during holidays and festivals. Waiting until the day of travel to book is not recommended.

➡ Bookings open 120 days before departure and you must make a reservation for all chair-car, sleeper, 1AC, 2AC and 3AC carriages. No reservations are required for general (2nd-class) compartments. Trains are always busy in India so it's wise to book as far in advance as possible; advance booking for overnight trains is strongly recommended. Train services to certain destinations are often increased during major festivals but it's still best to book well in advance.

➡ Reserved tickets show your seat/berth number and the carriage number. When the train pulls in, keep an eye out for your carriage number, written on the side of the train (station staff and porters can also point you in the right direction). A list of names and berths may be posted on the side of each reserved carriage, though this isn't always the case these days;

EXPRESS TRAIN FARES IN RUPEES

DISTANCE (KM)	1AC*	2AC*	3AC*	CHAIR CAR (CC)**	SLEEPER**	SECOND (II)**
100	1203	706	498	205	77	47
200	1203	706	498	282	136	73
300	1356	798	561	378	181	103
400	1678	978	687	467	222	128
500	2054	1209	846	577	276	151
1000	3362	1949	1352	931	446	258
1500	4320	2498	1708	1189	573	334
2000	5272	3025	2057	1443	698	412

* Rajdhani/Duronto Trains; ** Mail/Express Trains

CLASSIC TRAIN RIDES

South India offers some epic train experiences – as well as the following, consider the Golden Chariot, a luxurious round-trip journey from Bengaluru highlighting the romance of Karnataka, including spectacular Hampi and Badami. The train was under renovation at time of writing, with plans to introduce more affordable ticket options when it relaunches in October 2019 (see www.goldenchariottrain.com for the latest developments).

Nilgiri Mountain Railway (p414) One of India's most beloved rail lines, this Unesco-listed miniature ('toy') train trundles through dense forest and emerald tea-cloaked hills between Mettupalayam and Ooty (Udhagamandalam) in Tamil Nadu's Western Ghats (1st/2nd class ₹205/30; 3½ to 4¾ hours).

Goa Express: Vasco da Gama–Londa (www.irctc.co.in) Part of the superfast service between Goa's Vasco da Gama and Delhi's Nizamuddin station, the Goa Express sweeps from golden tropical beaches to the jungled hills of the Western Ghats; it's one of many Goa–Londa trains to chug past Dudhsagar Falls, India's second-highest falls at 603m (3AC/sleeper ₹495/160, 3½ hours).

Konkan Railway (www.irctc.co.in) Extending south from Mumbai through Goa and Karnataka almost to Kerala, this is a 765km sea-hugging beauty of a line. The Mandovi Express links Margao with Mumbai, crossing 200 bridges and India's highest viaduct, whizzing past rice paddies, coconut groves and mango plantations (3AC/sleeper ₹1070/390, 12½ hours).

Deccan Odyssey (www.deccan-odyssey-india.com) Seven-night luxury whirls around Maharashtra and beyond (single/double from US$6100/8750).

many stations have signs marking the approximate spot where each carriage stops (again, ask station staff for assistance).

➡ Refunds are available on any ticket, even after departure, with a penalty – the rules are complicated so check when you book.

➡ Be aware that train trips can be delayed at any point in the journey so, to avoid stress, factor some leeway into your travel plans.

If the train you want to travel on is sold out, make sure to enquire about the following possibilities:

➡ **Reservation Against Cancellation (RAC)** Even when a train is fully booked, Indian Railways sells a handful of RAC seats in each class. This means that if you have an RAC ticket and someone cancels before the departure date, you will get that seat (or berth). You'll have to check the reservation list at the station on the day of travel to see which seat you've been allocated. Even if no one cancels, as an RAC ticket holder you can still board the train, and even if you don't get a seat you can still travel.

➡ **Taktal Tickets** Indian Railways holds back a limited number of tickets on key trains and releases them at 10am (AC) and 11am (non-AC) one day before the train is due to depart. A charge of ₹100 to ₹500 is added to each ticket price depending on distance. 1AC tickets are excluded from the scheme.

➡ **Foreign Tourist Quota** As well as the regular general quota (GN), a special (albeit small) tourist quota is set aside for foreign tourists travelling between popular stations. These seats can now be booked up to 365 days ahead through the IRCTC website/app with an international card (in theory, though international cards weren't being accepted at research time – this may change) or, if you're very lucky, at dedicated reservation offices in major cities; you need to show your passport and visa as ID, and payment is in rupees (with ATM receipt), GBP or USD. Online, there's a ₹200 service charge per ticket plus a ₹100 registration fee, and you can book only 1AC, 2AC or Executive Chair tickets.

➡ **Waitlist (WL)** Trains are frequently overbooked, but many passengers cancel and there are regular no-shows. So if you buy a ticket on the waiting list you're quite likely to get a seat, even if there are a number of people ahead of you on the list. Check your booking status at www.indianrail.gov.in/pnr_Enq.html by entering your ticket's PNR number. A refund is available if you fail to get a seat – ask the ticket office about your chances.

Train-Travel Tips

➡ In all classes, a padlock and a length of chain are useful for securing your luggage to baggage racks.

➡ Be mindful of potential passenger drugging and theft (p504).

➡ RailYatri (www.railyatri.in) is handy for live-tracking train statuses.

Health

There is huge geographical variation in India, so environmental issues like heat, cold, altitude and, increasingly, pollution can cause health problems. Hygiene is poor in most regions so food- and water-borne illnesses are common. Many insect-borne diseases are present, particularly in tropical areas. Medical care is basic in many areas (especially beyond the larger cities) so it's essential to be well prepared.

Preexisting medical conditions and accidental injury (especially traffic accidents) account for most life-threatening problems. Becoming ill in some way, however, is very common. Fortunately, most travellers' illnesses can be prevented with some common-sense behaviour or treated with a well-stocked travellers' medical kit – however, never hesitate to consult a doctor while on the road.

Our advice is a general guide only and certainly does not replace the advice of a doctor trained in travel medicine.

BEFORE YOU GO

Medications

You can buy many medications over the counter in India without a doctor's prescription, but it can be difficult to find some of the newer drugs, particularly the latest antidepressant drugs, blood-pressure medications and contraceptives. Bring the following:

➡ medications in their original, labelled containers

➡ any regular medication – double your ordinary needs

➡ a signed, dated letter from your physician describing your medical conditions and medications, including generic names

➡ a physician's letter documenting the medical necessity of any syringes you bring

➡ if you have a heart condition, a copy of your ECG taken just prior to travelling

Health Insurance

Don't travel without health insurance. Emergency evacuation is expensive – bills of over US$100,000 are not uncommon. Consider the following when buying insurance:

➡ You may require extra cover for adventure activities such as rock climbing, trekking and scuba diving.

➡ In India, doctors usually require immediate payment in cash. Your insurance plan may make payments directly to providers or it will reimburse you later for overseas health expenditures. If you do have to claim later, make sure you keep all relevant documentation.

Vaccinations

Specialised travel-medicine clinics are your best source of up-to-date information. Most vaccines don't give immunity until *at least* two weeks after they're given, so visit a doctor six to eight weeks before departure. Ask your doctor for an International Certificate of Vaccination ('yellow booklet').

Medical Checklist

Recommended items for a personal medical kit:

➡ antibacterial cream, eg mupirocin

➡ antibiotic for skin infections, eg amoxycillin/clavulanate or cephalexin

➡ antifungal cream, eg clotrimazole

➡ antihistamine – there are many options, eg cetirizine for daytime and promethazine for night

➡ antiseptic, eg Betadine

➡ antispasmodic for stomach cramps, eg Buscopan

➡ contraceptives

➡ decongestant, eg pseudoephedrine

➡ DEET-based insect repellent

➡ diarrhoea medication – consider an oral rehydration solution (eg Gastrolyte), a diarrhoea 'stopper' (eg loperamide) – and antinausea medication (eg prochlorperazine). Antibiotics for diarrhoea include ciprofloxacin; for bacterial diarrhoea azithromycin; for giardiasis or amoebic dysentery, tinidazole.

➡ first-aid items such as scissors, sticking plasters (adhesive bandages), bandages, gauze, a thermometer (but not mercury), sterile needles and syringes, safety pins and tweezers

➡ high-factor sunscreen

➡ ibuprofen or another anti-inflammatory

➡ iodine tablets (unless you are pregnant or have a thyroid problem) to purify water

➡ paracetamol

➡ pyrethrin to impregnate clothing and mosquito nets

➡ steroid cream for allergic or itchy rashes, eg 1% to 2% hydrocortisone

➡ throat lozenges

➡ thrush (vaginal yeast infection) treatment, eg clotrimazole pessaries or Diflucan tablet

➡ Ural or equivalent if prone to urine infections

IN INDIA

Availability & Cost of Health Care

Medical care is hugely variable in India. Some cities now have clinics catering specifically to travellers and expatriates; these are usually more expensive than local medical facilities, and offer a higher standard of care. It is usually difficult to find reliable medical care in rural areas.

Self-treatment may be appropriate if your problem is minor (eg travellers'

diarrhoea), you are carrying the relevant medication and you cannot attend a recommended clinic. If you suspect a serious disease, especially malaria or dengue fever, travel to the nearest quality facility. Before buying medication over the counter, check the use-by date, and ensure the packet is sealed and properly stored (eg not exposed to sunshine).

Infectious Diseases

Malaria

Malaria is a serious and potentially deadly disease. Before you travel, seek expert advice according to your itinerary (rural areas are especially risky). At the time of writing, most of South India was considered a low to no risk area, apart from the Mangaluru (Mangalore) region, which was declared high risk in mid-2018.

Malaria is caused by a parasite transmitted by the bite of an infected mosquito. The most important symptom of malaria is fever, but general symptoms, such as headache, diarrhoea, cough or chills, may also occur. Diagnosis can only be properly made by taking a blood sample.

Two strategies should be combined to prevent malaria: mosquito avoidance and antimalarial medications.

➡ Use a DEET-containing insect repellent on exposed skin. Wash this off at night, as long as you are sleeping under a mosquito net. Natural repellents such as citronella can be effective, but must be applied more frequently than products containing DEET.

➡ Sleep under a mosquito net impregnated with pyrethrin.

➡ Choose accommodation with proper screens and fans (if not air-conditioned).

➡ Impregnate clothing with pyrethrin in high-risk areas.

➡ Wear long sleeves and trousers in light colours.

➡ Use mosquito coils and/or spray your room with insect repellent before going out for your evening meal.

There are a variety of medications available:

Chloroquine and Paludrine combination Limited effectiveness in many parts of South Asia. Common side effects include nausea (40% of people) and mouth ulcers.

Doxycycline (daily tablet) A broad-spectrum antibiotic that helps prevent a variety of tropical diseases, including leptospirosis, tick-borne disease and typhus. Potential side effects include photosensitivity (a tendency to sunburn), thrush (in women), indigestion, heartburn, nausea and interference with the contraceptive pill. More serious side effects include ulceration of the oesophagus – take your tablet with a meal and a large glass of water, and never lie down within half an hour of taking it. It must be taken for four weeks after leaving the risk area.

Lariam (mefloquine) This weekly tablet suits many people. Serious side effects are rare but include depression, anxiety, psychosis and seizures. Anyone with a history of depression, anxiety, other psychological disorders or epilepsy should not take Lariam. It is considered safe in the second and third trimesters of pregnancy. Tablets must be taken for four weeks after leaving the risk area.

WOMEN'S HEALTH

For gynaecological health issues, seek out a female doctor.

Birth control Bring adequate supplies of your own form of contraception.

Sanitary products Pads, but rarely tampons, are readily available.

Thrush Heat, humidity and antibiotics can all contribute to thrush. Treatment is with antifungal creams and pessaries such as clotrimazole. A practical alternative is a single tablet of fluconazole (Diflucan).

Urinary-tract infections These can be precipitated by dehydration or long bus journeys without toilet stops; bring suitable antibiotics.

REQUIRED & RECOMMENDED VACCINATIONS

The only vaccine required by international regulations is yellow fever. Proof of vaccination will only be required if you have visited a country in the yellow-fever zone within the six days prior to entering India. If you are travelling to India from Africa or South America, you should check to see if you require proof of vaccination. There is currently no vaccination against malaria (p531); prophylaxis is used instead. The World Health Organization (WHO) recommends the following vaccinations for India (as well as being up to date with measles, mumps and rubella vaccinations):

Adult diphtheria and tetanus Single booster recommended if none in the previous 10 years. Side effects include sore arm and fever.

Hepatitis A Provides almost 100% protection for up to a year; a booster after 12 months provides at least another 20 years' protection. Mild side effects such as headache and sore arm occur in 5% to 10% of people.

Hepatitis B Now considered routine for most travellers. Given as three shots over six months. A rapid schedule is also available, as is a combined vaccination with Hepatitis A. Side effects are mild and uncommon, usually headache and sore arm. In 95% of people lifetime protection results.

Polio Only one booster is required as an adult for lifetime protection. Inactivated polio vaccine is safe during pregnancy.

Typhoid Recommended for all travellers to India. The vaccine offers around 70% protection, lasts for two to three years and comes as a single shot. Tablets are also available, but the injection has fewer side effects. Sore arm and fever may occur.

Varicella If you haven't had chickenpox, discuss this vaccination with your doctor.

These immunisations are recommended for long-term travellers (more than one month) or those at special risk (seek further advice from your doctor):

Japanese B Encephalitis Two injections, plus a booster recommended after one to two years. Sore arm and headache are the most common side effects. In rare cases, an allergic reaction comprising hives and swelling can occur up to 10 days after any of the doses.

Meningitis Single injection. There are two types of vaccination: the quadrivalent vaccine gives two to three years' protection; meningitis group C vaccine gives around 10 years' protection. Recommended for long-term backpackers aged under 25.

Rabies Three injections in all. A booster after one year will then provide 10 years' protection. Side effects are rare – occasionally headache and sore arm.

Tuberculosis (TB) A complex issue. Adult long-term travellers are usually recommended to have a TB skin test before and after travel, rather than vaccination. Only one vaccine given in a lifetime, usually only to those under 16.

Malarone A combination of atovaquone and proguanil. Side effects are uncommon and mild, most commonly nausea and headache. It is the best tablet for scuba divers and for those on short trips to high-risk areas. It must be taken for one week after leaving the risk area.

Other Diseases

Avian Flu Influenza A (H5N1) is a subtype of the type A influenza virus. Contact with dead or sick birds is the principal source of infection and bird-to-human transmission does not easily occur.

Symptoms include high fever and flulike symptoms with rapid deterioration, leading to respiratory failure and death in many cases. Immediate medical care should be sought if bird flu is suspected. Check www.who.int/en/.

Coughs, colds and chest infections Around 25% of travellers to India will develop a respiratory infection. If a secondary bacterial infection occurs – marked by fever, chest pain and coughing up discoloured or blood-tinged sputum – seek medical advice or consider commencing a general antibiotic.

Dengue fever This mosquito-borne disease is becomingly increasingly problematic, especially in the cities. As there is no vaccine available it can only be prevented by avoiding mosquito bites at all times. Symptoms include high fever, severe headache and body ache, and sometimes a rash and diarrhoea. Treatment is rest and paracetamol – do not take aspirin or ibuprofen as it increases the likelihood of haemorrhaging. See a doctor.

Hepatitis A This food- and water-borne virus infects the liver, causing jaundice (yellow skin and eyes), nausea and lethargy. There is no specific treatment for hepatitis A. you just need to allow time for the liver to heal. All travellers to India should be vaccinated against hepatitis A.

Hepatitis B This sexually transmitted disease is spread by body fluids and can be prevented by vaccination. The long-term consequences can include liver cancer and cirrhosis.

Hepatitis E Transmitted through contaminated food and water, hepatitis E has similar symptoms to hepatitis A, but is far less common. It is a severe problem in pregnant women and can result in the death of both mother and baby. According to the WHO, a hepatitis E vaccine has been developed in China, but is not yet available elsewhere, so prevention is by following safe eating and drinking guidelines.

HIV Spread via contaminated body fluids. Avoid unsafe sex, unsterile needles (including in medical facilities) and procedures such as tattoos.

Influenza Present year-round in the tropics, influenza (flu) symptoms include fever, muscle aches, a runny nose, cough and sore throat. It can be severe in people over the age of 65 or in those with medical conditions such as heart disease or diabetes – vaccination is recommended for these individuals. There is no specific treatment, just rest, paracetamol and plenty of fluids.

Japanese B encephalitis This viral disease is transmitted by mosquitoes and is rare in travellers. Most cases occur in rural areas and vaccination is recommended for travellers spending more than one month outside of cities. There is no treatment, and it may result in permanent brain damage or death.

Rabies This fatal disease is spread by the bite or possibly even the lick of an infected animal – most commonly a dog or monkey. You should seek medical advice immediately after any animal bite and commence postexposure treatment. Having pretravel vaccination means the postbite treatment is greatly simplified. If an animal bites you,

gently wash the wound with soap and water, and apply iodine-based antiseptic. If you are not prevaccinated you will need to receive rabies immunoglobulin as soon as possible, and this is very difficult to obtain in much of India.

STDs Sexually transmitted diseases most common in India include herpes, warts, syphilis, gonorrhoea and chlamydia. Condoms will prevent gonorrhoea and chlamydia but not warts or herpes. If after a sexual encounter you develop any rash, lumps, discharge or pain when passing urine, seek immediate medical attention. If you have been sexually active during your travels, have an STD check on your return home.

Tuberculosis While TB is rare in travellers, those who have significant contact with the local population (such as medical and aid workers and long-term travellers) should take precautions. Vaccination is usually only given to those under 16, but adults at risk are recommended to have pre- and posttravel TB testing. The main symptoms are fever, cough, weight loss, night sweats and fatigue.

Typhoid This serious bacterial infection is spread via food and water. It gives a high and slowly progressive fever and headache, and may be accompanied by a dry cough and stomach pain. It

is diagnosed by blood tests and treated with antibiotics. Vaccination is recommended for all travellers who are spending more than a week in India. Be aware that vaccination is not 100% effective, so you must still be careful with what you eat and drink.

Zika At the time of writing, most of India has been categorised as having a moderate risk of Zika virus (except for Rajasthan, which has a high risk), though there have been recent cases in both Tamil Nadu and Ahmedabad. Check online for current updates.

Travellers' Diarrhoea

This is by far the most common problem affecting travellers in India – between 30% and 70% of people will suffer from it within two weeks of starting their trip. It's usually caused by a bacteria, and thus responds promptly to treatment with antibiotics.

Travellers' diarrhoea is defined as the passage of more than three watery bowel actions within 24 hours, plus at least one other symptom, such as fever, cramps, nausea, vomiting or feeling generally unwell.

Treatment consists of staying well hydrated; rehydration solutions like Gastrolyte are best for this. Antibiotics such as ciprofloxacin and

---

DRINKING WATER

⇒ Never drink tap water.

⇒ Bottled water is generally safe – check the seal is intact at purchase.

⇒ Avoid ice unless you know it has been safely made.

⇒ Be careful of fresh juices served at street stalls in particular – they may have been watered down or served in unhygienic jugs/glasses.

⇒ Boiling water is usually the most efficient method of purifying it.

⇒ The best chemical purifier is iodine. It should not be used by pregnant women or those with thyroid problems.

⇒ Water filters should also filter out viruses. Ensure your filter has a chemical barrier such as iodine and a small pore size (less than four microns).

⇒ Many places now offer filtered water or water refills.

azithromycin should kill the bacteria quickly. Seek medical attention quickly if you do not respond to an appropriate antibiotic.

Loperamide is just a 'stopper' and doesn't get to the cause of the problem. It can be helpful, though (eg if you have to go on a long bus ride). Don't take loperamide if you have a fever or blood in your stools.

Amoebic dysentery Amoebic dysentery is very rare in travellers but is often misdiagnosed by poor-quality labs. Symptoms are similar to bacterial diarrhoea: fever, bloody diarrhoea and generally feeling unwell. You should always seek reliable medical care if you have blood in your diarrhoea. Treatment involves two drugs: tinidazole or metronidazole to kill the parasite in your gut and then a second drug to kill the cysts. If left untreated, complications such as liver or gut abscesses can occur.

Giardiasis Giardia is a parasite that is relatively common in travellers. Symptoms include nausea, bloating, excess gas, fatigue and intermittent diarrhoea. The parasite will eventually go away if left untreated but this can take months; the best advice is to seek medical treatment. The treatment of choice is tinidazole, with metronidazole being a second-line option.

Environmental Hazards

Air & Noise Pollution

Air pollution, particularly vehicle pollution, is an increasing problem in most of India's urban hubs, as is noise pollution (which can have serious health repercussions). Travellers should consider earplugs and a mouth cover. If you have severe respiratory problems, speak with your doctor before travelling to India.

Diving & Surfing

➡ Divers and surfers should seek specialised advice before they travel to ensure their medical kit contains treatment for coral cuts and tropical ear infections.

➡ Divers should ensure their insurance covers them for decompression illness – get specialised dive insurance through an organisation such as Divers Alert Network (DAN; www.danap.org).

➡ Certain medical conditions are incompatible with diving; check with your doctor.

Heat

Much of South India is hot and humid throughout the year. For most people it takes at least two weeks to adapt to the hot climate. Swelling of the feet, ankles and hands is common, as are muscle cramps caused by excessive sweating. Prevent these by avoiding dehydration and excessive activity in the heat. Don't eat salt tablets (they aggravate the gut); drinking rehydration solution or eating salty food helps.

Dehydration is the main contributor to heat exhaustion. Recovery is usually rapid and it is common to feel weak for some days afterwards. Symptoms include:

➡ feeling weak

➡ headache

➡ irritability

➡ nausea or vomiting

➡ sweaty skin

➡ a fast, weak pulse

➡ normal or slightly elevated body temperature

Treatment:

➡ get out of the heat

➡ fan the sufferer

➡ apply cool, wet cloths to the skin

➡ lay the sufferer flat with their legs raised

➡ rehydrate with water containing one-quarter teaspoon of salt per litre

Heat stroke is a serious medical emergency. Symptoms include:

➡ weakness

➡ nausea

➡ a hot dry body

➡ temperature of over 41°C

➡ dizziness and confusion

➡ loss of coordination

➡ seizures

➡ eventual collapse

Treatment:

➡ get out of the heat

➡ fan the sufferer

➡ apply cool, wet cloths to the skin or ice to the body, especially to the groin and armpits

Prickly heat is a common skin rash in the tropics, caused by sweat trapped under the skin. Treat it by moving out of the heat and having cool showers. Creams and ointments clog the skin so they should be avoided. A local prickly-heat powder can be helpful.

Insect Bites & Stings

Leeches Found in humid rainforest areas. They do not transmit any disease but their bites are often intensely itchy for weeks and can easily become infected. Apply an iodine-based antiseptic to any leech bite to help prevent infection.

Ticks Contracted when walking in rural areas, and can carry serious diseases such as Kyasanur forest disease. If you have had a tick bite and have a rash at the site of the bite or elsewhere, fever or muscle aches, you should see a doctor. Doxycycline prevents tick-borne diseases.

Skin Problems

Cuts and scratches These easily become infected in humid climates. Immediately wash all wounds in clean water and apply antiseptic. If you develop signs of infection, see a doctor.

Fungal rashes There are two common fungal rashes that affect travellers. The first occurs in moist areas, such as the groin, armpits and between the toes. It starts as a red patch that slowly spreads and is usually itchy. Treatment involves keeping the skin dry, avoiding chafing and using an antifungal cream such as clotrimazole or Lamisil. The second, *Tinea versicolor*, causes light-coloured patches, most commonly on the back, chest and shoulders. Consult a doctor.

Language

The number of languages spoken in India helps explain why English is still widely spoken here, and why it's still in official use. Another 22 languages are recognised in the constitution, and more than 1600 other languages are spoken throughout the country.

While Hindi is the predominant language in the north, it bears little relation to the Dravidian languages of India's south and few people in the south speak Hindi. The native languages of the southern regions covered in this book (and in this chapter) are Tamil, Kannada, Konkani, Malayalam, Marathi and Telugu. Most of them belong to the Dravidian language family, although they have been influenced to varying degrees by Hindi and Sanskrit. As the predominant languages in specific geographic areas, they have in effect been used to determine the regional boundaries for the southern states.

Many educated Indians speak English as virtually their first language and for a large number of Indians it's often their second tongue, so you'll also find it very easy to get by in South India with English.

Pronunciation

The pronunciation systems of all languages covered in this chapter include a number of 'retroflex' consonants (pronounced with the tongue bent backwards), and all languages except for Tamil also have 'aspirated' consonants (pronounced with a puff of air). Our simplified pronunciation guides don't dis-

tinguish the retroflex consonants from their nonretroflex counterparts. The aspirated sounds are indicated with an apostrophe (') after the consonant. If you read our coloured pronunciation guides as if they were English, you'll be understood. The stressed syllables are indicated with italics for languages that have noticeable word stress; for others, all syllables should be equally stressed.

TAMIL

Tamil is the official language in the South Indian state of Tamil Nadu (as well as a national language in Sri Lanka, Malaysia and Singapore). It is one of the major Dravidian languages of South India, with records of its existence going back more than 2000 years. Tamil has about 62 million speakers in India.

A pronunciation tip: aw is pronounced as in 'law' and ow as in 'how'.

Basics

Hello.	வணக்கம்.	va·*nak*·kam
Goodbye.	போய். வருகிறேன்.	*po·*i va·*ru*·ki·reyn
Yes./No.	ஆமாம்./இல்லை.	aa·maam/*il*·lai
Excuse me.	தயவு செய்து.	ta·ya·*vu* sei·*du*
Sorry.	மன்னிக்கவும்.	*man*·nik·ka·vum
Please.	தயவு செய்து.	ta·ya·*vu* chey·*tu*
Thank you.	நன்றி.	*nan*·dri

How are you?
நீங்கள் நலமா? — neeng·kal na·*la*·maa

Fine, thanks. And you?
நலம், நன்றி. — na·*lam nan*·dri
நீங்கள்? — *neeng*·kal

What's your name?
உங்கள் பெயர் என்ன? — ung·kal pe·*yar en*·na

My name is ...
என் பெயர் ... — en pe·*yar* ...

Do you speak English?
நீங்கள் ஆங்கிலம் பேசுவீர்களா? — *neeng·kal aang·ki·lam pey·chu·veer·ka·la*

I don't understand.
எனக்கு விளங்கவில்லை. — *e·nak·ku vi·lang·ka·vil·lai*

Accommodation

Where's a ... nearby?
அருகே ஒரு ... எங்கே உள்ளது? — *a·ru·ke o·ru ... eng·ke ul·la·tu*

guesthouse — வீரந்தினர் இல்லம — *vi·run·ti·nar il·lam*

hotel — ஹோட்டல — *hot·tal*

Do you have a ... room?
உங்களிடம் ஓர் ... அறை உள்ளதா? — *ung·ka·li·tam awr ... a·rai ul·la·taa*

single — தன — *ta·ni*

double — இரட்டை — *i·rat·tai*

How much is it per ...?
ஓர் ... என்னவிலை? — *awr ... en·na·vi·lai*

night — இரவுக்கு — *i·ra·vuk·ku*

person — ஒருவருக்கு — *o·ru·va·ruk·ku*

bathroom — குளியலறை — *ku·li·ya·la·rai*

bed — படுக்கை — *pa·tuk·kai*

window — சன்னல — *chan·nal*

Directions

Where's the ...?
... எங்கே இருக்கிறது? — *... eng·key i·ruk·ki·ra·tu*

What's the address?
வீலாசம் என்ன? — *vi·laa·cham en·na*

Can you show me (on the map)?
எனக்கு (வரைரடத்தில்) காட்ட முடியுமா? — *e·nak·ku (va·rai·pa·tat·til) kaat·ta mu·ti·yu·maa*

How far is it?
எவ்வவவு தூரத்தில் இருக்கிறது? — *ev·va·la·vu too·rat·til i·ruk·ki·ra·tu*

It's ...
அது இருப்பது ... — *a·tu i·rup·pa·tu ...*

behind ... — ...க்குப் பின்னால — *... kup pin·naal*

in front of ... — ...க்கு முன்னால — *... ku mun·naal*

near (to ...) — (... க்கு) அருகே — *(... ku) a·ru·key*

on the corner — ஓரத்தில — *aw·rat·til*

straight ahead — நேரடியாக முன்புறம் — *ney·ra·di·yaa·ha mun·pu·ram*

Turn ...
... புறத்தில் திரும்புக. — *pu·rat·til ti·rum·pu·ka*

left — இடது — *i·ta·tu*

right — வலது — *va·la·tu*

Eating & Drinking

Can you recommend a ...?
நீங்கள் ஒரு ... பரிந்துரைக்க முடியுமா? — *neeng·kal o·ru ... pa·rin·tu·raik·ka mu·ti·yu·maa*

bar — பார் — *paar*

dish — உணவு வகை — *u·na·vu va·kai*

place to eat — உணவகம் — *u·na·va·ham*

I'd like (a/the) ..., please.
எனக்கு தயவு செய்து ... கொடுங்கள். — *e·nak·ku ta·ya·vu chey·tu ... ko·tung·kal*

bill — வீலைச்சீட்டு — *vi·laich·cheet·tu*

menu — உணவுப்– பட்டியல — *u·na·vup· pat·ti·yal*

that dish — அந்த உணவு வகை — *an·ta u·na·vu va·hai*

(cup of) coffee/tea ...
(கப்) காப்பி/ தேனீர் ... — *(kap) kaap·pi/ tey·neer ...*

with milk — பாலுடன் — *paa·lu·tan*

without sugar — சர்க்கரை– இல்லாமல — *chark·ka·rai· il·laa·mal*

a bottle/ glass of ... wine
ஒரு பாட்டில்/ கிளாஸ ... வைன் — *o·ru paat·til/ ki·laas ... vain*

red — சிவப்பு — *chi·vap·pu*

white — வெள்ளை — *vel·lai*

Do you have vegetarian food?
உங்களிடம சைவ உணவு உள்ளதா? — *ung·ka·li·tam chai·va u·na·vu ul·la·taa*

I'm allergic to (nuts).
எனக்கு (பருப்பு வகை) உணவு சேராது. — *e·nak·ku (pa·rup·pu va·kai) u·na·vu chey·raa·tu*

beer — பீர் — *peer*

breakfast — காலை உணவு — *kaa·lai u·na·vu*

dinner — இரவு உணவு — *i·ra·vu u·na·vu*

drink — பானம் — *paa·nam*

fish — மீன் — *meen*

food — உணவு — *u·na·vu*

fruit — பழம் — *pa·zam*

juice — சாறு — *chaa·ru*

lunch — மதிய உணவு — *ma·ti·ya u·na·vu*

meat — இறைச்சி — *i·raich·chi*

milk	பால்	paal
soft drink	குளிர் பானம்	ku·lir paa·nam
vegetable	காய்கறி	kai·ka·ri
water	தண்ணீர்	tan·neyr

Emergencies

Help! உதவ! u·ta·vi
Go away! போய் வீடு! pow·i vi·tu

Call a doctor!
ஐ அழைக்கவும் i a·zai·ka·vum
ஒரு மருத்துவர்! o·ru ma·rut·tu·var
Call the police!
ஐ அழைக்கவும் i a·zai·ka·vum
போலீஸ்! pow·lees
I'm lost.
நான் வழி தவறி naan va·zi ta·va·ri
போய்விட்டேன். pow·i·vit·teyn
I have to use the phone.
நான் தொலைபேசியை naan to·lai·pey·chi·yai
பயன்படுத்த வேண்டும். pa·yan·pa·tut·ta veyn·tum
Where are the toilets?
கழிவறைகள் எங்கே? ka·zi·va·rai·kal eng·key

Shopping & Services

Where's the market?
எங்கே சந்தை eng·key chan·tai
இருக்கிறது? i·ruk·ki·ra·tu
Can I look at it?
நான் இதைப் naan i·taip
பார்க்கலாமா? paark·ka·laa·maa
How much is it?
இது என்ன வீலை? i·tu en·na vi·lai
That's too expensive.
அது அதிக வீலையாக a·tu a·ti·ka vi·lai·yaa·ka
இருக்கிறது. i·ruk·ki·ra·tu
There's a mistake in the bill.
இந்த வீலைச்சீட்டில் in·ta vi·laich·cheet·til
ஒரு தவறு இருக்கிறது. o·ru ta·va·ru i·ruk·ki·ra·tu

bank	வங்கி	vang·ki
internet	இணையம்	i·nai·yam
post office	தபால்	ta·paal
	நிலையம்	ni·lai·yam
tourist office	சுற்றுப்பயண	chut·rup·pa·ya·na
	அலுவலகம்	a·lu·va·la·kam

Numbers

1	ஒன்று	on·dru
2	இரண்டு	i·ran·tu
3	மூன்று	moon·dru
4	நான்கு	naan·ku
5	ஐந்து	ain·tu
6	ஆறு	aa·ru
7	ஏழு	ey·zu
8	எட்டு	et·tu
9	ஒன்பது	on·pa·tu
10	பத்து	pat·tu
20	இருபது	i·ru pa·lu
30	முப்பது	mup·pa·tu
40	நாற்பது	naar·pa·tu
50	ஐம்பது	aim·pa·tu
60	அறுபது	a·ru·pa·tu
70	எழுபது	e·zu·pa·tu
80	எண்பது	en·pa·tu
90	தொன்னூறு	ton·noo·ru
100	நூறு	noo·ru
1000	ஓராயிரம்	aw·raa·yi·ram

Time & Dates

What time is it?
மணி என்ன? ma·ni en·na
It's (two) o'clock.
மணி (இரண்டு). ma·ni (i·ran·tu)
Half past (two).
(இரண்டு) முப்பது. (i·ran·tu) mup·pa·tu

morning	காலை	kaa·lai
evening	மாலை	maa·lai
yesterday	நேற்று	ncyt·lru
today	இன்று	in·dru
tomorrow	நாளை	naa·lai
Monday	திங்கள்	ting·kal
Tuesday	செவ்வாய்	chev·vai
Wednesday	புதன்	pu·tan
Thursday	வீயாழன்	vi·yaa·zan
Friday	வெள்ளி	vel·li
Saturday	சனி	cha·ni
Sunday	ஞாயிறு	nyaa·yi·ru

Transport

Is this the ... to (New Delhi)?
இது தானா i·tu taa·naa
(புது– (pu·tu
டில்லிக்குப்) til·lik·kup)
புறப்படும் ...? pu·rap·pa·tum ...
bus	பஸ்	pas
plane	வீமானம்	vi·maa·nam
train	இரயில்	i·ra·yil

One ... ticket (to Madurai), please.	(மதுரைக்கு) தயவு செய்து ... டிக்கட் கொடுங்கள்.	(ma·tu·raik·ku) ta·ya·vu chey·tu ... tik·kat ko·tung·kal
one-way	ஒரு வழிப்பயண	o·ru va·zip·pa·ya·na
return	இரு வழிப்பயண	i·ru va·zip·pa·ya·na

What time's the first/last bus?

| எத்தனை மணிக்கு முதல்/இறுதி பஸ் வரும்? | et·ta·nai ma·nik·ku mu·tal/i·ru·ti pas va·rum |

How long does the trip take?

| பயணம் எவ்வளவு நேரம் எடுக்கும்? | pa·ya·nam ev·va·la·vu ney·ram e·tuk·kum |

How long will it be delayed?

| எவ்வளவு நேரம் அது தாமதப்படும்? | ev·va·la·vu ney·ram a·tu taa·ma·tap·pa·tum |

Please tell me when we get to (Ooty).

| (ஊட்டிக்குப்) போனவுடன் தயவு செய்து எனக்குக கூறுங்கள். | (oot·tik·kup) paw·na·vu·tan ta·ya·vu chey·tu e·nak·kuk koo·rung·kal |

Please take me to (this address).

| தயவு செய்து என்னை இந்த (வீலாசத்துக்குக) கொண்டு செல்லுங்கள். | ta·ya·vu chey·tu en·nai in·ta (vi·laa·chat·tuk·kuk) kon·tu chel·lung·kal |

Please stop/wait here.

| தயவு செய்து இங்கே நிறுத்துங்கள்/ காத்திருங்கள். | ta·ya·vu chey·tu ing·key ni·rut·tung·kal/ kaat·ti·rung·kal |

I'd like to hire a car (with a driver).

| நான் ஒரு மோட்டார் வண்டை (ஓர் ஓட்டுநருடன்) வாடகைக்கு எடுக்க வீரும்புகிறேன். | naan o·ru mowt·taar van·ti (awr aw·tu·na·ru·tan) vaa·ta·haik·ku e·tuk·ka vi·rum·pu·ki·reyn |

Is this the road to (Mamallapuram)?

| இது தான் (மாமல்லபுரத்துக்கு) செல்லும் சாலையா? | i·tu taan (maa·mal·la·pu·rat·tuk·ku) chel·lum chaa·lai·yaa |

airport	வீமான நிலையம்	vi·maa·na ni·lai·yam
bicycle	சைக்கிள்	chaik·kil
boat	படகு	pa·ta·ku
bus stop	பஸ் நிறுத்தும்	pas ni·rut·tum
economy class	சீக்கன வகுப்பு	chik·ka·na va·kup·pu
first class	முதல் வகுப்பு	mu·tal va·kup·pu
motorcycle	மோட்டார் சைக்கிள்	mowt·taar chaik·kil
train station	நிலையம்	ni·lai·yam

KANNADA

Kannada is the official language of the state of Karnataka. It has 38 million speakers.

The symbol oh is pronounced as the 'o' in 'note' and ow as in 'how'.

Basics

Hello.	ನಮಸ್ಕಾರ.	na·mas·kaa·ra
Goodbye.	ಸಿಗೋಣ.	si·goh·na
Yes./No.	ಹೌದು./ಇಲ್ಲ.	how·du/il·la
Please.	ದಯವಿಟ್ಟು.	da·ya·vit·tu
Thank you.	ಥ್ಯಾಂಕ್ಯೂ.	t'ank·yoo
Excuse me.	ಸ್ವಲ್ಪ ದಾರಿ ಬಿಡಿ.	sval·pa daa·ri bi·di
Sorry.	ಕ್ಷಮಿಸಿ.	ksha·mi·si

What's your name?

| ನಿಮ್ಮ ಹೆಸರೇನು? | nim·ma he·sa·rey·nu |

My name is ...

| ನನ್ನ ಹೆಸರು ... | nan·na he·sa·ru ... |

Do you speak English?

| ನೀವ ಇಂಗ್ಲೀಷ್ ಮಾತಾಡುತ್ತೀರಾ? | nee·vu ing·lee·shu maa·taa·dut·tee·ra |

I don't understand.

| ನನಗೆ ಅರ್ಥವಾಗುವುದಿಲ್ಲ. | na·na·ge ar·t'a·aa·gu·vu·dil·la |

How much is it?

| ಎಷ್ಟು ಇದು? | esh·tu i·du |

Where are the toilets?

| ಟಾಯ್ಲೆಟ್ಟ್ಯುಗಳು ಎಲ್ಲಿ? | taay·let·tu·ga·lu el·li |

Emergencies

Help!	ಸಹಾಯ ಮಾಡಿ!	sa·haa·ya maa·di
Go away!	ದೂರ ಹೋಗಿ!	doo·ra hoh·gi
Call ...!	... ಕಾಲ್ ಮಾಡಿ!	... kaal maa·di
a doctor	ಡಾಕ್ಟರಿಗೆ	daak·ta·ri·ge
the police	ಪೋಲೀಸಿಗೆ	poh·lee·si·ge

I have to use the phone.

| ನಾನು ಫೋನು ಬಳಸಬೇಕು. | naa·nu foh·nu ba·la·sa·bey·ku |

I'm lost.

| ನಾನು ಕಳೆದುಹೋಗಿರುವೆ. | naa·nu ka·le·du·hoh·gi·ru·ve |

Numbers

1	ಒಂದು	on·du
2	ಎರಡು	e·ra·du
3	ಮೂರು	moo·ru
4	ನಾಲ್ಕು	naa·ku
5	ಐದು	ai·du
6	ಆರು	aa·ru

7	ಏಳು	ey·lu
8	ಎಂಟು	en·tu
9	ಒಂಬತ್ತು	om·bat·tu
10	ಹತ್ತು	hat·tu
20	ಇಪ್ಪತ್ತು	ip·pat·tu
30	ಮೂವತ್ತು	moo·vat·tu
40	ನಲವತ್ತು	na·la·vat·tu
50	ಐವತ್ತು	ai·vat·tu
60	ಆರವತ್ತು	a·ra·vat·tu
70	ಎಳ್ಪತ್ತು	ep·pat·tu
80	ಎಂಬತ್ತು	em·bat·tu
90	ತೊಂಬತ್ತು	tom·bat·tu
100	ನೂರು	noo·ru
1000	ಸಾವಿರ	saa·vi·ra

KONKANI

Konkani is the official language of the state of Goa. It has 2.5 million speakers. The Devanagari script (also used to write Hindi and Marathi) is the official writing system for Konkani in Goa. However, many Konkani speakers in Karnataka use the Kannada script, as given in this section.

Pronounce eu as the 'u' in 'nurse', oh as the 'o' in 'note' and ts as in 'hats'.

Basics

Hello.	ಹಲ್ಲೋ.	hal·lo
Goodbye.	ಮೆಳ್ಯಾಂ.	mel·yaang
Yes./No.	ವ್ಹಯ್./ನಾ.	weu·i/naang
Please.	ಉಪ್ಕಾರ್ ಕರ್ನ್.	up·kaar keurn
Thank you.	ದೇವ ಬರೆಂ ಕರುಂ.	day·u bo·reng ko·roong
Excuse me.	ಉಪ್ಕಾರ್ ಕರ್ನ್.	up·kaar keurn
Sorry.	ಚೂಕ್ ಝಾಲಿ, ಮಾಫ್ ಕರ್.	ts'ook zaa·li maaf keur

What's your name?
ತುಜೆಂ ನಾಂವ್ ಕಿತೆಂ? · tu·jeng naang·ung ki·teng

My name is ...
ಮ್ಹಜೆಂ ನಾಂವ್ ... · m'eu·jeng naang·ung ...

Do you speak English?
ಇಂಗ್ಲಿಶ್ ಉಲೈತ್ಯಾಯ್ಗೀ? · ing·leesh u·leuy·taay·gee

Do you understand?
ಸಮ್ಜಾಲೆಂಗೀ? · som·zaa·leng·gee

I understand.
ಸಮ್ಜಾಲೆಂ. · som·zaa·leng

I don't understand.
ನಾಂ, ಸಮ್ಜೊಂಕ್–ನಾಂ. · naang som·zonk·naang

How much is it?
ತಾಕಾ ಕಿತ್ಲೆ ಪೈಶೆ? · taa·kaa kit·le peuy·she

Where are the toilets?
ಟೊಯ್ಲೆಟ್ ಖೈಂಚರ್ ಆಸಾತ್? · toy·let k'eu·ing·ts'eur aa·saat

Emergencies

| Help! | ಮ್ಹಾಕಾ ಕುಮಕ್ ಕರ್! | m'aa·kaa ku·meuk keur |
| Go away! | ವೆಸ್! | weuts' |

Call ...!	... ಆಪೈ!	... aa·pai
a doctor	ಡಾಕ್ಟರಾಕ್	daak·te·raak
the police	ಪೊಲಿಸಾಂಕ್	po·li·saank

I have to use the phone.
ಮ್ಹಾಕಾ ಫೋನಾಚಿ ಘರ್ಜ್ ಆಸಾ. · m'aa·kaa fo·na·chi g'eurz aa·saa

I'm lost.
ಮ್ಹಜೆ ವಾಟ್ ಚುಕ್ಲ್ಯಾ · m'eu·ji waat ts'uk·lyaa

Could you help me, please?
ಮ್ಹಾಕಾ ಇಲ್ಲೊಜೊ ಉಪ್ಕಾರ್ ಕರ್ಶಿಗೀ? · m'aa·kaa il·lo·ts'o up·kaar keur·shi·gee

Numbers

1	ಏಕ್	ayk
2	ದೋನ್	dohn
3	ತೀನ್	teen
4	ಚಾರ್	chaar
5	ಪಾಂಚ್	paants'
6	ಸೊ	so
7	ಸಾತ್	saat
8	ಆಟ್	aat'
9	ನೊವ್	nohw
10	ಧಾ	d'aa
20	ವೀಸ್	wees
30	ತೀಸ್	tees
40	ಚಾಳೀಸ್	ts'aa·lees
50	ಪನ್ನಾಸ್	pon·naas
60	ಸಾಟ್	saat'
70	ಸತ್ತರ್	seut·teur
80	ಐಂಶಿಂ	euyng·shing
90	ನೊವ್ಪೋದ್	no·wod
100	ಶೆಂಭರ್	shem·bor
1000	ಹಜಾರ್	ha·zaar

MALAYALAM

Malayalam is the official language of the state of Kerala. It has around 33 million speakers.

Note that zh is pronounced as the 's' in 'measure'.

Basics

Hello.	ഹലോ.	ha·*lo*
Goodbye.	ഗുഡ് ബൈ.	good bai
Yes.	അതെ.	a·*t'e*
No.	അല്ല.	al·*la*
Please.	ദയവായി.	da·ya·va·*yi*
Thank you.	നന്ദി.	nan·*n'i*
Excuse me.	ക്ഷമിക്കണം.	ksha·mi·ka·*nam*
Sorry.	ക്ഷമിക്കുക.	ksha·mi·ku·*ka*

Do you speak English?
നിങ്ങൾ ഇംഗ്ലീഷ് സംസാരിക്കുമോ? ning·*al* in·*glish* sam·*saa*·ri·ku·*mo*

I don't understand.
എനിക്ക് മനസ്സിലാകില്ല. e·ni·*ku* ma·na·*si*·la·ki·la

What's your name?
താങ്കളുടെ പേര് എന്താണ്? t'ang·a·lu·*te* pey·*ru* en·t'aa·*nu*

My name is ...
എന്റെ പേര് ... en·*te* pey·*ru* ...

How much is it?
എത്രയാണ് ഇതിന്? et'·ra·yaa·*nu* i·t'i·*nu*

Where are the toilets?
എവിടെയാണ് കക്കൂസ്? e·vi·de·yaa·*nu* ka·koo·*su*

Emergencies

Help!	സഹായിക്കൂ!	sa·ha·yi·*koo*
Go away!	ഇവിടുന്ന് പോകൂ!	i·vi·du·*nu* po·*koo*

Call ...!	... വിളിക്കൂ!	... vi·li·*koo*
a doctor	ഒരു ഡോക്ടറെ	o·*ru* dok·ta·*re*
the police	പൊലീസിനെ	po·li·si·*ne*

I have to use the phone.
എനിക്ക് ഈ ഫോൺ ഒന്നു വേണമായിരുന്നു. e·ni·*ku* ee fon o·nu vey·na·maa·yi·ru·*nu*

I'm lost.
എനിക്ക് വഴി അറിഞ്ഞുകൂട. e·ni·*ku* va·*zhi* a·ri·*nyu*·koo·*da*

Numbers

1	ഒന്ന്	on·na
2	രണ്ട്	ran·d'a
3	മൂന്ന്	moo·na
4	നാല്	naa·la
5	അഞ്ച്	an·ja
6	ആറ്	aa·ra
7	ഏഴ്	e·zha

8	എട്ട്	e·t'a
9	ഒമ്പത്	on·pa·t'a
10	പത്ത്	pa·t'a
20	ഇരുപത്	i·ru·pa·t'a
30	മുപ്പത്	mu·p'a·t'a
40	നാൽപത്	naal·pa·t'a
50	അമ്പത്	an·ba·t'a
60	അറുപത്	a·ru·pa·t'a
70	എഴുപത്	e·zhu·pa·t'a
80	എൺപത്	en·pa·t'a
90	തൊണ്ണൂറ്	t'on·noo·ra
100	നൂറ്	n'oo·ra
1000	ആയിരം	aa·ye·ram

MARATHI

Marathi is the official language of the state of Maharashtra. It is spoken by an estimated 71 million people. Marathi is written in the Devanagari script (also used for Hindi).

Keep in mind that oh is pronounced as the 'o' in 'note'.

Basics

Hello.	नमस्कार.	na·mas·*kaar*
Goodbye.	बाय.	bai
Yes.	होय.	hoy
No.	नाही.	naa·*hee*
Please.	कृपया.	kri·pa·*yaa*
Thank you.	धन्यवाद.	d'an·ya·*vaad*
Excuse me.	क्षमस्व.	ksha·mas·*va*
Sorry.	खेद आहे.	k'ed aa·*he*

What's your name?
आपले नाव ? aa·pa·*le* naa·*nav*

My name is ...
माझे नाव ... maa·*j'e* naa·*nav* ...

Do you speak English?
आपण इंग्रजी बोलता का ? aa·*pan* ing·re·*jee* bol·*taa* kaa

I don't understand.
मला समजत नाही. ma·*laa* sam·*jat* naa·*hee*

How much is it?
याची काय किंमत आहे ? yaa·*chee* kaay ki·*mat* aa·*he*

Where are the toilets?
शौचालय कुठे आहे ? shoh·chaa·*lai* ku·*t'e* aa·*he*

Emergencies

Help!	मदत !	ma·*dat*
Go away!	दूर जा !	door jaa

Call ...!	कॉल करा ...!	kaal ka·*raa* ...
a doctor	डॉक्टरांना	dok·ta·raan·*naa*
the police	पोलिसांना	po·li·saa·*naa*

I have to use the phone.
मला फोन वापरायचा आहे. ma·*laa* fon vaa·pa·raa·ya·*chaa* aa·*he*

I'm lost.
मी हरवले आहे. mee ha·ra·va·*le* aa·*he*

Numbers

1	एक	ek
2	दोन	don
3	तीन	teen
4	चार	chaar
5	पाच	paach
6	सहा	sa·*haa*
7	सात	saat
8	आठ	aat'
9	नऊ	na·*oo*
10	दहा	da·*haa*
20	वीस	vees
30	तीस	tees
40	चाळीस	chaa·*lees*
50	पन्नास	pan·*naas*
60	साठ	saat'
70	सत्तर	sat·*tar*
80	ऐंशी	ain·*shee*
90	नव्वद	nav·*vad*
100	शंभर	sham·*b'ar*
1000	एक हजार	ek ha·*jaar*

TELUGU

Telugu is the official language of the states of Telengana and Andhra Pradesh. It has 70 million speakers.

Remember to pronounce oh as the 'o' in 'note'.

Basics

Hello.	నమస్కారం.	na·mas·kaa·ram
Goodbye.	వెళ్ళొస్తాను.	vel·loh·staa·nu
Yes./No.	అవును./కాదు.	a·vu·nu/kaa·du
Please.	దయచేసి.	da·ya·chay·si
Thank you.	ధన్యవాదాలు.	d'an·ya·vaa·daa·lu
Excuse me.	ఏమండి.	ay·an·di
Sorry.	క్షమించండి.	ksha·min·chan·di

What's your name?
మీ పేరేంటి? mee pay·rayn·ti

My name is ...
నా పేరు ... naa pay·ru ...

Do you speak English?
మీరు ఇంగ్లీషు మాట్లాడుతారా? mee·ru ing·lee·shu maat·laa·du·taa·raa

I don't understand.
అర్థం కాదు. ar·t'am kaa·du

How much is it?
అది ఎంత? a·di en·ta

Where are the toilets?
బాత్రూములు ఎక్కడ ఉన్నాయి? baat·room·lu ek·ka·da un·naa·yi

Emergencies

| Help! | సహాయం కావాలి! | sa·haa·yam kaa·vaa·li |
| Go away! | వెళ్ళిపో! | vel·li·poh |

Call ...!	... పిలవండి!	... pi·la·van·di
a doctor	డాక్టర్ని	daak·tar·ni
the police	పోలీసుల్ని	poh·lee·sul·ni

I have to use the phone.
నేను ఫోను వాడుకోవాలి. nay·nu p'oh·nu vaa·du·koh·vaa·li

I'm lost.
నేను దారి తప్పి పోయాను. nay·nu daa·ri tap·pi poh·yaa·nu

Numbers

1	ఒకటి	oh·ka·ti
2	రెండు	ren·du
3	మూడు	moo·du
4	నాలుగ	naa·lu·gu
5	ఐదు	ai·du
6	ఆరు	aa·ru
7	ఏడు	ay·du
8	ఎనిమిది	e·ni·mi·di
9	తొమ్మిది	tohm·mi·di
10	పది	pa·di
20	ఇరవై	i·ra·vai
30	ముప్పై	mup·p'ai
40	నలభై	na·la·b'ai
50	యాభై	yaa·b'ai
60	అరవై	a·ra·vai
70	డెబ్బై	deb·b'ai
80	ఎనభై	e·na·b'ai
90	తొంభై	tohm·b'ai
100	వంద	van·da
1000	వెయ్యి	vey·yi

GLOSSARY

Adivasi – tribal person

Agni – major deity in the *Vedas*; mediator between men and the gods; also fire

ahimsa – discipline of non-violence

air-cooler – noisy water-filled cooling fan

Ananta – serpent on whose coils *Vishnu* reclined

apsara – heavenly nymph

Arjuna – Mahabharata hero and military commander who married Subhadra

Aryan – Sanskrit for 'noble'; those who migrated from Persia and settled in northern India

Ashoka – ruler in the 3rd century BC; responsible for spreading Buddhism throughout South India

ashram – spiritual community or retreat

autorickshaw – noisy, three-wheeled, motorised contraption for transporting passengers, livestock etc for short distances; found throughout the country, they are cheaper than taxis

avatar – incarnation, usually of a deity

ayurveda – ancient and complex science of Indian herbal medicine and healing

azad – free (Urdu), as in Azad Jammu & Kashmir

baba – religious master or father; term of respect

bagh – garden

baksheesh – tip, donation (alms) or bribe

banyan – Indian fig tree; spiritual to many Indians

Bhagavad Gita – Hindu Song of the Divine One; *Krishna*'s lessons to *Arjuna*, the main thrust of which was to emphasise the philosophy of *bhakti*; it's part of the *Mahabharata*

bhajan – devotional song

bhakti – surrendering to the gods; faith

bhang – dried leaves and flowering shoots of the marijuana plant

bhavan – house, building; also spelt *bhawan*

BJP – Bharatiya Janata Party; political party

bodhisattva – literally 'one whose essence is perfected wisdom'; in Early Buddhism, bodhisattva refers only to *Buddha* during the period between his conceiving the intention to strive for Buddhahood and the moment he attained it; in *Mahayana* Buddhism, it is one who renounces nirvana in order to help others attain it

Bollywood – India's answer to Hollywood; the film industry of Mumbai (Bombay)

Brahma – Hindu god; worshipped as the creator in the *Trimurti*

Brahmin – member of the priest/scholar caste, the highest Hindu *caste*

Buddha – Awakened One; the originator of Buddhism; also regarded by Hindus as the ninth incarnation of *Vishnu*

cantonment – administrative and military area of a Raj-era town

Carnatic music – classical music of South India

caste – a Hindu's hereditary station (social standing) in life; there are four castes: the *Brahmins*, the *Kshatriyas*, the *Vaishyas* and the *Shudras*; the Brahmins occupy the top spot

chaitya – Sanskrit form of 'cetiya', meaning shrine or object of worship; has come to mean temple, and more specifically, a hall divided into a central nave and two side aisles by a line of columns, with a votive *stupa* at the end

chappals – sandals or leather thonglike footwear; flip-flops

charas – resin of the marijuana plant; also referred to as 'hashish'

chital – spotted deer

choli – sari blouse

chowk – town square, intersection or marketplace

dagoba – see *stupa*

Dalit – preferred term for India's *Untouchable* caste

dargah – shrine or place of burial of a Muslim saint

darshan – offering or audience with someone; auspicious viewing of a deity

Deccan – meaning 'South'; this refers to the central South Indian plateau

Devi – *Shiva*'s wife; goddess

dhaba – basic restaurant or snack bar; especially popular with truck drivers

dharamsala – pilgrims' rest house

dharma – for Hindus, the moral code of behaviour or social duty; for Buddhists, following the law of nature, or path, as taught by *Buddha*

dhobi – person who washes clothes; commonly referred to as *dhobi-wallah*

dhobi ghat – place where clothes are washed by the *dhobi*

dhoti – like a *lungi*, but the ankle-length cloth is then pulled up between the legs; worn by men

dhurrie – rug

dowry – money and/or goods given by a bride's parents to their son-in-law's family; it's illegal but still exists in many arranged marriages

Dravidian – general term for the cultures and languages of the deep south of India, including Tamil, Malayalam, Telugu and Kannada

dupatta – long scarf for women often worn with the *salwar kameez*

durbar – royal court; also a government

Durga – the Inaccessible; a form of *Shiva*'s wife, *Devi*, a beautiful, fierce goddess riding a tiger/lion

filmi – slang term describing anything to do with Indian movies

Ganesh – Hindu god of good fortune and remover of obstacles; popular elephant-headed son of *Shiva* and *Parvati*, he is also known as Ganpati; his vehicle is a ratlike creature

Ganga – Hindu goddess representing the sacred Ganges River; said to flow from *Vishnu*'s toe

Garuda – man-bird vehicle of *Vishnu*

gaur – Indian bison

ghat – steps or landing on a river, range of hills, or road up hills

giri – hill

gopuram – soaring pyramidal gateway tower of *Dravidian* temples

gurdwara – Sikh temple

guru – holy teacher; in Sanskrit literally *goe* (darkness) and *roe* (to dispel)

Hanuman – Hindu monkey god, prominent in the *Ramayana*, and a follower of *Rama*

Indo-Saracenic – style of colonial architecture that integrated Western designs with Islamic, Hindu and Jain influences

Indra – significant and prestigious Vedic god; god of rain, thunder, lightning and war

Jagannath – Lord of the Universe; a form of *Krishna*

ji – honorific that can be added to the end of almost anything as a form of respect; thus 'Babaji', 'Gandhiji'

Kailasa – sacred Himalayan mountain; home of *Shiva*

kalamkari – designs painted on cloth using vegetable dyes

Kali – the ominous-looking evil-destroying form of *Devi*; commonly depicted with dark skin, dripping with blood, and wearing a necklace of skulls

kameez – woman's shirtlike tunic

Kannada – state language of Karnataka

karma – Hindu, Buddhist and Sikh principle of retributive justice for past deeds

khadi – homespun cloth; Mahatma Gandhi encouraged people to spin this rather than buy English cloth

Khan – Muslim honorific title

kolam – elaborate chalk, rice-paste or coloured powder design; also known as *rangoli*

Konkani – state language of Goa

Krishna – *Vishnu*'s eighth incarnation, often coloured blue; he revealed the *Bhagavad Gita* to *Arjuna*

Kshatriya – Hindu *caste* of soldiers or administrators; second in the caste hierarchy

kurta – long shirt with either short collar or no collar

lakh – 100,000

Lakshmana – half-brother and aide of *Rama* in the *Ramayana*

Lakshmi – *Vishnu*'s consort, Hindu goddess of wealth; she sprang forth from the ocean holding a lotus

lama – Tibetan Buddhist priest or monk

lingam – phallic symbol; auspicious symbol of *Shiva;* plural 'linga'

lungi – worn by men, this loose, coloured garment (similar to a sarong) is pleated at the waist to fit the wearer

maha – prefix meaning 'great'

Mahabharata – Great Hindu Vedic epic poem of the Bharata dynasty; containing approximately 10,000 verses describing the battle between the Pandavas and the Kauravas

mahal – house or palace

maharaja – literally 'great king'; princely ruler

mahatma – literally 'great soul'

Mahavir – greater-vehicle of Buddhism

Mahayana – last *tirthankar*

mahout – elephant rider or master

maidan – open (often grassed) area; parade ground

Malayalam – state language of Kerala

mandapa – pillared pavilion; a temple forechamber

mandir – temple

Maratha – central Indian people who controlled much of India at various times and fought the *Mughals* and *Rajputs*

marg – road

masjid – mosque

mehndi – henna; ornate henna designs on women's hands (and often feet), traditionally for certain festivals or ceremonies (eg marriage)

mela – fair or festival

moksha – liberation from samsara

mudra – ritual hand movements used in Hindu religious dancing; gesture of *Buddha* figure

Mughal – Muslim dynasty of subcontinental emperors from Babur to Aurangzeb

Naga – mythical serpentlike beings capable of changing into human form

namaste – traditional Hindu greeting (hello or goodbye), often accompanied by a respectful small bow with the hands together at the chest or head level

Nandi – bull, vehicle of *Shiva*

Narasimha – man-lion incarnation of *Vishnu*

Narayan – incarnation of *Vishnu* the creator

Nataraja – *Shiva* as the cosmic dancer

nizam – hereditary title of the rulers of Hyderabad

NRI – Non-Resident Indian

Om – sacred invocation representing the essence of the divine principle; for Buddhists, if repeated often enough with complete concentration, it leads to a state of emptiness

Parsi – adherent of the Zoroastrian faith

Partition – formal division of British India in 1947 into two separate countries, India and Pakistan

Parvati – a form of *Devi*

PCO – Public Call Office from where to make local, interstate and international phone calls

Pongal – Tamil harvest festival

pradesh – state

prasad – temple-blessed food offering

puja – literally 'respect'; offering or prayers

Puranas – set of 18 encyclopaedic Sanskrit stories, written in verse, relating to the three gods, dating from the 5th century AD

Radha – favourite mistress of *Krishna* when he lived as a cowherd

raga – any of several conventional patterns of melody and rhythm that form the basis for freely interpreted compositions

raj – rule or sovereignty; British Raj (sometimes just Raj) refers to British rule

raja – king; sometimes *rana*

Rajput – Hindu warrior caste, former rulers of northwestern India

Rama – seventh incarnation of *Vishnu*

Ramadan – the Islamic holy month of sunrise-to-sunset fasting (no eating, drinking or smoking); also referred to as Ramazan

Ramayana – the story of *Rama* and *Sita* and their conflict with *Ravana* is one of India's best-known epics

rana – king; sometimes *raja*

rangoli – see *kolam*

rani – female ruler or wife of a king

rathas – rock-cut *Dravidian* temples

Ravana – demon king of Lanka (modern-day Sri Lanka)

rickshaw – small, two- or three-wheeled passenger vehicle

sadhu – ascetic, holy person; one who is trying to achieve enlightenment; often addressed as *swamiji* or *babaji*

sagar – lake, reservoir

sahib – respectful title applied to a gentleman

salwar – trousers usually worn with a *kameez*

salwar kameez – traditional dresslike tunic and trouser combination for women

sambar – deer

Saraswati – wife of *Brahma*; goddess of learning; sits on a white swan

Sati – wife of *Shiva*; became a *sati* ('honourable woman') by immolating herself; although banned more than a century ago, the act of *sati* is still (very) occasionally performed

satyagraha – nonviolent protest involving a hunger strike, popularised by Mahatma Gandhi; from Sanskrit, literally meaning 'insistence on truth'

Scheduled Castes – official term used for the *Untouchables* or *Dalits*

shahadah – Muslim declaration of faith ('There is no God but Allah; Mohammed is his prophet')

Shaivite – follower of *Shiva*

Shakti – creative energies perceived as female deities; devotees follow Shaktism

Shiv Sena – Hindu nationalist political party

Shiva – the Destroyer; also the Creator, in which form he is worshipped as a *lingam*

Shivaji – great Maratha leader of the 17th century

shola – virgin forest

Shudra – *caste* of labourers

sikhara – Hindu temple-spire or temple

Sita – the Hindu goddess of agriculture; more commonly associated with the *Ramayana*

sitar – Indian stringed instrument

Sivaganga – water tank in temple dedicated to *Shiva*

stupa – Buddhist religious monument composed of a solid hemisphere topped by a spire, containing relics of *Buddha*; also known as a *dagoba* or pagoda

Sufi – Muslim mystic

Surya – the sun; a major deity in the *Vedas*

swami – title of respect meaning 'lord of the self'; given to initiated Hindu monks

tabla – twin drums

Tamil – language of Tamil Nadu; people of *Dravidian* origin

tandava – *Shiva's* cosmic victory dance

tank – reservoir; pool or large receptacle of holy water found at some temples

tempo – noisy three-wheeler public-transport vehicle; bigger than an *autorickshaw*

Theravada – orthodox form of Buddhism practised in Sri Lanka and Southeast Asia that is char-

acterised by its adherence to the Pali canon; literally 'dwelling'

tilak – auspicious forehead mark of devout Hindu men

tirthankars – the 24 great Jain teachers

Trimurti – triple form; the Hindu triad of *Brahma*, *Shiva* and *Vishnu*

Untouchable – lowest *caste* or 'casteless', for whom the most menial tasks are reserved; the name derives from the belief that higher castes risk defilement if they touch one; now known as *Dalit*

Vaishya – member of the Hindu caste of merchants

Vedas – Hindu sacred books; collection of hymns composed in preclassical Sanskrit during the second millennium BC and divided into four books: Rig-Veda, Yajur-Veda, Sama-Veda and Atharva-Veda

vihara – Buddhist monastery, generally with central court or hall off which open residential cells, usually with a *Buddha* shrine at one end

vikram – *tempo* or a larger version of the standard *tempo*

vimana – principal part of Hindu temple; a tower over the sanctum

vipassana – insight meditation technique of *Theravada* Buddhism in which mind and body are closely examined as changing phenomena

Vishnu – part of the *Trimurti*; Vishnu is the Preserver and Restorer who so far has nine *avatars*: the fish Matsya, the tortoise Kurma, the wild boar Naraha, *Narasimha*, Vamana, Parasurama, *Rama*, *Krishna* and *Buddha*

wallah – man; added onto almost anything, eg *dhobi*-wallah, chai-wallah, taxi-wallah

yali – mythical lion creature

yatra – pilgrimage

zenana – area of a home where women are secluded; women's quarters

Behind the Scenes

SEND US YOUR FEEDBACK

We love to hear from travellers – your comments keep us on our toes and help make our books better. Our well-travelled team reads every word on what you loved or loathed about this book. Although we cannot reply individually to your submissions, we always guarantee that your feedback goes straight to the appropriate authors, in time for the next edition. Each person who sends us information is thanked in the next edition – the most useful submissions are rewarded with a selection of digital PDF chapters.

Visit **lonelyplanet.com/contact** to submit your updates and suggestions or to ask for help. Our award-winning website also features inspirational travel stories, news and discussions.

Note: We may edit, reproduce and incorporate your comments in Lonely Planet products such as guidebooks, websites and digital products, so let us know if you don't want your comments reproduced or your name acknowledged. For a copy of our privacy policy visit lonelyplanet.com/privacy.

OUR READERS

Many thanks to the travellers who used the last edition and wrote to us with helpful hints, useful advice and interesting anecdotes:

Francis John, Olivia Francis, Pierre Flener, Andy Hughes, D Steele, Daniel Biau, Olivia Veliyath, Peter Van Elsen, Ambar Duree, Katrin Glöckle, Luke Wingfield-Digby, Ricardo Losa Begue, John Marshall, Bob Put, Camilla Malvestiti, Jaroslav Ledvina, Anna Bernhardt.

WRITER THANKS

Isabella Noble

Huge thanks in Kerala: Paul, John, Roy, Lee, Kumar, Mariann and Philip, Johnson, Daniel, Roy Joseph, Dileep and Tomy, Beena and Varghese, Ajay, Suresh and Sulekha, Debra, Joseph, Yazer, the French yogis, and Mr Babu at Kochi's Vyttila Mobility Hub. Cheers to Norbu and Sangay in Darjeeling; and to Samit, Ashish, Sanjay, Rahul, Mark, Atalanta, Pawan, Jocelyn, Abnash and Shakti in the Andamans. Extra grateful to my fabulous India cowriters, and, at home, to Jack, Dan, Andrew and Paps.

Michael Benanav

I'd like to thank Isabella Noble – one of LP's own South India experts – for all of her Tamil Nadu advice. And as always, thanks to Luke and Kelly for their patience and understanding while I'm away.

Paul Harding

Thanks must go to the many friends I reconnected with in Goa and the new people I met on this trip. Big thanks to Jack, Ajit and family in Panaji; Ravi in Vagator; John, Jack and Kate in Palolem; and Joanna and Xavi in Patnem. Thanks also to friends in Kochi and Alappuzha (Alleppey), Philip, Maryann, Johnson, Shibu and Niaz, and to Joe at Lonely Planet for entrusting me with Goa. Biggest thanks goes to my travelling companions, Hannah and Layla.

Kevin Raub

Thanks to Joe Bindloss and all my fellow partners in crime at LP. On the road, Anil Whadwa and Bagpacker Travels, Pankil Shaw, Jas Charanjiva, Khaki Tours, Priyanka Jacob, Roxanne Bamboat, Sanil Kapse, Sudakshina Banerjee, Ashok Tours & Travels, Sakshi Chari, Sheetal Waradkar, Chirag Rupani, Zaid Purkars and Amrut and Aditya Dhanwatay.

Iain Stewart

Thanks to Jonty in Hyderabad for her insight and helpful tips. I was greatly aided by Prakash in Bengaluru (Bangalore), whose expertise of the craft beer scene and emerging restos is quite something. In Mysuru (Mysore) the folk from Gully Tours proved excellent company, as did the thousands of Hindu pilgrims I accompanied on the Tirumula trek. And thanks to all at LP, including Joe Bindloss and my fellow Team South India & Kerala writers.

ACKNOWLEDGEMENTS

Climate map data adapted from Peel MC, Finlayson BL & McMahon TA (2007) 'Updated World Map of the Köppen-Geiger Climate Classification', *Hydrology and Earth System Sciences*, 11, 1633–44.

Illustration on pp190-1 by Michael Weldon.

Cover photograph: Tea pickers, Munnar, Kerala; Peter Adams Photography Ltd/Alamy Stock Photo ©

THIS BOOK

This 10th edition of Lonely Planet's *South India & Kerala* guidebook was curated by Isabella Noble, and researched and written by Isabella, Michael Benanav, Paul Harding, Kevin Raub and Iain Stewart. The previous two editions were also written by Isabella, Paul, Kevin and Iain, along with Abigail Blasi, Trent Holden, John Noble and Sarina Singh.

This guidebook was produced by the following:

Destination Editor Joe Bindloss

Senior Product Editors Kate Chapman, Anne Mason

Regional Senior Cartographer Valentina Kremenchutskaya

Product Editor Amanda Williamson

Book Designer Mazzy Prinsep

Assisting Editors Sarah Bailey, James Bainbridge, Judith Bamber, Imogen Bannister, Nigel Chin, Joel Cotterell, Michelle Coxall, Melanie Dankel, Bruce Evans, Samantha Forge, Emma Gibbs, Kellie Langdon, Ali Lemer, Jodie Martire, Alison Morris, Rosie Nicholson, Lauren O'Connell, Kristen Odijk

Assisting Cartographers Anita Banh, James Leversha

Cover Researcher Naomi Parker

Thanks to Lauren Egan, James Hardy, Liz Heynes, Andi Jones, Catherine Naghten, Angela Tinson

Index

A

accessible travel 508
accommodation 16, 39, 283, 508-11, *see also individual locations*
accommodation costs
Andaman Islands 425
Andhra Pradesh 250
Goa 124
Kerala 273
Maharashtra 87
Mumbai 57
Tamil Nadu 358
Telangana 250
activities, *see individual activities*
Adivasis 460, *see also tribal peoples*
Agonda 153-5
Aihole 223-4
air travel 521, 522
airports 16
Ajanta Caves 10, 95-8, 169, **96, 10, 168, 169**
Alappuzha 278-83, **280**
alcohol 479-80
Alleppey, *see Alappuzha*
Amaravathi 251
Andaman Islands 13, 42, 417-38, **418**
accommodation 417
accommodation costs 425
beaches 417
cell phones 421
climate 417, 419
environment 419
geography 419
highlights 418
history 419
internet access 421
mobile phones 421

Map Pages **000**
Photo Pages **000**

Restricted Area Permit 419-20
safe travel 419
telephone services 421
travel to/from 420
travel within 420-1
tribal peoples 437-8
Andaman Trunk Road 434
Andamanese 437-8
Andhra Pradesh 41, 249-58, **229**
accommodation 228
accommodation costs 250
climate 228
festivals & events 230
food 228
highlights 229
history 230
Anegundi 220-1, **218**
animals 497-9, 500, *see also individual species*
Anjuna 135-9, **135**
antelope 498
antiques 514
apps 526
arak 480
Araku Valley 255-6
Arambol 147-9
architecture 11, 494-6, **11**
art deco 165
Chettinadu mansions 388
Chhatrapati Shivaji Maharaj Terminus 49
colonial-era 189
Mumbai 165
area codes 15, 519
art 484-6
art galleries
David Hall 298
Kalakriti Art Gallery 233-4
Kashi Art Gallery 298
Mario Gallery 121
Museum of Goa 131
Tara Books 337
arts 490-3

Ashoka, Emperor 445
ashrams 31, 34
Matha Amrithanandamayi Mission 278
Osho International Meditation Resort 112
Osho International Meditation Resort 109
Sivagiri Mutt 271-2
Sivananda Yoga Vedanta Dhanwantari Ashram 266
Sri Aurobindo Ashram 364-5
Sri Ramana Ashram 362
Surfing Ashram 209
Vivekanandapuram 396
Assagao 139-40
Asven 145-6
ATMs 515
Aurangabad 88-92, **89**
Auroville 373-4
autorickshaws 525
Avalanche Valley 413
avian flu 532
ayurveda 31-2, 291
Asven 145
Kochi 299
Kovalam 270
Madikeri 201
Mamallapuram 357
Mandrem 146
Ayyappan 467

B

backwaters 9, 286-7, 322, 328-9, **8-9, 328-9**
Badami 221-3
Baga 131-5, **132**
Bandipur National Park 199-200
Bangalore, *see Bengaluru*
bargaining 485
basilicas, *see churches & cathedrals*
bathrooms 510, 519
Bavikonda 255

bazaars 18
beach huts 509
beaches 17, **2, 9, 13, 326-7**
Alleppey Beach 279
Beach 1 (Shaheed Dweep) 431
Beach 2 (Shaheed Dweep) 432
Beach 3 (Swaraj Dweep) 427
Beach 3 (Shaheed Dweep) 432
Beach 4 (Shaheed Dweep) 432
Beach 5 (Swaraj Dweep) 427
Beach 5 (Shaheed Dweep) 432
Black Beach 271
Butler Bay 436
Cherai Beach 311
Cola 152
Elephant Beach 427
Girgaum Chowpatty 51
Havelock Island (Swaraj Dweep) 427
Juhu Beach 51
Kalapathar 427
Kalipur Beach 435
Kappil Beach 271, 323
Kerala 326-7
Kudle Beach 210
Marina Beach 341
Munda Pahar Beach 426
Neil's Cove 427
Netaji Nagar 436
Nileshwar Beach 323
Odayam Beach 271
Om Beach 210
Papanasham Beach 271
Paradise Beach 210-11
Radhanagar Beach 427
Ramakrishna Beach 252
Tarkali Beach 104
Thottada Beach 320-1
Wandoor Beach 425
beer 16, 70, 479

INDEX B-C

Bekal 322-3
Belur 204-5
Benaulim 152-3
Bengaluru 41, 172-87, **174-5**
  accommodation 178-9
  activities 177
  drinking & nightlife
    182-3
  entertainment 184-5
  festivals & events 178
  food 179-82
  history 173
  shopping 185
  sights 173-7
  tourist information 185-6
  tours 177
  travel to/from 186, 187
  travel within 186-7
betel nut 474
Bhagwan Shree Rajneesh
    109, 112
bhang lassi 517
Bheemunipatnam 254
Bhongir 248
bicycle travel, see cycling
Bidar 167, 227, **167**
Bijapur, see Vijapura
birds 498-9, 500
birdwatching
  Dandeli 222
  Hampi 216
  Ranganathittu Bird
    Sanctuary 199
  Thattekkad Bird
    Sanctuary 296
  Vedanthangal Bird
    Sanctuary 357
Blue Mountains 402
boat travel 522, 523, 525
boat trips 19, **8-9**, **328-9**
  Alappuzha 279
  Kerala backwaters 286-7,
  Kollam 276
  Periyar Tiger Reserve
    288
Bollywood 75, 492-3
Bombay, see Mumbai
booking trains 29-30
books 440, 459, 471,
    486, 491
  architecture 444, 496
  food 472, 473, 476, 477,
    478, 479
  history 443, 448, 455

Map Pages **000**
Photo Pages **000**

religion 465, 467, 469,
    470
  wildlife 501
border crossings 521-2
bouldering 215-16
Brahma 465
bread 473
bribes 514
British East India Company
    452-3
bronzeware 483
Buddhism 470
Buddhist temples & sites
    444, **168-9**
  Ajanta Caves 10, 95-8,
    169, **96**, **10**, **168**, **169**
  Amaravathi 251
  Aurangabad Caves 90
  Bavikonda 255
  Bhaja Caves 108
  Buddha Statue &
    Hussain Sagar 235-6
  Ellora Caves 92-5, 169,
    94, **168-9**
  Global Vipassana
    Pagoda 51
  Golden Temple 204-5
  Guntupalli 169, 252
  Karla Caves 108
  Nagarjunakonda 251
  Sankaram 255
  Thotlakonda 255
  Zangdogpalri Temple
    204-5
budget 15, 507
buffalo racing 210
bus travel 319, 523-4, 525
Bylakuppe 204

C
Calangute 131-5, **132**
Calicut, see Kozhikode
camping 509
Candolim 128-31, **130**
canoeing 329
Cape Comorin, see
    Kanyakumari
car travel 522, 524-5
carbon-monoxide
    poisoning 518
Carnival 20
carpets 483-4
car-sharing apps 526, see
    also taxis
Goa 119
Mumbai 80
cash 515
caste system 459-60

cathedrals, see churches &
    Cathedrals
caves 169
  Ajanta Caves 10, 95-8,
    169, **96**, **10**, **168**, **169**
  Aurangabad Caves 90
  Badami 222-3
  Baratang caves 434
  Bhaja Caves 108
  Borra Caves 255
  Buddhist Caves, Ellora
    94-5
  Edakkal Caves 318
  Ellora Caves 92-5, 169,
    94, **168-9**
  Guntupalli 169, 252
  Jain Caves, Ellora 95
  Kanheri Caves 77
  Karla Caves 108
  Lenyadri 114
  Undavalli Cave Temples
    249
cell phones 14, 421, 518
cemeteries 298, 299
chai 480
Chapora 140-4, **142**
Chennai 42, 335-53, **338-
    9**, **344-5**
  accommodation 342-5
  activities 341
  courses 341
  drinking & nightlife
    348-9
  entertainment 349
  food 345-8
  history 336
  shopping 349-50
  sights 336-7, 340-1, 342
  tourist information 350-1
  tours 341-2
  travel to/from 351
  travel within 352-3
Chennamangalam 311-12
Cherai Beach 311
Chettinadu 386-9
Chidambaram 374-5
Chidiya Tapu 426
children, travel with 37-9
  Mumbai 74
Chinnar Wildlife
    Sanctuary 297
Chola Temples 377
Christian sites 337
Christianity 470
churches & cathedrals
    495-6
  Basilica de Bom Jesus
    126

Basilica of Our Lady of
    Dolours 312
Chennai 342
Church of Our Lady
    of the Immaculate
    Conception 120
Church of South India
    314
Church of St Cajetan
    127-8
Church of St Francis of
    Assisi 127
CSI Christ Church 292
Lourdes Church 384
Marth Mariam Church
    312
New Jerusalem Church
    375
Our Lady of Immaculate
    Conception Cathedral
    366
Our Lady of Lourdes
    Cathedral 312
Puducherry 366
Sacred Heart Basilica
    366
San Thome Cathedral
    337
Santa Cruz Basilica 298
Sé Cathedral 126-7
St Aloysius College
    Chapel 207
St Francis Church 297
St John's Church 384
St Mary's Cathedral 391
St Mary's Orthodox
    Church 284
St Mary's Syrian
    Knanaya Church 284
St Stephen's Church 409
St Teresa's Church 51
St Thomas' Cathedral 50
St Thomas' Church 409
cinema 492-3
Cinque Island 426
climate 14, 442, 502, 534
Cochin, see Kochi
coffee 16, 480
Coimbatore 404-6, **405**
Colva 151-2
consulates 511-12
cooking classes 475
  Assagao 139
  Kochi 299
  Munnar 293
  Palolem 155-6
  Periyar Tiger Reserve
    288
Vagator 141

Coonoor 406-7
Coorg region, see Kodagu
   region
costs 15, 513, see also
   individual regions
courses
   art 341, 485
   cheesemaking 407
   cooking 55, 141, 189,
      366, 475
   diving 133, 267, 427, 432
   language 341
   martial arts 264
   massage 189
   meditation 18, 32,
      34, 251
   surfing 366
   yoga 17-18, 32, 107, 147,
      266, 341, 366, 404,
Covelong, see Kovalam
   (Tamil Nadu)
craft centres
   Kalakshetra Craft Centre
      341
Craggy Island 435
credit cards 515
   scams 504
cricket 463-4
culture 458-64
currency 14
customs regulations 511
cycle-rickshaws 525
cycling 300, 522-3

D
da Gama, Vasco 449
dabba-wallahs 69
dairy 474
dance 331, 490
dance classes
   around Thrissur 314
   Karnataka 187
   Kerala 263-4, 299-300,
      307-8
   Tamil Nadu 366
Dandeli 222
dangers, see safe travel
Daulatabad Fort 92
Deccan Odyssey 529
deer 498
deforestation 502
dehydration 534
dengue fever 532
dhal 473
Dhanushkodi 16, 394
Dharavi Slum 56
Dharmasthala 208
Diglipur 435-6

disabilities, travellers
   with 508
diving 19
   Baga 133
   Calangute 133
   Chidiya Tapu 426
   Kovalam 267
   Malvan 104
   safety 534
   Shaheed Dweep 432
   Swaraj Dweep 427, 432
Diwali 20
dolphin-watching 128
dosas 478
drinking water 533
drinks 479-80
   beer 16, 70, 479
   scams 504
   whisky 188
   wine 86, 188
drugs 504, 513-14, 517
Dussehra 193

E
economy 440
electricity 511
elephants 430, 497, 500
Ellora Caves 92-5, 169, **94**,
   168-9
embassies 511-12
emergencies 15
environmental issues 442,
   498, 501-2
   boat trips 287
   volunteering 36
Eravikulam National Park
   297
Ernakulam, see Kochi
etiquette 442
   food 473
   religion 471
   temple photography 95
Excelsior Island 435
exchange rates 15

F
ferries 329
festivals & events 19, 20-3,
   491, **23**
   Andhra Pradesh 230
   dance 491
   Elephanta Festival 47
   Ganesh Chaturthi 20, 47
   Goa 120
   Hampi 216
   Jio Mami Mumbai Film
      Festival 47

Kala Ghoda Arts Festival
   47
Karnataka 172
Kerala 261, 312
Kochi 300
Maharashtra 84
Mumbai Sanskruti 47
music 491
Mysuru 193
Nariyal Poornima 47
Nehru Trophy Boat
   Race 279
Tamil Nadu 336
Telangana 230
film industry sites 492-3
   Bollywood 37, 75
   Tollywood 237
films 75, 440
folk art 485
food 472-82, 512-13,
   see also individual
   locations
   books 472, 473, 476, 477,
      478, 479
   cooking courses 475
   dabba-wallahs 69
   etiquette 473
   glossary 481-2
   Hyderabadi cuisine 240
   Mumbai street food 66
   safety 477
   scams 504
   spirituality 479
   street food 348, 477-8
forts 17, 166-7, 496
   Bekal Fort 323
   Bidar Fort 167, 227, **167**
   Chalukyan hill fort 248
   Chandragiri Fort 258
   Chapora Fort 140
   Citadel (Vijapura) 224-5
   Dansborg fort 375-6
   Daulatabad Fort 92, 166
   Fort Aguada 128
   Fort St Angelo 320
   Fort St George 341
   Gingee Fort 167, 363, **167**
   Golconda Fort 166, 234-
      5, **166-7**
   Janjira 101-2, 167
   Kondapalli Fort 249
   Pratapgad Fort 116
   Raigad Fort 102-3
   Shaniwar Wada 109
   Shivneri Fort 114
   Sindhudurg Fort 104
   Sinhagad 113-14
   Warangal Fort 248

fruits 474-6

G
Galgibag 160
Gandhi, Mahatma 46,
   455-6, 488
   Gandhi Memorial
      Museum 390
   Gandhi National
      Memorial 108
Ganesh 466
Ganesh Chaturthi 20,
   47, **23**
Ganpatipule 103-4
gay travellers 73, 514
gems 505
geography 500-1
geology 500-1
ghee 475
Gingee Fort 167, 363, **167**
Goa 9, 41, 117-61, **118**, **9**
   accommodation 117
   accommodation costs
      124
   Central Goa 120-7
   climate 117
   festivals & events 120
   food 117
   highlights **118**
   history 119
   North Goa 127-49
   safe travel 139
   South Goa 150-61
   tourist information 119
   travel to/from 119
   travel within 119-20
Goa Express 529
gods 465-7
Gokarna 209-13
Golconda Fort 166, 234-5,
   166-7
Guntupalli 252

H
haggling 485
Halebid 205
Hampi 10, 164, **216**, **218**, **2**,
   10, **33**, **165**
   accommodation 216-19
   activities 215-16
   festivals & events 216
   food 219
   history 213-14
   shopping 219-20
   tickets 214
   tourist information 220
   travel to/from 220

Hanuman 466
Harmal, see Arambol
Hassan 203-4
health 506, 530-4
henna 462
hepatitis 532-3
Hesaraghatta 187
hijras 463
hiking, see trekking
hill stations 11, 18-19, 332,
   5, 11
   Coonoor 406-7
   Kotagiri 407-8
   Mahabaleshwar 115-16
   Udhagamandalam
      409-14
Himalaya, the 500
Hindu temples & sites 12,
   17, 365, 494, 495, 510
1000-Pillared Temple
   248
Achyutaraya Temple 215
Ajanta Caves 10, 95-8,
   169, **96**, **10**, **168**, **169**
Arjuna's Penance 355
Arunachaleshwar Temple
   362
Ayyappan Temple 292,
   442
Bhadrakali Temple 248
Birla Mandir 233
Brihadishwara Temple
   379
Channakeshava Temple
   205
Durga Temple 220, 223-4
Ekambareshwara Temple
   360
Elephanta Island 54
Ellora Caves 92-5, 169,
   94, 168-9
Five Rathas 355, 357
Ganesh Ratha 359
Hampi 164
Hanuman Temple 220
Hazarama Temple 215
Hoysaleswara Temple
   205
Iskcon Temple 51
Janardhana Temple 271
Kailasa Temple 93-4,
   168-9
Kailasanatha Temple 361
Kala Rama Temple 84
Kamakshi Amman
   Temple 360

Kanaka Durga Temple
   249
Kapaleeshwarar Temple
   337
Kashivishvanatha Temple
   376
Keshava Temple 199
Krishna Temple 208-9
Kumari Amman Temple
   396
Kumbeshwara Temple
   376
Lakshimi Narasmiha 215
Madurai 164, **12**, **164-5**
Mahabaleshwara Temple
   210
Mahaganapati temple
   210
Mahalaxmi Mandir 114
Mahishamardini
   Mandapa 359
Mamallapuram 165
Manjunatha Temple 208
Meenakshi Amman
   Temple 164, 389-90,
   12, 164-5
Nageshwara Temple 376
Nataraja Temple 374-5
Ramanathaswamy
   Temple 394
Ramappa Temple 248-9
Ramaswami Temple 376
Raya Gopura 359
Rock-Cut Temple 266-7
Rock Fort Temple 383
Sarangapani Temple 376
Shore Temple 355, **165**
Shri Krishna Temple 314
Shri Murudeshwar
   temple 211
Siddeshwara Temple 248
Simhachalam Temple
   252
Sri Chamundeswari
   Temple 189
Sri Jambukeshwara
   Temple 382-3
Sri Kalahasteeswara
   Temple 365
Sri Manakula Vinayagar
   Temple 366
Sri Ranganathaswamy
   Temple 382
Svayambhu Temple 248
Thanjavur 164-5
Thirunelly Temple 318
Tiger Cave 354
Trimurti Cave Temple
   355

Undavalli Cave Temples
   249
Vadakkunathan Kshe-
   tram Temple 312
Vaikunta Perumal
   Temple 360
Varadaraja Perumal
   Temple 360-1
Varaha Mandapa 359
Venkateshwara Temple
   256
Venugopala Swamy
   Temple 198
Vijayalaya Cholisvaram
   387
Virupaksha temple 214,
   223, **2**, **165**
Vittala Temple 214
historical sites 162-9
   Bahmani Tombs 227
   Cellular Jail National
      Memorial 421
   Colonel Bailey's Dungeon
      199
   Hemakuta Hill 215
   Madikeri Fort 201
   Malik-e-Maidan 225
   Paigah Tombs 235
   Qutb Shahi Tombs 235
   Sule Bazaar 215
   Upli Buruj 225
Hinduism 465-8
history 443-57
   British East India
      Company 452-3
   Chola Empire 446-7
   Christianity 448-50
   contemporary 457
   early civilisation 443-6
   European arrival 449-50
   Independence 454-6
   Mughals 450-2
   Muslim expansion 447-9
   Partition 454-7
   Portuguese 449
   Vijayanagar empire
      447-9
   War of Independence
      453-4
hitching 525
HIV 533
holidays 517
homestays 510
Hosapete 221
Hospet, see Hosapete
hostels 510
hotels 509
houseboats 328, **8-9**,
   328-9

Hubballi 221
Hubli, see Hubballi
Hyderabad 12, 230-47, **231**,
   233, **234**, **238**, **242**,
   12, **163**
   accommodation 236-8
   activities 236
   drinking & nightlife 241-4
   entertainment 244-5
   festivals & events 236
   food 239-41
   sights 231-6
   tourist information
      245-6
   tours 236
   travel to/from 246
   travel within 246-7

I
Indian classical dance 187
Indian clothing 461
influenza 533
insurance 513, 527, 530
internet access 421, 513
internet resources 15
   accessible travel 508
   LGBT+ 514
   wildlife 497
Islam 469, 495
Islamic calendar 20
Islamic sites 495, see also
   mosques
   Bidar 227
   Hyderabad 230-6
   Vijapura (Bijapur) 225-5
itineraries 26-8, **26**, **27**,
   28, see also individual
   regions
ivory 514

J
Jain temples & sites
   Badami 221-2
   Bhandari Basti 205
   Chandragupta Basti 205
   Ellora Caves 92-5, 169,
      94, 168-9
   Gomateshvara Statue
      205
   Sittannavasal 387
   Sultanbatheri 318
Jainism 470
Jalgaon 98
Japanese B encephalitis
   533
Jarawa 437-8
jeep safaris 500

Anamalai Tiger Reserve 416
Bandipur National Park 199
Dandeli Wildlife Sanctuary 222
Mudumalai Tiger Reserve 414-15
Nagarhole National Park 200
Parambikulam Tiger Reserve 295
Periyar Tiger Reserve 288
Tadoba-Andhari Tiger Reserve 100
Wayanad Wildlife Sanctuary 317-18
jewellery 484

K
Kailasa Temple 93-4, **168-9**
Kakkabe 203
kalamkari 341, 485
kalarippayat 264, 330, **331**
Kalipur 436
kambla 210
Kanchipuram 359-62, **360**
Kannada language 538-9
Kannur 320-2
Kanyakumari 395-8, **397**
Karnataka 41, 170-227, **171**
accommodation 170
accommodation costs 177
Central Karnataka 213-21
climate 170
festivals & events 172
food 170
highlights 171
history 172
Karnataka Coast 206-13
Northern Karnataka 221-7
permits 204
Southern Karnataka 187-206
kathakali 330, 490, **330-1**
Kochi 307-8
Thiruvananthapuram 263-4
Thrissur 314
Kattoor 283-4
kayaking 19, 279, 329
Kerala 41, 259-332, **260, 8-9, 33**
accommodation 259

accommodation costs 273
backwaters 286-7, 322
bus travel 319
Central Kerala 297-314
climate 259
drinking & nightlife 275
festivals & events 261, 312
floods 282, 311
food 259
highlights 260
homestays 283
Lakshadweep 323-4
Northern Kerala 314-23
Southern Kerala 261-86
Western Ghats 286-97
khadi 488
Khotachiwadi 51
kitesurfing 146
Kochi 297-310, **298, 302, 304, 307, 325, 330-1**
accommodation 300-3
accommodation costs 273
activities 299
courses 299-300
drinking 303, 305-7
eating 303, 305-7
entertainment 307-8
festivals & events 300
shopping 308
sights 297-9
tourist information 308-9
tours 300
travel to/from 309
travel within 309-10
Kochi-Muziris Biennale 491
Kodagu region 201-3
Kodaikanal 399-404, **400**
Kolhapur 114-15
Kollam 276-8, **277**
Konkan Coast 101
Konkan Railway 529
Konkani language 539
Kootiattam classes 263-4
Kotagiri 407-8
Kottayam 284-5
Kovalam (Kerala) 266-71, **268, 326-7**
Kovalam (Tamil Nadu) 354
Kozhikode 314-17, **315**
Krishna 466
Kumarakom 285-6
Kumbakonam 376-8, **378**

L
Lakshadweep 323-4, **327**
landmarks
Charminar 231
Chinese Fishing Nets 297, **324**
Taj Mahal Palace, Mumbai 47-8
languages 14, 441, 533-42
classes 341
food 481-2
Kannada 538-9
Konkari 539
Malayalam 539-40
Marathi 540-1
Tamil 535-8
Telugu 541
leatherwork 487
leeches 534
legal matters 513-14
leopards 77, 498
lesbian travellers 74, 514
LGBTQ+ travellers 73, 514
lighthouses
Alleppey Lighthouse 279
Little Andaman Lighthouse 436
Madras Lighthouse 341
Mamallapuram 359
Thangassery 276
Vizhinjam Lighthouse 266
literature, see books
Little Andaman 436-8
Lonar 99
Lonavla 106-7
Long Island 434-5
Lunar calandar 20

M
Madgaon, see Margao
Madikeri 201-2
Madras, see Chennai
Madurai 164, 389-93, **390, 164-5**
magazines 515
Mahabaleshwar 115-16
Mahabalipuram, see Mamallapuram
Mahabharata 467
Maharashtra 40, 82-116
accommodation 82
accommodation costs 87
climate 82
festivals & events 84
food 82

Northern Maharashtra 84-101
Southern Maharashtra 101-16
Mahatma Gandhi Marine National Park 425
Mahé 314
mahua 480
malaria 531-2
Malayalam language 539-40
Malpe 209
Malvan 104-5
Malvan Marine National Park 105
Mamallapuram 165, 355-9, **356, 165**
Mandrem 146-7
Mangalore, see Mangaluru
Mangaluru 206-8, **206**
maps 514
Mapusa 127-8
Marari 283-4
Marathi language 540-1
Margao 150-1
markets & bazaars 18, 483-9
Anjuna Flea Market 138
Charminar 244
Crawford Market 46
Devaraja Market 189
Krishnarajendra Market 174
Lalbaug Market 76
Mackie's 135
MMC New Market 151
Municipal Market (Panaji) 125
Saturday Night Market (Arpora) 135
marriage 458-9
Matha Amrithanandamayi Mission 278
Matheran 105-6
Mayabunder 438
meat 473-4
medical services 531
meditation 17-18, 32, 34, **33**
Chennai 341
Hyderabad 236
Kovalam 267
Pune 109, 112
Tiruvannamalai 362
Meenakshi Amman Temple 389-90, **12, 164-5**
mehndi 462
Melukote 199
Mercara, see Madikeri

metalware 487-8
Michinoku Coastal Trail 16
Middle Andaman 434-6
mobile phones 14, 421, 518
money 14, 15, 514-16
Morjim 144
mosques 495
  Haji Ali Dargah 50
  Jama Masjid 225
  Mecca Masjid 232
  Miskhal Masjid 314
motorcycle travel 522,
  526-7
Mudumalai Tiger Reserve
  414-15
Mumbai 11, 40, 44-81, **45**,
  48, **52-3**, **60-1**, **64**, **11**
  accommodation 44,
    56-62
  accommodation costs 57
  activities 55
  airports 78, 79
  autorickshaws 80
  boat trips 80
  Bollywood tours 75
  breweries 70
  bus travel 78-9, 80
  car-sharing services 80
  children, travel with 74
  climate 44
  costs 57
  courses 55
  dabba-wallahs 69
  Dharavi Slum 56
  drinking 69-72
  entertainment 72
  festivals 47
  food 44, 62-9
  highlights 45
  history 46
  internet access 76-7
  itineraries 46
  LGBTQ+ travellers 73
  medical services 77
  metro 80
  money 77
  nightlife 69-72
  Parsi cafes 63
  postal services 77
  safe travel 76
  shopping 73-6
  sights 47-54
  street food 66
  taxis 80

tourist information 77
tours 55-6
train travel 79, 81
travel agencies 78
travel to/from 78-9
travel within 79-81
walking tours 59
Munnar 292-6, 332, **293**,
  5, **332**
Murudeshwar 211
Murud-Janjira 101-2
Murugan 467
museums
  Aircraft Museum 252
  Anthropological Museum
    421
  Arakkal Museum 320
  Archaeological Museum
    (Badami) 222-3
  Archaeological Museum
    (Hampi) 215
  Archaeological Museum
    (Old Goa) 127
  Archaeological Museum
    (Vijapura) 224
  Archaeology Museum
    (Thrissur) 312
  Car Museum 208
  Chhatrapati Shivaji
    Maharaj Vastu
    Sangrahalaya 49
  Cholamandal Artists'
    Village 353-4
  coffee museum 256
  DAG 50
  Dr Bhau Daji Lad Mumbai
    City Museum 50
  Gandhi Memorial
    Museum 390
  Goa Chitra 152
  Goa State Museum &
    Secretariat Building
    120
  Government Museum
    336-7
  HEH The Nizam's
    Museum 232
  Indira Gandhi Rashtriya
    Manav Sangrahalaya
    189
  Indo-Portuguese
    Museum 298
  Jehangir Art Gallery 50
  Joshi's Museum of Min-
    iature Railway 108
  Kerala Folklore Museum
    299
  Kidzania 74
  Krishnapuram Palace
    Museum 278

Madurai Government
  Museum 390
Manjusha Museum 208
Maritime Museum 375
Mattancherry Palace 299
Museum of Habitat 255
Museum of History &
  Heritage 261-2
Nagarjunakonda
  Museum 251
Napier Museum 263
National Gallery of
  Modern Art 50
Nehru Centenary Tribal
  Museum 236
Puducherry Museum
  365
Pudukkottai Museum
  387
Puthe Maliga Palace
  Museum 263
Rail Museum 189
Railway Museum 383-4
Raja Dinkar Kelkar
  Museum 108
RKK Memorial Museum
  279
Sacred Heart Natural
  Science Museum 399
Salar Jung Museum 232
Samudrika Naval Marine
  Museum 421
San Thome Museum 152
Shree Chhatrapati Shahu
  Museum 114
St Joseph's College
  Museum 384
State Museum
  (Hyderabad) 232-3
Submarine Museum 252
Sudha Cars Museum 237
Sullivan Memorial 408
Swami Vivekananda
  Wandering Monk
  Exhibition 396
Tea Museum 292
Tribal Research Centre
  Museum 409
Vivekananda House 337
Wayanad Heritage
  Museum 318
music 245, 442, 490-1
musical instruments 488
Mysore, *see* Mysuru
Mysuru 13, 187-98, **192-3**,
  13, **162**, **190-1**
  accommodation 193-5
  activities 189
  ayurveda 192-3
  courses 189

drinking & nightlife 196
festivals & events 193
history 188
shopping 196-7
sights 188-9
tourist information 197
tours 193
travel to/from 197-8
travel within 198
Mysuru Palace 188-9,
  190-1, **162**, **190-1**

N

Nagarhole National Park
  200-1
Nagarjunakonda 251-2
Nagpur 98-9
name changes
  Andaman Islands 419
Nandi Hills 188
Nashik 84-8, **85**
national parks & reserves
  18, 499-500
  Bandipur National Park
    199-200
  Eravikulam National
    Park 297
  Mahatma Gandhi Marine
    National Park 425
  Malvan Marine National
    Park 105
  Nagarhole National Park
    200-1, 318
  Sanjay Gandhi National
    Park 77
  Wayanad Wildlife
    Sanctuary 332
Navratri & Dussehra 20
Nehru Trophy Boat Race
  279
Neil Island, *see* Shaheed
  Dweep
Netaji Subhas Chandra
  Bose Dweep 424
newspapers 515
Nicobarese 437-8
Nilgiri Hills 402, **408**
Nilgiri Mountain Railway
  529
North Andaman 434-6
North Paravur 311-12

O

Ola 80
Old Goa 126-7, **126**
Onge 437-8
Ooty, *see* Udhagamandalam
opening hours 15
Osho 109, 112

P

paan 474
painting 484-6, 491-2
palaces 17, 163, 496
    Aga Khan Palace 108
    Chowmahalla Palace 231-2
    Daria Daulat Bagh 198-9
    Jaganmohan Palace 189
    Mysuru Palace 188-9, 190-1, **13**, **162**, **190-1**
    Padmanabhapuram Palace 267, 395
    Royal Palace 379-80
    Tirumalai Nayak Palace 390
Palampet 248-9
Palolem 155-60, **156-7**, **2**
Panaji 120-6, **122**
    accommodation 121, 123
    activities 121
    drinking & nightlife 124
    entertainment 124-5
    food 123-4
    shopping 125
    sights 120-1
    tourist information 125
    travel to/from 125-6
    travel within 126
Panjim, see Panaji
paragliding 107, 147
Parambikulam Tiger Reserve 295
parks & gardens
    Botanical Gardens 409
    Brindavan Gardens 198
    Osho Teerth Gardens 109
    Rose Garden 409
    Theosophical Society 340-1
Parsis 63
passports 521
Patnem 160-1
Pattadakal 223
payphones 518
performing arts 330-1, **330-1**
Periyar Tiger Reserve 287-92, **289**
permits 204, 520
photography 505, 516
pilgrimages 460
    Ayyappan Temple 292
    Gomateshvara Statue 205
    Mt Arunachala 362
    Tirupati 256, 257
    Venkateshwara Temple 256

planning
    booking trains 29-30
    budgeting 15
    calendar of events 20-3
    children, travel with 37-9
    itineraries 26-8
    repeat visitors 16
    South India basics 14-15
    South India's regions 40-2
    travel seasons 20-3
plants 499
police 514
political violence 517-18
politics 440-2
pollution 502, 534
Ponda 121
Pondicherry, see Puducherry
Pongal 20, **23**
Ponnumthuruthu (Golden) Island 272
population 441
    indigenous 437
Port Blair 421-5, **422**
postal services 516-17
prickly heat 534
public holidays 517
Puducherry 12, 364-73, **368**, **12**
    accommodation 367-70
    activities 366
    churches & cathedrals 366
    courses 366-7
    drinking & nightlife 371-2
    food 370-1
    French Quarter 366
    shopping 372
    sights 364-6
    tourist information 372
    tours 367
    travel to/from 372-3
    travel within 373
Pune 108-13, **110**

Q

Qawwalia 245
Quilon, see Kollam
Qutb Shahi Tombs 163, 235, **12**, **163**

R

rabies 533
radio 515
rafting 288
Ramayana 467-8

Rameswaram 393-5
Ramtek 100-1
Rangat 434
rangolis 464
Rani Abbakka 212
rashes 534
religion 465-71
    books 465, 467, 469, 470, 471
    food 479
    Sufism 245
Restricted Area Permits 419-20, 438
rice 473
rockclimbing 223
Ross Island 435, see Netaji Subhas Chandra Bose Dweep

S

Sabarimala 292, 442
safe travel 517-18
    Andaman Islands 419
    diving & surfing 534
    drugs 139, 504
    food 477
    Hampi 220
    hitching 525
    Kerala floods 282
    Kovalam 267
    Mumbai 76
    sandflies 420
    scams 504-5
    solo travellers 507
    theft 139
    women travellers 506-7
sandflies 420
Sankaram 255
Sanriku Kaigan Railway 16
saris 486-7
scams 504-5
seafood 474
Sentinelese 437-8
Sevagram 101
Shaheed Dweep 431-4
shahtoosh shawls 514
Shakti 466
Shiva 466
Shivatri, Chhatrapati 451
Shivneri 114
Shompen 437-8
shopping 483-9, see also individual locations
Shore Temple 355, **165**
sikh temples 227
Sikhism 469
Sinhagad 113-14
Smith Island 435

smoking 513
snakes 501
solo travellers 507
Somnathpur 199
spas 34
spice farms 121
    Palolem 155
    Periyar Tiger Reserve 288
    Ponda 121
spices 472-3
spirituality 465-71, 479
sport 463-4
Sravanabelagola 205-6
Srirangapatna 198-9
Srirangapatnam, see Srirangapatna
STDs 533
street food 477-8
    Chennai 348
    Mumbai 66
Sufi shrines
    Dargah Hazrat Shah Khamosh 245
    Dargah Yousufain Sharifain 245
Sufism 245
surfing 19
    Agonda 154-5
    Arambol 147
    Asven 145
    Gorkana 211
    Kovalam (Kerala) 267
    Kovalam (Tamil Nadu) 354
    Little Andaman 436
    Mamallapuram 357
    Morjim 144
    Puducherry 366
    Tamil Nadu 354
    Varkala 272-3
    Visakhapatnam 253
sustainable travel 487
    Goa Foundation 129
    slum tours 56
Swaraj Dweep 426-31, 432, **428**, **13**
synagogues
    Chennamangalam Synagogue 312
    Keneseth Eliyahoo Synagogue 50
    Pardesi Synagogue 299

T

tabla classes 193
Tadoba-Andhari Tiger Reserve 100, **11**

Taj Mahal Palace, Mumbai 47-8
Talpona 160
Tamil language 535-8
Tamil Nadu 42, 333-416, **334**
  accommodation 333
  accommodation costs 358
  Central Tamil Nadu 374-86
  Chennai 335-53
  climate 333
  festivals & events 336
  food 333
  highlights 334
  Hindu temples 365
  history 335
  Northern Tamil Nadu 353-74
  religion 469
  Southern Tamil Nadu 386-98
  surfing 354
  Western Ghats 398-416
Tanjore, see Thanjavur
taxis 16, 525-6, see also car-sharing apps
tea 480
tea plantations **5**, **332**
  Coonoor 406
  Munnar 292-3
  Periyar Tiger Reserve 288
Telangana 41, 230-49, **229**
  accommodation 228
  accommodation costs 250
  climate 228
  festivals & events 230
  food 228
  highlights 229
  history 230
telephone services 14, 518
  Andaman Islands 421
Telugu language 541
terracotta ware 483
textiles 486-7
thalis 472
Thangassery 276
thangkas 486
Thanjavur 164-5, 378-82, **380**
Tharangambadi 375-6
Thattekkad Bird Sanctuary 296

theft 505
theyyam 320, 330-1, **331**
Thiruvananthapuram 261-6, **262**
Thotlakonda 255
Thrissur 312-14, **313**
Tibetan refugees 204
ticks 534
tiger reserves 11, 18
  Anamalai Tiger Reserve 415-16
  Mudumalai Tiger Reserve 414-15
  Parambikulam Tiger Reserve 295
  Periyar Tiger Reserve 287-92, 332
  Tadoba-Andhari Tiger Reserve 100
tigers 497-8, 500, 502, **11**
time 519
tipping 516
Tiruchirappalli, see Trichy
Tirumala 256-8
Tirupati 256-8
Tiruvannamalai 362-4
toilets 510, 519
Top Station 296
tourist information 519
tours 522, 527
train travel 29-30, 527-9
  bookings 29-30, 528
  classes 29
  Deccan Odyssey 529
  fares 528
  food 478
  Goa Express 529
  Konkan Railway 529
  luxury trains 30
  Nilgiri Mountain Railway 529
Tranquebar, see Tharangambadi
transport 505, 521-9
travel seasons 14, 20-3
travel to/from South India 521-2
travel within South India 15, 522-9
travellers' diarrhoea 533-4
trekking
  Andamans 435
  Kakkabe 203
  Kodagu (Coorg) Region 201
  Munnar 293
  Wayanad Region 318

tribal peoples 471, see also Adivasis
  Andaman Islands 421, 434, 437, 438
  Andhra Pradesh 255
  Chinnar Wildlife Santuary 297
  Hyderabad 236
  Karen 438
  Nilgri Hills 402, 409
  Toda 402, 489
Trichur, see Thrissur
Trichy 382-6, **386**, **383**
Trivandrum, see Thiruvananthapuram
tuberculosis 533
turtle-watching 436
TV 515
typhoid 533

U
Uber 80
Udhagamandalam 11, 409-14, **410-11**
Udupi 208-9
Unesco World Heritage Sites
  Ajanta Caves 10, 95-8, 169, **96**, **10**, **168**, **169**
  Chettinadu 386-7
  Elephanta Island 54
  Ellora Caves 92-5, 169, **94**, **168-9**
  Hampi 214
  Mumbai 7, 50, 165, 495, **7**
  Nilgiri Mountain Railway 414
  Niligris 402
  Western Ghats 11, 286-97, 398-416, 501, **11**

V
vacations 517
vaccinations 530, 532
Vagator 140-4, **142**, **9**
Varkala 271-6, **272**, **327**
vegetarian travellers 476
Vijapura 163, 224-7, **224**
Vijayawada 249-50
Virupaksha Temple 214, 223, **2**, **165**
Visakhapatnam 252-5
visas 14, 519-20
Vishnu 465-6
volunteering 35-6
  agencies 36

Andaman Islands 425
Arunachala Animal Sanctuary 362-3
Auroville 373-4
Kotagiri 408
Mumbai 55
vultures 499

W
walking tours 59, **59**
Wandoor 425-6
Warangal 248
water 502, 533
water sports 19
waterfalls
  Dudhsagar Falls 144
  Hampi 215
  Little Andaman 437-8
Wayanad region 317-20, **317**
Wayanad Wildlife Sanctuary 317-18
weather 14, 20-3, see also individual regions
weaving
  Chennamangalam 311
  Kalakshetra Craft Centre 341
  Kanchipuram 361
  Sri Mahalakshmi Handloom Weaving Centre 387
Western Ghats 11, 501, **11**
  Kerala 286-97
  Tamil Nadu 398-416
wildlife reserves & sanctuaries 11, 18, 332, 499-500
  Anamalai Tiger Reserve 415-16
  Arunachala Animal Sanctuary 362-3
  Bandipur National Park 199-200
  Chinnar Wildlife Sanctuary 297
  Dandeli 222
  Eravikulam National Park 297
  Kumarakom Bird Sanctuary 285
  Mudumalai Tiger Reserve 414-15
  Nagarhole National Park 200-1, 318
  Parambikulam Tiger Reserve 295

Periyar Tiger Reserve 287-92, **289**
Ranganathittu Bird Sanctuary 199
Tadoba-Andhari Tiger Reserve 100, **11**
Thattekkad Bird Sanctuary 296
Vedanthangal Bird Sanctuary 357
Wayanad Wildlife Sanctuary 317-18, 332
wildlife-watching 413, 497-9, 500, 522, *see also* tiger reserves, wildlife reserves & sanctuaries
wine 86, 188

wineries
  Nandi Hills 188
  Nashik 86
women in South India 441-2, 461-3
women travellers 506-7, 531
woodcarving 488
workshops
  Athangudi Palace Tiles 387
  Banana Fibre Craft Workshop 221
  Sri Mahalakshmi Handloom Weaving Centre 387
wrestling 114

Y
yatra 460
yoga 17-18, 32, **33**, **327**
  Anjuna 137, 141
  Arambol 147
  Assagao 141
  Chennai 341
  Coimbatore 404
  Gorkana 211
  Kochi 299
  Kovalam 267
  Lonavla 107
  Madurai 391
  Mandrem 146
  Mumbai 55
  Mysuru 194

Palolem 155-6
Puducherry 366, 367
Sivananda Yoga Vedanta Dhanwantari Ashram 266
Vagator 141
Varkala 272-3

Z
Zika virus 533
zoos
  Madras Crocodile Bank 354
  Zoological Gardens (Thiruvananthapuram) 263
Zoroastrianism 470-1

NOTES

Map Legend

Sights

- Beach
- Bird Sanctuary
- Buddhist
- Castle/Palace
- Christian
- Confucian
- Hindu
- Islamic
- Jain
- Jewish
- Monument
- Museum/Gallery/Historic Building
- Ruin
- Shinto
- Sikh
- Taoist
- Winery/Vineyard
- Zoo/Wildlife Sanctuary
- Other Sight

Activities, Courses & Tours

- Bodysurfing
- Diving
- Canoeing/Kayaking
- Course/Tour
- Sento Hot Baths/Onsen
- Skiing
- Snorkelling
- Surfing
- Swimming/Pool
- Walking
- Windsurfing
- Other Activity

Sleeping

- Sleeping
- Camping
- Hut/Shelter

Eating

- Eating

Drinking & Nightlife

- Drinking & Nightlife
- Cafe

Entertainment

- Entertainment

Shopping

- Shopping

Information

- Bank
- Embassy/Consulate
- Hospital/Medical
- Internet
- Police
- Post Office
- Telephone
- Toilet
- Tourist Information
- Other Information

Geographic

- Beach
- Gate
- Hut/Shelter
- Lighthouse
- Lookout
- Mountain/Volcano
- Oasis
- Park
- Pass
- Picnic Area
- Waterfall

Population

- Capital (National)
- Capital (State/Province)
- City/Large Town
- Town/Village

Transport

- Airport
- Border crossing
- Bus
- Cable car/Funicular
- Cycling
- Ferry
- Metro/MRT/MTR station
- Monorail
- Parking
- Petrol station
- Skytrain/Subway station
- Taxi
- Train station/Railway
- Tram
- Underground station
- Other Transport

Routes

- Tollway
- Freeway
- Primary
- Secondary
- Tertiary
- Lane
- Unsealed road
- Road under construction
- Plaza/Mall
- Steps
- Tunnel
- Pedestrian overpass
- Walking Tour
- Walking Tour detour
- Path/Walking Trail

Boundaries

- International
- State/Province
- Disputed
- Regional/Suburb
- Marine Park
- Cliff
- Wall

Hydrography

- River, Creek
- Intermittent River
- Canal
- Water
- Dry/Salt/Intermittent Lake
- Reef

Areas

- Airport/Runway
- Beach/Desert
- Cemetery (Christian)
- Cemetery (Other)
- Glacier
- Mudflat
- Park/Forest
- Sight (Building)
- Sportsground
- Swamp/Mangrove

Note: Not all symbols displayed above appear on the maps in this book